BUTTERWORTHS ENVIRONMENTAL LAW HANDBOOK

BUTTERWORTHS ENVIRONMENTAL LAW HANDBOOK

Edited by
ANDREW WAITE, MA, *Solicitor*
Partner, Planning and Environment Department,
Co-ordinator of the Environment Group, Berwin Leighton

BUTTERWORTHS
LONDON, EDINBURGH, DUBLIN
1997

United Kingdom	Butterworths a Division of Reed Elsevier (UK) Ltd, Halsbury House, 35 Chancery Lane, LONDON WC2A 1EL and 4 Hill Street, EDINBURGH EH2 3JZ
Australia	Butterworths, SYDNEY, MELBOURNE, BRISBANE, ADELAIDE, PERTH, CANBERRA and HOBART
Canada	Butterworths Canada Ltd, TORONTO and VANCOUVER
Ireland	Butterworth (Ireland) Ltd, DUBLIN
Malaysia	Malayan Law Journal Sdn Bhd, KUALA LUMPUR
Poland	Wydawnictwa Prawnicze PWN, WARSAW
New Zealand	Butterworths of New Zealand Ltd, WELLINGTON and AUCKLAND
Singapore	Butterworths Asia, SINGAPORE
South Africa	Butterworth Publishers (Pty) Ltd, DURBAN
USA	Michie, CHARLOTTESVILLE, Virginia

A CIP catalogue record for this book is available from the British Library.

ISBN 0 406 99154 5

Printed and bound in Great Britain by Clays Ltd, St Ives plc

INTRODUCTION

The numerous changes in environmental legislation since the first edition of this Handbook render a second edition appropriate. A number of the initiatives referred to in the introduction to the first edition have now been transposed into law whilst a number of new proposals are now being discussed. Perhaps the most significant legislative development since 1994 has been the passing of the Environment Act 1995 which not only contains new provisions on contaminated land, waste strategy and air pollution but has also enacted copious amendments to existing legislation, in particular the Environmental Protection Act 1990 and the Water Resources Act 1991. Of particular note are the changes made to the discharge consent licensing procedures and the new works notice provisions—both contained in the amendments to the Water Resources Act 1991.

The Surface Waters (Dangerous Substances) (Classification) Regulations 1997, SI 1997/2560, have recently introduced statutory environmental quality standards for 13 substances in water under the Dangerous Substances Directive (76/464/EEC).

The remainder of this introduction will comment on a few of the recent initiatives by the European Commission and the UK Government which may be reflected in future changes to the law.

Contaminated Land Legislation

Part II of the Environment Act 1995 inserted a new Part IIA into the Environmental Protection Act 1990 (which is included in this edition of the Handbook). However, the new legislation is not yet in force and awaits the enactment of Regulations and Statutory Guidance before it can take effect. Draft Guidance and Regulations were published for consultation in September and November 1996 respectively. However, the general election of 1997 delayed the implementation process. The present Labour Government is aware of the cost implications of the new legislation for local authorities and for that reason, implementation will probably be delayed until at least 1999 in view of the current expenditure freeze. However, it is intended to produce a final version of the Guidance and the Regulations well before this package of legislation is implemented so that local authorities and other interested parties have sufficient opportunity to become accustomed to it.

Contaminated Land Directive

Discussions have been held within DGXI of the European Commission as to the possibility of producing a proposal for a directive on contaminated land. This initiative is unlikely to proceed due to the generally accepted view that under the "subsidiarity" principle contaminated land is best dealt with by individual Member States.

The Works Notice Procedure

The Environment Act 1995 has amended the Water Resources Act 1991 by adding new ss 161A–D. These provide that the Environment Agency may serve a works notice on any person who causes or knowingly permits poisonous, noxious or polluting matter to be present in or to be in a position where it is likely to enter "controlled waters". These provisions overlap with the contaminated land legislation, although they are broader in scope since they also cover water pollution incidents unrelated to contaminated land. The new procedure is not yet in force and is awaiting Regulations for its implementation. Draft Regulations were issued for consultation in the summer of 1997. They have been criticised, inter alia, on the grounds that—

- there are no restraints against using the works notice procedure to circumvent the restrictions in the contaminated land draft Guidance as to which potentially liable parties should be served with a notice and when a notice should be served;

- the grounds of appeal are not specified;
- there is no provision for the suspension of a works notice pending the outcome of an appeal.

Proposed EC Framework Directive on Water Resources

This is designed to replace much of the existing specific EC legislation on water quality with a more general framework directive designed to ensure improvement. A key element of the proposal is that all waters should achieve the "good" status by the year 2010, although there will be provision for derogations in certain circumstances. It is also proposed that water resource management should be based on river basins.

Changes in the Hazardous Waste List

The European Commission proposes to add to the Hazardous Waste List after considering proposals from Member States. Proposals for additions to the list include—

- incineration residues;
- discarded vehicles which have not been "de-polluted";
- light fraction from automobile shredding;
- bottom ash from combustion of heavy fuel oil;
- equipment containing CFCs;
- electronic equipment with a certain content of dangerous components;
- lithium, zinc-manganese and alkaline batteries;
- packaging containing hazardous substances; and
- metal filings and turnings containing oil.

The precise impact of these proposals, if enacted, is unclear. Some substances would not satisfy the hazard criteria and would not, therefore, qualify as special waste.

Proposed Landfill Directive

A second proposal for a landfill directive was produced by the European Commission early in 1997 following the rejection of the earlier version by the European Parliament in 1996 on the ground that it was not sufficiently stringent. The main features of the new proposal include—

- a progressive reduction in the percentage of biodegradable municipal waste going to landfill by reference to the weight produced in 1993: to 75% by 2002, 50% by 2005 and 25% by 2010;
- a ban on landfilling the following wastes: non-inert liquid wastes, wastes which in landfill conditions are explosive, corrosive, oxidising, highly flammable or flammable, infectious clinical wastes, whole and shredded tyres;
- compulsory pre-treatment of waste;
- a ban on the co-disposal of hazardous and non-hazardous waste; and
- harmonisation of licensing procedures.

The Labour Government accepts the need for imposing high standards including the ban on co-disposal of hazardous and non-hazardous waste but does not agree with the aim of forcing higher rates of waste recovery through incineration which would be the likely result of the present draft directive.

Landfill Tax

HM Customs & Excise have recently announced a thorough review of the operation of landfill tax. They have asked interested parties to contribute their views on a range of topics including—

- Has the tax encouraged a reduction in the amounts of waste gas to landfill?
- What effect has the tax had on the use of demolition or construction waste?

- Is the current scope of the tax appropriate or should it include other deposits of waste presently exempt from environmental licensing?
- Are the exemptions for dredgings and mines and quarry waste consistent with environmental objectives?
- Are there other categories of waste that should be exempt from the tax?
- Has the exemption for wastes arising from the clearance of contaminated land achieved its objective of ensuring that the tax does not act as a disincentive to reclamation?
- Is there a case for the rates of landfill tax to be changed?
- Are two rates of tax sufficient to distinguish different waste streams? Are the categories of waste eligible for the lower rate of tax appropriate?
- How successful has the environmental bodies credit scheme been in encouraging donations to environmental projects? Can the scheme be improved?

Implementation of EC Directive (96/61/EEC) on Integrated Pollution Prevention and Control (IPPC)

IPPC is wider than the concept of Best Practicable Environmental Option (BPEO) under Part I of the Environmental Protection Act 1990. In particular, the basic obligations of the operator set out in the Directive include—
- causing no significant pollution including noise;
- avoiding the production of waste;
- using energy efficiently;
- preventing accidents; and
- avoiding any pollution risk and returning the site to a satisfactory state on definitive cessation of activities.

A Consultation Paper was issued by the Government in July 1997 on the implementation of the Directive. The Consultation Paper discusses the possibility of using a "Co-ordinated Pollution Control" approach to regulation under which two or more regulatory bodies may be involved with a particular process whilst ensuring that regulation is viewed in a holistic manner.

Civil Liability for Enforcing EC Environmental Law

The Green Paper of 1993 has been the subject of a number of meetings and studies carried out by and on behalf of the Commission, who propose to produce a White Paper in 1998. The principal aim seems to be to facilitate the enforceability of EC environmental law at Member State level. None of the proposals for implementing this initiative appears to have wide support so far.

Implementation of EC Directive (97/11/EC) on Environmental Assessment

The Directive substantially amends the original Directive (85/337/EEC), in particular by adding 12 new classes of project to Annex I and 8 new classes of project to Annex II. It also clarifies how Member States may determine whether Annex II projects require environmental assessment. Thresholds or criteria may be used or projects may be considered on a case by case basis, or alternatively a combination of both methods may be used. In implementing the Directive, the Government proposes to ensure that where an environmental assessment is necessary, it assists business to understand and minimise the environmental impact of its activities and thereby identify cost savings.

The contents of the Handbook take into account materials available as at 14 November 1997.

Andrew Waite
November 1997

CONTENTS

PART III EUROPEAN MATERIALS

PART I
STATUTES

CONTROL OF POLLUTION ACT 1974

(1974 c 40)

ARRANGEMENT OF SECTIONS
PART III
NOISE

An Act to make further provision with respect to waste disposal, water pollution, noise, atmospheric pollution and public health; and for purposes connected with the matters aforesaid

[31 July 1974]

1–56 (*(Pts I, II) outside the scope of this work.*)

PART III
NOISE

Periodical inspections by local authorities

57 Periodical inspections by local authorities

It shall be the duty of every local authority to cause its area to be inspected from time to time—

(a) ...

(b) to decide how to exercise its powers concerning noise abatement zones.

[1]

NOTES

Para (a) repealed by the Environmental Protection Act 1990, s 162(2), Sch 16, Pt III, and by the Environment Act 1995, s 120, Sch 24.

58, 59 (*Repealed by the Environmental Protection Act 1990, s 162(2), Sch 16, Pt III.*)

Construction sites

60 Control of noise on construction sites

(1) This section applies to works of the following description, that is to say—

(a) the erection, construction, alteration, repair or maintenance of buildings, structures or roads;

(b) breaking up, opening or boring under any road or adjacent land in connection with the construction, inspection, maintenance or removal of works;

(c) demolition or dredging work; and

(d) (whether or not also comprised in paragraph (a), (b) or (c) above) any work of engineering construction.

(2) Where it appears to a local authority that works to which this section applies are being, or are going to be, carried out on any premises, the local authority may serve a notice imposing requirements as to the way in which the works are to be carried out and may if it thinks fit publish notice of the requirements in such way as appears to the local authority to be appropriate.

(3) The notice may in particular—

(a) specify the plant or machinery which is or is not to be used;

(b) specify the hours during which the works may be carried out;

(c) specify the level of noise which may be emitted from the premises in question or at any specified point on those premises or which may be so emitted during specified hours; and

(d) provide for any change of circumstances.

(4) In acting under this section the local authority shall have regard—

(a) to the relevant provisions of any code of practice issued under this Part of this Act;

    (b) to the need for ensuring that the best practicable means are employed to minimise noise;

    (c) before specifying any particular methods or plant or machinery, to the desirability in the interests of any recipients of the notice in question of specifying other methods or plant or machinery which would be substantially as effective in minimising noise and more acceptable to them;

    (d) to the need to protect any persons in the locality in which the premises in question are situated from the effects of noise.

(5)   A notice under this section shall be served on the person who appears to the local authority to be carrying out, or going to carry out, the works, and on such other persons appearing to the local authority to be responsible for, or to have control over, the carrying out of the works as the local authority thinks fit.

(6)   A notice under this section may specify the time within which the notice is to be complied with, and may require the execution of such works, and the taking of such other steps, as may be necessary for the purpose of the notice, or as may be specified in the notice.

(7)   A person served with a notice under this section may appeal against the notice to a magistrates' court within twenty-one days from the service of the notice.

(8)   If a person on whom a notice is served under this section without reasonable excuse contravenes any requirement of the notice he shall be guilty of an offence against this Part of this Act.

[2]

61 Prior consent for work on construction sites

(1)   A person who intends to carry out works to which the preceding section applies may apply to the local authority for a consent under this section.

(2)   Where approval under building regulations . . . , or in Scotland a warrant under section 6 of the Building (Scotland) Act 1959, is required for the carrying out of the works, the application under this section must be made at the same time as, or later than, the request for the approval under building regulations or, as the case may be, the application for a warrant under the said Act of 1959.

(3)   An application under this section shall contain particulars of—

    (a) the works, and the method by which they are to be carried out; and

    (b) the steps proposed to be taken to minimise noise resulting from the works.

(4)   If the local authority considers that the application contains sufficient information for the purpose and that, if the works are carried out in accordance with the application, it would not serve a notice under the preceding section in respect of those works, the local authority shall give its consent to the application.

(5)   In acting under this section a local authority shall have regard to the considerations set out in subsection (4) of the preceding section and shall have power to—

    (a) attach any conditions to a consent; and

    (b) limit or qualify a consent to allow for any change in circumstances; and

    (c) limit the duration of a consent;

and any person who knowingly carries out the works, or permits the works to be carried out, in contravention of any conditions attached to a consent under this section shall be guilty of an offence against this Part of this Act.

(6)   The local authority shall inform the applicant of its decision on the application within twenty-eight days from receipt of the application; and if the local authority gives its consent to the application it may if it thinks fit publish notice of the consent, and of the works to which it relates, in such way as appears to the local authority to be appropriate.

(7) If—
  (a) the local authority does not give a consent within the said period of twenty-eight days; or
  (b) the local authority gives its consent within the said period of twenty-eight days but attaches any condition to the consent or limits or qualifies the consent in any way,

the applicant may appeal to a magistrates' court within twenty-one days from the end of that period.

(8) In any proceedings for an offence under section 60(8) of this Act it shall be a defence to prove that the alleged contravention amounted to the carrying out of the works in accordance with a consent given under this section.

(9) A consent given under this section shall contain a statement to the effect that the consent does not of itself constitute any ground of defence against any proceedings instituted under . . . [. . . section 82 of the Environmental Protection Act 1990 . . .].

(10) Where a consent has been given under this section and the works are carried out by a person other than the applicant for the consent, it shall be the duty of the applicant to take all reasonable steps to bring the consent to the notice of that other person; and if he fails to comply with this subsection he shall be guilty of an offence against this Part of this Act.

[3]

NOTES
  Sub-s (2): words omitted repealed by the Building Act 1984, s 133(2), Sch 7.
  Sub-s (9): words omitted repealed by the Environment Act 1995, s 120(3), Sch 24; words in square brackets added by the Environmental Protection Act 1990, s 162(1), Sch 15, para 15(1), (3).

Noise in streets

62 Noise in streets

(1) Subject to the provisions of this section, a loud-speaker in a street shall not be operated—
  (a) between the hours of nine in the evening and eight in the following morning, for any purpose;
  (b) at any other time, for the purpose of advertising any entertainment, trade or business;

and any person who operates or permits the operation of a loudspeaker in contravention of this subsection shall be guilty of an offence against this Part of this Act.

[In this section] "street" means a highway and any other road, footway, square or court which is for the time being open to the public.

[(1A) Subject to subsection (1B) of this section, the Secretary of State may by order amend the times specified in subsection (1)(a) of this section.

(1B) An order under subsection (1A) of this section shall not amend the times so as to permit the operation of a loudspeaker in a street at any time between the hours of nine in the evening and eight in the following morning.]

(2) [Subsection (1) of this section] shall not apply to the operation of a loudspeaker—
  (a) for police, fire brigade or ambulance purposes, by [the [Environment Agency], a water undertaker or a sewerage undertaker] in the exercise of any of its functions, or by a local authority within its area;
  (b) for communicating with persons on a vessel for the purpose of directing the movement of that or any other vessel;

    (c) if the loudspeaker forms part of a public telephone system;
    (d) if the loudspeaker—
        (i) is in or fixed to a vehicle, and
       (ii) is operated solely for the entertainment of or for communicating with the driver or a passenger of the vehicle or, where the loudspeaker is or forms part of the horn or similar warning instrument of the vehicle, solely for giving warning to other traffic, and
      (iii) is so operated as not to give reasonable cause for annoyance to persons in the vicinity;
    (e) otherwise than on a highway, by persons employed in connection with a transport undertaking used by the public in a case where the loudspeaker is operated solely for making announcements to passengers or prospective passengers or to other persons so employed;
    (f) by a travelling showman on land which is being used for the purposes of a pleasure fair;
    (g) in case of emergency.

(3)   Subsection (1)(b) of this section shall not apply to the operation of a loudspeaker between the hours of noon and seven in the evening on the same day if the loudspeaker—
    (a) is fixed to a vehicle which is being used for the conveyance of a perishable commodity for human consumption; and
    (b) is operated solely for informing members of the public (otherwise than by means of words) that the commodity is on sale from the vehicle; and
    (c) is so operated as not to give reasonable cause for annoyance to persons in the vicinity.

[(3A) Subsection (1) of this section shall not apply to the operation of a loudspeaker in accordance with a consent granted by a local authority under Schedule 2 to the Noise and Statutory Nuisance Act 1993.]

(4)   (*Applies to Scotland only.*)

[4]

NOTES
    Sub-s (1): words in square brackets substituted by the Noise and Statutory Nuisance Act 1993, s 7(2).
    Sub-ss (1A), (1B), (3A): inserted by the Noise and Statutory Nuisance Act 1993, s 7(3), (5).
    Sub-s (2): words in first pair of square brackets substituted by the Noise and Statutory Nuisance Act 1993, s 7(4); words in first (outer) pair of square brackets in para (a) substituted by the Water Act 1989, s 190(1), Sch 25, para 48, words in second (inner) pair of square brackets substituted by the Environment Act 1995, s 120, Sch 22, para 28.

Noise abatement zones

63 Designation of zones

(1)   A local authority may by order . . . designate all or any part of its area a noise abatement zone.

(2)   An order under this section shall specify the classes of premises to which it applies (that is to say, the classes of premises subject to control under the following provisions of this Part of this Act).

(3)   An order made . . . under this section may be revoked or varied by a subsequent order so made. . .

(4)   The provisions of Schedule 1 to this Act shall apply to the . . . coming into operation of an order under this section.

(5)   In this Part of this Act a "noise abatement order" means an order made under this section.

[5]

NOTES

Sub-ss (1), (3), (4): words omitted repealed by the Local Government, Planning and Land Act 1980, ss 1(2), 194, Sch 2, para 14, Sch 34, Pt II.

64 Register of noise levels

(1)   Every local authority which has designated its area or any part of its area a noise abatement zone shall measure the level of noise emanating from premises within the zone which are of any class to which the relevant noise abatement order relates.

(2)   The local authority shall record all measurements taken in pursuance of the preceding subsection in a register (in this Part of this Act referred to as a "noise level register") to be kept by the local authority for the purpose in accordance with regulations.

(3)   The local authority on recording any measurement in the noise level register shall serve a copy of that record on the owner and occupier of the premises in respect of which the measurement was taken; and any person on whom a copy of such a record is served may, within twenty-eight days of the date of service, appeal to the Secretary of State against the record.

(4)   On an appeal to the Secretary of State in pursuance of the preceding subsection the Secretary of State may give to the local authority in question such directions as he thinks fit as to the record of the measurement of noise which is the subject of the appeal, and it shall be the duty of the authority to comply with the directions.

(5)   Except as provided by the preceding provisions of this section the validity or accuracy of any entry in a noise level register shall not be questioned in any proceedings under this Part of this Act.

(6)   The premises as to which a local authority is to make measurements under this section shall include those which come within a class to which the relevant noise abatement order relates after the making of the order; and it shall be for the local authority to determine, both for those premises and all other premises of any class to which the relevant noise abatement order relates, where the measurements under this section are to be made.

(7)   A noise level register shall be open to public inspection at the principal office of the local authority free of charge at all reasonable hours, and the local authority shall afford members of the public reasonable facilities for obtaining from the authority, on payment of reasonable charges, copies of entries in the register.

(8)   Provision may be made by regulations—
    (a) for determining, or for authorising the Secretary of State to determine, the methods by which noise levels are to be measured for the purposes of any provision of this section and the three following sections; and
    (b) for enabling noise levels calculated in accordance with the regulations, or in accordance with the directions of the Secretary of State, to be treated for those purposes as measured by a method determined in pursuance of the preceding paragraph.

[6]

NOTES

Regulations: the Control of Noise (Measurement and Register) Regulations 1976, SI 1976/37.

65 Noise exceeding registered level

(1)   The level of noise recorded in the noise level register in respect of any premises shall not be exceeded except with the consent in writing of the local authority.

(2)   The local authority's consent may be made subject to such conditions, whether as to the amount by which the level of noise may be increased, or as to the period for which, or the periods during which, the level of noise may be increased, as may be specified in the consent; and the authority shall record particulars of the consent in the noise level register.

(3)   If within the period of two months beginning with the date on which a local authority receives an application for its consent under this section, or within such longer period as the authority and the applicant agree in writing, the authority has not notified the applicant of its decision on the application, the authority shall be deemed to have refused consent in pursuance of the application.

(4)   An applicant for consent under this section may appeal to the Secretary of State against the local authority's decision on the application within the period of three months beginning with the date on which the authority notifies him of the decision or, in a case falling within the preceding subsection, beginning with the expiration of the period or longer period there mentioned; and it shall be the duty of the local authority to act in accordance with the decision of the Secretary of State on the appeal.

(5)   If noise emitted from any premises constitutes a contravention of subsection (1) of this section or of a condition attached to a consent under this section, the person responsible shall be guilty of an offence against this Part of this Act.

(6)   The magistrates' court convicting a person of an offence under the preceding subsection may, if satisfied that the offence is likely to continue or recur, make an order requiring the execution of any works necessary to prevent it continuing or recurring; and if that person without reasonable excuse contravenes any requirement of the order he shall be guilty of an offence against this Part of this Act.

(7)   The magistrates' court may, after giving the local authority in whose area the premises are situated an opportunity of being heard, direct the local authority to do anything which the court has power under the preceding subsection to require the person convicted to do, either instead of, or in addition to, imposing any requirement on that person.

(8)   A consent given under this section shall contain a statement to the effect that the consent does not of itself constitute any ground of defence against any proceedings instituted under . . . [. . . section 82 of the Environmental Protection Act 1990 . . .].

[7]

NOTES
    Sub-s (8): words omitted repealed by the Environment Act 1995, s 120, Sch 24; words in square brackets added by the Environmental Protection Act 1990, s 162(1), Sch 15, para 15(1), (4).

66 Reduction of noise levels

(1)   If it appears to the local authority—
    (a) that the level of noise emanating from any premises to which a noise abatement order applies is not acceptable having regard to the purposes for which the order was made; and
    (b) that a reduction in that level is practicable at reasonable cost and would afford a public benefit,
the local authority may serve a notice on the person responsible.

(2)   The notice shall require that person—
   (a) to reduce the level of noise emanating from the premises to such level as may be specified in the notice;
   (b) to prevent any subsequent increase in the level of noise emanating from those premises without the consent of the local authority; and
   (c) to take such steps as may be specified in the notice to achieve those purposes.

(3)   A notice under this section (in this Part of this Act referred to as a "noise reduction notice") shall specify a time, not being less than six months from the date of service of the notice, within which the noise level is to be reduced to the specified level and, where the notice specifies any steps necessary to achieve that purpose, within which those steps shall be taken.

(4)   A noise reduction notice may specify particular times, or particular days, during which the noise level is to be reduced, and may require the noise level to be reduced to different levels for different times or days.

(5)   A notice under this section shall take effect whether or not a consent under the preceding section authorises a level of noise higher than that specified in the notice.

(6)   The local authority shall record particulars of a noise reduction notice in the noise level register.

(7)   A person who is served with a noise reduction notice may, within three months of the date of service, appeal to a magistrates' court against the notice.

(8)   A person who without reasonable excuse contravenes a noise reduction notice shall be guilty of an offence against this Part of this Act.

(9)   In proceedings for an offence under the preceding subsection in respect of noise caused in the course of a trade or business, it shall be a defence to prove that the best practicable means had been used for preventing, or for counteracting the effect of, the noise.

[8]

67 New buildings, etc

(1)   Where it appears to the local authority—
   (a) that a building is going to be constructed and that a noise abatement order will apply to it when it is erected; or
   (b) that any premises will, as the result of any works, become premises to which a noise abatement order applies,

the local authority may, on the application of the owner or occupier of the premises or a person who satisfies the authority that he is negotiating to acquire an interest in the premises or on its own initiative, determine the level of noise which will be acceptable as that emanating from the premises.

(2)   The local authority shall record in the noise level register the level of noise determined under this section for any premises.

(3)   The local authority shall give notice of its intention to the applicant or, in the case of a decision made on its own initiative, to the owner or the occupier of the premises, and the recipient of the notice may appeal to the Secretary of State against that decision within three months of the date on which the local authority notifies him of that decision; and it shall be the duty of the local authority to act in accordance with the decision of the Secretary of State on the appeal.

(4)   If within the period of two months beginning with the date when the local authority receives an application in pursuance of subsection (1) of this section, the

authority has not given notice to the applicant of its decision on the application, the authority shall be deemed to have given him notice on the expiration of that period that it has decided not to make a determination in pursuance of the application; and the applicant may accordingly appeal against the decision to the Secretary of State in pursuance of the preceding subsection.

(5)   Where at any time after the coming into force of a noise abatement order any premises become premises to which the order applies as a result of the construction of a building or as a result of any works carried out on the premises but no level of noise has been determined under this section as respects the premises, section 66 of this Act shall apply as if—
   (a) paragraph (b) of subsection (1) were omitted; and
   (b) three months were substituted for six months in subsection (3); and
   (c) subsection (9) were omitted.

                                                                              [9]

Noise from plant or machinery

68 Noise from plant or machinery

(1)   Provision may be made by regulations—
   (a) for requiring the use on or in connection with any plant or machinery of devices or arrangements for reducing the noise caused by the plant or machinery;
   (b) for limiting the level of noise which may be caused by any plant or machinery when used for works to which section 60 of this Act applies or which may be caused outside a factory within the meaning of the Factories Act 1961 by the use of plant or machinery in the factory;
and regulations under this section may apply standards, specifications, descriptions or tests laid down in documents not forming part of the regulations.

(2)   It shall be the duty of the Secretary of State, before he makes regulations under this section, to consult persons appearing to him to represent producers and users of plant and machinery with a view to ensuring that the regulations do not contain requirements which in his opinion would be impracticable or involve unreasonable expense.

(3)   Any person who contravenes or causes or permits another person to contravene regulations under this section shall be guilty of an offence against this Part of this Act; but in any proceedings for a contravention of regulations made in pursuance of paragraph (a) of subsection (1) of this section it shall be a defence to prove that means were used for the purpose of reducing the noise in question which were not less effective for that purpose than the means required by the regulations.

(4)   Without prejudice to the generality of section 104(1)(a) of this Act, different regulations may be made under this section for different localities, and it shall be the duty of each local authority to enforce the provisions of regulations under this section within its area; but nothing in this section shall be taken to authorise a local authority in Scotland to institute proceedings for any offence.

(5)   Nothing in this section or in regulations under this section shall be construed as derogating from any other provision of this Part of this Act.

                                                                             [10]

Supplemental

69 Execution of works by local authority

(1)   This section applies—
   (a) ...
   (b) to a noise reduction notice; and

(c) to an order of a magistrates' court under . . . section 65(6) of this Act,

being a notice or order which requires any person to execute any works.

(2)   If that person fails to execute all or any of the works in accordance with the notice or order, the local authority may execute those works.

(3)   Where a local authority execute works in pursuance of—
   (a) . . . section 65(7) of this Act; or
   (b) this section,

the local authority may recover from the person in default the expenditure incurred by the local authority in executing the works, except such of the expenditure as that person shows was unnecessary in the circumstances.

In this and the following subsection "the person in default" means—
   (i) . . . ,
   (ii) in a case under section 65(7), the person convicted of an offence under subsection (5) of that section, and
   (iii) in any other case, the person to whom the notice or order applies.

(4)   In proceedings to recover any amount due to a local authority under the preceding subsection in respect of works executed by the local authority in pursuance of this section, it shall not be open to the person in default to raise any question which he could have raised on an appeal against the notice or order.

[11]

NOTES

Sub-ss (1), (3): words omitted repealed by the Environmental Protection Act 1990, s 162(2), Sch 16, Pt III, and by the Environment Act 1995, s 120, Sch 24.

70 Appeals to Secretary of State and magistrates' court

(1)   Where any provision in this Part of this Act provides for an appeal to a magistrates' court, the procedure shall be by way of complaint for an order and the Magistrates' Courts Act 1952 shall apply to the proceedings.

(2)   The Secretary of State may make regulations as to appeals under this Part of this Act to the Secretary of State or, subject to the preceding subsection, to magistrates' courts; and the regulations may in particular—
   (a) include provisions comparable to those in section 290 of the Public Health Act 1936 (appeals against notices requiring the execution of works);
   (b) prescribe the cases in which a notice under this Part of this Act is, or is not, to be suspended until the appeal is decided, or until some other stage in the proceedings;
   (c) prescribe the cases in which the decision on appeal may in some respects be less favourable to the appellant than the decision from which he is appealing;
   (d) prescribe the cases in which the appellant may claim that a notice should have been served on some other person and prescribe the procedure to be followed in those cases.

(3)   Regulations under this section may prescribe the procedure and practice as respect appeals to the Secretary of State under this Part of this Act, and in particular may make provision as respects—
   (a) the particulars to be included in the notice of appeal;
   (b) the persons on whom notice of appeal is to be served and the particulars, if any, to accompany the notice; and
   (c) the abandonment of an appeal.

(4)   In entertaining any appeal under this Part of this Act the Secretary of State, or as the case may be the magistrates' court, shall have regard to any duty imposed by law on the appellant which concerns the activities in the course of which the noise is emitted.

(5)   (*Applies to Scotland only.*)

[12]

NOTES

Regulations: the Control of Noise (Appeals) Regulations 1975, SI 1975/2116, as amended by SI 1990/2276. Magistrates' Courts Act 1952: repealed by the Magistrates' Courts Act 1980, s 154, Sch 9, and replaced by provisions of that Act.

71 Codes of practice for minimising noise

(1)   For the purpose of giving guidance on appropriate methods (including the use of specified types of plant or machinery) for minimising noise, the Secretary of State may—
   (a)   prepare and approve and issue such codes of practice as in his opinion are suitable for the purpose; and
   (b)   approve such codes of practice issued or proposed to be issued otherwise than by the Secretary of State as in the opinion of the Secretary of State are suitable for the purpose.

(2)   The Secretary of State shall under paragraph (a) or paragraph (b) of the preceding subsection approve a code of practice for the carrying out of works to which section 60 of this Act applies.

(3)   The powers conferred by this section on the Secretary of State shall be exercisable by order, and shall include power to vary or revoke a previous order under this section.

[13]

NOTES

Orders: the Control of Noise (Code of Practice on Noise for Ice-Cream Van Chimes Etc) Order 1981, SI 1981/1828; the Control of Noise (Code of Practice on Noise from Audible Intruder Alarms) Order 1981, SI 1981/1829; the Control of Noise (Code of Practice on Noise from Model Aircraft) Order 1981, SI 1981/1830; the Control of Noise (Codes of Practice for Construction and Open Sites) Order 1984, SI 1984/1992; the Control of Noise (Code of Practice for Construction and Open Sites) Order 1987, SI 1987/1730.

72 "Best practicable means"

(1)   This section shall apply for the construction of references in this Part of this Act to best practicable means.

(2)   In that expression "practicable" means reasonably practicable having regard among other things to local conditions and circumstances, to the current state of technical knowledge and to the financial implications.

(3)   The means to be employed include the design, installation, maintenance and manner and periods of operation of plant and machinery, and the design, construction and maintenance of buildings and acoustic structures.

(4)   The test of best practicable means is to apply only so far as compatible with any duty imposed by law, and in particular is to apply to statutory undertakers only so far as compatible with the duties imposed on them in their capacity of statutory undertakers.

(5)   The said test is to apply only so far as compatible with safety and safe working conditions, and with the exigencies of any emergency or unforeseeable circumstances.

(6)   Subject to the preceding provisions of this section, regard shall be had, in construing references to "best practicable means", to any relevant provision of a code of practice approved under the preceding section.

73 Interpretation and other supplementary provisions

(1)   Except where the context otherwise requires, in this Part of this Act—
"contravention" includes a failure to comply with the provision in question, and "contravene" shall be construed accordingly;
[. . . . .]
"local authority" means—
  (a) in England . . . , the council of a district or a London borough, the Common Council of the City of London, the Sub-Treasurer of the Inner Temple and the Under Treasurer of the Middle Temple;
  [(aa) in Wales, the council of a county or a county borough;] and
  (b) (*applies to Scotland only*);
"noise" includes vibration;
"noise abatement order" and "noise abatement zone" have the meanings given by section 63 of this Act;
"noise level register" has the meaning given by section 64(2) of this Act;
"noise reduction notice" has the meaning given by section 66(3) of this Act;
"person responsible", in relation to
  [(a)] the emission of noise, means the person to whose act, default or sufferance the noise is attributable;
[(b), (c) . . .]
[. . . . .]
"statutory undertakers" means persons authorised by any enactment to carry on any railway, light railway, tramway, road transport, water transport, canal, inland navigation, dock, harbour, pier or lighthouse undertaking, or any undertaking for the supply of . . . , [or hydraulic power], and includes the Post Office;
"work of engineering construction" means the construction, structural alteration, maintenance or repair of any railway line or siding or any dock, harbour, inland navigation, tunnel, bridge, viaduct, waterworks, reservoir, pipeline, aqueduct, sewer, sewage works or gas-holder.

(2)   The area of a local authority which includes part of the seashore shall also include for the purposes of this Part of this Act, except sections 62 to 67, the territorial sea lying seawards from that part of the shore; and—
  (a) . . .
  (b) this Part of this Act (except sections 62 to 67 and this subsection) shall have effect, in relation to any area included in the area of a local authority by virtue of this subsection—
    (i) as if references to premises and the occupier of premises included respectively a vessel and the master of a vessel, and
    (ii) with such other modifications, if any, as are prescribed.

(3)   Where more than one person is responsible for noise, this Part of this Act shall apply to each of those persons whether or not what any one of them is responsible for would by itself amount to a nuisance, or would result in a level of noise justifying action under this Part of this Act [. . .].

(4)   This Part of this Act does not apply to noise caused by aircraft other than model aircraft and does not confer functions on port health authorities.

NOTES

Sub-s (1): first and final definitions omitted inserted, in relation to Scotland only, by the Noise and Statutory Nuisance Act 1993, s 6, Sch 1, para 7(a), subsequently repealed by the Environment Act 1995, s 120, Sch 24; in definition "local authority" first words omitted repealed, and para (aa) inserted, by the Local Government (Wales) Act 1994, ss 22(3), 66(8), Sch 9, para 10(3), Sch 18; in definition "person responsible" para (a) numbered as such and paras (b), (c) added, in relation to Scotland only, by the Noise and Statutory Nuisance Act 1993, s 6, Sch 1, para 7(a), paras (b), (c) subsequently repealed by the Environment Act 1995, s 120, Sch 24; in definition "statutory undertakers" words omitted repealed by the Electricity Act 1989, s 12(4), Sch 18 and the Gas Act 1986, s 67(4), Sch 9, Pt I, words in square brackets substituted by the Water Act 1989, s 190, Sch 25, para 48.

Sub-s (2): para (a) repealed by the Local Government, Planning and Land Act 1980, ss 1(2), 194, Sch 2, Sch 34, Pt II.

Sub-s (3): words omitted added, in relation to Scotland only, by the Noise and Statutory Nuisance Act 1993, s 6, Sch 1, para 7(b), subsequently repealed by the Environment Act 1995, s 120, Sch 24.

The Post Office: as from 5 August 1984 this reference no longer includes a reference to British Telecommunications by virtue of the Telecommunications Act 1984, s 109, Sch 4, para 3.

74 Penalties

(1) [. . .] A person guilty of an offence against this Part of this Act shall be liable on summary conviction [to a fine not exceeding level 5 on the standard scale] together, in any case, with a further fine not exceeding £50 for each day on which the offence continues after the conviction.

(2) In determining whether an offence is a second or subsequent offence against this Part of this Act, account shall be taken of any offence—
   (a) under section 24 of the Public Health (Scotland) Act 1897 by way of contravening a decree or interdict relating to noise; or
   (b) under section 95 of the Public Health Act 1936 by way of contravening a nuisance order relating to noise[; or
   (c) under section 80(4) of the Environmental Protection Act 1990],

as if it were an offence against this Part of this Act.

[16]

NOTES

Sub-s (1): words omitted inserted, in relation to Scotland only, by the Noise and Statutory Nuisance Act 1993, s 6, Sch 1, para 8, subsequently repealed by the Environment Act 1995, s 120, Sch 24; enhanced penalty on a subsequent conviction now abolished, maximum fine on any conviction increased and converted to level 5 on the standard scale by the Criminal Justice Act 1982, ss 35, 37, 38, 46.

Sub-s (2): words in square brackets inserted by the Environmental Protection Act 1990, s 162(1), Sch 15, para 15(5).

75–84 *((Pt IV) Repealed by the Clean Air Act 1993, s 67(3), Sch 6.)*

PART V
SUPPLEMENTARY PROVISIONS

Legal proceedings

85 Appeals to Crown Court or Court of Session against decisions of magistrates' court or sheriff

(1) An appeal against any decision of a magistrates' court in pursuance of this Act (other than a decision made in criminal proceedings) shall lie to the Crown

Court at the instance of any party to the proceedings in which the decision was given if such an appeal does not lie to the Crown Court by virtue of any other enactment.

(2)   (*Applies to Scotland only.*)

(3)   Where a person appeals to the Crown Court or the Court of Session against a decision of a magistrates' court or the sheriff dismissing an appeal against a notice served in pursuance of this Act which was suspended pending determination of that appeal, the notice shall again be suspended pending the determination of the appeal to the Crown Court or Court of Session.

[17]

86   (*Repealed by the Water Act 1989, s 190(3), Sch 27, Pt I.*)

87 Miscellaneous provisions relating to legal proceedings

(1)   When an offence under this Act which has been committed by a body corporate is proved to have been committed with the consent or connivance of, or to be attributable to any neglect on the part of, any director, manager, secretary or other similar officer of the body corporate or any person who was purporting to act in any such capacity, he as well as the body corporate shall be guilty of that offence and be liable to be proceeded against and punished accordingly.

Where the affairs of a body corporate are managed by its members the preceding provisions of this subsection shall apply in relation to the acts and defaults of a member in connection with his functions of management as if he were a director of the body corporate.

(2)   Where the commission by any person of an offence under this Act is due to the act or default of some other person, that other person shall be guilty of the offence; and a person may be charged with and convicted of an offence by virtue of this subsection whether or not proceedings for the offence are taken against any other person.

(3)   . . .

(4)   Where an appeal against a decision of a relevant authority lies to a magistrates court by virtue of any provision of this Act, it shall be the duty of the authority to include in any document by which it notifies the decision to the person concerned a statement indicating that such an appeal lies as aforesaid and specifying the time within which it must be brought.

(5)   Where on an appeal to any court against or arising out of a decision of a relevant authority in pursuance of this Act the court varies or reverses the decision it shall be the duty of the authority to act in accordance with the court's decision.

(6)   A judge of any court and a justice of the peace shall not be disqualified from acting in cases arising under this Act by reason of his being, as one of several ratepayers or as one of any other class of persons, liable in common with the others to contribute to or be benefited by any rate or fund out of which any expenses of a relevant authority are to be defrayed.

[18]–[19]

NOTES

Sub-s (3): repealed in part by the Environment Act 1995, s 120, Sch 24, and by the Criminal Law Act 1977, s 65, Sch 13, remainder applies to Scotland only.

88–90   (*S 88 outside the scope of this work; ss 89, 90 relate to financial matters, so far as unrepealed.*)

Miscellaneous

91 Rights of entry and inspection, etc

(1)   Any person authorised in writing in that behalf by a relevant authority may at any reasonable time—
  (a) enter upon any land or vessel for the purpose of—
     (i) performing any function conferred on the authority or that person by virtue of this Act, or
     (ii) determining whether, and if so in what manner, such a function should be performed, or
     (iii) determining whether any provision of this Act or of an instrument made by virtue of this Act is being complied with;
  (b) carry out such inspections, measurements and tests on the land or vessel or of any articles on it and take away such samples of the land or articles as he considers appropriate for such a purpose.

(2)   If it is shown to the satisfaction of a justice of the peace on sworn information in writing—
  (a) that admission to any land or vessel which a person is entitled to enter in pursuance of the preceding subsection has been refused to that person or that refusal is apprehended or that the land or vessel is unoccupied or that the occupier is temporarily absent or that the case is one of emergency or that an application for admission would defeat the object of the entry; and
  (b) that there is reasonable ground for entry upon the land or vessel for the purpose for which entry is required,

then, subject to the following subsection, the justice may by warrant under his hand authorise that person to enter the land or vessel, if need be by force.

(3)   A justice of the peace shall not issue a warrant in pursuance of the preceding subsection in respect of any land or vessel unless he is satisfied—
  (a) that admission to the land or vessel in pursuance of subsection (1) of this section was sought after not less than seven days notice of the intended entry had been served on the occupier; or
  (b) that admission to the land or vessel in pursuance of that subsection was sought in an emergency and was refused by or on behalf of the occupier; or
  (c) that the land or vessel is unoccupied; or
  (d) that an application for admission to the land or vessel would defeat the object of the entry.

(4)   A warrant issued in pursuance of this section shall continue in force until the purpose for which the entry is required has been satisfied.

(5)   (*Applies to Scotland only.*)

[20]

92 Provisions supplementary to s 91

(1)   A person authorised to enter upon any land or vessel in pursuance of the preceding section shall, if so required, produce evidence of his authority before he enters upon the land or vessel.

(2) A person so authorised may take with him on to the land or vessel in question such other persons and such equipment as may be necessary.

(3) Admission to any land or vessel used for residential purposes and admission with heavy equipment to any other land or vessel shall not, except in an emergency or in a case where the land or vessel is unoccupied, be demanded as of right in pursuance of subsection (1) of the preceding section unless a notice of the intended entry has been served on the occupier not less than seven days before the demand.

(4) A person who, in the exercise of powers conferred on him by virtue of the preceding section or this section, enters upon any land or vessel which is unoccupied or of which the occupier is temporarily absent shall leave the land or vessel as effectually secured against trespassers as he found it.

(5) It shall be the duty of a relevant authority to make full compensation to any person who has sustained damage by reason of—
(a) the exercise by a person authorised by the authority of any powers conferred on the person so authorised by virtue of the preceding section or this section; or
(b) the failure of a person so authorised to perform the duty imposed on him by the preceding subsection,

except where the damage is attributable to the default of the person who sustained it; and any dispute as to a person's entitlement to compensation in pursuance of this subsection or as to the amount of the compensation shall be determined by arbitration.

(6) A person who wilfully obstructs another person acting in the exercise of any powers conferred on the other person by virtue of the preceding section or this section shall be guilty of an offence and liable on summary conviction to a fine not exceeding [level 3 on the standard scale].

(7) In the preceding section and this section any reference to an emergency is a reference to a case where a person requiring entry to any land or vessel has reasonable cause to believe that circumstances exist which are likely to endanger life or health and that immediate entry to the land or vessel is necessary to verify the existence of those circumstances or to ascertain their cause or to effect a remedy.

[21]

NOTES

Sub-s (6): maximum fine increased and converted to a level on the standard scale by the Criminal Justice Act 1982, ss 37, 38, 46.

---

93 Power of authorities to obtain information

(1) Subject to the following subsection, a relevant authority may serve on any person a notice requiring him to furnish to the authority, within a period or at times specified in the notice and in a form so specified, any information so specified which the authority reasonably considers that it needs for the purposes of any function conferred on the authority by this Act.

(2) Provision may be made by regulations for restricting the information which may be required in pursuance of the preceding subsection and for determining the form in which the information is to be so required.

[(3) A person who—
(a) fails without reasonable excuse to comply with the requirements of a notice served on him in pursuance of this section; or

(b) in furnishing any information in compliance with such a notice, makes any statement which he knows to be false or misleading in a material particular or recklessly makes any statement which is false or misleading in a material particular,

shall be guilty of an offence.

(3A) A person guilty of an offence under this section shall be liable—
(a) on summary conviction, to a fine not exceeding the statutory maximum; or
(b) on conviction on indictment, to a fine or to imprisonment for a term not exceeding two years, or to both.]

(4) (*Applies to Scotland only.*)

[22]

NOTES

Sub-ss (3), (3A): substituted, for original sub-s (3), by the Environment Act 1995, s 112, Sch 19, para 1(3).

94 Prohibition of disclosure of information

(1) If a person discloses information relating to any trade secret used in carrying on a particular undertaking and the information has been given to him or obtained by him by virtue of this Act he shall, subject to the following subsection, be guilty of an offence and liable on summary conviction to a fine not exceeding [level 5 on the standard scale].

(2) A person shall not be guilty of an offence under the preceding subsection by virtue of the disclosure of any information if—
(a) the disclosure is made—
(i) in the performance of his duty, or
(ii) in pursuance of section 79(1)(b) of this Act, or
(iii) with the consent in writing of a person having a right to disclose the information; or
(b) the information is of a kind prescribed for the purposes of this paragraph and, if regulations made for those purposes provide that information of that kind may only be disclosed in pursuance of the regulations to prescribed persons, the disclosure is to a prescribed person.

(3) (*Applies to Scotland only.*)

[23]

NOTES

Sub-s (1): maximum fine increased and converted to a level on the standard scale by the Criminal Justice Act 1982, ss 37, 38, 46.

95 (*Relates to service of documents.*)

96 Local inquiries

(1) The Secretary of State may cause a local inquiry to be held in any case in which he considers it appropriate for such an inquiry to be held either in connection with a provision of this Act or with a view to preventing or dealing with pollution [other than air pollution] or noise at any place.

(2) Subsections (2) to (5) of section 250 of the Local Government Act 1972 (which contain supplementary provisions with respect to local inquiries held in pursuance of that section) shall, without prejudice to the generality of subsection (1) of that section, apply to inquiries in England and Wales in pursuance of the preceding subsection as they apply to inquiries in pursuance of that section . . .

(3)   *(Applies to Scotland only.)*

NOTES
   Sub-s (1): words in square brackets inserted by the Clean Air Act 1993, s 67(1), Sch 4, para 2.
   Sub-s (2): words omitted repealed by the Water Act 1989, s 190(3), Sch 27, Pt I.

97 Default powers

(1)   If the Secretary of State is satisfied that any other relevant authority has failed to perform any functions which it ought to have performed, he may make an order declaring the authority to be in default.

(2)   An order made by virtue of the preceding subsection which declares an authority to be in default may, for the purpose of remedying the default, direct the authority (hereafter in this section referred to as "the defaulting authority") to perform such of its functions as are specified in the order and may specify the manner in which and the time or times within which those functions are to be performed by the authority.

(3)   If the defaulting authority fails to comply with any direction contained in such an order the Secretary of State may, instead of enforcing the order by mandamus, make an order transferring to himself such of the functions of the authority as he thinks fit.

(4)   Where any functions of the defaulting authority are transferred in pursuance of the preceding subsection, the amount of any expenses which the Secretary of State certifies were incurred by him in performing those functions shall on demand be paid to him by the defaulting authority.

(5)   Any expenses which in pursuance of the preceding subsection are required to be paid by the defaulting authority in respect of any functions transferred in pursuance of this section shall be defrayed by the authority in the like manner, and shall be debited to the like account, as if the functions had not been transferred and the expenses had been incurred by the authority in performing them; and the authority shall have the like powers for the purpose of raising any money required in pursuance of this subsection as the authority would have had for the purpose of raising money required for defraying expenses incurred for the purposes of the functions in question.

(6)   An order transferring any functions of the defaulting authority in pursuance of subsection (3) of this section may provide for the transfer to the Secretary of State of such of the property, rights, liabilities and obligations of the authority as he considers appropriate; and where such an order is revoked the Secretary of State may, by the revoking order or a subsequent order, make such provision as he considers appropriate with respect to any property, rights, liabilities and obligations held by him for the purposes of the transferred functions.

(7)   The Secretary of State may by order vary or revoke any order previously made by him in pursuance of this section.

(8)   In this section "functions", in relation to an authority, means functions conferred on the authority by virtue of this Act.

(9)   This section shall not apply to Scotland.

[25]

98 Interpretation of Part V

In this Part of this Act—
   "functions" includes powers and duties; and

"relevant authority" means—
- (a) in England . . . , the Secretary of State, . . . a county council, . . ., a district council, a London borough council, the Common Council of the City of London, the Sub-Treasurer of the Inner Temple and the Under Treasurer of the Middle Temple [and, for the purposes of sections 91 to 93 of this Act, a sewerage undertaker][, any authority established by the Waste Regulation and Disposal (Authorities) Order 1985]; and
- [(aa) in Wales, the Secretary of State, a county council or a county borough council and, for the purposes of sections 91 to 93 of this Act, a sewerage undertaker; and]
- (b) (*applies to Scotland only*).

[26]

NOTES
In definition "relevant authority"words omitted in the first place repealed, and para (aa) inserted, by the Local Government (Wales) Act 1994, ss 22(3), 66(8), Sch 9, para 10(4), Sch 18, words omitted in the second place repealed by the Water Act 1989, s 190, Sch 27, Pt I, words omitted in the third place repealed by the Local Government Act 1985, s 102, Sch 17; words in first pair of square brackets inserted by the Water Act 1989, s 190(1), Sch 25, para 48, words in second pair of square brackets inserted by the Waste Regulation and Disposal (Authorities) Order 1985, SI 1985/1884, art 5, Sch 2, para 12.

PART VI
MISCELLANEOUS AND GENERAL

99–103 (*Relate to alteration of penalties (s 99); disposal of waste, etc, by the Atomic Energy Authority (s 101); power to give effect to international agreements (s 102); s 100 repealed by the Environmental Protection Act 1990, s 162(2), (5), Sch 16, Pt IX; s 103 repealed by the Clean Air Act 1993, s 67(3), Sch 6.*)

General

104   (*Relates to orders and regulations, so far as unrepealed.*)

105 Interpretation etc general

(1)   In this Act—

. . . . .

"county"[, "county borough"] and "district", except in relation to Scotland, have the same meanings as in the Local Government Act 1972;
"mine" and "quarry" have the same meanings as in the Mines and Quarries Act 1954;
"modifications" includes additions, omissions and amendments and "modify" and cognate expressions shall be construed accordingly;
"notice" means notice in writing;
"owner", except in relation to Scotland, means the person for the time being receiving the rackrent of the premises in connection with which the word is used, whether on his own account or as agent or trustee for another person, or who would so receive the rackrent if the premises were let at a rackrent;
"premises" includes land;
"prescribed" means prescribed by regulations;
"regulations" means regulations made by the Secretary of State;
[. . . . .]

. . . . .

(2)   Except so far as this Act expressly provides otherwise and subject to the provisions of section 33 of the Interpretation Act 1889 (which relates to offences under two or more laws), nothing in this Act—

(a) confers a right of action in any civil proceedings (other than proceedings for the recovery of a fine) in respect of any contravention of this Act or an instrument made in pursuance of this Act;

(b) affects any restriction imposed by or under any other enactment, whether public, local or private; or

(c) derogates from any right of action or other remedy (whether civil or criminal) in proceedings instituted otherwise than under this Act.

(3) In so far as any interest in Crown land is not an interest belonging to Her Majesty or a Crown interest or a Duchy interest, this Act shall apply to the land as if it were not Crown land; and expressions used in this subsection and [subsection (1) of section 293 of the Town and Country Planning Act 1990] or, in relation to Scotland, [subsections (1) to (3) of section 242 of the Town and Country Planning (Scotland) Act 1997] have the same meanings in this subsection as in that subsection.

(4) References in this Act to any enactment are references to it as amended by or under any other enactment.

[27]

NOTES

Sub-s (1): definitions omitted outside the scope of this work or apply to Scotland only; in definition beginning "county" words in square brackets inserted by the Local Government (Wales) Act 1994, s 22(3), Sch 9, para 10(5);

Sub-s (3): words in first pair of square brackets substituted by the Planning (Consequential Provisions) Act 1990, s 4, Sch 2, para 31(2); words in second pair of square brackets substituted by the Planning (Consequential Provisions) (Scotland) Act 1997, s 4, Sch 2, para 23(2).

106–108 (*s 106 applies to Scotland only; s 107 relates to the application to the Isles of Scilly; s 108 relates to minor and consequential amendments of enactments and repeals, so far as unrepealed.*)

109 Short title, commencement and extent

(1) This Act may be cited as the Control of Pollution Act 1974.

(2) This Act shall come into force on such day as the Secretary of State may by order appoint; and—

(a) without prejudice to the generality of section 104(1)(a) of this Act, different days may be appointed in pursuance of this subsection for different provisions of this Act and for such different purposes of the same provision as may be specified in the order;

(b) any provision appointing a day in pursuance of this subsection may be revoked or varied by an order made by the Secretary of State which comes into force before that day.

(3) This Act, except sections . . . 100 and 101 and this section, does not extend to Northern Ireland.

[28]

NOTES

Sub-s (3): figures omitted repealed by the Clean Air Act 1993, s 67(3), Sch 6.

[SCHEDULE 1
NOISE ABATEMENT ZONES

Section 63(4)

1. Before making a noise abatement order the local authority—

(a) shall serve on every owner, lessee and occupier (other than tenants for a month or any period less than a month) of any of the premises within the area and of a class to which the order will relate; and

   (b)   shall publish in the London Gazette and once at least in each of two successive weeks in some newspaper circulating in the area to which the order will relate,

a notice complying with the requirements set out in the following paragraph.

2.   The requirements referred to in the preceding paragraph are that the notice—
   (a)   shall state that the local authority propose to make the order, and its general effect;
   (b)   shall specify a place in the area of the local authority where a copy of the order and of any map or plan referred to in it may be inspected by any person free of charge at all reasonable times during a period of not less than six weeks from the date of the last publication of the notice; and
   (c)   shall state that within the said period any person who will be affected by the order may by notice in writing to the local authority object to the making of the order.

3.—(1) If an objection is duly made to the local authority within the said period, and is not withdrawn, the local authority shall not make the order without first considering the objection.

   (2) The local authority may make the order without complying with sub-paragraph (1) of this paragraph if they are satisfied that compliance is unnecessary having regard—
   (a)   to the nature of the premises to which the order will relate when it comes into force; or
   (b)   to the nature of the interests of the persons who have made objections which have not been withdrawn.

   (3) Where the order varies or revokes a previous order, the local authority may, in acting under this paragraph disregard any objection to the order which in their opinion amounts in substance to an objection which was made to the previous order.

4.—(1) Subject to paragraph 5 below, an order shall come into operation on such date after it is made as may be specified in it.

   (2) Except in the case of an order revoking an existing order or varying an existing order by excluding from it any specified class of premises, the date specified under sub-paragraph (1) above shall not be a date earlier than one month from the date on which the order is made.

5.   If, before the date on which the order is to come into operation, the local authority—
   (a)   passes a resolution postponing the coming into operation of the order; and
   (b)   publishes a notice stating the effect of the resolution in the London Gazette and once at least in each of two successive weeks in a newspaper circulating in the area to which the order relates,

the order shall, unless there is a further postponement under paragraph (a) above, come into operation on the date specified in the resolution.]

[29]

NOTES

   Substituted by the Local Government, Planning and Land Act 1980, s 1(2), Sch 2, para 18.

(Schs 1A–4 outside the scope of this work.)

WILDLIFE AND COUNTRYSIDE ACT 1981

(1981 c 69)

ARRANGEMENT OF SECTIONS

PART I
WILDLIFE

Protection of birds

PART II
NATURE CONSERVATION, COUNTRYSIDE AND NATIONAL PARKS

An Act to repeal and re-enact with amendments the Protection of Birds Acts 1954 to 1967 and the Conservation of Wild Creatures and Wild Plants Act 1975; to prohibit certain methods of killing or taking wild animals; to amend the law relating to protection of certain mammals; to restrict the introduction of certain animals and plants; to amend the Endangered Species (Import and Export) Act 1976; to amend the law relating to nature conservation, the countryside and National Parks and to make provision with respect to the Countryside Commission; to amend the law relating to public rights of way; and for connected purposes

[30 October 1981]

PART I
WILDLIFE

NOTES

Natural habitats: Pt I of this Act should be read in conjunction with the Conservation (Natural Habitats, &c) Regulations 1994, SI 1994/2716 at **[988]** (and in particular reg 3(1), (2) thereof), which make provision for implementing Council Directive 92/43/EEC on the conservation of natural habitats and of wild fauna and flora.

Protection of birds

1 Protection of wild birds, their nests and eggs

(1)   Subject to the provisions of this Part, if any person intentionally—
  (a) kills, injures or takes any wild bird;
  (b) takes, damages or destroys the nest of any wild bird while that nest is in use or being built; or
  (c) takes or destroys an egg of any wild bird,
he shall be guilty of an offence.

(2)   Subject to the provisions of this Part, if any person has in his possession or control—
  (a) any live or dead wild bird or any part of, or anything derived from, such a bird; or
  (b) an egg of a wild bird or any part of such an egg,
he shall be guilty of an offence.

(3)   A person shall not be guilty of an offence under subsection (2) if he shows that—
  (a) the bird or egg had not been killed or taken, or had been killed or taken otherwise than in contravention of the relevant provisions; or
  (b) the bird, egg or other thing in his possession or control had been sold (whether to him or any other person) otherwise than in contravention of those provisions;

and in this subsection "the relevant provisions" means the provisions of this Part and of orders made under it and, in the case of a bird or other thing falling within subsection (2)(a), the provisions of the Protection of Birds Acts 1954 to 1967 and of orders made under those Acts.

(4)   Any person convicted of an offence under subsection (1) or (2) in respect of—

    (a) a bird included in Schedule 1 or any part of, or anything derived from, such a bird;

    (b) the nest of such a bird; or

    (c) an egg of such a bird or any part of such an egg, shall be liable to a special penalty.

(5)   Subject to the provisions of this Part, if any person intentionally—

    (a) disturbs any wild bird included in Schedule 1 while it is building a nest or is in, on or near a nest containing eggs or young; or

    (b) disturbs dependent young of such a bird,

he shall be guilty of an offence and liable to a special penalty.

(6)   In this section "wild bird" does not include any bird which is shown to have been bred in captivity.

(7)   Any reference in this Part to any bird included in Schedule 1 is a reference to any bird included in Part I and, during the close season for the bird in question, any bird included in Part II of that Schedule.

2 Exceptions to s 1

(1)   Subject to the provisions of this section, a person shall not be guilty of an offence under section 1 by reason of the killing or taking of a bird included in Part I of Schedule 2 outside the close season for that bird, or the injuring of such a bird outside that season in the course of an attempt to kill it.

(2)   Subject to the provisions of this section, an authorised person shall not be guilty of an offence under section 1 by reason of—

    (a) the killing or taking of a bird included in Part II of Schedule 2, or the injuring of such a bird in the course of an attempt to kill it;

    (b) the taking, damaging or destruction of a nest of such a bird; or

    (c) the taking or destruction of an egg of such a bird.

(3)   Subsections (1) and (2) shall not apply in Scotland on Sundays or on Christmas Day; and subsection (1) shall not apply on Sundays in any area of England and Wales which the Secretary of State may by order prescribe for the purposes of that subsection.

(4)   In this section and section 1 "close season" means—

    (a) in the case of capercaillie and (except in Scotland) woodcock, the period in any year commencing with 1st February and ending with 30th September;

    (b) in the case of snipe, the period in any year commencing with 1st February and ending with 11th August;

    (c) in the case of wild duck and wild geese in or over any area below high-water mark of ordinary spring tides, the period in any year commencing with 21st February and ending with 31st August;

    (d) in any other case, subject to the provisions of this Part, the period in any year commencing with 1st February and ending with 31st August.

(5)   The Secretary of State may by order made with respect to the whole or any specified part of Great Britain vary the close season for any wild bird specified in the order.

(6) If it appears to the Secretary of State expedient that any wild birds included in Part II of Schedule 1 or Part I of Schedule 2 should be protected during any period outside the close season for those birds, he may by order made with respect to the whole or any specified part of Great Britain declare any period (which shall not in the case of any order exceed fourteen days) as a period of special protection for those birds; and this section and section 1 shall have effect as if any period of special protection declared under this subsection for any birds formed part of the close season for those birds.

(7) Before making an order under subsection (6) the Secretary of State shall consult a person appearing to him to be a representative of persons interested in the shooting of birds of the kind proposed to be protected by the order.

[31]

3 Areas of special protection

(1) The Secretary of State may by order make provision with respect to any area specified in the order providing for all or any of the following matters, that is to say—
 (a) that any person who, within that area or any part of it specified in the order, at any time or during any period so specified, intentionally—
  (i) kills, injures or takes any wild bird or any wild bird so specified;
  (ii) takes, damages or destroys the nest of such a bird while that nest is in use or being built;
  (iii) takes or destroys an egg of such a bird;
  (iv) disturbs such a bird while it is building a nest or is in, on or near a nest containing eggs or young; or
  (v) disturbs dependent young of such a bird,
  shall be guilty of an offence under this section;
 (b) that any person who, except as may be provided in the order, enters into that area or any part of it specified in the order at any time or during any period so specified shall be guilty of an offence under this section;
 (c) that where any offence under this Part, or any such offence under this Part as may be specified in the order, is committed within that area, the offender shall be liable to a special penalty.

(2) An authorised person shall not by virtue of any such order be guilty of an offence by reason of—
 (a) the killing or taking of a bird included in Part II of Schedule 2, or the injuring of such a bird in the course of an attempt to kill it;
 (b) the taking, damaging or destruction of the nest of such a bird;
 (c) the taking or destruction of an egg of such a bird; or
 (d) the disturbance of such a bird or dependent young of such a bird.

(3) The making of any order under this section with respect to any area shall not affect the exercise by any person of any right vested in him, whether as owner, lessee or occupier of any land in that area or by virtue of a licence or agreement.

(4) Before making any order under this section the Secretary of State shall give particulars of the intended order either by notice in writing to every owner and every occupier of any land included in the area with respect to which the order is to be made or, where the giving of such a notice is in his opinion impracticable, by advertisement in a newspaper circulating in the [locality] in which that area is situated.

(5) The Secretary of State shall not make an order under this section unless—
 (a) all the owners and occupiers aforesaid have consented thereto;
 (b) no objections thereto have been made by any of those owners or occupiers before the expiration of a period of three months from the date of the giving of the notice or the publication of the advertisement; or
 (c) any such objections so made have been withdrawn.

[32]

NOTES

Sub-s (4): word in square brackets substituted by the Local Government (Wales) Act 1994, s 66(6), Sch 16, para 65(1).

4 Exceptions to ss 1 and 3

(1)   Nothing in section 1 or in any order made under section 3 shall make unlawful—
  (a) anything done in pursuance of a requirement by the Minister of Agriculture, Fisheries and Food or the Secretary of State under section 98 of the Agriculture Act 1947, or by the Secretary of State under section 39 of the Agriculture (Scotland) Act 1948;
  (b) anything done under, or in pursuance of an order made under, section 21 or 22 of the Animal Health Act 1981; or
  (c) except in the case of a wild bird included in Schedule 1 or the nest or egg of such a bird, anything done under, or in pursuance of an order made under, any other provision of the said Act of 1981.

(2)   Notwithstanding anything in the provisions of section 1 or any order made under section 3, a person shall not be guilty of an offence by reason of—
  (a) the taking of any wild bird if he shows that the bird had been disabled otherwise than by his unlawful act and was taken solely for the purpose of tending it and releasing it when no longer disabled;
  (b) the killing of any wild bird if he shows that the bird had been so seriously disabled otherwise than by his unlawful act that there was no reasonable chance of its recovering; or
  (c) any act made unlawful by those provisions if he shows that the act was the incidental result of a lawful operation and could not reasonably have been avoided.

(3)   Notwithstanding anything in the provisions of section 1 or any order made under section 3, an authorised person shall not be guilty of an offence by reason of the killing or injuring of any wild bird, other than a bird included in Schedule 1, if he shows that his action was necessary for the purpose of—
  (a) preserving public health or public or air safety;
  (b) preventing the spread of disease; or
  (c) preventing serious damage to livestock, foodstuffs for livestock, crops, vegetables, fruit, growing timber[, fisheries or inland waters].

[(4)   An authorised person shall not be regarded as showing that any action of his was necessary for a purpose mentioned in subsection (3)(c) unless he shows that as regards that purpose, there was no other satisfactory solution.

(5)   An authorised person shall not be entitled to rely on the defence provided by subsection (3)(c) as respects any action taken at any time for any purpose mentioned in that paragraph if it had become apparent, before that time, that that action would prove necessary for that purpose and either—
  (a) a licence under section 16 authorising that action had not been applied for by him as soon as reasonably practicable after that fact had become apparent; or
  (b) an application by him for such a licence had been determined.

(6)   An authorised person shall not be entitled to rely on the defence provided by subsection (3)(c) as respects any action taken at any time unless he notified the agriculture Minister as soon as reasonably practicable after that time that he had taken the action.]

[33]

NOTES
   Sub-s (3): words in square brackets substituted by the Wildlife and Countryside Act 1981 (Amendment) Regulations 1995, SI 1995/2825, reg 2(1).
   Sub-ss (4)–(6): added by SI 1995/2825, reg 2(2).

5 Prohibition of certain methods of killing or taking wild birds

(1)   Subject to the provisions of this Part, if any person—
   (a) sets in position any of the following articles, being an article which is of such a nature and is so placed as to be calculated to cause bodily injury to any wild bird coming into contact therewith, that is to say, any springe, trap, gin, snare, hook and line, any electrical device for killing, stunning or frightening or any poisonous, poisoned or stupefying substance;
   (b) uses for the purpose of killing or taking any wild bird any such article as aforesaid, whether or not of such a nature and so placed as aforesaid, or any net, baited board, bird-lime or substance of a like nature to bird-lime;
   (c) uses for the purpose of killing or taking any wild bird—
         (i)   any bow or crossbow;
         (ii) any explosive other than ammunition for a firearm;
         (iii) any automatic or semi-automatic weapon;
         (iv) any shot-gun of which the barrel has an internal diameter at the muzzle of more than one and three-quarter inches;
         (iv) any device for illuminating a target or any sighting device for night shooting;
         (vi) any form of artificial lighting or any mirror or other dazzling device;
         (vii) any gas or smoke not falling within paragraphs (a) and (b); or
         (viii) any chemical wetting agent;
   (d) uses as a decoy, for the purpose of killing or taking any wild bird, any sound recording or any live bird or other animal whatever which is tethered, or which is secured by means of braces or other similar appliances, or which is blind, maimed or injured; . . .
   (e) uses any mechanically propelled vehicle in immediate pursuit of a wild bird for the purpose of killing or taking that bird[; or
   (f) knowingly causes or permits to be done an act which is mentioned in the foregoing provisions of this subsection and which is not lawful under subsection (5),]
he shall be guilty of an offence and be liable to a special penalty.

(2)   Subject to subsection (3), the Secretary of State may by order, either generally or in relation to any kind of wild bird specified in the order, amend subsection (1) by adding any method of killing or taking wild birds or by omitting any such method which is mentioned in that subsection.

(3)   The power conferred by subsection (2) shall not be exercisable, except for the purpose of complying with an international obligation, in relation to any method of killing or taking wild birds which involves the use of a firearm.

(4)   In any proceedings under subsection (1)(a) it shall be a defence to show that the article was set in position for the purpose of killing or taking, in the interests of public health, agriculture, forestry, fisheries or nature conservation, any wild animals which could be lawfully killed or taken by those means and that he took all reasonable precautions to prevent injury thereby to wild birds.

[(4A)In any proceedings under subsection (1)(f) relating to an act which is mentioned in subsection (1)(a) it shall be a defence to show that the article was set in position for the purpose of killing or taking, in the interests of public health, agriculture, forestry, fisheries or nature conservation, any wild animals which could be lawfully killed or taken by those means and that he took or caused to be taken all reasonable precautions to prevent injury thereby to wild birds.]

(5)   Nothing in subsection (1) shall make unlawful—
  (a) the use of a cage-trap or net by an authorised person for the purpose of taking a bird included in Part II of Schedule 2;
  (b) the use of nets for the purpose of taking wild duck in a duck decoy which is shown to have been in use immediately before the passing of the Protection of Birds Act 1954; or
  (c) the use of a cage-trap or net for the purpose of taking any game bird if it is shown that the taking of the bird is solely for the purpose of breeding;

but nothing in this subsection shall make lawful the use of any net for taking birds in flight or the use for taking birds on the ground of any net which is projected or propelled otherwise than by hand.

[34]

NOTES
  Sub-s (1): word omitted from para (d) repealed, and para (f) added, by the Wildlife and Countryside (Amendment) Act 1991, s 1(2), (3).
  Sub-s (4A): inserted by the Wildlife and Countryside (Amendment) Act 1991, s 1(4).

6 Sale etc of live or dead wild birds, eggs etc

(1)   Subject to the provisions of this Part, if any person—
  (a) sells, offers or exposes for sale, or has in his possession or transports for the purpose of sale, any live wild bird other than a bird included in Part I of Schedule 3, or an egg of a wild bird or any part of such an egg; or
  (b) publishes or causes to be published any advertisement likely to be understood as conveying that he buys or sells, or intends to buy or sell, any of those things,

he shall be guilty of an offence.

(2)   Subject to the provisions of this Part, if any person who is not for the time being registered in accordance with regulations made by the Secretary of State—
  (a) sells, offers or exposes for sale, or has in his possession or transports for the purpose of sale, any dead wild bird other than a bird included in Part II or III of Schedule 3, or any part of, or anything derived from, such a wild bird; or
  (b) publishes or causes to be published any advertisement likely to be understood as conveying that he buys or sells, or intends to buy or sell, any of those things,

he shall be guilty of an offence.

(3)   Subject to the provisions of this Part, if any person shows or causes or permits to be shown for the purposes of any competition or in any premises in which a competition is being held—
  (a) any live wild bird other than a bird included in Part I of Schedule 3; or
  (b) any live bird one of whose parents was such a wild bird,

he shall be guilty of an offence.

(4)   Any person convicted of an offence under this section in respect of—
  (a) a bird included in Schedule 1 or any part of, or anything derived from, such a bird; or
  (b) an egg of such bird or any part of such an egg,

shall be liable to a special penalty.

(5)   Any reference in this section to any bird included in Part I of Schedule 3 is a reference to any bird included in that Part which was bred in captivity and has been ringed or marked in accordance with regulations made by the Secretary of State; and regulations so made may make different provision for different birds or different provisions of this section.

(6)   Any reference in this section to any bird included in Part II or III of Schedule 3 is a reference to any bird included in Part II and, during the period commencing with 1st September in any year and ending with 28th February of the following year, any bird included in Part III of that Schedule.

(7)   The power of the Secretary of State to make regulations under subsection (2) shall include power—
  (a) to impose requirements as to the carrying out by a person registered in accordance with the regulations of any act which, apart from the registration, would constitute an offence under this section; and
  (b) to provide that any contravention of the regulations shall constitute such an offence.

(8)   Regulations under subsection (2) shall secure that no person shall become or remain registered—
  (a) within five years of his having been convicted of an offence under this Part for which a special penalty is provided; or
  (b) within three years of his having been convicted of any other offence under this Part so far as it relates to the protection of birds or other animals or any offence involving their ill-treatment,

no account being taken for this purpose of a conviction which has become spent by virtue of the Rehabilitation of Offenders Act 1974.

[(8A) The Secretary of State may charge such reasonable sum (if any) as he may determine in respect of any registration effected in accordance with regulations under subsection (2).]

(9)   Any person authorised in writing by the Secretary of State may, at any reasonable time and (if required to do so) upon producing evidence that he is authorised, enter and inspect any premises where a registered person keeps any wild birds for the purpose of ascertaining whether an offence under this section is being, or has been, committed on those premises.

(10) Any person who intentionally obstructs a person acting in the exercise of the power conferred by subsection (9) shall be guilty of an offence.

[35]

NOTES

Sub-s (8A): inserted by the Birds (Registration Charges) Act 1997, s 1(1).

Regulations: the Wildlife and Countryside (Registration to Sell, etc, Certain Dead Wild Birds) Regulations 1982, SI 1982/1219, as amended by SI 1991/479; the Wildlife and Countryside (Ringing of Certain Birds) Regulations 1982, SI 1982/1220.

---

7 Registration etc of certain captive birds

(1)   If any person keeps or has in his possession or under his control any bird included in Schedule 4 which has not been registered and ringed or marked in accordance with regulations made by the Secretary of State, he shall be guilty of an offence and be liable to a special penalty.

(2)   The power of the Secretary of State to make regulations under subsection (1) shall include power—
  (a) to impose requirements which must be satisfied in relation to a bird included in Schedule 4 before it can be registered in accordance with the regulations; and
  (b) to make different provision for different birds or different descriptions of birds.

[(2A) The Secretary of State may charge such reasonable sum (if any) as he may determine in respect of any registration effected in accordance with regulations under subsection (1).]

(3) If any person keeps or has in his possession or under his control any bird included in Schedule 4—
  (a) within five years of his having been convicted of an offence under this Part for which a special penalty is provided; or
  (b) within three years of his having been convicted of any other offence under this Part so far as it relates to the protection of birds or other animals or any offence involving their ill-treatment,
he shall be guilty of an offence.

(4) If any person knowingly disposes of or offers to dispose of any bird included in Schedule 4 to any person—
  (a) within five years of that person's having been convicted of such an offence as is mentioned in paragraph (a) of subsection (3); or
  (b) within three years of that person's having been convicted of such an offence as is mentioned in paragraph (b) of that subsection,
he shall be guilty of an offence.

(5) No account shall be taken for the purposes of subsections (3) and (4) of any conviction which has become spent for the purpose of the Rehabilitation of Offenders Act 1974.

(6) Any person authorised in writing by the Secretary of State may, at any reasonable time and (if required to do so) upon producing evidence that he is authorised, enter and inspect any premises where any birds included in Schedule 4 are kept for the purpose of ascertaining whether an offence under this section is being, or has been, committed on those premises.

(7) Any person who intentionally obstructs a person acting in the exercise of the power conferred by subsection (6) shall be guilty of an offence.

[36]

NOTES

Sub-s (2A): inserted by the Birds (Registration Charges) Act 1997, s 1(2).
Regulations: the Wildlife and Countryside (Registration and Ringing of Certain Captive Birds) Regulations 1982, SI 1982/1221, as amended by SI 1991/478, SI 1994/1152; the Marketing Authorisations for Veterinary Medicinal Products Regulations 1994, SI 1994/3142, as amended by SI 1997/654.

8 Protection of captive birds

(1) If any person keeps or confines any bird whatever in any cage or other receptacle which is not sufficient in height, length or breadth to permit the bird to stretch its wings freely, he shall be guilty of an offence and be liable to a special penalty.

(2) Subsection (1) does not apply to poultry, or to the keeping or confining of any bird—
  (a) while that bird is in the course of conveyance, by whatever means;
  (b) while that bird is being shown for the purposes of any public exhibition or competition if the time during which the bird is kept or confined for those purposes does not in the aggregate exceed 72 hours; or
  (c) while that bird is undergoing examination or treatment by a veterinary surgeon or veterinary practitioner.

(3) Every person who—
  (a) promotes, arranges, conducts, assists in, receives money for, or takes part in, any event whatever at or in the course of which captive birds are liberated by hand or by any other means whatever for the purpose of being shot immediately after their liberation; or
  (b) being the owner or occupier of any land, permits that land to be used for the purposes of such an event,
shall be guilty of an offence and be liable to a special penalty.

[37]

Protection of other animals

9 Protection of certain wild animals

(1)   Subject to the provisions of this Part, if any person intentionally kills, injures or takes any wild animal included in Schedule 5, he shall be guilty of an offence.

(2)   Subject to the provisions of this Part, if any person has in his possession or control any live or dead wild animal included in Schedule 5 or any part of, or anything derived from, such an animal, he shall be guilty of an offence.

(3)   A person shall not be guilty of an offence under subsection (2) if he shows that—
  (a) the animal had not been killed or taken, or had been killed or taken otherwise than in contravention of the relevant provisions; or
  (b) the animal or other thing in his possession or control had been sold (whether to him or any other person) otherwise than in contravention of those provisions;

and in this subsection "the relevant provisions" means the provisions of this Part and of the Conservation of Wild Creatures and Wild Plants Act 1975.

(4)   Subject to the provisions of this Part, if any person intentionally—
  (a) damages or destroys, or obstructs access to, any structure or place which any wild animal included in Schedule 5 uses for shelter or protection; or
  (b) disturbs any such animal while it is occupying a structure or place which it uses for that purpose,

he shall be guilty of an offence.

(5)   Subject to the provisions of this Part, if any person—
  (a) sells, offers or exposes for sale, or has in his possession or transports for the purpose of sale, any live or dead wild animal included in Schedule 5, or any part of, or anything derived from, such an animal; or
  (b) publishes or causes to be published any advertisement likely to be understood as conveying that he buys or sells, or intends to buy or sell, any of those things,

he shall be guilty of an offence.

(6)   In any proceedings for an offence under subsection (1), (2) or (5)(a), the animal in question shall be presumed to have been a wild animal unless the contrary is shown.

[38]

10 Exceptions to s 9

(1)   Nothing in section 9 shall make unlawful—
  (a) anything done in pursuance of a requirement by the Minister of Agriculture, Fisheries and Food or the Secretary of State under section 98 of the Agriculture Act 1947, or by the Secretary of State under section 39 of the Agriculture (Scotland) Act 1948; or
  (b) anything done under, or in pursuance of an order made under, the Animal Health Act 1981.

(2)   Nothing in subsection (4) of section 9 shall make unlawful anything done within a dwelling-house.

(3)   Notwithstanding anything in section 9, a person shall not be guilty of an offence by reason of—
  (a) the taking of any such animal if he shows that the animal had been disabled otherwise than by his unlawful act and was taken solely for the purpose of tending it and releasing it when no longer disabled;

(b) the killing of any such animal if he shows that the animal had been so seriously disabled otherwise than by his unlawful act that there was no reasonable chance of its recovering; or

(c) any act made unlawful by that section if he shows that the act was the incidental result of a lawful operation and could not reasonably have been avoided.

(4)   Notwithstanding anything in section 9, an authorised person shall not be guilty of an offence by reason of the killing or injuring of a wild animal included in Schedule 5 if he shows that his action was necessary for the purpose of preventing serious damage to livestock, foodstuffs for livestock, crops, vegetables, fruit, growing timber or any other form of property or to fisheries.

(5)   A person shall not be entitled to rely on the defence provided by subsection (2) or (3)(c) as respects anything done in relation to a bat otherwise than in the living area of a dwelling house unless he had notified the Nature Conservancy Council [for the area in which the house is situated or, as the case may be, the act is to take place] of the proposed action or operation and allowed them a reasonable time to advise him as to whether it should be carried out and, if so, the method to be used.

(6)   An authorised person shall not be entitled to rely on the defence provided by subsection (4) as respects any action taken at any time if it had become apparent, before that time, that that action would prove necessary for the purpose mentioned in that subsection and either—

(a) a licence under section 16 authorising that action had not been applied for as soon as reasonably practicable after that fact had become apparent; or

(b) an application for such a licence had been determined.

[39]

NOTES
Sub-s (5): words in square brackets inserted by the Environmental Protection Act 1990, s 132, Sch 9, para 11(2).

11 Prohibition of certain methods of killing or taking wild animals

(1)   Subject to the provisions of this Part, if any person—

(a) sets in position any self-locking snare which is of such a nature and so placed as to be calculated to cause bodily injury to any wild animal coming into contact therewith;

(b) uses for the purpose of killing or taking any wild animal any self-locking snare, whether or not of such a nature or so placed as aforesaid, any bow or crossbow or any explosive other than ammunition for a firearm; . . .

(c) uses as a decoy, for the purpose of killing or taking any wild animal, any live mammal or bird whatever[; or

(d) knowingly causes or permits to be done an act which is mentioned in the foregoing provisions of this section,]

he shall be guilty of an offence.

(2)   Subject to the provisions of this Part, if any person—

(a) sets in position any of the following articles, being an article which is of such a nature and so placed as to be calculated to cause bodily injury to any wild animal included in Schedule 6 which comes into contact therewith, that is to say, any trap or snare, any electrical device for killing or stunning or any poisonous, poisoned or stupefying substance;

(b) uses for the purpose of killing or taking any such wild animal any such article as aforesaid, whether or not of such a nature and so placed as aforesaid, or any net;

(c) uses for the purpose of killing or taking any such wild animal—

      (i) any automatic or semi-automatic weapon;

     (ii) any device for illuminating a target or sighting device for night shooting;

    (iii) any form of artificial light or any mirror or other dazzling device; or

    (iv) any gas or smoke not falling within paragraphs (a) and (b);

   (d) uses as a decoy, for the purpose of killing or taking any such wild animal, any sound recording; . . .

   (e) uses any mechanically propelled vehicle in immediate pursuit of any such wild animal for the purpose of driving, killing or taking that animal[; or

   (f) knowingly causes or permits to be done an act which is mentioned in the foregoing provisions of this subsection,]

he shall be guilty of an offence.

   (3)   Subject to the provisions of this Part, if any person—

   (a) sets in position [or knowingly causes or permits to be set in position] any snare which is of such a nature and so placed as to be calculated to cause bodily injury to any wild animal coming into contact therewith; and

   (b) while the snare remains in position fails, without reasonable excuse, to inspect it, or cause it to be inspected, at least once every day,

he shall be guilty of an offence.

   (4)   The Secretary of State may, for the purpose of complying with an international obligation, by order, either generally or in relation to any kind of wild animal specified in the order, amend subsection (1) or (2) by adding any method of killing or taking wild animals or by omitting any such method as is mentioned in that subsection.

   (5)   In any proceedings for an offence under subsection (1)(b) or (c) or (2)(b), (c), (d) or (e) [and in any proceedings for an offence under subsection (1)(d) or (2)(f) relating to an act which is mentioned in any of those paragraphs], the animal in question shall be presumed to have been a wild animal unless the contrary is shown.

   (6)   In any proceedings for an offence under subsection (2)(a) it shall be a defence to show that the article was set in position by the accused for the purpose of killing or taking, in the interests of public health, agriculture, forestry, fisheries or nature conservation, any wild animals which could be lawfully killed or taken by those means and that he took all reasonable precautions to prevent injury thereby to any wild animals included in Schedule 6.

   [(7)   In any proceedings for an offence under subsection (2)(f) relating to an act which is mentioned in subsection (2)(a) it shall be a defence to show that the article was set in position for the purpose of killing or taking, in the interests of public health, agriculture, forestry, fisheries or nature conservation, any wild animals which could be lawfully killed or taken by those means and that he took or caused to be taken all reasonable precautions to prevent injury thereby to any wild animals included in Schedule 6.]

[40]

NOTES

    Sub-s (1): word omitted from para (b) repealed and para (d) added, by the Wildlife and Countryside (Amendment) Act 1991, s 2(2).

    Sub-s (2): word omitted from para (d) repealed and para (f) added, by the Wildlife and Countryside (Amendment) Act 1991, s 2(3).

    Sub-ss (3), (5): words in square brackets inserted by the Wildlife and Countryside (Amendment) Act 1991, s 2(4), (5).

    Sub-s (7): added by the Wildlife and Countryside (Amendment) Act 1991, s 2(6).

12 Protection of certain mammals

Schedule 7, which amends the law relating to the protection of certain mammals, shall have effect.

[41]

Protection of plants

13 Protection of wild plants

(1)   Subject to the provisions of this Part, if any person—
   (a) intentionally picks, uproots or destroys any wild plant included in Schedule 8; or
   (b) not being an authorised person, intentionally uproots any wild plant not included in that Schedule,

he shall be guilty of an offence.

(2)   Subject to the provisions of this Part, if any person—
   (a) sells, offers or exposes for sale, or has in his possession or transports for the purpose of sale, any live or dead wild plant included in Schedule 8, or any part of, or anything derived from, such a plant; or
   (b) publishes or causes to be published any advertisement likely to be understood as conveying that he buys or sells, or intends to buy or sell, any of those things,

he shall be guilty of an offence.

(3)   Notwithstanding anything in subsection (1), a person shall not be guilty of an offence by reason of any act made unlawful by that subsection if he shows that the act was an incidental result of a lawful operation and could not reasonably have been avoided.

(4)   In any proceedings for an offence under subsection (2)(a), the plant in question shall be presumed to have been a wild plant unless the contrary is shown.

[42]

Miscellaneous

14 Introduction of new species etc

(1)   Subject to the provisions of this Part, if any person releases or allows to escape into the wild any animal which—
   (a) is of a kind which is not ordinarily resident in and is not a regular visitor to Great Britain in a wild state; or
   (b) is included in Part I of Schedule 9,

he shall be guilty of an offence.

(2)   Subject to the provisions of this Part, if any person plants or otherwise causes to grow in the wild any plant which is included in Part II of Schedule 9, he shall be guilty of an offence.

(3)   Subject to subsection (4), it shall be a defence to a charge of committing an offence under subsection (1) or (2) to prove that the accused took all reasonable steps and exercised all due diligence to avoid committing the offence.

(4)   Where the defence provided by subsection (3) involves an allegation that the commission of the offence was due to the act or default of another person, the person charged shall not, without leave of the court, be entitled to rely on the defence unless, within a period ending seven clear days before the hearing, he has served on the prosecutor a notice giving such information identifying or assisting in the identification of the other person as was then in his possession.

(5)   Any person authorised in writing by the Secretary of State may, at any reasonable time and (if required to do so) upon producing evidence that he is authorised, enter any land for the purpose of ascertaining whether an offence under subsection (1) or (2) is being, or has been, committed on that land; but nothing in this subsection shall authorise any person to enter a dwelling.

(6)   Any person who intentionally obstructs a person acting in the exercise of the power conferred by subsection (5) shall be guilty of an offence.

[43]

15 Endangered species (import and export)

(1)   The Endangered Species (Import and Export) Act 1976 shall have effect subject to the amendments provided for in Schedule 10; and in that Schedule "the 1976 Act" means that Act.

(2)   The functions of the Nature Conservancy [Councils] shall include power to advise or assist—
   (a) any constable;
   (b) any officer commissioned or other person appointed or authorised by the Commissioners of Customs and Excise to exercise any function conferred on the Commissioners by the said Act of 1976; or
   (c) any person duly authorised by the Secretary of State under section 7(3) of that Act,

in, or in connection with, the enforcement of that Act or any order made under it.

[44]

NOTES
   Sub-s (2): word in square brackets substituted by the Environmental Protection Act 1990, s 132, Sch 9, para 11(3).

Supplemental

16 Power to grant licences

(1)   Sections 1, 5, 6(3), 7 and 8 and orders under section 3 do not apply to anything done—
   [(a) for scientific, research or educational purposes;]
   (b) for the purpose of ringing or marking, or examining any ring or mark on, wild birds;
   (c) for the purpose of conserving wild birds;
   [(ca) for the purposes of the re-population of an area with, or the re-introduction into an area of, wild birds, including any breeding necessary for those purposes;
   (cb) for the purpose of conserving flora or fauna;]
   (d) for the purpose of protecting any collection of wild birds;
   (e) for the purposes of falconry or aviculture;
   (f) for the purposes of any public exhibition or competition;
   (g) for the purposes of taxidermy;
   (h) for the purpose of photography;
   (i) for the purposes of preserving public health or public or air safety;
   (j) for the purpose of preventing the spread of disease; or
   (k) for the purposes of preventing serious damage to livestock, foodstuffs for livestock, crops, vegetables, fruit, growing timber[, fisheries or inland waters],

if it is done under and in accordance with the terms of a licence granted by the appropriate authority.

[(1A) The appropriate authority—
(a) shall not grant a licence for any purpose mentioned in subsection (1) unless it is satisfied that, as regards that purpose, there is no other satisfactory solution; and
(b) shall not grant a licence for any purpose mentioned in paragraphs (e) to (h) of that subsection otherwise than on a selective basis and in respect of a small number of birds.]

(2) Section 1 and orders under section 3 do not apply to anything done for the purpose of providing food for human consumption in relation to—
(a) a gannet on the island of Sula Sgeir; or
(b) a gull's egg or, at any time before 15th April in any year, a lapwing's egg,

if it is done under and in accordance with the terms of a licence granted by the appropriate authority.

(3) Sections 9(1), (2) and (4), 11(1) and (2) and 13(1) do not apply to anything done—
(a) for scientific or educational purposes;
(b) for the purpose of ringing or marking, or examining any ring or mark on, wild animals;
(c) for the purpose of conserving wild animals or wild plants or introducing them to particular areas;
(d) for the purpose of protecting any zoological or botanical collection;
(e) for the purpose of photography;
(f) for the purpose of preserving public health or public safety;
(g) for the purpose of preventing the spread of disease; or
(h) for the purpose of preventing serious damage to livestock, foodstuffs for livestock, crops, vegetables, fruit, growing timber or any other form of property or to fisheries,

if it is done under and in accordance with the terms of a licence granted by the appropriate authority.

(4) The following provisions, namely—
(a) section 6(1) and (2);
(b) sections 9(5) and 13(2); and
(c) section 14,

do not apply to anything done under and in accordance with the terms of a licence granted by the appropriate authority.

(5) Subject to [subsections (5A) and (6)], a licence under the foregoing provisions of this section—
(a) may be, to any degree, general or specific;
(b) may be granted either to persons of a class or to a particular person;
(c) may be subject to compliance with any specified conditions;
(d) may be modified or revoked at any time by the appropriate authority; and
(e) subject to paragraph (d), shall be valid for the period stated in the licence;

and the appropriate authority may charge therefor such reasonable sum (if any) as they may determine.

[(5A) A licence under subsection (1) which authorises any action in respect of wild birds—
(a) shall specify the species of wild birds in respect of which, the circumstances in which, and the conditions subject to which, the action may be taken;
(b) shall specify the methods, means or arrangements which are authorised or required for the taking of the action; and
(c) subject to subsection (5)(d), shall be valid for the period, not exceeding two years, stated in the licence.]

(6)   A licence under subsection [(2) or (3)] which authorises any person to kill wild birds or wild animals—
    (a) shall specify the area within which, and the methods by which the wild birds or wild animals may be killed; and
    (b) subject to subsection (5)(d), shall be valid for the period, not exceeding two years, stated in the licence.

(7)   It shall be a defence in proceedings for an offence under section 8(b) of the Protection of Animals Act 1911 or section 7(b) of the Protection of Animals (Scotland) Act 1912 (which restrict the placing on land of poison and poisonous substances) to show that—
    (a) the act alleged to constitute the offence was done under and in accordance with the terms of a licence issued under subsection (1) or (3); and
    (b) any conditions specified in the licence were complied with.

(8)   For the purposes of a licence granted under the foregoing provisions of this section, the definition of a class of persons may be framed by reference to any circumstances whatever including, in particular, their being authorised by any other person.

(9)   In this section "the appropriate authority" means—
    (a) in the case of a licence under [any of paragraphs (a) to (cb)] of subsection (1), either the Secretary of State after consultation with whichever one of the advisory bodies he considers is best able to advise him as to whether the licence should be granted, or the [relevant] Nature Conservancy Council;
    (b) in the case of a licence under any of paragraphs (d) to (g) of subsection (1), subsection (2) or paragraph (a) or (b) of subsection (4), the Secretary of State after such consultation as aforesaid;
    (c) in the case of a licence under paragraph (h) of subsection (1) or any of paragraphs (a) to (e) of subsection (3), the [relevant] Nature Conservancy Council;
    (d) in the case of a licence under paragraph (i), (j) or (k) of subsection (1) or paragraph (f), (g) or (h) of subsection (3) or a licence under paragraph (c) of subsection (4) which authorises anything to be done in relation to fish or shellfish, the agriculture Minister; and
    (e) in the case of any other licence under paragraph (c) of subsection (4), the Secretary of State.

[(9A) In this section "re-population" and "re-introduction", in relation to wild birds, have the same meaning as in the Directive of the Council of the European Communities dated 2nd April 1979 (No 79/409/EEC) on the conservation of wild birds.]

(10) The Agricultural Minister—
    (a) shall from time to time consult with [each of the Nature Conservancy Councils] as to the exercise [in the area of that Council] of his functions under this section; and
    (b) shall not grant a licence of any description unless he has been advised by the [relevant Nature Conservancy] Council as to the circumstances in which, in their opinion, licences of that description should be granted.

[(11) For the purposes of this section a reference to a relevant Nature Conservancy Council is a reference to the Nature Conservancy Council for the area in which it is proposed to carry on the activity requiring a licence.]

[45]

NOTES
    Sub-s (1): para (a) substituted, paras (ca), (cb) inserted, and words in square brackets in para (k) substituted, by the Wildlife and Countryside Act 1981 (Amendment) Regulations 1995, SI 1995/2825, reg 3(2).
    Sub-ss (1A), (5A), (9A): inserted by SI 1995/2825, reg 3(3), (5), (8).
    Sub-ss (5), (6): words in square brackets substituted by SI 1995/2825, reg 3(4), (6).

Sub-s (9): words in first pair of square brackets substituted by SI 1995/2825, reg 3(7); words in second and third pairs of square brackets inserted by the Environmental Protection Act 1990, s 132, Sch 9, para 11(4)(a).

Sub-s (10): words in square brackets substituted or inserted by the Environmental Protection Act 1990, s 132, Sch 9, para 11(4)(b), (c).

Sub-s (11): added by the Environmental Protection Act 1990, s 132, Sch 9, para 11(4)(d).

17 False statements made for obtaining registration or licence etc

A person who, for the purposes of obtaining, whether for himself or another, a registration in accordance with regulations made under section 6(2) or 7(1) or the grant of a licence under section 16—

    (a) makes a statement or representation, or furnishes a document or information, which he knows to be false in a material particular; or

    (b) recklessly makes a statement or representation, or furnishes a document or information, which is false in a material particular,

shall be guilty of an offence.

[46]

18 Attempts to commit offences etc

    (1) Any person who attempts to commit an offence under the foregoing provisions of this Part shall be guilty of an offence and shall be punishable in like manner as for the said offence.

    (2) Any person who for the purposes of committing an offence under the foregoing provisions of this Part, has in his possession anything capable of being used for committing the offence shall be guilty of an offence and shall be punishable in like manner as for the said offence.

[47]

19 Enforcement

    (1) If a constable suspects with reasonable cause that any person is committing or has committed an offence under this Part, the constable may without warrant—

    (a) stop and search that person if the constable suspects with reasonable cause that evidence of the commission of the offence is to be found on that person;

    (b) search or examine any thing which that person may then be using or have in his possession if the constable suspects with reasonable cause that evidence of the commission of the offence is to be found on that thing;

    (c) . . .

    (d) seize and detain for the purposes of proceedings under this Part any thing which may be evidence of the commission of the offence or may be liable to be forfeited under section 21.

    (2) If a constable suspects with reasonable cause that any person is committing an offence under this Part, he may, for the purpose of exercising the powers conferred by subsection (1) [or arresting a person, in accordance with section 25 of the Police and Criminal Evidence Act 1984, for such an offence], enter any land other than a dwelling-house.

    (3) If a justice of the peace is satisfied by information on oath that there are reasonable grounds for suspecting that—

    (a) an offence under section 1, 3, 5, 7 or 8 in respect of which this Part or any order made under it provides for a special penalty; or

    (b) an offence under section 6, 9, 11(1) or (2), 13 or 14,

has been committed and that evidence of the offence may be found on any premises, he may grant a warrant to any constable (with or without other persons) to enter upon and search those premises for the purpose of obtaining that evidence.

. . .

[48]

NOTES

Sub-s (1): para (c) repealed by the Police and Criminal Evidence Act 1984, s 119, Sch 7, Part I.

Sub-s (2): words in square brackets inserted by the Police and Criminal Evidence Act 1984, s 119, Sch 6, para 25.

Sub-s (3): words omitted apply to Scotland only.

[19A (*Inserted, in relation to Scotland only, by the Prisoners and Criminal Proceedings (Scotland) Act 1993, s 36.*)]

20 Summary prosecutions

(1)   This section applies to—
  (a) any offence under section 1(1) or 3(1) involving the killing or taking of any wild bird or the taking of an egg of such a bird;
  (b) any offence under section 9(1) involving the killing or taking of any wild animal; and
  (c) any offence under section 13(1) involving the picking uprooting or destruction of any wild plant.

(2)   Summary proceedings for an offence to which this section applies may be brought within a period of six months from the date on which evidence sufficient in the opinion of the prosecutor to warrant the proceedings came to his knowledge; but no such proceedings shall be brought by virtue of this section more than two years after the commission of the offence.

(3)   For the purpose of this section a certificate signed by or on behalf of the prosecutor and stating the date on which such evidence as aforesaid came to his knowledge shall be conclusive evidence of that fact; and a certificate stating that matter and purporting to be so signed shall be deemed to be so signed unless the contrary is proved.

[49]

21 Penalties, forfeitures etc

(1)   Subject to subsection (5), a person guilty of an offence under section 1, 3, 5, 6, 7 or 8 shall be liable on summary conviction—
  (a) in a case where this Part or any order made under it provides that he shall be liable to a special penalty, to a fine not exceeding [level 5 on the standard scale];
  (b) in any other case, to a fine not exceeding [level 3 on the standard scale].

(2)   Subject to subsection (5), a person guilty of an offence under section 9 or 11(1) or (2) shall be liable on summary conviction to a fine not exceeding [level 5 on the standard scale].

(3)   Subject to subsection (5), a person guilty of an offence under section 11(3), 13 or 17 shall be liable on summary conviction to a fine not exceeding [level 4 on the standard scale].

(4)   A person guilty of an offence under section 14 shall be liable—
  (a) on summary conviction, to a fine not exceeding the statutory maximum;
  (b) on conviction on indictment, to a fine.

(5)   Where an offence to which subsection (1), (2) or (3) applies was committed in respect of more than one bird, nest, egg, other animal, plant or other thing, the maximum fine which may be imposed under that subsection shall be determined as if the person convicted had been convicted of a separate offence in respect of each bird, nest, egg, animal, plant or thing.

(6)   The court by which any person is convicted of an offence under this Part—
  (a) shall order the forfeiture of any bird, nest, egg, other animal, plant or other thing in respect of which the offence was committed; and
  (b) may order the forfeiture of any vehicle, animal, weapon or other thing which was used to commit the offence and, in the case of an offence under section 14, any animal or plant which is of the same kind as that in respect of which the offence was committed and was found in his possession.

(7)   Any offence under this Part shall, for the purpose of conferring jurisdiction, be deemed to have been committed in any place where the offender is found or to which he is first brought after the commission of the offence.

[50]

NOTES

Sub-ss (1)–(3): maximum fines converted to levels on the standard scale by the Criminal Justice Act 1982, ss 37, 46.

22 Power to vary Schedules

(1)   The Secretary of State may by order, either generally or with respect to particular provisions of this Part, particular areas of Great Britain or particular times of the year, add any bird to, or remove any bird from, any of or any Part of Schedules 1 to 4.

(2)   An order under subsection (1) adding any bird to Part II of Schedule 1 or Part I of Schedule 2 may prescribe a close season in the case of that bird for the purposes of sections 1 and 2; and any close season so prescribed shall commence on a date not later than 21st February and end on a date not earlier than 31st August.

(3)   The Secretary of State may, on a representation made [jointly to him by the Nature Conservancy Councils], by order, either generally or with respect to particular provisions of this Part, particular areas of Great Britain or particular times of the year—
  (a) add to Schedule 5 or Schedule 8 any animal or plant which, in his opinion, is in danger of extinction in Great Britain or is likely to become so endangered unless conservation measures are taken; and
  (b) remove from Schedule 5 or Schedule 8 any animal or plant which, in his opinion, is no longer so endangered or likely to become so endangered
[and the functions of the Nature Conservancy Councils under this subsection shall be special functions of the Councils for the purposes of section 133 of the Environmental Protection Act 1990].

(4)   The Secretary of State may, for the purpose of complying with an international obligation, by order, either generally or with respect to particular provisions of this Part or particular times of the year—
  (a) add any animals to, or remove any animals from, Schedule 5 or Schedule 6; and
  (b) add any plants to, or remove any plants from, Schedule 8.

(5)   The Secretary of State may by order, either generally or with respect to particular areas of Great Britain—
  (a) add any animals to, or remove any animals from, Part I of Schedule 9; and
  (b) add any plants to, or remove any plants from, Part II of that Schedule.

[51]

NOTES

Sub-s (3): words in first pair of square brackets substituted, words in final pair of square brackets added, by the Environmental Protection Act 1990, s 132, Sch 9, para 11(5).

Orders: the Wildlife and Countryside Act 1981 (Variation of Schedules) Order 1988, SI 1988/288; the Wildlife and Countryside Act 1981 (Variation of Schedule) Order 1989, SI 1989/906; the Wildlife and

Countryside Act 1981 (Variation of Schedule) Order 1991, SI 1991/367; the Wildlife and Countryside Act 1981 (Variation of Schedule) Order 1992, SI 1992/320; the Wildlife and Countryside Act 1981 (Variation of Schedules 5 and 8) Order 1992, SI 1992/2350; the Wildlife and Countryside Act 1981 (Variation of Schedule) (No 2) Order 1992, SI 1992/2674; the Wildlife and Countryside Act 1981 (Variation of Schedules 2 and 3) Order 1992, SI 1992/3010; the Wildlife and Countryside Act 1981 (Variation of Schedule 4) Order 1994, SI 1994/1151; the Wildlife and Countryside Act 1981 (Variation of Schedule 9) Order 1997, SI 1997/226.

23 Advisory bodies and their functions

(1)   The Secretary of State may—
   (a)   establish any body or bodies, consisting in each case of such members as he may from time to time appoint;
   (b)   assign to any body or bodies the duty referred to in subsection (4).

(2)   Without prejudice to his power under subsection (1), the Secretary of State shall, as soon as practicable after the commencement date,—
   (a)   establish at least one body under paragraph (a) of subsection (1); or
   (b)   assign to at least one body, under paragraph (b) of that subsection, the duty referred to in subsection (4).

(3)   A reference in this Part to an advisory body is a reference to a body which is established under subsection (1) or to which the duty there referred to is assigned under that subsection.

(4)   It shall be the duty of an advisory body to advise the Secretary of State on any question which he may refer to it or on which it considers it should offer its advice—
   (a)   in connection with the administration of this Part; or
   (b)   otherwise in connection with the protection of birds or other animals or plants.

(5)   In so far as it does not have power to do so apart from this subsection, an advisory body may publish reports relating to the performance by it of its duty under subsection (4).

(6)   Before appointing a person to be a member of an advisory body established under subsection (1)(a), the Secretary of State shall consult such persons or bodies as he thinks fit.

(7)   The Secretary of State may, out of moneys provided by Parliament and to such an extent as may be approved by the Treasury, defray or contribute towards the expenses of an advisory body established under subsection (1)(a).

24 Functions of Nature Conservancy Council

(1)   The Nature Conservancy [Councils, acting jointly,] may at any time and shall five years after [30th October 1991] and every five years thereafter, review Schedules 5 and 8 and advise the Secretary of State whether, in their opinion,—
   (a)   any animal should be added to, or removed from, Schedule 5;
   (b)   any plant should be added to, or removed from, Schedule 8;
[and the functions of the Nature Conservancy Councils under this subsection shall be special functions of the Councils for the purposes of section 133 of the Environmental Protection Act 1990].

(2)   Advice may be given under subsection (1) either generally or with respect to particular provisions of this Part, particular areas of Great Britain or particular times of the year; and any advice so given shall be accompanied by a statement of the reasons which led [to that advice being given.]

[(3) The Secretary of State shall lay before each House of Parliament a copy of any advice so given and the statements accompanying it.]

(4)   The functions of the [Nature Conservancy Councils] shall include power to advise or assist—
   (a) any constable;
   (b) any proper officer of a local authority; or
   (c) any person duly authorised by the Secretary of State under section 6(9), 7(6) or 14(5),

in, or in connection with, the enforcement of the provisions of this Part or any order or regulations made under it.

[53]

NOTES
   Sub-s (1): words in first and second pairs of square brackets substituted, words in final pair of square brackets added, by the Environmental Protection Act 1990, s 132, Sch 9, para 11(6)(a).
   Sub-ss (2), (4): words in square brackets substituted by the Environmental Protection Act 1990, s 132, Sch 9, para 11(6)(b), (d).
   Sub-s (3): substituted by the Environmental Protection Act 1990, s 132, Sch 9, para 11(6)(c).

25 Functions of local authorities

(1)   Every local authority shall take such steps as they consider expedient for bringing to the attention of the public and of schoolchildren in particular the effect of—
   (a) the provisions of this Part; and
   (b) any order made under this Part affecting the whole or any part of their area.

(2)   A local authority in England and Wales may institute proceedings for any offence under this Part or any order made under it which is committed within their area.

[54]

26 Regulations, orders, notices etc

(1)   Any power to make regulations or order under this Part shall be exercisable by statutory instrument.

(2)   A statutory instrument containing regulations under this Part, or an order under a provision of this Part other than sections 2(6), 3, 5 and 11, shall be subject to annulment in pursuance of a resolution of either House of Parliament.

(3)   No order under section 5 or 11 shall be made unless a draft of the order has been laid before and approved by a resolution of each House of Parliament.

(4)   Before making any order under this Part, the Secretary of State—
   (a) except in the case of an order under section 2(6), shall give to any local authority affected and, except in the case of an order under section 3, any other person affected, by such means as he may think appropriate, an opportunity to submit objections or representations with respect to the subject matter of the order;
   (b) except in the case of an order under section 22(3), shall consult with whichever one of the advisory bodies he considers is best able to advise him as to whether the order should be made; and
   (c) may, if he thinks fit, cause a public inquiry to be held.

(5)   Notice of the making of an order under this Part shall be published by the Secretary of State—
   (a) if the order relates in whole or in part to England and Wales, in the London Gazette; and
   (b) if the order relates in whole or in part to Scotland, in the Edinburgh Gazette.

(6)   The Secretary of State shall give consideration to any proposals for the making by him of an order under this Part with respect to any area which may be submitted to him by a local authority whose area includes that area.

[55]

27 Interpretation of Part I

(1)   In this Part, unless the context otherwise requires—
   "advertisement" includes a catalogue, a circular and a price list;
   "advisory body" has the meaning given by section 23;
   "agriculture Minister" means the Minister of Agriculture, Fisheries and Food or the Secretary of State;
   "authorised person" means—
      (a) the owner or occupier, or any person authorised by the owner or occupier, of the land on which the action authorised is taken;
      (b) any person authorised in writing by the local authority for the area within which the action authorised is taken;
      (c) as respects anything done in relation to wild birds, any person authorised in writing by any of the following bodies, that is to say, [any of the Nature Conservancy Councils], . . . a district board for a fishery district within the meaning of the Salmon Fisheries (Scotland) Act 1862 or a local fisheries committee constituted under the Sea Fisheries Regulation Act 1966;
      [(d) any person authorised in writing by the National Rivers Authority, a water undertakers or a sewerage undertaker;]
   so, however, that the authorisation of any person for the purposes of this definition shall not confer any right of entry upon any land;
   "automatic weapon" and "semi-automatic weapon" do not include any weapon the magazine of which is incapable of holding more than two rounds;
   "aviculture" means the breeding and rearing of birds in captivity;
   "destroy", in relation to an egg, includes doing anything to the egg which is calculated to prevent it from hatching, and "destruction" shall be construed accordingly;
   "domestic duck" means any domestic form of duck;
   "domestic goose" means any domestic form of goose;
   "firearm" has the same meaning as in the Firearms Act 1968;
   "game bird" means any pheasant, partridge, grouse (or moor game), black (or heath) game or ptarmigan;
   ["inland waters" means—
      (a) inland waters within the meaning of the Water Resources Act 1991;
      (b) any waters not falling within paragraph (a) above which are within the seaward limits of the territorial sea;
      (c) controlled waters within the meaning of Part II of the Control of Pollution Act 1974 other than ground waters as defined in section 30A(1)(d) of that Act.]
   "livestock" includes any animal which is kept—
      (a) for the provision of food, wool, skins or fur;
      (b) for the purpose of its use in the carrying on of any agricultural activity; or
      (c) for the provision or improvement of shooting or fishing;
   "local authority" means—
      (a) in relation to England . . . , a county, district or London borough council . . . ;
      [(aa) in relation to Wales, a county council or county borough council;]
      (b) (*applies to Scotland only*);
   "occupier", in relation to any land other than the foreshore, includes any person having any right of hunting, shooting, fishing or taking game or fish;

"pick", in relation to a plant, means gather or pluck any part of the plant without uprooting it;

"poultry" means domestic fowls, geese, ducks, guinea-fowls, pigeons and quails, and turkeys;

"sale" includes hire, barter and exchange and cognate expressions shall be construed accordingly;

"uproot", in relation to a plant, means dig up or otherwise remove the plant from the land on which it is growing;

"vehicle" includes aircraft, hovercraft and boat;

. . . . .

"wild animal" means any animal (other than a bird) which is or (before it was killed or taken) was living wild;

"wild bird" means any bird of a kind which is ordinarily resident in or is a visitor to Great Britain in a wild state but does not include poultry or, except in sections 5 and 16, any game bird;

"wild plant" means any plant which is or (before it was picked, uprooted or destroyed) was growing wild and is of a kind which ordinarily grows in Great Britain in a wild state.

(2)   A bird shall not be treated as bred in captivity for the purposes of this Part unless its parents were lawfully in captivity when the egg was laid.

(3)   Any reference in this Part to an animal of any kind includes, unless the context otherwise requires, a reference to an egg, larva, pupa, or other immature stage of an animal of that kind.

[(3A) Any reference in this Part to the Nature Conservancy Councils is a reference to the Nature Conservancy Council for England, [Scottish Natural Heritage] and the Countryside Council for Wales.]

(4)   This Part shall apply to the Isles of Scilly as if the Isles were a county and as if the Council of the Isles were a county council.

(5)   This Part extends to the territorial waters adjacent to Great Britain, and for the purposes of this Part any part of Great Britain which is bounded by territorial waters shall be taken to include the territorial waters adjacent to that part.

[56]

NOTES

Sub-s (1): in definition "authorised person" words in square brackets in para (c) substituted by the Environmental Protection Act 1990, s 132, Sch 9, para 11(7)(a), words omitted repealed by the Water Act 1989, s 190, Sch 27, Pt I, para (d) inserted by the Water Act 1989, s 190, Sch 25, para 66; definition "inland waters" inserted by the Wildlife and Countryside Act 1981 (Amendment) Regulations 1995, SI 1995/2825, reg 4; in definition "local authority" words omitted from para (a) in the first place repealed, and para (aa) inserted, by the Local Government (Wales) Act 1994, s 66(6), (8), Sch 16, para 65(2), Sch 18, words omitted from para (a) in the second place repealed by the Local Government Act 1985, s 102, Sch 17; definition omitted applies to Scotland only.

Sub-s (3A): inserted by the Environmental Protection Act 1990, s 132, Sch 9, para 11(7)(b); words in square brackets substituted by the Natural Heritage (Scotland) Act 1991, s 4, Sch 2, para 8(2).

National Rivers Authority: a reference to the National Rivers Authority is to be construed as a reference to the Environment Agency; by virtue of the Environment Act 1995 (Consequential Amendments) Regulations 1996, SI 1996/593, reg 2, Sch 1.

PART II
NATURE CONSERVATION, COUNTRYSIDE AND NATIONAL PARKS

NOTES

Ss 28–37 of this Act should be read in conjunction with the Conservation (Natural Habitats, &c) Regulations 1994, SI 1994/2716 at [988] (and in particular reg 3 thereof), which make provision for implementing Council Directive 92/43/EEC on the conservation of natural habitats and of wild fauna and flora.

Nature conservation

[27A Construction of references to Nature Conservancy Council

In this Part references to "the Nature Conservancy Council" are, unless the contrary intention appears, references—
   (a) in relation to land in, or land covered by waters adjacent to, England, to the Nature Conservancy Council for England;
   (b) in relation to land in, or land covered by waters adjacent to, Scotland, to [Scottish Natural Heritage]; and
   (c) in relation to land in, or land covered by waters adjacent to, Wales, to the Countryside Council for Wales;

and references to "the Council" shall be construed accordingly.]

[57]

NOTES
Inserted by the Environmental Protection Act 1990, s 132, Sch 9, para 11(8).
Words in square brackets substituted by the Natural Heritage (Scotland) Act 1991, s 4, Sch 2, para 8(3).

28 Areas of special scientific interest

   (1) Where the Nature Conservancy Council are of the opinion that any area of land is of special interest by reason of any of its flora, fauna, or geological or physiographical features, it shall be the duty of the Council to notify that fact—
   (a) to the local planning authority in whose area the land is situated;
   (b) to every owner and occupier of any of that land; and
   (c) to the Secretary of State.

   [(2) A notification under subsection (1) shall specify the time (not being less than three months from the date of the giving of the notification) within which, and the manner in which, representations or objections with respect thereto may be made; and the Council shall consider any representation or objection duly made.]

   (3) ...

   (4) A notification under subsection (1)(b) shall specify—
   (a) the flora, fauna, or geological or physiographical features by reason of which the land is of special interest; and
   (b) any operations appearing to the Council to be likely to damage that flora or fauna or those features.

   [(4A) Where a notification under subsection (1) has been given, the Council may within the period of nine months beginning with the date on which the notification was served on the Secretary of State either—
   (a) give notice to the persons mentioned in subsection (1) withdrawing the notification; or
   (b) give notice to those persons confirming the notification (with or without modifications);
and the notification shall cease to have effect—
   (i) on the giving of notice of its withdrawal under paragraph (a) of this subsection to any of the persons mentioned in subsection (1), or
   (ii) if not withdrawn or confirmed by notice under paragraph (a) or (b) of this subsection within the said period of nine months, at the end of that period.

   (4B) The Council's power under subsection (4A)(b) to confirm a notification under subsection (1) with modifications shall not be exercised so as to add to the operations specified in the notification or extend the area to which it applies.

   (4C) As from the time when there is served on the owner or occupier of any land which has been notified under subsection (1)(b) a notice under subsection (4A) confirming the notification with modifications, the notification shall have effect in its modified form in relation to so much (if any) of that land as remains subject to it].

(5) The owner or occupier of any land which has been notified under subsection (1)(b) shall not [while the notification remains in force] carry out, or cause or permit to be carried out, on that land any operation specified in the notification unless—
   (a) one of them has, [after service on him of the notification], given the Council written notice of a proposal to carry out the operation specifying its nature and the land on which it is proposed to carry it out; and
   (b) one of the conditions specified in subsection (6) is fulfilled.

(6) The said conditions are—
   (a) that the operation is carried out with the Council's written consent;
   (b) that the operation is carried out in accordance with the terms of an agreement under section 16 of the 1949 Act or section 15 of the 1968 Act; and
   (c) that [four months] have expired from the giving of the notice under subsection (5).

[(6A) If before the expiry of the four months referred to in subsection (6)(c) the relevant person agrees with the Council in writing that, subject to subsection (6B), the condition specified in paragraph (c) of subsection (6) shall not apply in relation to the operation mentioned in subsection (5)(a), then, subject to subsection (6B), subsection (5) shall as from the date of the agreement have effect in relation to the operation in question (as regards both the owner and the occupier of the land) as if paragraph (c) of subsection (6) were omitted.

(6B) If after an agreement has been made with the Council under subsection (6A) the relevant person (whether a party to the agreement or not) gives the Council written notice that he wishes to terminate the agreement, then as from the giving of the notice subsection (5) shall have effect in relation to the operation in question (as regards both the owner and the occupier of the land) as if paragraph (c) of subsection (6) specified the condition that one month or, if the notice under this subsection specifies a longer period, that longer period has expired from the giving of the notice under this subsection.

(6C) In subsections (6A) and (6B) "the relevant person"—
   (a) in a case where the notice under subsection (5) was given by the owner of the land in question, means the owner of that land;
   (b) in a case where that notice was given by the occupier of that land, means the occupier of that land.]

(7) A person who, without reasonable excuse, contravenes subsection (5) shall be liable on summary conviction to a fine not exceeding [level 4 on the standard scale].

(8) It is a reasonable excuse in any event for a person to carry out an operation if—
   (a) the operation was authorised by a planning permission granted on an application under [Part III of the Town and Country Planning Act 1990] or [Part III of the Town and Country Planning (Scotland) Act 1997]; or
   (b) the operation was an emergency operation particulars of which (including details of the emergency) were notified to the Council as soon as practicable after the commencement of the operation.

(9) The Council shall have power to enforce the provisions of this section; . . .

(10) Proceedings in England and Wales for an offence under subsection (7) shall not, without the consent of the Director of Public Prosecutions, be taken by a person other than the Council.

(11) A notification under subsection (1)(b) of land in England and Wales shall be a local land charge.

[(12)–(12B)](*Apply to Scotland only.*)

(13) Section 23 of the 1949 Act (which is superseded by this section) shall cease to have effect; but any notification given under that section shall have effect as if given under subsection (1)(a).

[(13A) For the purposes of this section "local planning authority, in relation to land within the Broads, includes the Broads Authority.]

(14) ...

[58]

NOTES

Sub-s (2): substituted with savings by the Wildlife and Countryside (Amendment) Act 1985, s 2(2).

Sub-s (3): repealed by the Wildlife and Countryside (Service of Notices) Act 1985, s 1(2).

Sub-ss (4A)–(4C), (6A)–(6C): inserted by the Wildlife and Countryside (Amendment) Act 1985, s 2(4), (7).

Sub-ss (5), (6): words in square brackets substituted by the Wildlife and Countryside (Amendment) Act 1985, s 2(5)(b), (6).

Sub-s (7): maximum fine converted to a level on the standard scale by virtue of the Criminal Justice Act 1982, s 46.

Sub-s (8): words in first pair of square brackets in para (a) substituted by the Planning (Consequential Provisions) Act 1990, s 4, Sch 2, para 54(1); words in second pair of square brackets substituted by the Planning (Consequential Provisions) (Scotland) Act 1997, s 4, Sch 2, para 34(1).

Sub-s (9): words omitted apply to Scotland only.

Sub-s (13A): inserted by the Norfolk and Suffolk Broads Act 1988, s 2(5), (6), Sch 3, Pt I.

Sub-s (14): repealed by the Wildlife and Countryside (Amendment) Act 1985, s 2(9), (10).

29 Special protection for certain areas of special scientific interest

(1) Where it appears to the Secretary of State expedient to do so—
 (a) in the case of any land to which this paragraph applies, for the purpose of securing the survival in Great Britain of any kind of animal or plant or of complying with an international obligation; or
 (b) in the case of any land to which this paragraph applies, for the purpose of conserving any of its flora, fauna, or geological or physiographical features,

he may, after consultation with the Nature Conservancy Council, by order apply subsection (3) to that land; and the provisions of Schedule 11 shall have effect as to the making, confirmation and coming into operation of orders under this section.

An order made under this section may be amended or revoked by a subsequent order so made.

(2) Paragraphs (a) and (b) of subsection (1) apply to any land which in the opinion of the Secretary of State is—
 (a) of special interest; and
 (b) in the case of paragraph (b) of that subsection, of national importance,

by reason of any of its flora, fauna, or geological or physiographical features.

(3) Subject to subsection (4), no person shall carry out on any land to which this subsection applies any operation which—
 (a) appears to the Secretary of State to be likely to destroy or damage the flora, fauna, or geological or physiographical features by reason of which the land is land to which paragraph (a) or, as the case may be, paragraph (b) of subsection (1) applies; and
 (b) is specified in the order applying this subsection to the land.

(4)   Subsection (3) shall not apply in relation to any operation carried out, or caused or permitted to be carried out, by the owner or occupier of the land if—
  (a) one of them has, after the [making of the order], given the Council [written] notice of a proposal to carry out the operation, specifying its nature and the land on which it is proposed to carry it out; and
  (b) one of the conditions specified in subsection (5) is fulfilled.

(5)   The said conditions are—
  (a) that the operation is carried out with the Council's written consent;
  (b) that the operation is carried out in accordance with the terms of an agreement under section 16 of the 1949 Act or section 15 of the 1968 Act; and
  (c) subject to subsections (6) and (7), that three months have expired from the giving of the notice under subsection (4).

(6)   If before the expiration of the period mentioned in paragraph (c) of subsection (5) the Council offer to enter into an agreement for the acquisition of the interest of the person who gave the notice under subsection (4) or an agreement under section 16 of the 1949 Act or section 15 of the 1968 Act providing for the making by them of payments to that person, that paragraph shall have effect as if for the said period there were substituted—
  (a) where the agreement is entered into before the expiration of twelve months from the giving of the notice, the period expiring on the day on which it is entered into;
  (b) in any other case, twelve months from the giving of the notice or three months from rejection or withdrawal of the offer to enter into the agreement, whichever period last expires.

(7)   If before the expiration of the period mentioned in paragraph (c) of subsection (5), or that paragraph as if it has effect by virtue of subsection (6), an order is made for the compulsory acquisition by the Council of the interest of the person who gave the notice under subsection (4), that paragraph shall have effect as if for the said period there were substituted the period expiring—
  (a) in the case of an order which is confirmed, on the day on which the Council enter on the land;
  (b) in any other case, on the day on which the order is withdrawn or the Secretary of State decides not to confirm it.

(8)   A person who, without reasonable excuse, contravenes subsection (3) shall be liable—
  (a) on summary conviction, to a fine not exceeding the statutory maximum;
  (b) on conviction on indictment, to a fine.

(9)   It is a reasonable excuse in any event for a person to carry out an operation if—
  (a) the operation was authorised by a planning permission granted on an application under [Part III of the Town and Country Planning Act 1990] or [Part III of the Town and Country Planning (Scotland) Act 1997]; or
  (b) the operation was an emergency operation particulars of which (including details of the emergency) were notified to the Council as soon as practicable after the commencement of the operation.

(10) (*Applies to Scotland only.*)

(11) A report submitted by the Council to the Secretary of State under [paragraph 20 of Schedule 6 to the Environmental Protection Act 1990] [or under section 10(2) of the Natural Heritage (Scotland) Act 1991] for any year shall set out particulars of any areas of land as respects which orders under this section have come into operation during that year.

NOTES

Sub-s (4): words in first pair of square brackets substituted, and word in second pair of square brackets inserted, by the Environmental Protection Act 1990, s 132, Sch 9, para 11(9), (10).

Sub-s (9): words in first pair of square brackets in para (a) substituted by the Planning (Consequential Provisions) Act 1990, s 4, Sch 2, para 54(1); words in second pair of square brackets in para (a) substituted by the Planning (Consequential Provisions) (Scotland) Act 1997, s 4, Sch 2, para 34(1).

Sub-s (11): words in first pair of square brackets substituted by the Environmental Protection Act 1990, s 132, Sch 9, para 11(11); words in second pair of square brackets inserted by the Natural Heritage (Scotland) Act 1991, s 4(10), Sch 2, para 8(1), (3).

30 Compensation where order is made under s 29

(1)   Subsection (2) applies where an order is made under section 29 and subsection (3) applies where—
  (a) notice of a proposal to carry out an operation is duly given to the Nature Conservancy Council under subsection (4) of that section; and
  (b) paragraph (c) of subsection (5) of that section has effect as modified by subsection (6) or (7) of that section.

(2)   The Council shall pay compensation to any person having at the time of the making of the order an interest in land comprised in an agricultural unit comprising land to which the order relates who, on a claim made to the Council within the time and in the manner prescribed by regulations under this section, shows that the value of his interest is less than what it would have been if the order had not been made; and the amount of the compensation shall be equal to the difference between the two values.

(3)   The Council shall pay compensation to any person having at the time of the giving of the notice an interest in land to which the notice relates who, on a claim made to the Council within the time and in the manner prescribed by regulations under this section, shows that—
  (a) he has reasonably incurred expenditure which has been rendered abortive, or expenditure in carrying out work which has been rendered abortive, by reason of paragraph (c) of subsection (5) of section 29 having effect as modified by subsection (6) or (7) of that section; or
  (b) he has incurred loss or damage which is directly attributable to that paragraph having effect as so modified;
but nothing in this subsection shall entitle any such person to compensation in respect of any reduction in the value of his interest in the land.

(4)   For the purposes of subsection (2)—
  (a) an interest in land shall be valued as at the time when the order is made;
  (b) where a person, by reason of his having more than one interest in land, makes more than one claim under that subsection in respect of the same order, his various interests shall be valued together;
  (c) section 10 of the Land Compensation Act 1973 (mortgages, [trusts of land] and settlements) or section 10 of the Land Compensation (Scotland) Act 1973 (restricted interests in land) shall apply in relation to compensation under that subsection as it applies in relation to compensation under Part I of that Act.

(5)   For the purposes of assessing any compensation payable under subsection (2), the rules set out in section 5 of the Land Compensation Act 1961 or section 12 of the Land Compensation (Scotland) Act 1963 shall, so far as applicable and subject to any necessary modifications, have effect as they have effect for the purpose of assessing compensation for the compulsory acquisition of an interest in land.

(6)   No claim shall be made under subsection (2) in respect of any order under section 29 unless the Secretary of State has given notice under paragraph 6(1) or (2)

of Schedule 11 of his decision in respect of the order; and, without prejudice to subsection (4)(a), that decision will be taken into account in assessing the compensation payable in respect of the order.

(7)   Compensation under this section shall carry interest, at the rate for the time being prescribed under section 32 of the Land Compensation Act 1961 or section 40 of the Land Compensation (Scotland) Act 1963, from the date of the claim until payment.

(8)   Except in so far as may be provided by regulations under this section, any question of disputed compensation under this section shall be referred to and determined by the Lands Tribunal or the Lands Tribunal for Scotland.

(9)   In relation to the determination of any such question, the provisions of sections 2 and 4 of the Land Compensation Act 1961 or sections 9 and 11 of the Land Compensation (Scotland) Act 1963 (procedure and costs) shall apply, subject to any necessary modifications and to the provisions of any regulations under this section.

(10)   Regulations under this section shall be made by the Secretary of State and shall be made by statutory instrument subject to annulment in pursuance of a resolution of either House of Parliament.

(11)   In this section "agricultural unit" means land which is occupied as a unit for agricultural purposes, including any dwelling-house or other building occupied by the same person for the purpose of farming the land.

[60]

NOTES

Sub-s (4): words in square brackets in para (c) substituted by the Trusts of Land and Appointment of Trustees Act 1996, s 25(1), Sch 3, para 20 (for savings see s 25(4), (5) of that Act).

Regulations: the Wildlife and Countryside (Claims for Compensation under Section 30) Regulations 1982, SI 1982/1346.

31 Restoration where order under s 29 is contravened

(1)   Where the operation in respect of which a person is convicted of an offence under section 29 has destroyed or damaged any of the flora, fauna, or geological or physiographical features by reason of which the land on which it was carried out is of special interest, the court by which he is convicted, in addition to dealing with him in any way, may make an order requiring him to carry out, within such period as may be specified in the order, such operations for the purpose of restoring the land to its former condition as may be so specified.

(2)   An order under this section made on conviction on indictment shall be treated for the purposes of sections 30 and 42(1) and (2) of the Criminal Appeal Act 1968 (effect of appeals on orders for the restitution of property) as an order for the restitution of property; and where by reason of the quashing by the Court of Appeal of a person's conviction any such order does not take effect, and on appeal to the House of Lords the conviction is restored by that House, the House may make any order under this section which could be made on his conviction by the court which convicted him.

(3)   In the case of an order under this section made by a magistrates' court the period specified in the order shall not begin to run—
   (a) in any case until the expiration of the period for the time being prescribed by law for the giving of notice of appeal against a decision of a magistrates' court;
   (b) where notice of appeal is given within the period so prescribed, until determination of the appeal.

(4)   At any time before an order under this section has been complied with or fully complied with, the court by which it was made may, on the application of the person against whom it was made, discharge or vary the order if it appears to the court that a change in circumstances has made compliance or full compliance with the order impracticable or unnecessary.

(5)   If, within the period specified in an order under this section, the person against whom it was made fails, without reasonable excuse, to comply with it, he shall be liable on summary conviction—
  (a) to a fine not exceeding [level 5 on the standard scale]; and
  (b) in the case of a continuing offence, to a further fine not exceeding £100 for each day during which the offence continues after conviction.

(6)   If, within the period specified in an order under this section, any operations specified in the order have not been carried out, the Nature Conservancy Council may enter the land and carry out those operations and recover from the person against whom the order was made any expenses reasonably incurred by them in doing so.

(7)   (*Applies to Scotland only.*)

[61]

NOTES
  Sub-s (5): maximum fine in para (a) converted to a level on the standard scale by virtue of the Criminal Justice Act 1982, s 46.

32 Duties of agriculture Ministers with respect to areas of special scientific interest

(1)   Where an application for [a farm capital grant] is made as respects expenditure incurred or to be incurred for the purpose of activities on land notified under section 28(1) or land to which section 29(3) applies, the appropriate Minister—
  (a) shall, so far as may be consistent with the purposes of [the grant provisions], so exercise his functions thereunder as to further the conservation of the flora, fauna, or geological or physiographical features by reason of which the land is of special interest; and
  (b) where the Nature Conservancy Council have objected to the making of the grant on the ground that the activities in question have destroyed or damaged or will destroy or damage that flora or fauna or those features, shall not make the grant except after considering the objection and, in the case of land in England, after consulting with the Secretary of State.

(2)   Where, in consequence of an objection by the Council, an application for a grant as respects expenditure to be incurred is refused on the ground that the activities in question will have such an effect as is mentioned in subsection (1)(b), the Council shall, within three months of their receiving notice of the appropriate Minister's decision, offer to enter into, in the terms of a draft submitted to the applicant, an agreement under section 16 of the 1949 Act or section 15 of the 1968 Act—
  (a) imposing restrictions as respects those activities; and
  (b) providing for the making by them of payments to the applicant.

[(3)   In this section—
    "the appropriate Minister" means the Minister responsible for determining the application;
    "farm capital grant" means—
      (a) a grant under a scheme made under section 29 of the Agriculture Act 1970; or
      (b) a grant under regulations made under section 2(2) of the European Communities Act 1972 to a person carrying on an agricultural

business within the meaning of those regulations in respect of expenditure incurred or to be incurred for the purposes of or in connection with that business, being expenditure of a capital nature or incurred in connection with expenditure of a capital nature;
"grant provisions" means—
    (i) in the case of such a grant as is mentioned in paragraph (a) above, the scheme under which the grant is made and section 29 of the Agriculture Act 1970; and
    (ii) in the case of such a grant as is mentioned in paragraph (b) above, the regulations under which the grant is made and the Community instrument in pursuance of which the regulations were made.]

[62]

NOTES

Sub-s (1): words in square brackets substituted by the Agriculture Act 1986, s 20(1), (2).
Sub-s (3): substituted by the Agriculture Act 1986, s 20(1), (3).

33 Ministerial guidance as respects areas of special scientific interest

(1)   The Ministers shall from time to time, after consultation with the Nature Conservancy [Councils] and such persons appearing to them to represent other interests concerned as they consider appropriate—
    (a) prepare codes containing such recommendations, advice and information as they consider proper for the guidance of—
        (i) persons exercising functions under sections 28 to 32; and
        (ii) persons affected or likely to be affected by the exercise of any of those functions; and
    (b) revise any such code by revoking, varying, amending or adding to the provisions of the code in such manner as the Ministers think fit.

(2)   A code prepared in pursuance of subsection (1) and any alterations proposed to be made on a revision of such a code shall be laid before both Houses of Parliament forthwith after being prepared; and the code or revised code, as the case may be, shall not be issued until the code or the proposed alterations have been approved by both Houses.

(3)   Subject to subsection (2), the Ministers shall cause every code prepared or revised in pursuance of subsection (1) to be printed, and may cause copies of it to be put on sale to the public at such price as the Ministers may determine.

[63]

NOTES

Sub-s (1): word in square brackets substituted by the Environmental Protection Act 1990, s 132, Sch 9, para 11(12).

34 Limestone pavement orders

(1)   Where the Nature Conservancy Council or the Commission are of the opinion that any land in the countryside which comprises a limestone pavement is of special interest by reason of its flora, fauna or geological or physiographical features, it shall be the duty of the Council or the Commission to notify that fact to the local planning authority in whose area the land is situated.

(2)   Where it appears to the Secretary of State or the relevant authority that the character or appearance of any land notified under subsection (1) would be likely to be adversely affected by the removal of the limestone or by its disturbance in any way whatever, the Secretary of State or that authority may make an order (in this section referred to as a "limestone pavement order") designating the land and prohibiting the removal or disturbance of limestone on or in it; and the provisions of

Schedule 11 shall have effect as to the making, confirmation and coming into operation of limestone pavement orders.

(3)   The relevant authority may, after consultation with the Council and the Commission, amend or revoke a limestone pavement order made by the authority; and the Secretary of State may, after such consultation as aforesaid, amend or revoke any such order made by him or that authority but, in the case of an order made by that authority, only after consultation with that authority.

(4)   If any person without reasonable excuse removes or disturbs limestone on or in any land designated by a limestone pavement order he shall be liable—
    (a) on summary conviction, to a fine not exceeding the statutory maximum;
    (b) on conviction on indictment, to a fine.

(5)   It is a reasonable excuse in any event for a person to remove or disturb limestone or cause or permit its removal or disturbance, if the removal or disturbance was authorised by a planning permission granted on an application under [Part III of the Town and Country Planning Act 1990] or [Part III of the Town and Country Planning (Scotland) Act 1997].

(6)   In this section—
    "the Commission" means the Countryside Commission in relation to England . . . ;
    "limestone pavement" means an area of limestone which lies wholly or partly exposed on the surface of the ground and has been fissured by natural erosion;
    ["the relevant authority" means—
        (a) in relation to a non-metropolitan county [in England], the county planning authority and, in relation to any other area in England, the local planning authority;
    [(aa) in relation to any area in Wales, the local planning authority;]
        (b) (*applies to Scotland only*).

[64]

NOTES

Sub-s (5): words in first pair of square brackets substituted by the Planning (Consequential Provisions) Act 1990, s 4, Sch 2, para 54(1); words in second pair of square brackets substituted by the Planning (Consequential Provisions) (Scotland) Act 1997, s 4, Sch 2, para 34(1).

Sub-s (6): in definition "the Commission" words omitted repealed by the Environmental Protection Act 1990, ss 130, 162, Sch 8, para 6(2), Sch 16, Pt VI and the Natural Heritage (Scotland) Act 1991, s 27(2), Sch 11; definition "the relevant authority" substituted by the Local Government Act 1985, s 7, Sch 3, para 7(2), words in square brackets therein inserted by the Local Government (Wales) Act 1994, s 66(6), Sch 16, para 65(3), as from a day to be appointed.

35 National nature reserves

(1)   Where the Nature Conservancy Council are satisfied that any land which—
    (a) is being managed as a nature reserve under an agreement entered into with the Council;
    (b) is held by the Council and is being managed by them as a nature reserve; or
    (c) is held by an approved body and is being managed by that body as a nature reserve,
is of national importance, they may declare that land to be a national nature reserve.

(2)   A declaration by the Council that any land is a national nature reserve shall be conclusive of the matters declared; and subsections (4) and (5) of section 19 of the 1949 Act shall apply in relation to any such declaration as they apply in relation to a declaration under that section.

(3)   On the application of the approved body concerned, the Council may, as respects any land which is declared to be a national nature reserve under subsection (1)(c), make byelaws for the protection of the reserve.

(4)   Subsections (2) and (3) of section 20 and section 106 of the 1949 Act shall apply in relation to byelaws under this section as they apply in relation to byelaws under the said section 20.

(5)   In this section—
"approved body" means a body approved by the Council for the purposes of this section;
"nature reserve" has the same meaning as in Part III of the 1949 Act.

[65]

36 Marine nature reserves

(1)   Where, in the case of any land covered (continuously or intermittently) by tidal waters or parts of the sea [which are landward of the baselines from which the breadth of the territorial sea adjacent to Great Britain is measured or are seaward of those baselines up to a distance of three nautical miles], it appears to the Secretary of State expedient, on an application made by the Nature Conservancy Council, that the land and waters covering it should be managed by the Council for the purpose of—
   (a) conserving marine flora or fauna or geological or physiographical features of special interest in the area; or
   (b) providing, under suitable conditions and control, special opportunities for the study of, and research into, matters relating to marine flora and fauna and the physical conditions in which they live, or for the study of geological and physiographical features of special interest in the area,

he may by order designate the area comprising that land and those waters as a marine nature reserve; and the Council shall manage any area so designated for either or both of those purposes.

(2)   An application for an order under this section shall be accompanied by—
   (a) a copy of the byelaws which, if an order is made, the Council propose making under section 37 for the protection of the area specified in the application; and
   (b) a copy of any byelaws made or proposed to be made for the protection of that area by a relevant authority;

and an order made on the application shall authorise the making under that section of such of the byelaws proposed to be made by the Council as may be set out in the order with or without modifications.

(3)   Byelaws the making of which is so authorised—
   (a) shall not require the Secretary of State's consent under subsection (1) of section 37; and
   (b) notwithstanding anything in the provisions applied by subsection (4) of that section, shall take effect on their being made.

(4)   The provisions of Schedule 12 shall have effect as to the making, validity and date of coming into operation of orders under this section; and an order made under this section may be amended or revoked by a subsequent order so made.

(5)   The powers exercisable by the Council for the purpose of managing an area designated as a marine nature reserve under this section shall include power to install markers indicating the existence and extent of the reserve.

(6)   Nothing in this section or in byelaws made under section 37 shall interfere with the exercise of any functions of a relevant authority, any functions conferred by or under an enactment (whenever passed) or any right of any person (whenever vested).

(7)   In this section—
"enactment" includes an enactment contained in a local Act;
"local authority" means—

(a) in relation to England and Wales, a county council, [a county borough council], a district council, . . . or a London borough council;

(b) (*applies to Scotland only*);

["nautical miles" means international-nautical miles of 1,852 metres;]

"relevant authority" means a local authority, [the National Rivers Authority, a water undertaker, a sewerage undertaker,] an internal drainage board, a navigation authority, a harbour authority, . . . , a lighthouse authority, a conservancy authority, [the Scottish Environment Protection Agency], a district board for a fishery district within the meaning of the Salmon Fisheries (Scotland) Act 1862, or a local fisheries committee constituted under the Sea Fisheries Regulation Act 1966.

[66]

NOTES

Sub-s (1): words in square brackets substituted by the Territorial Sea Act 1987, s 3(1), Sch 1, para 6.

Sub-s (7): in definition "local authority" words in square brackets inserted by the Local Government (Wales) Act 1994, s 66(6), Sch 16, para 65(4), as from a day to be appointed, words omitted repealed by the Local Government Act 1985, s 102(2), Sch 17; definition "nautical miles" inserted by the Territorial Sea Act 1987, s 3(1), Sch 1, para 6; in definition "relevant authority" words in first pair of square brackets substituted by the Water Act 1989, s 190, Sch 25, para 66(2), words omitted repealed by the Pilotage Act 1987, s 32(5), Sch 3, words in second pair of square brackets substituted by the Environment Act 1995 (Consequential and Transitional Provisions) (Scotland) Regulations 1996, SI 1996/973, reg 2, Schedule, para 6.

National Rivers Authority: a reference to the National Rivers Authority is to be construed as a reference to the Environment Agency; by virtue of the Environment Act 1995 (Consequential Amendments) Regulations 1996, SI 1996/593, reg 2, Sch 1.

37 Byelaws for protection of marine nature reserves

(1) The Nature Conservancy Council may, with the consent of the Secretary of State make byelaws for the protection of any area designated as a marine nature reserve under section 36.

(2) Without prejudice to the generality of subsection (1), byelaws made under this section as respects a marine nature reserve—

(a) may provide for prohibiting or restricting, either absolutely or subject to any exceptions—

(i) the entry into, or movement within, the reserve of persons and vessels;

(ii) the killing, taking, destruction, molestation or disturbance of animals or plants of any description in the reserve, or the doing of anything therein which will interfere with the sea bed or damage or disturb any object in the reserve; or

(iii) the depositing of rubbish in the reserve;

(b) may provide for the issue, on such terms and subject to such conditions as may be specified in the byelaws, of permits authorising entry into the reserve or the doing of anything which would otherwise be unlawful under the byelaws; and

(c) may be so made as to apply either generally or with respect to particular parts of the reserve or particular times of the year.

(3) Nothing in byelaws made under this section shall—

(a) prohibit or restrict the exercise of any right of passage by a vessel other than a pleasure boat; or

(b) prohibit, except with respect to particular parts of the reserve at particular times of the year, the exercise of any such right by a pleasure boat.

(4) Nothing in byelaws so made shall make unlawful—

(a) anything done for the purpose of securing the safety of any vessel, or of preventing damage to any vessel or cargo, or of saving life;

(b) the discharge of any substance from a vessel; or

(c) anything done more than 30 metres below the sea bed.

(5)   Sections 236 to 238 of the Local Government Act 1972 or sections 202 to 204 of the Local Government (Scotland) Act 1973 (which relate to the procedure for making byelaws, authorise byelaws to impose fines not exceeding the amount there specified and provide for the proof of byelaws in legal proceedings) shall apply to byelaws under this section as if the Council were a local authority within the meaning of the said Act of 1972 or the said Act of 1973, so however that in relation to such byelaws the said sections shall apply subject to such modifications (including modifications increasing the maximum fines which the byelaws may impose) as may be prescribed by regulations made by the Secretary of State.

Regulations under this subsection shall be made by statutory instrument which shall be subject to annulment in pursuance of a resolution of either House of Parliament.

(6)   In relation to byelaws under this section the confirming authority for the purposes of the said section 236 or the said section 202 shall be the Secretary of State.

(7)   The Secretary of State may, after consultation with the Council, direct them—

(a) to revoke any byelaws previously made under this section; or

(b) to make any such amendments of any byelaws so made as may be specified in the direction.

(8)   The Council shall have power to enforce byelaws made under this section; . . .

(9)   Proceedings in England and Wales for an offence under byelaws made under this section shall not, without the consent of the Director of Public Prosecutions, be taken by a person other than the Council.

(10) In this section "vessel" includes a hovercraft and any aircraft capable of landing on water and "pleasure boat" shall be construed accordingly.

(11) References in this section to animals or plants of any description include references to eggs, seeds, spores, larvae or other immature stages of animals or plants of that description.

[67]

NOTES

Sub-s (8): words omitted apply to Scotland only.

Regulations: the Wildlife and Countryside (Byelaws for Marine Nature Reserves) Regulations 1986, SI 1986/143.

---

38   *(Repealed by the Environmental Protection Act 1990, s 162(2), Sch 16, Pt VI.)*

Countryside

39 Management agreements with owners and occupiers of land

(1)   A relevant authority may, for the purpose of conserving or enhancing the natural beauty or amenity of any land which is both in the countryside and within their area or promoting its enjoyment by the public, make an agreement (in this section referred to as a "management agreement") with any person having an interest in the land with respect to the management of the land during a specified term or without limitation of the duration of the agreement.

(2)   Without prejudice to the generality of subsection (1), a management agreement—

(a) may impose on the person having an interest in the land restrictions as respects the method of cultivating the land, its use for agricultural purposes

or the exercise of rights over the land and may impose obligations on that
person to carry out works or agricultural or forestry operations or do other
things on the land;

(b) may confer on the relevant authority power to carry out works for the
purpose of performing their functions under the 1949 Act and the 1968
Act; and

(c) may contain such incidental and consequential provisions (including
provisions for the making of payments by either party to the other) as
appear to the relevant authority to be necessary or expedient for the
purposes of the agreement.

(3)   The provisions of a management agreement with any person interested in
the land shall, unless the agreement otherwise provides, be binding on persons
deriving title under or from that person and be enforceable by the relevant authority
against those persons accordingly.

(4)   Schedule 2 to the Forestry Act 1967 (power for tenant for life and others to
enter into forestry dedication covenants) shall apply to management agreements as it
applies to forestry dedication covenants.

(5)   In this section "the relevant authority" means—

(a) *as respects land [which is not in an area for which a National Park
authority is the local planning authority but is] in a National Park [and
outside a metropolitan county], the county planning authority;*

[(aa) as respects land within the Broads, the Broads Authority;]

(b) . . .

(c) as respects any other land, the local planning authority.

(6)   The powers conferred by this section on a relevant authority shall be in
addition to and not in derogation of any powers conferred on such an authority by or
under any enactment.

[68]

_____

NOTES

Sub-s (5): words in first pair of square brackets in para (a) inserted, and whole of para (a) as so
amended repealed, by the Environment Act 1995, s 78, Sch 10, para 22(1), (7), Sch 24, as from a day to
be appointed; words in second pair of square brackets in para (a) inserted and para (b) repealed by the
Local Government Act 1985, ss 7, 102(2), Sch 3, para 7(3), Sch 17; para (aa) inserted by the Norfolk and
Suffolk Broads Act 1988, s 2(5), Sch 3, Part I, para 31(2).

_____

40   (*Substitutes the Countryside Act 1968, s 4(1), for sub-ss (1), (2) of that section as
originally enacted.*)

41 Duties of agriculture Ministers with respect to the countryside

(1)   . . .

(2)   (*Applies to Scotland only.*)

(3)   Where an application for [a farm capital grant] is made as respects
expenditure incurred or to be incurred for the purposes of activities on land which is
in a National Park or an area specified for the purposes of this subsection by the
Ministers, the appropriate Minister—

(a) shall, so far as may be consistent with the purposes of [the grant
provisions], so exercise his functions thereunder as to further the
conservation and enhancement of the natural beauty and amenity of the
countryside and to promote its enjoyment by the public; and

(b) where the relevant authority have objected to the making of the grant on
the ground that the activities in question have had or will have an adverse
effect on the natural beauty or amenity of the countryside or its enjoyment

by the public, shall not make the grant except after considering the objection and, in the case of land in England, after consulting with the Secretary of State;

. . .

(4)   Where, in consequence of an objection by the relevant authority, an application for a grant as respects expenditure to be incurred is refused on the ground that the activities in question will have such an effect as is mentioned in subsection (3)(b), the relevant authority shall, within three months of their receiving notice of the appropriate Minister's decision, offer to enter into, in the terms of a draft submitted on the applicant, a management agreement—
  (a) imposing restrictions as respects those activities; and
  (b) providing for the making by them of payments to the applicant.

(5)   In this section—
  ["agricultural business" has the same meaning as in section 29 of the
       Agriculture Act 1970;
  "the appropriate Minister", "farm capital grant" and "grant provisions" have
       the same meanings as in section 32;]
  "management agreement"—
       (a) in relation to England and Wales, means an agreement under section 39;
       (b) (*applies to Scotland only*);
  "the relevant authority"—
       (a) in relation to England and Wales, has the same meaning as in section 39;
       (b) (*applies to Scotland only*).

[(5A) For the purposes of this section the Broads shall be treated as a National Park [(and, as respects land within the Broads, any reference in this section to the relevant authority is accordingly a reference to the Broads Authority).]

(6)   . . . subsection (2) extends only to Scotland.

[69]

_____

NOTES
  Sub-ss (1), (6): words omitted repealed by the Agriculture Act 1986, s 24(5), Sch 4.
  Sub-s (3): words in square brackets substituted by the Agriculture Act 1986, s 20(1), (4), words omitted apply to Scotland only.
  Sub-s (5): words in square brackets substituted by the Agriculture Act 1986, s 20(1), (5).
  Sub-s (5A): inserted by the Norfolk and Suffolk Broads Act 1988, s 2(5), Sch 3, Pt I, para 31(3), words in square brackets added by the Environment Act 1995, s 78, Sch 10, para 22(2), as from a day to be appointed.

_____

National Parks

42 Notification of agricultural operations on moor and heath in National Parks

(1)   The Ministers may, if satisfied that it is expedient to do so, by order apply subsection (2) to any land which is comprised in a National Park and which appears to them to consist of or include moor or heath.

(2)   Subject to subsection (3), no person shall—
  (a) by ploughing or otherwise convert into agricultural land any land to which
       this subsection applies and which is moor or heath which has not been
       agricultural land at any time within the preceding 20 years; or
  (b) carry out on any such land any other agricultural operation or any forestry
       operation which (in either case) appears to the Ministers to be likely to
       affect its character or appearance and is specified in the order applying this
       subsection to that land.

(3)   Subsection (2) shall not apply in relation to any operation carried out, or caused or permitted to be carried out, by the owner or occupier of the land if—

(a) one of them has, after the coming into force of the order, given the [National Park authority] written notice of a proposal to carry out the operation, specifying its nature and the land on which it is proposed to carry it out; and

(b) one of the conditions specified in subsection (4) is satisfied.

(4) The said conditions are—

(a) that the [National Park authority] have given their consent to the carrying out of the operation;

(b) where that authority have neither given nor refused their consent, that three months have expired from the giving of the notice; and

(c) where that authority have refused their consent, that twelve months have expired from the giving of the notice.

(5) A person who, without reasonable excuse, contravenes subsection (2) shall be liable—

(a) on summary conviction, to a fine not exceeding the statutory maximum;

(b) on conviction on indictment, to a fine.

(6) Where the [National Park authority] are given notice under this section in respect of any land, the authority shall forthwith send copies of the notice to the Ministers, the Nature Conservancy Council and the Countryside Commission.

(7) In considering for the purposes of this section whether land has been agricultural land within the preceding 20 years, no account shall be taken of any conversion of the land into agricultural land which was unlawful under the provisions of this section or section 14 of the 1968 Act.

(8) An order under this section shall be made by statutory instrument which shall be subject to annulment in pursuance of a resolution of either House of Parliament.

(9) The said section 14 (which is superseded by this section) shall cease to have effect; but this section shall have effect as if any order under that section in force immediately before the coming into force of this section had been made under this section.

[70]

NOTES

Sub-ss (3), (4), (6): words in square brackets substituted by the Environment Act 1995, s 78, Sch 10, para 22(3).

43 Maps of National Parks showing certain areas of moor or heath

(1) Every [local planning authority] whose area comprises the whole or any part of a National Park shall—

(a) before the expiration of the period of two years beginning with [the relevant date], prepare a map of the Park or the part thereof showing any areas [to which this section applies whose natural beauty] it is, in the opinion of the authority, particularly important to conserve; and

(b) [at intervals of not more than five years] review the particulars contained in the map and make such revisions thereof (if any) as may be requisite.

[(1A) In considering under subsection (1) whether any area to which this section applies is one whose natural beauty it is particularly important to conserve, a [local planning authority] shall act in accordance with the guide-lines from time to time issued . . . under subsection (1B).

(1B) The Countryside Commission [and the Countryside Council for Wales shall each] issue guidelines for the guidance of [local planning authorities] in considering as mentioned in subsection (1A), and [the Commission and the Council may each] from time to time revise any guidelines so issued.

(1C) Before issuing or revising any guidelines under subsection (1B) the Commission [or, as the case may be, the Council] shall consult such bodies as appear to them to represent interests concerned; and before preparing or revising any map under subsection (1) a [local planning authority] shall consult such bodies as appear to the authority to represent interests concerned with matters affecting the Park or part of the Park in question.]

(2) The authority shall cause a map prepared or revised in pursuance of subsection (1) to be printed, and shall cause copies thereof to be put on sale to the public at such price as the authority may determine.

[(3) This section applies to any area of mountain, moor, heath, woodland, down, cliff or foreshore (including any bank, barrier, dune, beach, flat or other land adjacent to the foreshore); and in this section "the relevant date" means the date of issue of the first guidelines under subsection (1B).]

[71]

NOTES
    Sub-s (1): words in first pair of square brackets substituted by the Local Government Act 1985, s 7, Sch 3, para 7(4); words in remaining pairs of square brackets substituted by the Wildlife and Countryside (Amendment) Act 1985, s 3.
    Sub-s (1A): inserted by the Wildlife and Countryside (Amendment) Act 1985, s 3; words in square brackets substituted by the Local Government Act 1985, s 7, Sch 3, para 7(4); words omitted repealed by the Environmental Protection Act 1990, ss 130, 162(2), Sch 8, para 6(1), (3), Sch 16, Pt VI.
    Sub-s (1B): inserted by the Wildlife and Countryside (Amendment) Act 1985, s 3; words in first and third pairs of square brackets substituted by the Environmental Protection Act 1990, s 130, Sch 8, para 6(1), (3); words in second pair of square brackets substituted by the Local Government Act 1985, s 7, Sch 3, para 7.
    Sub-s (1C): inserted by the Wildlife and Countryside (Amendment) Act 1985, s 3; words in first pair of square brackets inserted by the Environmental Protection Act 1990, s 130, Sch 8, para 6(1), (3); words in second pair of square brackets substituted by the Local Government Act 1985, s 7, Sch 3, para 7(4).
    Sub-s (3): added by the Wildlife and Countryside (Amendment) Act 1985, s 3.

44 Grants and loans for purposes of National Parks

(1)   Without prejudice to section 11 of the 1949 Act (general powers of local planning authorities in relation to National Parks), a [local planning authority] may give financial assistance by way of grant or loan, or partly in one way and partly in the other, to any person in respect of expenditure incurred by him in doing anything which in the opinion of the authority is conducive to the attainment, in any National Park the whole or part of which is comprised in that authority's area, of any of the following purposes, that is to say, the conservation and enhancement of the natural beauty of that Park and the promotion of its enjoyment by the public.

[(1A) *Subsection (1) above shall not apply in relation to any National Park for which a National Park authority is the local planning authority; but* the National Park authority for such a Park may give financial assistance by way of grant or loan, or partly in one way and partly in the other, to any person in respect of expenditure incurred by him in doing anything which, in the opinion of the authority, is conducive to the attainment in the Park in question of any of the purposes mentioned in section 5(1) of the 1949 Act (purposes of conserving and enhancing the natural beauty, wildlife and cultural heritage of National Parks and of promoting opportunities for the understanding and enjoyment of the special qualities of those Parks by the public).]

(2)   On making a grant or loan under this section [the authority in question] may impose such conditions as they think fit, including (in the case of a grant) conditions for repayment in specified circumstances.

(3)   [The authority in question] shall so exercise their powers under subsection (2) as to ensure that any person receiving a grant or loan under this section in respect of premises to which the public are to be admitted, whether on payment or otherwise,

shall, in the means of access both to and within the premises, and in the parking facilities and sanitary conveniences to be available (if any), make provision, insofar as it is in the circumstances both practicable and reasonable, for the needs of members of the public visiting the premises who are disabled.

[(4) For the purposes of this section the Broads Authority shall be treated as a *county planning authority and the Broads as a National Park.*]

[72]

_____

NOTES

Sub-s (1): words in square brackets substituted by the Local Government Act 1985, s 7, Sch 3, para 7; whole sub-section repealed by the Environment Act 1995, s 120(3), Sch 24, as from a day to be appointed.

Sub-s (1A): inserted by the Environment Act 1995, ss 69(4), 78, Sch 10, para 22(4)(a), (b), words in italics repealed by the Environment Act 1995, s 120(3), Sch 24, as from a day to be appointed.

Sub-ss (2), (3): words in square brackets substituted by the Environment Act 1995, ss 69(4), 78, Sch 10, para 22(4)(a), (b).

Sub-s (4): added by the Norfolk and Suffolk Broads Act 1988, s 2(5), Sch 3, Pt I, para 31(4), for the words in italics there are substituted the words "National Park authority and the Broads as a National Park for which it is the local planning authority" by the Environment Act 1995, s 78, Sch 10, para 22(4)(c), as from a day to be appointed.

_____

45 Power to vary orders designating National Park

[(1)] The Countryside Commission (as well as the Secretary of State) shall have power to make an order amending an order made under section 5 of the 1949 Act designating a National Park [in England], and—
  (a) section 7(5) and (6) of that Act (consultation and publicity in connection with orders under section 5 or 7) shall apply to an order under this section as they apply to an order under section 7(4) of that Act with the substitution for the reference in section 7(5) to the Secretary of State of a reference to the Countryside Commission; and
  (b) Schedule 1 to that Act (procedure in connection with the making and confirmation of orders under section 5 or 7) shall apply to an order under this section as it applies to an order designating a National Park.

[(2) Subsection (1) shall apply to the Countryside Council for Wales, in relation to any National Park in Wales, as it applies to the Countryside Commission in relation to any National Park in England.]

[73]

_____

NOTES

Sub-s (1): numbered as such and words in square brackets inserted by the Environmental Protection Act 1990, s 130, Sch 8, para 6(1), (4).

Sub-s (2): added by the Environmental Protection Act 1990, s 130, Sch 8, para 6(1), (4).

_____

46   (*Relates to membership of National Park Authorities.*)

Miscellaneous and supplemental

47–49   (*Relate to provisions with respect to the Countryside Commission (s 47), the extension of power to appoint wardens (s 49); s 48 repealed by the Water Act 1989, s 190(3), Sch 27, Pt 1.*)

50 Payments under certain agreements offered by authorities

  (1)   This section applies where—
  (a) the Nature Conservancy Council offer to enter into an agreement under section 16 of the 1949 Act or section 15 of the 1968 Act providing for the making by them of payments to—

      (i) a person who has given notice under section 28(5) or 29(4); or

     (ii) a person whose application for farm capital grant has been refused in consequence of an objection by the Council; or

  (b) the relevant authority offer to enter into a management agreement providing for the making by them of payments to a person whose application for a farm capital grant has been refused in consequence of an objection by the authority.

(2)   Subject to subsection (3), the said payments shall be of such amounts as may be determined by the offeror in accordance with guidance given by the Ministers.

(3)   If the offeree so requires within one month of receiving the offer, the determination of those amounts shall be referred to an arbitrator (or, in Scotland, an arbiter) to be appointed, in default of agreement, by the Secretary of State; and where the amounts determined by the arbitrator exceed those determined by the offeror, the offeror shall—

  (a) amend the offer so as to give effect to the arbitrator's (or, in Scotland, the arbiter's) determination; or

  (b) except in the case of an offer made to a person whose application for a farm capital grant has been refused in consequence of an objection by the offeror, withdraw the offer.

(4)   In this section—

["farm capital grant" has the same meaning as in section 32;]

"management agreement" and "the relevant authority" have the same meanings as in section 41.

[74]

NOTES

    Sub-s (4): words in square brackets substituted by the Agriculture Act 1986, s 20(1), (6).

51 Powers of entry

(1)   Any person authorised in writing by the relevant authority may, at any reasonable time and (if required to do so) upon producing evidence that he is authorised, enter any land for any of the following purposes—

  (a) to ascertain whether an order should be made in relation to that land under section 29 or if an offence under that section is being, or has been, committed on that land;

  (b) to ascertain the amount of any compensation payable under section 30 in respect of an interest in that land;

  (c) to ascertain whether an order should be made in relation to that land under section 34 or if an offence under that section is being, or has been, committed on that land;

  (d) to ascertain whether an order should be made in relation to that land under section 42 or if an offence under that section is being, or has been, committed on that land;

but nothing in this subsection shall authorise any person to enter a dwelling.

(2)   In subsection (1) "the relevant authority" means—

  (a) for the purposes of paragraphs (a) and (b) of that subsection, the Nature Conservancy Council;

  (b) for the purposes of paragraph (c) of that subsection, the Secretary of State or the relevant authority within the meaning of section 34;

  (c) for the purposes of paragraph (d) of that subsection, the Ministers or the [National Park authority].

(3)   A person shall not demand admission as of right to any land which is occupied unless either—

(a) 24 hours notice of the intended entry has been given to the occupier; or
(b) the purpose of the entry is to ascertain if an offence under section 29, 34 or 42 is being, or has been, committed on that land.

(4) Any person who intentionally obstructs a person acting in the exercise of any power conferred by subsection (1) shall be liable on summary conviction to a fine not exceeding [level 3 on the standard scale].

[75]

NOTES

Sub-s (2): words in square brackets in para (c) substituted by the Environment Act 1995, s 78, Sch 10, para 22(5).

Sub-s (4): maximum fine converted to a level on the standard scale by virtue of the Criminal Justice Act 1982, ss 37, 46.

52 Interpretation of Part II

(1) In this Part, unless the context otherwise requires,—
"agricultural land" does not include land which affords rough grazing for livestock but is not otherwise used as agricultural land;
"the Ministers", in the application of this Part to England, means the Secretary of State and the Minister of Agriculture, Fisheries and Food, and, in the application of this Part to Scotland or Wales, means the Secretary of State;
["the Nature Conservancy Councils" means the Nature Conservancy Council for England, [Scottish Natural Heritage] and the Countryside Council for Wales;

and references to "the Nature Conservancy Council" shall be construed in accordance with section 27A.]

(2) [In the application of this Part to England (except as respects [a National Park for which a National Park authority is the local planning authority,] a metropolitan county or Greater London) *and to Wales* references to a local planning authority shall be construed—
(a) in sections 42, 43, 44 and 51(2)(c) as references to a county planning authority; and
(b) *in any other provision*, as references to a county planning authority and a district planning authority;]

. . .

(3) References in this Part to the conservation of the natural beauty of any land shall be construed as including references to the conservation of its flora, fauna and geological and physiographical features.

(4) Section 114 of the 1949 Act shall apply for the construction of this Part.

(5) Any power or duty which under this Part (except sections 41 and 42(1)) falls to be exercised or performed by or in relation to the Ministers may, in England, be exercised or performed by or in relation to either of them.

[76]

NOTES

Sub-s (1): words in first (outer) pair of square brackets added by the Environmental Protection Act 1990, s 132, 133, Sch 9, para 11(1), (13), words in second (inner) pair of square brackets substituted by the Natural Heritage (Scotland) Act 1991, s 4, Sch 2, para 8(5).

Sub-s (2): words in first (outer) pair of square brackets substituted by the Local Government Act 1985, s 7, Sch 3, para 7(4), words in second (inner) pair of square brackets inserted, and words in italics repealed, by the Environment Act 1995, ss 78, 120(3), Sch 10, para 22(6), Sch 24, as from a day to be appointed; words omitted apply to Scotland only.

53–66 *((Pt III) relate to public rights of way, insofar as unrepealed.)*

PART IV
MISCELLANEOUS AND GENERAL

67–70A *(Relate to miscellaneous matters concerning application to the Crown (s 67); application to Isles of Scilly (s 68); offences by bodies corporate etc (s 69); financial provisions (s 70); service of notices (s 70A), so far as unrepealed.)*

71 General interpretation

In this Act—
"the 1949 Act" means the National Parks and Access to the Countryside Act 1949;
"the 1968 Act" means the Countryside Act 1968;
["the Broads" has the same meaning as in the Norfolk and Suffolk Broads Act 1988.]
"the commencement date", in relation to any provision of this Act and any area, means the date of the coming into force of that provision in that area;
"London borough council" includes the Common Council of the City of London;
"modifications" includes additions, alterations and omissions, and cognate expressions shall be construed accordingly;
. . . . .

[77]

NOTES
    Definition "the Broads" inserted by the Norfolk and Suffolk Broads Act 1988, s 2(5), (6), Sch 3, Pt I; definition omitted repealed by the Statute Law (Repeals) Act 1993.

72, 73 *(Relate to minor amendments (s 72); repeals and savings (s 73), so far as unrepealed.)*

74 Short title, commencement and extent

(1)   This Act may be cited as the Wildlife and Countryside Act 1981.

(2)   The following provisions of this Act, namely—
Part II, except sections 29 to 32, 41 and 46 to 48 and Schedule 13;
sections 59 to 62 and 65 and 66; and
Part IV, except section 72(4), (6) and (14) and section 73(1) so far as relating to Part II of Schedule 17,
shall come into force on the expiration of the period of one month beginning with the passing of this Act.

(3)   The remaining provisions of this Act shall come into force on such day as the Secretary of State may by order made by statutory instrument appoint and different days may be appointed under this subsection for different provisions, different purposes or different areas.

(4)   An order under subsection (3) may make such transitional provisions as appears to the Secretary of State to be necessary or expedient in connection with the provisions thereby brought into force.

(5)   *(Applies to Scotland only.)*

(6)   This Act, except section 15(1) and Schedule 10 and, so far as regards any enactment mentioned in Schedule 17 that so extends, section 73 and that Schedule, does not extend to Northern Ireland.

NOTES
Orders: the Wildlife and Countryside Act 1981 (Commencement No 1) Order 1982, SI 1982/44; the Wildlife and Countryside Act 1981 (Commencement No 2) Order 1982, SI 1982/327; the Wildlife and Countryside Act 1981 (Commencement No 3) Order 1982, SI 1982/990; the Wildlife and Countryside Act 1981 (Commencement No 4) Order 1982, SI 1982/1136; the Wildlife and Countryside Act 1981 (Commencement No 5) Order 1982, SI 1982/1217; the Wildlife and Countryside Act 1981 (Commencement No 6) Order 1982, SI 1983/20; the Wildlife and Countryside Act 1981 (Commencement No 7) Order 1982, 1983/87.

(Schs 1–10 outside the scope of this work.)

SCHEDULE 11
PROCEDURE IN CONNECTION WITH CERTAIN ORDERS UNDER PART II
Sections 29, 34

Coming into operation

1.—(1) An original order or a restrictive amending order shall take effect on its being made.

(2) It shall be the duty of the Secretary of State to consider every original order or restrictive amending order made by him or a relevant authority, and any such order shall cease to have effect nine months after it is made unless the Secretary of State has previously given notice under paragraph 6 that he has considered it and does not propose to amend or revoke it or he has amended or revoked it or, in the case of an order made by such an authority, the authority has revoked it.

(3) An amending or revoking order, other than a restrictive amending order, made by a relevant authority shall be submitted by the authority to the Secretary of State for confirmation and shall not take effect until confirmed by him.

(4) Subject to paragraphs 3(1) and 4(4), an amending or revoking order, other than a restrictive amending order, made by the Secretary of State shall not take effect until confirmed by him.

(5) An amending or revoking order requiring confirmation shall, by virtue of this sub-paragraph, stand revoked if the Secretary of State gives notice under paragraph 6 that the order is not to be confirmed.

Publicity for orders

2.—(1) Where an order takes effect immediately, the authority making the order (whether the relevant authority or the Secretary of State) shall give notice—
    (a)   setting out the order or describing its general effect and in either case stating that it has taken effect;
    (b)   naming a place in the area in which the land to which the order relates is situated where a copy of the order may be inspected free of charge at all reasonable hours; and
    (c)   specifying the time (not being less than 28 days from the date of the first publication of the notice) within which, and the manner in which, representations or objections with respect to the order may be made.

(2) Where an order requires confirmation, the authority making the order shall give notice—
    (a)   setting out the order or describing its general effect and in either case stating that it has been made and requires confirmation; and
    (b)   stating in relation to it the matters specified in sub-paragraph (1)(b) and (c).

(3) Subject to sub-paragraph (4), the notice to be given under sub-paragraph (1) or (2) shall be given—
    (a)   by publication in the Gazette and also at least one local newspaper circulating in the area in which the land to which the order relates is situated;
    (b)   by serving a like notice on every owner and occupier of any of that land; and
    (c)   in the case of a notice given by the Secretary of State, by serving a like notice on the relevant authority in whose area the land to which the order relates is situated.

(4) The Secretary of State may, in any particular case, direct that it shall not be necessary to comply with sub-paragraph (3)(b); but if he so directs in the case of any land, then in

addition to publication the notice shall be addressed to "The owners and any occupiers" of the land (describing it) and a copy or copies of the notice shall be affixed to some conspicuous object or objects on the land.

Unopposed orders

3.—(1) Where an order made by a relevant authority takes effect immediately and no representations or objections are duly made in respect of it or any so made are withdrawn,—
    (a)   the Secretary of State shall as soon as practicable after considering it decide either to take no action on the order or to make an order amending or revoking it (subject, however, to paragraph 5); and
    (b)   the amending or revoking order shall take effect immediately, but it shall not require confirmation and no representation or objection with respect to it shall be entertained.

(2) Where an order requiring confirmation is made and no representations or objections are duly made in respect of it or any so made are withdrawn, the Secretary of State may confirm the order (with or without modification).

Opposed orders

4.—(1) If any representation or objection duly made with respect to an order is not withdrawn, then, as soon as practicable in the case of an order having immediate effect and before confirming an order requiring confirmation, the Secretary of State shall either—
    (a)   cause a local inquiry to be held; or
    (b)   afford any person by whom a representation or objection has been duly made and not withdrawn an opportunity of being heard by a person appointed by the Secretary of State for the purpose.

(2) On considering any representations or objections duly made and the report of any person appointed to hold the inquiry or to hear representations or objections, the Secretary of State—
    (a)   shall, if the order has already taken effect, decide either to take no action on the order or to make an order (subject, however, to paragraph 5) amending or revoking the order as the Secretary of State thinks appropriate in the light of the report, representations or objections, without consulting the relevant authority where that authority made the order; or
    (b)   if the order requires confirmation, may confirm it (with or without modifications).

(3) The provisions of subsections (2) to (5) of section 250 of the Local Government Act 1972 or subsections (4) to (8) of section 210 of the Local Government (Scotland) Act 1973 (which relate to the giving of evidence at, and defraying the cost of, local inquiries) shall apply in relation to any inquiry held under this paragraph as they apply in relation to a local inquiry which a Minister causes to be held under subsection (1) of that section.

(4) An amending or revoking order made by virtue of this paragraph shall take effect immediately, but it shall not require confirmation and no representation or objection with respect to it shall be entertained.

Restriction on power to amend orders or confirm them with modifications

5. The Secretary of State shall not by virtue of paragraph 3(1) or 4(2) amend an order which has taken effect, or confirm any other order with modifications, so as to extend the area to which an original order applies.

Notice of final decision on orders

6.—(1) The Secretary of State shall as soon as practicable after making an order by virtue of paragraph 3(1) or 4(2) give notice—
    (a)   setting out the order or describing its general effect and in either case stating that it has taken effect; and
    (b)   stating the name of the place in the area in which the land to which the order relates is situated where a copy of the order may be inspected free of charge at all reasonable hours.

(2) The Secretary of State shall give notice of any of the following decisions of his as soon as practicable after making the decision—

(a) a decision under paragraph 3(1) or 4(2) to take no action on an order which has already taken effect;

(b) a decision to confirm or not to confirm an order requiring confirmation under this Schedule.

(3) A notice under this paragraph of a decision to confirm an order shall—

(a) set out the order as confirmed or describe its general effect, and in either case state the day on which the order took effect;

(b) state the name of the place in the area in which the land to which the order relates is situated where a copy of the order as confirmed may be inspected free of charge at all reasonable hours.

(4) A notice under this paragraph shall be given by publishing it in accordance with paragraph 2(3) and serving a copy of it on any person on whom a notice was required to be served under paragraph 2(3) or (4).

Proceedings for questioning validity of orders

7.—(1) This paragraph applies to any order which has taken effect and as to which the Secretary of State has given notice under paragraph 6 of a decision of his to take no action or to amend the order in accordance with paragraph 3 or 4; and in this paragraph "the relevant notice" means any such notice.

(2) If any person is aggrieved by an order to which this paragraph applies and desires to question its validity on the ground that it is not within the powers of section 29 or 34, as the case may be, or that any of the requirements of this Schedule have not been complied with in relation to it, he may within six weeks from the date of the relevant notice make an application to the Court under this paragraph.

(3) On any such application the Court may, if satisfied that the order is not within those powers or that the interests of the applicant have been substantially prejudiced by a failure to comply with any of those requirements—

(a) in England and Wales, quash the order, or any provision of the order, either generally or in so far as it affects the interests of the applicant; or

(b) *(applies to Scotland only).*

(4) Except as provided by this paragraph, the validity of an order shall not be questioned in any legal proceedings whatsoever.

(5) In this paragraph "the Court" means the High Court in relation to England and Wales and the Court of Session in relation to Scotland.

Interpretation

8. In this Schedule—

"amending order" and "revoking order" mean an order which amends or, as the case may be, revokes a previous order;

"the Gazette" means—

(a) if the order relates in whole or in part to England and Wales, the London Gazette;

(b) if the order relates in whole or in part to Scotland, the Edinburgh Gazette;

"order" means an order under section 29 or 34;

"original order" means an order other than an amending or revoking order;

"the relevant authority" has the same meaning as in section 34;

"restrictive amending order" means an amending order which extends the area to which a previous order applies.

[79]

SCHEDULE 12
PROCEDURE IN CONNECTION WITH ORDERS UNDER SECTION 36

Section 36

Consultation

1. Before making an order, the Secretary of State shall consult with such persons as he may consider appropriate.

Publicity for draft orders

2.—(1) Before making an order, the Secretary of State shall prepare a draft of the order and give notice—

(a)   stating that he proposes to make the order and the general effect of it;

(b)   naming a place in the area in which the land to which the draft order relates is situated where a copy of the draft order, and of any byelaws made or proposed to be made by a relevant authority for the protection of the area specified in the draft order, may be inspected free of charge, and copies thereof may be obtained at a reasonable charge, at all reasonable hours; and

(c)   specifying the time (not being less than 28 days from the date of the first publication of the notice) within which, and the manner in which, representations or objections with respect to the draft order may be made.

(2) Subject to sub-paragraph (3), the notice to be given under sub-paragraph (1) shall be given—

(a)   by publication in the Gazette and also at least one local newspaper circulating in the area in which the land to which the draft order relates is situated;

(b)   by serving a like notice on—
    (i)   every person in whom is vested an interest in or right over any of that land;
    (ii) every relevant authority whose area includes any of that land; and
    (iii) such other bodies as may be prescribed or as the Secretary of State may consider appropriate; and

(c)   by causing a copy of the notice to be displayed in a prominent position—
    (i)   at council offices in the locality of the land to which the draft order relates; and
    (ii) at such other places as the Secretary of State may consider appropriate.

(3) The Secretary of State may, in any particular case, direct that it shall not be necessary to comply with sub-paragraph (2)(b)(i).

(4) Subject to sub-paragraph (3), sub-paragraph (2)(b) and (c) shall be complied with not less than 28 days before the expiration of the time specified in the notice.

Unopposed orders

3. If no representations or objections are duly made, or if any so made are withdrawn, the Secretary of State may make the order with or without modifications.

Opposed orders

4.—(1) If any representation or objection duly made is not withdrawn the Secretary of State shall, before making the order, either—

(a)   cause a local inquiry to be held; or

(b)   afford any person by whom a representation or objection has been duly made and not withdrawn an opportunity of being heard by a person appointed by the Secretary of State for the purpose.

(2) On considering any representations or objections duly made and the report of the person appointed to hold the inquiry or hear representations or objections, the Secretary of State may make the order with or without modifications.

Restriction on power to make orders with modifications

5.—(1) The Secretary of State shall not make an order with modifications so as—

(a)   to affect land not affected by the draft order; or

(b)   to authorise the making of any byelaw not authorised by the draft order,

except after complying with the requirements of sub-paragraph (2).

(2) The said requirements are that the Secretary of State shall—

(a)   give such notice as appears to him requisite of his proposal so to modify the order, specifying the time (which shall not be less than 28 days from the date of the first publication of the notice) within which, and the manner in which, representations or objections with respect to the proposal may be made;

(b)   hold a local inquiry or afford any person by whom any representation or objection has been duly made and not withdrawn an opportunity of being heard by a person appointed by the Secretary of State for the purpose; and

(c)   consider the report of the person appointed to hold the inquiry or to hear representations or objections.

Local inquiries

6.—(1) The provisions of subsections (2) to (5) of section 250 of the Local Government Act 1972 or subsections (4) to (8) of section 210 of the Local Government (Scotland) Act 1973 (which relate to the giving of evidence at, and defraying the cost of, local inquiries) shall apply in relation to any inquiry held under paragraph 4 or 5 as they apply in relation to a local inquiry which a Minister causes to be held under subsection (1) of that section.

(2) A local inquiry caused to be held under paragraph 4 or 5 before the making of an order may be held concurrently with any local inquiry caused to be held before the confirmation of byelaws made by a relevant authority for the protection of the area specified in the order.

Notice of making of orders

7.—(1) As soon as practicable after an order is made, the Secretary of State shall give notice—
   (a)   describing the general effect of the order as made and stating the date on which it took effect; and
   (b)   naming a place in the area in which the land to which the order relates is situated where a copy of the order as made may be inspected free of charge, and copies thereof may be obtained at a reasonable charge, at all reasonable hours.

(2) A notice under sub-paragraph (1) shall be given—
   (a)   by publication in the manner required by paragraph 2(2)(a);
   (a)   by serving a like notice on any persons on whom notices were required to be served under paragraph 2(2)(b); and
   (c)   by causing like notices to be displayed in the like manner as the notices required to be displayed under paragraph 2(2)(c).

Proceedings for questioning validity of orders

8.—(1) If any person is aggrieved by an order which has taken effect and desires to question its validity on the ground that it is not within the powers of section 36 or that any of the requirements of this Schedule have not been complied with in relation to it, he may within 42 days from the date of publication of the notice under paragraph 7 make an application to the Court under this paragraph.

(2) On any such application the Court may, if satisfied that the order is not within those powers or that the interests of the applicant have been substantially prejudiced by a failure to comply with those requirements—
   (a)   in England and Wales, quash the order, or any provision of the order, either generally or in so far as it affects the interests of the applicant; or
   (b)   *(applies to Scotland only)*.

(3) Except as provided by this paragraph, the validity of an order shall not be questioned in any legal proceedings whatever.

(4) In this paragraph "the Court" means the High Court in relation to England and Wales and the Court of Session in relation to Scotland.

Supplemental

9.—(1) In this Schedule—
   "area" includes district [or Welsh county or county borough];
   "council offices" means offices or buildings acquired or provided by a local authority;
   "the Gazette" means—
      (a)   if the order relates in whole or in part to England and Wales, the London Gazette;
      (b)   if the order relates in whole or in part to Scotland, the Edinburgh Gazette;
   "order" means an order under section 36;
   "prescribed" means prescribed by regulations made by the Secretary of State;

and expressions to which a meaning is assigned by section 36 have the same meanings in this Schedule as in that section.

(2)   References in this Schedule to land include references to any waters covering it; and for the purposes of this Schedule any area in Great Britain which is bounded by tidal waters or parts of the sea shall be taken to include—
  (a)   the waters adjacent to that area up to the seaward limits of territorial waters; and
  (b)   the land covered by the said adjacent waters.

(3)   Regulations under this Schedule shall be made by statutory instrument which shall be subject to annulment in pursuance of a resolution of either House of Parliament.

[80]

NOTES
  Para 9: in sub-para (1) words in square brackets added by the Local Government (Wales) Act 1994, s 66(6), Sch 16, para 65(10), as from a day to be appointed.

(*Schs 13–17 outside the scope of this work.*)

CONTROL OF POLLUTION (AMENDMENT) ACT 1989

(1989 c 14)

ARRANGEMENT OF SECTIONS

An Act to provide for the registration of carriers of controlled waste and to make further provision with respect to the powers exercisable in relation to vehicles shown to have been used for illegal waste disposal

[6 July 1989]

1 Offence of transporting controlled waste without registering

(1)   Subject to the following provisions of this section, it shall be an offence for any person who is not a registered carrier of controlled waste, in the course of any business of his or otherwise with a view to profit, to transport any controlled waste to or from any place in Great Britain.

(2)   A person shall not be guilty of an offence under this section in respect of—
  (a)   the transport of controlled waste within the same premises between different places in those premises;
  (b)   the transport to a place in Great Britain of controlled waste which has been brought from a country or territory outside Great Britain and is not landed in Great Britain until it arrives at that place;
  (c)   the transport by air or sea of controlled waste from a place in Great Britain to a place outside Great Britain.

(3)   The Secretary of State may by regulations provide that a person shall not be required for the purposes of this section to be a registered carrier of controlled waste if—

(a) he is a prescribed person or a person of such a description as may be prescribed; or

(b) without prejudice to paragraph (a) above, he is a person in relation to whom the prescribed requirements under the law of any other member State are satisfied.

(4)   In proceedings against any person for an offence under this section in respect of the transport of any controlled waste it shall be a defence for that person to show—

(a) that the waste was transported in an emergency of which notice was given, as soon as practicable after it occurred, to the [regulation authority] in whose area the emergency occurred;

(b) that he neither knew nor had reasonable grounds for suspecting that what was being transported was controlled waste and took all such steps as it was reasonable to take for ascertaining whether it was such waste; or

(c) that he acted under instructions from his employer.

(5)   A person guilty of an offence under this section shall be liable on summary conviction to a fine not exceeding level 5 on the standard scale.

(6)   In this section "emergency", in relation to the transport of any controlled waste, means any circumstances in which, in order to avoid, remove or reduce any serious danger to the public or serious risk of damage to the environment, it is necessary for the waste to be transported from one place to another without the use of a registered carrier of such waste.

[81]

NOTES

Sub-s (4): words in square brackets in para (a) substituted by the Environmental Protection Act 1990, s 162(1), Sch 15, para 31(1), (2).

Regulations: the Controlled Waste (Registration of Carriers and Seizure of Vehicles) Regulations 1991, SI 1991/1624, reg 2, as amended by SI 1992/588, SI 1994/1056; the Waste Management Licensing Regulations 1994, SI 1994/1056, as amended by SI 1994/1137, SI 1995/288, SI 1995/1950, SI 1996/593, SI 1996/634, SI 1996/972, SI 1996/1279.

---

2 Registration of carriers

(1)   Subject to section 3 below, the Secretary of State may by regulations make provision for the registration of persons with [regulation authorities] as carriers of controlled waste and, for that purpose, for the establishment and maintenance by such authorities, in accordance with the regulations, of such registers as may be prescribed.

(2)   Regulations under this section may—

(a) make provision with respect to applications for registration;

(b) impose requirements with respect to the manner in which [regulation authorities] maintain registers of carriers of controlled waste;

(c) provide for the issue of a certificate of registration free of charge to a registered carrier of controlled waste both on his registration and on the making of any alteration of any entry relating to him in a register of such carriers;

(d) provide for such a certificate to be in such form and to contain such information as may be prescribed;

(e) provide that the provision by a [regulation authority] to a registered carrier of such copies of a certificate of registration as are provided in addition to the certificate provided free of charge in pursuance of provision made by virtue of paragraph (c) above is to be made subject to the payment of a charge imposed under the regulations.

(3)   Provision contained in any regulations under this section by virtue of subsection (2)(a) above may, in particular, include provision which—

(a) prescribes the manner of determining the [regulation authority] to which an application is to be made;

(b) prescribes the form on which and other manner in which an application is to be made;

(c) prescribes the period within which an application for the renewal of any registration which is due to expire is to be made;

(d) imposes requirements with respect to the information which is to be provided by an applicant to the authority to which his application is made;

(e) requires [regulation authorities] to impose charges in respect of their consideration of applications.

[(3A) Without prejudice to the generality of paragraphs (b) and (d) of subsection (3) above—

(a) the power to prescribe a form under paragraph (b) of that subsection includes power to require an application to be made on any form of any description supplied for the purpose by the regulation authority to which the application is to be made; and

(b) the power to impose requirements with respect to information under paragraph (d) of that subsection includes power to make provision requiring an application to be accompanied by such information as may reasonably be required by the regulation authority to which it is to be made.]

(4) Provision contained in any regulations under this section by virtue of subsection (2)(b) above may, in particular, include provision—

(a) specifying or describing the information to be incorporated in any register maintained by a [regulation authority] in pursuance of any such regulations;

(b) requiring a registered carrier of controlled waste to notify a [regulation authority] which maintains such a register of any change of circumstances affecting information contained in the entry relating to that carrier in that register;

(c) requiring a [regulation authority], to such extent and in such manner as may be prescribed, to make the contents of any such register available for public inspection free of charge; and

(d) requiring such an authority, on payment of such charges as may be imposed under the regulations, to provide such copies of the contents of any such register to any person applying for a copy as may be prescribed.

(5) Subsections (2) to (4) above are without prejudice to the generality of subsection (1) above.

[82]

NOTES

Sub-ss (1), (2), (4): words in square brackets substituted by the Environmental Protection Act 1990, s 162(1), Sch 15, para 31.

Sub-s (3): words in square brackets substituted by the Environmental Protection Act 1990, s 162(1), Sch 15, para 31; para (e) repealed (but without prejudice to the power of regulation authorities to impose a charge in respect of their consideration of any such application) by the Environment Act 1995, s 120, Sch 22, para 37(2)(a), Sch 24.

Sub-s (3A): inserted by the Environment Act 1995, s 120, Sch 22, para 37(2)(b).

Regulations: the Controlled Waste (Registration of Carriers and Seizure of Vehicles) Regulations 1991, SI 1991/1624, regs 3 et seq, as amended by SI 1994/1056, SI 1994/1137, SI 1996/593; the Waste Management Licensing Regulations 1994, SI 1994/1056, as amended by SI 1994/1137, SI 1995/288, SI 1995/1950, SI 1996/593, SI 1996/634, SI 1996/972, SI 1996/1279; the Transfrontier Shipment of Waste Regulations 1994, SI 1994/1137, as amended by SI 1996/593, SI 1996/972.

---

3 Restrictions on power under section 2

(1) Nothing in any regulations under section 2 above shall authorise a [regulation authority] to refuse an application for registration except where—

(a) there has, in relation to that application, been a contravention of the requirements of any regulations made by virtue of subsection (2)(a) of that section; or

(b) the applicant or another relevant person has been convicted of a prescribed offence and, in the opinion of the authority, it is undesirable for the applicant to be authorised to transport controlled waste.

(2)   Nothing in any regulations under section 2 above shall authorise any [regulation authority] to revoke any person's registration as a carrier of controlled waste except where—

(a) that person or another relevant person has been convicted of a prescribed offence; and

(b) in the opinion of the authority, it is undesirable for the registered carrier to continue to be authorised to transport controlled waste;

but registration in accordance with any regulations under that section shall cease to have effect after such period as may be prescribed or if the registered carrier gives written notice requiring the removal of his name from the register.

(3)   Regulations under section 2 above may require every registration in respect of a business which is or is to be carried on by a partnership to be a registration of all the partners and to cease to have effect if any of the partners ceases to be registered or if any person who is not registered becomes a partner.

(4)   Nothing in any regulations under section 2 above shall have the effect of bringing the revocation of any person's registration as a carrier of controlled waste into force except—

(a) after the end of such period as may be prescribed for appealing against the revocation under section 4 below; or

(b) where that person has indicated, within that period, that he does not intend to make or continue with an appeal.

(5)   In relation to any applicant for registration or registered carrier, another relevant person shall be treated for the purposes of any provision made by virtue of subsection (1) or (2) above as having been convicted of a prescribed offence if—

(a) any person has been convicted of a prescribed offence committed by him in the course of his employment by the applicant or registered carrier or in the course of the carrying on of any business by a partnership one of the members of which was the applicant or registered carrier;

(b) a body corporate has been convicted of a prescribed offence committed at a time when the applicant or registered carrier was a director, manager, secretary or other similar officer of that body corporate; or

(c) where the applicant or registered carrier is a body corporate, a person who is a director, manager, secretary or other similar officer of that body corporate—

(i) has been convicted of a prescribed offence; or

(ii) was a director, manager, secretary or other similar officer of another body corporate at a time when a prescribed offence for which that other body corporate has been convicted was committed.

(6)   In determining for the purposes of any provision made by virtue of subsection (1) or (2) above whether it is desirable for any individual to be or to continue to be authorised to transport controlled waste, a [regulation authority] shall have regard, in a case in which a person other than the individual has been convicted of a prescribed offence, to whether that individual has been a party to the carrying on of a business in a manner involving the commission of prescribed offences.

[83]

NOTES

Sub-ss (1), (2), (6): words in square brackets substituted by the Environmental Protection Act 1990, s 162(1), Sch 15, para 31.

Regulations: the Controlled Waste (Registration of Carriers and Seizure of Vehicles) Regulations 1991, SI 1991/1624, regs 3 et seq, as amended by SI 1994/1056, SI 1994/1137, SI 1996/593; the Transfrontier Shipment of Waste Regulations 1994, SI 1994/1137, as amended by SI 1996/593, SI 1996/972.

4 Appeals against refusal of registration etc

(1)   Where a person has applied to a [regulation authority] to be registered in accordance with any regulations under section 2 above, he may appeal to the Secretary of State if—

(a) his application is refused; or

(b) the relevant period from the making of the application has expired without his having been registered;

and for the purposes of this subsection the relevant period is two months or, except in the case of an application for the renewal of his registration by a person who is already registered, such longer period as may be agreed between the applicant and the [regulation authority] in question.

(2)   A person whose registration as a carrier of controlled waste has been revoked may appeal against the revocation to the Secretary of State.

(3)   On an appeal under this section the Secretary of State may, as he thinks fit, either dismiss the appeal or give the [regulation authority] in question a direction to register the appellant or, as the case may be, to cancel the revocation.

(4)   Where on an appeal made by virtue of subsection (1)(b) above the Secretary of State dismisses an appeal, he shall direct the [regulation authority] in question not to register the appellant.

(5)   It shall be the duty of a [regulation authority] to comply with any direction under this section.

(6)   The Secretary of State may by regulations make provision as to the manner in which and time within which an appeal under this section is to be made and as to the procedure to be followed on any such appeal.

(7)   Where an appeal under this section is made in accordance with regulations under this section—

(a) by a person whose appeal is in respect of such an application for the renewal of his registration as was made, in accordance with regulations under section 2 above, at a time when he was already registered; or

(b) by a person whose registration has been revoked,

that registration shall continue in force, notwithstanding the expiry of the prescribed period or the revocation, until the appeal is disposed of.

(8)   For the purposes of subsection (7) above an appeal is disposed of when any of the following occurs, that is to say—

(a) the appeal is withdrawn;

(b) the appellant is notified by the Secretary of State or the [regulation authority] in question that his appeal has been dismissed; or

(c) the [regulation authority] comply with any direction of the Secretary of State to renew the appellant's registration or to cancel the revocation.

[(9)   This section is subject to section 114 of the Environment Act 1995 (delegation or reference of appeals etc).]

NOTES

Sub-ss (1), (3)–(5), (8): words in square brackets substituted by the Environmental Protection Act 1990, s 162(1), Sch 15, para 31.

Sub-s (9): added by the Environment Act 1995, s 120, Sch 22, para 37(3).

Regulations: the Controlled Waste (Registration of Carriers and Seizure of Vehicles) Regulations 1991, SI 1991/1624, regs 15–18.

5 Duty to produce authority to transport controlled waste

(1)   If it reasonably appears to any duly authorised officer of a [regulation authority] or to a constable that any controlled waste is being or has been transported in contravention of section 1(1) above, he may—
   (a) stop any person appearing to him to be or to have been engaged in transporting that waste and require that person to produce his authority or, as the case may be, his employer's authority for transporting that waste; and
   (b) search any vehicle that appears to him to be a vehicle which is being or has been used for transporting that waste, carry out tests on anything found in any such vehicle and take away for testing samples of anything so found.

(2)   Nothing in subsection (1) above shall authorise any person other than a constable in uniform to stop a vehicle on any road.

(3)   Subject to the following provisions of this section, a person who is required by virtue of this section to produce an authority for transporting controlled waste shall do so by producing it forthwith to the person making the requirement, by producing it at the prescribed place and within the prescribed period or by sending it to that place within that period.

(4)   A person shall be guilty of an offence under this section if he—
   (a) intentionally obstructs any authorised officer of a [regulation authority] or constable in the exercise of the power conferred by subsection (1) above; or
   (b) subject to subsection (5) below, fails without reasonable excuse to comply with a requirement imposed in exercise of that power;

and in paragraph (b) above the words "without reasonable excuse" shall be construed in their application to Scotland, as in their application to England and Wales, as making it a defence for a person against whom proceedings for the failure are brought to show that there was a reasonable excuse for the failure, rather than as requiring the person bringing the proceedings to show that there was no such excuse.

(5)   A person shall not be guilty of an offence by virtue of subsection (4)(b) above unless it is shown—
   (a) that the waste in question was controlled waste; and
   (b) that that person did transport it to or from a place in Great Britain.

(6)   For the purposes of this section a person's authority for transporting controlled waste is—
   (a) his certificate of registration as a carrier of controlled waste or such a copy of that certificate as satisfies prescribed requirements; or
   (b) such evidence as may be prescribed that he is not required to be registered as a carrier of controlled waste.

(7)   A person guilty of an offence under this section shall be liable on summary conviction to a fine not exceeding level 5 on the standard scale.

[85]

NOTES

Sub-ss (1), (4): words in square brackets substituted by the Environmental Protection Act 1990, s 162(1), Sch 15, para 31(1), (2).

Regulations: the Controlled Waste (Registration of Carriers and Seizure of Vehicles) Regulations 1991, SI 1991/1624, reg 14, as amended by SI 1996/593.

6 Seizure and disposal of vehicles used for illegal waste disposal

(1) A justice of the peace or, in Scotland, a sheriff or a justice of the peace may issue a warrant to a [regulation authority] for the seizure of any vehicle if he is satisfied, on sworn information in writing—
  (a) that there are reasonable grounds for believing—
    (i) that an offence under section 3 of the Control of Pollution Act 1974 [or section 33 of the Environmental Protection Act 1990] (prohibition on unlicensed [deposit, treatment or] disposal of waste) has been committed; and
    (ii) that that vehicle was used in the commission of the offence;
  (b) that proceedings for that offence have not yet been brought against any person; and
  (c) that the authority have failed, after taking the prescribed steps, to ascertain the name and address of any person who is able to provide them with the prescribed information about who was using the vehicle at the time when the offence was committed.

(2) Subject to subsections (3) and (4) below, where a warrant under this section has been issued to a [regulation authority] in respect of any vehicle, any duly authorised officer of the [regulation authority] or any constable may stop the vehicle and, on behalf of the authority, seize the vehicle and its contents.

(3) Nothing in this section shall authorise any person other than a constable in uniform to stop a vehicle on any road; and a duly authorised officer of a [regulation authority] shall not be entitled to seize any property under this section unless he is accompanied by a constable.

(4) A warrant under this section shall continue in force until its purpose is fulfilled; and any person seizing any property under this section shall, if required to do so, produce both the warrant and any authority in pursuance of which he is acting under the warrant.

(5) Where any property has been seized under this section on behalf of a [regulation authority], the authority may, in accordance with regulations made by the Secretary of State, remove it to such place as the authority consider appropriate and may retain custody of it until either—
  (a) it is returned, in accordance with the regulations, to a person who establishes that he is entitled to it; or
  (b) it is disposed of by the authority in exercise of a power conferred by the regulations to sell or destroy the property or to deposit it at any place.

[(6) Regulations under this section shall not authorise a regulation authority to sell or destroy any property or to deposit any property at any place unless—
  (a) the following conditions are satisfied, that is to say—
    (i) the authority have published such notice, and taken such other steps (if any), as may be prescribed for informing persons who may be entitled to the property that it has been seized and is available to be claimed; and
    (ii) the prescribed period has expired without any obligation arising under the regulations for the regulation authority to return the property to any person; or
  (b) the condition of the property requires it to be disposed of without delay.]

(7) Regulations under this section may—
  (a) impose obligations on a [regulation authority] to return any property which has been seized under this section to a person who claims to be entitled to it and satisfies such requirements for establishing his entitlement, and such other requirements, as may be prescribed;
  (b) provide for the manner in which the person entitled to any such property is to be determined where there is more than one claim to it;

(c) provide for the proceeds of sale of any property sold by a [regulation authority] under the regulations to be applied towards meeting expenses incurred by the authority in exercising their functions by virtue of this section and, in so far as they are not so applied, to be applied in such other manner as may be prescribed;

(d) make provision which treats a person who establishes that he is entitled to a vehicle as having established for the purposes of regulations under this section that he is also entitled to its contents.

(8) Subject to their powers by virtue of any regulations under this section to sell or destroy any property or to dispose of it by depositing it at any place, it shall be the duty of a [regulation authority], while any property is in their custody by virtue of a warrant under this section, to take such steps as are reasonably necessary for the safe custody of that property.

(9) Any person who intentionally obstructs any authorised officer of a [regulation authority] or constable in the exercise of any power conferred by virtue of a warrant under this section shall be guilty of an offence and liable, on summary conviction, to a fine not exceeding level 5 on the standard scale.

[86]

NOTES

Sub-ss (1), (2), (3), (5)–(9): words in square brackets substituted by the Environmental Protection Act 1990, s 162(1), Sch 15, para 31(1), (2).

Sub-s (6): substituted by the Environment Act 1995, s 120, Sch 22, para 37(4).

Regulations: the Controlled Waste (Registration of Carriers and Seizure of Vehicles) Regulations 1991, SI 1991/1624, regs 21–25.

7 Further enforcement provisions

(1) Subject to subsection (2) below, the provisions of [[section 71] of the Environmental Protection Act 1990 (powers of entry, of dealing with imminent pollution and to obtain information)] shall have effect as if the provisions of this Act were provisions of that Act and as if, in those sections, references to a relevant authority were references to a [regulation authority].

(2) . . .

(3) A person shall be guilty of an offence under this subsection if he—

(a) fails, without reasonable excuse, to comply with any requirement in pursuance of regulations under this Act to provide information to the Secretary of State or a [regulation authority]; or

(b) in complying with any such requirement, provides information which he knows to be false [or misleading] in a material particular or recklessly provides information which is false [or misleading] in a material particular;

and in paragraph (a) above the words "without reasonable excuse" shall be construed in their application to Scotland, as in their application to England and Wales, as making it a defence for a person against whom proceedings for the failure are brought to show that there was a reasonable excuse for the failure, rather than as requiring the person bringing the proceedings to show that there was no such excuse.

(4) A person guilty of an offence under subsection (3) above shall be liable on summary conviction to a fine not exceeding level 5 on the standard scale.

(5) Where the commission by any person of an offence under this Act is due to the act or default of some other person, that other person shall also be guilty of the offence; and a person may be charged with and convicted of an offence by virtue of this subsection whether or not proceedings for the offence are taken against any other person.

(6)   Where a body corporate is guilty of an offence under this Act (including where it is so guilty by virtue of subsection (5) above) in respect of any act or omission which is shown to have been committed with the consent or connivance of, or to be attributable to any neglect on the part of, any director, manager, secretary or other similar officer of the body corporate or any person who was purporting to act in any such capacity, he, as well as the body corporate, shall be guilty of that offence and shall be liable to be proceeded against and punished accordingly.

(7)   Where the affairs of a body corporate are managed by its members, subsection (6) above shall apply in relation to the acts and defaults of a member in connection with his functions of management as if he were a director of the body corporate.

(8)   . . .

[87]

NOTES

Sub-s (1): words in first and final pairs of square brackets substituted by the Environmental Protection Act 1990, s 162(1), Sch 15, para 31(1), (2), (4); reference to "section 71" substituted by the Environment Act 1995, s 120, Sch 22, para 37(5).

Sub-ss (2), (8): repealed by the Environment Act 1995, s 120, Sch 22, para 37(6), (7), Sch 24.

Sub-s (3): words in first pair of square brackets substituted by the Environmental Protection Act 1990, s 162(1), Sch 15, para 31(1), (2); words in second and final pairs of square brackets inserted by the Environment Act 1995, s 112, Sch 19, para 3.

8 Regulations

(1)   The powers of the Secretary of State under this Act to make regulations shall be exercisable by statutory instrument subject to annulment in pursuance of a resolution of either House of Parliament.

(2)   Regulations made in exercise of any such power may—
  (a)   contain such supplemental, consequential and transitional provision as the Secretary of State considers appropriate; and
  (b)   make different provision for different cases (including different provision for different persons, circumstances or localities).

[88]

9 Interpretation

(1)   In this Act—
  "controlled waste" has[, at any time,] the same meaning as [for the purposes of Part II of the Environmental Protection Act 1990];

. . . . .

  "prescribed" means prescribed by regulations made by the Secretary of State;
  ["regulation authority" means—
      (a)   in relation to England and Wales, the Environment Agency; and
      (b)   in relation to Scotland, the Scottish Environment Protection Agency;
      and any reference to the area of a regulation authority shall accordingly be construed as a reference to any area in England and Wales or, as the case may be, in Scotland;]
  "road" has the same meaning as in the Road Traffic Act 1988;
  "transport", in relation to any controlled waste, includes the transport of that waste by road or rail or by air, sea or inland waterway but does not include moving that waste from one place to another by means of any pipe or other apparatus that joins those two places.
  "vehicle" means any motor vehicle or trailer within the meaning of the Road Traffic Regulation Act 1984.

(2)   . . .

[89]

NOTES
    Sub-s (1): in definition "controlled waste" words in square brackets substituted, and definition omitted repealed, by the Environmental Protection Act 1990, s 162(1), Sch 15, para 31(1), (5), Sch 16, Pt II; definition "regulation authority" inserted by the Environmental Protection Act 1990, s 162(1), Sch 15, para 31(1), (6), substituted by the Environment Act 1995, s 120, Sch 22, para 37(8).
    Sub-s (2): repealed by the Environmental Protection Act 1990, s 162, Sch 15, para 31, Sch 16, Pt II.

10 Expenses

There shall be paid out of money provided by Parliament—
    (a) any administrative expenses incurred by the Secretary of State in consequence of this Act; and
    (b) any increase attributable to this Act in the sums payable out of money so provided under any other Act.

[90]

[10A Application to the Isles of Scilly

(1)   Subject to the provisions of any order under this section, this Act shall not apply in relation to the Isles of Scilly.

(2)   The Secretary of State may, after consultation with the Council of the Isles of Scilly, by order provide for the application of any provisions of this Act to the Isles of Scilly; and any such order may provide for the application of those provisions to those Isles with such modifications as may be specified in the order.

(3)   An order under this section may—
    (a) make different provision for different cases, including different provision in relation to different persons, circumstances or localities; and
    (b) contain such supplemental, consequential and transitional provision as the Secretary of State considers appropriate, including provision saving provision repealed by or under any enactment.

(4)   The power of the Secretary of State to make an order under this section shall be exercisable by statutory instrument; and a statutory instrument containing such an order shall be subject to annulment in pursuance of a resolution of either House of Parliament.]

[91]

NOTES
    Commencement: 1 February 1996.
    Inserted by the Environment Act 1995, s 118(1).

11 Short title, commencement and extent

(1)   This Act may be cited as the Control of Pollution (Amendment) Act 1989.

(2)   This Act shall come into force on such day as the Secretary of State may by order made by statutory instrument appoint; and different days may be so appointed for different provisions and for different purposes.

(3)   . . .

(4)   This Act shall not extend to Northern Ireland.

[92]

NOTES
    Sub-s (3): repealed by the Environment Act 1995, ss 118(2), 120, Sch 24.
    Order: Control of Pollution (Amendment) Act 1989 (Commencement) Order 1991, SI 1991/1618.

ENVIRONMENTAL PROTECTION ACT 1990

(1990 c 43)

ARRANGEMENT OF SECTIONS

PART I
INTEGRATED POLLUTION CONTROL AND AIR POLLUTION CONTROL BY LOCAL AUTHORITIES

PART II
WASTE ON LAND

PART III
STATUTORY NUISANCES AND CLEAN AIR

Statutory nuisances

Termination of existing controls over offensive trades and businesses

PART IV
LITTER ETC

Provisions relating to litter

PART VI
GENETICALLY MODIFIED ORGANISMS

Preliminary

General controls

An Act to make provision for the improved control of pollution arising from certain industrial and other processes; to re-enact the provisions of the Control of Pollution Act 1974 relating to waste on land with modifications as respects the functions of the regulatory and other authorities concerned in the collection and disposal of waste and to make further provision in relation to such waste; to restate the law defining statutory nuisances and improve the summary procedures for dealing with them, to provide for the termination of the existing controls over offensive trades or businesses and to provide for the extension of the Clean Air Acts to prescribed gases; to amend the law relating to litter and make further provision imposing or conferring powers to impose duties to keep public places clear of litter and clean; to make provision conferring powers in relation to trolleys abandoned on land in the open air; to amend the Radioactive Substances Act 1960; to make provision for the control of genetically modified organisms; to make provision for the abolition of the Nature Conservancy Council and for the creation of councils to replace it and discharge the functions of that Council and, as respects Wales, of the Countryside Commission; to make further provision for the control of the importation, exportation, use, supply or storage of prescribed substances and articles and the importation or exportation of prescribed descriptions of waste; to confer powers to obtain information about potentially hazardous substances; to amend the law relating to the control of hazardous substances on, over or under land; to amend section 107(6) of the Water Act 1989 and sections 31(7)(a), 31A(c)(i) and 32(7)(a) of the Control of Pollution Act 1974; to amend the provisions of the Food and

Environment Protection Act 1985 as regards the dumping of waste at sea; to make further provision as respects the prevention of oil pollution from ships; to make provision for and in connection with the identification and control of dogs; to confer powers to control the burning of crop residues; to make provision in relation to financial or other assistance for purposes connected with the environment; to make provision as respects superannuation of employees of the Groundwork Foundation and for remunerating the chairman of the Inland Waterways Amenity Advisory Council; and for purposes connected with those purposes

[1 November 1990]

PART I
INTEGRATED POLLUTION CONTROL AND AIR POLLUTION CONTROL BY LOCAL AUTHORITIES

NOTES

This Part should be read in conjunction with the Conservation (Natural Habitats, &c) Regulations 1994, SI 1994/2716, regs 10, 48 et seq, 83, 84 (which make provision for implementing Council Directive 92/43/EEC on the conservation of natural habitats and of wild fauna and flora).

Modification: for the modification of this Part, see the Waste Management Licensing Regulations 1994, SI 1994/1056, regs 1(3), 19, Sch 4, Pt I, para 8 at **[937]**, **[954]**, **[959]**.

Preliminary

1 Preliminary

(1)   The following provisions have effect for the interpretation of this Part.

(2)   The "environment" consists of all, or any, of the following media, namely, the air, water and land; and the medium of air includes the air within buildings and the air within other natural or man-made structures above or below ground.

(3)   "Pollution of the environment" means pollution of the environment due to the release (into any environmental medium) from any process of substances which are capable of causing harm to man or any other living organisms supported by the environment.

(4)   "Harm" means harm to the health of living organisms or other interference with the ecological systems of which they form part and, in the case of man, includes offence caused to any of his senses or harm to his property; and "harmless" has a corresponding meaning.

(5)   "Process" means any activities carried on in Great Britain, whether on premises or by means of mobile plant, which are capable of causing pollution of the environment and "prescribed process" means a process prescribed under section 2(1) below.

(6)   For the purposes of subsection (5) above—
"activities" means industrial or commercial activities or activities of any other nature whatsoever (including, with or without other activities, the keeping of a substance);
"Great Britain" includes so much of the adjacent territorial sea as is, or is treated as, relevant territorial waters for the purposes of [Part III of the Water Resources Act 1991] or, as respects Scotland, Part II of the Control of Pollution Act 1974; and
"mobile plant" means plant which is designed to move or to be moved whether on roads or otherwise.

(7)   The "enforcing authority", in relation to England and Wales, is [the Environment Agency or the local authority by which], under section 4 below, the

functions conferred or imposed by this Part otherwise than on the Secretary of State are for the time being exercisable in relation respectively to releases of substances into the environment or into the air; and "local enforcing authority" means any such local authority.

[(8)   (*Applies to Scotland only.*)]

(9)   "Authorisation" means an authorisation for a process (whether on premises or by means of mobile plant) granted under section 6 below; and a reference to the conditions of an authorisation is a reference to the conditions subject to which at any time the authorisation has effect.

(10)   A substance is "released" into any environmental medium whenever it is released directly into that medium whether it is released into it within or outside Great Britain and "release" includes—

(a)   in relation to air, any emission of the substance into the air;

(b)   in relation to water, any entry (including any discharge) of the substance into water;

(c)   in relation to land, any deposit, keeping or disposal of the substance in or on land;

and for this purpose "water" and "land" shall be construed in accordance with subsections (11) and (12) below.

(11)   For the purpose of determining into what medium a substance is released—

(a)   any release into—

(i)   the sea or the surface of the seabed,

(ii)   any river, watercourse, lake, loch or pond (whether natural or artificial or above or below ground) or reservoir or the surface of the riverbed or of other land supporting such waters, or

(iii)   ground waters,

is a release into water;

(b)   any release into—

(i)   land covered by water falling outside paragraph (a) above or the water covering such land; or

(ii)   the land beneath the surface of the seabed or of other land supporting waters falling within paragraph (a)(ii) above,

is a release into land; and

(c)   any release into a sewer (within the meaning of [the Water Industry Act 1991] or, in relation to Scotland, of the Sewerage (Scotland) Act 1968) shall be treated as a release into water;

but a sewer and its contents shall be disregarded in determining whether there is pollution of the environment at any time.

(12)   In subsection (11) above "ground waters" means any waters contained in underground strata, or in—

(a)   a well, borehole or similar work sunk into underground strata, including any adit or passage constructed in connection with the well, borehole or work for facilitating the collection of water in the well, borehole or work; or

(b)   any excavation into underground strata where the level of water in the excavation depends wholly or mainly on water entering it from the strata.

(13)   "Substance" shall be treated as including electricity or heat and "prescribed substance" has the meaning given by section 2(7) below.

[(14) In this Part "the appropriate Agency" means—

(a)   in relation to England and Wales, the Environment Agency; and

(b)   (*applies to Scotland only.*)]

NOTES
    Commencement: 1 April 1996 (sub-ss (8), (14)); 1 January 1991 (remainder).
    Sub-ss (6), (11): words in square brackets substituted by the Water Consolidation (Consequential Provisions) Act 1991, s 2, Sch 1, para 56(1).
    Sub-s (7): words in square brackets substituted by the Environment Act 1995, s 120, Sch 22, para 45(2).
    Sub-s (8): substituted by the Environment Act 1995, s 120, Sch 22, para 45(3).
    Sub-s (14): added by the Environment Act 1995, s 120, Sch 22, para 45(4).

2 Prescribed processes and prescribed substances

(1)   The Secretary of State may, by regulations, prescribe any description of process as a process for the carrying on of which after a prescribed date an authorisation is required under section 6 below.

(2)   Regulations under subsection (1) above may frame the description of a process by reference to any characteristics of the process or the area or other circumstances in which the process is carried on or the description of person carrying it on.

(3)   Regulations under subsection (1) above may prescribe or provide for the determination under the regulations of different dates for different descriptions of persons and may include such transitional provisions as the Secretary of State considers necessary or expedient as respects the making of applications for authorisations and suspending the application of section 6(1) below until the determination of applications made within the period allowed by the regulations.

(4)   Regulations under subsection (1) above shall, as respects each description of process, designate it as one for central control or one for local control.

(5)   The Secretary of State may, by regulations, prescribe any description of substance as a substance the release of which into the environment is subject to control under sections 6 and 7 below.

(6)   Regulations under subsection (5) above may—
    (a)   prescribe separately, for each environmental medium, the substances the release of which into that medium is to be subject to control; and
    (b)   provide that a description of substance is only prescribed, for any environmental medium, so far as it is released into that medium in such amounts over such periods, in such concentrations or in such other circumstances as may be specified in the regulations;
and in relation to a substance of a description which is prescribed for releases into the air, the regulations may designate the substance as one for central control or one for local control.

(7)   In this Part "prescribed substance" means any substance of a description prescribed in regulations under subsection (5) above or, in the case of a substance of a description prescribed only for releases in circumstances specified under subsection (6)(b) above, means any substance of that description which is released in those circumstances.

[94]

NOTES
    Regulations: the Environmental Protection (Prescribed Processes and Substances) Regulations 1991, SI 1991/472, as amended by SI 1991/836, SI 1992/614, SI 1993/1749, SI 1993/2405, SI 1994/1271, SI 1995/3247, SI 1996/2678; the Environmental Protection (Prescribed Processes and Substances etc) (Amendment) Regulations 1994, SI 1994/1271, as amended by SI 1994/1329; the Environmental Protection (Prescribed Processes and Substances Etc) (Amendment) (Petrol Vapour Recovery) Regulations 1996, SI 1996/2678.

3 Emission etc limits and quality objectives

(1)   The Secretary of State may make regulations under subsection (2) or (4) below establishing standards, objectives or requirements in relation to particular prescribed processes or particular substances.

(2)   Regulations under this subsection may—
   (a) in relation to releases of any substance from prescribed processes into any environmental medium, prescribe standard limits for—
      (i) the concentration, the amount or the amount in any period of that substance which may be so released; and
      (ii) any other characteristic of that substance in any circumstances in which it may be so released;
   (b) prescribe standard requirements for the measurement or analysis of, or of releases of, substances for which limits have been set under paragraph (a) above; and
   (c) in relation to any prescribed process, prescribe standards or requirements as to any aspect of the process.

(3)   Regulations under subsection (2) above may make different provision in relation to different cases, including different provision in relation to different processes, descriptions of person, localities or other circumstances.

(4)   Regulations under this subsection may establish for any environmental medium (in all areas or in specified areas) quality objectives or quality standards in relation to any substances which may be released into that or any other medium from any process.

(5)   The Secretary of State may make plans for—
   (a) establishing limits for the total amount, or the total amount in any period, of any substance which may be released into the environment in, or in any area within, the United Kingdom;
   (b) allocating quotas as respects the release of substances to persons carrying on processes in respect of which any such limit is established;
   (c) establishing limits of the descriptions specified in subsection (2)(a) above so as progressively to reduce pollution of the environment;
   (d) the progressive improvement in the quality objectives and quality standards established by regulations under subsection (4) above;
and the Secretary of State may, from time to time, revise any plan so made.

(6)   Regulations or plans under this section may be made for any purposes of this Part or for other purposes.

(7)   The Secretary of State shall give notice in the London, Edinburgh and Belfast Gazettes of the making and the revision of any plan under subsection (5) above and shall make the documents containing the plan, or the plan as so revised, available for inspection by members of the public at the places specified in the notice.

(8)   Subject to any Order made after the passing of this Act by virtue of subsection (1)(a) of section 3 of the Northern Ireland Constitution Act 1973, the making and revision of plans under subsection (5) above shall not be a transferred matter for the purposes of that Act but shall for the purposes of subsection (2) of that section be treated as specified in Schedule 3 to that Act.

[95]

4 Discharge and scope of functions

(1)   This section determines the authority by whom the functions conferred or imposed by this Part otherwise than on the Secretary of State are exercisable and the purposes for which they are exercisable.

(2)   Those functions, in their application to prescribed processes designated for central control, shall be functions of [the appropriate Agency], and shall be exercisable for the purpose of preventing or minimising pollution of the environment due to the release of substances into any environmental medium.

(3)   Subject to subsection (4) below, those functions, in their application to prescribed processes designated for local control, shall be functions of—
    [(a) in the case of a prescribed process carried on (or to be carried on) by means
         of a mobile plant, where the person carrying on the process has his
         principal place of business—
          (i) in England and Wales, the local authority in whose area that place of
              business is;
         (ii) *(applies to Scotland only)*;
    (b) in any other cases, where the prescribed processes are (or are to be) carried
         on—
          (i) in England and Wales, the local authority in whose area they are (or
              are to be) carried on;
         (ii) *(applies to Scotland only)*;]
and the functions applicable to such processes shall be exercisable for the purpose of preventing or minimising pollution of the environment due to the release of substances into the air (but not into any other environmental medium).

(4)   The Secretary of State may, as respects the functions under this Part being exercised by a local authority specified in the direction, direct that those functions shall be exercised instead by [the Environment Agency] while the direction remains in force or during a period specified in the direction.

[(4A) In England and Wales, a local authority, in exercising the functions conferred or imposed on it under this Part by virtue of subsection (3) above, shall have regard to the strategy for the time being published pursuant to section 80 of the Environment Act 1995.]

(5)   A transfer of functions under subsection (4) above to [the Environment Agency] does not make them exercisable by [that Agency] for the purpose of preventing or minimising pollution of the environment due to releases of substances into any other environmental medium than the air.

(6)   A direction under subsection (4) above may transfer those functions as exercisable in relation to all or any description of prescribed processes carried on by all or any description of persons (a "general direction") or in relation to a prescribed process carried on by a specified person (a "specific direction").

(7)   A direction under subsection (4) above may include such saving and transitional provisions as the Secretary of State considers necessary or expedient.

(8)   The Secretary of State, on giving or withdrawing a direction under subsection (4) above, shall—
    (a) in the case of a general direction—
          (i) forthwith serve notice of it on [the Environment Agency] and on the
              local enforcing authorities affected by the direction; and
         (ii) cause notice of it to be published as soon as practicable in the London
              Gazette . . . and in at least one newspaper circulating in the area of
              each authority affected by the direction;
    (b) in the case of a specific direction—
          (i) forthwith serve notice of it on [the Environment Agency], the local
              enforcing authority and the person carrying on or appearing to the
              Secretary of State to be carrying on the process affected, and
         (ii) cause notice of it to be published as soon as practicable in the London
              Gazette . . . and in at least one newspaper circulating in the authority's
              area;

and any such notice shall specify the date at which the direction is to take (or took) effect and (where appropriate) its duration.

[(8A) The requirements of sub-paragraph (ii) of paragraph (a) or, as the case may be, of paragraph (b) of subsection (8) above shall not apply in any case where, in the opinion of the Secretary of State, the publication of notice in accordance with that sub-paragraph would be contrary to the interests of national security.

(8B) *(Applies to Scotland only.)*]

[(9) It shall be the duty of local authorities to follow such developments in technology and techniques for preventing or reducing pollution of the environment due to releases of substances from prescribed processes as concern releases into the air of substances from prescribed processes designated for local control.]

(10) It shall be the duty of [the Environment Agency, SEPA] and the local enforcing authorities to give effect to any directions given to them under any provision of this Part.

(11) In this Part "local authority" means, subject to subsection (12) below—
    (a) in Greater London, a London borough council, the Common Council of the City of London, the Sub-Treasurer of the Inner Temple and the Under Treasurer of the Middle Temple;
    (b) [in England . . .] outside Greater London, a district council and the Council of the Isles of Scilly;
  [(bb) in Wales, a county council or county borough council;] . . .
    (c) . . .

(12) Where, by an order under section 2 of the Public Health (Control of Disease) Act 1984, a port health authority has been constituted for any port health district, the port health authority shall have by virtue of this subsection, as respects its district, the functions conferred or imposed by this Part and no such order shall be made assigning those functions; and "local authority" and "area" shall be construed accordingly.

[96]

NOTES

Commencement: 1 April 1996 (sub-ss (8A), (8B), (9)); 1 January 1991 (sub-ss (1)–(4), (5)–(8), (10)–(12)); to be appointed (remainder).

Sub-ss (2), (4), (5), (10): words in square brackets substituted by the Environment Act 1995, s 120, Sch 22, para 46(2), (4), (6), (10).

Sub-s (3): paras (a), (b) substituted by the Environment Act 1995, s 120, Sch 22, para 46(3).

Sub-s (4A): inserted by the Environment Act 1995, s 120, Sch 22, para 46(5), (8), as from a day to be appointed.

Sub-s (8): words in square brackets substituted, and words omitted repealed, by the Environment Act 1995, s 120, Sch 22, para 46(7), Sch 24.

Sub-ss (8A), (8B): inserted by the Environment Act 1995, s 120, Sch 22, para 46(5), (8).

Sub-s (9): substituted by the Environment Act 1995, s 120, Sch 22, para 46(9).

Sub-s (11): words in square brackets in para (b) inserted by the Environment Act 1995, s 120, Sch 22, para 46(11), words omitted repealed by the Environment Act 1995, s 120, Sch 24; para (bb) inserted by the Local Government (Wales) Act 1994, s 22(3), Sch 9, para 17(1); para (c) and the word immediately preceding it repealed by the Environment Act 1995, s 120, Sch 22, para 46(11)(b), Sch 24.

---

5 *(Repealed by the Environment Act 1995, s 120(1), (3), Sch 22, para 47, Sch 24.)*

Authorisations

6 Authorisations: general provisions

(1)   No person shall carry on a prescribed process after the date prescribed or determined for that description of process by or under regulations under section 2(1)

above (but subject to any transitional provision made by the regulations) except under an authorisation granted by the enforcing authority and in accordance with the conditions to which it is subject.

(2)   An application for an authorisation shall be made to the enforcing authority in accordance with Part I of Schedule 1 to this Act and shall be accompanied by
[(a) in a case where, by virtue of section 41 of the Environment Act 1995, a charge prescribed by a charging scheme under that section is required to be paid to the appropriate Agency in respect of the application, the charge so prescribed; or
(b) in any other case,] the fee prescribed under section 8(2)(a) below.

(3)   Where an application is duly made to the enforcing authority, the authority shall either grant the authorisation subject to the conditions required or authorised to be imposed by section 7 below or refuse the application.

(4)   An application shall not be granted unless the enforcing authority considers that the applicant will be able to carry on the process so as to comply with the conditions which would be included in the authorisation.

(5)   The Secretary of State may, if he thinks fit in relation to any application for an authorisation, give to the enforcing authority directions as to whether or not the authority should grant the authorisation.

(6)   The enforcing authority shall, as respects each authorisation in respect of which it has functions under this Part, from time to time but not less frequently than once in every period of four years, carry out a review of the conditions of the authorisation.

(7)   The Secretary of State may, by regulations, substitute for the period for the time being specified in subsection (6) above such other period as he thinks fit.

(8)   Schedule 1 to this Act (supplementary provisions) shall have effect in relation to authorisations.

[97]

NOTES
    Sub-s (2): words in square brackets inserted by the Environment Act 1995, s 120, Sch 22, para 48.

7 Conditions of authorisations

(1)   There shall be included in an authorisation—
   (a) subject to paragraph (b) below, such specific conditions as the enforcing authority considers appropriate, when taken with the general condition implied by subsection (4) below, for achieving the objectives specified in subsection (2) below;
   (b) such conditions as are specified in directions given by the Secretary of State under subsection (3) below; and
   (c) such other conditions (if any) as appear to the enforcing authority to be appropriate;
but no conditions shall be imposed for the purpose only of securing the health of persons at work (within the meaning of Part I of the Health and Safety at Work etc Act 1974).

(2)   Those objectives are—
   (a) ensuring that, in carrying on a prescribed process, the best available techniques not entailing excessive cost will be used—
      (i) for preventing the release of substances prescribed for any environmental medium into that medium or, where that is not practicable by such means, for reducing the release of such substances

to a minimum and for rendering harmless any such substances which
are so released; and
   (ii) for rendering harmless any other substances which might cause harm
        if released into any environmental medium;
   (b) compliance with any directions by the Secretary of State given for the
       implementation of any obligations of the United Kingdom under the
       Community Treaties or international law relating to environmental
       protection;
   (c) compliance with any limits or requirements and achievement of any
       quality standards or quality objectives prescribed by the Secretary of State
       under any of the relevant enactments;
   (d) compliance with any requirements applicable to the grant of authorisations
       specified by or under a plan made by the Secretary of State under section 3(5)
       above.

(3)   Except as respects the general condition implied by subsection (4) below,
the Secretary of State may give directions to the enforcing authorities as to the
conditions which are, or are not, to be included in all authorisations, in
authorisations of any specified description or in any particular authorisation.

(4)   Subject to subsections (5) and (6) below, there is implied in every
authorisation a general condition that, in carrying on the process to which the
authorisation applies, the person carrying it on must use the best available
techniques not entailing excessive cost—
   (a) for preventing the release of substances prescribed for any environmental
       medium into that medium or, where that is not practicable by such means,
       for reducing the release of such substances to a minimum and for rendering
       harmless any such substances which are so released; and
   (b) for rendering harmless any other substances which might cause harm if
       released into any environmental medium.

(5)   In the application of subsections (1) to (4) above to authorisations granted
by a local enforcing authority references to the release of substances into any
environmental medium are to be read as references to the release of substances into
the air.

(6)   The obligation implied by virtue of subsection (4) above shall not apply in
relation to any aspect of the process in question which is regulated by a condition
imposed under subsection (1) above.

(7)   The objectives referred to in subsection (2) above shall, where the process—
   (a) is one designated for central control; and
   (b) is likely to involve the release of substances into more than one
       environmental medium;
include the objective of ensuring that the best available techniques not entailing
excessive cost will be used for minimising the pollution which may be caused to the
environment taken as a whole by the releases having regard to the best practicable
environmental option available as respects the substances which may be released.

(8)   An authorisation for carrying on a prescribed process may, without
prejudice to the generality of subsection (1) above, include conditions—
   (a) imposing limits on the amount or composition of any substance produced
       by or utilised in the process in any period; and
   (b) requiring advance notification of any proposed change in the manner of
       carrying on the process.

(9)   This section has effect subject to section 28 below . . .

(10) References to the best available techniques not entailing excessive cost, in
relation to a process, include (in addition to references to any technical means and

technology) references to the number, qualifications, training and supervision of persons employed in the process and the design, construction, lay-out and maintenance of the buildings in which it is carried on.

(11) It shall be the duty of enforcing authorities to have regard to any guidance issued to them by the Secretary of State for the purposes of the application of subsections (2) and (7) above as to the techniques and environmental options that are appropriate for any description of prescribed process.

(12) In subsection (2) above "the relevant enactments" are any enactments or instruments contained in or made for the time being under—
   (a) section 2 of the Clean Air Act 1968;
   (b) section 2 of the European Communities Act 1972;
   (c) Part I of the Health and Safety at Work etc. Act 1974;
   (d) Parts II, III or IV of the Control of Pollution Act 1974;
   [(e) the Water Resources Act 1991; and]
   (f) section 3 of this Act[; and
   (g) section 87 of the Environment Act 1995.]

[98]

NOTES
   Sub-s (9): words omitted repealed by the Environment Act 1995, s 120, Sch 22, para 49(1), Sch 24.
   Sub-s (12): para (e) substituted by the Water Consolidation (Consequential Provisions) Act 1991, s 2, Sch 1, para 56(2); para (g) and word immediately preceding it added by the Environment Act 1995, s 120, Sch 22, para 49(2).

8 Fees and charges for authorisations

(1)   There shall be charged by and paid to the [local enforcing authority] such fees and charges as may be prescribed from time to time by a scheme under subsection (2) below (whether by being specified in or made calculable under the scheme).

(2)   The Secretary of State may, with the approval of the Treasury, make, and from time to time revise, a scheme prescribing—
   (a) fees payable in respect of applications for authorisations;
   (b) fees payable by persons holding authorisations in respect of, or of applications for, the variation of authorisations; and
   (c) charges payable by such persons in respect of the subsistence of their authorisations.

(3)   The Secretary of State shall, on making or revising a scheme under subsection (2) above, lay a copy of the scheme or of the alterations made in the scheme or, if he considers it more appropriate, the scheme as revised, before each House of Parliament.

(4)   . . .

(5)   A scheme under subsection (2) above may, in particular—
   (a) make different provision for different cases, including different provision in relation to different persons, circumstances or localities;
   (b) allow for reduced fees or charges to be payable in respect of authorisations for a number of prescribed processes carried on by the same person;
   (c) provide for the times at which and the manner in which the payments required by the scheme are to be made; and
   (d) make such incidental, supplementary and transitional provision as appears to the Secretary of State to be appropriate.

(6)   The Secretary of State, in framing a scheme under subsection (2) above, shall, so far as practicable, secure that the fees and charges payable under the

scheme are sufficient, taking one financial year with another, to cover the relevant expenditure attributable to authorisations.

(7) The "relevant expenditure attributable to authorisations" is the expenditure incurred by the [local enforcing authorities] in exercising their functions under this Part in relation to authorisations . . .

(8) If it appears to the [local enforcing authority] that the holder of an authorisation has failed to pay a charge due in consideration of the subsistence of the authorisation, it may, by notice in writing served on the holder, revoke the authorisation.

(9) . . .

[(10) *(Applies to Scotland only.)*]

[99]

NOTES
Commencement: 1 April 1996 (sub-s (10)); 1 January 1991 (remainder).
Sub-ss (1), (8): words in square brackets substituted by the Environment Act 1995, s 120, Sch 22, para 50(2), (5).
Sub-ss (4), (9): repealed by the Environment Act 1995, s 120, Sch 22, para 50(3), (6), Sch 24.
Sub-s (7): words in square brackets substituted, and words omitted repealed, by the Environment Act 1995, s 120, Sch 22, para 50(4).

9 Transfer of authorisations

(1) An authorisation for the carrying on of any prescribed process may be transferred by the holder to a person who proposes to carry on the process in the holder's place.

(2) Where an authorisation is transferred under this section, the person to whom it is transferred shall notify the enforcing authority in writing of that fact not later than the end of the period of twenty-one days beginning with the date of the transfer.

(3) An authorisation which is transferred under this section shall have effect on and after the date of the transfer as if it had been granted to that person under section 6 above, subject to the same conditions as were attached to it immediately before that date.

[100]

10 Variation of authorisations by enforcing authority

(1) The enforcing authority may at any time, subject to the requirements of section 7 above, and, in cases to which they apply, the requirements of Part II of Schedule 1 to this Act, vary an authorisation and shall do so if it appears to the authority at that time that that section requires conditions to be included which are different from the subsisting conditions.

(2) Where the enforcing authority has decided to vary an authorisation under subsection (1) above the authority shall notify the holder of the authorisation and serve a variation notice on him.

(3) In this Part a "variation notice" is a notice served by the enforcing authority on the holder of an authorisation—
(a) specifying variations of the authorisation which the enforcing authority has decided to make; and
(b) specifying the date or dates on which the variations are to take effect;
and, unless the notice is withdrawn [or is varied under subsection (3A) below], the variations specified in a variation notice shall take effect on the date or dates so specified.

[(3A) An enforcing authority which has served a variation notice may vary that notice by serving on the holder of the authorisation in question a further notice—
  (a) specifying the variations which the enforcing authority has decided to make to the variation notice; and
  (b) specifying the date or dates on which the variations specified in the variation notice, as varied by the further notice, are to take effect;

and any reference in this Part to a variation notice, or to a variation notice served under subsection (2) above, includes a reference to such a notice as varied by a further notice served under this subsection.]

(4) A variation notice served under subsection (2) above shall also—
  (a) require the holder of the authorisation, within such period as may be specified in the notice, to notify the authority what action (if any) he proposes to take to ensure that the process is carried on in accordance with the authorisation as varied by the notice; and
  [(b) require the holder to pay, within such period as may be specified in the notice,—
    (i) in a case where the enforcing authority is the Environment Agency or SEPA, the charge (if any) prescribed for the purpose by a charging scheme under section 41 of the Environment Act 1995; or
    (ii) in any other case, the fee (if any) prescribed by a scheme under section 8 above.]

(5) Where in the opinion of the enforcing authority any action to be taken by the holder of an authorisation in consequence of a variation notice served under subsection (2) above will involve a substantial change in the manner in which the process is being carried on, the enforcing authority shall notify the holder of its opinion.

(6) The Secretary of State may, if he thinks fit in relation to authorisations of any description or particular authorisations, direct the enforcing authorities—
  (a) to exercise their powers under this section, or to do so in such circumstances as may be specified in the directions, in such manner as may be so specified; or
  (b) not to exercise those powers, or not to do so in such circumstances or such manner as may be so specified;

and the Secretary of State shall have the corresponding power of direction in respect of the powers of the enforcing authorities to vary authorisations under section 11 below.

(7) In this section and section 11 below a "substantial change", in relation to a prescribed process being carried on under an authorisation, means a substantial change in the circumstances released from the process or in the amount or any other characteristic of any substance so released; and the Secretary of State may give directions to the enforcing authorities as to what does or does not constitute a substantial change in relation to processes generally, any description of process or any particular process.

(8) In this section and section 11 below—
  "prescribed" means prescribed in regulations made by the Secretary of State;
  "vary",
    [(a)] in relation to the subsisting conditions or other provisions of an authorisation, means adding to them or varying or rescinding any of them; [and
    (b) in relation to a variation notice, means adding to, or varying or rescinding the notice or any of its contents;]
  and "variation" shall be construed accordingly.

[101]

NOTES

Commencement: 12 October 1995 (sub-s (3A)); 1 January 1991 (remainder).

Sub-s (3): words in square brackets inserted by the Environment Act 1995, s 120, Sch 22, para 51(2).

Sub-s (3A): inserted by the Environment Act 1995, s 120, Sch 22, para 51(3).

Sub-s (4): para (b) substituted by the Environment Act 1995, s 120, Sch 22, para 51(4).

Sub-s (8): in definition "vary" para (a) lettered as such and para (b) inserted by the Environment Act 1995, s 120, Sch 22, para 51(5).

Regulations: the Environmental Protection (Applications, Appeals and Registers) Regulations 1991, SI 1991/507, reg 3, as amended by SI 1991/836, SI 1996/667.

11 Variation of conditions etc: applications by holders of authorisations

(1)   A person carrying on a prescribed process under an authorisation who wishes to make a relevant change in the process may at any time—
  (a) notify the enforcing authority in the prescribed form of that fact, and
  (b) request the enforcing authority to make a determination, in relation to the proposed change, of the matters mentioned in subsection (2) below;

and a person making a request under paragraph (b) above shall furnish the enforcing authority with such information as may be prescribed or as the authority may by notice require.

(2)   On receiving a request under subsection (1) above the enforcing authority shall determine—
  (a) whether the proposed change would involve a breach of any condition of the authorisation;
  (b) if it would not involve such a breach, whether the authority would be likely to vary the conditions of the authorisation as a result of the change;
  (c) if it would involve such a breach, whether the authority would consider varying the conditions of the authorisation so that the change may be made; and
  (d) whether the change would involve a substantial change in the manner in which the process is being carried on;

and the enforcing authority shall notify the holder of the authorisation of its determination of those matters.

(3)   Where the enforcing authority has determined that the proposed change would not involve a substantial change, but has also determined under paragraph (b) or (c) of subsection (2) above that the change would lead to or require the variation of the conditions of the authorisation, then—
  (a) the enforcing authority shall (either on notifying its determination under that subsection or on a subsequent occasion) notify the holder of the authorisation of the variations which the authority is likely to consider making; and
  (b) the holder may apply in the prescribed form to the enforcing authority for the variation of the conditions of the authorisation so that he may make the proposed change.

(4)   Where the enforcing authority has determined that a proposed change would involve a substantial change that would lead to or require the variation of the conditions of the authorisation, then—
  (a) the authority shall (either on notifying its determination under subsection (2) above or on a subsequent occasion) notify the holder of the authorisation of the variations which the authority is likely to consider making; and
  (b) the holder of the authorisation shall, if he wishes to proceed with the change, apply in the prescribed form to the enforcing authority for the variation of the conditions of the authorisation.

(5)   The holder of an authorisation may at any time, unless he is carrying on a prescribed process under the authorisation and wishes to make a relevant change in the process, apply to the enforcing authority in the prescribed form for the variation of the conditions of the authorisation.

(6)   A person carrying on a process under an authorisation who wishes to make a relevant change in the process may, where it appears to him that the change will require the variation of the conditions of the authorisation, apply to the enforcing authority in the prescribed form for the variation of the conditions of the authorisation specified in the application.

(7)   A person who makes an application for the variation of the conditions of an authorisation shall furnish the authority with such information as may be prescribed or as the authority may by notice require.

(8)   On an application for variation of the conditions of an authorisation under any provision of this section—
    (a) the enforcing authority may, having fulfilled the requirements of Part II of Schedule 1 to this Act in cases to which they apply, as it thinks fit either refuse the application or, subject to the requirements of section 7 above, vary the conditions or, in the case of an application under subsection (6) above, treat the application as a request for a determination under subsection (2) above; and
    (b) if the enforcing authority decides to vary the conditions, it shall serve a variation notice on the holder of the authorisation.

[(9)   Any application to the enforcing authority under this section shall be accompanied—
    (a) in a case where the enforcing authority is the Environment Agency or SEPA, by the charge (if any) prescribed for the purpose by a charging scheme under section 41 of the Environment Act 1995; or
    (b) in any other case, by the fee (if any) prescribed by a scheme under section 8 above.]

(10)   This section applies to any provision other than a condition which is contained in an authorisation as it applies to a condition with the modification that any reference to the breach of a condition shall be read as a reference to acting outside the scope of the authorisation.

(11)   For the purposes of this section a relevant change in a prescribed process is a change in the manner of carrying on the process which is capable of altering the substances released from the process or of affecting the amount or any other characteristic of any substance so released.

[102]

NOTES

Commencement: 1 April 1996 (sub-s (9)); 1 January 1991 (remainder).

Sub-s (9): substituted by the Environment Act 1995, s 120, Sch 22, para 52.

Prescribed: see the Environmental Protection (Applications, Appeals and Registers) Regulations 1991, SI 1991/507, reg 3, as amended by SI 1991/836, SI 1996/667.

12 Revocation of authorisation

(1)   The enforcing authority may at any time revoke an authorisation by notice in writing to the person holding the authorisation.

(2)   Without prejudice to the generality of subsection (1) above, the enforcing authority may revoke an authorisation where it has reason to believe that a prescribed process for which the authorisation is in force has not been carried on or not for a period of twelve months.

(3)   The revocation of an authorisation under this section shall have effect from the date specified in the notice; and the period between the date on which the notice is served and the date so specified shall not be less than twenty-eight days.

(4)   The enforcing authority may, before the date on which the revocation of an authorisation takes effect, withdraw the notice or vary the date specified in it.

(5)   The Secretary of State may, if he thinks fit in relation to an authorisation, give to the enforcing authority directions as to whether the authority should revoke the authorisation under this section.

[103]

Enforcement

13 Enforcement notices

(1)   If the enforcing authority is of the opinion that the person carrying on a prescribed process under an authorisation is contravening any condition of the authorisation, or is likely to contravene any such condition, the authority may serve on him a notice ("an enforcement notice").

(2)   An enforcement notice shall—
   (a) state that the authority is of the said opinion;
   (b) specify the matters constituting the contravention or the matters making it likely that the contravention will arise, as the case may be;
   (c) specify the steps that must be taken to remedy the contravention or to remedy the matters making it likely that the contravention will arise, as the case may be; and
   (d) specify the period within which those steps must be taken.

(3)   The Secretary of State may, if he thinks fit in relation to the carrying on by any person of a prescribed process, give to the enforcing authority directions as to whether the authority should exercise its powers under this section and as to the steps which are to be required to be taken under this section.

[(4)   The enforcing authority may, as respects any enforcement notice it has issued to any person, by notice in writing served on that person, withdraw the notice.]

[104]

___

NOTES
   Commencement: 12 October 1995 (sub-s (4)); 1 January 1991 (remainder).
   Sub-s (4): added by the Environment Act 1995, s 120, Sch 22, para 53.
___

14 Prohibition notices

(1)   If the enforcing authority is of the opinion, as respects the carrying on of a prescribed process under an authorisation, that the continuing to carry it on, or the continuing to carry it on in a particular manner, involves an imminent risk of serious pollution of the environment the authority shall serve a notice (a "prohibition notice") on the person carrying on the process.

(2)   A prohibition notice may be served whether or not the manner of carrying on the process in question contravenes a condition of the authorisation and may relate to any aspects of the process, whether regulated by the conditions of the authorisation or not.

(3)   A prohibition notice shall—
   (a) state the authority's opinion;
   (b) specify the risk involved in the process;

(c) specify the steps that must be taken to remove it and the period within which they must be taken; and

(d) direct that the authorisation shall, until the notice is withdrawn, wholly or to the extent specified in the notice cease to have effect to authorise the carrying on of the process;

and where the direction applies to part only of the process it may impose conditions to be observed in carrying on the part which is authorised to be carried on.

(4)   The Secretary of State may, if he thinks fit in relation to the carrying on by any person of a prescribed process, give to the enforcing authority directions as to—

(a) whether the authority should perform its duties under this section; and

(b) the matters to be specified in any prohibition notice in pursuance of subsection (3) above which the authority is directed to issue.

(5)   The enforcing authority shall, as respects any prohibition notice it has issued to any person, by notice in writing served on that person, withdraw the notice when it is satisfied that the steps required by the notice have been taken.

[105]

15 Appeals as respects authorisations and against variation, enforcement and prohibition notices

(1)   The following persons, namely—

(a) a person who has been refused the grant of an authorisation under section 6 above;

(b) a person who is aggrieved by the conditions attached, under any provision of this Part, to his authorisation;

(c) a person who has been refused a variation of an authorisation on an application under section 11 above;

(d) a person whose authorisation has been revoked under section 12 above;

may appeal against the decision of the enforcing authority to the Secretary of State (except where the decision implements a direction of his).

(2)   A person on whom a variation notice, an enforcement notice or a prohibition notice is served may appeal against the notice to the Secretary of State [(except where the notice implements a direction of his).]

[(3)   This section is subject to section 114 of the Environment Act 1995 (delegation or reference of appeals etc).]

(4)   An appeal under this section shall, if and to the extent required by regulations under subsection (10) below, be advertised in such manner as may be prescribed by regulations under that subsection.

[(5)   Before determining an appeal under this section, the Secretary of State may, if he thinks fit—

(a) cause the appeal to take or continue in the form of a hearing (which may, if the person hearing the appeal so decides, be held, or held to any extent, in private); or

(b) cause a local inquiry to be held;

and the Secretary of State shall act as mentioned in paragraph (a) or (b) above if a request is made by either party to the appeal to be heard with respect to the appeal.]

(6)   On determining an appeal against a decision of an enforcing authority under subsection (1) above, the Secretary of State—

(a) may affirm the decision;

(b) where the decision was a refusal to grant an authorisation or a variation of an authorisation, may direct the enforcing authority to grant the authorisation or to vary the authorisation, as the case may be;

(c) where the decision was as to the conditions attached to an authorisation, may quash all or any of the conditions of the authorisation;

(d) where the decision was to revoke an authorisation, may quash the decision;

and where he exercises any of the powers in paragraphs (b), (c) or (d) above, he may give directions as to the conditions to be attached to the authorisation.

(7)   On the determination of an appeal under subsection (2) above the Secretary of State may either quash or affirm the notice and, if he affirms it, may do so either in its original form or with such modifications as he may in the circumstances think fit.

(8)   Where an appeal is brought under subsection (1) above against the revocation of an authorisation, the revocation shall not take effect pending the final determination or the withdrawal of the appeal.

(9)   Where an appeal is brought under subsection (2) above against a notice, the bringing of the appeal shall not have the effect of suspending the operation of the notice.

(10)   Provision may be made by the Secretary of State by regulations with respect to appeals under this section and in particular—

(a) as to the period within which and the manner in which appeals are to be brought; and

(b) as to the manner in which appeals are to be considered.

[and any such regulations may make different provision for different cases or different circumstances.]

[106]

NOTES

Commencement: 1 April 1996 (sub-ss (3), (5)); 1 January 1991 (remainder).

Sub-ss (2), (10): words in square brackets inserted by the Environment Act 1995, s 120, Sch 22, para 54(2), (5).

Sub-ss (3), (5): substituted by the Environment Act 1995, s 120, Sch 22, para 54(3), (4).

Regulations: the Environmental Protection (Applications, Appeals and Registers) Regulations 1991, SI 1991/507, regs 9–14, as amended by SI 1996/667.

16–18 (*Repealed by the Environment Act 1995, s 120(1), (3), Sch 22, para 55, Sch 24.*)

19 Obtaining of information from persons and authorities

(1)   For the purposes of the discharge of his functions under this Part, the Secretary of State may, by notice in writing served on an enforcing authority, require the authority to furnish such information about the discharge of its functions as an enforcing authority under this Part as he may require.

(2)   For the purposes of the discharge of their respective functions under this Part, the following authorities, that is to say—

(a) the Secretary of State,

(b) a local enforcing authority,

[(c) the Environment Agency, and

(d) (*applies to Scotland only.*)]

may, by notice in writing served on any person, require that person to furnish to the authority such information which the authority reasonably considers that it needs as is specified in the notice, in such form and within such period following service of the notice[, or at such time,] as is so specified.

(3)   For the purposes of this section the discharge by the Secretary of State of an obligation of the United Kingdom under the Community Treaties or any international agreement relating to environmental protection shall be treated as a function of his under this Part.

[107]

NOTES

Sub-s (2): paras (c), (d) substituted and words in final pair of square brackets inserted by the Environment Act 1995, s 120, Sch 22, para 56.

Publicity

20 Public registers of information

(1)   It shall be the duty of each enforcing authority, as respects prescribed processes for which it is the enforcing authority, to maintain, in accordance with regulations made by the Secretary of State, a register containing prescribed particulars of or relating to—

(a) applications for authorisations made to that authority;

(b) the authorisations which have been granted by that authority or in respect of which the authority has functions under this Part;

(c) variation notices, enforcement notices and prohibition notices issued by that authority;

(d) revocations of authorisations effected by that authority;

(e) appeals under section 15 above;

(f) convictions for such offences under section 23(1) below as may be prescribed;

(g) information obtained or furnished in pursuance of the conditions of authorisations or under any provision of this Part;

(h) directions given to the authority under any provision of this Part by the Secretary of State; and

(i) such other matters relating to the carrying on of prescribed processes or any pollution of the environment caused thereby as may be prescribed;

but that duty is subject to sections 21 and 22 below.

(2)   Subject to subsection (4) below, the register maintained by a local enforcing authority [in England and Wales] shall also contain prescribed particulars of such information contained in any register maintained by [the Environment Agency] as relates to the carrying on in the area of the authority of prescribed processes in relation to which [the Environment Agency] has functions under this Part; and [the Environment Agency] shall furnish each authority with the particulars which are necessary to enable it to discharge its duty under this subsection.

(3)   . . .

(4)   Subsection (2) above does not apply to port health authorities but each local enforcing authority [in England and Wales] whose area adjoins that of a port health authority shall include corresponding information in the register maintained by it; and [the Environment Agency] shall furnish each such local enforcing authority with the particulars which are necessary to enable it to discharge its duty under this subsection.

(5)   Where information of any description is excluded from any register by virtue of section 22 below, a statement shall be entered in the register indicating the existence of information of that description.

(6)   The Secretary of State may give to enforcing authorities directions requiring the removal from any register of theirs of any specified information not prescribed for inclusion under subsection (1) or (2) above or which, by virtue of section 21 or 22 below, ought to have been excluded from the register.

(7)   It shall be the duty of each enforcing authority—

(a) to secure that the registers maintained by them under this section are available, at all reasonable times, for inspection by the public free of charge; and

(b) to afford to members of the public facilities for obtaining copies of entries, on payment of reasonable charges

[and, for the purposes of this subsection, places may be prescribed by the Secretary of State at which any such registers or facilities as are mentioned in paragraph (a) or (b) above are to be available or afforded to the public in pursuance of the paragraph in question.]

(8) Registers under this section may be kept in any form.

(9) ...

(10) In this section "prescribed" means prescribed in regulations under this section.

[108]

NOTES
Sub-ss (2), (4): words in square brackets inserted or substituted by the Environment Act 1995, s 120, Sch 22, para 57(2), (4).
Sub-s (3): repealed by the Environment Act 1995, s 120, Sch 22, para 57(3), Sch 24.
Sub-s (7): words in square brackets added by the Environment Act 1995, s 120, Sch 22, para 57(5).
Sub-s (9): repealed by the Environment Act 1995, s 120, Sch 22, para 57(6), Sch 24.
Regulations: the Environmental Protection (Applications, Appeals and Registers) Regulations 1991, SI 1991/507, regs 15, 16, as amended by SI 1996/667, SI 1996/979.

21 Exclusion from registers of information affecting national security

(1) No information shall be included in a register maintained under section 20 above if and so long as, in the opinion of the Secretary of State, the inclusion in the register of that information, or information of that description, would be contrary to the interests of national security.

(2) The Secretary of State may, for the purpose of securing the exclusion from registers of information to which subsection (1) above applies, give to enforcing authorities directions—
   (a) specifying information, or descriptions of information, to be excluded from their registers; or
   (b) specifying descriptions of information to be referred to the Secretary of State for his determination;

and no information referred to the Secretary of State in pursuance of paragraph (b) above shall be included in any such register until the Secretary of State determines that it should be so included.

(3) The enforcing authority shall notify the Secretary of State of any information it excludes from the register in pursuance of directions under subsection (2) above.

(4) A person may, as respects any information which appears to him to be information to which subsection (1) above may apply, give a notice to the Secretary of State specifying the information and indicating its apparent nature; and, if he does so—
   (a) he shall notify the enforcing authority that he has done so; and
   (b) no information so notified to the Secretary of State shall be included in any such register until the Secretary of State has determined that it should be so included.

[109]

22 Exclusion from registers of certain confidential information

(1) No information relating to the affairs of any individual or business shall be included in a register maintained under section 20 above, without the consent of that individual or the person for the time being carrying on that business, if and so long as the information—

(a) is, in relation to him, commercially confidential; and
(b) is not required to be included in the register in pursuance of directions under subsection (7) below;

but information is not commercially confidential for the purposes of this section unless it is determined under this section to be so by the enforcing authority or, on appeal, by the Secretary of State.

(2)   Where information is furnished to an enforcing authority for the purpose of—
(a) an application for an authorisation or for the variation of an authorisation;
(b) complying with any condition of an authorisation; or
(c) complying with a notice under section 19(2) above;

then, if the person furnishing it applies to the authority to have the information excluded from the register on the ground that it is commercially confidential (as regards himself or another person), the authority shall determine whether the information is or is not commercially confidential.

(3)   A determination under subsection (2) above must be made within the period of fourteen days beginning with the date of the application and if the enforcing authority fails to make a determination within that period it shall be treated as having determined that the information is commercially confidential.

(4)   Where it appears to an enforcing authority that any information (other than information furnished in circumstances within subsection (2) above) which has been obtained by the authority under or by virtue of any provision of this Part might be commercially confidential, the authority shall—
(a) give to the person to whom or whose business it relates notice that that information is required to be included in the register unless excluded under this section; and
(b) give him a reasonable opportunity—
   (i) of objecting to the inclusion of the information on the ground that it is commercially confidential; and
   (ii) of making representations to the authority for the purpose of justifying any such objection;

and, if any representations are made, the enforcing authority shall, having taken the representations into account, determine whether the information is or is not commercially confidential.

(5)   Where, under subsection (2) or (4) above, an authority determines that information is not commercially confidential—
(a) the information shall not be entered [in the register] until the end of the period of twenty-one days beginning with the date on which the determination is notified to the person concerned;
(b) that person may appeal to the Secretary of State against the decision;

and, where an appeal is brought in respect of any information, the information shall not be entered [in the register until the end of the period of seven days following the day on which the appeal is finally determined or withdrawn].

[(6)   Subsections (5) and (10) of section 15 above shall apply in relation to an appeal under subsection (5) above as they apply in relation to an appeal under that section, but—
(a) subsection (5) of that section shall have effect for the purposes of this subsection with the substitution for the words from "(which may" onwards of the words "(which must be held in private)"; and
(b) subsection (5) above is subject to section 114 of the Environment Act 1995 (delegation or reference of appeals etc).]

(7)   The Secretary of State may give to the enforcing authorities directions as to specified information, or descriptions of information, which the public interest

requires to be included in registers maintained under section 20 above notwithstanding that the information may be commercially confidential.

(8) Information excluded from a register shall be treated as ceasing to be commercially confidential for the purposes of this section at the expiry of the period of four years beginning with the date of the determination by virtue of which it was excluded; but the person who furnished it may apply to the authority for the information to remain excluded from the register on the ground that it is still commercially confidential and the authority shall determine whether or not that is the case.

(9) Subsections (5) and (6) above shall apply in relation to a determination under subsection (8) above as they apply in relation to a determination under subsection (2) or (4) above.

(10) The Secretary of State may, by order, substitute for the period for the time being specified in subsection (3) above such other period as he considers appropriate.

(11) Information is, for the purposes of any determination under this section, commercially confidential, in relation to any individual or person, if its being contained in the register would prejudice to an unreasonable degree the commercial interests of that individual or person.

[110]

NOTES
Commencement: 1 April 1996 (sub-s (6)); 1 January 1991 (remainder).
Sub-s (5): words in square brackets substituted by the Environment Act 1995, s 120, Sch 22, para 58(2).
Sub-s (6): substituted by the Environment Act 1995, s 120, Sch 22, para 58(3).

Provisions as to offences

23 Offences

(1) It is an offence for a person—
  (a) to contravene section 6(1) above;
  (b) to fail to give the notice required by section 9(2) above;
  (c) to fail to comply with or contravene any requirement or prohibition imposed by an enforcement notice or a prohibition notice;
(d)–(f) . . .
  (g) to fail, without reasonable excuse, to comply with any requirement imposed by a notice under section 19(2) above;
  (h) to make a statement which he knows to be false or misleading in a material particular, or recklessly to make a statement which is false or misleading in a material particular, where the statement is made—
    (i) in purported compliance with a requirement to furnish any information imposed by or under any provision of this Part; or
    (ii) for the purpose of obtaining the grant of an authorisation to himself or any other person or the variation of an authorisation;
  (i) intentionally to make a false entry in any record required to be kept under section 7 above;
  (j) with intent to deceive, to forge or use a document issued or authorised to be issued under section 7 above or required for any purpose thereunder or to make or have in his possession a document so closely resembling any such document as to be likely to deceive;
  (k) . . .
  (l) to fail to comply with an order made by a court under section 26 below.

(2) A person guilty of an offence under paragraph (a), (c) or (l) of subsection (1) above shall be liable:

(a) on summary conviction, to a fine not exceeding £20,000 [or to imprisonment for a term not exceeding three months, or to both];

(b) on conviction on indictment, to a fine or to imprisonment for a term not exceeding two years, or to both.

(3) A person guilty of an offence under paragraph (b), (g), (h), (i) or (j) of subsection (1) above shall be liable—

(a) on summary conviction, to a fine not exceeding the statutory maximum;

(b) on conviction on indictment, to a fine or to imprisonment for a term not exceeding two years, or to both.

(4), (5). . .

[111]

NOTES

Sub-s (1): paras (d)–(f), (k) repealed by the Environment Act 1995, s 120, Sch 22, para 59(2), Sch 24.
Sub-s (2): words in square brackets inserted by the Environment Act 1995, s 59(3).
Sub-ss (4), (5): repealed by the Environment Act 1995, s 120, Sch 22, para 59(4), (5), Sch 24.

24 Enforcement by High Court

If the enforcing authority is of the opinion that proceedings for an offence under section 23(1)(c) above would afford an ineffectual remedy against a person who has failed to comply with the requirements of an enforcement notice or a prohibition notice, the authority may take proceedings in the High Court or, in Scotland, in any court of competent jurisdiction for the purpose of securing compliance with the notice.

[112]

25 Onus of proof as regards techniques and evidence

(1) In any proceedings for an offence under section 23(1)(a) above consisting in a failure to comply with the general condition implied in every authorisation by section 7(4) above, it shall be for the accused to prove that there was no better available technique not entailing excessive cost than was in fact used to satisfy the condition.

(2) Where—

(a) an entry is required under section 7 above to be made in any record as to the observance of any condition of an authorisation; and

(b) the entry has not been made;

that fact shall be admissible as evidence that that condition has not been observed.

[(3) Subsection (2) above shall not have effect in relation to any entry required to be made in any record by virtue of a condition of a relevant licence, within the meaning of section 111 of the Environment Act 1995 (which makes corresponding provision in relation to such licences).]

[113]

NOTES

Commencement: 1 April 1996 (sub-s (3)); 1 January 1991 (remainder).
Sub-s (3): added by the Environment Act 1995, s 111(6).

26 Power of court to order cause of offence to be remedied

(1) Where a person is convicted of an offence under section 23(1)(a) or (c) above in respect of any matters which appear to the court to be matters which it is in his power to remedy, the court may, in addition to or instead of imposing any punishment, order him, within such time as may be fixed by the order, to take such steps as may be specified in the order for remedying those matters.

(2) The time fixed by an order under subsection (1) above may be extended or further extended by order of the court on an application made before the end of the time as originally fixed or as extended under this subsection, as the case may be.

(3)   Where a person is ordered under subsection (1) above to remedy any matters, that person shall not be liable under section 23 above in respect of those matters in so far as they continue during the time fixed by the order or any further time allowed under subsection (2) above.

[114]

27 Power of chief inspector to remedy harm

(1)   Where the commission of an offence under section 23(1)(a) or (c) above causes any harm which it is possible to remedy, [the appropriate Agency] may, subject to subsection (2) below—
    (a) arrange for any reasonable steps to be taken towards remedying the harm; and
    (b) recover the cost of taking those steps from any person convicted of that offence.

(2)   [The Environment Agency or SEPA, as the case may be, shall not exercise its] powers under this section except with the approval in writing of the Secretary of State and, where any of the steps are to be taken on or will affect land in the occupation of any person other than the person on whose land the prescribed process is being carried on, with the permission of that person.

[115]

NOTES
    Sub-ss (1), (2): words in square brackets substituted by the Environment Act 1995, s 120, Sch 22, para 60.

Authorisations and other statutory controls

28 Authorisations and other statutory controls

(1)   No condition shall at any time be attached to an authorisation so as to regulate the final disposal by deposit in or on land of controlled waste (within the meaning of Part II), nor shall any condition apply to such a disposal; . . .

(2)   Where any of the activities comprising a prescribed process are regulated both by an authorisation granted by the enforcing authority under this Part and by a registration or authorisation under the [Radioactive Substances Act 1993], then, if different obligations are imposed as respects the same matter by a condition attached to the authorisation under this Part and a condition attached to the registration or authorisation under that Act, the condition imposed by the authorisation under this Part shall be treated as not binding the person carrying on the process.

(3), (4). . .

[116]

NOTES
    Sub-s (1): words omitted repealed by the Environment Act 1995, s 120, Sch 22, para 61(1), Sch 24.
    Sub-s (2): words in square brackets substituted by the Radioactive Substances Act 1993, s 49(1), Sch 4, para 6.
    Sub-ss (3), (4): repealed by the Environment Act 1995, s 120, Sch 22, para 61(2), Sch 24.

PART II
WASTE ON LAND

NOTES
    This Part should be read in conjunction with the Conservation (Natural Habitats, &c) Regulations 1994, SI 1994/2716, regs 10, 48 et seq, 83, 84 at **[997]**, **[1034]** et seq, **[1068]**, **[1069]** (which make provision for implementing Council Directive 92/43/EEC on the conservation of natural habitats and of wild fauna and flora).
    Modification: for the modification of this Part, see the Waste Management Licensing Regulations 1994, SI 1994/1056, regs 1(3), 19, Sch 4, Pt I, para 9 at **[937]**, **[954]**, **[959]**.

Preliminary

29 Preliminary

(1)   The following provisions have effect for the interpretation of this Part.

(2)   The "environment" consists of all, or any, of the following media, namely land, water and the air.

(3)   "Pollution of the environment" means pollution of the environment due to the release or escape (into any environmental medium) from—
  (a) the land on which controlled waste is treated,
  (b) the land on which controlled waste is kept,
  (c) the land in or on which controlled waste is deposited,
  (d) fixed plant by means of which controlled waste is treated, kept or disposed of,

of substances or articles constituting or resulting from the waste and capable (by reason of the quantity or concentrations involved) of causing harm to man or any other living organisms supported by the environment.

(4)   Subsection (3) above applies in relation to mobile plant by means of which controlled waste is treated or disposed of as it applies to plant on land by means of which controlled waste is treated or disposed of.

(5)   For the purposes of subsections (3) and (4) above "harm" means harm to the health of living organisms or other interference with the ecological systems of which they form part and in the case of man includes offence to any of his senses or harm to his property; and "harmless" has a corresponding meaning.

(6)   The "disposal" of waste includes its disposal by way of deposit in or on land and, subject to subsection (7) below, waste is "treated" when it is subjected to any process, including making it re-usable or reclaiming substances from it and "recycle" (and cognate expressions) shall be construed accordingly.

(7)   Regulations made by the Secretary of State may prescribe activities as activities which constitute the treatment of waste for the purposes of this Part or any provision of this Part prescribed in the regulations.

(8)   "Land" includes land covered by waters where the land is above the low water mark of ordinary spring tides and references to land on which controlled waste is treated, kept or deposited are references to the surface of the land (including any structure set into the surface).

(9)   "Mobile plant" means, subject to subsection (10) below, plant which is designed to move or be moved whether on roads or other land.

(10) Regulations made by the Secretary of State may prescribe descriptions of plant which are to be treated as being, or as not being, mobile plant for the purposes of this Part.

(11) "Substance" means any natural or artificial substance, whether in solid or liquid form or in the form of a gas or vapour.

[117]

NOTES
  Regulations: the Waste Management Licensing Regulations 1994, SI 1994/1056, as amended by SI 1994/1137, SI 1995/288, SI 1995/1950, SI 1996/593, SI 1996/634, SI 1996/972, SI 1996/1279; the Waste Management Regulations 1996, SI 1996/634 (made under sub-s (10)).

30 Authorities for purposes of this Part

[(1) Any reference in this Part to a waste regulation authority—
  (a) in relation to England and Wales, is a reference to the Environment Agency; and
  (b) *(applies to Scotland only)*,

and any reference in this Part to the area of a waste regulation authority shall accordingly be taken as a reference to the area over which the Environment Agency or the Scottish Environment Protection Agency, as the case may be, exercises its functions or, in the case of any particular function, the function in question.]

(2)   For the purposes of this Part the following authorities are waste disposal authorities, namely—
    (a) for any non-metropolitan county in England, the county council;
    (b) in Greater London, the following—
        (i) for the area of a London waste disposal authority, the authority constituted as the waste disposal authority for that area;
        (ii) for the City of London, the Common Council;
        (iii) for any other London borough, the council of the borough;
    (c) in the metropolitan county of Greater Manchester, the following—
        (i) for the metropolitan district of Wigan, the district council;
        (ii) for all other areas in the county, the authority constituted as the Greater Manchester Waste Disposal Authority;
    (d) for the metropolitan county of Merseyside, the authority constituted as the Merseyside Waste Disposal Authority;
    (e) for any district in any other metropolitan county in England, the council of the district;
    [(f) for any county or county borough in Wales, the council of the county or county borough;]
    (g) (*applies to Scotland only*).

(3)   For the purposes of this Part the following authorities are waste collection authorities—
    (a) for any district in England . . . not within Greater London, the council of the district;
    (b) in Greater London, the following—
        (i) for any London borough, the council of the borough;
        (ii) for the City of London, the Common Council;
        (iii) for the Temples, the Sub-Treasurer of the Inner Temple and the Under Treasurer of the Middle Temple respectively;
    [(bb) for any county or county borough in Wales, the council of the county or county borough;]
    (c) (*applies to Scotland only*).

(4)   In this section references to particular authorities having been constituted as waste disposal . . . authorities are references to their having been so constituted by the Waste Regulation and Disposal (Authorities) Order 1985 made by the Secretary of State under section 10 of the Local Government Act 1985 and the reference to London waste disposal authorities is a reference to the authorities named in Parts I, II, III, IV and V of Schedule 1 to that Order and this section has effect subject to any order made under the said section 10 . . .

(5)   In this Part "waste disposal contractor" means a person who in the course of a business collects, keeps, treats or disposes of waste, being either—
    (a) a company formed for all or any of those purposes by a waste disposal authority whether in pursuance of section 32 below or otherwise; or
    (b) either a company formed for all or any of those purposes by other persons or a partnership or an individual;
and "company" has the same meaning as in the Companies Act 1985 and "formed", in relation to a company formed by other persons, includes the alteration of the objects of the company.

(6)–(8). . .

NOTES

Commencement: 1 April 1996 (sub-s (1)); 31 May 1991 (remainder).

Sub-s (1): substituted by the Environment Act 1995, s 120, Sch 22, para 62(2).

Sub-s (2): para (f) substituted by the Local Government (Wales) Act 1994, s 22(3), Sch 9, para 17(2).

Sub-s (3): words omitted from para (a) repealed, and para (bb) inserted, by the Local Government (Wales) Act 1994, ss 22(3), 66(8), Sch 9, para 17(3), Sch 18; words in square brackets in para (c) substituted by the Local Government etc (Scotland) Act 1994, s 180(1), Sch 13, para 167(3).

Sub-s (4): words omitted repealed by the Environment Act 1995, s 120, Sch 22, para 62(3), Sch 24.

Sub-ss (6)–(8): repealed by the Environment Act 1995, s 120, Sch 22, para 62(4), Sch 24.

31   (*Repealed by the Environment Act 1995, s 120(1), (3), Sch 22, para 63, Sch 24.*)

32 Transition to waste disposal companies etc

(1)   In this section "existing disposal authority" means any authority (including any joint authority) constituted as a waste disposal authority for any area before the day appointed for this section to come into force.

(2)   The Secretary of State shall, subject to subsection (3) below, give directions to existing disposal authorities or, in the case of joint authorities, to the constituent authorities requiring them, before specified dates, to—

    (a) form or participate in forming waste disposal companies; and

    (b) transfer to the companies so formed, by and in accordance with a scheme made in accordance with Schedule 2 to this Act, the relevant part of their undertakings;

and a waste disposal authority shall accordingly have power to form, and hold securities in, any company so established.

(3)   Subject to subsection (4) below, the Secretary of State shall not give any direction under subsection (2) above to an existing disposal authority, or to the constituent authorities of an existing disposal authority, as respects which or each of which he is satisfied that the authority—

    (a) has formed or participated in forming a waste disposal company and transferred to it the relevant part of its undertaking;

    (b) has, in pursuance of arrangements made with other persons, ceased to carry on itself the relevant part of its undertaking;

    (c) has made arrangements with other persons to cease to carry on itself the relevant part of its undertaking; or

    (d) has, in pursuance of arrangements made with other persons, ceased to provide places at which and plant and equipment by means of which controlled waste can be disposed of or deposited for the purposes of disposal.

(4)   Subsection (3) above does not apply in a case falling within paragraph (a) unless it appears to the Secretary of State that—

    (a) the form of the company and the undertaking transferred are satisfactory; and

    (b) the requirements of subsections (8) and (9) below are fulfilled;

and "satisfactory" means satisfactory by reference to the corresponding arrangements to which he would give his approval for the purposes of a transfer scheme under Schedule 2 to this Act.

(5)   Where the Secretary of State is precluded from giving a direction under subsection (2) above to any authority by reason of his being satisfied as to the arrangements mentioned in subsection (3)(c) above, then, if those arrangements are not implemented within what appears to him to be a reasonable time, he may exercise his power to give directions under subsection (2) above as respects that authority.

(6)   Part I of Schedule 2 to this Act has effect for the purposes of this section and Part II for regulating the functions of waste disposal authorities and the activities of waste disposal contractors.

(7)   Subject to subsection (8) below, the activities of a company which a waste disposal authority has formed or participated in forming (whether in pursuance of subsection (2)(a) above or otherwise) may include activities which are beyond the powers of the authority to carry on itself, but, in the case of a company formed otherwise than in pursuance of subsection (2)(a) above, only if the Secretary of State has determined under subsection (4)(a) above that the form of the company and the undertaking transferred to it are satisfactory.

(8)   A waste disposal authority shall, for so long as it controls a company which it has formed or participated in forming (whether in pursuance of subsection (2)(a) above or otherwise), so exercise its control as to secure that the company does not engage in activities other than the following activities or any activities incidental or conducive to, or calculated to facilitate, them, that is to say, the disposal, keeping or treatment of waste and the collection of waste.

(9)   Subject to subsection (10) below, a waste disposal authority shall, for so long as it controls a company which it has formed or participated in forming (whether in pursuance of subsection (2)(a) above or otherwise), so exercise its control as to secure that, for the purposes of Part V of the Local Government and Housing Act 1989, the company is an arm's length company.

(10)   Subsection (9) above shall not apply in the case of a company which a waste disposal authority has formed or participated in forming in pursuance of subsection (2)(a) above until after the vesting date for that company.

(11)   In this section and Schedule 2 to this Act—
"control" (and cognate expressions) is to be construed in accordance with
    section 68 or, as the case requires, section 73 of the Local Government and
    Housing Act 1989;
"the relevant part" of the undertaking of an existing disposal authority is that part
    which relates to the disposal, keeping or treatment or the collection of waste;
and in this section "securities" and "vesting date" have the same meaning as in Schedule 2.

(12)   This section shall not apply to Scotland.

[119]

Prohibition on unauthorised or harmful depositing, treatment or disposal of waste

33 Prohibition on unauthorised or harmful depositing, treatment or disposal etc of waste

(1)   Subject to subsection (2) and (3) below *and, in relation to Scotland, to section 54 below,* a person shall not—
(a) deposit controlled waste, or knowingly cause or knowingly permit
    controlled waste to be deposited in or on any land unless a waste
    management licence authorising the deposit is in force and the deposit is in
    accordance with the licence;
(b) treat, keep or dispose of controlled waste, or knowingly cause or
    knowingly permit controlled waste to be treated, kept or disposed of—
    (i) in or on any land, or
    (ii) by means of any mobile plant,
    except under and in accordance with a waste management licence;
(c) treat, keep or dispose of controlled waste in a manner likely to cause
    pollution of the environment or harm to human health.

(2)   Subsection (1) above does not apply in relation to household waste from a domestic property which is treated, kept or disposed of within the curtilage of the dwelling by or with the permission of the occupier of the dwelling.

(3)   Subsection (1)(a), (b) or (c) above do not apply in cases prescribed in regulations made by the Secretary of State and the regulations may make different exceptions for different areas.

(4)   The Secretary of State, in exercising his power under subsection (3) above, shall have regard in particular to the expediency of excluding from the controls imposed by waste management licences—
  (a) any deposits which are small enough or of such a temporary nature that they may be so excluded;
  (b) any means of treatment or disposal which are innocuous enough to be so excluded;
  (c) cases for which adequate controls are provided by another enactment than this section.

(5)   Where controlled waste is carried in and deposited from a motor vehicle, the person who controls or is in a position to control the use of the vehicle shall, for the purposes of subsection (1)(a) above, be treated as knowingly causing the waste to be deposited whether or not he gave any instructions for this to be done.

(6)   A person who contravenes subsection (1) above or any condition of a waste management licence commits an offence.

(7)   It shall be a defence for a person charged with an offence under this section to prove—
  (a) that he took all reasonable precautions and exercised all due diligence to avoid the commission of the offence; or
  (b) that he acted under instructions from his employer and neither knew nor had reason to suppose that the acts done by him constituted a contravention of subsection (1) above; or
  [(c) that the acts alleged to constitute the contravention were done in an emergency in order to avoid danger to human health in a case where—
      (i) he took all such steps as were reasonably practicable in the circumstances for minimising pollution of the environment and harm to human health; and
      (ii) particulars of the acts were furnished to the waste regulation authority as soon as reasonably practicable after they were done.]

(8)   Except in a case falling within subsection (9) below, a person who commits an offence under this section shall be liable—
  (a) on summary conviction, to imprisonment for a term not exceeding six months or a fine not exceeding £20,000 or both; and
  (b) on conviction on indictment, to imprisonment for a term not exceeding two years or a fine or both.

(9)   A person who commits an offence under this section in relation to special waste shall be liable—
  (a) on summary conviction, to imprisonment for a term not exceeding six months or a fine not exceeding £20,000 or both;
  (b) on conviction on indictment, to imprisonment for a term not exceeding five years or a fine or both.

[120]

NOTES
  Commencement: 1 May 1994 (sub-s (1) in part, sub-ss (2), (5), (6)–(9) certain purposes); 1 April 1992 (sub-s (1) in part, sub-ss (2), (6)–(9), certain purposes); 13 December 1991 (sub-ss (3), (4)); for commencement dates for remaining purposes see the Environmental Protection Act 1990 (Commencement No 15) Order 1994, SI 1994/1096.

Sub-s (1): words in italics repealed by the Environment Act 1995, s 120, Sch 24, as from a day to be appointed.

Sub-s (7): para (c) substituted by the Environment Act 1995, s 120, Sch 22, para 64.

Regulations: the Waste Management Licensing Regulations 1994, SI 1994/1056, as amended by SI 1994/1137, SI 1995/288, SI 1995/1950, SI 1996/593, SI 1996/634, SI 1996/972, SI 1996/1279; the Waste Management Regulations 1996, SI 1996/634; the Special Waste Regulations 1996, SI 1996/972 (made under sub-s (3)), as amended by SI 1996/2019, SI 1997/251.

Duty of care etc as respects waste

34 Duty of care etc as respects waste

(1) Subject to subsection (2) below, it shall be the duty of any person who imports, produces, carries, keeps, treats or disposes of controlled waste or, as a broker, has control of such waste, to take all such measures applicable to him in that capacity as are reasonable in the circumstances—

(a) to prevent any contravention by any other person of section 33 above;

(b) to prevent the escape of the waste from his control or that of any other person; and

(c) on the transfer of the waste, to secure—

(i) that the transfer is only to an authorised person or to a person for authorised transport purposes; and

(ii) that there is transferred such a written description of the waste as will enable other persons to avoid a contravention of that section and to comply with the duty under this subsection as respects the escape of waste.

(2) The duty imposed by subsection (1) above does not apply to an occupier of domestic property as respects the household waste produced on the property.

(3) The following are authorised persons for the purpose of subsection (1)(c) above—

(a) any authority which is a waste collection authority for the purposes of this Part;

(b) any person who is the holder of a waste management licence under section 35 below *or of a disposal licence under section 5 of the Control of Pollution Act 1974*;

(c) any person to whom section 33(1) above does not apply by virtue of regulations under subsection (3) of that section;

(d) any person registered as a carrier of controlled waste under section 2 of the Control of Pollution (Amendment) Act 1989;

(e) any person who is not required to be so registered by virtue of regulations under section 1(3) of that Act; and

(f) (*applies to Scotland only*).

[(3A) The Secretary of State may by regulations amend subsection (3) above so as to add, whether generally or in such circumstances as may be prescribed in the regulations, any person specified in the regulations, or any description of person so specified, to the persons who are authorised persons for the purposes of subsection (1)(c) above.]

(4) The following are authorised transport purposes for the purposes of subsection (1)(c) above—

(a) the transport of controlled waste within the same premises between different places in those premises;

(b) the transport to a place in Great Britain of controlled waste which has been brought from a country or territory outside Great Britain not having been landed in Great Britain until it arrives at that place; and

(c) the transport by air or sea of controlled waste from a place in Great Britain to a place outside Great Britain;

and "transport" has the same meaning in this subsection as in the Control of Pollution (Amendment) Act 1989.

[(4A) For the purposes of subsection (1)(c)(ii) above—
(a) a transfer of waste in stages shall be treated as taking place when the first stage of the transfer takes place, and
(b) a series of transfers between the same parties of waste of the same description shall be treated as a single transfer taking place when the first of the transfers in the series takes place.]

(5) The Secretary of State may, by regulations, make provision imposing requirements on any person who is subject to the duty imposed by subsection (1) above as respects the making and retention of documents and the furnishing of documents or copies of documents.

(6) Any person who fails to comply with the duty imposed by subsection (1) above or with any requirement imposed under subsection (5) above shall be liable—
(a) on summary conviction, to a fine not exceeding the statutory maximum; and
(b) on conviction on indictment, to a fine.

(7) The Secretary of State shall, after consultation with such persons or bodies as appear to him representative of the interests concerned, prepare and issue a code of practice for the purpose of providing to persons practical guidance on how to discharge the duty imposed on them by subsection (1) above.

(8) The Secretary of State may from time to time revise a code of practice issued under subsection (7) above by revoking, amending or adding to the provisions of the code.

(9) The code of practice prepared in pursuance of subsection (7) above shall be laid before both Houses of Parliament.

(10) A code of practice issued under subsection (7) above shall be admissible in evidence and if any provision of such a code appears to the court to be relevant to any question arising in the proceedings it shall be taken into account in determining that question.

(11) Different codes of practice may be prepared and issued under subsection (7) above for different areas.

[121]

NOTES

Commencement: 1 April 1996 (sub-s (3A)); 1 April 1992 (sub-ss (1)–(3), (4), (6), (10), sub-s (4A) (for effect see below)); 13 December 1991 (remainder).

Sub-s (3): words in italics in para (b) repealed by s 162 of, and Sch 16, Pt II to, this Act, as from a day to be appointed.

Sub-s (3A): inserted by the Environment Act 1995, s 120, Sch 22, para 65.

Sub-s (4A): inserted, subject to the provisions below, by the Deregulation and Contracting Out Act 1994, s 33(1). Sub-ss 33(2), (3) of the 1994 Act provide as follows—

"(2) Subsection (1) above shall be deemed always to have had effect, except in relation to any proceedings for failure to comply with the duty imposed by section 34(1) of that Act which were commenced before the coming into force of subsection (1) above.

(3) Where any such proceedings have not been disposed of before the coming into force of subsection (1) above, it shall be a defence to show that the conduct in question would not have constituted a breach of the duty concerned had subsection (1) above been in force at the time.".

Regulations: the Environmental Protection (Duty of Care) Regulations 1991, SI 1991/2839, as amended by SI 1996/972; the Special Waste Regulations 1996, SI 1996/972, as amended by SI 1996/2019, SI 1997/251.

Waste Management Licences

35 Waste management licences: general

(1)   A waste management licence is a licence granted by a waste regulation authority authorising the treatment, keeping or disposal of any specified description of controlled waste in or on specified land or the treatment or disposal of any specified description of controlled waste by means of specified mobile plant.

(2)   A licence shall be granted to the following person, that is to say—
 (a) in the case of a licence relating to the treatment, keeping or disposal of waste in or on land, to the person who is in occupation of the land; and
 (b) in the case of a licence relating to the treatment or disposal of waste by means of mobile plant, to the person who operates the plant.

(3)   A licence shall be granted on such terms and subject to such conditions as appear to the waste regulation authority to be appropriate and the conditions may relate—
 (a) to the activities which the licence authorises, and
 (b) to the precautions to be taken and works to be carried out in connection with or in consequence of those activities;

and accordingly requirements may be imposed in the licence which are to be complied with before the activities which the licence authorises have begun or after the activities which the licence authorises have ceased.

(4)   Conditions may require the holder of a licence to carry out works or do other things notwithstanding that he is not entitled to carry out the works or to do the thing and any person whose consent would be required shall grant, or join in granting, the holder of the licence such rights in relation to the land as will enable the holder of the licence to comply with any requirements imposed on him by the licence.

(5)   Conditions may relate, where waste other than controlled waste is to be treated, kept or disposed of, to the treatment, keeping or disposal of that other waste.

(6)   The Secretary of State may, by regulations, make provision as to the conditions which are, or are not, to be included in a licence; and regulations under this subsection may make different provision for different circumstances.

(7)   The Secretary of State may, as respects any licence for which an application is made to a waste regulation authority, give to the authority directions as to the terms and conditions which are, or are not, to be included in the licence; and it shall be the duty of the authority to give effect to the directions.

[(7A) In any case where—
 (a) an entry is required under this section to be made in any record as to the observance of any condition of a licence, and
 (b) the entry has not been made,

that fact shall be admissible as evidence that condition has not been observed.

(7B) Any person who
 (a) intentionally makes a false entry in any record required to be kept under any condition of a licence, or
 (b) with intent to deceive, forges or uses a licence or makes or has in his possession a document so closely resembling a licence as to be likely to deceive,

shall be guilty of an offence.

(7C) A person guilty of an offence under subsection (7B) above shall be liable—
 (a) on summary conviction, to a fine not exceeding the statutory maximum;
 (b) on conviction on indictment, to a fine or to imprisonment for a term not exceeding two years, or to both.]

(8)   It shall be the duty of waste regulation authorities to have regard to any guidance issued to them by the Secretary of State with respect to the discharge of their functions in relation to licences.

(9)   A licence may not be surrendered by the holder except in accordance with section 39 below.

(10) A licence is not transferable by the holder but the waste regulation authority may transfer it to another person under section 40 below.

(11) A licence shall continue in force until it is revoked entirely by the waste regulation authority under section 38 below or it is surrendered or its surrender is accepted under section 39 below.

(12) In this Part "licence" means a waste management licence and "site licence" and "mobile plant licence" mean, respectively, a licence authorising the treatment, keeping or disposal of waste in or on land and a licence authorising the treatment or disposal of waste by means of mobile plant.

[122]

NOTES

   Commencement: 1 April 1996 (sub-ss (7A)–(7C)); 1 May 1994 (sub-ss (1)–(5), (7)–(12), certain purposes); for commencement dates for remaining purposes see the Environmental Protection Act 1990 (Commencement No 15) Order 1994, SI 1994/1096; 18 February 1993 (sub-s (6)).

   Sub-ss (7A)–(7C): inserted by the Environment Act 1995, s 120, Sch 22, para 66.

   Regulations: the Waste Management Licensing Regulations 1994, SI 1994/1056, as amended by SI 1994/1137, SI 1995/288, SI 1995/1950, SI 1996/593, SI 1996/634, SI 1996/972, SI 1996/1279.

[35A Compensation where rights granted pursuant to section 35(4) or 38(9A)

(1)   This section applies in any case where—
   (a) the holder of a licence is required—
      (i) by the conditions of the licence; or
      (ii) by a requirement imposed under section 38(9) below,
      to carry out any works or do any other thing which he is not entitled to carry out or do;
   (b) a person whose consent would be required has, pursuant to the requirements of section 35(4) above or 38(9A) below, granted, or joined in granting, to the holder of the licence any rights in relation to any land; and
   (c) those rights, or those rights together with other rights, are such as will enable the holder of the licence to comply with any requirements imposed on him by the licence or, as the case may be, under section 38(9) below.

(2)   In a case where this section applies, any person who has granted, or joined in granting, the rights in question shall be entitled to be paid compensation under this section by the holder of the licence.

(3)   The Secretary of State shall by regulations provide for the descriptions of loss and damage for which compensation is payable under this section.

(4)   The Secretary of State may by regulations—
   (a) provide for the basis on which any amount to be paid by way of compensation under this section is to be assessed;
   (b) without prejudice to the generality of subsection (3) and paragraph (a) above, provide for compensation under this section to be payable in respect of—
      (i) any effect of any rights being granted, or
      (ii) any consequence of the exercise of any rights which have been granted;
   (c) provide for the times at which any entitlement to compensation under this section is to arise or at which any such compensation is to become payable;

(d) provide for the persons or bodies by whom, and the manner in which, any dispute—
  (i) as to whether any, and (if so) how much and when, compensation under this section is payable; or
  (ii) as to the person to or by whom it shall be paid,
  is to be determined;
(e) provide for when or how applications may be made for compensation under this section;
(f) without prejudice to the generality of paragraph (d) above, provide for when or how applications may be made for the determination of any such disputes as are mentioned in that paragraph;
(g) without prejudice to the generality of paragraphs (e) and (f) above, prescribe the form in which any such applications as are mentioned in those paragraphs are to be made;
(h) make provision similar to any provision made by paragraph 8 of Schedule 19 to the Water Resources Act 1991;
(j) make different provision for different cases, including different provision in relation to different persons or circumstances;
(k) include such incidental, supplemental, consequential or transitional provision as the Secretary of State considers appropriate.]

[123]

NOTES

Commencement: 1 February 1996 (certain purposes); to be appointed (remaining purposes).

Inserted by the Environment Act 1995, s 120, Sch 22, para 67, and in force only in so far as it confers power to make regulations or makes provision in relation to the exercise of that power (the Environment Act 1995 (Commencement No 5) Order 1996, SI 1996/186, art 2).

36 Grant of licences

(1) An application for a licence shall be made—
  (a) in the case of an application for a site licence, to the waste regulation authority in whose area the land is situated; and
  (b) in the case of an application for a mobile plant licence, to the waste regulation authority in whose area the operator of the plant has his principal place of business;
and shall be made in the form prescribed by the Secretary of State in regulations and accompanied by the prescribed fee payable under section 41 below.

(2) A licence shall not be issued for a use of land for which planning permission is required in pursuance of the Town and Country Planning Act 1990 or the Town and Country Planning (Scotland) Act 1972 unless—
  (a) such planning permission is in force in relation to that use of the land, or
  (b) an established use certificate is in force under section 192 of the said Act of 1990 or section 90 of the said Act of 1972 in relation to that use of the land.

(3) Subject to subsection (2) above and subsection (4) below, a waste regulation authority to which an application for a licence has been duly made shall not reject the application if it is satisfied that the applicant is a fit and proper person unless it is satisfied that its rejection is necessary for the purpose of preventing—
  (a) pollution of the environment;
  (b) harm to human health; or
  (c) serious detriment to the amenities of the locality;
but paragraph (c) above is inapplicable where planning permission is in force in relation to the use to which the land will be put under the licence.

(4) Where the waste regulation authority proposes to issue a licence, the authority must, before it does so,—

(a) refer the proposal to [the appropriate planning authority] and the Health and Safety Executive; and

(b) consider any representations about the proposal which the [authority] or the Executive makes to it during the allowed period.

(5), (6). . .

(7)   Where any part of the land to be used is land which has been notified under section 28(1) of the Wildlife and Countryside Act 1981 (protection for certain areas) and the waste regulation authority proposes to issue a licence, the authority must, before it does so—

(a) refer the proposal to the appropriate nature conservation body; and

(b) consider any representations about the proposal which the body makes to it during the allowed period;

and in this section any reference to the appropriate nature conservation body is a reference to the Nature Conservancy Council for England, [Scottish Natural Heritage] or the Countryside Council for Wales, according as the land is situated in England, Scotland or Wales.

(8)   Until the date appointed under section 131(3) below any reference in subsection (7) above to the appropriate nature conservation body is a reference to the Nature Conservancy Council.

(9)   If within the period of four months beginning with the date on which a waste regulation authority received an application for the grant of a licence, or within such longer period as the authority and the applicant may at any time agree in writing, the authority has neither granted the licence in consequence of the application nor given notice to the applicant that the authority has rejected the application, the authority shall be deemed to have rejected the application.

[(9A) Subsection (9) above—

(a) shall not have effect in any case where, by virtue of subsection (1A) above, the waste regulation authority refuses to proceed with the application in question, and

(b) shall have effect in any case where, by virtue of subsection (1A) above, the waste regulation authority refuses to proceed with it until the required information is provided, with the substitution for the period of four months there mentioned of the period of four months beginning with the date on which the authority received the information.]

[(10) The period allowed to the appropriate planning authority, the Health and Safety Executive or the appropriate nature conservancy body for the making of representations under subsection (4) or (7) above about a proposal is the period of twenty-eight days beginning with the day on which the proposal is received by the waste regulation authority or such longer period as the waste regulation authority, the appropriate planning authority, the Executive or the body, as the case may be, agree in writing.

(11)   In this section—

"the appropriate planning authority" means—

(a) where the relevant land is situated in the area of a London borough council, that London borough council;

(b) where the relevant land is situated in the City of London, the Common Council of the City of London;

(c) where the relevant land is situated in a non-metropolitan county in England, the council of that county;

(d) where the relevant land is situated in a National Park or the Broads, the National Park authority for that National Park or, as the case may be, the Broads Authority;

(e) where the relevant land is situated elsewhere in England or Wales, the council of the district or, in Wales, the county or county borough, in which the land is situated;

(f) where the relevant land is situated in Scotland, the council constituted under section 2 of the Local Government etc (Scotland) Act 1994 for the area in which the land is situated;

"the Broads" has the same meaning as in the Norfolk and Suffolk Broads Act 1988;

"National Park authority", . . . , means a National Park authority established under section 63 of the Environment Act 1995 which has become the local planning authority for the National Park in question;

"the relevant land" means—

(a) in relation to a site licence, the land to which the licence relates; and

(b) in relation to a mobile plant licence, the principal place of business of the operator of the plant to which the licence relates.

(12) . . .

(13) The Secretary of State may by regulations amend the definition of "appropriate planning authority" in subsection (11) above.

(14) This section shall have effect subject to section 36A below.]

[124]

NOTES

Commencement: 1 April 1996 (sub-ss (1A), (10)–(14)); 1 May 1994 (sub-ss (2)–(10), certain purposes), for commencement dates for remaining purposes see the Environmental Protection Act 1990 (Commencement No 15) Order 1994, SI 1994/1096; 18 February 1993 (sub-s (1)); to be appointed (remainder).

Sub-s (1): words in italics substituted as from a day to be appointed, by the Environment Act 1995, s 120, Sch 22, para 68(2) , as follows—

"and shall be made on a form provided for the purpose by the waste regulation authority and accompanied by such information as that authority reasonably requires and the charge prescribed for the purpose by a charging scheme under section 41 of the Environment Act 1995.

(1A) Where an applicant for a licence fails to provide the waste regulation authority with any information required under subsection (1) above, the authority may refuse to proceed with the application, or refuse to proceed with it until the information is provided."

This amendment is in force from 1 April 1996 in so far as it requires an application to be accompanied by the prescribed charge (by virtue of the Environment Act 1995 (Commencement No 5) Order 1996, SI 1996/186, art 3); subject to savings in art 4 relating to an application for a licence under this section made, but not finally disposed of, before that date.

In relation to such licences, art 4 provides that this section has effect as if—

(a) those amendments had not been made;

(b) in subsection (4)(a) the words "National Rivers Authority and" were omitted; and

(c) in subsection (4)(b) the words "the Authority or" were omitted."

Sub-s (4): words in square brackets substituted for original words "National Rivers Authority" and "the Authority" by the Environment Act 1995, s 120, Sch 22, para 68(3), except as set out in note to sub-s (1) above.

Sub-s (5), (6): repealed by the Environment Act 1995, s 120, Sch 22, para 68(4), Sch 24.

Sub-s (7): words in square brackets substituted by the Natural Heritage (Scotland) Act 1991, s 4, Sch 2, para 10(2).

Sub-s (8): repealed by s 162 of, and Sch 16, Pt II to, this Act, as from a day to be appointed.

Sub-s (9A): inserted by the Environment Act 1995, s 120, Sch 22, para 68(5), as from a day to be appointed.

Sub-ss (10), (13), (14): substituted together with sub-ss (11), (12), for original sub-s (10), by the Environment Act 1995, s 120, Sch 22, para 68(6).

Sub-s (11): substituted, together with sub-ss (10), (12)–(14), for original sub-s (10), by the Environment Act 1995, s 120, Sch 22, para 68(5); words omitted repealed by the Environment Act 1995, s 120, Sch 24.

Sub-s (12): repealed by the Environment Act 1995, s 120, Sch 24.

Regulations: the Waste Management Licensing Regulations 1994, SI 1994/1056, as amended by SI 1994/1137, SI 1995/288, SI 1995/1950, SI 1996/593, SI 1996/634, SI 1996/972, SI 1996/1279.

[36A Consultation before the grant of certain licences

(1)   This section applies where an application for a licence has been duly made to a waste regulation authority, and the authority proposes to issue a licence subject

(by virtue of section 35(4) above) to any condition which might require the holder of the licence to—

(a) carry out any works, or

(b) do any other thing,

which he might not be entitled to carry out or do.

(2) Before issuing the licence, the waste regulation authority shall serve on every person appearing to the authority to be a person falling within subsection (3) below a notice which complies with the requirements set out in subsection (4) below.

(3) A person falls within this subsection if—

(a) he is the owner, lessee or occupier of any land; and

(b) that land is land in relation to which it is likely that, as a consequence of the licence being issued subject to the condition in question, rights will have to be granted by virtue of section 35(4) above to the holder of the licence.

(4) A notice served under subsection (2) above shall—

(a) set out the condition in question;

(b) indicate the nature of the works or other things which that condition might require the holder of the licence to carry out or do; and

(c) specify the date by which, and the manner in which, any representations relating to the condition or its possible effects are to be made to the waste regulation authority by the person on whom the notice is served.

(5) The date which, pursuant to subsection (4)(c) above, is specified in a notice shall be a date not earlier than the date on which expires the period—

(a) beginning with the date on which the notice is served, and

(b) of such length as may be prescribed in regulations made by the Secretary of State.

(6) Before the waste regulation authority issues the licence it must, subject to subsection (7) below, consider any representations made in relation to the condition in question, or its possible effects, by any person on whom a notice has been served under subsection (2) above.

(7) Subsection (6) above does not require the waste regulation authority to consider any representations made by a person after the date specified in the notice served on him under subsection (2) above as the date by which his representations in relation to the condition or its possible effects are to be made.

(8) In subsection (3) above—

"owner", in relation to any land in England and Wales, means the person who—

(a) is for the time being receiving the rack-rent of the land, whether on his own account or as agent or trustee for another person; or

(b) would receive the rack-rent if the land were let at a rack-rent,

but does not include a mortgagee not in possession; and

. . .]

[125]

NOTES

Commencement: to be appointed.

Inserted by the Environment Act 1995, s 120, Sch 22, para 69, as from a day to be appointed.

Sub-s (8): words omitted relate to Scotland only.

37 Variation of licences

(1) While a licence issued by a waste regulation authority is in force, the authority may, subject to regulations under section 35(6) above and to subsection (3) below,—

(a) on its own initiative, modify the conditions of the licence to any extent which, in the opinion of the authority, is desirable and is unlikely to require unreasonable expense on the part of the holder; and

(b) on the application of the licence holder accompanied by [the charge prescribed for the purpose by a charging scheme under section 41 of the Environment Act 1995,] modify the conditions of his licence to the extent requested in the application.

(2) While a licence issued by a waste regulation authority is in force, the authority shall, except where it revokes the licence entirely under section 38 below, modify the conditions of the licence—

(a) to the extent which in the opinion of the authority is required for the purpose of ensuring that the activities authorised by the licence do not cause pollution of the environment or harm to human health or become seriously detrimental to the amenities of the locality affected by the activities; and

(b) to the extent required by any regulations in force under section 35(6) above.

(3) The Secretary of State may, as respects any licence issued by a waste regulation authority, give to the authority directions as to the modifications which are to be made in the conditions of the licence under subsection (1)(a) or (2)(a) above; and it shall be the duty of the authority to give effect to the directions.

(4) Any modification of a licence under this section shall be effected by notice served on the holder of the licence and the notice shall state the time at which the modification is to take effect.

(5) Section 36(4), . . . (7), . . . and (10) above shall with the necessary modifications apply to a proposal by a waste regulation authority to modify a licence under subsection (1) or (2)(a) above as they apply to a proposal to issue a licence, except that—

(a) the authority may postpone the reference so far as the authority considers that by reason of an emergency it is appropriate to do so; and

(b) the authority need not consider any representations as respects a modification which, in the opinion of the waste regulation authority, will not affect any authority mentioned in the subsections so applied.

(6) If within the period of two months beginning with the date on which a waste regulation authority received an application by the holder of a licence for a modification of it, or within such longer period as the authority and the applicant may at any time agree in writing, the authority has neither granted a modification of the licence in consequence of the application nor given notice to the applicant that the authority has rejected the application, the authority shall be deemed to have rejected the application.

[(7) This section shall have effect subject to section 37A below.]

[126]

NOTES

Commencement: 1 May 1994 (sub-ss (1), (2), (4)–(6), sub-s (3) certain purposes); 18 February 1993 (sub-s (3), certain purposes); to be appointed (remainder); for commencement dates for remaining purposes see the Environmental Protection Act 1990 (Commencement No 15) Order 1994, SI 1994/1096.

Sub-s (1): words in square brackets substituted by the Environment Act 1995, s 120, Sch 22, para 70(1).

Sub-s (5): words omitted repealed by the Environment Act 1995, s 120, Sch 22, para 70(2), Sch 24.

Sub-s (7): added by the Environment Act 1995, s 120, Sch 22, para 70(3), as from a day to be appointed.

[37A Consultation before certain variations

(1) This section applies where—

(a) a waste regulation authority proposes to modify a licence under section 37(1) or (2)(a) above; and

(b) the licence, if modified as proposed, would be subject to a relevant new condition.

(2)   For the purposes of this section, a "relevant new condition" is any condition by virtue of which the holder of the licence might be required to carry out any works or do any other thing—
  (a) which he might not be entitled to carry out or do, and
  (b) which he could not be required to carry out or do by virtue of the conditions to which, prior to the modification, the licence is subject.

(3)   Before modifying the licence, the waste regulation authority shall serve on every person appearing to the authority to be a person falling within subsection (4) below a notice which complies with the requirements set out in subsection (5) below.

(4)   A person falls within this subsection if—
  (a) he is the owner, lessee or occupier of any land; and
  (b) that land is land in relation to which it is likely that, as a consequence of the licence being modified so as to be subject to the relevant new condition in question, rights will have to be granted by virtue of section 35(4) above to the holder of the licence.

(5)   A notice served under subsection (3) above shall—
  (a) set out the relevant new condition in question;
  (b) indicate the nature of the works or other things which that condition might require the holder of the licence to carry out or do but which he could not be required to carry out or do by virtue of the conditions (if any) to which, prior to the modification, the licence is subject; and
  (c) specify the date by which, and the manner in which, any representations relating to the condition or its possible effects are to be made to the waste regulation authority by the person on whom the notice is served.

(6)   The date which, pursuant to subsection (5)(c) above, is specified in a notice shall be a date not earlier than the date on which expires the period—
  (a) beginning with the date on which the notice is served, and
  (b) of such length as may be prescribed in regulations made by the Secretary of State.

(7)   Before the waste regulation authority issues the licence it must, subject to subsection (8) below, consider any representations made in relation to the condition in question, or its possible effects, by any person on whom a notice has been served under subsection (3) above.

(8)   Subsection (7) above does not require the waste regulation authority to consider any representations made by a person after the date specified in the notice served on him under subsection (3) above as the date by which his representations in relation to the condition or its possible effects are to be made.

(9)   A waste regulation authority may postpone the service of any notice or the consideration of any representations required under the foregoing provisions of this section so far as the authority considers that by reason of an emergency it is appropriate to do so.

(10) In subsection (3) above, "owner" has the same meaning as it has in subsection (3) of section 36A above by virtue of subsection (8) of that section.]

[127]

NOTES
  Commencement: to be appointed.
  Inserted by the Environment Act 1995, s 120, Sch 22, para 71, as from a day to be appointed.

38 Revocation and suspension of licences

(1)   Where a licence granted by a waste regulation authority is in force and it appears to the authority—
  (a) that the holder of the licence has ceased to be a fit and proper person by reason of his having been convicted of a relevant offence; or

(b) that the continuation of the activities authorised by the licence would cause pollution of the environment or harm to human health or would be seriously detrimental to the amenities of the locality affected; and

(c) that the pollution, harm or detriment cannot be avoided by modifying the conditions of the licence;

the authority may exercise, as it thinks fit, either of the powers conferred by subsections (3) and (4) below.

(2)   Where a licence granted by a waste regulation authority is in force and it appears to the authority that the holder of the licence has ceased to be a fit and proper person by reason of the management of the activities authorised by the licence having ceased to be in the hands of a technically competent person, the authority may exercise the power conferred by subsection (3) below.

(3)   The authority may, under this subsection, revoke the licence so far as it authorises the carrying on of the activities specified in the licence or such of them as the authority specifies in revoking the licence.

(4)   The authority may, under this subsection, revoke the licence entirely.

(5)   A licence revoked under subsection (3) above shall cease to have effect to authorise the carrying on of the activities specified in the licence or, as the case may be, the activities specified by the authority in revoking the licence but shall not affect the requirements imposed by the licence which the authority, in revoking the licence, specify as requirements which are to continue to bind the licence holder.

(6)   Where a licence granted by a waste regulation authority is in force and it appears to the authority—

(a) that the holder of the licence has ceased to be a fit and proper person by reason of the management of the activities authorised by the licence having ceased to be in the hands of a technically competent person; or

(b) that serious pollution of the environment or serious harm to human health has resulted from, or is about to be caused by, the activities to which the licence relates or the happening or threatened happening of an event affecting those activities; and

(c) that the continuing to carry on those activities, or any of those activities, in the circumstances will continue or, as the case may be, cause serious pollution of the environment or serious harm to human health;

the authority may suspend the licence so far as it authorises the carrying on of the activities specified in the licence or such of them as the authority specifies in suspending the licence.

(7)   The Secretary of State may, if he thinks fit in relation to a licence granted by a waste regulation authority, give to the authority directions as to whether and in what manner the authority should exercise its powers under this section; and it shall be the duty of the authority to give effect to the directions.

(8)   A licence suspended under subsection (6) above shall, while the suspension has effect, be of no effect to authorise the carrying on of the activities specified in the licence or, as the case may be, the activities specified by the authority in suspending the licence.

(9)   Where a licence is suspended under subsection (6) above, the authority, in suspending it or at any time while it is suspended, may require the holder of the licence to take such measures to deal with or avert the pollution or harm as the authority considers necessary.

[(9A) A requirement imposed under subsection (9) above may require the holder of a licence to carry out works or do other things notwithstanding that he is not entitled to carry out the works or do the thing and any person whose consent would be required shall grant, or join in granting, the holder of the licence such rights in relation to the land as will enable the holder of the licence to comply with any requirements imposed on him under that subsection.

(9B) Subsections (2) to (8) of section 36A above shall, with the necessary modifications, apply where the authority proposes to impose a requirement under subsection (9) above which may require the holder of a licence to carry out any such works or do any such thing as is mentioned in subsection (9A) above as they apply where the authority proposes to issue a licence subject to any such condition as is mentioned in subsection (1) of that section, but as if—

> (a) the reference in subsection (3) of that section to section 35(4) above were a reference to subsection (9A) above; and
> (b) any reference in those subsections—
> > (i) to the condition, or the condition in question, were a reference to the requirement; and
> > (ii) to issuing a licence were a reference to serving a notice, under subsection (12) below, effecting the requirement.

(9C) The authority may postpone the service of any notice or the consideration of any representations required under section 36A above, as applied by subsection (9B) above, so far as the authority considers that by reason of an emergency it is appropriate to do so.]

(10) A person who, without reasonable excuse, fails to comply with any requirement imposed under subsection (9) above otherwise than in relation to special waste shall be liable—

> (a) on summary conviction, to a fine of an amount not exceeding the statutory maximum; and
> (b) on conviction on indictment, to imprisonment for a term not exceeding two years or a fine or both.

(11) A person who, without reasonable excuse, fails to comply with any requirement imposed under subsection (9) above in relation to special waste shall be liable—

> (a) on summary conviction, to imprisonment for a term not exceeding six months or a fine not exceeding the statutory maximum or both; and
> (b) on conviction on indictment, to imprisonment for a term not exceeding five years or a fine or both.

(12) Any revocation or suspension of a licence or requirement imposed during the suspension of a licence under this section shall be effected by notice served on the holder of the licence and the notice shall state the time at which the revocation or suspension or the requirement is to take effect and, in the case of suspension, the period at the end of which, or the event on the occurrence of which, the suspension is to cease.

[(13) If a waste regulation authority is of the opinion that proceedings for an offence under subsection (10) or (11) above would afford an ineffectual remedy against a person who has failed to comply with any requirement imposed under subsection (9) above, the authority may take proceedings in the High Court or, in Scotland, in any court of competent jurisdiction for the purpose of securing compliance with the requirement.]

[128]

NOTES

Commencement: 1 April 1996 (sub-s (13)); 1 May 1994 (sub-ss (1)–(12), certain purposes); 18 February 1993 (sub-s (7), certain purposes); to be appointed (remainder); for commencement dates for remaining purposes see the Environmental Protection Act 1990 (Commencement No 15) Order 1994, SI 1994/1096.

Sub-ss (9A)–(9C): inserted by the Environment Act 1995, s 120, Sch 22, para 72(1), as from a day to be appointed.

Sub-s (13): added by the Environment Act 1995, s 120, Sch 22, para 72(2).

39 Surrender of licences

(1)   A licence may be surrendered by its holder to the authority which granted it but, in the case of a site licence, only if the authority accepts the surrender.

(2)   The following provisions apply to the surrender and acceptance of the surrender of a site licence.

(3)   The holder of a site licence who desires to surrender it shall make an application for that purpose to the authority *in such form, giving such information and accompanied by such evidence as the Secretary of State prescribes by regulations and accompanied by the prescribed fee payable under section 41 below.*

(4)   An authority which receives an application for the surrender of a site licence—
  (a) shall inspect the land to which the licence relates, and
  (b) may require the holder of the licence to furnish to it further information or further evidence.

(5)   The authority shall determine whether it is likely or unlikely that the condition of the land, so far as that condition is the result of the use of the land for the treatment, keeping or disposal of waste (whether or not in pursuance of the licence), will cause pollution of the environment or harm to human health.

(6)   If the authority is satisfied that the condition of the land is unlikely to cause the pollution or harm mentioned in subsection (5) above, the authority shall, subject to subsection (7) below, accept the surrender of the licence; but otherwise the authority shall refuse to accept it.

(7)   Where the authority proposes to accept the surrender of a site licence, the authority must, before it does so,—
  (a) refer the proposal to [the appropriate planning authority]; and
  (b) consider any representations about the proposal which [the appropriate planning authority] makes to it during the allowed period;

. . .

(8)   . . .

(9)   Where the surrender of a licence is accepted under this section the authority shall issue to the applicant, with the notice of its determination, a certificate (a "certificate of completion") stating that it is satisfied as mentioned in subsection (6) above and, on the issue of that certificate, the licence shall cease to have effect.

(10) If within the period of three months beginning with the date on which an authority receives an application to surrender a licence, or within such longer period as the authority and the applicant may at any time agree in writing, the authority has neither issued a certificate of completion nor given notice to the applicant that the authority has rejected the application, the authority shall be deemed to have rejected the application.

(11) Section 36(10) above applies for the interpretation of the "allowed period" in [subsection (7) above].

[(12) In this section—
    "the appropriate planning authority" means—
      (a) where the relevant land is situated in the area of a London borough council, that London borough council;
      (b) where the relevant land is situated in the City of London, the Common Council of the City of London;
      (c) where the relevant land is situated in a non-metropolitan county in England, the council of that county;

(d) where the relevant land is situated in a National Park or the Broads, the National Park authority for that National Park or, as the case may be, the Broads Authority;

(e) where the relevant land is situated elsewhere in England or Wales, the council of the district or, in Wales, the county or county borough, in which the land is situated;

(f) where the relevant land is situated in Scotland, the council constituted under section 2 of the Local Government etc (Scotland) Act 1994 for the area in which the land is situated;

"the Broads" has the same meaning as in the Norfolk and Suffolk Broads Act 1988;

"National Park authority", . . . , means a National Park authority established under section 63 of the Environment Act 1995 which has become the local planning authority for the National Park in question;

"the relevant land", in the case of any site licence, means the land to which the licence relates.

(13) . . .

(14) The Secretary of State may by regulations amend the definition of "appropriate planning authority" in subsection (12) above.]

[129]

NOTES

Commencement: 1 April 1996 (sub-ss (12)–(14)); 1 May 1994 (sub-ss (1), (2), (4)–(11) certain purposes), for commencement dates for remaining purposes see the Environmental Protection Act 1990 (Commencement No 15) Order 1994, SI 1994/1096; 18 February 1993 (remainder).

Sub-s (3): words in italics substituted, as from a day to be appointed, by the Environment Act 1995, s 120, Sch 22, para 73(2) , as follows—

"on a form provided by the authority for the purpose, giving such information and accompanied by such evidence as the authority reasonably requires and accompanied by the charge prescribed for the purpose by a charging scheme under section 41 of the Environment Act 1995".

This amendment is in force from 1 April 1996 in so far as it requires an application to be accompanied by the prescribed charge (by virtue of the Environment Act 1995 (Commencement No 5) Order 1996, SI 1996/186, art 3).

Sub-s (7): words in square brackets substituted and words omitted repealed by the Environment Act 1995, s 120, Sch 22, para 73(3),Sch 24.

Sub-s (8): repealed by the Environment Act 1995, s 120, Sch 22, para 73(4), Sch 24.

Sub-s (11): words in square brackets substituted by the Environment Act 1995, s 120, Sch 22, para 73(5).

Sub-s (12): added by the Environment Act 1995, s 120, Sch 22, para 73(6); in the definition "National Park authority" words omitted repealed by the Environment Act 1995, s 120, Sch 24.

Sub-s (13): added by the Environment Act 1995, s 120, Sch 22, para 73(6); repealed by the Environment Act 1995, s 120, Sch 24.

Sub-s (14): added by the Environment Act 1995, s 120, Sch 22, para 73(6).

Regulations: the Waste Management Licensing Regulations 1994, SI 1994/1056, as amended by SI 1994/1137, SI 1995/288, SI 1995/1950, SI 1996/593, SI 1996/634, SI 1996/972, SI 1996/1279.

40 Transfer of licences

(1) A licence may be transferred to another person in accordance with subsections (2) to (6) below and may be so transferred whether or not the licence is partly revoked or suspended under any provision of this Part.

(2) Where the holder of a licence desires that the licence be transferred to another person ("the proposed transferee") the licence holder and the proposed transferee shall jointly make an application to the waste regulation authority which granted the licence for a transfer of it.

(3) An application under subsection (2) above for the transfer of a licence shall be made *in such form and shall include such information as the Secretary of State prescribes by regulations and shall be accompanied by the prescribed fee payable under section 41 below.*

(4)   If, on such an application, the authority is satisfied that the proposed transferee is a fit and proper person the authority shall effect a transfer of the licence to the proposed transferee.

(5)   The authority shall effect a transfer of a licence under the foregoing provisions of this section by causing the licence to be endorsed with the name and other particulars of the proposed transferee as the holder of the licence from such date specified in the endorsement as may be agreed with the applicants.

(6)   If within the period of two months beginning with the date on which the authority receives an application for the transfer of a licence, or within such longer period as the authority and the applicants may at any time agree in writing, the authority has neither effected a transfer of the licence nor given notice to the applicants that the authority has rejected the application, the authority shall be deemed to have rejected the application.

[130]

―――――――――――

NOTES

Commencement: 1 May 1994 (sub-ss (1), (2), (4)–(6), certain purposes), for commencement dates for remaining purposes see the Environmental Protection Act 1990 (Commencement No 15) Order 1994, SI 1994/1096; 18 February 1993 (sub-s (3)).

Sub-s (3): words in italics substituted, as from a day to be appointed, by the Environment Act 1995, s 120, Sch 22, para 74, as follows―

"on a form provided by the authority for the purpose, accompanied by such information as the authority may reasonably require, the charge prescribed for the purpose by a charging scheme under section 41 of the Environment Act 1995".

This amendment is in force from 1 April 1996 in so far as it requires an application to be accompanied by the prescribed charge (by virtue of the Environment Act 1995 (Commencement No 5) Order 1996, SI 1996/186, art 3).

Regulations: the Waste Management Licensing Regulations 1994, SI 1994/1056, as amended by SI 1994/1137, SI 1995/288, SI 1995/1950, SI 1996/593, SI 1996/634, SI 1996/972, SI 1996/1279.

―――――――――――

41   (*Repealed by the Environment Act 1995, s 120(1), (3), Sch 22, para 75, Sch 24.*)

42 Supervision of licensed activities

(1)   While a licence is in force it shall be the duty of the waste regulation authority which granted the licence to take the steps needed―
  (a) for the purpose of ensuring that the activities authorised by the licence do not cause pollution of the environment or harm to human health or become seriously detrimental to the amenities of the locality affected by the activities; and
  (b) for the purpose of ensuring that the conditions of the licence are complied with.

(2)   . . .

(3)   For the purpose of performing the duty imposed on it by subsection (1) above, any officer of the authority authorised in writing for the purpose by the authority may, if it appears to him that by reason of an emergency it is necessary to do so, carry out work on the land or in relation to plant or equipment on the land to which the licence relates or, as the case may be, in relation to the mobile plant to which the licence relates.

(4)   Where a waste regulation authority incurs any expenditure by virtue of subsection (3) above, the authority may recover the amount of the expenditure from [the holder, or (as the case may be) the former holder, of the licence], except where the holder or former holder of the licence shows that there was no emergency requiring any work or except such of the expenditure as he shows was unnecessary.

(5)   Where it appears to a waste regulation authority that a condition of a licence granted by it is not being complied with [or is likely not to be complied with], then, without prejudice to any proceedings under section 33(6) above, the authority may―

[(a) serve on the holder of the licence a notice—
    (i) stating that the authority is of the opinion that a condition of the licence is not being complied with or, as the case may be, is likely not to be complied with;
    (ii) specifying the matters which constitute the non-compliance or, as the case may be, which make the anticipated non-compliance likely;
    (iii) specifying the steps which must be taken to remedy the non-compliance or, as the case may be, to prevent the anticipated non-compliance from occurring; and
    (iv) specifying the period within which those steps must be taken; and]
  (b) if in the opinion of the authority the licence holder [has not taken the steps specified in the notice within the period so specified,] exercise any of the powers specified in subsection (6) below.

(6) The powers which become exercisable in the event mentioned in subsection (5)(b) above are the following—
  (a) to revoke the licence so far as it authorises the carrying on of the activities specified in the licence or such of them as the authority specifies in revoking the licence;
  (b) to revoke the licence entirely; and
  (c) to suspend the licence so far as it authorises the carrying on of the activities specified in the licence or, as the case may be, the activities specified by the authority in suspending the licence.

[(6A) If a waste regulation authority is of the opinion that revocation or suspension of the licence, whether entirely or to any extent, under subsection (6) above would afford an ineffectual remedy against a person who has failed to comply with any requirement imposed under subsection (5)(a) above, the authority may take proceedings in the High Court or, in Scotland, in any court of competent jurisdiction for the purpose of securing compliance with the requirement.]

(7) Where a licence is revoked or suspended under subsection (6) above, [subsections (5) and (12) or, as the case may be, subsections (8) to (12) of section 38] above shall apply with the necessary modifications as they respectively apply to revocations or suspensions of licences under that section; . . .

(8) The Secretary of State may, if he thinks fit in relation to a licence granted by a waste regulation authority, give to the authority directions as to whether and in what manner the authority should exercise its powers under this section; and it shall be the duty of the authority to give effect to the directions.

[131]

NOTES
    Commencement: 1 April 1996 (sub-s (6A)); 1 May 1994 (sub-ss (1)–(6), (7), sub-s (8) certain purposes); 18 February 1993 (sub-s (8), certain purposes); for commencement dates for remaining purposes see the Environmental Protection Act 1990 (Commencement No 15) Order 1994, SI 1994/1096.
    Sub-s (2): repealed by the Environment Act 1995, s 120, Sch 22, para 76(2), Sch 24.
    Sub-s (4): words in square brackets substituted by the Environment Act 1995, s 120, Sch 22, para 76(3).
    Sub-s (5): words in first pair of square brackets inserted, para (a) substituted, and words in square brackets in para (b) substituted, by the Environment Act 1995, s 120, Sch 22, para 76(4)–(6).
    Sub-s (6A): inserted by the Environment Act 1995, s 120, Sch 22, para 76(7).
    Sub-s (7): words in square brackets substituted, and words omitted repealed, by the Environment Act 1995, s 120, Sch 22, para 76(8), Sch 24.

43 Appeals to Secretary of State from decisions with respect to licences

(1) Where, except in pursuance of a direction given by the Secretary of State,—
  (a) an application for a licence or a modification of the conditions of a licence is rejected;
  (b) a licence is granted subject to conditions;

    (c) the conditions of a licence are modified;
    (d) a licence is suspended;
    (e) a licence is revoked under section 38 or 42 above;
    (f) an application to surrender a licence is rejected; or
    (g) an application for the transfer of a licence is rejected;

then, except in the case of an application for a transfer, the applicant for the licence or, as the case may be, the holder or former holder of it may appeal from the decision to the Secretary of State and, in the case of an application for a transfer, the proposed transferee may do so.

    (2)   Where an appeal is made to the Secretary of State—
(a), (b) ...
    (c) if a party to the appeal so requests, or the Secretary of State so decides, the appeal shall be or continue in the form of a hearing (which may, if the person hearing the appeal so decides, be held or held to any extent in private).

[(2A) This section is subject to section 114 of the Environment Act 1995 (delegation or reference of appeals etc).]

    (3)   Where, on such an appeal, the Secretary of State or other person determining the appeal determines that the decision of the authority shall be altered it shall be the duty of the authority to give effect to the determination.

    (4)   While an appeal is pending in a case falling within subsection (1)(c) or (e) above, the decision in question shall, subject to subsection (6) below, be ineffective; and if the appeal is dismissed or withdrawn the decision shall become effective from the end of the day on which the appeal is dismissed or withdrawn.

    (5)   Where an appeal is made in a case falling within subsection (1)(d) above, the bringing of the appeal shall have no effect on the decision in question.

    (6)   Subsection (4) above shall not apply to a decision modifying the conditions of a licence under section 37 above or revoking a licence under section 38 or 42 above in the case of which the notice effecting the modification or revocation includes a statement that in the opinion of the authority it is necessary for the purpose of preventing or, where that is not practicable, minimising pollution of the environment or harm to human health that that subsection should not apply.

    (7)   Where the decision under appeal is one falling within subsection (6) above or is a decision to suspend a licence, if, on the application of the holder or former holder of the licence, the Secretary of State or other person determining the appeal determines that the authority acted unreasonably in excluding the application of subsection (4) above or, as the case may be, in suspending the licence, then—
    (a) if the appeal is still pending at the end of the day on which the determination is made, subsection (4) above shall apply to the decision from the end of that day; and
    (b) the holder or former holder of the licence shall be entitled to recover compensation from the authority in respect of any loss suffered by him in consequence of the exclusion of the application of that subsection or the suspension of the licence;

and any dispute as to a person's entitlement to such compensation or as to the amount of it shall be determined by arbitration or in Scotland by a single arbiter appointed, in default of agreement between the parties concerned, by the Secretary of State on the application of any of the parties.

    (8)   Provision may be made by the Secretary of State by regulations with respect to appeals under this section and in particular—
    (a) as to the period within which and the manner in which appeals are to be brought; and
    (b) as to the manner in which appeals are to be considered.

NOTES
Commencement: 1 April 1996 (sub-s (2A)); 1 May 1994 (sub-ss (1), (2), (3)–(7), certain purposes), for commencement dates for remaining purposes see the Environmental Protection Act 1990 (Commencement No 15) Order 1994, SI 1994/1096; 18 February 1993 (sub-s (8)).
Sub-s (2): paras (a), (b) repealed by the Environment Act 1995, s 120, Sch 22, para 77, Sch 24.
Sub-s (2A): inserted by the Environment Act 1995, s 120, Sch 22, para 77.
Regulations: the Waste Management Licensing Regulations 1994, SI 1994/1056, as amended by SI 1994/1137, SI 1995/288, SI 1995/1950, SI 1996/593, SI 1996/634, SI 1996/972, SI 1996/1279.

[44 Offences of making false or misleading statements or false entries

(1)   A person who—
(a) in purported compliance with a requirement to furnish any information imposed by or under any provision of this Part, or
(b) for the purpose of obtaining for himself or another any grant of a licence, any modification of the conditions of a licence, any acceptance of the surrender of a licence or any transfer of a licence,

makes a statement which he knows to be false or misleading in a material particular, or recklessly makes any statement which is false or misleading in a material particular, commits an offence.

(2)   A person who intentionally makes a false entry in any record required to be kept by virtue of a licence commits an offence.

(3)   A person who commits an offence under this section shall be liable—
(a) on summary conviction, to a fine not exceeding the statutory maximum;
(b) on conviction on indictment, to a fine or to imprisonment for a term not exceeding two years, or to both.]

[133]

NOTES
Commencement: 1 April 1996.
Substituted by the Environment Act 1995, s 112, Sch 19, para 4(1).

Collection, disposal or treatment of controlled waste

[44A National waste strategy: England and Wales

(1)   The Secretary of State shall as soon as possible prepare a statement ("the strategy") containing his policies in relation to the recovery and disposal of waste in England and Wales.

(2)   The strategy shall consist of or include—
(a) a statement which relates to the whole of England and Wales; or
(b) two or more statements which between them relate to the whole of England and Wales.

(3)   The Secretary of State may from time to time modify the strategy.

(4)   Without prejudice to the generality of what may be included in the strategy, the strategy must include—
(a) a statement of the Secretary of State's policies for attaining the objectives specified in Schedule 2A to this Act;
(b) provisions relating to each of the following, that is to say—
   (i) the type, quantity and origin of waste to be recovered or disposed of;
   (ii) general technical requirements; and
   (iii) any special requirements for particular wastes.

(5)   In preparing the strategy or any modification of it, the Secretary of State—
(a) shall consult the Environment Agency,

   (b) shall consult—
        (i) such bodies or persons appearing to him to be representative of the
             interests of local government, and
        (ii) such bodies or persons appearing to him to be representative of the
             interests of industry,
        as he may consider appropriate, and
   (c) may consult such other bodies or persons as he considers appropriate.

   (6)   Without prejudice to any power to give directions conferred by section 40 of
the Environment Act 1995, the Secretary of State may give directions to the
Environment Agency requiring it—
   (a) to advise him on the policies which are to be included in the strategy;
   (b) to carry out a survey of or investigation into—
        (i)   the kinds or quantities of waste which it appears to that Agency is
              likely to be situated in England and Wales,
        (ii) the facilities which are or appear to that Agency likely to be available
              or needed in England and Wales for recovering or disposing of any
              such waste,
        (iii) any other matter upon which the Secretary of State wishes to be
              informed in connection with his preparation of the strategy or any
              modification of it,
        and to report its findings to him.

   (7)   A direction under subsection (6)(b) above—
   (a) shall specify or describe the matters or the areas which are to be the subject
        of the survey or investigation; and
   (b) may make provision in relation to the manner in which—
        (i)   the survey or investigation is to be carried out, or
        (ii) the findings are to be reported or made available to other persons.

   (8)   Where a direction is given under subsection (6)(b) above, the Environment
Agency shall, in accordance with any requirement of the direction,—
   (a) before carrying out the survey or investigation, consult—
        (i)   such bodies or persons appearing to it to be representative of local
              planning authorities, and
        (ii) such bodies or persons appearing to it to be representative of the
              interests of industry,
        as it may consider appropriate; and
   (b) make its findings available to those authorities.

   (9)   In this section—
        "local planning authority" has the same meaning as in the Town and Country
             Planning Act 1990;
        "strategy" includes the strategy as modified from time to time and "statement"
             shall be construed accordingly.

   (10) This section makes provision for the purpose of implementing Article 7 of
the directive of the Council of the European Communities, dated 15th July 1975, on
waste, as amended by—
   (a) the directive of that Council, dated 18th March 1991, amending directive
        75/442/EEC on waste; and
   (b) the directive of that Council, dated 23rd December 1991, standardising and
        rationalising reports on the implementation of certain Directives relating to
        the environment.]

                                                                                    [134]

_____

NOTES
   Commencement: 1 April 1996.
   Inserted, together with s 44B, by the Environment Act 1995, s 92(1).

[44B (*Inserted, in relation to Scotland only, by the Environment Act 1995, s 92(1).*)**]**

45 Collection of controlled waste

(1)   It shall be the duty of each waste collection authority—
  (a) to arrange for the collection of household waste in its area except waste—
    (i)   which is situated at a place which in the opinion of the authority is so isolated or inaccessible that the cost of collecting it would be unreasonably high, and
    (ii) as to which the authority is satisfied that adequate arrangements for its disposal have been or can reasonably be expected to be made by a person who controls the waste; and
  (b) if requested by the occupier of premises in its area to collect any commercial waste from the premises, to arrange for the collection of the waste.

(2)   Each waste collection authority may, if requested by the occupier of premises in its area to collect any industrial waste from the premises, arrange for the collection of the waste; but a collection authority in England and Wales shall not exercise the power except with the consent of the waste disposal authority whose area includes the area of the waste collection authority.

(3)   No charge shall be made for the collection of household waste except in cases prescribed in regulations made by the Secretary of State; and in any of those cases—
  (a) the duty to arrange for the collection of the waste shall not arise until a person who controls the waste requests the authority to collect it; and
  (b) the authority may recover a reasonable charge for the collection of the waste from the person who made the request.

(4)   A person at whose request waste other than household waste is collected under this section shall be liable to pay a reasonable charge for the collection and disposal of the waste to the authority which arranged for its collection; and it shall be the duty of that authority to recover the charge unless in the case of a charge in respect of commercial waste the authority considers it inappropriate to do so.

(5)   It shall be the duty of each waste collection authority—
  (a) to make such arrangements for the emptying, without charge, of privies serving one or more private dwellings in its area as the authority considers appropriate;
  (b) if requested by the person who controls a cesspool serving only one or more private dwellings in its area to empty the cesspool, to remove such of the contents of the cesspool as the authority considers appropriate on payment, if the authority so requires, of a reasonable charge.

(6)   A waste collection authority may, if requested by the person who controls any other privy or cesspool in its area to empty the privy or cesspool, empty the privy or, as the case may be, remove from the cesspool such of its contents as the authority consider appropriate on payment, if the authority so requires, of a reasonable charge.

(7)   A waste collection authority may—
  (a) construct, lay and maintain, within or outside its area, pipes and associated works for the purpose of collecting waste;
  (b) contribute towards the cost incurred by another person in providing or maintaining pipes or associated works connecting with pipes provided by the authority under paragraph (a) above.

(8)   A waste collection authority may contribute towards the cost incurred by another person in providing or maintaining plant or equipment intended to deal with

commercial or industrial waste before it is collected under arrangements made by the authority under subsection (1)(b) or (2) above.

(9)   Subject to section 48(1) below, anything collected under arrangements made by a waste collection authority under this section shall belong to the authority and may be dealt with accordingly.

(10), (11)   (*Apply to Scotland only.*)

(12) In this section "privy" means a latrine which has a moveable receptacle and "cesspool" includes a settlement tank or other tank for the reception or disposal of foul matter from buildings.

[135]

NOTES
    Commencement: 1 April 1992 (sub-s (1), sub-s (3) certain purposes, sub-ss (4)–(12)); 14 February 1992 (sub-s (3), remaining purposes); to be appointed (sub-s (2)).
    Regulations: the Controlled Waste Regulations 1992, SI 1992/588, reg 4, Sch 2; the Waste Management Licensing Regulations 1994, SI 1994/1056, as amended by SI 1994/1137, SI 1995/288, SI 1995/1950, SI 1996/593, SI 1996/634, SI 1996/972, SI 1996/1279.

46 Receptacles for household waste

(1)   Where a waste collection authority has a duty by virtue of section 45(1)(a) above to arrange for the collection of household waste from any premises, the authority may, by notice served on him, require the occupier to place the waste for collection in receptacles of a kind and number specified.

(2)   The kind and number of the receptacles required under subsection (1) above to be used shall be such only as are reasonable but, subject to that, separate receptacles or compartments of receptacles may be required to be used for waste which is to be recycled and waste which is not.

(3)   In making requirements under subsection (1) above the authority may, as respects the provision of the receptacles—
    (a) determine that they be provided by the authority free of charge;
    (b) propose that they be provided, if the occupier agrees, by the authority on payment by him of such a single payment or such periodical payments as he agrees with the authority;
    (c) require the occupier to provide them if he does not enter into an agreement under paragraph (b) above within a specified period; or
    (d) require the occupier to provide them.

(4)   In making requirements as respects receptacles under subsection (1) above, the authority may, by the notice under that subsection, make provision with respect to—
    (a) the size, construction and maintenance of the receptacles;
    (b) the placing of the receptacles for the purpose of facilitating the emptying of them, and access to the receptacles for that purpose;
    (c) the placing of the receptacles for that purpose on highways or, in Scotland, roads;
    (d) the substances or articles which may or may not be put into the receptacles or compartments of receptacles of any description and the precautions to be taken where particular substances or articles are put into them; and
    (e) the steps to be taken by occupiers of premises to facilitate the collection of waste from the receptacles.

(5)   No requirement shall be made under subsection (1) above for receptacles to be placed on a highway or, as the case may be, road, unless—
    (a) the relevant highway authority or roads authority have given their consent to their being so placed; and

(b) arrangements have been made as to the liability for any damage arising out of their being so placed.

(6) A person who fails, without reasonable excuse, to comply with any requirements imposed under subsection (1), (3)(c) or (d) or (4) above shall be liable on summary conviction to a fine not exceeding level 3 on the standard scale.

(7) Where an occupier is required under subsection (1) above to provide any receptacles he may, within the period allowed by subsection (8) below, appeal to a magistrates' court or, in Scotland, to the sheriff by way of summary application against any requirement imposed under subsection (1), subsection (3)(c) or (d) or (4) above on the ground that—
(a) the requirement is unreasonable; or
(b) the receptacles in which household waste is placed for collection from the premises are adequate.

(8) The period allowed to the occupier of premises for appealing against such a requirement is the period of twenty-one days beginning—
(a) in a case where a period was specified under subsection (3)(c) above, with the end of that period; and
(b) where no period was specified, with the day on which the notice making the requirement was served on him.

(9) Where an appeal against a requirement is brought under subsection (7) above—
(a) the requirement shall be of no effect pending the determination of the appeal;
(b) the court shall either quash or modify the requirement or dismiss the appeal; and
(c) no question as to whether the requirement is, in any respect, unreasonable shall be entertained in any proceedings for an offence under subsection (6) above.

(10) In this section—
"receptacle" includes a holder for receptacles; and
"specified" means specified in a notice under subsection (1) above.

[136]

47 Receptacles for commercial or industrial waste

(1) A waste collection authority may, at the request of any person, supply him with receptacles for commercial or industrial waste which he has requested the authority to arrange to collect and shall make a reasonable charge for any receptacle supplied unless in the case of a receptacle for commercial waste the authority considers it appropriate not to make a charge.

(2) If it appears to a waste collection authority that there is likely to be situated, on any premises in its area, commercial waste or industrial waste of a kind which, if the waste is not stored in receptacles of a particular kind, is likely to cause a nuisance or to be detrimental to the amenities of the locality, the authority may, by notice served on him, require the occupier of the premises to provide at the premises receptacles for the storage of such waste of a kind and number specified.

(3) The kind and number of the receptacles required under subsection (2) above to be used shall be such only as are reasonable.

(4) In making requirements as respects receptacles under subsection (2) above, the authority may, by the notice under that subsection, make provision with respect to—
(a) the size, construction and maintenance of the receptacles;
(b) the placing of the receptacles for the purpose of facilitating the emptying of them, and access to the receptacles for that purpose;

(c) the placing of the receptacles for that purpose on highways or, in Scotland, roads;

(d) the substances or articles which may or may not be put into the receptacles and the precautions to be taken where particular substances or articles are put into them; and

(e) the steps to be taken by occupiers of premises to facilitate the collection of waste from the receptacles.

(5) No requirement shall be made under subsection (2) above for receptacles to be placed on a highway or, as the case may be, road unless—

(a) the relevant highway authority or roads authority have given their consent to their being so placed; and

(b) arrangements have been made as to the liability for any damage arising out of their being so placed.

(6) A person who fails, without reasonable excuse, to comply with any requirements imposed under subsection (2) or (4) above shall be liable on summary conviction to a fine not exceeding level 3 on the standard scale.

(7) Where an occupier is required under subsection (2) above to provide any receptacles he may, within the period allowed by subsection (8) below, appeal to a magistrates' court or, in Scotland, to the sheriff by way of summary application against any requirement imposed under subsection (2) or (4) above on the ground that—

(a) the requirement is unreasonable; or

(b) the waste is not likely to cause a nuisance or be detrimental to the amenities of the locality.

(8) The period allowed to the occupier of premises for appealing against such a requirement is the period of twenty-one days beginning with the day on which the notice making the requirement was served on him.

(9) Where an appeal against a requirement is brought under subsection (7) above—

(a) the requirement shall be of no effect pending the determination of the appeal;

(b) the court shall either quash or modify the requirement or dismiss the appeal; and

(c) no question as to whether the requirement is, in any respect, unreasonable shall be entertained in any proceedings for an offence under subsection (6) above.

(10) In this section—

"receptacle" includes a holder for receptacles; and

"specified" means specified in a notice under subsection (2) above.

[137]

48 Duties of waste collection authorities as respects disposal of waste collected

(1) Subject to subsections (2) and (6) below, it shall be the duty of each waste collection authority to deliver for disposal all waste which is collected by the authority under section 45 above to such places as the waste disposal authority for its area directs.

(2) The duty imposed on a waste collection authority by subsection (1) above does not, except in cases falling within subsection (4) below, apply as respects household waste or commercial waste for which the authority decides to make arrangements for recycling the waste; and the authority shall have regard, in deciding what recycling arrangements to make, to its waste recycling plan under section 49 below.

(3)   A waste collection authority which decides to make arrangements under subsection (2) above for recycling waste collected by it shall, as soon as reasonably practicable, by notice in writing, inform the waste disposal authority for the area which includes its area of the arrangements which it proposes to make.

(4)   Where a waste disposal authority has made with a waste disposal contractor arrangements, as respects household waste or commercial waste in its area or any part of its area, for the contractor to recycle the waste, or any of it, the waste disposal authority may, by notice served on the waste collection authority, object to the waste collection authority having the waste recycled; and the objection may be made as respects all the waste, part only of the waste or specified descriptions of the waste.

(5)   Where an objection is made under subsection (4) above, subsection (2) above shall not be available to the waste collection authority to the extent objected to.

(6)   A waste collection authority may, subject to subsection (7) below, provide plant and equipment for the sorting and baling of waste retained by the authority under subsection (2) above.

(7)   Subsection (6) above does not apply to an authority which is also a waste disposal authority; but, in such a case, the authority may make arrangements with a waste disposal contractor for the contractor to deal with the waste as mentioned in that subsection.

(8)   A waste collection authority may permit another person to use facilities provided by the authority under subsection (6) above and may provide for the use of another person any such facilities as the authority has power to provide under that subsection; and—
   (a)   subject to paragraph (b) below, it shall be the duty of the authority to make a reasonable charge in respect of the use by another person of the facilities, unless the authority considers it appropriate not to make a charge;
   (b)   no charge shall be made under this subsection in respect of household waste; and
   (c)   anything delivered to the authority by another person in the course of using the facilities shall belong to the authority and may be dealt with accordingly.

(9)   This section shall not apply to Scotland.

[138]

NOTES

Commencement: 1 April 1992 (sub-ss (1)–(6), (8), (9)); to be appointed (remainder).

49 Waste recycling plans by collection authorities

(1)   It shall be the duty of each waste collection authority, as respects household and commercial waste arising in its area—
   (a)   to carry out an investigation with a view to deciding what arrangements are appropriate for dealing with the waste by separating, baling or otherwise packaging it for the purpose of recycling it;
   (b)   to decide what arrangements are in the opinion of the authority needed for that purpose;
   (c)   to prepare a statement ("the plan") of the arrangements made and proposed to be made by the authority and other persons for dealing with waste in those ways;
   (d)   to carry out from time to time further investigations with a view to deciding what changes in the plan are needed; and
   (e)   to make any modification of the plan which the authority thinks appropriate in consequence of any such further investigation.

(2)   In considering any arrangements or modification for the purposes of subsection (1)(c) or (e) above it shall be the duty of the authority to have regard to the effect which the arrangements or modification would be likely to have on the amenities of any locality and the likely cost or saving to the authority attributable to the arrangements or modification.

(3)   It shall be the duty of a waste collection authority to include in the plan information as to—
   (a) the kinds and quantities of controlled waste which the authority expects to collect during the period specified in the plan;
   (b) the kinds and quantities of controlled waste which the authority expects to purchase during that period;
   (c) the kinds and quantities of controlled waste which the authority expects to deal with in the ways specified in subsection (1)(a) above during that period;
   (d) the arrangements which the authority expects to make during that period with waste disposal contractors or, in Scotland, waste disposal authorities and waste disposal contractors for them to deal with waste in those ways;
   (e) the plant and equipment which the authority expects to provide under section 48(6) above or 53 below; and
   (f) the estimated costs or savings attributable to the methods of dealing with the waste in the ways provided for in the plan.

(4)   It shall be the duty of a waste collection authority, before finally determining the content of the plan or a modification, to send a copy of it in draft to the Secretary of State for the purpose of enabling him to determine whether subsection (3) above has been complied with; and, if the Secretary of State gives any directions to the authority for securing compliance with that subsection, it shall be the duty of the authority to comply with the direction.

(5)   When a waste collection authority has determined the content of the plan or a modification it shall be the duty of the authority—
   (a) to take such steps as in the opinion of the authority will give adequate publicity in its area to the plan or modification; and
   (b) to send to the waste disposal authority and waste regulation authority for the area which includes its area a copy of the plan or, as the case may be, particulars of the modification.

(6)   It shall be the duty of each waste collection authority to keep a copy of the plan and particulars of any modifications to it available at all reasonable times at its principal offices for inspection by members of the public free of charge and to supply a copy of the plan and of the particulars of any modifications to it to any person who requests one, on payment by that person of such reasonable charge as the authority requires.

(7)   The Secretary of State may give to any waste collection authority directions as to the time by which the authority is to perform any duty imposed by this section specified in the direction; and it shall be the duty of the authority to comply with the direction.

[139]

50   (*Repealed by the Environment Act 1995, s 120(1), (3), Sch 22, para 78, Sch 24; for savings see, in particular, s 120(2) of, and Sch 23, Pt I, para 16 to, the 1995 Act at* **[564]**, **[570]**.)

51 Functions of waste disposal authorities

(1)   It shall be the duty of each waste disposal authority to arrange—
   (a) for the disposal of the controlled waste collected in its area by the waste collection authorities; and

(b) for places to be provided at which persons resident in its area may deposit their household waste and for the disposal of waste so deposited;

in either case by means of arrangements made (in accordance with Part II of Schedule 2 to this Act) with waste disposal contractors, but by no other means.

(2) The arrangements made by a waste disposal authority under subsection (1)(b) above shall be such as to secure that—

    (a) each place is situated either within the area of the authority or so as to be reasonably accessible to persons resident in its area;

    (b) each place is available for the deposit of waste at all reasonable times (including at least one period on the Saturday or following day of each week except a week in which the Saturday is 25th December or 1st January);

    (c) each place is available for the deposit of waste free of charge by persons resident in the area;

but the arrangements may restrict the availability of specified places to specified descriptions of waste.

(3) A waste disposal authority may include in arrangements made under subsection (1)(b) above arrangements for the places provided for its area for the deposit of household waste free of charge by residents in its area to be available for the deposit of household or other controlled waste by other persons on such terms as to payment (if any) as the authority determines.

(4) For the purpose of discharging its duty under subsection (1)(a) above as respects controlled waste collected as mentioned in that paragraph a waste disposal authority—

    (a) shall give directions to the waste collection authorities within its area as to the persons to whom and places at which such waste is to be delivered;

    (b) may arrange for the provision, within or outside its area, by waste disposal contractors of places at which such waste may be treated or kept prior to its removal for treatment or disposal;

    (c) may make available to waste disposal contractors (and accordingly own) plant and equipment for the purpose of enabling them to keep such waste prior to its removal for disposal or to treat such waste in connection with so keeping it or for the purpose of facilitating its transportation;

    (d) may make available to waste disposal contractors (and accordingly hold) land for the purpose of enabling them to treat, keep or dispose of such waste in or on the land;

    (e) may contribute towards the cost incurred by persons who produce commercial or industrial waste in providing and maintaining plant or equipment intended to deal with such waste before it is collected; and

    (f) may contribute towards the cost incurred by persons who produce commercial or industrial waste in providing or maintaining pipes or associated works connecting with pipes provided by a waste collection authority within the area of the waste disposal authority.

(5) For the purpose of discharging its duties under subsection (1)(b) above as respects household waste deposited as mentioned in that paragraph a waste disposal authority—

    (a) may arrange for the provision, within or outside its area, by waste disposal contractors of places at which such waste may be treated or kept prior to its removal for treatment or disposal;

    (b) may make available to waste disposal contractors (and accordingly own) plant and equipment for the purpose of enabling them to keep such waste prior to its removal for disposal or to treat such waste in connection with so keeping it or for the purpose of facilitating its transportation; and

    (c) may make available to waste disposal contractors (and accordingly hold) land for the purpose of enabling them to treat, keep or dispose of such waste in or on the land.

(6)   Where the arrangements made under subsection (1)(b) include such arrangements as are authorised by subsection (3) above, subsection (5) above applies as respects household or other controlled waste as it applies as respects household waste.

(7)   Subsection (1) above is subject to section 77.

(8)   This section shall not apply to Scotland.

[140]

52 Payments for recycling and disposal etc of waste

(1)   Where, under section 48(2) above, a waste collection authority retains for recycling waste collected by it under section 45 above, the waste disposal authority for the area which includes the area of the waste collection authority shall make to that authority payments, in respect of the waste so retained, of such amounts representing its net saving of expenditure on the disposal of the waste as the authority determines.

(2)   Where, by reason of the discharge by a waste disposal authority of its functions, waste arising in its area does not fall to be collected by a waste collection authority under section 45 above, the waste collection authority shall make to the waste disposal authority payments, in respect of the waste not falling to be so collected, of such amounts representing its net saving of expenditure on the collection of the waste as the authority determines.

(3)   Where a person other than a waste collection authority, for the purpose of recycling it, collects waste arising in the area of a waste disposal authority which would fall to be collected under section 45 above, the waste disposal authority may make to that person payments, in respect of the waste so collected, of such amounts representing its net saving of expenditure on the disposal of the waste as the authority determines.

(4)   Where a person other than a waste collection authority, for the purpose of recycling it, collects waste which would fall to be collected under section 45 above, the waste collection authority may make to that person payments, in respect of the waste so collected, of such amounts representing its net saving of expenditure on the collection of the waste as the authority determines.

(5)   The Secretary of State may, by regulations, impose on waste disposal authorities a duty to make payments corresponding to the payments which are authorised by subsection (3) above to such persons in such circumstances and in respect of such descriptions or quantities of waste as are specified in the regulations.

(6)   For the purposes of subsections (1), (3) and (5) above the net saving of expenditure of a waste disposal authority on the disposal of any waste retained or collected for recycling is the amount of the expenditure which the authority would, but for the retention or collection, have incurred in having it disposed of less any amount payable by the authority to any person in consequence of the retention or collection for recycling (instead of the disposal) of the waste.

(7)   For the purposes of subsections (2) and (4) above the net saving of expenditure of a waste collection authority on the collection of any waste not falling to be collected by it is the amount of the expenditure which the authority would, if it had had to collect the waste, have incurred in collecting it.

(8)   The Secretary of State shall, by regulations, make provision for the determination of the net saving of expenditure for the purposes of subsections (1), (2), (3), (4) and (5) above.

(9)   A waste disposal authority shall be entitled to receive from a waste collection authority such sums as are needed to reimburse the waste disposal

authority the reasonable cost of making arrangements under section 51(1) above for the disposal of commercial and industrial waste collected in the area of the waste disposal authority.

(10) A waste disposal authority shall pay to a waste collection authority a reasonable contribution towards expenditure reasonably incurred by the waste collection authority in delivering waste, in pursuance of a direction under section 51(4)(a) above, to a place which is unreasonably far from the waste collection authority's area.

(11) Any question arising under subsection (9) or (10) above shall, in default of agreement between the two authorities in question, be determined by arbitration.

[141]

NOTES

Commencement: 1 April 1992 (sub-ss (1), (3)–(7), (9)–(11)); 13 December 1991 (sub-s (8), certain purposes); to be appointed (sub-s (2), sub-s (8) remaining purposes).

Regulations: the Environmental Protection (Waste Recycling Payments) Regulations 1992, SI 1992/462, as amended by SI 1993/445, SI 1994/522, SI 1995/476, SI 1996/634, SI 1997/351; the Waste Management Regulations 1996, SI 1996/634; the Waste Management (Miscellaneous Provisions) Regulations 1997, SI 1997/351.

53, 54 *(Apply to Scotland only. S 54 repealed by the Environment Act 1995, s 120(3), Sch 24, as from a day to be appointed.)*

55 Powers for recycling waste

(1) This section has effect for conferring on waste disposal authorities and waste collection authorities powers for the purposes of recycling waste.

(2) A waste disposal authority may—
 (a) make arrangements with waste disposal contractors for them to recycle waste as respects which the authority has duties under section 51(1) above or agrees with another person for its disposal or treatment;
 (b) make arrangements with waste disposal contractors for them to use waste for the purpose of producing from it heat or electricity or both;
 (c) buy or otherwise acquire waste with a view to its being recycled;
 (d) use, sell or otherwise dispose of waste as respects which the authority has duties under section 51(1) above or anything produced from such waste.

(3) A waste collection authority may—
 (a) buy or otherwise acquire waste with a view to recycling it;
 (b) use, or dispose of by way of sale or otherwise to another person, waste belonging to the authority or anything produced from such waste.

(4) This section shall not apply to Scotland.

[142]

56 *(Applies to Scotland only.)*

57 Powers of Secretary of State to require waste to be accepted, treated, disposed of or delivered

(1) The Secretary of State may, by notice in writing, direct the holder of any waste management licence to accept and keep, or accept and treat or dispose of, controlled waste at specified places on specified terms.

(2) The Secretary of State may, by notice in writing, direct any person who is keeping controlled waste on any land to deliver the waste to a specified person on specified terms with a view to its being treated or disposed of by that other person.

(3) A direction under this section may impose a requirement as respects waste of any specified kind or as respects any specified consignment of waste.

(4) A direction under subsection (2) above may require the person who is directed to deliver the waste to pay to the specified person his reasonable costs of treating or disposing of the waste.

(5) A person who fails, without reasonable excuse, to comply with a direction under this section shall be liable on summary conviction to a fine not exceeding level 5 on the standard scale.

(6) A person shall not be guilty of an offence under any other enactment prescribed by the Secretary of State by regulations made for the purposes of this subsection by reason only of anything necessarily done or omitted in order to comply with a direction under this section.

(7) The Secretary of State may, where the costs of the treatment or disposal of waste are not paid or not fully paid in pursuance of subsection (4) above to the person treating or disposing of the waste, pay the costs or the unpaid costs, as the case may be, to that person.

(8) In this section "specified" means specified in a direction under this section.

[143]

NOTES

Commencement: 1 May 1994 (certain purposes); for commencement dates for remaining purposes see the Environmental Protection Act 1990 (Commencement No 15) Order 1994, SI 1994/1096.

58 (*Applies to Scotland only.*)

59 Powers to require removal of waste unlawfully deposited

(1) If any controlled waste is deposited in or on any land in the area of a waste regulation authority or waste collection authority in contravention of section 33(1) above, the authority may, by notice served on him, require the occupier to do either or both of the following, that is—
  (a) to remove the waste from the land within a specified period not less than a period of twenty-one days beginning with the service of the notice;
  (b) to take within such a period specified steps with a view to eliminating or reducing the consequences of the deposit of the waste.

(2) A person on whom any requirements are imposed under subsection (1) above may, within the period of twenty-one days mentioned in that subsection, appeal against the requirement to a magistrates' court or, in Scotland, to the sheriff by way of summary application.

(3) On any appeal under subsection (2) above the court shall quash the requirement if it is satisfied that—
  (a) the appellant neither deposited nor knowingly caused nor knowingly permitted the deposit of the waste; or
  (b) there is a material defect in the notice;
and in any other case shall either modify the requirement or dismiss the appeal.

(4) Where a person appeals against any requirement imposed under subsection (1) above, the requirement shall be of no effect pending the determination of the appeal; and where the court modifies the requirement or dismisses the appeal it may extend the period specified in the notice.

(5) If a person on whom a requirement imposed under subsection (1) above fails, without reasonable excuse, to comply with the requirement he shall be liable,

on summary conviction, to a fine not exceeding level 5 on the standard scale and to a further fine of an amount equal to one-tenth of level 5 on the standard scale for each day on which the failure continues after conviction of the offence and before the authority has begun to exercise its powers under subsection (6) below.

(6)   Where a person on whom a requirement has been imposed under subsection (1) above by an authority fails to comply with the requirement the authority may do what that person was required to do and may recover from him any expenses reasonably incurred by the authority in doing it.

(7)   If it appears to a waste regulation authority or waste collection authority that waste has been deposited in or on any land in contravention of section 33(1) above and that—

    (a) in order to remove or prevent pollution of land, water or air or harm to human health it is necessary that the waste be forthwith removed or other steps taken to eliminate or reduce the consequences of the deposit or both; or

    (b) there is no occupier of the land; or

    (c) the occupier neither made nor knowingly permitted the deposit of the waste;

the authority may remove the waste from the land or take other steps to eliminate or reduce the consequences of the deposit or, as the case may require, to remove the waste and take those steps.

(8)   Where an authority exercises any of the powers conferred on it by subsection (7) above it shall be entitled to recover the cost incurred by it in removing the waste or taking the steps or both and in disposing of the waste—

    (a) in a case falling within subsection (7)(a) above, from the occupier of the land unless he proves that he neither made nor knowingly caused nor knowingly permitted the deposit of the waste;

    (b) in any case, from any person who deposited or knowingly caused or knowingly permitted the deposit of any of the waste;

except such of the cost as the occupier or that person shows was incurred unnecessarily.

(9)   Any waste removed by an authority under subsection (7) above shall belong to that authority and may be dealt with accordingly.

[144]

NOTES

    Commencement: 1 May 1994.

---

60 Interference with waste sites and receptacles for waste

(1)   No person shall sort over or disturb—

    (a) anything deposited at a place for the deposit of waste provided by a waste collection authority, by a waste disposal contractor under arrangements made with a waste disposal authority or by any other local authority or person or, in Scotland, by a waste disposal authority;

    (b) anything deposited in a receptacle for waste, whether for public or private use, provided by a waste collection authority, by a waste disposal contractor under arrangements made with a waste disposal authority, by a parish or community council or by a holder of a waste management licence or, in Scotland, by a waste disposal authority or a roads authority; or

    (c) the contents of any receptacle for waste which, in accordance with a requirement under section 46 or 47 above, is placed on any highway or, in Scotland, road or in any other place with a view to its being emptied;

unless he has the relevant consent or right to do so specified in subsection (2) below.

(2)   The consent or right that is relevant for the purposes of subsection (1)(a), (b) or (c) above is—

(a)   in the case of paragraph (a), the consent of the authority, contractor or other person who provides the place for the deposit of the waste;

(b)   in the case of paragraph (b), the consent of the authority, contractor or other person who provides the receptacle for the deposit of the waste;

(c)   in the case of paragraph (c), the right to the custody of the receptacle, the consent of the person having the right to the custody of the receptacle or the right conferred by the function by or under this Part of emptying such receptacles.

(3)   A person who contravenes subsection (1) above shall be liable on summary conviction to a fine of an amount not exceeding level 3 on the standard scale.

[145]

NOTES

Commencement: 1 May 1994 (certain purposes); 31 May 1991 (remaining purposes).

61 Duty of waste regulation authorities as respects closed landfills

(1)   Except as respects land in relation to which a site licence is in force, it shall be the duty of every waste regulation authority to cause its area to be inspected from time to time to detect whether any land is in such a condition, by reason of the relevant matters affecting the land, that it may cause pollution of the environment or harm to human health.

(2)   The matters affecting land relevant for the purposes of this section are the concentration or accumulation in, and emission or discharge from, the land of noxious gases or noxious liquids caused by deposits of controlled waste in the land.

(3)   For the purpose of discharging the duty imposed by subsection (1) above on a waste regulation authority, the authority may enter and inspect any land—

(a)   in or on which controlled waste has been deposited at any time under the authority of a waste management licence or a disposal licence under section 5 of the Control of Pollution Act 1974; or

(b)   as respects which the authority has reason to believe that controlled waste has been deposited in the land at any time (whether before or after 1st January 1976); or

(c)   in which there are, or the authority has reason to believe there may be, concentrations or accumulations of noxious gases or noxious liquids.

In this subsection "controlled waste" means household, industrial or commercial waste as defined in section 75(5), (6) and (7) below (subject, if the regulations so provide, to regulations under section 63(1) or 75(8) below).

(4)   Where it appears to a waste regulation authority that the condition of any land in its area is such as is specified in subsection (1) above it shall be the duty of the authority, from time to time during the period of its responsibility for the land, to enter and inspect the land for the purpose of keeping its condition under review.

(5)   Where, at any time during the period of its responsibility for any land, it appears to a waste regulation authority that the condition of the land is, by reason of the relevant matters affecting the land, such that pollution of water is likely to be caused, it shall be the duty of the authority to consult the National Rivers Authority or, in Scotland, the river purification authority whose area includes the land in question as to the discharge by the authority of the duty imposed on it in relation to the land by subsection (7) below.

(6)   The "period of responsibility" for any land for the purposes of subsections (4) and (5) above extends from the time at which the condition of the land first appears to

the authority to be such as is referred to in that subsection until the authority is satisfied that no pollution of the environment or harm to human health will be caused by reason of the relevant matters affecting the land.

(7)   Where, on an inspection by a waste regulation authority of any land under this section, it appears to the authority that the condition of the land is, by reason of the relevant matters affecting the land, such that pollution of the environment or harm to human health is likely to be caused it shall be the duty of the authority to do such works and take such other steps (whether on the land affected or on adjacent land) as appear to the authority to be reasonable to avoid such pollution or harm.

(8)   Where an authority exercises in relation to waste on any land the duty imposed by subsection (7) above, the authority shall, except in a case falling within subsection (9) below, be entitled to recover the cost or part of the cost incurred in doing so from the person who is for the time being the owner of the land, except such of the cost as that person shows was incurred unreasonably.

(9)   Subsection (8) above does not apply in a case where the authority accepted the surrender under section 39 above of the waste management licence which authorised the activities in the course of which the waste was deposited.

(10)   In deciding whether to recover the cost and, if so, how much to recover of the cost which it is entitled to recover under subsection (8) above, the authority shall have regard to any hardship which the recovery may cause to the owner of the land.

(11)   It shall be the duty of waste regulation authorities to have regard to any guidance issued to them by the Secretary of State as respects the discharge of their functions under this section.

[146]

NOTES

Commencement: to be appointed.
Repealed by the Environment Act 1995, s 120, Sch 22, para 79, Sch 24, as from a day to be appointed.

Special waste and non-controlled waste

62 Special provision with respect to certain dangerous or intractable waste

(1)   If the Secretary of State considers that controlled waste of any kind is or may be so dangerous or difficult to treat, keep or dispose of that special provision is required for dealing with it he shall make provision by regulations for the treatment, keeping or disposal of waste of that kind ("special waste").

(2)   Without prejudice to the generality of subsection (1) above, the regulations may include provision—
  (a) for the giving of directions by waste regulation authorities with respect to matters connected with the treatment, keeping or disposal of special waste;
  (b) for securing that special waste is not, while awaiting treatment or disposal in pursuance of the regulations, kept at any one place in quantities greater than those which are prescribed and in circumstances which differ from those which are prescribed;
  (c) in connection with requirements imposed on consignors or consignees of special waste, imposing, in the event of non-compliance, requirements on any person carrying the consignment to re-deliver it as directed;
  (d) for requiring the occupier of premises on which special waste is situated to give notice of that fact and other prescribed information to a prescribed authority;
  (e) for the keeping of records by waste regulation authorities and by persons who import, export, produce, keep, treat or dispose of special waste or deliver it to another person for treatment or disposal, for the inspection of

the records and for the furnishing by such persons to waste regulation authorities of copies of or information derived from the records;

(f) for the keeping in the register under section 64(1) below of copies of such of those records, or such information derived from those records, as may be prescribed;

(g) providing that a contravention of the regulations shall be an offence and prescribing the maximum penalty for the offence, which shall not exceed, on summary conviction, a fine at level 5 on the standard scale and, on conviction on indictment, imprisonment for a term of two years or a fine or both.

(3) Without prejudice to the generality of subsection (1) above, the regulations may include provision—

[(a) for the supervision by waste regulation authorities—

(i) of activities authorised by virtue of the regulations or of activities by virtue of carrying on which persons are subject to provisions of the regulations, or

(ii) of persons who carry on activities authorised by virtue of the regulations or who are subject to provisions of the regulations,

and for the recovery from persons falling within sub-paragraph (ii) above of the costs incurred by waste regulation authorities in performing functions conferred upon those authorities by the regulations;]

(b) as to the recovery of expenses or other charges for the treatment, keeping or disposal or the re-delivery of special waste in pursuance of the regulations;

(c) as to appeals to the Secretary of State from decisions of waste regulation authorities under the regulations.

[(3A) This section is subject to section 114 of the Environment Act 1995 (delegation or reference of appeals etc).]

(4) In the application of this section to Northern Ireland "waste regulation authority" means a district council established under the Local Government Act (Northern Ireland) 1972.

[147]

NOTES
Commencement: 1 April 1996 (sub-s (3A)); 11 August 1995 (remainder).
Sub-s (3): para (a) substituted by the Environment Act 1995, s 120, Sch 22, para 80(2).
Sub-s (3A): inserted by the Environment Act 1995, s 120, Sch 22, para 80(3).
Regulations: the Special Waste Regulations 1996, SI 1996/972, as amended by SI 1996/2019, SI 1997/251.

63 Waste other than controlled waste

(1) The Secretary of State may, after consultation with such bodies as he considers appropriate, make regulations providing that prescribed provisions of this Part shall have effect in a prescribed area—

(a) as if references in those provisions to controlled waste or controlled waste of a kind specified in the regulations included references to such waste as is mentioned in section 75(7)(c) below which is of a kind so specified; and

(b) with such modifications as may be prescribed;

and the regulations may make such modifications of other enactments as the Secretary of State considers appropriate.

(2) *A person who—*

(a) *deposits any waste other than controlled waste, or*

(b) *knowingly causes or knowingly permits the deposit of any waste other than controlled waste, in a case where, if the waste were special waste and any waste management licence were not in force, he would be guilty of an offence under section 33 above shall, subject to subsection (3) below, be guilty of that offence and punishable accordingly.*

(3)　No offence is committed by virtue of subsection (2) above if the act charged was done under and in accordance with any consent, licence, approval or authority granted under any enactment (excluding any planning permission under the enactments relating to town and country planning).

(4)　Section 45(2) and section 47(1) above shall apply to waste other than controlled waste as they apply to controlled waste.

[148]

NOTES

Commencement: 18 February 1993 (sub-s (1)); to be appointed (remainder).

Sub-s (2): substituted by the Environment Act 1995, s 120, Sch 22, para 81, as from a day to be appointed, as follows—

"(2)　A person who deposits, or knowingly causes or knowingly permits the deposit of, any waste—
  (a)　which is not controlled waste, but
  (b)　which, if it were controlled waste, would be special waste,

in a case where he would be guilty of an offence under section 33 above if the waste were special waste and any waste management licence were not in force, shall, subject to subsection (3) below, be guilty of that offence and punishable as if the waste were special waste."

Publicity

64　Public registers

(1)　Subject to sections 65 and 66 below, it shall be the duty of each waste regulation authority to maintain a register containing prescribed particulars of or relating to—
  (a)　current or recently current licences ("licences") granted by the authority;
  (b)　current or recently current applications to the authority for licences;
  (c)　applications made to the authority under section 37 above for the modification of licences;
  (d)　notices issued by the authority under section 37 above effecting the modification of licences;
  (e)　notices issued by the authority under section 38 above effecting the revocation or suspension of licences or imposing requirements on the holders of licences;
  (f)　appeals under section 43 above relating to decisions of the authority;
  (g)　certificates of completion issued by the authority under section 39(9) above;
  (h)　notices issued by the authority imposing requirements on the holders of licences under section 42(5) above;
  (i)　convictions of the holders of licences granted by the authority for any offence under this Part (whether in relation to a licence so granted or not);
  (j)　the occasions on which the authority has discharged any function under section 42 or 61 above;
  (k)　directions given to the authority under any provision of this Part by the Secretary of State;
  (l)　. . .
  (m)　such matters relating to the treatment, keeping or disposal of waste in the area of the authority or any pollution of the environment caused thereby as may be prescribed;

and any other document or information required to be kept in the register under any provision of this Act.

(2)　Where information of any description is excluded from any register by virtue of section 66 below, a statement shall be entered in the register indicating the existence of information of that description.

[(2A) The Secretary of State may give to a waste regulation authority directions requiring the removal from any register of its of any specified information not prescribed for inclusion under subsection (1) above or which, by virtue of section 65 or 66 below, ought to be excluded from the register.]

(3)   For the purposes of subsection (1) above licences are "recently" current for the period of twelve months after they cease to be in force and applications for licences are "recently" current if they relate to a licence which is current or recently current or, in the case of an application which is rejected, for the period of twelve months beginning with the date on which the waste regulation authority gives notice of rejection or, as the case may be, on which the application is deemed by section 36(9) above to have been rejected.

(4)   It shall be the duty of each waste collection authority in England [or Wales] . . . to maintain a register containing prescribed particulars of such information contained in any register maintained under subsection (1) above as relates to the treatment, keeping or disposal of controlled waste in the area of the authority.

[(5)   The waste regulation authority in relation to England and Wales shall furnish any waste collection authorities in its area with the particulars necessary to enable them to discharge their duty under subsection (4) above.]

(6)   Each waste regulation authority and waste collection authority
   [(a)]   shall secure that any register maintained under this section is open to inspection . . . by members of the public free of charge at all reasonable hours and
   [(b)]   shall afford to members of the public reasonable facilities for obtaining, on payment of reasonable charges, copies of entries in the register

[and, for the purposes of this subsection, places may be prescribed by the Secretary of State at which any such registers or facilities as are mentioned in paragraph (a) or (b) above are to be available or afforded to the public in pursuance of the paragraph in question.]

(7)   Registers under this section may be kept in any form.

(8)   In this section "prescribed" means prescribed in regulations by the Secretary of State.

[149]

NOTES
   Commencement: 1 April 1996 (sub-ss (2A), (5)); 1 May 1994 (sub-ss (2), (3), (6), (7)); 18 February 1993 (remainder).
   Sub-s (1): para (l) repealed by the Environment Act 1995, s 120, Sch 24.
   Sub-s (2A): inserted by the Environment Act 1995, s 120, Sch 22, para 82(2).
   Sub-s (4): words in square brackets inserted and words omitted repealed by the Environment Act 1995, s 120, Sch 22, para 82(3), Sch 24.
   Sub-s (5): substituted by the Environment Act 1995, s 120, Sch 22, para 82(4).
   Sub-s (6): words in square brackets inserted by the Environment Act 1995, s 120, Sch 22, para 82(5); words omitted repealed by the Environment Act 1995 (Consequential Amendments) Regulations 1996, SI 1996/593, reg 3, Sch 2, para 6.
   Regulations: the Waste Management Licensing Regulations 1994, SI 1994/1056, as amended by SI 1994/1137, SI 1995/288, SI 1995/1950, SI 1996/593, SI 1996/634, SI 1996/972, SI 1996/1279.

65 Exclusion from registers of information affecting national security

(1)   No information shall be included in a register maintained under section 64 above (a "register") if and so long as, in the opinion of the Secretary of State, the inclusion in the register of that information, or information of that description, would be contrary to the interests of national security.

(2)   The Secretary of State may, for the purpose of securing the exclusion from registers of information to which subsection (1) above applies, give to the authorities maintaining registers directions—

(a) specifying information, or descriptions of information, to be excluded from their registers; or

(b) specifying descriptions of information to be referred to the Secretary of State for his determination;

and no information referred to the Secretary of State in pursuance of paragraph (*b*) above shall be included in any such register until the Secretary of State determines that it should be so included.

(3) An authority maintaining a register shall notify the Secretary of State of any information it excludes from the register in pursuance of directions under subsection (2) above.

(4) A person may, as respects any information which appears to him to be information to which subsection (1) above may apply, give a notice to the Secretary of State specifying the information and indicating its apparent nature; and, if he does so—

(a) he shall notify the authority concerned that he has done so; and

(b) no information so notified to the Secretary of State shall be included in the register kept by that authority until the Secretary of State has determined that it should be so included.

[150]

NOTES

Commencement: 1 May 1994 (sub-ss (1), (3), (4), sub-s (2) certain purposes); 18 February 1993 (sub-s (2), remaining purposes).

66 Exclusion from registers of certain confidential information

(1) No information relating to the affairs of any individual or business shall be included in a register maintained under section 64 above (a "register"), without the consent of that individual or the person for the time being carrying on that business, if and so long as the information—

(a) is, in relation to him, commercially confidential; and

(b) is not required to be included in the register in pursuance of directions under subsection (7) below;

but information is not commercially confidential for the purposes of this section unless it is determined under this section to be so by the authority maintaining the register or, on appeal, by the Secretary of State.

(2) Where information is furnished to an authority maintaining a register for the purpose of—

(a) an application for, or for the modification of, a licence;

(b) complying with any condition of a licence; or

(c) complying with a notice under section 71(2) below;

then, if the person furnishing it applies to the authority to have the information excluded from the register on the ground that it is commercially confidential (as regards himself or another person), the authority shall determine whether the information is or is not commercially confidential.

(3) A determination under subsection (2) above must be made within the period of fourteen days beginning with the date of the application and if the authority fails to make a determination within that period it shall be treated as having determined that the information is commercially confidential.

(4) Where it appears to an authority maintaining a register that any information (other than information furnished in circumstances within subsection (2) above) which has been obtained by the authority under or by virtue of any provision of this Part might be commercially confidential, the authority shall—

(a) give to the person to whom or whose business it relates notice that that information is required to be included in the register unless excluded under this section; and

(b) give him a reasonable opportunity—
   (i) of objecting to the inclusion of the information on the grounds that it is commercially confidential; and
   (ii) of making representations to the authority for the purpose of justifying any such objection;

and, if any representations are made, the authority shall, having taken the representations into account, determine whether the information is or is not commercially confidential.

(5) Where, under subsection (2) or (4) above, an authority determines that information is not commercially confidential—

(a) the information shall not be entered in the register until the end of the period of twenty-one days beginning with the date on which the determination is notified to the person concerned;

(b) that person may appeal to the Secretary of State against the decision;

and, where an appeal is brought in respect of any information, the information shall not be entered in the register [until the end of the period of seven days following the day on which the appeal is finally determined or withdrawn].

[(6) Subsections (2) and (8) of section 43 above shall apply in relation to appeals under subsection (5) above as they apply in relation to appeals under that section; but—

(a) subsection (2)(c) of that section shall have effect for the purposes of this subsection with the substitution for the words from "(which may" onwards of the words "(which must be held in private)"; and

(b) subsection (5) above is subject to section 114 of the Environment Act 1995 (delegation or reference of appeals etc).]

(7) The Secretary of State may give to the authorities maintaining registers directions as to specified information, or descriptions of information, which the public interest requires to be included in the registers notwithstanding that the information may be commercially confidential.

(8) Information excluded from a register shall be treated as ceasing to be commercially confidential for the purposes of this section at the expiry of the period of four years beginning with the date of the determination by virtue of which it was excluded; but the person who furnished it may apply to the authority for the information to remain excluded from the register on the ground that it is still commercially confidential and the authority shall determine whether or not that is the case.

(9) Subsections (5) and (6) above shall apply in relation to a determination under subsection (8) above as they apply in relation to a determination under subsection (2) or (4) above.

(10) The Secretary of State may, by order, substitute for the period for the time being specified in subsection (3) above such other period as he considers appropriate.

(11) Information is, for the purposes of any determination under this section, commercially confidential, in relation to any individual or person, if its being contained in the register would prejudice to an unreasonable degree the commercial interests of that individual or person.

[151]

NOTES

Commencement: 1 April 1996 (sub-s (6)); 1 May 1994 (sub-ss (1)–(5), (8)–(11), sub-s (7) certain purposes); 18 February 1993 (sub-s (7), remaining purposes).

Sub-s (5): words in square brackets substituted by the Environment Act 1995, s 120, Sch 22, para 83(1).

Sub-s (6): substituted by the Environment Act 1995, s 120, Sch 22, para 83(2).

67–70   (*Repealed by the Environment Act 1995, s 120(1), (3), Sch 22, paras 84, 85, Sch 24.*)

Supervision and enforcement

71 Obtaining of information from persons and authorities

(1)   . . .

(2)   For the purpose of the discharge of their respective functions under this Part—
   (a)   the Secretary of State, and
   (b)   a waste regulation authority,
may, by notice in writing served on him, require any person to furnish such information specified in the notice as the Secretary of State or the authority, as the case may be, reasonably considers he or it needs, in such form and within such period following service of the notice[, or at such time,] as is so specified.

(3)   A person who—
   (a)   fails, without reasonable excuse, to comply with a requirement imposed under subsection (2) above; . . .
   (b)   . . .
shall be liable—
   (i)   on summary conviction, to a fine not exceeding the statutory maximum;
   (ii)   on conviction on indictment, to a fine or to imprisonment for a term not exceeding two years, or to both.

[152]

NOTES
   Sub-s (1): repealed by the Environment Act 1995, s 120, Sch 22, para 86(1), Sch 24.
   Sub-s (2): words in square brackets inserted by the Environment Act 1995, s 120, Sch 22, para 86(2).
   Sub-s (3): words omitted repealed by the Environment Act 1995, ss 112, 120, Sch 19, para 4(2), Sch 24.

72   (*Repealed by the Environment Act 1995, s 120(1), (3), Sch 22, para 87, Sch 24.*)

Supplemental

73 Appeals and other provisions relating to legal proceedings and civil liability

(1)   An appeal against any decision of a magistrates' court under this Part (other than a decision made in criminal proceedings) shall lie to the Crown Court at the instance of any party to the proceedings in which the decision was given if such an appeal does not lie to the Crown Court by virtue of any other enactment.

(2)   (*Applies to Scotland only.*)

(3)   Where a person appeals to the Crown Court or the Court of Session against a decision of a magistrates' court or the sheriff dismissing an appeal against any requirement imposed under this Part which was suspended pending determination of that appeal, the requirement shall again be suspended pending the determination of the appeal to the Crown Court or Court of Session.

(4)   Where an appeal against a decision of any authority lies to a magistrates' court or to the sheriff by virtue of any provision of this Part, it shall be the duty of the authority to include in any document by which it notifies the decision to the person concerned a statement indicating that such an appeal lies and specifying the time within which it must be brought.

(5)   Where on an appeal to any court against or arising out of a decision of any authority under this Part the court varies or reverses the decision it shall be the duty of the authority to act in accordance with the court's decision.

(6)   Where any damage is caused by waste which has been deposited in or on land, any person who deposited it, or knowingly caused or knowingly permitted it to be deposited, in either case so as to commit an offence under section 33(1) or 63(2) above, is liable for the damage except where the damage—
  (a) was due wholly to the fault of the person who suffered it; or
  (b) was suffered by a person who voluntarily accepted the risk of the damage being caused;
but without prejudice to any liability arising otherwise than under this subsection.

(7)   The matters which may be proved by way of defence under section 33(7) above may be proved also by way of defence to an action brought under subsection (6) above.

(8)   In subsection (6) above—
  "damage" includes the death of, or injury to, any person (including any disease and any impairment of physical or mental condition); and
  "fault" has the same meaning as in the Law Reform (Contributory Negligence) Act 1945.

(9)   For the purposes of the following enactments—
  (a) the Fatal Accidents Act 1976;
  (b) the Law Reform (Contributory Negligence) Act 1945; and
  (c) the Limitation Act 1980;
and for the purposes of any action of damages in Scotland arising out of the death of, or personal injury to, any person, any damage for which a person is liable under subsection (6) above shall be treated as due to his fault.

[153]

NOTES
    Commencement: 1 May 1994 (sub-ss (6)–(9)); 1 April 1992 (remainder).

74 Meaning of "fit and proper person"

(1)   The following provisions apply for the purposes of the discharge by a waste regulation authority of any function under this Part which requires the authority to determine whether a person is or is not a fit and proper person to hold a waste management licence.

(2)   Whether a person is or is not a fit and proper person to hold a licence is to be determined by reference to the carrying on by him of the activities which are or are to be authorised by the licence and the fulfilment of the requirements of the licence.

(3)   Subject to subsection (4) below, a person shall be treated as not being a fit and proper person if it appears to the authority—
  (a) that he or another relevant person has been convicted of a relevant offence;
  (b) that the management of the activities which are or are to be authorised by the licence are not or will not be in the hands of a technically competent person; or
  (c) that the person who holds or is to hold the licence has not made and either has no intention of making or is in no position to make financial provision adequate to discharge the obligations arising from the licence.

(4)   The authority may, if it considers it proper to do so in any particular case, treat a person as a fit and proper person notwithstanding that subsection (3)(a) above applies in his case.

(5)   It shall be the duty of waste regulation authorities to have regard to any guidance issued to them by the Secretary of State with respect to the discharge of their functions of making the determinations to which this section applies.

(6)   The Secretary of State may, by regulations, prescribe the offences that are relevant for the purposes of subsection (3)(a) above and the qualifications and experience required of a person for the purposes of subsection (3)(b) above.

(7)   For the purposes of subsection (3)(a) above, another relevant person shall be treated, in relation to the licence holder or proposed licence holder, as the case may be, as having been convicted of a relevant offence if—

    (a)   any person has been convicted of a relevant offence committed by him in the course of his employment by the holder or, as the case may be, the proposed holder of the licence or in the course of the carrying on of any business by a partnership one of the members of which was the holder or, as the case may be, the proposed holder of the licence;

    (b)   a body corporate has been convicted of a relevant offence committed when the holder or, as the case may be, the proposed holder of the licence was a director, manager, secretary or other similar officer of that body corporate; or

    (c)   where the holder or, as the case may be, the proposed holder of the licence is a body corporate, a person who is a director, manager, secretary or other similar officer of that body corporate—

       (i)   has been convicted of a relevant offence; or

      (ii)   was a director, manager, secretary or other similar officer of another body corporate at a time when a relevant offence for which that other body corporate has been convicted was committed.

[154]

NOTES

Commencement: 1 May 1994 (sub-ss (1)–(5), (7)); 18 February 1993 (remainder).

Regulations: the Waste Management Licensing Regulations 1994, SI 1994/1056, as amended by SI 1994/1137, SI 1995/288, SI 1995/1950, SI 1996/593, SI 1996/634, SI 1996/972, SI 1996/1279; the Transfrontier Shipment of Waste Regulations 1994, SI 1994/1137, as amended by SI 1996/593, SI 1996/972; the Waste Management Regulations 1996, SI 1996/634; the Special Waste Regulations 1996, SI 1996/972, as amended by SI 1996/2019, SI 1997/251; the Waste Management (Miscellaneous Provisions) Regulations 1997, SI 1997/351.

75 Meaning of "waste" and household, commercial and industrial waste and special waste

(1)   The following provisions apply for the interpretation of this Part.

(2)   "Waste" includes—

    (a)   any substance which constitutes a scrap material or an effluent or other unwanted surplus substance arising from the application of any process; and

    (b)   any substance or article which requires to be disposed of as being broken, worn out, contaminated or otherwise spoiled;

but does not include a substance which is an explosive within the meaning of the Explosives Act 1875.

(3)   Any thing which is discarded or otherwise dealt with as if it were waste shall be presumed to be waste unless the contrary is proved.

(4)   "Controlled waste" means household, industrial and commercial waste or any such waste.

(5)   Subject to subsection (8) below, "household waste" means waste from—

    (a)   domestic property, that is to say, a building or self-contained part of a building which is used wholly for the purposes of living accommodation;

    (b)   a caravan (as defined in section 29(1) of the Caravan Sites and Control of Development Act 1960) which usually and for the time being is situated on a caravan site (within the meaning of that Act);

(c) a residential home;
(d) premises forming part of a university or school or other educational establishment;
(e) premises forming part of a hospital or nursing home.

(6)   Subject to subsection (8) below, "industrial waste" means waste from any of the following premises—
(a) any factory (within the meaning of the Factories Act 1961);
(b) any premises used for the purposes of, or in connection with, the provision to the public of transport services by land, water or air;
(c) any premises used for the purposes of, or in connection with, the supply to the public of gas, water or electricity or the provision of sewerage services; or
(d) any premises used for the purposes of, or in connection with, the provision to the public of postal or telecommunications services.

(7)   Subject to subsection (8) below, "commercial waste" means waste from premises used wholly or mainly for the purposes of a trade or business or the purposes of sport, recreation or entertainment excluding—
(a) household waste;
(b) industrial waste;
(c) waste from any mine or quarry and waste from premises used for agriculture within the meaning of the Agriculture Act 1947 or, in Scotland, the Agriculture (Scotland) Act 1948; and
(d) waste of any other description prescribed by regulations made by the Secretary of State for the purposes of this paragraph.

(8)   Regulations made by the Secretary of State may provide that waste of a description prescribed in the regulations shall be treated for the purposes of provisions of this Part prescribed in the regulations as being or not being household waste or industrial waste or commercial waste; but no regulations shall be made in respect of such waste as is mentioned in subsection (7)(c) above and references to waste in subsection (7) above and this subsection do not include sewage (including matter in or from a privy) except so far as the regulations provide otherwise.

(9)   "Special waste" means controlled waste as respects which regulations are in force under section 62 above.

[(10) Schedule 2B to this Act (which reproduces Annex I to the Waste Directive) shall have effect.

(11) Subsection (2) above is substituted, and Schedule 2B to this Act is inserted, for the purpose of assigning to "waste" in this Part the meaning which it has in the Waste Directive by virtue of paragraphs (a) to (c) of Article 1 of, and Annex I to, that Directive, and those provisions shall be construed accordingly.

(12) In this section "the Waste Directive" means the directive of the Council of the European Communities, dated 15th July 1975, on waste, as amended by—
(a) the directive of that Council, dated 18th March 1991, amending directive 75/442/EEC on waste; and
(b) the directive of that Council, dated 23rd December 1991, standardising and rationalising reports on the implementation of certain Directives relating to the environment.]

NOTES
Commencement: 31 May 1991 (sub-ss (1)–(9)); to be appointed (remainder).
   Sub-s (2): substituted by the Environment Act 1995, s 120, Sch 22, para 88(2), as from a day to be appointed, as follows—
   "(2)"Waste" means any substance or object in the categories set out in Schedule 2B to this Act which the holder discards or intends or is required to discard; and for the purposes of this definition—
   "holder" means the producer of the waste or the person who is in possession of it; and

"producer" means any person whose activities produce waste or any person who carries out pre-processing, mixing or other operations resulting in a change in the nature or composition of this waste.".

Sub-s (3): repealed by the Environment Act 1995, s 120, Sch 22, para 88(3), Sch 24, as from a day to be appointed.

Sub-ss (10)–(12): added by the Environment Act 1995, s 120, Sch 22, para 88(4) as from a day to be appointed.

Regulations: the Controlled Waste Regulations 1992, SI 1992/588, regs 2, 3, 5–7, Schs 1, 3, 4, as amended by SI 1993/566, SI 1994/1056, SI 1995/288, SI 1996/972; the Waste Management Licensing Regulations 1994, SI 1994/1056, as amended by SI 1994/1137, SI 1995/288, SI 1995/1950, SI 1996/593, SI 1996/634, SI 1996/972, SI 1996/1279; the Special Waste Regulations 1996, SI 1996/972, as amended by SI 1996/2019, SI 1997/251.

[76 Application to the Isles of Scilly

(1)   Subject to the provisions of any order under this section, this Part shall not apply in relation to the Isles of Scilly.

(2)   The Secretary of State may, after consultation with the Council of the Isles of Scilly, by order provide for the application of any provisions of this Part to the Isles of Scilly; and any such order may provide for the application of those provisions to those Isles with such modifications as may be specified in the order.

(3)   An order under this section may—
   (a) make different provision for different cases, including different provision in relation to different persons, circumstances or localities; and
   (b) contain such supplemental, consequential and transitional provision as the Secretary of State considers appropriate, including provision saving provision repealed by or under any enactment.]

[156]

NOTES
Commencement: 1 February 1996.
Substituted by the Environment Act 1995, s 118(3).

77 Transition from Control of Pollution Act 1974 to this Part

(1)   This section has effect for the purposes of the transition from the provisions of Part I of the Control of Pollution Act 1974 ("the 1974 Act") to the corresponding provisions of this Part of this Act and in this section—
   "existing disposal authority" has the same meaning as in section 32 above;
   "existing disposal licence" means a disposal licence under section 5 of the 1974 Act subsisting on the day appointed under section 164(3) below for the repeal of sections 3 to 10 of the 1974 Act and "relevant appointed day for licences" shall be construed accordingly;
   "existing disposal plan" means a plan under section 2 of the 1974 Act subsisting on the day appointed under section 164(3) below for the repeal of that section and "relevant appointed day for plans" shall be construed accordingly;
   "relevant part of its undertaking", in relation to an existing disposal authority, has the same meaning as in section 32 above; and
   "the vesting date", in relation to an existing disposal authority and its waste disposal contractors, means the vesting date under Schedule 2 to this Act.

(2)   An existing disposal licence shall, on and after the relevant appointed day for licences, be treated as a site licence until it expires or otherwise ceases to have effect; and accordingly it shall be variable and subject to revocation or suspension under this Part of this Act and may not be surrendered or transferred except under this Part of this Act.

(3)   The restriction imposed by section 33(1) above shall not apply in relation to land occupied by an existing disposal authority for which a resolution of the authority subsists under section 11 of the 1974 Act on the relevant appointed day for licences until the following date, that is to say—

    (a) in the case of an authority which transfers the relevant part of its undertaking in accordance with a scheme under Schedule 2 to this Act, the date which is the vesting date for that authority; and

    (b) in any other case, the date on which the authority transfers, or ceases itself to carry on, the relevant part of its undertaking or ceases to provide places at which and plant and equipment by means of which controlled waste can be disposed of or deposited for the purposes of disposal.

(4)   Any existing disposal plan of an existing disposal authority shall, on and after the relevant appointed day for plans, be treated as the plan of that authority under section 50 above and that section shall accordingly have effect as if references in it to "the plan" included the existing disposal plan of that authority.

(5)   *(Applies to Scotland only.)*

(6)   Subject to subsection (7) below, as respects any existing disposal authority—

    (a) the restriction imposed by section 51(1) of this Act on the means whereby the authority arranges for the disposal of controlled waste shall not apply to the authority—

        (i) in the case of an authority which transfers the relevant part of its undertaking in accordance with a scheme under Schedule 2 to this Act, until the date which is the vesting date for that authority; and

        (ii) in any other case, until the date on which the authority transfers, or ceases itself to carry on, the relevant part of its undertaking or ceases to provide places at which and plant and equipment by means of which controlled waste can be disposed of or deposited for the purposes of disposal; and

    (b) on and after that date, section 14(4) of the 1974 Act shall not authorise the authority to arrange for the disposal of controlled waste except by means of arrangements made (in accordance with Part II of Schedule 2 to this Act) with waste disposal contractors.

(7)   The Secretary of State may, as respects any existing disposal authority, direct that the restriction imposed by section 51(1) above shall not apply in the case of that authority until such date as he specifies in the direction and where he does so paragraph (a) of subsection (6) above shall not apply and paragraph (b) shall be read as referring to the date so specified.

(8)   . . .

(9)   As respects any existing disposal authority, until the date which is, under subsection (6)(a) above, the date until which the restriction imposed by section 51(1) of this Act is disapplied,—

    (a) the powers conferred on a waste disposal authority by section 55(2)(a) and (b) of this Act as respects the recycling of waste and the use of waste to produce heat or electricity shall be treated as powers which the authority may exercise itself; and

    (b) the power conferred on a waste disposal authority by section 48(4) of this Act to object to a waste collection authority having waste recycled where the disposal authority has made arrangements with a waste disposal contractor for the contractor to recycle the waste shall be available to the waste disposal authority where it itself has the waste recycled.

[157]

NOTES

Sub-s (8): amends the Control of Pollution Act 1974, s 14(4).

78 This Part and radioactive substances

Except as provided by regulations made by the Secretary of State under this section, nothing in this Part applies to radioactive waste within the meaning of the [Radioactive Substances Act 1993]; but regulations may—
 (a) provide for prescribed provisions of this Part to have effect with such modifications as the Secretary of State considers appropriate for the purposes of dealing with such radioactive waste;
 (b) make such modifications of the [Radioactive Substances Act 1993] and any other Act as the Secretary of State considers appropriate.

[158]

NOTES

Words in square brackets substituted by the Radioactive Substances Act 1993, s 49(1), Sch 4, para 7.
Regulations: the Special Waste Regulations 1996, SI 1996/972, as amended by SI 1996/2019, SI 1997/251.

[PART IIA
CONTAMINATED LAND

78A Preliminary

(1)   The following provisions have effect for the interpretation of this Part.

(2)   "Contaminated land" is any land which appears to the local authority in whose area it is situated to be in such a condition, by reason of substances in, on or under the land, that—
 (a) significant harm is being caused or there is a significant possibility of such harm being caused; or
 (b) pollution of controlled waters is being, or is likely to be, caused;

and, in determining whether any land appears to be such land, a local authority shall, subject to subsection (5) below, act in accordance with guidance issued by the Secretary of State in accordance with section 78YA below with respect to the manner in which that determination is to be made.

(3)   A "special site" is any contaminated land—
 (a) which has been designated as such a site by virtue of section 78C(7) or 78D(6) below; and
 (b) whose designation as such has not been terminated by the appropriate Agency under section 78Q(4) below.

(4)   "Harm" means harm to the health of living organisms or other interference with the ecological systems of which they form part and, in the case of man, includes harm to his property.

(5)   The questions—
 (a) what harm is to be regarded as "significant",
 (b) whether the possibility of significant harm being caused is "significant",
 (c) whether pollution of controlled waters is being, or is likely to be caused,

shall be determined in accordance with guidance issued for the purpose by the Secretary of State in accordance with section 78YA below.

(6)   Without prejudice to the guidance that may be issued under subsection (5) above, guidance under paragraph (a) of that subsection may make provision for different degrees of importance to be assigned to, or for the disregard of,—
 (a) different descriptions of living organisms or ecological systems;
 (b) different descriptions of places; or
 (c) different descriptions of harm to health or property, or other interference;

and guidance under paragraph (b) of that subsection may make provision for different degrees of possibility to be regarded as "significant" (or as not being "significant") in relation to different descriptions of significant harm.

(7)   "Remediation" means—
    (a)   the doing of anything for the purpose of assessing the condition of—
        (i)   the contaminated land in question;
        (ii) any controlled waters affected by that land; or
        (iii) any land adjoining or adjacent to that land;
    (b)   the doing of any works, the carrying out of any operations or the taking of any steps in relation to any such land or waters for the purpose—
        (i)   of preventing or minimising, or remedying or mitigating the effects of, any significant harm, or any pollution of controlled waters, by reason of which the contaminated land is such land; or
        (ii) of restoring the land or waters to their former state; or
    (c)   the making of subsequent inspections from time to time for the purpose of keeping under review the condition of the land or waters;
and cognate expressions shall be construed accordingly.

(8)   Controlled waters are "affected by" contaminated land if (and only if) it appears to the enforcing authority that the contaminated land in question is, for the purposes of subsection (2) above, in such a condition, by reason of substances in, on or under the land, that pollution of those waters is being, or is likely to be caused.

(9)   The following expressions have the meaning respectively assigned to them—
    "the appropriate Agency" means—
        (a) in relation to England and Wales, the Environment Agency;
        (b) *(applies to Scotland only)*;
    "appropriate person" means any person who is an appropriate person, determined in accordance with section 78F below, to bear responsibility for any thing which is to be done by way of remediation in any particular case;
    "charging notice" has the meaning given by section 78P(3)(b) below;
    "controlled waters"—
        (a) in relation to England and Wales, has the same meaning as in Part III of the Water Resources Act 1991; and
        (b) *(applies to Scotland only)*;

        . . . . .

    "enforcing authority" means—
        (a) in relation to a special site, the appropriate Agency;
        (b) in relation to contaminated land other than a special site, the local authority in whose area the land is situated;

        . . . . .

    "local authority" in relation to England and Wales means—
        (a) any unitary authority;
        (b) any district council, so far as it is not a unitary authority;
        (c) the Common Council of the City of London and, as respects the Temples, the Sub-Treasurer of the Inner Temple and the Under-Treasurer of the Middle Temple respectively;
    and in relation to Scotland means a council for an area constituted under section 2 of the Local Government etc (Scotland) Act 1994;
    "notice" means notice in writing;
    "notification" means notification in writing;
    "owner", in relation to any land in England and Wales, means a person (other than a mortgagee not in possession) who, whether in his own right or as trustee for any other person, is entitled to receive the rack rent of the land, or, where the land is not let at a rack rent, would be so entitled if it were so let;

        . . . . .

"pollution of controlled waters" means the entry into controlled waters of any
poisonous, noxious or polluting matter or any solid waste matter;
"prescribed" means prescribed by regulations;
"regulations" means regulations made by the Secretary of State;
"remediation declaration" has the meaning given by section 78H(6) below;
"remediation notice" has the meaning given by section 78E(1) below;
"remediation statement" has the meaning given by section 78H(7) below;
"required to be designated as a special site" shall be construed in accordance
with section 78C(8) below;
"substance" means any natural or artificial substance, whether in solid or liquid
form or in the form of a gas or vapour;
"unitary authority" means—
  (a) the council of a county, so far as it is the council of an area for which
      there are no district councils;
  (b) the council of any district comprised in an area for which there is no
      county council;
  (c) the council of a London borough;
  (d) the council of a county borough in Wales.]

                                                                    [159]

NOTES

Commencement: 21 September 1995 (certain purposes); to be appointed (remaining purposes).

Inserted, together with ss 78A–78YC, by the Environment Act 1995, s 57, and in force only in so far
as to confer power on the Secretary of State to make regulations or orders, give directions or issue
guidance, or in so far as to make provision with respect to the excercise of any such power (the
Environment Act 1995 (Commencement No 1) Order 1995, SI 1995/1983, art 3).

Sub-s (9): definitions omitted apply to Scotland only.

[78B Identification of contaminated land

(1)   Every local authority shall cause its area to be inspected from time to time
for the purpose—
  (a) of identifying contaminated land; and
  (b) of enabling the authority to decide whether any such land is land which is
      required to be designated as a special site.

(2)   In performing its functions under subsection (1) above a local authority shall
act in accordance with any guidance issued for the purpose by the Secretary of State
in accordance with section 78YA below.

(3)   If a local authority identifies any contaminated land in its area, it shall give
notice of that fact to—
  (a) the appropriate Agency;
  (b) the owner of the land;
  (c) any person who appears to the authority to be in occupation of the whole or
      any part of the land; and
  (d) each person who appears to the authority to be an appropriate person;

and any notice given under this subsection shall state by virtue of which of
paragraphs (a) to (d) above it is given.

(4)   If, at any time after a local authority has given any person a notice pursuant
to subsection (3)(d) above in respect of any land, it appears to the enforcing
authority that another person is an appropriate person, the enforcing authority shall
give notice to that other person—
  (a) of the fact that the local authority has identified the land in question as
      contaminated land; and
  (b) that he appears to the enforcing authority to be an appropriate person.]

                                                                    [160]

NOTES

Commencement: 21 September 1995 (certain purposes); to be appointed (remaining purposes).
Inserted as noted to s 78A at **[159]**.

[78C Identification and designation of special sites

(1)   If at any time it appears to a local authority that any contaminated land in its area might be land which is required to be designated as a special site, the authority—
(a) shall decide whether or not the land is land which is required to be so designated; and
(b) if the authority decides that the land is land which is required to be so designated, shall give notice of that decision to the relevant persons.

(2)   For the purposes of this section, "the relevant persons" at any time in the case of any land are the persons who at that time fall within paragraphs (a) to (d) below, that is to say—
(a) the appropriate Agency;
(b) the owner of the land;
(c) any person who appears to the local authority concerned to be in occupation of the whole or any part of the land; and
(d) each person who appears to that authority to be an appropriate person.

(3)   Before making a decision under paragraph (a) of subsection (1) above in any particular case, a local authority shall request the advice of the appropriate Agency, and in making its decision shall have regard to any advice given by that Agency in response to the request.

(4)   If at any time the appropriate Agency considers that any contaminated land is land which is required to be designated as a special site, that Agency may give notice of that fact to the local authority in whose area the land is situated.

(5)   Where notice under subsection (4) above is given to a local authority, the authority shall decide whether the land in question—
(a) is land which is required to be designated as a special site, or
(b) is not land which is required to be so designated,
and shall give notice of that decision to the relevant persons.

(6)   Where a local authority makes a decision falling within subsection (1)(b) or (5)(a) above, the decision shall, subject to section 78D below, take effect on the day after whichever of the following events first occurs, that is to say—
(a) the expiration of the period of twenty-one days beginning with the day on which the notice required by virtue of subsection (1)(b) or, as the case may be, (5)(a) above is given to the appropriate Agency; or
(b) if the appropriate Agency gives notification to the local authority in question that it agrees with the decision, the giving of that notification;
and where a decision takes effect by virtue of this subsection, the local authority shall give notice of that fact to the relevant persons.

(7)   Where a decision that any land is land which is required to be designated as a special site takes effect in accordance with subsection (6) above, the notice given under subsection (1)(b) or, as the case may be, (5)(a) above shall have effect, as from the time when the decision takes effect, as the designation of that land as such a site.

(8)   For the purposes of this Part, land is required to be designated as a special site if, and only if, it is land of a description prescribed for the purposes of this subsection.

(9)   Regulations under subsection (8) above may make different provision for different cases or circumstances or different areas or localities and may, in particular, describe land by reference to the area or locality in which it is situated.

(10)   Without prejudice to the generality of his power to prescribe any description of land for the purposes of subsection (8) above, the Secretary of State, in deciding whether to prescribe a particular description of contaminated land for those purposes, may, in particular, have regard to—
    (a)   whether land of the description in question appears to him to be land which is likely to be in such a condition, by reason of substances in, on or under the land that—
        (i)   serious harm would or might be caused, or
        (ii)   serious pollution of controlled waters would be, or would be likely to be, caused; or
    (b)   whether the appropriate Agency is likely to have expertise in dealing with the kind of significant harm, or pollution of controlled waters, by reason of which land of the description in question is contaminated land.]

[161]

NOTES

Commencement: 21 September 1995 (certain purposes); to be appointed (remaining purposes).
Inserted as noted to s 78A at **[159]**.

[78D   Referral of special site decisions to the Secretary of State

(1)   In any case where—
    (a)   a local authority gives notice of a decision to the appropriate Agency pursuant to subsection (1)(b) or (5)(b) of section 78C above, but
    (b)   before the expiration of the period of twenty-one days beginning with the day on which that notice is so given, that Agency gives the local authority notice that it disagrees with the decision, together with a statement of its reasons for disagreeing,
the authority shall refer the decision to the Secretary of State and shall send to him a statement of its reasons for reaching the decision.

(2)   Where the appropriate Agency gives notice to a local authority under paragraph (b) of subsection (1) above, it shall also send to the Secretary of State a copy of the notice and of the statement given under that paragraph.

(3)   Where a local authority refers a decision to the Secretary of State under subsection (1) above, it shall give notice of that fact to the relevant persons.

(4)   Where a decision of a local authority is referred to the Secretary of State under subsection (1) above, he—
    (a)   may confirm or reverse the decision with respect to the whole or any part of the land to which it relates; and
    (b)   shall give notice of his decision on the referral—
        (i)   to the relevant persons; and
        (ii)   to the local authority.

(5)   Where a decision of a local authority is referred to the Secretary of State under subsection (1) above, the decision shall not take effect until the day after that on which the Secretary of State gives the notice required by subsection (4) above to the persons there mentioned and shall then take effect as confirmed or reversed by him.

(6)   Where a decision which takes effect in accordance with subsection (5) above is to the effect that at least some land is land which is required to be designated as a special site, the notice given under subsection (4)(b) above shall have effect, as from the time when the decision takes effect, as the designation of that land as such a site.

(7)   In this section "the relevant persons" has the same meaning as in section 78C above.]

[162]

NOTES
    Commencement: 21 September 1995 (certain purposes); to be appointed (remaining purposes).
    Inserted as noted to s 78A at [159].

[78E Duty of enforcing authority to require remediation of contaminated land etc

(1)   In any case where—
  (a) any land has been designated as a special site by virtue of section 78C(7) or 78D(6) above, or
  (b) a local authority has identified any contaminated land (other than a special site) in its area,

the enforcing authority shall, in accordance with such procedure as may be prescribed and subject to the following provisions of this Part, serve on each person who is an appropriate person a notice (in this Part referred to as a "remediation notice") specifying what that person is to do by way of remediation and the periods within which he is required to do each of the things so specified.

(2)   Different remediation notices requiring the doing of different things by way of remediation may be served on different persons in consequence of the presence of different substances in, on or under any land or waters.

(3)   Where two or more persons are appropriate persons in relation to any particular thing which is to be done by way of remediation, the remediation notice served on each of them shall state the proportion, determined under section 78F(7) below, of the cost of doing that thing which each of them respectively is liable to bear.

(4)   The only things by way of remediation which the enforcing authority may do, or require to be done, under or by virtue of this Part are things which it considers reasonable, having regard to—
  (a) the cost which is likely to be involved; and
  (b) the seriousness of the harm, or pollution of controlled waters, in question.

(5)   In determining for any purpose of this Part—
  (a) what is to be done (whether by an appropriate person, the enforcing authority or any other person) by way of remediation in any particular case,
  (b) the standard to which any land is, or waters are, to be remediated pursuant to the notice, or
  (c) what is, or is not, to be regarded as reasonable for the purposes of subsection (4) above,

the enforcing authority shall have regard to any guidance issued for the purpose by the Secretary of State.

(6)   Regulations may make provision for or in connection with—
  (a) the form or content of remediation notices; or
  (b) any steps of a procedural nature which are to be taken in connection with, or in consequence of, the service of a remediation notice.]

[163]

NOTES
    Commencement: 21 September 1995 (certain purposes); to be appointed (remaining purposes).
    Inserted as noted to s 78A at [159].

[78F Determination of the appropriate person to bear responsibility for remediation

(1)   This section has effect for the purpose of determining who is the appropriate person to bear responsibility for any particular thing which the enforcing authority determines is to be done by way of remediation in any particular case.

(2)   Subject to the following provisions of this section, any person, or any of the persons, who caused or knowingly permitted the substances, or any of the substances, by reason of which the contaminated land in question is such land to be in, on or under that land is an appropriate person.

(3)   A person shall only be an appropriate person by virtue of subsection (2) above in relation to things which are to be done by way of remediation which are to any extent referable to substances which he caused or knowingly permitted to be present in, on or under the contaminated land in question.

(4)   If no person has, after reasonable inquiry, been found who is by virtue of subsection (2) above an appropriate person to bear responsibility for the things which are to be done by way of remediation, the owner or occupier for the time being of the contaminated land in question is an appropriate person.

(5)   If, in consequence of subsection (3) above, there are things which are to be done by way of remediation in relation to which no person has, after reasonable inquiry, been found who is an appropriate person by virtue of subsection (2) above, the owner or occupier for the time being of the contaminated land in question is an appropriate person in relation to those things.

(6)   Where two or more persons would, apart from this subsection, be appropriate persons in relation to any particular thing which is to be done by way of remediation, the enforcing authority shall determine in accordance with guidance issued for the purpose by the Secretary of State whether any, and if so which, of them is to be treated as not being an appropriate person in relation to that thing.

(7)   Where two or more persons are appropriate persons in relation to any particular thing which is to be done by way of remediation, they shall be liable to bear the cost of doing that thing in proportions determined by the enforcing authority in accordance with guidance issued for the purpose by the Secretary of State.

(8)   Any guidance issued for the purposes of subsection (6) or (7) above shall be issued in accordance with section 78YA below.

(9)   A person who has caused or knowingly permitted any substance ("substance A") to be in, on or under any land shall also be taken for the purposes of this section to have caused or knowingly permitted there to be in, on or under that land any substance which is there as a result of a chemical reaction or biological process affecting substance A.

(10)   A thing which is to be done by way of remediation may be regarded for the purposes of this Part as referable to the presence of any substance notwithstanding that the thing in question would not have to be done—
    (a)   in consequence only of the presence of that substance in any quantity; or
    (b)   in consequence only of the quantity of that substance which any particular person caused or knowingly permitted to be present.]

                                                                                    [164]

NOTES
    Commencement: 21 September 1995 (certain purposes); to be appointed (remaining purposes).
    Inserted as noted to s 78A at **[159]**.

[78G Grant of, and compensation for, rights of entry etc

(1) A remediation notice may require an appropriate person to do things by way of remediation, notwithstanding that he is not entitled to do those things.

(2) Any person whose consent is required before any thing required by a remediation notice may be done shall grant, or join in granting, such rights in relation to any of the relevant land or waters as will enable the appropriate person to comply with any requirements imposed by the remediation notice.

(3) Before serving a remediation notice, the enforcing authority shall reasonably endeavour to consult every person who appears to the authority—
  (a) to be the owner or occupier of any of the relevant land or waters, and
  (b) to be a person who might be required by subsection (2) above to grant, or join in granting, any rights,
concerning the rights which that person may be so required to grant.

(4) Subsection (3) above shall not preclude the service of a remediation notice in any case where it appears to the enforcing authority that the contaminated land in question is in such a condition, by reason of substances in, on or under the land, that there is imminent danger of serious harm, or serious pollution of controlled waters, being caused.

(5) A person who grants, or joins in granting, any rights pursuant to subsection (2) above shall be entitled, on making an application within such period as may be prescribed and in such manner as may be prescribed to such person as may be prescribed, to be paid by the appropriate person compensation of such amount as may be determined in such manner as may be prescribed.

(6) Without prejudice to the generality of the regulations that may be made by virtue of subsection (5) above, regulations by virtue of that subsection may make such provision in relation to compensation under this section as may be made by regulations by virtue of subsection (4) of section 35A above in relation to compensation under that section.

(7) In this section, "relevant land or waters" means—
  (a) the contaminated land in question;
  (b) any controlled waters affected by that land; or
  (c) any land adjoining or adjacent to that land or those waters.]

[165]

NOTES
  Commencement: 21 September 1995 (certain purposes); to be appointed (remaining purposes).
  Inserted as noted to s 78A at **[159]**.

[78H Restrictions and prohibitions on serving remediation notices

(1) Before serving a remediation notice, the enforcing authority shall reasonably endeavour to consult—
  (a) the person on whom the notice is to be served,
  (b) the owner of any land to which the notice relates,
  (c) any person who appears to that authority to be in occupation of the whole or any part of the land, and
  (d) any person of such other description as may be prescribed,
concerning what is to be done by way of remediation.

(2) Regulations may make provision for, or in connection with, steps to be taken for the purposes of subsection (1) above.

(3) No remediation notice shall be served on any person by reference to any contaminated land during any of the following periods, that is to say—

(a) the period—
    (i) beginning with the identification of the contaminated land in question pursuant to section 78B(1) above, and
    (ii) ending with the expiration of the period of three months beginning with the day on which the notice required by subsection (3)(d) or, as the case may be, (4) of section 78B above is given to that person in respect of that land;

(b) if a decision falling within paragraph (b) of section 78C(1) above is made in relation to the contaminated land in question, the period beginning with the making of the decision and ending with the expiration of the period of three months beginning with—
    (i) in a case where the decision is not referred to the Secretary of State under section 78D above, the day on which the notice required by section 78C(6) above is given, or
    (ii) in a case where the decision is referred to the Secretary of State under section 78D above, the day on which he gives the notice required by subsection (4)(b) of that section;

(c) if the appropriate Agency gives a notice under subsection (4) of section 78C above to a local authority in relation to the contaminated land in question, the period beginning with the day on which that notice is given and ending with the expiration of the period of three months beginning with—
    (i) in a case where notice is given under subsection (6) of that section, the day on which that notice is given;
    (ii) in a case where the authority makes a decision falling within subsection (5)(b) of that section and the appropriate Agency fails to give notice under paragraph (b) of section 78D(1) above, the day following the expiration of the period of twenty-one days mentioned in that paragraph; or
    (iii) in a case where the authority makes a decision falling within section 78C(5)(b) above which is referred to the Secretary of State under section 78D above, the day on which the Secretary of State gives the notice required by subsection (4)(b) of that section.

(4) Neither subsection (1) nor subsection (3) above shall preclude the service of a remediation notice in any case where it appears to the enforcing authority that the land in question is in such a condition, by reason of substances in, on or under the land, that there is imminent danger of serious harm, or serious pollution of controlled waters, being caused.

(5) The enforcing authority shall not serve a remediation notice on a person if and so long as any one or more of the following conditions is for the time being satisfied in the particular case, that is to say—
(a) the authority is satisfied, in consequence of section 78E(4) and (5) above, that there is nothing by way of remediation which could be specified in a remediation notice served on that person;
(b) the authority is satisfied that appropriate things are being, or will be, done by way of remediation without the service of a remediation notice on that person;
(c) it appears to the authority that the person on whom the notice would be served is the authority itself; or
(d) the authority is satisfied that the powers conferred on it by section 78N below to do what is appropriate by way of remediation are exercisable.

(6) Where the enforcing authority is precluded by virtue of section 78E(4) or (5) above from specifying in a remediation notice any particular thing by way of remediation which it would otherwise have specified in such a notice, the authority shall prepare and publish a document (in this Part referred to as a "remediation declaration") which shall record—

(a) the reasons why the authority would have specified that thing; and
(b) the grounds on which the authority is satisfied that it is precluded from specifying that thing in such a notice.

(7) In any case where the enforcing authority is precluded, by virtue of paragraph (b), (c) or (d) of subsection (5) above, from serving a remediation notice, the responsible person shall prepare and publish a document (in this Part referred to as a "remediation statement") which shall record—
(a) the things which are being, have been, or are expected to be, done by way of remediation in the particular case;
(b) the name and address of the person who is doing, has done, or is expected to do, each of those things; and
(c) the periods within which each of those things is being, or is expected to be, done.

(8) For the purposes of subsection (7) above, the "responsible person" is—
(a) in a case where the condition in paragraph (b) of subsection (5) above is satisfied, the person who is doing or has done, or who the enforcing authority is satisfied will do, the things there mentioned; or
(b) in a case where the condition in paragraph (c) or (d) of that subsection is satisfied, the enforcing authority.

(9) If a person who is required by virtue of subsection (8)(a) above to prepare and publish a remediation statement fails to do so within a reasonable time after the date on which a remediation notice specifying the things there mentioned could, apart from subsection (5) above, have been served, the enforcing authority may itself prepare and publish the statement and may recover its reasonable costs of doing so from that person.

(10) Where the enforcing authority has been precluded by virtue only of subsection (5) above from serving a remediation notice on an appropriate person but—
(a) none of the conditions in that subsection is for the time being satisfied in the particular case, and
(b) the authority is not precluded by any other provision of this Part from serving a remediation notice on that appropriate person,

the authority shall serve a remediation notice on that person; and any such notice may be so served without any further endeavours by the authority to consult persons pursuant to subsection (1) above, if and to the extent that that person has bean consulted pursuant to that subsection concerning the things which will be specified in the notice.]

[166]

NOTES
   Commencement: 21 September 1995 (certain purposes); to be appointed (remaining purposes).
   Inserted as noted to s 78A at [159].

[78J Restrictions on liability relating to the pollution of controlled waters

(1) This section applies where any land is contaminated land by virtue of paragraph (b) of subsection (2) of section 78A above (whether or not the land is also contaminated land by virtue of paragraph (a) of that subsection).

(2) Where this section applies, no remediation notice given in consequence of the land in question being contaminated land shall require a person who is an appropriate person by virtue of section 78F(4) or (5) above to do anything by way of remediation to that or any other land, or any waters, which he could not have been required to do by such a notice had paragraph (b) of section 78A(2) above (and all other references to pollution of controlled waters) been omitted from this Part.

(3)   If, in a case where this section applies, a person permits, has permitted, or might permit, water from an abandoned mine or part of a mine—
   (a) to enter any controlled waters, or
   (b) to reach a place from which it is or, as the case may be, was likely, in the opinion of the enforcing authority, to enter such waters,
no remediation notice shall require him in consequence to do anything by way of remediation (whether to the contaminated land in question or to any other land or waters) which he could not have been required to do by such a notice had paragraph (b) of section 78A(2) above (and all other references to pollution of controlled waters) been omitted from this Part.

(4)   Subsection (3) above shall not apply to the owner or former operator of any mine or part of a mine if the mine or part in question became abandoned after 31st December 1999.

(5)   In determining for the purposes of subsection (4) above whether a mine or part of a mine became abandoned before, on or after 31st December 1999 in a case where the mine or part has become abandoned on two or more occasions, of which—
   (a) at least one falls on or before that date, and
   (b) at least one falls after that date,
the mine or part shall be regarded as becoming abandoned after that date (but without prejudice to the operation of subsection (3) above in relation to that mine or part at, or in relation to, any time before the first of those occasions which falls after that date).

(6)   Where, immediately before a part of a mine becomes abandoned, that part is the only part of the mine not falling to be regarded as abandoned for the time being, the abandonment of that part shall not be regarded for the purposes of subsection (4) or (5) above as constituting the abandonment of the mine, but only of that part of it.

(7)   Nothing in subsection (2) or (3) above prevents the enforcing authority from doing anything by way of remediation under section 78N below which it could have done apart from that subsection, but the authority shall not be entitled under section 78P below to recover from any person any part of the cost incurred by the authority in doing by way of remediation anything which it is precluded by subsection (2) or (3) above from requiring that person to do.

(8)   In this section "mine" has the same meaning as in the Mines and Quarries Act 1954.]

[167]

NOTES
   Commencement: 21 September 1995 (certain purposes); to be appointed (remaining purposes).
   Inserted as noted to s 78A at **[159]**.

[78K Liability in respect of contaminating substances which escape to other land

(1)   A person who has caused or knowingly permitted any substances to be in, on or under any land shall also be taken for the purposes of this Part to have caused or, as the case may be, knowingly permitted those substances to be in, on or under any other land to which they appear to have escaped.

(2)   Subsections (3) and (4) below apply in any case where it appears that any substances are or have been in, on or under any land (in this section referred to as "land A") as a result of their escape, whether directly or indirectly, from other land in, on or under which a person caused or knowingly permitted them to be.

(3)   Where this subsection applies, no remediation notice shall require a person—
   (a) who is the owner or occupier of land A, and

(b) who has not caused or knowingly permitted the substances in question to be in, on or under that land,

to do anything by way of remediation to any land or waters (other than land or waters of which he is the owner or occupier) in consequence of land A appearing to be in such a condition, by reason of the presence of those substances in, on or under it, that significant harm is being caused, or there is a significant possibility of such harm being caused, or that pollution of controlled waters is being, or is likely to be caused.

(4) Where this subsection applies, no remediation notice shall require a person—
   (a) who is the owner or occupier of land A, and
   (b) who has not caused or knowingly permitted the substances in question to be in, on or under that land,

to do anything by way of remediation in consequence of any further land in, on or under which those substances or any of them appear to be or to have been present as a result of their escape from land A ("land B") appearing to be in such a condition; by reason of the presence of those substances in, on or under it, that significant harm is being caused, or there is a significant possibility of such harm being caused, or that pollution of controlled waters is being, or is likely to be caused, unless he is also the owner or occupier of land B.

(5) In any case where—
   (a) a person ("person A") has caused or knowingly permitted any substances to be in, on, or under any land,
   (b) another person ("person B") who has not caused or knowingly permitted those substances to be in, on, or under that land becomes the owner or occupier of that land, and
   (c) the substances, or any of the substances, mentioned in paragraph (a) above appear to have escaped to other land,

no remediation notice shall require person B to do anything by way of remediation to that other land in consequence of the apparent acts or omissions of person A, except to the extent that person B caused or knowingly permitted the escape.

(6) Nothing in subsection (3), (4) or (5) above prevents the enforcing authority from doing anything by way of remediation under section 78N below which it could have done apart from that subsection, but the authority shall not be entitled under section 78P below to recover from any person any part of the cost incurred by the authority in doing by way of remediation anything which it is precluded by subsection (3), (4) or (5) above from requiring that person to do.

(7) In this section, "appear" means appear to the enforcing authority, and cognate expressions shall be construed accordingly.]

[168]

NOTES
   Commencement: 21 September 1995 (certain purposes); to be appointed (remaining purposes).
   Inserted as noted to s 78A at **[159]**.

[78L Appeals against remediation notices

(1) A person on whom a remediation notice is served may, within the period of twenty-one days beginning with the day on which the notice is served, appeal against the notice—
   (a) if it was served by a local authority, to a magistrates' court or, in Scotland, to the sheriff by way of summary application; or
   (b) if it was served by the appropriate Agency, to the Secretary of State;

and in the following provisions of this section "the appellate authority" means the magistrates' court, the sheriff or the Secretary of State, as the case may be.

(2)   On any appeal under subsection (1) above the appellate authority—
   (a) shall quash the notice, if it is satisfied that there is a material defect in the notice; but
   (b) subject to that, may confirm the remediation notice, with or without modification, or quash it.

(3)   Where an appellate authority confirms a remediation notice, with or without modification, it may extend the period specified in the notice for doing what the notice requires to be done.

(4)   Regulations may make provision with respect to—
   (a) the grounds on which appeals under subsection (1) above may be made;
   (b) the cases in which, grounds on which, court or tribunal to which, or person at whose instance, an appeal against a decision of a magistrates' court or sheriff court in pursuance of an appeal under subsection (1) above shall lie; or
   (c) the procedure on an appeal under subsection (1) above or on an appeal by virtue of paragraph (b) above.

(5)   Regulations under subsection (4) above may (among other things)—
   (a) include provisions comparable to those in section 290 of the Public Health Act 1936 (appeals against notices requiring the execution of works);
   (b) prescribe the cases in which a remediation notice is, or is not, to be suspended until the appeal is decided, or until some other stage in the proceedings;
   (c) prescribe the cases in which the decision on an appeal may in some respects be less favourable to the appellant than the remediation notice against which he is appealing;
   (d) prescribe the cases in which the appellant may claim that a remediation notice should have been served on some other person and prescribe the procedure to be followed in those cases;
   (e) make provision as respects—
      (i)   the particulars to be included in the notice of appeal;
      (ii) the persons on whom notice of appeal is to be served and the particulars, if any, which are to accompany the notice; and
      (iii) the abandonment of an appeal;
   (f) make different provision for different cases or classes of case.

(6)   This section, so far as relating to appeals to the Secretary of State, is subject to section 114 of the Environment Act 1995 (delegation or reference of appeals etc).]

[169]

NOTES

Commencement: 21 September 1995 (certain purposes); to be appointed (remaining purposes).

Inserted as noted to s 78A at **[159]**.

[78M Offences of not complying with a remediation notice

(1)   If a person on whom an enforcing authority serves a remediation notice fails, without reasonable excuse, to comply with any of the requirements of the notice, he shall be guilty of an offence.

(2)   Where the remediation notice in question is one which was required by section 78E(3) above to state, in relation to the requirement which has not been complied with, the proportion of the cost involved which the person charged with the offence is liable to bear, it shall be a defence for that person to prove that the only reason why he has not complied with the requirement is that one or more of the other persons who are liable to bear a proportion of that cost refused, or was not able, to comply with the requirement.

(3) Except in a case falling within subsection (4) below, a person who commits an offence under subsection (1) above shall be liable, on summary conviction, to a fine not exceeding level 5 on the standard scale and to a further fine of an amount equal to one-tenth of level 5 on the standard scale for each day on which the failure continues after conviction of the offence and before the enforcing authority has begun to exercise its powers by virtue of section 78N(3)(c) below.

(4) A person who commits an offence under subsection (1) above in a case where the contaminated land to which the remediation notice relates is industrial, trade or business premises shall be liable on summary conviction to a fine not exceeding £20,000 or such greater sum as the Secretary of State may from time to time by order substitute and to a further fine of an amount equal to one-tenth of that sum for each day on which the failure continues after conviction of the offence and before the enforcing authority has begun to exercise its powers by virtue of section 78N(3)(c) below.

(5) If the enforcing authority is of the opinion that proceedings for an offence under this section would afford an ineffectual remedy against a person who has failed to comply with any of the requirements of a remediation notice which that authority has served on him, that authority may take proceedings in the High Court or, in Scotland, in any court of competent jurisdiction, for the purpose of securing compliance with the remediation notice.

(6) In this section, "industrial, trade or business premises" means premises used for any industrial, trade or business purposes or premises not so used on which matter is burnt in connection with any industrial, trade or business process, and premises are used for industrial purposes where they are used for the purposes of any treatment or process as well as where they are used for the purpose of manufacturing.

(7) No order shall be made under subsection (4) above unless a draft of the order has been laid before, and approved by a resolution of, each House of Parliament.]

[170]

NOTES

Commencement: 21 September 1995 (certain purposes); to be appointed (remaining purposes).
Inserted as noted to s 78A at **[159]**.

[78N Powers of the enforcing authority to carry out remediation

(1) Where this section applies, the enforcing authority shall itself have power, in a case falling within paragraph (a) or (b) of section 78E(1) above, to do what is appropriate by way of remediation to the relevant land or waters.

(2) Subsection (1) above shall not confer power on the enforcing authority to do anything by way of remediation if the authority would, in the particular case, be precluded by section 78YB below from serving a remediation notice requiring that thing to be done.

(3) This section applies in each of the following cases, that is to say—
   (a) where the enforcing authority considers it necessary to do anything itself by way of remediation for the purpose of preventing the occurrence of any serious harm, or serious pollution of controlled waters, of which there is imminent danger;
   (b) where an appropriate person has entered into a written agreement with the enforcing authority for that authority to do, at the cost of that person, that which he would otherwise be required to do under this Part by way of remediation;
   (c) where a person on whom the enforcing authority serves a remediation notice fails to comply with any of the requirements of the notice;
   (d) where the enforcing authority is precluded by section 78J or 78K above from including something by way of remediation in a remediation notice;

(e) where the enforcing authority considers that, were it to do some particular thing by way of remediation, it would decide, by virtue of subsection (2) of section 78P below or any guidance issued under that subsection,—
  (i) not to seek to recover under subsection (1) of that section any of the reasonable cost incurred by it in doing that thing; or
  (ii) to seek so to recover only a portion of that cost;
(f) where no person has, after reasonable inquiry, been found who is an appropriate person in relation to any particular thing.

(4)   Subject to section 78E(4) and (5) above, for the purposes of this section, the things which it is appropriate for the enforcing authority to do by way of remediation are—
  (a) in a case falling within paragraph (a) of subsection (3) above, anything by way of remediation which the enforcing authority considers necessary for the purpose mentioned in that paragraph;
  (b) in a case falling within paragraph (b) of that subsection, anything specified in, or determined under, the agreement mentioned in that paragraph;
  (c) in a case falling within paragraph (c) of that subsection, anything which the person mentioned in that paragraph was required to do by virtue of the remediation notice;
  (d) in a case falling within paragraph (d) of that subsection, anything by way of remediation which the enforcing authority is precluded by section 78J or 78K above from including in a remediation notice;
  (e) in a case falling within paragraph (e) or (f) of that subsection, the particular thing mentioned in the paragraph in question.

(5)   In this section "the relevant land or waters" means—
  (a) the contaminated land in question;
  (b) any controlled waters affected by that land; or
  (c) any land adjoining or adjacent to that land or those waters.]

[171]

___

NOTES
    Commencement: 21 September 1995 (certain purposes); to be appointed (remaining purposes).
    Inserted as noted to s 78A at **[159]**.
___

[78P Recovery of, and security for, the cost of remediation by the enforcing authority

(1)   Where, by virtue of section 78N(3)(a), (c), (e) or (f) above, the enforcing authority does any particular thing by way of remediation, it shall be entitled, subject to sections 78J(7) and 78K(6) above, to recover the reasonable cost incurred in doing it from the appropriate person or, if there are two or more appropriate persons in relation to the thing in question, from those persons in proportions determined pursuant to section 78F(7) above.

(2)   In deciding whether to recover the cost, and, if so, how much of the cost, which it is entitled to recover under subsection (1) above, the enforcing authority shall have regard—
  (a) to any hardship which the recovery may cause to the person from whom the cost is recoverable; and
  (b) to any guidance issued by the Secretary of State for the purposes of this subsection.

(3)   Subsection (4) below shall apply in any case where—
  (a) any cost is recoverable under subsection (1) above from a person—
    (i) who is the owner of any premises which consist of or include the contaminated land in question; and
    (ii) who caused or knowingly permitted the substances, or any of the substances, by reason of which the land is contaminated land to be in, on or under the land; and

    (b) the enforcing authority serves a notice under this subsection (in this Part referred to as a "charging notice") on that person.

(4)   Where this subsection applies—
    (a) the cost shall carry interest, at such reasonable rate as the enforcing authority may determine, from the date of service of the notice until the whole amount is paid; and
    (b) subject to the following provisions of this section, the cost and accrued interest shall be a charge on the premises mentioned in subsection (3)(a)(i) above.

(5)   A charging notice shall—
    (a) specify the amount of the cost which the enforcing authority claims is recoverable;
    (b) state the effect of subsection (4) above and the rate of interest determined by the authority under that subsection; and
    (c) state the effect of subsections (7) and (8) below.

(6)   On the date on which an enforcing authority serves a charging notice on a person, the authority shall also serve a copy of the notice on every other person who, to the knowledge of the authority, has an interest in the premises capable of being affected by the charge.

(7)   Subject to any order under subsection (9)(b) or (c) below, the amount of any cost specified in a charging notice and the accrued interest shall be a charge on the premises—
    (a) as from the end of the period of twenty-one days beginning with the service of the charging notice, or
    (b) where an appeal is brought under subsection (8) below, as from the final determination or (as the case may be) the withdrawal, of the appeal,
until the cost and interest are recovered.

(8)   A person served with a charging notice or a copy of a charging notice may appeal against the notice to a county court within the period of twenty-one days beginning with the date of service.

(9)   On an appeal under subsection (8) above, the court may—
    (a) confirm the notice without modification;
    (b) order that the notice is to have effect with the substitution of a different amount for the amount originally specified in it; or
    (c) order that the notice is to be of no effect.

(10) Regulations may make provision with respect to—
    (a) the grounds on which appeals under this section may be made; or
    (b) the procedure on any such appeal.

(11) An enforcing authority shall, for the purpose of enforcing a charge under this section, have all the same powers and remedies under the Law of Property Act 1925, and otherwise, as if it were a mortgagee by deed having powers of sale and lease, of accepting surrenders of leases and of appointing a receiver.

(12) Where any cost is a charge on premises under this section, the enforcing authority may by order declare the cost to be payable with interest by instalments within the specified period until the whole amount is paid.

(13) In subsection (12) above—
    "interest" means interest at the rate determined by the enforcing authority under subsection (4) above; and
    "the specified period" means such period of thirty years or less from the date of service of the charging notice as is specified in the order.

(14)   Subsections (3) to (13) above do not extend to Scotland.]

[172]

NOTES
   Commencement: 21 September 1995 (certain purposes); to be appointed (remaining purposes).
   Inserted as noted to s 78A at **[159]**.

[78Q Special sites

(1)   If, in a case where a local authority has served a remediation notice, the contaminated land in question becomes a special site, the appropriate Agency may adopt the remediation notice and, if it does so,—
   (a)   it shall give notice of its decision to adopt the remediation notice to the appropriate person and to the local authority;
   (b)   the remediation notice shall have effect, as from the time at which the appropriate Agency decides to adopt it, as a remediation notice given by that Agency; and
   (c)   the validity of the remediation notice shall not be affected by—
        (i)   the contaminated land having become a special site;
        (ii)   the adoption of the remediation notice by the appropriate Agency; or
        (iii)   anything in paragraph (b) above.

(2)   Where a local authority has, by virtue of section 78N above, begun to do any thing, or any series of things, by way of remediation—
   (a)   the authority may continue doing that thing, or that series of things, by virtue of that section, notwithstanding that the contaminated land in question becomes a special site; and
   (b)   section 78P above shall apply in relation to the reasonable cost incurred by the authority in doing that thing or those things as if that authority were the enforcing authority.

(3)   If and so long as any land is a special site, the appropriate Agency may from time to time inspect that land for the purpose of keeping its condition under review.

(4)   If it appears to the appropriate Agency that a special site is no longer land which is required to be designated as such a site, the appropriate Agency may give notice—
   (a)   to the Secretary of State, and
   (b)   to the local authority in whose area the site is situated,
terminating the designation of the land in question as a special site as from such date as may be specified in the notice.

(5)   A notice under subsection (4) above shall not prevent the land, or any of the land, to which the notice relates being designated as a special site on a subsequent occasion.

(6)   In exercising its functions under subsection (3) or (4) above, the appropriate Agency shall act in accordance with any guidance given for the purpose by the Secretary of State.]

[173]

NOTES
   Commencement: 21 September 1995 (certain purposes); to be appointed (remaining purposes).
   Inserted as noted to s 78A at **[159]**.

[78R Registers

(1)   Every enforcing authority shall maintain a register containing prescribed particulars of or relating to—
   (a)   remediation notices served by that authority;

(b) appeals against any such remediation notices;

(c) remediation statements or remediation declarations prepared and published under section 78H above;

(d) in relation to an enforcing authority in England and Wales, appeals against charging notices served by that authority;

(e) notices under subsection (1)(b) or (5)(a) of section 78C above which have effect by virtue of subsection (7) of that section as the designation of any land as a special site;

(f) notices under subsection (4)(b) of section 78D above which have effect by virtue of subsection (6) of that section as the designation of any land as a special site;

(g) notices given by or to the enforcing authority under section 78Q(4) above terminating the designation of any land as a special site;

(h) notifications given to that authority by persons—

    (i) on whom a remediation notice has been served, or

    (ii) who are or were required by virtue of section 78H(8)(a) above to prepare and publish a remediation statement,

of what they claim has been done by them by way of remediation;

(j) notifications given to that authority by owners or occupiers of land—

    (i) in respect of which a remediation notice has been served, or

    (ii) in respect of which a remediation statement has been prepared and published,

of what they claim has been done on the land in question by way of remediation;

(k) convictions for such offences under section 78M above as may be prescribed;

(l) such other matters relating to contaminated land as may be prescribed;

but that duty is subject to sections 78S and 78T below.

(2) The form of, and the descriptions of information to be contained in, notifications for the purposes of subsection (1)(h) or (j) above may be prescribed by the Secretary of State.

(3) No entry made in a register by virtue of subsection (1)(h) or (j) above constitutes a representation by the body maintaining the register or, in a case where the entry is made by virtue of subsection (6) below, the authority which sent the copy of the particulars in question pursuant to subsection (4) or (5) below—

(a) that what is stated in the entry to have been done has in fact been done; or

(b) as to the manner in which it has been done.

(4) Where any particulars are entered on a register maintained under this section by the appropriate Agency, the appropriate Agency shall send a copy of those particulars to the local authority in whose area is situated the land to which the particulars relate.

(5) In any case where—

(a) any land is treated by virtue of section 78X(2) below as situated in the area of a local authority other than the local authority in whose area it is in fact situated, and

(b) any particulars relating to that land are entered on the register maintained under this section by the local authority in whose area the land is so treated as situated,

that authority shall send a copy of those particulars to the local authority in whose area the land is in fact situated.

(6) Where a local authority receives a copy of any particulars sent to it pursuant to subsection (4) or (5) above, it shall enter those particulars on the register maintained by it under this section.

(7)   Where information of any description is excluded by virtue of section 78T below from any register maintained under this section, a statement shall be entered in the register indicating the existence of information of that description.

(8)   It shall be the duty of each enforcing authority—
  (a) to secure that the registers maintained by it under this section are available, at all reasonable times, for inspection by the public free of charge; and
  (b) to afford to members of the public facilities for obtaining copies of entries, on payment of reasonable charges;

and, for the purposes of this subsection, places may be prescribed by the Secretary of State at which any such registers or facilities as are mentioned in paragraph (a) or (b) above are to be available or afforded to the public in pursuance of the paragraph in question.

(9)   Registers under this section may be kept in any form.]

[174]

NOTES

Commencement: 21 September 1995 (certain purposes); to be appointed (remaining purposes).
Inserted as noted to s 78A at **[159]**.

[78S Exclusion from registers of information affecting national security

(1)   No information shall be included in a register maintained under section 78R above if and so long as, in the opinion of the Secretary of State, the inclusion in the register of that information, or information of that description, would be contrary to the interests of national security.

(2)   The Secretary of State may, for the purpose of securing the exclusion from registers of information to which subsection (1) above applies, give to enforcing authorities directions—
  (a) specifying information, or descriptions of information, to be excluded from their registers; or
  (b) specifying descriptions of information to be referred to the Secretary of State for his determination;

and no information referred to the Secretary of State in pursuance of paragraph (b) above shall be included in any such register until the Secretary of State determines that it should be so included.

(3)   The enforcing authority shall notify the Secretary of State of any information which it excludes from the register in pursuance of directions under subsection (2) above.

(4)   A person may, as respects any information which appears to him to be information to which subsection (1) above may apply, give a notice to the Secretary of State specifying the information and indicating its apparent nature; and, if he does so—
  (a) he shall notify the enforcing authority that he has done so; and
  (b) no information so notified to the Secretary of State shall be included in any such register until the Secretary of State has determined that it should be so included.]

[175]

NOTES

Commencement: 21 September 1995 (certain purposes); to be appointed (remaining purposes).
Inserted as noted to s 78A at **[159]**.

[78T Exclusion from registers of certain confidential information

(1)   No information relating to the affairs of any individual or business shall be included in a register maintained under section 78R above, without the consent of that individual or the person for the time being carrying on that business, if and so long as the information—
  (a) is, in relation to him, commercially confidential; and
  (b) is not required to be included in the register in pursuance of directions under subsection (7) below;

but information is not commercially confidential for the purposes of this section unless it is determined under this section to be so by the enforcing authority or, on appeal, by the Secretary of State.

(2)   Where it appears to an enforcing authority that any information which has been obtained by the authority under or by virtue of any provision of this Part might be commercially confidential, the authority shall—
  (a) give to the person to whom or whose business it relates notice that that information is required to be included in the register unless excluded under this section; and
  (b) give him a reasonable opportunity—
     (i) of objecting to the inclusion of the information on the ground that it is commercially confidential; and
     (ii) of making representations to the authority for the purpose of justifying any such objection;

and, if any representations are made, the enforcing authority shall, having taken the representations into account, determine whether the information is or is not commercially confidential.

(3)   Where, under subsection (2) above, an authority determines that information is not commercially confidential—
  (a) the information shall not be entered in the register until the end of the period of twenty-one days beginning with the date on which the determination is notified to the person concerned;
  (b) that person may appeal to the Secretary of State against the decision;

and, where an appeal is brought in respect of any information, the information shall not be entered in the register until the end of the period of seven days following the day on which the appeal is finally determined or withdrawn.

(4)   An appeal under subsection (3) above shall, if either party to the appeal so requests or the Secretary of State so decides, take or continue in the form of a hearing (which must be held in private).

(5)   Subsection (10) of section 15 above shall apply in relation to an appeal under subsection (3) above as it applies in relation to an appeal under that section.

(6)   Subsection (3) above is subject to section 114 of the Environment Act 1995 (delegation or reference of appeals etc).

(7)   The Secretary of State may give to the enforcing authorities directions as to specified information, or descriptions of information, which the public interest requires to be included in registers maintained under section 78R above notwithstanding that the information may be commercially confidential.

(8)   Information excluded from a register shall be treated as ceasing to be commercially confidential for the purposes of this section at the expiry of the period of four years beginning with the date of the determination by virtue of which it was excluded; but the person who furnished it may apply to the authority for the information to remain excluded from the register on the ground that it is still commercially confidential and the authority shall determine whether or not that is the case.

(9)   Subsections (3) to (6) above shall apply in relation to a determination under subsection (8) above as they apply in relation to a determination under subsection (2) above.

(10) Information is, for the purposes of any determination under this section, commercially confidential, in relation to any individual or person, if its being contained in the register would prejudice to an unreasonable degree the commercial interests of that individual or person.

(11) For the purposes of subsection (10) above, there shall be disregarded any prejudice to the commercial interests of any individual or person so far as relating only to the value of the contaminated land in question or otherwise to the ownership or occupation of that land.]

[176]

NOTES
Commencement: 21 September 1995 (certain purposes); to be appointed (remaining purposes).
Inserted as noted to s 78A at **[159]**.

[78U Reports by the appropriate Agency on the state of contaminated land

(1)   The appropriate Agency shall—
   (a) from time to time, or
   (b) if the Secretary of State at any time so requests,
prepare and publish a report on the state of contaminated land in England and Wales or in Scotland, as the case may be.

(2)   A local authority shall, at the written request of the appropriate Agency, furnish the appropriate Agency with such information to which this subsection applies as the appropriate Agency may require for the purpose of enabling it to perform its functions under subsection (1) above.

(3)   The information to which subsection (2) above applies is such information as the local authority may have, or may reasonably be expected to obtain, with respect to the condition of contaminated land in its area, being information which the authority has acquired or may acquire in the exercise of its functions under this Part.]

[177]

NOTES
Commencement: to be appointed.
Inserted as noted to s 78A at **[159]**.

[78V Site-specific guidance by the appropriate Agency concerning contaminated land

(1)   The appropriate Agency may issue guidance to any local authority with respect to the exercise or performance of the authority's powers or duties under this Part in relation to any particular contaminated land; and in exercising or performing those powers or duties in relation to that land the authority shall have regard to any such guidance so issued.

(2)   If and to the extent that any guidance issued under subsection (1) above to a local authority is inconsistent with any guidance issued under this Part by the Secretary of State, the local authority shall disregard the guidance under that subsection.

(3)   A local authority shall, at the written request of the appropriate Agency, furnish the appropriate Agency with such information to which this subsection applies as the appropriate Agency may require for the purpose of enabling it to issue guidance for the purposes of subsection (1) above.

(4)   The information to which subsection (3) above applies is such information as the local authority may have, or may reasonably be expected to obtain, with respect to any contaminated land in its area, being information which the authority has acquired, or may acquire, in the exercise of its functions under this Part.]

[178]

NOTES
   Commencement: 21 September 1995 (certain purposes); to be appointed (remaining purposes).
   Inserted as noted to s 78A at **[159]**.

[78W The appropriate Agency to have regard to guidance given by the Secretary of State

(1)   The Secretary of State may issue guidance to the appropriate Agency with respect to the exercise or performance of that Agency's powers or duties under this Part; and in exercising or performing those powers or duties the appropriate Agency shall have regard to any such guidance so issued.

(2)   The duty imposed on the appropriate Agency by subsection (1) above is without prejudice to any duty imposed by any other provision of this Part on that Agency to act in accordance with guidance issued by the Secretary of State.]

[179]

NOTES
   Commencement: 21 September 1995 (certain purposes); to be appointed (remaining purposes).
   Inserted as noted to s 78A at **[159]**.

[78X Supplementary provisions

(1)   Where it appears to a local authority that two or more different sites, when considered together, are in such a condition, by reason of substances in, on or under the land, that—
   (a) significant harm is being caused or there is a significant possibility of such harm being caused, or
   (b) pollution of controlled waters is being, or is likely to be, caused,
this Part shall apply in relation to each of those sites, whether or not the condition of the land at any of them, when considered alone, appears to the authority to be such that significant harm is being caused, or there is a significant possibility of such harm being caused, or that pollution of controlled waters is being or is likely to be caused.

(2)   Where it appears to a local authority that any land outside, but adjoining or adjacent to, its area is in such a condition, by reason of substances in, on or under the land, that significant harm is being caused, or there is a significant possibility of such harm being caused, or that pollution of controlled waters is being, or is likely to be, caused within its area—
   (a) the authority may, in exercising its functions under this Part, treat that land as if it were land situated within its area; and
   (b) except in this subsection, any reference—
      (i) to land within the area of a local authority, or
      (ii) to the local authority in whose area any land is situated,
      shall be construed accordingly;
but this subsection is without prejudice to the functions of the local authority in whose area the land is in fact situated.

(3)   A person acting in a relevant capacity—
   (a) shall not thereby be personally liable, under this Part, to bear the whole or any part of the cost of doing any thing by way of remediation, unless that thing is to any extent referable to substances whose presence in, on or

under the contaminated land in question is a result of any act done or omission made by him which it was unreasonable for a person acting in that capacity to do or make; and

(b) shall not thereby be guilty of an offence under or by virtue of section 78M above unless the requirement which has not been complied with is a requirement to do some particular thing for which he is personally liable to bear the whole or any part of the cost.

(4) In subsection (3) above, "person acting in a relevant capacity" means—
   (a) a person acting as an insolvency practitioner, within the meaning of section 388 of the Insolvency Act 1986 (including that section as it applies in relation to an insolvent partnership by virtue of any order made under section 421 of that Act);
   (b) the official receiver acting in a capacity in which he would be regarded as acting as an insolvency practitioner within the meaning of section 388 of the Insolvency Act 1986 if subsection (5) of that section were disregarded;
   (c) the official receiver acting as receiver or manager;
   (d) a person acting as a special manager under section 177 or 370 of the Insolvency Act 1986;
   (e) (*applies to Scotland only*);
   (f) a person acting as a receiver or receiver and manager—
      (i) under or by virtue of any enactment; or
      (ii) by virtue of his appointment as such by an order of a court or by any other instrument.

(5) Regulations may make different provision for different cases or circumstances.]

[180]

NOTES
Commencement: 21 September 1995 (certain purposes); to be appointed (remaining purposes).
Inserted as noted to s 78A at **[159]**.

[78Y Application to the Isles of Scilly

(1) Subject to the provisions of any order under this section, this Part shall not apply in relation to the Isles of Scilly.

(2) The Secretary of State may, after consultation with the Council of the Isles of Scilly, by order provide for the application of any provisions of this Part to the Isles of Scilly; and any such order may provide for the application of those provisions to those Isles with such modifications as may be specified in the order.

(3) An order under this section may—
   (a) make different provision for different cases, including different provision in relation to different persons, circumstances or localities; and
   (b) contain such supplemental, consequential and transitional provision as the Secretary of State considers appropriate, including provision saving provision repealed by or under any enactment.]

[181]

NOTES
Commencement: 21 September 1995 (certain purposes); to be appointed (remaining purposes).
Inserted as noted to s 78A at **[159]**.

[78YA Supplementary provisions with respect to guidance by the Secretary of State

(1) Any power of the Secretary of State to issue guidance under this Part shall only be exercisable after consultation with the appropriate Agency and such other

bodies or persons as he may consider it appropriate to consult in relation to the guidance in question.

(2)   A draft of any guidance proposed to be issued under section 78A(2) or (5), 78B(2) or 78F(6) or (7) above shall be laid before each House of Parliament and the guidance shall not be issued until after the period of 40 days beginning with the day on which the draft was so laid or, if the draft is laid on different days, the later of the two days.

(3)   If, within the period mentioned in subsection (2) above, either House resolves that the guidance, the draft of which was laid before it, should not be issued, the Secretary of State shall not issue that guidance.

(4)   In reckoning any period of 40 days for the purposes of subsection (2) or (3) above, no account shall be taken of any time during which Parliament is dissolved or prorogued or during which both Houses are adjourned for more than four days.

(5)   The Secretary of State shall arrange for any guidance issued by him under this Part to be published in such manner as he considers appropriate.]

[182]

NOTES
Commencement: 21 September 1995.
Inserted as noted to s 78A at **[159]**.

[78YB   Interaction of this Part with other enactments

(1)   A remediation notice shall not be served if and to the extent that it appears to the enforcing authority that the powers of the appropriate Agency under section 27 above may be exercised in relation to—
    (a) the significant harm (if any), and
    (b) the pollution of controlled waters (if any),
by reason of which the contaminated land in question is such land.

(2)   Nothing in this Part shall apply in relation to any land in respect of which there is for the time being in force a site licence under Part II above, except to the extent that any significant harm, or pollution of controlled waters, by reason of which that land would otherwise fall to be regarded as contaminated land is attributable to causes other than—
    (a) breach of the conditions of the licence; or
    (b) the carrying on, in accordance with the conditions of the licence, of any
         activity authorised by the licence.

(3)   If, in a case falling within subsection (1) or (7) of section 59 above, the land in question is contaminated land, or becomes such land by reason of the deposit of the controlled waste in question, a remediation notice shall not be served in respect of that land by reason of that waste or any consequences of its deposit, if and to the extent that it appears to the enforcing authority that the powers of a waste regulation authority or waste collection authority under that section may be exercised in relation to that waste or the consequences of its deposit.

(4)   No remediation notice shall require a person to do anything the effect of which would be to impede or prevent the making of a discharge in pursuance of a consent given under Chapter II of Part III of the Water Resources Act 1991 (pollution offences) or, in relation to Scotland, in pursuance of a consent given under Part II of the Control of Pollution Act 1974.]

[183]

NOTES
Commencement: to be appointed.
Inserted as noted to s 78A at **[159]**.

[78YC This Part and radioactivity

Except as provided by regulations, nothing in this Part applies in relation to harm, or pollution of controlled waters, so far as attributable to any radioactivity possessed by any substance; but regulations may—

(a) provide for prescribed provisions of this Part to have effect with such modifications as the Secretary of State considers appropriate for the purpose of dealing with harm, or pollution of controlled waters, so far as attributable to any radioactivity possessed by any substances; or

(b) make such modifications of the Radioactive Substances Act 1993 or any other Act as the Secretary of State considers appropriate.]

[184]

NOTES
Commencement: 21 September 1995 (certain purposes); to be appointed (remaining purposes).
Inserted as noted to s 78A at **[159]**.

PART III
STATUTORY NUISANCES AND CLEAN AIR

Statutory nuisances . . .

79 Statutory nuisances and inspections therefor

(1) [*Subject to subsections (2) to (6A) below*], the following matters constitute "statutory nuisances" for the purposes of this Part, that is to say—

(a) any premises in such a state as to be prejudicial to health or a nuisance;

(b) smoke emitted from premises so as to be prejudicial to health or a nuisance;

(c) fumes or gases emitted from premises so as to be prejudicial to health or a nuisance;

(d) any dust, steam, smell or other effluvia arising on industrial, trade or business premises and being prejudicial to health or a nuisance;

(e) any accumulation or deposit which is prejudicial to health or a nuisance;

(f) any animal kept in such a place or manner as to be prejudicial to health or a nuisance;

(g) noise emitted from premises so as to be prejudicial to health or a nuisance;

[(ga) noise that is prejudicial to health or a nuisance and is emitted from or caused by a vehicle, machinery or equipment in a street [or in Scotland, road];]

(h) any other matter declared by any enactment to be a statutory nuisance;

and it shall be the duty of every local authority to cause its area to be inspected from time to time to detect any statutory nuisances which ought to be dealt with under section 80 below [or sections 80 and 80A below] and, where a complaint of a statutory nuisance is made to it by a person living within its area, to take such steps as are reasonably practicable to investigate the complaint.

[(1A) No matter shall constitute a statutory nuisance to the extent that it consists of, or is caused by, any land being in a contaminated state.

(1B) Land is in a "contaminated state" for the purposes of subsection (1A) above if, and only if, it is in such a condition, by reason of substances in, on or under the land, that—

(a) harm is being caused or there is a possibility of harm being caused; or

(b) pollution of controlled waters is being, or is likely to be, caused;

and in this subsection "harm", "pollution of controlled waters" and "substance" have the same meaning as in Part IIA of this Act.]

(2)   Subsection (1)(b) and (g) above do not apply in relation to premises—
    (a) occupied on behalf of the Crown for naval, military or air force purposes or for the purposes of the department of the Secretary of State having responsibility for defence, or
    (b) occupied by or for the purposes of a visiting force;

and "visiting force" means any such body, contingent or detachment of the forces of any country as is a visiting force for the purposes of any of the provisions of the Visiting Forces Act 1952.

(3)   Subsection (1)(b) above does not apply to—
    (i)   smoke emitted from a chimney of a private dwelling within a smoke control area,
    (ii) dark smoke emitted from a chimney of a building or a chimney serving the furnace of a boiler or industrial plant attached to a building or for the time being fixed to or installed on any land,
    (iii) smoke emitted from a railway locomotive steam engine, or
    (iv) dark smoke emitted otherwise than as mentioned above from industrial or trade premises.

(4)   Subsection (1)(c) above does not apply in relation to premises other than private dwellings.

(5)   Subsection (1)(d) above does not apply to steam emitted from a railway locomotive engine.

(6)   Subsection (1)(g) above does not apply to noise caused by aircraft other than model aircraft.

[(6A) Subsection (1)(ga) above does not apply to noise made—
    (a) by traffic,
    (b) by any naval, military or air force of the Crown or by a visiting force (as defined in subsection (2) above), or
    (c) by a political demonstration or a demonstration supporting or opposing a cause or campaign.]

(7)   In this Part—
    "chimney" includes structures and openings of any kind from or through which smoke may be emitted;
    "dust" does not include dust emitted from a chimney as an ingredient of smoke;
    ["equipment" includes a musical instrument;]
    "fumes" means any airborne solid matter smaller than dust;
    "gas" includes vapour and moisture precipitated from vapour;
    "industrial, trade or business premises" means premises used for any industrial, trade or business purposes or premises not so used on which matter is burnt in connection with any industrial, trade or business process, and premises are used for industrial purposes where they are used for the purposes of any treatment or process as well as where they are used for the purposes of manufacturing;
    "local authority" means, subject to subsection (8) below,—
        (a) in Greater London, a London borough council, the Common Council of the City of London and, as respects the Temples, the Sub-Treasurer of the Inner Temple and the Under-Treasurer of the Middle Temple respectively;
        (b) [in England] outside Greater London, a district council;
        [(bb) in Wales, a county council or county borough council;] . . .
        (c) the Council of the Isles of Scilly; [and
        (d) in Scotland, a district or islands council or a council constituted under section 2 of the Local Government etc (Scotland) Act 1994;]
    "noise" includes vibration;

["person responsible"—
    (a) in relation to a statutory nuisance, means the person to whose act, default or sufferance the nuisance is attributable;
    (b) in relation to a vehicle, includes the person in whose name the vehicle is for the time being registered under [the Vehicle Excise and Registration Act 1994] and any other person who is for the time being the driver of the vehicle;
    (c) in relation to machinery or equipment, includes any person who is for the time being the operator of the machinery or equipment;]
"prejudicial to health" means injurious, or likely to cause injury, to health;
"premises" includes land and, subject to subsection (12) [and[, in relation to England and Wales] section 81A(9)] below, any vessel;
"private dwelling" means any building, or part of a building, used or intended to be used, as a dwelling;
["road" has the same meaning as in Part IV of the New Roads and Street Works Act 1991;]
"smoke" includes soot, ash, grit and gritty particles emitted in smoke;
["street" means a highway and any other road, footway, square or court that is for the time being open to the public;]
and any expressions used in this section and in [the Clean Air Act 1993] have the same meaning in this section as in that Act and [section 3 of the Clean Air Act 1993] shall apply for the interpretation of the expression "dark smoke" and the operation of this Part in relation to it.

(8)   Where, by an order under section 2 of the Public Health (Control of Disease) Act 1984, a port health authority has been constituted for any port health district [or in Scotland where by an order under section 172 of the Public Health (Scotland) Act 1897 a port local authority or a joint port local authority has been constituted for the whole or part of a port,], the port health authority[, port local authority or joint port local authority, as the case may be] shall have by virtue of this subsection, as respects its district, the functions conferred or imposed by this Part in relation to statutory nuisances other than a nuisance falling within paragraph (g) [or (ga)] of subsection (1) above and no such order shall be made assigning those functions; and "local authority" and "area" shall be construed accordingly.

(9)   In this Part "best practicable means" is to be interpreted by reference to the following provisions—
    (a) "practicable" means reasonably practicable having regard among other things to local conditions and circumstances, to the current state of technical knowledge and to the financial implications;
    (b) the means to be employed include the design, installation, maintenance and manner and periods of operation of plant and machinery, and the design, construction and maintenance of buildings and structures;
    (c) the test is to apply only so far as compatible with any duty imposed by law;
    (d) the test is to apply only so far as compatible with safety and safe working conditions, and with the exigencies of any emergency or unforeseeable circumstances;
and, in circumstances where a code of practice under section 71 of the Control of Pollution Act 1974 (noise minimisation) is applicable, regard shall also be had to guidance given in it.

(10)   A local authority shall not without the consent of the Secretary of State institute summary proceedings under this Part in respect of a nuisance falling within paragraph (b), (d) or (e) [and, in relation to Scotland, paragraph (g) or (ga),] of subsection (1) above if proceedings in respect thereof might be instituted under Part I . . .

(11)   The area of a local authority which includes part of the seashore shall also include for the purposes of this Part the territorial sea lying seawards from that part

of the shore; and subject to subsection (12) [and[, in relation to England and Wales,] section 81A] below, this Part shall have effect, in relation to any area included in the area of a local authority by virtue of this subsection—

(a) as if references to premises and the occupier of premises included respectively a vessel and the master of a vessel; and

(b) with such other modifications, if any, as are prescribed in regulations made by the Secretary of State.

(12) A vessel powered by steam reciprocating machinery is not a vessel to which this Part of this Act applies.

[185]

NOTES

Commencement: 5 January 1994 (sub-s (6A)); 1 January 1991 (sub-ss (1), (2)–(6), (7)–(12)): to be appointed (remainder).

Cross-heading: words omitted repealed by the Environment Act 1995, s 120, Sch 24.

Sub-s (1): words in first pair of square brackets substituted, para (ga) and words in final pair of square brackets inserted, by the Noise and Statutory Nuisance Act 1993, s 2(2); words in italics substituted by the words "Subject to subsections (1A) to (6A) below", as from a day to be appointed, and words in square brackets in para (ga) inserted, by the Environment Act 1995, ss 107, 120, Sch 17, para 2(a), Sch 22, para 89(2).

Sub-ss (1A), (1B): inserted by the Environment Act 1995, s 120, Sch 22, para 89(3), as from a day to be appointed.

Sub-s (6A): inserted by the Noise and Statutory Nuisance Act 1993, s 2(3).

Sub-s (7): definitions "equipment" and "street" inserted, and definition "person responsible" substituted, by the Noise and Statutory Nuisance Act 1993, s 2(4); in definition "local authority" words in first and third pairs of square brackets inserted by the Local Government (Wales) Act 1994, s 22(3), Sch 9, para 17(5), words in second and final pairs of square brackets inserted, and word omitted repealed, by the Environment Act 1995, ss 107, 120, Sch 17, para 2(b)(i), Sch 24; in definition "person responsible" words in square brackets substituted by the Vehicle Excise and Registration Act 1994, s 63, Sch 3, para 27; in definition "premises" words in first (outer) pair of square brackets inserted by the Noise and Statutory Nuisance Act 1993, s 10(1), words in second (inner) pair of square brackets inserted by the Environment Act 1995, s 107, Sch 17, para 2(b)(ii); definition "road" inserted by the Environment Act 1995, s 107, Sch 17, para 2(b)(iii); words in remaining pairs of square brackets substituted by the Clean Air Act 1993, s 67(1), Sch 4, para 4.

Sub-s (8): words in first and second pairs of square brackets inserted by the Environment Act 1995, s 107, Sch 17, para 2(c); words in final pair of square brackets inserted by the Noise and Statutory Nuisance Act 1993, s 2(5).

Sub-s (10): words in square brackets inserted by the Environment Act 1995, s 107, Sch 17, para 2(d); words omitted repealed by the Environmental Protection Act 1990, s 162, Sch 16, Pt I.

Sub-s (11): words in first (outer) pair of square brackets inserted by the Noise and Statutory Nuisance Act 1993, s 10(1), words in second (inner) pair of square brackets inserted by the Environment Act 1995, s 107, Sch 17, para 2(e).

Modified, in relation to London boroughs, by the London Local Authorities Act 1996, s 24(1).

80 Summary proceedings for statutory nuisances

(1) Where a local authority is satisfied that a statutory nuisance exists, or is likely to occur or recur, in the area of the authority, the local authority shall serve a notice ("an abatement notice") imposing all or any of the following requirements—

(a) requiring the abatement of the nuisance or prohibiting or restricting its occurrence or recurrence;

(b) requiring the execution of such works, and the taking of such other steps, as may be necessary for any of those purposes,

and the notice shall specify the time or times within which the requirements of the notice are to be complied with.

(2) [Subject to section 80A(1) below, the abatement notice] shall be served—

(a) except in a case falling within paragraph (b) or (c) below, on the person responsible for the nuisance;

(b) where the nuisance arises from any defect of a structural character, on the owner of the premises;

(c) where the person responsible for the nuisance cannot be found or the nuisance has not yet occurred, on the owner or occupier of the premises.

(3) [A person served with an abatement notice] may appeal against the notice to a magistrates' court [or in Scotland, the sheriff] within the period of twenty-one days beginning with the date on which he was served with the notice.

(4) If a person on whom an abatement notice is served, without reasonable excuse, contravenes or fails to comply with any requirement or prohibition imposed by the notice, he shall be guilty of an offence.

(5) Except in a case falling within subsection (6) below, a person who commits an offence under subsection (4) above shall be liable on summary conviction to a fine not exceeding level 5 on the standard scale together with a further fine of an amount equal to one-tenth of that level for each day on which the offence continues after the conviction.

(6) A person who commits an offence under subsection (4) above on industrial, trade or business premises shall be liable on summary conviction to a fine not exceeding £20,000.

(7) Subject to subsection (8) below, in any proceedings for an offence under subsection (4) above in respect of a statutory nuisance it shall be a defence to prove that the best practicable means were used to prevent, or to counteract the effects of, the nuisance.

(8) The defence under subsection (7) above is not available—
(a) in the case of a nuisance falling within paragraph (a), (d), (e), (f) or (g) of section 79(1) above except where the nuisance arises on industrial, trade or business premises;
[(aa) in the case of a nuisance falling within paragraph (ga) of section 79(1) above except where the noise is emitted from or caused by a vehicle, machinery or equipment being used for industrial, trade or business purposes;]
(b) in the case of a nuisance falling within paragraph (b) of section 79(1) above except where the smoke is emitted from a chimney; and
(c) in the case of a nuisance falling within paragraph (c) or (h) of section 79(1) above.

(9) In proceedings for an offence under subsection (4) above in respect of a statutory nuisance falling within paragraph (g) [or (ga)] of section 79(1) above where the offence consists in contravening requirements imposed by virtue of subsection (1)(a) above it shall be a defence to prove—
(a) that the alleged offence was covered by a notice served under section 60 or a consent given under section 61 or 65 of the Control of Pollution Act 1974 (construction sites, etc); or
(b) where the alleged offence was committed at a time when the premises were subject to a notice under section 66 of that Act (noise reduction notice), that the level of noise emitted from the premises at that time was not such as to constitute a contravention of the notice under that section; or
(c) where the alleged offence was committed at a time when the premises were not subject to a notice under section 66 of that Act, and when a level fixed under section 67 of that Act (new buildings liable to abatement order) applied to the premises, that the level of noise emitted from the premises at that time did not exceed that level.

(10) Paragraphs (b) and (c) of subsection (9) above apply whether or not the relevant notice was subject to appeal at the time when the offence was alleged to have been committed.

NOTES

Sub-s (2): words in square brackets substituted by the Noise and Statutory Nuisance Act 1993, s 3(2), (3).

Sub-s (3): words in first pair of square brackets substituted by the Noise and Statutory Nuisance Act 1993, s 3(2), (3); words in second pair of square brackets inserted by the Environment Act 1995, s 107, Sch 17, para 3.

Sub-s (8): para (aa) inserted by the Noise and Statutory Nuisance Act 1993, s 3(4).

Sub-s (9): words in square brackets inserted by the Noise and Statutory Nuisance Act 1993, s 3(5).

[80A Abatement notice in respect of noise in the street

(1)   In the case of a statutory nuisance within section 79(1)(ga) above that—
  (a) has not yet occurred, or
  (b) arises from noise emitted from or caused by an unattended vehicle or unattended machinery or equipment,
the abatement notice shall be served in accordance with subsection (2) below.

(2)   The notice shall be served—
  (a) where the person responsible for the vehicle, machinery or equipment can be found, on that person;
  (b) where that person cannot be found or where the local authority determines that this paragraph should apply, by fixing the notice to the vehicle, machinery or equipment.

(3)   Where—
  (a) an abatement notice is served in accordance with subsection (2)(b) above by virtue of a determination of the local authority, and
  (b) the person responsible for the vehicle, machinery or equipment can be found and served with a copy of the notice within an hour of the notice being fixed to the vehicle, machinery or equipment,
a copy of the notice shall be served on that person accordingly.

(4)   Where an abatement notice is served in accordance with subsection (2)(b) above by virtue of a determination of the local authority, the notice shall state that, if a copy of the notice is subsequently served under subsection (3) above, the time specified in the notice as the time within which its requirements are to be complied with is extended by such further period as is specified in the notice.

(5)   Where an abatement notice is served in accordance with subsection (2)(b) above, the person responsible for the vehicle, machinery or equipment may appeal against the notice under section 80(3) above as if he had been served with the notice on the date on which it was fixed to the vehicle, machinery or equipment.

(6)   Section 80(4) above shall apply in relation to a person on whom a copy of an abatement notice is served under subsection (3) above as if the copy were the notice itself.

(7)   A person who removes or interferes with a notice fixed to a vehicle, machinery or equipment in accordance with subsection (2)(b) above shall be guilty of an offence, unless he is the person responsible for the vehicle, machinery or equipment or he does so with the authority of that person.

(8)   A person who commits an offence under subsection (7) above shall be liable on summary conviction to a fine not exceeding level 3 on the standard scale.]

[187]

NOTES

Commencement: 5 January 1994.

Inserted by the Noise and Statutory Nuisance Act 1993, s 3(6).

Sub-s (1) modified, in relation to London boroughs, by the London Local Authorities Act 1996, s 24(2).

81 Supplementary provisions

(1)   [Subject to subsection (1A) below, where] more than one person is responsible for a statutory nuisance section 80 above shall apply to each of those persons whether or not what any one of them is responsible for would by itself amount to a nuisance.

[(1A) In relation to a statutory nuisance within section 79(1)(ga) above for which more than one person is responsible (whether or not what any one of those persons is responsible for would by itself amount to such a nuisance), section 80(2)(a) above shall apply with the substitution of "any one of the persons" for "the person".

(1B) In relation to a statutory nuisance within section 79(1)(ga) above caused by noise emitted from or caused by an unattended vehicle or unattended machinery or equipment for which more than one person is responsible, section 80A above shall apply with the substitution—

   (a) in subsection (2)(a), of "any of the persons" for "the person" and of "one such person" for "that person",
   (b) in subsection (2)(b), of "such a person" for "that person",
   (c) in subsection (3), of "any of the persons" for "the person" and of "one such person" for "that person",
   (d) in subsection (5), of "any person" for "the person", and
   (e) in subsection (7), of "a person" for "the person" and of "such a person" for "that person"]

(2)   Where a statutory nuisance which exists or has occurred within the area of a local authority, or which has affected any part of that area, appears to the local authority to be wholly or partly caused by some act or default committed or taking place outside the area, the local authority may act under section 80 above as if the act or default were wholly within that area, except that any appeal shall be heard by a magistrates' court [or in Scotland, the sheriff] having jurisdiction where the act or default is alleged to have taken place.

(3)   Where an abatement notice has not been complied with the local authority may, whether or not they take proceedings for an offence [or, in Scotland, whether or not proceedings have been taken for an offence,] under section 80(4) above, abate the nuisance and do whatever may be necessary in execution of the notice.

(4)   Any expenses reasonably incurred by a local authority in abating, or preventing the recurrence of, a statutory nuisance under subsection (3) above may be recovered by them from the person by whose act or default the nuisance was caused and, if that person is the owner of the premises, from any person who is for the time being the owner thereof; and the court [or sheriff] may apportion the expenses between persons by whose acts or defaults the nuisance is caused in such manner as the court consider [or sheriff considers] fair and reasonable.

(5)   If a local authority is of opinion that proceedings for an offence under section 80(4) above would afford an inadequate remedy in the case of any statutory nuisance, they may, subject to subsection (6) below, take proceedings in the High Court [or, in Scotland, in any court of competent jurisdiction] for the purpose of securing the abatement, prohibition or restriction of the nuisance, and the proceedings shall be maintainable notwithstanding the local authority have suffered no damage from the nuisance.

(6)   In any proceedings under subsection (5) above in respect of a nuisance falling within paragraph (g) [or (ga)] of section 79(1) above, it shall be a defence to prove that the noise was authorised by a notice under section 60 or a consent under section 61 (construction sites) of the Control of Pollution Act 1974.

(7)   The further supplementary provisions in Schedule 3 to this Act shall have effect.

NOTES
Commencement: 5 January 1994 (sub-s (1A), (1B)); 1 January 1991 (remainder).
Sub-s (1): words in square brackets substituted by the Noise and Statutory Nuisance Act 1993, s 4(2).
Sub-ss (1A), (1B): inserted by the Noise and Statutory Nuisance Act 1993, s 4(3).
Sub-ss (2)–(5): words in square brackets inserted by the Environment Act 1995, s 107, Sch 17, para 4.
Sub-s (6): words in square brackets inserted by the Noise and Statutory Nuisance Act 1993, s 4(4).

[81A Expenses recoverable from owner to be a charge on premises

(1) Where any expenses are recoverable under section 81(4) above from a person who is the owner of the premises there mentioned and the local authority serves a notice on him under this section—
    (a) the expenses shall carry interest, at such reasonable rate as the local authority may determine, from the date of service of the notice until the whole amount is paid, and
    (b) subject to the following provisions of this section, the expenses and accrued interest shall be a charge on the premises.

(2) A notice served under this section shall—
    (a) specify the amount of the expenses that the local authority claims is recoverable,
    (b) state the effect of subsection (1) above and the rate of interest determined by the local authority under that subsection, and
    (c) state the effect of subsections (4) to (6) below.

(3) On the date on which a local authority serves a notice on a person under this section the authority shall also serve a copy of the notice on every other person who, to the knowledge of the authority, has an interest in the premises capable of being affected by the charge.

(4) Subject to any order under subsection (7)(b) or (c) below, the amount of any expenses specified in a notice under this section and the accrued interest shall be a charge on the premises—
    (a) as from the end of the period of twenty-one days beginning with the date of service of the notice, or
    (b) where an appeal is brought under subsection (6) below, as from the final determination of the appeal,
until the expenses and interest are recovered.

(5) For the purposes of subsection (4) above, the withdrawal of an appeal has the same effect as a final determination of the appeal.

(6) A person served with a notice or copy of a notice under this section may appeal against the notice to the county court within the period of twenty-one days beginning with the date of service.

(7) On such an appeal the court may—
    (a) confirm the notice without modification,
    (b) order that the notice is to have effect with the substitution of a different amount for the amount originally specified in it, or
    (c) order that the notice is to be of no effect.

(8) A local authority shall, for the purpose of enforcing a charge under this section, have all the same powers and remedies under the Law of Property Act 1925, and otherwise, as if it were a mortgagee by deed having powers of sale and lease, of accepting surrenders of leases and of appointing a receiver.

(9) In this section—
    "owner", in relation to any premises, means a person (other than a mortgagee not in possession) who, whether in his own right or as trustee for any other

person, is entitled to receive the rack rent of the premises or, where the premises are not let at a rack rent, would be so entitled if they were so let, and

"premises" does not include a vessel.

[(10) (*Applies to Scotland only.*)]]

[189]

NOTES
Commencement: 1 April 1996 (sub-s (10)); 5 January 1994 (remainder).
Inserted by the Noise and Statutory Nuisance Act 1993, s 10(1).

[81B Payment of expenses by instalments

(1)   Where any expenses are a charge on premises under section 81A above, the local authority may by order declare the expenses to be payable with interest by instalments within the specified period, until the whole amount is paid.

(2)   In subsection (1) above—
"interest" means interest at the rate determined by the authority under section 81A(1) above, and
"the specified period" means such period of thirty years or less from the date of service of the notice under section 81A above as is specified in the order.

(3)   Subject to subsection (5) below, the instalments and interest, or any part of them, may be recovered from the owner or occupier for the time being of the premises.

(4)   Any sums recovered from an occupier may be deducted by him from the rent of the premises.

(5)   An occupier shall not be required to pay at any one time any sum greater than the aggregate of—
(a) the amount that was due from him on account of rent at the date on which he was served with a demand from the local authority together with a notice requiring him not to pay rent to his landlord without deducting the sum demanded, and
(b) the amount that has become due from him on account of rent since that date.

[(6)   (*Applies to Scotland only.*)]]

[190]

NOTES
Commencement: 1 April 1996 (sub-s (6)); 5 January 1994 (remainder).
Inserted by the Noise and Statutory Nuisance Act 1993, s 10(2).

82 Summary proceedings by persons aggrieved by statutory nuisances

(1)   A magistrates' court may act under this section on a complaint [or, in Scotland, the sheriff may act under this section on a summary application,] made by any person on the ground that he is aggrieved by the existence of a statutory nuisance.

(2)   If the magistrates' court [or, in Scotland, the sheriff] is satisfied that the alleged nuisance exists, or that although abated it is likely to recur on the same premises[or, in the case of a nuisance within section 79(1)(ga) above, in the same street] [or, in Scotland, road], the court [or the sheriff] shall make an order for either or both of the following purposes—
(a) requiring the defendant [or, in Scotland, defender] to abate the nuisance, within a time specified in the order, and to execute any works necessary for that purpose;

(b) prohibiting a recurrence of the nuisance, and requiring the defendant [or defender], within a time specified in the order, to execute any works necessary to prevent the recurrence;

and[, in England and Wales,] may also impose on the defendant a fine not exceeding level 5 on the standard scale.

(3) If the magistrates' court [or the sheriff] is satisfied that the alleged nuisance exists and is such as, in the opinion of the court [or of the sheriff], to render premises unfit for human habitation, an order under subsection (2) above may prohibit the use of the premises for human habitation until the premises are, to the satisfaction of the court [or of the sheriff], rendered fit for that purpose.

(4) Proceedings for an order under subsection (2) above shall be brought—
  (a) except in a case falling within [paragraph (b), (c) or (d) below], against the person responsible for the nuisance;
  (b) where the nuisance arises from any defect of a structural character, against the owner of the premises;
  (c) where the person responsible for the nuisance cannot be found, against the owner or occupier of the premises.
  [(d) in the case of a statutory nuisance within section 79(1)(ga) above caused by noise emitted from or caused by an unattended vehicle or unattended machinery or equipment, against the person responsible for the vehicle, machinery or equipment.]

(5) [Subject to subsection (5A) below, where] more than one person is responsible for a statutory nuisance, subsections (1) to (4) above shall apply to each of those persons whether or not what any one of them is responsible for would by itself amount to a nuisance.

[(5A) In relation to a statutory nuisance within section 79(1)(ga) above for which more than one person is responsible (whether or not what any one of those persons is responsible for would by itself amount to such a nuisance), subsection (4)(a) above shall apply with the substitution of "each person responsible for the nuisance who can be found" for "the person responsible for the nuisance".

(5B) In relation to a statutory nuisance within section 79(1)(ga) above caused by noise emitted from or caused by an unattended vehicle or unattended machinery or equipment for which more than one person is responsible, subsection (4)(d) above shall apply with the substitution of "any person" for "the person"]

(6) Before instituting proceedings for an order under subsection (2) above against any person, the person aggrieved by the nuisance shall give to that person such notice in writing of his intention to bring the proceedings as is applicable to proceedings in respect of a nuisance of that description and the notice shall specify the matter complained of.

(7) The notice of the bringing of proceedings in respect of a statutory nuisance required by subsection (6) above which is applicable is—
  (a) in the case of a nuisance falling within paragraph (g) [or (ga)] of section 79(1) above, not less than three days' notice; and
  (b) in the case of a nuisance of any other description, not less than twenty-one days' notice;

but the Secretary of State may, by order, provide that this subsection shall have effect as if such period as is specified in the order were the minimum period of notice applicable to any description of statutory nuisance specified in the order.

(8) A person who, without reasonable excuse, contravenes any requirement or prohibition imposed by an order under subsection (2) above shall be guilty of an offence and liable on summary conviction to a fine not exceeding level 5 on the standard scale together with a further fine of an amount equal to one-tenth of that level for each day on which the offence continues after the conviction.

(9)   Subject to subsection (10) below, in any proceedings for an offence under subsection (8) above in respect of a statutory nuisance it shall be a defence to prove that the best practicable means were used to prevent, or to counteract the effects of, the nuisance.

(10)   The defence under subsection (9) above is not available—
   (a)   in the case of a nuisance falling within paragraph (a), (d), (e), (f) or (g) of section 79(1) above except where the nuisance arises on industrial, trade or business premises;
   [(aa)   in the case of a nuisance falling within paragraph (ga) of section 79(1) above except where the noise is emitted from or caused by a vehicle, machinery or equipment being used for industrial, trade or business purposes;]
   (b)   in the case of a nuisance falling within paragraph (b) of section 79(1) above except where the smoke is emitted from a chimney;
   (c)   in the case of a nuisance falling within paragraph (c) or (h) of section 79(1) above; and
   (d)   in the case of a nuisance which is such as to render the premises unfit for human habitation.

(11)   If a person is convicted of an offence under subsection (8) above, a magistrates' court [or the sheriff] may, after giving the local authority in whose area the nuisance has occurred an opportunity of being heard, direct the authority to do anything which the person convicted was required to do by the order to which the conviction relates.

(12)   Where on the hearing of proceedings for an order under subsection (2) above it is proved that the alleged nuisance existed at the date of the making of the complaint [or summary application], then, whether or not at the date of the hearing it still exists or is likely to recur, the court [or the sheriff] shall order the [defendant or defender (or defendants or defenders] in such proportions as appears fair and reasonable) to pay to the person bringing the proceedings such amount as the court [or the sheriff] considers reasonably sufficient to compensate him for any expenses properly incurred by him in the proceedings.

(13)   If it appears to the magistrates' court [or to the sheriff] that neither the person responsible for the nuisance nor the owner or occupier of the premises [or (as the case may be) the person responsible for the vehicle, machinery or equipment] can be found the court [or the sheriff] may, after giving the local authority in whose area the nuisance has occurred an opportunity of being heard, direct the authority to do anything which the court [or the sheriff] would have ordered that person to do.

[191]

NOTES
    Sub-ss (1), (3), (11): words in square brackets inserted by the Environment Act 1995, s 107, Sch 17, para 6(a), (c), (d).
    Sub-s (2): words in second pair of square brackets inserted by the Noise and Statutory Nuisance Act 1993, s 5(2); words in remaining pairs of square brackets inserted by the Environment Act 1995, s 107, Sch 17, para 6(b).
    Sub-s (4): words in square brackets in para (a) substituted and para (d) inserted by the Noise and Statutory Nuisance Act 1993.
    Sub-s (5): words in square brackets substituted by the Noise and Statutory Nuisance Act 1993, s 5(4).
    Sub-ss (5A), (5B): inserted by the Noise and Statutory Nuisance Act 1993, s 5(5).
    Sub-s (7): words in square brackets inserted by the Noise and Statutory Nuisance Act 1993, s 5(6).
    Sub-s (10): para (aa) inserted by the Noise and Statutory Nuisance Act 1993, s 5(7).
    Sub-s (12): words in first, second and final pairs of square brackets inserted, and words in third pair of square brackets substituted, by the Environment Act 1995, s 107, Sch 17, para 6(e).
    Sub-s (13): words in first, third and final pairs of square brackets inserted by the Environment Act 1995, s 107, Sch 17, para 6(f); words in second pair of square brackets inserted by the Noise and Statutory Nuisance Act 1993, s 5(6).

83   *(Applied to Scotland only; repealed by the Environmental Protection Act 1995, s 120(3), Sch 24.)*

Termination of existing controls over offensive trades and businesses

84 Termination of Public Health Act controls over offensive trades etc

(1)   Where a person carries on, in the area or part of the area of any local authority—
  (a) in England or Wales, a trade which—
      (i) is an offensive trade within the meaning of section 107 of the Public Health Act 1936 in that area or part of that area, and
      (ii) constitutes a prescribed process designated for local control for the carrying on of which an authorisation is required under section 6 of this Act; or
  (b) *(applies to Scotland only)*,

(2)   Where this subsection applies in relation to the trade or business carried on by any person—
  (a) nothing in section 107 of the Public Health Act 1936 or in section 32 of the Public Health (Scotland) Act 1897 shall apply in relation to it, and
  (b) no byelaws or further byelaws made under section 108(2) of the said Act of 1936, or under subsection (2) of the said section 32, with respect to a trade or business of that description shall apply in relation to it;

but without prejudice to the continuance of, and imposition of any penalty in, any proceedings under the said section 107 or the said section 32 which were instituted before the date as from which this subsection has effect in relation to the trade or business.

(3)   Subsection (2)(b) above shall apply in relation to the trade of fish frying as it applies in relation to an offensive trade.

(4)   When the Secretary of State considers it expedient to do so, having regard to the operation of Part I and the preceding provisions of this Part of this Act in relation to offensive trades or businesses, he may by order repeal—
  (a) sections 107 and 108 of the Public Health Act 1936; and
  (b) *(applies to Scotland only)*,

and different days may be so appointed in relation to trades or businesses which constitute prescribed processes and those which do not.

(5)   In this section—
  "prescribed process" has the same meaning as in Part I of this Act; and
  "offensive trade" or "trade" has the same meaning as in section 107 of the Public Health Act 1936.

[192]

NOTES
  Orders: the Repeal of Offensive Trade or Businesses Provisions Order 1995, SI 1995/2054.

85   *(Repealed by the Clean Air Act 1993, s 67(3), Sch 6, Pt I.)*

PART IV
LITTER ETC

Provisions relating to litter

86 Preliminary

(1)   The following provisions have effect for the purposes of this Part.

(2)   In England and Wales the following are "principal litter authorities"—
  (a) a county council,
  [(aa) a county borough council,]

    (b) a district council,
    (c) a London borough council,
    (d) the Common Council of the City of London, and
    (e) the Council of the Isles of Scilly;

but the Secretary of State may, by order, designate other descriptions of local authorities as litter authorities for the purposes of this Part; and any such authority shall also be a principal litter authority.

(3)   *(Applies to Scotland only.)*

(4)   Subject to subsection (8) below, land is "relevant land" of a principal litter authority if, not being relevant land falling within subsection (7) below, it is open to the air and is land (but not a highway or in Scotland a public road) which is under the direct control of such an authority to which the public are entitled or permitted to have access with or without payment.

(5)   Land is "Crown land" if it is land—
    (a) occupied by the Crown Estate Commissioners as part of the Crown Estate,
    (b) occupied by or for the purposes of a government department or for naval, military or air force purposes, or
    (c) occupied or managed by any body acting on behalf of the Crown;

is "relevant Crown land" if it is Crown land which is open to the air and is land (but not a highway or in Scotland a public road) to which the public are entitled or permitted to have access with or without payment; and "the appropriate Crown authority" for any Crown land is the Crown Estate Commissioners, the Minister in charge of the government department or the body which occupies or manages the land on the Crown's behalf, as the case may be.

(6)   Subject to subsection (8) below, land is "relevant land" of a designated statutory undertaker if it is land which is under the direct control of any statutory undertaker or statutory undertaker of any description which may be designated by the Secretary of State, by order, for the purposes of this Part, being land to which the public are entitled or permitted to have access with or without payment or, in such cases as may be prescribed in the designation order, land in relation to which the public have no such right or permission.

(7)   Subject to subsection (8) below, land is "relevant land" of a designated educational institution if it is open to the air and is land which is under the direct control of the governing body of or, in Scotland, of such body or of the education authority responsible for the management of, any educational institution or educational institution of any description which may be designated by the Secretary of State, by order, for the purposes of this Part.

(8)   The Secretary of State may, by order, designate descriptions of land which are not to be treated as relevant Crown land or as relevant land of principal litter authorities, of designated statutory undertakers or of designated educational institutions or of any description of any of them.

(9)   Every highway maintainable at the public expense other than a trunk road which is a special road is a "relevant highway" and the local authority which is, for the purposes of this Part, "responsible" for so much of it as lies within its area is, subject to any order under subsection (11) below—
    (a) in Greater London, the council of the London borough or the Common Council of the City of London;
    (b) [in England] outside Greater London, the council of the district; and
  [(bb) in Wales, the council of the county or county borough;]
    (c) the Council of the Isles of Scilly.

(10) In Scotland, every public road other than a trunk road which is a special road is a "relevant road" and the local authority which is, for the purposes of this

Part, "responsible" for so much of it as lies within [their] area is, subject to any order under subsection (11) below, [the council constituted under section 2 of the Local Government etc (Scotland) Act 1994].

(11) The Secretary of State may, by order, as respects relevant highways or relevant roads, relevant highways or relevant roads of any class or any part of a relevant highway or relevant road specified in the order, transfer the responsibility for the discharge of the duties imposed by section 89 below from the local authority to the highway or roads authority; but he shall not make an order under this subsection unless—

   (a) (except where he is the highway or roads authority) he is requested to do so by the highway or roads authority;

   (b) he consults the local authority; and

   (c) it appears to him to be necessary or expedient to do so in order to prevent or minimise interference with the passage or with the safety of traffic along the highway or, in Scotland, road in question;

and where, by an order under this subsection, responsibility for the discharge of those duties is transferred, the authority to which the transfer is made is, for the purposes of this Part, "responsible" for the highway, road or part specified in the order.

(12) Land is "relevant land within a litter control area of a local authority" if it is land included in an area designated by the local authority under section 90 below to which the public are entitled or permitted to have access with or without payment.

(13) A place on land shall be treated as "open to the air" notwithstanding that it is covered if it is open to the air on at least one side.

(14) The Secretary of State may, by order, apply the provisions of this Part which apply to refuse to any description of animal droppings in all or any prescribed circumstances subject to such modifications as appear to him to be necessary.

(15) Any power under this section may be exercised differently as respects different areas, different descriptions of land or for different circumstances.

                                                                      [193]

NOTES

Sub-ss (2), (9): words in square brackets inserted by the Local Government (Wales) Act 1994, s 22(3), Sch 9, para 17(6), (7).

Sub-s (3): para (a) substituted for original paras (a), (b), by the Local Government etc (Scotland) Act 1994, s 180(1), Sch 13, para 167(10)(a).

Sub-s (10): words in square brackets substituted by the Local Government etc (Scotland) Act 1994, s 180(1), Sch 13, para 167(10)(b).

Orders: the Highway Litter Clearance and Cleaning (Transfer of Duties) Order 1991, SI 1991/337; the Litter (Relevant Land of Principal Litter Authorities and Relevant Crown Land) Order 1991, SI 1991/476; the Litter (Designated Educational Institutions) Order 1991, SI 1991/561; the Litter (Animal Droppings) Order 1991, SI 1991/961; the Litter (Statutory Undertakers) (Designation and Relevant Land) Order 1991, SI 1991/1043, as amended by SI 1992/406.

Regulations: the Litter Etc (Transitional Provisions) Regulations 1991, SI 1991/719.

87 Offence of leaving litter

(1)   If any person throws down, drops or otherwise deposits in, into or from any place to which this section applies, and leaves, any thing whatsoever in such circumstances as to cause, or contribute to, or tend to lead to, the defacement by litter of any place to which this section applies, he shall, subject to subsection (2) below, be guilty of an offence.

(2)   No offence is committed under this section where the depositing and leaving of the thing was—

    (a) authorised by law, or
    (b) done with the consent of the owner, occupier or other person or authority having control of the place in or into which that thing was deposited.

(3)   This section applies to any public open place and, in so far as the place is not a public open place, also to the following places—
    (a) any relevant highway or relevant road and any trunk road which is a special road;
    (b) any place on relevant land of a principal litter authority;
    (c) any place on relevant Crown land;
    (d) any place on relevant land of any designated statutory undertaker;
    (e) any place on relevant land of any designated educational institution;
    (f) any place on relevant land within a litter control area of a local authority.

(4)   In this section "public open place" means a place in the open air to which the public are entitled or permitted to have access without payment; and any covered place open to the air on at least one side and available for public use shall be treated as a public open place.

(5)   A person who is guilty of an offence under this section shall be liable on summary conviction to a fine not exceeding level 4 on the standard scale.

(6)   A local authority, with a view to promoting the abatement of litter, may take such steps as the authority think appropriate for making the effect of subsection (5) above known to the public in their area.

(7)   *(Applies to Scotland only.)*

[194]

88 Fixed penalty notices for leaving litter

(1)   Where on any occasion an authorised officer of a litter authority finds a person who he has reason to believe has on that occasion committed an offence under section 87 above in the area of that authority, he may give that person a notice offering him the opportunity of discharging any liability to conviction for that offence by payment of a fixed penalty.

(2)   Where a person is given a notice under this section in respect of an offence—
    (a) no proceedings shall be instituted for that offence before the expiration of fourteen days following the date of the notice; and
    (b) he shall not be convicted of that offence if he pays the fixed penalty before the expiration of that period.

(3)   A notice under this section shall give such particulars of the circumstances alleged to constitute the offence as are necessary for giving reasonable information of the offence and shall state—
    (a) the period during which, by virtue of subsection (2) above, proceedings will not be taken for the offence;
    (b) the amount of the fixed penalty; and
    (c) the person to whom and the address at which the fixed penalty may be paid;
and, without prejudice to payment by any other method, payment of the fixed penalty may be made by pre-paying and posting to that person at that address a letter containing the amount of the penalty (in cash or otherwise).

(4)   Where a letter is sent in accordance with subsection (3) above payment shall be regarded as having been made at the time at which that letter would be delivered in the ordinary course of post.

(5)   The form of notices under this section shall be such as the Secretary of State may by order prescribe.

(6)   The fixed penalty payable to a litter authority in pursuance of a notice under this section shall, subject to subsection (7) below, be [£25]; and as respects the sums received by the authority, those sums—
    (a) if received by an authority in England and Wales, shall be paid to the Secretary of State;
    (b) *(applies to Scotland only)*.

(7)   The Secretary of State may by order substitute a different amount for the amount for the time being specified as the amount of the fixed penalty in subsection (6) above.

(8)   In any proceedings a certificate which—
    (a) purports to be signed by or on behalf of—
        (i) in England and Wales, the chief finance officer of the litter authority; or
        (ii) *(applies to Scotland only)*.
    (b) states that payment of a fixed penalty was or was not received by a date specified in the certificate,
shall be evidence of the facts stated.

(9)   For the purposes of this section the following are "litter authorities"—
    (a) any principal litter authority, other than [an English county] council . . . or a joint board;
    (b) any [English] county council . . . or joint board designated by the Secretary of State, by order, in relation to such area as is specified in the order (not being an area in a National Park);
    (c), (d). . .
    (e) the Broads Authority.

(10) In this section—
    "authorised officer" means an officer of, . . . , a litter authority who is authorised in writing by the authority for the purpose of issuing notices under this section;
    "chief finance officer", in relation to a litter authority, means the person having responsibility for the financial affairs of the authority;
. . . . .

[195]

NOTES
    Sub-s (6): sum in square brackets substituted by the Litter (Fixed Penalty) Order 1996, SI 1996/3055, art 2.
    Sub-s (9): words in square brackets in para (a) substituted by the Local Government (Wales) Act 1994, s 22(3), Sch 9, para 17(8), words omitted repealed by the Local Government etc (Scotland) Act 1994, s 180(1), (2), Sch 13, para 167(11), Sch 14; word in square brackets in para (b) inserted by the Local Government (Wales) Act 1994, s 22(3), Sch 9, para 17(8), words omitted repealed by the Local Government etc (Scotland) Act 1994, s 180(1), (2), Sch 13, para 167(11), Sch 14; paras (c), (d) repealed by the Environment Act 1995, s 120, Sch 24.
    Sub-s (10): in definition "authorised officer" words omitted repealed and definitions omitted repealed by the Environment Act 1995, s 120, Sch 24 (or apply to Scotland only) .
    Modification: this section has effect as if a National Park authority were a litter authority and as if the relevant Park were the authority's area, by virtue of the Environment Act 1995, Sch 9, para 12.
    Modification: sub-s (6) modified, in relation to fixed penalty notices made under the Dogs (Fouling of Land) Act 1996, s 4(1), by the Dog Fouling (Fixed Penalties) Order 1996, SI 1996/2763, art 3.
    Order: the Litter (Fixed Penalty Notices) Order 1991, SI 1991/111; the Dog Fouling (Fixed Penalties) Order 1996, SI 1996/2763; the Litter (Fixed Penalty) Order 1996, SI 1996/3055.

89 Duty to keep land and highways clear of litter etc

(1)   It shall be the duty of—

(a) each local authority, as respects any relevant highway or, in Scotland, relevant road for which it is responsible,

(b) the Secretary of State, as respects any trunk road which is a special road and any relevant highway or relevant road for which he is responsible,

(c) each principal litter authority, as respects its relevant land,

(d) the appropriate Crown authority, as respects its relevant Crown land,

(e) each designated statutory undertaker, as respects its relevant land,

(f) the governing body of each designated educational institution or in Scotland such body or, as the case may be, the education authority responsible for the management of the institution, as respects its relevant land, and

(g) the occupier of any relevant land within a litter control area of a local authority,

to ensure that the land is, so far as is practicable, kept clear of litter and refuse.

(2)   Subject to subsection (6) below, it shall also be the duty of—

(a) each local authority, as respects any relevant highway or relevant road for which it is responsible,

(b) the Secretary of State, as respects any trunk road which is a special road and any relevant highway or relevant road for which he is responsible,

to ensure that the highway or road is, so far as is practicable, kept clean.

(3)   In determining what standard is required, as respects any description of land, highway or road, for compliance with subsections (1) and (2) above, regard shall be had to the character and use of the land, highway or road as well as the measures which are practicable in the circumstances.

(4)   Matter of any description prescribed by regulations made by the Secretary of State for the purposes of subsections (1)(a) and (2) above shall be litter or refuse to which the duties imposed by those subsections apply as respects relevant highways or relevant roads whether or not it would be litter or refuse apart from this subsection.

(5)   It shall be the duty of a local authority, when discharging its duty under subsection (1)(a) or (2) above as respects any relevant highway or relevant road, to place and maintain on the highway or road such traffic signs and barriers may be necessary for giving warning and preventing danger to traffic or for regulating it and afterwards to remove them as soon as they cease to be necessary for those purposes; but this subsection has effect subject to any directions given under subsection (6) below.

(6)   In discharging its duty under subsection (1)(a) or (2) above to keep clear of litter and refuse or to clean any relevant highway or relevant road for which it is responsible, the local authority shall comply with any directions given to it by the highway or roads authority with respect to—

(a) the placing and maintenance of any traffic signs or barriers;

(b) the days or periods during which clearing or cleaning shall not be undertaken or undertaken to any extent specified in the direction;

and for the purpose of enabling it to discharge its duty under subsection (1)(a) or (2) above as respects any relevant highway or relevant road the local authority may apply to the highway authority or roads authority for that authority to exercise its powers under [section 14(1) or (2)] of the Road Traffic Regulation Act 1984 (temporary prohibition or restriction of traffic).

(7)   The Secretary of State shall prepare and issue a code of practice for the purpose of providing practical guidance on the discharge of the duties imposed by subsections (1) and (2) above.

(8)   Different codes of practice may be prepared and issued under subsection (7) above for different areas.

(9)   The Secretary of State may issue modifications of, or withdraw, a code issued under subsection (7) above; but where a code is withdrawn, he shall prepare and issue a new code under that subsection in substitution for it.

(10)   Any person subject to any duty imposed by subsection (1) or (2) above shall have regard to the code of practice in force under subsection (7) above in discharging that duty.

(11)   A draft code prepared under subsection (7) above shall be laid before both Houses of Parliament and shall not be issued until after the end of the period of 40 days beginning with the day on which the code was so laid, or if the draft is laid on different days, the later of the two days.

(12)   If, within the period mentioned in subsection (11) above, either House resolves that the code the draft of which was laid before it should not be issued, the Secretary of State shall not issue that code.

(13)   No account shall be taken in reckoning any period of 40 days for the purposes of this section of any time during which Parliament is dissolved or prorogued or during which both Houses are adjourned for more than four days.

(14)   In this section "traffic sign" has the meaning given in section 64(1) of the Road Traffic Regulation Act 1984.

[196]

NOTES
    Sub-s (6): words in square brackets substituted by the Road Traffic (Temporary Restrictions) Act 1991, s 2(6).

90–105   *(Relate to litter control areas (s 90); summary proceedings by persons aggrieved by litter (s 91); summary proceedings by litter authorities (s 92); street litter control notices (s 93); street litter: supplementary provisions (s 94); public registers (s 95); application of Part II (s 96); transitional provision relating to s 89 (s 97); definitions (s 98); powers in relation to abandoned shopping and luggage trolleys (s 99); ss 100–105 (Pt V) repealed by the Radioactive Substances Act 1993, s 50, Sch 6, Pt I.)*

PART VI
GENETICALLY MODIFIED ORGANISMS

Preliminary

106 Purpose of Part VI and meaning of "genetically modified organisms" and related expressions

(1)   This Part has effect for the purpose of preventing or minimising any damage to the environment which may arise from the escape or release from human control of genetically modified organisms.

(2)   In this Part the term "organism" means any acellular, unicellular or multicellular entity (in any form), other than humans or human embryos; and, unless the context otherwise requires, the term also includes any article or substance consisting of or including biological matter.

(3)   For the purpose of subsection (2) above "biological matter" means anything (other than an entity mentioned in that subsection) which consists of or includes—
      (a)   tissue or cells (including gametes or propagules) or subcellular entities, of any kind, capable of replication or of transferring genetic material, or
      (b)   genes or other genetic material, in any form, which are so capable,

and it is immaterial, in determining if something is or is not an organism or biological matter, whether it is the product of natural or artificial processes of reproduction and, in the case of biological matter, whether it has ever been part of a whole organism.

(4)   For the purposes of this Part an organism is "genetically modified" if any of the genes or other genetic material in the organism—

   (a) have been modified by means of an artificial technique prescribed in regulations by the Secretary of State; or

   (b) are inherited or otherwise derived, through any number of replications, from genes or other genetic material (from any source) which were so modified.

(5)   The techniques which may be prescribed for the purposes of subsection (4) above include—

   (a) any technique for the modification of any genes or other genetic material by the recombination, insertion or deletion of, or of any component parts of, that material from its previously occurring state, and

   (b) any other technique for modifying genes or other genetic material which in the opinion of the Secretary of State would produce organisms which should for the purposes of this Part be treated as having been genetically modified,

but do not include techniques which involve no more than, or no more than the assistance of, naturally occurring processes of reproduction (including selective breeding techniques or *in vitro* fertilisation).

(6)   It is immaterial for the purposes of subsections (4) and (5) above whether the modifications of genes or other genetic material effected by a prescribed technique are produced by direct operations on that genetic material or are induced by indirect means (including in particular the use of viruses, microbial plasmids or other vector systems or of mutation inducing agents).

(7)   In this Part, where the context permits, a reference to "reproduction", in relation to an organism, includes a reference to its replication or its transferring genetic material.

[197]

NOTES

   Commencement: 1 February 1993 (sub-ss (1)–(3), (6), (7)); 1 April 1991 (remainder).

   Regulations: the Genetically Modified Organisms (Deliberate Release) Regulations 1992, SI 1992/3280, reg 3.

---

107 Meaning of "damage to the environment", "control" and related expressions in Part VI

(1)   The following provisions have effect for the interpretation of this Part.

(2)   The "environment" consists of land, air and water or any of those media.

(3)   "Damage to the environment" is caused by the presence in the environment of genetically modified organisms which have (or of a single such organism which has) escaped or been released from a person's control and are (or is) capable of causing harm to the living organisms supported by the environment.

(4)   An organism shall be regarded as present in the environment notwithstanding that it is present in or on any human or other organism, or any other thing, which is itself present in the environment.

(5)   Genetically modified organisms present in the environment are capable of causing harm if—

(a) they are individually capable, or are present in numbers such that together they are capable, of causing harm; or

(b) they are able to produce descendants which will be capable, or which will be present in numbers such that together they will be capable, of causing harm;

and a single organism is capable of causing harm either if it is itself capable of causing harm or if it is able to produce descendants which will be so capable.

(6) "Harm" means harm to the health of humans or other living organisms or other interference with the ecological systems of which they form part and, in the case of man, includes offence caused to any of his senses or harm to his property.

(7) "Harmful" and "harmless" mean respectively, in relation to genetically modified organisms, their being capable or their being incapable of causing harm.

(8) The Secretary of State may by regulations provide, in relation to genetically modified organisms of any description specified in the regulations, that—

(a) the capacity of those organisms for causing harm of any description so specified, or

(b) harm of any description so specified,

shall be disregarded for such purposes of this Part as may be so specified.

(9) Organisms of any description are under the "control" of a person where he keeps them contained by any system of physical, chemical or biological barriers (or combination of such barriers) used for either or both of the following purposes, namely—

(a) for ensuring that the organisms do not enter the environment or produce descendants which are not so contained; or

(b) for ensuring that any of the organisms which do enter the environment, or any descendants of the organisms which are not so contained, are harmless.

(10) An organism under a person's control is "released" if he deliberately causes or permits it to cease to be under his control or the control of any other person and to enter the environment; and such an organism "escapes" if, otherwise than by being released, it ceases to be under his control or that of any other person and enters the environment.

(11) Genetically modified organisms of any description are "marketed" when products consisting of or including such organisms are placed on the market.

[198]

NOTES

Commencement: 1 February 1993 (sub-ss (1)–(7), (9)–(11)); 1 April 1991 (remainder).

Regulations: the Genetically Modified Organisms (Deliberate Release) Regulations 1992, SI 1992/3280, reg 4.

General controls

108 Risk assessment and notification requirements

(1) Subject to subsections (2) and (7) below, no person shall import or acquire, release or market any genetically modified organisms unless, before doing that act—

(a) he has carried out an assessment of any risks there are (by reference to the nature of the organisms and the manner in which he intends to keep them after their importation or acquisition or, as the case may be, to release or market them) of damage to the environment being caused as a result of doing that act; and

(b) in such cases and circumstances as may be prescribed, he has given the Secretary of State such notice of his intention of doing that act and such information as may be prescribed.

(2)   Subsection (1) above does not apply to a person proposing to do an act mentioned in that subsection who is required under section 111(1)(a) below to have a consent before doing that act.

(3)   Subject to subsections (4) and (7) below, a person who is keeping genetically modified organisms shall, in such cases or circumstances and at such times or intervals as may be prescribed—
   (a) carry out an assessment of any risks there are of damage to the environment being caused as a result of his continuing to keep them;
   (b) give the Secretary of State notice of the fact that he is keeping the organisms and such information as may be prescribed.

(4)   Subsection (3) above does not apply to a person who is keeping genetically modified organisms and is required under section 111(2) below to have a consent authorising him to continue to keep the organisms.

(5)   It shall be the duty of a person who carries out an assessment under subsection (1)(a) or (3)(a) above to keep, for the prescribed period, such a record of the assessment as may be prescribed.

(6)   A person required by subsection (1)(b) or (3)(b) above to give notice to the Secretary of State shall give the Secretary of State such further information as the Secretary of State may by notice in writing require.

(7)   Regulations under this section may provide for exemptions, or for the granting by the Secretary of State of exemptions to particular persons or classes of person, from the requirements of subsection (1) or (3) above in such cases or circumstances, and to such extent, as may be prescribed.

(8)   The Secretary of State may at any time—
   (a) give directions to a person falling within subsection (1) above requiring that person to apply for a consent before doing the act in question; or
   (b) give directions to a person falling within subsection (3) above requiring that person, before such date as may be specified in the direction, to apply for a consent authorising him to continue keeping the organisms in question;

and a person given directions under paragraph (a) above shall then, and a person given directions under paragraph (b) above shall from the specified date, be subject to section 111 below in place of the requirements of this section.

(9)   Regulations under this section may—
   (a) prescribe the manner in which assessments under subsection (1) or (3) above are to be carried out and the matters which must be investigated and assessed;
   (b) prescribe minimum periods of notice between the giving of a notice under subsection (1)(b) above and the doing of the act in question;
   (c) make provision allowing the Secretary of State to shorten or to extend any such period;
   (d) prescribe maximum intervals at which assessments under subsection (3)(a) above must be carried out;

and the regulations may make different provision for different cases and different circumstances.

(10) In this section "prescribed" means prescribed by the Secretary of State in regulations under this section.

[199]

NOTES
   Commencement: 1 February 1993 (sub-s (1) (in part)); 1 January 1993 (sub-s (10)); 1 April 1991 (sub-ss (1), (3) (in part), (5), (7), (9)); to be appointed (remainder).
   Regulations: the Genetically Modified Organisms (Risk Assessment) (Records and Exemptions) Regulations 1996, SI 1996/1106, as amended by SI 1997/1900.

109 General duties relating to importation, acquisition, keeping, release or marketing of organisms

(1)   A person who—
    (a) is proposing to import or acquire any genetically modified organisms, or
    (b) is keeping any such organisms, or
    (c) is proposing to release or market any such organisms,

shall, subject to subsection (5) below, be subject to the duties specified in subsection (2), (3) or (4) below, as the case may be.

(2)   A person who proposes to import or acquire genetically modified organisms—
    (a) shall take all reasonable steps to identify, by reference to the nature of the organisms and the manner in which he intends to keep them (including any precautions to be taken against their escaping or causing damage to the environment), what risks there are of damage to the environment being caused as a result of their importation or acquisition; and
    (b) shall not import or acquire the organisms if it appears that, despite any precautions which can be taken, there is a risk of damage to the environment being caused as a result of their importation or acquisition.

(3)   A person who is keeping genetically modified organisms—
    (a) shall take all reasonable steps to keep himself informed of any damage to the environment which may have been caused as a result of his keeping the organisms and to identify what risks there are of damage to the environment being caused as a result of his continuing to keep them;
    (b) shall cease keeping the organisms if, despite any additional precautions which can be taken, it appears, at any time, that there is a risk of damage to the environment being caused as a result of his continuing to keep them; and
    (c) shall use the best available techniques not entailing excessive cost for keeping the organisms under his control and for preventing any damage to the environment being caused as a result of his continuing to keep the organisms;

and where a person is required by paragraph (b) above to cease keeping the organisms he shall dispose of them as safely and as quickly as practicable and paragraph (c) above shall continue to apply until he has done so.

(4)   A person who proposes to release genetically modified organisms—
    (a) shall take all reasonable steps to keep himself informed, by reference to the nature of the organisms and the extent and manner of the release (including any precautions to be taken against their causing damage to the environment), what risks there are of damage to the environment being caused as a result of their being released;
    (b) shall not release the organisms if it appears that, despite the precautions which can be taken, there is a risk of damage to the environment being caused as a result of their being released; and
    (c) subject to paragraph (b) above, shall use the best available techniques not entailing excessive cost for preventing any damage to the environment being caused as a result of their being released;

and this subsection applies, with the necessary modifications, to a person proposing to market organisms as it applies to a person proposing to release organisms.

(5)   This section does not apply—
    (a) to persons proposing to import or acquire, to release or to market any genetically modified organisms, in cases or circumstances where, under section 108 above, they are not required to carry out a risk assessment before doing that act;

> (b) to persons who are keeping any genetically modified organisms and who—
>> (i) were not required under section 108 above to carry out a risk assessment before importing or acquiring them;
>> (ii) have not been required under that section to carry out a risk assessment in respect of the keeping of those organisms since importing or acquiring them; or
> (c) to holders of consents, in the case of acts authorised by those consents.

[200]

NOTES
Commencement: to be appointed.

110 Prohibition notices

(1) The Secretary of State may serve a notice under this section (a "prohibition notice") on any person he has reason to believe—
> (a) is proposing to import or acquire, release or market any genetically modified organisms; or
> (b) is keeping any such organisms;

if he is of the opinion that doing any such act in relation to those organisms or continuing to keep them, as the case may be, would involve a risk of causing damage to the environment.

(2) A prohibition notice may prohibit a person from doing an act mentioned in subsection (1)(a) above in relation to any genetically modified organisms or from continuing to keep them; and the prohibition may apply in all cases or circumstances or in such cases or circumstances as may be specified in the notice.

(3) A prohibition notice shall—
> (a) state that the Secretary of State is, in relation to the person on whom it is served, of the opinion mentioned in subsection (1) above;
> (b) specify what is, or is to be, prohibited by the notice; and
> (c) if the prohibition is not to be effective on being served, specify the date on which the prohibition is to take effect;

and a notice may be served on a person notwithstanding that he may have a consent authorising any act which is, or is to be, prohibited by the notice.

(4) Where a person is prohibited by a prohibition notice from continuing to keep any genetically modified organisms, he shall dispose of them as quickly and safely as practicable or, if the notice so provides, as may be specified in the notice.

(5) The Secretary of State may at any time withdraw a prohibition notice served on any person by notice given to that person.

[201]

NOTES
Commencement: 1 February 1993 (certain purposes); to be appointed (remaining purposes).

Consents

111 Consents required by certain persons

(1) Subject to subsection (7) below, no person shall import or acquire, release or market any genetically modified organisms—
> (a) in such cases or circumstances as may be prescribed in relation to that act, or
> (b) in any case where he has been given directions under section 108(8)(a) above,

except in pursuance of a consent granted by the Secretary of State and in accordance with any limitations and conditions to which the consent is subject.

(2)   Subject to subsection (7) below, no person who has imported or acquired any genetically modified organisms (whether under a consent or not) shall continue to keep the organisms—

    (a) in such cases or circumstances as may be prescribed, after the end of the prescribed period, or

    (b) if he has been given directions under section 108(8)(b) above, after the date specified in the directions,

except in pursuance of a consent granted by the Secretary of State and in accordance with any limitations or conditions to which the consent is subject.

(3)   A person who is required under subsection (2) above to cease keeping any genetically modified organisms shall dispose of them as quickly and safely as practicable.

(4)   An application for a consent must contain such information and be made and advertised in such manner as may be prescribed and shall be accompanied by the fee required under section 113 below.

(5)   The applicant shall, in prescribed circumstances, give such notice of his application to such persons as may be prescribed.

(6)   The Secretary of State may by notice to the applicant require him to furnish such further information specified in the notice, within such period as may be so specified, as he may require for the purpose of determining the application; and if the applicant fails to furnish the information within the specified period the Secretary of State may refuse to proceed with the application.

[(6A) Where an applicant for consent for releasing or marketing genetically modified organisms becomes aware, before his application is either granted or rejected, of any new information with regard to any risks there are of damage to the environment being caused as a result of the organisms being released or marketed, he shall notify the Secretary of State of that new information forthwith.]

(7)   Regulations under this section may provide for exemptions, or for the granting by the Secretary of State of exemptions to particular persons or classes of person, from—

    (a) any requirement under subsection (1) or (2) above to have a consent, or

    (b) any of the requirements to be fulfilled under the regulations by an applicant for a consent,

in such cases or circumstances as may be prescribed.

(8)   Where an application for a consent is duly made to him, the Secretary of State may grant the consent subject to such limitations and conditions as may be imposed under section 112 below or he may refuse the application.

(9)   The conditions attached to a consent may include conditions which are to continue to have effect notwithstanding that the holder has completed or ceased the act or acts authorised by the consent.

(10) The Secretary of State may at any time, by notice given to the holder of a consent, revoke the consent or vary the consent (whether by attaching new limitations and conditions or by revoking or varying any limitations and conditions to which it is at that time subject).

(11) Regulations under this section may make different provision for different cases and different circumstances; and in this section "prescribed" means prescribed in regulations under this section.

[202]

NOTES

    Commencement: 1 February 1993 (sub-ss (6), (6A), (8)–(10)); 1 April 1991 (sub-ss (1), (2), (4), (5), (7), (11)); to be appointed (remainder).

Sub-s (6A): inserted by the Genetically Modified Organisms (Deliberate Release) Regulations 1992, SI 1992/3280, reg 13(1).
Regulations: the Genetically Modified Organisms (Deliberate Release) Regulations 1992, SI 1992/3280, as amended by SI 1995/304, SI 1997/1900.

112 Consents: limitations and conditions

(1)   The Secretary of State may include in a consent such limitations and conditions as he may think fit . . .

(2)   Without prejudice to the generality of subsection (1) above, the conditions included in a consent may—
    (a) require the giving of notice of any fact to the Secretary of State; or
    (b) prohibit or restrict the keeping, releasing or marketing of genetically modified organisms under the consent in specified cases or circumstances;

and where, under any condition, the holder of a consent is required to cease keeping any genetically modified organisms, he shall dispose of them, if no manner is specified in the conditions, as quickly and safely as practicable.

(3)   Subject to subsection (6) below, there is implied in every consent for the importation or acquisition of genetically modified organisms a general condition that the holder of the consent shall—
    (a) take all reasonable steps to keep himself informed (by reference to the nature of the organisms and the manner in which he intends to keep them after their importation or acquisition) of any risks there are of damage to the environment being caused as a result of their importation or acquisition; and
    (b) if at any time it appears that any such risks are more serious than were apparent when the consent was granted, notify the Secretary of State forthwith.

(4)   Subject to subsection (6) below, there is implied in every consent for keeping genetically modified organisms a general condition that the holder of the consent shall—
    (a) take all reasonable steps to keep himself informed of any damage to the environment which may have been caused as a result of his keeping the organisms and of any risks there are of such damage being caused as a result of his continuing to keep them;
    (b) if at any time it appears that any such risks are more serious than were apparent when the consent was granted, notify the Secretary of State forthwith; and
    (c) use the best available techniques not entailing excessive cost for keeping the organisms under his control and for preventing any damage to the environment being caused as a result of his continuing to keep them.

(5)   Subject to subsection (6) below, there is implied in every consent for releasing or marketing genetically modified organisms a general condition that the holder of the consent shall—
    (a) take all reasonable steps to keep himself informed (by reference to the nature of the organisms and the extent and manner of the release or marketing) of any risks there are of damage to the environment being caused as a result of their being released or, as the case may be, marketed;
    [(b) notify the Secretary of State of—
       (i) any new information which becomes available with regard to any risks there are of damage to the environment being so caused, and
      (ii) the effects of any releases by him for the assessment of any risks there are of damage to the environment being so caused by such organisms being released or marketed;]

(c) use the best available techniques not entailing excessive cost for preventing any damage to the environment being caused as a result of their being released or, as the case may be, marketed.

(6) The general condition implied into a consent under subsection (3), (4) or (5) above has effect subject to any conditions imposed under subsection (1) above; and the obligations imposed by virtue of subsection (4)(c) or (5)(c) above shall not apply to any aspect of an act authorised by a consent which is regulated by such a condition.

(7) There shall be implied in every consent for keeping, releasing or marketing genetically modified organisms of any description a general condition that the holder of the consent—
　(a) shall take all reasonable steps to keep himself informed of developments in the techniques which may be available in his case for preventing damage to the environment being caused as a result of the doing of the act authorised by the consent in relation to organisms of that description; and
　(b) if it appears at any time that any better techniques are available to him than is required by any condition included in the consent under subsection (1) above, shall notify the Secretary of State of that fact forthwith.

But this general condition shall have effect subject to any conditions imposed under subsection (1) above.

[203]

NOTES
　Commencement: 1 February 1993 (sub-ss (1), (2), (5)–(7)); to be appointed (remainder).
　Sub-s (1): words omitted repealed by the Environmental Protection Act 1990 (Modification of section 112) Regulations 1992, SI 1992/2617, reg 2.
　Sub-s (5): para (b) substituted by the Genetically Modified Organisms (Deliberate Release) Regulations 1992, SI 1992/3280, reg 9.

113 Fees and charges

(1) The Secretary of State may, with the approval of the Treasury, make and from time to time revise a scheme prescribing—
　(a) fees payable in respect of applications for consents; and
　(b) charges payable by persons holding consents in respect of the subsistence of their consents;
and it shall be a condition of any such consent that any applicable prescribed charge is paid in accordance with that scheme.

(2) A scheme under this section may, in particular—
　(a) provide for different fees or charges to be payable in different cases or circumstances;
　(b) provide for the times at which and the manner in which payments are to be made; and
　(c) make such incidental, supplementary and transitional provision as appears to the Secretary of State to be appropriate.

(3) The Secretary of State shall so frame a scheme under this section as to secure, so far as practicable, that the amounts payable under it will be sufficient, taking one financial year with another, to cover the expenditure of the Secretary of State in discharging his functions under this Part in relation to consents.

(4) The Secretary of State shall, on making or revising a scheme under this section, lay a copy of the scheme or of the scheme as revised before each House of Parliament.

[204]

Inspectors

114 Appointment etc of inspectors

(1)   The Secretary of State may appoint as inspectors, for carrying this Part into effect, such number of persons appearing to him to be qualified for the purpose as he may consider necessary.

(2)   The Secretary of State may make to or in respect of any person so appointed such payments by way of remuneration, allowances or otherwise as he may with the approval of the Treasury determine.

(3)   An inspector shall not be personally liable in any civil or criminal proceedings for anything done in the purported exercise of any power under section 115 or 117 below if the court is satisfied that the act was done in good faith and that there were reasonable grounds for doing it.

(4)   In England and Wales an inspector, if authorised to do so by the Secretary of State, may, although not of counsel or a solicitor, prosecute before a magistrates' court proceedings for an offence under section 118(1) below.

(5)   In this Part "inspector" means, subject to section 125 below, a person appointed as an inspector under subsection (1) above.

[205]

NOTES

Commencement: 1 February 1993 (sub-ss (4), (5)); 1 April 1991 (remainder).

115 Rights of entry and inspection

(1)   An inspector may, on production (if so required) of his authority, exercise any of the powers specified in subsection (3) below for the purposes of the discharge of the functions of the Secretary of State under this Part.

(2)   Those powers are exercisable—
    (a) in relation to premises—
        (i) on which the inspector has reason to believe a person is keeping or has kept any genetically modified organisms, or
        (ii) from which he has reason to believe any such organisms have been released or have escaped; and
    (b) in relation to premises on which the inspector has reason to believe there may be harmful genetically modified organisms or evidence of damage to the environment caused by genetically modified organisms;

but they are not exercisable in relation to premises used wholly or mainly for domestic purposes.

(3)   The powers of an inspector are—
    (a) at any reasonable time (or, in a situation in which in his opinion there is an immediate risk of damage to the environment, at any time)—
        (i) to enter premises which he has reason to believe it is necessary for him to enter and to take with him any person duly authorised by the Secretary of State and, if the inspector has reasonable cause to apprehend any serious obstruction in the execution of his duty, a constable; and
        (ii) to take with him any equipment or materials required for any purpose for which the power of entry is being exercised;
    (b) to carry out such tests and inspections (and to make such recordings), as may in any circumstances be necessary;
    (c) to direct that any, or any part of, premises which he has power to enter, or anything in or on such premises, shall be left undisturbed (whether

generally or in particular respects) for so long as is reasonably necessary for the purpose of any test or inspection;

(d) to take samples of any organisms, articles or substances found in or on any premises which he has power to enter, and of the air, water or land in, on, or in the vicinity of, the premises;

(e) in the case of anything found in or on any premises which he has power to enter, which appears to him to contain or to have contained genetically modified organisms which have caused or are likely to cause damage to the environment, to cause it to be dismantled or subjected to any process or test (but not so as to damage or destroy it unless this is necessary);

(f) in the case of anything mentioned in paragraph (e) above or anything found on premises which he has power to enter which appears to be a genetically modified organism or to consist of or include genetically modified organisms, to take possession of it and detain it for so long as is necessary for all or any of the following purposes, namely—

  (i) to examine it and do to it anything which he has power to do under that paragraph;

  (ii) to ensure that it is not tampered with before his examination of it is completed; and

  (iii) to ensure that it is available for use as evidence in any proceedings for an offence under section 118 below;

(g) to require any person whom he has reasonable cause to believe to be able to give any information relevant to any test or inspection under this subsection to answer (in the absence of persons other than a person nominated to be present and any persons whom the inspector may allow to be present) such questions as the inspector thinks fit to ask and to sign a declaration of the truth of his answers;

(h) to require the production of, or where the information is recorded in computerised form, the furnishing of extracts from, any records which are required to be kept under this Part or it is necessary for him to see for the purposes of any test or inspection under this subsection and to inspect, and take copies of, or of any entry in, the records;

(i) to require any person to afford him such facilities and assistance with respect to any matters or things within that person's control or in relation to which that person has responsibilities as are necessary to enable the inspector to exercise any of the powers conferred on him by this section;

(j) any other power for the purpose mentioned in subsection (1) above which is conferred by regulations made by the Secretary of State.

(4)   The Secretary of State may by regulations make provision as to the procedure to be followed in connection with the taking of, and the dealing with, samples under subsection (3)(d) above.

(5)   Where an inspector proposes to exercise the power conferred by subsection (3)(e) above, he shall, if so requested by a person who at the time is present on and has responsibilities in relation to those premises, cause anything which is to be done by virtue of that power to be done in the presence of that person.

(6)   Before exercising the power conferred by subsection (3)(e) above, an inspector shall consult such persons as appear to him appropriate for the purpose of ascertaining what dangers, if any, there may be in doing anything which he proposes to do under the power.

(7)   Where under the power conferred by subsection (3)(f) above an inspector takes possession of anything found on any premises, he shall leave there, either with a responsible person or, if that is impracticable, fixed in a conspicuous position, a notice giving particulars sufficient to identify what he has seized and stating that he has taken possession of it under that power; and before taking possession under that power of—

(a) any thing that forms part of a batch of similar things, or
(b) any substance,

an inspector shall, if it is practical and safe for him to do so, take a sample of it and give to a responsible person at the premises a portion of the sample marked in a manner sufficient to identify it.

(8)   No answer given by a person in pursuance of a requirement imposed under subsection (3)(g) above shall be admissible in evidence—
(a) in any proceedings in England and Wales against that person; or
(b) *(applies to Scotland only)*.

(9)   The powers conferred by subsection (3)(a), (b), (c), (d), (e) and (h) above shall also be exercisable (subject to subsections (4), (5) and (6) above) by any person authorised for the purpose in writing by the Secretary of State.

(10) Nothing in this section shall be taken to compel the production by any person of a document of which he would on grounds of legal professional privilege be entitled to withhold production on an order for discovery in an action in the High Court or, in relation to Scotland, on an order for the production of documents in an action in the Court of Session.

[206]

NOTES
Commencement: 1 February 1993 (sub-ss (1)–(3), (5)–(10)); 1 April 1991 (remainder).

Enforcement powers and offences

116 Obtaining of information from persons

(1)   For the purposes of the discharge of his functions under this Part, the Secretary of State may, by notice in writing served on any person who appears to him—
(a) to be involved in the importation, acquisition, keeping, release or marketing of genetically modified organisms; or
(b) to be about to become, or to have been, involved in any of those activities;

require that person to furnish such relevant information available to him as is specified in the notice, in such form and within such period following service of the notice as is so specified.

(2)   For the purposes of this section "relevant information" means information concerning any aspects of the activities in question, including any damage to the environment which may be or have been caused thereby; and the discharge by the Secretary of State of an obligation of the United Kingdom under the Community Treaties or any international agreement concerning the protection of the environment from harm caused by genetically modified organisms shall be treated as a function of his under this Part.

[207]

NOTES
Commencement: 1 February 1993 (certain purposes); to be appointed (remaining purposes).

117 Power to deal with cause of imminent danger of damage to the environment

(1)   Where, in the case of anything found by him on any premises which he has power to enter, an inspector has reason to believe that it is a genetically modified organism or that it consists of or includes genetically modified organisms and that, in the circumstances in which he finds it, is a cause of imminent danger of damage

to the environment, he may seize it and cause it to be rendered harmless (whether by destruction, by bringing it under proper control or otherwise).

(2) Before there is rendered harmless under this section—
(a) any thing that forms part of a batch of similar things, or
(b) any substance,

the inspector shall, if it is practicable and safe for him to do so, take a sample of it and give to a responsible person at the premises a portion of the sample marked in a manner sufficient to identify it.

(3) As soon as may be after anything has been seized and rendered harmless under this section, the inspector shall prepare and sign a written report giving particulars of the circumstances in which it was seized and so dealt with by him, and shall—
(a) give a signed copy of the report to a responsible person at the premises where it was found by him; and
(b) unless that person is the owner of it, also serve a signed copy of the report on the owner;

and if, where paragraph (b) above applies, the inspector cannot after reasonable inquiry ascertain the name or address of the owner, the copy may be served on him by giving it to the person to whom a copy was given under paragraph (a) above.

[208]

NOTES
Commencement: 1 February 1993.

118 Offences

(1) It is an offence for a person—
(a) to do anything in contravention of section 108(1) above in relation to something which is, and which he knows or has reason to believe is, a genetically modified organism;
(b) to fail to comply with section 108(3) above when keeping something which is, and which he knows or has reason to believe is, a genetically modified organism;
(c) to do anything in contravention of section 111(1) or (2) above in relation to something which is, and which he knows or has reason to believe is, a genetically modified organism;
(d) to fail to comply with any requirement of subsection (2), (3)(a), (b) or (c) or (4) of section 109 above in relation to something which is, and which he knows or has reason to believe is, a genetically modified organism;
(e) to fail, without reasonable excuse, to comply with section 108(5) or (6) [or section 111(6A)] above;
(f) to contravene any prohibition imposed on him by a prohibition notice;
(g) without reasonable excuse, to fail to comply with any requirement imposed under section 115 above;
(h) to prevent any other person from appearing before or from answering any question to which an inspector may, by virtue of section 115(3) above, require an answer;
(i) intentionally to obstruct an inspector in the exercise or performance of his powers or duties, other than his powers or duties under section 117 above;
(j) intentionally to obstruct an inspector in the exercise of his powers or duties under section 117 above;
(k) to fail, without reasonable excuse, to comply with any requirement imposed by a notice under section 116 above;
(l) to make a statement which he knows to be false or misleading in a material particular, or recklessly to make a statement which is false or misleading in a material particular, where the statement is made—
(i) in purported compliance with a requirement to furnish any information imposed by or under any provision of this Part; or

(ii) for the purpose of obtaining the grant of a consent to himself or any other person or the variation of a consent;

(m) intentionally to make a false entry in any record required to be kept under section 108 or 111 above;

(n) with intent to deceive, to forge or use a document purporting to be issued under section 111 above or required for any purpose thereunder or to make or have in his possession a document so closely resembling any such document as to be likely to deceive;

(o) falsely to pretend to be an inspector.

(2) It shall be a defence for a person charged with an offence under paragraph (a), (b), (c), (d) or (f) of subsection (1) above to prove that he took all reasonable precautions and exercised all due diligence to avoid the commission of the offence.

(3) A person guilty of an offence under paragraph (c) or (d) of subsection (1) above shall be liable—

(a) on summary conviction, to a fine not exceeding £20,000 or to imprisonment for a term not exceeding six months, or to both;

(b) on conviction on indictment, to a fine or to imprisonment for a term not exceeding five years, or to both.

(4) A person guilty of an offence under paragraph (f) of subsection (1) above shall be liable—

(a) on summary conviction, to a fine not exceeding £20,000 or to imprisonment for a term not exceeding six months, or to both;

(b) on conviction on indictment, to a fine or to imprisonment for a term not exceeding two years, or to both.

(5) A person guilty of an offence under paragraph (a) or (b) of subsection (1) above shall be liable—

(a) on summary conviction, to a fine not exceeding the statutory maximum or to imprisonment for a term not exceeding six months, or to both;

(b) on conviction on indictment, to a fine or to imprisonment for a term not exceeding five years, or to both.

(6) A person guilty of an offence under paragraph (e), (j), (k), (l), (m) or (n) of subsection (1) above shall be liable—

(a) on summary conviction, to a fine not exceeding the statutory maximum or to imprisonment for a term not exceeding six months, or to both;

(b) on conviction on indictment, to a fine or to imprisonment for a term not exceeding two years, or to both.

(7) A person guilty of an offence under paragraph (g), (h) or (i) of subsection (1) above shall be liable on summary conviction to a fine not exceeding the statutory maximum or to imprisonment for a term not exceeding three months, or to both.

(8) A person guilty of an offence under paragraph (o) of subsection (1) above shall be liable on summary conviction to a fine not exceeding level 5 on the standard scale.

(9) Where a person is convicted of an offence under paragraph (b) of subsection (1) above in respect of his keeping any genetically modified organism, then, if the contravention in respect of which he was convicted is continued after he was convicted he shall be guilty of a further offence and liable on summary conviction to a fine of one-fifth of level 5 on the standard scale for each day on which the contravention is so continued.

(10) Proceedings in respect of an offence under this section shall not be instituted in England and Wales except by the Secretary of State or with the consent of the Director of Public Prosecutions or in Northern Ireland except with the consent of the Director of Public Prosecutions for Northern Ireland.

NOTES
Commencement: 1 February 1993 (sub-ss (1) (in part), (2)–(10)); to be appointed (remainder).
Sub-s (1): words in square brackets in para (e) inserted by the Genetically Modified Organisms (Deliberate Release) Regulations 1992, SI 1992/3280, reg 13(2).

119 Onus of proof as regards techniques and evidence

(1)   In any proceedings for either of the following offences, that is to say—
(a) an offence under section 118(1)(c) above consisting in a failure to comply with the general condition implied by section 112(4)(c) or (5)(c) above; or
(b) an offence under section 118(1)(d) above consisting in a failure to comply with section 109(3)(c) or (4)(c) above;

it shall be for the accused to prove that there was no better available technique not entailing excessive cost than was in fact used to satisfy the condition or to comply with that section.

(2)   Where an entry is required by a condition in a consent to be made in any record as to the observance of any other condition and the entry has not been made, that fact shall be admissible as evidence that that other condition has not been observed.

[210]

NOTES
Commencement: 1 February 1993.

120 Power of court to order cause of offence to be remedied

(1)   Where a person is convicted of an offence under section 118(1)(a), (b), (c), (d), (e) or (f) above in respect of any matters which appear to the court to be matters which it is in his power to remedy, the court may, in addition to or instead of imposing any punishment, order him, within such time as may be fixed by the order, to take such steps as may be specified in the order for remedying those matters.

(2)   The time fixed by an order under subsection (1) above may be extended or further extended by order of the court on an application made before the end of the time as originally fixed or as extended under this subsection, as the case may be.

(3)   Where a person is ordered under subsection (1) above to remedy any matters, that person shall not be liable under section 118 above in respect of those matters, in so far as they continue during the time fixed by the order or any further time allowed under subsection (2) above.

[211]

NOTES
Commencement: 1 February 1993.

121 Power of Secretary of State to remedy harm

(1)   Where the commission of an offence under section 118(1)(a), (b), (c), (d), (e) or (f) above causes any harm which it is possible to remedy, the Secretary of State may, subject to subsection (2) below—
(a) arrange for any reasonable steps to be taken towards remedying the harm; and
(b) recover the cost of taking those steps from any person convicted of that offence.

(2)   The Secretary of State shall not exercise his powers under this section, where any of the steps are to be taken on or will affect land in the occupation of any

person other than a person convicted of the offence in question, except with the permission of that person.

[212]

NOTES
Commencement: 1 February 1993.

Publicity

122 Public register of information

(1)	The Secretary of State shall maintain a register ("the register") containing prescribed particulars of or relating to—
  (a)	notices given or other information furnished under section 108 above;
  (b)	directions given under section 108(8) above;
  (c)	prohibition notices;
  (d)	applications for consents (and any further information furnished in connection with them) and any advice given by the committee appointed under section 124 below in relation to such applications;
  (e)	consents granted by the Secretary of State and any information furnished to him in pursuance of consent conditions;
  (f)	any other information obtained or furnished under any provision of this Part;
  (g)	convictions for such offences under section 118 above as may be prescribed;
  (h)	such other matters relating to this Part as may be prescribed;
but that duty is subject to section 123 below.

(2)	It shall be the duty of the Secretary of State—
  (a)	to secure that the register is open to inspection by members of the public free of charge at all reasonable hours; and
  (b)	to afford to members of the public facilities for obtaining copies of entries, on payment of reasonable charges.

(3)	The register may be kept in any form.

(4)	The Secretary of State may make regulations with respect to the keeping of the register; and in this section "prescribed" means prescribed in regulations made by the Secretary of State.

[213]

NOTES
Commencement: 1 February 1993 (sub-s (1), certain purposes, sub-ss (2), (3)); 1 April 1991 (sub-s (1), certain purposes, sub-s (4)); to be appointed (remaining purposes).
  Regulations: the Genetically Modified Organisms (Deliberate Release) Regulations 1992, SI 1992/3280, regs 17, 18, as amended (in the case of reg 18) by SI 1993/152, SI 1995/304.

123 Exclusion from register of certain information

(1)	No information shall be included in the register under section 122 above if and so long as, in the opinion of the Secretary of State, the inclusion of the information would be contrary to the interests of national security.

(2)	No information shall be included in the register if and so long as, in the opinion of the Secretary of State, it ought to be excluded on the ground that its inclusion might result in damage to the environment.

(3)	No information relating to the affairs of any individual or business shall be included in the register without the consent of that individual or the person for the time being carrying on that business, if the Secretary of State has determined that the information—

(a) is, in relation to him, commercially confidential; and

(b) is not information of a description to which subsection (7) below applies;

unless the Secretary of State is of the opinion that the information is no longer commercially confidential in relation to him.

(4) Nothing in subsection (3) above requires the Secretary of State to determine whether any information is or is not commercially confidential except where the person furnishing the information applies to have it excluded on the ground that it is (in relation to himself or another person) commercially confidential.

(5) Where an application has been made for information to be excluded under subsection (3) above, the Secretary of State shall make a determination and inform the applicant of it as soon as is practicable.

(6) Where it appears to the Secretary of State that any information (other than information furnished by the person to whom it relates) which has been obtained under or by virtue of any provision of this Part might be commercially confidential, the Secretary of State shall—

(a) give to the person to whom or to whose business it relates notice that the information is required to be included in the register unless excluded under subsection (3) above; and

(b) give him a reasonable opportunity—

(i) of objecting to the inclusion of the information on the ground that it is commercially confidential; and

(ii) of making representations to the Secretary of State for the purpose of justifying any such objection;

and the Secretary of State shall take any representations into account before determining whether the information is or is not commercially confidential.

(7) The prescribed particulars of or relating to the matters mentioned in section 122(1)(a), (d) and (e) above shall be included in the register notwithstanding that they may be commercially confidential if and so far as they are of any of the following descriptions, namely—

(a) the name and address of the person giving the notice or furnishing the information;

(b) the description of any genetically modified organisms to which the notice or other information relates;

(c) the location at any time of those organisms;

(d) the purpose for which those organisms are being imported, acquired, kept, released or marketed (according to whichever of those acts the notice or other information relates);

(e) results of any assessment of the risks of damage to the environment being caused by the doing of any of those acts;

(f) notices under section 112(3), (4), (5) or (7) above;

and the Secretary of State may by regulations prescribe any other description of information as information which the public interest requires to be included in the register notwithstanding that it may be commercially confidential.

(8) Information excluded from the register under subsection (3) above shall be treated as ceasing to be commercially confidential for the purposes of that subsection at the expiry of a period of four years beginning with the date of the determination by virtue of which it was excluded; but the person who furnished it or to whom or to whose business it relates may apply to the Secretary of State for the information to remain excluded on the ground that it is still commercially confidential.

(9) The Secretary of State may by order substitute for the period for the time being specified in subsection (8) above such other period as he considers appropriate.

NOTES
Commencement: 1 February 1993 (sub-ss (1)–(6), (8)); 1 April 1991 (remainder).

Supplementary

124 Advisory committee for purposes of Part VI

(1)   The Secretary of State shall appoint a committee to provide him with advice—

(a) on the exercise of his powers under sections 111, 112 and 113 above;

(b) on the exercise of any power under this Part to make regulations;

and on such other matters concerning his functions under this Part as he may from time to time direct.

(2)   The chairman and other members of the committee shall hold and vacate office in accordance with the terms of their appointment.

(3)   The Secretary of State shall pay to the members of the committee such remuneration (if any) and such allowances as he may, with the consent of the Treasury, determine.

[215]

125 Delegation of enforcement functions

(1)   The Secretary of State may, by an agreement made with any public authority, delegate to that authority or to any officer appointed by an authority exercising functions on behalf of that authority any of his enforcement functions under this Part, subject to such restrictions and conditions as may be specified in the agreement.

(2)   For the purposes of this section the following are "enforcement functions" of the Secretary of State, that is to say, his functions under—

section 110;
section 114(1) and (4);
section 116;
section 118(10); and
section 121;

and "inspector" in sections 115 and 117 includes, to the extent of the delegation, any inspector appointed by an authority other than the Secretary of State by virtue of an agreement under this section.

(3)   The Secretary of State shall, if and so far as an agreement under this section so provides, make payments to the authority to reimburse the authority the expenses incurred in the performance of functions delegated under this section; but no such agreement shall be made without the approval of the Treasury.

[216]

126 Exercise of certain functions jointly by Secretary of State and Minister of Agriculture, Fisheries and Food

(1)   Subject to subsection (2) below, any reference in this Part to a function exercisable by the Secretary of State shall, in any case where the function is to be exercised in relation to a matter with which the Minister of Agriculture, Fisheries and Food is concerned, be exercisable by the Secretary of State and that Minister acting jointly.

(2)   The validity of anything purporting to be done in pursuance of the exercise of any such function shall not be affected by any question whether that thing fell, by

virtue of this section, to be done by the Secretary of State and the Minister of Agriculture, Fisheries and Food.

[217]

127 Definitions

(1)   In this Part—
"acquire", in relation to genetically modified organisms, includes any method by which such organisms may come to be in a person's possession, other than by their being imported;
"consent" means a consent granted under section 111 above, and a reference to the limitations or conditions to which a consent is subject is a reference to the limitations or conditions subject to which the consent for the time being has effect;
"descendant", in relation to a genetically modified organism, means any other organism whose genes or other genetic material is derived, through any number of generations, from that organism by any process of reproduction;
"import" means import into the United Kingdom;
"premises" includes any land;
"prohibition notice" means a notice under section 110 above.

(2)   This Part, except in so far as it relates to importations of genetically modified organisms, applies to the territorial sea adjacent to Great Britain, and to any area for the time being designated under section 1(7) of the Continental Shelf Act 1964, as it applies in Great Britain.

[218]

NOTES
Commencement: 1 February 1993.

PART VII
NATURE CONSERVATION IN GREAT BRITAIN AND COUNTRYSIDE MATTERS IN WALES

New Councils for England, Scotland and Wales

128 Creation and constitution of new Councils

(1)   There shall be [two] councils, to be called the Nature Conservancy Council for England, . . . and the Countryside Council for Wales (in this Part referred to as "the Councils").

(2)   The Councils shall have the following membership, that is to say—
   (a) the Nature Conservancy Council for England shall have not less than 10 nor more than 14 members;
   (b) . . . ; and
   (c) the Countryside Council for Wales shall have not less than 8 nor more than 12 members;
and those members shall be appointed by the Secretary of State.

(3)   The Secretary of State may by order amend paragraph (a), (b) or (c) of subsection (2) above so as to substitute for the number for the time being specified as the maximum membership of a Council such other number as he thinks appropriate.

(4)   The Councils shall establish a committee to be called the Joint Nature Conservation Committee (in this Part referred to as "the joint committee").

(5)   Schedules 6 and 7 to this Act shall have effect with respect to the constitution and proceedings of the Councils and of the joint committee and related matters.

[219]

NOTES
    Sub-s (1): word in first pair of square brackets substituted and words omitted repealed, by the Natural
Heritage (Scotland) Act 1991, ss 4, 27, Sch 2, para 10(4), Sch 11.
    Sub-s (2): words omitted repealed by the Natural Heritage (Scotland) Act 1991, s 27, Sch 11.

129   (*Relates to grants by the Secretary of State to new councils.*)

Countryside matters

130 Countryside functions of Welsh Council

(1)   The Countryside Council for Wales shall, in place of the Commission established under section 1 of the National Parks and Access to the Countryside Act 1949 (so far as concerns Wales), have such of the functions under the Acts amended by Schedule 8 to this Act (which relates to countryside matters) as are assigned to them in accordance with the amendments effected by that Schedule.

(2)   The Countryside Council for Wales shall discharge those functions—
    (a) for the conservation and enhancement of natural beauty in Wales and of the natural beauty and amenity of the countryside in Wales, both in the areas designated under the National Parks and Access to the Countryside Act 1949 as National Parks or as areas of outstanding natural beauty and elsewhere;
    (b) for encouraging the provision or improvement, for persons resorting to the countryside in Wales, of facilities for the enjoyment thereof and for the enjoyment of the opportunities for open-air recreation and the study of nature afforded thereby;
and shall have regard to the social and economic interests of rural areas in Wales.

(3)   The reference in subsection (2) above to the conservation of the natural beauty of the countryside includes the conservation of its flora, fauna and geological and physiographical features.

(4)   The Countryside Council for Wales and the Countryside Commission shall discharge their respective functions under those Acts (as amended by Schedule 8) on and after a day to be appointed by an order made by the Secretary of State.

[220]

NOTES
    Order: the Environmental Protection Act 1990 (Commencement No 6 and Appointed Day) Order 1991,
SI 1991/685.

Nature conservation in Great Britain

131 Nature conservation functions: preliminary

(1)   For the purposes of nature conservation, and fostering the understanding thereof, the Councils shall, in place of the Nature Conservancy Council established under the Nature Conservancy Council Act 1973, have the functions conferred on them by sections 132 to 134 below (which are in this Part referred to as "nature conservation functions").

(2)   It shall be the duty of the Councils in discharging their nature conservation functions to take appropriate account of actual or possible ecological changes.

(3)   The Councils shall discharge their nature conservation functions on and after a day to be appointed by an order made by the Secretary of State.

(4)   The Secretary of State may give the Councils, or any of them, directions of a general or specific character with regard to the discharge of any of their nature conservation functions other than those conferred on them by section 132(1)(a) below.

(5)   Any reference in this section to the Councils includes a reference to the joint committee and, accordingly, directions under subsection (4) above may be given to the joint committee as respects any of the functions dischargeable by them (other than under section 133(2)(a)).

(6)   In this Part "nature conservation" means the conservation of flora, fauna or geological or physiographical features.

[221]

NOTES
Order: the Environmental Protection Act 1990 (Commencement No 6 and Appointed Day) Order 1991, SI 1991/685.

132 General functions of the Councils

(1)   The Councils shall each have the following functions, namely—
   (a) such of the functions previously discharged by the Nature Conservancy Council under the Acts amended by Schedule 9 to this Act as are assigned to them in accordance with the amendments effected by that Schedule;
   (b) the establishment, maintenance and management of nature reserves (within the meaning of section 15 of the National Parks and Access to the Countryside Act 1949) in their area;
   (c) the provision of advice for the Secretary of State or any other Minister on the development and implementation of policies for or affecting nature conservation in their area;
   (d) the provision of advice and the dissemination of knowledge to any persons about nature conservation in their area or about matters arising from the discharge of their functions under this section or section 134 below;
   (e) the commissioning or support (whether by financial means or otherwise) of research which in their opinion is relevant to any of their functions under this section or section 134 below;
and the Councils shall, in discharging their functions under this section, have regard to any advice given to them by the joint committee under section 133(3) below.

(2)   The Councils shall each have power—
   (a) to accept any gift or contribution made to them for the purposes of any of the functions conferred on them by subsection (1) above or section 134 below and, subject to the terms of the gift or contribution, to apply it to those purposes;
   (b) to initiate and carry out such research directly related to those functions as it is appropriate that they should carry out instead of commissioning or supporting other persons under paragraph (e) of that subsection;
and they may do all such other things as are incidental or conducive to those functions including (without prejudice to the generality of this provision) making charges and holding land or any interest in or right over land.

(3)   Nothing in this section [or in the Natural Heritage (Scotland) Act 1991 (in so far as it relates to the nature conservation functions of Scottish Natural Heritage)] shall be taken as preventing any of the Councils—
   (a) if consulted by another of the Councils about a matter relating to the functions of that other Council, from giving that other Council any advice or information which they are able to give; or
   (b) from giving advice or information to the joint committee about any matter relating to any of the functions conferred by section 133(2) and (3) below.

[222]

NOTES
Sub-s (3): words in square brackets inserted by the Natural Heritage (Scotland) Act 1991, s 4(10), Sch 2, para 10(1), (5).

133 Special functions of Councils

(1) The Councils shall jointly have the following functions which may, however, be discharged only through the joint committee; and in this section the functions so dischargeable are referred to as "special functions".

(2) The special functions of the Councils are—
  (a) such of the functions previously discharged by the Nature Conservancy Council under the Wildlife and Countryside Act 1981 as are assigned to the Councils jointly as special functions in accordance with the amendments to that Act effected by Schedule 9 to this Act;
  (b) the provision of advice for the Secretary of State or any other Minister on the development and implementation of policies for or affecting nature conservation for Great Britain as a whole or nature conservation outside Great Britain;
  (c) the provision of advice and the dissemination of knowledge to any persons about nature conservation for Great Britain as a whole or nature conservation outside Great Britain;
  (d) the establishment of common standards throughout Great Britain for the monitoring of nature conservation and for research into nature conservation and the analysis of the resulting information;
  (e) the commissioning or support (whether by financial means or otherwise) of research which in the opinion of the joint committee is relevant to any matter mentioned in paragraphs (a) to (d) above;

and section 132(2) above shall apply to the special functions as it applies to the functions conferred by subsection (1) of that section.

(3) The joint committee may give advice or information to any of the Councils on any matter arising in connection with the functions of that Council under section 132 above which, in the opinion of the committee, concerns nature conservation for Great Britain as a whole or nature conservation outside Great Britain.

(4) For the purposes of this section, references to nature conservation for Great Britain as a whole are references to—
  (a) any nature conservation matter of national or international importance or which otherwise affects the interests of Great Britain as a whole; or
  (b) any nature conservation matter which arises throughout Great Britain and raises issues common to England, Scotland and Wales,

and it is immaterial for the purposes of paragraph (a) above that a matter arises only in relation to England, to Scotland or to Wales.

(5) The Secretary of State may, as respects any matter arising in connection with—
  (a) any special function of the Councils, or
  (b) the function of the joint committee under subsection (3) above,

give directions to any of the Councils requiring that Council (instead of the joint committee) to discharge that function in relation to that matter.

[223]

134 Grants and loans by the Councils

(1) The Councils may each, with the consent of or in accordance with a general authorisation given by the Secretary of State, give financial assistance by way of

grant or loan (or partly in one way and partly in the other) to any person in respect of expenditure incurred or to be incurred by him in doing anything which in their opinion is conducive to nature conservation or fostering the understanding of nature conservation.

(2)   No consent or general authorisation shall be given by the Secretary of State under subsection (1) above without the approval of the Treasury.

(3)   On making a grant or loan a Council may impose such conditions as they think fit, including (in the case of a grant) conditions for repayment in specified circumstances.

(4)   The Councils shall exercise their powers under subsection (3) above so as to ensure that any person receiving a grant or loan under this section in respect of premises to which the public are to be admitted (on payment or otherwise) shall, in the means of access both to and within the premises, and in the parking facilities and sanitary conveniences to be available (if any), make provision, so far as it is in the circumstances both practicable and reasonable, for the needs of members of the public visiting the premises who are disabled.

[224]

135–138   (*Relate to transfer of property, rights and liabilities to new councils (ss 135, 136); employment by new councils of staff of existing bodies (s 137); dissolution of Nature Conservancy Council (s 138).*)

Transitional provisions and savings

139 Transitional provisions and savings

Schedule 11 to this Act (which contains transitional provisions and savings relating to this Part) shall have effect.

[225]

PART VIII
MISCELLANEOUS

Other controls on substances, articles or waste

140 Power to prohibit or restrict the importation, use, supply or storage of injurious substances or articles

(1)   The Secretary of State may by regulations prohibit or restrict—
   (a) the importation into and the landing and unloading in the United Kingdom,
   (b) the use for any purpose,
   (c) the supply for any purpose, and
   (d) the storage,
of any specified substance or article if he considers it appropriate to do so for the purpose of preventing the substance or article from causing pollution of the environment or harm to human health or to the health of animals or plants.

(2)   Any such prohibition or restriction may apply—
   (a) in all, or only in specified, areas;
   (b) in all, or only in specified, circumstances or if conditions imposed by the regulations are not complied with; and
   (c) to all, or only to specified descriptions of, persons.

(3)   Regulations under this section may—
   (a) confer on the Secretary of State power to direct that any substance or article whose use, supply or storage is prohibited or restricted is to be

treated as waste or controlled waste of any description and in relation to any such substance or article—

    (i) to apply, with or without modification, specified provisions of Part II; or

    (ii) to direct that it be disposed of or treated in accordance with the direction;

(b) confer on the Secretary of State power, where a substance or article has been imported, landed or unloaded in contravention of a prohibition or restriction imposed under subsection (1)(a) above, to require that the substance or article be disposed of or treated in or removed from the United Kingdom;

(c) confer powers corresponding to those conferred by section 17 above on persons authorised for any purpose of the regulations by the Secretary of State or any local or other authority; and

(d) include such other incidental and supplemental, and such transitional provisions, as the Secretary of State considers appropriate.

(4) The Secretary of State may, by regulations under this section, direct that, for the purposes of any power conferred on him under subsection (3)(b) above, any prohibition or restriction on the importation into or the landing and unloading in the United Kingdom imposed—

(a) by or under any Community instrument, or

(b) by or under any enactment,

shall be treated as imposed under subsection (1)(a) above and any power conferred on him under subsection (3)(b) above shall be exercisable accordingly.

(5) The Secretary of State may by order establish a committee to give him advice in relation to the exercise of the power to make regulations under this section and Schedule 12 to this Act shall have effect in relation to it.

(6) Subject to subsection (7) below, it shall be the duty of the Secretary of State before he makes any regulations under this section other than regulations under subsection (4) above—

(a) to consult the committee constituted under subsection (5) above about the proposed regulations;

(b) having consulted the committee, to publish in the London Gazette and, if the regulations apply in Scotland or Northern Ireland, the Edinburgh Gazette or, as the case may be, Belfast Gazette and in any other publication which he considers appropriate, a notice indicating the effect of the proposed regulations and specifying—

    (i) the date on which it is proposed that the regulations will come into force;

    (ii) a place where a draft of the proposed regulations may be inspected free of charge by members of the public during office hours; and

    (iii) a period of not less than fourteen days, beginning with the date on which the notice is first published, during which representations in writing may be made to the Secretary of State about the proposed regulations; and

(c) to consider any representations which are made to him in accordance with the notice.

(7) The Secretary of State may make regulations under this section in relation to any substance or article without observing the requirements of subsection (6) above where it appears to him that there is an imminent risk, if those requirements are observed, that serious pollution of the environment will be caused.

(8) The Secretary of State may, after performing the duty imposed on him by subsection (6) above with respect to any proposed regulations, make the regulations either—

(a) in the form of the draft mentioned in subsection (6)(b) above, or

(b) in that form with such modifications as he considers appropriate;

but the Secretary of State shall not make any regulations incorporating modifications unless he is of opinion that it is appropriate for the requirements of subsection (6) above to be disregarded.

(9) Regulations under this section may provide that a person who contravenes or fails to comply with a specified provision of the regulations or causes or permits another person to contravene or fail to comply with a specified provision of the regulations commits an offence and may prescribe the maximum penalty for the offence.

(10) No offence under the regulations shall be made punishable with imprisonment for more than two years or punishable on summary conviction with a fine exceeding level 5 on the standard scale (if not calculated on a daily basis) or, in the case of a continuing offence, exceeding one-tenth of the level on the standard scale specified as the maximum penalty for the original offence.

(11) In this section—

"the environment" means the air, water and land, or any of those media, and the medium of air includes the air within buildings and the air within other natural or man-made structures above or below ground;

"specified" means specified in the regulations; and

"substance" means any natural or artificial substance, whether in solid or liquid form or in the form of a gas or vapour and it includes mixtures of substances.

[226]

NOTES

Order: the Advisory Committee on Hazardous Substances Order 1991, SI 1991/1487.

Regulations: the Control of Pollution (Supply and Use of Injurious Substances) Regulations 1986, SI 1986/902, as amended by SI 1992/31; the Control of Pollution (Anglers' Lead Weights) Regulations 1986, SI 1986/1992, as amended by SI 1993/49; the Control of Pollution (Anti-Fouling Paints and Treatments) Regulations 1987, SI 1987/783; the Environmental Protection (Controls on Injurious Substances) Regulations 1992, SI 1992/31; the Environmental Protection (Controls on Injurious Substances) (No 2) Regulations 1992, SI 1992/1583; and the Environmental Protection (Controls on Injurious Substances) Regulations 1993, SI 1993/1; the Environmental Protection (Non-Refillable Refrigerant Containers) Regulations 1994, SI 1994/199; the Environmental Protection (Non-Refillable Refrigerant Containers) Regulations 1994, SI 1994/199, as amended by SI 1996/506; the Environmental Protection (Controls on Substances that Deplete the Ozone Layer) Regulations 1996, SI 1996/506 (all made under this section or have effect thereunder by virtue of s 162(5) of this Act).

141 Power to prohibit or restrict the importation or exportation of waste

(1) The Secretary of State may, for the purpose of preventing any risk of pollution of the environment or of harm to human health arising from waste being imported or exported or of conserving the facilities or resources for dealing with waste, make regulations prohibiting or restricting, or providing for the prohibition or restriction of—

(a) the importation into and the landing and unloading in the United Kingdom, or

(b) the exportation, or the loading for exportation, from the United Kingdom,

of waste of any description.

(2) Regulations under this section may make different provision for different descriptions of waste or waste of any description in different circumstances.

(3) Regulations under this section may, as respects any description of waste, confer or impose on waste regulation authorities or any of them such functions in relation to the importation of waste as appear to be appropriate to the Secretary of State, subject to such limitations and conditions as are specified in the regulations.

(4)   Regulations under this section may confer or impose on waste regulation authorities or any of them functions of enforcing any of the regulations on behalf of the Secretary of State whether or not the functions fall within subsection (3) above.

(5)   Regulations under this section may—
  (a) as respects functions conferred or imposed on waste regulation authorities—
       (i) make them exercisable in relation to individual consignments or consignments in a series by the same person but not in relation to consignments or descriptions of consignments generally; . . .
       (ii) . . .
  (b) impose or provide for the imposition of prohibitions either absolutely or only if conditions or procedures prescribed in or under the regulations are not complied with;
  (c) impose duties to be complied with before, on or after any importation or exportation of waste by persons who are, or are to be, consignors, consignees, carriers or holders of the waste or any waste derived from it;
  (d) confer powers corresponding to those conferred by section 69(3) above;
  (e) provide for appeals to the Secretary of State from determinations made by authorities under the regulations;
  (f) provide for the keeping by the Secretary of State, waste regulation authorities and waste collection authorities of public registers of information relating to the importation and exportation of waste and for the transmission of such information between any of those persons;
  (g) create offences, subject to the limitation that no offence shall be punishable with imprisonment for more than two years or punishable on summary conviction with imprisonment for more than six months or a fine exceeding level 5 on the standard scale (if not calculated on a daily basis) or, in the case of a continuing offence, exceeding one-tenth of the level on the standard scale specified as the maximum penalty for the original offence.

(6)   In this section—
  "the environment" means land, water and air or any of them;
  "harm" includes offence to any of man's senses;
  "waste", "waste collection authority", and "waste regulation authority" have the same meaning as in Part II; and
  "the United Kingdom" includes its territorial sea.

(7)   In the application of this section to Northern Ireland and the territorial sea of the United Kingdom adjacent to Northern Ireland "waste regulation authority" means a district council established under the Local Government Act (Northern Ireland) 1972.

[227]

NOTES

Sub-s (5): words omitted repealed by the Environment Act 1995, s 120, Sch 22, para 90, Sch 24.

---

142 Powers to obtain information about potentially hazardous substances

(1)   The Secretary of State may, for the purpose of assessing their potential for causing pollution of the environment or harm to human health, by regulations make provision for and in connection with the obtaining of relevant information relating to substances which may be specified by him by order for the purposes of this section.

(2)   The Secretary of State shall not make an order under subsection (1) above specifying any substance—
  (a) which was first supplied in any member State on or after 18th September 1981; or
  (b) in so far as it is a regulated substance for the purposes of any relevant enactment.

(3)   The Secretary of State shall not make an order under subsection (1) above specifying any substance without consulting the committee established under section 140(5) except where it appears to him that information about the substance needs to be obtained urgently under this section.

(4)   Regulations under this section may—
    (a)   prescribe the descriptions of relevant information which are to be furnished under this section in relation to specified substances;
    (b)   impose requirements on manufacturers, importers or suppliers generally to furnish information prescribed under paragraph (a) above;
    (c)   provide for the imposition of requirements on manufacturers, importers or suppliers generally to furnish relevant information relating to products or articles containing specified substances in relation to which information has been furnished in pursuance of paragraph (b) above;
    (d)   provide for the imposition of requirements on particular manufacturers, importers or suppliers to furnish further information relating to specified substances in relation to which information has been furnished in pursuance of paragraph (b) above;
    (e)   provide for the imposition of requirements on particular manufacturers or importers to carry out tests of specified substances and to furnish information of the results of the tests;
    (f)   authorise persons to comply with requirements to furnish information imposed on them by or under the regulations by means of representative persons or bodies;
    (g)   impose restrictions on the disclosure of information obtained under this section and provide for determining what information is, and what information is not, to be treated as furnished in confidence;
    (h)   create offences, subject to the limitation that no offence shall be punishable with imprisonment or punishable on summary conviction with a fine exceeding level 5 on the standard scale;
    (i)   make any public authority designated by the regulations responsible for the enforcement of the regulations to such extent as may be specified in the regulations;
    (j)   include such other incidental and supplemental, and such transitional, provisions as the Secretary of State considers appropriate.

(5)   The Secretary of State shall have regard, in imposing or providing for the imposition of any requirement under subsection (4)(b), (c), (d) or (e) above, to the cost likely to be involved in complying with the requirement.

(6)   In this section—
"the environment" means the air, water and land or any of them;
"relevant information", in relation to substances, products or articles, means information relating to their properties, production, distribution, importation or use or intended use and, in relation to products or articles, to their disposal as waste;
"substance" means any natural or artificial substance, whether in solid or liquid form or in the form of a gas or vapour and it includes mixtures of substances.

(7)   The enactments which are relevant for the purposes of subsection (2)(b) above are the following—
the Explosive Substances Act 1875;
[the Radioactive Substances Act 1993];
Parts II, III and VIII of the Medicines Act 1968;
Part IV of the Agriculture Act 1970;
the Misuse of Drugs Act 1971;
Part III of the Food and Environment Protection Act 1985; and
the Food Safety Act 1960;

and a substance is a regulated substance for the purposes of any such enactment in so far as any prohibition, restriction or requirement is imposed in relation to it by or under the enactment for the purposes of that enactment.

[228]

NOTES

Sub-s (7): words in square brackets substituted by the Radioactive Substances Act 1993, s 49(1), Sch 4, para 8.

143 Public registers of land which may be contaminated

(1)   For the purposes of the registers to be maintained under this section, the Secretary of State may, by regulations—
>   *(a)   specify contaminative uses of land;*
>   *(b)   prescribe the form of the registers and the particulars to be included in them; and*
>   *(c)   make such other provision as appears to him to be appropriate in connection with the maintenance of the registers.*

(2)   It shall be the duty of a local authority, as respects land in its area subject to contamination, to maintain, in accordance with the regulations, a register in the prescribed form and containing the prescribed particulars.

(3)   The duty imposed by subsection (2) above on a local authority is a duty to compile and maintain the register from the information available to the authority from time to time.

(4)   A local authority shall secure that the register is open to inspection at its principal office by members of the public free of charge at all reasonable hours and shall afford to members of the public reasonable facilities for obtaining, on payment of reasonable charges, copies of entries in the register.

(5)   Regulations under subsection (1)(c) above may prescribe the measures to be taken by local authorities for informing persons whose land is the subject of entries in a register about the entries or for enabling them to inform themselves about them.

(6)   In this section—
>   *"contaminative use" means any use of land which may cause it to be contaminated with noxious substances;*
>   *"land subject to contamination" means land which is being or has been put to a contaminative use;*
>   *"local authority" means—*
>>   *(a)   in Greater London, a London borough council or the Common Council of the City of London;*
>>   *(b)   in England . . . outside Greater London, a district council;*
>>   *[(bb)   in Wales, a county council or county borough council;]*
>>   *(c)   (applies to Scotland only); and*
>>   *(d)   the Council of the Isles of Scilly; and*
>   *"substance" means any natural or artificial substance, whether in solid or liquid form or in the form of a gas or vapour.*

[229]

NOTES

Commencement: 14 February 1992 (sub-ss (1), (5), (6), England and Wales); to be appointed (remainder).

Repealed by the Environment Act 1995, s 120, Sch 22, para 91, Sch 24, as from a day to be appointed.

Sub-s (6): in definition "local authority" words omitted from para (b) repealed, and para (bb) inserted, by the Local Government (Wales) Act 1994, ss 22(3), 66(8), Sch 9, para 17(12), Sch 18.

144–148 *(Relate to amendments of hazardous substances legislation (s 144); amendments to the Food and Environment Protection Act 1985 (ss 146, 147); s 145, so far as unrepealed, relates to Scotland only; s 148 repealed by the Merchant Shipping Act 1995, s 314(1), Sch 12.)*

Control of dogs

149 Seizure of stray dogs

(1)   Every local authority shall appoint an officer (under whatever title the authority may determine) for the purpose of discharging the functions imposed or conferred by this section for dealing with stray dogs found in the area of the authority.

(2)   The officer may delegate the discharge of his functions to another person but he shall remain responsible for securing that the functions are properly discharged.

(3)   Where the officer has reason to believe that any dog found in a public place or on any other land or premises is a stray dog, he shall (if practicable) seize the dog and detain it, but, where he finds it on land or premises which is not a public place, only with the consent of the owner or occupier of the land or premises.

(4)   Where any dog seized under this section wears a collar having inscribed thereon or attached thereto the address of any person, or the owner of the dog is known, the officer shall serve on the person whose address is given on the collar, or on the owner, a notice in writing stating that the dog has been seized and where it is being kept and stating that the dog will be liable to be disposed of if it is not claimed within seven clear days after the service of the notice and the amounts for which he would be liable under subsection (5) below are not paid.

(5)   A person claiming to be the owner of a dog seized under this section shall not be entitled to have the dog returned to him unless he pays all the expenses incurred by reason of its detention and such further amount as is for the time being prescribed.

(6)   Where any dog seized under this section has been detained for seven clear days after the seizure or, where a notice has been served under subsection (4) above, the service of the notice and the owner has not claimed the dog and paid the amounts due under subsection (5) above the officer may dispose of the dog—
  (a) by selling it or giving it to a person who will, in his opinion, care properly for the dog;
  (b) by selling it or giving it to an establishment for the reception of stray dogs; or
  (c) by destroying it in a manner to cause as little pain as possible;

but no dog seized under this section shall be sold or given for the purposes of vivisection.

(7)   Where a dog is disposed of under subsection (6)(a) or (b) above to a person acting in good faith, the ownership of the dog shall be vested in the recipient.

(8)   The officer shall keep a register containing the prescribed particulars of or relating to dogs seized under this section and the register shall be available, at all reasonable times, for inspection by the public free of charge.

(9)   The officer shall cause any dog detained under this section to be properly fed and maintained.

(10) Notwithstanding anything in this section, the officer may cause a dog detained under this section to be destroyed before the expiration of the period mentioned in subsection (6) above where he is of the opinion that this should be done to avoid suffering.

(11) In this section—
  "local authority", in relation to England . . . , means a district council, a London borough council, the Common Council of the City of London or the Council of the Isles of Scilly [in relation to Wales, means a county council or a county borough council] and, in relation to Scotland, means [a council constituted under section 2 of the Local Government etc (Scotland) Act 1994];
  "officer" means an officer appointed under subsection (1) above;
  "prescribed" means prescribed in regulations made by the Secretary of State; and
  "public place" means—
    (i) as respects England and Wales, any highway and any other place to which the public are entitled or permitted to have access;
    (ii) as respects Scotland, any road (within the meaning of the Roads (Scotland) Act 1984) and any other place to which the public are entitled or permitted to have access;

and, for the purposes of section 160 below in its application to this section, the proper address of the owner of a dog which wears a collar includes the address given on the collar.

[230]

NOTES
  Sub-s (11): in definition "local authority" words omitted repealed, and words in first pair of square brackets inserted, by the Local Government (Wales) Act 1994, ss 22(3), 66(8), Sch 9, para 17(13), Sch 18, words in final pair of square brackets substituted by the Local Government etc (Scotland) Act 1994, s 180(1), Sch 13, para 167(17).
  Regulations: the Environmental Protection (Stray Dogs) Regulations 1992, SI 1992/288.

150 Delivery of stray dogs to police or local authority officer

(1) Any person (in this section referred to as "the finder") who takes possession of a stray dog shall forthwith either—
  (a) return the dog to its owner; or
  (b) take the dog—
    (i) to the officer of the local authority for the area in which the dog was found; or
    (ii) to the police station which is nearest to the place where the dog was found;
and shall inform the officer of the local authority or the police officer in charge of the police station, as the case may be, where the dog was found.

(2) Where a dog has been taken under subsection (1) above to the officer of a local authority, then—
  (a) if the finder desires to keep the dog, he shall inform the officer of this fact and shall furnish his name and address and the officer shall, having complied with the procedure (if any) prescribed under subsection (6) below, allow the finder to remove the dog;
  (b) if the finder does not desire to keep the dog, the officer shall, unless he has reason to believe it is not a stray, treat it as if it had been seized by him under section 149 above.

(3) Where the finder of a dog keeps the dog by virtue of this section he must keep it for not less than one month.

(4) In Scotland a person who keeps a dog by virtue of this section for a period of two months without its being claimed by the person who has right to it shall at the end of that period become the owner of the dog.

(5) If the finder of a dog fails to comply with the requirements of subsection (1) or (3) above he shall be liable on summary conviction to a fine not exceeding level 2 on the standard scale.

(6)   The Secretary of State may, by regulations, prescribe the procedure to be followed under subsection (2)(a) above.

(7)   In this section "local authority" and "officer" have the same meaning as in section 149 above.

[231]

NOTES

Regulations: the Environmental Protection (Stray Dogs) Regulations 1992, SI 1992/288.

151   (*Amends the Animal Health Act 1981, ss 13, 50(1), 60(1).*)

Straw and stubble burning

152 Burning of straw and stubble etc

(1)   The appropriate Minister may by regulations prohibit or restrict the burning of crop residues on agricultural land by persons engaged in agriculture and he may (by the same or other regulations) provide exemptions from any prohibition or restriction so imposed.

(2)   Regulations providing an exemption from any prohibition or restriction may make the exemption applicable—
   (a) in all, or only in specified, areas;
   (b) to all, or only to specified, crop residues; or
   (c) in all, or only in specified, circumstances.

(3)   Any power to make regulations under this section includes power—
   (a) to make different provision for different areas or circumstances;
   (b) where burning of a crop residue is restricted, to impose requirements to be complied with before or after the burning;
   (c) to create offences subject to the limitation that no offence shall be made punishable otherwise than on summary conviction and the fine prescribed for the offence shall not exceed level 5 on the standard scale; and
   (d) to make such incidental, supplemental and transitional provision as the appropriate Minister considers appropriate.

(4)   Where it appears to the appropriate Minister appropriate to do so in consequence of any regulations made under the foregoing provisions of this section, the appropriate Minister may, by order, repeal any byelaws of local authorities dealing with the burning of crop residues on agricultural land.

(5)   In this section—
   "agriculture" and "agricultural land" have, as respects England or as respects Wales, the same meaning as in the Agriculture Act 1947 and, as respects Scotland, the same meaning as in the Agriculture (Scotland) Act 1948;
   "crop residue" means straw or stubble or any other crop residue;
   "the appropriate Minister" means the Minister of Agriculture, Fisheries and Food or the Secretary of State or both of them.

[232]

NOTES

Order: the Burning of Crop Residues (Repeal of Byelaws) Order 1992, SI 1992/693.
Regulations: the Crop Residues (Burning) Regulations 1993, SI 1993/1366.

153–155   (*Relate to environmental expenditure (ss 153, 154); ss 155 inserts the Transport Act 1968, s 110(7).*)

PART IX
GENERAL

156 Power to give effect to Community and other international obligations etc

(1)   The Secretary of State may by regulations provide that the provisions to which this section applies shall have effect with such modifications as may be prescribed for the purpose of enabling Her Majesty's Government in the United Kingdom—

   (a) to give effect to any Community obligation or exercise any related right; or

   (b) to give effect to any obligation or exercise any related right under any international agreement to which the United Kingdom is for the time being a party.

(2)   This section applies to the following provisions of this Act—

   (a) Part I;

   (b) Part II;

   (c) Part VI; and

   (d) in Part VIII, sections 140, 141 or 142;

and the provisions of the [Radioactive Substances Act 1993].

(3)   In this section—

"modifications" includes additions, alterations and omissions;

"prescribed" means prescribed in regulations under this section; and

"related right", in relation to an obligation, includes any derogation or other right to make more onerous provisions available in respect of that obligation.

(4)   This section, in its application to Northern Ireland, has effect subject to the following modifications, that is to say—

   (a) in its application in relation to Part VI and sections 140, 141, and 142, the reference to Her Majesty's Government in the United Kingdom includes a reference to Her Majesty's Government in Northern Ireland; and

   (b) in its application in relation to the [Radioactive Substances Act 1993], the reference to the Secretary of State shall be construed as a reference to the Department of the Environment for Northern Ireland and the reference to Her Majesty's Government in the United Kingdom shall be construed as a reference to Her Majesty's Government in Northern Ireland;

and regulations under it made by that Department shall be a statutory rule for the purposes of the Statutory Rules (Northern Ireland) Order 1979 and shall be subject to negative resolution within the meaning of section 41(6) of the Interpretation Act (Northern Ireland) 1954.

[233]

NOTES

   Sub-ss (2), (4): words in square brackets substituted by the Radioactive Substances Act 1993, s 49(1), Sch 4, para 9.

   Regulations: the Environmental Protection Act 1990 (Modification of s 112) Regulations 1992, SI 1992/2617; the Genetically Modified Organisms (Deliberate Release) Regulations 1992, SI 1992/3280, regs 9, 13; the Waste Management Licensing Regulations 1994, SI 1994/1056, as amended by SI 1994/1137, SI 1995/288, SI 1995/1950, SI 1996/593, SI 1996/634, SI 1996/972, SI 1996/1279.

157 Offences by bodies corporate

(1)   Where an offence under any provision of this Act committed by a body corporate is proved to have been committed with the consent or connivance of, or to have been attributable to any neglect on the part of, any director, manager, secretary or other similar officer of the body corporate or a person who was purporting to act in any such capacity, he as well as the body corporate shall be guilty of that offence and shall be liable to be proceeded against and punished accordingly.

(2)   Where the affairs of a body corporate are managed by its members, subsection (1) above shall apply in relation to the acts or defaults of a member in connection with his functions of management as if he were a director of the body corporate.

[234]

158 Offences under Parts I, II, IV, VI, etc due to fault of others

Where the commission by any person of an offence under Part I, II, IV, or VI, or section 140, 141 or 142 above is due to the act or default of some other person, that other person may be charged with and convicted of the offence by virtue of this section whether or not proceedings for the offence are taken against the first-mentioned person.

[235]

159 Application to Crown

(1)   Subject to the provisions of this section, the provisions of this Act and of regulations and orders made under it shall bind the Crown.

(2)   No contravention by the Crown of any provision of this Act or of any regulations or order made under it shall make the Crown criminally liable; but the High Court or, in Scotland, the Court of Session may, on the application of any public or local authority charged with enforcing that provision, declare unlawful any act or omission of the Crown which constitutes such a contravention.

(3)   Notwithstanding anything in subsection (2) above, the provisions of this Act and of regulations and orders made under it shall apply to persons in the public service of the Crown as they apply to other persons.

(4)   If the Secretary of State certifies that it appears to him, as respects any Crown premises and any powers of entry exercisable in relation to them specified in the certificate that it is requisite or expedient that, in the interests of national security, the powers should not be exercisable in relation to the premises, those powers shall not be exercisable in relation to those premises; and in this subsection "Crown premises" means premises held or used by or on behalf of the Crown.

(5)   Nothing in this section shall be taken as in any way affecting Her Majesty in her private capacity; and this subsection shall be construed as if section 38(3) of the Crown Proceedings Act 1947 (interpretation of references in that Act to Her Majesty in her private capacity) were contained in this Act.

(6)   References in this section to regulations or orders are references to regulations or orders made by statutory instrument.

(7)   For the purposes of this section in its application to Part II and Part IV the authority charged with enforcing the provisions of those Parts in its area is—
   (a) in the case of Part II, any waste regulation authority, and
   (b) in the case of Part IV, any principal litter authority.

[236]

160 Service of notices

(1)   Any notice required or authorised by or under this Act to be served on or given to an inspector may be served or given by delivering it to him or by leaving it at, or sending it by post to, his office.

(2)   Any such notice required or authorised to be served on or given to a person other than an inspector may be served or given by delivering it to him, or by leaving it at his proper address, or by sending it by post to him at that address.

(3)   Any such notice may—
(a) in the case of a body corporate, be served on or given to the secretary or clerk of that body;
(b) in the case of a partnership, be served on or given to a partner or a person having the control or management of the partnership business.

(4)   For the purposes of this section and of section 7 of the Interpretation Act 1978 (service of documents by post) in its application to this section, the proper address of any person on or to whom any such notice is to be served or given shall be his last known address, except that—
(a) in the case of a body corporate or their secretary or clerk, it shall be the address of the registered or principal office of that body;
(b) in the case of a partnership or person having the control or the management of the partnership business, it shall be the principal office of the partnership;

and for the purposes of this subsection the principal office of a company registered outside the United Kingdom or of a partnership carrying on business outside the United Kingdom shall be their principal office within the United Kingdom.

(5)   If the person to be served with or given any such notice has specified an address in the United Kingdom other than his proper address within the meaning of subsection (4) above as the one at which he or someone on his behalf will accept notices of the same description as that notice, that address shall also be treated for the purposes of this section and section 7 of the Interpretation Act 1978 as his proper address.

(6)   The preceding provisions of this section shall apply to the sending or giving of a document as they apply to the giving of a notice.

[237]

161 Regulations, orders and directions

(1)   Any power of the Secretary of State or the Minister of Agriculture, Fisheries and Food under this Act to make regulations or orders shall be exercisable by statutory instrument; but this subsection does not apply to orders under section 72 above or paragraph 4 of Schedule 3.

(2)   A statutory instrument containing regulations under this Act shall be subject to annulment in pursuance of a resolution of either House of Parliament.

(3)   Except in the cases specified in subsection (4) below, a statutory instrument containing an order under this Act shall be subject to annulment in pursuance of a resolution of either House of Parliament.

(4)   Subsection (3) above does not apply to [a statutory instrument—
(a) which contains an order under section 78M(4) above, or
(b) by reason only that it contains] an order under section 130(4), 131(3) or 138(2) above or section 164(3) below.

(5)   Any power conferred by this Act to give a direction shall include power to vary or revoke the direction.

(6)   Any direction given under this Act shall be in writing.

[238]

NOTES
Sub-s (4): words in square brackets inserted by the Environment Act 1995, s 120, Sch 22, para 92, as from a day to be appointed.

162 Consequential and minor amendments and repeals

(1) ...

(2)   The enactments specified in Schedule 16 to this Act shall have effect subject to section 77 above, Schedule 11 to this Act and any provision made by way of a note in Schedule 16.

(3)   *(Applies to Scotland only.)*

(4), (5) ...

NOTES
Commencement: see Sch 16 at **[252]–[260]**.
Sub-ss (1), (4), (5): outside the scope of this work.

163   *(Relates to financial provisions.)*

164 Short title, commencement and extent

(1)   This Act may be cited as the Environmental Protection Act 1990.

(2)   The following provisions of the Act shall come into force at the end of the period of two months beginning with the day on which it is passed, namely—
sections 79 to 85;
section 97;
section 99;
section 105 in so far as it relates to paragraphs 7, 13, 14 and 15 of Schedule 5;
section 140;
section 141;
section 142;
section 145;
section 146;
section 148;
section 153;
section 154;
section 155;
section 157;
section 160;
section 161;
section 162(1) in so far as it relates to paragraphs 4, 5, 7, 8, 9, 18, 22, 24 and 31(4)(b) of Schedule 15; but, in the case of paragraph 22, in so far only as that paragraph inserts a paragraph (m) into section 7(4) of the Act of 1984;
section 162(2) in so far as it relates to Part III of Schedule 16 and, in Part IX of that Schedule, the repeal of section 100 of the Control of Pollution Act 1974;
section 162(5);
section 163.

(3)   The remainder of this Act (except this section) shall come into force on such day as the Secretary of State may by order appoint and different days may be appointed for different provisions or different purposes.

(4)   Only the following provisions of this Act (together with this section) extend to Northern Ireland, namely—
section 3(5) to (8);
section 62(2)(e) in so far as it relates to importation;
Part V;
Part VI in so far as it relates to importation and, without that restriction, section 127(2) in so far as it relates to the continental shelf;

section 140 in so far as it relates to importation;
section 141;
section 142 in so far as it relates to importation;
section 146;
section 147;
section 148;
section 153 except subsection (1)(k) and (m);
section 156 in so far as it relates to Part VI and sections 140, 141 and 142 in so far as they extend to Northern Ireland and in so far as it relates to the Radioactive Substances Act 1960;
section 158 in so far as it relates to Part VI and sections 140, 141 and 142 in so far as they extend to Northern Ireland.

(5)   Where any enactment amended or repealed by this Act extends to any part of the United Kingdom, the amendment or repeal extends to that part, subject, however, to any express provision in Schedule 15 or 16.

[240]

NOTES
Sub-s (4): words in italics repealed, in relation to Northern Ireland, by the Genetically Modified Organisms (Northern Ireland) Order 1991, SI 1991/1714, art 25, as from a day to be appointed.
Orders: SI 1990/2226; SI 1990/2243; SI 1990/2565, as amended by SI 1990/2635; SI 1990/2635; SI 1991/96; SI 1991/685; SI 1991/1042; SI 1991/1319; SI 1991/1577; SI 1991/2829; SI 1992/266; SI 1992/3253; SI 1993/274; SI 1994/780; SI 1994/1096, as amended by SI 1994/2487, SI 1994/3234, SI 1994/2854, SI 1995/2152, SI 1996/3056.

SCHEDULE 1
AUTHORISATIONS FOR PROCESSES: SUPPLEMENTARY PROVISIONS
Section 6

PART I
GRANT OF AUTHORISATIONS

Applications for authorisations

1.—(1) An application to the enforcing authority for an authorisation must contain such information, and be made in such manner, as may be prescribed in regulations made by the Secretary of State.

(2)   An application to the enforcing authority for an authorisation must also, unless regulations made by the Secretary of State exempt applications of that class, be advertised in such manner as may be prescribed in regulations so made.

(3)   The enforcing authority may, by notice in writing to the applicant, require him to furnish such further information specified in the notice, within the period so specified, as the authority may require for the purpose of determining the application.

(4)   If a person fails to furnish any information required under sub-paragraph (3) above within the period specified thereunder the enforcing authority may refuse to proceed with the application.

(5)   Regulations under this paragraph may make different provision for different classes of applications.

Determination of applications

2.—(1) Subject to sub-paragraph (2) below, the enforcing authority shall give notice of any application for an authorisation, enclosing a copy of the application, to the persons who are prescribed or directed to be consulted under this paragraph and shall do so within the specified period for notification.

(2)   The Secretary of State may, by regulations, exempt any class of application from the requirements of this paragraph or exclude any class of information contained in applications

for authorisations from those requirements, in all cases or as respects specified classes only of persons to be consulted.

(3) Any representations made by the persons so consulted within the period allowed shall be considered by the enforcing authority in determining the application.

(4) For the purposes of sub-paragraph (1) above—
    (a) persons are prescribed to be consulted on any description of application for an authorisation if they are persons specified for the purposes of applications of that description in regulations made by the Secretary of State;
    (b) persons are directed to be consulted on any particular application if the Secretary of State specifies them in a direction given to the enforcing authority;

and the "specified period for notification" is the period specified in the regulations or in the direction.

(5) Any representations made by any other persons within the period allowed shall also be considered by the enforcing authority in determining the application.

(6) Subject to sub-paragraph (7) below, the period allowed for making representations is—
    (a) in the case of persons prescribed or directed to be consulted, the period of twenty-eight days beginning with the date on which notice of the application was given under sub-paragraph (1) above, and
    (b) in the case of other persons, the period of twenty-eight days beginning with the date on which the making of the application was advertised in pursuance of paragraph 1(2) above.

(7) The Secretary of State may, by order, substitute for the period for the time being specified in sub-paragraph (6)(a) or (b) above, such other period as he considers appropriate.

3.—(1) The Secretary of State may give directions to the enforcing authority requiring that any particular application or any class of applications for an authorisation shall be transmitted to him for determination pending a further direction under sub-paragraph (5) below.

(2) The enforcing authority shall inform the applicant of the fact that his application is being transmitted to the Secretary of State.

(3) Where an application for an authorisation is referred to him under sub-paragraph (1) above the Secretary of State may—
    (a) cause a local inquiry to be held in relation to the application; or
    (b) afford the applicant and the authority concerned an opportunity of appearing before and being heard by a person appointed by the Secretary of State;

and he shall exercise one of the powers under this sub-paragraph in any case where, in the manner prescribed by regulations made by the Secretary of State, a request is made to be heard with respect to the application by the applicant or [the enforcing authority] concerned.

(4) Subsections (2) to (5) of section 250 of the Local Government Act 1972 (supplementary provisions about local inquiries under that section) or, in relation to Scotland, subsections (2) to (8) of section 210 of the Local Government (Scotland) Act 1973 (which make similar provision) shall, without prejudice to the generality of subsection (1) of either of those sections, apply to inquiries in pursuance of sub-paragraph (3) above as they apply to inquiries in pursuance of either of those sections and, in relation to England and Wales, as if the reference to a local authority in subsection (4) of the said section 250 included a reference to the enforcing authority.

(5) The Secretary of State shall, on determining any application transferred to him under this paragraph, give to the enforcing authority such a direction as he thinks fit as to whether it is to grant the application and, if so, as to the conditions that are to be attached to the authorisation.

4. The Secretary of State may give the enforcing authority a direction with respect to any particular application or any class of applications for an authorisation requiring the authority not to determine or not to proceed with the application or applications of that class until the expiry of any such period as may be specified in the direction, or until directed by the Secretary of State that they may do so, as the case may be.

5.—(1) Except in a case where an application has been referred to the Secretary of State under paragraph 3 above and subject to sub-paragraph (3) below, the enforcing authority shall determine an application for an authorisation within the period of four months beginning with the day on which it received the application or within such longer period as may be agreed with the applicant.

(2) If the enforcing authority fails to determine an application for an authorisation within the period allowed by or under this paragraph the application shall, if the applicant notifies the authority in writing that he treats the failure as such, be deemed to have been refused at the end of that period.

(3) The Secretary of State may, by order, substitute for the period for the time being specified in sub-paragraph (1) above such other period as he considers appropriate and different periods may be substituted for different classes of application.

[241]

NOTES
Para 3: words in square brackets substituted by the Environment Act 1995, s 120, Sch 22, para 93(2).
Modification: the Environmental Protection (Authorisation of Processes) (Determination Periods) Order 1991, SI 1991/513, arts 2, 3(6) provides for the extension of the period of four months referred to in para 5.
Order: the Environmental Protection (Authorisation of Processes) (Determination Periods) Order 1991, SI 1991/513, as amended by SI 1994/2847.
Regulations: the Environmental Protection (Applications, Appeals and Registers) Regulations 1991, SI 1991/507, regs 2, 4–8, as amended by SI 1991/836 (amending reg 5), SI 1994/1271 (amending reg 4(1)), SI 1996/667 (amending regs 2, 4, 5), SI 1996/2678 (amending regs 4, 5, and inserting reg 6A); the Environmental Protection (Prescribed Processes and Substances etc) (Amendment) Regulations 1994, SI 1994/1271, as amended by SI 1994/1329; the Environmental Protection (Prescribed Processes and Substances) (Amendment) Regulations 1995, SI 1995/3247; the Environmental Protection (Prescribed Processes and Substances Etc) (Amendment) (Petrol Vapour Recovery) Regulations 1996/2678.

PART II
VARIATION OF AUTHORISATIONS

Variations by the enforcing authority

6.—(1) [Except as provided by sub-paragraph (1A) below,] the requirements of this paragraph apply where an enforcing authority has decided to vary an authorisation under section 10 and is of the opinion that any action to be taken by the holder of the authorisation in consequence of the variation will involve a substantial change in the manner in which the process is being carried on.

[(1A) The requirements of this paragraph shall not apply in relation to any variations of an authorisation which an enforcing authority has decided to make in consequence of representations made in accordance with this paragraph and which are specified by way of variation of a variation notice by a further notice under section 10(3A) of this Act.]

(2) Subject to sub-paragraph (3) below, the enforcing authority shall give notice of the action to be taken by the holder of the authorisation to the persons who are prescribed or directed to be consulted under this paragraph and shall do so within the specified period for notification; and the holder shall advertise the action in the manner prescribed in regulations made by the Secretary of State.

(3) The Secretary of State may, by regulations, exempt any class of variation from all or any of the requirements of this paragraph or exclude any class of information relating to action to be taken by holders of authorisations from all or any of those requirements, in all cases or as respects specified classes only of persons to be consulted.

(4) Any representations made by the persons so consulted within the period allowed shall be considered by the enforcing authority in taking its decision.

(5) For the purposes of sub-paragraph (2) above—
  (a) persons are prescribed to be consulted on any description of variation if they are persons specified for the purposes of variations of that description in regulations made by the Secretary of State;
  (b) persons are directed to be consulted on any particular variation if the Secretary of State specifies them in a direction given to the enforcing authority;

and the "specified period for notification" is the period specified in the regulations or in the direction.

(6) Any representations made by any other persons within the period allowed shall also be considered by the enforcing authority in taking its decision.

(7) Subject to sub-paragraph (8) below, the period allowed for making representations is—
    (a) in the case of persons prescribed or directed to be consulted, the period of twenty-eight days beginning with the date on which notice was given under sub-paragraph (2) above, and
    (b) in the case of other persons, the period of twenty-eight days beginning with the date of the advertisement under sub-paragraph (2) above.

(8) The Secretary of State may, by order, substitute for the period for the time being specified in sub-paragraph (7)(a) or (b) above, such other period as he considers appropriate.

Applications for variation

7.—(1) The requirements of this paragraph apply where an application is made to an enforcing authority under section 11(4) for the variation of an authorisation.

(2) Subject to sub-paragraph (3) below, the enforcing authority shall give notice of any such application for a variation of an authorisation, enclosing a copy of the application, to the persons who are prescribed or directed to be consulted under this paragraph and shall do so within the specified period for notification; and the holder of the authorisation shall advertise the application in the manner prescribed in regulations made by the Secretary of State.

(3) The Secretary of State may, by regulations, exempt any class of application from all or any of the requirements of this paragraph or exclude any class of information furnished with applications for variations of authorisations from all or any of those requirements, in all cases or as respects specified classes only of persons to be consulted.

(4) Any representations made by the persons so consulted within the period allowed shall be considered by the enforcing authority in determining the application.

(5) For the purposes of sub-paragraph (2) above—
    (a) persons are prescribed to be consulted on any description of application for a variation if they are persons specified for the purposes of applications of that description in regulations made by the Secretary of State;
    (b) persons are directed to be consulted on any particular application if the Secretary of State specifies them in a direction given to the enforcing authority;

and the "specified period for notification" is the period specified in the regulations or in the direction.

(6) Any representation made by any other persons within the period allowed shall also be considered by the enforcing authority in determining the application.

(7) Subject to sub-paragraph (8) below, the period allowed for making representations is—
    (a) in the case of persons prescribed or directed to be consulted, the period of twenty-eight days beginning with the date on which notice of the application was given under sub-paragraph (2) above; and
    (b) in the case of other persons, the period of twenty-eight days beginning with the date on which the making of the application was advertised in pursuance of sub-paragraph (2) above.

(8) The Secretary of State may, by order, substitute for the period for the time being specified in sub-paragraph (7)(a) or (b) above, such other period as he considers appropriate.

[Call in of applications for variation

8.—(1) The Secretary of State may give directions to the enforcing authority requiring that any particular application or any class of applications for the variation of an authorisation shall be transmitted to him for determination pending a further direction under sub-paragraph (5) below.

(2) The enforcing authority shall inform the applicant of the fact that his application is being transmitted to the Secretary of State.

(3) Where an application for the variation of an authorisation is referred to him under sub-paragraph (1) above the Secretary of State may—
    (a) cause a local inquiry to be held in relation to the application; or
    (b) afford the applicant and the authority concerned an opportunity of appearing before and being heard by a person appointed by the Secretary of State;

and he shall exercise one of the powers under this sub-paragraph in any case where, in the manner prescribed by regulations made by the Secretary of State, a request is made to be heard with respect to the application by the applicant or the enforcing authority concerned.

(4) Subsections (2) to (5) of section 250 of the Local Government Act 1972 (supplementary provisions about local inquiries under that section) or, in relation to Scotland, subsections (2) to (8) of section 210 of the Local Government (Scotland) Act 1973 (which make similar provision) shall, without prejudice to the generality of subsection (1) of either of those sections, apply to local inquiries or other hearings in pursuance of sub-paragraph (3) above as they apply to inquiries in pursuance of either of those sections and, in relation to England and Wales, as if the reference to a local authority in subsection (4) of the said section 250 included a reference to the enforcing authority.

(5) The Secretary of State shall, on determining any application transferred to him under this paragraph, give to the enforcing authority such a direction as he thinks fit as to whether it is to grant the application and, if so, as to the conditions that are to be attached to the authorisation by means of the variation notice.

9. The Secretary of State may give the enforcing authority a direction with respect to any particular application or any class of applications for the variation of an authorisation requiring the authority not to determine or not to proceed with the application or applications of that class until the expiry of any such period as may be specified in the direction, or until directed by the Secretary of State that they may do so, as the case may be.

10.—(1) Except in a case where an application for the variation of an authorisation has been referred to the Secretary of State under paragraph 8 above and subject to sub-paragraph (3) below, the enforcing authority shall determine an application for the variation of an authorisation within the period of four months beginning with the day on which it received the application or within such longer period as may be agreed with the applicant.

(2) If the enforcing authority fails to determine an application for the variation of an authorisation within the period allowed by or under this paragraph the application shall, if the applicant notifies the authority in writing that he treats the failure as such, be deemed to have been refused at the end of that period.

(3) The Secretary of State may, by order, substitute for the period for the time being specified in sub-paragraph (1) above such other period as he considers appropriate and different periods may be substituted for different classes of application.]

[242]

NOTES
Commencement: 1 April 1996 (paras 8–10); 1 January 1991 (remainder).
Para 6: words in square brackets in sub-para (1) inserted, and sub-para (1A) inserted, by the Environment Act 1995, s 120, Sch 22, para 93(3), (4).
Paras 8–10: added by the Environment Act 1995, s 120, Sch 22, para 93(5).
Regulations: the Environmental Protection (Applications, Appeals and Registers) Regulations 1991, SI 1991/507, regs 4–7, as amended by SI 1991/836 (amending reg 5); SI 1994/1271 (amending reg 4(1)), SI 1996/667 (amending regs 4, 5), SI 1996/2678 (amending regs 4, 5 and inserting reg 6A); the Environmental Protection (Prescribed Processes and Substances Etc) (Amendment) Regulations 1994, SI 1994/1271, as amended by SI 1994/1329; the Environmental Protection (Prescribed Processes and Substances Etc) (Amendment) (Petrol Vapour Recovery) Regulations 1996, SI 1996/2678.

SCHEDULE 2
WASTE DISPOSAL AUTHORITIES AND COMPANIES

Section 32

PART I
TRANSITION TO COMPANIES

Preliminary

1. In this Part of this Schedule—
    "authority" means an existing disposal authority as defined in section 32(1);
    "company" means a waste disposal contractor formed under the Companies Act 1985 by a waste disposal authority as mentioned in section 30(5);

"direction" means a direction under section 32(2);

"joint company" means a company in which more than one authority holds securities;

"securities", in relation to a company includes shares, debentures, bonds or other securities of the company, whether or not constituting a charge on the assets of the company; and

"the vesting date" means the date on which property, rights and liabilities vest in a company by virtue of a transfer scheme under paragraph 6 below.

Notice of direction

2.—(1) The Secretary of State, before giving any directions to any authority or constituent authority, shall give notice of his intention to do so to that authority.

(2) A notice under this paragraph shall give a general indication of the provisions to be included in the direction, indicating in particular whether the proposed direction will require the formation of one or more than one company and the authority or authorities who are to form or control the company or companies and whether any existing disposal authority will be abolished.

(3) A notice under this paragraph shall state that the authority to whom it is given is entitled, within a period specified in the notice, to make to the Secretary of State applications or representations with respect to the proposed direction under paragraph 3 below.

Applications for exemption from and representations about directions

3.—(1) An authority which has been given notice under paragraph 2 above of a proposed direction may, within the period specified in the notice, make to the Secretary of State either an application under sub-paragraph (2) below or representations under sub-paragraph (3) below.

(2) An authority may, under this sub-paragraph, apply to the Secretary of State requesting him not to make a direction in its case on the ground that the authority falls within any of paragraphs (a), (b), (c) or (d) of section 32(3).

(3) An authority may, under this sub-paragraph, make representations to the Secretary of State requesting him to make, in the direction, other provision than that proposed in the notice.

(4) It shall be the duty of the Secretary of State to consider any application duly made under sub-paragraph (2) above and to notify the authority of his decision.

(5) It shall be the duty of the Secretary of State to consider any representations duly made under sub-paragraph (3) above before he gives a direction.

Directions

4.—(1) A direction may require the authority or authorities to whom it is given to form or participate in forming one or more than one company or to form or participate in forming one or more than one joint company and it shall specify the date before which the company or companies is or are to be formed.

(2) Where a direction is to require a joint company to be formed the direction may be given to such of the authorities as the Secretary of State considers appropriate (the "representative authority").

(3) Where a direction is given to an authority as the representative authority it shall be the duty of that representative authority to consult the other authorities concerned before forming a company in accordance with the direction.

(4) The Secretary of State may exercise his powers to vary or revoke a direction and give a further direction at any time before the vesting date, whether before or after a company has been formed in accordance with the direction or previous direction, as the case may be.

Formation and status of companies

5.—(1) An authority which has been directed to form a company shall do so by forming it under the Companies Act 1985 as a company which—

(a) is limited by shares, and

(b) is a wholly-owned subsidiary of the authority or authorities forming it;

and it shall do so before such date as the Secretary of State specifies in the direction.

(2) The authority shall so exercise its control of the company as to secure that, at some time before the vesting date, the conditions specified in section 68(6)(a) to (h) of the Local Government and Housing Act 1989 (conditions for "arm's length companies") apply in relation to the company and shall, at some time before the vesting date, resolve that the company shall be an arm's length company for the purposes of Part V of that Act.

(3) In this paragraph "wholly-owned subsidiary", in relation to a company and an authority, is to be construed in accordance with section 736 of the Companies Act 1985.

Transfer schemes

6.—(1) Where an authority has formed a company or companies in pursuance of a direction, the authority shall, before such date as the Secretary of State may specify in a direction given to the authority under this sub-paragraph, submit to the Secretary of State a scheme providing for the transfer to the company or companies of any property, rights or liabilities of that or that and any other authority, or of any subsidiary of its or theirs, which appear to be appropriate to transfer as representing the relevant part of the undertaking of that authority or of that authority and the other authorities.

(2) In preparing a scheme in pursuance of sub-paragraph (1) above the authority shall take into account any advice given by the Secretary of State as to the provisions he regards as appropriate for inclusion in the scheme (and in particular any advice as to the description of property, rights and liabilities which it is in his view appropriate to transfer to the company).

(3) A scheme under this paragraph shall not come into force until it has been approved by the Secretary of State and the date on which it is to come into force shall be such date as the Secretary of State may, either in giving his approval or subsequently, specify in writing to the authority; and the Secretary of State may approve a scheme either without modifications or with such modifications as he thinks fit after consulting the authority who submitted the scheme.

(4) If it appears to the Secretary of State that a scheme submitted under sub-paragraph (1) above does not accord with any advice given by him, he may do one or other of the following things, as he thinks fit, namely—
  (a)   approve the scheme under sub-paragraph (3) above with modifications; or
  (b)   after consulting the authority who submitted the scheme, substitute for it a scheme of his own, to come into force on such date as may be specified in the scheme.

(5) In the case of a scheme for the transfer to a company or joint company of the relevant part of the undertaking of two or more authorities, the representative authority shall consult the other authority or authorities before submitting the scheme under sub-paragraph (1) above; and the Secretary of State shall not approve the scheme (whether with or without modifications), or substitute a scheme of his own unless—
  (a)   he has given that other authority or (as the case may be) those other authorities an opportunity of making, within such time as he may allow for the purpose, written representations with respect to the scheme; and
  (b)   he has considered any such representations made to him within that time.

(6) The Secretary of State shall not specify the date on which the scheme is to come into force without consulting the authority which submitted the scheme and, where the scheme was submitted by a representative authority, the other authorities concerned.

(7) On the coming into force of a scheme under this paragraph the property, rights and liabilities affected by the scheme shall be transferred and vest in accordance with the scheme.

(8) As a consequence of the vesting by virtue of the scheme of property, rights and liabilities of an authority in a company, that company shall issue to the authority such securities of the company as are specified in the transfer scheme.

Transfer schemes: supplementary provisions

7. A scheme under paragraph 6 above may define the property, rights and liabilities to be transferred by the scheme—
  (a)   by specifying the property, rights and liabilities in question; or
  (b)   by referring to all the property, rights and liabilities comprised in any specified part of the undertaking or undertakings to be transferred; or
  (c)   partly in the one way and partly in the other;
and may make such supplemental, incidental and consequential provision as the authority making the scheme considers appropriate.

8.—(1) The provisions of this paragraph apply to the transfer to a company of the property, rights and liabilities representing the relevant part of an authority's undertaking.

(2) Any property, rights or liabilities held or subsisting partly for the purpose of the relevant part of the authority's undertaking and partly for the purpose of another part shall, where the nature of the property, rights or liabilities permits, be divided or apportioned between the authority and the company in such proportions as may be appropriate; and where any estate or interest in land falls to be so divided, any rent payable under a lease in respect of that estate or interest, and any rent charged on that estate or interest, shall be correspondingly apportioned or divided so that the one part is payable in respect of, or charged on, only one part of the estate or interest and the other part is payable in respect of, or charged on, only the other part of the estate or interest.

(3) Any property, rights or liabilities held or subsisting as mentioned in sub-paragraph (2) above the nature of which does not permit their division or apportionment as so mentioned shall be transferred to the company or retained by the authority according to which of them appear at the vesting date likely to make use of the property, or, as the case may be, to be affected by the right or liability, to the greater extent, subject to such arrangements for the protection of the other of them as may be agreed between them.

(4) It shall be the duty of the authority and the company, before or after the vesting date, so far as practicable to enter into such written agreements, and to execute such other instruments, as are necessary or expedient to identify or define the property, rights and liabilities transferred to the company or retained by the authority and as will—
- (a) afford to the authority and the company as against one another such rights and safeguards as they may require for the proper discharge of the authority's functions and the proper carrying on of the company's undertaking; and
- (b) make, as from such date (not being earlier than the vesting date) as may be specified in that agreement or instrument, such clarifications and modifications of the division of the authority's undertaking as will best serve the proper discharge of the authority's functions and the proper carrying on of the company's undertaking.

(5) Any such agreement shall provide so far as it is expedient—
- (a) for the granting of leases and for the creation of other liabilities and rights over land whether amounting in law to interests in land or not, and whether involving the surrender of any existing interest or the creation of a new interest or not;
- (b) for the granting of indemnities in connection with the severance of leases and other matters;
- (c) for responsibility for complying with any statutory requirements as respects matters to be registered and any licences, authorisations or permissions which need to be obtained.

(6) If the authority or the company represents to the Secretary of State, or if it appears to him without such a representation, that it is unlikely in the case of any matter on which agreement is required under sub-paragraph (4) above that such agreement will be reached, the Secretary of State may, whether before or after the vesting date, give a direction determining the manner in which the property, rights or liabilities in question are to be divided between the authority and the company, and may include in the direction any provision which might have been included in an agreement under that sub-paragraph; and any property, rights or liabilities required by the direction to be transferred to the company shall be regarded as having been transferred to, and by virtue of the transfer scheme vested in, the company accordingly.

Tax and company provisions

9.—(1) Any shares in a company which are issued as a consequence of the vesting by a transfer scheme of property, rights and liabilities in the company shall—
- (a) be issued as fully paid; and
- (b) be treated for the purposes of the application of the Companies Act 1985 in relation to that company as if they had been paid up by virtue of the payment to the company of their nominal value in cash.

(2) For the purposes of Chapter I of Part II of the Capital Allowances Act 1990 (capital allowance in respect of machinery and plant) property which is vested in a company by virtue of a transfer scheme shall be treated as if—
- (a) it had been acquired by the company on the transfer date for the purposes for which it is used by the company on and after that date; and

(b)   capital expenditure of an amount equal to the price which the property would have fetched if sold in the open market had been incurred on that date by the company on the acquisition of the property for the purposes mentioned in paragraph (a) above.

Benefit of certain planning permission

10.—(1) This paragraph applies in relation to planning permission deemed to have been granted to the authority under regulation 4 of the Town and Country Planning General Regulations 1976 (deemed planning permission for development by local authorities) which subsists at the vesting date.

(2) Any planning permission to which this paragraph applies which authorises the use of land by the authority for the treatment, keeping or disposal of waste shall, on the transfer of the land to the company by the scheme, endure for the benefit of the land.

Right to production of documents of title

11. Where on any transfer by virtue of a transfer scheme the authority is entitled to retain possession of any documents relating to the title to, or to the management of, any land or other property transferred to the company, the authority shall be deemed to have given to the company an acknowledgment in writing of the right of the company to production of that document and to delivery of copies thereof; and, in England and Wales, section 64 of the Law of Property Act 1925 shall have effect accordingly, and on the basis that the acknowledgement did not contain any such expression of contrary intention as is mentioned in that section.

Proof of title by certificate

12.—(1) A joint certificate by or on behalf of the authority and the company that any property specified in the certificate, or any such interest in or right over any such property as may be specified in the certificate, is by virtue of the transfer scheme for the time being vested in the authority or in the company shall be conclusive evidence for all purposes of that fact.

(2) If on the expiration of one month after a request from the authority or the company for the preparation of such a joint certificate the authority and the company have failed to agree on the terms of the certificate, they shall refer the matter to the Secretary of State and issue the certificate in such terms as the Secretary of State may direct.

Construction of agreements

13. Where any of the rights or liabilities transferred by a transfer scheme are rights or liabilities under an agreement to which the authority was a party immediately before the vesting date, whether in writing or not, and whether or not of such a nature that rights and liabilities thereunder could be assigned by the authority, that agreement shall have effect on and after the vesting date as if—

(a)   the company had been a party to the agreement; and

(b)   for any reference (however worded and whether express or implied) to the authority there were substituted a reference, as respects anything falling to be done on or after the vesting date, to the company; and

(c)   any reference (however worded and whether express or implied) to any officer or servant of the authority were, as respects anything falling to be done on or after the vesting date, a reference to such person as the company may appoint or, in default of appointment, to the officer or servant of the company who corresponds as nearly as may be to that officer or servant of the authority; and

(d)   where the agreement refers to property, rights or liabilities which fall to be apportioned or divided between the authority and the company, as if the agreement constituted two separate agreements separately enforceable by and against the authority and the company respectively as regards the part of the property, rights and liabilities retained by the authority or, as the case may be, the part of the property, rights and liabilities vesting in the company and not as regards the other part;

and sub-paragraph (d) above shall apply in particular to the covenants, stipulations and conditions of any lease by or to the authority.

14. Without prejudice to the generality of the provisions of paragraph 13 above, the company and any other person shall, as from the vesting date, have the same rights, powers and remedies

(and in particular the same rights and powers as to the taking or resisting of legal proceedings or the making or resisting of applications to any authority) for ascertaining, perfecting or enforcing any right or liability transferred to and vested in the company by a transfer scheme as he would have had if that right or liability had at all times been a right or liability of the company, and any legal proceedings or applications to any authority pending on the vesting date by or against the authority, in so far as they relate to any property, right or liability transferred to the company by the scheme, or to any agreement to any such property, right or liability, shall be continued by or against the company to the exclusion of the authority.

Third parties affected by vesting provisions

15.—(1)   Without prejudice to the provisions of paragraphs 13 and 14 above, any transaction effected between the authority and the company in pursuance of paragraph 8(4) above or of a direction under paragraph 8(6) above shall be binding on all other persons, and notwithstanding that it would, apart from this sub-paragraph, have required the consent or concurrence of any other person.

(2)   It shall be the duty of the authority and the company, if they effect any transaction in pursuance of paragraph 8(4) above or of a direction under paragraph 8(6) above, to notify any person who has rights or liabilities which thereby become enforceable as to part by or against the authority and as to part by or against the company; and if such a person applies to the Secretary of State and satisfies him that the transaction operated unfairly against him the Secretary of State may give such directions to the authority and the company as appear to him to be appropriate for varying the transaction.

(3)   If in consequence of a transfer by a transfer scheme or of anything done in pursuance of paragraphs 8 to 14 above the rights or liabilities of any person other than the authority which were enforceable against or by the authority become enforceable as to part against or by the authority and as to part against or by the company, and the value of any property or interest of that person is thereby diminished, such compensation as may be just shall be paid to that person by the authority, the company or both, and any dispute as to whether and if so how much compensation is payable, or as to the person by whom it shall be paid, shall be referred to, and determined by, the Lands Tribunal.

Transfer of staff

16.—(1)   The Transfer of Undertakings (Protection of Employment) Regulations 1981 shall apply in relation to the relevant employees of an authority in accordance with sub-paragraph (2) below.

(2)   For the purposes of the application of those Regulations in relation to any of the relevant employees of an authority, the relevant part of the undertaking of the authority shall (whether or not it would otherwise be so regarded) be regarded—
  (a)   as a part of an undertaking within the meaning of those Regulations which is transferred from the authority to the company on the vesting date, and
  (b)   as being so transferred by a transfer to which those Regulations apply and which is completed on that date.

(3)   Where a person is, in pursuance of section 32, to cease to be employed by an authority and to become employed by a company, none of the agreed redundancy procedures applicable to persons employed by waste disposal authorities shall apply to him.

(4)   For the purposes of this paragraph persons are "relevant employees" of an authority if they are to become, in pursuance of section 32, employees of a company to which the relevant part of the undertaking of the authority is to be transferred.

Information for purposes of transfer scheme

17.—(1)   The Secretary of State may, by directions, prescribe descriptions of information which are to be furnished for purposes connected with the transfer by authorities to companies of the relevant part of the undertakings of authorities.

(2)   It shall be the duty of . . . waste disposal authority, on being requested to do so by a written notice served on it by the Secretary of State, to furnish to the Secretary of State such information of a description prescribed under sub-paragraph (1) above as may be specified in the notice.

PART II
PROVISIONS REGULATING WASTE DISPOSAL AUTHORITIES AND COMPANIES

Terms of waste disposal contracts

18. A waste disposal authority shall, in determining the terms and conditions of any contract which the authority proposes to enter into for the keeping, treatment or disposal of waste, so frame the terms and conditions as to avoid undue discrimination in favour of one description of waste disposal contractor as against other descriptions of waste disposal contractors.

19.—(1) A waste disposal authority shall have regard to the desirability of including in any contract which the authority proposes to enter into for the keeping, treatment or disposal of waste terms or conditions designed to—
    (a) minimise pollution of the environment or harm to human health due to the disposal or treatment of the waste under the contract; and
    (b) maximise the recycling of waste under the contract.

(2) A waste disposal authority shall be entitled—
    (a) to invite tenders for any such contract, and
    (b) to accept or refuse to accept any tender for such a contract and accordingly to enter or not to enter into a contract,

by reference to acceptance or refusal of acceptance by persons tendering for the contract of any terms or conditions included in the draft contract in pursuance of sub-paragraph (1) above.

Procedure for putting waste disposal contracts out to tender

20.—(1) A waste disposal authority which proposes to enter into a contract for the keeping, treatment or disposal of controlled waste shall comply with the following requirements before making the contract and if it does not any contract which is made shall be void.

(2) The authority shall publish, in at least two publications circulating among waste disposal contractors, a notice containing—
    (a) a brief description of the contract work;
    (b) a statement that during a specified period any person may inspect a detailed specification of the contract work free of charge at a specified place and time;
    (c) a statement that during that period any person will be supplied with a copy of the detailed specification on request and on payment of the specified charge;
    (d) a statement that any person who wishes to submit a tender for the contract must notify the authority of his wish within a specified period; and
    (e) a statement that the authority intend to invite tenders for the contract, in accordance with sub-paragraph (4) below.

(3) The authority shall—
    (a) ensure that the periods, place and time and the charge specified in the notice are such as are reasonable;
    (b) make the detailed specification available for inspection in accordance with the notice; and
    (c) make copies of the detailed specification available for supply in accordance with the notice.

(4) If any persons notified the authority, in accordance with the notice, of their wish to submit tenders for the contract, the authority shall—
    (a) if more than four persons did so, invite at least four of them to tender for the contract;
    (b) if less than four persons did so, invite each of them to tender for the contract.

(5) In this paragraph—
    "the contract work", in relation to a contract for the keeping, treatment or disposal of waste, means the work comprising the services involved in the keeping, treatment or disposal of the waste under the contract; and
    "specified" means specified in the notice under sub-paragraph (2) above.

21. A waste disposal authority, in taking any of the following decisions, namely—
    (a)   who to invite to tender for the contract under paragraph 20(4)(a) above, and
    (b)   who to enter into the contract with,

shall disregard the fact that any waste disposal contractor tendering for the contract is, or is not, controlled by the authority.

Variation of waste disposal contracts

22. Where a waste disposal authority has entered into a contract with a waste disposal contractor under the authority's control, paragraph 18 above shall, with the necessary modifications, apply on any proposed variation of the contract during the subsistence of that control, in relation to the terms and conditions that would result from the variation as it applies to the original contract.

Avoidance of restrictions on transfer of securities of companies

23.—(1) Subject to sub-paragraph (3) below, any provision to which this paragraph applies shall be void in so far as it operates—
    (a)   to preclude the holder of any securities of a waste disposal contractor from disposing of those securities; or
    (b)   to require the holder of any such securities to dispose, or offer to dispose, of those securities to particular persons or to particular classes of persons; or
    (c)   to preclude the holder of any securities from disposing of those securities except—
        (i)   at a particular time or at particular times; or
        (ii)   on the fulfilment of particular conditions or in other particular circumstances.

(2) This paragraph applies to any provision relating to any securities of a waste disposal contractor which is controlled by a waste disposal authority or to which the authority has transferred the relevant part of its undertaking and contained in—
    (a)   the memorandum or articles of association of the company or any other instrument purporting to regulate to any extent the respective rights and liabilities of the members of the company;
    (b)   any resolution of the company; or
    (c)   any instrument issued by the company and embodying terms and conditions on which any such securities are to be held by persons for the time being holding them.

(3) No provision shall be void by reason of its operating as mentioned in sub-paragraph (1) above if the Secretary of State has given his approval in writing to that provision.

[244]

[SCHEDULE 2A
OBJECTIVES FOR THE PURPOSES OF THE NATIONAL WASTE STRATEGY
Sections 44A, 44B

1. Ensuring that waste is recovered or disposed of without endangering human health and without using processes or methods which could harm the environment and, in particular, without—
    (a)   risk to water, air, soil, plants or animals;
    (b)   causing nuisance through noise or odours; or
    (c)   adversely affecting the countryside or places of special interest.

2. Establishing an integrated and adequate network of waste disposal installations, taking account of the best available technology not involving excessive costs.

3. Ensuring that the network referred to in paragraph 2 above enables—
    (a)   the European Community as a whole to become self-sufficient in waste disposal, and the Member States individually to move towards that aim, taking into account geographical circumstances or the need for specialised installations for certain types of waste; and
    (b)   waste to be disposed of in one of the nearest appropriate installations, by means of the most appropriate methods and technologies in order to ensure a high level of protection for the environment and public health.

4. Encouraging the prevention or reduction of waste production and its harmfulness, in particular by—
    (a)   the development of clean technologies more sparing in their use of natural resources;
    (b)   the technical development and marketing of products designed so as to make no contribution or to make the smallest possible contribution, by the nature of their manufacture, use or final disposal, to increasing the amount or harmfulness of waste and pollution hazards; and
    (c)   the development of appropriate techniques for the final disposal of dangerous substances contained in waste destined for recovery.

5. Encouraging—
    (a)   the recovery of waste by means of recycling, reuse or reclamation or any other process with a view to extracting secondary raw materials; and
    (b)   the use of waste as a source of energy.]

[245]

NOTES
Commencement: 1 April 1996.
Inserted by the Environment Act 1995, s 92, Sch 12.

[SCHEDULE 2B
CATEGORIES OF WASTE

Section 75

1. Production or consumption residues not otherwise specified below.

2. Off-specification products.

3. Products whose date for appropriate use has expired.

4. Materials spilled, lost or having undergone other mishap, including any materials, equipment, etc, contaminated as a result of the mishap.

5. Materials contaminated or soiled as a result of planned actions (eg residues from cleaning operations, packing materials, containers, etc).

6. Unusable parts (eg reject batteries, exhausted catalysts, etc).

7. Substances which no longer perform satisfactorily (eg contaminated acids, contaminated solvents, exhausted tempering salts, etc).

8. Residues of industrial processes (eg slags, still bottoms, etc).

9. Residues from pollution abatement processes (eg scrubber sludges, baghouse dusts, spent filters, etc).

10. Machining or finishing residues (eg lathe turnings, mill scales, etc).

11. Residues from raw materials extraction and processing (eg mining residues, oil field slops, etc).

12. Adulterated materials (eg oils contaminated with PCBs, etc).

13. Any materials, substances or products whose use has been banned by law.

14. Products for which the holder has no further use (eg agricultural, household, office, commercial and shop discards, etc).

15. Contaminated materials, substances or products resulting from remedial action with respect to land.

16. Any materials, substances or products which are not contained in the above categories.]

[246]

NOTES
Commencement: to be appointed.
Inserted by the Environment Act 1995, s 120, Sch 22, para 95, as from a day to be appointed.

SCHEDULE 3
STATUTORY NUISANCES: SUPPLEMENTARY PROVISIONS

Section 81

Appeals to magistrates' court

1.—(1) This paragraph applies in relation to appeals under section 80(3) against an abatement notice to a magistrates' court.

(2) An appeal to which this paragraph applies shall be by way of complaint for an order and the Magistrates' Courts Act 1980 shall apply to the proceedings.

(3) An appeal against any decision of a magistrates' court in pursuance of an appeal to which this paragraph applies shall lie to the Crown Court at the instance of any party to the proceedings in which the decision was given.

(4) The Secretary of State may make regulations as to appeals to which this paragraph applies and the regulations may in particular—
  (a) include provisions comparable to those in section 290 of the Public Health Act 1936 (appeals against notices requiring the execution of works);
  (b) prescribe the cases in which an abatement notice is, or is not, to be suspended until the appeal is decided, or until some other stage in the proceedings;
  (c) prescribe the cases in which the decision on appeal may in some respects be less favourable to the appellant than the decision from which he is appealing;
  (d) prescribe the cases in which the appellant may claim that an abatement notice should have been served on some other person and prescribe the procedure to be followed in those cases.

[Appeals to Sheriff

1A.—(1) This paragraph applies in relation to appeals to the sheriff under section 80(3) against an abatement notice.

(2) An appeal to which this paragraph applies shall be by way of a summary application.

(3) The Secretary of State may make regulations as to appeals to which this paragraph applies and the regulations may in particular include or prescribe any of the matters referred to in sub-paragraphs (4)(a) to (d) of paragraph 1 above.]

Powers of entry etc

2.—(1) Subject to sub-paragraph (2) below, any person authorised by a local authority may, on production (if so required) of his authority, enter any premises at any reasonable time—
  (a) for the purpose of ascertaining whether or not a statutory nuisance exists; or
  (b) for the purpose of taking any action, or executing any work, authorised or required by Part III.

(2) Admission by virtue of sub-paragraph (1) above to any premises used wholly or mainly for residential purposes shall not except in an emergency be demanded as of right unless twenty-four hours notice of the intended entry has been given to the occupier.

(3) If it is shown to the satisfaction of a justice of the peace on sworn information in writing—
  (a) that admission to any premises has been refused, or that refusal is apprehended, or that the premises are unoccupied or the occupier is temporarily absent, or that the case is one of emergency, or that an application for admission would defeat the object of the entry; and
  (b) that there is reasonable ground for entry into the premises for the purpose for which entry is required,

the justice may by warrant under his hand authorise the local authority by any authorised person to enter the premises, if need be by force.

(4) An authorised person entering any premises by virtue of sub-paragraph (1) or a warrant under sub-paragraph (3) above may—
  (a) take with him such other persons and such equipment as may be necessary;
  (b) carry out such inspections, measurements and tests as he considers necessary for the discharge of any of the local authority's functions under Part III; and
  (c) take away such samples or articles as he considers necessary for that purpose.

(5) On leaving any unoccupied premises which he has entered by virtue of sub-paragraph (1) above or a warrant under sub-paragraph (3) above the authorised person shall leave them as effectually secured against trespassers as he found them.

(6) A warrant issued in pursuance of sub-paragraph (3) above shall continue in force until the purpose for which the entry is required has been satisfied.

(7) Any reference in this paragraph to an emergency is a reference to a case where the person requiring entry has reasonable cause to believe that circumstances exist which are likely to endanger life or health and that immediate entry is necessary to verify the existence of those circumstances or to ascertain their cause and to effect a remedy.

[(8) In the application of this paragraph to Scotland, a reference to a justice of the peace or to a justice includes a reference to the sheriff.]

[2A.—(1) Any person authorised by a local authority may on production (if so required) of his authority—
- (a)   enter or open a vehicle, machinery or equipment, if necessary by force, or
- (b)   remove a vehicle, machinery or equipment from a street [or, in Scotland, road] to a secure place,

for the purpose of taking any action, or executing any work, authorised by or required under Part III in relation to a statutory nuisance within section 79(1)(ga) above caused by noise emitted from or caused by the vehicle, machinery or equipment.

(2) On leaving any unattended vehicle, machinery or equipment that he has entered or opened under sub-paragraph (1) above, the authorised person shall (subject to sub-paragraph (3) below) leave it secured against interference or theft in such manner and as effectually as he found it.

(3) If the authorised person is unable to comply with sub-paragraph (2) above, he shall for the purpose of securing the unattended vehicle, machinery or equipment either—
- (a)   immobilise it by such means as he considers expedient, or
- (b)   remove it from the street to a secure place.

(4) In carrying out any function under sub-paragraph (1), (2) or (3) above, the authorised person shall not cause more damage than is necessary.

(5) Before a vehicle, machinery or equipment is entered, opened or removed under sub-paragraph (1) above, the local authority shall notify the police of the intention to take action under that sub-paragraph.

(6) After a vehicle, machinery or equipment has been removed under sub-paragraph (1) or (3) above, the local authority shall notify the police of its removal and current location.

(7) Notification under sub-paragraph (5) or (6) above may be given to the police at any police station in the local authority's area or, in the case of the Temples, at any police station of the City of London Police.

(8) For the purposes of section 81(4) above, any expenses reasonably incurred by a local authority under sub-paragraph (2) or (3) above shall be treated as incurred by the authority under section 81(3) above in abating or preventing the recurrence of the statutory nuisance in question.]

Offences relating to entry

3.—(1) A person who wilfully obstructs any person acting in the exercise of any powers conferred by paragraph 2 [or 2A] above shall be liable, on summary conviction, to a fine not exceeding level 3 on the standard scale.

(2) If a person discloses any information relating to any trade secret obtained in the exercise of any powers conferred by paragraph 2 above he shall, unless the disclosure was made in the performance of his duty or with the consent of the person having the right to disclose the information, be liable, on summary conviction, to a fine not exceeding level 5 on the standard scale.

Default powers

4.—(1) This paragraph applies to the following functions of a local authority, that is to say its duty under section 79 to cause its area to be inspected to detect any statutory nuisance which ought to be dealt with under section 80 [or sections 80 and 80A] and its powers under paragraph 2 [or 2A] above.

(2) If the Secretary of State is satisfied that any local authority has failed, in any respect, to discharge the function to which this paragraph applies which it ought to have discharged, he may make an order declaring the authority to be in default.

(3) An order made under sub-paragraph (2) above which declares an authority to be in default may, for the purpose of remedying the default, direct the authority ("the defaulting authority") to perform the function specified in the order and may specify the manner in which and the time or times within which the function is to be performed by the authority.

(4) If the defaulting authority fails to comply with any direction contained in such an order the Secretary of State may, instead of enforcing the order by mandamus, make an order transferring to himself the function of the authority specified in the order.

(5) Where the function of a defaulting authority is transferred under sub-paragraph (4) above, the amount of any expenses which the Secretary of State certifies were incurred by him in performing the function shall on demand be paid to him by the defaulting authority.

(6) Any expenses required to be paid by a defaulting authority under sub-paragraph (5) above shall be defrayed by the authority in like manner, and shall be debited to the like account, as if the function had not been transferred and the expenses had been incurred by the authority in performing them.

(7) The Secretary of State may by order vary or revoke any order previously made by him under this paragraph.

(8) Any order under this paragraph may include such incidental, supplemental and transitional provisions as the Secretary of State considers appropriate.

[(9) This paragraph does not apply to Scotland.]

Protection from personal liability

5.   Nothing done by, or by a member of, a local authority or by an officer of or other person authorised by a local authority shall, if done in good faith for the purpose of executing Part III, subject them or any of them personally to any action, liability, claim or demand whatsoever (other than any liability under section 19 or 20 of the Local Government Finance Act 1982 (powers of district auditor and court)).

Statement of right of appeal in notices

6.   Where an appeal against a notice served by a local authority lies to a magistrates' court [or, in Scotland, the sheriff] by virtue of section 80, it shall be the duty of the authority to include in such a notice a statement indicating that such an appeal lies as aforesaid and specifying the time within which it must be brought.

[247]

NOTES

Commencement: 1 April 1996 (para 1A); 5 January 1994 (para 2A); 1 January 1991 (remainder).
Para 1A: inserted by the Environment Act 1995, s 107, Sch 17, para 7(a).
Para 2: sub-para (8) inserted by the Environment Act 1995, s 107, Sch 17, para 7(b).
Para 2A: inserted by the Noise and Statutory Nuisance Act 1993, s 4(5); words in square brackets inserted by the Environment Act 1995, s 107, Sch 17, para 7(c).
Para 3: words in square brackets inserted by the Noise and Statutory Nuisance Act 1993, s 4(6), (7).
Para 4: words in square brackets in sub-para (1) inserted by the Noise and Statutory Nuisance Act 1993, s 4(6), (7); sub-para (9) inserted by the Environment Act 1995, s 107, Sch 17, para 7(d).
Para 6: words in square brackets inserted by the Environment Act 1995, s 107, Sch 17, para 7(e).
Regulations: the Statutory Nuisance (Appeals) Regulations 1995, SI 1995/2644.

SCHEDULE 4
ABANDONED SHOPPING AND LUGGAGE TROLLEYS

Section 99

Application

1.—(1) Subject to sub-paragraph (2) below, this Schedule applies where any shopping or luggage trolley is found by an authorised officer of the local authority on any land in the open air and appears to him to be abandoned.

(2) This Schedule does not apply in relation to a shopping or luggage trolley found on the following descriptions of land, that is to say—
  (a) land in which the owner of the trolley has a legal estate or, in Scotland, of which the owner of the trolley is the owner or occupier;
  (b) where an off-street parking place affords facilities to the customers of shops for leaving there shopping trolleys used by them, land on which those facilities are afforded;
  (c) where any other place designated by the local authority for the purposes of this Schedule affords like facilities, land on which those facilities are afforded; and
  (d) as respects luggage trolleys, land which is used for the purposes of their undertaking by persons authorised by an enactment to carry on any railway, light railway, tramway or road transport undertaking or by a relevant airport operator (within the meaning of Part V of the Airports Act 1986).

Power to seize and remove trolleys

2.—(1) Where this Schedule applies in relation to a shopping or luggage trolley, the local authority may, subject to sub-paragraph (2) below,—
  (a) seize the trolley; and
  (b) remove it to such place under its control as the authority thinks fit.

(2) When a shopping or luggage trolley is found on any land appearing to the authorised officer to be occupied by any person, the trolley shall not be removed without the consent of that person unless—
  (a) the local authority has served on that person a notice stating that the authority proposes to remove the trolley; and
  (b) no notice objecting to its removal is served by that person on the local authority within the period of fourteen days beginning with the day on which the local authority served the notice of the proposed removal on him.

Retention, return and disposal of trolleys

3.—(1) Subject to the following sub-paragraphs, the local authority, as respects any shopping or luggage trolley it has seized and removed,—
  (a) shall keep the trolley for a period of six weeks; and
  (b) may sell or otherwise dispose of the trolley at any time after the end of that period.

(2) The local authority shall, as respects any trolley it has seized or removed, as soon as reasonably practicable (but not later than fourteen days) after its removal, serve on the person (if any) who appears to the authority to be the owner of the trolley a notice stating—
  (a) that the authority has removed the trolley and is keeping it;
  (b) the place where it is being kept; and
  (c) that, if it is not claimed, the authority may dispose of it.

(3) Subject to sub-paragraph (4) below, if, within the period mentioned in sub-paragraph (1)(a) above, any person claims to be the owner of a shopping or luggage trolley being kept by the authority under that sub-paragraph, the local authority shall, if it appears that the claimant is the owner, deliver the trolley to him.

(4) A person claiming to be the owner of a shopping or luggage trolley shall not be entitled to have the trolley delivered to him unless he pays the local authority, on demand, such charge as the authority requires.

(5) No shopping or luggage trolley shall be disposed of by the local authority unless (where it has not been claimed) the authority has made reasonable enquiries to ascertain who owns it.

Charges

4.—(1) The local authority, in fixing the charge to be paid under paragraph 3 above by the claimant of a shopping or luggage trolley, shall secure that the charges so payable by claimants shall be such as are sufficient, taking one financial year with another, to cover the cost of removing, storing and disposing of such trolleys under this Schedule.

(2) The local authority may agree with persons who own shopping or luggage trolleys and make them available for use in its area a scheme for the collection by them of trolleys

they make available for use; and where such an agreement is in force with any person, no charge may be demanded under paragraph 3 above by the local authority in respect of any trolley within the scheme in relation to which the provisions of the scheme are complied with.

Definitions

5. In this Schedule—
> "luggage trolley" means a trolley provided by a person carrying on an undertaking mentioned in paragraph 1(2)(d) above to travellers for use by them for carrying their luggage to, from or within the premises used for the purposes of his undertaking, not being a trolley which is power-assisted; and
> "shopping trolley" means a trolley provided by the owner of a shop to customers for use by them for carrying goods purchased at the shop, not being a trolley which is power-assisted.

[248]

(Sch 5 repealed by the Radioactive Substances Act 1993, s 50, Sch 6, Pt I; Schs 6–10 outside the scope of this work.)

SCHEDULE 11
TRANSITIONAL PROVISIONS AND SAVINGS FOR PART VII
Section 139

PART I
COUNTRYSIDE FUNCTIONS

Preliminary

1. In this Part of this Schedule—
> "the appointed day" means the day appointed under section 130(4) of this Act;
> "the Commission" means the Countryside Commission;
> "the Council" means the Countryside Council for Wales;
> "relevant", in relation to anything done by or in relation to the Commission before the appointed day, means anything which, if it were to be done on or after the appointed day, would be done by or in relation to the Council or, as the case may be, by or in relation to both the Commission (so far as concerning England) and the Council (so far as concerning Wales).

Continuity of exercise of functions

2.—(1) Any relevant thing done by or in relation to the Commission before the appointed day shall, so far as is required for continuing its effect on and after that date, have effect as if done by or in relation to the Council or, as the case may be, by or in relation to both the Council and the Commission.

(2) Any relevant thing which, immediately before the appointed day, is in the process of being done by or in relation to the Commission may be continued by or in relation to the Council or, as the case may be, by or in relation to both the Council and the Commission.

Construction of references to the Countryside Commission

3.—(1) This paragraph applies to any provision of any agreement, or of any instrument or other document, subsisting immediately before the appointed day which refers (in whatever terms) to the Commission and does so (or is to be construed as doing so) in relation to, or to things being done in or in connection with, Wales.

(2) Any provision to which this paragraph applies shall, subject to sub-paragraphs (3) and (4) below, have effect on and after the appointed day with the substitution for, or the inclusion in, any reference to the Commission of a reference to the Council, according as the reference concerns Wales only or concerns both England and Wales.

(3) Any provision to which this paragraph applies which refers in general terms to members of or to persons employed by or agents of the Commission shall have effect on and after the appointed day with the substitution for, or the inclusion in, any such reference of a reference to members of or persons employed by or agents of the Council, according as the reference concerns Wales only or concerns both England and Wales.

(4) Any provision to which this paragraph applies which refers to a member or employee of the Commission shall have effect on and after the appointed day with the substitution for, or the inclusion in, any such reference of—

(a)   a reference to such person as the Council may appoint, or

(b)   in default of appointment, to the member or employee of the Council who corresponds as nearly as may be to the member or employee in question,

according as the reference concerns Wales only or concerns both England and Wales.

4.—(1) This paragraph applies to any provision of a local Act passed, or subordinate legislation made, before the appointed day which refers (in whatever terms) to the Commission and relates to, or to things being done in or in connection with, Wales.

(2) The Secretary of State may by order make such consequential modifications of any provision to which this paragraph applies as appear to him to be necessary or expedient.

(3) Subject to any exercise of the power conferred by sub-paragraph (2) above, any provision to which this paragraph applies shall have effect on and after the appointed day with the substitution for, or inclusion in, any reference to the Commission of a reference to the Council, according as the reference concerns Wales only or concerns both England and Wales.

Existing areas of outstanding natural beauty and long distance routes

5.—(1) This paragraph applies to—

(a)   any area of land which immediately before the appointed day is an area of outstanding natural beauty designated under section 87 of the 1949 Act of which part is in England and part is in Wales (referred to as "the two parts" of such an area); and

(b)   any long distance route under Part IV of that Act of which some parts are in England and other parts in Wales.

(2) On and after the appointed day the two parts of an area to which this paragraph applies shall be treated as if each were a distinct area of outstanding natural beauty; and accordingly, so far as may be necessary for the purpose of applying paragraphs 2 and 3 above, anything done by or in relation to the Commission in relation to both parts of that area shall be treated as having been done in relation to the part in Wales by or in relation to the Council.

(3) On and after the appointed day any route to which this paragraph applies shall not cease, by virtue of this Part of this Act to be a single route for the purposes of Part IV of the 1949 Act; but any function which before that day is exercisable by or in relation to the Commission shall, on and after that day be exercisable by or in relation to the Commission (so far as concerns parts of the route in England) and by or in relation to the Council (so far as concerns parts of the route in Wales).

(4) On or after the appointed day the Commission and the Council shall each exercise any function of theirs in relation to an area or route to which this paragraph applies only after consultation with the other; and the Commission and the Council may make arrangements for discharging any of their functions in relation to such an area or route jointly.

[249]

PART II
NATURE CONSERVATION FUNCTIONS

Preliminary

6.   In this Part of this Schedule—

"appointed day" means the date appointed under section 131(3) of this Act;

"appropriate new council" shall be construed in accordance with paragraph 7 below; and

"new council" means a council established by section 128(1) of this Act.

7.—(1) In this Part of this Schedule a reference to "the appropriate new council" is, in relation to or to things done in connection with property, rights or liabilities of the Nature Conservancy Council which are transferred by section 135(2) of this Act to a new council, a reference to that new council.

(2) Subject to sub-paragraph (1) above, a reference in this Part of this Schedule to "the appropriate new council" is, in relation to anything else done before the appointed day by or in

relation to the Nature Conservancy Council in the exercise of or in connection with any function of theirs (other than a function corresponding to a special function of the new councils)—

(a)   a reference to the new council by whom the nature conservation function corresponding to that function is exercisable on and after that date; or

(b)   where the thing done relates to a matter affecting the area of more than one new council, a reference to each new council by whom the nature conservation function corresponding to that function is exercisable on and after that date;

and in relation to anything done in the exercise of or in connection with any function of the Nature Conservancy Council corresponding to a special function of the new councils a reference to "the appropriate new council" is a reference to the joint committee or, where directions under section 133(5) of this Act have been given, the new council by whom the corresponding special function is dischargeable (on behalf of the new councils) on and after that day.

(3)   Any question arising under this paragraph as to which new council is the appropriate new council in relation to any particular function of the Nature Conservancy Council may be determined by a direction given by the Secretary of State .

Continuity of exercise of functions

8.—(1)   Anything done (or deemed by any enactment to have been done) by or in relation to the Nature Conservancy Council before the appointed day shall, so far as is required for continuing its effect on and after that date, have effect as if done by or in relation to the appropriate new council.

(2)   Anything which immediately before the appointed day is in the process of being done by or in relation to the Nature Conservancy Council may be continued by or in relation to the appropriate new council as if it had been done by or in relation to that council.

Construction of references to the Nature Conservancy Council

9.—(1)   This paragraph applies to any agreement, any instrument and any other document subsisting immediately before the appointed day which refers (in whatever terms) to the Nature Conservancy Council, other than a scheme provided by that Council under paragraph 12 of Schedule 3 to the Nature Conservancy Council Act 1973.

(2)   Any agreement, instrument or other document to which this paragraph applies shall have effect on and after the appointed day with the substitution—

(a)   for any reference to the Nature Conservancy Council of a reference to the appropriate new council;

(b)   for any reference in general terms to members of or to persons employed by or agents of the Nature Conservancy Council of a reference to members of or persons employed by or agents of the appropriate new council; and

(c)   for any reference to a member or officer of the Nature Conservancy Council of a reference to such person as the appropriate new council may appoint or, in default of appointment, to the member or employee of that council who corresponds as nearly as may be to the member or officer in question.

10.—(1)   This paragraph applies to any provision of a local Act passed, or subordinate legislation made, before the appointed day which refers (in whatever terms) to the Nature Conservancy Council.

(2)   The Secretary of State may by order make such consequential modifications of any provision to which this paragraph applies as appear to him to be necessary or expedient.

(3)   Subject to any exercise of the power conferred by sub-paragraph (2) above, any provision to which this paragraph applies shall have effect on and after the appointed day with the substitution for each reference to the Nature Conservancy Council of a reference to such one or more of the new councils as may be appropriate, according as the provision relates to, or to things being done in or in connection with, England, Scotland or Wales.

Pensions for Nature Conservancy Council staff

11.—(1)   The repeal by this Act of paragraph 12 of Schedule 3 to the Nature Conservancy Council Act 1973 shall not affect the operation on and after the appointed day of any scheme provided by the Nature Conservancy Council for the payment to or in respect of its officers of pensions, allowances or gratuities.

(2) Any such scheme shall have effect on and after the appointed day with the substitution for any reference to the Nature Conservancy Council of a reference to the Secretary of State.

Existing nature reserves and areas of special scientific interest

12.—(1) This paragraph applies to any land which, immediately before the appointed day is—
  (a) a nature reserve (within the meaning of Part III of the 1949 Act) which is managed by, or under an agreement entered into with, the Nature Conservancy Council or which is the subject of a declaration under section 35 of the 1981 Act; or
  (b) an area of special scientific interest which has been notified by the Nature Conservancy Council under section 28(1) of the 1981 Act or is treated by section 28(13) of that Act as having been notified under section 28(1)(a) of that Act or is an area to which an order under section 29(1) of that Act relates;

and of which part is in England and part is in Wales or, as the case may be, part is in England and part is in Scotland (referred to as "the two parts" of such a reserve or area).

(2) On and after the appointed day, the two parts of any reserve or area to which this paragraph applies shall be treated as if each were a distinct nature reserve or area of special scientific interest; and accordingly, so far as may be necessary for the purpose of applying paragraphs 8 and 9 above, anything done by or in relation to the Nature Conservancy Council affecting both parts of that reserve or area shall be treated as having been done by or in relation to each of the two parts separately.

(3) On and after the appointed day the new council exercising functions as respects either part of a reserve or area to which this paragraph applies shall exercise those functions only after consultation with the new council exercising functions as respects the other part; and those councils may make arrangements for discharging any of those functions jointly.

[250]

PART III
SUPPLEMENTARY

13. Paragraphs 3, 4, 5, 8, 9, 10 and 12 above are without prejudice to any provision made by or under this Part of this Act in relation to any particular functions, property, rights or liabilities; and, in particular, nothing in this Schedule applies in relation to contracts of employment made by the Countryside Commission or the Nature Conservancy Council.

14. The Secretary of State may, in relation to any particular functions of the Countryside Commission or the Nature Conservancy Council, by order exclude, or modify or supplement any provision of this Schedule or make such other transitional provision as he may think necessary or expedient.

15. In this Schedule "the 1949 Act" means the National Parks and Access to the Countryside Act 1949 and "the 1981 Act" means the Wildlife and Countryside Act 1981.

[251]

(*Sch 12, 13, 15 outside the scope of this work; Sch 14 repealed, subject to an exception, by the Merchant Shipping Act 1995, s 314(1), Sch 12.*)

SCHEDULE 16
REPEALS

Section 162

PART I
ENACTMENTS RELATING TO PROCESSES

Chapter	Short title	Extent of repeal
1906 c 14.	Alkali, &c Works Regulation Act 1906.	The whole Act so far as unrepealed.
1956 c 52.	Clean Air Act 1956.	Section 17(4).

Chapter	Short title	Extent of repeal
		In section 29(1), in the proviso, paragraph (a).
		In section 31(1), the words from "(other" to "1906)".
		Schedule 2.
1968 c 62.	Clean Air Act 1968.	Section 11.
1972 c 70.	Local Government Act 1972.	In section 180(3), paragraph (b).
1973 c 65.	Local Government (Scotland) Act 1973.	In section 142(2), paragraph (b).
1974 c 37.	Health and Safety at Work etc Act 1974.	Section 1(1)(d) and the word "and" preceding it.
		Section 5.
1974 c 40.	Control of Pollution Act 1974.	In section 76(4), the words "or work subject to the Alkali Act".
		In section 78(1), the words "or work subject to the Alkali Act".
		In section 79(4), the words "or work subject to the Alkali Act".
		In section 80(3), the words "or work subject to the Alkali Act".
		In section 84(1), the definition of "a work subject to the Alkali Act".
		In section 103(1)(a), the words "Alkali Act or the".
		In section 105(1), the definition of "the Alkali Act".
1990 c 43.	Environmental Protection Act 1990.	In section 79(10), the words following "Part I".

Note: The repeal of the Alkali, &c Works Regulation Act 1906 does not extend to Northern Ireland.

[252]

NOTES
    Commencement: 16 December 1996 (in part); 1 December 1994 (in part) (for more information see the Environmental Protection Act 1990 (Commencement No 16) Order 1994, SI 1994/2854); to be appointed (remainder).

PART II
ENACTMENTS RELATING TO WASTE ON LAND

Chapter	Short title	Extent of repeal
1974 c 40.	Control of Pollution Act 1974.	Sections 1 to 21.
		Sections 27 to 30.
1978 c 3.	Refuse Disposal (Amenity) Act 1978.	Section 1.
1982 c 45.	Civic Government (Scotland) Act 1982.	Sections 124 and 125 and in section 126, subsections (1) and (3).

Chapter	Short title	Extent of repeal
1988 c 9.	Local Government Act 1988.	In Schedule 1, in paragraph 1, in sub-paragraph (1) the words "in the application of this Part to England and Wales," and sub-paragraph (4).
1989 c 14.	Control of Pollution (Amendment) Act 1989.	In section 7(2), paragraph (b) and the word "and" preceding it.
		In section 9, in subsection (1), the definition of "disposal authority" and subsection (2).
1989 c 15.	Water Act 1989.	In Schedule 25, in paragraph 48, sub-paragraphs (1) to (6).
1989 c 29.	Electricity Act 1989.	In Schedule 16, paragraph 18.
1990 c 43.	Environmental Protection Act 1990.	In section 34(3)(b), the words following "below".
		Section 36(8).

Note: The repeal in the Refuse Disposal (Amenity) Act 1978 does not extend to Scotland.

[253]

NOTES

Commencement: on or after 1 May 1994 (in part) (for more information see the Environmental Protection Act 1990 (Commencement No 15) Order 1994, SI 1994/1096, as amended by SI 1994/2487, SI 1994/3234); 1 April 1992 (in part); 31 May 1991 (in part); to be appointed (remainder).

PART III
ENACTMENTS RELATING TO STATUTORY NUISANCES

Chapter	Short title	Extent of repeal
1936 c 49.	Public Health Act 1936.	Sections 91 to 100.
		Sections 107 and 108.
		Sections 109 and 110.
		In section 267(4), "III"
1956 c 52.	Clean Air Act 1956.	Section 16.
		In section 30(1), the words from "or a nuisance" to "existed".
1960 c 34.	Radioactive Substances Act 1960.	In Schedule 1—
		(a) In paragraph 3, the words "and ninety-two";
		(b) in paragraph 3, the words "subsection (2) of section one hundred and eight"; and
		(c) in paragraph 8, the words "and sixteen".
1961 c 64.	Public Health Act 1961.	Section 72.
1963 c 33.	London Government Act 1963.	In Schedule 11, in Part I, paragraph 20.

Chapter	Short title	Extent of repeal
1963 c 41.	Offices, Shops and Railway Premises Act 1963.	Section 76(3).
1969 c 25.	Public Health (Recurring Nuisances) Act 1969.	The whole Act.
1972 c 70.	Local Government Act 1972.	In section 180(3), paragraph (j).
		In Schedule 14—
		(a) in paragraph 4, the words "107(1) and (2), 108";
		(b) paragraph 11; and
		(c) paragraph 12.
1974 c 40.	Control of Pollution Act 1974.	In section 57, paragraph (a).
		Sections 58 and 59.
		In section 69, in subsection (1), paragraph (a) and, in paragraph (c), the words "section 59(2) or", and in subsection (3) the words "section 59(6) or" and paragraph (i).
		In Schedule 2, paragraphs 11 and 12.
1982 c 30.	Local Government (Miscellaneous Provisions) Act 1982.	Section 26(1) and (2).
1989 c 17.	Control of Smoke Pollution Act 1989.	Section 1.
1990 c 8.	Town and Country Planning Act 1990.	In Schedule 17, paragraph 1.

Note: The repeals in the Clean Air Act 1956, the Control of Pollution Act 1974 and the Control of Smoke Pollution Act 1989 do not extend to Scotland.

[254]

PART IV
ENACTMENTS RELATING TO LITTER

Chapter	Short title	Extent of repeal
1974 c 40.	Control of Pollution Act 1974.	Section 22(1) and (2).
1982 c 43.	Local Government and Planning (Scotland) Act 1982.	Section 25(1).
1983 c 35.	Litter Act 1983.	Sections 1 and 2.
		Section 12(1).
1986 c ii.	Berkshire Act 1986.	Section 13.
1987 c xi.	Exeter City Council Act 1987.	Section 24.
1988 c viii.	City of Westminster Act 1988.	The whole Act.
1990 c vii.	London Local Authorities Act 1990.	Section 43.

[255]

PART V
ENACTMENTS RELATING TO RADIOACTIVE SUBSTANCES

Chapter	Short title	Extent of repeal
1960 c 34.	Radioactive Substances Act 1960.	Section 2(1).
		In section 4, subsection (1) and in subsection (2) the word "further".
		Section 7(3)(a).
		Section 8(1)(a).
		In section 12, subsection (1), in subsection (2)(b) the words "of waste" and, at the end "and", and in subsection (3)(b) the words "subsection (1) or".
		In section 19(1) the definition of "the Minister".
		Section 21(4).
		In Schedule 1, paragraphs 9 and 11.

[256]

PART VI
ENACTMENTS RELATING TO NATURE CONSERVATION AND COUNTRYSIDE MATTERS

Chapter	Short title	Extent of repeal
1968 c 41.	Countryside Act 1968.	In section 15(2), the words "in the national interest".
		Section 19.
		In section 46(2), the words "and (2)".
1973 c 54.	Nature Conservancy Council Act 1973.	In section 1, subsections (1), (2) and (4) to (8).
		Sections 2 and 4.
		In Schedule 1, paragraphs 6, 10 and 12.
		In Schedule 3, Parts I and II.
1981 c 69	Wildlife and Countryside Act 1981.	In section 34(6) the words "and Wales".
		Section 38.
		In section 43(1A) the words "by the Countryside Commission".
		In Schedule 13, paragraph 5.

[257]

NOTES

Commencement: 1 April 1992 (in part); 1 April 1991 (in part); to be appointed (remainder).

PART VII
ENACTMENTS RELATING TO HAZARDOUS SUBSTANCES

Chapter	Short title	Extent of repeal
1972 c 52.	Town and Country Planning (Scotland) Act 1972.	In section 56A(1), the words "and to section 56B below".
		Section 56B.
		In section 56E(2)(e) and 56K(5)(b), the words "or Health and Safety Commission".
		In section 56F(1), the words "and (3)".
		Section 56F(3).
		Section 56H(5).
		In section 56J(5), the words from "other" to "applies".
		In section 56M(3), the words "Subject to subsection (4) below,".
		Section 56M(4).
		In section 56N, in subsection (1)(b), the words from "or" to "would be" and subsection (2).
		In section 56O, the definition of "the appropriate body" and the word "and" immediately following.
1986 c 63.	Housing and Planning Act 1986.	In Part II of Schedule 7, in paragraph 8 the word "56B,".
1989 c 29.	Electricity Act 1989.	In Schedule 17, paragraph 37(1)(b).
1990 c 10.	Planning (Hazardous Substances) Act 1990.	In section 1, the words "2 or".
		Section 2.
		Section 3(6).
		In section 9(2)(e) and 18(2)(b), the words "or Health and Safety Commission".
		In section 11(7), the words "to the conditions that".
		Section 13(7).
		In section 15(1), the words from "other" to "applies)".
		Section 20(6).
		Section 21(7).
		Section 27(4).
		In section 28(1), the words "authority who are a" and the words "by virtue of section 1 or 3".

Chapter	Short title	Extent of repeal
		In section 28(1)(b), the words "or but for section 2 would be".
		Section 28(2).
		In section 29(6), the definition of "the appropriate body" and the word "and" immediately following that definition.
		In section 30(1), the words "by virtue of section 1 or 3".
		Section 33.
		In section 38(2), the words "(being a local planning authority)".
		In section 39(2), the entries for "the 1971 Act", "the appropriate Minister" and "operational land".
		In section 39(4), the words "2," and "and his undertaking a statutory undertaking".
		In section 39(5), the word "2,", in the first place it occurs and the words following "undertaker" in the second place it occurs.
		In section 39(6), the words "and their undertakings statutory undertakings".
		Section 39(7) and (8).
1990 c 11.	Planning (Consequential Provisions) Act 1990.	In Schedule 2, paragraph 82(2).

[258]

NOTES

Commencement: 1 May 1993 (in part); 18 February 1993 (in part); 1 January 1992 (in part); to be appointed (remainder).

PART VIII
ENACTMENTS RELATING TO DEPOSITS AT SEA

Chapter	Short title	Extent of repeal
1985 c 48.	Food and Environment Protection Act 1985.	Section 5(c), (d) and (e)(iii).
		Section 6(1)(a)(iii).
		Schedule 4.

[259]

NOTES

Commencement: to be appointed.

PART IX
MISCELLANEOUS ENACTMENTS

Chapter	Short title	Extent of repeal
1906 c 32.	Dogs Act 1906.	Section 4(1).
1974 c 40.	Control of Pollution Act 1974.	Section 100.
1982 c 45.	Civic Government (Scotland) Act 1982.	Section 128(1).
1982 c 48.	Criminal Justice Act 1982.	Section 43.
1988 c 9.	Local Government Act 1988.	Section 39(2) and (4).
1988 c 33.	Criminal Justice Act 1988.	Section 58.

[260]

NOTES
    Commencement: 18 February 1993 (in part); 1 April 1992 (in part); 1 January 1991 (in part); to be appointed (remainder).

WATER INDUSTRY ACT 1991

(1991 c 56)

ARRANGEMENT OF SECTIONS

PART IV
SEWERAGE SERVICES

CHAPTER III
TRADE EFFLUENT

PART VII
INFORMATION PROVISIONS

PART VIII
MISCELLANEOUS AND SUPPLEMENTAL

An Act to consolidate enactments relating to the supply of water and the provision of sewerage services, with amendments to give effect to recommendations of the Law Commission

[25 July 1991]

1–93 *((Pts I–III) outside the scope of this work.)*

PART IV
SEWERAGE SERVICES

94–117 *(Outside the scope of this work.)*

CHAPTER III
TRADE EFFLUENT

Consent for discharge of trade effluent into public sewer

118 Consent required for discharge of trade effluent into public sewer

(1)   Subject to the following provisions of this Chapter, the occupier of any trade premises in the area of a sewerage undertaker may discharge any trade effluent

proceeding from those premises into the undertaker's public sewers if he does so with the undertaker's consent.

(2) Nothing in this Chapter shall authorise the discharge of any effluent into a public sewer otherwise than by means of a drain or sewer.

(3) The following, that is to say—

(a) the restrictions imposed by paragraphs (a) and (b) of section 106(2) above; and

(b) section 111 above so far as it relates to anything falling within paragraph (a) or (b) of subsection (1) of that section,

shall not apply to any discharge of trade effluent which is lawfully made by virtue of this Chapter.

(4) Accordingly, subsections (3) to (8) of section 106 above and sections 108 and 109 above shall have effect in relation to communication with a sewer for the purpose of making any discharge which is lawfully made by virtue of this Chapter as they have effect in relation to communication with a sewer for the purpose of making discharges which are authorised by subsection (1) of section 106 above.

(5) If, in the case of any trade premises, any trade effluent is discharged without such consent or other authorisation as is necessary for the purposes of this Chapter, the occupier of the premises shall be guilty of an offence and liable—

(a) on summary conviction, to a fine not exceeding the statutory maximum; and

(b) on conviction on indictment, to a fine.

[261]

Consents on an application

119 Application for consent

(1) An application to a sewerage undertaker for a consent to discharge trade effluent from any trade premises into a public sewer of that undertaker shall be by notice served on the undertaker by the owner or occupier of the premises.

(2) An application under this section with respect to a proposed discharge of any such effluent shall state—

(a) the nature or composition of the trade effluent;

(b) the maximum quantity of the trade effluent which it is proposed to discharge on any one day; and

(c) the highest rate at which it is proposed to discharge the trade effluent.

[262]

120 Applications for the discharge of special category effluent

(1) Subject to subsection (3) below, where a notice containing an application under section 119 above is served on a sewerage undertaker with respect to discharges of any special category effluent, it shall be the duty of the undertaker to refer to [the Environment Agency] the questions—

(a) whether the discharges to which the notice relates should be prohibited; and

(b) whether, if they are not prohibited, any requirements should be imposed as to the conditions on which they are made.

(2) Subject to subsection (3) below, a reference which is required to be made by a sewerage undertaker by virtue of subsection (1) above shall be made before the end of the period of two months beginning with the day after the notice containing the application is served on the undertaker.

(3)   There shall be no obligation on a sewerage undertaker to make a reference under this section in respect of any application if, before the end of the period mentioned in subsection (2) above, there is a refusal by the undertaker to give any consent on the application.

(4)   It shall be the duty of a sewerage undertaker where it has made a reference under this section not to give any consent, or enter into any agreement, with respect to the discharges to which the reference relates at any time before [the Environment Agency] serves notice on the undertaker of his determination on the reference.

(5)   Every reference under this section shall be made in writing and shall be accompanied by a copy of the notice containing the application in respect of which it is made.

(6)   It shall be the duty of a sewerage undertaker, on making a reference under this section, to serve a copy of the reference on the owner or the occupier of the trade premises in question, according to whether the discharges to which the reference relates are to be by the owner or by the occupier.

[(9)   If a sewerage undertaker fails, within the period provided by subsection (2) above, to refer to the Environment Agency any question which he is required by subsection (1) above to refer to the Agency, the undertaker shall be guilty of an offence and liable—
  (a) on summary conviction, to a fine not exceeding the statutory maximum;
  (b) on conviction on indictment, to a fine.

(10)   If the Environment Agency becomes aware of any such failure as is mentioned in subsection (9) above, the Agency may—
  (a) if a consent under this Chapter to make discharges of any special category effluent has been granted on the application in question, exercise its powers of review under section 127 or 131 below, notwithstanding anything in subsection (2) of the section in question; or
  (b) in any other case, proceed as if the reference required by this section had been made.]

                                                                       [263]

_____

NOTES
   Sub-ss (1), (4): words in square brackets substituted by the Environment Act 1995, s 120, Sch 22, para 105(2), (3).
   Sub-ss (9), (10): substituted, for original sub-ss (7), (8), by the Environment Act 1995, s 120, Sch 22, para 105(4).

_____

121 Conditions of consent

(1)   The power of a sewerage undertaker, on an application under section 119 above, to give a consent with respect to the discharge of any trade effluent shall be a power to give a consent either unconditionally or subject to such conditions as the sewerage undertaker thinks fit to impose with respect to—
  (a) the sewer or sewers into which the trade effluent may be discharged;
  (b) the nature or composition of the trade effluent which may be discharged;
  (c) the maximum quantity of trade effluent which may be discharged on any one day, either generally or into a particular sewer; and
  (d) the highest rate at which trade effluent may be discharged, either generally or into a particular sewer.

(2)   Conditions with respect to all or any of the following matters may also be attached under this section to a consent to the discharge of trade effluent from any trade premises—
  (a) the period or periods of the day during which the trade effluent may be discharged from the trade premises into the sewer;

(b) the exclusion from the trade effluent of all condensing water;

(c) the elimination or diminution, in cases falling within subsection (3) below, of any specified constituent of the trade effluent, before it enters the sewer;

(d) the temperature of the trade effluent at the time when it is discharged into the sewer, and its acidity or alkalinity at that time;

(e) the payment by the occupier of the trade premises to the undertaker of charges for the reception of the trade effluent into the sewer and for the disposal of the effluent;

(f) the provision and maintenance of such an inspection chamber or manhole as will enable a person readily to take samples, at any time, of what is passing into the sewer from the trade premises;

(g) the provision, testing and maintenance of such meters as may be required to measure the volume and rate of discharge of any trade effluent being discharged from the trade premises into the sewer;

(h) the provision, testing and maintenance of apparatus for determining the nature and composition of any trade effluent being discharged from the premises into the sewer;

(i) the keeping of records of the volume, rate of discharge, nature and composition of any trade effluent being discharged and, in particular, the keeping of records of readings of meters and other recording apparatus provided in compliance with any other condition attached to the consent; and

(j) the making of returns and giving of other information to the sewerage undertaker concerning the volume, rate of discharge, nature and composition of any trade effluent discharged from the trade premises into the sewer.

(3) A case falls within this subsection where the sewerage undertaker is satisfied that the constituent in question, either alone or in combination with any matter with which it is likely to come into contact while passing through any sewers—

(a) would injure or obstruct those sewers, or make the treatment or disposal of the sewage from those sewers specially difficult or expensive; or

(b) in the case of trade effluent which is to be or is discharged—

(i) into a sewer having an outfall in any harbour or tidal water; or

(ii) into a sewer which connects directly or indirectly with a sewer or sewage disposal works having such an outfall,

would cause or tend to cause injury or obstruction to the navigation on, or the use of, the harbour or tidal water.

(4) In the exercise of the power conferred by virtue of subsection (2)(e) above, regard shall be had—

(a) to the nature and composition and to the volume and rate of discharge of the trade effluent discharged;

(b) to any additional expense incurred or likely to be incurred by a sewerage undertaker in connection with the reception or disposal of the trade effluent; and

(c) to any revenue likely to be derived by the undertaker from the trade effluent.

(5) If, in the case of any trade premises, a condition imposed under this section is contravened, the occupier of the premises shall be guilty of an offence and liable—

(a) on summary conviction, to a fine not exceeding the statutory maximum; and

(b) on conviction on indictment, to a fine.

(6) In this section "harbour" and "tidal water" have the same meanings as in the [Merchant Shipping Act 1995].

(7) This section has effect subject to the provisions of sections 133 and 135(3) below.

NOTES

Sub-s (6): words in square brackets substituted by the Merchant Shipping Act 1995, s 314(2), Sch 13, para 89(a).

122 Appeals to the Director with respect to decisions on applications etc

(1) Any person aggrieved by—
  (a) the refusal of a sewerage undertaker to give a consent for which application has been duly made to the undertaker under section 119 above;
  (b) the failure of a sewerage undertaker to give such a consent within the period of two months beginning with the day after service of the notice containing the application; or
  (c) any condition attached by a sewerage undertaker to such a consent,
may appeal to the Director.

(2) On an appeal under this section in respect of a refusal or failure to give a consent, the Director may give the necessary consent, either unconditionally or subject to such conditions as he thinks fit to impose for determining any of the matters as respects which the undertaker has power to impose conditions under section 121 above.

(3) On an appeal under this section in respect of a condition attached to a consent, the Director may take into review all the conditions attached to the consent, whether appealed against or not, and may—
  (a) substitute for them any other set of conditions, whether more or less favourable to the appellant; or
  (b) annul any of the conditions.

(4) The Director may, under subsection (3) above, include provision as to the charges to be made in pursuance of any condition attached to a consent for any period before the determination of the appeal.

(5) On any appeal under this section, the Director may give a direction that the trade effluent in question shall not be discharged until a specified date.

(6) Any consent given or conditions imposed by the Director under this section in respect of discharges of trade effluent shall have effect for the purposes of this Chapter as if given or imposed by the sewerage undertaker in question.

(7) The powers of the Director under this section shall be subject to the provisions of sections 123, 128, 133, 135 and 137 below.

[265]

123 Appeals with respect to the discharge of special category effluent

(1) Where a reference is made to [the Environment Agency] under section 120 above, the period mentioned in paragraph (b) of subsection (1) of section 122 above shall not begin to run for the purposes of that subsection, in relation to the application to which the reference relates, until the beginning of the day after [the Environment Agency] serves notice on the sewerage undertaker in question of his determination on the reference.

(2) If, on an appeal under section 122 above, it appears to the Director—
  (a) that the case is one in which the sewerage undertaker in question is required to make a reference under section 120 above before giving a consent; and
  (b) that the undertaker has not made such a reference, whether because the case falls within subsection (3) of that section or otherwise,
the Director shall not be entitled to determine the appeal, otherwise than by upholding a refusal, except where the conditions set out in subsection (3) below are satisfied.

(3)   The conditions mentioned in subsection (2) above are satisfied if the Director—

    (a) has himself referred the questions mentioned in section 120(1) above to [the Environment Agency]; and

    (b) has been sent a copy of the notice of [the Environment Agency's] determination on the reference.

(4)   Every reference under this section shall be made in writing and shall be accompanied by a copy of the notice containing the application in respect of which the appeal and reference is made.

(5)   It shall be the duty of the Director, on making a reference under this section, to serve a copy of the reference—

    (a) on the owner or the occupier of the trade premises in question, according to whether the discharges to which the reference relates are to be by the owner or by the occupier; and

    (b) on the sewerage undertaker in question.

[266]

NOTES

Sub-ss (1), (3): words in square brackets substituted by the Environment Act 1995, s 120, Sch 22, para 106.

124 Variation of consents

(1)   Subject to sections 128, 133 and 135(3) below, a sewerage undertaker may from time to time give a direction varying the conditions which have been attached to any of its consents under this Chapter to the discharge of trade effluent into a public sewer.

(2)   Subject to subsections (3) and (4) and section 125 below, no direction shall be given under this section with respect to a consent under this Chapter—

    (a) within two years from the date of the consent; or

    (b) where a previous direction has been given under this section with respect to that consent, within two years from the date on which notice was given of that direction.

(3)   Subsection (2) above shall not prevent a direction being given before the time specified in that subsection if it is given with the consent of the owner and occupier of the trade premises in question.

(4)   A direction given with the consent mentioned in subsection (3) above shall not affect the time at which any subsequent direction may be given.

(5)   The sewerage undertaker shall give to the owner and occupier of the trade premises to which a consent under this Chapter relates notice of any direction under this section with respect to that consent.

(6)   A notice under subsection (5) above shall—

    (a) include information as to the right of appeal conferred by subsection (1) of section 126 below; and

    (b) state the date, being a date not less than two months after the giving of the notice, on which (subject to subsection (2) of that section) the direction is to take effect.

(7)   For the purposes of this section references to the variation of conditions include references to the addition or annulment of a condition and to the attachment of a condition to a consent to which no condition was previously attached.

[267]

125 Variations within time limit

(1)   A sewerage undertaker may give a direction under section 124 above before the time specified in subsection (2) of that section and without the consent required by subsection (3) of that section if it considers it necessary to do so in order to provide proper protection for persons likely to be affected by the discharges which could lawfully be made apart from the direction.

(2)   Subject to section 134(3) below, where a sewerage undertaker gives a direction by virtue of subsection (1) above, the undertaker shall be liable to pay compensation to the owner and occupier of the trade premises to which the direction relates, unless the undertaker is of the opinion that the direction is required—
-    (a)   in consequence of a change of circumstances which—
     -    (i)   has occurred since the beginning of the period of two years in question; and
     -    (ii)   could not reasonably have been foreseen at the beginning of that period;

     and
-    (b)   otherwise than in consequence of consents for discharges given after the beginning of that period.

(3)   Where a sewerage undertaker gives a direction by virtue of subsection (1) above and is of the opinion mentioned in subsection (2) above, it shall be the duty of the undertaker to give notice of the reasons for its opinion to the owner and occupier of the premises in question.

(4)   For the purposes of this section the circumstances referred to in subsection (2)(a) above may include the information available as to the discharges to which the consent in question relates or as to the interaction of those discharges with other discharges or matter.

(5)   The Secretary of State may by regulations make provision as to the manner of determining the amount of any compensation payable under this section, including the factors to be taken into account in determining that amount.

[268]

126 Appeals with respect to variations of consent

(1)   The owner or occupier of any trade premises may—
-    (a)   within two months of the giving to him under subsection (5) of section 124 above of a notice of a direction under that section; or
-    (b)   with the written permission of the Director, at any later time,

appeal to the Director against the direction.

(2)   Subject to subsection (3) below, if an appeal against a direction is brought under subsection (1) above before the date specified under section 124(6)(b) above in the notice of the direction, the direction shall not take effect until the appeal is withdrawn or finally disposed of.

(3)   In so far as the direction which is the subject of an appeal relates to the making of charges payable by the occupier of any trade premises, it may take effect on any date after the giving of the notice.

(4)   On an appeal under subsection (1) above with respect to a direction, the Director shall have power—
-    (a)   to annul the direction given by the sewerage undertaker; and
-    (b)   to substitute for it any other direction, whether more or less favourable to the appellant;

and any direction given by the Director may include provision as to the charges to be made for any period between the giving of the notice by the sewerage undertaker and the determination of the appeal.

(5)   A person to whom notice is given in pursuance of section 125(3) above may, in accordance with regulations made by the Secretary of State, appeal to the Director against the notice on the ground that compensation should be paid in consequence of the direction to which the notice relates.

(6)   On an appeal under subsection (5) above the Director may direct that section 125 above shall have effect as if the sewerage undertaker in question were not of the opinion to which the notice relates.

(7)   Any consent given or conditions imposed by the Director under this section in respect of discharges of trade effluent shall have effect for the purposes of this Chapter as if given or imposed by the sewerage undertaker in question.

(8)   The powers of the Director under this section shall be subject to the provisions of sections 133, 135 and 137 below.

[269]

127 Review by [the Environment Agency] of consents relating to special category effluent

(1)   Where any person, as the owner or occupier of any trade premises, is (whether or not in accordance with a notice under section 132 below) for the time being authorised by virtue of a consent under this Chapter to make discharges of any special category effluent from those premises into a sewerage undertaker's public sewer, [the Environment Agency] may review the questions—
  (a) whether the discharges authorised by the consent should be prohibited; and
  (b) whether, if they are not prohibited, any requirements should be imposed as to the conditions on which they are made.

(2)   Subject to subsection (3) below, [the Environment Agency] shall not review any question under this section unless—
  (a) the consent or variation by virtue of which the discharges in question are made has not previously been the subject-matter of a review and was given or made—
    (i) before 1st September 1989; or
    (ii) in contravention of section 133 below;
  (b) a period of more than two years has elapsed since the time, or last time, when notice of [the Environment Agency's] determination on any reference or review relating to that consent or the consent to which that variation relates was served under section 132 below on the owner or occupier of the trade premises in question; or
  (c) there has, since the time, or last time, when such a notice was so served, been a contravention of any provision which was included in compliance with a requirement of a notice under section 132 below in the consent or variation by virtue of which the discharges in question are made.

(3)   Subsection (2) above shall not apply if the review is carried out—
  (a) for the purpose of enabling Her Majesty's Government in the United Kingdom to give effect to any Community obligation or to any international agreement to which the United Kingdom is for the time being a party; or
  (b) for the protection of public health or of flora and fauna dependent on an aquatic environment.

[270]

NOTES

Section heading: words in square brackets substituted by the Environment Act 1995, s 120, Sch 22, para 107.

Sub-ss (1), (2): words in square brackets substituted by the Environment Act 1995, s 120, Sch 22, para 107.

Application for variation of time for discharge

128 Application for variation of time for discharge

(1)   If, after a direction has been given under any of the preceding provisions of this Chapter requiring that trade effluent shall not be discharged until a specified date, it appears to the sewerage undertaker in question that in consequence—
  (a) of a failure to complete any works required in connection with the reception and disposal of the trade effluent; or
  (b) of any other exceptional circumstances,
a later date ought to be substituted for the date so specified in the direction, the undertaker may apply to the Director for such a substitution.

(2)   The Director shall have power, on an application under subsection (1) above, to vary the direction so as to extend the period during which the trade effluent may not be discharged until the date specified in the application or, if he thinks fit, any earlier date.

(3)   Not less than one month before making an application under subsection (1) above a sewerage undertaker shall give notice of its intention to the owner and occupier of the trade premises from which the trade effluent is to be discharged.

(4)   The Director, before varying a direction on an application under subsection (1) above, shall take into account any representations made to him by the owner or occupier of the trade premises in question.

[271]

Agreements with respect the disposal etc of trade effluent

129 Agreements with respect to the disposal etc of trade effluent

(1)   Subject to sections 130 and 133 below, a sewerage undertaker may enter into and carry into effect—
  (a) an agreement with the owner or occupier of any trade premises within its area for the reception and disposal by the undertaker of any trade effluent produced on those premises;
  (b) an agreement with the owner or occupier of any such premises under which it undertakes, on such terms as may be specified in the agreement, to remove and dispose of substances produced in the course of treating any trade effluent on or in connection with those premises.

(2)   Without prejudice to the generality of subsection (1) above, an agreement such as is mentioned in paragraph (a) of that subsection may, in particular, provide—
  (a) for the construction or extension by the sewerage undertaker of such works as may be required for the reception or disposal of the trade effluent; and
  (b) for the repayment by the owner or occupier, as the case may be, of the whole or part of the expenses incurred by the undertaker in carrying out its obligations under the agreement.

(3)   It is hereby declared that the power of a sewerage undertaker to enter into an agreement under this section includes a power, by that agreement, to authorise such a discharge as apart from the agreement would require a consent under this Chapter.

[272]

130 Reference to [the Environment Agency] of agreements relating to special category effluent

(1)   Where a sewerage undertaker and the owner or occupier of any trade premises are proposing to enter into an agreement under section 129 above with

respect to, or to any matter connected with, the reception or disposal of any special category effluent, it shall be the duty of the undertaker to refer to [the Environment Agency] the questions—

  (a) whether the operations which would, for the purposes of or in connection with the reception or disposal of that effluent, be carried out in pursuance of the proposed agreement should be prohibited; and

  (b) whether, if they are not prohibited, any requirements should be imposed as to the conditions on which they are carried out.

(2)   It shall be the duty of a sewerage undertaker where it has made a reference under this section not to give any consent or enter into any agreement with respect to any such operations as are mentioned in subsection (1)(a) above at any time before [the Environment Agency] serves notice on the undertaker of his determination on the reference.

(3)   Every reference under this section shall be made in writing and shall be accompanied by a copy of the proposed agreement.

(4)   It shall be the duty of a sewerage undertaker, on making a reference under this section, to serve a copy of the reference on the owner or the occupier of the trade premises in question, according to whether it is the owner or occupier who is proposing to be a party to the agreement.

[(7)   If a sewerage undertaker fails, before giving any consent or entering into any agreement with respect to any such operations as are mentioned in paragraph (a) of subsection (1) above, to refer to the Environment Agency any question which he is required by that subsection to refer to the Agency, the undertaker shall be guilty of an offence and liable—

  (a) on summary conviction, to a fine not exceeding the statutory maximum;

  (b) on conviction on indictment, to a fine.

(8)   If the Environment Agency becomes aware—

  (a) that a sewerage undertaker and the owner or occupier of any trade premises are proposing to enter into any such agreement as is mentioned in subsection (1) above, and

  (b) that the sewerage undertaker has not referred to the Agency any question which it is required to refer to the Agency by that subsection,

the Agency may proceed as if the reference required by that subsection had been made.

(9)   If the Environment Agency becomes aware that any consent has been given or agreement entered into with respect to any such operations as are mentioned in paragraph (a) of subsection (1) above without the sewerage undertaker in question having referred to the Environment Agency any question which he is required by that subsection to refer to the Agency, the Agency may exercise its powers of review under section 127 above or, as the case may be, section 131 below, notwithstanding anything in subsection (2) of the section in question.]

[273]

NOTES

  Section heading, sub-ss (1), (2): words in square brackets substituted by the Environment Act 1995, s 120, Sch 22, para 108(2).

  Sub-ss (7)–(9): substituted, for original sub-ss (5), (6), by the Environment Act 1995, s 120, Sch 22, para 108(3).

131 Review by [the Environment Agency] of agreements relating to special category effluent

(1)   Where any person, as the owner or occupier of any trade premises, is (whether or not in accordance with a notice under section 132 below) for the time

being a party to any agreement under section 129 above with respect to, or to any matter connected with, the reception or disposal of special category effluent, [the Environment Agency] may review the questions—
> (a) whether the operations which, for the purposes of or in connection with the reception or disposal of that effluent, are carried out in pursuance of the agreement should be prohibited; and
> (b) whether, if they are not prohibited, any requirements should be imposed as to the conditions on which they are carried out.

(2) Subject to subsection (3) below, [the Environment Agency] shall not review any question under this section unless—
> (a) the agreement by virtue of which the operations in question are carried out has not previously been the subject-matter of a review and was entered into—
>> (i) before 1st September 1989; or
>> (ii) in contravention of section 133 below;
> (b) a period of more than two years has elapsed since the time, or last time, when notice of [the Environment Agency's] determination on any reference or review relating to that agreement was served under section 132 below on the owner or occupier of the trade premises in question; or
> (c) there has, since the time, or last time, when such a notice was so served, been a contravention of any provision which was included in compliance with a requirement of a notice under section 132 below in the agreement by virtue of which the operations in question are carried out.

(3) Subsection (2) above shall not apply if the review is carried out—
> (a) for the purpose of enabling Her Majesty's Government in the United Kingdom to give effect to any Community obligation or to any international agreement to which the United Kingdom is for the time being a party; or
> (b) for the protection of public health or of flora and fauna dependent on an aquatic environment.

(4) References in this section to an agreement include references to an agreement as varied from time to time by a notice under section 132 below.

[274]

NOTES
Section heading: words in square brackets substituted by the Environment Act 1995, s 120, Sch 22, para 109.
Sub-ss (1), (2): words in square brackets substituted by the Environment Act 1995, s 120, Sch 22, para 109.

References and reviews relating to special category effluent

132 Powers and procedure on references and reviews

(1) This section applies to—
> (a) any reference to [the Environment Agency] under section 120, 123 or 130 above; and
> (b) any review by [the Environment Agency] under section 127 or 131 above.

(2) On a reference or review to which this section applies, it shall be the duty of [the Environment Agency], before determining the questions which are the subject-matter of the reference or review—
> (a) to give an opportunity of making representations or objections to [the Environment Agency]—
>> (i) to the sewerage undertaker in question; and
>> (ii) to the following person, that is to say, the owner or the occupier of the trade premises in question, according to whether it is the owner or the

occupier of those premises who is proposing to be, or is, the person
making the discharges or, as the case may be, a party to the
agreement;

and

(b) to consider any representations or objections which are duly made to [the
Agency] with respect to those questions by a person to whom [the Agency]
is required to give such an opportunity and which are not withdrawn.

(3)   On determining any question on a reference or review to which this section
applies, [the Environment Agency] shall serve notice on the sewerage undertaker in
question and on the person specified in subsection (2)(a)(ii) above.

(4)   A notice under this section shall state, according to what has been
determined—

(a) that the discharges or operations to which, or to the proposals for which,
the reference or review relates, or such of them as are specified in the
notice, are to be prohibited; or

(b) that those discharges or operations, or such of them as are so specified, are
to be prohibited except in so far as they are made or carried out in
accordance with conditions which consist in or include conditions so
specified; or

(c) that [the Environment Agency] has no objection to those discharges or
operations and does not intend to impose any requirements as to the
conditions on which they are made or carried out.

(5)   Without prejudice to section 133 below, a notice under this section, in
addition to containing such provision as is specified in sub-paragraph (4) above,
may do one or both of the following, that is to say—

(a) vary or revoke the provisions of a previous notice with respect to the
discharges or operations in question; and

(b) for the purpose of giving effect to any prohibition or other requirement
contained in the notice, vary or revoke any consent under this Chapter or
any agreement under section 129 above.

(6)   Nothing in subsection (1) or (2) of section 121 above shall be construed as
restricting the power of [the Environment Agency], by virtue of subsection (4)(b)
above, to specify such conditions as [the Agency] considers appropriate in a notice
under this section.

(7)   . . .

(8)   [The Environment Agency] shall send a copy of every notice served under
this section to the Director.

[275]

NOTES

Sub-ss (1)–(4), (6), (8): words in square brackets substituted by the Environment Act 1995, s 120,
Sch 22, para 110(2)–(4).

Sub-s (7): repealed by the Environment Act 1995, s 120, Sch 22, para 110(5), Sch 24.

133 Effect of determination on reference or review

(1)   Where a notice under section 132 above has been served on a sewerage
undertaker, it shall be the duty—

(a) of the undertaker; and

(b) in relation to that undertaker, of the Director,

so to exercise the powers to which this section applies as to secure compliance with
the provisions of the notice.

(2)   This paragraph applies to the following powers, that is to say—

(a) in relation to a sewerage undertaker, its power to give a consent under this Chapter, any of its powers under section 121 or 124 above and any power to enter into or vary an agreement under section 129 above; and

(b) in relation to the Director, any of his powers under this Chapter.

(3) Nothing in subsection (1) or (2) of section 121 above shall be construed as restricting the power of a sewerage undertaker, for the purpose of complying with this section, to impose any condition specified in a notice under section 132 above.

[(5) A sewerage undertaker which fails to perform its duty under subsection (1) above shall be guilty of an offence and liable—

(a) on summary conviction, to a fine not exceeding the statutory maximum;

(b) on conviction on indictment, to a fine.

(6) The Environment Agency may, for the purpose of securing compliance with the provisions of a notice under section 132 above, by serving notice on the sewerage undertaker in question and on the person specified in section 132(2)(a)(ii) above, vary or revoke—

(a) any consent given under this Chapter to make discharges of any special category effluent, or

(b) any agreement under section 129 above.]

[276]

NOTES

Sub-ss (5), (6): substituted, for original sub-s (4), by the Environment Act 1995, s 120, Sch 22, para 111.

134 Compensation in respect of determinations made for the protection of public health etc

(1) Subject to subsection (2) below, [the Environment Agency] shall be liable to pay compensation to the relevant person in respect of any loss or damage sustained by that person as a result of any notice under section 132 above containing [the Environment Agency's] determination on a review which—

(a) has been carried out for the protection of public health or of flora and fauna dependent on an aquatic environment; and

(b) but for being so carried out would have been prohibited by virtue of section 127(2) or 131(2) above.

(2) [The Environment Agency] shall not be required to pay any compensation under this section if the determination in question is shown to have been given in consequence of—

(a) a change of circumstances which could not reasonably have been foreseen at the time when the period of two years mentioned in section 127(2) or, as the case may be, section 131(2) above began to run; or

(b) consideration by [the Environment Agency] of material information which was not reasonably available to [the Agency] at that time.

(3) No person shall be entitled to any compensation under section 125 above in respect of anything done in pursuance of section 133 above.

(4) In this section "the relevant person", in relation to a review, means the owner or the occupier of the trade premises in question, according to whether it is the owner or the occupier who makes the discharges to which the review relates or, as the case may be, is a party to the agreement to which it relates.

[277]

NOTES

Sub-ss (1), (2): words in square brackets substituted by the Environment Act 1995, s 120, Sch 22, para 112.

Supplemental provisions of Chapter III

135 Restrictions on power to fix charges under Chapter III

(1)   On any appeal under section 122 or 126(1) above conditions providing for the payment of charges to the sewerage undertaker in question shall not be determined by the Director except in so far as no provision is in force by virtue of a charges scheme under section 143 below in respect of any such receptions, discharges, removals or disposals of effluent or substances as are of the same description as the reception, discharge, removal or disposal which is the subject-matter of the appeal.

(2)   In so far as any such conditions as are mentioned in subsection (1) above do fall to be determined by the Director, they shall be determined having regard to the desirability of that undertaker's—
   (a) recovering the expenses of complying with its obligations in consequence of the consent or agreement to which the conditions relate; and
   (b) securing a reasonable return on its capital.

(3)   To the extent that subsection (1) above excludes any charges from a determination on an appeal those charges shall be fixed from time to time by a charges scheme under section 143 below but not otherwise.

[278]

[135A Power of the Environment Agency to acquire information for the purpose of its functions in relation to special category effluent

(1)   For the purpose of the discharge of its functions under this Chapter, the Environment Agency may, by notice in writing served on any person, require that person to furnish such information specified in the notice as that Agency reasonably considers it needs, in such form and within such period following service of the notice, or at such time, as is so specified.

(2)   A person who—
   (a) fails, without reasonable excuse, to comply with a requirement imposed under subsection (1) above, or
   (b) in furnishing any information in compliance with such a requirement, makes any statement which he knows to be false or misleading in a material particular, or recklessly makes a statement which is false or misleading in a material particular,
shall be guilty of an offence.

(3)   A person guilty of an offence under subsection (2) above shall be liable—
   (a) on summary conviction, to a fine not exceeding the statutory maximum;
   (b) on conviction on indictment, to a fine or to imprisonment for a term not exceeding two years, or to both.]

[279]

NOTES
Commencement: 1 April 1996.
Inserted by the Environment Act 1995, s 120, Sch 22, para 113.

136 Evidence from meters etc

Any meter or apparatus provided in pursuance of this Chapter in any trade premises for the purpose of measuring, recording or determining the volume, rate of discharge, nature or composition of any trade effluent discharged from those premises shall be presumed in any proceedings to register accurately, unless the contrary is shown.

[280]

137 Statement of case on appeal

(1)   At any stage of the proceedings on an appeal under section 122 or 126(1) above, the Director may, and if so directed by the High Court shall, state in the form of a special case for the decision of the High Court any question of law arising in those proceedings.

(2)   The decision of the High Court on a special case under this section shall be deemed to be a judgment of the Court within the meaning of section 16 of the Supreme Court Act 1981 (which relates to the jurisdiction of the Court of Appeal); but no appeal to the Court of Appeal shall be brought by virtue of this subsection except with the leave of the High Court or of the Court of Appeal.

[281]

138 Meaning of "special category effluent"

(1)   Subject to subsection (2) below, trade effluent shall be special category effluent for the purposes of this Chapter if—
  (a) such substances as may be prescribed under this Act are present in the effluent or are present in the effluent in prescribed concentrations; or
  (b) the effluent derives from any such process as may be so prescribed or from a process involving the use of prescribed substances or the use of such substances in quantities which exceed the prescribed amounts.

(2)   Trade effluent shall not be special category effluent for the purposes of this Chapter if it is produced, or to be produced, in any process which is a prescribed process designated for central control as from the date which is the determination date for that process.

(3)   In subsection (2) above "determination date", in relation to a prescribed process, means—
  (a) in the case of a process for which authorisation is granted, the date on which the enforcing authority grants it, whether in pursuance of the application or, on an appeal, of a direction to grant it;
  (b) in the case of a process for which authorisation is refused, the date of refusal or, on appeal, of the affirmation of the refusal.

(4)   In this section—
  (a) "authorisation", "enforcing authority" and "prescribed process" have the meanings given by section 1 of the Environmental Protection Act 1990; and
  (b) the references to designation for central control and to an appeal are references, respectively, to designation under section 4 of that Act and to an appeal under section 15 of that Act.

(5)   Without prejudice to the power in subsection (3) of section 139 below, nothing in this Chapter shall enable regulations under this section to prescribe as special category effluent any liquid or matter which is not trade effluent but falls to be treated as such for the purposes of this Chapter by virtue of an order under that section.

[282]

NOTES

    Regulations: the Trade Effluents (Prescribed Processes and Substances) Regulations 1989, SI 1989/1156, as amended by SI 1990/1629 (having effect under this section by virtue of the Water Consolidation (Consequential Provisions) Act 1991, s 2(2), Sch 2, Pt I, para 1(1), (2)); the Trade Effluents (Prescribed Processes and Substances) Regulations 1992, SI 1992/339.

139 Power to apply Chapter III to other effluents

(1)   The Secretary of State may by order provide that, subject to section 138(5) above, this Chapter shall apply in relation to liquid or other matter of any description specified in the order which is discharged into public sewers as it applies in relation to trade effluent.

(2)   An order applying the provisions of this Chapter in relation to liquid or other matter of any description may provide for it to so apply subject to such modifications (if any) as may be specified in the order and, in particular, subject to any such modification of the meaning for the purposes of this Chapter of the expression "trade premises" as may be so specified.

(3)   The Secretary of State may include in an order under this section such provisions as appear to him expedient for modifying any enactment relating to sewage as that enactment applies in relation to the discharge into sewers of any liquid or other matter to which any provisions of this Chapter are applied by an order under this section.

(4)   The Secretary of State may include in an order under this section such other supplemental, incidental and transitional provision as appears to him to be expedient.

(5)   The power to make an order under this section shall be exercisable by statutory instrument; and no order shall be made under this section unless a draft of it has been laid before, and approved by a resolution of, each House of Parliament.

[283]

140 Pre-1989 Act authority for trade effluent discharges etc

Schedule 8 to this Act shall have effect (without prejudice to the provisions of the Water Consolidation (Consequential Provisions) Act 1991 or to sections 16 and 17 of the Interpretation Act 1978) for the purpose of making provision in respect of certain cases where trade effluent was discharged in accordance with provision made before the coming into force of the Water Act 1989.

[284]

Interpretation of Chapter III

141 Interpretation of Chapter III

(1)   In this Chapter, except in so far as the context otherwise requires—
"special category effluent" has the meaning given by section 138 above;
"trade effluent"—
  (a) means any liquid, either with or without particles of matter in suspension in the liquid, which is wholly or partly produced in the course of any trade or industry carried on at trade premises; and
  (b) in relation to any trade premises, means any such liquid which is so produced in the course of any trade or industry carried on at those premises,
  but does not include domestic sewage;
"trade premises" means, subject to subsection (2) below, any premises used or intended to be used for carrying on any trade or industry.

(2)   For the purposes of this Chapter any land or premises used or intended for use (in whole or in part and whether or not for profit)—
  (a) for agricultural or horticultural purposes or for the purposes of fish farming; or
  (b) for scientific research or experiment,
shall be deemed to be premises used for carrying on a trade or industry; and the references to a trade or industry in the definition of "trade effluent" in subsection (1)

above shall include references to agriculture, horticulture, fish farming and scientific research or experiment.

(3)   Every application or consent made or given under this Chapter shall be made or given in writing.

(4)   Nothing in this Chapter shall affect any right with respect to water in a river stream or watercourse, or authorise any infringement of such a right, except in so far as any such right would dispense with the requirements of this Chapter so far as they have effect by virtue of any regulations under section 138 above.

[285]

142–192 (*(Pts V, VI) outside the scope of this work.*)

PART VII
INFORMATION PROVISIONS

193–194 (*Relate to reports by the Director (s 193); reports by customer service committees (s 194).*)

Registers, maps etc

195   (*Relates to the register.*)

196 Trade effluent registers

(1)   It shall be the duty of every sewerage undertaker to secure that copies of—
   (a) every consent given or having effect as if given by the undertaker under Chapter III of Part IV of this Act;
   (b) every direction given or having effect as if given by the undertaker under that Chapter;
   (c) every agreement entered into or having effect as if entered into by the undertaker under section 129 above; and
   (e) every notice served on the undertaker under section 132 above,

are kept available, at all reasonable times, for inspection by the public free of charge at the offices of the undertaker.

(2)   It shall be the duty of every sewerage undertaker, on the payment of such sum as may be reasonable, to furnish a person who requests it with a copy of, or of an extract from, anything kept available for inspection under this section.

(3)   The duties of a sewerage undertaker under this section shall be enforceable under section 18 above by the Director.

[286]

NOTES

Note: sub-s (1)(d) is missing in the Queen's Printers' copy of this Act.

197–205 (*Relate to registers, maps etc (ss 197–200); publication of certain information and advice (s 201); and powers to acquire and duties to provide information (ss 202–205).*)

Restriction on disclosure of information

206 Restriction on disclosure of information

(1)   Subject to the following provisions of this section, no information with respect to any particular business which—

(a) has been obtained by virtue of any of the provisions of this Act; and

(b) relates to the affairs of any individual or to any particular business,

shall, during the lifetime of that individual or so long as that business continues to be carried on, be disclosed without the consent of that individual or the person for the time being carrying on that business.

(2) No person shall disclose any information furnished to him under section . . . 204 above or under Chapter III of Part IV of this Act except—

(a) with the consent of the person by whom the information was furnished;

(b) in connection with the execution of that Chapter;

(c) for the purposes of any proceedings arising under that Chapter (including any appeal, application to the Secretary of State or the Director or an arbitration);

(d) for the purposes of any criminal proceedings (whether or not so arising); or

(e) for the purposes of any report of any proceedings falling within paragraph (c) or (d) above.

(3) Subsection (1) above does not apply to any disclosure of information which is made—

(a) for the purpose of facilitating the carrying out by the Secretary of State, the Minister, [the Environment Agency, the Scottish Environment Protection Agency], the Director, the Monopolies Commission or a county council or local authority of any of his, its or, as the case may be, their functions by virtue of this Act, any of the other consolidation Acts[, the Water Act 1989, Part I or IIA of the Environmental Protection Act 1990 or the Environment Act 1995];

(b) for the purpose of facilitating the performance by a relevant undertaker of any of the duties imposed on it by or under this Act, any of the other consolidation Acts or the Water Act 1989;

(c) in pursuance of any arrangements made by the Director under section 29(6) above or of any duty imposed by section 197(1)(a) or (2) or 203(1) or (2) of the Water Resources Act 1991 (information about water flow and pollution);

(d) for the purpose of facilitating the carrying out by any person mentioned in Part I of Schedule 15 to this Act of any of his functions under any of the enactments or instruments specified in Part II of that Schedule;

(e) for the purpose of enabling or assisting the Secretary of State to exercise any powers conferred on him by the Financial Services Act 1986 or by the enactments relating to companies, insurance companies or insolvency or for the purpose of enabling or assisting any inspector appointed by him under the enactments relating to companies to carry out his functions;

(f) for the purpose of enabling an official receiver to carry out his functions under the enactments relating to insolvency or for the purpose of enabling or assisting a recognised professional body for the purposes of section 391 of the Insolvency Act 1986 to carry out its functions as such;

(g) for the purpose of facilitating the carrying out by the Health and Safety Commission or the Health and Safety Executive of any of its functions under any enactment or of facilitating the carrying out by any enforcing authority, within the meaning of Part I of the Health and Safety at Work etc Act 1974, of any functions under a relevant statutory provision, within the meaning of that Act;

(h) for the purpose of facilitating the carrying out by the Comptroller and Auditor General of any of his functions under any enactment;

(i) in connection with the investigation of any criminal offence or for the purposes of any criminal proceedings;

(j) for the purposes of any civil proceedings brought under or by virtue of this Act, any of the other consolidation Acts, the Water Act 1989 or any of the enactments or instruments specified in Part II of Schedule 15 to this Act, or of any arbitration under this Act, any of the other consolidation Acts or that Act of 1989; or

(k)　in pursuance of a Community obligation.

(4)　Nothing in subsection (1) above shall be construed—

(a)　as limiting the matters which may be published under section [38A, 95A or] 201 above or may be included in, or made public as part of, a report of [the Environment Agency, the Scottish Environment Protection Agency], the Director, a customer service committee or the Monopolies Commission under any provision of this Act[, Part I or IIA of the Environmental Protection Act 1990, the Water Resources Act 1991 or the Environment Act 1995]; or

(b)　as applying to any information which has been so published or has been made public as part of such a report or to any information exclusively of a statistical nature.

(5)　Subject to subsection (6) below, nothing in subsection (1) above shall preclude the disclosure of information—

(a)　if the disclosure is of information relating to a matter connected with the carrying out of the functions of a relevant undertaker and is made by one Minister of the Crown or government department to another; or

(b)　if the disclosure is for the purpose of enabling or assisting any public or other authority for the time being designated for the purposes of this section by an order made by the Secretary of State to discharge any functions which are specified in the order.

(6)　The power to make an order under subsection (5) above shall be exercisable by statutory instrument subject to annulment in pursuance of a resolution of either House of Parliament; and where such an order designates an authority for the purposes of paragraph (b) of that subsection, the order may—

(a)　impose conditions subject to which the disclosure of information is permitted by virtue of that paragraph; and

(b)　otherwise restrict the circumstances in which disclosure is so permitted.

(7)　Any person who discloses any information in contravention of the preceding provisions of this section shall be guilty of an offence.

(8)　A person who is guilty of an offence under this section by virtue of subsection (1) above shall be liable—

(a)　on summary conviction, to a fine not exceeding the statutory maximum;

(b)　on conviction on indictment, to imprisonment for a term not exceeding two years or to a fine or to both.

(9)　A person who is guilty of an offence under this section by virtue of subsection (2) above shall be liable, on summary conviction, to imprisonment for a term not exceeding three months or to a fine not exceeding level 3 on the standard scale or to both.

(10)　In this section "the other consolidation Acts" means the Water Resources Act 1991, the Statutory Water Companies Act 1991, the Land Drainage Act 1991 and the Water Consolidation (Consequential Provisions) Act 1991.

[287]

NOTES

Sub-s (2): words omitted repealed by the Environment Act 1995, s 120, Sch 22, para 121(1), Sch 24.

Sub-s (3): words in square brackets substituted by the Environment Act 1995, s 120, Sch 22, para 121(2).

Sub-s (4): words in first pair of square brackets added by the Competition and Service (Utilities) Act 1992, s 56(6), Sch 1, para 27; words in remaining pairs of square brackets substituted by the Environment Act 1995, s 120, Sch 22, para 121(3).

207　*(Relates to provision of false information.)*

PART VIII
MISCELLANEOUS AND SUPPLEMENTAL

208, 209 *(Relate to miscellaneous provisions concerning national security (s 208), civil liability, etc (s 209).)*

Offences

210 Offences by bodies corporate

(1) Where a body corporate is guilty of an offence under this Act and that offence is proved to have been committed with the consent or connivance of, or to be attributable to any neglect on the part of, any director, manager, secretary or other similar officer of the body corporate or any person who was purporting to act in any such capacity, then he, as well as the body corporate, shall be guilty of that offence and shall be liable to be proceeded against and punished accordingly.

(2) Where the affairs of a body corporate are managed by its members, subsection (1) above shall apply in relation to the acts and defaults of a member in connection with his functions of management as if he were a director of the body corporate.

[288]

211 Limitation on right to prosecute in respect of sewerage offences

Proceedings in respect of an offence created by or under any of the relevant sewerage provisions shall not, without the written consent of the Attorney-General, be taken by any person other than—
    (a) a party aggrieved;
    (b) a sewerage undertaker; or
    (c) a body whose function it is to enforce the provisions in question.

[289]

212–215 *(Relate to judicial disqualification (s 212); powers to make regulations (ss 213, 214); and local inquiries (s 215).)*

Construction of Act

216 Provisions relating to the service of documents

(1) Any document required or authorised by virtue of this Act to be served on any person may be served—
    (a) by delivering it to him or by leaving it at his proper address or by sending it by post to him at that address; or
    (b) if the person is a body corporate, by serving it in accordance with paragraph (a) above on the secretary or clerk of that body; or
    (c) if the person is a partnership, by serving it in accordance with paragraph (a) above on a partner or a person having the control of management of the partnership business.

(2) For the purposes of this section and section 7 of the Interpretation Act 1978 (which relates to the service of documents by post) in its application to this section, the proper address of any person on whom a document is to be served shall be his last known address, except that—
    (a) in the case of service on a body corporate or its secretary or clerk, it shall be the address of the registered or principal office of the body;
    (b) in the case of service on a partnership or a partner or a person having the control or management of a partnership business, it shall be the principal office of the partnership;

and for the purposes of this subsection the principal office of a company registered outside the United Kingdom or of a partnership carrying on business outside the United Kingdom is its principal office within the United Kingdom.

(3)   If a person to be served by virtue of this Act with any document by another has specified to that other an address within the United Kingdom other than his proper address (as determined in pursuance of subsection (2) above) as the one at which he or someone on his behalf will accept documents of the same description as that document, that address shall also be treated as his proper address for the purposes of this section and for the purposes of the said section 7 in its application to this section.

(4)   Where under any provision of this Act any document is required to be served on the owner, on a lessee or on the occupier of any premises then—
   (a)   if the name or address of the owner, of the lessee or, as the case may be, of the occupier of the premises cannot after reasonable inquiry be ascertained; or
   (b)   in the case of service on the occupier, if the premises appear to be or are unoccupied,
that document may be served either by leaving it in the hands of a person who is or appears to be resident or employed on the land or by leaving it conspicuously affixed to some building or object on the land.

(5)   This section shall not apply to any document in relation to the service of which provision is made by rules of court.

[290]

217, 218 (*Relate to construction of provisions conferring powers by reference to undertakers' functions (s 217); and the meaning of "domestic purposes" (s 218).*)

219 General interpretation

(1)   In this Act, except in so far as the context otherwise requires—
   "accessories", in relation to a water main, sewer or other pipe, includes any manholes, ventilating shafts, inspection chambers, settling tanks, wash-out pipes, pumps, ferrules or stopcocks for the main, sewer or other pipe, or any machinery or other apparatus which is designed or adapted for use in connection with the use or maintenance of the main, sewer or other pipe or of another accessory for it, but does not include any telecommunication apparatus (within the meaning of Schedule 2 to the Telecommunications Act 1984) unless it—
      (a)   is or is to be situated inside or in the close vicinity of the main, sewer or other pipe or inside or in the close vicinity of another accessory for it; and
      (b)   is intended to be used only in connection with the use or maintenance of the main, sewer or other pipe or of another accessory for it;
   "analyse", in relation to any sample of land, water or effluent, includes subjecting the sample to a test of any description, and cognate expressions shall be construed accordingly;
   "conservancy authority" means any person who has a duty or power under any enactment to conserve, maintain or improve the navigation of a tidal water, and is not a harbour authority or navigation authority;
   "contravention" includes a failure to comply, and cognate expressions shall be construed accordingly;
   "customer or potential customer", in relation to a company holding an appointment under Chapter I of Part II of this Act, means—
      (a)   any person for or to whom that company provides any services in the course of carrying out the functions of a water undertaker or sewerage undertaker; or

(b) any person who might become such a person on making an application for the purpose to the company;

"damage", in relation to individuals, includes death and any personal injury, including any disease or impairment of physical or mental condition;

"the Director" means the Director General of Water Services;

"disposal"—

(a) in relation to land or any interest or right in or over land, includes the creation of such an interest or right and a disposal effected by means of the surrender or other termination of any such interest or right; and

(b) in relation to sewage, includes treatment;

and cognate expressions shall be construed accordingly;

"disposal main" means (subject to subsection (2) below) any outfall pipe or other pipe which—

(a) is a pipe for the conveyance of effluent to or from any sewage disposal works, whether of a sewerage undertaker or of any other person; and

(b) is not a public sewer;

"domestic purposes", except in relation to sewers, shall be construed in accordance with section 218 above;

"drain" means (subject to subsection (2) below) a drain used for the drainage of one building or of any buildings or yards appurtenant to buildings within the same curtilage;

"effluent" means any liquid, including particles of matter and other substances in suspension in the liquid;

"enactment" includes an enactment contained in this Act or in any Act passed after this Act;

"engineering or building operations", without prejudice to the generality of that expression, includes—

(a) the construction, alteration, improvement, maintenance or demolition of any building or structure or of any reservoir, watercourse, dam, weir, well, borehole or other works; and

(b) the installation, modification or removal of any machinery or apparatus;

"financial year" means the twelve months ending with 31st March;

"functions", in relation to a relevant undertaker, means the functions of the undertaker under or by virtue of any enactment and shall be construed subject to section 217 above;

"harbour authority" means a person who is a harbour authority within the meaning of [Chapter II of Part VI of the Merchant Shipping Act 1995] and is not a navigation authority;

"highway" and "highway authority" have the same meanings as in the Highways Act 1980;

"house" means any building or part of a building which is occupied as a dwelling-house, whether or not a private dwelling-house, or which, if unoccupied, is likely to be so occupied;

"information" includes anything contained in any records, accounts, estimates or returns;

"inland waters", has the same meaning as in the Water Resources Act 1991;

"limited company" means a company within the meaning of the Companies Act 1985 which is limited by shares;

"local authority" means the council of a district or of a London borough or the Common Council of the City of London [but, in relation to Wales, means the council of a county or county borough];

"local statutory provision" means—

(a) a provision of a local Act (including an Act confirming a provisional order);

(b) a provision of so much of any public general Act as has effect with respect to a particular area, with respect to particular persons or works or with respect to particular provisions falling within any paragraph of this definition;

(c) a provision of an instrument made under any provision falling within paragraph (a) or (b) above; or

(d) a provision of any other instrument which is in the nature of a local enactment;

"meter" means any apparatus for measuring or showing the volume of water supplied to, or of effluent discharged from, any premises;

"micro-organism" includes any microscopic biological entity which is capable of replication;

"modifications" includes additions, alterations and omissions, and cognate expressions shall be construed accordingly;

"the Monopolies Commission" means the Monopolies and Mergers Commission;

. . . . .

"navigation authority" means any person who has a duty or power under any enactment to work, maintain, conserve, improve or control any canal or other inland navigation, navigable river, estuary, harbour or dock;

"notice" means notice in writing;

"owner", in relation to any premises, means the person who—

(a) is for the time being receiving the rack-rent of the premises, whether on his own account or as agent or trustee for another person; or

(b) would receive the rack-rent if the premises were let at a rack-rent,

and cognate expressions shall be construed accordingly;

"prescribed" means prescribed by regulations made by the Secretary of State;

"protected land", in relation to a company holding an appointment under Chapter I of Part II of this Act, means any land which, or any interest or right in or over which—

(a) was transferred to that company in accordance with a scheme under Schedule 2 to the Water Act 1989 or, where that company is a statutory water company, was held by that company at any time during the financial year ending with 31st March 1990;

(b) is or has at any time on or after 1st September 1989 been held by that company for purposes connected with the carrying out of its functions as a water undertaker or sewerage undertaker (including any functions which for the purposes for which section 218 above has effect are taken to be such functions by virtue of subsection (6) or (7) of that section); or

(c) has been transferred to that company in accordance with a scheme under Schedule 2 to this Act from another company in relation to which that land was protected land when the other company held an appointment under that Chapter;

"public authority" means any Minister of the Crown or government department, [the Environment Agency], any local authority or county council or any person certified by the Secretary of State to be a public authority for the purposes of this Act;

"public sewer" means a sewer for the time being vested in a sewerage undertaker in its capacity as such, whether vested in that undertaker by virtue of a scheme under Schedule 2 to the Water Act 1989 or Schedule 2 to this Act or under section 179 above or otherwise, and "private sewer" shall be construed accordingly;

"railway undertakers" means the British Railways Board, London Regional Transport or any other person authorised by any enactment, or by any order, rule or regulation made under any enactment, to construct, work or carry on any railway;

"records" includes computer records and any other records kept otherwise than in a document;

"the relevant sewerage provisions" means the following provisions of this Act, that is to say—

(a) Chapters II and III of Part IV (except sections 98 to 101 and 110 and so much of Chapter III of that Part as provides for regulations under section 138 or has effect by virtue of any such regulations);

(b) sections 160, 171, 172(4), 178, 184, 189, 196 and 204 and paragraph 4 of Schedule 12; and

(c) the other provisions of this Act so far as they have effect for the purposes of any provision falling within paragraph (a) or (b) of this definition;

"relevant undertaker" means a water undertaker or sewerage undertaker;

"resource main" means (subject to subsection (2) below) any pipe, not being a trunk main, which is or is to be used for the purpose of—

(a) conveying water from one source of supply to another, from a source of supply to a regulating reservoir or from a regulating reservoir to a source of supply; or

(b) giving or taking a supply of water in bulk;

"service pipe" means (subject to subsection (2) below) so much of a pipe which is, or is to be, connected with a water main for supplying water from that main to any premises as—

(a) is or is to be subject to water pressure from that main; or

(b) would be so subject but for the closing of some valve,

and includes part of any service pipe;

"services" includes facilities;

"sewer" includes (without prejudice to subsection (2) below) all sewers and drains (not being drains within the meaning given by this subsection) which are used for the drainage of buildings and yards appurtenant to buildings;

"sewerage services" includes the disposal of sewage and any other services which are required to be provided by a sewerage undertaker for the purpose of carrying out its functions;

"special administration order" has the meaning given by section 23 above;

"statutory water company" means any company which was a statutory water company for the purposes of the Water Act 1973 immediately before 1st September 1989;

"stopcock" includes any box or pit in which a stopcock is enclosed and the cover to any such box or pit;

"street" has, subject to subsection (5) below, the same meaning as in Part III of the New Roads and Street Works 1991;

"subordinate legislation" has the same meaning as in the Interpretation Act 1978;

"substance" includes micro-organisms and any natural or artificial substance or other matter, whether it is in solid or liquid form or in the form of a gas or vapour;

"supply of water in bulk" means a supply of water for distribution by a water undertaker taking the supply;

"surface water" includes water from roofs;

"trunk main" means a water main which is or is to be used by a water undertaker for the purpose of—

(a) conveying water from a source of supply to a filter or reservoir or from one filter or reservoir to another filter or reservoir; or

(b) conveying water in bulk, whether in the course of taking a supply of water in bulk or otherwise, between different places outside the area of the undertaker, from such a place to any part of that area or from one part of that area to another part of that area;

"underground strata" means strata subjacent to the surface of any land;

"vessel" includes a hovercraft within the meaning of the Hovercraft Act 1968;

"water main" means (subject to subsection (2) below) any pipe, not being a pipe for the time being vested in a person other than the undertaker, which is used or to be used by a water undertaker for the purpose of making a general supply of water available to customers or potential customers of the undertaker, as distinct from for the purpose of providing a supply to particular customers;

"watercourse" includes all rivers, streams, ditches, drains, cuts, culverts, dykes, sluices, sewers and passages through which water flows except mains and other pipes which belong to [the Environment Agency] or a water undertaker or are used by a water undertaker or any other person for the purpose only of providing a supply of water to any premises.

(2)   In this Act—
   (a) references to a pipe, including references to a main, a drain or a sewer, shall include references to a tunnel or conduit which serves or is to serve as the pipe in question and to any accessories for the pipe; and
   (b) references to any sewage disposal works shall include references to the machinery and equipment of those works and any necessary pumping stations and outfall pipes;

and, accordingly, references to the laying of a pipe shall include references to the construction of such a tunnel or conduit, to the construction or installation of any such accessories and to the making of a connection between one pipe and another.

(3)   Nothing in Part III or IV of this Act by virtue of which a relevant undertaker owes a duty to any particular person to lay any water main, resource main or service pipe or any sewer, disposal main or discharge pipe shall be construed—
   (a) as conferring any power in addition to the powers conferred apart from those Parts; or
   (b) as requiring the undertaker to carry out any works which it has no power to carry out.

(4)   References in this Act to the fixing of charges in relation to any premises by reference to volume are references to the fixing of those charges by reference to the volume of water supplied to those premises, to the volume of effluent discharged from those premises, to both of those factors or to one or both of those factors taken together with other factors.

(5)   Until the coming into force of Part III of the New Roads and Street Works Act 1991, the definition of "street" in subsection (1) above shall have effect as if the reference to that Part were a reference to the Public Utilities Street Works Act 1950; but nothing in this section shall be taken—
   (a) to prejudice the power of the Secretary of State under that Act of 1991 to make an order bringing Part III of that Act into force on different days for different purposes (including the purposes of this section); or
   (b) in the period before the coming into force of that Part, to prevent references in this Act to a street, where the street is a highway which passes over a bridge or through a tunnel, from including that bridge or tunnel.

(6)   For the purposes of any provision of this Act by or under which power is or may be conferred on any person to recover the expenses incurred by that person in doing anything, those expenses shall be assumed to include such sum as may be reasonable in respect of establishment charges or overheads.

(7)   References in this Act to the later or latest of two or more different times or days are, in a case where those times or days coincide, references to the time at which or, as the case may be, the day on which they coincide.

(8)   Where by virtue of any provision of this Act any function of a Minister of the Crown is exercisable concurrently by different Ministers, that function shall also be exercisable jointly by any two or more of those Ministers.

(9)   Sub-paragraph (1) of paragraph 1 of Schedule 2 to the Water Consolidation (Consequential Provisions) Act 1991 has effect (by virtue of sub-paragraph (2)(b) of that paragraph) so that references in this Act to things done under or for the purposes of provisions of this Act or the Water Resources Act 1991 include references to things done, or treated as done, under or for the purposes of the corresponding provisions of the law in force before the commencement of this Act.

[291]

NOTES

Sub-s (1): in definition "harbour authority" words in square brackets substituted by the Merchant Shipping Act 1995, s 314(2), Sch 13, para 89(b); in definition "local authority" words in square brackets inserted by the Local Government (Wales) Act 1994, s 22(5), Sch 11, para 2(2); definition omitted repealed and in definitions "public authority" and "watercourse" words in square brackets substituted by the Environment Act 1995, s 120, Sch 22, para 125, Sch 24.

220   (*Relates to the effect of local Acts.*)

Other supplemental provisions

221, 222   (*Relates to crown application (s 221); and application to Isles of Scilly (s 222).*)

223 Short title, commencement and extent

(1)   This Act may be cited as the Water Industry Act 1991.

(2)   This Act shall come into force on 1st December 1991.

(3)   Except for the purpose of giving effect to any scheme under Schedule 2 to this Act, this Act extends to England and Wales only.

[292]

(*Schs 1–14 outside the scope of this work.*)

SCHEDULE 15
DISCLOSURE OF INFORMATION

Section 206

PART I
PERSONS IN RESPECT OF WHOSE FUNCTIONS DISCLOSURE MAY BE MADE

Any Minister of the Crown.

The Director General of Fair Trading.

The Monopolies Commission.

The Director General of Telecommunications.

The Civil Aviation Authority.

The Director General of Gas Supply.

The Director General of Electricity Supply.

[The Rail Regulator]

A local weights and measures authority in England and Wales.

[293]

NOTES

Words in square brackets inserted by the Railways Act 1993, s 152(1), Sch 12, para 30(a).

PART II
ENACTMENTS ETC IN RESPECT OF WHICH DISCLOSURE MAY BE MADE

The Trade Descriptions Act 1968.

The Fair Trading Act 1973.

The Consumer Credit Act 1974.

The Restrictive Trade Practices Act 1976.

The Resale Prices Act 1976.

The Estate Agents Act 1979.

The Competition Act 1980.

The Telecommunications Act 1984.

The Airports Act 1986.

The Gas Act 1986.

The Consumer Protection Act 1987.

The Electricity Act 1989.

[The Railways Act 1993]

Any subordinate legislation made for the purpose of securing compliance with the Directive of the Council of the European Communities dated 10th September 1984 (No 84/450/EEC) on the approximation of the laws, regulations and administrative provisions of the member States concerning misleading advertising.

[294]

NOTES
Words in square brackets inserted by the Railways Act 1993, s 152, Sch 12, para 30(b).

WATER RESOURCES ACT 1991

(1991 c 57)

ARRANGEMENT OF SECTIONS

PART II
WATER RESOURCES MANAGEMENT

CHAPTER I
GENERAL MANAGEMENT FUNCTIONS

PART III
CONTROL OF POLLUTION OF WATER RESOURCES

CHAPTER I
QUALITY OBJECTIVES

CHAPTER II
POLLUTION OFFENCES

Principal offences

Offences in connection with deposits and vegetation in rivers

Consents for the purposes of sections 88 to 90

Appeals in respect of consents under Chapter II

CHAPTER IIA
ABANDONED MINES

CHAPTER III
POWERS TO PREVENT AND CONTROL POLLUTION

CHAPTER IV
SUPPLEMENTAL PROVISIONS WITH RESPECT TO WATER POLLUTION

PART VII
LAND AND WORKS POWERS

CHAPTER I
POWERS OF THE AGENCY

PART VIII
INFORMATION PROVISIONS

PART IX
MISCELLANEOUS AND SUPPLEMENTAL

An Act to consolidate enactments relating to the National Rivers Authority and the matters in relation to which it exercises functions, with amendments to give effect to recommendations of the Law Commission

[25 July 1991]

1–18 (*Outside the scope of this work.*)

PART II
WATER RESOURCES MANAGEMENT

CHAPTER I
GENERAL MANAGEMENT FUNCTIONS

19, 20 (*S 19 repealed by the Environment Act 1995, s 120(1), (3), Sch 22, para 131, Sch 24, subject to transitional provisions (see s 120(2) of, and Sch 23, Pt I, paras 1, 2 to, the 1995 Act); s 20 relates to water resources management schemes.*)

21 Minimum acceptable flows

(1) The [Agency] may, if it thinks it appropriate to do so, submit a draft statement to the Secretary of State containing, in relation to any inland waters that are not discrete waters—

  (a) provision for determining the minimum acceptable flow for those waters; or

  (b) where any provision for determining such a flow is for the time being in force in relation to those waters, provision for amending that provision or for replacing it with different provision for determining the minimum acceptable flow for those waters.

(2) The provision contained in any statement for determining the minimum acceptable flow for any inland waters shall, in relation to the inland waters to which it relates, set out—

  (a) the control points at which the flow in the waters is to be measured;

  (b) the method of measurement which is to be used at each control point; and

  (c) the flow which is to be the minimum acceptable flow at each control point or, where appropriate, the flows which are to be the minimum acceptable flows at each such point for the different times or periods specified in the statement.

(3) Before preparing so much of any draft statement under this section as relates to any particular inland waters, the [Agency] shall consult—

  (a) any water undertaker having the right to abstract water from those waters;

  (b) any other water undertaker having the right to abstract water from any related underground strata;

  (c) the drainage board for any internal drainage district from which water is discharged into those waters or in which any part of those waters is situated;

  (d) any navigation authority, harbour authority or conservancy authority having functions in relation to those waters or any related inland waters;

  (e) if those waters or any related inland waters are tidal waters in relation to which there is no such navigation authority, harbour authority or conservancy authority, the Secretary of State for Transport; and

  (f) any person authorised by a licence under Part I of the Electricity Act 1989 to generate electricity [who has a right to abstract water from those waters].

(4) In determining the flow to be specified in relation to any inland waters under subsection (2)(c) above, the [Agency] shall have regard—

  (a) to the flow of water in the inland waters from time to time;

  (b) in the light of its duties under [sections 6(1), 7 and 8 of the 1995 Act], to the character of the inland waters and their surroundings; and

  (c) to any water quality objectives established under Chapter I of Part III of this Act in relation to the inland waters or any other inland waters which may be affected by the flow in the inland waters in question.

(5)   The flow specified in relation to any inland waters under subsection (2)(c) above shall be not less than the minimum which, in the opinion of the [Agency], is needed for safeguarding the public health and for meeting (in respect of both quantity and quality of water)—
  (a) the requirements of existing lawful uses of the inland waters, whether for agriculture, industry, water supply or other purposes; and
  (b) the requirements, in relation to both those waters and other inland waters whose flow may be affected by changes in the flow of those waters, of navigation, fisheries or land drainage.

(6)   The provisions of Schedule 5 to this Act shall have effect with respect to draft statements under this section and with respect to the approval of statements submitted as draft statements.

(7)   The approval under Schedule 5 to this Act of a draft statement under this section shall bring into force, on the date specified in that approval, so much of that statement, as approved, as contains provision for determining, amending or replacing the minimum acceptable flow for any inland waters.

(8)   For the purposes of subsection (3) above—
  (a) underground strata are related underground strata in relation to any inland waters if—
    (i) a water undertaker has a right to abstract water from the strata; and
    (ii) it appears to the [Agency], having regard to the extent to which the level of water in the strata depends on the flow of those waters, that the exercise of that right may be substantially affected by so much of the draft statement in question as relates to those waters;
  (b) inland waters are related inland waters in relation to any other inland waters, where it appears to the [Agency] that changes in the flow of the other waters may affect the flow of the first-mentioned inland waters.

(9)   For the purposes of subsection (5) above the [Agency] shall be entitled (but shall not be bound) to treat as lawful any existing use of any inland waters unless—
  (a) by a decision given in any legal proceedings, it has been held to be unlawful; and
  (b) that decision has not been quashed or reversed;

and in that subsection the reference to land drainage includes a reference to defence against water (including sea water), irrigation other than spray irrigation, warping and the provision of flood warning systems.

[295]

NOTES
   Sub-ss (1), (4), (5), (8), (9): words in square brackets substituted by the Environment Act 1995, s 120, Sch 22, paras 128, 133(2).
   Sub-s (3): words in first pair of square brackets substituted, and words in final pair of square brackets added, by the Environment Act 1995, s 120, Sch 22, paras 128, 131(1).

---

22 Directions to the [Agency] to consider minimum acceptable flow

(1)   If the [Agency] is directed by the Secretary of State to consider whether the minimum acceptable flow for any particular inland waters ought to be determined or reviewed, the [Agency] shall consider that matter as soon as reasonably practicable after being directed to do so.

(2)   After considering any matter under subsection (1) above the [Agency] shall submit to the Secretary of State with respect to the inland waters in question either—
  (a) such a draft statement as is mentioned in subsection (1) of section 21 above; or

(b) a draft statement that no minimum acceptable flow ought to be determined for those waters or, as the case may require, that the minimum acceptable flow for those waters does not need to be changed,

and subsections (6) and (7) of that section shall apply in relation to a draft statement under this subsection as they apply in relation to a draft statement under that section.

(3) Without prejudice to the generality of paragraph 4 of Schedule 5 to this Act, the power of the Secretary of State under that paragraph to alter a draft statement before approving it shall include power to substitute a statement containing or amending any such provision as is mentioned in subsection (2) of section 21 above for such a draft statement as is mentioned in subsection (2)(b) of this section.

[296]

NOTES

Section heading: word in square brackets substituted by the Environment Act 1995, s 120, Sch 22, para 128.

Sub-ss (1), (2): words in square brackets substituted by the Environment Act 1995, s 120, Sch 22, para 128.

23 Minimum acceptable level or volume of inland waters

(1) Where it appears to the [Agency], in the case of any particular inland waters, that it would be appropriate to measure the level or the volume (either instead of or in addition to the flow) the [Agency] may determine that sections 21 and 22 above shall apply in relation to those inland waters as if any reference to the flow were or, as the case may be, included a reference to the level or to the volume.

(2) Where the [Agency] makes a determination under subsection (1) above with respect to any inland waters, any draft statement prepared for the purposes of section 21 or 22 above, in so far as it relates to those waters, shall state—
  (a) whether the level or the volume is to be measured; and
  (b) whether it is to be measured instead of, or in addition to, the flow.

(3) Chapter II of this Part shall apply in relation to any inland waters with respect to which a determination has been made under subsection (1) above as if any reference in that Chapter to the flow were, or (as the case may be) included, a reference to the level or, as the case may be, the volume.

[297]

NOTES

Sub-ss (1), (2): words in square brackets substituted by the Environment Act 1995, s 120, Sch 22, para 128.

CHAPTER II
ABSTRACTION AND IMPOUNDING

Restrictions on abstraction and impounding

24 Restrictions on abstraction

(1) Subject to the following provisions of this Chapter and to any drought order [or drought permit] under Chapter III of this Part, no person shall—
  (a) abstract water from any source of supply; or
  (b) cause or permit any other person so to abstract any water,

except in pursuance of a licence under this Chapter granted by the [Agency] and in accordance with the provisions of that licence.

(2) Where by virtue of subsection (1) above the abstraction of water contained in any underground strata is prohibited except in pursuance of a licence under this Chapter, no person shall begin, or cause or permit any other person to begin—

(a) to construct any well, borehole or other work by which water may be abstracted from those strata;

(b) to extend any such well, borehole or other work; or

(c) to install or modify any machinery or apparatus by which additional quantities of water may be abstracted from those strata by means of a well, borehole or other work,

unless the conditions specified in subsection (3) below are satisfied.

(3) The conditions mentioned in subsection (2) above are—

(a) that the abstraction of the water or, as the case may be, of the additional quantities of water is authorised by a licence under this Chapter; and

(b) that—

(i) the well, borehole or work, as constructed or extended; or

(ii) the machinery or apparatus, as installed or modified,

fulfils the requirements of that licence as to the means by which water is authorised to be abstracted.

(4) A person shall be guilty of an offence if—

(a) he contravenes subsection (1) or (2) above; or

(b) he is for the purposes of this section the holder of a licence under this Chapter and, in circumstances not constituting such a contravention, does not comply with a condition or requirement imposed by the provisions, as for the time being in force, of that licence.

(5) A person who is guilty of an offence under this section shall be liable—

(a) on summary conviction, to a fine not exceeding the statutory maximum;

(b) on conviction on indictment, to a fine.

(6) The restrictions imposed by this section shall have effect notwithstanding anything in any enactment contained in any Act passed before the passing of the Water Resources Act 1963 on 31st July 1963 or in any statutory provision made or issued, whether before or after the passing of that Act, by virtue of such an enactment.

[298]

NOTES

Sub-s (1): words in first pair of square brackets inserted by the Environment Act 1995 (Consequential Amendments) Regulations 1996, SI 1996/593, reg 3, Sch 2, para 8; word in final pair of square brackets substituted by the Environment Act 1995, s 120, Sch 22, para 128.

---

25 Restrictions on impounding

(1) Subject to the following provisions of this Chapter and to any drought order [or drought permit] under Chapter III of this Part, no person shall begin, or cause or permit any other person to begin, to construct or alter any impounding works at any point in any inland waters which are not discrete waters unless—

(a) a licence under this Chapter granted by the [Agency] to obstruct or impede the flow of those inland waters at that point by means of impounding works is in force;

(b) the impounding works will not obstruct or impede the flow of the inland waters except to the extent, and in the manner, authorised by the licence; and

(c) any other requirements of the licence, whether as to the provision of compensation water or otherwise, are complied with.

(2) A person shall be guilty of an offence if—

(a) he contravenes subsection (1) above; or

(b) he is for the purposes of this section the holder of a licence under this Chapter and, in circumstances not constituting such a contravention, does not comply with a condition or requirement imposed by the provisions, as for the time being in force, of that licence.

(3)   A person who is guilty of an offence under this section shall be liable—
    (a) on summary conviction, to a fine not exceeding the statutory maximum;
    (b) on conviction on indictment, to a fine.

(4)   Subject to subsection (5) below, the restrictions imposed by this section shall have effect notwithstanding anything in any enactment contained in any Act passed before the passing of the Water Resources Act 1963 on 31st July 1963 or in any statutory provision made or issued, whether before or after the passing of that Act, by virtue of such an enactment.

(5)   Subject to subsection (6) below, the restriction on impounding works shall not apply to the construction or alteration of any impounding works, if—
    (a) the construction or alteration of those works; or
    (b) the obstruction or impeding of the flow of the inland waters resulting from the construction or alteration of the works,

is authorised (in whatsoever terms, and whether expressly or by implication) by virtue of any such statutory provision as at the coming into force of this Act was an alternative statutory provision for the purposes of section 36(2) of the Water Resources Act 1963.

(6)   The provisions of this Chapter shall have effect in accordance with subsection (7) below where by virtue of any such provision as is mentioned in subsection (5) above and is for the time being in force—
    (a) any water undertaker or sewerage undertaker to which rights under that provision have been transferred in accordance with a scheme under Schedule 2 to the Water Act 1989 or Schedule 2 to the Water Industry Act 1991; or
    (b) any other person,

is authorised (in whatsoever terms, and whether expressly or by implication) to obstruct or impede the flow of any inland waters by means of impounding works (whether those works have already been constructed or not).

(7)   Where subsection (6) above applies, the provisions of this Chapter shall have effect (with the necessary modifications), where the reference is to the revocation or variation of a licence under this Chapter, as if—
    (a) any reference in those provisions to a licence under this Chapter included a reference to the authorisation mentioned in that subsection; and
    (b) any reference to the holder of such a licence included a reference to the undertaker or other person so mentioned.

(8)   In this Chapter "impounding works" means either of the following, that is to say—
    (a) any dam, weir or other works in any inland waters by which water may be impounded;
    (b) any works for diverting the flow of any inland waters in connection with the construction or alteration of any dam, weir or other works falling within paragraph (a) above.

[299]

NOTES

Sub-s (1): words in first pair of square brackets inserted by the Environment Act 1995 (Consequential Amendments) Regulations 1996, SI 1996/593, reg 3, Sch 2, para 8; word in final pair of square brackets substituted by the Environment Act 1995, s 120, Sch 22, para 128.

Rights to abstract or impound

26 Rights of navigation, harbour and conservancy authorities

(1)   The restriction on abstraction shall not apply to any transfer of water from one area of inland waters to another in the course of, or resulting from, any operations carried out by a navigation authority, harbour authority or conservancy authority in the carrying out of their functions as such an authority.

(2)   The restriction on impounding works shall not apply to the construction or alteration of impounding works in the course of the performance by a navigation authority, harbour authority or conservancy authority of their functions as such an authority.

[300]

27 Rights to abstract small quantities

(1)   The restriction on abstraction shall not apply to any abstraction of a quantity of water not exceeding five cubic metres if it does not form part of a continuous operation, or of a series of operations, by which a quantity of water which, in aggregate, is more than five cubic metres is abstracted.

(2)   The restriction on abstraction shall not apply to any abstraction of a quantity of water not exceeding twenty cubic metres if the abstraction—
  (a) does not form part of a continuous operation, or of a series of operations, by which a quantity of water which, in aggregate, is more than twenty cubic metres is abstracted; and
  (b) is with the consent of the [Agency].

(3)   The restriction on abstraction shall not apply to so much of any abstraction from any inland waters by or on behalf of an occupier of contiguous land as falls within subsection (4) below, unless the abstraction is such that the quantity of water abstracted from the inland waters by or on behalf of the occupier by virtue of this subsection exceeds twenty cubic metres, in aggregate, in any period of twenty-four hours.

(4)   Subject to section 28 below, an abstraction of water falls within this subsection in so far as the water-
  (a) is abstracted for use on a holding consisting of the contiguous land with or without other land held with that land; and
  (b) is abstracted for use on that holding for either or both of the following purposes, that is to say—
    (i) the domestic purposes of the occupier's household;
    (ii) agricultural purposes other than spray irrigation.

(5)   The restriction on abstraction shall not apply to the abstraction of water from underground strata, in so far as the water is abstracted by or on behalf of an individual as a supply of water for the domestic purposes of his household, unless the abstraction is such that the quantity of water abstracted from the strata by or on behalf of that individual by virtue of this subsection exceeds twenty cubic metres, in aggregate, in any period of twenty-four hours.

(6)   For the purposes of this Chapter a person who is in a position to abstract water in such circumstances that, by virtue of subsection (3) or (5) above, the restriction on abstraction does not apply shall be taken to have a right to abstract water to the extent specified in that subsection.

(7)   In the case of any abstraction of water from underground strata which falls within subsection (5) above, the restriction imposed by section 24(2) above shall not apply—

(a) to the construction or extension of any well, borehole or other work; or
(b) to the installation or modification of machinery or other apparatus,

if the well, borehole or other work is constructed or extended, or the machinery or apparatus is installed or modified, for the purpose of abstracting the water.

(8) In this section "contiguous land", in relation to the abstraction of any water from inland waters, means land contiguous to those waters at the place where the abstraction is effected.

[301]

NOTES

28 Curtailment of rights under section 27

(1) The provisions of this section shall have effect where a person ("the occupier") is entitled, by virtue of subsection (6) of section 27 above, to a protected right for the purposes of this Chapter by reason of his being the occupier of such a holding as is mentioned in subsection (4) of that section in relation to an abstraction falling within that subsection ("the holding").

(2) If it appears to the [Agency] that the occupier is entitled, as against other occupiers of land contiguous to the inland waters in question, to abstract water from those waters for use on part of the holding ("the relevant part"), but is not so entitled to abstract water for use on other parts of the holding—
  (a) the [Agency] may serve on him a notice specifying the relevant part of the holding; and
  (b) subject to the following provisions of this section, the notice shall have effect so as to require subsections (3) and (4) of section 27 above to be construed in relation to the holding as if the references in subsection (4) to use on the holding were references to use on the part of the holding specified in the notice.

(3) Where a notice is served under subsection (2) above and the occupier objects to the notice on the grounds—
  (a) that he is entitled, as against other occupiers of land contiguous to the inland waters in question, to abstract water from those waters for use on every part of the holding; or
  (b) that he is so entitled to abstract water for use on a larger part of the holding than that specified in the notice,

he may, within such period (not being less than twenty-eight days from the date of service of the notice) and in such manner as may be prescribed, appeal to the court against the notice.

(4) On any appeal under subsection (3) above, the court shall determine the matter in dispute and, in accordance with its decision, confirm, quash or vary the [Agency's] notice and—
  (a) where the court quashes a notice served under subsection (2) above, paragraph (b) of that subsection shall not have effect; and
  (b) where the court varies such a notice, that paragraph shall have effect, but with the substitution, for the reference to the part of the holding specified in the notice, of a reference to the part specified in the notice as varied by the court.

(5) In this section—
  "the court" means the county court for the district in which the holding, or the part of the holding which is contiguous to the inland waters in question, is situated; and
  "entitled" (except in subsection (1) above) means entitled apart from this Chapter or any other statutory provision.

[302]

NOTES
Sub-ss (2), (4): words in square brackets substituted by the Environment Act 1995, s 120, Sch 22, para 128.

29 Rights to abstract for drainage purposes etc

(1)   The restriction on abstraction shall not apply to any abstraction of water from a source of supply in the course of, or resulting from, any operations for purposes of land drainage.

(2)   The restriction on abstraction shall not apply to any abstraction of water from a source of supply in so far as the abstraction (where it does not fall within subsection (1) above) is necessary—
> (a)   to prevent interference with any mining, quarrying, engineering, building or other operations (whether underground or on the surface); or
> (b)   to prevent damage to works resulting from any such operations.

(3)   Where—
> (a)   water is abstracted, in the course of any such operations as are mentioned in subsection (2) above, from any excavation into underground strata in a case in which the level of water in the underground strata depends wholly or mainly on water entering it from those strata; and
> (b)   the abstraction is necessary as mentioned in that subsection,

the exemption conferred by that subsection shall apply notwithstanding that the water is used for the purposes of the operations.

(4)   In the case of any abstraction of water from underground strata which falls within subsection (1) or (2) above, the restriction imposed by section 24(2) above shall not apply—
> (a)   to the construction or extension of any well, borehole or other work; or
> (b)   to the installation or modification of machinery or other apparatus,

if the well, borehole or other work is constructed or extended, or the machinery or apparatus is installed or modified, for the purpose of abstracting the water.

(5)   In this section, "land drainage" includes the protection of land against erosion or encroachment by water, whether from inland waters or from the sea, and also includes warping and irrigation other than spray irrigation.

[303]

30 Notices with respect to borings not requiring licences

(1)   Where any person—
> (a)   proposes to construct a well, borehole or other work which is to be used solely for the purpose of abstracting, to the extent necessary to prevent interference with the carrying out or operation of any underground works, water contained in underground strata; or
> (b)   proposes to extend any such well, borehole or other work,

he shall, before he begins to construct or extend the work, give to the [Agency] a notice of his intention in the prescribed form.

(2)   Where a notice under subsection (1) above is given to the [Agency] by any person, the [Agency] may (subject to section 31 below) by notice to that person require him, in connection with the construction, extension or use of the work to which that person's notice relates, to take such reasonable measures for conserving water as are specified in the notice.

(3)   The measures that may be specified in a notice under subsection (2) above shall be measures which, in the opinion of the [Agency], will not interfere with the protection of the underground works in question.

(4)   Any person who contravenes subsection (1) above or fails to comply with a notice under subsection (2) above shall be guilty of an offence and liable—
(a) on summary conviction, to a fine not exceeding the statutory maximum;
(b) on conviction on indictment, to a fine.

[304]

NOTES
Sub-ss (1)–(3): words in square brackets substituted by the Environment Act 1995, s 120, Sch 22, para 128.
Regulations: the Water Resources (Miscellaneous Provisions) Regulations 1965, SI 1965/1092, reg 7(1), Schedule (having effect under this section by virtue of the Water Consolidation (Consequential Provisions) Act 1991, s 2(2), Sch 2, Pt I, para 16).

31 Appeals against conservation notices under section 30

(1)   The person on whom a notice under section 30(2) above ("a conservation notice") is served may, by notice to the Secretary of State, appeal to him against the conservation notice on either or both of the following grounds, that is to say—
(a) that the measures required by the conservation notice are not reasonable;
(b) that those measures would interfere with the protection of the underground works in question.

(2)   Any notice of appeal against a conservation notice shall be served within such period (not being less than twenty-eight days from the date of service of the conservation notice) and in such manner as may be prescribed.

(3)   Before determining an appeal against a conservation notice, the Secretary of State may, if he thinks fit—
(a) cause a local inquiry to be held; or
(b) afford to the appellant and the [Agency] an opportunity of appearing before, and being heard by, a person appointed by the Secretary of State for the purpose;
and the Secretary of State shall act as mentioned in paragraph (a) or (b) above if a request is made by the appellant or the [Agency] to be heard with respect to the appeal.

(4)   On an appeal against a conservation notice the Secretary of State may confirm, quash or vary the notice as he may consider appropriate.

(5)   The decision of the Secretary of State on any appeal against a conservation notice shall be final.

(6)   The Secretary of State may by regulations make provision as to the manner in which appeals against conservation notices are to be dealt with, including provision requiring the giving of notices of, and information relating to, the making of such appeals or decisions on any such appeals.

[305]

NOTES
Sub-s (3): words in square brackets substituted by the Environment Act 1995, s 120, Sch 22, para 128.
Regulations: the Water Resources (Miscellaneous Provisions) Regulations 1965, SI 1965/1092, reg 8, (having effect under this section by virtue of the Water Consolidation (Consequential Provisions) Act 1991, s 2(2), Sch 2, para 1).

32 Miscellaneous rights to abstract

(1)   The restriction on abstraction shall not apply to any abstraction by machinery or apparatus installed on a vessel, where the water is abstracted for use on that, or any other, vessel.

(2)   The restriction on abstraction and the other restrictions imposed by section 24 above shall not apply to the doing of anything—

(a) for fire-fighting purposes (within the meaning of the Fire Services Act 1947); or

(b) for the purpose of testing apparatus used for those purposes or of training or practice in the use of such apparatus.

(3) The restriction on abstraction and the other restrictions imposed by section 24 above shall not apply—

(a) to any abstraction of water;

(b) to the construction or extension of any well, borehole or other work; or

(c) to the installation or modification of machinery or other apparatus,

if the abstraction, construction, extension, installation or modification is for any of the purposes specified in subsection (4) below and takes place with the consent of the [Agency] and in compliance with any conditions imposed by the [Agency].

(4) The purposes mentioned in subsection (3) above are—

(a) the purpose of ascertaining the presence of water in any underground strata or the quality or quantity of any such water; and

(b) the purpose of ascertaining the effect of abstracting water from the well, borehole or other work in question on the abstraction of water from, or the level of water in, any other well, borehole or other work or any inland waters.

[306]

NOTES

Sub-s (3): words in square brackets substituted by the Environment Act 1995, s 120, Sch 22, para 128.

33 Power to provide for further rights to abstract

(1) Any of the relevant authorities, after consultation with the other relevant authorities (if any), may apply to the Secretary of State for an order excepting any one or more sources of supply from the restriction on abstraction, on the grounds that that restriction is not needed in relation to that source of supply or, as the case may be, those sources of supply.

(2) An application under this section may be made in respect of—

(a) any one or more areas of inland waters specified in the application or any class of inland waters so specified; or

(b) any underground strata described in the application, whether by reference to their formation or their location in relation to the surface of the land or in relation to other strata subjacent to that surface or partly in one way and partly in another;

and an order may be made under this section accordingly.

(3) For the purposes of this section—

(a) the [Agency] is a relevant authority in relation to every source of supply; and

(b) a navigation authority, harbour authority or conservancy authority having functions in relation to any inland waters is a relevant authority in relation to those inland waters.

(4) If, in the case of any source of supply—

(a) it appears to the Secretary of State, after consultation with the [Agency], that the question whether the restriction on abstraction is needed in relation to that source of supply ought to be determined; but

(b) no application for an order under this section has been made,

the Secretary of State may direct the [Agency] to make an application under this section in respect to that source of supply.

(5) Schedule 6 to this Act shall have effect with respect to applications for orders under this section and with respect to the making of such orders; and the power to make any such order shall be exercisable by statutory instrument.

(6)　On the coming into force of an order under this section—
 (a)　the restriction on abstraction and, in the case of any underground strata, the restriction imposed by subsection (2) of section 24 above shall cease to apply to any source of supply to which the order relates; and
 (b)　any licence granted under this Chapter which is for the time being in force shall cease to have effect in so far as it authorises abstraction from any such source of supply.

[307]

NOTES
　Sub-ss (3), (4): words in square brackets substituted by the Environment Act 1995, s 120, Sch 22, para 128.

Applications for a licence

34 Regulations with respect to applications

(1)　Any application for a licence under this Chapter shall be made in such manner as may be prescribed, and shall include such particulars, and be verified by such evidence, as may be prescribed.

(2)　The Secretary of State may by regulations make provision as to the manner in which applications for the grant of licences under this Chapter are to be dealt with, including provision requiring the giving of notices of, and information relating to, the making of such applications or decisions on such applications.

(3)　Without prejudice to the generality of subsection (2) above, provision shall be made by regulations under this section for securing that, in such circumstances as may be prescribed (being circumstances in which it appears to the Secretary of State that applications for licences under this Chapter would be of special concern to National Park . . . authorities)—
 (a)　notice of any such application will be given to such one or more National Park . . . authorities as may be determined in accordance with the regulations; and
 (b)　the matters to which the [Agency] or, as the case may be, the Secretary of State is to have regard in dealing with the application will include any representations made by any such National Park . . . authority within such period and in such manner as may be prescribed.

(4)　The preceding provisions of this section shall have effect subject to any express provision contained in, or having effect by virtue of, any other enactment contained in this Chapter; and any regulations made under this section shall have effect subject to any such express provision.

(5)　. . .

[308]

NOTES
　Sub-s (3): words omitted repealed, and word in square brackets substituted, by the Environment Act 1995, s 120, Sch 22, para 128, Sch 24.
　Sub-s (5): repealed by the Environment Act 1995, s 120, Sch 24.
　Modification: references to a National Park planning authority modified by the Environment Act 1995, s 78, Sch 10, para 34.
　Regulations: the Water Resources (Licences) Regulations 1965, SI 1965/534, Pt II (regs 4–12) (partly having effect under sub-ss (1)–(3) of this section by virtue of the Water Consolidation (Consequential Provisions) Act 1991, s 2(2), Sch 2, para 1(1), (2)).

35 Restrictions on persons who may make applications for abstraction licences

(1)　No application for a licence under this Chapter to abstract water shall be entertained unless it is made by a person entitled to make the application in accordance with the following provisions of this section.

(2)   In relation to abstractions from any inland waters, a person shall be entitled to make the application if, at the place (or, if more than one, at each of the places) at which the proposed abstractions are to be effected, either—
  (a) he is the occupier of land contiguous to the inland waters; or
  (b) he satisfies the [Agency] that he has, or at the time when the proposed licence is to take effect will have, a right of access to such land.

(3)   In relation to abstractions from underground strata, a person shall be entitled to make the application if either—
  (a) he is the occupier of land consisting of or comprising those underground strata; or
  (b) the following two conditions are satisfied, that is to say—
    (i) the case is one in which water contained in an excavation into underground strata is to be treated as water contained in those strata by virtue of the level of water in the excavation depending wholly or mainly on water entering it from those strata; and
    (ii) that person satisfies the [Agency] that he has, or at the time when the proposed licence is to take effect will have, a right of access to land consisting of, or comprising, those underground strata.

(4)   Any reference in this section to a person who is the occupier of land of any description—
  (a) includes a reference to a person who satisfies the [Agency] that he has entered into negotiations for the acquisition of an interest in land of that description such that, if the interest is acquired by him, he will be entitled to occupy that land; and
  (b) without prejudice to the application of paragraph (a) above to a person who is or can be authorised to acquire land compulsorily, also includes any person who satisfies the [Agency] that by virtue of any enactment, the compulsory acquisition by that person of land of that description either has been authorised or can be authorised and has been initiated.

(5)   In subsection (4) above the reference to initiating the compulsory acquisition of land by a person is a reference to—
  (a) the submission to the relevant Minister of a draft of an order which, if made by that Minister in the form of the draft, will authorise that person to acquire that land compulsorily, with or without other land; or
  (b) the submission to the relevant Minister of an order which, if confirmed by that Minister as submitted will authorise that person to acquire that land compulsorily, with or without other land.

(6)   In subsection (5) above "the relevant Minister", in relation to the compulsory acquisition of land by any person, means the Minister who, in accordance with the enactment mentioned in subsection (4)(b) above, is empowered to authorise that person to acquire land compulsorily.

[309]

NOTES
  Sub-ss (2), (3), (4): words in square brackets substituted by the Environment Act 1995, s 120, Sch 22, para 128.

---

36 Application for combined abstraction and impounding licence

Where a licence under this Chapter is required by virtue of section 25 above for constructing or altering impounding works at a point in any inland waters, for the purpose of abstracting water from those waters at or near that point—
  (a) an application may be made to the [Agency] for a combined licence under this Chapter to obstruct or impede the flow of those inland waters by means of impounding works at that point and to abstract the water; and

(b) the [Agency] shall have power (subject to the provisions of this Chapter as
to procedure and as to the matters to be taken into account in dealing with
applications for licences) to grant such a licence accordingly.

[310]

NOTES

Words in square brackets substituted by the Environment Act 1995, s 120, Sch 22, para 128.

37 Publication of application for licence

(1)   The [Agency] shall not entertain an application for a licence under this
Chapter to abstract water or to obstruct or impede the flow of any inland waters by
means of impounding works or for a combined licence, unless the application is
accompanied—
(a) by a copy of a notice in the prescribed form; and
(b) by the prescribed evidence that the necessary notices of the application
have been given.

(2)   Subject to subsection (3) below, the necessary notices of an application have
been given for the purposes of subsection (1) above if—
(a) the notice mentioned in paragraph (a) of that subsection has been
published—
(i) in the London Gazette; and
(ii) at least once in each of two successive weeks, in one or more
newspapers (other than the London Gazette) circulating in the
relevant locality; and

and
(b) a copy of that notice has been served, not later than the date on which it
was first published as mentioned in paragraph (a)(ii) above—
(i) on any navigation authority, harbour authority or conservancy
authority having functions in relation to any inland waters at a
proposed point of abstraction or impounding;
(ii) on the drainage board for any internal drainage district within which
any such proposed point is situated; and
(iii) on any water undertaker within whose area any such proposed point is
situated.

(3)   Where the licence applied for is exclusively for the abstraction of water from
a source of supply that does not form part of any inland waters, the giving of the
necessary notices shall not for the purposes of subsection (1) above require the
service of any copy of the notice mentioned in paragraph (a) of that subsection on any
navigation authority, harbour authority, conservancy authority or drainage board.

(4)   A notice for the purposes of the preceding provisions of this section, in
addition to containing any other matters required to be contained in that notice, shall—
(a) name a place within the relevant locality where a copy of the application,
and of any map, plan or other document submitted with it, will be open to
inspection by the public, free of charge, at all reasonable hours during a
period specified in the notice in accordance with subsection (5) below; and
(b) state that any person may make representations in writing to the [Agency]
with respect to the application at any time before the end of that period.

(5)   The period specified in a notice for the purposes of the preceding provisions
of this section shall be a period which—
(a) begins not earlier than the date on which the notice is first published in a
newspaper other than the London Gazette; and
(b) ends not less than twenty-eight days from that date and not less than
twenty-five days from the date on which the notice is published in the
London Gazette.

(6) Where—

(a) an application for a licence under this Chapter to abstract water is made to the [Agency]; and

(b) the application proposes that the quantity of water abstracted in pursuance of the licence should not in any period of twenty-four hours exceed, in aggregate, twenty cubic metres or any lesser amount specified in the application,

the [Agency] may dispense with the requirements imposed by virtue of the preceding provisions of this section if and to the extent that it appears to the [Agency] appropriate to do so.

(7) In this section—

"proposed point of abstraction or impounding", in relation to any application for a licence under this Chapter, means a place where a licence, if granted in accordance with the application, would authorise water to be abstracted or, as the case may be, would authorise inland waters to be obstructed or impeded by means of impounding works; and

"relevant locality", in relation to an application for a licence under this Act, means the locality in which any proposed point of abstraction or impounding is situated.

[311]

NOTES

Sub-ss (1), (4), (6): words in square brackets substituted by the Environment Act 1995, s 120, Sch 22, para 128.

Regulations: the Water Resources (Licences) Regulations 1965, SI 1965/534, regs 4(4), 6(4), Sch 2, Forms N1–N3 (having effect under this section by virtue of the Water Consolidation (Consequential Provisions) Act 1991, s 2(2), Sch 2, Pt I, para 2).

Consideration of licence applications

38 General consideration of applications

(1) The [Agency] shall not determine any application for a licence under this Chapter before the end of the period specified for the purposes of the application in accordance with section 37(5) above.

(2) Subject to the following provisions of this Chapter, on any application to the [Agency] for a licence under this Chapter, the [Agency]—

(a) may grant a licence containing such provisions as the [Agency] considers appropriate; or

(b) if, having regard to the provisions of this Chapter, the [Agency] considers it necessary or expedient to do so, may refuse to grant a licence.

(3) Without prejudice to section 39(1) below, the [Agency], in dealing with any application for a licence under this Chapter, shall have regard to—

(a) any representations in writing relating to the application which are received by the [Agency] before the end of the period mentioned in subsection (1) above; and

(b) the requirements of the applicant, in so far as they appear to the [Agency] to be reasonable requirements.

[312]

NOTES

Sub-ss (1)–(3): words in square brackets substituted by the Environment Act 1995, s 120, Sch 22, para 128.

39 Obligation to have regard to existing rights and privileges

(1) The [Agency] shall not, except with the consent of the person entitled to the rights, grant a licence so authorising—

(a) the abstraction of water; or

(b) the flow of any inland waters to be obstructed or impeded by means of impounding works,

as to derogate from any rights which, at the time when the application is determined by the [Agency], are protected rights for the purposes of this Chapter.

(2) In a case where an application for a licence under this Chapter relates to abstraction from underground strata, the [Agency], in dealing with the application, shall have regard to the requirements of existing lawful uses of water abstracted from those strata, whether for agriculture, industry, water supply or other purposes.

(3) For the purposes of this Chapter a right is a protected right if it is such a right as a person is taken to have by virtue of section 27(6) above or section 48(1) below; and any reference in this Chapter to the person entitled to such a right shall be construed accordingly.

(4) Any reference in this Chapter, in relation to the abstraction of water or obstructing or impeding the flow of any inland waters by means of impounding works, to derogating from a right which is a protected right for the purposes of this Chapter is a reference to, as the case may be—

(a) abstracting water; or

(b) so obstructing or impeding the flow of any such waters,

in such a way, or to such an extent, as to prevent the person entitled to that right from abstracting water to the extent mentioned in section 27(6) above or, as the case may be, section 48(1) below.

(5) For the purposes of subsection (2) above the [Agency] shall be entitled (but shall not be bound) to treat as lawful any existing use of water from underground strata unless—

(a) by a decision given in any legal proceedings, it has been held to be unlawful; and

(b) that decision has not been quashed or reversed.

[313]

NOTES

Sub-ss (1), (2), (5): words in square brackets substituted by the Environment Act 1995, s 120, Sch 22, para 128.

40 Obligations to take river flow etc into account

(1) Without prejudice to sections 38(3) and 39(1) above, subsection (2) or, as the case may be, subsection (3) below shall apply where any application for a licence under this Chapter relates to abstraction from any inland waters or to obstructing or impeding the flow of any inland waters by means of impounding works.

(2) If, in the case of such an application as is mentioned in subsection (1) above, the application is made at a time when no minimum acceptable flow for the inland waters in question has been determined under Chapter I of this Part, the [Agency], in dealing with the application, shall have regard to the considerations by reference to which, in accordance with section 21(4) and (5) above, a minimum acceptable flow for those waters would fall to be determined.

(3) If, in the case of such an application as is mentioned in subsection (1) above, the application is made at a time after a minimum acceptable flow for the waters in

question has been determined under Chapter I of this Part, the [Agency], in dealing with the application, shall have regard to the need to secure or, as the case may be, secure in relation to the different times or periods for which the flow is determined—

    (a) that the flow at any control point will not be reduced below the minimum acceptable flow at that point; or

    (b) if it is already less than that minimum acceptable flow, that the flow at any control point will not be further reduced below the minimum acceptable flow at that point.

    (4) Without prejudice to sections 38(3) and 39(1) above, where—

    (a) an application for a licence under this Chapter relates to abstraction from underground strata; and

    (b) it appears to the [Agency] that the proposed abstraction is likely to affect the flow, level or volume of any inland waters which are neither discrete waters nor waters comprised in an order under section 33 above,

subsection (2) or, as the case may be, subsection (3) above shall apply as if the application related to abstraction from those waters.

[314]

NOTES

Sub-ss (2)–(4): words in square brackets substituted by the Environment Act 1995, s 120, Sch 22, para 128.

Call-in of applications

41 Secretary of State's power to call in applications

    (1) The Secretary of State may give directions to the [Agency] requiring applications for licences under this Chapter to be referred to him, instead of being dealt with by the [Agency].

    (2) A direction under this section—

    (a) may relate either to a particular application or to applications of a class specified in the direction; and

    (b) may except from the operation of the direction such classes of applications as may be specified in the direction in such circumstances as may be so specified.

[315]

NOTES

Sub-s (1): words in square brackets substituted by the Environment Act 1995, s 120, Sch 22, para 128.

42 Consideration of called-in applications

    (1) Subject to the following provisions of this section and to section 46 below, the Secretary of State, on considering a called-in application—

    (a) may determine that a licence shall be granted containing such provisions as he considers appropriate; or

    (b) if, having regard to the provisions of this Act, he considers it necessary or expedient to do so, may determine that no licence shall be granted.

    (2) Before determining a called-in application, the Secretary of State may, if he thinks fit—

    (a) cause a local inquiry to be held; or

    (b) afford to the applicant and the [Agency] an opportunity of appearing before, and being heard by, a person appointed by the Secretary of State for the purpose;

and the Secretary of State shall act as mentioned in paragraph (a) or (b) above if a request is made by the applicant or the [Agency] to be heard with respect to the application.

(3)	The provisions of sections 37, 38(1) and (3), 39(2) and 40 above shall apply in relation to any called-in application as if—

(a)	any reference in those provisions to the [Agency], except the references in sections 37(4)(b) and (6)(a) and 38(3)(a), were a reference to the Secretary of State; and

(b)	any reference to section 39(1) above were a reference to subsection (4) below.

(4)	In determining any called-in application and, in particular, in determining what (if any) direction to give under subsection (5) below, the Secretary of State shall consider whether any such direction would require the grant of a licence which would so authorise—

(a)	the abstraction of water; or

(b)	the flow of any inland waters to be obstructed or impeded by means of impounding works,

as to derogate from rights which, at the time when the direction in question is given, are protected rights for the purposes of this Chapter.

(5)	Where the decision of the Secretary of State on a called-in application is that a licence is to be granted, the decision shall include a direction to the [Agency] to grant a licence containing such provisions as may be specified in the direction.

(6)	The decision of the Secretary of State on any called-in application shall be final.

(7)	In this section "called-in application" means an application referred to the Secretary of State in accordance with directions under section 41 above.

[316]

NOTES

Sub-ss (2), (3), (5): words in square brackets substituted by the Environment Act 1995, s 120, Sch 22, para 128.

Appeals with respect to decisions on licence applications

43 Appeals to the Secretary of State

(1)	Where an application has been made to the [Agency] for a licence under this Chapter, the applicant may by notice appeal to the Secretary of State if—

(a)	the applicant is dissatisfied with the decision of the [Agency] on the application; or

(b)	the [Agency] fails within the period specified in subsection (2) below to give to the applicant either—

(i)	notice of the [Agency's] decision on the application; or

(ii)	notice that the application has been referred to the Secretary of State in accordance with any direction under section 41 above.

[(1A) This section is subject to section 114 of the 1995 Act (delegation or reference of appeals etc).]

(2)	The period mentioned in subsection (1)(b) above is—

(a)	except in a case falling within paragraph (b) below, such period as may be prescribed; and

(b)	where an extended period is at any time agreed in writing between the applicant and the [Agency], the extended period.

(3)	A notice of appeal under this section shall be served—

(a)	in such manner as may be prescribed; and

(b)	within such period as may be prescribed, being a period of not less than 28 days from, as the case may be—

      (i) the date on which the decision to which it relates was notified to the applicant; or

      (ii) the end of the period which, by virtue of subsection (2) above, is applicable for the purposes of subsection (1)(b) above.

(4) Where a notice is served under this section in respect of any application, the applicant shall, within the period prescribed for the purposes of subsection (3)(b) above, serve a copy of the notice on the [Agency].

(5) Where any representations in writing with respect to an application were made within the period specified for the purposes of the application in accordance with section 37(5) above, the Secretary of State shall, before determining an appeal under this section in respect of the application, require the [Agency] to serve a copy of the notice of appeal on each of the persons who made those representations.

[317]

NOTES

    Sub-ss (1), (2), (4), (5): words in square brackets substituted by the Environment Act 1995, s 120, Sch 22, para 128.

    Sub-s (1A): inserted by the Environment Act 1995, s 120, Sch 22, para 134.

    Regulations: see the Water Resources (Licences) Regulations 1965, SI 1965/534, regs 10(4), 12(1) (as construed in accordance with the Water Consolidation (Consequential Provisions) Act 1991, s 2(2), Sch 2, para 1(3)).

44 Determination of appeals

(1) Subject to the following provisions of this Chapter, where an appeal is brought under section 43 above, the Secretary of State—

    (a) may allow or dismiss the appeal or reverse or vary any part of the decision of the [Agency], whether the appeal relates to that part of the decision or not; and

    (b) may deal with the application as if it had been made to him in the first instance;

and for the purposes of this section an appeal by virtue of section 43(1)(b) above shall be taken to be an appeal against a refusal of the application.

(2) Before determining an appeal under section 43 above, the Secretary of State may, if he thinks fit—

    (a) cause a local inquiry to be held; or

    (b) afford to the applicant and the [Agency] an opportunity of appearing before, and being heard by, a person appointed by the Secretary of State for the purpose;

and the Secretary of State shall act as mentioned in paragraph (a) or (b) above if a request is made by the applicant or the [Agency] to be heard with respect to the appeal.

(3) The Secretary of State, in determining an appeal under section 43 above, shall take into account—

    (a) any further representations in writing received by him, within the prescribed period, from the persons mentioned in section 43(5) above; and

    (b) the requirements of the applicant, in so far as they appear to the Secretary of State to be reasonable requirements.

(4) In determining any appeal under section 43 above and, in particular, in determining what (if any) direction to give under subsection (6) below, the Secretary of State shall consider whether any such direction would require such a grant or variation of a licence as would so authorise—

    (a) the abstraction of water; or

    (b) the flow of any inland waters to be obstructed or impeded by means of impounding works, as to derogate from rights which, at the time when the direction in question is given, are protected rights for the purposes of this Chapter.

(5)   The provisions of sections 39(2) and 40 above shall apply in relation to any appeal under section 43 above as if—

(a) any reference in those provisions to the [Agency], were a reference to the Secretary of State; and

(b) the references to sections 38(3) and 39(1) above were references to subsections (3) and (4) above.

(6)   Where the decision on an appeal under section 43 above is that a licence is to be granted or to be varied or revoked, the decision shall include a direction to the [Agency], as the case may be—

(a) to grant a licence containing such provisions as may be specified in the direction;

(b) to vary the licence so as to contain such provisions as may be so specified; or

(c) to revoke the licence.

(7)   The decision of the Secretary of State on any appeal under section 43 above shall be final.

[318]

NOTES

Sub-ss (1), (2), (5), (6): words in square brackets substituted by the Environment Act 1995, s 120, Sch 22, para 128.

Regulations: see the Water Resources (Licences) Regulations 1965, SI 1965/534, reg 12(4) (as construed in accordance with the Water Consolidation (Consequential Provisions) Act 1991, s 2(2), Sch 2, para 1(3)).

45 Regulations with respect to appeals

(1)   The Secretary of State may by regulations make provision as to the manner in which appeals against decisions on applications for the grant, revocation or variation of licences under this Chapter are to be dealt with, including provision requiring the giving of notices of, and information relating to, the making of such appeals or decisions on any such appeals.

(2)   Without prejudice to the generality of subsection (1) above, provision shall be made by regulations under this section for securing that, in prescribed circumstances (being circumstances in which it appears to the Secretary of State that applications for licences under this Chapter would be of special concern to National Park . . . authorities)—

(a) notice of any appeal against the decision on such an application, will be served on any National Park . . . authority who made representations falling within paragraph (b) of section 34(3) above; and

(b) the Secretary of State, in determining the appeal, will take account of any further representations made by such an authority within such period and in such manner as may be prescribed.

(3)   Subsections (4) . . . of section 34 above shall apply for the purposes of this section as they apply for the purposes of that section.

[319]

NOTES

Sub-ss (2), (3): words omitted repealed by the Environment Act 1995, s 120, Sch 24.

Modification: references to a National Park planning authority modified by the Environment Act 1995, s 78, Sch 10, para 34.

Regulations: the Water Resources (Licences) Regulations 1965, SI 1965/534, reg 12 (partly having effect under this section by virtue of the Water Consolidation (Consequential Provisions) Act 1991, s 2(2), Sch 2, para 1(1), (2)).

Form, contents and effect of licences

46 Form and contents of licences

(1)   The Secretary of State may by regulations make provision as to the form of licences under this Chapter or of any class of such licences; but any regulations under this subsection shall have effect subject to the following provisions of this section and to any other express provision contained in, or having effect by virtue of, any other enactment contained in this Chapter.

(2)   Every licence under this Chapter to abstract water shall make—
    (a) provision as to the quantity of water authorised to be abstracted in pursuance of the licence from the source of supply to which the licence relates during a period or periods specified in the licence, including provision as to the way in which that quantity is to be measured or assessed for the purposes of this Chapter; and
    (b) provision for determining, by measurement or assessment, what quantity of water is to be taken to have been abstracted during any such period by the holder of the licence from the source of supply to which the licence relates.

(3)   Every licence under this Chapter to abstract water shall indicate the means by which water is authorised to be abstracted in pursuance of the licence, by reference either to specified works, machinery or apparatus or to works, machinery or apparatus fulfilling specified requirements.

(4)   Every licence under this Chapter to abstract water, except a licence granted to the [Agency], to a water undertaker or sewerage undertaker or to any person (not being a water undertaker) who proposes to abstract the water for the purpose of supplying it to others shall also specify the land on which, and the purposes for which, water abstracted in pursuance of the licence is to be used.

(5)   Every licence under this Chapter to abstract water shall state whether the licence is to remain in force until revoked or is to expire at a time specified in the licence.

(6)   Different provision may be made by the same licence with respect to any one or more of the following matters, that is to say—
    (a) the abstraction of water during different periods;
    (b) the abstraction of water from the same source of supply but at different points or by different means;
    (c) the abstraction of water for use for different purposes;
and any such provision as is mentioned in subsection (2) above may be made separately in relation to each of the matters for which (in accordance with this subsection) different provision is made in the licence.

(7)   Nothing in subsection (6) above shall be construed as preventing two or more licences from being granted to the same person to be held concurrently in respect of the same source of supply, if the licences authorise the abstraction of water at different points or by different means.

[320]

NOTES
    Sub-s (4): word in square brackets substituted by the Environment Act 1995, s 120, Sch 22, para 128.
    Regulations: the Water Resources (Licences) Regulations 1965, SI 1965/534, reg 10(6), Sch 3 (partly having effect under sub-s (1) of this section by virtue of the Water Consolidation (Consequential Provisions) Act 1991, s 2(2), Sch 2, para 1(1), (2)).

47 Holders of licence

(1)   Every licence under this Chapter to abstract water shall specify the person to whom the licence is granted.

(2)   The person to whom a licence under this Chapter is granted to abstract water or to obstruct or impede any inland waters and, in the case of a licence to obstruct or impede any inland waters, no other person is the holder of the licence for the purposes of this Act.

(3)   This section has effect subject to sections 49, 50 and 67 below and to any power under this Chapter to vary licences.

[321]

48 General effect of licence

(1)   For the purposes of this Chapter a person who is for the time being the holder of a licence under this Chapter to abstract water shall be taken to have a right to abstract water to the extent authorised by the licence and in accordance with the provisions contained in it.

(2)   In any action brought against a person in respect of the abstraction of water from a source of supply, it shall be a defence, subject to paragraph 2 of Schedule 7 to this Act, for him to prove—
  (a) that the water was abstracted in pursuance of a licence under this Chapter; and
  (b) that the provisions of the licence were complied with.

(3)   In any action brought against a person in respect of any obstruction or impeding of the flow of any inland waters at any point by means of impounding works, it shall be a defence for him to prove—
  (a) that the flow was so obstructed or impeded in pursuance of a licence under this Chapter;
  (b) that the obstructing or impeding was in the manner specified in that licence and to an extent not exceeding the extent so specified; and
  (c) that the other requirements of the licence (if any) were complied with.

(4)   Nothing in subsection (2) or (3) above shall exonerate a person from any action for negligence or breach of contract.

[322]

Succession to licences

49 Succession to licences to abstract where person ceases to occupy the relevant land

(1)   This section applies to a case where the holder of a licence under this Chapter to abstract water ("the prior holder") is the occupier of the whole of the land specified in the licence as the land on which water abstracted in pursuance of the licence is to be used ("the relevant land").

(2)   If—
  (a) the prior holder dies or, by reason of any other act or event, ceases to be the occupier of the whole of the relevant land and does not continue to be the occupier of any part of that land; and
  (b) either immediately after the death of the prior holder or the occurrence of that other act or event or subsequently, another person ("the successor") becomes the occupier of the whole of the relevant land,

the prior holder shall cease (if he would not otherwise do so) to be the holder of the licence and the successor shall become the holder of the licence.

(3)   Where the successor becomes the holder of a licence under subsection (2) above, he shall cease to be the holder of the licence at the end of the period of fifteen months beginning with the date on which he became the occupier of the relevant land unless before the end of that period he has given to the [Agency] notice of the change in the occupation of the relevant land.

(4)   Where any person who becomes the holder of a licence by virtue of the provisions of this section gives notice to the [Agency] in accordance with those provisions, the [Agency] shall vary the licence accordingly.

(5)   Where, by virtue of the provisions of this section, any person ceases to be the holder of a licence in such circumstances that no other person thereupon becomes the holder of it, the licence shall cease to have effect.

(6)   The preceding provisions of this section shall have effect without prejudice to any power to revoke or vary licences under this Chapter or to the powers conferred by section 50 below.

[323]

NOTES

Sub-ss (3), (4): words in square brackets substituted by the Environment Act 1995, s 120, Sch 22, para 128.

50 Succession where person becomes occupier of part of the relevant land

(1)   The Secretary of State may by regulations make provision, in relation to [cases in which the holder of a licence under this Chapter to abstract water ("the prior holder") is the occupier of the whole or part of the land specified in the licence as the land on which water abstracted in pursuance of the licence is to be used ("the relevant land")], for conferring succession rights, in such circumstances as may be specified in the regulations, on a person who becomes the occupier of part of the relevant land after—
    (a) the death of the prior holder; or
    (b) the occurrence of any other act or event whereby the prior holder ceases to be the occupier of the relevant land or of part of that land.

(2)   For the purposes of subsection (1) above succession rights are—
    (a) a right to become the holder of the licence, subject to provisions corresponding to subsection (3) of section 49 above; or
    (b) a right to apply for, and to the grant of, a new licence containing provisions (as to quantities of water and otherwise) determined, in accordance with the regulations made by the Secretary of State, by reference to the provisions of the original licence.

(3)   The Secretary of State may by regulations make provision for conferring on the prior holder, where he—
    (a) continues to be the occupier of part of the relevant land; but
    (b) ceases to be the occupier of another part of that land,
a right, in such circumstances as may be specified in the regulations, to apply for, and to the grant of, a new licence containing such provisions as are mentioned in subsection (2)(b) above.

(4)   Regulations under this section may provide that the provisions of this Chapter shall have effect in relation—
    (a) to an application for a licence made by virtue of the regulations; or
    (b) to a person entitled to make such an application,
subject to such modifications as may be specified in the regulations.

(5)   Where any person who becomes the holder of a licence by virtue of the provisions of any regulations under this section gives notice to the [Agency] in accordance with those provisions, the [Agency] shall vary the licence accordingly.

(6) Where, by virtue of the provisions of any regulations under this section, any person ceases to be the holder of a licence in such circumstances that no other person thereupon becomes the holder of it, the licence shall cease to have effect.

(7) The preceding provisions of this section shall have effect without prejudice to the exercise of any power to revoke or vary licences under this Chapter.

[324]

NOTES

Sub-s (1): words in square brackets substituted with retrospective effect by the Environment Act 1995, s 120, Sch 22, para 135.

Sub-s (5): words in square brackets substituted by the Environment Act 1995, s 120, Sch 22, para 128.

Regulations: the Water Resources (Succession to Licences) Regulations 1969, SI 1969/976 (having effect under this section by virtue of the Water Consolidation (Consequential Provisions) Act 1991, s 2(2), Sch 2, para 1(1), (2)).

Modification of licences

51 Modification on application of licence holder

(1) The holder of a licence under this Chapter may apply to the [Agency] to revoke the licence and, on any such application, the [Agency] shall revoke the licence accordingly.

(2) The holder of a licence under this Chapter may apply to the [Agency] to vary the licence.

(3) Subject to subsection (4) below, the provisions of sections 37 to 44 above shall apply (with the necessary modifications) to applications under subsection (2) above, and to the variation of licences in pursuance of such applications, as they apply to applications for, and the grant of, licences under this Chapter.

(4) Where the variation proposed in an application under subsection (2) above is limited to reducing the quantity of water authorised to be abstracted in pursuance of the licence during one or more periods—
   (a) sections 37 and 38(1) above shall not apply by virtue of subsection (3) above; and
   (b) sections 43 and 44 above, as applied by that subsection, shall have effect as if subsection (5) of section 43 and paragraph (a) of section 44(3) were omitted.

[325]

NOTES

Sub-ss (1), (2): words in square brackets substituted by the Environment Act 1995, s 120, Sch 22, para 128.

52 Proposals for modification at instance of the [Agency] or Secretary of State

(1) Where it appears to the [Agency] that a licence under this Chapter should be revoked or varied, the [Agency] may formulate proposals for revoking or varying the licence.

(2) Where—
   (a) it appears to the Secretary of State (either in consequence of representations made to the Secretary of State or otherwise) that a licence under this Chapter ought to be reviewed; but
   (b) no proposals for revoking or varying the licence have been formulated by the [Agency] under subsection (1) above,

the Secretary of State may, as he may consider appropriate in the circumstances, give the [Agency] a direction under subsection (3) below.

(3) A direction under this subsection may—
  (a) direct the [Agency] to formulate proposals for revoking the licence in question; or
  (b) direct the [Agency] to formulate proposals for varying that licence in such manner as may be specified in the direction.

(4) Notice in the prescribed form of any proposals formulated under this section with respect to any licence shall—
  (a) be served on the holder of the licence; and
  (b) be published in the London Gazette and, at least once in each of two successive weeks, in one or more newspapers (other than the London Gazette) circulating in the relevant locality.

(5) If—
  (a) a licence with respect to which any proposals are formulated under this section relates to any inland waters; and
  (b) the proposals provide for variation of that licence,
a copy of the notice for the purposes of subsection (4) above shall, not later than the date on which it is first published otherwise than in the London Gazette, be served on any navigation authority, harbour authority or conservancy authority having functions in relation to those waters at a place where the licence, if varied in accordance with the proposals, would authorise water to be abstracted or impounded.

(6) A notice for the purposes of subsection (4) above, in addition to any other matters required to be contained in that notice, shall—
  (a) name a place within the relevant locality where a copy of the proposals, and of any map, plan or other document prepared in connection with them, will be open to inspection by the public, free of charge, at all reasonable hours during a period specified in the notice in accordance with subsection (7) below; and
  (b) state that, at any time before the end of that period—
    (i) the holder of the licence may give notice in writing to the [Agency] objecting to the proposals; and
    (ii) any other person may make representations in writing to the [Agency] with respect to the proposals.

(7) The period specified in a notice for the purposes of subsection (6) above shall be a period which—
  (a) begins not earlier than the date on which the notice is first published in a newspaper other than the London Gazette; and
  (b) ends not less than twenty-eight days from that date and not less than twenty-five days from the date on which the notice is published in the London Gazette.

(8) In this section "the relevant locality" means the locality in which the place or places where the licence authorises water to be abstracted or impounded is or are situated.

[326]

NOTES

Section heading: word in square brackets substituted by the Environment Act 1995, s 120, Sch 22, para 128.

Sub-ss (1)–(3), (6): words in square brackets substituted by the Environment Act 1995, s 120, Sch 22, para 128.

Regulations: see the Water Resources (Licences) Regulations 1965, SI 1965/534, reg 18, Sch 2, Form N5 (as construed in accordance with the Water Consolidation (Consequential Provisions) Act 1991, s 2(2), Sch 2, para 1(3)).

---

53 Modification in pursuance of proposals under section 52

(1)   Subject to the following provisions of this section, where the [Agency] has formulated any proposals under section 52 above with respect to any licence under this Chapter, it may—

(a) if the proposals are for the revocation of the licence, revoke the licence; and

(b) if the proposals are proposals for varying the licence, vary the licence in accordance with those proposals or, with the consent of the holder of the licence, in any other way.

(2)   The [Agency] shall not proceed with any proposals formulated under section 52 above before the end of the period specified, in accordance with subsection (7) of that section, for the purposes in relation to those proposals of subsection (6) of that section.

(3)   If no notice under subsection (4) below is given to the [Agency] before the end of the period mentioned in subsection (2) above, the [Agency] may proceed with the proposals.

(4)   If the holder of the licence gives notice to the [Agency] objecting to the proposals before the end of the period mentioned in subsection (2) above, the [Agency] shall refer the proposals to the Secretary of State, with a copy of the notice of objection.

(5)   Where the [Agency] proceeds with any proposals under subsection (3) above and the proposals are proposals for varying the licence, the provisions of sections 38(3), 39(1) and (2) and 40 above shall apply (with the necessary modifications) to any action of the [Agency] in proceeding with the proposals as they apply to the action of the [Agency] in dealing with an application for a licence.

[327]

NOTES

Sub-ss (1)–(5): words in square brackets substituted by the Environment Act 1995, s 120, Sch 22, para 128.

54 Reference of modification proposals to the Secretary of State

(1)   Where any proposals of the [Agency] with respect to a licence are referred to the Secretary of State in accordance with subsection (4) of section 53 above, the Secretary of State shall consider—

(a) the proposals;

(b) the objection of the holder of the licence; and

(c) any representations in writing relating to the proposals which were received by the [Agency] before the end of the period mentioned in subsection (2) of that section,

and, subject to subsection (2) below, shall determine (according to whether the proposals are for the revocation or variation of the licence) the question whether the licence should be revoked or the question whether it should be varied as mentioned in subsection (1)(b) of that section.

(2)   Before determining under this section whether a licence should be revoked or varied in a case in which proposals have been formulated under section 52 above, the Secretary of State may, if he thinks fit—

(a) cause a local inquiry to be held; or

(b) afford to the holder of the licence and the [Agency] an opportunity of appearing before, and being heard by, a person appointed by the Secretary of State for the purpose;

and the Secretary of State shall act as mentioned in paragraph (a) or (b) above if a request is made by the holder of the licence or the [Agency] to be heard with respect to the proposals.

(3)   In determining under this section whether a licence should be varied and, if so, what directions should be given under subsection (5) below, the Secretary of State shall consider whether any such direction would require such a variation of the licence as would so authorise—

(a) the abstraction of water; or

(b) the flow of any inland waters to be obstructed or impeded by means of impounding works,

as to derogate from rights which, at the time when the direction is given, are protected rights for the purposes of this Chapter.

(4)   The provisions of sections 39(2) and 40 above shall apply in relation to any proposals referred to the Secretary of State in accordance with section 53(4) above as if in those provisions—

(a) any reference to the [Agency] were a reference to the Secretary of State;

(b) any reference to the application were a reference to the proposals; and

(c) the references to sections 38(3) and 39(1) were references to subsections (1) and (3) above.

(5)   Where the decision of the Secretary of State on a reference in accordance with section 53(4) above is that the licence in question should be revoked or varied, the decision shall include a direction to the [Agency] to revoke the licence or, as the case may be, to vary it so as to contain such provisions as may be specified in the direction.

(6)   A decision of the Secretary of State under this section with respect to any proposals shall be final.

[328]

NOTES
    Sub-ss (1), (2), (4), (5): words in square brackets substituted by the Environment Act 1995, s 120, Sch 22, para 128.

55 Application for modification of licence by owner of fishing rights

(1)   Subject to the following provisions of this section and to Schedule 7 to this Act, where a licence under this Chapter authorises abstraction from any inland waters in respect of which no minimum acceptable flow has been determined under Chapter I of this Part, any person who is the owner of fishing rights in respect of those inland waters may apply to the Secretary of State for the revocation or variation of the licence.

(2)   No application shall be made under this section in respect of any licence except at a time after the end of the period of one year beginning with the date on which the licence was granted but before a minimum acceptable flow has been determined in relation to the waters in question.

(3)   Any application under this section made by a person as owner of fishing rights in respect of any inland waters shall be made on the grounds that, in his capacity as owner of those rights, he has sustained loss or damage which is directly attributable to the abstraction of water in pursuance of the licence in question and either—

(a) he is not entitled to a protected right for the purposes of this Chapter in respect of those inland waters; or

(b) the loss or damage which he has sustained in his capacity as owner of those rights is not attributable to any such breach of statutory duty as is mentioned in subsection (2) or (3) of section 60 below or is in addition to any loss or damage attributable to any such breach.

(4)   Where an application is made under this section in respect of any licence, the applicant shall serve notice in the prescribed form on the [Agency] and on the

holder of the licence, stating that each of them is entitled, at any time before the end of the period of twenty-eight days beginning with the date of service of the notice, to make representations in writing to the Secretary of State with respect to the application.

(5) In this section and section 56 below "fishing rights", in relation to any inland waters, means any right (whether it is an exclusive right or a right in common with one or more other persons) to fish in those waters, where the right in question—
(a) constitutes or is included in an interest in land; or
(b) is exercisable by virtue of an exclusive licence granted for valuable consideration;

and any reference to an owner of fishing rights is a reference to the person for the time being entitled to those rights.

(6) In this section any reference to a right included in an interest in land is a reference to a right which is exercisable only by virtue of, and as a right incidental to, the ownership of that interest.

[329]

NOTES
Sub-s (4): word in square brackets substituted by the Environment Act 1995, s 120, Sch 22, para 128.
Regulations: see the Water Resources (Licences) Regulations 1965, SI 1965/534, reg 19, Sch 2, Form N6 (as construed in accordance with the Water Consolidation (Consequential Provisions) Act 1991, s 2(2), Sch 2, para 1(3)).

56 Determination of application under section 55

(1) The Secretary of State, in determining any application under section 55 above in respect of any licence, shall take into account any representations in writing received by him, within the period mentioned in subsection (4) of that section, from the [Agency] or from the holder of the licence.

(2) Before determining on an application under section 55 above whether a licence should be revoked or varied the Secretary of State may, if he thinks fit—
(a) cause a local inquiry to be held, or
(b) afford to the applicant, the holder of the licence and the [Agency] an opportunity of appearing before, and being heard by, a person appointed by the Secretary of State for the purpose;

and the Secretary of State shall act as mentioned in paragraph (a) or (b) above if a request is made by the applicant, the holder of the licence or the [Agency] to be heard with respect to the proposals.

(3) Subject to subsections (4) and (5) below, on an application under section 55 above in respect of any licence, the Secretary of State shall not determine that the licence shall be revoked or varied unless—
(a) the grounds of the application, as mentioned in subsection (3) of that section, are established to his satisfaction; and
(b) he is satisfied that the extent of the loss or damage which the applicant has sustained, as mentioned in that subsection, is such as to justify the revocation or variation of the licence.

(4) On an application under section 55 above in respect of any licence, the Secretary of State shall not determine that the licence shall be revoked or varied if he is satisfied that the fact that the abstraction of water in pursuance of the licence caused the loss or damage which the applicant has sustained, as mentioned in subsection (3) of that section, was wholly or mainly attributable to exceptional shortage of rain or to an accident or other unforeseen act or event not caused by, and outside the control of, the [Agency].

(5)   Where the Secretary of State determines, on an application under section 55 above, that a licence shall be varied, the variation shall be limited to that which, in the opinion of the Secretary of State, is requisite having regard to the loss or damage which the applicant has sustained as mentioned in subsection (3) of that section.

(6)   Where the decision of the Secretary of State on an application under section 55 above in respect of any licence is that the licence should be revoked or varied, the decision shall include a direction to the [Agency] to revoke the licence or, as the case may be, to vary it so as to contain such provisions as may be specified in the direction.

(7)   A decision of the Secretary of State on an application under section 55 above shall be final.

[330]

NOTES
    Sub-ss (1), (2), (4), (6): words in square brackets substituted by the Environment Act 1995, s 120, Sch 22, para 128.

57 Emergency variation of licences for spray irrigation purposes

(1)   This section applies where at any time—
    (a) one or more licences under this Chapter are in force in relation to a source of supply authorising water abstracted in pursuance of the licences to be used for the purpose of spray irrigation, or for that purpose together with other purposes; and
    (b) by reason of exceptional shortage of rain or other emergency, it appears to the [Agency] that it is necessary to impose a temporary restriction on the abstraction of water for use for that purpose.

(2)   Subject to subsections (3) and (4) below, where this section applies the [Agency] may serve a notice on the holder of any of the licences reducing, during such period as may be specified in the notice, the quantity of water authorised to be abstracted in pursuance of the licence from the source of supply for use for the purpose of spray irrigation; and, in relation to that period, the licence shall have effect accordingly subject to that reduction.

(3)   The [Agency] shall not serve a notice under this section in respect of abstraction of water from underground strata unless it appears to the [Agency] that such abstraction is likely to affect the flow, level or volume of any inland waters which are neither discrete waters nor inland waters comprised in an order under section 33 above.

(4)   In the exercise of the power conferred by this section in a case where there are two or more licences under this Chapter in force authorising abstraction from the same source of supply either at the same point or at points which, in the opinion of the [Agency], are not far distant from each other—
    (a) the [Agency] shall not serve a notice under this section on the holder of one of the licences unless a like notice is served on the holders of the other licences in respect of the same period; and
    (b) the reductions imposed by the notices on the holders of the licences shall be so calculated as to represent, as nearly as appears to the [Agency] to be practicable, the same proportion of the quantity of water authorised by the licences (apart from the notices) to be abstracted for use for the purpose of spray irrigation.

(5)   The provisions of this section shall have effect without prejudice to the exercise of any power conferred by sections 51 to 54 above.

[331]

NOTES
    Sub-ss (1)–(4): words in square brackets substituted by the Environment Act 1995, s 120, Sch 22, para 128.

58   (*Repealed by the Environment Act 1995, s 120(1), (3), Sch 22, para 136, Sch 24.*)

59 Regulations with respect to modification applications

(1)   The Secretary of State may by regulations make provision as to the manner in which applications for the revocation or variation of licences under this Chapter are to be dealt with, including provision requiring the giving of notices of, and information relating to, the making of such applications or decisions on any such applications.

(2)   Subsection (1) above shall have effect subject to any express provision contained in, or having effect by virtue of, any other enactment contained in this Chapter; and any regulations made under this section shall have effect subject to any such express provision.

[332]

NOTES
Regulations: the Water Resources (Licences) Regulations 1965, SI 1965/534, Pt II (regs 4–12) (partly having effect under this section by virtue of the Water Consolidation (Consequential Provisions) Act 1991, s 2(2), Sch 2, para 1(1), (2)).

Remedies and compensation in respect of infringement of protected rights etc

60 Liability of the [Agency] for derogation from protected right

(1)   A breach of the duty imposed by subsection (1) of section 39 above (including that duty as applied by section 51(3) or 53(5) above) shall neither invalidate the grant or variation of a licence nor be enforceable by any criminal proceedings, by prohibition or injunction or by action against any person other than the [Agency].

(2)   Instead, the duty referred to in subsection (1) above shall be enforceable, at the suit of any person entitled to a protected right for the purposes of this Chapter, by an action against the [Agency] for damages for breach of statutory duty.

(3)   Where under any provision of this Chapter, the [Agency] is directed by the Secretary of State to grant or vary a licence, and the licence, as granted or varied in compliance with the direction, authorises derogation from protected rights, then—
   (a) the grant or variation of the licence shall, as between the [Agency] and the person entitled to those rights, have effect as a breach on the part of the [Agency] of a statutory duty not to authorise derogation from those rights; and
   (b) subsection (2) above shall apply in relation to that statutory duty as it applies in relation to the duty imposed by section 39(1) above.

(4)   Subsection (3) above shall be without prejudice to the duty of the [Agency], to comply with the direction in question, but that duty shall not afford any defence in an action brought by virtue of paragraph (b) of that subsection.

(5)   In any action brought against the [Agency] in pursuance of this section it shall be a defence for the [Agency] to show that the fact, as the case may be—
   (a) that the abstraction of water authorised by the licence, as granted or varied by the [Agency], derogated from the plaintiff's protected right; or
   (b) that the obstruction or impeding of the flow of the inland waters authorised by the licence, as so granted or varied, derogated from the plaintiff's protected right,
was wholly or mainly attributable to exceptional shortage of rain or to an accident or other unforeseen act or event not caused by, and outside the control of, the [Agency].

(6)   This section has effect subject to the provision made by Schedule 7 to this Act.

(7)   In this section any reference to authorising a derogation from protected rights is a reference to so authorising—
   (a) the abstraction of water; or
   (b) the flow of any inland waters to be obstructed or impeded by means of impounding works,

as to derogate from rights which, at the time of the authorisation, are protected rights for the purposes of this Chapter.

[333]

NOTES
   Section heading: word in square brackets substituted by the Environment Act 1995, s 120, Sch 22, para 128.
   Sub-ss (1)–(5): words in square brackets substituted by the Environment Act 1995, s 120, Sch 22, para 128.

61 Compensation where licence modified on direction of the Secretary of State

(1)   Where a licence is revoked or varied in pursuance of a direction under section 54 or 55 above and it is shown that the holder of the licence—
   (a) has incurred expenditure in carrying out work which is rendered abortive by the revocation or variation; or
   (b) has otherwise sustained loss or damage which is directly attributable to the revocation or variation,

the [Agency] shall pay him compensation in respect of that expenditure, loss or damage.

(2)   For the purposes of this section, any expenditure incurred in the preparation of plans for the purposes of any work, or upon other similar matters preparatory to any work, shall be taken to be included in the expenditure incurred in carrying out that work.

(3)   Subject to subsection (2) above and to Schedule 7 to this Act, no compensation shall be paid under this section—
   (a) in respect of any work carried out before the grant of the licence which is revoked or varied; or
   (b) in respect of any other loss or damage arising out of anything done or omitted to be done before the grant of that licence.

(4)   No compensation shall be payable under this section in respect of a licence to abstract water, if it is shown that no water was abstracted in pursuance of the licence during the period of seven years ending with the date on which notice of the proposals for revoking or varying the licence was served on the holder of the licence.

(5)   Any question of disputed compensation under this section shall be referred to and determined by the Lands Tribunal; and in relation to the determination of any such compensation the provisions of sections 2 and 4 of the Land Compensation Act 1961 shall apply, subject to any necessary modifications.

(6)   For the purpose of assessing any compensation under this section, in so far as that compensation is in respect of loss or damage consisting of depreciation of the value of an interest in land, the rules set out in section 5 of the Land Compensation Act 1961 shall, so far as applicable and subject to any necessary modifications, have effect as they have effect for the purpose of assessing compensation for the compulsory acquisition of an interest in land.

(7)   Where the interest in land, in respect of which any compensation falls to be assessed in accordance with subsection (6) above, is subject to a mortgage—

(a) the compensation shall be assessed as if the interest were not subject to the mortgage;

(b) a claim for the compensation may be made by any mortgagee of the interest, but without prejudice to the making of a claim by the person entitled to the interest;

(c) no such compensation shall be payable in respect of the interest of the mortgagee (as distinct from the interest which is subject to the mortgage);

(d) any such compensation which is payable in respect of the interest which is subject to the mortgage shall be paid to the mortgagee or, if there is more than one mortgagee, to the first mortgagee, and shall in either case be applied by him as if it were proceeds of sale.

[334]

NOTES

Sub-s (1): word in square brackets substituted by the Environment Act 1995, s 120, Sch 22, para 128.

62 Compensation for owner of fishing rights applying under section 55

(1)   Where a licence is revoked or varied on an application under section 55 above, the applicant shall be entitled to compensation from the [Agency] in respect of the loss or damage which he has sustained as mentioned in subsection (3) of that section.

(2)   Where, on an application under section 55 above for the revocation or variation of a licence, the Secretary of State determines—

(a) that the grounds of the application (as mentioned in subsection (3) of that section) have been established to his satisfaction; but

(b) that the licence shall not be revoked or varied in pursuance of that application,

he shall certify accordingly for the purposes of the following provisions of this section.

(3)   Unless within the period of six months from the date on which a certificate under subsection (2) above is granted either—

(a) notice to treat for the acquisition of the fishing rights of the applicant, or of an interest in land which includes those rights, has been served by the [Agency]; or

(b) an offer has been made by the [Agency] to the owner of those rights to acquire them on compulsory purchase terms or, where the rights subsist only as rights included in an interest in land, to acquire that interest on such terms,

the owner of the fishing rights shall be entitled to compensation from the [Agency].

(4)   The amount of the compensation payable under subsection (3) above in respect of any fishing rights shall be the amount by which—

(a) the value of those rights; or

(b) where they subsist only as rights included in an interest in land, the value of that interest,

is depreciated by the operation of section 48(2) above in relation to the licence to which the application related.

(5)   Any question of disputed compensation under this section shall be referred to and determined by the Lands Tribunal; and in relation to the determination of any such compensation the provisions of sections 2 and 4 of the Land Compensation Act 1961 shall apply, subject to any necessary modifications.

(6)   For the purposes of this section a right or interest is acquired on compulsory purchase terms if it is acquired on terms that the price payable shall be equal to and shall, in default of agreement, be determined in like manner as the compensation

which would be payable in respect thereof if the right or interest were acquired compulsorily by the [Agency].

(7) Where—
    (a) the Secretary of State, on an application under section 55 above, determines that the licence to which the application relates shall not be revoked or varied and grants a certificate under subsection (2) above; and
    (b) notice to treat for the acquisition of the fishing rights to which the application related, or of an interest in land in which those rights are included, has been served by the [Agency] within the period of six months from the date on which that certificate is granted,

then, for the purpose of assessing compensation in respect of any compulsory acquisition in pursuance of that notice to treat, no account shall be taken of any depreciation of the value of the fishing rights, or of the interest in question, which is applicable to the operation, in relation to that licence, of section 48(2) above.

(8) Subsections (5) and (6) of section 55 above shall apply for construing references in this section to fishing rights or to rights included in an interest in land as they have effect for construing such references in that section.

[335]

NOTES
    Sub-ss (1), (3), (6), (7): words in square brackets substituted by the Environment Act 1995, s 120, Sch 22, para 128.

63 Secretary of State to indemnify [Agency] in certain cases

(1) Where—
    (a) the [Agency] is liable under section 60 above to pay damages to any person in consequence of the grant or variation of a licence in compliance with a direction given by the Secretary of State; and
    (b) the [Agency] pay to that person any sum in satisfaction of that liability,

then, whether an action for recovery of those damages has been brought or not, the Secretary of State may, if he thinks fit, pay to the [Agency] the whole or such part as he considers appropriate of the relevant amount.

(2) If—
    (a) proposals for revoking or varying the licence, in a case falling within subsection (1) above, are formulated by the [Agency], or an application with respect to any licence is made under section 55 above;
    (b) in consequence of those proposals or that application, the licence is revoked or varied; and
    (c) compensation in respect of the revocation or variation is payable by the [Agency] under section 61 above,

the Secretary of State may, if he thinks fit, pay to the [Agency] the whole or such part as he considers appropriate of the relevant amount.

(3) Where—
    (a) the Secretary of State determines under section 55 above—
        (i) that a licence granted in compliance with a direction given by the Secretary of State shall be revoked or varied; or
        (ii) that a licence shall not be revoked or varied;
        and
    (b) in consequence of that determination, compensation is payable by the [Agency] under section 62 above,

the Secretary of State may, if he thinks fit, pay to the [Agency] the whole or such part as he considers appropriate of the relevant amount.

(4)   In this section "the relevant amount" means—

(a) for the purposes of subsection (1) above, the amount of the sum paid by the [Agency] and, if an action has been brought against the [Agency] in respect of the liability mentioned in that subsection, the amount of any costs reasonably incurred by the [Agency] in connection with the action (including any costs of the plaintiff which the [Agency] was required to pay); and

(b) for the purposes of subsections (2) and (3) above, the amount of the compensation and, if any question relating to that compensation is referred to the Lands Tribunal, the amount of any costs reasonably incurred by the [Agency] in connection with that reference (including any costs of the claimant which the [Agency] is required to pay).

[336]

NOTES

Section heading: word in square brackets substituted by the Environment Act 1995, s 120, Sch 22, para 128.

Sub-ss (1)–(4): words in square brackets substituted by the Environment Act 1995, s 120, Sch 22, para 128.

Supplemental provisions of Chapter II

64 Abstracting and impounding by the [Agency]

(1)   The provisions of this Chapter shall have effect—

(a) in relation to the abstraction of water by the [Agency] from sources of supply; and

(b) in relation to the construction or alteration by the [Agency] of impounding works,

subject to such exceptions and modifications as may be prescribed.

(2)   Regulations under this section may, in particular, provide for securing—

(a) that any licence required by the [Agency] in relation to the matters mentioned in subsection (1) above shall be granted (or be deemed to be granted) by the Secretary of State, and not be granted by the [Agency];

(b) that, in such cases and subject to such conditions as may be prescribed, any licence so required by the [Agency] shall be deemed to be granted by the Secretary of State unless the Secretary of State requires an application for the licence to be made to him by the [Agency]; and

(c) that where a licence is deemed to be granted as mentioned in paragraph (b) above, the [Agency] shall give such notice of that fact as may be prescribed.

(3)   Without prejudice to the preceding provisions of this section, section 52 above shall not apply in relation to any licence which by virtue of any regulations under this section is granted or deemed to have been granted by the Secretary of State, except in accordance with regulations under this section.

[337]

NOTES

Section heading: word in square brackets substituted by the Environment Act 1995, s 120, Sch 22, para 128.

Sub-ss (1), (2): words in square brackets substituted by the Environment Act 1995, s 120, Sch 22, para 128.

Regulations: the Water Resources (Licences) Regulations 1965, SI 1965/534, regs 13–15 (partly having effect under this section by virtue of the Water Consolidation (Consequential Provisions) Act 1991, s 2(2), Sch 2, para 1(1), (2)).

65 Licences of right

Schedule 7 to this Act shall have effect for the purposes of giving effect to provisions conferring an entitlement to licences under this Chapter and with respect to licences granted in pursuance of that entitlement or the entitlement conferred by section 33 of the Water Resources Act 1963 or paragraph 30 or 31 of Schedule 26 to the Water Act 1989.

[338]

66 Inland waters owned or managed by British Waterways Board

(1)   This section applies to all inland waters owned or managed by the British Waterways Board ("the Board"), except any such inland waters to which the Secretary of State may by order made by statutory instrument direct that this section shall not apply.

(2)   In respect of abstraction from any inland waters to which this section applies—
   (a)   no person other than the Board or a person authorised for the purpose by the Board may be given a consent for the purposes of section 27(2) above;
   (b)   no person other than the Board shall be entitled to apply for a licence under this Chapter;
   (c)   in relation to any application by the Board for a licence under this Chapter—
      (i)   section 35 above shall not apply; and
      (ii) section 37 above shall apply as if subsection (1) of that section did not require the service of any copy of the notice mentioned in paragraph (a) of that subsection on any navigation authority, harbour authority, conservancy authority or drainage board.

(3)   Before making an order under subsection (1) above, the Secretary of State shall consult the Board and the [Agency].

[339]

NOTES

Sub-s (3): word in square brackets substituted by the Environment Act 1995, s 120, Sch 22, para 128.

Orders: the Inland Waters of the British Waterways Board Order 1965, SI 1965/1193 (having effect under this section by virtue of the Water Consolidation (Consequential Provisions) Act 1991, s 2(2), Sch 2, para 1(1), (2)).

67 Ecclesiastical property

(1)   Where the relevant land belongs to a benefice—
   (a)   an application for a licence under this Chapter may be made by the Church Commissioners if the benefice is for the time being vacant; and
   (b)   any reference in this Chapter to the applicant for a licence shall be construed—
      (i)   in relation to any time when the benefice in question is vacant, as a reference to the Church Commissioners; and
      (ii) in relation to any time when there is an incumbent of the benefice, as a reference to that incumbent.

(2)   Where the relevant land belongs to a benefice, any licence under this Chapter shall provide that (notwithstanding anything in the preceding provisions of this Chapter) whoever is for the time being the incumbent of the benefice shall be the holder of the licence.

(3)   Where a licence under this Chapter provides as mentioned in subsection (2) above—
   (a)   the licence shall not be required to specify the person to whom the licence is granted; and

(b) the licence shall be deemed to be held by the Church Commissioners at any time when the benefice in question is vacant.

(4) So much of any compensation falling to be paid under this Chapter as is payable—

(a) in respect of damage to land which is ecclesiastical property and to the owner of the fee simple in the land; or

(b) in respect of depreciation of the value of the fee simple in land which is ecclesiastical property,

shall be paid (where the fee simple is vested in any person other than the Church Commissioners) to them, instead of to the person in whom the fee simple is vested.

(5) Any sums paid under subsection (4) above to the Church Commissioners with reference to any land shall—

(a) if the land is not consecrated, be applied by them for the purposes for which the proceeds of a sale by agreement of the fee simple in the land would be applicable under any enactment or Measure authorising such a sale or disposing of the proceeds of such a sale; and

(b) if the land is consecrated, be applied by them in such manner as they may determine.

(6) Where—

(a) the Church Commissioners are required, by virtue of subsection (3)(b) above, to pay any fee or other charge in respect of a licence under this Chapter; and

(b) any moneys are then payable by the Commissioners to the incumbent of the benefice in question or subsequently become so payable,

the Commissioners shall be entitled to retain out of those moneys an amount not exceeding the amount of that fee or other charge.

(7) Where under any provision of this Chapter a document is required to be served on an owner of land and the land is ecclesiastical property, a copy of the document shall be served on the Church Commissioners.

(8) In this section —

"benefice" means an ecclesiastical benefice of the Church of England;

"ecclesiastical property" means land which—

(a) belongs to a benefice;

(b) is or forms part of a church subject to the jurisdiction of the bishop of any diocese of the Church of England or the site of a church so subject; or

(c) is or forms part of a burial ground so subject;

and

"the relevant land", in relation to a licence under this Chapter or an application for such a licence, means—

(a) the land on which water abstracted in pursuance of the licence is to be, or is proposed to be, used; or

(b) in the case of a licence for the purposes of section 25 above or an application for such a licence—

(i) the land on which any part of the impounding works is to be, or is proposed to be, constructed; or

(ii) in relation to an alteration of impounding works, the land on which any part of those works is situated or is to be, or is proposed to be, situated.

[340]

68 *(Repealed by the Environment Act 1995, s 120(1), (3), Sch 22, para 137, Sch 24.)*

69 Validity of decisions of Secretary of State and related proceedings

(1)   Except as provided by the following provisions of this section, the validity of a decision of the Secretary of State on—
   (a) any appeal to the Secretary of State under this Chapter; or
   (b) any reference to the Secretary of State in pursuance of a direction under section 41 above or in pursuance of section 53(4) above,
shall not be questioned in any legal proceedings whatsoever.

(2)   If, in the case of any such appeal or reference, the [Agency] or the other party desires to question the validity of the decision of the Secretary of State on the grounds—
   (a) that the decision is not within the powers of this Act; or
   (b) that any of the requirements of, or of any regulations made under, this Chapter which are applicable to the appeal or reference have not been complied with,
the [Agency] or, as the case may be, the other party may, at any time within the period of six weeks beginning with the date on which the decision is made, make an application to the High Court under this section.

(3)   On any application under this section, the High Court may by interim order suspend the operation of the decision to which the application relates until the final determination of the proceedings.

(4)   If the High Court is satisfied, on an application under this section—
   (a) that the decision to which the application relates is not within the powers of this Act; or
   (b) that the interests of the person making the application under this section have been substantially prejudiced by a failure to comply with any of the requirements mentioned in subsection (2)(b) above,
the High Court may quash the decision.

(5)   . . .

(6)   In this section—
      "decision" includes a direction; and
      "other party"—
         (a) in relation to an appeal, means the appellant;
         (b) in relation to a reference in pursuance of a direction under section 41 above, means the applicant for the licence or, where that section applies by virtue of section 51(3) above, for the revocation or variation; and
         (c) in relation to a reference in pursuance of section 53(4) above, means (subject, without prejudice to their application to the other provisions of this Chapter, to subsections (6) and (7) of section 25 above) the holder of the licence.

[341]

NOTES
   Sub-s (2): words in square brackets substituted by the Environment Act 1995, s 120, Sch 22, para 128.
   Sub-s (5): repealed by the Environment Act 1995, s 120, Sch 22, para 138, Sch 24.

70 Civil liability under Chapter II

Except in so far as this Act otherwise expressly provides and subject to the provisions of section 18 of the Interpretation Act 1978 (which relates to offences under two or more laws), the restrictions imposed by sections 24, 25 and 30 above shall not be construed as—
   (a) conferring a right of action in any civil proceedings (other than proceedings for the recovery of a fine) in respect of any contravention of those restrictions;

(b) affecting any restriction imposed by or under any other enactment, whether contained in a public general Act or in a local or private Act; or

(c) derogating from any right of action or other remedy (whether civil or criminal) in proceedings instituted otherwise than under this Chapter.

[342]

71 Modification of local enactments

(1)   If it appears to the Secretary of State by whom an order is made under a provision of this Chapter to which this section applies that any local enactment passed or made before the relevant date—

(a) is inconsistent with any of the provisions of that order; or

(b) requires to be amended or adapted, having regard to any of the provisions of that order,

the Secretary of State may by order repeal, amend or adapt that enactment to such extent, or in such manner, as he may consider appropriate.

(2)   Any order under this section may include such transitional, incidental, supplementary and consequential provisions as the Secretary of State may consider necessary or expedient.

(3)   The power to make an order under this section shall be exercisable by statutory instrument subject to annulment in pursuance of a resolution of either House of Parliament.

(4)   This section applies to the following provisions of this Chapter, that is to say, sections 33, 66, 68 and 72(5).

(5)   In this section—
"local enactment" means—

(a) a local or private Act;

(b) a public general Act relating to London;

(c) an order or scheme made under an Act, confirmed by Parliament or brought into operation in accordance with special parliamentary procedure; or

(d) an enactment in a public general Act amending a local or private Act or any such order or scheme;

"relevant date" means the date which was the second appointed day for the purposes of section 133 of the Water Resources Act 1963.

(6)   The provisions of this section shall have effect without prejudice to the exercise of any other power to repeal, amend or adapt local enactments which is conferred by any other enactment.

[343]

72 Interpretation of Chapter II

(1)   In this Chapter—
"derogate", in relation to a protected right, shall be construed in accordance with section 39(4) above;
"flow" shall be construed subject to section 23(3) above;
"impounding works" has the meaning given by section 25(8) above;
"licence", in relation to the variation or revocation of a licence, shall be construed subject to section 25(6) and (7) above;
"protected right" shall be construed in accordance with section 39(3) above;
"the restriction on abstraction" means the restriction imposed by section 24(1) above;
"the restriction on impounding works" means the restriction imposed by section 25(1) above;

"spray irrigation" means (subject to subsection (5) below) the irrigation of land or plants (including seeds) by means of water or other liquid emerging (in whatever form) from apparatus designed or adapted to eject liquid into the air in the form of jets or spray; and

"statutory provision" means a provision (whether of a general or special nature) which is contained in, or in any document made or issued under, any Act (whether of a general or special nature).

(2)   References in this Chapter to a watercourse shall not include references—
  (a) to any sewer or part of a sewer vested in—
      (i)   a sewerage undertaker;
      (ii) a local authority or joint planning board;
      (iii) the Commission for the New Towns or a development corporation for a new town;
      (iv) a harbour board within the meaning of the Railway and Canal Traffic Act 1888;
      or
  (b) to any adit or passage constructed in connection with a well, borehole or other similar work for facilitating the collection of water in the well, borehole or work.

(3)   Any reference in this Chapter to the doing of anything in pursuance of a licence under this Chapter is a reference to its being done—
  (a) by the holder of such a licence: or
  (b) by a person acting as a servant or agent of, or otherwise under the authority of, the holder of such a licence,
at a time when the licence is in force and in circumstances such that, if no such licence were in force, the doing of that thing would contravene a restriction imposed by this Chapter.

(4)   For the purposes of this Chapter land shall be taken to be contiguous to any inland waters notwithstanding that it is separated from those waters by a towpath or by any other land used, or acquired for use, in connection with the navigation of the inland waters, unless that other land comprises any building or works other than a lock, pier, wharf, landing-stage or similar works.

(5)   The Ministers may by order direct that references to spray irrigation in this Chapter, and in any other enactments in which "spray irrigation" is given the same meaning as in this Chapter, or such of those references as may be specified in the order—
  (a) shall be construed as not including spray irrigation if carried out by such methods or in such circumstances or for such purposes as may be specified in the order; and
  (b) without prejudice to the exercise of the power conferred by virtue of paragraph (a) above, shall be construed as including references to the carrying out, by such methods or in such circumstances or for such purposes as may be specified in the order, of irrigation of any such description, other than spray irrigation, as may be so specified.

(6)   The power of the Ministers to make an order under subsection (5) above shall be exercisable by statutory instrument subject to annulment in pursuance of a resolution of either House of Parliament.

[344]

NOTES

Modification: by virtue of the National Park Authorities (Wales) Order 1995, SI 1995/2803, art 18, Sch 5, para 2C(a), and the National Park Authorities (England) Order 1996, SI 1996/1243, art 18, Sch 5, para 6(2)(a), sub-s (2)(a) is to have effect, in relation to National Park authorities, as if there were added the words—

"(v) a National Park authority;".

Orders: the Spray Irrigation (Definition) Order 1992, SI 1992/1096.

73–81   *(Relate to drought.)*

PART III
CONTROL OF POLLUTION OF WATER RESOURCES

CHAPTER I
QUALITY OBJECTIVES

82 Classification of quality of waters

(1)   The Secretary of State may, in relation to any description of controlled waters (being a description applying to some or all of the waters of a particular class or of two or more different classes), by regulations prescribe a system of classifying the quality of those waters according to criteria specified in the regulations.

(2)   The criteria specified in regulations under this section in relation to any classification shall consist of one or more of the following, that is to say—
    (a) general requirements as to the purposes for which the waters to which the classification is applied are to be suitable;
    (b) specific requirements as to the substances that are to be present in or absent from the water and as to the concentrations of substances which are or are required to be present in the water;
    (c) specific requirements as to other characteristics of those waters;

and for the purposes of any such classification regulations under this section may provide that the question whether prescribed requirements are satisfied may be determined by reference to such samples as may be prescribed.

[345]

NOTES

Regulations: the Surface Waters (Dangerous Substances) (Classification) Regulations 1989, SI 1989/2286; the Bathing Waters (Classification) Regulations 1991, SI 1991/1597 (both taking effect, wholly or partly, under this section by virtue of the Water Consolidation (Consequential Provisions) Act 1991, s 2(2), Sch 2, para 1(1), (2)); the Surface Waters (Dangerous Substances) (Classification) Regulations 1992, SI 1992/337; the Surface Waters (River Ecosystems) (Classification) Regulations 1994, SI 1994/1057; the Surface Waters (Abstraction for Drinking Water) (Classification) Regulations 1996, SI 1996/3001; the Surface Waters (Fishlife) (Classification) Regulations 1997, SI 1997/1331; the Surface Waters (Shellfish) (Classification) Regulations 1997, SI 1997/1332.

---

83 Water quality objectives

(1)   For the purpose of maintaining and improving the quality of controlled waters the Secretary of State may, by serving a notice on the [Agency] specifying—
    (a) one or more of the classifications for the time being prescribed under section 82 above; and
    (b) in relation to each specified classification, a date,

establish the water quality objectives for any waters which are, or are included in, waters of a description prescribed for the purposes of that section.

(2)   The water quality objectives for any waters to which a notice under this section relates shall be the satisfaction by those waters, on and at all times after each date specified in the notice, of the requirements which at the time of the notice were the requirements for the classification in relation to which that date is so specified.

(3)   Where the Secretary of State has established water quality objectives under this section for any waters he may review objectives for those waters if—
    (a) five years or more have elapsed since the service of the last notice under subsection (1) or (6) of this section to be served in respect of those waters; or

    (b) the [Agency], after consultation with such water undertakers and other persons as it considers appropriate, requests a review;

and the Secretary of State shall not exercise his power to establish objectives for any waters by varying the existing objectives for those waters except in consequence of such a review.

(4)   Where the Secretary of State proposes to exercise his power under this section to establish or vary the objectives for any waters he shall—

    (a) give notice setting out his proposal and specifying the period (not being less than three months from the date of publication of the notice) within which representations or objections with respect to the proposal may be made; and

    (b) consider any representations or objections which are duly made and not withdrawn;

and, if he decides, after considering any such representations or objections, to exercise his power to establish or vary those objectives, he may do so either in accordance with the proposal contained in the notice or in accordance with that proposal as modified in such manner as he considers appropriate.

(5)   A notice under subsection (4) above shall be given—

    (a) by publishing the notice in such manner as the Secretary of State considers appropriate for bringing it to the attention of persons likely to be affected by it; and

    (b) by serving a copy of the notice on the [Agency].

(6)   If, on a review under this section or in consequence of any representations or objections made following such a review for the purposes of subsection (4) above, the Secretary of State decides that the water quality objectives for any waters should remain unchanged, he shall serve notice of that decision on the [Agency].

                                                            [346]

NOTES

Sub-ss (1), (3), (5), (6): words in square brackets substituted by the Environment Act 1995, s 120, Sch 22, para 128.

Modifications: the Surface Waters (Dangerous Substances) (Classification) Regulations 1989, SI 1989/2286, reg 4, provides that sub-ss (4), (5) above do not apply to the initial establishment of water quality objectives so far as they involve the specification of a classification prescribed by those regulations.

The Bathing Waters (Classification) Regulations 1991, SI 1991/1597, reg 3, provides that this section has effect as if—

    (a) it imposed a duty on the Secretary of State to exercise his powers under this section to apply the classification BW1 (criteria for which are specified in the 1991 regulations) to relevant territorial waters, coastal waters and inland waters which are bathing waters within the meaning of Council Directive 76/160/EEC, Art 1.2;

    (b) in relation to the establishment of water quality objectives under that duty, sub-ss (4), (5) above were omitted.

The Surface Waters (Dangerous Substances) (Classification) Regulations 1992, SI 1992/337, reg 4, provides that, in relation to the application of the classification DS3, this section has effect as if it imposed a duty on the Secretary of State to exercise his powers under this section to apply the classification DS3 to all relevant territorial waters, coastal waters and inland freshwaters, and, in relation to the establishment of water quality objectives in pursuance of that duty, as if sub-ss (4), (5) above were omitted.

The Surface Waters (Abstraction for Drinking Water) (Classification) Regulations 1996, SI 1996/3001, reg 7(1), provides that this section has effect as if—

    (a) it imposed a duty on the Secretary of State to exercise the powers conferred on him by this section to classify appropriately under the said Regulations such waters as are necessary to give effect to Directive 75/440/EEC in England and Wales; and

    (b) in relation to the performance of that duty, sub-ss (4), (5) above were omitted.

The Surface Waters (Fishlife) (Classification) Regulations 1997, SI 1997/1331, reg 6(1), provides that this section has effect as if—

    (a) it imposed a duty on the Secretary of State to exercise the powers conferred on him by this section to classify appropriately under these Regulations such waters as are appropriate for the purpose of giving effect to Directive 78/659/EEC in England and Wales; and

    (b) in relation to the performance of that duty, sub-ss (4), (5) above were omitted.

The Surface Waters (Shellfish) (Classification) Regulations 1997, SI 1997/1332, reg 6(1), provides that this section has effect as if—

    (a) it imposed a duty on the Secretary of State to exercise the powers conferred on him under this section to classify under these Regulations such waters as are appropriate for the purpose of giving effect to Directive 79/923/EEC in relation to waters in or adjacent to England and Wales; and

    (b) in relation to the performance of that duty, sub-ss (4), (5) above were omitted.

84 General duties to achieve and maintain objectives etc

    (1)   It shall be the duty of the Secretary of State and of the [Agency] to exercise the powers conferred on him or it by or under the water pollution provisions of this Act (other than the preceding provisions of this Chapter and sections 104 and 192 below) in such manner as ensures, so far as it is practicable by the exercise of those powers to do so, that the water quality objectives specified for any waters in—

    (a) a notice under section 83 above; or

    (b) a notice under section 30C of the Control of Pollution Act 1974 (which makes corresponding provision for Scotland),

are achieved at all times.

    (2)   It shall be the duty of the [Agency], for the purposes of the carrying out of its functions under the water pollution provisions of this Act—

    (a) to monitor the extent of pollution in controlled waters; and

    (b) to consult, in such cases as it may consider appropriate, with [the Scottish Environment Protection Agency] in Scotland.

[347]

NOTES

    Sub-s (1): words in square brackets substituted by the Environment Act 1995, s 120, Sch 22, para 128.

    Sub-s (2): word in first pair of square brackets substituted by the Environment Act 1995, s 120, Sch 22, para 128; words in second pair of square brackets substituted by the Environment Act 1995 (Consequential and Transitional Provisions) (Scotland) Regulations 1996, SI 1996/973, reg 2, Schedule, para 11.

CHAPTER II
POLLUTION OFFENCES

NOTES

    This Chapter should be read in conjunction with the Conservation (Natural Habitats, &c) Regulations 1994, SI 1994/2716, regs 10, 48 et seq, 85 at **[997]**, **[1034]** et seq, **[1070]** (which make provision for implementing Council Directive 92/43/EEC on the conservation of natural habitats and of wild fauna and flora), and the Urban Waste Water Treatment (England and Wales) Regulations 1994, SI 1994/2841, regs 6 et seq (which make provision for implementing Council Directive 91/271/EEC concerning urban waste water treatment).

    Modification: for the modification of this Chapter, see the Waste Management Licensing Regulations 1994, SI 1994/1056, regs 1(3), 19, Sch 4, Pt I, para 11 at **[937]**, **[954]** and **[959]**.

Principal offences

85 Offences of polluting controlled waters

    (1)   A person contravenes this section if he causes or knowingly permits any poisonous, noxious or polluting matter or any solid waste matter to enter any controlled waters.

    (2)   A person contravenes this section if he causes or knowingly permits any matter, other than trade effluent or sewage effluent, to enter controlled waters by being discharged from a drain or sewer in contravention of a prohibition imposed under section 86 below.

(3) A person contravenes this section if he causes or knowingly permits any trade effluent or sewage effluent to be discharged—

(a) into any controlled waters; or

(b) from land in England and Wales, through a pipe, into the sea outside the seaward limits of controlled waters.

(4) A person contravenes this section if he causes or knowingly permits any trade effluent or sewage effluent to be discharged, in contravention of any prohibition imposed under section 86 below, from a building or from any fixed plant—

(a) on to or into any land; or

(b) into any waters of a lake or pond which are not inland freshwaters.

(5) A person contravenes this section if he causes or knowingly permits any matter whatever to enter any inland freshwaters so as to tend (either directly or in combination with other matter which he or another person causes or permits to enter those waters) to impede the proper flow of the waters in a manner leading, or likely to lead, to a substantial aggravation of—

(a) pollution due to other causes; or

(b) the consequences of such pollution.

(6) Subject to the following provisions of this Chapter, a person who contravenes this section or the conditions of any consent given under this Chapter for the purposes of this section shall be guilty of an offence and liable—

(a) on summary conviction, to imprisonment for a term not exceeding three months or to a fine not exceeding £20,000 or to both;

(b) on conviction on indictment, to imprisonment for a term not exceeding two years or to a fine or to both.

[348]

NOTES

Modification: references to waste modified by the Waste Management Licensing Regulations 1994, SI 1994/1056, reg 19, Sch 4, Pt I, para 11, to include "Directive Waste" as defined by reg 1(3), Sch 4, Pt II thereof.

86 Prohibition of certain discharges by notice or regulations

(1) For the purposes of section 85 above a discharge of any effluent or other matter is, in relation to any person, in contravention of a prohibition imposed under this section if, subject to the following provisions of this section—

(a) the [Agency] has given that person notice prohibiting him from making or, as the case may be, continuing the discharge; or

(b) the [Agency] has given that person notice prohibiting him from making or, as the case may be, continuing the discharge unless specified conditions are observed, and those conditions are not observed.

(2) For the purposes of section 85 above a discharge of any effluent or other matter is also in contravention of a prohibition imposed under this section if the effluent or matter discharged—

(a) contains a prescribed substance or a prescribed concentration of such a substance; or

(b) derives from a prescribed process or from a process involving the use of prescribed substances or the use of such substances in quantities which exceed the prescribed amounts.

(3) Nothing in subsection (1) above shall authorise the giving of a notice for the purposes of that subsection in respect of discharges from a vessel; and nothing in any regulations made by virtue of subsection (2) above shall require any discharge from a vessel to be treated as a discharge in contravention of a prohibition imposed under this section.

(4) A notice given for the purposes of subsection (1) above shall expire at such time as may be specified in the notice.

(5) The time specified for the purposes of subsection (4) above shall not be before the end of the period of three months beginning with the day on which the notice is given, except in a case where the [Agency] is satisfied that there is an emergency which requires the prohibition in question to come into force at such time before the end of that period as may be so specified.

(6) Where, in the case of such a notice for the purposes of subsection (1) above as (but for this subsection) would expire at a time at or after the end of the said period of three months, an application is made before that time for a consent under this Chapter in respect of the discharge to which the notice relates, that notice shall be deemed not to expire until the result of the application becomes final—
  (a) on the grant or withdrawal of the application;
  (b) on the expiration, without the bringing of an appeal with respect to the decision on the application, of any period prescribed as the period within which any such appeal must be brought; or
  (c) on the withdrawal or determination of any such appeal.

[349]

NOTES
Sub-ss (1), (5): words in square brackets substituted by the Environment Act 1995, s 120, Sch 22, para 128.

87 Discharges into and from public sewers etc

[(1) This section applies for the purpose of determining liability where sewage effluent is discharged as mentioned in subsection (3) or (4) of section 85 above from any sewer or works ("the discharging sewer") vested in a sewerage undertaker ("the discharging undertaker").

(1A) If the discharging undertaker did not cause, or knowingly permit, the discharge it shall nevertheless be deemed to have caused the discharge if—
  (a) matter included in the discharge was received by it into the discharging sewer or any other sewer or works vested in it;
  (b) it was bound (either unconditionally or subject to conditions which were observed) to receive that matter into that sewer or works; and
  (c) subsection (1B) below does not apply.

(1B) This subsection applies where the sewage effluent was, before being discharged from the discharging sewer, discharged through a main connection into that sewer or into any other sewer or works vested in the discharging undertaker by another sewerage undertaker ("the sending undertaker") under an agreement having effect between the discharging undertaker and the sending undertaker under section 110A of the Water Industry Act 1991.

(1C) Where subsection (1B) above applies, the sending undertaker shall be deemed to have caused the discharge if, although it did not cause, or knowingly permit, the sewage effluent to be discharged into the discharging sewer, or into any other sewer or works of the discharging undertaker—
  (a) matter included in the discharge was received by it into a sewer or works vested in it; and
  (b) it was bound (either unconditionally or subject to conditions which were observed) to receive that matter into that sewer or works.]

(2) A sewerage undertaker shall not be guilty of an offence under section 85 above by reason only of the fact that a discharge from a sewer or works vested in the undertaker contravenes conditions of a consent relating to the discharge if—
  (a) the contravention is attributable to a discharge which another person caused or permitted to be made into the sewer or works;

(b) the undertaker either was not bound to receive the discharge into the sewer or works or was bound to receive it there subject to conditions which were not observed; and

(c) the undertaker could not reasonably have been expected to prevent the discharge into the sewer or works.

(3) A person shall not be guilty of an offence under section 85 above in respect of a discharge which he caused or permitted to be made into a sewer or works vested in a sewerage undertaker if the undertaker was bound to receive the discharge there either unconditionally or subject to conditions which were observed.

[(4) In this section "main connection" has the same meaning as in section 110A of the Water Industry Act 1991.]

[350]

NOTES
Sub-ss (1), (1A)–(1C): substituted for original sub-s (1), by the Competition and Service (Utilities) Act 1992, s 46(1).
Sub-s (4): added by the Competition and Service (Utilities) Act 1992, s 46(2).

88 Defence to principal offences in respect of authorised discharges

(1) Subject to the following provisions of this section, a person shall not be guilty of an offence under section 85 above in respect of the entry of any matter into any waters or any discharge if the entry occurs or the discharge is made under and in accordance with, or as a result of any act or omission and in accordance with—

(a) a consent given under this Chapter or under Part II of the Control of Pollution Act 1974 (which makes corresponding provision for Scotland);

(b) an authorisation for a prescribed process designated for central control granted under Part I of the Environmental Protection Act 1990;

(c) a waste management or disposal licence;

(d) a licence granted under Part II of the Food and Environment Protection Act 1985;

(e) section 163 below or section 165 of the Water Industry Act 1991 (discharges for works purposes);

(f) any local statutory provision or statutory order which expressly confers power to discharge effluent into water; or

(g) any prescribed enactment.

(2) Schedule 10 to this Act shall have effect, subject to section 91 below, with respect to the making of applications for consents under this Chapter for the purposes of subsection (1)(a) above and with respect to the giving, revocation and modification of such consents.

(3) Nothing in any disposal licence shall be treated for the purposes of subsection (1) above as authorising—

(a) any entry or discharge as is mentioned in subsections (2) to (4) of section 85 above; or

(b) any act or omission so far as it results in any such entry or discharge.

(4) In this section—
"disposal licence" means a licence issued in pursuance of section 5 of the Control of Pollution Act 1974;
"statutory order" means—
(a) any order under section 168 below or section 167 of the Water Industry Act 1991 (compulsory works orders); or
(b) any order, byelaw, scheme or award made under any other enactment, including an order or scheme confirmed by Parliament or brought into operation in accordance with special parliamentary procedure;
and

"waste management licence" means such a licence granted under Part II of the Environmental Protection Act 1990.

[351]

NOTES

Modification: references to waste modified by the Waste Management Licensing Regulations 1994, SI 1994/1056, reg 19, Sch 4, Pt I, para 11, to include "Directive Waste" as defined by reg 1(3), Sch 4, Pt II thereof.

89 Other defences to principal offences

(1)   A person shall not be guilty of an offence under section 85 above in respect of the entry of any matter into any waters or any discharge if—

(a) the entry is caused or permitted, or the discharge is made, in an emergency in order to avoid danger to life or health;

(b) that person takes all such steps as are reasonably practicable in the circumstances for minimising the extent of the entry or discharge and of its polluting effects; and

(c) particulars of the entry or discharge are furnished to the [Agency] as soon as reasonably practicable after the entry occurs.

(2)   A person shall not be guilty of an offence under section 85 above by reason of his causing or permitting any discharge of trade or sewage effluent from a vessel.

(3)   A person shall not be guilty of an offence under section 85 above by reason only of his permitting water from an abandoned mine [or an abandoned part of a mine] to enter controlled waters.

[(3A) Subsection (3) above shall not apply to the owner or former operator of any mine or part of a mine if the mine or part in question became abandoned after 31st December 1999.

(3B) In determining for the purposes of subsection (3A) above whether a mine or part of a mine became abandoned before, on or after 31st December 1999 in a case where the mine or part has become abandoned on two or more occasions, of which—

(a) at least one falls on or before that date, and

(b) at least one falls after that date,

the mine or part shall be regarded as becoming abandoned after that date (but without prejudice to the operation of subsection (3) above in relation to that mine or part at, or in relation to, any time before the first of those occasions which falls after that date).

(3C) Where, immediately before a part of a mine becomes abandoned, that part is the only part of the mine not falling to be regarded as abandoned for the time being, the abandonment of that part shall not be regarded for the purposes of subsection (3A) or (3B) above as constituting the abandonment of the mine, but only of that part of it.]

(4)   A person shall not, otherwise than in respect of the entry of any poisonous, noxious or polluting matter into any controlled waters, be guilty of an offence under section 85 above by reason of his depositing the solid refuse of a mine or quarry on any land so that it falls or is carried into inland freshwaters if—

(a) he deposits the refuse on the land with the consent of the [Agency];

(b) no other site for the deposit is reasonably practicable; and

(c) he takes all reasonably practicable steps to prevent the refuse from entering those inland freshwaters.

(5)   A highway authority or other person entitled to keep open a drain by virtue of section 100 of the Highways Act 1980 shall not be guilty of an offence under section 85 above by reason of his causing or permitting any discharge to be made

from a drain kept open by virtue of that section unless the discharge is made in contravention of a prohibition imposed under section 86 above.

(6) In this section "mine" and "quarry" have the same meanings as in the Mines and Quarries Act 1954.

[352]

NOTES

Sub-ss (1), (4): words in square brackets substituted by the Environment Act 1995, s 120, Sch 22, para 128.

Sub-s (3): words in square brackets inserted by the Environment Act 1995, s 60(1), as from a day to be appointed.

Sub-ss (3A)–(3C): inserted by the Environment Act 1995, s 60(2), as from a day to be appointed.

Offences in connection with deposits and vegetation in rivers

90 Offences in connection with deposits and vegetation in rivers

(1) A person shall be guilty of an offence under this section if, without the consent of the [Agency], he—
  (a) removes from any part of the bottom, channel or bed of any inland freshwaters a deposit accumulated by reason of any dam, weir or sluice holding back the waters; and
  (b) does so by causing the deposit to be carried away in suspension in the waters.

(2) A person shall be guilty of an offence under this section if, without the consent of the [Agency], he—
  (a) causes or permits a substantial amount of vegetation to be cut or uprooted in any inland freshwaters, or to be cut or uprooted so near to any such waters that it falls into them; and
  (b) fails to take all reasonable steps to remove the vegetation from those waters.

(3) A person guilty of an offence under this section shall be liable, on summary conviction, to a fine not exceeding level 4 on the standard scale.

(4) Nothing in subsection (1) above applies to anything done in the exercise of any power conferred by or under any enactment relating to land drainage, flood prevention or navigation.

(5) In giving a consent for the purposes of this section the [Agency] may make the consent subject to such conditions as it considers appropriate.

(6) The Secretary of State may by regulations provide that any reference to inland freshwaters in subsection (1) or (2) above shall be construed as including a reference to such coastal waters as may be prescribed.

[353]

NOTES

Sub-ss (1), (2), (5): words in square brackets substituted by the Environment Act 1995, s 120, Sch 22, para 128.

[Consents for the purposes of sections 88 to 90

90A Applications for consent under section 89 or 90

(1) Any application for a consent for the purposes of section 89(4)(a) or 90(1) or (2) above—
  (a) must be made on a form provided for the purpose by the Agency, and
  (b) must be advertised in such manner as may be required by regulations made by the Secretary of State,

except that paragraph (b) above shall not have effect in the case of an application of any class or description specified in the regulations as being exempt from the requirements of that paragraph.

(2)   The applicant for such a consent must, at the time when he makes his application, provide the Agency—
(a) with all such information as it reasonably requires; and
(b) with all such information as may be prescribed for the purpose by the Secretary of State.

(3)   The information required by subsection (2) above must be provided either on, or together with, the form mentioned in subsection (1) above.

(4)   The Agency may give the applicant notice requiring him to provide it with all such further information of any description specified in the notice as it may require for the purpose of determining the application.

(5)   If the applicant fails to provide the Agency with any information required under subsection (4) above, the Agency may refuse to proceed with the application or refuse to proceed with it until the information is provided.]

[354]

NOTES
Commencement: 31 December 1996 (certain purposes); 21 November 1996 (remaining purposes).
Inserted, together with s 90B, by the Environment Act 1995, s 120, Sch 22, para 142.
Regulations: the Control of Pollution (Applications, Appeals and Registers) Regulations 1996, SI 1996/2971.

[90B Enforcement notices

(1)   If the Agency is of the opinion that the holder of a relevant consent is contravening any condition of the consent, or is likely to contravene any such condition, the Agency may serve on him a notice (an "enforcement notice").

(2)   An enforcement notice shall—
(a) state that the Agency is of the said opinion;
(b) specify the matters constituting the contravention or the matters making it likely that the contravention will arise;
(c) specify the steps that must be taken to remedy the contravention or, as the case may be, to remedy the matters making it likely that the contravention will arise; and
(d) specify the period within which those steps must be taken.

(3)   Any person who fails to comply with any requirement imposed by an enforcement notice shall be guilty of an offence and liable—
(a) on summary conviction, to imprisonment for a term not exceeding three months or to a fine not exceeding £20,000 or to both;
(b) on conviction on indictment, to imprisonment for a term not exceeding two years or to a fine or to both.

(4)   If the Agency is of the opinion that proceedings for an offence under subsection (3) above would afford an ineffectual remedy against a person who has failed to comply with the requirements of an enforcement notice, the Agency may take proceedings in the High Court for the purpose of securing compliance with the notice.

(5)   The Secretary of State may, if he thinks fit in relation to any person, give to the Agency directions as to whether the Agency should exercise its powers under this section and as to the steps which must be taken.

(6)   In this section—
"relevant consent" means—

(a) a consent for the purposes of section 89(4)(a) or 90(1) or (2) above; or
(b) a discharge consent, within the meaning of section 91 below; and
"the holder", in relation to a relevant consent, is the person who has the consent in question.]

[355]

NOTES
Commencement: 31 December 1996 (certain purposes); 21 November 1996 (remaining purposes).
Inserted as noted to s 90A at **[354]**.

Appeals in respect of consents under Chapter II

91 Appeals in respect of consents under Chapter II

(1) This section applies where the [Agency], otherwise than in pursuance of a direction of the Secretary of State—
  (a) on an application for a consent under this Chapter for the purposes of section 88(1)(a) above, has refused a consent for any discharges;
  (b) in giving a discharge consent, has made that consent subject to conditions;
  (c) has revoked a discharge consent, modified the conditions of any such consent or provided that any such consent which was unconditional shall be subject to conditions;
  (d) has, for the purposes of paragraph [8(1)] or (2) of Schedule 10 to this Act, specified a period in relation to a discharge consent without the agreement of the person who proposes to make, or makes, discharges in pursuance of that consent;
  (e) has refused a consent for the purposes of section 89(4)(a) above for any deposit; *or*
  (f) has refused a consent for the purposes of section 90 above for the doing of anything by any person or, in giving any such consent, made that consent subject to conditions.
  [(g) has refused a person a variation of any such consent as is mentioned in paragraphs (a) to (f) above or, in allowing any such variation, has made the consent subject to conditions; or
  (h) has served an enforcement notice on any person.]

(2) The person, if any, who applied for the consent [or variation] in question, or any person whose deposits, discharges or other conduct is or would be authorised by the consent[, or the person on whom the enforcement notice was served,] may appeal against the decision to the Secretary of State.

[(2A) This section is subject to section 114 of the 1995 Act (delegation or reference of appeals etc).

(2B) An appeal under this section shall, if and to the extent required by regulations under subsection (2K) below, be advertised in such manner as may be prescribed by regulations under that subsection.

(2C) If either party to the appeal so requests or the Secretary of State so decides, an appeal shall be or continue in the form of a hearing (which may, if the person hearing the appeal so decides, be held, or held to any extent, in private).

(2D) On determining an appeal brought by virtue of any of paragraphs (a) to (g) of subsection (1) above against a decision of the Agency, the Secretary of State—
  (a) may affirm the decision;
  (b) where the decision was a refusal to grant a consent or a variation of a consent, may direct the Agency to grant the consent or to vary the consent, as the case may be;
  (c) where the decision was as to the conditions of a consent, may quash all or any of those conditions;

(d) where the decision was to revoke a consent, may quash the decision;

(e) where the decision relates to a period specified for the purposes of paragraph 8(1) or (2) of Schedule 10 to this Act, may modify any provisions specifying that period;

and where he exercises any of the powers in paragraphs (b), (c) or (d) above, he may give directions as to the conditions to which the consent is to be subject.

(2E) On the determination of an appeal brought by virtue of paragraph (h) of subsection (1) above, the Secretary of State may either quash or affirm the enforcement notice and, if he affirms it, may do so either in its original form or with such modifications as he may in the circumstances think fit.

(2F) Subject to subsection (2G) below, where an appeal is brought by virtue of subsection (1)(c) above against a decision—

(a) to revoke a discharge consent,

(b) to modify the conditions of any such consent, or

(c) to provide that any such consent which was unconditional shall be subject to conditions,

the revocation, modification or provision shall not take effect pending the final determination or the withdrawal of the appeal.

(2G) Subsection (2F) above shall not apply to a decision in the case of which the notice effecting the revocation, modification or provision in question includes a statement that in the opinion of the Agency it is necessary for the purpose of preventing or, where that is not practicable, minimising—

(a) the entry into controlled waters of any poisonous, noxious or polluting matter or any solid waste matter, or

(b) harm to human health,

that that subsection should not apply.

(2H) Where the decision under appeal is one falling within subsection (2G) above, if, on the application of the holder or former holder of the consent, the Secretary of State or other person determining the appeal determines that the Agency acted unreasonably in excluding the application of subsection (2F) above, then—

(a) if the appeal is still pending at the end of the day on which the determination is made, subsection (2F) above shall apply to the decision from the end of that day; and

(b) the holder or former holder of the consent shall be entitled to recover compensation from the Agency in respect of any loss suffered by him in consequence of the exclusion of the application of that subsection;

and any dispute as to a person's entitlement to such compensation or as to the amount of it shall be determined by arbitration.

(2J) Where an appeal is brought under this section against an enforcement notice, the bringing of the appeal shall not have the effect of suspending the operation of the notice.

(2K) Provision may be made by the Secretary of State by regulations with respect to appeals under this section and in particular—

(a) as to the period within which and the manner in which appeals are to be brought; and

(b) as to the manner in which appeals are to be considered.]

(8) In this section "discharge consent" means such a consent under this Chapter for any discharges or description of discharges as is given for the purposes of section 88(1)(a) above either on an application for a consent or, by virtue of paragraph [6] of Schedule 10 to this Act, without such an application having been made.

NOTES

Sub-s (1): words in first pair of square brackets substituted, numbers in square brackets in para (d) substituted for numbers "7(1)", word in italics in para (e) repealed, and paras (g), (h) added, by the Environment Act 1995, s 120, Sch 22, paras 128, 143(1), Sch 24, except in relation to any appeal made under this section in relation to a decision made before 31 December 1996, by virtue of the Environment Act 1995 (Commencement No 8 and Saving Provisions) Order 1996, SI 1996/2909, art 4(1).

Sub-s (2): words in square brackets inserted by the Environment Act 1995, s 120, Sch 22, para 143(2), except in relation to any appeal made under this section in relation to a decision made before 31 December 1996, by virtue of SI 1996/2909, art 4(1).

Sub-ss (2A)–(2K): substituted, for original sub-ss (3)–(7), by the Environment Act 1995, s 120, Sch 22, para 143(3), except in relation to any appeal made under this section in relation to a decision made before 31 December 1996, by virtue of SI 1996/2909, art 4(1). Sub-ss (3)–(7) of this section, as originally enacted, read as follows—

"(3)   The Secretary of State may by regulations provide for the conduct and disposal of appeals under this section.

(4)   Without prejudice to the generality of the power conferred by subsection (3) above, regulations under that subsection may, with prescribed modifications, apply any provision of paragraphs 1(3) to (6), 2(1) and 4(4) to (6) of Schedule 10 to this Act in relation to appeals under this section.

(5)   If, on an appeal under this section the Secretary of State is of the opinion that the decision of the Authority should be modified or reversed, he may give the Authority such directions as he thinks appropriate for requiring it—
    (a)   to give a consent, either unconditionally or, in the case of a discharge consent or a consent for the purposes of section 90 above, subject to such conditions as may be specified in the direction;
    (b)   to modify the conditions of any discharge consent or any consent for the purposes of section 90 above or to provide that any discharge consent which is unconditional shall be subject to such conditions as may be specified in the direction;
    (c)   to modify in accordance with the direction any provision specifying a period for the purposes of paragraph 7 of Schedule 10 to this Act.

(6)   In complying with a direction under subsection (5) above to give a consent the Authority shall not be required to comply with any requirement imposed by paragraph 3 of Schedule 10 to this Act.

(7)   Nothing in any direction under subsection (5) above or in anything done in pursuance of any such direction shall be taken to affect the lawfulness or validity of anything which was done—
    (a)   in pursuance of any decision of the Authority which is to be modified or reversed under the direction; and
    (b)   before the direction is complied with.".

Sub-s (8): number in square brackets substituted for number "5" by the Environment Act 1995, s 120, Sch 22, para 143(4), except in relation to any appeal made under this section in relation to a decision made before 31 December 1996, by virtue of SI 1996/2909, art 4(1).

Regulations: the Control of Pollution (Consents for Discharges etc) (Secretary of State Functions) Regulations 1989, SI 1989/1151, are revoked, subject to savings, by SI 1996/2971; the Control of Pollution (Applications, Appeals and Registers) Regulations 1996, SI 1996/2971.

[CHAPTER IIA
ABANDONED MINES

91A Introductory

(1)   For the purposes of this Chapter, "abandonment", in relation to a mine,—
    (a) subject to paragraph (b) below, includes—
        (i)   the discontinuance of any or all of the operations for the removal of water from the mine;
        (ii) the cessation of working of any relevant seam, vein or vein-system;
        (iii) the cessation of use of any shaft or outlet of the mine;
        (iv) in the case of a mine in which activities other than mining activities are carried on (whether or not mining activities are also carried on in the mine)—
            (A) the discontinuance of some or all of those other activities in the mine; and
            (B) any substantial change in the operations for the removal of water from the mine; but

(b) does not include—
　　(i) any disclaimer under section 178 or 315 of the Insolvency Act 1986 (power of liquidator, or trustee of a bankrupt's estate, to disclaim onerous property) by the official receiver acting in a compulsory capacity; or
　　(ii) the abandonment of any rights, interests or liabilities by the Accountant in Bankruptcy acting as permanent or interim trustee in a sequestration (within the meaning of the Bankruptcy (Scotland) Act 1985);

and cognate expressions shall be construed accordingly.

(2) In this Chapter, except where the context otherwise requires—
"the 1954 Act" means the Mines and Quarries Act 1954;
"acting in a compulsory capacity", in the case of the official receiver, means acting as—
　　(a) liquidator of a company;
　　(b) receiver or manager of a bankrupt's estate, pursuant to section 287 of the Insolvency Act 1986;
　　(c) trustee of a bankrupt's estate;
　　(d) liquidator of an insolvent partnership;
　　(e) trustee of an insolvent partnership;
　　(f) trustee, or receiver or manager, of the insolvent estate of a deceased person;
"mine" has the same meaning as in the 1954 Act;
"the official receiver" has the same meaning as it has in the Insolvency Act 1986 by virtue of section 399(1) of that Act;
"prescribed" means prescribed in regulations;
"regulations" means regulations made by the Secretary of State;
"relevant seam, vein or vein-system", in the case of any mine, means any seam, vein or vein-system for the purpose of, or in connection with, whose working any excavation constituting or comprised in the mine was made.]
　　　　　　　　　　　　　　　　　　　　　　　　　　　　[357]

NOTES

Commencement: 21 September 1995 (certain purposes); to be appointed (remaining purposes).

Chapter IIA (ss 91A, 91B) inserted by the Environment Act 1995, s 58, and in force only in so far as to confer power on the Secretary of State to make regulations or orders, give directions or issue guidance, or in so far as to make provision with respect to the excercise of any such power (the Environment Act 1995 (Commencement No 1) Order 1995, SI 1995/1983, art 3).

[91B Mine operators to give the Agency six months' notice of any proposed abandonment

(1) If, in the case of any mine, there is to be an abandonment at any time after the expiration of the initial period, it shall be the duty of the operator of the mine to give notice of the proposed abandonment to the Agency at least six months before the abandonment takes effect.

(2) A notice under subsection (1) above shall contain such information (if any) as is prescribed for the purpose, which may include information about the operator's opinion as to any consequences of the abandonment.

(3) A person who fails to give the notice required by subsection (1) above shall be guilty of an offence and liable—
　　(a) on summary conviction, to a fine not exceeding the statutory maximum;
　　(b) on conviction on indictment, to a fine.

(4) A person shall not be guilty of an offence under subsection (3) above if—
　　(a) the abandonment happens in an emergency in order to avoid danger to life or health; and

(b) notice of the abandonment, containing such information as may be prescribed, is given as soon as reasonably practicable after the abandonment has happened.

(5)   Where the operator of a mine is—
(a) the official receiver acting in a compulsory capacity, or
(b) the Accountant in Bankruptcy acting as permanent or interim trustee in a sequestration (within the meaning of the Bankruptcy (Scotland) Act 1985),

he shall not be guilty of an offence under subsection (3) above by reason of any failure to give the notice required by subsection (1) above if, as soon as reasonably practicable (whether before or after the abandonment), he gives to the Agency notice of the abandonment or proposed abandonment, containing such information as may be prescribed.

(6)   Where a person gives notice under subsection (1), (4)(b) or (5) above, he shall publish prescribed particulars of, or relating to, the notice in one or more local newspapers circulating in the locality where the mine is situated.

(7)   Where the Agency—
(a) receives notice under this section or otherwise learns of an abandonment or proposed abandonment in the case of any mine, and
(b) considers that, in consequence of the abandonment or proposed abandonment taking effect, any land has or is likely to become contaminated land, within the meaning of Part IIA of the Environmental Protection Act 1990,

it shall be the duty of the Agency to inform the local authority in whose area that land is situated of the abandonment or proposed abandonment.

(8)   In this section—
"the initial period" means the period of six months beginning with the day on which subsection (1) above comes into force;
"local authority" means—
(a) any unitary authority;
(b) any district council, so far as it is not a unitary authority;
(c) the Common Council of the City of London and, as respects the Temples, the Sub-Treasurer of the Inner Temple and the Under-Treasurer of the Middle Temple respectively;
"unitary authority" means—
(a) the council of a county, so far as it is the council of an area for which there are no district councils;
(b) the council of any district comprised in an area for which there is no county council;
(c) the council of a London borough;
(d) the council of a county borough in Wales.]

[358]

NOTES

Commencement: 21 September 1995 (certain purposes); to be appointed (remaining purposes).
Inserted as noted to s 91A at [357].

CHAPTER III
POWERS TO PREVENT AND CONTROL POLLUTION

92 Requirements to take precautions against pollution

(1)   The Secretary of State may by regulations make provision—
(a) for prohibiting a person from having custody or control of any poisonous, noxious or polluting matter unless prescribed works and prescribed

precautions and other steps have been carried out or taken for the purpose of preventing or controlling the entry of the matter into any controlled waters;

(b) for requiring a person who already has custody or control of, or makes use of, any such matter to carry out such works for that purpose and to take such precautions and other steps for that purpose as may be prescribed.

(2) Without prejudice to the generality of the power conferred by subsection (1) above, regulations under that subsection may—

(a) confer power on the [Agency]—

  (i) to determine for the purposes of the regulations the circumstances in which a person is required to carry out works or to take any precautions or other steps; and

  (ii) by notice to that person, to impose the requirement and to specify or describe the works, precautions or other steps which that person is required to carry out or take;

(b) provide for appeals to the Secretary of State against notices served by the [Agency] in pursuance of provision made by virtue of paragraph (a) above; and

(c) provide that a contravention of the regulations shall be an offence the maximum penalties for which shall not exceed the penalties specified in subsection (6) of section 85 above.

[(3) This section is subject to section 114 of the 1995 Act (delegation or reference of appeals etc).]

[359]

NOTES

Sub-s (2): words in square brackets substituted by the Environment Act 1995, s 120, Sch 22, para 128.

Sub-s (3): added by the Environment Act 1995, s 120, Sch 22, para 144.

Regulations: the Control of Pollution (Silage, Slurry and Agricultural Fuel Oil) Regulations 1991, SI 1991/324 (having effect under this section by virtue of the Water Consolidation (Consequential Provisions) Act 1991, s 2(2), Sch 2, para 1(1), (2)), as amended by SI 1996/2044, SI 1997/547.

---

93 Water protection zones

(1) Where the Secretary of State considers, after consultation (in the case of an area wholly or partly in England) with the Minister, that subsection (2) below is satisfied in relation to any area, he may by order make provision—

(a) designating that area as a water protection zone; and

(b) prohibiting or restricting the carrying on in the designated area of such activities as may be specified or described in the order.

(2) For the purposes of subsection (1) above this subsection is satisfied in relation to any area if (subject to subsection (3) below) it is appropriate, with a view to preventing or controlling the entry of any poisonous, noxious or polluting matter into controlled waters, to prohibit or restrict the carrying on in that area of activities which the Secretary of State considers are likely to result in the pollution of any such waters.

(3) The reference in subsection (2) above to the entry of poisonous, noxious or polluting matter into controlled waters shall not include a reference to the entry of nitrate into controlled waters as a result of, or of anything done in connection with, the use of any land for agricultural purposes

(4) Without prejudice to the generality of the power conferred by virtue of subsection (1) above, an order under this section may—

(a) confer power on the [Agency] to determine for the purposes of the order the circumstances in which the carrying on of any activities is prohibited or restricted and to determine the activities to which any such prohibition or restriction applies;

(b) apply a prohibition or restriction in respect of any activities to cases where the activities are carried on without the consent of the [Agency] or in contravention of any conditions subject to which any such consent is given;

(c) provide that a contravention of a prohibition or restriction contained in the order or of a condition of a consent given for the purposes of any such prohibition or restriction shall be an offence the maximum penalties for which shall not exceed the penalties specified in subsection (6) of section 85 above;

(d) provide (subject to any regulations under section 96 below) for anything falling to be determined under the order by the [Agency] to be determined in accordance with such procedure and by reference to such matters and to the opinion of such persons as may be specified in the order;

(e) make different provision for different cases, including different provision in relation to different persons, circumstances or localities; and

(f) contain such supplemental, consequential and transitional provision as the Secretary of State considers appropriate.

(5) The power of the Secretary of State to make an order under this section shall be exercisable by statutory instrument subject to annulment in pursuance of a resolution of either House of Parliament; but the Secretary of State shall not make such an order except on an application made by the [Agency] in accordance with Schedule 11 to this Act and otherwise in accordance with that Schedule.

[360]

NOTES

Sub-ss (4), (5): words in square brackets substituted by the Environment Act 1995, s 120, Sch 22, para 128.

94 Nitrate sensitive areas

(1) Where the relevant Minister considers that it is appropriate to do so with a view to achieving the purpose specified in subsection (2) below in relation to any land, he may by order make provision designating that land, together with any other land to which he considers it appropriate to apply the designation, as a nitrate sensitive area.

(2) The purpose mentioned in subsection (1) above is preventing or controlling the entry of nitrate into controlled waters as a result of, or of anything done in connection with, the use for agricultural purposes of any land.

(3) Where it appears to the relevant Minister, in relation to any area which is or is to be designated by an order under this section as a nitrate sensitive area, that it is appropriate for provision for the imposition of requirements, prohibitions or restrictions to be contained in an order under this section (as well as for him to be able to enter into such agreements as are mentioned in section 95 below), he may, by a subsequent order under this section or, as the case may be, by the order designating that area—

(a) with a view to achieving the purpose specified in subsection (2) above, require, prohibit or restrict the carrying on, either on or in relation to any agricultural land in that area, of such activities as may be specified or described in the order; and

(b) provide for such amounts (if any) as may be specified in or determined under the order to be paid by one of the Ministers, to such persons as may be so specified or determined, in respect of the obligations imposed in relation to that area on those persons by virtue of paragraph (a) above.

(4) Without prejudice to the generality of subsection (3) above, provision contained in an order under this section by virtue of that subsection may—

(a) confer power on either of the Ministers to determine for the purposes of the order the circumstances in which the carrying on of any activities is required, prohibited or restricted and to determine the activities to which any such requirement, prohibition or restriction applies;

(b) provide for any requirement to carry on any activity not to apply in cases where one of the Ministers has consented to a failure to carry on that activity and any conditions on which the consent has been given are complied with;

(c) apply a prohibition or restriction in respect of any activities to cases where the activities are carried on without the consent of one of the Ministers or in contravention of any conditions subject to which any such consent is given;

(d) provide that a contravention of a requirement, prohibition or restriction contained in the order or in a condition of a consent given in relation to or for the purposes of any such requirement, prohibition or restriction shall be an offence the maximum penalties for which shall not exceed the penalties specified in subsection (6) of section 85 above;

(e) provide for amounts paid in pursuance of any provision contained in the order to be repaid at such times and in such circumstances, and with such interest, as may be specified in or determined under the order; and

(f) provide (subject to any regulations under section 96 below) for anything falling to be determined under the order by any person to be determined in accordance with such procedure and by reference to such matters and to the opinion of such persons as may be specified in the order.

(5) An order under this section may—
 (a) make different provision for different cases, including different provision in relation to different persons, circumstances or localities; and
 (b) contain such supplemental, consequential and transitional provision as the relevant Minister considers appropriate.

(6) The power of the relevant Minister to make an order under this section shall be exercisable by statutory instrument subject to annulment in pursuance of a resolution of either House of Parliament; but the relevant Minister shall not make such an order except in accordance with any applicable provisions of Schedule 12 to this Act.

(7) In this section and in Schedule 12 to this Act "the relevant Minister"—
 (a) in relation to the making of an order in relation to an area which is wholly in England or which is partly in England and partly in Wales, means the Ministers; and
 (b) in relation to the making of an order in relation to an area which is wholly in Wales, means the Secretary of State.

[361]

95 Agreements in nitrate sensitive areas

(1) Where—
 (a) any area has been designated as a nitrate sensitive area by an order under section 94 above; and
 (b) the relevant Minister considers that it is appropriate to do so with a view to achieving the purpose mentioned in subsection (2) of that section,

he may, subject to such restrictions (if any) as may be set out in the order, enter into an agreement falling within subsection (2) below.

(2) An agreement falls within this subsection if it is one under which, in consideration of payments to be made by the relevant Minister—
 (a) the owner of the freehold interest in any agricultural land in a nitrate sensitive area; or
 (b) where the owner of the freehold interest in any such land has given his written consent to the agreement being entered into by any person having another interest in that land, that other person,

accepts such obligations with respect to the management of that land or otherwise as may be imposed by the agreement.

(3)   An agreement such as is mentioned in subsection (2) above between the relevant Minister and a person having an interest in any land shall bind all persons deriving title from or under that person to the extent that the agreement is expressed to bind that land in relation to those persons.

(4)   In this section "the relevant Minister"—
  (a) in relation to an agreement with respect to land which is wholly in England, means the Minister;
  (b) in relation to an agreement with respect to land which is wholly in Wales, means the Secretary of State; and
  (c) in relation to an agreement with respect to land which is partly in England and partly in Wales, means either of the Ministers.

[362]

96 Regulations with respect to consents required by virtue of section 93 or 94

(1)   The Secretary of State may, for the purposes of any orders under section 93 above which require the consent of the [Agency] to the carrying on of any activities, by regulations make provision with respect to—
  (a) applications for any such consent;
  (b) the conditions of any such consent;
  (c) the revocation or variation of any such consent;
  (d) appeals against determinations on any such application;
  (e) the exercise by the Secretary of State of any power conferred on the [Agency] by the orders;
  (f) the imposition of charges where such an application has been made, such a consent has been given or anything has been done in pursuance of any such consent; and
  (g) the registration of any such application or consent.

(2)   The Ministers may, for the purposes of any orders under section 94 above which require the consent of either of those Ministers to the carrying on of any activities or to any failure to carry on any activity, by regulations make provision with respect to—
  (a) applications for any such consent;
  (b) the conditions of any such consent;
  (c) the revocation or variation of any such consent;
  (d) the reference to arbitration of disputes about determinations on any such application;
  (e) the imposition of charges where such an application has been made, such a consent has been given or there has been any act or omission in pursuance of any such consent; and
  (f) the registration of any such application or consent.

(3)   Without prejudice to the generality of the powers conferred by the preceding provisions of this section, regulations under subsection (1) above may apply (with or without modifications) any enactment having effect in relation to consents under Chapter II of this Part.

[(4)   This section is subject to section 114 of the 1995 Act (delegation or reference of appeals etc).]

[363]

NOTES

97 Codes of good agricultural practice

(1)   The Ministers may by order made by statutory instrument approve any code of practice issued (whether by either or both of the Ministers or by another person) for the purpose of—
  (a) giving practical guidance to persons engaged in agriculture with respect to activities that may affect controlled waters; and
  (b) promoting what appear to them to be desirable practices by such persons for avoiding or minimising the pollution of any such waters,

and may at any time by such an order approve a modification of such a code or withdraw their approval of such a code or modification.

(2)   A contravention of a code of practice as for the time being approved under this section shall not of itself give rise to any criminal or civil liability, but the [Agency] shall take into account whether there has been or is likely to be any such contravention in determining when and how it should exercise—
  (a) its power, by giving a notice under subsection (1) of section 86 above, to impose a prohibition under that section; and
  (b) any powers conferred on the [Agency] by regulations under section 92 above.

(3)   The Ministers shall not make an order under this section unless they have first consulted the [Agency].

[364]

NOTES
    Sub-ss (2), (3): words in square brackets substituted by the Environment Act 1995, s 120, Sch 22, para 128.
    Orders: the Water (Prevention of Pollution) (Code of Practice) Order 1991, SI 1991/2285 (having effect under this section by virtue of the Water Consolidation (Consequential Provisions Act 1991, s 2(2), Sch 2, para 1(1), (2)).

CHAPTER IV
SUPPLEMENTAL PROVISIONS WITH RESPECT TO WATER POLLUTION

98 Radioactive substances

(1)   Except as provided by regulations made by the Secretary of State under this section, nothing in this Part shall apply in relation to radioactive waste within the meaning of the [Radioactive Substances Act 1993].

(2)   The Secretary of State may by regulations—
  (a) provide for prescribed provisions of this Part to have effect with such modifications as he considers appropriate for dealing with such waste;
  (b) make such modifications of the said Act of [1993] or, in relation to such waste, of any other enactment as he considers appropriate in consequence of the provisions of this Part and of any regulations made by virtue of paragraph (a) above.

[365]

NOTES
    Words in square brackets substituted by the Radioactive Substances Act 1993, s 49(1), Sch 4, para 11.
    Regulations: the Control of Pollution (Radioactive Waste) Regulations 1989, SI 1989/1158 (having effect under sub-s (2) of this section by virtue of the Water Consolidation (Consequential Provisions) Act 1991, s 2(2), Sch 2, para 1(1), (2)).

99 Consents required by the [Agency]

(1)   The Secretary of State may by regulations—
  (a) make provision modifying the water pollution provisions of this Act in relation to cases in which consents under Chapter II of this Part are required by the [Agency]; and

(b) for the purposes of the application of the provisions of this Part in relation to discharges by the [Agency], make such other modifications of those provisions as may be prescribed.

(2) Without prejudice to the generality of subsection (1) above, regulations under this section may provide for such consents as are mentioned in paragraph (a) of that subsection to be required to be given by the Secretary of State (instead of by the [Agency]) and, in prescribed cases, to be deemed to have been so given.

[366]

NOTES

Section heading: word in square brackets substituted by the Environment Act 1995, s 120, Sch 22, para 128.

Sub-ss (1), (2): words in square brackets substituted by the Environment Act 1995, s 120, Sch 22, para 128.

Regulations: the Control of Pollution (Applications, Appeals and Registers) Regulations 1996, SI 1996/2971.

100 Civil liability in respect of pollution and savings

Except in so far as this Part expressly otherwise provides and subject to the provisions of section 18 of the Interpretation Act 1978 (which relates to offences under two or more laws), nothing in this Part—

(a) confers a right of action in any civil proceedings (other than proceedings for the recovery of a fine) in respect of any contravention of this Part or any subordinate legislation, consent or other instrument made, given or issued under this Part;

(b) derogates from any right of action or other remedy (whether civil or criminal) in proceedings instituted otherwise than under this Part; or

(c) affects any restriction imposed by or under any other enactment, whether public, local or private.

[367]

101 Limitation for summary offences under Part III

Notwithstanding anything in section 127 of the Magistrates' Courts Act 1980 (time limit for summary proceedings), a magistrates' court may try any summary offence under this Part, or under any subordinate legislation made under this Part, if the information is laid not more than twelve months after the commission of the offence.

[368]

102 Power to give effect to international obligations

The Secretary of State shall have power by regulations to provide that the water pollution provisions of this Act shall have effect with such modifications as may be prescribed for the purpose of enabling Her Majesty's Government in the United Kingdom to give effect—

(a) to any Community obligations; or

(b) to any international agreement to which the United Kingdom is for the time being a party.

[369]

NOTES

Regulations: the Surface Waters (Dangerous Substances) (Classification) Regulations 1989, SI 1989/2286, the Bathing Waters (Classification) Regulations 1991, SI 1991/1597, the Surface Waters (Dangerous Substances) (Classification) Regulations 1992, SI 1992/337; the Surface Waters (Abstraction of Drinking Water) (Classification) Regulations 1996, SI 1996/3001; the Surface Waters (Fishlife) (Classification) Regulations 1997, SI 1997/1331; the Surface Waters (Shellfish) (Classification) Regulations 1997, SI 1997/1332.

103 Transitional pollution provisions

The provisions of this Part shall have effect subject to the provisions of Schedule 13 to this Act (which reproduce transitional provision originally made in connection with the coming into force of provisions of the Water Act 1989).

[370]

104 Meaning of "controlled waters" etc in Part III

(1)   References in this Part to controlled waters are references to waters of any of the following classes—
  (a) relevant territorial waters, that is to say, subject to subsection (4) below, the waters which extend seaward for three miles from the baselines from which the breadth of the territorial sea adjacent to England and Wales is measured;
  (b) coastal waters, that is to say, any waters which are within the area which extends landward from those baselines as far as—
    (a) the limit of the highest tide; or
    (b) in the case of the waters of any relevant river or watercourse, the fresh-water limit of the river or watercourse,
  together with the waters of any enclosed dock which adjoins waters within that area;
  (c) inland freshwaters, that is to say, the waters of any relevant lake or pond or of so much of any relevant river or watercourse as is above the fresh-water limit;
  (d) ground waters, that is to say, any waters contained in underground strata;

and, accordingly, in this Part "coastal waters", "controlled waters", "ground waters", "inland freshwaters" and "relevant territorial waters" have the meanings given by this subsection.

(2)   In this Part any reference to the waters of any lake or pond or of any river or watercourse includes a reference to the bottom, channel or bed of any lake, pond, river or, as the case may be, watercourse which is for the time being dry.

(3)   In this section—
  "fresh-water limit", in relation to any river or watercourse, means the place for the time being shown as the fresh-water limit of that river or watercourse in the latest map deposited for that river or watercourse under section 192 below;
  "miles" means international nautical miles of 1,852 metres;
  "lake or pond" includes a reservoir of any description;
  "relevant lake or pond" means (subject to subsection (4) below) any lake or pond which (whether it is natural or artificial or above or below ground) discharges into a relevant river or watercourse or into another lake or pond which is itself a relevant lake or pond;
  "relevant river or watercourse" means (subject to subsection (4) below) any river or watercourse (including an underground river or watercourse and an artificial river or watercourse) which is neither a public sewer nor a sewer or drain which drains into a public sewer.

(4)   The Secretary of State may by order provide—
  (a) that any area of the territorial sea adjacent to England and Wales is to be treated as if it were an area of relevant territorial waters for the purposes of this Part and of any other enactment in which any expression is defined by reference to the meanings given by this section;
  (b) that any lake or pond which does not discharge into a relevant river or watercourse or into a relevant lake or pond is to be treated for those purposes as a relevant lake or pond;

(c) that a lake or pond which does so discharge and is of a description specified in the order is to be treated for those purposes as if it were not a relevant lake or pond;

(d) that a watercourse of a description so specified is to be treated for those purposes as if it were not a relevant river or watercourse.

(5) An order under this section may—

   (a) contain such supplemental, consequential and transitional provision as the Secretary of State considers appropriate; and

   (b) make different provision for different cases, including different provision in relation to different persons, circumstances or localities.

(6) The power of the Secretary of State to make an order under this section shall be exercisable by statutory instrument subject to annulment in pursuance of a resolution of either House of Parliament.

[371]

NOTES

Modifications: sub-s (1)(c) has effect as if "inland freshwaters" included all waters which need to be classified under the Surface Waters (Abstraction for Drinking Water) (Classification) Regulations 1996, SI 1996/3001, to give effect to Directive 75/440/EEC in England and Wales, by reg 7(2) of the 1996 Regulations.

Sub-s (1) has effect as if "inland freshwaters" included all waters which are fresh waters which need to be classified under the Surface Waters (Fishlife) (Classification) Regulations 1997, SI 1997/1331, to give effect to Directive 78/659/EEC in England and Wales, by reg 6(2) of the 1997 Regulations.

Sub-s (1) has effect as if "controlled waters" included all waters which are coastal or brackish waters which need to be classified under the Surface Waters (Shellfish) (Classification) Regulations 1997, SI 1997/1332, to give effect to Directive 79/923/EEC in England and Wales, by reg 6(2) of the 1997 Regulations.

Orders: the Controlled Waters (Lakes and Ponds) Order 1989, SI 1989/1149 (having effect under sub-s (4)(b) of this section by virtue of the Water Consolidation (Consequential Provisions) Act 1991, s 2(2), Sch 2, para 1(1), (2)).

105–153 *((Pts IV–VI) outside the scope of this work.)*

PART VII
LAND AND WORKS POWERS

CHAPTER I
POWERS OF THE [AGENCY]

154–160 *(Relate to provisions concerning land (ss 154–157); works agreements for water resources purposes (s 158); pipe-laying powers (ss 159, 160).)*

Anti-pollution works

161 Anti-pollution works and operations

(1) *Subject to subsection (2) below,* where it appears to the [Agency] that any poisonous, noxious or polluting matter or any solid waste matter is likely to enter, or to be or to have been present in, any controlled waters, the [Agency] shall be entitled to carry out the following works and operations, that is to say—

   (a) in a case where the matter appears likely to enter any controlled waters, works and operations for the purpose of preventing it from doing so; or

   (b) in a case where the matter appears to be or to have been present in any controlled waters, works and operations for the purpose—

      (i) of removing or disposing of the matter;

      (ii) of remedying or mitigating any pollution caused by its presence in the waters; or

      (iii) so far as it is reasonably practicable to do so, of restoring the waters, including any flora and fauna dependent on the aquatic environment of the waters, to their state immediately before the matter became present in the waters

[and, in either case, the Agency shall be entitled to carry out investigations for the purpose of establishing the source of the matter and the identity of the person who has caused or knowingly permitted it to be present in controlled waters or at a place from which it was likely, in the opinion of the Agency, to enter controlled waters].

[(1A) Without prejudice to the power of the Agency to carry out investigations under subsection (1) above, the power conferred by that subsection to carry out works and operations shall only be exercisable in a case where—

(a) the Agency considers it necessary to carry out forthwith any works or operations falling within paragraph (a) or (b) of that subsection; or

(b) it appears to the Agency, after reasonable inquiry, that no person can be found on whom to serve a works notice under section 161A below.]

(2) Nothing in subsection (1) above shall entitle the [Agency] to impede or prevent the making of any discharge in pursuance of a consent given under Chapter II of Part III of this Act.

(3) Where the [Agency] carries out any such works [operations or investigations] as are mentioned in subsection (1) above, it shall, subject to subsection (4) below, be entitled to recover the expenses reasonably incurred in doing so from any person who, as the case may be—

(a) caused or knowingly permitted the matter in question to be present at the place from which it was likely, in the opinion of the [Agency], to enter any controlled waters; or

(b) caused or knowingly permitted the matter in question to be present in any controlled waters.

(4) No such expenses shall be recoverable from a person for any works [operations or investigations] in respect of water from an abandoned mine which that person permitted to reach such a place as is mentioned in subsection (3) above or to enter any controlled waters.

(5) Nothing in this section—

(a) derogates from any right of action or other remedy (whether civil or criminal) in proceedings instituted otherwise than under this section; or

(b) affects any restriction imposed by or under any other enactment, whether public, local or private.

(6) In this section—

"controlled waters" has the same meaning as in Part III of this Act; and

["expenses" includes costs;]

"mine" has the same meaning as in the Mines and Quarries Act 1954.

[372]

NOTES

Chapter-heading: word in square brackets substituted by the Environment Act 1995, s 120, Sch 22, para 128.

Sub-s (1): words in italics substituted by words "Subject to subsections (1A) and (2) below," as from a day to be appointed, and words in first and second pairs of square brackets substituted, by the Environment Act 1995, s 120, Sch 22, paras 128, 161(2); words in final pair of square brackets added by the Environment Act 1995, s 60(3).

Sub-s (1A): inserted by the Environment Act 1995, s 120, Sch 22, para 161(3), as from a day to be appointed.

Sub-s (2): words in square brackets substituted by the Environment Act 1995, s 120, Sch 22, para 128.

Sub-s (3): words in first and final pairs of square brackets substituted by the Environment Act 1995, s 120, Sch 22, para 128; words in second pair of square brackets substituted by the Environment Act 1995, s 60(4).

Sub-s (4): words in square brackets substituted by the Environment Act 1995, s 60(5)(a).

Sub-s (6): definition "expenses" inserted by the Environment Act 1995, s 60(7).

[161A Notices requiring persons to carry out anti-pollution works and operations

(1)   Subject to the following provisions of this section, where it appears to the Agency that any poisonous, noxious or polluting matter or any solid waste matter is likely to enter, or to be or to have been present in, any controlled waters, the Agency shall be entitled to serve a works notice on any person who, as the case may be,—
   (a) caused or knowingly permitted the matter in question to be present at the place from which it is likely, in the opinion of the Agency, to enter any controlled waters; or
   (b) caused or knowingly permitted the matter in question to be present in any controlled waters.

(2)   For the purposes of this section, a "works notice" is a notice requiring the person on whom it is served to carry out such of the following works or operations as may be specified in the notice, that is to say—
   (a) in a case where the matter in question appears likely to enter any controlled waters, works or operations for the purpose of preventing it from doing so; or
   (b) in a case where the matter appears to be or to have been present in any controlled waters, works or operations for the purpose—
      (i)   of removing or disposing of the matter;
      (ii) of remedying or mitigating any pollution caused by its presence in the waters; or
      (iii) so far as it is reasonably practicable to do so, of restoring the waters, including any flora and fauna dependent on the aquatic environment of the waters, to their state immediately before the matter became present in the waters.

(3)   A works notice—
   (a) must specify the periods within which the person on whom it is served is required to do each of the things specified in the notice; and
   (b) is without prejudice to the powers of the Agency by virtue of section 161(1A)(a) above.

(4)   Before serving a works notice on any person, the Agency shall reasonably endeavour to consult that person concerning the works or operations which are to be specified in the notice.

(5)   The Secretary of State may by regulations make provision for or in connection with—
   (a) the form or content of works notices;
   (b) requirements for consultation, before the service of a works notice, with . persons other than the person on whom that notice is to be served;
   (c) steps to be taken for the purposes of any consultation required under subsection (4) above or regulations made by virtue of paragraph (b) above; or
   (d) any other steps of a procedural nature which are to be taken in connection with, or in consequence of, the service of a works notice.

(6)   A works notice shall not be regarded as invalid, or as invalidly served, by reason only of any failure to comply with the requirements of subsection (4) above or of regulations made by virtue of paragraph (b) of subsection (5) above.

(7)   Nothing in subsection (1) above shall entitle the Agency to require the carrying out of any works or operations which would impede or prevent the making of any discharge in pursuance of a consent given under Chapter II of Part III of this Act.

(8)   No works notice shall be served on any person requiring him to carry out any works or operations in respect of water from an abandoned mine or an abandoned part of a mine which that person permitted to reach such a place as is mentioned in subsection (1)(a) above or to enter any controlled waters.

(9)   Subsection (8) above shall not apply to the owner or former operator of any mine or part of a mine if the mine or part in question became abandoned after 31st December 1999.

(10) Subsections (3B) and (3C) of section 89 above shall apply in relation to subsections (8) and (9) above as they apply in relation to subsections (3) and (3A) of that section.

(11) Where the Agency—
   (a) carries out any such investigations as are mentioned in section 161(1) above, and
   (b) serves a works notice on a person in connection with the matter to which the investigations relate,

it shall (unless the notice is quashed or withdrawn) be entitled to recover the costs or expenses reasonably incurred in carrying out those investigations from that person.

(12) The Secretary of State may, if he thinks fit in relation to any person, give directions to the Agency as to whether or how it should exercise its powers under this section.

(13) In this section—
   "controlled waters" has the same meaning as in Part III of this Act;
   "mine" has the same meaning as in the Mines and Quarries Act 1954.]

[373]

NOTES
   Commencement: 21 September 1995 (certain purposes); to be appointed (remaining purposes).
   Inserted, together with ss 161B–161D, by the Environment Act 1995, s 120, Sch 22, para 162, and in force only in so far as to confer power on the Secretary of State to make regulations or orders, give directions or issue guidance, or in so far as to make provision with respect to the excercise of any such power (the Environment Act 1995 (Commencement No 1) Order 1995, SI 1995/1983, art 3).

[161B Grant of, and compensation for, rights of entry etc

(1)   A works notice may require a person to carry out works or operations in relation to any land or waters notwithstanding that he is not entitled to carry out those works or operations.

(2)   Any person whose consent is required before any works or operations required by a works notice may be carried out shall grant, or join in granting, such rights in relation to any land or waters as will enable the person on whom the works notice is served to comply with any requirements imposed by the works notice.

(3)   Before serving a works notice, the Agency shall reasonably endeavour to consult every person who appears to it—
   (a) to be the owner or occupier of any relevant land, and
   (b) to be a person who might be required by subsection (2) above to grant, or join in granting, any rights,
concerning the rights which that person may be so required to grant.

(4)   A works notice shall not be regarded as invalid, or as invalidly served, by reason only of any failure to comply with the requirements of subsection (3) above.

(5)   A person who grants, or joins in granting, any rights pursuant to subsection (2) above shall be entitled, on making an application within such period as may be prescribed and in such manner as may be prescribed to such person as may be prescribed, to be paid by the person on whom the works notice in question is served compensation of such amount as may be determined in such manner as may be prescribed.

(6)   Without prejudice to the generality of the regulations that may be made by virtue of subsection (5) above, regulations by virtue of that subsection may make

such provision in relation to compensation under this section as may be made by regulations by virtue of subsection (4) of section 35A of the Environmental Protection Act 1990 in relation to compensation under that section.

(7)   In this section—
"prescribed" means prescribed in regulations made by the Secretary of State;
"relevant land" means—
    (a) any land or waters in relation to which the works notice in question requires, or may require, works or operations to be carried out; or
    (b) any land adjoining or adjacent to that land or those waters;
"works notice" means a works notice under section 161A above.]

[374]

NOTES
Commencement: 21 September 1995 (certain purposes); to be appointed (remaining purposes).
Inserted as noted to s 161A at **[373]**.

[161C Appeals against works notices

(1)   A person on whom a works notice is served may, within the period of twenty-one days beginning with the day on which the notice is served, appeal against the notice to the Secretary of State.

(2)   On any appeal under this section the Secretary of State—
    (a) shall quash the notice, if he is satisfied that there is a material defect in the notice; but
    (b) subject to that, may confirm the notice, with or without modification, or quash it.

(3)   The Secretary of State may by regulations make provision with respect to—
    (a) the grounds on which appeals under this section may be made; or
    (b) the procedure on any such appeal.

(4)   Regulations under subsection (3) above may (among other things)—
    (a) include provisions comparable to those in section 290 of the Public Health Act 1936 (appeals against notices requiring the execution of works);
    (b) prescribe the cases in which a works notice is, or is not, to be suspended until the appeal is decided, or until some other stage in the proceedings;
    (c) prescribe the cases in which the decision on an appeal may in some respects be less favourable to the appellant than the works notice against which he is appealing;
    (d) prescribe the cases in which the appellant may claim that a works notice should have been served on some other person and prescribe the procedure to be followed in those cases;
    (e) make provision as respects—
        (i) the particulars to be included in the notice of appeal;
        (ii) the persons on whom notice of appeal is to be served and the particulars, if any, which are to accompany the notice; or
        (iii) the abandonment of an appeal.

(5)   In this section "works notice" means a works notice under section 161A above.

(6)   This section is subject to section 114 of the 1995 Act (delegation or reference of appeals).]

[375]

NOTES
Commencement: 21 September 1995 (certain purposes); to be appointed (remaining purposes).
Inserted as noted to s 161A at **[373]**.

[161D Consequences of not complying with a works notice

(1)   If a person on whom the Agency serves a works notice fails to comply with any of the requirements of the notice, he shall be guilty of an offence.

(2)   A person who commits an offence under subsection (1) above shall be liable—
  (a) on summary conviction, to imprisonment for a term not exceeding three months or to a fine not exceeding £20,000 or to both;
  (b) on conviction on indictment to imprisonment for a term not exceeding two years or to a fine or to both.

(3)   If a person on whom a works notice has been served fails to comply with any of the requirements of the notice, the Agency may do what that person was required to do and may recover from him any costs or expenses reasonably incurred by the Agency in doing it.

(4)   If the Agency is of the opinion that proceedings for an offence under subsection (1) above would afford an ineffectual remedy against a person who has failed to comply with the requirements of a works notice, the Agency may take proceedings in the High Court for the purpose of securing compliance with the notice.

(5)   In this section "works notice" means a works notice under section 161A above.]

[376]

NOTES
Inserted as noted to s 161A at [373].

162–186 *(Relate to powers to deal with foul water and pollution (s 162); powers to discharge water (ss 163, 164); flood defence and drainage works (ss 165–167); compulsory works orders (s 168); powers of entry (ss 169–174); provisions supplemental to land and works powers (ss 175–186).)*

PART VIII
INFORMATION PROVISIONS

187, 188 *(S 187 repealed by the Environment Act 1995, s 120(1), (3), Sch 22, para 168, Sch 24; s 188 relates to the duty of the Authority to publish certain information.)*

Registers etc to be kept by the [Agency]

189 Register of abstraction and impounding licences

(1)   The [Agency] shall keep, in such manner as may be prescribed, registers containing such information as may be prescribed with respect—
  (a) to applications made for the grant, revocation or variation of licences under Chapter II of Part II of this Act, including information as to the way in which such applications have been dealt with; and
  (b) to persons becoming the holders of such licences by virtue of section 49 above of this Act or regulations made under section 50 above.

(2)   Every register kept by the [Agency] under this section shall also contain such information as may be prescribed with respect—
  (a) to applications made in accordance with regulations under section 64 above; and
  (b) to licences granted or deemed to be granted, and licences revoked or varied, in accordance with regulations made under that section.

(3)   Subject to any regulations under this section, the information which the [Agency] is required to keep in registers under this section shall continue to include the information which immediately before 1st September 1989 was contained in a register kept by a water authority under section 53 of the Water Resources Act 1963.

(4)   The contents of every register kept under this section shall be available, at such place as may be prescribed, for inspection by the public at all reasonable hours.

[377]

NOTES

Cross-heading: word in square brackets substituted by the Environment Act 1995, s 120, Sch 22, para 128.

Sub-ss (1)–(3): words in square brackets substituted by the Environment Act 1995, s 120, Sch 22, para 128.

Regulations: the Water Resources (Licences) Regulations 1965, SI 1965/534, reg 17 (as construed with the Water Consolidation (Consequential Provisions) Act 1991, s 2(2), Sch 2, para 1(1), (2)).

190 Pollution control register

(1)   It shall be the duty of the [Agency] to maintain, in accordance with regulations made by the Secretary of State, registers containing prescribed particulars of [or relating to]—

   (a) any notices of water quality objectives or other notices served under section 83 above;
   (b) applications made for consents under Chapter II of Part III of this Act;
   (c) consents given under that Chapter and the conditions to which the consents are subject;
   (d) *certificates issued under paragraph 1(7) of Schedule 10 to this Act;*
   (e) the following, that is to say—
       (i)   samples of water or effluent taken by the [Agency] for the purposes of any of the water pollution provisions of this Act;
       (ii) information produced by analyses of those samples;
       (iii) such information with respect to samples of water or effluent taken by any other person, and the analyses of those samples, as is acquired by the [Agency] from any person under arrangements made by the [Agency] for the purposes of any of those provisions; and
       (iv) the steps taken in consequence of any such information as is mentioned in any of sub-paragraphs (i) to (iii) above;
       and
   (f) *any matter about which particulars are required to be kept in any register under section 20 of the Environmental Protection Act 1990 (particulars about authorisations for prescribed processes etc) by the chief inspector under Part I of that Act.*
   [(g) applications made to the Agency for the variation of discharge consents;
   (h) enforcement notices served under section 90B above;
   (j) revocations, under paragraph 7 of Schedule 10 to this Act, of discharge consents;
   (k) appeals under section 91 above;
   (l) directions given by the Secretary of State in relation to the Agency's functions under the water pollution provisions of this Act;
   (m) convictions, for offences under Part III of this Act, of persons who have the benefit of discharge consents;
   (n) information obtained or furnished in pursuance of conditions of discharge consents;
   (o) works notices under section 161A above;
   (p) appeals under section 161C above;
   (q) convictions for offences under section 161D above;
   (r) such other matters relating to the quality of water or the pollution of water as may be prescribed by the Secretary of State.

(1A) Where information of any description is excluded from any register by virtue of section 191B below, a statement shall be entered in the register indicating the existence of information of that description.]

(2)   It shall be the duty of the [Agency]—

   (a) to secure that the contents of registers maintained by the [Agency] under this section are available, at all reasonable times, for inspection by the public free of charge; and

   (b) to afford members of the public reasonable facilities for obtaining from the [Agency], on payment of reasonable charges, copies of entries in any of the registers.

[and, for the purposes of this subsection, places may be prescribed by the Secretary of State at which any such registers or facilities as are mentioned in paragraph (a) or (b) above are to be available or afforded to the public in pursuance of the paragraph in question.]

(3)   Section 101 above shall have effect in relation to any regulations under this section as it has effect in relation to any subordinate legislation under Part III of this Act.

[(4)   The Secretary of State may give to the Agency directions requiring the removal from any register maintained by it under this section of any specified information which is not prescribed for inclusion under subsection (1) above or which, by virtue of section 191A or 191B below, ought to have been excluded from the register.

(5)   In this section "discharge consent" has the same meaning as in section 91 above.]

[378]

NOTES

   Sub-s (1): references to "Agency" in square brackets substituted, words in second pair of square brackets and paras (g)–(r) inserted, and paras (d), (f) and word immediately preceding para (f) repealed, by the Environment Act 1995, s 120, Sch 22, paras 128, 169(2)–(4), Sch 24, as from 21 November 1996 so far as to confer power to make regulations, and from 31 December 1996 otherwise (Environment Act 1995 (Commencement No 8 and Saving Provisions) Order 1996, SI 1996/2909, art 2).

   Sub-ss (1A), (4), (5): added with savings by the Environment Act 1995, s 120, Sch 22, para 169(4), (6); for savings see SI 1996/2909, art 4(1).

   Sub-s (2): words in first, second and third pairs of square brackets substituted; words in final pair of square brackets inserted as from a day to be appointed, by the Environment Act 1995, s 120, Sch 22, paras 128, 169(5).

   Regulations: the Control of Pollution (Applications, Appeals and Registers) Regulations 1996, SI 1996/2971.

191–195 *(Relate to the register for the purposes of works discharges (s 191); maps of fresh- water limits (s 192); main river maps (s 193); amendment of main river maps (s 194); maps of waterworks (s 195).)*

Provision and acquisition of information etc

196, 197 *(S 196 repealed by the Environment Act 1995, s 120(1), (3), Sch 22, para 171, Sch 24; s 197 relates to the provision of information about water flow, etc.)*

198 Information about underground water

(1)   Any person who, for the purpose of searching for or abstracting water, proposes to sink a well or borehole intended to reach a depth of more than fifty feet below the surface shall, before he begins to do so, give notice to the Natural Environment Research Council of his intention to do so.

(2)   Any person sinking any such well or borehole as is mentioned in subsection (1) above shall—
  (a) keep a journal of the progress of the work and, on completion or abandonment of the work, send a complete copy of the journal to the Natural Environment Research Council;
  (b) send to that Council particulars of any test made before completion or abandonment of the work of the flow of water;
  (c) allow any person authorised by that Council for the purpose, on production of some duly authenticated document showing his authority, at all reasonable times to exercise any of the rights specified in subsection (5) below.

(3)   The journal required to be kept under this section shall include measurements of—
  (a) the strata passed through; and
  (b) the levels at which water is struck and subsequently rests.

(4)   The particulars required to be sent to the Natural Environment Research Council under subsection (2)(b) above shall specify—
  (a) the rate of flow throughout the test;
  (b) the duration of the test;
  (c) where practicable, the water levels during the test and afterwards until the water returns to its natural level; and
  (d) where the well or borehole is sunk in connection with an existing pumping station, the rate of pumping at the existing works during the test.

(5)   The rights mentioned in subsection (2)(c) above are the rights, subject to section 205 below—
  (a) to have free access to the well or borehole;
  (b) to inspect the well or borehole and the material extracted from it;
  (c) to take specimens of any such material and of water abstracted from the well or borehole; and
  (d) to inspect and take copies of or extracts from the journal required to be kept under this section.

(6)   Where the person sinking a well or borehole on any land is not the occupier of the land, the obligation imposed on that person by virtue of subsection (2)(c) above shall be the obligation of the occupier as well.

(7)   Where—
  (a) any person contracts to sink any well or borehole on land belonging to or occupied by another; and
  (b) the carrying out of the work is under the control of the contractor,
the contractor and no other person shall be deemed for the purposes of this section to be the person sinking the well or borehole.

(8)   Any person who fails to comply with any obligation imposed on him by this section shall be guilty of an offence and liable, on summary conviction—
  (a) to a fine not exceeding level 3 on the standard scale; and
  (b) where the offence continues after conviction, to a further fine of £20 for every day during which it so continues.

[379]

199, 200   (*Relate to notice etc of mining operations which might affect water conservation (s 199); gauges and records kept by other persons (s 200).*)

201 Power to require information with respect to abstraction

(1)   The [Agency] may give directions requiring any person who is abstracting water from a source of supply, at such times and in such form as may be specified in

the directions, to give such information to the [Agency] as to the abstraction as may be so specified.

(2) Where—
(a) directions are given to any person under this section; and
(b) that person considers that they are unreasonable or unduly onerous,

he may make representations to the Secretary of State with respect to the directions.

(3) Subject to subsection (4) below, where representations are made to the Secretary of State under subsection (2) above, he may, if he thinks fit, give a direction under this section requiring the [Agency] to revoke or modify the direction.

(4) Subsection (3) above shall not apply to any directions in so far as they require the occupier of any land to give any prescribed particulars as to the quantity or quality of water abstracted by him or on his behalf from any source of supply.

(5) Any person who fails to comply with any directions given by the [Agency] under this section shall be guilty of an offence and liable, on summary conviction, to a fine not exceeding level 1 on the standard scale.

[380]

NOTES
Sub-ss (1), (3), (5): words in square brackets substituted by the Environment Act 1995, s 120, Sch 22, para 128.

202 Information and assistance required in connection with the control of pollution

(1) It shall be the duty of the [Agency], if and so far as it is requested to do so by either of the Ministers, to give him all such advice and assistance as appears to it to be appropriate for facilitating the carrying out by him of his functions under the water pollution provisions of this Act.

(2) Subject to subsection (3) below, either of the Ministers or the [Agency] may serve on any person a notice requiring that person to furnish him or, as the case may be, it, within a period or at times specified in the notice and in a form and manner so specified, with such information as is reasonably required by the Minister in question or by the [Agency] for the purpose of carrying out any of his or, as the case may be, its functions under the water pollution provisions of this Act.

(3) Each of the Ministers shall have power by regulations to make provision for restricting the information which may be required under subsection (2) above and for determining the form in which the information is to be so required.

(4) A person who fails without reasonable excuse to comply with the requirements of a notice served on him under this section shall be guilty of an offence and [liable—
(a) on summary conviction, to a fine not exceeding the statutory maximum;
(b) on conviction on indictment, to a fine or to imprisonment for a term not exceeding two years, or to both.]

(5) . . .

[381]

NOTES
Sub-ss (1), (2), (4): words in square brackets substituted by the Environment Act 1995, s 120, Sch 22, paras 128, 172(1).
Sub-s (5): repealed by the Environment Act 1995, s 120, Sch 22, para 172(2), Sch 24.
Modifications: sub-s (2) has effect as if it conferred power on the Environment Agency to require the furnishing of information reasonably required by the Agency for the purposes of giving effect to Directives 75/440/EEC and 79/869/EEC, by the Surface Waters (Abstraction for Drinking Water) (Classification) Regulations 1996, SI 1996/3001, art 7(3).

Sub-s (2) has effect as if it conferred power on the Secretary of State and the Environment Agency to require the furnishing of information reasonably required for the purposes of giving effect to Directive 78/659/EEC, by the Surface Waters (Fishlife) (Classification) Regulations 1997, SI 1997/1331, reg 6(3), and to Directive 79/923/EEC, by the Surface Waters (Shellfish) (Classification) Regulations 1997, SI 1997/1332, reg 6(3).

203   (*Relates to exchange of information with respect to pollution incidents etc.*)

Restriction on disclosure of information

204 Restriction on disclosure of information

(1)   Subject to the following provisions of this section, no information with respect to any particular business which—
  (a) has been obtained by virtue of any of the provisions of this Act; and
  (b) relates to the affairs of any individual or to any particular business,

shall, during the lifetime of that individual or so long as that business continues to be carried on, be disclosed without the consent of that individual or the person for the time being carrying on that business.

(2)   Subsection (1) above does not apply to any disclosure of information which is made—
  (a) for the purpose of facilitating the carrying out by either of the Ministers, [the Agency, the Scottish Environment Protection Agency], the Director General of Water Services, the Monopolies Commission or a local authority of any of his, its or, as the case may be, their functions by virtue of this Act, any of the other consolidation Acts[, the Water Act 1989, Part I or IIA of the Environmental Protection Act 1990 or the 1995 Act];
  (b) for the purpose of facilitating the performance by a water undertaker or sewerage undertaker of any of the duties imposed on it by or under this Act, any of the other consolidation Acts or the Water Act 1989;
  (c) in pursuance of any duty imposed by section 197(1)(a) or (2) or 203(1) or (2) above or of any arrangements made by the Director General of Water Services under section 29(6) of the Water Industry Act 1991;
  (d) for the purpose of facilitating the carrying out by any person mentioned in Part I of Schedule 24 to this Act of any of his functions under any of the enactments or instruments specified in Part II of that Schedule;
  (e) for the purpose of enabling or assisting the Secretary of State to exercise any powers conferred on him by the Financial Services Act 1986 or by the enactments relating to companies, insurance companies or insolvency or for the purpose of enabling or assisting any inspector appointed by him under the enactments relating to companies to carry out his functions;
  (f) for the purpose of enabling an official receiver to carry out his functions under the enactments relating to insolvency or for the purpose of enabling or assisting a recognised professional body for the purposes of section 391 of the Insolvency Act 1986 to carry out its functions as such;
  (g) for the purpose of facilitating the carrying out by the Health and Safety Commission or the Health and Safety Executive of any of its functions under any enactment or of facilitating the carrying out by any enforcing authority, within the meaning of Part I of the Health and Safety at Work etc Act 1974, of any functions under a relevant statutory provision, within the meaning of that Act;
  (h) for the purpose of facilitating the carrying out by the Comptroller and Auditor General of any of his functions under any enactment;
  (i) in connection with the investigation of any criminal offence or for the purposes of any criminal proceedings;
  (j) for the purposes of any civil proceedings brought under or by virtue of this Act, any of the other consolidation Acts, the Water Act 1989 or any of the

enactments or instruments specified in Part II of Schedule 24 to this Act, or of any arbitration under this Act, any of the other consolidation Acts or that Act of 1989; or

(k) in pursuance of a Community obligation.

(3) Nothing in subsection (1) above shall be construed—

(a) as limiting the matters which may be included in, or made public as part of, a report of—

(i) the [Agency];

[(ia) the Scottish Environment Protection Agency;]

(ii) the Director General of Water Services;

(iii) a customer service committee maintained under the Water Industry Act 1991; or

(iv) the Monopolies Commission,

under any provision of this Act[, Part I or IIA of the Environmental Protection Act 1990, that Act of 1991 or the 1995 Act];

(b) as limiting the matters which may be published under section 201 of that Act [of 1991]; or

(c) as applying to any information which has been made public as part of such a report or has been so published or to any information exclusively of a statistical nature.

(4) Subject to subsection (5) below, nothing in subsection (1) above shall preclude the disclosure of information—

(a) if the disclosure is of information relating to a matter connected with the carrying out of the functions of a water undertaker or sewerage undertaker and is made by one Minister of the Crown or government department to another; or

(b) if the disclosure is for the purpose of enabling or assisting any public or other authority for the time being designated for the purposes of this section by an order made by the Secretary of State to discharge any functions which are specified in the order.

(5) The power to make an order under subsection (4) above shall be exercisable by statutory instrument subject to annulment in pursuance of a resolution of either House of Parliament; and where such an order designates an authority for the purposes of paragraph (b) of that subsection, the order may—

(a) impose conditions subject to which the disclosure of information is permitted by virtue of that paragraph; and

(b) otherwise restrict the circumstances in which disclosure is so permitted.

(6) Any person who discloses any information in contravention of the preceding provisions of this section shall be guilty of an offence and liable—

(a) on summary conviction, to a fine not exceeding the statutory maximum;

(b) on conviction on indictment, to imprisonment for a term not exceeding two years or to a fine or to both.

(7) In this section "the other consolidation Acts" means the Water Industry Act 1991, the Statutory Water Companies Act 1991, the Land Drainage Act 1991 and the Water Consolidation (Consequential Provisions) Act 1991.

[382]

NOTES

Sub-s (2): words in square brackets substituted by the Environment Act 1995, s 120, Sch 22, para 173(2).

Sub-s (3): words in first and third pair of square brackets substituted, and para (a)(ia) and words in square brackets in para (b) inserted, by the Environment Act 1995, s 120, Sch 22, paras 128, 173(3).

205 Confidentiality of information relating to underground water etc

(1) The person sinking any such well or borehole as is mentioned in section 198 above or, if it is a different person, the owner or occupier of the land on which any such well or borehole is sunk may by notice to the Natural Environment Research Council require that Council to treat as confidential—

(a) any copy of or extract from the journal required to be kept under that section; or

(b) any specimen taken in exercise of the rights specified in subsection (5) of that section.

(2) Subject to subsections (3) and (4) below, the Natural Environment Research Council shall not, without the consent of the person giving the notice, allow any matter to which any notice under subsection (1) above relates to be published or shown to any person who is not an officer of that Council or of a department of the Secretary of State.

(3) Subsection (2) above shall not prohibit any matter from being published or shown to any person in so far as it contains or affords information as to water resources and supplies.

(4) If at any time the Natural Environment Research Council give notice to any person that in their opinion his consent for the purposes of subsection (2) above is being unreasonably withheld—

(a) that person may, within three months after the giving of the notice, appeal to the High Court for an order restraining that Council from acting as if consent had been given; and

(b) that Council may proceed as if consent had been given if either no such appeal is brought within that period or the High Court, after hearing the appeal, do not make such an order.

(5) Any person who fails to comply with any obligation imposed on him by the preceding provisions of this section shall be guilty of an offence and liable, on summary conviction—

(a) to a fine not exceeding level 3 on the standard scale; and

(b) where the offence continues after conviction, to a further fine of £20 for every day during which it so continues.

(6) If any person who is admitted to any premises in compliance with section 198(2)(c) above discloses to any person any information obtained by him there with regard to any manufacturing process or trade secret, he shall, unless the disclosure is in performance of his duty, be guilty of an offence and liable—

(a) on summary conviction, to imprisonment for a term not exceeding three months or to a fine not exceeding the statutory maximum or to both;

(b) on conviction on indictment, to imprisonment for a term not exceeding three months or to a fine or to both.

[383]

206 *(Relates to the making of false statements etc.)*

PART IX
MISCELLANEOUS AND SUPPLEMENTAL

Miscellaneous

207, 208 *(Relate to miscellaneous matters concerning national security (s 207), civil liability, etc (s 208).)*

209 Evidence of samples and abstractions

(1), (2). . .

(3) Where, in accordance with the provisions contained in a licence in pursuance of paragraph (b) of subsection (2) of section 46 above, or in pursuance of that paragraph as read with subsection (6) of that section, it has been determined what quantity of water is to be taken—

    (a) to have been abstracted during any period from a source of supply by the holder of the licence; or

    (b) to have been so abstracted at a particular point or by particular means, or for use for particular purposes,

that determination shall, for the purposes of any proceedings under Chapter II of Part II of this Act or any of the related water resources provisions, be conclusive evidence of the matters to which it relates.

(4)   . . .

[384]

NOTES

Sub-ss (1), (2), (4): repealed by the Environment Act 1995, ss 111(1), 120, Sch 24.

210–215 (*Relate to byelaws (ss 210–212); ss 213–215 repealed by the Environment Act 1995, s 120(1), (3), Sch 22, para 174, Sch 24).*)

Offences etc

216 Enforcement: powers and duties

(1)   Without prejudice to its powers of enforcement in relation to the other provisions of this Act, it shall be the duty of the [Agency] to enforce the provisions to which this section applies.

(2)   No proceedings for any offence under any provision to which this section applies shall be instituted except—

    (a) by the [Agency]; or

    (b) by, or with the consent of, the Director of Public Prosecutions.

(3)   This section applies to Chapter II of Part II of this Act and the related water resources provisions.

[385]

NOTES

Sub-ss (1), (2): words in square brackets substituted by the Environment Act 1995, s 120, Sch 22, para 128.

217 Criminal liabilities of directors and other third parties

(1)   Where a body corporate is guilty of an offence under this Act and that offence is proved to have been committed with the consent or connivance of, or to be attributable to any neglect on the part of, any director, manager, secretary or other similar officer of the body corporate or any person who was purporting to act in any such capacity, then he, as well as the body corporate, shall be guilty of that offence and shall be liable to be proceeded against and punished accordingly.

(2)   Where the affairs of a body corporate are managed by its members, subsection (1) above shall apply in relation to the acts and defaults of a member in connection with his functions of management as if he were a director of the body corporate.

(3)   Without prejudice to subsections (1) and (2) above, where the commission by any person of an offence under the water pollution provisions of this Act is due to the act or default of some other person, that other person may be charged with and convicted of the offence whether or not proceedings for the offence are taken against the first-mentioned person.

[386]

218, 219   (*S 218 repealed by the Environment Act 1995, s 120(1), (3), Sch 22, para 175, Sch 24; s 219 relates to powers to make regulations.*)

Construction of Act

220 Provisions relating to service of documents

(1)   Any document required or authorised by virtue of this Act to be served on any person may be served—
   (a) by delivering it to him or by leaving it at his proper address or by sending it by post to him at that address; or
   (b) if the person is a body corporate, by serving it in accordance with paragraph (a) above on the secretary or clerk of that body; or
   (c) if the person is a partnership, by serving it in accordance with paragraph (a) above on a partner or a person having the control or management of the partnership business.

(2)   For the purposes of this section and section 7 of the Interpretation Act 1978 (which relates to the service of documents by post) in its application to this section, the proper address of any person on whom a document is to be served shall be his last known address, except that—
   (a) in the case of service on a body corporate or its secretary or clerk, it shall be the address of the registered or principal office of the body;
   (b) in the case of service on a partnership or a partner or a person having the control or management of a partnership business, it shall be the address of the principal office of the partnership;
and for the purposes of this subsection the principal office of a company registered outside the United Kingdom, or of a partnership carrying on business outside the United Kingdom is its principal office within the United Kingdom.

(3)   If a person to be served by virtue of this Act with any document by another has specified to that other an address within the United Kingdom other than his proper address (as determined in pursuance of subsection (2) above) as the one at which he or someone on his behalf will accept documents of the same description as that document, that address shall also be treated as his proper address for the purposes of this section and for the purposes of the said section 7 in its application to this section.

(4)   Where under any provision of this Act any document is required to be served on the owner, on a lessee or on the occupier of any premises then—
   (a) if the name or address of the owner, of the lessee or, as the case may be, of the occupier of the premises cannot after reasonable inquiry be ascertained; or
   (b) in the case of service on the occupier, if the premises appear to be or are unoccupied,
that document may be served either by leaving it in the hands of a person who is or appears to be resident or employed on the land or by leaving it conspicuously affixed to some building or object on the land.

(5)   This section shall not apply to any document in relation to the service of which provision is made by rules of court.

[387]

221 General interpretation

(1)   In this Act, except in so far as the context otherwise requires—

["the 1995 Act" means the Environment Act 1995;]

"abstraction", in relation to water contained in any source of supply, means the doing of anything whereby any of that water is removed from that source of supply, whether temporarily or permanently, including anything whereby the water is so removed for the purpose of being transferred to another source of supply; and "abstract" shall be construed accordingly;

"accessories", in relation to a main, sewer or other pipe, includes any manholes, ventilating shafts, inspection chambers, settling tanks, wash-out pipes, pumps, ferrules or stopcocks for the main, sewer or other pipe, or any machinery or other apparatus which is designed or adapted for use in connection with the use or maintenance of the main, sewer or other pipe or of another accessory for it, but does not include any telecommunication apparatus (within the meaning of Schedule 2 to the Telecommunications Act 1984) unless it—

(a) is or is to be situated inside or in the close vicinity of the main, sewer or other pipe or inside or in the close vicinity of another accessory for it; and

(b) is intended to be used only in connection with the use or maintenance of the main, sewer or other pipe or of another accessory for it;

and in this definition "stopcock" has the same meaning as in the Water Industry Act 1991;

["the Agency" means the Environment Agency;]

"agriculture" has the same meaning as in the Agriculture Act 1947 and "agricultural" shall be construed accordingly;

"analyse", in relation to any sample of land, water or effluent, includes subjecting the sample to a test of any description, and cognate expressions shall be construed accordingly;

. . . . .

"conservancy authority" means any person who has a duty or power under any enactment to conserve, maintain or improve the navigation of a tidal water and is not a navigation authority or harbour authority;

. . . . .

"contravention" includes a failure to comply, and cognate expressions shall be construed accordingly;

"damage", in relation to individuals, includes death and any personal injury (including any disease or impairment of physical or mental condition);

"discrete waters" means inland waters so far as they comprise—

(a) a lake, pond or reservoir which does not discharge to any other inland waters; or

(b) one of a group of two or more lakes, ponds or reservoirs (whether near to or distant from each other) and of watercourses or mains connecting them, where none of the inland waters in the group discharges to any inland waters outside the group;

"disposal"—

(a) in relation to land or any interest or right in or over land, includes the creation of such an interest or right and a disposal effected by means of the surrender or other termination of any such interest or right; and

(b) in relation to sewage, includes treatment;

and cognate expressions shall be construed accordingly;

"drain" has, subject to subsection (2) below, the same meaning as in the Water Industry Act 1991;

"drainage" in the expression "drainage works" has the meaning given by section 113 above for the purposes of Part IV of this Act;

"drought order" means an ordinary drought order under subsection (1) of section 73 above or an emergency drought order under subsection (2) of that section;

"effluent" means any liquid, including particles of matter and other substances in suspension in the liquid;

"enactment" includes an enactment contained in this Act or in any Act passed after this Act;

["enforcement notice" has the meaning given by section 90B above;]

"engineering or building operations", without prejudice to the generality of that expression, includes—

    (a) the construction, alteration, improvement, maintenance or demolition of any building or structure or of any reservoir, watercourse, dam, weir, well, borehole or other works; and

    (b) the installation, modification or removal of any machinery or apparatus;

"financial year" means the twelve months ending with 31st March;

["flood defence functions", in relation to the Agency, means—

    (a) its functions with respect to flood defence and land drainage by virtue of Part IV of this Act, the Land Drainage Act 1991 and section 6 of the 1995 Act;

    (b) those functions transferred to the Agency by section 2(1)(a)(iii) of the 1995 Act which were previously transferred to the Authority by virtue of section 136(8) of the Water Act 1989 and paragraph 1(3) of Schedule 15 to that Act (transfer of land drainage functions under local statutory provisions and subordinate legislation); and

    (c) any other functions of the Agency under any of the flood defence provisions of this Act;]

["flood defence provisions", in relation to this Act, means—

    (a) any of the following provisions of this Act, that is to say—

        (i) Part IV;

        (ii) sections 133 to 141 (including Schedule 15), 143, 147 to 149, 155, 165 to 167, 180, 193, 194 and paragraph 5 of Schedule 25;

    (b) any of the following provisions of the 1995 Act, that is to say—

        (i) section 6(4) (general supervision of flood defence);

        (ii) section 53 (inquiries and other hearings); and

        (iii) Schedule 5 (membership and proceedings of regional and local flood defence committees); and

    (c) any other provision of this Act or the 1995 Act so far as it relates to a provision falling within paragraph (a) or (b) above;]

"harbour" has the same meaning for the purposes of the flood defence provisions of this Act as in [section 313 of the Merchant Shipping Act 1995];

"harbour authority" (except in the flood defence provisions of this Act, in which it has the same meaning as in [section 313 of the Merchant Shipping Act 1995]) means a person who is a harbour authority [as defined in section 151 for the purposes of Chapter II of Part VI of that Act] and is not a navigation authority;

"highway" has the same meaning as in the Highways Act 1980;

"information" includes anything contained in any records, accounts, estimates or returns;

"inland waters" means the whole or any part of—

    (a) any river, stream or other watercourse (within the meaning of Chapter II of Part II of this Act), whether natural or artificial and whether tidal or not;

    (b) any lake or pond, whether natural or artificial, or any reservoir or dock, in so far as the lake, pond, reservoir or dock does not fall within paragraph (a) of this definition; and

(c) so much of any channel, creek, bay, estuary or arm of the sea as does not fall within paragraph (a) or (b) of this definition;

"joint planning board" has the same meaning as in the Town and Country Planning Act 1990;

"local authority" means the council of any county, [county borough,] district or London borough or the Common Council of the City of London;

"local statutory provision" means—

(a) a provision of a local Act (including an Act confirming a provisional order);

(b) a provision of so much of any public general Act as has effect with respect to a particular area, with respect to particular persons or works or with respect to particular provisions falling within any paragraph of this definition;

(c) a provision of an instrument made under any provision falling within paragraph (a) or (b) above; or

(d) a provision of any other instrument which is in the nature of a local enactment;

"main river" means a main river within the meaning of Part IV of this Act;

"main river map" has, subject to section 194 above, the meaning given by section 193(2) above;

"micro-organism" includes any microscopic, biological entity which is capable of replication;

"minimum acceptable flow", in relation to any inland waters, means (except in sections 21 and 22 above and subject to section 23(3) above) the minimum acceptable flow as for the time being contained in provisions which are in force under section 21(7) above in relation to those waters;

"the Minister" means the Minister of Agriculture, Fisheries and Food;

"the Ministers" means the Secretary of State and the Minister;

"modifications" includes additions, alterations and omissions, and cognate expressions shall be construed accordingly;

"mortgage" includes any charge or lien on any property for securing money or money's worth, and "mortgagee" shall be construed accordingly;

"navigation authority" means any person who has a duty or power under any enactment to work, maintain, conserve, improve or control any canal or other inland navigation, navigable river, estuary, harbour or dock;

"notice" means notice in writing;

"owner", in relation to any premises, means the person who

(a) is for the time being receiving the rack-rent of the premises, whether on his own account or as agent or trustee for another person; or

(b) would receive the rack-rent if the premises were let at a rack-rent,

but for the purposes of Schedule 2 to this Act, Chapter II of Part II of this Act and the related water resources provisions does not include a mortgagee not in possession, and cognate expressions shall be construed accordingly;

"prescribed" means prescribed by regulations made by the Secretary of State or, in relation to regulations made by the Minister, by those regulations;

"public authority" means any Minister of the Crown or government department, the Authority, any local authority or any person certified by the Secretary of State to be a public authority for the purposes of this Act;

"public sewer" means a sewer for the time being vested in a sewerage undertaker in its capacity as such, whether vested in that undertaker by virtue of a scheme under Schedule 2 to the Water Act 1989, section 179 of or Schedule 2 to the Water Industry Act 1991 or otherwise;

"records" includes computer records and any other records kept otherwise than in a document;

["the related water resources provisions", in relation to Chapter II of Part II of this Act, means—

    (a) the following provisions of this Act, that is to say, the provisions—
        (i) of sections 21 to 23 (including Schedule 5);
        (ii) of sections 120, 125 to 130, 158, 189, 199 to 201, 206(3), 209(3), 211(1) and 216; and
        (iii) of paragraph 1 of Schedule 25; and
    (b) the following provisions of the 1995 Act, that is to say, the provisions—
        (i) of sections 41 and 42 (charging schemes) as they have effect by virtue of subsection (1)(a) of section 41 (licences under Chapter II of Part II of this Act); and
        (ii) of subsections (1) and (2) of section 53 (inquiries and other hearings);]

"sewage effluent" includes any effluent from the sewage disposal or sewerage works of a sewerage undertaker but does not include surface water;

"sewer" has, subject to subsection (2) below, the same meaning as in the Water Industry Act 1991;

"source of supply" means—
    (a) any inland waters except, without prejudice to subsection (3) below in its application to paragraph (b) of this definition, any which are discrete waters; or
    (b) any underground strata in which water is or at any time may be contained;

"street" has, subject to subsection (4) below, the same meaning as in Part III of the New Roads and Street Works 1991;

"subordinate legislation" has the same meaning as in the Interpretation Act 1978;

"substance" includes micro-organisms and any natural or artificial substance or other matter, whether it is in solid or liquid form or in the form of a gas or vapour;

"surface water" includes water from roofs;

"trade effluent" includes any effluent which is discharged from premises used for carrying on any trade or industry, other than surface water and domestic sewage, and for the purposes of this definition any premises wholly or mainly used (whether for profit or not) for agricultural purposes or for the purposes of fish farming or for scientific research or experiment shall be deemed to be premises used for carrying on a trade;

"underground strata" means strata subjacent to the surface of any land;

"vessel" includes a hovercraft within the meaning of the Hovercraft Act 1968;

"watercourse" includes (subject to sections 72(2) and 113(1) above) all rivers, streams, ditches, drains, cuts, culverts, dykes, sluices, sewers and passages through which water flows, except mains and other pipes which—
    (a) belong to the Authority or a water undertaker; or
    (b) are used by a water undertaker or any other person for the purpose only of providing a supply of water to any premises;

"water pollution provisions", in relation to this Act, means the following provisions of this Act—
    (a) the provisions of Part III of this Act;
    (b) sections 161 [to 161D], 190, 202, [and 203]; and
    (c) paragraph 4 of Schedule 25 to this Act and section 211 above so far as it relates to byelaws made under that paragraph

[and the following provisions of the 1995 Act, that is to say, the provisions of subsections (1) and (2) of section 53.].

(2) References in this Act to a pipe, including references to a main, a drain or a sewer, shall include references to a tunnel or conduit which serves or is to serve as the pipe in question and to any accessories for the pipe; and, accordingly, references to the laying of a pipe shall include references to the construction of such a tunnel or

conduit, to the construction or installation of any such accessories and to the making of a connection between one pipe and another.

(3)   Any reference in this Act to water contained in underground strata is a reference to water so contained otherwise than in a sewer, pipe, reservoir, tank or other underground works constructed in any such strata; but for the purposes of this Act water for the time being contained in—

(a) a well, borehole or similar work, including any adit or passage constructed in connection with the well, borehole or work for facilitating the collection of water in the well, borehole or work; or

(b) any excavation into underground strata, where the level of water in the excavation depends wholly or mainly on water entering it from those strata,

shall be treated as water contained in the underground strata into which the well, borehole or work was sunk or, as the case may be, the excavation was made.

(4)   Until the coming into force of Part III of the New Roads and Street Works Act 1991, the definition of "street" in subsection (1) above shall have effect as if the reference to that Part were a reference to the Public Utilities Street Works Act 1950; but nothing in this section shall be taken—

(a) to prejudice the power of the Secretary of State under that Act of 1991 to make an order bringing Part III of that Act into force on different days for different purposes (including the purposes of this section); or

(b) in the period before the coming into force of that Part, to prevent references in this Act to a street, where the street is a highway which passes over a bridge or through a tunnel, from including that bridge or tunnel.

(5)   For the purposes of any provision of this Act by or under which power is or may be conferred on any person to recover the expenses incurred by that person in doing anything, those expenses shall be assumed to include such sum as may be reasonable in respect of establishment charges or overheads.

(6)   References in this Act to the later or latest of two or more different times or days are, in a case where those times or days coincide, references to the time at which or, as the case may be, the day on which they coincide.

(7)   For the purposes of this Act—

(a) references in this Act to more than one Minister of the Crown, in relation to anything falling to be done by those Ministers, are references to those Ministers acting jointly; and

(b) any provision of this Act by virtue of which any function of a Minister of the Crown is exercisable concurrently by different Ministers, shall have effect as providing for that function also to be exercisable jointly by any two or more of those Ministers.

(8)   Sub-paragraph (1) of paragraph 1 of Schedule 2 to the Water Consolidation (Consequential Provisions) Act 1991 has effect (by virtue of sub-paragraph (2)(b) of that paragraph) so that references in this Act to things done under or for the purposes of provisions of this Act, the Water Industry Act 1991 or the Land Drainage Act 1991 include references to things done, or treated as done, under or for the purposes of the corresponding provisions of the law in force before the commencement of this Act.

(9)   Subject to any provision to the contrary which is contained in Schedule 26 to the Water Act 1989 or in the Water Consolidation (Consequential Provisions) Act 1991, nothing in any local statutory provision passed or made before 1st September 1989 shall be construed as relieving any water undertaker or sewerage undertaker from any liability arising by virtue of this Act in respect of any act or omission occurring on or after that date.

[388]

NOTES

Sub-s (1): definitions "the 1995 Act", "the Agency" and "enforcement notice" inserted, definitions omitted repealed, and definitions "flood defence functions", "flood defence provisions" and "the related water resources provisions" substituted, and in definition "water pollution provisions" words in first and final pairs of square brackets inserted, and words in other pairs of square brackets substituted, by the Environment Act 1995, s 120, Sch 22, para 177, Sch 24; in definitions "harbour" and "harbour authority" words in square brackets substituted by the Merchant Shipping Act 1995, s 314(2), Sch 13, para 90; in definition "local authority" words in square brackets inserted by the Local Government (Wales) Act 1994, s 22(5), Sch 11, para 3(6).

Other supplemental provisions

222–224 (*Relate to application to Crown (s 222); exemption for visiting forces (s 223); application to Isles of Scilly (s 224).*)

225 Short title, commencement and extent

(1)   This Act may be cited as the Water Resources Act 1991.

(2)   This Act shall come into force on 1st December 1991.

(3)   Subject to subsections (4) to (6) of section 2 and to section 224 above, to the extension of section 166(3) above to Scotland and to the extension, by virtue of any other enactment, of any provision of this Act to the territorial sea, this Act extends to England and Wales only.

(4)   Nothing in this Act, so far as it extends to Scotland, shall authorise the [Agency] to acquire any land in Scotland compulsorily.

[389]

NOTES

Sub-s (4): word in square brackets substituted by the Environment Act 1995, s 120, Sch 22, para 128.

(*Schs 1–5 outside the scope of this work.*)

SCHEDULE 6
ORDERS PROVIDING FOR EXEMPTION FROM RESTRICTIONS ON ABSTRACTION

Section 33

Notice of draft order

1.—(1) An application to the Secretary of State for an order under section 33 of this Act ("an exemption order") shall be accompanied by a draft of the proposed order.

(2) Before submitting a draft exemption order to the Secretary of State, the applicant authority shall publish a notice—
    (a)   stating the general effect of the draft order;
    (b)   specifying the place where a copy of the draft order, and of any relevant map or plan, may be inspected by any person free of charge at all reasonable times during the period of twenty-eight days beginning with the date of first publication of the notice; and
    (c)   stating that any person may within that period, by notice to the Secretary of State, object to the making of the order.

(3) A notice under this paragraph shall be published either—
    (a)   at least once in each of two successive weeks, in one or more newspapers circulating in the locality in which the sources of supply to which the draft order relates are situated; or
    (b)   in any other manner which, in any particular case, may be certified by the Secretary of State to be expedient in that case.

(4) Not later than the date on which the notice is first published in pursuance of sub-paragraph (2) above, the applicant authority shall serve a copy of the notice on—

(a)   the [Agency], if it is not the applicant;

(b)   every local authority or joint planning board whose area comprises any source of supply to which the draft order relates;

(c)   any water undertaker having the right to abstract water from any such source of supply;

(d)   any other water undertaker having the right to abstract water from any related underground strata;

(e)   the drainage board for any internal drainage district which comprises any such source of supply or from which water is discharged into any such source of supply;

(f)   any navigation authority, harbour authority or conservancy authority having functions in relation to any such source of supply or any related inland waters;

(g)   if any such source of supply or any related inland waters are tidal waters in relation to which there is no such navigation authority, harbour authority or conservancy authority, the Secretary of State for Transport; and

(h)   any person authorised by a licence under Part I of the Electricity Act 1989 to generate electricity [who has a right to abstract water from any such source of supply or related inland waters].

(5) Where an application for an exemption order is made, the applicant authority shall also publish a notice in the London Gazette—

(a)   stating that the draft exemption order has been submitted to the Secretary of State;

(b)   naming the areas in respect of which a copy of a notice is required to be served under sub-paragraph (4)(b) above;

(c)   specifying a place where a copy of the draft order and of any relevant map or plan may be inspected; and

(d)   where the notice required by sub-paragraph (1) above is published in a newspaper, giving the name of the newspaper and the date of an issue containing the notice.

(6) For the purposes of this paragraph—

(a)   underground strata are related underground strata in relation to any source of supply if—

(i)   a water undertaker has a right to abstract water from the strata; and

(ii)   it appears to the applicant authority, having regard to the extent to which the level of water in those strata depends on the flow of the waters in that source of supply, that the exercise of that right may be substantially affected by so much of the draft order in question as relates to that source of supply;

(b)   inland waters are related inland waters in relation to any source of supply, where it appears to the applicant authority that changes in the flow of the waters of the source of supply may affect the flow of the waters in the inland waters in question.

Duty to provide copy of draft order

2.   Where an application for an exemption order is made, the applicant authority shall, at the request of any person, furnish him with a copy of the draft exemption order on payment of such charge as the authority thinks reasonable.

Making of order

3.—(1) Where an application for an exemption order is made, the Secretary of State may make the exemption order either in the form of the draft or in that form as altered in such manner as he thinks fit.

(2) Where the Secretary of State—

(a)   proposes to make any alteration of an exemption order before making it; and

(b)   considers that any persons are likely to be adversely affected by it,

the applicant authority shall give and publish such additional notices, in such manner, as the Secretary of State may require.

(3) Sub-paragraph (4) below shall apply if before the end of—

(a)   the period of twenty-eight days referred to in sub-paragraph (2) of paragraph 1 above;

(b)   the period of twenty-five days from the publication in the London Gazette of the notice under sub-paragraph (5) of that paragraph; or

(c)   any period specified in notices under sub-paragraph (2) above, notice of an objection is received by the Secretary of State from any person on whom a notice is required by this Schedule to be served, from any other person appearing to the Secretary of State to be affected by the exemption order (either as prepared in draft or as proposed to be altered) or, in the case of a draft order submitted under section 33(4) of this Act, from the [Agency].

(4) Where this sub-paragraph applies and the objection in question is not withdrawn, the Secretary of State, before making the order, shall either—

(a)   cause a local inquiry to be held; or

(b)   afford to the objector and to the applicant authority an opportunity of appearing before, and being heard by, a person appointed by the Secretary of State for the purpose.

(5) Where the exemption order (whether as prepared in draft or as proposed to be altered) relates to any tidal water in respect of which there is no relevant authority for the purposes of section 33 of this Act except the [Agency], sub-paragraphs (1) to (4) above and paragraph 4 below shall have effect as if references to the Secretary of State (except the first reference in sub-paragraph (3) above) were references to the Secretary of State and the Secretary of State for Transport.

Notice and inspection of final order

4.—(1)   Where an exemption order is made under section 33 of this Act, whether in the form of the draft proposed by the applicant authority or with alterations, the Secretary of State shall give notice to the applicant authority and (if it is not the applicant authority) to the [Agency]—

(a)   stating that the exemption order has been made, either without alteration or with alterations specified in the notice; and

(b)   specifying the date (not being earlier than twenty-eight days after the date of the notice under this paragraph) on which the order shall have effect;

and the [Agency] shall forthwith publish the notice.

(2) The [Agency] shall keep a copy of every order made under section 33 of this Act available at its offices for inspection by the public, free of charge, at all reasonable times.

[390]

NOTES

Para 1: word in square brackets in sub-para (4)(a) substituted, and words in square brackets in sub-para (4)(h) inserted, by the Environment Act 1995, s 120, Sch 22, paras 128, 181.

Paras 3, 4: words in square brackets substituted by the Environment Act 1995, s 120, Sch 22, para 128.

Modifications: para 1(4)(b) has effect, in relation to a National Park authority in Wales, as if after the words "joint planning board" there were inserted the words "or National Park authority", by virtue of the National Park Authorities (Wales) Order 1995, SI 1995/2803, art 18, Sch 5, para 2C(e).

Para 1(4)(b) has effect, in relation to a National Park authority in England, as if after the words "local authority" there were inserted the words "National Park authority,", by virtue of the National Park Authorities (England) Order 1996, SI 1996/1243, art 18, Sch 5, para 6(2)(b).

SCHEDULE 7
LICENCES OF RIGHT

Sections 48, 55, 60, 61, 65

Applications for licences of right under paragraph 30 or 31 of Schedule 26 to the Water Act 1989

1.—(1)   Paragraphs 30 and 31 of Schedule 26 to the Water Act 1989 shall continue to apply (notwithstanding the repeals made by the Water Consolidation (Consequential Provisions) Act 1991 but subject to the following provisions of this Schedule) in relation—

(a)   to any application made under either of those paragraphs which is outstanding immediately before the coming into force of this Act; and

(b)   to any appeal against a determination made, on an application under either of those paragraphs, either before the coming into force of this Act or, thereafter, by virtue of paragraph (a) above;

but for the purposes of any such application or appeal any reference in those paragraphs to a provision of the Water Resources Act 1963 which is re-enacted in this Act shall have effect, in relation to a time after the coming into force of this Act, as a reference to the corresponding provision of this Act.

(2) Where an application for the grant of a licence by virtue of paragraph 30 or 31 of Schedule 26 to the Water Act 1989 has been made before the end of the period within which such an application was required to be made under that paragraph, then—

(a) sections 24 and 48 of this Act and Part II of the Gas Act 1965 shall have effect, until the application is disposed of, as if the licence had been granted on the date of the application and the provisions of the licence had been in accordance with the proposals contained in the application; and

(b) for the purposes of those sections and Part II of the said Act of 1965 any licence granted on the application shall be treated as not having effect until the application has been disposed of.

(3) For the purposes of this paragraph an application for the grant of a licence by virtue of paragraph 30 or 31 of Schedule 26 to the Water Act 1989 above shall be taken to be disposed of on (but not before) the occurrence of whichever of the following events last occurs, that is to say—

(a) the grant, on the determination of the application by the [Agency], of a licence the provisions of which are in accordance with the proposals contained in the application;

(b) the expiration, without a notice of appeal having been given, of the period (if any) within which the applicant is entitled to give notice of appeal against the decision on the application;

(c) the determination or withdrawal of an appeal against that decision;

(d) the grant, variation or revocation, in compliance with a direction given by the Secretary of State in consequence of such an appeal, of any licence;

and in this sub-paragraph any reference to a decision includes a reference to a decision which is to be treated as having been made by virtue of any failure of the [Agency] to make a decision within a specified time.

(4) Subject to the other provisions of this Schedule, any licence granted by virtue of this paragraph shall have effect as a licence under Chapter II of Part II of this Act; and, so far as necessary for the purposes of this paragraph, anything done under or for the purposes of a provision of the Water Resources Act 1963 applied by paragraph 30 or 31 of Schedule 26 to the 1989 Act, shall have effect as if that paragraph applied the corresponding provision of this Act and that thing had been done under or for the purposes of that corresponding provision.

Section 48 of this Act

2. Subsection (2) of section 48 of this Act shall not afford any defence to an action brought before 1st September 1992 if the licence referred to in that subsection is a 1989 Act licence of right; and there shall be no defence afforded to such an action by that subsection as applied by paragraph 1(2) above.

Section 55 of this Act

3. No application shall be made under section 55 of this Act (variation of licence on application of owner of fishing rights) in respect of any 1989 Act licence of right.

Section 60 of this Act

4.—(1) Where the plaintiff in any action brought against the [Agency] in pursuance of section 60 of this Act (liability of the [Agency] for derogation from protected right) is entitled to a protected right for the purposes of Chapter II of Part II of this Act by reason only that he is the holder of, or has applied for, a licence of right, it shall be a defence for the [Agency] to prove—

(a) that the plaintiff could have carried out permissible alterations in the means whereby he abstracted water from the source of supply in question; and

(b) that, if he had carried out such alterations, the abstraction or, as the case may be, the obstruction or impeding of the flow of the inland waters authorised by the licence to which the action relates would not have derogated from his protected right for the purposes of that Chapter;

and subsection (3) of that section (liability of [Agency] for compliance with direction requiring derogation from protected rights) shall not apply to a direction given in consequence of an appeal against the decision of the [Agency] on an application for the grant of a 1989 Act licence of right.

(2) In this paragraph "permissible alterations"—

(a) in relation to a person who is the holder of a licence of right, means any alteration of works, or modification of machinery or apparatus, which would fulfil the requirements of the licence as to the means whereby water is authorised to be abstracted;

(b) in relation to a person who is not the holder of a licence of right, but to whose application for such a licence paragraph 1 above applies, means any alteration of works, or modification of machinery or apparatus, by means of which he abstracted water from the source of supply in question during the period of five years ending with 1st September 1989, being an alteration or modification which would be within the scope of the licence if granted in accordance with the application.

Section 61 of this Act

5.—(1) No compensation shall be payable under section 61 of this Act (compensation for revocation or variation of a licence) in respect of the revocation or variation of a 1989 Act licence of right if the revocation or variation is for giving effect to the decision of the court in an action in respect of which paragraph 2 above has effect or in any proceedings in consequence of such an action.

(2) Nothing in section 61(3) of this Act (compensation not payable in respect of works etc carried out before the grant of a licence) shall apply in relation to any licence of right.

Licences of right

6.—(1) In this Schedule references to a licence of right are references to—

(a) any 1989 Act licence of right, that is to say, a licence granted (whether or not by virtue of paragraph 1 above) under paragraph 30 or 31 of Schedule 26 to the Water Act 1989; or

(b) any licence which, having been granted in pursuance of an application under section 33 of the Water Resources Act 1963 (or in pursuance of an appeal consequential on such an application), has effect after the coming into force of this Act by virtue of sub-paragraph (2) below.

(2) The repeal by the Water Consolidation (Consequential Provisions) Act 1991 of paragraph 29(4) of schedule 26 to the Water Act 1989 shall not prevent any licence granted as mentioned in paragraph (b) of sub-paragraph (1) above from continuing (in accordance with paragraph 1 of Schedule 2 to that Act of 1991 and subject to the preceding provisions of this Schedule) to have effect after the coming into force of this Act as a licence under Chapter II of Part II of this Act.

[391]

NOTES

Paras 1, 4: words in square brackets substituted by the Environment Act 1995, s 120, Sch 22, para 128.

(Schs 8, 9 outside the scope of this work.)

SCHEDULE 10
DISCHARGE CONSENTS

Section 88

[Application for consent

1.—(1) An application for a consent, for the purposes of section 88(1)(a) of this Act, for any discharges—

(a) shall be made to the Agency on a form provided for the purpose by the Agency; and

(b) must be advertised by or on behalf of the applicant in such manner as may be required by regulations made by the Secretary of State.

(2) Regulations made by the Secretary of State may make provision for enabling the Agency to direct or determine that any such advertising of an application as is required under

sub-paragraph (1)(b) above may, in any case, be dispensed with if, in that case, it appears to the Agency to be appropriate for that advertising to be dispensed with.

(3) The applicant for such a consent must provide to the Agency, either on, or together with, the form mentioned in sub-paragraph (1) above—
    (a)   such information as the Agency may reasonably require; and
    (b)   such information as may be prescribed for the purpose by the Secretary of State;

but, subject to paragraph 3(3) below and without prejudice to the effect (if any) of any other contravention of the requirements of this Schedule in relation to an application under this paragraph, a failure to provide information in pursuance of this sub-paragraph shall not invalidate an application.

(4) The Agency may give the applicant notice requiring him to provide it with such further information of any description specified in the notice as it may require for the purpose of determining the application.

(5) An application made in accordance with this paragraph which relates to proposed discharges at two or more places may be treated by the Agency as separate applications for consents for discharges at each of those places.

Consultation in connection with applications

2.—(1) Subject to sub-paragraph (2) below, the Agency shall give notice of any application under paragraph 1 above, together with a copy of the application, to the persons who are prescribed or directed to be consulted under this paragraph and shall do so within the specified period for notification.

(2) The Secretary of State may, by regulations, exempt any class of application from the requirements of this paragraph or exclude any class of information contained in applications from those requirements, in all cases or as respects specified classes only of persons to be consulted.

(3) Any representations made by the persons so consulted within the period allowed shall be considered by the Agency in determining the application.

(4) For the purposes of sub-paragraph (1) above—
    (a)   persons are prescribed to be consulted on any description of application if they are persons specified for the purposes of applications of that description in regulations made by the Secretary of State;
    (b)   persons are directed to be consulted on any particular application if the Secretary of State specifies them in a direction given to the Agency;

and the "specified period for notification" is the period specified in the regulations or in the direction.

(5) Any representations made by any other persons within the period allowed shall also be considered by the Agency in determining the application.

(6) Subject to sub-paragraph (7) below, the period allowed for making representations is—
    (a)   in the case of persons prescribed or directed to be consulted, the period of six weeks beginning with the date on which notice of the application was given under sub-paragraph (1) above, and
    (b)   in the case of other persons, the period of six weeks beginning with the date on which the making of the application was advertised in pursuance of paragraph 1(1)(b) above.

(7) The Secretary of State may, by regulations, substitute for any period for the time being specified in sub-paragraph (6)(a) or (b) above, such other period as he considers appropriate.

Consideration and determination of applications

3.—(1) On an application under paragraph 1 above the Agency shall be under a duty, if the requirements—
    (a)   of that paragraph, and
    (b)   of any regulations made under paragraph 1 or 2 above or of any directions under paragraph 2 above,

are complied with, to consider whether to give the consent applied for, either unconditionally or subject to conditions, or to refuse it.

(2) Subject to the following provisions of this Schedule, on an application made in accordance with paragraph 1 above, the applicant may treat the consent applied for as having been refused if it is not given within the period of four months beginning with the day on which the application is received or within such longer period as may be agreed in writing between the Agency and the applicant.

(3) Where any person, having made an application to the Agency for a consent, has failed to comply with his obligation under paragraph 1(3) or (4) above to provide information to the Agency, the Agency may refuse to proceed with the application, or refuse to proceed with it until the information is provided.

(4) The conditions subject to which a consent may be given under this paragraph shall be such conditions as the Agency may think fit and, in particular, may include conditions—
    (a) as to the places at which the discharges to which the consent relates may be made and as to the design and construction of any outlets for the discharges;
    (b) as to the nature, origin, composition, temperature, volume and rate of the discharges and as to the periods during which the discharges may be made;
    (c) as to the steps to be taken, in relation to the discharges or by way of subjecting any substance likely to affect the description of matter discharged to treatment or any other process, for minimising the polluting effects of the discharges on any controlled waters;
    (d) as to the provision of facilities for taking samples of the matter discharged and, in particular, as to the provision, maintenance and use of manholes, inspection chambers, observation wells and boreholes in connection with the discharges;
    (e) as to the provision, maintenance and testing of meters for measuring or recording the volume and rate of the discharges and apparatus for determining the nature, composition and temperature of the discharges;
    (f) as to the keeping of records of the nature, origin, composition, temperature, volume and rate of the discharges and, in particular, of records of readings of meters and other recording apparatus provided in accordance with any other condition attached to the consent; and
    (g) as to the making of returns and the giving of other information to the Authority about the nature, origin, composition, temperature, volume and rate of the discharges;

and it is hereby declared that a consent may be given under this paragraph subject to different conditions in respect of different periods.

(5) The Secretary of State may, by regulations, substitute for any period for the time being specified in sub-paragraph (2) above, such other period as he considers appropriate.

4. The Secretary of State may give the Agency a direction with respect to any particular application, or any description of applications, for consent under paragraph 1 above requiring the Agency not to determine or not to proceed with the application or applications of that description until the expiry of any such period as may be specified in the direction, or until directed by the Secretary of State that it may do so, as the case may be.

Reference to Secretary of State of certain applications for consent

5.—(1) The Secretary of State may, either in consequence of representations or objections made to him or otherwise, direct the Agency to transmit to him for determination such applications for consent under paragraph 1 above as are specified in the direction or are of a description so specified.

(2) Where a direction is given to the Agency under this paragraph, the Agency shall comply with the direction and inform every applicant to whose application the direction relates of the transmission of his application to the Secretary of State.

(3) Paragraphs 1(1) and 2 above shall have effect in relation to an application transmitted to the Secretary of State under this paragraph with such modifications as may be prescribed.

(4) Where an application is transmitted to the Secretary of State under this paragraph, the Secretary of State may at any time after the application is transmitted and before it is granted or refused—
    (a) cause a local inquiry to be held with respect to the application; or
    (b) afford the applicant and the Agency an opportunity of appearing before, and being heard by, a person appointed by the Secretary of State for the purpose.

(5) The Secretary of State shall exercise his power under sub-paragraph (4) above in any case where a request to be heard with respect to the application is made to him in the prescribed manner by the applicant or by the Agency.

(6) It shall be the duty of the Secretary of State, if the requirements of this paragraph and of any regulations made under it are complied with, to determine an application for consent transmitted to him by the Agency under this paragraph by directing the Agency to refuse its consent or to give its consent under paragraph 3 above (either unconditionally or subject to such conditions as are specified in the direction).

(7) Without prejudice to any of the preceding provisions of this paragraph, the Secretary of State may by regulations make provision for the purposes of, and in connection with, the consideration and disposal by him of applications transmitted to him under this paragraph.

Consents without applications

6.—(1) If it appears to the Agency—
  (a)   that a person has caused or permitted effluent or other matter to be discharged in contravention—
    (i)   of the obligation imposed by virtue of section 85(3) of this Act; or
    (ii)   of any prohibition imposed under section 86 of this Act; and
  (b)   that a similar contravention by that person is likely,
the Agency may, if it thinks fit, serve on him an instrument in writing giving its consent, subject to any conditions specified in the instrument, for discharges of a description so specified.

(2) A consent given under this paragraph shall not relate to any discharge which occurred before the instrument containing the consent was served on the recipient of the instrument.

(3) Sub-paragraph (4) of paragraph 3 above shall have effect in relation to a consent given under this paragraph as it has effect in relation to a consent given under that paragraph.

(4) Where a consent has been given under this paragraph, the Agency shall publish notice of the consent in such manner as may be prescribed by the Secretary of State and send copies of the instrument containing the consent to such bodies or persons as may be so prescribed.

(5) It shall be the duty of the Agency to consider any representations or objections with respect to a consent under this paragraph as are made to it in such manner, and within such period, as may be prescribed by the Secretary of State and have not been withdrawn.

(6) Where notice of a consent is published by the Agency under sub-paragraph (4) above, the Agency shall be entitled to recover the expenses of publication from the person on whom the instrument containing the consent was served.

Revocation of consents and alteration and imposition of conditions

7.—(1) The Agency may from time to time review any consent given under paragraph 3 or 6 above and the conditions (if any) to which the consent is subject.

(2) Subject to such restrictions on the exercise of the power conferred by this sub-paragraph as are imposed under paragraph 8 below, where the Agency has reviewed a consent under this paragraph, it may by a notice served on the person making a discharge in pursuance of the consent—
  (a)   revoke the consent;
  (b)   make modifications of the conditions of the consent; or
  (c)   in the case of an unconditional consent, provide that it shall be subject to such conditions as may be specified in the notice.

(3) If on a review under sub-paragraph (1) above it appears to the Agency that no discharge has been made in pursuance of the consent to which the review relates at any time during the preceding twelve months, the Agency may revoke the consent by a notice served on the holder of the consent.

(4) If it appears to the Secretary of State appropriate to do so—
  (a)   for the purpose of enabling Her Majesty's Government in the United Kingdom to give effect to any Community obligation or to any international agreement to which the United Kingdom is for the time being a party;
  (b)   for the protection of public health or of flora and fauna dependent on an aquatic environment; or
  (c)   in consequence of any representations or objections made to him or otherwise,

he may, subject to such restrictions on the exercise of the power conferred by virtue of paragraph (c) above as are imposed under paragraph 8 below, at any time direct the Agency, in relation to a consent given under paragraph 3 or 6 above, to do anything mentioned in sub-paragraph (2)(a) to (c) above.

(5) The Agency shall be liable to pay compensation to any person in respect of any loss or damage sustained by that person as a result of the Agency's compliance with a direction given in relation to any consent by virtue of sub-paragraph (4)(b) above if—
  (a) in complying with that direction the Agency does anything which, apart from that direction, it would be precluded from doing by a restriction imposed under paragraph 8 below; and
  (b) the direction is not shown to have been given in consequence of—
      (i) a change of circumstances which could not reasonably have been foreseen at the beginning of the period to which the restriction relates; or
      (ii) consideration by the Secretary of State of material information which was not reasonably available to the Agency at the beginning of that period.

(6) For the purposes of sub-paragraph (5) above information is material, in relation to a consent, if it relates to any discharge made or to be made by virtue of the consent, to the interaction of any such discharge with any other discharge or to the combined effect of the matter discharged and any other matter.

Restriction on variation and revocation of consent and previous variation

8.—(1) Each instrument signifying the consent of the Agency under paragraph 3 or 6 above shall specify a period during which no notice by virtue of paragraph 7(2) or (4)(c) above shall be served in respect of the consent except, in the case of a notice doing anything mentioned in paragraph 7(2)(b) or (c), with the agreement of the holder of the consent.

(2) Each notice served by the Agency by virtue of paragraph 7(2) or (4)(c) above (except a notice which only revokes a consent) shall specify a period during which a subsequent such notice which alters the effect of the first-mentioned notice shall not be served except, in the case of a notice doing anything mentioned in paragraph 7(2)(b) or (c) above, with the agreement of the holder of the consent.

(3) The period specified under sub-paragraph (1) or (2) above in relation to any consent shall not, unless the person who proposes to make or makes discharges in pursuance of the consent otherwise agrees, be less than the period of four years beginning—
  (a) in the case of a period specified under sub-paragraph (1) above, with the day on which the consent takes effect; and
  (b) in the case of a period specified under sub-paragraph (2) above, with the day on which the notice specifying that period is served.

(4) A restriction imposed under sub-paragraph (1) or (2) above shall not prevent the service by the Agency of a notice by virtue of paragraph 7(2) or (4)(c) above in respect of a consent given under paragraph 6 above if—
  (a) the notice is served not more than three months after the beginning of the period prescribed under paragraph 6(5) above for the making of representations and objections with respect to the consent; and
  (b) the Agency or, as the case may be, the Secretary of State considers, in consequence of any representations or objections received by it or him within that period, that it is appropriate for the notice to be served.

(5) A restriction imposed under sub-paragraph (1) or (2) above shall not prevent the service by the Agency of a notice by virtue of paragraph 7(2)(b) or (c) or (4)(c) above in respect of a consent given under paragraph 6 above if the holder has applied for a variation under paragraph 10 below.

General review of consents

9.—(1) If it appears appropriate to the Secretary of State to do so he may at any time direct the Agency to review—
  (a) the consents given under paragraph 3 or 6 above, or
  (b) any description of such consents,

and the conditions (if any) to which those consents are subject.

(2) A direction given by virtue of sub-paragraph (1) above—
   (a)   shall specify the purpose for which, and
   (b)   may specify the manner in which,
the review is to be conducted.

(3) After carrying out a review pursuant to a direction given by virtue of sub-paragraph (1) above, the Agency shall submit to the Secretary of State its proposals (if any) for—
   (a)   the modification of the conditions of any consent reviewed pursuant to the direction, or
   (b)   in the case of any unconditional consent reviewed pursuant to the direction, subjecting the consent to conditions.

(4) Where the Secretary of State has received any proposals from the Agency under sub-paragraph (3) above in relation to any consent he may, if it appears appropriate to him to do so, direct the Agency to do, in relation to that consent, anything mentioned in paragraph 7(2)(b) or (c) above.

(5) A direction given by virtue of sub-paragraph (4) above may only direct the Agency to do, in relation to any consent,—
   (a)   any such thing as the Agency has proposed should be done in relation to that consent, or
   (b)   any such thing with such modifications as appear to the Secretary of State to be appropriate.

Applications for variation

10.—(1) The holder of a consent under paragraph 3 or 6 above may apply to the Agency, on a form provided for the purpose by the Agency, for the variation of the consent.

(2) The provisions of paragraphs 1 to 5 above shall apply (with the necessary modifications) to applications under sub-paragraph (1) above, and to the variation of consents in pursuance of such applications, as they apply to applications for, and the grant of, consents.

Transfer of consents

11.—(1) A consent under paragraph 3 or 6 above may be transferred by the holder to a person who proposes to carry on the discharges in place of the holder.

(2) On the death of the holder of a consent under paragraph 3 or 6 above, the consent shall, subject to sub-paragraph (4) below, be regarded as property forming part of the deceased's personal estate, whether or not it would be so regarded apart from this sub-paragraph, and shall accordingly vest in his personal representatives.

(3) If a bankruptcy order is made against the holder of a consent under paragraph 3 or 6 above, the consent shall, subject to sub-paragraph (4) below, be regarded for the purposes of any of the Second Group of Parts of the Insolvency Act 1986 (insolvency of individuals; bankruptcy), as property forming part of the bankrupt's estate, whether or not it would be so regarded apart from this sub-paragraph, and shall accordingly vest as such in the trustee in bankruptcy.

(4) Notwithstanding anything in the foregoing provisions of this paragraph, a consent under paragraph 3 or 6 above (and the obligations arising out of, or incidental to, such a consent) shall not be capable of being disclaimed.

(5) A consent under paragraph 3 or 6 above which is transferred to, or which vests in, a person under this section shall have effect on and after the date of the transfer or vesting as if it had been granted to that person under paragraph 3 or 6 above, subject to the same conditions as were attached to it immediately before that date.

(6) Where a consent under paragraph 3 or 6 above is transferred under sub-paragraph (1) above, the person from whom it is transferred shall give notice of that fact to the Agency not later than the end of the period of twenty-one days beginning with the date of the transfer.

(7) Where a consent under paragraph 3 or 6 above vests in any person as mentioned in sub-paragraph (2) or (3) above, that person shall give notice of that fact to the Agency not later than the end of the period of fifteen months beginning with the date of the vesting.

(8) If—
   (a)   a consent under paragraph 3 or 6 above vests in any person as mentioned in sub-paragraph (2) or (3) above, but

(b)   that person fails to give the notice required by sub-paragraph (7) above within the period there mentioned,

the consent, to the extent that it permits the making of any discharges, shall cease to have effect.

(9)   A person who fails to give a notice which he is required by sub-paragraph (6) or (7) above to give shall be guilty of an offence and liable—
    (a)   on summary conviction, to a fine not exceeding the statutory maximum;
    (b)   on conviction on indictment, to a fine or to imprisonment for a term not exceeding two years, or to both.]

[392]

NOTES
    Commencement: 31 December 1996 (certain purposes); 21 November 1996 (remaining purposes).
    Substituted with savings by the Environment Act 1995, s 120, Sch 22, para 183; for savings see the Environment Act 1995 (Commencement No 8 and Saving Provisions) Order 1996, SI 1996/2909, art 4(1). Paras 1–5 of this Schedule, as originally enacted, read as follows—

"Application for consents

1.—(1)   An application for a consent, for the purposes of section 88(1)(a) of this Act, for any discharges shall be made to the Authority.

(2)   An application under this paragraph shall be accompanied or supplemented by all such information as the Authority may reasonably require; but, subject to paragraph 2(4) below and without prejudice to the effect (if any) of any other contravention of the requirements of this Schedule in relation to such an application, a failure to provide information in pursuance of this sub-paragraph, shall not invalidate an application.

(3)   An application made in accordance with this paragraph which relates to proposed discharges at two or more places may be treated by the Authority as separate applications for consents for discharges at each of those places.

(4)   Where an application is made in accordance with this paragraph the Authority shall—
    (a)   publish notice of the application, at least once in each of two successive weeks, in a newspaper or newspapers circulating in—
        (i)   the locality or localities in which the places are situated at which it is proposed in the application that the discharges should be made; and
        (ii)   the locality or localities appearing to the Authority to be in the vicinity of any controlled waters which the Authority considers likely to be affected by the proposed discharges;
    (b)   publish a copy of that notice in an edition of the London Gazette published no earlier than the day after the publication of the last of the notices to be published by virtue of paragraph (a) above;
    (c)   send a copy of the application to every local authority or water undertaker within whose area any of the proposed discharges is to occur;
    (d)   in the case of an application which relates to proposed discharges into coastal waters, relevant territorial waters or waters outside the seaward limits of relevant territorial waters, serve a copy of the application on each of the Ministers.

(5)   The Authority shall be entitled, on an application made in accordance with this paragraph, to disregard the provisions of paragraphs (a) to (c) of sub-paragraph (4) above if it proposes to give the consent applied for and considers that the discharges in question will have no appreciable effect on the waters into which it is proposed that they should be made.

(6)   Where notice of an application under this paragraph is published by the Authority under sub-paragraph (4) above, the Authority shall be entitled to recover the expenses of publication from the applicant.

(7)   If a person who proposes to make or has made an application under this paragraph ("the relevant application")—
    (a)   applies to the Secretary of State within the prescribed period for a certificate providing that the provisions of sub-paragraph (4) above and subsection (1) of section 190 of this Act shall not apply to—
        (i)   the relevant application;
        (ii)   any consent given or conditions imposed on the relevant application;
        (iii) any sample of effluent taken from a discharge for which consent is given on the relevant application; or
        (iv)   information produced by analysis of such a sample;
        and
    (b)   satisfies the Secretary of State that it would be contrary to the public interest or would prejudice, to an unreasonable degree, some private interest, by disclosing information about a trade secret, if a certificate were not issued under this sub-paragraph,

the Secretary of State may issue a certificate to that person providing that those provisions shall not apply to such of the things mentioned in paragraph (a) above as are specified in the certificate.

Consideration and determination of applications

2.—(1) It shall be the duty of the Authority to consider any written representations or objections with respect to an application under paragraph 1 above which are made to it in the period of six weeks beginning with the day of the publication of notice of the application in the London Gazette and are not withdrawn.

(2) On an application under paragraph 1 above the Authority shall be under a duty, if the requirements of that paragraph are complied with, to consider whether to give the consent applied for, either unconditionally or subject to conditions, or to refuse it.

(3) Subject to sub-paragraph (4) and paragraph 3(5) below, on an application made in accordance with paragraph 1 above, the consent applied for shall be deemed to have been refused if it is not given within the period of four months beginning with the day on which the application is received or within such longer period as may be agreed in writing between the Authority and the applicant.

(4) Where—
   (a) any person, having made an application to the Authority for a consent, has failed to comply with his obligation under paragraph 1(2) above to supplement that application with information required by the Authority; and
   (b) that requirement was made by the Authority at such a time before the end of the period within which the Authority is required to determine the application as gave that person a reasonable opportunity to provide the required information within that period,

the Authority may delay its determination of the application until a reasonable time after the required information is provided.

(5) The conditions subject to which a consent may be given under this paragraph shall be such conditions as the Authority may think fit and, in particular, may include conditions—
   (a) as to the places at which the discharges to which the consent relates may be made and as to the design and construction of any outlets for the discharges;
   (b) as to the nature, origin, composition, temperature, volume and rate of the discharges and as to the periods during which the discharges may be made;
   (c) as to the steps to be taken, in relation to the discharges or by way of subjecting any substance likely to affect the description of matter discharged to treatment or any other process, for minimising the polluting effects of the discharges on any controlled waters;
   (d) as to the provision of facilities for taking samples of the matter discharged and, in particular, as to the provision, maintenance and use of manholes, inspection chambers, observation wells and boreholes in connection with the discharges;
   (e) as to the provision, maintenance and testing of meters for measuring or recording the volume and rate of the discharges and apparatus for determining the nature, composition and temperature of the discharges;
   (f) as to the keeping of records of the nature, origin, composition, temperature, volume and rate of the discharges and, in particular, of records of readings of meters and other recording apparatus provided in accordance with any other condition attached to the consent; and
   (g) as to the making of returns and the giving of other information to the Authority about the nature, origin, composition, temperature, volume and rate of the discharges;

and it is hereby declared that a consent may be given under this paragraph subject to different conditions in respect of different periods.

(6) A consent for any discharges which is given under this paragraph is not limited to discharges by a particular person and, accordingly, extends to discharges which are made by any person.

Notification of proposal to give consent

3.—(1) This paragraph applies where the Authority proposes to give its consent under paragraph 2 above on an application in respect of which such representations or objections as the Authority is required to consider under sub-paragraph (1) of that paragraph have been made.

(2) It shall be the duty of the Authority to serve notice of the proposal on every person who made any such representations or objection; and any such notice shall include a statement of the effect of sub-paragraph (3) below.

(3) Any person who made any such representations or objection may, within the period of twenty-one days beginning with the day on which the notice of the proposal is served on him, in the prescribed manner request the Secretary of State to give a direction under paragraph 4(1) below in respect of the application.

(4) It shall be the duty of the Authority not to give its consent on the application before the end of the period of twenty-one days mentioned in sub-paragraph (3) above and, if within that period—
   (a) a request is made under sub-paragraph (3) above in respect of the application; and
   (b) the person who makes that request serves notice of it on the Authority,

the Authority shall not give its consent on the application unless the Secretary of State has served notice on the Authority stating that he declines to comply with the request.

(5) Any period during which the Authority is prohibited by virtue of sub-paragraph (4) above from giving its consent on the application shall be disregarded in determining whether the application is deemed to have been refused under paragraph 2(3) above.

Reference to Secretary of State of certain applications for consent

4.—(1) The Secretary of State may, either in consequence of representations or objections made to him or otherwise, direct the Authority to transmit to him for determination such applications for consent under paragraph 1 above as are specified in the direction or are of a description so specified.

(2) Where a direction is given to the Authority under this paragraph, the Authority shall comply with the direction and inform every applicant to whose application the direction relates of the transmission of his application to the Secretary of State.

(3) Paragraphs 1(4) to (6) and 2(1) above shall have effect in relation to an application transmitted to the Secretary of State under this paragraph with such modifications as may be prescribed.

(4) Where an application is transmitted to the Secretary of State under this paragraph, the Secretary of State may at any time after the application is transmitted and before it is granted or refused—
    (a)   cause a local inquiry to be held with respect to the application; or
    (b)   afford the applicant and the Authority an opportunity of appearing before, and being heard by, a person appointed by the Secretary of State for the purpose.

(5) The Secretary of State shall exercise his power under sub-paragraph (4) above in any case where a request to be heard with respect to the application is made to him in the prescribed manner by the applicant or by the Authority.

(6) Where under this paragraph the Secretary of State affords to an applicant and the Authority an opportunity of appearing before, and being heard by, a person appointed for the purpose, it shall be the duty of the Secretary of State to afford an opportunity of appearing before, and being heard by, that person to every person who has made any representations or objection to the Secretary of State with respect to the application in question.

(7) It shall be the duty of the Secretary of State, if the requirements of this paragraph and of any regulations made under it are complied with, to determine an application for consent transmitted to him by the Authority under this paragraph by directing the Authority to refuse its consent or to give its consent under paragraph 2 above (either unconditionally or subject to such conditions as are specified in the direction).

(8) In complying with a direction under sub-paragraph (7) above to give a consent the Authority shall not be required to comply with any requirement imposed by paragraph 3 above.

(9) Without prejudice to any of the preceding provisions of this paragraph, the Secretary of State may by regulations make provision for the purposes of, and in connection with, the consideration and disposal by him of applications transmitted to him under this paragraph.

Consents without applications

5.—(1) If it appears to the Authority—
    (a)   that a person has caused or permitted effluent or other matter to be discharged in contravention—
        (i)   of the obligation imposed by virtue of section 85(3) of this Act; or
        (ii)   of any prohibition imposed under section 86 of this Act;
        and
    (b)   that a similar contravention by that person is likely,
the Authority may, if it thinks fit, serve on him an instrument in writing giving its consent, subject to any conditions specified in the instrument, for discharges of a description so specified.

(2) A consent given under this paragraph shall not relate to any discharge which occurred before the instrument containing the consent was served on the recipient of the instrument.

(3) Sub-paragraphs (5) and (6) of paragraph 2 above shall have effect in relation to a consent given under this paragraph as they have effect in relation to a consent given under that paragraph.

(4) Where a consent has been given under this paragraph, the Authority shall, as soon as practicable after giving it—
    (a)   publish notice of the consent, at least once in each of two successive weeks, in a newspaper or newspapers circulating in—
        (i)   the locality or localities in which the places are situated at which discharges may be made in pursuance of the consent; and
        (ii)   the locality or localities appearing to the Authority to be in the vicinity of any controlled waters which it considers likely to be affected by the discharges;
    (b)   publish a copy of that notice in an edition of the London Gazette published no earlier than the day after the publication of the last of the notices to be published by virtue of paragraph (a) above;

(c)   send a copy of the instrument containing the consent to every local authority within whose area any of the discharges authorised by the consent may occur;

(d)   in the case of a consent which relates to discharges into coastal waters, relevant territorial waters or waters outside the seaward limits of relevant territorial waters, serve a copy of the instrument containing the consent on each of the Ministers.

(5)   It shall be the duty of the Authority to consider any written representations or objections with respect to a consent under this paragraph which are made to it in the period of six weeks beginning with the day of the publication of notice of the consent in the London Gazette and are not withdrawn.

(6)   Where notice of a consent is published by the Authority under sub-paragraph (4) above, the Authority shall be entitled to recover the expenses of publication from the person on whom the instrument containing the consent was served.".

Regulations: the Control of Pollution (Consents for Discharges etc) (Secretary of State Functions) Regulations 1989, SI 1989/1151, are revoked, subject to savings, by SI 1996/2971; the Control of Pollution (Applications, Appeals and Registers) Regulations 1996, SI 1996/2971.

SCHEDULE 11
WATER PROTECTION ZONE ORDERS

Section 93

Applications for orders

1.—(1) Where the [Agency] applies to the Secretary of State for an order under section 93 of this Act, it shall—

(a)   submit to the Secretary of State a draft of the order applied for;

(b)   publish a notice with respect to the application, at least once in each of two successive weeks, in one or more newspapers circulating in the locality proposed to be designated as a water protection zone by the order;

(c)   not later than the date on which that notice is first published serve a copy of the notice on every local authority and water undertaker whose area includes the whole or any part of that locality; and

(d)   publish a notice in the London Gazette which—

    (i)   states that the draft order has been submitted to the Secretary of State;

    (ii)   names every local authority on whom a notice is required to be served under this paragraph;

    (iii)   specifies a place where a copy of the draft order and of any relevant map or plan may be inspected; and

    (iv)   gives the name of every newspaper in which the notice required by virtue of paragraph (b) above was published and the date of an issue containing the notice.

(2)   The notice required by virtue of sub-paragraph (1)(b) above to be published with respect to an application for an order shall—

(a)   state the general effect of the order applied for;

(b)   specify a place where a copy of the draft order and of any relevant map or plan may be inspected by any person free of charge at all reasonable times during the period of twenty-eight days beginning with the date of the first publication of the notice; and

(c)   state that any person may, within that period, by notice to the Secretary of State object to the making of the order.

Supply of copies of draft orders

2.   Where the [Agency] has applied for an order under section 93 of this Act, it shall, at the request of any person and on payment by that person of such charge (if any) as the [Agency] may reasonably require, furnish that person with a copy of the draft order submitted to the Secretary of State under paragraph 1 above.

Modifications of proposals

3.—(1) On an application for an order under section 93 of this Act, the Secretary of State may make the order either in the terms of the draft order submitted to him or, subject to sub-paragraph (2) below, in those terms as modified in such manner as he thinks fit, or may refuse to make an order.

(2) The Secretary of State shall not make such a modification of a draft order submitted to him as he considers is likely adversely to affect any persons unless he is satisfied that the [Agency] has given and published such additional notices, in such manner, as the Secretary of State may have required.

(3) Subject to sub-paragraph (2) above and to the service of notices of the proposed modification on such local authorities as appear to him to be likely to be interested in it, the modifications that may be made by the Secretary of State of any draft order include any modification of the area designated by the draft order as a water protection zone.

Consideration of objections etc

4. Without prejudice to [section 53 of the 1995 Act (inquiries and other hearings)], where an application for an order under section 93 of this Act has been made, the Secretary of State may, if he considers it appropriate to do so, hold a local inquiry before making any order on the application.

[393]

NOTES

Paras 1–4: words in square brackets substituted by the Environment Act 1995, s 120, Sch 22, paras 128, 184.

SCHEDULE 12
NITRATE SENSITIVE AREA ORDERS

Section 94

PART I
APPLICATIONS BY THE [AGENCY] FOR DESIGNATION ORDERS

Orders made only on application

1.—(1) Subject to sub-paragraphs (2) and (3) below, the relevant Minister shall not make an order under section 94 of this Act by virtue of which any land is designated as land comprised in a nitrate sensitive area, except with the consent of the Treasury and on an application which—

   (a)   has been made by the [Agency] in accordance with paragraph 2 below; and
   (b)   in identifying controlled waters by virtue of sub-paragraph (2)(a) of that paragraph, identified the controlled waters with respect to which that land is so comprised by the order.

(2) This paragraph shall not apply to an order which reproduces or amends an existing order without adding any land appearing to the relevant Minister to constitute a significant area to the land already comprised in the areas for the time being designated as nitrate sensitive areas.

Procedure for applications

2.—(1) The [Agency] shall not for the purposes of paragraph 1 above apply for the making of any order under section 94 of this Act by which any land would be comprised in the areas for the time being designated as nitrate sensitive areas unless it appears to the [Agency]—

   (a)   that pollution is or is likely to be caused by the entry of nitrate into controlled waters as a result of, or of anything done in connection with, the use of particular land in England and Wales for agricultural purposes; and
   (b)   that the provisions for the time being in force in relation to those waters and that land are not sufficient, in the opinion of the [Agency], for preventing or controlling such an entry of nitrate into those waters.

(2) An application under this paragraph shall identify—

   (a)   the controlled waters appearing to the [Agency] to be the waters which the nitrate is or is likely to enter; and
   (b)   the land appearing to the [Agency] to be the land the use of which for agricultural purposes, or the doing of anything in connection with whose use for agricultural purposes, is resulting or is likely to result in the entry of nitrate into those waters.

(3) An application under this paragraph shall be made—
  (a) where the land identified in the application is wholly in Wales, by serving a notice containing the application on the Secretary of State; and
  (b) in any other case, by serving such a notice on each of the Ministers.

[394]

NOTES

Part heading: word in square brackets substituted by the Environment Act 1995, s 120, Sch 22, para 128.
Paras 1, 2: words in square brackets substituted by the Environment Act 1995, s 120, Sch 22, para 128.

PART II
ORDERS CONTAINING MANDATORY PROVISIONS

Publication of proposal for order containing mandatory provisions

3.—(1) This paragraph applies where the relevant Minister proposes to make an order under section 94 of this Act which—
  (a) makes or modifies any such provision as is authorised by subsection (3)(a) of that section; and
  (b) in doing so, contains provision which is not of one of the following descriptions, that is to say—
    (i) provision reproducing existing provisions without modification and in relation to substantially the same area; and
    (ii) provision modifying any existing provisions so as to make them less onerous.

(2) The relevant Minister shall, before making any such order as is mentioned in sub-paragraph (1) above—
  (a) publish a notice with respect to the proposed order, at least once in each of two successive weeks, in one or more newspapers circulating in the locality in relation to which the proposed order will have effect;
  (b) not later than the date on which that notice is first published, serve a copy of the notice on—
    (i) the [Agency];
    (ii) every local authority and water undertaker whose area includes the whole or any part of that locality; and
    (iii) in the case of an order containing any such provision as is authorised by section 94(3)(b) of this Act, such owners and occupiers of agricultural land in that locality as appear to the relevant Minister to be likely to be affected by the obligations in respect of which payments are to be made under that provision;
    and
  (c) publish a notice in the London Gazette which—
    (i) names every local authority on whom a notice is required to be served under this paragraph;
    (ii) specifies a place where a copy of the proposed order and of any relevant map or plan may be inspected; and
    (iii) gives the name of every newspaper in which the notice required by virtue of paragraph (a) above was published and the date of an issue containing the notice.

(3) The notice required by virtue of sub-paragraph (2)(a) above to be published with respect to any proposed order shall—
  (a) state the general effect of the proposed order;
  (b) specify a place where a copy of the proposed order, and of any relevant map or plan, may be inspected by any person free of charge at all reasonable times during the period of forty-two days beginning with the date of the first publication of the notice; and
  (c) state that any person may, within that period, by notice to the Secretary of State or, as the case may be, to one of the Ministers object to the making of the order.

Supply of copies of proposed orders

4.   The Secretary of State and, in a case where he is proposing to join in making the order, the Minister shall, at the request of any person and on payment by that person of such charge (if any) as the Secretary of State or the Minister may reasonably require, furnish that person with a copy of any proposed order of which notice has been published under paragraph 3 above.

Modifications of proposals

5.—(1)   Where notices with respect to any proposed order have been published and served in accordance with paragraph 3 above and the period of forty-two days mentioned in sub-paragraph (3)(b) of that paragraph has expired, the relevant Minister may—
  (a)   make the order either in the proposed terms or, subject to sub-paragraph (2) below (but without any further compliance with paragraph 3 above), in those terms as modified in such manner as he thinks fit; or
  (b)   decide not to make any order.

  (2)   The relevant Minister shall not make such a modification of a proposed order of which notice has been so published and served as he considers is likely adversely to affect any persons unless he has given such notices as he considers appropriate for enabling those persons to object to the modification.

  (3)   Subject to sub-paragraph (2) above and to the service of notices of the proposed modification on such local authorities as appear to him to be likely to be interested in it, the modifications that may be made by the relevant Minister include any modification of any area designated by the proposed order as a nitrate sensitive area.

  (4)   For the purposes of this Schedule it shall be immaterial, in a case in which a modification such as is mentioned in sub-paragraph (3) above incorporates land in England in an area which (but for the modification) would have been wholly in Wales, that any requirements of paragraph 3 above in relation to the proposed order have been complied with by the Secretary of State, rather than by the Ministers.

Consideration of objections etc

6.   Without prejudice to [section 53 of the 1995 Act (inquiries and other hearings)], where notices with respect to any proposed order have been published and served in accordance with paragraph 3 above, the Secretary of State or, as the case may be, the Ministers may, if he or they consider it appropriate to do so, hold a local inquiry before deciding whether or not to make the proposed order or to make it with modifications.

Consent of Treasury for payment provisions

7.   The consent of the Treasury shall be required for the making of any order under section 94 of this Act the making of which does not require the consent of the Treasury by virtue of paragraph 1 above but which contains any such provision as is authorised by subsection (3)(b) of that section.

[395]

NOTES
  Paras 3, 6: words in square brackets substituted by the Environment Act 1995, s 120, Sch 22, paras 128, 185.

(Schs 13–23 outside the scope of this work.)

SCHEDULE 24
DISCLOSURE OF INFORMATION

Section 204

PART I
PERSONS IN RESPECT OF WHOSE FUNCTIONS DISCLOSURE MAY BE MADE

Any Minister of the Crown.

The Director General of Fair Trading.

The Monopolies and Mergers Commission.

The Director General of Telecommunications.

The Civil Aviation Authority.

The Director General of Gas Supply.

The Director General of Electricity Supply.

[The Coal Authority.]

[The Rail Regulator.]

A local weights and measures authority in England and Wales.

[396]

NOTES

Entry "The Coal Authority" inserted by the Coal Industry Act 1994, s 67, Sch 9, para 43(2)(a); entry "The Rail Regulator" inserted by the Railways Act 1993, s 152, Sch 12, para 31(a).

PART II
ENACTMENTS ETC IN RESPECT OF WHICH DISCLOSURE MAY BE MADE

The Trade Descriptions Act 1968.

The Fair Trading Act 1973.

The Consumer Credit Act 1974.

The Restrictive Trade Practices Act 1976.

The Resale Prices Act 1976.

The Estate Agents Act 1979.

The Competition Act 1980.

The Telecommunications Act 1984.

The Airports Act 1986.

The Gas Act 1986.

The Consumer Protection Act 1987.

The Electricity Act 1989.

[The Coal Industry Act 1994.]

[The Railways Act 1993.]

Any subordinate legislation made for the purpose of securing compliance with the Directive of the Council of the European Communities dated 10th September 1984 (No 84/450/EEC) on the approximation of the laws, regulations and administrative provisions of the member States concerning misleading advertising.

[397]

NOTES

Entry "The Coal Industry Act 1994" inserted by the Coal Industry Act 1994, s 67, Sch 9, para 43(2)(b); entry "The Railways Act 1993" inserted by the Railways Act 1993, s 152, Sch 12, para 31(b).

(Schs 25, 26: outside the scope of this work.)

CLEAN AIR ACT 1993

(1993 c 11)

ARRANGEMENT OF SECTIONS

PART I
DARK SMOKE

PART II
SMOKE, GRIT, DUST AND FUMES

Installation of furnaces

Limits on rate of emission of grit and dust

Arrestment plant for furnaces

Measurement of grit, dust and fumes

Outdoor furnaces

Height of chimneys

PART III
SMOKE CONTROL AREAS

Creation of smoke control areas

Prohibition on emission of smoke in smoke control area

Dealings with unauthorised fuel

Adaptation of fireplaces

An Act to consolidate the Clean Air Acts 1956 and 1968 and certain related enactments, with amendments to give effect to recommendations of the Law Commission and the Scottish Law Commission

[27 May 1993]

PART I
DARK SMOKE

NOTES

Exclusion: this Part of this Act does not apply: (a) to any process which is a prescribed process within the meaning of the Environmental Protection Act 1990, s 1; (b) in relation to smoke, grit or dust from the combustion of refuse deposited from any mine or quarry to which s 42 of this Act applies (see s 42(1), (4), (6) of this Act, at **[438]**); (c) to any smoke, grit or dust from any railway locomotive engine, except as provided by s 43(1)–(4) (see s 43(5) of this Act, at **[439]**; (d) to smoke, grit or dust from any vessel except as provided by ss 44(1)–(5), 46(4) (see s 44(6) of this Act) at **[440]**, **[442]** respectively).

1 Prohibition of dark smoke from chimneys

(1)   Dark smoke shall not be emitted from a chimney of any building, and if, on any day, dark smoke is so emitted, the occupier of the building shall be guilty of an offence.

(2)   Dark smoke shall not be emitted from a chimney (not being a chimney of a building) which serves the furnace of any fixed boiler or industrial plant, and if, on any day, dark smoke is so emitted, the person having possession of the boiler or plant shall be guilty of an offence.

(3)   This section does not apply to emissions of smoke from any chimney, in such classes of case and subject to such limitations as may be prescribed in regulations made by the Secretary of State, lasting for not longer than such periods as may be so prescribed.

(4)   In any proceedings for an offence under this section, it shall be a defence to prove—
(a) that the alleged emission was solely due to the lighting up of a furnace which was cold and that all practicable steps had been taken to prevent or minimise the emission of dark smoke;
(b) that the alleged emission was solely due to some failure of a furnace, or of apparatus used in connection with a furnace, and that—
(i) the failure could not reasonably have been foreseen, or, if foreseen, could not reasonably have been provided against; and
(ii) the alleged emission could not reasonably have been prevented by action taken after the failure occurred; or

(c) that the alleged emission was solely due to the use of unsuitable fuel and that—
  (i) suitable fuel was unobtainable and the least unsuitable fuel which was available was used; and
  (ii) all practicable steps had been taken to prevent or minimise the emission of dark smoke as the result of the use of that fuel;

or that the alleged emission was due to the combination of two or more of the causes specified in paragraphs (a) to (c) and that the other conditions specified in those paragraphs are satisfied in relation to those causes respectively.

(5) A person guilty of an offence under this section shall be liable on summary conviction—
  (a) in the case of a contravention of subsection (1) as respects a chimney of a private dwelling, to a fine not exceeding level 3 on the standard scale; and
  (b) in any other case, to a fine not exceeding level 5 on the standard scale.

(6) This section has effect subject to section 51 (duty to notify offences to occupier or other person liable).

[398]

NOTES
Commencement: 27 August 1993.
Sub-s (1) derived from the Clean Air Act 1956, s 1(1) (in part); sub-s (2) derived from the Clean Air Act 1956, s 1(4) (in part); sub-ss (3), (4) derived from the Clean Air Act 1956, s 1(2), (3); sub-s (5) derived from the Clean Air Act 1956, s 27(1) (in part), the Control of Pollution Act 1974, s 99, Sch 2, para 19(1), the Criminal Justice Act 1982, ss 38, 46; sub-s (6) derived from the Clean Air Act 1956, s 1(1) (in part).
Regulations: the Dark Smoke (Permitted Periods) Regulations 1958, SI 1958/498; the Dark Smoke (Permitted Periods) (Vessels) Regulations 1958, SI 1958/878 (having effect under this section by virtue of the Interpretation Act 1978, s 17(2)(b)).

2 Prohibition of dark smoke from industrial or trade premises

(1) Dark smoke shall not be emitted from any industrial or trade premises and if, on any day, dark smoke is so emitted the occupier of the premises and any person who causes or permits the emission shall be guilty of an offence.

(2) This section does not apply—
  (a) to the emission of dark smoke from any chimney to which section 1 above applies; or
  (b) to the emission of dark smoke caused by the burning of any matter prescribed in regulations made by the Secretary of State, subject to compliance with such conditions (if any) as may be so prescribed.

(3) In proceedings for an offence under this section, there shall be taken to have been an emission of dark smoke from industrial or trade premises in any case where—
  (a) material is burned on those premises; and
  (b) the circumstances are such that the burning would be likely to give rise to the emission of dark smoke,

unless the occupier or any person who caused or permitted the burning shows that no dark smoke was emitted.

(4) In proceedings for an offence under this section, it shall be a defence to prove—
  (a) that the alleged emission was inadvertent; and
  (b) that all practicable steps had been taken to prevent or minimise the emission of dark smoke.

(5) A person guilty of an offence under this section shall be liable on summary conviction to a fine not exceeding [£20,000].

(6)   In this section "industrial or trade premises" means—
  (a) premises used for any industrial or trade purposes; or
  (b) premises not so used on which matter is burnt in connection with any industrial or trade process.

(7)   This section has effect subject to section 51 (duty to notify offences to occupier or other person liable).

[399]

NOTES

Commencement: 27 August 1993.

Sub-s (1) derived from the Clean Air Act 1968, s 1(1) (in part), the Control of Smoke Pollution Act 1989, s 2(1); sub-s (2) derived from the Clean Air Act 1968, s 1(2), (3) (as read with s 12(1) of that Act); sub-s (3) derived from the Clean Air Act 1968, s 1(1A), the Control of Smoke Pollution Act 1989, s 2(2); sub-ss (4), (6) derived from the Clean Air Act 1968, s 1(4), (5); sub-s (5) derived from the Clean Air Act 1968, s 1(1) (in part), the Control of Pollution Act 1974, s 99, Sch 2, para 26(a), the Criminal Justice Act 1982, ss 38, 46.

Sub-s (5): sum in square brackets substituted by the Environment Act 1995, s 120, Sch 22, para 195.

Regulations: the Clean Air (Emission of Dark Smoke) (Exemption) Regulations 1969, SI 1969/1263 (having effect under this section by virtue of the Interpretation Act 1978, s 17(2)(b)).

3 Meaning of "dark smoke"

(1)   In this Act "dark smoke" means smoke which, if compared in the appropriate manner with a chart of the type known on 5th July 1956 (the date of the passing of the Clean Air Act 1956) as the Ringelmann Chart, would appear to be as dark as or darker than shade 2 on the chart.

(2)   For the avoidance of doubt it is hereby declared that in proceedings—
  (a) for an offence under section 1 or 2 (prohibition of emissions of dark smoke); . . .
  (b) . . .
the court may be satisfied that smoke is or is not dark smoke as defined in subsection (1) notwithstanding that there has been no actual comparison of the smoke with a chart of the type mentioned in that subsection.

(3)   Without prejudice to the generality of subsections (1) and (2), if the Secretary of State by regulations prescribes any method of ascertaining whether smoke is dark smoke as defined in subsection (1), proof in any such proceedings as are mentioned in subsection (2)—
  (a) that that method was properly applied, and
  (b) that the smoke was thereby ascertained to be or not to be dark smoke as so defined,
shall be accepted as sufficient.

[400]

NOTES

Commencement: 27 August 1993.

This section derived from the Clean Air Act 1956, s 34(2), the Clean Air Act 1968, s 14(1), Sch 1, para 11.

Sub-s (2): words omitted repealed by the Environment Act 1995, s 120, Sch 24.

PART II
SMOKE, GRIT, DUST AND FUMES

NOTES

Exclusion: this Part of this Act does not apply: (a) to any process which is a prescribed process within the meaning of the Environmental Protection Act 1990, s 1 (see s 41 of this Act, at [437]); (b) in relation to smoke, grit or dust from the combustion of refuse deposited from any mine or quarry to which s 42 of this Act applies (see s 42(1), (4), (6) of this Act, at [438]); (c) any smoke, grit or dust from any railway locomotive engine (see s 43(5) of this Act, at [439]); (d) smoke, grit or dust from any vessel (see ss 44(6), 46(4) of this Act, at [440], [442] respectively).

Installation of furnaces

4 Requirement that new furnaces shall be so far as practicable smokeless

(1)   No furnace shall be installed in a building or in any fixed boiler or industrial plant unless notice of the proposal to install it has been given to the local authority.

(2)   No furnace shall be installed in a building or in any fixed boiler or industrial plant unless the furnace is so far as practicable capable of being operated continuously without emitting smoke when burning fuel of a type for which the furnace was designed.

(3)   Any furnace installed in accordance with plans and specifications submitted to, and approved for the purposes of this section by, the local authority shall be treated as complying with the provisions of subsection (2).

(4)   Any person who installs a furnace in contravention of subsection (1) or (2) or on whose instructions a furnace is so installed shall be guilty of an offence and liable on summary conviction—
  (a) in the case of a contravention of subsection (1), to a fine not exceeding level 3 on the standard scale; and
  (b) in the case of a contravention of subsection (2), to a fine not exceeding level 5 on that scale.

(5)   This section does not apply to the installation of domestic furnaces.

(6)   This section applies in relation to—
  (a) the attachment to a building of a boiler or industrial plant which already contains a furnace; or
  (b) the fixing to or installation on any land of any such boiler or plant;

as it applies in relation to the installation of a furnace in any fixed boiler or industrial plant.

[401]

NOTES
Commencement: 27 August 1993.

Sub-s (1) derived from the Clean Air Act 1956, s 3(3) (in part); sub-s (2) derived from the Clean Air Act 1956, s 3(1) (in part); sub-s (3) derived from the Clean Air Act 1956, s 3(2); sub-s (4) derived from the Clean Air Act 1956, ss 3(1), (3) 27(2), (4) (all in part), the Control of Pollution Act 1974, s 99, Sch 2, para 19(2), (4), the Criminal Justice Act 1982, ss 38, 46, and gives effect to the first recommendation of the Law Commission Report on this consolidation (Law Com 209; Cm 2085); sub-ss (5), (6) derived from the Clean Air Act 1956, s 3(4), (5), the Clean Air (Units of Measurement) Regulations 1992, SI 1992/36, reg 2(2).

Limits on rate of emission of grit and dust

5 Emission of grit and dust from furnaces

(1)   This section applies to any furnace other than a domestic furnace.

(2)   The Secretary of State may by regulations prescribe limits on the rates of emission of grit and dust from the chimneys of furnaces to which this section applies.

(3)   If on any day grit or dust is emitted from a chimney serving a furnace to which this section applies at a rate exceeding the relevant limit prescribed under subsection (2), the occupier of any building in which the furnace is situated shall be guilty of an offence.

(4)   In proceedings for an offence under subsection (3) it shall be a defence to prove that the best practicable means had been used for minimising the alleged emission.

(5)   If, in the case of a building containing a furnace to which this section applies and which is served by a chimney to which there is no limit applicable under subsection (2), the occupier fails to use any practicable means there may be for minimising the emission of grit or dust from the chimney, he shall be guilty of an offence.

(6)   A person guilty of an offence under this section shall be liable on summary conviction to a fine not exceeding level 5 on the standard scale.

[402]

NOTES
Commencement: 27 August 1993.

Sub-s (1) derived from the Clean Air Act 1968, s 2(5); sub-s (2) derived from the Clean Air Act 1968, s 2(1) (in part); sub-s (3) derived from the Clean Air Act 1968, s 2(2) (in part); sub-s (4) derived from the Clean Air Act 1968, s 2(3); sub-s (5) derived from the Clean Air Act 1968, s 2(4) (in part); sub-s (6) derived from the Clean Air Act 1968, s 2(2), (4), the Control of Pollution Act 1974, s 99, Sch 2, para 26(b), (c), the Criminal Justice Act 1982, ss 38, 46.

Regulations: the Clean Air (Emission of Grit and Dust from Furnaces) Regulations 1971, SI 1971/162 (having effect under this section by virtue of the Interpretation Act 1978, s 17(2)(b)).

Arrestment plant for furnaces

6 Arrestment plant for new non-domestic furnaces

(1)   A furnace other than a domestic furnace shall not be used in a building—
    (a) to burn pulverised fuel; or
    (b) to burn, at a rate of 45.4 kilograms or more an hour, any other solid matter; or
    (c) to burn, at a rate equivalent to 366.4 kilowatts or more, any liquid or gaseous matter,

unless the furnace is provided with plant for arresting grit and dust which has been approved by the local authority or which has been installed in accordance with plans and specifications submitted to and approved by the local authority, and that plant is properly maintained and used.

(2)   Subsection (1) has effect subject to any exemptions prescribed or granted under section 7.

(3)   The Secretary of State may by regulations substitute for any rate mentioned in subsection (1)(b) or (c) such other rate as he thinks fit: but no regulations shall be made so as to reduce any rate unless a draft of the regulations has been laid before and approved by each House of Parliament.

(4)   Regulations under subsection (3) reducing any rate shall not apply to a furnace which has been installed, the installation of which has been begun, or an agreement for the purchase or installation of which has been entered into, before the date on which the regulations come into force.

(5)   If on any day a furnace is used in contravention of subsection (1), the occupier of the building shall be guilty of an offence and liable on summary conviction to a fine not exceeding level 5 on the standard scale.

[403]

NOTES
Commencement: 27 August 1993.

Sub-ss (1), (2) derived from the Clean Air Act 1968, s 3(1), the Clean Air (Units of Measurement) Regulations 1992, SI 1992/36, reg 3(1), (3), (4); sub-s (3) derived from the Clean Air Act 1968, s 3(2); sub-s (4) derived from the Clean Air Act 1968, s 3(4) (in part); sub-s (5) derived from the Clean Air Act 1968, s 3(3), the Control of Pollution Act 1974, s 99, Sch 2, para 26(d), the Criminal Justice Act 1982, ss 38, 46.

7 Exemptions from section 6

(1)   The Secretary of State may by regulations provide that furnaces of any class prescribed in the regulations shall, while used for a purpose so prescribed, be exempted from the operation of section 6(1).

(2)   If on the application of the occupier of a building a local authority are satisfied that the emission of grit and dust from any chimney serving a furnace in the building will not be prejudicial to health or a nuisance if the furnace is used for a particular purpose without compliance with section 6(1), they may exempt the furnace from the operation of that subsection while used for that purpose.

(3)   If a local authority to whom an application is duly made for an exemption under subsection (2) fail to determine the application and to give a written notice of their decision to the applicant within—
    (a)   eight weeks of receiving the application; or
    (b)   such longer period as may be agreed in writing between the applicant and the authority,
the furnace shall be treated as having been granted an exemption from the operation of section 6(1) while used for the purpose specified in the application.

(4)   If a local authority decide not to grant an exemption under subsection (2), they shall give the applicant a written notification of their decision stating their reasons, and the applicant may within twenty-eight days of receiving the notification appeal against the decision to the Secretary of State.

(5)   On an appeal under this section the Secretary of State—
    (a)   may confirm the decision appealed against; or
    (b)   may grant the exemption applied for or vary the purpose for which the furnace to which the application relates may be used without compliance with section 6(1);
and shall give the appellant a written notification of his decision, stating his reasons for it.

(6)   If on any day a furnace which is exempt from the operation of section 6(1) is used for a purpose other than a prescribed purpose or, as the case may be, a purpose for which the furnace may be used by virtue of subsection (2), (3) or (5), the occupier of the building shall be guilty of an offence and liable on summary conviction to a fine not exceeding level 5 on the standard scale.

[404]

NOTES

Commencement: 27 August 1993.

Sub-ss (1), (2), (3) derived from the Clean Air Act 1968, s 4(1), (2), (4); sub-ss (4), (5) derived from the Clean Air Act 1968, s 4(5), (6) (as read with s 13(1) (in part) of that Act); sub-s (6) derived from the Clean Air Act 1968, s 4(7), the Control of Pollution Act 1974, s 99, Sch 2, para 26(e), the Criminal Justice Act 1982, ss 38, 46.

Regulations: the Clean Air (Arrestment Plant) (Exemption) Regulations 1969, SI 1969/1262 (having effect under this section by virtue of the Interpretation Act 1978, s 17(2)(b)).

---

8 Requirement to fit arrestment plant for burning solid fuel in other cases

(1)   A domestic furnace shall not be used in a building—
    (a)   to burn pulverised fuel; or
    (b)   to burn, at a rate of 1.02 tonnes an hour or more, solid fuel in any other form or solid waste;
unless the furnace is provided with plant for arresting grit and dust which has been approved by the local authority or which has been installed in accordance with plans and specifications submitted to and approved by the local authority, and that plant is properly maintained and used.

(2)   If a furnace is used in a building in contravention of subsection (1), the occupier of the building shall be guilty of an offence and liable on summary conviction to a fine not exceeding level 5 on the standard scale.

[405]

NOTES
Commencement: 27 August 1993.
This section derived from the Clean Air Act 1956, ss 6(1), 27(4), the Control of Pollution Act 1974, s 99, Sch 2, para 19(4), the Criminal Justice Act 1982, ss 38, 46, the Clean Air (Units of Measurement) Regulations 1992, SI 1992/36, reg 2(1), (3), and gives effect to the first recommendation of the Law Commission Report on this consolidation (Law Com No 209; Cm 2085).

9 Appeal to Secretary of State against refusal of approval

(1)   Where a local authority determine an application for approval under section 6 or 8, they shall give the applicant a written notification of their decision and, in the case of a decision not to grant approval, shall state their reasons for not doing so.

(2)   A person who—
    (a) has made such an application to a local authority; or
    (b) is interested in a building with respect to which such an application has been made,

may, if he is dissatisfied with the decision of the authority on the application, appeal within twenty-eight days after he is notified of the decision to the Secretary of State; and the Secretary of State may give any approval which the local authority might have given.

(3)   An approval given by the Secretary of State under this section shall have the like effect as an approval of the local authority.

[406]

NOTES
Commencement: 27 August 1993.
Sub-s (1) derived from the Clean Air Act 1968, s 3(6); sub-ss (2), (3) derived from the Clean Air Act 1956, s 6(4), (5), the Clean Air Act 1968, s 3(5), (7), the Local Government, Planning and Land Act 1980, ss 1(2), Sch 2, para 6(a).

Measurement of grit, dust and fumes

10 Measurement of grit, dust and fumes by occupiers

(1)   If a furnace in a building is used—
    (a) to burn pulverised fuel;
    (b) to burn, at a rate of 45.4 kilograms or more an hour, any other solid matter; or
    (c) to burn, at a rate equivalent to 366.4 kilowatts or more, any liquid or gaseous matter,

the local authority may, by notice in writing served on the occupier of the building, direct that the provisions of subsection (2) below shall apply to the furnace, and those provisions shall apply accordingly.

(2)   In the case of a furnace to which this subsection for the time being applies, the occupier of the building shall comply with such requirements as may be prescribed as to—
    (a) making and recording measurements from time to time of the grit, dust and fumes emitted from the furnace;
    (b) making adaptations for that purpose to the chimney serving the furnace;
    (c) providing and maintaining apparatus for making and recording the measurements; and

(d) informing the local authority of the results obtained from the measurements or otherwise making those results available to them;

and in this subsection "prescribed" means prescribed (whether generally or for any class of furnace) by regulations made by the Secretary of State.

(3)   If the occupier of the building fails to comply with those requirements, he shall be guilty of an offence and liable on summary conviction—
   (a) to a fine not exceeding level 5 on the standard scale; or
   (b) to cumulative penalties on continuance in accordance with section 50.

(4)   The occupier of a building who by virtue of subsection (2) is under a duty to make and record measurements of grit, dust and fumes emitted from a furnace in the building shall permit the local authority to be represented during the making and recording of those measurements.

(5)   The Secretary of State may by regulations substitute for any rate mentioned in subsection (1)(b) or (c) such other rate as he thinks fit; but regulations shall not be made under this subsection so as to reduce any rate unless a draft of the regulations has been laid before and approved by each House of Parliament.

(6)   Any direction given by a local authority under subsection (1) with respect to a furnace in a building may be revoked by the local authority by a subsequent notice in writing served on the occupier of the building, without prejudice, however, to their power to give another direction under that subsection.

[407]

NOTES
   Commencement: 27 August 1993.
   Sub-ss (1), (6) derived from the Clean Air Act 1956, s 7(1), and the proviso to that Act, the Clean Air Act 1968, ss 5(1), the Clean Air (Units of Measurement) Regulations 1992, SI 1992/36, reg 2(1), (4), (5); sub-s (2) derived from the Clean Air Act 1956, s 7(2), (3), the Clean Air Act 1968, s 14(1), Sch 1, para 2; sub-s (3) derived from the Clean Air Act 1956, s 27(4), the Control of Pollution Act 1974, s 99, Sch 2, para 19(4), the Criminal Justice Act 1982, ss 38, 46; sub-ss (4), (5) derived from the Clean Air Act 1968, s 5(7), (2), respectively.
   Regulations: the Clean Air (Measurement of Grit and Dust from Furnaces) Regulations 1971, SI 1971/161 (having effect under sub-s (2) by virtue of the Interpretation Act 1978, s 17(2)(b)).

11 Measurement of grit, dust and fumes by local authorities

(1)   This section applies to any furnace to which section 10(2) (duty to comply with prescribed requirements) for the time being applies and which is used—
   (a) to burn, at a rate less than 1.02 tonnes an hour, solid matter other than pulverised fuel; or
   (b) to burn, at a rate of less than 8.21 Megawatts, any liquid or gaseous matter.

(2)   The occupier of the building in which the furnace is situated may, by notice in writing given to the local authority, request that authority to make and record measurements of the grit, dust and fumes emitted from the furnace.

(3)   While a notice is in force under subsection (2)—
   (a) the local authority shall from time to time make and record measurements of the grit, dust and fumes emitted from the furnace; and
   (b) the occupier shall not be under a duty to comply with any requirements of regulations under subsection (2) of section 10 in relation to the furnace, except those imposed by virtue of paragraph (b) of that subsection;

and any such notice given by the occupier of a building may be withdrawn by a subsequent notice in writing given to the local authority by him or any subsequent occupier of that building.

(4)   A direction under section 10(1) applying section 10(2) to a furnace which is used as mentioned in subsection (1)(a) or (b) of this section shall contain a statement of the effect of subsections (1) to (3) of this section.

[408]

NOTES

Commencement: 27 August 1993.

Sub-ss (1), (2) derived from the Clean Air Act 1968, s 5(3), the Clean Air (Units of Measurement) Regulations 1992, SI 1992/36, reg 3(1), (5), (6); sub-s (3) derived from the Clean Air Act 1968, s 5(4), (5); sub-s (4) derived from the Clean Air Act 1968, s 5(6).

12 Information about furnaces and fuel consumed

(1)   For the purpose of enabling the local authority properly to perform their functions under and in connection with sections 5 to 11, the local authority may, by notice in writing served on the occupier of any building, require the occupier to furnish to them, within fourteen days or such longer time as may be limited by the notice, such information as to the furnaces in the building and the fuel or waste burned in those furnaces as they may reasonably require for that purpose.

(2)   Any person who, having been duly served with a notice under subsection (1)—
  (a) fails to comply with the requirements of the notice within the time limited, or
  (b) furnishes any information in reply to the notice which he knows to be false in a material particular,

shall be guilty of an offence and liable on summary conviction to a fine not exceeding level 5 on the standard scale.

[409]

NOTES

Commencement: 27 August 1993.

Sub-s (1) derived from the Clean Air Act 1956, s 8(1), the Clean Air Act 1968, s 14(1), Sch 1, para 3; sub-s (2) derived from the Clean Air Act 1956, ss 8(2), 27(4), the Control of Pollution Act 1974, s 99, Sch 2, para 19(4), the Criminal Justice Act 1982, ss 38, 46.

Outdoor furnaces

13 Grit and dust from outdoor furnaces, etc

(1)   Sections 5 to 12 shall apply in relation to the furnace of any fixed boiler or industrial plant as they apply in relation to a furnace in a building.

(2)   References in those sections to the occupier of the building shall, in relation to a furnace falling within subsection (1), be read as references to the person having possession of the boiler or plant.

(3)   The reference in section 6(4) (and the reference in paragraph 6(1) and (3) of Schedule 5) to the installation and to the purchase of a furnace shall, in relation to a furnace which is already contained in any fixed boiler or industrial plant, be read as a reference to attaching the boiler or plant to the building or fixing it to or installing it on any land and to purchasing it respectively.

[410]

NOTES

Commencement: 27 August 1993.

This section derived from the Clean Air Act 1956, s 9, the Clean Air Act 1968, s 14(1), Sch 1, para 4, and gives effect to the second recommendation of the Law Commission Report on this consolidation (Law Com No 209; Cm 2085).

Height of chimneys

14 Height of chimneys for furnaces

(1)   This section applies to any furnace served by a chimney.

(2)   An occupier of a building shall not knowingly cause or permit a furnace to be used in the building—

    (a) to burn pulverised fuel;

    (b) to burn, at a rate of 45.4 kilograms or more an hour, any other solid matter; or

    (c) to burn, at a rate equivalent to 366.4 kilowatts or more, any liquid or gaseous matter,

unless the height of the chimney serving the furnace has been approved for the purposes of this section and any conditions subject to which the approval was granted are complied with.

(3)   If on any day the occupier of a building contravenes subsection (2), he shall be guilty of an offence.

(4)   A person having possession of any fixed boiler or industrial plant, other than an exempted boiler or plant, shall not knowingly cause or permit a furnace of that boiler or plant to be used as mentioned in subsection (2), unless the height of the chimney serving the furnace has been approved for the purposes of this section and any conditions subject to which the approval was granted are complied with.

(5)   If on any day a person having possession of any boiler or plant contravenes subsection (3), he shall be guilty of an offence.

(6)   A person guilty of an offence under this section shall be liable on summary conviction to a fine not exceeding level 5 on the standard scale.

(7)   In this section "exempted boiler or plant" means a boiler or plant which is used or to be used wholly for any purpose prescribed in regulations made by the Secretary of State; and the height of a chimney is approved for the purposes of this section if approval is granted by the local authority or the Secretary of State under section 15.

[411]

NOTES

    Commencement: 27 August 1993.

    Sub-s (1) derived from the Clean Air Act 1968, s 6(10) (in part); sub-ss (2)–(6) derived from the Clean Air Act 1968, s 6(1), (2), the Control of Pollution Act 1974, s 99, Sch 2, para 26(f), the Criminal Justice Act 1982, ss 38, 46; sub-s (7) derived from the Clean Air Act 1968, s 6(11) (in part).

    Regulations: the Clean Air (Height of Chimneys) (Exemption) Regulations 1969, SI 1969/411 (having effect under this section by virtue of the Interpretation Act 1978, s 17(2)(b)).

---

15 Applications for approval of height of chimneys of furnaces

(1)   This section applies to the granting of approval of the height of a chimney for the purposes of section 14.

(2)   Approval shall not be granted by a local authority unless they are satisfied that the height of the chimney will be sufficient to prevent, so far as practicable, the smoke, grit, dust, gases or fumes emitted from the chimney from becoming prejudicial to health or a nuisance having regard to—

    (a) the purpose of the chimney;

    (b) the position and descriptions of buildings near it;

    (c) the levels of the neighbouring ground; and

    (d) any other matters requiring consideration in the circumstances.

(3)   Approval may be granted without qualification or subject to conditions as to the rate or quality, or the rate and quality, of emissions from the chimney.

(4)   If a local authority to whom an application is duly made for approval fail to determine the application and to give a written notification of their decision to the applicant within four weeks of receiving the application or such longer period as

may be agreed in writing between the applicant and the authority, the approval applied for shall be treated as having been granted without qualification.

(5)   If a local authority decide not to approve the height of a chimney, or to attach conditions to their approval, they shall give the applicant a written notification of their decision which—
  (a) states their reasons for that decision; and
  (b) in the case of a decision not to approve the height of the chimney, specifies—
    (i) the lowest height (if any) which they are prepared to approve without qualification; or
    (ii) the lowest height which they are prepared to approve if approval is granted subject to any specified conditions,
  or (if they think fit) both.

(6)   The applicant may within twenty-eight days of receiving a notification under subsection (5) appeal against the local authority's decision to the Secretary of State.

(7)   On an appeal under this section the Secretary of State may confirm the decision appealed against or he may—
  (a) approve the height of the chimney without qualification or subject to conditions as to the rate or quality, or the rate and quality, of emissions from the chimney; or
  (b) cancel any conditions imposed by the local authority or substitute for any conditions so imposed any other conditions which the authority had power to impose.

(8)   The Secretary of State shall give the appellant a written notification of his decision on an appeal under this section which—
  (a) states his reasons for the decision; and
  (b) in the case of a decision not to approve the height of the chimney, specifies—
    (i) the lowest height (if any) which he is prepared to approve without qualification; or
    (ii) the lowest height which he is prepared to approve if approval is granted subject to any specified conditions,
  or (if he thinks fit) both.

(9)   References in this section to "the applicant" shall, in a case where the original applicant notifies the local authority that his interest in the application has been transferred to another person, be read as references to that other person.

[412]

NOTES

Commencement: 27 August 1993.

Sub-ss (2)–(4) derived from the Clean Air Act 1968, s 6(4)–(6), respectively; sub-ss (5)–(8) derived from the Clean Air Act 1968, s 6(7)–(9) (as read with s 13(1) (in part) of that Act); sub-s (9) derived from the Clean Air Act 1968, s 6(11) (in part).

16 Height of other chimneys

(1)   This section applies where plans for the erection or extension of a building outside Greater London or in an outer London borough, other than a building used or to be used wholly for one or more of the following purposes, that is to say—
  (a) as a residence or residences;
  (b) as a shop or shops; or
  (c) as an office or offices,
are in accordance with building regulations deposited with the local authority and the plans show that it is proposed to construct a chimney, other than one serving a furnace, for carrying smoke, grit, dust or gases from the building.

(2)   The local authority shall reject the plans unless they are satisfied that the height of the chimney as shown on the plans will be sufficient to prevent, so far as practicable, the smoke, grit, dust or gases from becoming prejudicial to health or a nuisance having regard to—

(a) the purpose of the chimney;
(b) the position and descriptions of buildings near it;
(c) the levels of the neighbouring ground; and
(d) any other matters requiring consideration in the circumstances.

(3)   If a local authority reject plans under the authority of this section—

(a) the notice given under section 16(6) of the Building Act 1984 shall specify that the plans have been so rejected; and
(b) any person interested in the building may appeal to the Secretary of State.

(4)   On an appeal under subsection (3) the Secretary of State may confirm or cancel the rejection and, where he cancels the rejection, may, if he thinks it necessary, direct that the time for rejecting the plans otherwise than under the authority of this section shall be extended so as to run from the date on which his decision is notified to the local authority.

(5)   *(Applies to Scotland only.)*

[413]

NOTES

Commencement: 27 August 1993.

Sub-ss (1), (2) derived from the Clean Air Act 1956, s 10(1), the Public Health Act 1961, ss 5(1), 11(2), Sch 1, Pt III (as saved by the Building Act 1984, ss 89(1), 132, Sch 5, para 2), the London Government Act 1963, s 40(1), Sch 11, Pt I, para 31 (as excluded (as respects chimneys serving furnaces) by the Clean Air Act 1968, s 6(12)); sub-ss (3), (4) derived from the Clean Air Act 1956, s 10(2), (3), the Building Act 1984, s 133(1), Sch 6, para 5.

See further, in relation to provision made regarding radioactivity possessed by any substance or article or by any part of any premises, the Radioactive Substances Act 1993, s 40 at **[506]**.

17 *(Repealed by the Environment Act 1995, s 120(3), Sch 24.)*

PART III
SMOKE CONTROL AREAS

NOTES

Exclusion: this Part of this Act does not apply: (a) to any process which is a prescribed process within the meaning of the Environmental Protection Act 1990, s 1 (see s 41 of this Act, at **[437]**); (b) in relation to smoke, grit or dust from the combustion of refuse deposited from any mine or quarry to which s 42 of this Act applies (see s 42(1), (4), (6) of this Act, at **[438]**); (c) to any smoke, grit or dust from any railway locomotive engine (see s 43(5) of this Act, at **[439]**); (d) to smoke, grit or dust from any vessel (see ss 44(6), 46(4) of this Act, at **[440]**, **[442]** respectively).

Creation of smoke control areas

18 Declaration of smoke control area by local authority

(1)   A local authority may by order declare the whole or any part of the district of the authority to be a smoke control area; and any order made under this section is referred to in this Act as a "smoke control order".

(2)   A smoke control order—

(a) may make different provision for different parts of the smoke control area;
(b) may limit the operation of section 20 (prohibition of emissions of smoke) to specified classes of building in the area; and

(c) may exempt specified buildings or classes of building or specified fireplaces or classes of fireplace in the area from the operation of that section, upon such conditions as may be specified in the order;

and the reference in paragraph (c) to specified buildings or classes of building include a reference to any specified, or to any specified classes of, fixed boiler or industrial plant.

(3)   A smoke control order may be revoked or varied by a subsequent order.

(4)   The provisions of Schedule 1 apply to the coming into operation of smoke control orders.

[414]

NOTES
Commencement: 27 August 1993.
Sub-s (1) derived from the Clean Air Act 1956, s 11(1); sub-s (2) derived from the Clean Air Act 1956, s 11(3), (10) (in part); sub-ss (3), (4) derived from the Clean Air Act 1956, s 11(5), (6).

19 Power of Secretary of State to require creation of smoke control areas

(1)   If, after consultation with a local authority, the [Scottish Environment Protection Agency (in this section referred to as "the Agency")] is satisfied—
> (a) that it is expedient to abate the pollution of the air by smoke in the district or part of the district of the authority; and
> (b) that the authority have not exercised, or have not sufficiently exercised, their powers under section 18 (power to declare smoke control area) to abate the pollution,

[the Agency] may direct the authority to prepare and submit to [it] for [its] approval, within such period not being less than six months from the direction as may be specified in the direction, proposals for making and bringing into operation one or more smoke control orders within such period or periods as the authority think fit.

(2)   Any proposals submitted by a local authority in pursuance of a direction under subsection (1) may be varied by further proposals submitted by the authority within the period specified for the making of the original proposals or such longer period as the [Agency] may allow.

(3)   The [Agency] may reject any proposals submitted to [it] under this section or may approve them in whole or in part, with or without modifications.

(4)   Where a local authority to whom a direction under subsection (1) has been given—
> (a) fail to submit proposals to the [Agency] within the period specified in the direction; or
> (b) submit proposals which are rejected in whole or in part,

[the Agency, with the consent of] the Secretary of State may make an order declaring them to be in default and directing them for the purposes of removing the default to exercise their powers under section 18 in such manner and within such period as may be specified in the order.

(5)   An order made under subsection (4) may be varied or revoked by a subsequent order so made.

(6)   While proposals submitted by a local authority and approved by the [Agency] under this section are in force, it shall be the duty of the authority to make such order or orders under section 18 as are necessary to carry out the proposals.

[415]

NOTES
Commencement: 27 August 1993.
This section derived from the Clean Air Act 1968, s 8(1)–(6) (as read with s 13(1) (in part) of that Act).

Sub-ss (1)–(3), (6): words in square brackets substituted by the Environment Act 1995, s 120, Sch 22, para 196.

Sub-s (4): word in first pair of square brackets substituted, and words in final pair of square brackets inserted, by the Environment Act 1995, s 120, Sch 22, para 196.

Prohibition on emission of smoke in smoke control area

20 Prohibition on emission of smoke in smoke control area

(1)   If, on any day, smoke is emitted from a chimney of any building within a smoke control area, the occupier of the building shall be guilty of an offence.

(2)   If, on any day, smoke is emitted from a chimney (not being a chimney of a building) which serves the furnace of any fixed boiler or industrial plant within a smoke control area, the person having possession of the boiler or plant shall be guilty of an offence.

(3)   Subsections (1) and (2) have effect—
   (a)   subject to any exemptions for the time being in force under section 18, 21 or 22;
   (b)   subject to section 51 (duty to notify offences to occupier or other person liable).

(4)   In proceedings for an offence under this section it shall be a defence to prove that the alleged emission was not caused by the use of any fuel other than an authorised fuel.

(5)   A person guilty of an offence under this section shall be liable on summary conviction to a fine not exceeding level 3 on the standard scale.

(6)   In this Part "authorised fuel" means a fuel declared by regulations of the Secretary of State to be an authorised fuel for the purposes of this Part.

[416]

NOTES

Commencement: 27 August 1993.

Sub-ss (1), (2), derived from the Clean Air Act 1956, s 11(2), (10) (both in part); sub-s (3) derived in part from the Clean Air Act 1956, s 11(2); sub-s (4) derived from the Clean Air Act 1956, s 11(2), proviso; sub-s (5) derived from the Clean Air Act 1956, s 27(2) (in part), the Control of Pollution Act 1974, s 99, Sch 2, para 19(2), the Criminal Justice Act 1982, ss 38, 46; sub-s (6) derived from the Clean Air Act 1956, s 34(1).

Regulations: the Smoke Control Areas (Authorised Fuels) Regulations 1991, SI 1991/1282, as amended by SI 1992/72, SI 1992/3148, SI 1993/2499, SI 1996/1145 (having effect under sub-s (6) by virtue of the Interpretation Act 1978, s 17(2)(b)).

21 Power by order to exempt certain fireplaces

The Secretary of State may by order exempt any class of fireplace, upon such conditions as may be specified in the order, from the provisions of section 20 (prohibition of smoke emissions in smoke control area), if he is satisfied that such fireplaces can be used for burning fuel other than authorised fuels without producing any smoke or a substantial quantity of smoke.

[417]

NOTES

Commencement: 27 August 1993.

This section derived from the Clean Air Act 1956, s 11(4).

Orders: the Smoke Control Areas (Exempted Fireplaces) Order 1970, SI 1970/615, as amended by SI 1974/855; the Smoke Control Areas (Exempted Fireplaces) (No 2) Order 1970, SI 1970/1667, as amended by SI 1974/762; the Smoke Control Areas (Exempted Fireplaces) Order 1971, SI 1971/1265, as amended by SI 1974/762; the Smoke Control Areas (Exempted Fireplaces) Order 1972, SI 1972/438, as amended by SI 1974/762; the Smoke Control Areas (Exempted Fireplaces) (No 2) Order 1972, SI 1972/955, as amended by SI 1974/762; the Smoke Control Areas (Exempted Fireplaces) Order 1973, SI 1973/2166, as amended by SI 1974/762; the Smoke Control Areas (Exempted Fireplaces) (No 2) Order 1975, SI 1975/1001; the Smoke Control Areas (Exempted Fireplaces) (No 3) Order 1975, SI 1975/1111; the Smoke Control Areas (Exempted Fireplaces) Order 1978, SI 1978/1609; the Smoke Control Areas (Exempted Fireplaces) Order 1982, SI 1982/1615; the Smoke Control Areas (Exempted Fireplaces) Order 1983, SI 1983/277; the Smoke Control Areas (Exempted Fireplaces) (No 2) Order 1983, SI 1983/426; the Smoke Control Areas (Exempted Fireplaces) (No 3) Order 1983, SI 1983/1018; the Smoke Control Areas (Exempted Fireplaces) Order 1984, SI 1984/1649, as amended by SI 1985/864; the Smoke Control Areas (Exempted Fireplaces) Order 1986, SI 1986/638; the Smoke Control Areas (Exempted Fireplaces) Order 1988, SI 1988/2282; the Smoke Control Areas (Exempted Fireplaces) Order 1989, SI 1989/1769; the Smoke Control Areas (Exempted Fireplaces) Order 1990, SI 1990/345; the Smoke Control Areas (Exempted Fireplaces) (No 2) Order 1990, SI 1990/2457; the Smoke Control Areas (Exempted Fireplaces) Order 1991, SI 1991/2892, as amended by SI 1996/1108; and the Smoke Control Areas (Exempted Fireplaces) Order 1992, SI 1992/2811 (all having effect under this section by virtue of the Interpretation Act 1978, s 17(2)(b)); the Smoke Control Areas (Exempted Fireplaces) Order 1993, SI 1993/2277; the Smoke Control Areas (Exempted Fireplaces) Order 1996, SI 1996/1108.

22 Exemptions relating to particular areas

(1)   The Secretary of State may, if it appears to him to be necessary or expedient so to do, by order suspend or relax the operation of section 20 (prohibition of smoke emissions in smoke control area) in relation to the whole or any part of a smoke control area.

(2)   Before making an order under subsection (1) the Secretary of State shall consult with the local authority unless he is satisfied that, on account of urgency, such consultation is impracticable.

(3)   As soon as practicable after the making of such an order the local authority shall take such steps as appear to them suitable for bringing the effect of the order to the notice of persons affected.

[418]

NOTES
Commencement: 27 August 1993.
This section derived from the Clean Air Act 1956, s 11(7), (9).

Dealings with unauthorised fuel

23 Acquisition and sale of unauthorised fuel in a smoke control area

(1)   Any person who—
  (a) acquires any solid fuel for use in a building in a smoke control area otherwise than in a building or fireplace exempted from the operation of section 20 (prohibition of smoke emissions in smoke control area);
  (b) acquires any solid fuel for use in any fixed boiler or industrial plant in a smoke control area, not being a boiler or plant so exempted; or
  (c) sells by retail any solid fuel for delivery by him or on his behalf to—
    (i) a building in a smoke control area; or
    (ii) premises in such an area in which there is any fixed boiler or industrial plant,
shall be guilty of an offence and liable on summary conviction to a fine not exceeding level 3 on the standard scale.

(2)   In subsection (1), "solid fuel" means any solid fuel other than an authorised fuel.

(3)   Subsection (1) shall, in its application to a smoke control area in which the operation of section 20 is limited by a smoke control order to specified classes of buildings, boilers or plant, have effect as if references to a building, boiler or plant were references to a building, boiler or plant of a class specified in the order.

(4)   The power of the Secretary of State under section 22 (exemptions relating to particular areas) to suspend or relax the operation of section 20 in relation to the whole or any part of a smoke control area includes power to suspend or relax the operation of subsection (1) in relation to the whole or any part of such an area.

(5)   In proceedings for an offence under this section consisting of the sale of fuel for delivery to a building or premises, it shall be a defence for the person accused to prove that he believed and had reasonable grounds for believing—

(a)   that the building was exempted from the operation of section 20 or, in a case where the operation of that section is limited to specified classes of building, was not of a specified class; or

(b)   that the fuel was acquired for use in a fireplace, boiler or plant so exempted or, in a case where the operation of that section is limited to specified classes of boilers or plant, in a boiler or plant not of a specified class.

[419]

NOTES

Commencement: 27 August 1993.

This section derived from the Clean Air Act 1968, s 9, the Control of Pollution Act 1974, s 99, Sch 2, para 27, the Criminal Justice Act 1982, ss 38, 46.

Adaptation of fireplaces

24 Power of local authority to require adaptation of fireplaces in private dwellings

(1)   The local authority may, by notice in writing served on the occupier or owner of a private dwelling which is, or when a smoke control order comes into operation will be, within a smoke control area, require the carrying out of adaptations in or in connection with the dwelling to avoid contraventions of section 20 (prohibition of smoke emissions in smoke control area).

(2)   The provisions of Part XII of the Public Health Act 1936 with respect to appeals against, and the enforcement of, notices requiring the execution of works shall apply in relation to any notice under subsection (1).

(3)   Any reference in those provisions to the expenses reasonably incurred in executing the works shall, in relation to a notice under subsection (1), be read as a reference to three-tenths of those expenses or such smaller fraction of those expenses as the local authority may in any particular case determine.

(4)   *(Applies to Scotland only.)*

[420]

NOTES

Commencement: 27 August 1993.

Sub-ss (1)–(3) derived from the Clean Air Act 1956, s 12(2); sub-s (4) derived from the Clean Air Act 1956, s 12(3), the Housing (Scotland) Act 1987, Sch 23, para 6(1).

25 Expenditure incurred in relation to adaptations in private dwellings

(1)   Schedule 2 to this Act shall have effect with respect to certain expenditure incurred in adapting old private dwellings in smoke control areas.

(2)   In this Part "old private dwelling" means any private dwelling other than one which either—

(a)   was erected after 15th August 1964 (which was the date immediately preceding the time when the enactment replaced by this subsection came into force), or

(b)   was produced by the conversion, after that date, of other premises, with or without the addition of premises erected after that date;

and for the purposes of this subsection a dwelling or premises shall not be treated as erected or converted after that date unless the erection or conversion was begun after it.

[421]

NOTES
Commencement: 27 August 1993.
Sub-s (2) derived from the Housing Act 1964, s 95(1) (as read with s 108(4) of that Act).

26 Power of local authority to make grants towards adaptations to fireplaces in churches, chapels, buildings used by charities etc

(1)   If, after the making of a smoke control order, the owner or occupier of any premises or part of any premises to which this section applies and which will be within a smoke control area as the result of the order incurs expenditure on adaptations in or in connection with the premises or part to avoid contraventions of section 20 (prohibition of smoke emissions in smoke control area), the local authority may, if they think fit, repay to him the whole or any part of that expenditure.

(2)   This section applies to any premises or part of any premises which fall within one or more of the following paragraphs, that is to say—
  (a) any place of public religious worship, being, in the case of a place in England or Wales, a place which belongs to the Church of England or to the Church in Wales (within the meaning of the Welsh Church Act 1914) or which is for the time being certified as required by law as a place of religious worship;
  (b) any church hall, chapel hall or similar premises used in connection with any such place of public religious worship, and so used for the purposes of the organisation responsible for the conduct of public religious worship in that place;
  (c) any premises or part of any premises occupied for the purposes of an organisation (whether corporate or unincorporated) which is not established or conducted for profit and whose main objects are charitable or are otherwise concerned with the advancement of religion, education or social welfare.

[422]

NOTES
Commencement: 27 August 1993.
   This section derived from the Clean Air Act 1956, s 15(1), (2), the Local Government, Planning and Land Act 1980, s 1(2), Sch 2, para 2.

Supplementary provisions

27 References to adaptations for avoiding contraventions of section 20

(1)   References in this Part to adaptations in or in connection with a dwelling to avoid contraventions of section 20 (prohibition of smoke emissions from smoke control area) shall be read as references to the execution of any of the following works (whether in or outside the dwelling), that is to say—
  (a) adapting or converting any fireplace;
  (b) replacing any fireplace by another fireplace or by some other means of heating or cooking;
  (c) altering any chimney which serves any fireplace;
  (d) providing gas ignition, electric ignition or any other special means of ignition; or
  (e) carrying out any operation incidental to any of the operations mentioned in paragraphs (a) to (d);

being works which are reasonably necessary in order to make what is in all the circumstances suitable provision for heating and cooking without contraventions of section 20.

(2)   For the purposes of this section the provision of any igniting apparatus or appliance (whether fixed or not) operating by means of gas, electricity or other special means shall be treated as the execution of works.

(3)   Except for the purposes of section 24 (power of local authority to require certain adaptations), works which make such suitable provision as is mentioned in subsection (1) shall not be treated as not being adaptations to avoid contraventions of section 20 of this Act by reason that they go beyond what is reasonably necessary for that purpose, but any expenditure incurred in executing them in excess of the expenditure which would have been reasonably incurred in doing what was reasonably necessary shall be left out of account.

(4)   References in this section to a dwelling include references to any premises or part of any premises to which section 26 (grants towards certain adaptations in churches and other buildings) applies.

[423]

NOTES
Commencement: 27 August 1993.
Sub-ss (1)–(3) derived from the Clean Air Act 1956, s 14(1), the Housing Act 1964, s 95(9); sub-s (4) derived from the Clean Air Act 1956, s 15(3).

28 Cases where expenditure is taken to be incurred on execution of works

(1)   References in this Part to expenses incurred in the execution of works include references to the cost of any fixed cooking or heating appliance installed by means of the execution of the works, notwithstanding that the appliance can be readily removed from the dwelling without injury to itself or the fabric of the dwelling.

(2)   For the purposes of this Part a person who enters into either—
(a) a conditional sale agreement for the sale to him, or
(b) (*applies to Scotland only*)

of a cooking or heating appliance shall be treated as having incurred on the date of the agreement expenditure of an amount equal to the price which would have been payable for the appliance if he had purchased it for cash on that date.

(3)   References in this section to a dwelling include references to any premises or part of any premises to which section 26 (grants towards certain adaptations in churches and other buildings) applies.

[424]

NOTES
Commencement: 27 August 1993.
Sub-ss (1), (2) derived from the Clean Air Act 1956, s 14(2), the Consumer Credit Act 1974, s 192(3)(a), Sch 4, Pt I, para 15; sub-s (3) derived from the Clean Air Act 1956, s 15(3).

29 Interpretation of Part III

In this Part, except so far as the context otherwise requires—
"authorised fuel" has the meaning given in section 20(6);
"conditional sale agreement" means an agreement for the sale of goods under which—
(a) the purchase price or part of it is payable by instalments; and
(b) the property in the goods is to remain in the seller (notwithstanding that the buyer is to be in possession of the goods) until such

conditions as to the payment of instalments or otherwise as may be specified in the agreement are fulfilled;

"heating", in relation to a dwelling, includes the heating of water;

"hire-purchase agreement" means an agreement, other than a conditional sale agreement, under which—

    (a) goods are bailed or (in Scotland) hired in return for periodical payments by the person to whom they are bailed or hired; and

    (b) the property in the goods will pass to that person if the terms of the agreement are complied with and one or more of the following occurs—

        (i) the exercise of an option to purchase by that person;

        (ii) the doing of any other specified act by any party to the agreement; and

        (iii) the happening of any other specified event;

"old private dwelling" has the meaning given in section 25; and

"smoke control order" means an order made by a local authority under section 18.

[425]

NOTES

Commencement: 27 August 1993.

This section derived from the Clean Air Act 1956, s 34(1) (in part), the Consumer Credit Act 1974, s 192(3)(a), Sch 4, para 16.

PART IV
CONTROL OF CERTAIN FORMS OF AIR POLLUTION

30 Regulations about motor fuel

(1) For the purpose of limiting or reducing air pollution, the Secretary of State may by regulations—

    (a) impose requirements as to the composition and contents of any fuel of a kind used in motor vehicles; and

    (b) where such requirements are in force, prevent or restrict the production, treatment, distribution, import, sale or use of any fuel which in any respect fails to comply with the requirements, and which is for use in the United Kingdom.

(2) It shall be the duty of the Secretary of State, before he makes any regulations under this section, to consult—

    (a) such persons appearing to him to represent manufacturers and users of motor vehicles;

    (b) such persons appearing to him to represent the producers and users of fuel for motor vehicles; and

    (c) such persons appearing to him to be conversant with problems of air pollution,

as he considers appropriate.

(3) Regulations under this section—

    (a) in imposing requirements as to the composition and contents of any fuel, may apply standards, specifications, descriptions or tests laid down in documents not forming part of the regulations; and

    (b) where fuel is subject to such requirements, may, in order that persons to whom the fuel is supplied are afforded information as to its composition or contents, impose requirements for securing that the information is displayed at such places and in such manner as may be prescribed by the regulations.

(4) It shall be duty of every local weights and measures authority to enforce the provisions of regulations under this section within its area; and subsections (2) and (3)

of section 26 of the Trade Descriptions Act 1968 (reports and inquiries) shall apply as respects those authorities' functions under this subsection as they apply to their functions under that Act.

(5)   The following provisions of the Trade Descriptions Act 1968 shall apply in relation to the enforcement of regulations under this section as they apply to the enforcement of that Act, that is to say—

section 27 (power to make test purchases);
section 28 (power to enter premises and inspect and seize goods and documents);
section 29 (obstruction of authorised officers);
section 30 (notice of test);

and section 33 of that Act shall apply to the exercise of powers under section 28 as applied by this subsection.

References to an offence under that Act in those provisions as applied by this subsection, except the reference in section 30(2) to an offence under section 28(5) or 29 of that Act, shall be construed as references to an offence under section 32 of this Act (provisions supplementary to this section) relating to regulations under this section.

(6)   *(Applies to Scotland only.)*

(7)   In Northern Ireland it shall be the duty of the Department of Economic Development to enforce the provisions of regulations under this section; and accordingly this section shall have effect in relation to Northern Ireland with the omission of subsection (4).

(8)   It is hereby declared that in relation to Northern Ireland the references in subsection (5) to provisions of the Trade Descriptions Act 1968 are references to those provisions as modified by section 40(1)(b) and (c) of that Act.

(9)   The Secretary of State shall for each financial year pay into the Consolidated Fund of Northern Ireland such sum as the Secretary of State and the Department of Economic Development for Northern Ireland may agree to be appropriate as representing the expenses incurred by that Department in enforcing the provisions of any regulations made under this section.

[426]

NOTES

Commencement: 27 August 1993.

Sub-ss (1), (2), (4), (5) derived from the Control of Pollution Act 1974, s 75(1), (2), (5), (6) respectively; sub-s (3) derived from the Control of Pollution Act 1974, s 75(3)(a), (4); sub-ss (7)–(9) derived from the Control of Pollution Act 1974, s 75(8), (9) (as read with the Departments (No 2) (Northern Ireland) Order 1982, SI 1982/846 (NI 11)).

Regulations: the Motor Fuel (Composition and Content) Regulations 1994, SI 1994/2295.

---

31 Regulations about sulphur content of oil fuel for furnaces or engines

(1)   For the purpose of limiting or reducing air pollution, the Secretary of State may by regulations impose limits on the sulphur content of oil fuel which is used in furnaces or engines.

(2)   It shall be the duty of the Secretary of State, before he makes any regulations in pursuance of this section, to consult—

(a) such persons appearing to him to represent producers and users of oil fuel;
(b) such persons appearing to him to represent manufacturers and users of plant and equipment for which oil fuel is used; and
(c) such persons appearing to him to be conversant with problems of air pollution,

as he considers appropriate.

(3)   Regulations under this section may—

(a)   prescribe the kinds of oil fuel, and the kinds of furnaces and engines, to which the regulations are to apply;

(b)   apply standards, specifications, descriptions or tests laid down in documents not forming part of the regulations; and

(c)   without prejudice to the generality of section 63(1)(a), make different provision for different areas.

(4)   It shall be the duty—

(a)   of every local authority to enforce the provisions of regulations under this section within its area, except in relation to a furnace which is part of a process subject to Part I of the Environmental Protection Act 1990; and

(b)   of the inspectors appointed under that Part to enforce those provisions in relation to such furnaces;

but nothing in this section shall be taken to authorise a local authority in Scotland to institute proceedings for any offence.

(5)   In this section "oil fuel" means any liquid petroleum product produced in a refinery.

[427]

NOTES

Commencement: 27 August 1993.

Sub-ss (1), (2), (5) derived from the Control of Pollution Act 1974, s 76(1), (2), (5); sub-s (3) derived from the Control of Pollution Act 1974, s 76(3)(a), (b), (d); sub-s (4) derived from the Control of Pollution Act 1974, s 76(4), the Environmental Protection Act 1990, s 162(1), Sch 15, para 15(1), (6).

32   Provisions supplementary to section 30 and 31

(1)   Regulations under section 30 or 31 (regulation of content of motor fuel and fuel oil) may authorise the Secretary of State to confer exemptions from any provision of the regulations.

(2)   A person who contravenes or fails to comply with any provision of regulations under section 30 or 31 shall be guilty of an offence and liable—

(a)   on conviction on indictment, to a fine; and

(b)   on summary conviction, to a fine not exceeding the statutory maximum;

but the regulations may in any case exclude liability to conviction on indictment or reduce the maximum fine on summary conviction.

(3)   Regulations under section 30 or 31 shall, subject to any provision to the contrary in the regulations, apply to fuel used for, and to persons in, the public service of the Crown as they apply to fuel used for other purposes and to other persons.

(4)   A local authority shall not be entitled by virtue of subsection (3) to exercise, in relation to fuel used for and persons in that service, any power conferred on the authority by virtue of sections 56 to 58 (rights of entry and inspection and other local authority powers).

[428]

NOTES

Commencement: 27 August 1993.

Sub-s (1) derived from the Control of Pollution Act 1974, ss 75(3)(b), 76(3)(c); sub-s (2) derived from the Control of Pollution Act 1974, s 77(1), the Magistrates' Courts Act 1980, s 32(2); sub-ss (3), (4) derived from the Control of Pollution Act 1974, s 77(2).

33 Cable burning

(1)   A person who burns insulation from a cable with a view to recovering metal from the cable shall be guilty of an offence unless the burning is part of a process subject to Part I of the Environmental Protection Act 1990.

(2)   A person guilty of an offence under this section shall be liable on summary conviction to a fine not exceeding level 5 on the standard scale.

[429]

NOTES

Commencement: 27 August 1993.

Sub-s (1) derived from the Control of Pollution Act 1974, s 78(1), the Environmental Protection Act 1990, s 162(1), Sch 15, para 15(1), (7); sub-s (2) derived from the Control of Pollution Act 1974, s 78(2), the Clean Air Enactments (Repeals and Modifications) Regulations 1974, SI 1974/2170, reg 10, the Criminal Justice Act 1982, s 46.

PART V
INFORMATION ABOUT AIR POLLUTION

34 Research and publicity

(1)   A local authority may—
  (a) undertake, or contribute towards the cost of, investigation and research relevant to the problem of air pollution;
  (b) arrange for the publication of information on that problem;
  (c) arrange for the delivery of lectures and addresses, and the holding of discussions, on that problem;
  (d) arrange for the display of pictures, cinematograph films or models, or the holding of exhibitions, relating to that problem; and
  (e) prepare, or join in or contribute to the cost of the preparation of, pictures, films, models or exhibitions to be displayed or held as mentioned in paragraph (d).

(2)   In acting under subsection (1)(b), a local authority shall ensure that the material published is presented in such a way that no information relating to a trade secret is disclosed, except with the consent in writing of a person authorised to disclose it.

(3)   Breach of a duty imposed by subsection (2) shall be actionable.

(4)   In any civil or criminal proceedings (whether or not arising under this Act) brought against a local authority, or any member or officer of a local authority, on the grounds that any information has been published it shall be a defence to show that it was published, in compliance with subsections (1) and (2).

[430]

NOTES

Commencement: 27 August 1993.

Sub-s (1) derived from the Clean Air Act 1956, s 25(c)–(e), the Control of Pollution Act 1974, s 79(1), (10); sub-s (2) derived from the Control of Pollution Act 1974, s 79(5); sub-ss (3), (4) derived from the Control of Pollution Act 1974, s 79(6), (7).

35 Obtaining information

(1)   Without prejudice to the generality of section 34 (research, etc by local authorities), local authorities may obtain information about the emission of pollutants and other substances into the air—
  (a) by issuing notices under section 36 (information about emissions from premises);

(b) by measuring and recording the emissions, and for that purpose entering on any premises, whether by agreement or in exercise of the power conferred by section 56 (rights of entry and inspection); and

(c) by entering into arrangements with occupiers of premises under which they measure and record emissions on behalf of the local authority;

but references to premises in paragraphs (b) and (c) do not include private dwellings or caravans.

(2) A local authority shall not be entitled to exercise the power of entry mentioned in subsection (1)(b) for the purpose of measuring and recording such emissions on any premises unless—

(a) the authority has given to the occupier of the premises a notice in writing—

(i) specifying the kind of emissions in question and the steps it proposes to take on the premises for the purpose of measuring and recording emissions of that kind; and

(ii) stating that it proposes to exercise that power for that purpose unless the occupier requests the authority to serve on him a notice under section 36 (information about emissions from premises) with respect to the emissions; and

(b) the period of twenty-one days beginning with the day on which the notice was given has expired;

and the authority shall not be entitled to exercise that power if, during that period, the occupier gives a notice to the authority requesting it to serve on him a notice under section 36.

(3) Nothing in this section shall authorise a local authority to investigate emissions from any process subject to Part I of the Environmental Protection Act 1990 otherwise than—

(a) by issuing notices under section 36; or

(b) by exercising the powers conferred on the authority by section 34(1)(a) (investigation and research etc) without entering the premises concerned.

(4) So long as a local authority exercises any of its powers under subsection (1), it shall from time to time consult the persons mentioned in subsection (5)—

(a) about the way in which the local authority exercises those powers (under this section and section 36); and

(b) about the extent to which, and the manner in which, any information collected under those powers should be made available to the public.

(5) The consultations required by subsection (4) shall be with—

(a) such persons carrying on any trade or business in the authority's area or such organisations appearing to the authority to be representative of those persons; and

(b) such persons appearing to the authority to be conversant with problems of air pollution or to have an interest in local amenity;

as appear to the authority to be appropriate.

(6) The consultations shall take place as the authority think necessary, but not less than twice in each financial year.

[431]

36 Notices requiring information about air pollution

(1)   A local authority may by notice in writing require the occupier of any premises in its area to furnish, whether by periodical returns or by other means, such estimates or other information as may be specified or described in the notice concerning the emission of pollutants and other substances into the air from the premises.

(2)   This section does not apply to premises in so far as they consist of a private dwelling or a caravan.

(3)   If the notice relates to a process subject to Part I of the Environmental Protection Act 1990, the person on whom the notice is served shall not be obliged to supply any information which, as certified by an inspector appointed under that Part, is not of a kind which is being supplied to the inspector for the purposes of that Part.

(4)   The person on whom a notice is served under this section shall comply with the notice within six weeks of the date of service, or within such longer period as the local authority may by notice allow.

(5)   A notice under this section shall not require returns at intervals of less than three months, and no one notice (whether or not requiring periodical returns) shall call for information covering a period of more than twelve months.

(6)   Except so far as regulations made by the Secretary of State provide otherwise, this section applies to premises used for, and to persons in, the public service of the Crown as it applies to other premises and persons.

(7)   A local authority shall not be entitled by virtue of subsection (6) to exercise, in relation to premises used for and persons in the public service of the Crown, any power conferred on the authority by virtue of sections 56 to 58 (rights of entry and other local authority powers).

(8)   A person who—
(a) fails without reasonable excuse to comply with the requirements of a notice served on him in pursuance of this section; or
(b) in furnishing any estimate or other information in compliance with a notice under this section, makes any statement which he knows to be false in a material particular or recklessly makes any statement which is false in a material particular,

shall be guilty of an offence and liable on summary conviction to a fine not exceeding level 5 on the standard scale.

(9)   Where a person is convicted of an offence under subsection (8) in respect of any premises and information of any kind, nothing in section 35(2) (limits on exercise of power of entry) shall prevent a local authority from exercising the power of entry there mentioned for the purpose of obtaining information of that kind in respect of the premises.

[432]

NOTES

Commencement: 27 August 1993.

Sub-s (1) derived from the Control of Pollution Act 1974, s 80(1) (as read with s 105(1) (in part) of that Act); sub-s (2) derived from the Control of Pollution Act 1974, s 80(2) (as read with s 84(1) (in part) of that Act); sub-s (3) derived from the Control of Pollution Act 1974, s 80(3), the Environmental Protection Act 1990, s 162(1), Sch 15, para 15(1), (9); sub-ss (4), (5), (9) derived from the Control of Pollution Act 1974, s 80(4), (5), (8), respectively; sub-s (6) derived from the Control of Pollution Act 1974, s 80(6) (in part) (as read with s 105(1) (in part) of that Act); sub-s (7) derived from the Control of Pollution Act 1974, s 80(6) (in part); sub-s (8) derived from the Control of Pollution Act 1974, s 80(7), the Criminal Justice Act 1982, ss 38, 46.

Regulations: the Control of Atmospheric Pollution (Exempted Premises) Regulations 1977, SI 1977/18 (having effect under sub-s (6) by virtue of the Interpretation Act 1978, s 17(2)(b)).

37 Appeals against notices under section 36

(1)   A person served with a notice under section 36 (information about air pollution), or any other person having an interest in the premises to which the notice relates, may appeal to the Secretary of State—

    (a) on the ground that the giving to the authority or the disclosure to the public of all or part of the information required by the notice would—

        (i) prejudice to an unreasonable degree some private interest by disclosing information about a trade secret; or

        (ii) be contrary to the public interest; or

    (b) on the ground that the information required by the notice is not immediately available and cannot readily be collected or obtained by the recipient of the notice without incurring undue expenditure for the purpose.

(2)   If the Secretary of State allows the appeal he may direct the local authority to withdraw or modify the notice, or to take such steps as he may specify to ensure that prejudicial information is not disclosed to the public; and it shall be the duty of the authority to comply with the direction.

(3)   The Secretary of State may make regulations as to appeals under this section, including regulations about the time for bringing an appeal and the circumstances in which all or any part of the appellant's case is to be withheld from the respondent.

(4)   It shall be the duty of the Secretary of State, before he makes any regulations under subsection (3), to consult—

    (a) such persons appearing to him to represent local authorities;

    (b) such persons appearing to him to represent industrial interests; and

    (c) such persons appearing to him to be conversant with problems of air pollution,

as he considers appropriate.

[433]

NOTES

Commencement: 27 August 1993.

Sub-ss (1), (2) derived from the Control of Pollution Act 1974, s 81(1), (2); sub-ss (3), (4) derived from the Control of Pollution Act 1974, s 81(3).

Regulations: the Control of Atmospheric Pollution (Appeals) Regulations 1977, SI 1977/17 (having effect under this section by virtue of the Interpretation Act 1978, s 17(2)(b)).

38 Regulations about local authority functions under sections 34, 35 and 36

(1)   The Secretary of State shall by regulations prescribe the manner in which, and the methods by which, local authorities are to perform their functions under sections 34(1)(a) and (b), 35 and 36 (investigation and research etc into, and the obtaining of information about, air pollution).

(2)   It shall be the duty of the Secretary of State, before he makes regulations under this section, to consult—

    (a) such persons appearing to him to represent local authorities;

    (b) such persons appearing to him to represent industrial interests; and

    (c) such persons appearing to him to be conversant with problems of air pollution,

as he considers appropriate.

(3)   Regulations under this section may in particular—

    (a) prescribe the kinds of emissions to which notices under section 36 (power to require information about air pollution) may relate;

    (b) prescribe the kinds of information which may be required by those notices;

(c) prescribe the manner in which any such notice is to be given, and the evidence which is to be sufficient evidence of its having been given, and of its contents and authenticity;

(d) require each local authority to maintain in a prescribed form a register containing—

(i) information obtained by the authority by virtue of section 35(1) (powers of local authorities to obtain information), other than information as to which a direction under section 37(2) (appeals against notices under section 36) provides that the information is not to be disclosed to the public; and

(ii) such information (if any) as the Secretary of State may determine, or as may be determined by or under regulations, with respect to any appeal under section 37 against a notice served by the authority which the Secretary of State did not dismiss;

(e) specify the circumstances in which local authorities may enter into arrangements with owners or occupiers of premises under which they will record and measure emissions on behalf of the local authorities; and

(f) specify the kinds of apparatus which local authorities are to have power to provide and use for measuring and recording emissions, and for other purposes.

(4) Regulations made by virtue of subsection (3)(b) may in particular require returns of—

(a) the total volume of gases, whether pollutant or not, discharged from the premises in question over any period;

(b) the concentration of pollutant in the gases discharged;

(c) the total of the pollutant discharged over any period;

(d) the height or heights at which discharges take place;

(e) the hours during which discharges take place; or

(f) the concentration of pollutants at ground level.

(5) A register maintained by a local authority in pursuance of regulations made by virtue of subsection (3)(d) shall be open to public inspection at the principal office of the authority free of charge at all reasonable hours, and the authority shall afford members of the public reasonable facilities for obtaining from the authority, on payment of reasonable charges, copies of entries in the register.

[434]

NOTES

Commencement: 27 August 1993.

This section derived from the Control of Pollution Act 1974, s 82.

Regulations: the Control of Pollution (Research and Publicity) Regulations 1977, SI 1977/19 (having effect under this section by virtue of the Interpretation Act 1978, s 17(2)(b)).

39 Provision by local authorities of information for Secretary of State

(1) The Secretary of State may, for the purpose of obtaining information about air pollution, direct a local authority to make such arrangements as may be specified in the direction—

(a) for the provision, installation, operation and maintenance by the local authority of apparatus for measuring and recording air pollution; and

(b) for transmitting the information so obtained to the Secretary of State;

but before giving the direction under this section the Secretary of State shall consult the local authority.

(2) Where apparatus is provided in pursuance of a direction under this section, the Secretary of State shall defray the whole of the capital expenditure incurred by the local authority in providing and installing the apparatus.

(3)   It shall be the duty of the local authority to comply with any direction given under this section.

NOTES

Commencement: 27 August 1993.

Sub-s (1) derived from the Control of Pollution Act 1974, s 83(1), (3) (in part); sub-s (2) derived from the Control of Pollution Act 1974, s 83(2); sub-s (3) derived from the Control of Pollution Act 1974, s 83(3) (in part).

40 Interpretation of Part V

In this Part—
(a) references to the emission of substances into the atmosphere are to be construed as applying to substances in a gaseous or liquid or solid state; or any combination of those states; and
(b) any reference to measurement includes a reference to the taking of samples.

[436]

NOTES

Commencement: 27 August 1993.

This section derived from the Control of Pollution Act 1974, s 84(2), (3).

PART VI
SPECIAL CASES

41 Relation to Environmental Protection Act 1990

(1)   Parts I to III shall not apply to any process which is a prescribed process as from the date which is the determination date for that process.

(2)   The "determination date" for a prescribed process is—
(a) in the case of a process for which an authorisation is granted, the date on which the enforcing authority grants it, whether in pursuance of the application or, on an appeal, of a direction to grant it, and
(b) in the case of a process for which an authorisation is refused, the date of the refusal or, on an appeal, of the affirmation of the refusal.

(3)   In this section "authorisation", "enforcing authority" and "prescribed process" have the meaning given in section 1 of the Environmental Protection Act 1990 and the reference to an appeal is a reference to an appeal under section 15 of that Act.

[437]

NOTES

Commencement: 27 August 1993.

This section derived from the Clean Air Act 1956, s 16A, the Clean Air Act 1968, s 11A, the Environmental Protection Act 1990, s 162(1), Sch 15, paras 6, 12.

42 Colliery spoilbanks

(1)   This section applies to any mine or quarry from which coal or shale has been, is being or is to be got.

(2)   The owner of a mine or quarry to which this section applies shall employ all practicable means—
(a) for preventing combustion of refuse deposited from the mine or quarry; and

(b) for preventing or minimising the emission of smoke and fumes from such refuse;

and, if he fails to do so, he shall be guilty of an offence.

(3) A person guilty of an offence under subsection (2) shall be liable on summary conviction—

(a) to a fine not exceeding level 5 on the standard scale; or

(b) to cumulative penalties on continuance in accordance with section 50.

(4) Neither the provisions of Part III of the Environmental Protection Act 1990 nor any provision of Parts I to III of this Act shall apply in relation to smoke, grit or dust from the combustion of refuse deposited from any mine or quarry to which this section applies.

(5) . . .

(6) In this section, "mine", "quarry" and "owner" have the same meaning as in the Mines and Quarries Act 1954.

[438]

NOTES

Commencement: 27 August 1993.

Sub-ss (1), (2) derived from the Clean Air Act 1956, s 18(1); sub-s (3) derived from the Clean Air Act 1956, s 27(4) (in part), the Control of Pollution Act 1974, s 99, Sch 2, para 19(4), the Criminal Justice Act 1982, ss 38, 46; sub-s (4) derived from the Clean Air Act 1956, s 18(2), the Clean Air Act 1968, s 14(1), Sch 1, para 1 (in part), the Environmental Protection Act 1990, s 162(1), Sch 15, para 7(1), (2); sub-s (5) derived from the Clean Air Act 1956, s 18(5), the Environmental Protection Act 1990, s 162(1), Sch 15, para 7(2); sub-s (6) derived from the Clean Air Act 1956, s 18(4).

Sub-s (5): repealed by the Environment Act 1995, s 120, Sch 24.

43 Railway engines

(1) Section 1 (prohibition of emissions of dark smoke) shall apply in relation to railway locomotive engines as it applies in relation to buildings.

(2) In the application of section 1 to such engines, for the reference in subsection (1) of that section to the occupier of the building there shall be substituted a reference to the owner of the engine.

(3) The owner of any railway locomotive engine shall use any practicable means there may be for minimising the emission of smoke from the chimney on the engine and, if he fails to do so, he shall, if smoke is emitted from that chimney, be guilty of an offence.

(4) A person guilty of an offence under subsection (3) shall be liable on summary conviction—

(a) to a fine not exceeding level 5 on the standard scale; or

(b) to cumulative penalties on continuance in accordance with section 50.

(5) Except as provided in this section, nothing in Parts I to III applies to smoke, grit or dust from any railway locomotive engine.

[439]

NOTES

Commencement: 27 August 1993.

Sub-ss (1), (2) derived from the Clean Air Act 1956, s 19(1); sub-s (3) derived from the Clean Air Act 1956, s 19(2); sub-s (4) derived from the Clean Air Act 1956, s 27(4) (in part), the Control of Pollution Act 1974, s 99, Sch 2, para 19(4), the Criminal Justice Act 1982, ss 38, 46; sub-s (5) derived from the Clean Air Act 1956, s 19(3), the Clean Air Act 1968, s 14(1), Sch 1, para 1 (in part).

44 Vessels

(1)   Section 1 (prohibition of emissions of dark smoke) shall apply in relation to vessels in waters to which this section applies as it applies in relation to buildings.

(2)   In the application of section 1 to a vessel—
 (a) for the reference in subsection (1) of that section to the occupier of the building there shall be substituted a reference to the owner of, and to the master or other officer or person in charge of, the vessel;
 (b) references to a furnace shall be read as including references to an engine of the vessel; and
 (c) subsection (5) of that section shall be omitted;

and a person guilty of an offence under that section in relation to a vessel shall be liable on summary conviction to a fine not exceeding level 5 on the standard scale.

(3)   For the purposes of this Act a vessel in any waters to which this section applies which are not within the district of any local authority shall be deemed to be within the district of the local authority whose district includes that point on land which is nearest to the spot where the vessel is.

(4)   The waters to which this section applies are—
 (a) all waters not navigable by sea-going ships; and
 (b) all waters navigable by sea-going ships which are within the seaward limits of the territorial waters of the United Kingdom and are contained within any port, harbour, river, estuary, haven, dock, canal or other place so long as a person or body of persons is empowered by or under any Act to make charges in respect of vessels entering it or using facilities in it.

(5)   In subsection (4) "charges" means any charges with the exception of light dues, local light dues and any other charges payable in respect of lighthouses, buoys or beacons and of charges in respect of pilotage.

(6)   Except as provided in this section, nothing in Parts I to III applies to smoke, grit or dust from any vessel.

[440]

NOTES
Commencement: 27 August 1993.

Sub-s (1) derived from the Clean Air Act 1956, s 20(1) (in part); sub-s (2) derived from the Clean Air Act 1956, ss 20(1), 27(1) (both in part), the Control of Pollution Act 1974, s 99, Sch 2, para 19(1), the Criminal Justice Act 1982, ss 38, 46; sub-s (3) derived from the Clean Air Act 1956, s 20(2); sub-ss (4), (5) derived from the Clean Air Act 1956, s 20(3); sub-s (6) derived from the Clean Air Act 1956, s 20(4), the Clean Air Act 1968, s 14(1), Sch 1, para 1 (in part).

45 Exemption for purposes of investigations and research

(1)   If the local authority are satisfied, on the application of any person interested, that it is expedient to do so for the purpose of enabling investigations or research relevant to the problem of the pollution of the air to be carried out without rendering the applicant liable to proceedings brought under or by virtue of any of the provisions of this Act or the Environmental Protection Act 1990 mentioned below, the local authority may by notice in writing given to the applicant exempt, wholly or to a limited extent,—
 (a) any chimney from the operation of sections 1 (dark smoke), 5 (grit and dust), 20 (smoke in smoke control area) and 43 (railway engines) of this Act and Part III of the Environmental Protection Act 1990 (statutory nuisances);
 (b) any furnace, boiler or industrial plant from the operation of section 4(2) (new furnaces to be as far as practicable smokeless);
 (c) any premises from the operation of section 2 (emissions of dark smoke);

(d) any furnace from the operation of sections 6 or 8 (arrestment plant) and 10 (measurement of grit, dust and fumes by occupier), and

(e) the acquisition or sale of any fuel specified in the notice from the operation of section 23 (acquisition and sale of unauthorised fuel in smoke control area),

in each case subject to such conditions, if any, and for such period as may be specified in the notice.

(2)   Any person who has applied to the local authority for an exemption under this section may, if he is dissatisfied with the decision of the authority on the application, appeal to the Secretary of State; and the Secretary of State may, if he thinks fit, by notice in writing given to the applicant and the local authority, give any exemption which the authority might have given or vary the terms of any exemption which they have given.

[441]

NOTES

Commencement: 27 August 1993.

This section derived from the Clean Air Act 1956, s 21, the Clean Air Act 1968, s 14(1), Sch 1, para 6, the Environmental Protection Act 1990, s 162(1), Sch 15, para 7(1), (3).

---

46 Crown premises, etc

(1)   It shall be part of the functions of the local authority, in cases where it seems to them proper to do so, to report to the responsible Minister any cases of—

(a) emissions of dark smoke, or of grit or dust, from any premises which are under the control of any Government department and are occupied for the public service of the Crown or for any of the purposes of any Government department;

(b) emissions of smoke, whether dark smoke or not, from any such premises which are within a smoke control area;

(c) emissions of smoke, whether dark smoke or not, from any such premises which appear to them to constitute a nuisance to the inhabitants of the neighbourhood; or

(d) emissions of dark smoke from any vessel of Her Majesty's navy, or any Government ship in the service of the Secretary of State while employed for the purposes of Her Majesty's navy, which appear to them to constitute a nuisance to the inhabitants of the neighbourhood,

and on receiving any such report the responsible Minister shall inquire into the circumstances and, if his inquiry reveals that there is cause for complaint, shall employ all practicable means for preventing or minimising the emission of the smoke, grit or dust or for abating the nuisance and preventing a recurrence of it, as the case may be.

(2)   Subsection (1) shall apply to premises occupied for the purposes of the Duchy of Lancaster or the Duchy of Cornwall as it applies to premises occupied for the public service of the Crown which are under the control of a Government department, with the substitution, in the case of the Duchy of Cornwall, for references to the responsible Minister of references to such person as the Duke of Cornwall or the possessor for the time being of the Duchy of Cornwall appoints.

(3)   The fact that there subsists in any premises an interest belonging to Her Majesty in right of the Crown or of the Duchy of Lancaster, or to the Duchy of Cornwall, or belonging to a Government department or held in trust for Her Majesty for the purposes of a Government department, shall not affect the application of this Act to those premises so long as that interest is not the interest of the occupier of the premises, and this Act shall have effect accordingly in relation to the premises and that and all other interests in the premises.

(4)   Section 44 (vessels) shall, with the omission of the reference in subsection (2) of that section to the owner, apply to vessels owned by the Crown, except that it shall not apply to vessels of Her Majesty's navy or to Government ships in the service of the Secretary of State while employed for the purposes of Her Majesty's navy.

(5)   This Act (except Parts IV and V) shall have effect in relation to premises occupied for the service of a visiting force as if the premises were occupied for the public service of the Crown and were under the control of the Government department by arrangement with whom the premises are occupied.

(6)   In this section—
   "Government ship" has the same meaning as in [the Merchant Shipping Act 1995]; and
   "visiting force" means any such body, contingent or detachment of the forces of any country as is a visiting force for the purposes of any of the provisions of the Visiting Forces Act 1952.

[442]

NOTES

Commencement: 27 August 1993.

Sub-ss (1), (2) derived from the Clean Air Act 1956, s 22(1), the Defence (Transfer of Functions) (No 1) Order 1964, SI 1964/488, art 2, Sch 1, Pt I; sub-s (3) derived from the Clean Air Act 1956, s 22(2), the Clean Air Act 1968, s 14(1), Sch 1, para 1 (in part); sub-s (4) derived from the Clean Air Act 1956, s 22(3), the Defence (Transfer of Functions) (No 1) Order 1964, SI 1964/488, art 2, Sch 1, Pt I; sub-s (5) derived from the Clean Air Act 1956, s 22(4) (in part), the Clean Air Act 1968, s 14(1), Sch 1, para 1 (in part); sub-s (6) derived from the Clean Air Act 1956, s 22(4) (in part), (5).

Sub-s (6): in definition "Government ship" words in square brackets substituted by the Merchant Shipping Act 1995, s 314(2), Sch 13, para 94(a).

PART VII
MISCELLANEOUS AND GENERAL

Power to apply certain provisions to fumes and gases

47 Application to fumes and gases of certain provisions as to grit, dust and smoke

(1)   The Secretary of State may by regulations—
   (a) apply all or any of the provisions of sections 5, 6, 7, 42(4), 43(5), 44(6) and 46(1) to fumes or prescribed gases or both as they apply to grit and dust;
   (b) apply all or any of the provisions of section 4 to fumes or prescribed gases or both as they apply to smoke; and
   (c) apply all or any of the provisions of section 11 to prescribed gases as they apply to grit and dust,

subject, in each case, to such exceptions and modifications as he thinks expedient.

(2)   No regulations shall be made under this section unless a draft of the regulations has been laid before and approved by each House of Parliament.

(3)   In the application of any provision of this Act to prescribed gases by virtue of regulations under this section, any reference to the rate of emission of any substance shall be construed as a reference to the percentage by volume or by mass of the gas which may be emitted during a period specified in the regulations.

(4)   In this section—
   "gas" includes vapour and moisture precipitated from vapour; and
   "prescribed" means prescribed in regulations under this section.

[443]

NOTES

Commencement: 27 August 1993.

Sub-ss (1), (2) derived from the Clean Air Act 1968, ss 7(1), (3), 7A(1), (3), the Environmental Protection Act 1990, s 85; sub-ss (3), (4) derived from the Clean Air Act 1968, s 7A(4), (5), the Environmental Protection Act 1990, s 85.

Power to give effect to international agreements

48 Power to give effect to international agreements

The Secretary of State may by regulations provide that any provision of Parts IV and V, or of this Part (apart from this section) so far as relating to those Parts, shall have effect with such modifications as are prescribed in the regulations with a view to enabling the Government of the United Kingdom to give effect to any provision made by or under any international agreement to which the Government is for the time being a party.

[444]

NOTES

Commencement: 27 August 1993.

This section derived from the Control of Pollution Act 1974, s 102(1) (as read with s 105(1) (in part) of that Act).

Administration and enforcement

49 Unjustified disclosures of information

(1)   If a person discloses any information relating to any trade secret used in carrying on any particular undertaking which has been given to him or obtained by him by virtue of this Act, he shall, subject to subsection (2), be guilty of an offence and liable on summary conviction to a fine not exceeding level 5 on the standard scale.

(2)   A person shall not be guilty of an offence under subsection (1) by reason of the disclosure of any information if the disclosure is made—
    (a) in the performance of his duty;
    (b) in pursuance of section 34(1)(b); or
    (c) with the consent of a person having a right to disclose the information.

[445]

NOTES

Commencement: 27 August 1993.

This section derived from the Clean Air Act 1956, ss 26, 27(3), the Clean Air Act 1968, s 14(1), Sch 1, para 1 (in part), the Control of Pollution Act 1974, s 94(1), (2)(a), Sch 2, para 19(3), the Criminal Justice Act 1982, ss 38, 46, and gives effect to the third recommendation of the Law Commission Report on this consolidation (Law Com No 209; Cm 2085).

50 Cumulative penalties on continuance of certain offences

(1)   Where—
    (a) a person is convicted of an offence which is subject to cumulative penalties on continuance in accordance with this section; and
    (b) it is shown to the satisfaction of the court that the offence was substantially a repetition or continuation of an earlier offence by him after he had been convicted of the earlier offence,

the penalty provided by subsection (2) shall apply instead of the penalty otherwise specified for the offence.

(2)   Where this subsection applies the person convicted shall be liable on summary conviction to a fine not exceeding—

(a) level 5 on the standard scale; or

(b) £50 for every day on which the earlier offence has been so repeated or continued by him within the three months next following his conviction of that offence,

whichever is the greater.

(3)   Where an offence is subject to cumulative penalties in accordance with this section—

(a) the court by which a person is convicted of the original offence may fix a reasonable period from the date of conviction for compliance by the defendant with any directions given by the court; and

(b) where a court has fixed such a period, the daily penalty referred to in subsection (2) is not recoverable in respect of any day before the end of that period.

[446]

NOTES

Commencement: 27 August 1993.

Sub-ss (1), (2) derived from the Clean Air Act 1956, s 27(4) (in part), the Control of Pollution Act 1974, s 99, Sch 2, para 19(4), the Criminal Justice Act 1982, ss 38, 46; sub-s (3) derived from the Public Health Act 1936, s 297, the Clean Air Act 1956, s 31(1) (as modified by Sch 3, Pt 1, para 2 of that Act).

51 Duty to notify occupiers of offences

(1)   If, in the opinion of an authorised officer of the local authority—

(a) an offence is being or has been committed under section 1, 2 or 20 (prohibition of certain emissions of smoke); . . .

(b) . . .

he shall, unless he has reason to believe that notice of it has already been given by or on behalf of the local authority, as soon as may be notify the appropriate person, and, if his notification is not in writing, shall before the end of the four days next following the day on which he became aware of the offence, confirm the notification in writing.

(2)   For the purposes of subsection (1), the appropriate person to notify is the occupier of the premises, the person having possession of the boiler or plant, the owner of the railway locomotive engine or the owner or master or other officer or person in charge of the vessel concerned, as the case may be.

(3)   In any proceedings for an offence under section 1, 2 or 20 it shall be a defence to prove that the provisions of subsection (1) have not been complied with in the case of the offence; and if no such notification as is required by that subsection has been given before the end of the four days next following the day of the offence, that subsection shall be taken not to have been complied with unless the contrary is proved.

[447]

NOTES

Commencement: 27 August 1993.

Sub-ss (1), (2) derived from the Clean Air Act 1956, s 30(1), the Clean Air Act 1968, s 14(1), Sch 1, para 9 (in part), the Control of Pollution Act 1974, s 108(1), Sch 3, para 16(1); sub-s (3) derived from the Clean Air Act 1956, s 30(2), the Clean Air Act 1968, s 14(1), Sch 1, para 9 (in part), the Control of Pollution Act 1974, s 108(1), Sch 3, para 16(2).

Sub-s (1): words omitted repealed by the Environment Act 1995, s 120, Sch 24.

52 Offences committed by bodies corporate

(1)　Where an offence under this Act which has been committed by a body corporate is proved to have been committed with the consent or connivance of, or to be attributable to any neglect on the part of, any director, manager, secretary or other similar officer of the body corporate or any person who was purporting to act in any such capacity, he as well as the body corporate shall be guilty of that offence and be liable to be proceeded against and punished accordingly.

(2)　Where the affairs of a body corporate are managed by its members this section shall apply in relation to the acts and defaults of a member in connection with his functions of management as if he were a director of the body corporate.

[448]

NOTES
Commencement: 27 August 1993.

This section derived from the Control of Pollution Act 1974, s 87(1), and gives effect to the fourth recommendation of the Law Commission Report on this consolidation (Law Com No 209; Cm 2085).

53 Offence due to act or default of another

(1)　Where the commission by any person of an offence under this Act is due to the act or default of some other person, that other person shall be guilty of the offence.

(2)　A person may be charged with and convicted of an offence by virtue of this section whether or not proceedings for the offence are taken against any other person.

[449]

NOTES
Commencement: 27 August 1993.

This section derived from the Control of Pollution Act 1974, s 87(2), and gives effect to the fourth recommendation of the Law Commission Report on this consolidation (Law Com No 209; Cm 2085).

54 Power of county court to authorise works and order payments

(1)　If works are reasonably necessary in or in connection with a building in order to enable the building to be used for some purpose without contravention of any of the provisions of this Act (apart from Parts IV and V), the occupier of the building—
  (a) may, if by reason of a restriction affecting his interest in the building he is unable to carry out the works without the consent of the owner of the building or some other person interested in the building and is unable to obtain that consent, apply to the county court for an order to enable the works to be carried out by him; and
  (b) may, if he considers that the whole or any proportion of the cost of carrying out the works should be borne by the owner of the building or some other person interested in the building, apply to the county court for an order directing the owner or other person to indemnify him, either wholly or in part, in respect of that cost;

and on an application under paragraph (a) or (b) the court may make such order as may appear to the court to be just.

(2)　*(Applies to Scotland only.)*

[450]

NOTES
Commencement: 27 August 1993.

This section derived from the Clean Air Act 1956, s 28, the Clean Air Act 1968, s 14(1), Sch 1, para 1 (in part).

55 General provisions as to enforcement

(1)   It shall be the duty of the local authority to enforce—
  (a) the provisions of Parts I to III, section 33 and Part VI; and
  (b) the provisions of this Part so far as relating to those provisions;
but nothing in this section shall be taken as extending to the enforcement of any building regulations.

(2)   A local authority in England and Wales may institute proceedings for an offence under section 1 or 2 (prohibition of emissions of dark smoke) in the case of any smoke which affects any part of their district notwithstanding, in the case of an offence under section 1, that the smoke is emitted from a chimney outside their district and, in the case of an offence under section 2, that the smoke is emitted from premises outside their district.

(3)   *(Applies to Scotland only.)*

NOTES

Commencement: 27 August 1993.

Sub-s (1) derived from the Clean Air Act 1956, s 29(1), the Public Health Act 1961, ss 5(1), 11(2), Sch 1, Pt III (as saved by the Building Act 1984, ss 89(1), 132, Sch 5, para 2), the Clean Air Act 1968, s 14(1), Sch 1, para 1 (in part), and gives effect to the fifth recommendation of the Law Commission Report on this consolidation (Law Com No 209; Cm 2085); sub-s (2) derived from the Clean Air Act 1956, s 29(2), the Clean Air Act 1968, s 14(1), Sch 1, paras 1 (in part), 8.

----

56 Rights of entry and inspection etc

(1)   Any person authorised in that behalf by a local authority may at any reasonable time—
  (a) enter upon any land or vessel for the purpose of—
      (i) performing any function conferred on the authority or that person by virtue of this Act,
      (ii) determining whether, and if so in what manner, such a function should be performed, or
      (iii) determining whether any provision of this Act or of an instrument made under this Act is being complied with; and
  (b) carry out such inspections, measurements and tests on the land or vessel or of any articles on it and take away such samples of the land or articles as he considers appropriate for such a purpose.

(2)   Subsection (1) above does not, except in relation to work under section 24(1) (adaptations to dwellings in smoke control area), apply in relation to a private dwelling.

(3)   If it is shown to the satisfaction of a justice of the peace on sworn information in writing—
  (a) that admission to any land or vessel which a person is entitled to enter in pursuance of subsection (1) has been refused to that person or that refusal is apprehended or that the land or vessel is unoccupied or that the occupier is temporarily absent or that the case is one of emergency or that an application for admission would defeat the object of the entry; and
  (b) that there is reasonable ground for entry upon the land or vessel for the purpose for which entry is required,
then, subject to subsection (4), the justice may by warrant under his hand authorise that person to enter the land or vessel, if need be by force.

(4)   A justice of the peace shall not issue a warrant in pursuance of subsection (3) in respect of any land or vessel unless he is satisfied—

(a) that admission to the land or vessel in pursuance of subsection (1) was sought after not less than seven days notice of the intended entry had been served on the occupier; or
(b) that admission to the land or vessel in pursuance of that subsection was sought in an emergency and was refused by or on behalf of the occupier; or
(c) that the land or vessel is unoccupied; or
(d) that an application for admission to the land or vessel would defeat the object of the entry.

(5) A warrant issued in pursuance of this section shall continue in force until the purpose for which the entry is required has been satisfied.

(6) (*Applies to Scotland only.*)

[452]

NOTES

Commencement: 27 August 1993.

This section derived from the Public Health (Scotland) Act 1897, s 18, the Public Health Act 1936, s 287, the Clean Air Act 1956, s 31(1), Sch 3, Pt I, para 1(a), Pt III, the Control of Pollution Act 1974, s 91, and gives effect to the sixth recommendation of the Law Commission Report on this consolidation (Law Com No 209; Cm 2085).

---

57 Provisions supplementary to section 56

(1) A person authorised to enter upon any land or vessel in pursuance of section 56 shall, if so required, produce evidence of his authority before he enters upon the land or vessel.

(2) A person so authorised may take with him on to the land or vessel in question such other persons and such equipment as may be necessary.

(3) Admission to any land or vessel used for residential purposes and admission with heavy equipment to any other land or vessel shall not, except in an emergency or in a case where the land or vessel is unoccupied, be demanded as of right in pursuance of section 56(1) unless notice of the intended entry has been served on the occupier not less than seven days before the demand.

(4) A person who, in the exercise of powers conferred on him by virtue of section 56 or this section, enters upon any land or vessel which is unoccupied or of which the occupier is temporarily absent shall leave the land or vessel as effectually secured against unauthorised entry as he found it.

(5) It shall be the duty of a local authority to make full compensation to any person who has sustained damage by reason of—
(a) the exercise by a person authorised by the authority of any of the powers conferred on the person so authorised by virtue of section 56 or this section; or
(b) the failure of a person so authorised to perform the duty imposed on him by subsection (4),

except where the damage is attributable to the default of the person who sustained it; and any dispute as to a person's entitlement to compensation in pursuance of this subsection or as to the amount of the compensation shall be determined by arbitration.

(6) A person who wilfully obstructs another person acting in the exercise of any powers conferred on the other person by virtue of section 56 or this section shall be guilty of an offence and liable on summary conviction to a fine not exceeding level 3 on the standard scale.

(7) In section 56 and this section any reference to an emergency is a reference to a case where a person requiring entry to any land or vessel has reasonable cause to

believe that circumstances exist which are likely to endanger life or health and that immediate entry to the land or vessel is necessary to verify the existence of those circumstances or to ascertain their cause or to effect a remedy.

[453]

NOTES
Commencement: 27 August 1993.
This section derived from the Control of Pollution Act 1974, s 92, the Criminal Justice Act 1982, ss 38, 46, and gives effect to the sixth recommendation of the Law Commission Report on this consolidation (Law Com No 209; Cm 2085).

58 Power of local authorities to obtain information

(1)   A local authority may serve on any person a notice requiring him to furnish to the authority, within a period or at times specified in the notice and in a form so specified, any information so specified which the authority reasonably considers that it needs for the purposes of any function conferred on the authority by Part IV or V of this Act (or by this Part of this Act so far as relating to those Parts).

(2)   The Secretary of State may by regulations provide for restricting the information which may be required in pursuance of subsection (1) and for determining the form in which the information is to be so required.

(3)   Any person who—
    (a) fails without reasonable excuse to comply with the requirements of a notice served on him in pursuance of this section; or
    (b) in furnishing any information in compliance with such a notice, makes any statement which he knows to be false in a material particular or recklessly makes any statement which is false in a material particular,
shall be guilty of an offence and liable on summary conviction to a fine not exceeding level 5 on the standard scale.

[454]

NOTES
Commencement: 27 August 1993.
Sub-s (1) derived from the Control of Pollution Act 1974, s 93(1); sub-s (2) derived from the Control of Pollution Act 1974, s 93(2) (as read with s 105(1) (in part) of that Act); sub-s (3) derived from the Control of Pollution Act 1974, s 93(3), the Criminal Justice Act 1982, ss 38, 46.

[59 Inquiries]

(1)   The Secretary of State may cause [an inquiry] to be held in any case in which he considers it appropriate for [an inquiry] to be held either in connection with a provision of this Act or with a view to preventing or dealing with air pollution at any place.

(2)   Subsections (2) to (5) of section 250 of the Local Government Act 1972 (which contains supplementary provisions with respect to local inquiries held in pursuance of that section) shall, without prejudice to the generality of subsection (1) of that section, apply to inquiries in England and Wales in pursuance of subsection (1) as they apply to inquiries in pursuance of that section.

(3)   *(Applies to Scotland only.)*

[455]

NOTES
Commencement: 27 August 1993.
This section derived from the Public Health Act 1936, s 318, the Clean Air Act 1956, s 31(1), the Clean Air Act 1968, s 14(1), Sch 1, para 1 (in part), the Control of Pollution Act 1974, s 96(1), (2).
Section heading: substituted by the Environment Act 1995, s 120, Sch 22, para 197.
Sub-s (1): words in square brackets substituted by the Environment Act 1995, s 120, Sch 22, para 197.

60 Default powers

(1) If the Secretary of State is satisfied that any local authority (in this section referred to as the "defaulting authority") have failed to perform any functions which they ought to have performed, he may make an order—

 (a) declaring the authority to be in default; and

 (b) directing the authority to perform such of their functions as are specified in the order;

and he may specify the manner in which and the time or times within which those functions are to be performed by the authority.

(2) If the defaulting authority fails to comply with any direction contained in such an order, the Secretary of State may, instead of enforcing the order by mandamus, make an order transferring to himself such of the functions of the authority as he thinks fit.

(3) Where any functions of the defaulting authority are transferred in pursuance of subsection (2) above, the amount of any expenses which the Secretary of State certifies were incurred by him in performing those functions shall on demand be paid to him by the defaulting authority.

(4) Where any expenses are in pursuance of subsection (3) required to be paid by the defaulting authority in respect of any functions transferred in pursuance of this section—

 (a) the expenses shall be defrayed by the authority in the like manner, and shall be debited to the like account, as if the functions had not been transferred and the expenses had been incurred by the authority in performing them; and

 (b) the authority shall have the like powers for the purpose of raising any money required for the purpose of paragraph (a) as the authority would have had for the purpose of raising money required for defraying expenses incurred for the purposes of the functions in question.

(5) An order transferring any functions of the defaulting authority in pursuance of subsection (2) may provide for the transfer to the Secretary of State of such of the property, rights, liabilities and obligations of the authority as he considers appropriate; and where such an order is revoked the Secretary of State may, by the revoking order or a subsequent order, make such provision as he considers appropriate with respect to any property, rights, liabilities and obligations held by him for the purposes of the transferred functions.

(6) An order made under this section may be varied or revoked by a subsequent order so made.

(7) This section does not apply to a failure by a local authority—

 (a) to discharge their functions under section 18 (declaration of smoke control areas);

 (b) to submit proposals to the Secretary of State in pursuance of a direction under subsection (1) of section 19 (Secretary of State's power to require creation of smoke control area); or

 (c) to perform a duty imposed on them by or by virtue of subsection (4) or (6) of that section.

(8) In this section "functions", in relation to an authority, means functions conferred on the authority by virtue of this Act.

                     [456]

NOTES

Commencement: 27 August 1993.

This section derived from the Clean Air Act 1968, s 8(7), the Control of Pollution Act 1974, s 97(1)–(8), and gives effect to the eighth recommendation of the Law Commission Report on this consolidation (Law Com No 209; Cm 2085).

61 Joint exercise of local authority functions

(1)   Sections 6, 7, 9 and 10 of the Public Health Act 1936 (provisions relating to joint boards) shall, so far as applicable, have effect in relation to this Act as if the provisions of this Act were provisions of that Act.

(2)   *(Applies to Scotland only.)*

(3)   Without prejudice to subsections (1) and (2), any two or more local authorities may combine for the purpose of declaring an area to be a smoke control area and in that event—
   (a) the smoke control area may be the whole of the districts of those authorities or any part of those districts;
   (b) the references in section 18, Schedule 1 and paragraph 1 of Schedule 2 to the local authority shall be read as references to the local authorities acting jointly;
   (c) the reference in paragraph 1 of Schedule 1 to a place in the district of the local authority shall be construed as a reference to a place in each of the districts of the local authorities;

but, except as provided in this subsection, references in this Act to the local authority shall, in relation to a building or dwelling, or to a boiler or industrial plant, in the smoke control area, be read as references to that one of the local authorities within whose district the building, dwelling, boiler or plant is situated.

(4)   For the avoidance of doubt it is hereby declared that where a port health authority or joint board has functions, rights or liabilities under this Act—
   (a) any reference in this Act to a local authority or its district includes, in relation to those functions, rights or liabilities, a reference to the port health authority or board or its district;
   (b) for the purposes of this Act, no part of the district of any such port health authority or board is to be treated, in relation to any matter falling within the competence of the authority or board, as forming part of the district of any other authority.

(5)   Any premises which extend into the districts of two or more authorities shall be treated for the purposes of this Act as being wholly within such one of those districts—
   (a) in England and Wales, as may from time to time be agreed by those authorities; or
   (b) *(applies to Scotland only)*.

[457]

NOTES
Commencement: 27 August 1993.

Sub-s (1) derived from the Clean Air Act 1956, s 31(1) (in part), the Clean Air Act 1968, s 14(1), Sch 1, para 1 (in part), and gives effect to the ninth recommendation of the Law Commission Report on this consolidation (Law Com No 209; Cm 2085); sub-ss (3), (4), (5)(a) derived from the Clean Air Act 1956, s 31(3), (4), (6).

62 Application of certain provisions of Part XII of Public Health Act 1936 and corresponding Scottish legislation

(1)   In the application of this Act to England and Wales, the following provisions of Part XII of the Public Health Act 1936 shall have effect in relation to the provisions of this Act (apart from Parts IV and V) as if those provisions were provisions of that Act—
   section 275 (power of local authority to execute works);
   section 276 (power of local authority to sell materials);
   section 278 (compensation to individuals for damage resulting from exercise of powers under Act);

section 283 (form of notices);

section 284 (authentication of documents);

section 285 (service of notices);

section 289 (power to require occupier to permit works to be executed by owner);

section 291 (expenses to be a charge on the premises);

section 293 (recovery of expenses);

section 294 (limitation of liability of certain owners);

. . .

section 305 (protection of members and officers of local authorities from personal liability).

(2)   (*Applies to Scotland only.*)

                                                       [458]

NOTES

Commencement: 27 August 1993.

Sub-s (1) derived from the Clean Air Act 1956, s 31(1), the Clean Air Act 1968, s 14(1), Sch 1, para 1 (in part); sub-s (2) derived from the Clean Air Act 1956, s 31(7), Sch 3, Pt III, the Clean Air Act 1968, s 14(1), Sch 1, para 1, the Housing (Scotland) Act 1987, Sch 23, para 6(2), (3).

Sub-s (1): words omitted repealed by the Statute Law (Repeals) Act 1993.

General

63 Regulations and orders

(1)   Any power of the Secretary of State under this Act to make an order or regulations—

    (a)   includes power to make different provision in the order or regulations for different circumstances;

    (b)   includes power to make such incidental, supplemental and transitional provision as the Secretary of State considers appropriate; and

    (c)   is exercisable by statutory instrument except in the case of the powers conferred by sections 19(4) and 60 and paragraph 3 of Schedule 3.

(2)   Any statutory instrument containing regulations made under this Act, except an instrument containing regulations a draft of which is required by section 6(3), 10(5) or 47(2) to be approved by a resolution of each House of Parliament, shall be subject to annulment in pursuance of a resolution of either House of Parliament.

(3)   Any statutory instrument containing an order under section 21 or 22 shall be subject to annulment in pursuance of a resolution of either House of Parliament.

                                                       [459]

NOTES

Commencement: 27 August 1993.

Sub-s (1)(a), (b) derived from the Control of Pollution Act 1974, s 104(1)(a) and gives effect to the tenth recommendation of the Law Commission Report on this consolidation (Law Com No 209; Cm 2085); sub-s (1)(c) derived from the Clean Air Act 1956, s 33(1), the Clean Air Act 1968, s 12(1); sub-ss (2), (3) derived in part from the Clean Air Act 1956, s 33(1) (in part), the Clean Air Act 1968, s 12(2).

64 General provisions as to interpretation

(1)   In this Act, except so far as the context otherwise requires,—

"authorised officer" means any officer of a local authority authorised by them in writing, either generally or specially, to act in matters of any specified kind or in any specified matter;

. . . . .

"caravan" means a caravan within the meaning of Part I of the Caravan Sites and Control of Development Act 1960, disregarding the amendment made by section 13(2) of the Caravan Sites Act 1968, which usually and for the time being is situated on a caravan site within the meaning of that Act;

"chimney" includes structures and openings of any kind from or through which smoke, grit, dust or fumes may be emitted, and, in particular, includes flues, and references to a chimney of a building include references to a chimney which serves the whole or a part of a building but is structurally separate from the building;

"dark smoke" has the meaning given by section 3(1);

"day" means a period of twenty-four hours beginning at midnight;

"domestic furnace" means any furnace which is—

(a) designed solely or mainly for domestic purposes, and

(b) used for heating a boiler with a maximum heating capacity of less than 16.12 kilowatts;

"fireplace" includes any furnace, grate or stove, whether open or closed;

"fixed boiler or industrial plant" means any boiler or industrial plant which is attached to a building or is for the time being fixed to or installed on any land;

"fumes" means any airborne solid matter smaller than dust;

"industrial plant" includes any still, melting pot or other plant used for any industrial or trade purposes, and also any incinerator used for or in connection with any such purposes;

"local authority" means—

(a) in England . . . , the council of a district or a London borough, the Common Council of the City of London, the Sub-Treasurer of the Inner Temple and the Under Treasurer of the Middle Temple;

[(aa) in Wales, the council of a county or county borough;] and

(b) (applies to Scotland only);

"owner", in relation to premises—

(a) as respects England and Wales, means the person for the time being receiving the rackrent of the premises, whether on his own account or as agent or trustee for another person, or who would so receive the rackrent if the premises were let at a rackrent; and

(b) (applies to Scotland only);

. . . . .

"practicable" means reasonably practicable having regard, amongst other things, to local conditions and circumstances, to the financial implications and to the current state of technical knowledge, and "practicable means" includes the provision and maintenance of plant and its proper use;

"premises" includes land;

"smoke" includes soot, ash, grit and gritty particles emitted in smoke; and

"vessel" has the same meaning as ["ship" in the Merchant Shipping Act 1995].

(2) Any reference in this Act to the occupier of a building shall, in relation to any building different parts of which are occupied by different persons, be read as a reference to the occupier or other person in control of the part of the building in which the relevant fireplace is situated.

(3) In this Act any reference to the rate of emission of any substance or any reference which is to be understood as such a reference shall, in relation to any regulations or conditions, be construed as a reference to the quantities of that substance which may be emitted during a period specified in the regulations or conditions.

(4) In this Act, except so far as the context otherwise requires, "private dwelling" means any building or part of a building used or intended to be used as such, and a building or part of a building is not to be taken for the purposes of this

Act to be used or intended to be used otherwise than as a private dwelling by reason that a person who resides or is to reside in it is or is to be required or permitted to reside in it in consequence of his employment or of holding an office.

(5)   In considering for the purposes of this Act whether any and, if so, what works are reasonably necessary in order to make suitable provision for heating and cooking in the case of a dwelling or are reasonably necessary in order to enable a building to be used for a purpose without contravention of any of the provisions of this Act, regard shall be had to any difficulty there may be in obtaining, or in obtaining otherwise than at a high price, any fuels which would have to be used but for the execution of the works.

(6)   Any furnaces which are in the occupation of the same person and are served by a single chimney shall, for the purposes of sections 5 to 12, 14 and 15, be taken to be one furnace.

[460]

NOTES
Commencement: 27 August 1993.
Sub-s (1) derived in part from the Public Health Act 1936, s 343(1) (in part), the Clean Air Act 1956, s 31(1), 34(1) (in part), the Clean Air Act 1968, ss 13(1) (in part), 14(1), Sch 1, para 10, the Local Government Act 1972, s 180(1), (3)(f), the Control of Pollution Act 1974, s 30(1), 84(1), 105(1) (all in part), and gives effect to the eleventh recommendation of the Law Commission Report on this consolidation (Law Com No 209; Cm 2085); sub-s (2) derived from the Clean Air Act 1956, s 34(3); sub-s (3) derived from the Clean Air Act 1968, s 13(2); sub-s (4) derived from the Clean Air Act 1956, s 34(4), and gives effect to the twelfth recommendation of the Law Commission Report on this consolidation (Law Com No 209; Cm 2085); sub-s (5) derived from the Clean Air Act 1956, s 34(6); sub-s (6) derived from the Clean Air Act 1956, s 34(7), the Clean Air Act 1968, s 14(1), Sch 1, para 12.
Sub-s (1): in definition "local authority" in para (a) words omitted repealed, and para (aa) inserted, by the Local Government (Wales) Act 1994, ss 22(3), 66(8), Sch 9, para 18, Sch 18, in definition "vessel" words in square brackets substituted by the Merchant Shipping Act 1995, s 314(2), Sch 13, para 94(b).

65 Application to Isles of Scilly

Parts IV and V, and this Part so far as relating to those Parts, shall have effect in their application to the Isles of Scilly with such modifications as the Secretary of State may by order specify.

[461]

NOTES
Commencement: 27 August 1993.
This section derived from the Control of Pollution Act 1974, s 107.

66   *(Repealed by sub-s (2) of this section, as originally enacted, in consequence of the repeal by the Environmental Protection Act 1990, s 162, Sch 16, Pt I, of the Alkali, &c Works Regulation Act 1906.)*

67 Consequential amendments, transitional provisions and repeals

(1)   The enactments specified in Schedule 4 shall have effect subject to the amendments set out in that Schedule, being amendments consequential on the preceding provisions of this Act.

(2)   The transitional provisions and savings contained in Schedule 5 (which include provisions preserving the effect of transitional or saving provisions in enactments repealed by this Act) shall have effect.

(3)   The enactments specified in Schedule 6 (which include spent enactments) are repealed to the extent specified in the third column of that Schedule.

[462]

NOTES
Commencement: 27 August 1993.

68 Short title, commencement and extent

(1)   This Act may be cited as the Clean Air Act 1993.

(2)   This Act shall come into force at the end of the period of three months beginning with the day on which it is passed.

(3)   The following provisions of this Act (apart from this section) extend to Northern Ireland—
  (a)   section 30;
  (b)   section 32 so far as it relates to regulations under section 30; and
  (c)   section 67(3) and Schedule 6, so far as they relate to the repeal of sections 75 and 77 of the Control of Pollution Act 1974;

but otherwise this Act does not extend to Northern Ireland.

[463]

NOTES
Commencement: 27 August 1993.
  Sub-s (3) derived in part from the Clean Air Act 1956, s 36, the Clean Air Act 1968, s 15(6), the Control of Smoke Pollution Act 1989, s 3(3), the Control of Pollution Act 1974, s 109(3) (in part).

SCHEDULE 1
COMING INTO OPERATION OF SMOKE CONTROL ORDERS
Section 18(4)

1.   Before making a smoke control order the local authority shall publish in the London Gazette and once at least in each of two successive weeks in some newspaper circulating in the area to which the order will relate a notice—
  (a)   stating that the local authority propose to make the order, and its general effect;
  (b)   specifying a place in the district of the local authority where a copy of the order and of any map or plan referred to in it may be inspected by any person free of charge at all reasonable times during a period of not less than six weeks from the date of the last publication of the notice; and
  (c)   stating that within that period any person who will be affected by the order may by notice in writing to the local authority object to the making of the order.

2.   Besides publishing such a notice, the local authority shall post, and keep posted throughout the period mentioned in paragraph 1(b), copies of the notice in such number of conspicuous places within the area to which the order will relate as appear to them necessary for the purpose of bringing the proposal to make the order to the notice of persons who will be affected.

3.   If an objection is duly made to the local authority within the period mentioned in paragraph 1(b), and is not withdrawn, the local authority shall not make the order without first considering the objection.

4.   Subject to paragraphs 5 and 6, an order shall come into operation on such date not less than six months after it is made as may be specified in it.

5.   An order varying a previous order so as to exempt specified buildings or classes of building or specified fireplaces or classes of fireplace from the operation of section 20 (prohibition of smoke emissions in smoke control area) may come into operation on, or at any time after, the date on which it is made.

6.   If, before the date on which the order is to come into operation, the local authority—
  (a)   pass a resolution postponing its coming into operation; and
  (b)   publish a notice stating the effect of the resolution in the London Gazette and once at least in each of two successive weeks in some newspaper circulating in the area to which the order will relate,

the order shall, unless its coming into operation is again postponed under this paragraph, come into operation on the date specified in the resolution.

7. (*Applies to Scotland only.*)

[464]

NOTES

Commencement: 27 August 1993.

This Schedule derived from the Clean Air Act 1956, Sch 1, the Local Government, Planning and Land Act 1980, s 1(2), Sch 2, para 5.

Transitional provisions: see s 67(2) of, and Sch 5, Pt II, paras 8, 9, Pt III to, this Act, at [462], [468], [469].

SCHEDULE 2
SMOKE CONTROL ORDERS: EXPENDITURE ON OLD PRIVATE DWELLINGS
Section 25(1)

Grants for expenditure incurred in adaptation of fireplaces

1.—(1) This paragraph applies if, after the making of a smoke control order by a local authority, the owner or occupier of, or any person interested in, an old private dwelling which is or will be within a smoke control area as a result of the order incurs relevant expenditure.

(2) For the purposes of this paragraph "relevant expenditure" is expenditure on adaptations in or in connection with an old private dwelling to avoid contraventions of section 20 (prohibition of smoke emissions in smoke control area) which—

(a)   is incurred before the coming into operation of the order and with the approval of the local authority given for the purposes of this paragraph; or

(b)   is reasonably incurred in carrying out adaptations required by a notice given under section 24(1) (power of local authority to require certain adaptations).

(3) If the adaptations in question are carried out to the satisfaction of the local authority, the local authority—

(a)   shall repay to him seven-tenths of the relevant expenditure; and

(b)   may, if they think fit, also repay to him the whole or any part of the remainder of that expenditure.

(4) Where relevant expenditure is incurred by the occupier of a private dwelling who is not an owner of the dwelling and the adaptations in question consist of or include the provision of any cooking or heating appliance which can be readily removed from the dwelling without injury to itself or the fabric of the dwelling, the following provisions shall have effect as respects so much of the expenditure as represents the cost of the appliance, that is to say—

(a)   not more than seven-twentieths of that part of that expenditure shall be repaid until two years from the coming into operation of the order; and

(b)   any further repayment of that part of that expenditure shall be made only if the appliance has not by then been removed from the dwelling and, if made, shall be made to the person who is the occupier of the dwelling at the end of the two years.

(5) The approval of a local authority to the incurring of expenditure may be given for the purposes of this paragraph, if the authority think fit in the circumstances of any particular case, after the expenditure has been incurred.

(6) This paragraph has effect subject to paragraph 4.

Exclusion of grants in case of unsuitable appliances

2. For the purposes of this Schedule, an appliance is unsuitable for installation in any area or (as the case may be) in any district or part of Great Britain if it tends, by reason of its consumption of fuel (of whatever kind) or its consumption of fuel at times when it is generally used, to impose undue strain on the fuel resources available for that area, district or part.

3.—(1) Sub-paragraph (2) applies if—

(a)   after a local authority have resolved to make a smoke control order declaring a smoke control area (not being an order varying a previous order so made); and

(b)   before notice of the making of the order is first published in accordance with Schedule 1,

the authority pass a resolution designating any class of heating appliance as being, in their opinion, unsuitable for installation in that area.

(2) No payment shall be made by the authority under paragraph 1 in respect of expenditure incurred in providing, or in executing works for the purpose of the installation of, any heating appliance of the class designated by the resolution in or in connection with a dwelling within the area to which the order relates.

(3) No payment shall be made under paragraph 1 by a local authority in respect of expenditure incurred in providing, or in executing works for the purpose of the installation of, any heating appliance which, when the expenditure was incurred, fell within any class of appliance for the time being designated for the purposes of this paragraph by the Secretary of State as being in his opinion—

    (a)   unsuitable for installation in the district of that authority; or

    (b)   generally unsuitable for installation in the part of Great Britain with which the Secretary of State is concerned,

unless the approval of the local authority in respect of that expenditure was given for the purposes of paragraph 1 at a time when the appliance in question did not fall within any class of appliance so designated.

(4) Retrospective approval of expenditure may only be given by a local authority by virtue of paragraph 1(5) in the case of expenditure incurred in providing, or in executing works for the purpose of the installation of, a heating appliance, if the appliance—

    (a)   did not at the time when the expenditure was incurred; and

    (b)   does not when the approval is given,

fall within a class of appliance for the time being designated by the Secretary of State for the purposes of this paragraph as regards the district of that authority or generally.

(5) In accordance with the preceding provisions of this Schedule, expenditure within sub-paragraph (3) or (4) shall be left out of account for the purposes of paragraph 1.

Exchequer contributions to certain expenditure

4.—(1) The Secretary of State may, out of money provided by Parliament, make a contribution towards the following expenses, of any local authority (if approved by him), that is to say—

    (a)   any expenses of the local authority in making payments under paragraph 1;

    (b)   any expenses incurred by them in making, in or in connection with old private dwellings owned by them or under their control, adaptations to avoid contraventions of section 20; and

    (c)   any expenses incurred by them in carrying out adaptations required by notices under section 24 in or in connection with old private dwellings.

(2) A contribution under this paragraph in respect of any expenses shall be a single payment equal—

    (a)   in the case of expenses mentioned in sub-paragraph (1)(a), to four-sevenths of the amount of the expenses; and

    (b)   in the case of expenses mentioned in sub-paragraph (1)(b), to two-fifths of the amount of the expenses; and

    (c)   in the case of expenses mentioned in sub-paragraph (1)(c), to four-sevenths of the amount arrived at by deducting the recoverable amount from the amount of those expenses.

(3) In subparagraph (2)(c), "the recoverable amount" means, in relation to any expenses, the fraction of those expenses (whether three-tenths or some smaller fraction determined by the local authority, in the case of those expenses, under section 24(2) or (3)) which the local authority have power to recover from the occupier or owner by virtue of section 24(2) or (3).

[465]

NOTES

Commencement: 27 August 1993.

Para 1(1)–(4) derived from the Clean Air Act 1956, s 12(1), the Local Government, Planning and Land Act 1980, s 1(2), Sch 2, para 2; para 1(5), (6) derived from the Housing Act 1964, s 95(4)(a) (as read with s 108(4) of that Act); paras 2, 3(1), (2) derived from the Housing Act 1964, s 95(2) (in part), the Clean Air Act 1968, s 10(5); para 3(3), (4) derived from the Housing Act 1964, s 95(3) (in part), (4)(b), respectively; para 3(5) derived from the Housing Act 1964, s 95(2), (3) (both in part); para 4 derived from the Clean Air Act 1956, s 13(1), (2), the Housing Act 1964, s 95(7), (8).

Transitional provisions: see s 67(2) of, and Sch 5, Pt II, paras 8, 9, Pt III to, this Act, at [462], [468], [469].

(Sch 3 repealed by virtue of s 66(2) of this Act, as originally enacted, in consequence of the repeal by the Environmental Protection Act 1990, s 162, Sch 16, Pt I, of the Alkali, &c Works Regulation Act 1906.)

SCHEDULE 4
CONSEQUENTIAL AMENDMENTS

Section 67(1)

The Health and Safety at Work etc Act 1974 (c 37)

1.   Section 80(1) of the Health and Safety at Work etc Act 1974 shall apply to provisions in this Act which re-enact provisions previously contained in an Act passed before or in the same Session as that Act as it applies to provisions so contained.

2–6.. . .

[466]

NOTES
Commencement: 27 August 1993.
Para 2: amends the Control of Pollution Act 1974, s 96(1).
Paras 3, 5: outside the scope of this work.
Para 4: amends the Environmental Protection Act 1990, s 79(7).
Para 6: amends the Radioactive Substances Act 1993, Sch 3, paras 2, 12.

SCHEDULE 5
TRANSITIONAL PROVISIONS

Section 67(2)

PART I
GENERAL TRANSITIONAL PROVISIONS AND SAVINGS

Continuity of the law

1.   The substitution of this Act for the enactments repealed by this Act does not affect the continuity of the law.

2.   Any reference, whether express or implied, in this Act or any other enactment, instrument or document to a provision of this Act shall, so far as the context permits, be construed as including, in relation to the times, circumstances and purposes in relation to which the corresponding provision of the enactments repealed by this Act has effect, a reference to that corresponding provision.

3.   Any document made, served or issued after the commencement of this Act which contains a reference to any of the enactments repealed by this Act shall be construed, except so far as a contrary intention appears, as referring or, as the case may require, including a reference to the corresponding provision of this Act.

4.   Paragraphs 2 and 3 have effect without prejudice to the operation of sections 16 and 17 of the Interpretation Act 1978 (which relate to the effect of repeals).

General saving for old transitional provisions and savings

5.—(1)   The repeal by this Act of a transitional provision or saving relating to the coming into force of a provision reproduced in this Act does not affect the operation of the transitional provision or saving, in so far as it is not specifically reproduced in this Act but remains capable of having effect in relation to the corresponding provision of this Act.

(2)   The repeal by this Act of an enactment previously repealed subject to savings does not affect the continued operation of those savings.

(3)   The repeal by this Act of a saving on the previous repeal of an enactment does not affect the operation of the saving in so far as it is not specifically reproduced in this Act but remains capable of having effect.

[467]

PART II
EXCLUSION AND MODIFICATION OF CERTAIN PROVISIONS OF THIS ACT

Requirements to fit arrestment plant: sections 6 & 8

6.—(1) Section 6(1) (arrestment plant for new non-domestic furnaces) does not apply to a furnace which was installed, the installation of which began or an agreement for the purchase or installation of which was entered into before 1st October 1969 (which was the day appointed for the coming into force of the enactments replaced by section 6).

(2) Subject to sub-paragraph (3), section 8(1) (arrestment plant for furnaces burning solid fuel in other cases) applies in relation to a furnace to which, by virtue of sub-paragraph (1), section 6 does not apply as it applies to a domestic furnace.

(3) Section 8(1) does not apply to a furnace which was installed, the installation of which began or an agreement for the purchase or installation of which was entered into—
  (a)   in relation to a furnace in England and Wales, before 1st June 1958 (which was the day appointed as respects England and Wales for the coming into force of the enactments replaced by section 8); and
  (b)   in relation to a furnace in Scotland, before 15th November 1958 (which was the day so appointed as respects Scotland).

Height of chimneys for furnaces: section 14

7.—(1) Subject to sub-paragraph (2) below, section 14 (height of chimneys for furnaces) does not apply to any furnace served by a chimney the construction of which was begun or the plans for which were passed before 1st April 1969 (which was the day appointed for the coming into force of the enactments replaced by section 14).

(2) Notwithstanding sub-paragraph (1), section 14 does apply to—
  (a)   any furnace the combustion space of which has been increased on or after 1st April 1969; or
  (b)   any furnace the installation of which was begun on or after that day and which replaces a furnace which had a smaller combustion space.

Smoke control orders

8.—(1) In relation to any smoke control order made by a local authority under section 18 of this Act which revokes or varies an order made under section 11 of the Clean Air Act 1956 before 13th November 1980 (which was the date of the passing of the Local Government, Planning and Land Act 1980, which amended section 11 of that Act to omit the requirement that an order made by a local authority should be confirmed by the Secretary of State) the provisions of this Act mentioned in the following provisions of this paragraph shall have effect subject to the modifications there mentioned.

(2) In section 18—
  (a)   in subsection (1) after the word "order" where it first appears there shall be inserted the words "confirmed by the Secretary of State";
  (b)   in subsection (3), after the word "order" where it first appears there shall be inserted the words "confirmed by the Secretary of State" and at the end there shall be inserted the words "so confirmed"; and
  (c)   in subsection (4), after the words "to the" there shall be inserted the words "confirmation and".

(3) In section 26(1) and paragraph 1(1) of Schedule 2, for the word "making" there shall be substituted the word "confirmation".

9.   The provisions of Part III of this Schedule (which are derived from Schedule 1 to the Clean Air Act 1956 as that Schedule had effect immediately before the date mentioned in paragraph 8(1) of this Schedule) shall apply in substitution for Schedule 1 to this Act in relation to any such order; and references in this Act, as it applies in relation to any such order, to Schedule 1 to this Act or to any specified provision of that Schedule shall be read as referring to Part III of this Schedule or the corresponding provision of that Part (as the case may be).

Colliery spoilbanks: section 42

10. Subsections (2) to (4) of section 42 (colliery spoilbanks) shall not apply to any deposit of refuse deposited from a mine or quarry before 5th July 1956 (the date of the passing of the

Clean Air Act 1956) if at that date the deposit was not longer in use as such and was not under the control of the owner of the mine or quarry.

[468]

NOTES
Commencement: 27 August 1993.
Para 6 derived from the Clean Air Act 1956, s 6(2), as repealed in part by s 14(2) of, Sch 2 to, the 1968 Act, the Clean Air Act (Appointed Day) Order 1958/167, the Clean Air Act 1968, s 3(4) (in part), the Clean Air Act (Commencement No 2) Order 1969, SI 1969/995; para 7 derived from the Clean Air Act 1968, s 6(10) (in part), the Clean Air Act 1968 (Commencement No 1) Order 1968, SI 1968/1922; paras 8, 9 derived from the Local Government, Planning and Land Act 1980, s 1(2), Sch 2, paras 2(b), 5(b) (both in part); para 10 derived from the Clean Air Act 1956, s 18(3).

PART III
CONFIRMATION AND COMING INTO OPERATION OF CERTAIN SMOKE
CONTROL ORDERS

11. In this Part of this Schedule "order" means a smoke control order.

12. After making an order, the local authority shall publish in the London Gazette and also once at least in each of two successive weeks in some newspaper circulating in the area to which the order relates a notice—
    (a)   stating that the order has been made and its general effect;
    (b)   specifying a place in the district of the local authority where a copy of the order and of any map or plan referred to in the order may be inspected by any person free of charge at all reasonable times during a period of not less than six weeks from the date of the last publication of the notice; and
    (c)   stating that within that period any person who will be affected by the order may by notice in writing to the Secretary of State object to the confirmation of the order.

13. Besides publishing a notice as required by paragraph 12, the local authority who have made an order shall post, and keep posted throughout the period mentioned in that paragraph, copies of the notice in such number of conspicuous places within the area to which the order relates as appear to them necessary for the purpose of bringing the making of the order to the notice of persons affected.

14. If no objection is duly made to the Secretary of State within the period mentioned in paragraph 12(b), or if every objection so made is withdrawn, the Secretary of State may, if he thinks fit, confirm the order either with or without modifications.

15. In any case other than one within paragraph 14 the Secretary of State shall, before confirming the order, either—
    (a)   cause a local inquiry to be held; or
    (b)   afford to any person by whom an objection has been duly made in accordance with paragraph 12(c) and not withdrawn an opportunity of appearing before and being heard by a person appointed by him for the purpose;

and, after considering the objection and the report of the person who held the inquiry or the person so appointed, may confirm the order with or without modifications.

16. Section 250(2) to (5) of the Local Government Act 1972 (summoning of witnesses and production of documents before, and costs incurred at, local government inquiries held under that section) shall apply to an inquiry held under this Part of this Schedule by the Secretary of State as they apply to inquiries held under that section.

17. Subject to paragraphs 18 and 19, an order when confirmed shall come into operation on such date as may be specified in the order, not being earlier than six months from the date of the confirmation.

18. An order varying a previous order so as to exempt specified buildings or classes of building or specified fireplaces or classes of fireplace from the operation of section 18 may come into operation on, or at any time after, the date of its confirmation.

19.—(1) If, before the date on which an order is to come into operation, the local authority—

(a)   pass a resolution postponing its operation; and

(b)   publish a notice stating the effect of the resolution in the London Gazette and also once at least in each of two successive weeks in some newspaper circulating in the area to which the order relates;

the order shall, unless its coming into operation is again postponed under this paragraph, come into operation on the date specified in the resolution.

(2)   A local authority shall not without the consent of the Secretary of State exercise their power under sub-paragraph (1) of postponing the coming into operation of an order for a period of more than twelve months or for periods amounting in all to more than twelve months.

20. (*Applies to Scotland only.*)

[469]

NOTES
Commencement: 27 August 1993.
Paras 11–13 derived from the Clean Air Act 1956, Sch 1, paras 1–3 (as originally enacted); paras 14, 15 derived from the Clean Air Act 1956, Sch 1, para 4 (as originally enacted), the Clean Air Act 1968, s 10(4); para 16 derived from the Clean Air Act 1956, Sch 1, para 5 (as originally enacted) (as read with the Interpretation Act 1978, s 17(2)(a)); para 17 derived from the Clean Air Act 1956, Sch 1, para 6 (as originally enacted); para 18 derived from the Clean Air Act 1968, s 10(1); para 19 derived from the Clean Air Act 1956, Sch 1, para 6 (as originally enacted), the Clean Air Act 1968, s 10(2).

SCHEDULE 6
REPEALS

Section 67(3)

Chapter	Short title	Extent of repeal
4 & 5 Eliz 2 c 52	The Clean Air Act 1956	The whole Act.
1963 c 33	The London Government Act 1963	Section 40(4)(e).
		In Schedule 11, paragraphs 30 and 31.
1964 c 56	The Housing Act 1964	Section 95.
1968 c 62	The Clean Air Act 1968	The whole Act.
1970 c 38	The Building (Scotland) Act 1970	In Schedule 1, paragraph 5.
1972 c 70	The Local Government Act 1972	Section 180(3)(f).
1973 c 65	The Local Government (Scotland) Act 1973	In Schedule 15, paragraph 28.
		In Schedule 27, paragraph 128.
1974 c 39	The Consumer Credit Act 1974	In Schedule 4, paragraphs 15 and 16.
1974 c 40	The Control of Pollution Act 1974	Sections 75 to 84.
		Section 103.
		In section 109(3), the words "75, 77".
		In Schedule 2, paragraphs 19, 26 and 27.
		In Schedule 3, paragraph 16.
1980 c 65	The Local Government, Planning and Land Act 1980	Section 189.
		In Schedule 2, paragraphs 1 to 6 and 16.

Chapter	Short title	Extent of repeal
1984 c 55	The Building Act 1984	In Schedule 5, paragraph 2.
		In Schedule 6, paragraph 5.
1987 c 26	The Housing (Scotland) Act 1987	In Schedule 23, paragraphs 6 and 14.
1989 c 17	The Control of Smoke Pollution Act 1989	The whole Act.
1990 c 43	The Environmental Protection Act 1990	Section 85.
		In Schedule 15, paragraphs 6, 7, 12 and 15(6) to (9).
1991 c 46	The Atomic Weapons Establishment Act 1991	In the Schedule, paragraphs 4 and 8(1).

[470]

NOTES

Commencement: 27 August 1993.

RADIOACTIVE SUBSTANCES ACT 1993

(1993 c 12)

ARRANGEMENT OF SECTIONS

An Act to consolidate certain enactments relating to radioactive substances with corrections and minor improvements made under the Consolidation of Enactments (Procedure) Act 1949

[27 May 1993]

NOTES

Transitional provisions: see s 49(2) of, and Sch 5, Pt I to, this Act, at **[514]**, **[520]**.

Preliminary

1 Meaning of "radioactive material"

(1)   In this Act "radioactive material" means anything which, not being waste, is either a substance to which this subsection applies or an article made wholly or partly from, or incorporating, such a substance.

(2)   Subsection (1) applies to any substance falling within either or both of the following descriptions, that is to say,—
   (a) a substance containing an element specified in the first column of Schedule 1, in such a proportion that the number of becquerels of that element contained in the substance, divided by the number of grams which the substance weighs, is a number greater than that specified in relation to that element in the appropriate column of that Schedule;
   (b) a substance possessing radioactivity which is wholly or partly attributable to a process of nuclear fission or other process of subjecting a substance to bombardment by neutrons or to ionising radiations, not being a process occurring in the course of nature, or in consequence of the disposal of radioactive waste, or by way of contamination in the course of the application of a process to some other substance.

(3)   In subsection (2)(a) "the appropriate column"—
   (a) in relation to a solid substance, means the second column,
   (b) in relation to a liquid substance, means the third column, and
   (c) in relation to a substance which is a gas or vapour, means the fourth column.

(4)   For the purposes of subsection (2)(b), a substance shall not be treated as radioactive material if the level of radioactivity is less than such level as may be prescribed for substances of that description.

(5)   The Secretary of State may by order vary the provisions of Schedule 1, either by adding further entries to any column of that Schedule or by altering or deleting any entry for the time being contained in any column.

(6)   In the application of this section to Northern Ireland, the reference in subsection (5) to the Secretary of State shall have effect as a reference to the Department of the Environment for Northern Ireland.

[471]

NOTES

Commencement: 27 August 1993.

Sub-ss (1)–(3) derived from the Radioactive Substances Act 1960, s 18(1)–(3); sub-s (4) derived from the Radioactive Substances Act 1960, s 18(3A), the Environmental Protection Act 1990, s 105, Sch 5, Pt I, para 17; sub-s (5) derived from the Radioactive Substances Act 1960, s 18(6) (in part), the Environmental Protection Act 1990, s 100(3); sub-s (6) derived from the Radioactive Substances Act 1960, s 21(2)(a) (in part); the Environmental Protection Act 1990, s 105, Sch 5, Pt II, para 20(a)(i).

2 Meaning of "radioactive waste"

In this Act "radioactive waste" means waste which consists wholly or partly of—
   (a) a substance or article which, if it were not waste, would be radioactive material, or
   (b) a substance or article which has been contaminated in the course of the production, keeping or use of radioactive material, or by contact with or proximity to other waste falling within paragraph (a) or this paragraph.

[472]

NOTES

Commencement: 27 August 1993.

This section derived from the Radioactive Substances Act 1960, s 18(4).

3 Meaning of "mobile radioactive apparatus"

In this Act "mobile radioactive apparatus" means any apparatus, equipment, appliance or other thing which is radioactive material and—
   (a) is constructed or adapted for being transported from place to place, or
   (b) is portable and designed or intended to be used for releasing radioactive material into the environment or introducing it into organisms.

[473]

NOTES
Commencement: 27 August 1993.
This section derived from the Radioactive Substances Act 1960, s 18(5), the Environmental Protection Act 1990, s 105, Sch 5, Pt I, para 7(2).

4, 5 (*Repealed by the Environment Act 1995, s 120(1), (3), Sch 22, para 201, Sch 24.*)

Registration relating to use of radioactive material and mobile radioactive apparatus

6 Prohibition of use of radioactive material without registration

No person shall, on any premises which are used for the purposes of an undertaking carried on by him, keep or use, or cause or permit to be kept or used, radioactive material of any description, knowing or having reasonable grounds for believing it to be radioactive material, unless either—
   (a) he is registered under section 7 in respect of those premises and in respect of the keeping and use on those premises of radioactive material of that description, or
   (b) he is exempted from registration under that section in respect of those premises and in respect of the keeping and use on those premises of radioactive material of that description, or
   (c) the radioactive material in question consists of mobile radioactive apparatus in respect of which a person is registered under section 10 or is exempted from registration under that section.

[474]

NOTES
Commencement: 27 August 1993.
This section derived from the Radioactive Substances Act 1960, s 1(1).

7 Registration of users of radioactive material

   (1) Any application for registration under this section shall be made to the [appropriate Agency] and shall—
   (a) specify the particulars mentioned in subsection (2),
   (b) contain such other information as may be prescribed, and
   (c) be accompanied by the [charge prescribed for the purpose by a charging scheme under section 41 of the Environment Act 1995].

   (2) The particulars referred to in subsection (1)(a) are—
   (a) the premises to which the application relates,
   (b) the undertaking for the purposes of which those premises are used,
   (c) the description or descriptions of radioactive material proposed to be kept or used on the premises, and the maximum quantity of radioactive material of each such description likely to be kept or used on the premises at any one time, and
   (d) the manner (if any) in which radioactive material is proposed to be used on the premises.

(3)   On any application being made under this section, the [appropriate Agency] shall, subject to directions under section 25, send a copy of the application to each local authority in whose area the premises are situated.

(4)   Subject to the following provisions of this section, where an application is made to the [appropriate Agency] for registration under this section in respect of any premises, the [appropriate Agency] may either—

(a) register the applicant in respect of those premises and in respect of the keeping and use on those premises of radioactive material of the description to which the application relates, or

(b) if the application relates to two or more descriptions of radioactive material, register the applicant in respect of those premises and in respect of the keeping and use on those premises of such one or more of those descriptions of radioactive material as may be specified in the registration, or

(c) refuse the application.

(5)   An application for registration under this section which is duly made to the [appropriate Agency] may be treated by the applicant as having been refused if it is not determined within the prescribed period for determinations or within such longer period as may be agreed with the applicant.

(6)   Any registration under this section in respect of any premises may (subject to subsection (7)) be effected subject to such limitations or conditions as the [appropriate Agency] thinks fit, and in particular (but without prejudice to the generality of this subsection) may be effected subject to conditions of any of the following descriptions—

(a) conditions imposing requirements (including, if the [appropriate Agency] thinks fit, requirements involving structural or other alterations) in respect of any part of the premises, or in respect of any apparatus, equipment or appliance used or to be used on any part of the premises for the purposes of any use of radioactive material from which radioactive waste is likely to arise,

(b) conditions requiring the person to whom the registration relates, at such times and in such manner as may be specified in the registration, to furnish the [appropriate Agency] with information as to the removal of radioactive material from those premises to any other premises, and

(c) conditions prohibiting radioactive material from being sold or otherwise supplied from those premises unless it (or the container in which it is supplied) bears a label or other mark—

(i) indicating that it is radioactive material, or

(ii) if the conditions so require, indicating the description of radioactive material to which it belongs,

and (in either case) complying with any relevant requirements specified in the conditions.

(7)   In the exercise of any power conferred on [it] by subsection (4) or (6), the [appropriate Agency], except in determining whether to impose any conditions falling within paragraph (b) or (c) of subsection (6), shall have regard exclusively to the amount and character of the radioactive waste likely to arise from the keeping or use of radioactive material on the premises in question.

(8)   On registering a person under this section in respect of any premises, the [appropriate Agency]—

(a) shall furnish him with a certificate containing all material particulars of the registration, and

(b) subject to directions under section 25, shall send a copy of the certificate to each local authority in whose area the premises are situated.

NOTES

Commencement: 27 August 1993.

Sub-ss (1)–(3) derived from the Radioactive Substances Act 1960, s 1(2), the Environmental Protection Act 1990, ss 100(2), 105, Sch 5, Pt I, paras 4(1), 6(1)(a); sub-s (4) derived from the Radioactive Substances Act 1960, s 1(3), the Environmental Protection Act 1990 s 100(2); sub-s (5) derived from the Radioactive Substances Act 1960, s 1(3A), the Environmental Protection Act 1990, s 105, Sch 5, Pt I, para 11(1); sub-ss (6), (7) derived from the Radioactive Substances Act 1960, s 1(4), (5) respectively, the Environmental Protection Act 1990, s 100(2); sub-s (8) derived from the Radioactive Substances Act 1960, s 1(6), the Environmental Protection Act 1990, ss 100(2), 105, Sch 5, Pt I, para 6(1)(b).

Sub-ss (1), (3)–(8): words in square brackets substituted by the Environment Act 1995, s 120, Sch 22, paras 200, 202.

8 Exemptions from registration under s 7

(1)   At any time while a nuclear site licence is in force in respect of a site, and at any time after the revocation or surrender of such a licence but before the period of responsibility of the licensee has come to an end, the licensee (subject to subsection (2)) is exempted from registration under section 7 in respect of any premises situated on that site and in respect of the keeping and use on those premises of radioactive material of every description.

(2)   Where, in the case of any such premises as are mentioned in subsection (1), it appears to the [appropriate Agency] that, if the licensee had been required to apply for registration under section 7 in respect of those premises, the [appropriate Agency] would have imposed conditions such as are mentioned in paragraph (b) or (c) of subsection (6) of that section, the [appropriate Agency] may direct that the exemption conferred by subsection (1) of this section shall have effect subject to such conditions (being conditions which in the opinion of the [appropriate Agency] correspond to those which [it] would so have imposed) as may be specified in the direction.

(3)   On giving a direction under subsection (2) in respect of any premises, the [appropriate Agency] shall furnish the licensee with a copy of the direction.

(4)   Except as provided by subsection (5), in respect of all premises all persons are exempted from registration under section 7 in respect of the keeping and use on the premises of clocks and watches which are radioactive material.

(5)   Subsection (4) does not exempt from registration under section 7 any premises on which clocks or watches are manufactured or repaired by processes involving the use of luminous material.

(6)   The Secretary of State may by order grant further exemptions from registration under section 7, by reference to such classes of premises and undertakings, and such descriptions of radioactive material, as may be specified in the order.

(7)   Any exemption granted by an order under subsection (6) may be granted subject to such limitations or conditions as may be specified in the order.

(8)   In the application of this section to Northern Ireland, the reference in subsection (6) to the Secretary of State shall have effect as a reference to the Department of the Environment for Northern Ireland.

[476]

NOTES

Commencement: 27 August 1993.

Sub-ss (1), (7) derived from the Radioactive Substances Act 1960, s 2(2), (7), respectively; sub-ss (2), (3) derived from the Radioactive Substances Act 1960, s 2(3), (4), the Environmental Protection Act 1990, s 100(2); sub-ss (4), (5) derived from the Radioactive Substances Act 1960, s 2(5); sub-s (6) derived from the Radioactive Substances Act 1960, s 2(6), the Environmental Protection Act 1990, s 100(3); sub-s (8) derived from the Radioactive Substances Act 1960, s 21(2)(a) (in part), the Environmental Protection Act 1990, s 105, Sch 5, Pt II, para 20(a)(i).

Sub-ss (2), (3): words in square brackets substituted by the Environment Act 1995, s 120, Sch 22, paras 200, 203.

Orders: the Radioactive Substances (Exhibitions) Exemption Order 1962, SI 1962/2645; the Radioactive Substances (Storage in Transit) Exemption Order 1962, SI 1962/2646; the Radioactive Substances (Phosphatic Substances, Rare Earths, etc) Exemption Order 1962, SI 1962/2648; the Radioactive Substances (Lead) Exemption Order 1962, SI 1962/2649; the Radioactive Substances (Uranium and Thorium) Exemption Order 1962, SI 1962/2710; the Radioactive Substances (Prepared Uranium and Thorium Compounds) Exemption Order 1962, SI 1962/2711; the Radioactive Substances (Geological Specimens) Exemption Order 1962, SI 1962/2712; the Radioactive Substances (Waste Closed Sources) Exemption Order 1963, SI 1963/1831; the Radioactive Substances (Schools, etc) Exemption Order 1963, SI 1963/1832; the Radioactive Substances (Precipitated Phosphate) Exemption Order 1963, SI 1963/1836; the Radioactive Substances (Electronic Valves) Exemption Order 1967, SI 1967/1797; the Radioactive Substances (Smoke Detectors) Exemption Order 1980, SI 1980/953, as amended by SI 1991/477; the Radioactive Substances (Gaseous Tritium Light Devices) Exemption Order 1985, SI 1985/1047; the Radioactive Substances (Luminous Articles) Exemption Order 1985, SI 1985/1048; the Radioactive Substances (Testing Instruments) Exemption Order 1985, SI 1985/1049; the Radioactive Substances (Substances of Low Activity) Exemption Order 1986, SI 1986/1002, as amended by SI 1992/647; and the Radioactive Substances (Hospitals) Exemption Order 1990, SI 1990/2512, as amended by SI 1995/2395 (all having effect under sub-s (6) by virtue of the Interpretation Act 1978, s 17(2)(b)).

9 Prohibition of use of mobile radioactive apparatus without registration

(1)   No person shall, for the purpose of any activities to which this section applies—
   (a) keep, use, lend or let on hire mobile radioactive apparatus of any description, or
   (b) cause or permit mobile radioactive apparatus of any description to be kept, used, lent or let on hire,

unless he is registered under section 10 in respect of that apparatus or is exempted from registration under that section in respect of mobile radioactive apparatus of that description.

(2)   This section applies to activities involving the use of the apparatus concerned for—
   (a) testing, measuring or otherwise investigating any of the characteristics of substances or articles, or
   (b) releasing quantities of radioactive material into the environment or introducing such material into organisms.

[477]

NOTES

Commencement: 27 August 1993.

This section derived from the Radioactive Substances Act 1960, s 3(1), (2), the Environmental Protection Act 1990, s 105, Sch 5, Pt I, para 7(1).

10 Registration of mobile radioactive apparatus

(1)   Any application for registration under this section shall be made to the [appropriate Agency] and—
   (a) shall specify—
       (i) the apparatus to which the application relates, and
       (ii) the manner in which it is proposed to use the apparatus,
   (b) shall contain such other information as may be prescribed, and
   (c) shall be accompanied by the [charge prescribed for the purpose by a charging scheme under section 41 of the Environment Act 1995].

(2)   Where an application is made to the [appropriate Agency] for registration under this section in respect of any apparatus, the [appropriate Agency] may register the applicant in respect of that apparatus, either unconditionally or subject to such

limitations or conditions as the [appropriate Agency] thinks fit, or may refuse the application.

(3) On any application being made the [appropriate Agency] shall, subject to directions under section 25, send a copy of the application to each local authority in whose area it appears to [the appropriate Agency] the apparatus will be kept or will be used for releasing radioactive material into the environment.

(4) An application for registration under this section which is duly made to the [appropriate Agency] may be treated by the applicant as having been refused if it is not determined within the prescribed period for determinations or within such longer period as may be agreed with the applicant.

(5) On registering a person under this section in respect of any mobile radioactive apparatus, the [appropriate Agency]—

(a) shall furnish him with a certificate containing all material particulars of the registration, and

(b) shall, subject to directions under section 25, send a copy of the certificate to each local authority in whose area it appears to [the appropriate Agency] the apparatus will be kept or will be used for releasing radioactive material into the environment.

[478]

NOTES

Commencement: 27 August 1993.

Sub-s (1) derived from the Radioactive Substances Act 1960, s 3(3), the Environmental Protection Act 1990, s 105, Sch 5, Pt I, para 7(1); sub-s (2) derived from the Radioactive Substances Act 1960, s 3(4), the Environmental Protection Act 1990, s 100(2); sub-ss (3), (4) derived from the Radioactive Substances Act 1960, s 3(4A), (4B) respectively, the Environmental Protection Act 1990, s 105, Sch 5, Pt I, paras 6(2)(a), 11(2), respectively; sub-s (5) derived from the Radioactive Substances Act 1960, s 3(5), the Environmental Protection Act 1990, ss 100(2), 105, Sch 5, Pt I, para 6(2)(b).

Sub-ss (1)–(5): words in square brackets substituted by the Environment Act 1995, s 120, Sch 22, paras 200, 204.

11 Exemptions from registration under s 10

(1) The Secretary of State may by order grant exemptions from registration under section 10, by reference to such classes of persons, and such descriptions of mobile radioactive apparatus, as may be specified in the order.

(2) Any exemption granted by an order under subsection (1) may be granted subject to such limitations or conditions as may be specified in the order.

(3) In the application of this section to Northern Ireland, the reference to the Secretary of State shall have effect as a reference to the Department of the Environment for Northern Ireland.

[479]

NOTES

Commencement: 27 August 1993.

Sub-s (1) derived from the Radioactive Substances Act 1960, s 4(2), the Environmental Protection Act 1990, s 100(3); sub-s (2) derived from the Radioactive Substances Act 1960, s 4(3); sub-s (3) derived from the Radioactive Substances Act 1960, s 21(2)(a) (in part), the Environmental Protection Act 1990, s 105, Sch 5, Pt II, para 20(a)(i).

Orders: the Radioactive Substances (Electronic Valves) Exemption Order 1967, SI 1967/1797; the Radioactive Substances (Testing Instruments) Exemption Order 1985, SI 1985/1049 (both having effect under this section by virtue of the Interpretation Act 1978, s 17(2)(b)).

12 Cancellation and variation of registration

(1) Where any person is for the time being registered under section 7 or 10, the chief inspector may at any time cancel the registration, or may vary it—

(a) where the registration has effect without limitations or conditions, by attaching limitations or conditions to it, or

(b) where the registration has effect subject to limitations or conditions, by revoking or varying any of those limitations or conditions or by attaching further limitations or conditions to the registration.

(2) On cancelling or varying a registration by virtue of this section, the chief inspector shall—

(a) give notice of the cancellation or variation to the person to whom the registration relates, and

(b) if a copy of the certificate was sent to a local authority in accordance with section 7(8) or 10(5), send a copy of the notice to that local authority.

[480]

NOTES

Commencement: 27 August 1993.

This section derived from the Radioactive Substances Act 1960, s 5, the Environmental Protection Act 1990, ss 100(2), 105, Sch 5, Pt I, para 6(3).

Authorisation of disposal and accumulation of radioactive waste

13 Disposal of radioactive waste

(1) Subject to section 15, no person shall, except in accordance with an authorisation granted in that behalf under this subsection, dispose of any radioactive waste on or from any premises which are used for the purposes of any undertaking carried on by him, or cause or permit any radioactive waste to be so disposed of, if (in any such case) he knows or has reasonable grounds for believing it to be radioactive waste.

(2) Where any person keeps any mobile radioactive apparatus for the purpose of its being used in activities to which section 9 applies, he shall not dispose of any radioactive waste arising from any such apparatus so kept by him, or cause or permit any such radioactive waste to be disposed of, except in accordance with an authorisation granted in that behalf under this subsection.

(3) Subject to subsection (4) and to section 15, where any person, in the course of the carrying on by him of an undertaking, receives any radioactive waste for the purpose of its being disposed of by him, he shall not, except in accordance with an authorisation granted in that behalf under this subsection, dispose of that waste, or cause or permit it to be disposed of, knowing or having reasonable grounds for believing it to be radioactive waste.

(4) The disposal of any radioactive waste does not require an authorisation under subsection (3) if it is waste which falls within the provisions of an authorisation granted under subsection (1) or (2), and it is disposed of in accordance with the authorisation so granted.

(5) In relation to any premises which—

(a) are situated on a nuclear site, but

(b) have ceased to be used for the purposes of an undertaking carried on by the licensee,

subsection (1) shall apply (subject to section 15) as if the premises were used for the purposes of an undertaking carried on by the licensee.

[481]

NOTES

Commencement: 27 August 1993.

Sub-s (1) derived from the Radioactive Substances Act 1960, s 6(1); sub-s (2) derived from the Radioactive Substances Act 1960, s 6(2), the Environmental Protection Act 1990, s 105, Sch 5, Pt I, para 7(3); sub-ss (3), (4) derived from the Radioactive Substances Act 1960, s 6(3); sub-s (5) derived from the Radioactive Substances Act 1960, s 6(6) (in part).

14 Accumulation of radioactive waste

(1)   Subject to the provisions of this section and section 15, no person shall, except in accordance with an authorisation granted in that behalf under this section, accumulate any radioactive waste (with a view to its subsequent disposal) on any premises which are used for the purposes of an undertaking carried on by him, or cause or permit any radioactive waste to be so accumulated, if (in any such case) he knows or has reasonable grounds for believing it to be radioactive waste.

(2)   Where the disposal of any radioactive waste has been authorised under section 13, and in accordance with that authorisation the waste is required or permitted to be accumulated with a view to its subsequent disposal, no further authorisation under this section shall be required to enable the waste to be accumulated in accordance with the authorisation granted under section 13.

(3)   Subsection (1) shall not apply to the accumulation of radioactive waste on any premises situated on a nuclear site.

(4)   For the purposes of this section, where radioactive material is produced, kept or used on any premises, and any substance arising from the production, keeping or use of that material is accumulated in a part of the premises appropriated for the purpose, and is retained there for a period of not less than three months, that substance shall, unless the contrary is proved, be presumed—
    (a) to be radioactive waste, and
    (b) to be accumulated on the premises with a view to the subsequent disposal of the substance.

[482]

NOTES
Commencement: 27 August 1993.
Sub-s (1) derived from the Radioactive Substances Act 1960, s 7(1); sub-ss (2), (4) derived from the Radioactive Substances Act 1960, s 7(2), (5) respectively; sub-s (3) derived from the Radioactive Substances Act 1960, s 7(3)(b), (c).

15 Further exemptions from ss 13 and 14

(1)   Sections 13(1) and (3) and 14(1) shall not apply to the disposal or accumulation of any radioactive waste arising from clocks or watches, but this subsection does not affect the operation of section 13(1) or section 14(1) in relation to the disposal or accumulation of radioactive waste arising from clocks or watches on or from premises which, by virtue of subsection (5) of section 8, are excluded from the operation of subsection (4) of that section.

(2)   Without prejudice to subsection (1), the Secretary of State may by order exclude particular descriptions of radioactive waste from any of the provisions of section 13 or 14, either absolutely or subject to limitations or conditions; and accordingly such of those provisions as may be specified in an order under this subsection shall not apply to a disposal or accumulation of radioactive waste if it is radioactive waste of a description so specified, and (where the exclusion is subject to limitations or conditions) the limitations or conditions specified in the order are complied with.

(3)   In the application of this section to Northern Ireland, the reference to the Secretary of State shall have effect as a reference to the Department of the Environment for Northern Ireland.

[483]

NOTES
Commencement: 27 August 1993.
Sub-s (1) derived from the Radioactive Substances Act 1960, ss 6(4), 7(4) (in part); sub-s (2) derived from the Radioactive Substances Act 1960, ss 6(5), 7(4) (in part), the Environmental Protection Act 1990,

s 100(3); sub-s (3) derived from the Radioactive Substances Act 1960, s 21(2)(a) (in part), the Environmental Protection Act 1990, s 105, Sch 5, Pt II, para 20(a)(i).

Orders: the Radioactive Substances (Storage in Transit) Exemption Order 1962, SI 1962/2646; the Radioactive Substances (Phosphatic Substances, Rare Earths, etc) Exemption Order 1962, SI 1962/2648; the Radioactive Substances (Lead) Exemption Order 1962, SI 1962/2649; the Radioactive Substances (Uranium and Thorium) Exemption Order 1962, SI 1962/2710; the Radioactive Substances (Prepared Uranium and Thorium Compounds) Exemption Order 1962, SI 1962/2711; the Radioactive Substances (Geological Specimens) Exemption Order 1962, SI 1962/2712; the Radioactive Substances (Waste Closed Sources) Exemption Order 1963, SI 1963/1831; the Radioactive Substances (Schools, etc) Exemption Order 1963, SI 1963/1832; the Radioactive Substances (Electronic Valves) Exemption Order 1967, SI 1967/1797; the Radioactive Substances (Smoke Detectors) Exemption Order 1980, SI 1980/953, as amended by SI 1991/477; the Radioactive Substances (Gaseous Tritium Light Devices) Exemption Order 1985, SI 1985/1047; the Radioactive Substances (Luminous Articles) Exemption Order 1985, SI 1985/1048; the Radioactive Substances (Testing Instruments) Exemption Order 1985, SI 1985/1049; the Radioactive Substances (Substances of Low Activity) Exemption Order 1986, SI 1986/1002, as amended by SI 1992/647; and the Radioactive Substances (Hospitals) Exemption Order 1990, SI 1990/2512, as amended by SI 1995/2395 (all having effect under this section by virtue of the Interpretation Act 1978, s 17(2)(b)).

16 Grant of authorisations

(1) In this section, unless a contrary intention appears, "authorisation" means an authorisation granted under section 13 or 14.

(2) . . . , the power to grant authorisations shall be exercisable by the [appropriate Agency].

(3) . . .

(4) An application for an authorisation shall be accompanied by the [charge prescribed for the purpose by a charging scheme under section 41 of the Environment Act 1995];

[(4A) Without prejudice to subsection (5), on any application for an authorisation under section 13(1) in respect of the disposal of radioactive waste on or from any premises situated on a nuclear site in any part of Great Britain, the appropriate Agency—

  (a) shall consult the relevant Minister and the Health and Safety Executive before deciding whether to grant an authorisation on that application and, if so, subject to what limitations or conditions, and

  (b) shall consult the relevant Minister concerning the terms of the authorisation, for which purpose that Agency shall, before granting any authorisation on that application, send that Minister a copy of any authorisation which it proposes so to grant.]

(5) Before granting an authorisation under section 13(1) in respect of the disposal of radioactive waste on or from premises situated on a nuclear site, the [appropriate Agency] [shall] consult with such local authorities, relevant water bodies or other public or local authorities as appear to [that Agency] to be proper to be consulted by [that Agency].

(6) On any application being made, the [appropriate Agency] shall, subject to directions under section 25, send a copy of the application to each local authority in whose area, in accordance with the authorisation applied for, radioactive waste is to be disposed of or accumulated.

(7) An application for an authorisation [(other than an application for an authorisation under section 13(1) in respect of the disposal of radioactive waste on or from any premises situated on a nuclear site in any part of Great Britain)] which is duly made to the [appropriate Agency] may be treated by the applicant as having been refused if it is not determined within the prescribed period for determinations or such longer period as may be agreed with the applicant.

(8)   An authorisation may be granted—
  (a)   either in respect of radioactive waste generally or in respect of such one or more descriptions of radioactive waste as may be specified in the authorisation, and
  (b)   subject to such limitations or conditions as the [appropriate Agency] [thinks] fit.

(9)   Where any authorisation is granted, the [appropriate Agency]—
  (a)   shall furnish the person to whom the authorisation is granted with a certificate containing all material particulars of the authorisation, and
  (b)   shall, subject to directions under section 25, send a copy of the certificate—
    (i)   to each local authority in whose area, in accordance with the authorisation, radioactive waste is to be disposed of or accumulated, and
    (ii)   in the case of an authorisation to which subsection (5) applies, to any other public or local authority consulted in relation to the authorisation in accordance with that subsection.

(10)   An authorisation shall have effect as from such date as may be specified in it; and in fixing that date, in the case of an authorisation where copies of the certificate are required to be sent as mentioned in subsection (9)(b), the [appropriate Agency] . . .—
  (a)   shall have regard to the time at which those copies may be expected to be sent, and
  (b)   shall fix a date appearing to [it] to be such as will allow an interval of not less than twenty-eight days after that time before the authorisation has effect,

unless in [its] opinion it is necessary that the coming into operation of the authorisation should be immediate or should otherwise be expedited.

[(11) In this section, "the relevant Minister" means—
  (a)   in relation to premises in England, the Minister of Agriculture, Fisheries and Food, and
  (b)   in relation to premises in Wales or Scotland, the Secretary of State.]

NOTES

Commencement: 1 April 1996 (sub-ss (4A), (11)); 27 August 1993 (remainder).

Sub-ss (1), (2) derived from the Radioactive Substances Act 1960, s 8(3), the Environmental Protection Act 1990, s 100(2); sub-s (3) derived from the Radioactive Substances Act 1960, s 8(1), the Environmental Protection Act 1990, ss 100(2), 105, Sch 5, Pt I, para 1(1), (2) (as read with the Radioactive Substances Act 1960, s 21(2)(a), the Environmental Protection Act 1990, s 105, Sch 5, Pt II, para 20(a)(i)); sub-ss (4), (6), (7) derived from the Radioactive Substances Act 1960, s 8(3A), (4A), (3B), respectively, the Environmental Protection Act 1990, s 105, Sch 5, Pt I, paras 4(2), 6(4)(a), 11(3); sub-s (5) derived from the Radioactive Substances Act 1960, s 8(2), the Water Act 1989, s 190(1), Sch 25, para 27(1), the Environmental Protection Act 1990, s 100(2) (as read with the Water Act 1989, s 4(1)(a)); sub-ss (8), (10) derived from the Radioactive Substances Act 1960, s 8(4), (6), the Environmental Protection Act 1990, s 105, Sch 5, Pt I, para 1(1), (3), (5) (as read with the Radioactive Substances Act 1960, s 21(2)(a), the Environmental Protection Act 1990, s 105, Sch 5, Pt II, para 20(a)(i)); sub-s (9) derived from the Radioactive Substances Act 1960, s 8(5), the Environmental Protection Act 1990, s 105, Sch 5, Pt I, paras 1(1), (4), 6(4)(b) and gives effect to the second proposal of the Lord Chancellor in the Memorandum under the Consolidation of Enactments (Procedure) Act 1949 (16 December 1991, HC 148).

Sub-ss (2), (10): words omitted repealed, and words in square brackets substituted, by the Environment Act 1995, s 120, Sch 22, paras 200, 205(2), (9), Sch 24.

Sub-ss (4), (5), (6)–(9): words in square brackets substituted by the Environment Act 1995, s 120, Sch 22, paras 200, 205(4), (6)–(8).

Sub-s (3): repealed by the Environment Act 1995, s 120, Sch 22, para 205(3), Sch 24.

Sub-ss (4A), (11): inserted and added by the Environment Act 1995, s 120, Sch 22, para 205(5), (10).

17 Revocation and variation of authorisations

(1) The [appropriate Agency] may at any time revoke an authorisation granted under section 13 or 14.

(2) The [appropriate Agency] may at any time vary an authorisation granted under section 13 or 14—

(a) where the authorisation has effect without limitations or conditions, by attaching limitations or conditions to it, or

(b) where the authorisation has effect subject to limitations or conditions, by revoking or varying any of those limitations or conditions or by attaching further limitations or conditions to the authorisation.

[(2A) On any proposal to vary an authorisation granted under section 13(1) in respect of the disposal of radioactive waste on or from any premises situated on a nuclear site in any part of Great Britain, the appropriate Agency—

(a) shall consult the relevant Minister and the Health and Safety Executive before deciding whether to vary the authorisation and, if so, whether by attaching, revoking or varying any limitations or conditions or by attaching further limitations or conditions, and

(b) shall consult the relevant Minister concerning the terms of any variation, for which purpose that Agency shall, before varying the authorisation, send that Minister a copy of any variations which it proposes to make.]

(3) Where any authorisation granted under section 13 or 14 is revoked or varied, the [appropriate Agency]—

(a) shall give notice of the revocation or variation to the person to whom the authorisation was granted, and

(b) if a copy of the certificate of authorisation was sent to a public or local authority in accordance with section 16(9)(b), shall send a copy of the notice to that authority.

(4) . . .

[(5) In this section, "the relevant Minister" has the same meaning as in section 16 above.]

[485]

NOTES

Commencement: 1 April 1996 (sub-ss (2A), (5)); 27 August 1993 (remainder).

Sub-ss (1), (2), (4) derived from the Radioactive Substances Act 1960, s 8(7), the Environmental Protection Act 1990, s 105, Sch 5, Pt I, para 1(1), (5) (as read with the Radioactive Substances Act 1960, s 21(2)(a), the Environmental Protection Act 1990, s 105, Sch 5, Pt II, para 20(a)(i)); sub-s (3) derived from the Radioactive Substances Act 1960, s 8(8), the Environmental Protection Act 1990, s 105, Sch 5, Pt I, para 1(1), (5) and gives effect to the second proposal of the Lord Chancellor in the Memorandum under the Consolidation of Enactments (Procedure) Act 1949 (16 December 1991, HC 148).

Sub-ss (1), (2), (3): words in square brackets substituted by the Environment Act 1995, s 120, Sch 22, para 200.

Sub-ss (2A), (5): inserted and added by the Environment Act 1995, s 120, Sch 22, para 206(1), (3).

Sub-s (4): repealed by the Environment Act 1995, s 120, Sch 22, para 206(2), Sch 24.

---

18 Functions of public and local authorities in relation to authorisations under s 13

(1) If, in considering an application for an authorisation under section 13, it appears to the [appropriate Agency] . . . that the disposal of radioactive waste to which the application relates is likely to involve the need for special precautions to be taken by a local authority, relevant water body or other public or local authority, the [appropriate Agency] . . . shall consult with that public or local authority before granting the authorisation.

(2) Where a public or local authority take any special precautions in respect of radioactive waste disposed of in accordance with an authorisation granted under section 13, and those precautions are taken—

   (a) in compliance with the conditions subject to which the authorisation was
       granted, or
   (b) with the prior approval of the [appropriate Agency] . . . as being
       precautions which in the circumstances ought to be taken by that public or
       local authority,

the public or local authority shall have power to make such charges, in respect of the
taking of those precautions, as may be agreed between that authority and the person
to whom the authorisation was granted, or as, in default of such agreement, may be
determined by the [appropriate Agency], and to recover the charges so agreed or
determined from that person.

(3)   Where an authorisation granted under section 13 requires or permits
radioactive waste to be removed to a place provided by a local authority as a place
for the deposit of refuse, it shall be the duty of that local authority to accept any
radioactive waste removed to that place in accordance with the authorisation, and, if
the authorisation contains any provision as to the manner in which the radioactive
waste is to be dealt with after its removal to that place, to deal with it in the manner
indicated in the authorisation.

[486]

NOTES
Commencement: 27 August 1993.
   Sub-s (1) derived from the Radioactive Substances Act 1960, s 9(3), the Water Act 1989, s 190(1),
Sch 25, para 27(2), the Environmental Protection Act 1990, ss 100(2), 105, Sch 5, Pt I, para 2(1) (as read
with the Radioactive Substances Act 1960, s 21(2)(a), the Environmental Protection Act 1990, s 105,
Sch 5, Pt II, para 20(a)(i), the Water Act 1989, s 4(1)(a)); sub-s (2) derived from the Radioactive
Substances Act 1960, s 9(4), the Environmental Protection Act 1990, ss 100(2), 105, Sch 5, Pt I, para 2(1)
(as read with the Radioactive Substances Act 1960, s 21(2)(a), the Environmental Protection Act 1990,
s 105, Sch 5, Pt II, para 20(a)(i)); sub-s (3) derived from the Radioactive Substances Act 1960, s 9(5).
   Sub-ss (1), (2): words in square brackets substituted, and words omitted repealed, by the Environment
Act 1995, s 120, Sch 22, paras 200, 207, Sch 24.

Further obligations relating to registration or authorisation

19 Duty to display documents

At all times while—
   (a) a person is registered in respect of any premises under section 7, or
   (b) an authorisation granted in respect of any premises under section 13(1) or
       14 is for the time being in force,

the person to whom the registration relates, or to whom the authorisation was granted,
as the case may be, shall cause copies of the certificate of registration or authorisation
issued to him under this Act to be kept posted on the premises, in such characters and
in such positions as to be conveniently read by persons having duties on those
premises which are or may be affected by the matters set out in the certificate.

[487]

NOTES
Commencement: 27 August 1993.
   This section derived from the Radioactive Substances Act 1960, s 11(3).

20 Retention and production of site or disposal records

(1)   The [appropriate Agency] may, by notice served on any person to whom a
registration under section 7 or 10 relates or an authorisation under section 13 or 14
has been granted, impose on him such requirements authorised by this section in
relation to site or disposal records kept by that person as the [appropriate Agency]
may specify in the notice.

(2)   The requirements that may be imposed on a person under this section in relation to site or disposal records are—
(a) to retain copies of the records for a specified period after he ceases to carry on the activities regulated by his registration or authorisation, or
(b) to furnish the [appropriate Agency] with copies of the records in the event of his registration being cancelled or his authorisation being revoked or in the event of his ceasing to carry on the activities regulated by his registration or authorisation.

(3)   . . .

(4)   In this section, in relation to a registration and the person registered or an authorisation and the person authorised—
"the activities regulated" by his registration or authorisation means—
(a) in the case of registration under section 7, the keeping or use of radioactive material,
(b) in the case of registration under section 10, the keeping, using, lending or hiring of the mobile radioactive apparatus,
(c) in the case of an authorisation under section 13, the disposal of radioactive waste, and
(d) in the case of an authorisation under section 14, the accumulation of radioactive waste,
"records" means records required to be kept by virtue of the conditions attached to the registration or authorisation relating to the activities regulated by the registration or authorisation, and "site records" means records relating to the condition of the premises on which those activities are carried on or, in the case of registration in respect of mobile radioactive apparatus, of any place where the apparatus is kept and "disposal records" means records relating to the disposal of radioactive waste on or from the premises on which the activities are carried on, and
"specified" means specified in a notice under this section.

[488]

NOTES

Commencement: 27 August 1993.

This section derived from the Radioactive Substances Act 1960, s 8A, the Environmental Protection Act 1990, s 105, Sch 5, Pt I, para 8 (as read with the Radioactive Substances Act 1960, s 21(2)(a), the Environmental Protection Act 1990, s 105, Sch 5, Pt II, para 20(a)(i)).

Sub-ss (1), (2): words in square brackets substituted by the Environment Act 1995, s 120, Sch 22, para 200.

Sub-s (3): repealed by the Environment Act 1995, s 120, Sch 22, para 208, Sch 24.

Enforcement notices and prohibition notices

21 Enforcement notices

(1)   Subject to the provisions of this section, if the [appropriate Agency] is of the opinion that a person to whom a registration under section 7 or 10 relates or to whom an authorisation was granted under section 13 or 14—
(a) is failing to comply with any limitation or condition subject to which the registration or authorisation has effect, or
(b) is likely to fail to comply with any such limitation or condition,
[it] may serve a notice under this section on that person.

(2)   A notice under this section shall—
(a) state that the [appropriate Agency] is of that opinion,
(b) specify the matters constituting the failure to comply with the limitations or conditions in question or the matters making it likely that such a failure will occur, as the case may be, and

    (c) specify the steps that must be taken to remedy those matters and the period within which those steps must be taken.

(3) ...

(4) Where a notice is served under this section the [appropriate Agency] . . . shall—

    (a) in the case of a registration, if a certificate relating to the registration was sent to a local authority under section 7(8) or 10(5), or

    (b) in the case of an authorisation, if a copy of the authorisation was sent to a public or local authority under section 16(9)(b),

send a copy of the notice to that authority.

NOTES

Commencement: 27 August 1993.

Sub-ss (1), (2) derived from the Radioactive Substances Act 1960, s 11B(1), (2), the Environmental Protection Act 1990, s 102; sub-ss (3), (4) derived from the Radioactive Substances Act 1960, s 11B(4), (3), respectively, the Environmental Protection Act 1990, s 102, (as read with the Radioactive Substances Act 1960, s 21(2)(a), the Environmental Protection Act 1990, s 105, Sch 5, Pt II, para 20(a)(i)).

Sub-ss (1), (2), (4): words omitted repealed and words in square brackets substituted by the Environment Act 1995, s 120, Sch 22, paras 200, 209(1), (3), Sch 24.

Sub-s (3): repealed by the Environment Act 1995, s 120, Sch 22, para 209(2), Sch 24.

22 Prohibition notices

(1) Subject to the provisions of this section, if the [appropriate Agency] is of the opinion, as respects the keeping or use of radioactive material or of mobile radioactive apparatus, or the disposal or accumulation of radioactive waste, by a person in pursuance of a registration or authorisation under this Act, that the continuing to carry on that activity (or the continuing to do so in a particular manner) involves an imminent risk of pollution of the environment or of harm to human health, [it] may serve a notice under this section on that person.

(2) A notice under this section may be served whether or not the manner of carrying on the activity in question complies with any limitations or conditions to which the registration or authorisation in question is subject.

(3) A notice under this section shall—

    (a) state the [appropriate Agency's] opinion,

    (b) specify the matters giving rise to the risk involved in the activity, the steps that must be taken to remove the risk and the period within which those steps must be taken, and

    (c) direct that the registration or authorisation shall, until the notice is withdrawn, wholly or to the extent specified in the notice cease to have effect.

(4) Where the registration or authorisation is not wholly suspended by the direction given under subsection (3), the direction may specify limitations or conditions to which the registration or authorisation is to be subject until the notice is withdrawn.

(5) ...

(6) Where a notice is served under this section the [appropriate Agency] . . . shall—

    (a) in the case of a registration, if a certificate relating to the registration was sent to a local authority under section 7(8) or 10(5), or

    (b) in the case of an authorisation, if a copy of the authorisation was sent to a public or local authority under section 16(9)(b),

send a copy of the notice to that authority.

(7)   The [appropriate Agency] . . . shall, by notice to the recipient, withdraw a notice under this section when [that Agency] is satisfied that the risk specified in it has been removed; and on so doing [that Agency] shall send a copy of the withdrawal notice to any public or local authority to whom a copy of the notice under this section was sent.

[490]

NOTES

Commencement: 27 August 1993.

Sub-ss (1)–(4) derived from the Radioactive Substances Act 1960, s 11C(1)–(4), the Environmental Protection Act 1990, s 102; sub-s (5) derived from the Radioactive Substances Act 1960, s 11C(7), the Environmental Protection Act 1990, s 102 (as read with the Radioactive Substances Act 1960, s 21(2)(a), the Environmental Protection Act 1990, s 105, Sch 5, Pt II, para 20(a)(i)); sub-ss (6), (7) derived from the Radioactive Substances Act 1960, s 11C(5), (6), the Environmental Protection Act 1990, s 102.

Sub-ss (1), (3): words in square brackets substituted by the Environment Act 1995, s 120, Sch 22, paras 200, 210(1).

Sub-s (5): repealed by the Environment Act 1995, s 120, Sch 22, para 210(2), Sch 24.

Sub-ss (6), (7): words omitted repealed and words in square brackets substituted by the Environment Act 1995, s 120, Sch 22, paras 200, 210(3), (4), Sch 24.

Powers of Secretary of State in relation to applications etc

23 Power of Secretary of State to give directions to [appropriate Agency]

(1)   The Secretary of State may, if he thinks fit in relation to—
  (a) an application for registration under section 7 or 10,
  (b) an application for an authorisation under section 13 or 14, or
  (c) any such registration or authorisation,

give directions to the [appropriate Agency] requiring [it] to take any of the steps mentioned in the following subsections in accordance with the directions.

(2)   A direction under subsection (1) may require the [appropriate Agency] so to exercise [its] powers under this Act as—
  (a) to refuse an application for registration or authorisation, or
  (b) to effect or grant a registration or authorisation, attaching such limitations or conditions (if any) as may be specified in the direction, or
  (c) to vary a registration or authorisation, as may be so specified, or
  (d) to cancel or revoke (or not to cancel or revoke) a registration or authorisation.

(3)   The Secretary of State may give directions to the [appropriate Agency], as respects any registration or authorisation, requiring [it] to serve a notice under section 21 or 22 in such terms as may be specified in the directions.

(4)   The Secretary of State may give directions requiring the [appropriate Agency] to send such written particulars relating to, or to activities carried on in pursuance of, registrations effected or authorisations granted under any provision of this Act as may be specified in the directions to such local authorities as may be so specified.

[(4A) In the application of this section in relation to authorisations, and applications for authorisations, under section 13 in respect of premises situated on a nuclear site in England, references to the Secretary of State shall have effect as references to the Secretary of State and the Minister of Agriculture, Fisheries and Food.]

(5)   In the application of this section to Northern Ireland, references to the Secretary of State shall have effect as references to the Department of the Environment for Northern Ireland.

[491]

NOTES
Commencement: 1 April 1996 (sub-s (4A)); 27 August 1993 (remainder).

Sub-ss (1)–(4) derived from the Radioactive Substances Act 1960, s 12A(1)–(4), the Environmental Protection Act 1990, s 105, Sch 5, Pt I, para 12; sub-s (5) derived from the Radioactive Substances Act 1960, s 21(2)(a) (in part), the Environmental Protection Act 1990, s 105, Sch 5, Pt II, para 20(a)(i).

Section heading: words in square brackets substituted by the Environment Act 1995, s 120, Sch 22, para 200.

Sub-ss (1)–(4): words in square brackets substituted by the Environment Act 1995, s 120, Sch 22, paras 200, 211(1).

Sub-s (4A): inserted by the Environment Act 1995, s 120, Sch 22, para 211(2).

24 Power of Secretary of State to require certain applications to be determined by him

(1)   The Secretary of State may—

(a) give general directions to the [appropriate Agency] requiring [it] to refer applications under this Act for registrations or authorisations of any description specified in the directions to the Secretary of State for his determination, and

(b) give directions to the [appropriate Agency] in respect of any particular application requiring [it] to refer the application to the Secretary of State for his determination.

(2)   Where an application is referred to the Secretary of State in pursuance of directions given under this section, the Secretary of State may cause a local inquiry to be held in relation to the application.

(3)   The following provisions shall apply to inquiries in pursuance of subsection (2)—

(a) in England and Wales, subsections (2) to (5) of section 250 of the Local Government Act 1972 (supplementary provisions about local inquiries under that section) but with the omission, in subsection (4) of that section, of the words "such local authority or",

(b) *(applies to Scotland only)*, and

(c) in Northern Ireland, Schedule 8 to the Health and Personal Services (Northern Ireland) Order 1972 (provisions as to inquiries).

(4)   After determining any application so referred, the Secretary of State may give the [appropriate Agency] directions under section 23 as to the steps to be taken by [it] in respect of the application.

[(4A) In the application of this section in relation to authorisations, and applications for authorisations, under section 13 in respect of premises situated on a nuclear site in England, references to the Secretary of State shall have effect as references to the Secretary of State and the Minister of Agriculture, Fisheries and Food.]

(5)   In the application of this section to Northern Ireland, references to the Secretary of State shall have effect as references to the Department of the Environment for Northern Ireland.

NOTES
Commencement: 1 April 1996 (sub-s (4A)); 27 August 1993 (remainder).

Sub-ss (1), (2), (4) derived from the Radioactive Substances Act 1960, s 12B(1), (2), (5), the Environmental Protection Act 1990, s 105, Sch 5, Pt I, para 12; sub-s (3) derived from the Radioactive Substances Act 1960, ss 12B(3), (4), 21(2)(m), the Environmental Protection Act 1990, s 105, Sch 5, Pt II, para 20(a)(ii) ; sub-s (5) derived from the Radioactive Substances Act 1960, s 21(2)(a) (in part), the Environmental Protection Act 1990, s 105, Sch 5, Pt I, para 20(a)(i).

Sub-ss (1), (4): words in square brackets substituted by the Environment Act 1995, s 120, Sch 22, paras 200, 212(1).

Sub-s (4A): inserted by the Environment Act 1995, s 120, Sch 22, para 212(2).

25 Power of Secretary of State to restrict knowledge of applications etc

(1)	The Secretary of State may direct the [appropriate Agency] that in his opinion, on grounds of national security, it is necessary that knowledge of [such information as may be specified or described in the directions, being information contained in or relating to]—
    (a)	any particular application for registration under section 7 or 10 or applications of any description specified in the directions, or
    (b)	any particular registration or registrations of any description so specified,
should be restricted.

(2)	The Secretary of State . . . may direct the [appropriate Agency] that in his . . . opinion, on grounds of national security, it is necessary that knowledge of [such information as may be specified or described in the directions, being information contained in or relating to]—
    (a)	any particular application for authorisation under section 13 or 14 or applications of any description specified in the directions, or
    (b)	any particular authorisation under either of those sections or authorisations of any description so specified,
should be restricted.

(3)	Where it appears to the [appropriate Agency] that an application, registration or authorisation is the subject of any directions under this section, the [appropriate Agency] shall not send a copy of [so much of] the application or the certificate of registration or authorisation, as the case may be [as contains the information specified or described in the directions]—
    (a)	to any local authority under any provision of section 7 or 10, or
    (b)	to any public or local authority under any provision of section 16.

[(3A)	No direction under this section shall affect—
    (a)	any power or duty of the Agency to which it is given to consult the relevant Minister; or
    (b)	the information which is to be sent by that Agency to that Minister.]

(4)	In the application of this section to Northern Ireland—
    (a)	references to the Secretary of State shall have effect as references to the Department of the Environment for Northern Ireland, and
    (b)	in subsection (2), the reference to England shall have effect as a reference to Northern Ireland and the reference to the Minister of Agriculture, Fisheries and Food shall have effect as a reference to the Department of Agriculture for Northern Ireland.

[(5)	In this section "the relevant Minister" has the same meaning as in section 16 above.]

[493]

NOTES

Commencement: 1 April 1996 (sub-ss (3A), (5)); 27 August 1993 (remainder).

Sub-s (1) derived from the Radioactive Substances Act 1960, ss 1(7), 3(6) (both in part), the Environmental Protection Act 1990, s 105, Sch 5, Pt I, para 6(1)(c), (2)(c); sub-s (2) derived from the Radioactive Substances Act 1960, s 8(5A) (in part), the Environmental Protection Act 1990, s 105, Sch 5, Pt I, para 6(4)(c); sub-s (3) derived from the Radioactive Substances Act 1960, ss 1(7), 3(6), 8(5A) (all in part), the Environmental Protection Act 1990, s 105, Sch 5, Pt I, para 6(4)(c); sub-s (4) derived from the Radioactive Substances Act 1960, s 21(2)(a) (in part), the Environmental Protection Act 1990, s 105, Sch 5, Pt II, para 20(a)(i).

Sub-s (1): words in first pair of square brackets substituted, and words in second pair of square brackets inserted, by the Environment Act 1995, s 120, Sch 22, paras 200, 213(1).

Sub-s (2): words omitted repealed, words in first pair of square brackets substituted, and words in second pair of square brackets inserted, by the Environment Act 1995, s 120, Sch 22, paras 200, 213(2).

Sub-s (3): words in first and second pair of square brackets substituted, and words in third and final pairs of square brackets inserted, by the Environment Act 1995, s 120, Sch 22, paras 200, 213(3).

Sub-ss (3A), (5): inserted and added by the Environment Act 1995, s 120, Sch 22, para 213(4), (5).

Appeals

26 Registrations, authorisations and notices: appeals from decisions of [appropriate Agency]

(1)   Where the [appropriate Agency]—

(a)   refuses an application for registration under section 7 or 10, or refuses an application for an authorisation under section 13 or 14,

(b)   attaches any limitations or conditions to such a registration or to such an authorisation, or

(c)   varies such a registration or such an authorisation, otherwise than by revoking a limitation or condition subject to which it has effect, or

(d)   cancels such a registration or revokes such an authorisation,

the person directly concerned may, subject to subsection (3), appeal to the Secretary of State.

(2)   A person on whom a notice under section 21 or 22 is served may, subject to subsections (3) and (4), appeal against the notice to the Secretary of State.

(3)   No appeal shall lie—

(a)   . . .

(b)   under subsection (1) or (2) in respect of any decision taken by the [appropriate Agency] in pursuance of a direction of the Secretary of State under section 23 or 24.

(4)   No appeal shall lie under subsection (2) in respect of any notice served in . . . Northern Ireland by the appropriate Minister in exercise of the power under section 21 or 22.

(5)   In this section "the person directly concerned" means—

(a)   in relation to a registration under section 7 or 10, the person applying for the registration or to whom the registration relates;

(b)   in relation to an authorisation under section 13 or 14, the person applying for the authorisation or to whom it was granted;

and any reference to attaching limitations or conditions to a registration or authorisation is a reference to attaching limitations or conditions to it either in effecting or granting it or in exercising any power to vary it.

[(5A) In the application of this section in relation to authorisations, and applications for authorisations, under section 13 in respect of premises situated on a nuclear site in England, references in subsection (1) to (3) to the Secretary of State shall have effect as references to the Secretary of State and the Minister of Agriculture, Fisheries and Food.]

(6)   In the application of this section to Northern Ireland, references to the Secretary of State shall have effect as references to the Department of the Environment for Northern Ireland.

NOTES

Commencement: 1 April 1996 (sub-s (5A)); 27 August 1993 (remainder).

Sub-ss (1)–(5) derived from the Radioactive Substances Act 1960, s 11D(1)–(4), (12), the Environmental Protection Act 1990, s 105, Sch 5, Pt I, para 10 (as read with the Radioactive Substances Act 1960, s 21(2)(a), the Environmental Protection Act 1990, s 105, Sch 5, Pt II, para 20(a)(i)); sub-s (6) derived from the Radioactive Substances Act 1960, s 21(2)(a) (in part), the Environmental Protection Act 1990, s 105, Sch 5, Pt I, para 20(a)(i).

Section heading, sub-s (1): words in square brackets substituted by the Environment Act 1995, s 120, Sch 22, para 200.

Sub-s (3): para (a) repealed, and words in square brackets substituted, by the Environment Act 1995, s 120, Sch 22, paras 200, 214(2), Sch 24.

Sub-s (4): words omitted repealed by the Environment Act 1995, s 120, Sch 22, para 214(3), Sch 24.

Sub-s (5A): inserted by the Environment Act 1995, s 120, Sch 22, para 214(4).

27 Procedure on appeals under s 26

(1) The Secretary of State may refer any matter involved in an appeal under section 26[, other than an appeal against any decision of, or notice served by, SEPA,] to a person appointed by him for the purpose.

[(1A) As respects an appeal against any decision of, or notice served by, SEPA, this section is subject to section 114 of the Environment Act 1995 (delegation or reference of appeals).]

(2) An appeal under section 26 shall, if and to the extent required by regulations under subsection (7) of this section, be advertised in such manner as may be prescribed.

(3) If either party to the appeal so requests, an appeal shall be in the form of a hearing (which may, if the person hearing the appeal so decides, be held, or held to any extent, in private).

(4) On determining an appeal from a decision of the [appropriate Agency] under section 26 the Secretary of State—
   (a) may affirm the decision,
   (b) where that decision was the refusal of an application, may direct the [appropriate Agency] to grant the application,
   (c) where that decision involved limitations or conditions attached to a registration or authorisation, may quash those limitations or conditions wholly or in part, or
   (d) where that decision was a cancellation or revocation of a registration or authorisation, may quash the decision,

and where the Secretary of State does any of the things mentioned in paragraph (b), (c) or (d) he may give directions to the [appropriate Agency] as to the limitations and conditions to be attached to the registration or authorisation in question.

(5) On the determination of an appeal in respect of a notice under section 26(2), the Secretary of State may either cancel or affirm the notice and, if he affirms it, may do so either in its original form or with such modifications as he may think fit.

(6) The bringing of an appeal against a cancellation or revocation of a registration or authorisation shall, unless the Secretary of State otherwise directs, have the effect of suspending the operation of the cancellation or revocation pending the determination of the appeal; but otherwise the bringing of an appeal shall not, unless the Secretary of State so directs, affect the validity of the decision or notice in question during that period.

(7) The Secretary of State may by regulations make provision with respect to appeals under section 26 (including in particular provision as to the period within which appeals are to be brought).

[(7A) In the application of this section in relation to authorisations, and applications for authorisations, under section 13 in respect of premises situated on a nuclear site in England, references in subsections (1) to (6) to the Secretary of State shall have effect as references to the Secretary of State and the Minister of Agriculture, Fisheries and Food.]

(8) In the application of this section to Northern Ireland, references to the Secretary of State shall have effect as references to the Department of the Environment for Northern Ireland.

[495]

NOTES

Commencement: 1 April 1996 (sub-ss (1A), (7A)); 27 August 1993 (remainder).

Sub-ss (1)–(7) derived from the Radioactive Substances Act 1960, s 11D(5)–(11), the Environmental Protection Act 1990, s 105, Sch 5, Pt I, para 10; sub-s (8) derived from the Radioactive Substances Act 1960, s 21(2)(a) (in part), the Environmental Protection Act 1990, s 105, Sch 5, Pt II, para 20(a)(i).

Sub-s (1): words in square brackets inserted by the Environment Act 1995, s 120, Sch 22, para 215(2).

Sub-ss (1A), (7A): inserted by the Environment Act 1995, s 120, Sch 22, para 215(3), (4).

Sub-s (4): words in square brackets substituted by the Environment Act 1995, s 120, Sch 22, para 200.

Regulations: the Radioactive Substances (Appeals) Regulations 1990, SI 1990/2504 (having effect under this section by virtue of the Interpretation Act 1978, s 17(2)(b)).

28 *(Repealed by the Environment Act 1995, s 120(1), (3), Sch 22, para 216, Sch 24.)*

Further powers of Secretary of State in relation to radioactive waste

29 Provision of facilities for disposal or accumulation of radioactive waste

(1)   If it appears to the Secretary of State that adequate facilities are not available for the safe disposal or accumulation of radioactive waste, the Secretary of State may provide such facilities, or may arrange for their provision by such persons as the Secretary of State may think fit.

(2)   Where, in the exercise of the power conferred by this section, the Secretary of State proposes to provide, or to arrange for the provision of, a place for the disposal or accumulation of radioactive waste, the Secretary of State, before carrying out that proposal, shall consult with any local authority in whose area that place would be situated, and with such other public or local authorities (if any) as appear to him to be proper to be consulted by him.

(3)   The Secretary of State may make reasonable charges for the use of any facilities provided by him, or in accordance with arrangements made by him, under this section, or, in the case of facilities provided otherwise than by the Secretary of State, may direct that reasonable charges for the use of the facilities may be made by the person providing them in accordance with any such arrangements.

(4)   In the application of this section to Northern Ireland, references to the Secretary of State shall have effect as references to the Department of the Environment for Northern Ireland.

[496]

NOTES

Commencement: 27 August 1993.

Sub-ss (1)–(3) derived from the Radioactive Substances Act 1960, s 10(1)–(3), the Environmental Protection Act 1990, s 100(3); sub-s (4) derived from the Radioactive Substances Act 1960, s 21(2)(a) (in part), the Environmental Protection Act 1990, s 105, Sch 5, Pt II, para 20(a)(i).

30 Power of Secretary of State to dispose of radioactive waste

(1)   If there is radioactive waste on any premises, and [the appropriate Agency] is satisfied that—

(a) the waste ought to be disposed of, but

(b) by reason that the premises are unoccupied, or that the occupier is absent, or is insolvent, or for any other reason, it is unlikely that the waste will be lawfully disposed of unless the Secretary of State exercises [its] powers under this section,

[that Agency] shall have power to dispose of that radioactive waste as [that Agency] may think fit, and to recover from the occupier of the premises, or, if the premises are unoccupied, from the owner of the premises, any expenses reasonably incurred by [that Agency] in disposing of it.

(2)   In the application of subsection (1) to Northern Ireland, references to the Secretary of State shall have effect as references to the Department of the Environment for Northern Ireland.

(3)   For the purposes of this section in its application to England and Wales and Northern Ireland, the definition of "owner" in section 343 of the Public Health Act 1936, and the provisions of section 294 of that Act (which limits the liability of owners who are only agents or trustees), shall apply—

(a) with the substitution in section 294 for references to a council of references to the [Environment Agency] or, in Northern Ireland, the Department of the Environment for Northern Ireland, and

(b) in relation to Northern Ireland, as if that Act extended to Northern Ireland.

(4)   *(Applies to Scotland only.)*

[497]

NOTES

Commencement: 27 August 1993.

Sub-s (1) derived from the Radioactive Substances Act 1960, s 10(4), the Environmental Protection Act 1990, s 100(3); sub-s (2) derived from the Radioactive Substances Act 1960, s 21(2)(a) (in part), the Environmental Protection Act 1990, s 105, Sch 5, Pt I, para 20(a)(i); sub-s (3) derived from the Radioactive Substances Act 1960, s 10(5), the Environmental Protection Act 1990, s 100(3) (as read with the Radioactive Substances Act 1960, s 21(2)(a), (j), the Environmental Protection Act 1990, s 105, Sch 5, Pt II, para 20(a)(i)); sub-s (4) derived from the Radioactive Substances Act 1960, s 20(e).

Sub-ss (1), (3), (4): words in square brackets substituted by the Environment Act 1995, s 120, Sch 22, para 217.

31   *(Repealed by the Environment Act 1995, s 120(1), (3), Sch 22, para 218, Sch 24.)*

Offences

32 Offences relating to registration or authorisation

(1)   Any person who—

(a) contravenes section 6, 9, 13(1), (2) or (3) or 14(1), or

(b) being a person registered under section 7 or 10, or being (wholly or partly) exempted from registration under either of those sections, does not comply with a limitation or condition subject to which he is so registered or exempted, or

(c) being a person to whom an authorisation under section 13 or 14 has been granted, does not comply with a limitation or condition subject to which that authorisation has effect, or

(d) being a person who is registered under section 7 or 10 or to whom an authorisation under section 13 or 14 has been granted, fails to comply with any requirement of a notice served on him under section 21 or 22,

shall be guilty of an offence.

(2)   A person guilty of an offence under this section shall be liable—

(a) on summary conviction, to a fine not exceeding £20,000 or to imprisonment for a term not exceeding six months, or both;

(b) on conviction on indictment, to a fine or to imprisonment for a term not exceeding five years, or both.

[(3) If the appropriate Agency is of the opinion that proceedings for an offence under subsection (1)(d) would afford an ineffectual remedy against a person who has failed to comply with the requirements of a notice served on him under section 21 or 22, that Agency may take proceedings in the High Court or, in Scotland, in any court of competent jurisdiction, for the purpose of securing compliance with the notice.]

[498]

NOTES

Commencement: 1 April 1996 (sub-s (3)); 27 August 1993 (remainder).

This section derived from the Radioactive Substances Act 1960, s 13(1), (2), the Environmental Protection Act 1990, s 105, Sch 5, Pt I, para 14(1)–(3).

Sub-s (3): added by the Environment Act 1995, s 120, Sch 22, para 219.

33 Offences relating to ss 19 and 20

(1)   Any person who contravenes section 19 shall be guilty of an offence and liable—
    (a) on summary conviction, to a fine not exceeding the statutory maximum;
    (b) on conviction on indictment, to a fine.

(2)   Any person who without reasonable cause pulls down, injures or defaces any document posted in pursuance of section 19 shall be guilty of an offence and liable on summary conviction to a fine not exceeding level 2 on the standard scale.

(3)   Any person who fails to comply with a requirement imposed on him under section 20 shall be guilty of an offence and liable—
    (a) on summary conviction, to a fine not exceeding the statutory maximum or to imprisonment for a term not exceeding three months, or both;
    (b) on conviction on indictment, to a fine or to imprisonment for a term not exceeding two years, or both.

[499]

NOTES

Commencement: 27 August 1993.

Sub-ss (1), (2) derived from the Radioactive Substances Act 1960, s 13(5) (in part), (6), the Environmental Protection Act 1990, s 105, Sch 5, Pt I, para 14(1), (7), (8); sub-s (3) derived from the Radioactive Substances Act 1960, s 13(4A), the Environmental Protection Act 1990, s 105, Sch 5, Pt I, para 14(1), (5).

34 Disclosure of trade secrets

(1)   If any person discloses any information relating to any relevant process or trade secret used in carrying on any particular undertaking which has been given to or obtained by him under this Act or in connection with the execution of this Act, he shall be guilty of an offence, unless the disclosure is made—
    (a) with the consent of the person carrying on that undertaking, or
    (b) in accordance with any general or special directions given by the Secretary of State, or
  [(bb) under or by virtue of section 113 of the Environment Act 1995, or]
    (c) in connection with the execution of this Act, or
    (d) for the purposes of any legal proceedings arising out of this Act or of any report of any such proceedings.

(2)   A person guilty of an offence under this section shall be liable—
    (a) on summary conviction, to a fine not exceeding the statutory maximum or to imprisonment for a term not exceeding three months, or both;
    (b) on conviction on indictment, to a fine or to imprisonment for a term not exceeding two years, or both.

(3)   In this section "relevant process" means any process applied for the purposes of, or in connection with, the production or use of radioactive material.

(4)   In the application of this section to Northern Ireland, the reference in subsection (1)(b) to the Secretary of State shall have effect as a reference to the Department of the Environment for Northern Ireland.

[500]

NOTES

Commencement: 27 August 1993.

Sub-ss (1), (3) derived from the Radioactive Substances Act 1960, s 13(3), the Environmental Protection Act 1990, s 100(3); sub-s (2) derived from the Radioactive Substances Act 1960, s 13(4), the Environmental Protection Act 1990, s 105, Sch 5, Pt I, para 14(1), (4); sub-s (4) derived from the Radioactive Substances Act 1960, s 21(2)(a) (in part), the Environmental Protection Act 1990, s 105, Sch 5, Pt II, para 20(a)(i).

Sub-s (1): para (bb) inserted by the Environment Act 1995, s 120, Sch 22, para 220.

[34A Offences of making false or misleading statements or false entries

(1)   Any person who—
  (a) for the purpose of obtaining for himself or another any registration under section 7 or 10, any authorisation under section 13 or 14 or any variation of such an authorisation under section 17, or
  (b) in purported compliance with a requirement to furnish information imposed under section 31(1)(d),

makes a statement which he knows to be false or misleading in a material particular, or recklessly makes a statement which is false or misleading in a material particular, shall be guilty of an offence.

(2)   Any person who intentionally makes a false entry in any record—
  (a) which is required to be kept by virtue of a registration under section 7 or 10 or an authorisation under section 13 or 14, or
  (b) which is kept in purported compliance with a condition which must be complied with if a person is to have the benefit of an exemption under section 8, 11 or 15,

shall be guilty of an offence.

(3)   A person guilty of an offence under this section shall be liable—
  (a) on summary conviction, to a fine not exceeding the statutory maximum;
  (b) on conviction on indictment, to a fine or to imprisonment for a term not exceeding two years, or to both.]

[501]

NOTES
Commencement: 1 April 1996.
Inserted by the Environment Act 1995, s 112, Sch 19, para 6.

35 *(Repealed by the Environment Act 1995, s 120(1), (3), Sch 22, para 221, Sch 24.)*

36 Offences by bodies corporate

(1)   Where a body corporate is guilty of an offence under this Act, and that offence is proved to have been committed with the consent or connivance of, or to be attributable to any neglect on the part of, any director, manager, secretary or other similar officer of the body corporate, or any person who was purporting to act in any such capacity, he, as well as the body corporate, shall be guilty of that offence, and shall be liable to be proceeded against and punished accordingly.

(2)   In this section "director", in relation to a body corporate established by or under any enactment for the purpose of carrying on under national ownership any industry or part of an industry or undertaking, being a body corporate whose affairs are managed by its members, means a member of that body corporate.

[502]

NOTES
Commencement: 27 August 1993.
This section derived from the Radioactive Substances Act 1960, s 13(8).

37 Offence due to another's fault

Where the commission by any person of an offence under this Act is due to the act or default of some other person, that other person may by virtue of this section be charged with and convicted of the offence whether or not proceedings for the offence are taken against the first-mentioned person.

[503]

NOTES

Commencement: 27 August 1993.

This section derived from the Radioactive Substances Act 1960, s 13(9), the Environmental Protection Act 1990, s 105, Sch 5, Pt I, para 14(1), (10).

38 Restriction on prosecutions

(1)   Proceedings in respect of any offence under this Act shall not be instituted in England or Wales except—
   (a) by the Secretary of State,
   [(b) by the Environment Agency, or]
   (c) by or with the consent of the Director of Public Prosecutions.

(2)   Proceedings in respect of any offence under this Act shall not be instituted in Northern Ireland except—
   (a) by the head of the Department of the Environment for Northern Ireland, or
   (b) by or with the consent of the Attorney General for Northern Ireland.

(3)   This section shall be deemed to have been enacted before the coming into operation of the Prosecution of Offences (Northern Ireland) Order 1972.

[504]

NOTES

Commencement: 27 August 1993.

Sub-s (1) derived from the Radioactive Substances Act 1960, s 13(7), the Environmental Protection Act 1990, s 105, Sch 5, Pt I, para 14(1), (9); sub-s (2) derived from the Radioactive Substances Act 1960, s 21(3), the Northern Ireland Constitution Act 1973, s 40, Sch 5, para 7(1).

Sub-s (1): para (b) substituted by the Environment Act 1995, s 120, Sch 22, para 222.

Public access to documents and records

39 Public access to documents and records

(1)   The [appropriate Agency] shall keep copies of—
   (a) all applications made to [it] under any provision of this Act,
   (b) all documents issued by [it] under any provision of this Act,
   (c) all other documents sent by [it] to any local authority in pursuance of directions of the Secretary of State, and
   (d) such records of convictions under section 32, 33, 34 or 35 as may be prescribed in regulations;

and [the appropriate Agency] shall make copies of those documents available to the public except to the extent that that would involve the disclosure of information relating to any relevant process or trade secret or would involve the disclosure of [information] as respects which the Secretary of State has directed that knowledge should be restricted on grounds of national security.

(2)   Each local authority shall keep and make available to the public copies of all documents sent to the authority under any provision of this Act unless directed by the chief inspector . . . that all or any part of any such document is not to be available for inspection.

(3)   Directions under subsection (2) shall only be given for the purpose of preventing disclosure of relevant processes or trade secrets and may be given generally in respect of all, or any description of, documents or in respect of specific documents.

(4)   The copies of documents required to be made available to the public by this section need not be kept in documentary form.

(5)   The public shall have the right to inspect the copies of documents required to be made available under this section at all reasonable times and, on payment of a reasonable fee, to be provided with a copy of any such document.

(6)   In this section "relevant process" has the same meaning as in section 34.

(7)   In the application of this section to Northern Ireland, references to the Secretary of State shall have effect as references to the Department of the Environment for Northern Ireland.

[505]

NOTES
Commencement: 27 August 1993.
Sub-ss (1)–(6) derived from the Radioactive Substances Act 1960, s 13A, the Environmental Protection Act 1990, s 105, Sch 5, Pt I, para 15 (as read with the Radioactive Substances Act 1960, s 21(2)(a), the Environmental Protection Act 1990, s 105, Sch 5, Pt II, para 20(a)(i)); sub-s (7) derived from the Radioactive Substances Act 1960, s 21(2)(a) (in part), the Environmental Protection Act 1990, s 105, Sch 5, Pt II, para 20(a)(i).
Sub-s (1): words in square brackets substituted by the Environment Act 1995, s 120, Sch 22, paras 200, 223(1).
Sub-s (2): words omitted repealed by the Environment Act 1995, s 120, Sch 22, para 223(2), Sch 24.

Operation of other statutory provisions

40 Radioactivity to be disregarded for purposes of certain statutory provisions

(1)   For the purposes of the operation of any statutory provision to which this section applies, and for the purposes of the exercise or performance of any power or duty conferred or imposed by, or for the enforcement of, any such statutory provision, no account shall be taken of any radioactivity possessed by any substance or article or by any part of any premises.

(2)   This section applies—
  (a) to any statutory provision contained in, or for the time being having effect by virtue of, any of the enactments specified in Schedule 3, or any enactment for the time being in force whereby an enactment so specified is amended, extended or superseded, and
  (b) to any statutory provision contained in, or for the time being having effect by virtue of, a local enactment whether passed or made before or after the passing of this Act (in whatever terms the provision is expressed) in so far as—
    (i) the disposal or accumulation of waste or any description of waste, or of any substance which is a nuisance, or so as to be a nuisance, or of any substance which is, or so as to be, prejudicial to health, noxious, polluting or of any similar description, is prohibited or restricted by the statutory provision, or
    (ii) a power or duty is conferred or imposed by the statutory provision on [the Environment Agency or SEPA or on] any local authority, relevant water body or other public or local authority, or on any officer of a public or local authority, to take any action (whether by way of legal proceedings or otherwise) for preventing, restricting or abating such disposals or accumulations as are mentioned in sub-paragraph (i).

(3)   In this section—
  "statutory provision"—
    (a) in relation to Great Britain, means a provision, whether of a general or a special nature, contained in, or in any document made or issued under, any Act, whether of a general or a special nature, and
    (b) in relation to Northern Ireland, has the meaning given by section 1(f) of the Interpretation Act (Northern Ireland) 1954,

"local enactment" means—

    (a) a local or private Act (including a local or private Act of the Parliament of Northern Ireland or a local or private Measure of the Northern Ireland Assembly), or

    (b) an order confirmed by Parliament (or by the Parliament of Northern Ireland or the Northern Ireland Assembly) or brought into operation in accordance with special parliamentary procedure,

and any reference to disposal, in relation to a statutory provision, is a reference to discharging or depositing a substance or allowing a substance to escape or to enter a stream or other place, as may be mentioned in that provision.

(4) The references to provisions of the Water Resources Act 1991 in Part I of Schedule 3 shall have effect subject to the power conferred by section 98 of that Act.

[506]

NOTES

Commencement: 27 August 1993.

Sub-s (1) derived from the Radioactive Substances Act 1960, s 9(1); sub-s (2) derived from the Radioactive Substances Act 1960, s 9(2), the Water Act 1989, s 190(1), Sch 25, para 27(2) (as read with the Water Act 1989, s 4(1)(a)); sub-s (3) derived from the Radioactive Substances Act 1960, ss 9(6), 21(2)(i) (as read with the Northern Ireland Constitution Act 1973, s 40, Sch 5, para 1);

sub-s (4) derived from the Water Consolidation (Consequential Provisions) Act 1991, Sch 1, para 9(2).

Sub-s (2): words in square brackets inserted by the Environment Act 1995, s 120, Sch 22, para 224.

General

41 Service of documents

(1) Any notice required or authorised by or under this Act to be served on or given to any person may be served or given by delivering it to him, or by leaving it at his proper address, or by sending it by post to him at that address.

(2) Any such notice may—

    (a) in the case of a body corporate, be served on or given to the secretary or clerk of that body;

    (b) in the case of a partnership, be served on or given to a partner or a person having the control or management of the partnership business.

(3) For the purposes of this section and of section 7 of the Interpretation Act 1978 (service of documents by post) in its application to this section, the proper address of any person on or to whom any such notice is to be served or given shall be his last known address, except that—

    (a) in the case of a body corporate or their secretary or clerk, it shall be the address of the registered or principal office of that body;

    (b) in the case of a partnership or person having the control or the management of the partnership business, it shall be the principal office of the partnership;

and for the purposes of this subsection the principal office of a company registered outside the United Kingdom or of a partnership carrying on business outside the United Kingdom shall be their principal office within the United Kingdom.

(4) If the person to be served with or given any such notice has specified an address in the United Kingdom other than his proper address within the meaning of subsection (3) as the one at which he or someone on his behalf will accept notices of the same description as that notice, that address shall also be treated for the purposes of this section and section 7 of the Interpretation Act 1978 as his proper address.

(5) The preceding provisions of this section shall apply to the sending or giving of a document as they apply to the giving of a notice.

[507]

NOTES

Commencement: 27 August 1993.

This section derived from the Environmental Protection Act 1990, s 160(2)–(6) and gives effect to proposal 4 in the Memorandum under the Consolidation of Enactments (Procedure) Act 1949 (16 December 1991, HC 148).

42 Application of Act to Crown

(1)   Subject to the following provisions of this section, the provisions of this Act shall bind the Crown.

(2)   Subsection (1) does not apply in relation to premises—
    (a)   occupied on behalf of the Crown for naval, military or air force purposes or for the purposes of the department of the Secretary of State having responsibility for defence, or
    (b)   occupied by or for the purposes of a visiting force.

(3)   No contravention by the Crown of any provision of this Act shall make the Crown criminally liable; but the High Court or, in Scotland, the Court of Session may, on the application of any authority charged with enforcing that provision, declare unlawful any act or omission of the Crown which constitutes such a contravention.

(4)   Notwithstanding anything in subsection (3), the provisions of this Act shall apply to persons in the public service of the Crown as they apply to other persons.

(5)   . . .

(6)   Where, in the case of any such premises as are mentioned in subsection (2)—
    (a)   arrangements are made whereby radioactive waste is not to be disposed of from those premises except with the approval of the [appropriate Agency], and
    (b)   in pursuance of those arrangements the [appropriate Agency] proposes to approve, or approves, the removal of radioactive waste from those premises to a place provided by a local authority as a place for the deposit of refuse,

the provisions of section 18 shall apply as if the proposal to approve the removal of the waste were an application for an authorisation under section 13 to remove it, or (as the case may be) the approval were such an authorisation.

(7)   Nothing in this section shall be taken as in any way affecting Her Majesty in her private capacity; and this subsection shall be construed as if section 38(3) of the Crown Proceedings Act 1947 (interpretation of references in that Act to Her Majesty in her private capacity) were contained in this Act.

(8)   In this section "visiting force" means any such body, contingent or detachment of the forces of any country as is a visiting force for the purposes of any of the provisions of the Visiting Forces Act 1952.

(9)   In the application of this section to Northern Ireland—
    (a)   references to the Crown shall include references to the Crown in right of Her Majesty's Government in Northern Ireland, and
    (b)   the reference in subsection (5) to the Secretary of State shall have effect as a reference to the Department of the Environment for Northern Ireland.

[508]

NOTES

Commencement: 27 August 1993.

Sub-ss (1)–(8) derived from the Radioactive Substances Act 1960, s 14(1)–(8), the Environmental Protection Act 1990, s 104; sub-s (9) derived from the Radioactive Substances Act 1960, s 21(2)(a), (o), the Environmental Protection Act 1990, s 105, Sch 5, Pt II, para 20(a).

Sub-s (5): repealed by the Environment Act 1995, s 120, Sch 22, para 225, Sch 24.
Sub-s (6): words in square brackets substituted by the Environment Act 1995, s 120, Sch 22, para 200.

43 *(Repealed by the Environment Act 1995, s 120(1), (3), Sch 22, para 225, Sch 24.)*

44 Regulations and orders: Great Britain

(1)   The Secretary of State may make regulations under this Act for any purpose for which regulations are authorised or required to be made under this Act.

(2)   For the purpose of facilitating the exercise of any power under this Act to effect registrations, or grant authorisations, subject to limitations or conditions, the Secretary of State may make regulations setting out general limitations or conditions applicable to such classes of cases as may be specified in the regulations; and any limitations or conditions so specified shall, for the purposes of this Act, be deemed to be attached to any registration or authorisation falling within the class of cases to which those limitations or conditions are expressed to be applicable, subject to such exceptions or modifications (if any) as may be specified in any such registration or authorisation.

(3)   Any power conferred by this Act to make regulations or orders shall be exercisable by statutory instrument.

(4)   Any statutory instrument containing regulations or an order made under this Act, other than an order under Schedule 5, shall be subject to annulment in pursuance of a resolution of either House of Parliament.

(5)   This section does not extend to Northern Ireland.

[509]

NOTES
    Commencement: 27 August 1993.
    Sub-ss (1), (2) derived from the Radioactive Substances Act 1960, s 15(1), (2), the Environmental Protection Act 1990, s 103(3); sub-ss (3), (4) derived (in part) from the Radioactive Substances Act 1960, s 15(4), (5).

45 Regulations and orders: Northern Ireland

(1)   The Department of the Environment for Northern Ireland may make regulations under this Act for any purpose for which regulations are authorised or required to be made under this Act.

(2)   For the purpose of facilitating the exercise of any power under this Act to effect registrations, or grant authorisations, subject to limitations or conditions, the Department of the Environment for Northern Ireland may make regulations setting out general limitations or conditions applicable to such classes of cases as may be specified in the regulations; and any limitations or conditions so specified shall, for the purposes of this Act, be deemed to be attached to any registration or authorisation falling within the class of cases to which those limitations or conditions are expressed to be applicable, subject to such exceptions or modifications (if any) as may be specified in any such registration or authorisation.

(3)   Any power conferred by this Act to make regulations or orders shall be exercisable by statutory rule for the purposes of the Statutory Rules (Northern Ireland) Order 1979.

(4)   Any regulations or orders made under this Act shall be subject to negative resolution within the meaning of section 41(6) of the Interpretation Act (Northern Ireland) 1954.

(5)   This section extends to Northern Ireland only.

[510]

NOTES
Commencement: 27 August 1993.

Sub-ss (1), (2) derived from the Radioactive Substances Act 1960, s 15(1), (2), the Environmental Protection Act 1990, s 100(3) (as read with the Radioactive Substances Act 1960, s 21(2)(a) (in part), the Environmental Protection Act 1990, s 105, Sch 5, Pt II, para 20(a)(i)); sub-ss (3), (4) derived from the Radioactive Substances Act 1960, s 21(2)(b), (c).

46 Effect of Act on other rights and duties

Subject to the provisions of section 40 of this Act, and of section 18 of the Interpretation Act 1978 (which relates to offences under two or more laws), nothing in this Act shall be construed as—

    (a) conferring a right of action in any civil proceedings (other than proceedings for the recovery of a fine) in respect of any contravention of this Act, or

    (b) affecting any restriction imposed by or under any other enactment, whether contained in a public general Act or in a local or private Act, or

    (c) derogating from any right of action or other remedy (whether civil or criminal) in proceedings instituted otherwise than under this Act.

[511]

NOTES
Commencement: 27 August 1993.

This section derived from the Radioactive Substances Act 1960, s 19(5), as read with the Interpretation Act 1978, s 17(2)(a).

47 General interpretation provisions

    (1)   In this Act, except in so far as the context otherwise requires—

    ["the appropriate Agency" means—

        (a) in relation to England and Wales, the Environment Agency; and

        (b) in relation to Scotland, SEPA;]

    "the appropriate Minister" means—

    (a), (b) . . .

        (c) in relation to Northern Ireland, the Department of Agriculture for Northern Ireland,

    "article" includes a part of an article,

    "the chief inspector" means—

    (a), (b) . . .

        (c) in relation to Northern Ireland, the chief inspector for Northern Ireland appointed under section 4(7),

    "disposal", in relation to waste, includes its removal, deposit, destruction, discharge (whether into water or into the air or into a sewer or drain or otherwise) or burial (whether underground or otherwise) and "dispose of" shall be construed accordingly,

    "local authority" (except where the reference is to a public or local authority) means—

        (a) in England . . . , the council of a county, district or London borough or the Common Council of the City of London or an authority established by the Waste Regulation and Disposal (Authorities) Order 1985, and

    [(aa) in Wales, the council of a county or county borough;]

        (b) *(applies to Scotland only)*, and

        (c) in Northern Ireland, a district council,

    "nuclear site" means—

        (a) any site in respect of which a nuclear site licence is for the time being in force, or

  (b) any site in respect of which, after the revocation or surrender of a nuclear site licence, the period of responsibility of the licensee has not yet come to an end,

"nuclear site licence", "licensee" and "period of responsibility" have the same meaning as in the Nuclear Installations Act 1965,

"premises" includes any land, whether covered by buildings or not, including any place underground and any land covered by water,

"prescribed" means prescribed by regulations under this Act . . . ,

"the prescribed period for determinations", in relation to any application under this Act, means, subject to subsection (2), the period of four months beginning with the day on which the application was received,

"public or local authority", in relation to England and Wales, includes a water undertaker or a sewerage undertaker,

"relevant water body" means—

  (a) in England and Wales, . . . , a water undertaker, a sewerage undertaker or a local fisheries committee,

  (b) (*applies to Scotland only*), and

  (c) in Northern Ireland, the Fisheries Conservation Board for Northern Ireland,

["SEPA" means the Scottish Environment Protection Agency;]

"substance" means any natural or artificial substance, whether in solid or liquid form or in the form of a gas or vapour,

"undertaking" includes any trade, business or profession and—

  (a) in relation to a public or local authority, includes any of the powers or duties of that authority, and

  (b) in relation to any other body of persons, whether corporate or unincorporate, includes any of the activities of that body, and

"waste" includes any substance which constitutes scrap material or an effluent or other unwanted surplus substance arising from the application of any process, and also includes any substance or article which requires to be disposed of as being broken, worn out, contaminated or otherwise spoilt.

(2) The Secretary of State may by order substitute for the period for the time being specified in subsection (1) as the prescribed period for determinations such other period as he considers appropriate.

(3) In determining, for the purposes of this Act, whether any radioactive material is kept or used on any premises, no account shall be taken of any radioactive material kept or used in or on any railway vehicle, road vehicle, vessel or aircraft if either—

  (a) the vehicle, vessel or aircraft is on those premises in the course of a journey, or

  (b) in the case of a vessel which is on those premises otherwise than in the course of a journey, the material is used in propelling the vessel or is kept in or on the vessel for use in propelling it.

(4) Any substance or article which, in the course of the carrying on of any undertaking, is discharged, discarded or otherwise dealt with as if it were waste shall, for the purposes of this Act, be presumed to be waste unless the contrary is proved.

(5) Any reference in this Act to the contamination of a substance or article is a reference to its being so affected by either or both of the following, that is to say,—

  (a) absorption, admixture or adhesion of radioactive material or radioactive waste, and

  (b) the emission of neutrons or ionising radiations,

as to become radioactive or to possess increased radioactivity.

(6) In the application of this section to Northern Ireland, the reference in subsection (2) to the Secretary of State shall have effect as a reference to the Department of the Environment for Northern Ireland.

NOTES

Commencement: 27 August 1993.

Sub-s (1) derived from the Radioactive Substances Act 1960, ss 19(1), 21(2)(a) (in part), 21(2)(f), (g) (as read with the Interpretation Act 1978, s 17(2)(a), the Local Government Act 1972, ss 1(9), (10), 20(6), 179(1), (3)), the Fisheries Act (Northern Ireland) 1966, s 210, Sch 7, the Local Government (Modifications and Repeals) Order (Northern Ireland) 1973, SI 1973/285, art 3, Schedule, the Local Government Act 1985, s 102(2), Sch 17, the Waste Regulation and Disposal (Authorities) Order 1985, SI 1985/1884, art 5, Sch 2, the Water Act 1989, s 190(1), Sch 25, para 27(3), the Environmental Protection Act 1990, s 105, Sch 5, Pt I, paras 3, 5, 11(4)(a), Pt II, para 20(a)(i); sub-s (2) derived from the Radioactive Substances Act 1960, s 19(1A), the Environmental Protection Act 1990, s 105, Sch 5, Pt I, para 11(4)(b); sub-ss (3)–(5) derived from the Radioactive Substances Act 1960, s 19(2)–(4); sub-s (6) derived from the Radioactive Substances Act 1960, s 21(2)(a) (in part), the Environmental Protection Act 1990, s 105, Sch 5, Pt II, para 20(a)(i).

Sub-s (1): definitions "the appropriate Agency", "SEPA" inserted by the Environment Act 1995, s 120, Sch 22, para 227(2), (7); in definitions "the appropriate minister" and "the chief inspector" paras (a), (b) repealed by the Environment Act 1995, s 120, Sch 22, para 227(3), (4), Sch 24; in definition "local authority" words omitted repealed, and para (aa) inserted, by the Local Government (Wales) Act 1994, s 66(6), (8), Sch 16, para 102, Sch 18, words in square brackets in para (b) substituted by the Local Government etc (Scotland) Act 1994, s 180(1), Sch 13, para 181; in definition "prescribed" words omitted repealed by the Environment Act 1995, s 120, Sch 22, para 227(5), Sch 24; in definition "relevant water body" words omitted repealed by the Environment Act 1995, s 120, Sch 22, para 227(6), Sch 24.

48 Index of defined expressions

The following Table shows provisions defining or otherwise explaining expressions for the purposes of this Act—

[the appropriate Agency	section 47(1)]
the appropriate Minister	section 47(1)
article	section 47(1)
. . .	. . .
contamination	section 47(5)
disposal	section 47(1)
licensee (in relation to a nuclear site licence)	section 47(1)
local authority	section 47(1)
mobile radioactive apparatus	section 3
nuclear site	section 47(1)
nuclear site licence	section 47(1)
period of responsibility (in relation to a nuclear site licence)	section 47(1)
premises	section 47(1)
prescribed	section 47(1)
the prescribed period for determinations	section 47(1) and (2)
public or local authority	section 47(1)
radioactive material	section 1
radioactive waste	section 2
relevant water body	section 47(1)
[SEPA	section 47(1)]
substance	section 47(1)
undertaking	section 47(1)
waste	section 47(1) and (4)

NOTES
   Commencement: 27 August 1993.
   Entries "the appropriate Agency" and "SEPA" inserted and entry omitted repealed by the Environment Act 1995, s 120, Sch 22, para 228, Sch 24.

49 Consequential amendments and transitional and transitory provisions

   (1)   The enactments specified in Schedule 4 shall have effect subject to the amendments set out in that Schedule, being amendments consequential on the preceding provisions of this Act.

   (2)   The transitional and transitory provisions contained in Schedule 5 shall have effect.

[514]

NOTES
   Commencement: 27 August 1993.

50 Repeals

The enactments and instruments specified in Schedule 6 (which include spent enactments) are repealed or, as the case may be, revoked to the extent specified in the third column of that Schedule, but subject to any provision at the end of any Part of that Schedule.

[515]

NOTES
   Commencement: 27 August 1993.

51 Short title, commencement and extent

   (1)   This Act may be cited as the Radioactive Substances Act 1993.

   (2)   This Act shall come into force at the end of the period of three months beginning with the day on which it is passed.

   (3)   This Act extends to Northern Ireland.

[516]

NOTES
   Commencement: 27 August 1993.
   Sub-s (3) derived from the Radioactive Substances Act 1960, s 21(1).

SCHEDULE 1
SPECIFIED ELEMENTS

Section 1

ELEMENT		BECQUERELS PER GRAM (BQ G-1))	
	Solid	Liquid	Gas or Vapour
1. Actinium	0.37	7.40×10^{-2}	2.59×10^{-6}
2. Lead	0.74	3.70×10^{-3}	1.11×10^{-4}
3. Polonium	0.37	2.59×10^{-2}	2.22×10^{-4}
4. Protoactinium	0.37	3.33×10^{-2}	1.11×10^{-6}
5. Radium	0.37	3.70×10^{-4}	3.70×10^{-5}
6. Radon	—	—	3.70×10^{-2}
7. Thorium	2.59	3.70×10^{-2}	2.22×10^{-5}
8. Uranium	11.1	0.74	7.40×10^{-5}

[517]

NOTES
Commencement: 27 August 1993.
This Schedule derived from the Radioactive Substances Act 1960, Sch 3.

(Sch 2 repealed by the Environment Act 1995, s 120(1), (3), Sch 22, para 229, Sch 24.)

SCHEDULE 3
ENACTMENTS, OTHER THAN LOCAL ENACTMENTS, TO WHICH S 40 APPLIES

Section 40

PART I
ENGLAND AND WALES

1.   Sections 48, [79], 81, 82, 141, 259 and 261 of the Public Health Act 1936.

[2.   Section 16 of the Clean Air Act 1993.]

[2A.   Sections 2, 5 and 7 of the Rivers (Prevention of Pollution) Act 1961.]

3.   Section 5 of the Sea Fisheries Regulation Act 1966.

4.   Section 4 of the Salmon and Freshwater Fisheries Act 1975.

[4B.   The Control of Pollution (Special Waste) Regulations 1980.]

5.   Section 59 of the Building Act 1984.

6.   The Planning (Hazardous Substances) Act 1990.

7.   Part III of the Environmental Protection Act 1990.

8.   Sections 72, 111 and 113(6) and Chapter III of Part IV of the Water Industry Act 1991 and paragraphs 2 to 4 of Schedule 8 to that Act so far as they re-enact provisions of sections 43 and 44 of the Control of Pollution Act 1974.

9.   Sections 82, 84, 85, 86, 87(1), 88(2), 92, 93, 99, 161, 190, 202, [and 203] of and paragraph 6 of Schedule 25 to the Water Resources Act 1991.

10.   Section 18 of the Water Act 1945 so far as it continues to have effect by virtue of Schedule 2 to the Water Consolidation (Consequential Provisions) Act 1991 or by virtue of provisions of the Control of Pollution Act 1974 not having been brought into force.

[518]

NOTES
Commencement: 27 August 1993.
Para 1 derived from the Radioactive Substances Act 1960, Sch 1, Pt I, para 3; para 2 derived from the Radioactive Substances Act 1960, Sch 1, Pt I, para 8; paras 3, 4 derived from the Radioactive Substances Act 1960, Sch 1, Pt I, paras 1, 2 (as read with the Interpretation Act 1978, s 17(2)(a)); para 5 derived from the Radioactive Substances Act 1960, Sch 1, Pt I, para 8D, the Building Act 1984, s 133(1), Sch 6, para 7; para 6 derived from the Radioactive Substances Act 1960, Sch 1, Pt I, para 8AA, the Planning (Consequential Provisions) Act 1990, s 4, Sch 2, para 7; para 7 derived from the Radioactive Substances Act 1960, Sch 1, Pt I, para 9, the Environmental Protection Act 1990, s 162(1), Sch 15, para 8; paras 8–10 derived from the Radioactive Substances Act 1960, Sch 1, Pt I, paras 10–12, the Water Consolidation (Consequential Provisions) Act 1991, s 2, Sch 1, para 9(1).
Para 1: number in square brackets temporarily inserted by the Radioactive Substances Act 1993, s 49(2), Sch 5, para 9, until a day to be appointed.
Para 2: substituted by the Clean Air Act 1993, s 67(1), Sch 4, para 6(a).
Para 2A: temporarily inserted by the Radioactive Substances Act 1993, s 49(2), Sch 5, para 9, until a day to be appointed.
Para 4B: temporarily inserted by the Radioactive Substances Act 1993, s 49(2), Sch 5, para 11(a), until the date appointed for the repeal by the Environmental Protection Act 1990, Sch 16, Pt II of the Control of Pollution Act 1974, s 30(5).
Para 6: temporarily omitted by the Radioactive Substances Act 1993, s 49(2), Sch 5, para 10, until a date to be appointed.
Para 9: words in square brackets substituted by the Environment Act 1995, s 120, Sch 22, para 230(1).

(Pt II (paras 11–17A) apply to Scotland only.)

PART III
NORTHERN IRELAND

18. Sections 50, 51, 58, 107 and 129 of the Public Health (Ireland) Act 1878.

19. Section 26 of the Public Health Acts Amendment Act 1890.

20. Sections 35, 46, 49 and 51 of the Public Health Acts Amendment Act 1907.

21. Sections 26, 47 and 124 of the Fisheries Act (Northern Ireland) 1966.

22. Sections 5, 7 and 8 of the Water Act (Northern Ireland) 1972.

23. Article 34 of the Water and Sewerage Services (Northern Ireland) Order 1973.

24. The Clean Air (Northern Ireland) Order 1981.

25. The Pollution Control (Special Waste) Regulations (Northern Ireland) 1981.

[519]

NOTES
Commencement: 27 August 1993.
Para 18 derived from the Radioactive Substances Act 1960, Sch 1, Pt III, para 21; para 19 derived from the Radioactive Substances Act 1960, Sch 1, Pt III, para 22, the Water and Sewerage Services (Northern Ireland) Order 1973, SI 1973/70, art 60(1), Sch 3; para 20 derived from the Radioactive Substances Act 1960, Sch 1, Pt III, para 24; para 21 derived from the Radioactive Substances Act 1960, Sch 1, Pt III, para 27, the Fisheries Act (Northern Ireland) 1966, s 210, Sch 7; para 22 derived from the Radioactive Substances Act 1960, Sch 1, Pt III, para 28, the Water Act (Northern Ireland) 1972, s 31(1); para 23 derived from the Radioactive Substances Act 1960, Sch 1, Pt III, para 29, the Water and Sewerage Services (Northern Ireland) Order 1973, SI 1973/70, art 60(1), Sch 3; para 24 derived from the Radioactive Substances Act 1960, Sch 1, Pt III, para 26; para 25 derived from the Radioactive Substances Act 1960, Sch 1, Pt III, para 27, the Pollution Control (Special Waste) Regulations (Northern Ireland) Order 1981, SR (NI) 1981/252, reg 4.

(Sch 4 outside the scope of this work.)

SCHEDULE 5
TRANSITIONAL AND TRANSITORY PROVISIONS

Section 49(2)

PART I
GENERAL TRANSITIONAL PROVISIONS AND SAVINGS

1. The substitution of this Act for the enactments repealed by this Act does not affect the continuity of the law.

2. Any reference, whether express or implied, in this Act or any other enactment, instrument or document to a provision of this Act shall, so far as the context permits, be construed as including, in relation to the times, circumstances and purposes in relation to which the corresponding provision of the enactments repealed by this Act has effect, a reference to that corresponding provision.

3. Any document made, served or issued after the commencement of this Act which contains a reference to any of the enactments repealed by this Act shall be construed, except so far as a contrary intention appears, as referring or, as the case may require, including a reference to the corresponding provision of this Act.

4. Paragraphs 2 and 3 have effect without prejudice to the operation of sections 16 and 17 of the Interpretation Act 1978 (which relate to the effect of repeals).

5. The power to amend or revoke the subordinate legislation reproduced in the definition of "local authority" in section 47(1) shall be exercisable in relation to the provision reproduced to the same extent as it was exercisable in relation to the subordinate legislation.

6. Subsection (1) of section 80 of the Health and Safety at Work etc Act 1974 (general power to repeal or modify Acts or instruments) shall apply to provisions of this Act which re-enact provisions previously contained in the Radioactive Substances Act 1960 as it applies to provisions contained in Acts passed before the Health and Safety at Work etc Act 1974.

7. In the application of paragraph 6 to Northern Ireland—
  (a) the reference to subsection (1) of section 80 of the Health and Safety at Work etc Act 1974 shall have effect as a reference to paragraph (1) of Article 54 of the Health and Safety at Work (Northern Ireland) Order 1978, and
  (b) the reference to Acts passed before that Act shall have effect as a reference to statutory provisions passed or made before the making of that Order.

[520]

NOTES
Commencement: 27 August 1993.

PART II
TRANSITORY MODIFICATIONS OF SCHEDULE 3

8.—(1) If—
  (a) no date has been appointed before the commencement of this Act as the date on which paragraph 8 of Schedule 15 of the Environmental Protection Act 1990 (in this paragraph referred to as "the 1990 provision") is to come into force, or
  (b) a date has been appointed which is later than that commencement,
paragraph 7 of Schedule 3 to this Act shall be omitted until the appointed day.

  (2) In this paragraph "the appointed day" means—
  (a) in the case mentioned in paragraph (a) of sub-paragraph (1) above, such day as may be appointed by the Secretary of State by order, and
  (b) in the case mentioned in paragraph (b) of that sub-paragraph, the date appointed as the day on which the 1990 provision is to come into force.

9.—(1) If—
  (a) no date has been appointed before the commencement of this Act as the date on which the repeal by Schedule 4 to the Control of Pollution Act 1974 of the provisions of the Radioactive Substances Act 1960 specified in sub-paragraph (2) below (in this paragraph referred to as "the 1974 repeal") is to come into force, or
  (b) a date has been appointed which is later than that commencement,
Schedule 3 to this Act shall have effect until the appointed day with the modifications specified in sub-paragraph (3) below.

  (2) The provisions of the Radioactive Substances Act 1960 referred to in sub-paragraph (1)(a) above are—
  (a) in paragraph 3 of Schedule 1, the words "seventy-nine", and
  (b) paragraph 8A of Schedule 1.

  (3) The modifications of Schedule 3 to this Act referred to in sub-paragraph (1) are as follows—
  (a) in paragraph 3 after "48" there shall be inserted "79", and
  (b) after paragraph 2 there shall be inserted—

  "2A. Sections 2, 5 and 7 of the Rivers (Prevention of Pollution) Act 1961."

  (4) In this paragraph "the appointed day" means—
  (a) in the case mentioned in paragraph (a) of sub-paragraph (1), such day as may be appointed by the Secretary of State by order, and
  (b) in the case mentioned in paragraph (b) of that sub-paragraph, the date appointed as the day on which the 1974 repeal is to come into force.

10.—(1) If—
  (a) no date has been appointed before the commencement of this Act for the purposes of paragraph 17 of Schedule 4 to the Planning (Consequential Provisions) Act 1990, or
  (b) a date has been appointed which is later than that commencement,
paragraph 6 of Schedule 3 to this Act shall be omitted until the appointed day.

  (2) In this paragraph "the appointed day" means—
  (a) in the case mentioned in paragraph (a) of sub-paragraph (1), such day as may be appointed by the Secretary of State by order made by statutory instrument, and
  (b) in the case mentioned in paragraph (b) of that sub-paragraph, the date appointed for the purposes of paragraph 17 of Schedule 4 to the Planning (Consequential Provisions) Act 1990.

11. Until the commencement of the repeal by Part II of Schedule 16 to the Environmental Protection Act 1990 of subsection (5) of section 30 of the Control of Pollution Act 1974 (or, if the repeal of that subsection comes into force on different days, until the last of those days) Schedule 3 to this Act shall have effect—

    (a)   with the insertion after paragraph 4 of the following paragraph—

       "4B. The Control of Pollution (Special Waste) Regulations 1980.", and

    (b)   with the insertion after paragraph 17 of the following paragraph—

       "17A. The Control of Pollution (Special Waste) Regulations 1980."

12. (*Applies to Scotland only.*)

[521]

NOTES

    Commencement: 27 August 1993.

SCHEDULE 6
REPEALS AND REVOCATIONS

Section 50

PART I
ACTS OF THE PARLIAMENT OF THE UNITED KINGDOM

Chapter	Short title	Extent of repeal
11 & 12 Geo 6 c 37	The Radioactive Substances Act 1948	The whole Act so far as unrepealed.
8 & 9 Eliz 2 c 34	The Radioactive Substances Act 1960	The whole Act.
1968 c 47	The Sewerage (Scotland) Act 1968	In Schedule 1, paragraph 4.
1973 c 65	The Local Government (Scotland) Act 1973	In Schedule 27, in Part II, paragraph 144.
1979 c 2	The Customs and Excise Management Act 1979	In Schedule 4, in Part I of the Table following paragraph 12, the entry relating to the Radioactive Substances Act 1948.
1980 c 45	The Water (Scotland) Act 1980	In Schedule 10, in Part II, the entry relating to the Radioactive Substances Act 1960.
1984 c 55	The Building Act 1984	In Schedule 6. paragraph 7.
1986 c 63	The Housing and Planning Act 1986	In Part II of Schedule 7, paragraph 1.
1989 c 15	The Water Act 1989	In Schedule 25, paragraph 27.
1990 c 11	The Planning (Consequential Provisions) Act 1990	In Schedule 2, paragraph 7.
		In Schedule 4, paragraph 17 and the entry relating to it in the Table in paragraph 1(1).
1990 c 43	The Environmental Protection Act 1990	Sections 100 to 105. Schedule 5.
		In Schedule 15, paragraph 8.
1991 c 46	The Atomic Weapons Establishment Act 1991	In the Schedule, paragraph 5.
1991 c 60	The Water Consolidation (Consequential Provisions) Act 1991	In Schedule 1, paragraph 9.

    Note: Except as provided in Part II of this Schedule, the repeal of the Radioactive Substances Act 1948 does not extend to Northern Ireland.

[522]

NOTES

    Commencement: 27 August 1993.

PART II
REPEALS IN RADIOACTIVE SUBSTANCES ACT 1948 EXTENDING TO NORTHERN IRELAND

Chapter	Short title	Extent of repeal
11 & 12 Geo. 6 c 37.	The Radioactive Substances Act 1948	Section 2.
		Section 5(1)(b).
		In section 7, in subsection (1), the words "except section two" and in subsection (2)(b), the words "(except section two)".
		Section 8(7).
		In section 9(1), the words "or orders".
		In section 10, the words "or order" in both places.
		In section 11, the words from the beginning to "under this Act and".
		In section 12, the definitions of "registered dental practitioner", "registered pharmacist" and "sale by way of wholesale dealing".
		Section 14(2)(f).

Note: These repeals extend to Northern Ireland only.

[523]

NOTES

Commencement: 27 August 1993.

PART III
NORTHERN IRELAND LEGISLATION

Chapter or number	Short title	Extent of repeal
1966 c 17 (NI)	The Fisheries Act (Northern Ireland) 1966	In Schedule 7, the amendments of the Radioactive Substances Act 1960.
1972 c 5 (NI)	The Water Act (Northern Ireland) 1972	Section 31(1).
SI 1973/70 (NI 2)	The Water and Sewerage Services (Northern Ireland) Order 1973	In Schedule 3, paragraph 1.
SI 1978/1049 (NI 19)	The Pollution Control and Local Government (Northern Ireland) Order 1978	In Schedule 4, paragraph 5.

[524]

NOTES

Commencement: 27 August 1993.

PART IV
SUBORDINATE LEGISLATION

Number	Title	Extent of revocation
SI 1974/1821	The Radioactive Substances Act 1948 (Modification) Regulations 1974	The whole instrument.
SI 1980/170	The Control of Pollution (Special Waste) Regulations 1980	Regulation 3(2).
SR (NI) 1981/ 252	The Pollution Control (Special Waste) Regulations (Northern Ireland) 1981	Regulation 4(2).
SI 1985/1884	The Waste Regulation and Disposal (Authorities) Order 1985	In Schedule 2, paragraph 2.
SI 1991/2539	The Control of Pollution (Radioactive Waste) (Scotland) Regulations 1991	Regulation 4.

[525]

NOTES

Commencement: 27 August 1993.

NOISE AND STATUTORY NUISANCE ACT 1993

(1993 c 40)

ARRANGEMENT OF SECTIONS

An Act to make provision for noise in a street to be a statutory nuisance; to make provision with respect to the operation of loudspeakers in a street; to make provision with respect to audible intruder alarms; to make provision for expenses incurred by local authorities in abating, or preventing the recurrence of, a statutory nuisance to be a charge on the premises to which they relate; and for connected purposes

[5 November 1993]

Preliminary

1 Interpretation

In this Act "the 1974 Act" means the Control of Pollution Act 1974 and "the 1990 Act" means the Environmental Protection Act 1990.

[526]

NOTES
Commencement: 5 January 1994.

2–6 *(S 2 amends the Environmental Protection Act 1990, s 79, and inserts s 79(6A) thereof; s 3 amends s 80 of that Act and inserts s 80A thereof; s 4 amends s 81 of, and Sch 3, paras 3(1), 4(1) to, that Act and inserts s 81(1A), (1B) of, and Sch 3, para 2A to, that Act; s 5 amends s 82 of that Act and inserts s 82(5A), (10)(aa) thereof; s 6 repealed by the Environment Act 1995, s 120(3), Sch 24; s 7.)*

Loudspeakers

7 *(Amends the Control of Pollution Act 1974, s 62, and inserts s 62(1A), (1B), (3A) of that Act, with modifications in relation to Scotland.)*

8 Consent of local authorities to the operation of loudspeakers in streets or roads

(1)   A local authority may resolve that Schedule 2 is to apply to its area.

(2)   If a local authority does so resolve, Schedule 2 shall come into force in its area on such date as may be specified for that purpose in the resolution, being a date at least one month after the date on which the resolution is passed.

(3)   Where a local authority has passed a resolution under this section, the authority shall cause a notice to be published, in two consecutive weeks before the Schedule comes into force in its area, in a local newspaper circulating in the area.

(4)   The notice shall—
  (a) state that the resolution has been passed, and
  (b) set out the general effect of Schedule 2 and, in particular, the procedure for applying for a consent under that Schedule.

(5)   In this section "local authority" means—
  (a) in relation to England and Wales—
    (i)   the council of a district,
    (ii) the council of a London borough,
    (iii) the Common Council of the City of London,
    (iv) the Sub-Treasurer of the Inner Temple, or
    (v)   the Under Treasurer of the Middle Temple, and
  (b) *(applies to Scotland only)*.

[527]

NOTES
Commencement: 5 January 1994.

Audible intruder alarms

9 Audible intruder alarms

(1)   A local authority may, after consulting the chief officer of police, resolve that Schedule 3 is to apply to its area.

(2)   If a local authority does so resolve—

    (a)   Schedule 3 (other than paragraph 4) shall come into force in its area on such date as may be specified for that purpose in the resolution ("the first appointed day"), and

    (b)   paragraph 4 of Schedule 3 shall come into force in its area, and accordingly paragraphs 2 and 3 of that Schedule shall cease to have effect in its area, on such later date as may be so specified ("the second appointed day").

(3)   The first appointed day shall be at least four months after the date on which the resolution is passed.

(4)   The second appointed day shall be at least nine months after the first appointed day.

(5)   Where a local authority has passed a resolution under this section, the authority shall cause a notice to be published, in two consecutive weeks ending at least three months before the first appointed day, in a local newspaper circulating in its area.

(6)   The notice shall—

    (a)   state that the resolution has been passed,

    (b)   state the first and second appointed days, and

    (c)   set out the general effect of Schedule 3 as it will apply from each of those days.

(7)   In this section—

"chief officer of police", in relation to a local authority, means—

    (a)   the chief officer of police for the police area in which the area of the local authority is situated, or

    (b)   where part of the local authority's area is situated in one police area and part in another, the chief officer of police for each police area in which a part of the local authority's area is situated;

"local authority" means—

    (a)   in relation to England and Wales, the council of a district, and

    (b)   *(applies to Scotland only).*

                                                                                [528]

NOTES

Commencement: to be appointed.

10 (*Amends the Environmental Protection Act 1990, s 79, and inserts ss 81A, 81B of that Act.*)

General

11 Expenses

There shall be paid out of money provided by Parliament any increase attributable to this Act in the sums payable out of money so provided under any other enactment.

                                                                                [529]

NOTES

Commencement: 5 January 1994.

12 Commencement

(1)   Subject to subsection (2), this Act shall come into force at the end of the period of two months beginning with the day on which it is passed.

(2)   Section 9 and Schedule 3 shall come into force on such day as the Secretary of State may by order made by statutory instrument appoint; and different days may be so appointed in respect of different areas.

[530]

NOTES
Commencement: 5 January 1994.

13 Extent

(1)   Sections 2 to 5 and 10 do not extend to Scotland.

(2)   . . .

(3)   No provision of this Act extends to Northern Ireland.

[531]

NOTES
Commencement: 5 January 1994.
Sub-s (2): repealed by the Environment Act 1995, s 120, Sch 24.

14 Short title

This Act may be cited as the Noise and Statutory Nuisance Act 1993.

[532]

NOTES
Commencement: 5 January 1994.

(Sch 1 repealed by the Environment Act 1995, s 120(3), Sch 24.)

SCHEDULE 2
CONSENT TO THE OPERATION OF LOUDSPEAKERS IN STREETS OR ROADS
Section 8

Local authority consent

1.—(1) Subject to sub-paragraph (2), on an application made by any person, the local authority may consent to the operation in its area of a loudspeaker in contravention of section 62(1) of the 1974 Act.

(2)   A consent shall not be given to the operation of a loudspeaker in connection with any election or for the purpose of advertising any entertainment, trade or business.

2.   A consent may be granted subject to such conditions as the local authority considers appropriate.

Procedure

3.   An application for a consent shall be made in writing and shall contain such information as the local authority may reasonably require.

4.—(1) Where an application is duly made to the local authority for a consent, the authority shall determine the application and notify the applicant in writing of its decision within the period of twenty-one days beginning with the day on which the application is received by the authority.

(2)   In a case where a consent is granted, the notification under sub-paragraph (1) shall specify the conditions, if any, subject to which the consent is granted.

5.   An applicant for a consent shall pay such reasonable fee in respect of his application as the local authority may determine.

Publication of consent

6. Where the local authority grants a consent, the authority may cause a notice giving details of that consent to be published in a local newspaper circulating in its area.

Interpretation

7. In this Schedule "a consent" means a consent under paragraph 1.

NOTES
Commencement: 5 January 1994.

SCHEDULE 3
AUDIBLE INTRUDER ALARMS

Section 9

Installation of new alarms

1.—(1) A person who installs an audible intruder alarm on or in any premises shall ensure—
   (a) that the alarm complies with any prescribed requirements, and
   (b) that the local authority is notified within 48 hours of the installation.

(2) A person who without reasonable excuse contravenes sub-paragraph (1) shall be guilty of an offence and liable on summary conviction—
   (a) where the alarm does not comply with any prescribed requirements, to a fine not exceeding level 5 on the standard scale, and
   (b) in any other case, to a fine not exceeding level 2 on the standard scale.

Operation of alarms before second appointed day

2.—(1) A person who is the occupier of any premises when (on or after the first appointed day) an audible intruder alarm is installed on or in the premises shall not permit the alarm to be operated unless paragraph 5 is satisfied.

(2) A person who without reasonable excuse contravenes sub-paragraph (1) shall be guilty of an offence and liable on summary conviction—
   (a) where the alarm does not comply with any prescribed requirements, to a fine not exceeding level 5 on the standard scale, and
   (b) in any other case, to a fine not exceeding level 2 on the standard scale.

3.—(1) A person who (on or after the first appointed day) becomes the occupier of any premises on or in which an audible intruder alarm has been installed, shall not permit the alarm to be operated unless paragraph 5 is satisfied.

(2) A person who without reasonable excuse contravenes sub-paragraph (1) shall be guilty of an offence and liable on summary conviction—
   (a) where the alarm does not comply with any prescribed requirements, to a fine not exceeding level 4 on the standard scale, and
   (b) in any other case, to a fine not exceeding level 2 on the standard scale.

Operation of alarms on or after second appointed day

4.—(1) The occupier of any premises shall not permit any audible intruder alarm installed on or in those premises to be operated unless paragraph 5 is satisfied.

(2) A person who without reasonable excuse contravenes sub-paragraph (1) shall be guilty of an offence and liable on summary conviction—
   (a) where the alarm does not comply with any prescribed requirements, to a fine not exceeding level 5 on the standard scale, and
   (b) in any other case, to a fine not exceeding level 2 on the standard scale.

Requirements for operation of alarms

5.—(1) This paragraph is satisfied if—
   (a) the alarm complies with any prescribed requirements,
   (b) the police have been notified in writing of the names, addresses and telephone numbers of the current key-holders, and
   (c) the local authority has been informed of the address of the police station to which notification has been given under paragraph (b).

(2) Notification under sub-paragraph (1)(b) may be given to the police at any police station in the local authority's area.

Entry to premises

6.—(1) Where—
    (a)   an intruder alarm installed on or in any premises is operating audibly more than one hour after it was activated, and
    (b)   the audible operation of the alarm is such as to give persons living or working in the vicinity of the premises reasonable cause for annoyance,

an officer of the local authority who has been authorised (whether generally or specially) for that purpose may, on production (if so required) of his authority, enter the premises to turn off the alarm.

(2) An officer may not enter premises by force under this paragraph.

7.—(1) If, on an application made by an officer of the local authority who has been authorised (whether generally or specially) for that purpose, a justice of the peace is satisfied—
    (a)   that an intruder alarm installed on or in any premises is operating audibly more than one hour after it was activated,
    (b)   that the audible operation of the alarm is such as to give persons living or working in the vicinity of the premises reasonable cause for annoyance,
    (c)   where notification of any current key-holders has been given in accordance with paragraph 5(1)(b), that the officer has taken steps to obtain access to the premises with their assistance, and
    (d)   that the officer has been unable to obtain access to the premises without the use of force,

the justice may issue a warrant authorising the officer to enter the premises, if need be by force.

(2) Before applying for such a warrant, an officer shall leave a notice at the premises stating—
    (a)   that the audible operation of the alarm is such as to give persons living or working in the vicinity reasonable cause for annoyance, and
    (b)   that an application is to be made to a justice of the peace for a warrant authorising the officer to enter the premises and turn off the alarm.

(3) An officer shall not enter premises by virtue of this paragraph unless he is accompanied by a constable.

(4) A warrant under this paragraph shall continue in force until the alarm has been turned off and the officer has complied with paragraph 10.

8. An officer who enters premises by virtue of paragraph 6 or 7 may take with him such other persons and such equipment as may be necessary to turn off the alarm.

9. A person who enters premises by virtue of paragraph 6, 7 or 8 shall not cause more damage or disturbance than is necessary.

10. An officer who has entered premises by virtue of paragraph 6 or 7 which are unoccupied or from which the occupier is temporarily absent shall—
    (a)   after the alarm has been turned off, re-set it if reasonably practicable,
    (b)   leave a notice at the premises stating what action has been taken on the premises under this Schedule, and
    (c)   leave the premises, so far as reasonably practicable, as effectually secured against trespassers as he found them.

Recovery of expenses

11. Where any premises are entered by virtue of paragraph 6 or 7 in a case where the occupier of those premises has committed an offence under paragraph 2, 3 or 4, any expenses reasonably incurred by the local authority in connection with the entry, turning off the alarm or complying with paragraph 10 may be recovered by the authority from that occupier.

Protection from personal liability

12. Nothing done by, or by a member of, a local authority or by an officer of or another person authorised by a local authority shall, if done in good faith for the purposes of this Schedule, subject them or any of them personally to any action, liability, claim or demand whatsoever, other than any liability under section 19 or 20 of the Local Government Finance Act 1982 (powers of district auditor and court).

Interpretation

13.—(1)   In this Schedule references to the first appointed day or the second appointed day are to be read in accordance with section 9(2).

(2)   In this Schedule—
"justice of the peace", in relation to Scotland, includes a sheriff;
"key-holders", in relation to an alarm, means—
   (a)   two persons, other than the occupier of the premises on or in which the alarm is installed, each of whom holds keys sufficient to obtain access to those premises, or
   (b)   a company which holds keys sufficient to obtain access to those premises, from which those keys can be obtained at any time and the business of which consists of or includes the service of holding keys for occupiers of premises;
"occupier"—
   (a)   in relation to premises that are unoccupied, means any person entitled to occupy the premises, and
   (b)   in relation to premises comprising a building that is being erected, constructed, altered, improved, maintained, cleaned or repaired, does not include a person whose occupancy—
      (i)   is connected with the erection, construction, alteration, improvement, maintenance, cleaning or repair, and
      (ii)   is by virtue of a licence granted for less than four weeks;
"prescribed" means prescribed in regulations made by the Secretary of State for the purposes of this Schedule.

(3)   The Secretary of State's power to make such regulations shall be exercisable by statutory instrument, and an instrument containing such regulations shall be subject to annulment in pursuance of a resolution of either House of Parliament.

(4)   Such regulations may make different provision for different cases, circumstances or areas.

(5)   Nothing in this Schedule applies to an audible intruder alarm installed on or in a vehicle.

[534]

NOTES
Commencement: 5 January 1994.

ENVIRONMENT ACT 1995

(1995 c 25)

ARRANGEMENT OF SECTIONS

PART I
THE ENVIRONMENT AGENCY AND THE SCOTTISH ENVIRONMENT PROTECTION AGENCY

CHAPTER I
THE ENVIRONMENT AGENCY

CHAPTER III
MISCELLANEOUS, GENERAL AND SUPPLEMENTAL PROVISIONS RELATING TO THE NEW AGENCIES

An Act to provide for the establishment of a body corporate to be known as the Environment Agency and a body corporate to be known as the Scottish Environment Protection Agency; to provide for the transfer of functions, property, rights and liabilities to those bodies and for the conferring of other functions on them; to make provision with respect to contaminated land and abandoned mines; to make further provision in relation to National Parks; to make further provision for the control of pollution, the conservation of natural resources and the conservation or enhancement of the environment; to make provision for imposing obligations on certain persons in respect of certain products or materials; to make provision in relation to fisheries; to make provision for certain enactments to bind the Crown; to make provision with respect to the application of certain enactments in relation to the Isles of Scilly; and for connected purposes.

[19 July 1995]

PART I
THE ENVIRONMENT AGENCY AND THE SCOTTISH
ENVIRONMENT PROTECTION AGENCY

CHAPTER I
THE ENVIRONMENT AGENCY

1 (*Relates to the establishment of the Environment Agency.*)

Transfer of functions, property etc to the Agency

2 Transfer of functions to the Agency

(1)   On the transfer date there shall by virtue of this section be transferred to the Agency—
    (a) the functions of the National Rivers Authority, that is to say—
        (i) its functions under or by virtue of Part II (water resources management) of the Water Resources Act 1991 (in this Part referred to as "the 1991 Act");
        (ii) its functions under or by virtue of Part III of that Act (control of pollution of water resources);
        (iii) its functions under or by virtue of Part IV of that Act (flood defence) and the Land Drainage Act 1991 and the functions transferred to the Authority by virtue of section 136(8) of the Water Act 1989 and paragraph 1(3) of Schedule 15 to that Act (transfer of land drainage functions under local statutory provisions and subordinate legislation);
        (iv) its functions under or by virtue of Part VII of the 1991 Act (land and works powers);
        (v) its functions under or by virtue of the Diseases of Fish Act 1937, the Sea Fisheries Regulation Act 1966, the Salmon and Freshwater Fisheries Act 1975, Part V of the 1991 Act or any other enactment relating to fisheries;
        (vi) the functions as a navigation authority, harbour authority or conservancy authority which were transferred to the Authority by virtue of Chapter V of Part III of the Water Act 1989 or paragraph 23(3) of Schedule 13 to that Act or which have been transferred to the Authority by any order or agreement under Schedule 2 to the 1991 Act;
        (vii) its functions under Schedule 2 to the 1991 Act;
        (viii) the functions assigned to the Authority by or under any other enactment, apart from this Act;
    (b) the functions of waste regulation authorities, that is to say, the functions conferred or imposed on them by or under—

> (i) the Control of Pollution (Amendment) Act 1989, or
>
> (ii) Part II of the Environmental Protection Act 1990 (in this Part referred to as "the 1990 Act"),
>
> or assigned to them by or under any other enactment, apart from this Act;

(c) the functions of disposal authorities under or by virtue of the waste regulation provisions of the Control of Pollution Act 1974;

(d) the functions of the chief inspector for England and Wales constituted under section 16(3) of the 1990 Act, that is to say, the functions conferred or imposed on him by or under Part I of that Act or assigned to him by or under any other enactment, apart from this Act;

(e) the functions of the chief inspector for England and Wales appointed under section 4(2)(a) of the Radioactive Substances Act 1993, that is to say, the functions conferred or imposed on him by or under that Act or assigned to him by or under any other enactment, apart from this Act;

(f) the functions conferred or imposed by or under the Alkali, &c, Works Regulation Act 1906 (in this section referred to as "the 1906 Act") on the chief, or any other, inspector (within the meaning of that Act), so far as exercisable in relation to England and Wales;

(g) so far as exercisable in relation to England and Wales, the functions in relation to improvement notices and prohibition notices under Part I of the Health and Safety at Work etc Act 1974 (in this section referred to as "the 1974 Act") of inspectors appointed under section 19 of that Act by the Secretary of State in his capacity as the enforcing authority responsible in relation to England and Wales for the enforcement of the 1906 Act and section 5 of the 1974 Act; and

(h) the functions of the Secretary of State specified in subsection (2) below.

(2) The functions of the Secretary of State mentioned in subsection (1)(h) above are the following, that is to say—

(a) so far as exercisable in relation to England and Wales, his functions under section 30(1) of the Radioactive Substances Act 1993 (power to dispose of radioactive waste);

(b) his functions under Chapter III of Part IV of the Water Industry Act 1991 in relation to special category effluent, within the meaning of that Chapter, other than any function of making regulations or of making orders under section 139 of that Act;

(c) so far as exercisable in relation to England and Wales, the functions conferred or imposed on him by virtue of his being, for the purposes of Part I of the 1974 Act, the authority which is by any of the relevant statutory provisions made responsible for the enforcement of the 1906 Act and section 5 of the 1974 Act;

(d) so far as exercisable in relation to England and Wales, his functions under, or under regulations made by virtue, of section 9 of the 1906 Act (registration of works), other than any functions of his as an appellate authority or any function of making regulations;

(e) so far as exercisable in relation to England and Wales, his functions under regulations 7(1) and 8(2) of and paragraph 2(2)(c) of Schedule 2 to, the Sludge (Use in Agriculture) Regulations 1989 (which relate to the provision of information and the testing of soil).

(3) The National Rivers Authority and the London Waste Regulation Authority are hereby abolished.

[535]

NOTES

Commencement: 1 April 1996.

3–36 (*Relate to the transfer of functions, property etc to the Agency (ss 3–10); advisory committees (ss 11–13); flood defence committees (ss 14–19); Chapter II (ss 20–36) applies to Scotland only.*)

CHAPTER III
MISCELLANEOUS, GENERAL AND SUPPLEMENTAL PROVISIONS RELATING TO THE NEW AGENCIES

Additional general powers and duties

37, 38 (*Relate to incidental general functions (s 37); delegation of functions by Ministers etc to the new Agencies (s 38).*)

39 General duty of the new Agencies to have regard to costs and benefits in exercising powers

    (1)   Each new Agency—
        (a) in considering whether or not to exercise any power conferred upon it by or under any enactment, or
        (b) in deciding the manner in which to exercise any such power,
shall, unless and to the extent that it is unreasonable for it to do so in view of the nature or purpose of the power or in the circumstances of the particular case, take into account the likely costs and benefits of the exercise or non-exercise of the power or its exercise in the manner in question.

    (2)   The duty imposed upon a new Agency by subsection (1) above does not affect its obligation, nevertheless, to discharge any duties, comply with any requirements, or pursue any objectives, imposed upon or given to it otherwise than under this section.

[536]

NOTES
Commencement: 28 July 1995.

---

40 Ministerial directions to the new Agencies

    (1)   The appropriate Minister may give a new Agency directions of a general or specific character with respect to the carrying out of any of its functions.

    (2)   The appropriate Minister may give a new Agency such directions of a general or specific character as he considers appropriate for the implementation of—
        (a) any obligations of the United Kingdom under the Community Treaties, or
        (b) any international agreement to which the United Kingdom is for the time being a party.

    (3)   Any direction under subsection (2) above shall be published in such manner as the Minister giving it considers appropriate for the purpose of bringing the matters to which it relates to the attention of persons likely to be affected by them; and—
        (a) copies of the direction shall be made available to the public; and
        (b) notice shall be given—
            (i) in the case of a direction given to the Agency, in the London Gazette, or
           (ii) (*applies to Scotland only*),
        of the giving of the direction and of where a copy of the direction may be obtained.

(4)   The provisions of subsection (3) above shall have effect in relation to any direction given to a new Agency under an enactment other than subsection (2) above for the implementation of—

(a) any obligations of the United Kingdom under the Community Treaties, or

(b) any international agreement to which the United Kingdom is for the time being a party,

as those provisions have effect in relation to a direction given under subsection (2) above.

(5)   In determining—

(a) any appeal against, or reference or review of, a decision of a new Agency, or

(b) any application transmitted from a new Agency,

the body or person making the determination shall be bound by any direction given under this section or any other enactment by a Minister of the Crown to the new Agency to the same extent as the new Agency.

(6)   Any power to give a direction under this section shall be exercisable, except in an emergency, only after consultation with the new Agency concerned.

(7)   Any power of the appropriate Minister to give directions to a new Agency otherwise than by virtue of this section shall be without prejudice to any power to give directions conferred by this section.

(8)   It is the duty of a new Agency to comply with any direction which is given to that new Agency by a Minister of the Crown under this section or any other enactment.

[537]

NOTES

Commencement: 28 July 1995.

Charging schemes

41 Power to make schemes imposing charges

(1)   Subject to the following provisions of this section and section 42 below—

(a) in the case of any particular licence under Chapter II of Part II of the 1991 Act (abstraction and impounding), the Agency may require the payment to it of such charges as may from time to time be prescribed:

(b) in relation to other environmental licences, there shall be charged by and paid to a new Agency such charges as may from time to time be prescribed; and

(c) as a means of recovering costs incurred by it in performing functions conferred by regulations under section 62 of the 1990 Act (dangerous or intractable waste) each of the new Agencies may require the payment to it of such charges as may from time to time be prescribed:

and in this section "prescribed" means specified in, or determined under, a scheme (in this section referred to as a "charging scheme") made under this section by the new Agency in question.

(2)   As respects environmental licences, charges may be prescribed in respect of—

(a) the grant or variation of an environmental licence, or any application for, or for a variation of, such a licence;

(b) the subsistence of an environmental licence;

(c) the transfer (where permitted) of an environmental licence to another person, or any application for such a transfer;

(d) the renewal (where permitted) of an environmental licence, or any application for such a renewal;
(e) the surrender (where permitted) of an environmental licence, or any application for such a surrender; or
(f) any application for the revocation (where permitted) of an environmental licence.

(3) A charging scheme may, for the purposes of subsection (2)(b) above, impose—
(a) a single charge in respect of the whole of any relevant licensed period;
(b) separate charges in respect of different parts of any such period; or
(c) both such a single charge and such separate charges;

and in this subsection "relevant licensed period" means the period during which an environmental licence is in force or such part of that period as may be prescribed.

(4) Without prejudice to subsection (7)(a) below, a charging scheme may, as respects environmental licences, provide for different charges to be payable according to—
(a) the description of environmental licence in question;
(b) the description of authorised activity in question;
(c) the scale on which the authorised activity in question is carried on;
(d) the description or amount of the substance to which the authorised activity in question relates;
(e) the number of different authorised activities carried on by the same person.

(5) A charging scheme—
(a) shall specify, in relation to any charge prescribed by the scheme, the description of person who is liable to pay the charge; and
(b) may provide that it shall be a condition of an environmental licence of any particular description that any charge prescribed by a charging scheme in relation to an environmental licence of that description is paid in accordance with the scheme.

(6) Without prejudice to subsection (5)(b) above, if it appears to a new Agency that any charges due and payable to it in respect of the subsistence of an environmental licence have not been paid, it may, in accordance with the appropriate procedure, suspend or revoke the environmental licence to the extent that it authorises the carrying on of an authorised activity.

(7) A charging scheme may—
(a) make different provision for different cases, including different provision in relation to different persons, circumstances or localities;
(b) provide for the times at which, and the manner in which, the charges prescribed by the scheme are to be paid;
(c) revoke or amend any previous charging scheme;
(d) contain supplemental, incidental, consequential or transitional provision for the purposes of the scheme.

(8) If and to the extent that a charging scheme relates to licences under Chapter II of Part II of the 1991 Act (abstraction and impounding), the scheme shall have effect subject to any provision made by or under sections 125 to 130 of that Act (exemption from charges, imposition of special charges for spray irrigation, and charges in respect of abstraction from waters of the British Waterways Board).

(9) A new Agency shall not make a charging scheme unless the provisions of the scheme have been approved by the Secretary of State under section 42 below.

(10) In this section—
"the appropriate procedure" means such procedure as may be specified or described in regulations made for the purpose by the Secretary of State;
"authorised activity" means any activity to which an environmental licence relates.

(11) Any power to make regulations under this section shall be exercisable by statutory instrument; and a statutory instrument containing any such regulations shall be subject to annulment pursuant to a resolution of either House of Parliament.

[538]

NOTES

Commencement: 1 April 1996 (certain purposes); 1 February 1996 (certain purposes); 21 September 1995 (remaining purposes).

Regulations: the Environmental Licences (Suspension and Revocation) Regulations 1996, SI 1996/508.

42 Approval of charging schemes

(1) Before submitting a proposed charging scheme to the Secretary of State for his approval, a new Agency shall, in such manner as it considers appropriate for bringing it to the attention of persons likely to be affected by the scheme, publish a notice—

(a) setting out its proposals; and

(b) specifying the period within which representations or objections with respect to the proposals may be made to the Secretary of State.

(2) Where any proposed charging scheme has been submitted to the Secretary of State for his approval, he shall, in determining whether or not to approve the scheme or to approve it subject to modifications,—

(a) consider any representations or objections duly made to him and not withdrawn; and

(b) have regard to the matter specified in subsection (3) below.

(3) The matter mentioned in subsection (2)(b) above is the desirability of ensuring that, in the case of each of the descriptions of environmental licence specified in the paragraphs of the definition of that expression in section 56 below, the amounts recovered by the new Agency in question by way of charges prescribed by charging schemes are the amounts which, taking one year with another, need to be recovered by that new Agency to meet such of the costs and expenses (whether of a revenue or capital nature)—

(a) which it incurs in carrying out its functions,

(b) in the case of environmental licences which are authorisations under section 13(1) of the Radioactive Substances Act 1993—

(i) which the Minister incurs in carrying out his functions under or in consequence of that Act, and

(ii) which the Secretary of State incurs under that Act in carrying out in relation to Scotland or Wales such of his functions under or in consequence of that Act as are exercised by the Minister in relation to England,

as the Secretary of State may consider it appropriate to attribute to the carrying out of those functions in relation to activities to which environmental licences of the description in question relate.

(4) Without prejudice to the generality of the expression "costs and expenses", in determining for the purposes of subsection (3) above the amounts of the costs and expenses which the Secretary of State considers it appropriate to attribute to the carrying out of a new Agency's or the Minister's or the Secretary of State's functions in relation to the activities to which environmental licences of any particular description relate, the Secretary of State—

(a) shall take into account any determination of the new Agency's financial duties under section 44 below; and

(b) may include amounts in respect of the depreciation of, and the provision of a return on, such assets as are held by the new Agency, the Minister or the Secretary of State, as the case may be, for purposes connected with the carrying out of the functions in question.

(5)   If and to the extent that a charging scheme relates to any licence order under Chapter II of Part II of the 1991 Act (abstraction and impounding), the Secretary of State may consider it appropriate to attribute to the carrying out of the Agency's functions in relation to activities to which such a licence relates any costs and expenses incurred by the Agency in carrying out any of its functions under Part II of that Act or under section 6(2) above.

(6)   Subsection (5) above is without prejudice to what costs and expenses the Secretary of State may consider it appropriate to attribute to the carrying out of any functions of a new Agency, the Minister or the Secretary of State in relation to activities to which environmental licences of any particular description relate.

(7)   The consent of the Treasury shall be required for the giving of approval to a charging scheme and, if and to the extent that the scheme relates to authorisations by the Agency under section 13 of the Radioactive Substances Act 1993 (disposal of radioactive waste), the consent of the Minister shall also be required.

(8)   It shall be the duty of a new Agency to take such steps as it considers appropriate for bringing the provisions of any charging scheme made by it which is for the time being in force to the attention of persons likely to be affected by them.

(9)   If and to the extent that any sums recovered by a new Agency by way of charges prescribed by charging schemes may fairly be regarded as so recovered for the purpose of recovering the amount required to meet (whether in whole or in part)—

   (a) such of the costs and expenses incurred by the Secretary of State as fall within subsection (3) above, or
   (b) such of the costs and expenses incurred by the Minister as fall within that subsection,

those sums shall be paid by that new Agency to the Secretary of State or, as the case may be, to the Minister.

(10) For the purposes of subsection (9) above, any question as to the extent to which any sums may fairly be regarded as recovered for the purpose of recovering the amount required to meet the costs and expenses falling within paragraph (a) or paragraph (b) of that subsection shall be determined—

   (a) in the case of costs and expenses falling within paragraph (a) of that subsection, by the Secretary of State; and
   (b) in the case of costs and expenses falling within paragraph (b) of that subsection, by the Secretary of State and the Minister.

(11) In this section "charging scheme" has the same meaning as in section 41 above.

[539]

NOTES

Commencement: 21 September 1995.

Incidental power to impose charges

43 Incidental power of the new Agencies to impose charges

Without prejudice to the generality of its powers by virtue of section 37(1)(a) above and subject to any such express provision with respect to charging by a new Agency as is contained in the preceding provisions of this Chapter or any other enactment, each new Agency shall have power to fix and recover charges for services and facilities provided in the course of carrying out its functions.

[540]

NOTES

Commencement: 28 July 1995.

44–52   *(Relate to general financial provisions (ss 44–50); information (ss 51, 52).)*

Supplemental provisions

53–55   *(Relate to inquiries and other hearings (s 53); appearance in legal proceedings (s 54); continuity of exercise of functions: the new Agencies (s 55).)*

56 Interpretation of Part I

(1)   In this Part of this Act, except where the context otherwise requires—

. . . . .

"the 1990 Act" means the Environmental Protection Act 1990;

"the 1991 Act" means the Water Resources Act 1991;

"the appropriate Minister"—
(a) in the case of the Agency, means the Secretary of State or the Minister; and
(b) *(applies to Scotland only)*;

"the appropriate Ministers"—
(a) in the case of the Agency, means the Secretary of State and the Minister; and
(b) *(applies to Scotland only)*;

"conservancy authority" has the meaning given by section 221(1) of the 1991 Act;

"costs" includes—
(a) costs to any person; and
(b) costs to the environment;

"disposal authority"—
(a) in the application of this Part in relation to the Agency, has the same meaning as it has in Part I of the Control of Pollution Act 1974 by virtue of section 30(1) of that Act; and
(b) *(applies to Scotland only)*;

"the environment" has the same meaning as in Part I of the 1990 Act;

"environmental licence", in the application of this Part in relation to the Agency, means any of the following—
(a) registration of a person as a carrier of controlled waste under section 2 of the Control of Pollution (Amendment) Act 1989,
(b) an authorisation under Part I of the 1990 Act, other than any such authorisation granted by a local enforcing authority,
(c) a waste management licence under Part II of that Act,
(d) a licence under Chapter II of Part II of the 1991 Act,
(e) a consent for the purposes of section 88(1)(a), 89(4)(a) or 90 of that Act,
(f) registration under the Radioactive Substances Act 1993,
(g) an authorisation under that Act,
(h) registration of a person as a broker of controlled waste under the Waste Management Licensing Regulations 1994,
(j) registration in respect of an activity falling within paragraph 45(1) or (2) of Schedule 3 to those Regulations,
so far as having effect in relation to England and Wales;

. . . . .

"flood defence functions", in relation to the Agency, has the same meaning as in the 1991 Act;

"harbour authority" has the meaning given by section 221(1) of the 1991 Act;

"local authority", in the application of this Part in relation to SEPA, means a
district or islands council in Scotland;
"the Minister" means the Minister of Agriculture, Fisheries and Food;
"the Ministers" means the Secretary of State and the Minister;
"navigation authority" has the meaning given by section 221(1) of the 1991 Act;
"new Agency" means the Agency or SEPA;

. . . . .

"river purification board" means a river purification board established by virtue
of section 135 of the Local Government (Scotland) Act 1973;
"the transfer date" means such date as the Secretary of State may by order
made by statutory instrument appoint as the transfer date for the purposes
of this Part; and different dates may be appointed for the purposes of this
Part—
    (i) as it applies for or in connection with transfers under or by virtue of
        Chapter I above, and
   (ii) *(applies to Scotland only)*;
"waste regulation authority"—
    (a) in the application of this Part in relation to the Agency, means any
        authority in England or Wales which, by virtue of section 30(1) of the
        1990 Act, is a waste regulation authority for the purposes of Part II of
        that Act; and
    (b) *(applies to Scotland only)*.

(2)   *(Applies to Scotland only.)*

(3)   Where by virtue of any provision of this Part any function of a Minister of
the Crown is exercisable concurrently by different Ministers, that function shall also
be exercisable jointly by any two or more of those Ministers.

[541]

NOTES
  Commencement: 28 July 1995.
  Sub-s (1): definitions omitted apply to Scotland only.
  Orders: the Environment Agency (Transfer Date) Order 1996, SI 1996/234 (appointing 1 April 1996 for
the purposes of Pt I of this Act, as it applies for or in connection with transfers under or by virtue of Chapter I
of that Part); the Scottish Environment Protection Agency (Transfer Date) Order 1996, SI 1996/139.

57–79 *(Pt II (ss 57–60): s 57 inserts the Environmental Protection Act 1990, Pt IIA,
ss 78A–78YC at* **[159]–[184]**; *s 58 inserts the Water Resources Act 1991, Pt III, ss 91A,
91B at* **[357]**, **[358]**; *s 59 applies to Scotland only; s 60 amends the Water Resources Act
1991, ss 89, 161 at* **[352]**, **[372]**; *Pt III (ss 61–79) outside the scope of this work.)*

PART IV
AIR QUALITY

80 National air quality strategy

(1)   The Secretary of State shall as soon as possible prepare and publish a
statement (in this Part referred to as "the strategy") containing policies with respect
to the assessment or management of the quality of air.

(2)   The strategy may also contain policies for implementing—
    (a) obligations of the United Kingdom under the Community Treaties, or
    (b) international agreements to which the United Kingdom is for the time
        being a party,
so far as relating to the quality of air.

(3)   The strategy shall consist of or include—
   (a) a statement which relates to the whole of Great Britain; or
   (b) two or more statements which between them relate to every part of Great Britain.

(4)   The Secretary of State—
   (a) shall keep under review his policies with respect to the quality of air; and
   (b) may from time to time modify the strategy.

(5)   Without prejudice to the generality of what may be included in the strategy, the strategy must include statements with respect to—
   (a) standards relating to the quality of air;
   (b) objectives for the restriction of the levels at which particular substances are present in the air; and
   (c) measures which are to be taken by local authorities and other persons for the purpose of achieving those objectives.

(6)   In preparing the strategy or any modification of it, the Secretary of State shall consult—
   (a) the appropriate new Agency;
   (b) such bodies or persons appearing to him to be representative of the interests of local government as he may consider appropriate;
   (c) such bodies or persons appearing to him to be representative of the interests of industry as he may consider appropriate; and
   (d) such other bodies or persons as he may consider appropriate.

(7)   Before publishing the strategy or any modification of it, the Secretary of State—
   (a) shall publish a draft of the proposed strategy or modification, together with notice of a date before which, and an address at which, representations may be made to him concerning the draft so published; and
   (b) shall take into account any such representations which are duly made and not withdrawn.

                                                                      [542]

NOTES
Commencement: 1 February 1996.

81 Functions of the new Agencies

(1)   In discharging its pollution control functions, each new Agency shall have regard to the strategy.

(2)   In this section "pollution control functions", in relation to a new Agency, means—
   (a) in the case of the Agency, the functions conferred on it by or under the enactments specified in section 5(5) above; or
   (b) (*applies to Scotland only*).

                                                                      [543]

NOTES
Commencement: 1 April 1996.

82 Local authority reviews

(1)   Every local authority shall from time to time cause a review to be conducted of the quality for the time being, and the likely future quality within the relevant period, of air within the authority's area.

(2)   Where a local authority causes a review under subsection (1) above to be conducted, it shall also cause an assessment to be made of whether air quality standards and objectives are being achieved, or are likely to be achieved within the relevant period, within the authority's area.

(3) If, on an assessment under subsection (2) above, it appears that any air quality standards or objectives are not being achieved, or are not likely within the relevant period to be achieved, within the local authority's area, the local authority shall identify any parts of its area in which it appears that those standards or objectives are not likely to be achieved within the relevant period.

[544]

NOTES
Commencement: to be appointed.

83 Designation of air quality management areas

(1) Where, as a result of an air quality review, it appears that any air quality standards or objectives are not being achieved, or are not likely within the relevant period to be achieved, within the area of a local authority, the local authority shall by order designate as an air quality management area (in this Part referred to as a "designated area") any part of its area in which it appears that those standards or objectives are not being achieved, or are not likely to be achieved within the relevant period.

(2) An order under this section may, as a result of a subsequent air quality review,—
  (a) be varied by a subsequent order; or
  (b) be revoked by such an order, if it appears on that subsequent air quality review that the air quality standards and objectives are being achieved, and are likely throughout the relevant period to be achieved, within the designated area.

[545]

NOTES
Commencement: to be appointed.

84 Duties of local authorities in relation to designated areas

(1) Where an order under section 83 above comes into operation, the local authority which made the order shall, for the purpose of supplementing such information as it has in relation to the designated area in question, cause an assessment to be made of—
  (a) the quality for the time being, and the likely future quality within the relevant period, of air within the designated area to which the order relates; and
  (b) the respects (if any) in which it appears that air quality standards or objectives are not being achieved, or are not likely within the relevant period to be achieved, within that designated area.

(2) A local authority which is required by subsection (1) above to cause an assessment to be made shall also be under a duty—
  (a) to prepare, before the expiration of the period of twelve months beginning with the coming into operation of the order mentioned in that subsection, a report of the results of that assessment; and
  (b) to prepare, in accordance with the following provisions of this Part, a written plan (in this Part referred to as an "action plan") for the exercise by the authority, in pursuit of the achievement of air quality standards and objectives in the designated area, of any powers exercisable by the authority.

(3) An action plan shall include a statement of the time or times by or within which the local authority in question proposes to implement each of the proposed measures comprised in the plan.

(4) A local authority may from time to time revise an action plan.

(5) This subsection applies in any case where the local authority preparing an action plan or a revision of an action plan is the council of a district in England which is comprised in an area for which there is a county council; and if, in a case where this subsection applies, the county council disagrees with the authority about the contents of the proposed action plan or revision of the action plan—

(a) either of them may refer the matter to the Secretary of State;

(b) on any such reference the Secretary of State may confirm the authority's proposed action plan or revision of the action plan, with or without modifications (whether or not proposed by the county council) or reject it and, if he rejects it, he may also exercise any powers of his under section 85 below; and

(c) the authority shall not finally determine the content of the action plan, or the revision of the action plan, except in accordance with his decision on the reference or in pursuance of directions under section 85 below.

[546]

NOTES

Commencement: to be appointed.

85 Reserve powers of the Secretary of State or SEPA

(1) In this section, "the appropriate authority" means—

(a) in relation to England and Wales, the Secretary of State; and

(b) *(applies to Scotland only)*.

(2) The appropriate authority may conduct or make, or cause to be conducted or made,—

(a) a review of the quality for the time being, and the likely future quality within the relevant period, of air within the area of any local authority;

(b) an assessment of whether air quality standards and objectives are being achieved, or are likely to be achieved within the relevant period, within the area of a local authority;

(c) an identification of any parts of the area of a local authority in which it appears that those standards or objectives are not likely to be achieved within the relevant period; or

(d) an assessment of the respects (if any) in which it appears that air quality standards or objectives are not being achieved, or are not likely within the relevant period to be achieved, within the area of a local authority or within a designated area.

(3) If it appears to the appropriate authority—

(a) that air quality standards or objectives are not being achieved, or are not likely within the relevant period to be achieved, within the area of a local authority,

(b) that a local authority has failed to discharge any duty imposed on it under or by virtue of this Part,

(c) that the actions, or proposed actions, of a local authority in purported compliance with the provisions of this Part are inappropriate in all the circumstances of the case, or

(d) that developments in science or technology, or material changes in circumstances, have rendered inappropriate the actions or proposed actions of a local authority in pursuance of this Part,

the appropriate authority may give directions to the local authority requiring it to take such steps as may be specified in the directions.

(4) Without prejudice to the generality of subsection (3) above, directions under that subsection may, in particular, require a local authority—

(a) to cause an air quality review to be conducted under section 82 above in accordance with the directions;

(b) to cause an air quality review under section 82 above to be conducted afresh, whether in whole or in part, or to be so conducted with such differences as may be specified or described in the directions;

(c) to make an order under section 83 above designating as an air quality management area an area specified in, or determined in accordance with, the directions;

(d) to revoke, or modify in accordance with the directions, any order under that section;

(e) to prepare in accordance with the directions an action plan for a designated area;

(f) to modify, in accordance with the directions, any action plan prepared by the authority; or

(g) to implement, in accordance with the directions, any measures in an action plan.

(5)   The Secretary of State shall also have power to give directions to local authorities requiring them to take such steps specified in the directions as he considers appropriate for the implementation of—

(a) any obligations of the United Kingdom under the Community Treaties, or

(b) any international agreement to which the United Kingdom is for the time being a party,

so far as relating to the quality of air.

(6)   Any direction given under this section shall be published in such manner as the body or person giving it considers appropriate for the purpose of bringing the matters to which it relates to the attention of persons likely to be affected by them; and—

(a) copies of the direction shall be made available to the public; and

(b) notice shall be given—

(i) in the case of a direction given to a local authority in England and Wales, in the London Gazette, or

(ii) *(applies to Scotland only)*,

of the giving of the direction and of where a copy of the direction may be obtained.

(7)   It is the duty of a local authority to comply with any direction given to it under or by virtue of this Part.

[547]

NOTES

Commencement: to be appointed.

86 Functions of county councils for areas for which there are district councils

(1)   This section applies in any case where a district in England for which there is a district council is comprised in an area for which there is a county council; and in this paragraph—

(a) any reference to the county council is a reference to the council of that area; and

(b) any reference to a district council is a reference to the council of a district comprised in that area.

(2)   The county council may make recommendations to a district council with respect to the carrying out of—

(a) any particular air quality review,

(b) any particular assessment under section 82 or 84 above, or

(c) the preparation of any particular action plan or revision of an action plan,

and the district council shall take into account any such recommendations.

(3)   Where a district council is preparing an action plan, the county council shall, within the relevant period, submit to the district council proposals for the exercise (so far as relating to the designated area) by the county council, in pursuit of the achievement of air quality standards and objectives, of any powers exercisable by the county council.

(4)   Where the county council submits proposals to a district council in pursuance of subsection (3) above, it shall also submit a statement of the time or times by or within which it proposes to implement each of the proposals.

(5)   An action plan shall include a statement of—
(a) any proposals submitted pursuant to subsection (3) above; and
(b) any time or times set out in the statement submitted pursuant to subsection (4) above.

(6)   If it appears to the Secretary of State—
(a) that air quality standards or objectives are not being achieved, or are not likely within the relevant period to be achieved, within the area of a district council,
(b) that the county council has failed to discharge any duty imposed on it under or by virtue of this Part,
(c) that the actions, or proposed actions, of the county council in purported compliance with the provisions of this Part are inappropriate in all the circumstances of the case, or
(d) that developments in science or technology, or material changes in circumstances, have rendered inappropriate the actions or proposed actions of the county council in pursuance of this Part,

the Secretary of State may give directions to the county council requiring it to take such steps as may be specified in the directions.

(7)   Without prejudice to the generality of subsection (6) above, directions under that subsection may, in particular, require the county council—
(a) to submit, in accordance with the directions, proposals pursuant to subsection (3) above or a statement pursuant to subsection (4) above;
(b) to modify, in accordance with the directions, any proposals or statement submitted by the county council pursuant to subsection (3) or (4) above;
(c) to submit any proposals or statement so modified to the district council in question pursuant to subsection (3) or (4) above; or
(d) to implement, in accordance with the directions, any measures included in an action plan.

(8)   The Secretary of State shall also have power to give directions to county councils for areas for which there are district councils requiring them to take such steps specified in the directions as he considers appropriate for the implementation of—
(a) any obligations of the United Kingdom under the Community Treaties, or
(b) any international agreement to which the United Kingdom is for the time being a party,

so far as relating to the quality of air.

(9)   Any direction given under this section shall be published in such manner as the Secretary of State considers appropriate for the purpose of bringing the matters to which it relates to the attention of persons likely to be affected by them; and—
(a) copies of the direction shall be made available to the public; and
(b) notice of the giving of the direction, and of where a copy of the direction may be obtained, shall be given in the London Gazette.

(10) It is the duty of a county council for an area for which there are district councils to comply with any direction given to it under or by virtue of this Part.

NOTES
Commencement: to be appointed.

87 Regulations for the purposes of Part IV

(1) Regulations may make provision—
    (a) for, or in connection with, implementing the strategy;
    (b) for, or in connection with, implementing—
        (i) obligations of the United Kingdom under the Community Treaties, or
        (ii) international agreements to which the United Kingdom is for the time being a party,
    so far as relating to the quality of air; or
    (c) otherwise with respect to the assessment or management of the quality of air.

(2) Without prejudice to the generality of subsection (1) above, regulations under that subsection may make provision—
    (a) prescribing standards relating to the quality of air;
    (b) prescribing objectives for the restriction of the levels at which particular substances are present in the air;
    (c) conferring powers or imposing duties on local authorities;
    (d) for or in connection with—
        (i) authorising local authorities (whether by agreements or otherwise) to exercise any functions of a Minister of the Crown on his behalf;
        (ii) directing that functions of a Minister of the Crown shall be exercisable concurrently with local authorities; or
        (iii) transferring functions of a Minister of the Crown to local authorities;
    (e) prohibiting or restricting, or for or in connection with prohibiting or restricting,—
        (i) the carrying on of prescribed activities, or
        (ii) the access of prescribed vehicles or mobile equipment to prescribed areas,
    whether generally or in prescribed circumstances;
    (f) for or in connection with the designation of air quality management areas by orders made by local authorities in such cases or circumstances not falling within section 83 above as may be prescribed;
    (g) for the application, with or without modifications, of any provisions of this Part in relation to areas designated by virtue of paragraph (f) above or in relation to orders made by virtue of that paragraph;
    (h) with respect to—
        (i) air quality reviews;
        (ii) assessments under this Part;
        (iii) orders designating air quality management areas; or
        (iv) action plans;
    (j) prescribing measures which are to be adopted by local authorities (whether in action plans or otherwise) or other persons in pursuance of the achievement of air quality standards or objectives;
    (k) for or in connection with the communication to the public of information relating to quality for the time being, or likely future quality, of the air;
    (l) for or in connection with the obtaining by local authorities from any person of information which is reasonably necessary for the discharge of functions conferred or imposed on them under or by virtue of this Part;
    (m) for or in connection with the recovery by a local authority from prescribed persons in prescribed circumstances, and in such manner as may be prescribed, of costs incurred by the authority in discharging functions conferred or imposed on the authority under or by virtue of this Part;

(n) for a person who contravenes, or fails to comply with, any prescribed provision of the regulations to be guilty of an offence and liable on summary conviction to a fine not exceeding level 5 on the standard scale or such lower level on that scale as may be prescribed in relation to the offence;

(o) for or in connection with arrangements under which a person may discharge any liability to conviction for a prescribed offence by payment of a penalty of a prescribed amount;

(p) for or in connection with appeals against determinations or decisions made, notices given or served, or other things done under or by virtue of the regulations.

(3) Without prejudice to the generality of paragraph (h) of subsection (2) above, the provision that may be made by virtue of that paragraph includes provision for or in connection with any of the following, that is to say—

(a) the scope or form of a review or assessment;

(b) the scope, content or form of an action plan;

(c) the time at which, period within which, or manner in which a review or assessment is to be carried out or an action plan is to be prepared;

(d) the methods to be employed—
    (i) in carrying out reviews or assessments; or
    (ii) in monitoring the effectiveness of action plans;

(e) the factors to be taken into account in preparing action plans;

(f) the actions which must be taken by local authorities or other persons in consequence of reviews, assessments or action plans;

(g) requirements for consultation;

(h) the treatment of representations or objections duly made;

(j) the publication of, or the making available to the public of, or of copies of,—
    (i) the results, or reports of the results, of reviews or assessments; or
    (ii) orders or action plans;

(k) requirements for—
    (i) copies of any such reports, orders or action plans, or
    (ii) prescribed information, in such form as may be prescribed, relating to reviews or assessments,
    to be sent to the Secretary of State or to the appropriate new Agency.

(4) In determining—

(a) any appeal against, or reference or review of, a decision of a local authority under or by virtue of regulations under this Part, or

(b) any application transmitted from a local authority under or by virtue of any such regulations,

the body or person making the determination shall be bound by any direction given by a Minister of the Crown or SEPA to the local authority to the same extent as the local authority.

(5) The provisions of any regulations under this Part may include—

(a) provision for anything that may be prescribed by the regulations to be determined under the regulations and for anything falling to be so determined to be determined by such persons, in accordance with such procedure and by reference to such matters, and to the opinion of such persons, as may be prescribed;

(b) different provision for different cases, including different provision in relation to different persons, circumstances, areas or localities; and

(c) such supplemental, consequential, incidental or transitional provision (including provision amending any enactment or any instrument made under any enactment) as the Secretary of State considers appropriate.

(6) Nothing in regulations under this Part shall authorise any person other than a constable in uniform to stop a vehicle on any road.

(7)   Before making any regulations under this Part, the Secretary of State shall consult—
  (a) the appropriate new Agency;
  (b) such bodies or persons appearing to him to be representative of the interests of local government as he may consider appropriate;
  (c) such bodies or persons appearing to him to be representative of the interests of industry as he may consider appropriate; and
  (d) such other bodies or persons as he may consider appropriate.

(8)   Any power conferred by this Part to make regulations shall be exercisable by statutory instrument; and no statutory instrument containing regulations under this Part shall be made unless a draft of the instrument has been laid before, and approved by a resolution of, each House of Parliament.

(9)   If, apart from this subsection, the draft of an instrument containing regulations under this Part would be treated for the purposes of the Standing Orders of either House of Parliament as a hybrid instrument, it shall proceed in that House as if it were not such an instrument.

[549]

NOTES
   Commencement: 1 February 1996.

88 Guidance for the purposes of Part IV

(1)   The Secretary of State may issue guidance to local authorities with respect to, or in connection with, the exercise of any of the powers conferred, or the discharge of any of the duties imposed, on those authorities by or under this Part.

(2)   A local authority, in carrying out any of its functions under or by virtue of this Part, shall have regard to any guidance issued by the Secretary of State under this Part.

(3)   This section shall apply in relation to county councils for areas for which there are district councils as it applies in relation to local authorities.

[550]

NOTES
   Commencement: 1 February 1996.

89 Application of Part IV to the Isles of Scilly

(1)   Subject to the provisions of any order under this section, this Part, other than section 80, shall not apply in relation to the Isles of Scilly.

(2)   The Secretary of State may, after consultation with the Council of the Isles of Scilly, by order provide for the application of any provisions of this Part (other than section 80) to the Isles of Scilly; and any such order may provide for the application of those provisions to those Isles with such modifications as may be specified in the order.

(3)   An order under this section may—
  (a) make different provision for different cases, including different provision in relation to different persons, circumstances or localities; and
  (b) contain such supplemental, consequential and transitional provision as the Secretary of State considers appropriate, including provision saving provision repealed by or under any enactment.

(4)   The power of the Secretary of State to make an order under this section shall be exercisable by statutory instrument; and a statutory instrument containing such an order shall be subject to annulment in pursuance of a resolution of either House of Parliament.

[551]

90 Supplemental provisions

Schedule 11 to this Act shall have effect.

[552]

91 Interpretation of Part IV

(1)   In this Part—
"action plan" shall be construed in accordance with section 84(2)(b) above;
"air quality objectives" means objectives prescribed by virtue of section 87(2)(b) above;
"air quality review" means a review under section 82 or 85 above;
"air quality standards" means standards prescribed by virtue of section 87(2)(a) above;
"the appropriate new Agency" means—
  (a) in relation to England and Wales, the Agency;
  (b) (*applies to Scotland only*);
"designated area" has the meaning given by section 83(1) above;
"local authority", in relation to England and Wales, means—
  (a) any unitary authority,
  (b) any district council, so far as it is not a unitary authority,
  (c) the Common Council of the City of London and, as respects the Temples, the Sub-Treasurer of the Inner Temple and the Under-Treasurer of the Middle Temple respectively,
and, in relation to Scotland, means a council for an area constituted under section 2 of the Local Government etc (Scotland) Act 1994;
"new Agency" means the Agency or SEPA;
"prescribed" means prescribed, or of a description prescribed, by or under regulations;
"regulations" means regulations made by the Secretary of State;
"the relevant period", in the case of any provision of this Part, means such period as may be prescribed for the purposes of that provision;
"the strategy" has the meaning given by section 80(1) above;
"unitary authority" means—
  (a) the council of a county, so far as it is the council of an area for which there are no district councils;
  (b) the council of any district comprised in an area for which there is no county council;
  (c) the council of a London borough;
  (d) the council of a county borough in Wales.

(2)   Any reference in this Part to it appearing that any air quality standards or objectives are not likely within the relevant period to be achieved includes a reference to it appearing that those standards or objectives are likely within that period not to be achieved.

[553]–[554]

PART V
MISCELLANEOUS, GENERAL AND SUPPLEMENTAL PROVISIONS

Waste

92 (*Amends the Environmental Protection Act 1990, ss 44A at* **[134]**, *44B, Sch 2A at* **[245]**.)

93 Producer responsibility: general

(1)   For the purpose of promoting or securing an increase in the re-use, recovery or recycling of products or materials, the Secretary of State may by regulations make provision for imposing producer responsibility obligations on such persons, and in respect of such products or materials, as may be prescribed.

(2)   The power of the Secretary of State to make regulations shall be exercisable only after consultation with bodies or persons appearing to him to be representative of bodies or persons whose interests are, or are likely to be, substantially affected by the regulations which he proposes to make.

(3)   Except in the case of regulations for the implementation of—
   (a) any obligations of the United Kingdom under the Community Treaties, or
   (b) any international agreement to which the United Kingdom is for the time being a party,

the power to make regulations shall be exercisable only where the Secretary of State, after such consultation as is required by subsection (2) above, is satisfied as to the matters specified in subsection (6) below.

(4)   The powers conferred by subsection (1) above shall also be exercisable, in a case falling within paragraph (a) or (b) of subsection (3) above, for the purpose of sustaining at least a minimum level of (rather than promoting or securing an increase in) re-use, recovery or recycling of products or materials.

(5)   In making regulations by virtue of paragraph (a) or (b) of subsection (3) above, the Secretary of State shall have regard to the matters specified in subsection (6) below; and in its application in relation to the power conferred by virtue of subsection (4) above, subsection (6) below shall have effect as if—
   (a) any reference to an increase in the re-use, recovery or recycling of products or materials were a reference to the sustaining of at least a minimum level of re-use, recovery or recycling of the products or materials in question, and
   (b) any reference to the production of environmental or economic benefits included a reference to the sustaining of at least a minimum level of any such existing benefits,

and any reference in this section or section 94 below to securing or achieving any such benefits shall accordingly include a reference to sustaining at least a minimum level of any such existing benefits.

(6)   The matters mentioned in subsections (3) and (5) above are—
   (a) that the proposed exercise of the power would be likely to result in an increase in the re-use, recovery or recycling of the products or materials in question;
   (b) that any such increase would produce environmental or economic benefits;
   (c) that those benefits are significant as against the likely costs resulting from the imposition of the proposed producer responsibility obligation;
   (d) that the burdens imposed on businesses by the regulations are the minimum necessary to secure those benefits; and

(e) that those burdens are imposed on persons most able to make a contribution to the achievement of the relevant targets—
(i) having regard to the desirability of acting fairly between persons who manufacture, process, distribute or supply products or materials; and
(ii) taking account of the need to ensure that the proposed producer responsibility obligation is so framed as to be effective in achieving the purposes for which it is to be imposed;

but nothing in sub-paragraph (i) of paragraph (e) above shall be taken to prevent regulations imposing a producer responsibility obligation on any class or description of person to the exclusion of any others.

(7) The Secretary of State shall have a duty to exercise the power to make regulations in the manner which he considers best calculated to secure that the exercise does not have the effect of restricting, distorting or preventing competition or, if it is likely to have any such effect, that the effect is no greater than is necessary for achieving the environmental or economic benefits mentioned in subsection (6) above.

(8) In this section—
"prescribed" means prescribed in regulations;
"product" and "material" include a reference to any product or material (as the case may be) at a time when it becomes, or has become, waste;
"producer responsibility obligation" means the steps which are required to be taken by relevant persons of the classes or descriptions to which the regulations in question apply in order to secure attainment of the targets specified or described in the regulations;
"recovery", in relation to products or materials, includes—
(a) composting, or any other form of transformation by biological processes, of products or materials; or
(b) the obtaining, by any means, of energy from products or materials;
"regulations" means regulations under this section;
"relevant persons", in the case of any regulations or any producer responsibility obligation, means persons of the class or description to which the producer responsibility obligation imposed by the regulations applies;
"relevant targets" means the targets specified or described in the regulations imposing the producer responsibility obligation in question;

and regulations may prescribe, in relation to prescribed products or materials, activities, or the activities, which are to be regarded for the purposes of this section and sections 94 and 95 below or any regulations as re-use, recovery or recycling of those products or materials.

(9) The power to make regulations shall be exercisable by statutory instrument.

(10) Subject to the following provisions of this section, a statutory instrument containing regulations shall not be made unless a draft of the instrument has been laid before and approved by a resolution of each House of Parliament.

(11) Subsection (10) above shall not apply to a statutory instrument by reason only that it contains regulations varying any relevant targets.

(12) A statutory instrument which, by virtue of subsection (11) above, is not subject to any requirement that a draft of the instrument be laid before and approved by a resolution of each House of Parliament shall be subject to annulment in pursuance of a resolution of either House of Parliament.

[555]

NOTES

Commencement: 21 September 1995.

Regulations: the Producer Responsibility Obligations (Packaging Waste) Regulations 1997, SI 1997/648.

94 Producer responsibility: supplementary provisions

(1)   Without prejudice to the generality of section 93 above, regulations may, in particular, make provision for or with respect to—
   (a) the classes or descriptions of person to whom the producer responsibility obligation imposed by the regulations applies;
   (b) the classes or descriptions of products or materials in respect of which the obligation applies;
   (c) the targets which are to be achieved with respect to the proportion (whether by weight, volume or otherwise) of the products or materials in question which are to be re-used, recovered or recycled, whether generally or in any prescribed way;
   (d) particulars of the obligation imposed by the regulations;
   (e) the registration of persons who are subject to a producer responsibility obligation and who are not members of registered exemption schemes, the imposition of requirements in connection with such registration, the variation of such requirements, the making of applications for such registration, the period for which any such registration is to remain in force and the cancellation of any such registration;
   (f) the approval, or withdrawal of approval, of exemption schemes by the Secretary of State;
   (g) the imposition of requirements on persons who are not members of registered exemption schemes to furnish certificates of compliance to the appropriate Agency;
   (h) the approval of persons by the appropriate Agency for the purpose of issuing certificates of compliance;
   (j) the registration of exemption schemes, the imposition of conditions in connection with such registration, the variation of such conditions, the making of applications for such registration and the period for which any such registration is to remain in force;
   (k) the requirements which must be fulfilled, and the criteria which must be met, before an exemption scheme may be registered;
   (l) the powers of the appropriate Agency in relation to applications received by it for registration of exemption schemes;
   (m) the cancellation of the registration of an exemption scheme;
   (n) competition scrutiny of registered exemption schemes or of exemption schemes in whose case applications for registration have been received by the appropriate Agency;
   (o) the exclusion or modification of any provision of the Restrictive Trade Practices Acts 1976 and 1977 in relation to exemption schemes or in relation to agreements where at least one of the parties is an operator of an exemption scheme;
   (p) the fees, or the method of determining the fees, which are to be paid to the appropriate Agency—
      (i) in respect of the approval of persons for the purpose of issuing certificates of compliance;
      (ii) on the making of an application for registration of an exemption scheme;
      (iii) in respect of the subsistence of the registration of that scheme;
      (iv) on submission to the appropriate Agency of a certificate of compliance;
      (v) on the making of an application for, or for the renewal of, registration of a person required to register under the regulations;
      (vi) in respect of the renewal of the registration of that person;

(q) appeals against the refusal of registration, the imposition of conditions in connection with registration, or the cancellation of the registration, of any exemption scheme;

(r) the procedure on any such appeal;

(s) cases, or classes of case,—
  (i) in which an exemption scheme is, or is not, to be treated as registered, or
  (ii) in which a person is, or is not, to be treated as a member of a registered exemption scheme,

  pending the determination or withdrawal of an appeal, and otherwise with respect to the position of persons and exemption schemes pending such determination or withdrawal;

(t) the imposition on the appropriate Agency of a duty to monitor compliance with any of the obligations imposed by the regulations.;

(u) the imposition on prescribed persons of duties to maintain records, and furnish to the Secretary of State or to the appropriate Agency returns, in such form as may be prescribed of such information as may be prescribed for any purposes of, or for any purposes connected with, or related to, sections 93 to 95 of this Act or any regulations;

(w) the imposition on the appropriate Agency of a duty to maintain, and make available for inspection by the public, a register containing prescribed information relating to registered exemption schemes or persons required to register under the regulations;

(y) the powers of entry and inspection which are exercisable by a new Agency for the purposes of its functions under the regulations;

(ya) the conferring on prescribed persons of power to require, for the purposes of or otherwise in connection with competition scrutiny, the provision by any person of any information which he has, or which he may at any future time acquire, relating to any exemption scheme or to any acts or omissions of an operator of such a scheme or of any person dealing with such an operator.

(2) If it appears to the Secretary of State—
  (a) that any action proposed to be taken by the operator of a registered exemption scheme would be incompatible with—
    (i) any obligations of the United Kingdom under the Community Treaties, or
    (ii) any international agreement to which the United Kingdom is for the time being a party, or
  (b) that any action which the operator of such a scheme has power to take is required for the purpose of implementing any such obligations or agreement,

he may direct that operator not to take or, as the case may be, to take the action in question.

(3) Regulations may make provision as to which of the new Agencies is the appropriate Agency for the purposes of any function conferred or imposed by or under this section or section 93 above, or for the purposes of the exercise of that function in relation to the whole or a prescribed part of Great Britain, and may make provision for things done or omitted to be done by either new Agency in relation to any part of Great Britain to be treated for prescribed purposes as done or omitted to be done by the other of them in relation to some other part of Great Britain.

(4) Persons issuing certificates of compliance shall act in accordance with guidance issued for the purpose by the appropriate Agency, which may include guidance as to matters which are, or are not, to be treated as evidence of compliance or as evidence of non-compliance.

(5)   In making any provision in relation to fees, regard shall be had to the desirability of securing that the fees received by each new Agency under the regulations are sufficient to meet the costs and expenses incurred by that Agency in the performance of its functions under the regulations.

(6)   In this section—
"the appropriate Agency", subject to regulations made by virtue of subsection (3) above, means—
  (a) in relation to England and Wales, the Agency;
  (b) *(applies to Scotland only)*;
"certificate of compliance" means a certificate issued by a person approved for the purpose by the appropriate Agency to the effect that that person is satisfied that the person in respect of whom the certificate is issued is complying with any producer responsibility obligation to which he is subject;
"competition scrutiny", in the case of any scheme, means scrutiny of the scheme for the purpose of enabling the Secretary of State to satisfy himself—
  (i) whether or not the scheme has or is likely to have the effect of restricting, distorting or preventing competition or, if it appears to him that the scheme has or is likely to have any such effect, that the effect is or is likely to be no greater than is necessary for achieving the environmental or economic benefits mentioned in section 93(6) above; or
  (ii) whether or not the scheme leads or is likely to lead to an abuse of market power;
"exemption scheme" means a scheme which is (or, if it were to be registered in accordance with the regulations, would be) a scheme whose members for the time being are, by virtue of the regulations and their membership of that scheme, exempt from the requirement to comply with the producer responsibility obligation imposed by the regulations;
"new Agency" means the Agency or SEPA;
"operator", in relation to an exemption scheme, includes any person responsible for establishing, maintaining or managing the scheme;
"registered exemption scheme" means an exemption scheme which is registered pursuant to regulations;

and expressions used in this section and in section 93 above have the same meaning in this section as they have in that section.

(7)   Regulations—
  (a) may make different provision for different cases;
  (b) without prejudice to the generality of paragraph (a) above, may impose different producer responsibility obligations in respect of different classes or descriptions of products or materials and for different classes or descriptions of person or exemption scheme;
  (c) may include incidental, consequential, supplemental or transitional provision.

(8)   Any direction under this section—
  (a) may include such incidental, consequential, supplemental or transitional provision as the Secretary of State considers necessary or expedient; and
  (b) shall, on the application of the Secretary of State, be enforceable by injunction or, in Scotland, by interdict or by an order for specific performance under section 45 of the Court of Session Act 1988.

[556]

NOTES
Commencement: 21 September 1995.
Regulations: the Producer Responsibility Obligations (Packaging Waste) Regulations 1997, SI 1997/648.

95 Producer responsibility: offences

(1)   Regulations may make provision for a person who contravenes a prescribed requirement of the regulations to be guilty of an offence and liable—
    (a) on summary conviction, to a fine not exceeding the statutory maximum;
    (b) on conviction on indictment, to a fine.

(2)   Where an offence under any provision of the regulations committed by a body corporate is proved to have been committed with the consent or connivance of, or to have been attributable to any neglect on the part of, any director, manager, secretary or other similar officer of the body corporate or a person who was purporting to act in any such capacity, he as well as the body corporate shall be guilty of that offence and shall be liable to be proceeded against and punished accordingly.

(3)   Where the affairs of a body corporate are managed by its members, subsection (2) above shall apply in relation to the acts or defaults of a member in connection with his functions of management as if he were a director of the body corporate.

(4)   Where the commission by any person of an offence under the regulations is due to the act or default of some other person, that other person may be charged with and convicted of the offence by virtue of this section whether or not proceedings for the offence are taken against the first-mentioned person.

(5)   Expressions used in this section and in section 93 or 94 above have the same meaning in this section as they have in that section.

[557]

NOTES

Commencement: 21 September 1995.

96–107   *(Relate to mineral planning permissions (s 96); hedgerows etc (ss 97–99); ss 100, 101 amend the Water Resources Act 1991, ss 113(1), 147, the Land Drainage Act 1991, ss 59, 72(1); s 102 amends the Sea Fisheries Regulation Act 1966, ss 2, 8, and inserts s 5A of that Act; s 103 inserts the Sea Fish (Conservation) Act 1967, s 5A, the Water Resources Act 1991, Sch 25, para 6A, remainder applies to Scotland only; s 104 inserts the Salmon and Freshwater Fisheries Act 1975, s 37A and amends ss 35, 41(1) of that Act; s 105 introduces Sch 15 to this Act; s 106 applies to Scotland only; s 107 introduces Sch 17 to this Act.)*

Powers of entry

108 Powers of enforcing authorities and persons authorised by them

(1)   A person who appears suitable to an enforcing authority may be authorised in writing by that authority to exercise, in accordance with the terms of the authorisation, any of the powers specified in subsection (4) below for the purpose—
    (a) of determining whether any provision of the pollution control enactments in the case of that authority is being, or has been, complied with;
    (b) of exercising or performing one or more of the pollution control functions of that authority; or
    (c) of determining whether and, if so, how such a function should be exercised or performed.

(2)   A person who appears suitable to the Agency or SEPA may be authorised in writing by the Agency or, as the case may be, SEPA to exercise, in accordance with the terms of the authorisation, any of the powers specified in subsection (4) below

for the purpose of enabling the Agency or, as the case may be, SEPA to carry out any assessment or prepare any report which the Agency or, as the case may be, SEPA is required to carry out or prepare under section 5(3) or 33(3) above.

(3) Subsection (2) above only applies where the Minister who required the assessment to be carried out, or the report to be prepared, has, whether at the time of making the requirement or at any later time, notified the Agency or, as the case may be, SEPA that the assessment or report appears to him to relate to an incident or possible incident involving or having the potential to involve—
  (a) serious pollution of the environment,
  (b) serious harm to human health, or
  (c) danger to life or health.

(4) The powers which a person may be authorised to exercise under subsection (1) or (2) above are—
  (a) to enter at any reasonable time (or, in an emergency, at any time and, if need be, by force) any premises which he has reason to believe it is necessary for him to enter;
  (b) on entering any premises by virtue of paragraph (a) above, to take with him—
    (i) any other person duly authorised by the enforcing authority and, if the authorised person has reasonable cause to apprehend any serious obstruction in the execution of his duty, a constable; and
    (ii) any equipment or materials required for any purpose for which the power of entry is being exercised;
  (c) to make such examination and investigation as may in any circumstances be necessary;
  (d) as regards any premises which he has power to enter, to direct that those premises or any part of them, or anything in them, shall be left undisturbed (whether generally or in particular respects) for so long as is reasonably necessary for the purpose of any examination or investigation under paragraph (c) above;
  (e) to take such measurements and photographs and make such recordings as he considers necessary for the purpose of any examination or investigation under paragraph (c) above;
  (f) to take samples, or cause samples to be taken, of any articles or substances found in or on any premises which he has power to enter, and of the air, water or land in, on, or in the vicinity of, the premises;
  (g) in the case of any article or substance found in or on any premises which he has power to enter, being an article or substance which appears to him to have caused or to be likely to cause pollution of the environment or harm to human health, to cause it to be dismantled or subjected to any process or test (but not so as to damage or destroy it, unless that is necessary);
  (h) in the case of any such article or substance as is mentioned in paragraph (g) above, to take possession of it and detain it for so long as is necessary for all or any of the following purposes, namely—
    (i) to examine it, or cause it to be examined, and to do, or cause to be done, to it anything which he has power to do under that paragraph;
    (ii) to ensure that it is not tampered with before examination of it is completed;
    (iii) to ensure that it is available for use as evidence in any proceedings for an offence under the pollution control enactments in the case of the enforcing authority under whose authorisation he acts or in any other proceedings relating to a variation notice, enforcement notice or prohibition notice under those enactments;
  (j) to require any person whom he has reasonable cause to believe to be able to give any information relevant to any examination or investigation under paragraph (c) above to answer (in the absence of persons other than a

person nominated by that person to be present and any persons whom the authorised person may allow to be present) such questions as the authorised person thinks fit to ask and to sign a declaration of the truth of his answers;

(k) to require the production of, or where the information is recorded in computerised form, the furnishing of extracts from, any records—

    (i) which are required to be kept under the pollution control enactments for the enforcing authority under whose authorisation he acts, or

    (ii) which it is necessary for him to see for the purposes of an examination or investigation under paragraph (c) above,

and to inspect and take copies of, or of any entry in, the records;

(l) to require any person to afford him such facilities and assistance with respect to any matters or things within that person's control or in relation to which that person has responsibilities as are necessary to enable the authorised person to exercise any of the powers conferred on him by this section;

(m) any other power for—

    (i) a purpose falling within any paragraph of subsection (1) above, or

    (ii) any such purpose as is mentioned in subsection (2) above,

which is conferred by regulations made by the Secretary of State.

(5)   The powers which by virtue of subsections (1) and (4) above are conferred in relation to any premises for the purpose of enabling an enforcing authority to determine whether any provision of the pollution control enactments in the case of that authority is being, or has been, complied with shall include power, in order to obtain the information on which that determination may be made,—

(a) to carry out experimental borings or other works on those premises; and

(b) to install, keep or maintain monitoring and other apparatus there.

(6)   Except in an emergency, in any case where it is proposed to enter any premises used for residential purposes, or to take heavy equipment on to any premises which are to be entered, any entry by virtue of this section shall only be effected—

(a) after the expiration of at least seven days' notice of the proposed entry given to a person who appears to the authorised person in question to be in occupation of the premises in question, and

(b) either—

    (i) with the consent of a person who is in occupation of those premises; or

    (ii) under the authority of a warrant by virtue of Schedule 18 to this Act.

(7)   Except in an emergency, where an authorised person proposes to enter any premises and—

(a) entry has been refused and he apprehends on reasonable grounds that the use of force may be necessary to effect entry, or

(b) he apprehends on reasonable grounds that entry is likely to be refused and that the use of force may be necessary to effect entry,

any entry on to those premises by virtue of this section shall only be effected under the authority of a warrant by virtue of Schedule 18 to this Act.

(8)   In relation to any premises belonging to or used for the purposes of the United Kingdom Atomic Energy Authority, subsections (1) to (4) above shall have effect subject to section 6(3) of the Atomic Energy Authority Act 1954 (which restricts entry to such premises where they have been declared to be prohibited places for the purposes of the Official Secrets Act 1911).

(9)   The Secretary of State may by regulations make provision as to the procedure to be followed in connection with the taking of, and the dealing with, samples under subsection (4)(f) above.

(10) Where an authorised person proposes to exercise the power conferred by subsection (4)(g) above in the case of an article or substance found on any premises, he shall, if so requested by a person who at the time is present on and has responsibilities in relation to those premises, cause anything which is to be done by virtue of that power to be done in the presence of that person.

(11) Before exercising the power conferred by subsection (4)(g) above in the case of any article or substance, an authorised person shall consult—
   (a) such persons having duties on the premises where the article or substance is to be dismantled or subjected to the process or test, and
   (b) such other persons,
as appear to him appropriate for the purpose of ascertaining what dangers, if any, there may be in doing anything which he proposes to do or cause to be done under the power.

(12) No answer given by a person in pursuance of a requirement imposed under subsection (4)(j) above shall be admissible in evidence in England and Wales against that person in any proceedings, or in Scotland against that person in any criminal proceedings.

(13) Nothing in this section shall be taken to compel the production by any person of a document of which he would on grounds of legal professional privilege be entitled to withhold production on an order for discovery in an action in the High Court or, in relation to Scotland, on an order for the production of documents in an action in the Court of Session.

(14) Schedule 18 to this Act shall have effect with respect to the powers of entry and related powers which are conferred by this section.

(15) In this section—
   "authorised person" means a person authorised under subsection (1) or (2) above;
   "emergency" means a case in which it appears to the authorised person in question—
      (a) that there is an immediate risk of serious pollution of the environment or serious harm to human health, or
      (b) that circumstances exist which are likely to endanger life or health,
      and that immediate entry to any premises is necessary to verify the existence of that risk or those circumstances or to ascertain the cause of that risk or those circumstances or to effect a remedy;
   "enforcing authority" means—
      (a) the Secretary of State;
      (b) the Agency;
      (c) *(applies to Scotland only)*; or
      (d) a local enforcing authority;
   "local enforcing authority" means—
      (a) a local enforcing authority, within the meaning of Part I of the Environmental Protection Act 1990;
      (b) a local authority, within the meaning of Part IIA of that Act, in its capacity as an enforcing authority for the purposes of that Part;
      (c) a local authority for the purposes of Part IV of this Act or regulations under that Part;
   "mobile plant" means plant which is designed to move or to be moved whether on roads or otherwise;
   "pollution control enactments", in relation to an enforcing authority, means the enactments and instruments relating to the pollution control functions of that authority;
   "pollution control functions", in relation to the Agency or SEPA, means the functions conferred or imposed on it by or under—

    (a) the Alkali, &c, Works Regulation Act 1906;
(b), (c) (*apply to Scotland only*);
    (d) Part I of the Health and Safety at Work etc Act 1974;
    (e) Parts I, IA and II of the Control of Pollution Act 1974;
    (f) the Control of Pollution (Amendment) Act 1989;
    (g) Parts I, II and IIA of the Environmental Protection Act 1990 (integrated pollution control, waste on land and contaminated land);
    (h) Chapter III of Part IV of the Water Industry Act 1991 (special category effluent);
    (j) Part III and sections 161 to 161D of the Water Resources Act 1991;
    (k) section 19 of the Clean Air Act 1993;
    (l) the Radioactive Substances Act 1993;
    (m) regulations made by virtue of section 2(2) of the European Communities Act 1972, to the extent that the regulations relate to pollution;
"pollution control functions", in relation to a local enforcing authority, means the functions conferred or imposed on, or transferred to, that authority—
    (a) by or under Part I or IIA of the Environmental Protection Act 1990;
    (b) by or under regulations made by virtue of Part IV of this Act; or
    (c) by or under regulations made by virtue of section 2(2) of the European Communities Act 1972, to the extent that the regulations relate to pollution;
"pollution control functions", in relation to the Secretary of State, means any functions which are conferred or imposed upon him by or under any enactment or instrument and which relate to the control of pollution;
"premises" includes any land, vehicle, vessel or mobile plant.

(16) Any power to make regulations under this section shall be exercisable by statutory instrument; and a statutory instrument containing any such regulations shall be subject to annulment pursuant to a resolution of either House of Parliament.

[558]

NOTES
   Commencement: 1 April 1996.

109 Power to deal with cause of imminent danger of serious pollution etc

(1)   Where, in the case of any article or substance found by him on any premises which he has power to enter, an authorised person has reasonable cause to believe that, in the circumstances in which he finds it, the article or substance is a cause of imminent danger of serious pollution of the environment or serious harm to human health, he may seize it and cause it to be rendered harmless (whether by destruction or otherwise).

(2)   As soon as may be after any article or substance has been seized and rendered harmless under this section, the authorised person shall prepare and sign a written report giving particulars of the circumstances in which the article or substance was seized and so dealt with by him, and shall—
    (a) give a signed copy of the report to a responsible person at the premises where the article or substance was found by him; and
    (b) unless that person is the owner of the article or substance, also serve a signed copy of the report on the owner;
and if, where paragraph (b) above applies, the authorised person cannot after reasonable inquiry ascertain the name or address of the owner, the copy may be served on him by giving it to the person to whom a copy was given under paragraph (a) above.

(3)   In this section, "authorised person" has the same meaning as in section 108 above.

[559]

NOTES
Commencement: 1 April 1996.

110 Offences

(1)   It is an offence for a person intentionally to obstruct an authorised person in the exercise or performance of his powers or duties.

(2)   It is an offence for a person, without reasonable excuse,—
    (a) to fail to comply with any requirement imposed under section 108 above;
    (b) to fail or refuse to provide facilities or assistance or any information or to permit any inspection reasonably required by an authorised person in the execution of his powers or duties under or by virtue of that section; or
    (c) to prevent any other person from appearing before an authorised person, or answering any question to which an authorised person may require an answer, pursuant to subsection (4) of that section.

(3)   It is an offence for a person falsely to pretend to be an authorised person.

(4)   A person guilty of an offence under subsection (1) above shall be liable—
    (a) in the case of an offence of obstructing an authorised person in the execution of his powers under section 109 above—
        (i) on summary conviction, to a fine not exceeding the statutory maximum;
        (ii) on conviction on indictment, to a fine or to imprisonment for a term not exceeding two years, or to both;
    (b) in any other case, on summary conviction, to a fine not exceeding level 5 on the standard scale.

(5)   A person guilty of an offence under subsection (2) or (3) above shall be liable on summary conviction to a fine not exceeding level 5 on the standard scale.

(6)   In this section—
"authorised person" means a person authorised under section 108 above and includes a person designated under paragraph 2 of Schedule 18 to this Act;
"powers and duties" includes powers or duties exercisable by virtue of a warrant under Schedule 18 to this Act.

[560]

NOTES
Commencement: 1 April 1996.

Evidence

111 Evidence in connection with certain pollution offences

(1)   . . .

(2)   Information provided or obtained pursuant to or by virtue of a condition of a relevant licence (including information so provided or obtained, or recorded, by means of any apparatus) shall be admissible in evidence in any proceedings, whether against the person subject to the condition or any other person.

(3)   For the purposes of subsection (2) above, apparatus shall be presumed in any proceedings to register or record accurately, unless the contrary is shown or the relevant licence otherwise provides.

(4)   Where—
    (a) by virtue of a condition of a relevant licence, an entry is required to be made in any record as to the observance of any condition of the relevant licence, and
    (b) the entry has not been made,

that fact shall be admissible in any proceedings as evidence that that condition has not been observed.

(5)   In this section—

"apparatus" includes any meter or other device for measuring, assessing, determining, recording or enabling to be recorded, the volume, temperature, radioactivity, rate, nature, origin, composition or effect of any substance, flow, discharge, emission, deposit or abstraction;

"condition of a relevant licence" includes any requirement to which a person is subject under, by virtue of or in consequence of a relevant licence;

"environmental licence" has the same meaning as it has in Part I above as it applies in relation to the Agency or SEPA, as the case may be;

"relevant licence" means—

(a) any environmental licence;

(b), (c) (*apply to Scotland only*);

(d) any consent under Chapter III of Part IV of the Water Industry Act 1991 to make discharges of special category effluent; or

(e) any agreement under section 129 of that Act with respect to, or to any matter connected with, the reception or disposal of such effluent.

(6)   . . .

[561]

NOTES

Commencement: 1 April 1996.

Sub-s (1): repeals the Water Industry Act 1991, s 171(4), (5) and the Water Resources Act 1991, s 209(1), (2), (4); remainder applies to Scotland only.

Sub-s (6): amends the Environmental Protection Act 1990, s 25.

---

112   (*Introduces Sch 19 to this Act.*)

Information

113 Disclosure of information

(1)   Notwithstanding any prohibition or restriction imposed by or under any enactment or rule of law, information of any description may be disclosed—

(a) by a new Agency to a Minister of the Crown, the other new Agency or a local enforcing authority,

(b) by a Minister of the Crown to a new Agency, another Minister of the Crown or a local enforcing authority, or

(c) by a local enforcing authority to a Minister of the Crown, a new Agency or another local enforcing authority,

for the purpose of facilitating the carrying out by either of the new Agencies of any of its functions, by any such Minister of any of his environmental functions or by any local enforcing authority of any of its relevant functions; and no person shall be subject to any civil or criminal liability in consequence of any disclosure made by virtue of this subsection.

(2)   Nothing in this section shall authorise the disclosure to a local enforcing authority by a new Agency or another local enforcing authority of information—

(a) disclosure of which would, in the opinion of a Minister of the Crown, be contrary to the interests of national security; or

(b) which was obtained under or by virtue of the Statistics of Trade Act 1947 and which was disclosed to a new Agency or any of its officers by the Secretary of State.

(3)   No information disclosed to any person under or by virtue of this section shall be disclosed by that person to any other person otherwise than in accordance

with the provisions of this section, or any provision of any other enactment which authorises or requires the disclosure, if that information is information—

(a) which relates to a trade secret of any person or which otherwise is or might be commercially confidential in relation to any person; or

(b) whose disclosure otherwise than under or by virtue of this section would, in the opinion of a Minister of the Crown, be contrary to the interests of national security.

(4) Any authorisation by or under this section of the disclosure of information by or to any person shall also be taken to authorise the disclosure of that information by or, as the case may be, to any officer of his who is authorised by him to make the disclosure or, as the case may be, to receive the information.

(5) In this section—

"new Agency" means the Agency or SEPA;

"the environment" has the same meaning as in Part I of the Environmental Protection Act 1990;

"environmental functions", in relation to a Minister of the Crown, means any function of that Minister, whether conferred or imposed under or by virtue of any enactment or otherwise, relating to the environment; and

"local enforcing authority" means—

(a) any local authority within the meaning of Part IIA of the Environmental Protection Act 1990, and the "relevant functions" of such an authority are its functions under or by virtue of that Part;

(b) any local authority within the meaning of Part IV of this Act, and the "relevant functions" of such an authority are its functions under or by virtue of that Part;

(c) in relation to England, any county council for an area for which there are district councils, and the "relevant functions" of such a county council are its functions under or by virtue of Part IV of this Act; or

(d) in relation to England and Wales, any local enforcing authority within the meaning of section 1(7) of the Environmental Protection Act 1990, and the "relevant functions" of such an authority are its functions under or by virtue of Part I of that Act.

[562]

NOTES

Commencement: 1 April 1996.

114 (*Relates to appeals.*)

Crown application

115 Application of this Act to the Crown

(1) Subject to the provisions of this section, this Act shall bind the Crown.

(2) Part III of this Act and any amendments, repeals and revocations made by other provisions of this Act (other than those made by Schedule 21, which shall bind the Crown) bind the Crown to the extent that the enactments to which they relate bind the Crown.

(3) No contravention by the Crown of any provision made by or under this Act shall make the Crown criminally liable; but the High Court or, in Scotland, the Court of Session may, on the application of the Agency or, in Scotland, SEPA, declare unlawful any act or omission of the Crown which constitutes such a contravention.

(4) Notwithstanding anything in subsection (3) above, any provision made by or under this Act shall apply to persons in the public service of the Crown as it applies to other persons.

(5)   If the Secretary of State certifies that it appears to him, as respects any Crown premises and any powers of entry exercisable in relation to them specified in the certificate, that it is requisite or expedient that, in the interests of national security, the powers should not be exercisable in relation to those premises, those powers shall not be exercisable in relation to those premises; and in this subsection "Crown premises" means premises held or used by or on behalf of the Crown.

(6)   Nothing in this section shall be taken as in any way affecting Her Majesty in her private capacity; and this subsection shall be construed as if section 38(3) of the Crown Proceedings Act 1947 (interpretation of references to Her Majesty in her private capacity) were contained in this Act.

[563]

NOTES
Commencement: 1 April 1996.

116–118 (*S 116 introduces Sch 21 to this Act; ss 117, 118 relate to the Isles of Scilly.*)

Miscellaneous and supplemental

119 (*Relates to stamp duty.*)

120 Minor and consequential amendments, transitional and transitory provisions, savings and repeals

(1)   ...

(2)   The transitional provisions, transitory provisions and savings contained in Schedule 23 to this Act shall have effect; but those provisions are without prejudice to sections 16 and 17 of the Interpretation Act 1978 (effect of repeals).

(3)–(6). . .

[564]

NOTES
Commencement: 1 January 1999 (sub-ss (2), (3), certain purposes); 1 April 1997 (sub-s (3) certain purposes); 1 January 1997 (sub-s (3) certain purposes); 31 December 1996 (sub-ss (1), (3), certain purposes); 21 November 1996 (sub-s (1) certain purposes); 1 April 1996 (sub-ss (1)–(3) certain purposes); 1 February 1996 (sub-ss (1), (3), certain purposes); 1 November 1995 (sub-s (3) certain purposes); 12 October 1995 (sub-s (1) certain purposes); 21 September 1995 (sub-ss (1), (3), certain purposes); 28 July 1995 (sub-ss (4)–(6), sub-s (1) certain purposes); to be appointed (sub-ss (1)–(3) remaining purposes).
Sub-ss (1), (3)–(6): introduce Schs 22, 23 to this Act and make provision as to the power to make regulations.

121, 122 (*Relate to local statutory provisions and consequential amendments etc (s 121); directions (s 122).*)

123 Service of documents

(1)   Without prejudice to paragraph 17(2)(d) of Schedule 7 to this Act, any notice required or authorised by or under this Act to be served (whether the expression "serve" or the expression "give" or "send" or any other expression is used) on any person may be served by delivering it to him, or by leaving it at his proper address, or by sending it by post to him at that address.

(2)   Any such notice may—
(a) in the case of a body corporate, be served on the secretary or clerk of that body;

(b) in the case of a partnership, be served on a partner or a person having the control or management of the partnership business.

(3) For the purposes of this section and of section 7 of the Interpretation Act 1978 (service of documents by post) in its application to this section, the proper address of any person on whom any such notice is to be served shall be his last known address, except that—

(a) in the case of a body corporate or their secretary or clerk, it shall be the address of the registered or principal office of that body;

(b) in the case of a partnership or person having the control or the management of the partnership business, it shall be the principal office of the partnership;

and for the purposes of this subsection the principal office of a company registered outside the United Kingdom or of a partnership carrying on business outside the United Kingdom shall be their principal office within the United Kingdom.

(4) If the person to be served with any such notice has specified an address in the United Kingdom other than his proper address within the meaning of subsection (3) above as the one at which he or someone on his behalf will accept notices of the same description as that notice, that address shall also be treated for the purposes of this section and section 7 of the Interpretation Act 1978 as his proper address.

(5) Where under any provision of this Act any notice is required to be served on a person who is, or appears to be, in occupation of any premises then—

(a) if the name or address of such a person cannot after reasonable inquiry be ascertained, or

(b) if the premises appear to be or are unoccupied,

that notice may be served either by leaving it in the hands of a person who is or appears to be resident or employed on the premises or by leaving it conspicuously affixed to some building or object on the premises.

(6) This section shall not apply to any notice in relation to the service of which provision is made by rules of court.

(7) The preceding provisions of this section shall apply to the service of a document as they apply to the service of a notice.

(8) In this section—

"premises" includes any land, vehicle, vessel or mobile plant;

"serve" shall be construed in accordance with subsection (1) above.

                                                                                    [565]
_____

NOTES

Commencement: 28 July 1995.
_____

124 General interpretation

(1) In this Act, except in so far as the context otherwise requires—

"the Agency" means the Environment Agency;

"financial year" means a period of twelve months ending with 31st March;

"functions" includes powers and duties;

"modifications" includes additions, alterations and omissions and cognate expressions shall be construed accordingly;

"notice" means notice in writing;

"records", without prejudice to the generality of the expression, includes computer records and any other records kept otherwise than in a document;

"SEPA" means the Scottish Environment Protection Agency.

(2) The amendment by this Act of any provision contained in subordinate legislation shall not be taken to have prejudiced any power to make further subordinate legislation amending or revoking that provision.

(3)   In subsection (2) above, "subordinate legislation" has the same meaning as in the Interpretation Act 1978.

[566]

NOTES
Commencement: 28 July 1995.

125 Short title, commencement, extent, etc

(1)   This Act may be cited as the Environment Act 1995.

(2)   Part III of this Act, except for section 78, paragraph 7(2) of Schedule 7 and Schedule 10, shall come into force at the end of the period of two months beginning with the day on which this Act is passed.

(3)   Except as provided in subsection (2) above and except for this section, section 74 above and paragraphs 76(8)(a) and 135 of Schedule 22 to this Act (which come into force on the passing of this Act) and the repeal of sub-paragraph (1) of paragraph 22 of Schedule 10 to this Act (which comes into force in accordance with sub-paragraph (7) of that paragraph) this Act shall come into force on such day as the Secretary of State may specify by order made by statutory instrument; and different days may be so specified for different provisions or for different purposes of the same provision.

(4)   Without prejudice to the provisions of Schedule 23 to this Act, an order under subsection (3) above may make such transitional provisions and savings as appear to the Secretary of State necessary or expedient in connection with any provision brought into force by the order.

(5)   The power conferred by subsection (4) above includes power to modify any enactment contained in this or any other Act.

(6)   An Order in Council under paragraph 1(1)(b) of Schedule 1 to the Northern Ireland Act 1974 (legislation for Northern Ireland in the interim period) which states that it is made only for purposes corresponding to those of section 98 of this Act—
   (a) shall not be subject to paragraph 1(4) and (5) of that Schedule (affirmative resolution of both Houses of Parliament); but
   (b) shall be subject to annulment in pursuance of a resolution of either House of Parliament.

(7)   Except for this section and any amendment or repeal by this Act of any provision contained in—
   (a) the Parliamentary Commissioner Act 1967,
   (b) the Sea Fish (Conservation) Act 1967,
   (c) the House of Commons Disqualification Act 1975, or
   (d) the Northern Ireland Assembly Disqualification Act 1975,
this Act shall not extend to Northern Ireland.

(8)   Part III of this Act, and Schedule 24 to this Act so far as relating to that Part, extends to England and Wales only.

(9)   Section 106 of, and Schedule 16 to, this Act extend to Scotland only.

(10) Subject to the foregoing provisions of this section and to any express provision made by this Act to the contrary, any amendment, repeal or revocation made by this Act shall have the same extent as the enactment or instrument to which it relates.

[567]

NOTES
Commencement: 28 July 1995.
   Orders: the Environment Act 1995 (Commencement No 1) Order 1995, SI 1995/1983; the Environment Act 1995 (Commencement No 2) Order 1995, SI 1995/2649; the Environment Act 1995

(Commencement No 3) Order 1995, SI 1995/2765; the Environment Act 1995 (Commencement No 4 and Saving Provisions) Order 1995, SI 1995/2950, as amended by SI 1996/2560; the Environment Act 1995 (Commencement No 5) Order 1996, SI 1996/186; the Environment Act (Commencement No 6 and Repeal Provisions) Order 1996, SI 1996/2560; the Environment Act 1995 (Commencement No 7) (Scotland) Order 1996, SI 1996/2857; the Environment Act 1995 (Commencement No 8 and Savings Provisions) Order 1996, SI 1996/2909; the Environment Act 1995 (Commencement No 9 and Transitional Provisions) Order 1997, SI 1997/1626.

(Schs 1–10 outside the scope of this work.)

SCHEDULE 11
AIR QUALITY: SUPPLEMENTAL PROVISIONS

Section 90

Consultation requirements

1.—(1) A local authority in carrying out its functions in relation to—
    (a) any air quality review,
    (b) any assessment under section 82 or 84 of this Act, or
    (c) the preparation of an action plan or any revision of an action plan,

shall consult such other persons as fall within sub-paragraph (2) below.

    (2) Those persons are—
    (a) the Secretary of State;
    (b) the appropriate new Agency;
    (c) in England and Wales, the highway authority for any highway in the area to which the review or, as the case may be, the action plan or revision relates;
    (d) every local authority whose area is contiguous to the authority's area;
    (e) any county council in England whose area consists of or includes the whole or any part of the authority's area;
    (f) any National Park authority for a National Park whose area consists of or includes the whole or any part of the authority's area;
    (g) such public authorities exercising functions in, or in the vicinity of, the authority's area as the authority may consider appropriate;
    (h) such bodies appearing to the authority to be representative of persons with business interests in the area to which the review or action plan in question relates as the authority may consider appropriate;
    (j) such other bodies or persons as the authority considers appropriate.

    (3) In this paragraph "National Park authority" . . . means a National Park authority established under section 63 of this Act which has become the local planning authority for the National Park in question.

    (4) . . .

Exchange of information with county councils in England

2.—(1) This paragraph applies in any case where a district in England for which there is a district council is comprised in an area for which there is a county council; and in this paragraph—
    (a) any reference to the county council is a reference to the council of that area; and
    (b) any reference to a district council is a reference to the council of a district comprised in that area.

    (2) It shall be the duty of the county council to provide a district council with all such information as is reasonably requested by the district council for purposes connected with the carrying out of its functions under or by virtue of this Part.

    (3) It shall be the duty of a district council to provide the county council with all such information as is reasonably requested by the county council for purposes connected with the carrying out of any of its functions relating to the assessment or management of the quality of air.

    (4) Information provided to a district council or county council under sub-paragraph (2) or (3) above shall be provided in such form and in such manner and at such times as the district council or, as the case may be, the county council may reasonably require.

(5) A council which provides information under sub-paragraph (2) or (3) above shall be entitled to recover the reasonable cost of doing so from the council which requested the information.

(6) The information which a council may be required to provide under this paragraph shall include information which, although it is not in the possession of the council or would not otherwise come into the possession of the council, is information which it is reasonable to require the council to obtain.

Joint exercise of local authority functions

3.—(1) The appropriate authority may give directions to any two or more local authorities requiring them to exercise the powers conferred by—
  (a) section 101(5) of the Local Government Act 1972 (power of two or more local authorities to discharge functions jointly), or
  (b) section 56(5) of the Local Government (Scotland) Act 1973 (which makes similar provision for Scotland),
in relation to functions under or by virtue of this Part in accordance with the directions.

(2) The appropriate authority may give directions to a local authority requiring it—
  (a) not to exercise those powers, or
  (b) not to exercise those powers in a manner specified in the directions,
in relation to functions under or by virtue of this Part.

(3) Where two or more local authorities have exercised those powers in relation to functions under or by virtue of this Part, the appropriate authority may give them directions requiring them to revoke, or modify in accordance with the directions, the arrangements which they have made.

(4) In this paragraph, "the appropriate authority" means—
  (a) in relation to England and Wales, the Secretary of State; and
  (b) *(applies to Scotland only)*.

Public access to information about air quality

4.—(1) It shall be the duty of every local authority—
  (a) to secure that there is available at all reasonable times for inspection by the public free of charge a copy of each of the documents specified in sub-paragraph (2) below; and
  (b) to afford to members of the public facilities for obtaining copies of those documents on payment of a reasonable charge.

(2) The documents mentioned in sub-paragraph (1)(a) above are—
  (a) a report of the results of any air quality review which the authority has caused to be conducted;
  (b) a report of the results of any assessment which the authority has caused to be made under section 82 or 84 of this Act;
  (c) any order made by the authority under section 83 of this Act;
  (d) any action plan prepared by the authority;
  (e) any proposals or statements submitted to the authority pursuant to subsection (3) or (4) of section 86 of this Act;
  (f) any directions given to the authority under this Part;
  (g) in a case where section 86 of this Act applies, any directions given to the county council under this Part.

Fixed penalty offences

5.—(1) Without prejudice to the generality of paragraph (o) of subsection (2) of section 87 of this Act, regulations may, in particular, make provision—
  (a) for the qualifications, appointment or authorisation of persons who are to issue fixed penalty notices;
  (b) for the offences in connection with which, the cases or circumstances in which, the time or period at or within which, or the manner in which fixed penalty notices may be issued;
  (c) prohibiting the institution, before the expiration of the period for paying the fixed penalty, of proceedings against a person for an offence in connection with which a fixed penalty notice has been issued;

(d) prohibiting the conviction of a person for an offence in connection with which a fixed penalty notice has been issued if the fixed penalty is paid before the expiration of the period for paying it;

(e) entitling, in prescribed cases, a person to whom a fixed penalty notice is issued to give, within a prescribed period, notice requesting a hearing in respect of the offence to which the fixed penalty notice relates;

(f) for the amount of the fixed penalty to be increased by a prescribed amount in any case where the person liable to pay the fixed penalty fails to pay it before the expiration of the period for paying it, without having given notice requesting a hearing in respect of the offence to which the fixed penalty notice relates;

(g) for or in connection with the recovery of an unpaid fixed penalty as a fine or as a civil debt or as if it were a sum payable under a county court order;

(h) for or in connection with execution or other enforcement in respect of an unpaid fixed penalty by prescribed persons;

(j) for a fixed penalty notice, and any prescribed proceedings or other prescribed steps taken by reference to the notice, to be rendered void in prescribed cases where a person makes a prescribed statutory declaration, and for the consequences of any notice, proceedings or other steps being so rendered void (including extension of any time limit for instituting criminal proceedings);

(k) for or in connection with the extension, in prescribed cases or circumstances, by a prescribed person of the period for paying a fixed penalty;

(l) for or in connection with the withdrawal, in prescribed circumstances, of a fixed penalty notice, including—

    (i) repayment of any amount paid by way of fixed penalty in pursuance of a fixed penalty notice which is withdrawn; and

    (ii) prohibition of the institution or continuation of proceedings for the offence in connection with which the withdrawn notice was issued;

(m) for or in connection with the disposition of sums received by way of fixed penalty;

(n) for a certificate purporting to be signed by or on behalf of a prescribed person and stating either—

    (i) that payment of a fixed penalty was, or (as the case may be) was not, received on or before a date specified in the certificate, or

    (ii) that an envelope containing an amount sent by post in payment of a fixed penalty was marked as posted on a date specified in the certificate,

to be received as evidence of the matters so stated and to be treated, without further proof, as being so signed unless the contrary is shown;

(o) requiring a fixed penalty notice to give such reasonable particulars of the circumstances alleged to constitute the fixed penalty offence to which the notice relates as are necessary for giving reasonable information of the offence and to state—

    (i) the monetary amount of the fixed penalty which may be paid;

    (ii) the person to whom, and the address at which, the fixed penalty may be paid and any correspondence relating to the fixed penalty notice may be sent;

    (iii) the method or methods by which payment of the fixed penalty may be made;

    (iv) the period for paying the fixed penalty;

    (v) the consequences of the fixed penalty not being paid before the expiration of that period;

(p) similar to any provision made by section 79 of the Road Traffic Offenders Act 1988 (statements by constables in fixed penalty cases);

(q) for presuming, in any proceedings, that any document of a prescribed description purporting to have been signed by a person to whom a fixed penalty notice has been issued has been signed by that person;

(r) requiring or authorising a fixed penalty notice to contain prescribed information relating to, or for the purpose of facilitating, the administration of the fixed penalty system;

(s) with respect to the giving of fixed penalty notices, including, in particular, provision with respect to—

    (i) the methods by which,

    (ii) the officers, servants or agents by, to or on whom, and

    (iii) the places at which,

fixed penalty notices may be given by, or served on behalf of, a prescribed person;

(t) prescribing the method or methods by which fixed penalties may be paid;

(u) for or with respect to the issue of prescribed documents to persons to whom fixed penalty notices are or have been given;

(w) for a fixed penalty notice to be treated for prescribed purposes as if it were an information or summons or any other document of a prescribed description.

(2) The provision that may be made by regulations prescribing fixed penalty offences includes provision for an offence to be a fixed penalty offence—

(a) only if it is committed in such circumstances or manner as may be prescribed; or

(b) except if it is committed in such circumstances or manner as may be prescribed.

(3) Regulations may provide for any offence which is a fixed penalty offence to cease to be such an offence.

(4) An offence which, in consequence of regulations made by virtue of sub-paragraph (3) above, has ceased to be a fixed penalty offence shall be eligible to be prescribed as such an offence again.

(5) Regulations may make provision for such exceptions, limitations and conditions as the Secretary of State considers necessary or expedient.

(6) In this paragraph—

"fixed penalty" means a penalty of such amount as may be prescribed (whether by being specified in, or made calculable under, regulations);

"fixed penalty notice" means a notice offering a person an opportunity to discharge any liability to conviction for a fixed penalty offence by payment of a penalty of a prescribed amount;

"fixed penalty offence" means, subject to sub-paragraph (2) above, any offence (whether under or by virtue of this Part or any other enactment) which is for the time being prescribed as a fixed penalty offence;

"the fixed penalty system" means the system implementing regulations made under or by virtue of paragraph (o) of subsection (2) of section 87 of this Act;

"the period for paying", in relation to any fixed penalty, means such period as may be prescribed for the purpose;

"regulations" means regulations under or by virtue of paragraph (o) of subsection (2) of section 87 of this Act.

[568]

NOTES

Commencement: 1 February 1996 (paras 2, 3, 5); to be appointed (remainder).

Para 1: words omitted from sub-para (3) repealed, and sub-para (4) repealed, by s 120, Sch 24, of this Act.

(Sch 12 inserts the Environmental Protection Act 1990, Sch 2A at **[245]**; *Schs 13–17 outside the scope of this work.)*

SCHEDULE 18
SUPPLEMENTAL PROVISIONS WITH RESPECT TO POWERS OF ENTRY
Section 108

Interpretation

1.—(1) In this Schedule—

"designated person" means an authorised person, within the meaning of section 108 of this Act and includes a person designated by virtue of paragraph 2 below;

"relevant power" means a power conferred by section 108 of this Act, including a power exercisable by virtue of a warrant under this Schedule.

(2) Expressions used in this Schedule and in section 108 of this Act have the same meaning in this Schedule as they have in that section.

Issue of warrants

2.—(1) If it is shown to the satisfaction of a justice of the peace or, in Scotland, the sheriff or a justice of the peace, on sworn information in writing—

(a) that there are reasonable grounds for the exercise in relation to any premises of a relevant power; and

    (b)   that one or more of the conditions specified in sub-paragraph (2) below is fulfilled in relation to those premises,

the justice or sheriff may by warrant authorise an enforcing authority to designate a person who shall be authorised to exercise the power in relation to those premises, in accordance with the warrant and, if need be, by force.

    (2) The conditions mentioned in sub-paragraph (1)(b) above are—
       (a)   that the exercise of the power in relation to the premises has been refused;
       (b)   that such a refusal is reasonably apprehended;
       (c)   that the premises are unoccupied;
       (d)   that the occupier is temporarily absent from the premises and the case is one of urgency; or
       (e)   that an application for admission to the premises would defeat the object of the proposed entry.

    (3) In a case where subsection (6) of section 108 of this Act applies, a justice of the peace or sheriff shall not issue a warrant under this Schedule by virtue only of being satisfied that the exercise of a power in relation to any premises has been refused, or that a refusal is reasonably apprehended, unless he is also satisfied that the notice required by that subsection has been given and that the period of that notice has expired.

    (4) Every warrant under this Schedule shall continue in force until the purposes for which the warrant was issued have been fulfilled.

Manner of exercise of powers

3. A person designated as the person who may exercise a relevant power shall produce evidence of his designation and other authority before he exercises the power.

Information obtained to be admissible in evidence

4.—(1) Subject to section 108(12) of this Act, information obtained in consequence of the exercise of a relevant power, with or without the consent of any person, shall be admissible in evidence against that or any other person.

    (2) Without prejudice to the generality of sub-paragraph (1) above, information obtained by means of monitoring or other apparatus installed on any premises in the exercise of a relevant power, with or without the consent of any person in occupation of the premises, shall be admissible in evidence in any proceedings against that or any other person.

Duty to secure premises

5. A person who, in the exercise of a relevant power enters on any premises which are unoccupied or whose occupier is temporarily absent shall leave the premises as effectually secured against trespassers as he found them.

Compensation

6.—(1) Where any person exercises any power conferred by section 108(4)(a) or (b) or (5) of this Act, it shall be the duty of the enforcing authority under whose authorisation he acts to make full compensation to any person who has sustained loss or damage by reason of—
       (a)   the exercise by the designated person of that power; or
       (b)   the performance of, or failure of the designated person to perform, the duty imposed by paragraph 5 above.

    (2) Compensation shall not be payable by virtue of sub-paragraph (1) above in respect of any loss or damage if the loss or damage—
       (a)   is attributable to the default of the person who sustained it; or
       (b)   is loss or damage in respect of which compensation is payable by virtue of any other provision of the pollution control enactments.

    (3) Any dispute as to a person's entitlement to compensation under this paragraph, or as to the amount of any such compensation, shall be referred to the arbitration of a single arbitrator or, in Scotland, arbiter appointed by agreement between the enforcing authority in question and the person who claims to have sustained the loss or damage or, in default of agreement, by the Secretary of State.

(4) A designated person shall not be liable in any civil or criminal proceedings for anything done in the purported exercise of any relevant power if the court is satisfied that the act was done in good faith and that there were reasonable grounds for doing it.

[569]

NOTES
Commencement: 1 April 1996.

(Sch 19 partly amends the Control of Pollution Act 1974, s 93 at **[22]**, *the Control of Pollution (Amendment) Act 1989, s 7 at* **[87]**, *the Environmental Protection Act 1990, s 71 at* **[152]**, *adds the Radioactive Substances Act 1993, s 34A at* **[501]**, *and substitutes the Environmental Protection Act 1990, s 44 at* **[133]**; *remainder outside the scope of this work. Schs 20–22 outside the scope of this work.)*

SCHEDULE 23
TRANSITIONAL AND TRANSITORY PROVISIONS AND SAVINGS

Section 120

PART I
GENERAL TRANSITIONAL PROVISIONS AND SAVINGS

1.–3. . . .

Charging schemes

4.—(1) Without prejudice to section 55 of this Act, any charging scheme—
    (a)   which relates to any transferred functions,
    (b)   which was made before the transfer date, and
    (c)   which is in force immediately before that date or would (apart from this Act) have come into force at any time after that date,
shall, subject to the provisions of section 41 of this Act, have effect on and after the transfer date, with any necessary modifications, and for the remainder of the period for which the charging scheme would have been in force apart from any repeal made by this Act, as a scheme made under that section by the transferee in accordance with section 42 of this Act.

(2) Any costs or expenses incurred before the transfer date by any person in carrying out functions transferred to a new Agency by or under this Act may be treated for the purposes of subsections (3) and (4) of section 42 of this Act as costs or expenses incurred by that new Agency in carrying out those functions.

    (3) In this paragraph—
    "charging scheme" means a scheme specifying, or providing for the determination of, any fees or charges;
    "new Agency" means the Agency or SEPA;
    "transferred functions" means any functions which, by virtue of any provision made by or under this Act, become functions of a new Agency and "the transferee" means the new Agency whose functions they so become.

5.–15.. . .

The Environmental Protection Act 1990

16.—(1) Subject to sub-paragraph (2) below, if, at the transfer date, the content of the strategy required by section 44A of the Environmental Protection Act 1990 has not been finally determined, any plan or modification under section 50 of that Act, in its application to England and Wales, whose content has been finally determined before that date shall continue in force until the contents of the strategy are finally determined, notwithstanding the repeal by this Act of that section.

(2) If the strategy required by section 44A of that Act consists, or is to consist, of more than one statement, sub-paragraph (1) above shall apply as if—
    (a)   references to the strategy were references to any such statement; and
    (b)   references to a plan or modification under section 50 of that Act were references to such plans or modifications as relate to the area covered, or to be covered, by that statement.

17. If, at the transfer date, the content of the strategy required by section 44B of that Act has not been finally determined, any plan or modification under section 50 of that Act, in its application to Scotland, whose content has been finally determined before that date shall continue in force until the contents of the strategy are finally determined, notwithstanding the repeal by this Act of that section.

18.—(1) This paragraph applies to—
    (a)   any resolution of a waste regulation authority under section 54 of that Act (special provision for land occupied by disposal authorities in Scotland);
    (b)   any resolution of a waste disposal authority having effect by virtue of subsection (16) of that section as if it were a resolution of a waste regulation authority under that section,

which is in force on the transfer date.

(2) A resolution to which this paragraph applies shall continue in force—
    (a)   where no application is made under section 36(1) of that Act for a waste management licence in respect of the site or mobile plant covered by the resolution, until the end of the period of 6 months commencing with the transfer date;
    (b)   where an application as mentioned in sub-paragraph (a) above is made, until—
        (i)   the application is withdrawn;
        (ii)   the application is rejected and no appeal against the rejection is timeously lodged under section 43 of that Act;
        (iii)   any appeal against a rejection of the application is withdrawn or rejected; or
        (iv)   the application is granted.

(3) In relation to a resolution continued in force by sub-paragraph (2) above, the said section 54 shall have effect subject to the amendments set out in the following provisions of this paragraph.

(4) In subsection (2), for paragraph (b) there shall be substituted—

    "(b) specified in a resolution passed by a waste regulation authority, or by a waste disposal authority under Part I of the Control of Pollution Act 1974, before the transfer date within the meaning of section 56(1) of the Environment Act 1995".

(5) In subsection (3) for paragraph (b) there shall be substituted—

    "(b) by another person, that it is on land which is the subject of a resolution, that it is with the consent of the waste disposal authority and that any conditions to which such consent is subject are within the terms of the resolution."

(6) Subsections (4) to (7) shall cease to have effect.

(7) For subsections (8) and (9) there shall be substituted—

    "(8)   Subject to subsection (9) below, a resolution continued in force by paragraph 18 of Schedule 23 to the Environment Act 1995 may be varied or rescinded by SEPA by a resolution passed by it.

    (9)   Before passing a resolution under subsection (8) above varying a resolution, SEPA shall—
        (a)   prepare a statement of the variation which it proposes to make;
        (b)   refer that statement to the Health and Safety Executive and to the waste disposal authority in whose area the site is situated or, as the case may be, which is operating the plant; and
        (c)   consider any representations about the variation which the Health and Safety Executive or the waste disposal authority makes to it during the allowed period.

    (9A)   The period allowed to the Health and Safety Executive and the waste disposal authority for the making of representations under subsection (9)(c) above is the period of 28 days beginning with that on which the statement is received by that body, or such longer period as SEPA and that body agree in writing.

    (9B)   SEPA may—
        (a)   postpone the reference under subsection (9)(b) above so far as it considers that by reason of an emergency it is appropriate to do so;

(b) disregard the Health and Safety Executive in relation to a resolution which in SEPA's opinion will not affect the Health and Safety Executive."

(8) In subsection (10)—
(a) for the words "the authority which passed the resolution" and "the waste regulation authority" there shall be substituted the words "SEPA";
(b) the words "the waste disposal authority to discontinue the activities and of" shall cease to have effect.

(9) Subsections (11) to (15) shall cease to have effect.

19., 20.   . . .

21.—(1) This paragraph applies to any consent—
(a) which was given under paragraph 2 of Schedule 10 to the Water Resources Act 1991 (discharge consents), as in force before the transfer date; and
(b) which is in force immediately before that date.

(2) On and after the transfer date, a consent to which this paragraph applies—
(a) shall, for so long as it would have continued in force apart from this Act, have effect as a consent given under paragraph 3 of Schedule 10 to that Act, as substituted by this Act, subject to the same conditions as were attached to the consent immediately before the transfer date; and
(b) shall—
(i) during the period of six months beginning with the transfer date, not be limited to discharges by any particular person but extend to discharges made by any person; and
(ii) after that period, extend, but be limited, to discharges made by any person who before the end of that period gives notice to the Agency that he proposes to rely on the consent after that period.

22.–24.. . .

[570]

NOTES
Commencement: 1 January 1999 (in part); 1 April 1996 (in part); to be appointed (remainder).
Paras 1–3, 5–15, 19, 20, 22–24: outside the scope of this work.

(Sch 24 outside the scope of this work.)

FINANCE ACT 1996

(1996 c 8)

ARRANGEMENT OF SECTIONS

PART III
LANDFILL TAX

PART VII
MISCELLANEOUS AND SUPPLEMENTAL

An Act to grant certain duties, to alter other duties, and to amend the law relating to the National Debt and the Public Revenue, and to make further provision in connection with Finance.

[29 April 1996]

1–38 (*Outside the scope of this work.*)

PART III
LANDFILL TAX

The basic provisions

39 Landfill tax

(1)   A tax, to be known as landfill tax, shall be charged in accordance with this Part.

(2)   The tax shall be under the care and management of the Commissioners of Customs and Excise.

[571]

NOTES
Commencement: 29 April 1996.

40 Charge to tax

(1)   Tax shall be charged on a taxable disposal.

(2)   A disposal is a taxable disposal if—
   (a) it is a disposal of material as waste,
   (b) it is made by way of landfill,
   (c) it is made at a landfill site, and
   (d) it is made on or after 1st October 1996.

(3)   For this purpose a disposal is made at a landfill site if the land on or under which it is made constitutes or falls within land which is a landfill site at the time of the disposal.

[572]

NOTES
Commencement: 29 April 1996.

41 Liability to pay tax

(1)   The person liable to pay tax charged on a taxable disposal is the landfill site operator.

(2)   The reference here to the landfill site operator is to the person who is at the time of the disposal the operator of the landfill site which constitutes or contains the land on or under which the disposal is made.

[573]

NOTES
Commencement: 29 April 1996.

42 Amount of tax

(1)   The amount of tax charged on a taxable disposal shall be found by taking—
   (a) £7 for each whole tonne disposed of and a proportionately reduced sum for any additional part of a tonne, or
   (b) a proportionately reduced sum if less than a tonne is disposed of.

(2)   Where the material disposed of consists entirely of qualifying material this section applies as if the reference to £7 were to £2.

(3) Qualifying material is material for the time being listed for the purposes of this section in an order.

(4) The Treasury must have regard to the object of securing that material is listed if it is of a kind commonly described as inactive or inert.

[574]

NOTES
Commencement: 29 April 1996.
Orders: the Landfill Tax (Qualifying Material) Order 1996, SI 1996/1528.

Exemptions

43 Material removed from water

(1) A disposal is not a taxable disposal for the purposes of this Part if it is shown to the satisfaction of the Commissioners that the disposal is of material all of which—
   (a) has been removed (by dredging or otherwise) from water falling within subsection (2) below, and
   (b) formed part of or projected from the bed of the water concerned before its removal.

(2) Water falls within this subsection if it is—
   (a) a river, canal or watercourse (whether natural or artificial), or
   (b) a dock or harbour (whether natural or artificial).

(3) A disposal is not a taxable disposal for the purposes of this Part if it is shown to the satisfaction of the Commissioners that the disposal is of material all of which—
   (a) has been removed (by dredging or otherwise) from water falling within the approaches to a harbour (whether natural or artificial),
   (b) has been removed in the interests of navigation, and
   (c) formed part of or projected from the bed of the water concerned before its removal.

(4) A disposal is not a taxable disposal for the purposes of this Part if it is shown to the satisfaction of the Commissioners that the disposal is of material all of which—
   (a) consists of naturally occurring mineral material, and
   (b) has been removed (by dredging or otherwise) from the sea in the course of commercial operations carried out to obtain substances such as sand or gravel from the seabed.

[575]

NOTES
Commencement: 29 April 1996.

[43A Contaminated land

(1) A disposal is not a taxable disposal for the purposes of this Part if it is a disposal within subsection (2) below.

(2) A disposal is within this subsection if—
   (a) it is of material all of which has been removed from land in relation to which a certificate issued under section 43B below was in force at the time of the removal;
   (b) none of that material has been removed from a part of the land in relation to which, as at the time of the removal, the qualifying period has expired;

(c) it is a disposal in relation to which any conditions to which the certificate was made subject are satisfied; and

(d) it is not a disposal within subsection (4) below.

(3) For the purpose of subsection (2)(b) above the qualifying period expires, in relation to the part of the land in question—

(a) in the case of a reclamation which qualified under section 43B(7)(a) below, where the object involves the construction of—

(i) a building; or

(ii) a civil engineering work,

when the construction commences;

(b) in any other case of a reclamation which qualified under section 43B(7)(a) below, when pollutants have been cleared to the extent that they no longer prevent the object from being fulfilled; or

(c) in the case of a reclamation which qualified under section 43B(7)(b) below, when pollutants have been cleared to the extent that the potential for harm has been removed.

(4) Subject to subsection (5) below, a disposal is within this subsection if it is of material the removal of any of which is required in order to comply with—

(a) a works notice served under section 46A of the Control of Pollution Act 1974;

(b) an enforcement notice served under section 13 of the Environmental Protection Act 1990;

(c) a prohibition notice served under section 14 of the Environmental Protection Act 1990;

(d) an order under section 26 of the Environmental Protection Act 1990;

(e) a remediation notice served under section 78E of the Environmental Protection Act 1990;

(f) an enforcement notice served under section 90B of the Water Resources Act 1991; or

(g) a works notice served under section 161A of the Water Resources Act 1991.

(5) A disposal shall not be regarded as falling within subsection (4) above where the removal of the material has been carried out by or on behalf of any of the following bodies:

(a) a local authority;

(b) a development corporation;

(c) the Environment Agency;

(d) the Scottish Environment Protection Agency;

(e) English Partnerships;

(f) Scottish Enterprise;

(g) Highlands and Islands Enterprise;

(h) the Welsh Development Agency.

(6) In this section—

"development corporation" means—

(a) in England and Wales, a corporation established under section 135 of the Local Government, Planning and Land Act 1980;

(b) in Scotland, a corporation established under section 2 of the New Towns (Scotland) Act 1968;

"English Partnerships" means the Urban Regeneration Agency established by section 158 of the Leasehold Reform, Housing and Urban Development Act 1993;

"Highlands and Islands Enterprise" means the body established by section 1(b) of the Enterprise and New Towns (Scotland) Act 1990;

"land" includes land covered by water;

"Scottish Enterprise" means the corporation established by section 1(a) of the Enterprise and New Towns (Scotland) Act 1990;

"the Welsh Development Agency" means the body established by section 1 of the Welsh Development Agency Act 1975.

(7) For the purposes of this section—
   (a) the removal of material includes its removal from one part of the land for disposal on another part of the same land;
   (b) the clearing of pollutants includes their being cleared from one part of the land for disposal on another part of the same land.]

[576]

NOTES
Commencement: 1 August 1996.
Inserted, together with s 43B, by the Landfill Tax (Contaminated Land) Order 1996, SI 1996/1529, art 3.

[43B Contaminated land: certificates

(1) Subject to subsection (2) below, the Commissioners shall issue a certificate in relation to any land where—
   (a) an application in writing is made by a person carrying out, or intending to carry out, a reclamation of that land (the applicant);
   (b) the applicant provides to them such information as they may direct, whether generally or as regards that particular case;
   (c) the application is made not less than 30 days before the date from which the certificate is to take effect; and
   (d) the reclamation qualifies under subsection (7) below.

(2) The Commissioners shall not refuse an application for a certificate in a case where the conditions specified in subsection (1)(a) to (d) above are satisfied unless it appears to them—
   (a) necessary to do so for the protection of the revenue; or
   (b) except where the applicant is one of the bodies mentioned in subsection (5) of section 43A above, that all or part of the reclamation of land to which the application relates is required in order to comply with a notice or order mentioned in subsection (4) of that section.

(3) The Commissioners may make a certificate subject to such conditions set out in the certificate as they think fit, including (but not restricted to) conditions—
   (a) that the certificate is to be in force only in relation to a particular quantity of material;
   (b) that the certificate is to be in force only in relation to disposals made at a particular landfill site or sites;
   (c) that the certificate is to be in force in relation to part only of the land to which the application relates.

(4) A certificate issued under this section—
   (a) shall have effect from the date it is issued to the applicant or such later date as the Commissioners may specify in the certificate; and
   (b) shall cease to have effect on such date as the Commissioners may set out in the certificate, but in any event no later than the day on which the person to whom the certificate was issued ceases to have the intention to carry out any activity involving reclamation of the land in relation to which the certificate was issued.

(5) Where a certificate has been issued to a person, the Commissioners—
   (a) may vary it by issuing a further certificate to that person; or
   (b) may withdraw it by giving notice in writing to that person; but this is subject to subsection (6) below.

(6) The Commissioners shall not withdraw a certificate unless it appears to them—

(a) necessary to do so for the protection of the revenue;
(b) that the reclamation did not in fact qualify under subsection (7) below or no longer so qualifies;
(c) that there will not be any or any more disposals within section 43A(2) above of material from the land to which the certificate relates; or
(d) except where the person to whom the certificate was issued is one of the bodies mentioned in subsection (5) of section 43A above, that the removal of material from the land to which the certificate relates is required in order to comply with a notice or order mentioned in subsection (4) of that section.

(7) A reclamation qualifies under this subsection if—
(a) it is, or is to be, carried out with the object of facilitating development, conservation, the provision of a public park or other amenity, or the use of the land for agriculture or forestry; or
(b) in a case other than one within paragraph (a) above, it is, or is to be, carried out with the object of reducing or removing the potential of pollutants to cause harm,

and, in either case, the conditions specified in subsection (8) below are satisfied.

(8) The conditions mentioned in subsection (7) above are—
(a) that the reclamation constitutes or includes clearing the land of pollutants which are causing harm or have the potential for causing harm;
(b) that, in a case within subsection (7)(a) above, those pollutants would (unless cleared) prevent the object concerned being fulfilled; and
(c) that all relevant activities have ceased or have ceased to give rise to any pollutants in relation to that land.

(9) For the purposes of subsection (8) above the clearing of pollutants—
(a) need not be such that all pollutants are removed;
(b) need not be such that pollutants are removed from every part of the land in which they are present;
(c) may involve their being cleared from one part of the land and disposed of on another part of the same land.

(10) For the purposes of subsection (8)(c) above an activity is relevant if—
(a) it has at any time resulted in the presence of pollutants in, on or under the land in question otherwise than—
    (i) without the consent of the person who was the occupier of the land at the time, or
    (ii) by allowing pollutants to be carried onto the land by air or water, and
(b) at that time it was carried out—
    (i) by the applicant or a person connected with him, or
    (ii) by any person on the land in question.

(11) For the purposes of subsection (10) above—
(a) any question whether a person is connected with another shall be determined in accordance with section 839 of the Taxes Act 1988;
(b) the occupier of land that is not in fact occupied is the person entitled to occupy it.

(12) In this section "land" has the meaning given by section 43A(6) above.]
[577]

NOTES
Commencement: 1 August 1996.
Inserted as noted to s 43A at [576].

44 Mining and quarrying

(1)   A disposal is not a taxable disposal for the purposes of this Part if it is shown to the satisfaction of the Commissioners that the disposal is of material all of which fulfils each of the conditions set out in subsections (2) to (4) below.

(2)   The material must result from commercial mining operations (whether the mining is deep or open-cast) or from commercial quarrying operations.

(3)   The material must be naturally occurring material extracted from the earth in the course of the operations.

(4)   The material must not have been subjected to, or result from, a non-qualifying process carried out at any stage between the extraction and the disposal.

(5)   A non-qualifying process is—
 (a) a process separate from the mining or quarrying operations, or
 (b) a process forming part of those operations and permanently altering the material's chemical composition.

[578]

NOTES
Commencement: 29 April 1996.

45 Pet cemeteries

(1)   A disposal is not a taxable disposal for the purposes of this Part if—
 (a) the disposal is of material consisting entirely of the remains of dead domestic pets, and
 (b) the landfill site at which the disposal is made fulfils the test set out in subsection (2) below.

(2)   The test is that during the relevant period—
 (a) no landfill disposal was made at the site, or
 (b) the only landfill disposals made at the site were of material consisting entirely of the remains of dead domestic pets.

(3)   For the purposes of subsection (2) above the relevant period—
 (a) begins with 1st October 1996 or (if later) with the coming into force in relation to the site of the licence or resolution mentioned in section 66 below, and
 (b) ends immediately before the disposal mentioned in subsection (1) above.

[579]

NOTES
Commencement: 29 April 1996.

46 Power to vary

(1)   Provision may be made by order to produce the result that—
 (a) a disposal which would otherwise be a taxable disposal (by virtue of this Part as it applies for the time being) is not a taxable disposal;
 (b) a disposal which would otherwise not be a taxable disposal (by virtue of this Part as it applies for the time being) is a taxable disposal.

(2)   Without prejudice to the generality of subsection (1) above, an order under this section may—
 (a) confer exemption by reference to certificates issued by the Commissioners and to conditions set out in certificates;
 (b) allow the Commissioners to direct requirements to be met before certificates can be issued;

(c) provide for the review of decisions about certificates and for appeals relating to decisions on review.

(3)   Provision may be made under this section in such way as the Treasury think fit (whether by amending this Part or otherwise).

[580]

NOTES
Commencement: 29 April 1996.
Orders: the Landfill Tax (Contaminated Land) Order 1996, SI 1996/1529.

Administration

47 Registration

(1)   The register kept under this section may contain such information as the Commissioners think is required for the purposes of the care and management of the tax.

(2)   A person who—
   (a) carries out taxable activities, and
   (b) is not registered,
is liable to be registered.

(3)   Where—
   (a) a person at any time forms the intention of carrying out taxable activities, and
   (b) he is not registered,
he shall notify the Commissioners of his intention.

(4)   A person who at any time ceases to have the intention of carrying out taxable activities shall notify the Commissioners of that fact.

(5)   Where a person is liable to be registered by virtue of subsection (2) above the Commissioners shall register him with effect from the time when he begins to carry out taxable activities; and this subsection applies whether or not he notifies the Commissioners under subsection (3) above.

(6)   Where the Commissioners are satisfied that a person has ceased to carry out taxable activities they may cancel his registration with effect from the earliest practicable time after he so ceased; and this subsection applies whether or not he notifies the Commissioners under subsection (4) above.

(7)   Where—
   (a) a person notifies the Commissioners under subsection (4) above,
   (b) they are satisfied that he will not carry out taxable activities,
   (c) they are satisfied that no tax which he is liable to pay is unpaid,
   (d) they are satisfied that no credit to which he is entitled under regulations made under section 51 below is outstanding, and
   (e) subsection (8) below does not apply,
the Commissioners shall cancel his registration with effect from the earliest practicable time after he ceases to carry out taxable activities.

(8)   Where—
   (a) a person notifies the Commissioners under subsection (4) above, and
   (b) they are satisfied that he has not carried out, and will not carry out, taxable activities,
the Commissioners shall cancel his registration with effect from the time when he ceased to have the intention to carry out taxable activities.

(9)   For the purposes of this section regulations may make provision—

(a) as to the time within which a notification is to be made;

(b) as to the form and manner in which any notification is to be made and as to the information to be contained in or provided with it;

(c) requiring a person who has made a notification to notify the Commissioners if any information contained in or provided in connection with it is or becomes inaccurate;

(d) as to the correction of entries in the register.

(10) References in this Part to a registrable person are to a person who—

(a) is registered under this section, or

(b) is liable to be registered under this section.

[581]

NOTES

Commencement: 29 April 1996.

Regulations: the Landfill Tax Regulations 1996, SI 1996/1527, as amended by SI 1996/2100, SI 1997/1431.

48 Information required to keep register up to date

(1) Regulations may make provision requiring a registrable person to notify the Commissioners of particulars which—

(a) are of changes in circumstances relating to the registrable person or any business carried on by him,

(b) appear to the Commissioners to be required for the purpose of keeping the register kept under section 47 above up to date, and

(c) are of a prescribed description.

(2) Regulations may make provision—

(a) as to the time within which a notification is to be made;

(b) as to the form and manner in which a notification is to be made;

(c) requiring a person who has made a notification to notify the Commissioners if any information contained in it is inaccurate.

[582]

NOTES

Commencement: 29 April 1996.

Regulations: the Landfill Tax Regulations 1996, SI 1996/1527, as amended by SI 1996/2100, SI 1997/1431.

49 Accounting for tax and time for payment

Regulations may provide that a registrable person shall—

(a) account for tax by reference to such periods (accounting periods) as may be determined by or under the regulations;

(b) make, in relation to accounting periods, returns in such form as may be prescribed and at such times as may be so determined;

(c) pay tax at such times and in such manner as may be so determined.

[583]

NOTES

Commencement: 29 April 1996.

Regulations: the Landfill Tax Regulations 1996, SI 1996/1527, as amended by SI 1996/2100, SI 1997/1431.

50 Power to assess

(1) Where—

(a) a person has failed to make any returns required to be made under this Part,

(b) a person has failed to keep any documents necessary to verify returns required to be made under this Part,

(c) a person has failed to afford the facilities necessary to verify returns required to be made under this Part, or

(d) it appears to the Commissioners that returns required to be made by a person under this Part are incomplete or incorrect,

the Commissioners may assess the amount of tax due from the person concerned to the best of their judgment and notify it to him.

(2)   Where a person has for an accounting period been paid an amount to which he purports to be entitled under regulations made under section 51 below, then, to the extent that the amount ought not to have been paid or would not have been paid had the facts been known or been as they later turn out to be, the Commissioners may assess the amount as being tax due from him for that period and notify it to him accordingly.

(3)   Where a person is assessed under subsections (1) and (2) above in respect of the same accounting period the assessments may be combined and notified to him as one assessment.

(4)   Where the person failing to make a return, or making a return which appears to the Commissioners to be incomplete or incorrect, was required to make the return as a personal representative, trustee in bankruptcy, receiver, liquidator or person otherwise acting in a representative capacity in relation to another person, subsection (1) above shall apply as if the reference to tax due from him included a reference to tax due from that other person.

(5)   An assessment under subsection (1) or (2) above of an amount of tax due for an accounting period shall not be made after the later of the following—

(a) two years after the end of the accounting period;

(b) one year after evidence of facts, sufficient in the Commissioners' opinion to justify the making of the assessment, comes to their knowledge;

but where further such evidence comes to their knowledge after the making of an assessment under subsection (1) or (2) above another assessment may be made under the subsection concerned in addition to any earlier assessment.

(6)   Where—

(a) as a result of a person's failure to make a return in relation to an accounting period the Commissioners have made an assessment under subsection (1) above for that period,

(b) the tax assessed has been paid but no proper return has been made in relation to the period to which the assessment related, and

(c) as a result of a failure to make a return in relation to a later accounting period, being a failure by the person referred to in paragraph (a) above or a person acting in a representative capacity in relation to him, as mentioned in subsection (4) above, the Commissioners find it necessary to make another assessment under subsection (1) above,

then, if the Commissioners think fit, having regard to the failure referred to in paragraph (a) above, they may specify in the assessment referred to in paragraph (c) above an amount of tax greater than that which they would otherwise have considered to be appropriate.

(7)   Where an amount has been assessed and notified to any person under subsection (1) or (2) above it shall be deemed to be an amount of tax due from him and may be recovered accordingly unless, or except to the extent that, the assessment has subsequently been withdrawn or reduced.

(8)   For the purposes of this section notification to—

(a) a personal representative, trustee in bankruptcy, receiver or liquidator, or

(b) a person otherwise acting in a representative capacity in relation to another person,

shall be treated as notification to the person in relation to whom the person mentioned in paragraph (a) above, or the first person mentioned in paragraph (b) above, acts.

(9) Subsection (5) above has effect subject to paragraph 33 of Schedule 5 to this Act.

(10) In this section "trustee in bankruptcy" means, as respects Scotland, an interim or permanent trustee (within the meaning of the Bankruptcy (Scotland) Act 1985) or a trustee acting under a trust deed (within the meaning of that Act).

[584]

NOTES

Commencement: 29 April 1996.

Credit

51 Credit: general

(1) Regulations may provide that where—
    (a) a person has paid or is liable to pay tax, and
    (b) prescribed conditions are fulfilled,
the person shall be entitled to credit of such an amount as is found in accordance with prescribed rules.

(2) Regulations may make provision as to the manner in which a person is to benefit from credit, and in particular may make provision—
    (a) that a person shall be entitled to credit by reference to accounting periods;
    (b) that a person shall be entitled to deduct an amount equal to his total credit for an accounting period from the total amount of tax due from him for the period;
    (c) that if no tax is due from a person for an accounting period but he is entitled to credit for the period, the amount of the credit shall be paid to him by the Commissioners;
    (d) that if the amount of credit to which a person is entitled for an accounting period exceeds the amount of tax due from him for the period, an amount equal to the excess shall be paid to him by the Commissioners;
    (e) for the whole or part of any credit to be held over to be credited for a subsequent accounting period;
    (f) as to the manner in which a person who has ceased to be registrable is to benefit from credit.

(3) Regulations under subsection (2)(c) or (d) above may provide that where at the end of an accounting period an amount is due to a person who has failed to submit returns for an earlier period as required by this Part, the Commissioners may withhold payment of the amount until he has complied with that requirement.

(4) Regulations under subsection (2)(e) above may provide for credit to be held over either on the person's application or in accordance with directions given by the Commissioners from time to time; and the regulations may allow directions to be given generally or with regard to particular cases.

(5) Regulations may provide that—
    (a) no benefit shall be conferred in respect of credit except on a claim made in such manner and at such time as may be determined by or under regulations;
    (b) payment in respect of credit shall be made subject to such conditions (if any) as the Commissioners think fit to impose, including conditions as to repayment in specified circumstances;
    (c) deduction in respect of credit shall be made subject to such conditions (if any) as the Commissioners think fit to impose, including conditions as to the payment to the Commissioners, in specified circumstances, of an amount representing the whole or part of the amount deducted.

(6)   Regulations may require a claim by a person to be made in a return required by provision made under section 49 above.

(7)   Nothing in section 52 or 53 below shall be taken to derogate from the power to make regulations under this section (whether with regard to bad debts, the environment or any other matter).

[585]

NOTES
Commencement: 29 April 1996.
Regulations: the Landfill Tax Regulations 1996, SI 1996/1527, as amended by SI 1996/2100, SI 1997/1431.

52 Bad debts

(1)   Regulations may be made under section 51 above with a view to securing that a person is entitled to credit if—
    (a) he carries out a taxable activity as a result of which he becomes entitled to a debt which turns out to be bad (in whole or in part), and
    (b) such other conditions as may be prescribed are fulfilled.

(2)   The regulations may include provision under section 51(5)(b) or (c) above requiring repayment or payment if it turns out that it was not justified to regard a debt as bad (or to regard it as bad to the extent that it was so regarded).

(3)   The regulations may include provision for determining whether, and to what extent, a debt is to be taken to be bad.

[586]

NOTES
Commencement: 29 April 1996.
Regulations: the Landfill Tax Regulations 1996, SI 1996/1527, as amended by SI 1996/2100, SI 1997/1431.

53 Bodies concerned with the environment

(1)   Regulations may be made under section 51 above with a view to securing that a person is entitled to credit if—
    (a) he pays a sum to a body whose objects are or include the protection of the environment, and
    (b) such other conditions as may be prescribed are fulfilled.

(2)   The regulations may in particular prescribe conditions—
    (a) requiring bodies to which sums are paid (environmental bodies) to be approved by another body (the regulatory body);
    (b) requiring the regulatory body to be approved by the Commissioners;
    (c) requiring sums to be paid with the intention that they be expended on such matters connected with the protection of the environment as may be prescribed.

(3)   The regulations may include provision under section 51(5)(b) or (c) above requiring repayment or payment if—
    (a) a sum is not in fact expended on matters prescribed under subsection (2)(c) above, or
    (b) a prescribed condition turns out not to have been fulfilled.

(4)   The regulations may include—
    (a) provision for determining the amount of credit (including provision for limiting it);
    (b) provision that matters connected with the protection of the environment include such matters as overheads (including administration) of environmental bodies and the regulatory body;

(c) provision as to the matters by reference to which an environmental body or the regulatory body can be, and remain, approved (including matters relating to the functions and activities of any such body);

(d) provision allowing approval of an environmental body or the regulatory body to be withdrawn (whether prospectively or retrospectively);

(e) provision that, if approval of the regulatory body is withdrawn, another body may be approved in its place or its functions may be performed by the Commissioners;

(f) provision allowing the Commissioners to disclose to the regulatory body information which relates to the tax affairs of persons carrying out taxable activities and which is relevant to the credit scheme established by the regulations.

[587]

NOTES
Commencement: 29 April 1996.
Regulations: the Landfill Tax Regulations 1996, SI 1996/1527, as amended by SI 1996/2100, SI 1997/1431.

Review and appeal

54 Review of Commissioners' decisions

(1) This section applies to the following decisions of the Commissioners—

(a) a decision as to the registration or cancellation of registration of any person under this Part;

(b) a decision as to whether tax is chargeable in respect of a disposal or as to how much tax is chargeable;

[(ba) a decision to refuse an application for a certificate under section 43B above, or to withdraw such a certificate;

(bb) a decision to make a certificate issued under section 43B above subject to a condition that it is to be in force in relation to part only of the land to which the application for the certificate related;]

(c) a decision as to whether a person is entitled to credit by virtue of regulations under section 51 above or as to how much credit a person is entitled to or as to the manner in which he is to benefit from credit;

(d) a decision as to an assessment falling within subsection (2) below or as to the amount of such an assessment;

(e) a decision to refuse a request under section 58(3) below;

(f) a decision to refuse an application under section 59 below;

(g) a decision as to whether conditions set out in a specification under the authority of provision made under section 68(4)(b) below are met in relation to a disposal;

(h) a decision to give a direction under any provision contained in regulations by virtue of section 68(5) below;

(i) a decision as to a claim for the repayment of an amount under paragraph 14 of Schedule 5 to this Act;

(j) a decision as to liability to a penalty under Part V of that Schedule or as to the amount of such a penalty;

(k) a decision under paragraph 19 of that Schedule (as mentioned in paragraph 19(5));

(l) a decision as to any liability to pay interest under paragraph 26 or 27 of that Schedule or as to the amount of the interest payable;

(m) a decision as to any liability to pay interest under paragraph 29 of that Schedule or as to the amount of the interest payable;

(n) a decision to require any security under paragraph 31 of that Schedule or as to its amount;

(o) a decision as to the amount of any penalty or interest specified in an assessment under paragraph 32 of that Schedule.

(2)   An assessment falls within this subsection if it is an assessment under section 50 above in respect of an accounting period in relation to which a return required to be made by virtue of regulations under section 49 above has been made.

(3)   Any person who is or will be affected by any decision to which this section applies may by notice in writing to the Commissioners require them to review the decision.

(4)   The Commissioners shall not be required under this section to review any decision unless the notice requiring the review is given before the end of the period of 45 days beginning with the day on which written notification of the decision, or of the assessment containing the decision, was first given to the person requiring the review.

(5)   For the purposes of subsection (4) above it shall be the duty of the Commissioners to give written notification of any decision to which this section applies to any person who—
    (a) requests such a notification,
    (b) has not previously been given written notification of that decision, and
    (c) if given such a notification, will be entitled to require a review of the decision under this section.

(6)   A person shall be entitled to give a notice under this section requiring a decision to be reviewed for a second or subsequent time only if—
    (a) the grounds on which he requires the further review are that the Commissioners did not, on any previous review, have the opportunity to consider certain facts or other matters, and
    (b) he does not, on the further review, require the Commissioners to consider any facts or matters which were considered on a previous review except in so far as they are relevant to any issue not previously considered.

(7)   Where the Commissioners are required in accordance with this section to review any decision it shall be their duty to do so; and on the review they may withdraw, vary or confirm the decision.

(8)   Where—
    (a) it is the duty under this section of the Commissioners to review any decision, and
    (b) they do not, within the period of 45 days beginning with the day on which the review was required, give notice to the person requiring it of their determination on the review,

they shall be deemed for the purposes of this Part to have confirmed the decision.

[588]

NOTES
    Commencement: 1 October 1996 (subject to s 57(b) at **[591]**).
    Sub-s (1): paras (ba), (bb) inserted by the Landfill Tax (Contaminated Land) Order 1996, SI 1996/1529, art 4.

---

55 Appeals: general

(1)   Subject to the following provisions of this section, an appeal shall lie to an appeal tribunal with respect to any of the following decisions—
    (a) any decision by the Commissioners on a review under section 54 above (including a deemed confirmation under subsection (8) of that section);
    (b) any decision by the Commissioners on such review of a decision referred to in section 54(1) above as the Commissioners have agreed to undertake in consequence of a request made after the end of the period mentioned in section 54(4) above.

(2)   Where an appeal is made under this section by a person who is required to make returns by virtue of regulations under section 49 above, the appeal shall not be entertained unless the appellant—

    (a) has made all the returns which he is required to make by virtue of those regulations, and

    (b) has paid the amounts shown in those returns as payable by him.

(3)   Where an appeal is made under this section with respect to a decision falling within section 54(1)(b) or (d) above the appeal shall not be entertained unless—

    (a) the amount which the Commissioners have determined to be payable as tax has been paid or deposited with them, or

    (b) on being satisfied that the appellant would otherwise suffer hardship the Commissioners agree or the tribunal decides that it should be entertained notwithstanding that that amount has not been so paid or deposited.

(4)   On an appeal under this section against an assessment to a penalty under paragraph 18 of Schedule 5 to this Act, the burden of proof as to the matters specified in paragraphs (a) and (b) of sub-paragraph (1) of paragraph 18 shall lie upon the Commissioners.

[589]

NOTES

    Commencement: 1 October 1996 (subject to s 57(b) at **[591]**).

56 Appeals: other provisions

(1)   Subsection (2) below applies where the Commissioners make a decision falling within section 54(1)(d) above and on a review of it there is a further decision with respect to which an appeal is made under section 55 above; and the reference here to a further decision includes a reference to a deemed confirmation under section 54(8) above.

(2)   Where on the appeal—

    (a) it is found that the amount specified in the assessment is less than it ought to have been, and

    (b) the tribunal gives a direction specifying the correct amount,

the assessment shall have effect as an assessment of the amount specified in the direction and that amount shall be deemed to have been notified to the appellant.

(3)   Where on an appeal under section 55 above it is found that the whole or part of any amount paid or deposited in pursuance of section 55(3) above is not due, so much of that amount as is found not to be due shall be repaid with interest at such rate as the tribunal may determine.

(4)   Where on an appeal under section 55 above it is found that the whole or part of any amount due to the appellant by virtue of regulations under section 51(2)(c) or (d) or (f) above has not been paid, so much of that amount as is found not to have been paid shall be paid with interest at such rate as the tribunal may determine.

(5)   Where an appeal under section 55 above has been entertained notwithstanding that an amount determined by the Commissioners to be payable as tax has not been paid or deposited and it is found on the appeal that that amount is due the tribunal may, if it thinks fit, direct that that amount shall be paid with interest at such rate as may be specified in the direction.

(6)   Without prejudice to paragraph 25 of Schedule 5 to this Act, nothing in section 55 above shall be taken to confer on a tribunal any power to vary an amount assessed by way of penalty except in so far as it is necessary to reduce it to the amount which is appropriate under paragraphs 18 to 24 of that Schedule.

(7)   Without prejudice to paragraph 28 of Schedule 5 to this Act, nothing in section 55 above shall be taken to confer on a tribunal any power to vary an amount assessed by way of interest except in so far as it is necessary to reduce it to the amount which is appropriate under paragraph 26 or 27 of that Schedule.

(8)   Sections 85 and 87 of the Value Added Tax Act 1994 (settling of appeals by agreement and enforcement of certain decisions of tribunal) shall have effect as if—
   (a)   the references to section 83 of that Act included references to section 55 above, and
   (b)   the references to value added tax included references to landfill tax.

[590]

NOTES
   Commencement: 1 October 1996 (subject to s 57(b) at **[591]**).

57 Review and appeal: commencement

Sections 54 to 56 above shall come into force on—
   (a)   1st October 1996, or
   (b)   such earlier day as may be appointed by order.

[591]

NOTES
   Commencement: 29 April 1996.

Miscellaneous

58 Partnership, bankruptcy, transfer of business, etc

(1)   As regards any case where a business is carried on in partnership or by another unincorporated body, regulations may make provision for determining by what persons anything required by this Part to be done by a person is to be done.

(2)   The registration under this Part of an unincorporated body other than a partnership may be in the name of the body concerned; and in determining whether taxable activities are carried out by such a body no account shall be taken of any change in its members.

(3)   The registration under this Part of a body corporate carrying on a business in several divisions may, if the body corporate so requests and the Commissioners see fit, be in the names of those divisions.

(4)   As regards any case where a person carries on a business of a person who has died or become bankrupt or incapacitated or whose estate has been sequestrated, or of a person which is in liquidation or receivership or in relation to which an administration order is in force, regulations may—
   (a)   require the first-mentioned person to inform the Commissioners of the fact that he is carrying on the business and of the event that has led to his carrying it on;
   (b)   make provision allowing the person to be treated for a limited time as if he were the other person;
   (c)   make provision for securing continuity in the application of this Part where a person is so treated.

(5)   Regulations may make provision for securing continuity in the application of this Part in cases where a business carried on by a person is transferred to another person as a going concern.

(6)   Regulations under subsection (5) above may in particular—
   (a)   require the transferor to inform the Commissioners of the transfer;

(b) provide for liabilities and duties under this Part of the transferor to become, to such extent as may be provided by the regulations, liabilities and duties of the transferee;

(c) provide for any right of either of them to repayment or credit in respect of tax to be satisfied by making a repayment or allowing a credit to the other;

but the regulations may provide that no such provision as is mentioned in paragraph (b) or (c) of this subsection shall have effect in relation to any transferor and transferee unless an application in that behalf has been made by them under the regulations.

[592]

NOTES

Commencement: 29 April 1996.

Regulations: the Landfill Tax Regulations 1996, SI 1996/1527, as amended by SI 1996/2100, SI 1997/1431.

59 Groups of companies

(1) Where under the following provisions of this section any bodies corporate are treated as members of a group, for the purposes of this Part—

(a) any liability of a member of the group to pay tax shall be taken to be a liability of the representative member;

(b) the representative member shall be taken to carry out any taxable activities which a member of the group would carry out (apart from this section) by virtue of section 69 below;

(c) all members of the group shall be jointly and severally liable for any tax due from the representative member.

(2) Two or more bodies corporate are eligible to be treated as members of a group if the condition mentioned in subsection (3) below is fulfilled and—

(a) one of them controls each of the others,

(b) one person (whether a body corporate or an individual) controls all of them, or

(c) two or more individuals carrying on a business in partnership control all of them.

(3) The condition is that the prospective representative member has an established place of business in the United Kingdom.

(4) Where an application to that effect is made to the Commissioners with respect to two or more bodies corporate eligible to be treated as members of a group, then—

(a) from the beginning of an accounting period they shall be so treated, and

(b) one of them shall be the representative member,

unless the Commissioners refuse the application; and the Commissioners shall not refuse the application unless it appears to them necessary to do so for the protection of the revenue.

(5) Where any bodies corporate are treated as members of a group and an application to that effect is made to the Commissioners, then, from the beginning of an accounting period—

(a) a further body eligible to be so treated shall be included among the bodies so treated,

(b) a body corporate shall be excluded from the bodies so treated,

(c) another member of the group shall be substituted as the representative member, or

(d) the bodies corporate shall no longer be treated as members of a group,

unless the application is to the effect mentioned in paragraph (a) or (c) above and the Commissioners refuse the application.

(6)   The Commissioners may refuse an application under subsection (5)(a) or (c) above only if it appears to them necessary to do so for the protection of the revenue.

(7)   Where a body corporate is treated as a member of a group as being controlled by any person and it appears to the Commissioners that it has ceased to be so controlled, they shall, by notice given to that person, terminate that treatment from such date as may be specified in the notice.

(8)   An application under this section with respect to any bodies corporate must be made by one of those bodies or by the person controlling them and must be made not less than 90 days before the date from which it is to take effect, or at such later time as the Commissioners may allow.

(9)   For the purposes of this section a body corporate shall be taken to control another body corporate if it is empowered by statute to control that body's activities or if it is that body's holding company within the meaning of section 736 of the Companies Act 1985; and an individual or individuals shall be taken to control a body corporate if he or they, were he or they a company, would be that body's holding company within the meaning of that section.

[593]

NOTES
Commencement: 29 April 1996.

60 Information, powers, penalties, etc

Schedule 5 to this Act (which contains provisions relating to information, powers, penalties and other matters) shall have effect.

[594]

NOTES
Commencement: 29 April 1996.

61 Taxable disposals: special provisions

(1)   Where—
  (a) a taxable disposal is in fact made on a particular day,
  (b) within the period of 14 days beginning with that day the person liable to pay tax in respect of the disposal issues a landfill invoice in respect of the disposal, and
  (c) he has not notified the Commissioners in writing that he elects not to avail himself of this subsection,

for the purposes of this Part the disposal shall be treated as made at the time the invoice is issued.

(2)   The reference in subsection (1) above to a landfill invoice is to a document containing such particulars as regulations may prescribe for the purposes of that subsection.

(3)   The Commissioners may at the request of a person direct that subsection (1) above shall apply—
  (a) in relation to disposals in respect of which he is liable to pay tax, or
  (b) in relation to such of them as may be specified in the direction,

as if for the period of 14 days there were substituted such longer period as may be specified in the direction.

[595]

NOTES
Commencement: 29 April 1996.
Regulations: the Landfill Tax Regulations 1996, SI 1996/1527, as amended by SI 1996/2100, SI 1997/1431.

62 Taxable disposals: regulations

(1)   For the purposes of this Part, regulations may make provision under this section in relation to a disposal which is a taxable disposal (or would be apart from the regulations).

(2)   The regulations may provide that if particular conditions are fulfilled—
(a) the disposal shall be treated as not being a taxable disposal, or
(b) the disposal shall, to the extent found in accordance with prescribed rules, be treated as not being a taxable disposal.

(3)   The regulations may provide that if particular conditions are fulfilled—
(a) the disposal shall be treated as made at a time which is found in accordance with prescribed rules and which falls after the time when it would be regarded as made apart from the regulations, or
(b) the disposal shall, to the extent found in accordance with prescribed rules, be treated as made at a time which is found in accordance with prescribed rules and which falls after the time when it would be regarded as made apart from the regulations.

(4)   In finding the time when the disposal would be regarded as made apart from the regulations, section 61(1) above and any direction under section 61(3) above shall be taken into account.

(5)   The regulations may be framed by reference to—
(a) conditions specified in the regulations or by the Commissioners or by an authorised person, or
(b) any combination of such conditions;
and the regulations may specify conditions, or allow conditions to be specified, generally or with regard to particular cases.

(6)   The regulations may make provision under subsections (2)(b) and (3)(b) above in relation to the same disposal.

(7)   The regulations may only provide that a disposal is to be treated as not being a taxable disposal if or to the extent that—
(a) the disposal is a temporary one pending the incineration or recycling of the material concerned, or pending the removal of the material for use elsewhere, or pending the sorting of the material with a view to its removal elsewhere or its eventual disposal, and
(b) the temporary disposal is made in an area designated for the purpose by an authorised person.

[596]

NOTES
Commencement: 29 April 1996.
Regulations: the Landfill Tax Regulations 1996, SI 1996/1527, as amended by SI 1996/2100, SI 1997/1431.

63 Qualifying material: special provisions

(1)   This section applies for the purposes of section 42 above.

(2)   The Commissioners may direct that where material is disposed of it must be treated as qualifying material if it would in fact be such material but for a small quantity of non-qualifying material; and whether a quantity of non-qualifying material is small must be determined in accordance with the terms of the direction.

(3)   The Commissioners may at the request of a person direct that where there is a disposal in respect of which he is liable to pay tax the material disposed of must be treated as qualifying material if it would in fact be such material but for a small quantity of non-qualifying material, and—

(a) a direction may apply to all disposals in respect of which a person is liable to pay tax or to such of them as are identified in the direction;
(b) whether a quantity of non-qualifying material is small must be determined in accordance with the terms of the direction.

(4) If a direction under subsection (3) above applies to a disposal any direction under subsection (2) above shall not apply to it.

(5) An order may provide that material must not be treated as qualifying material unless prescribed conditions are met.

(6) A condition may relate to any matter the Treasury think fit (such as the production of a document which includes a statement of the nature of the material).
[597]

NOTES
Commencement: 29 April 1996.
Orders: the Landfill Tax (Qualifying Material) Order 1996, SI 1996/1528.

Interpretation

64 Disposal of material as waste

(1) A disposal of material is a disposal of it as waste if the person making the disposal does so with the intention of discarding the material.

(2) The fact that the person making the disposal or any other person could benefit from or make use of the material is irrelevant.

(3) Where a person makes a disposal on behalf of another person, for the purposes of subsections (1) and (2) above the person on whose behalf the disposal is made shall be treated as making the disposal.

(4) The reference in subsection (3) above to a disposal on behalf of another person includes references to a disposal—
(a) at the request of another person;
(b) in pursuance of a contract with another person.
[598]

NOTES
Commencement: 29 April 1996.

65 Disposal by way of landfill

(1) There is a disposal of material by way of landfill if—
(a) it is deposited on the surface of land or on a structure set into the surface, or
(b) it is deposited under the surface of land.

(2) Subsection (1) above applies whether or not the material is placed in a container before it is deposited.

(3) Subsection (1)(b) above applies whether the material—
(a) is covered with earth after it is deposited, or
(b) is deposited in a cavity (such as a cavern or mine).

(4) If material is deposited on the surface of land (or on a structure set into the surface) with a view to it being covered with earth the disposal must be treated as made when the material is deposited and not when it is covered.

(5) An order may provide that the meaning of the disposal of material by way of landfill (as it applies for the time being) shall be varied.

(6)   An order under subsection (5) above may make provision in such way as the Treasury think fit, whether by amending any of subsections (1) to (4) above or otherwise.

(7)   In this section "land" includes land covered by water where the land is above the low water mark of ordinary spring tides.

(8)   In this section "earth" includes similar matter (such as sand or rocks).

[599]

NOTES
Commencement: 29 April 1996.

66 Landfill sites

Land is a landfill site at a given time if at that time—
- (a) a licence which is a site licence for the purposes of Part II of the Environmental Protection Act 1990 (waste on land) is in force in relation to the land and authorises disposals in or on the land,
- (b) a resolution under section 54 of that Act (land occupied by waste disposal authorities in Scotland) is in force in relation to the land and authorises deposits or disposals in or on the land,
- (c) a disposal licence issued under Part II of the Pollution Control and Local Government (Northern Ireland) Order 1978 (waste on land) is in force in relation to the land and authorises deposits on the land,
- (d) a resolution passed under Article 13 of that Order (land occupied by district councils in Northern Ireland) is in force in relation to the land and relates to deposits on the land, or
- (e) a licence under any provision for the time being having effect in Northern Ireland and corresponding to section 35 of the Environmental Protection Act 1990 (waste management licences) is in force in relation to the land and authorises disposals in or on the land.

[600]

NOTES
Commencement: 29 April 1996.

67 Operators of landfill sites

The operator of a landfill site at a given time is—
- (a) the person who is at the time concerned the holder of the licence, where section 66(a) above applies;
- (b) the waste disposal authority which at the time concerned occupies the landfill site, where section 66(b) above applies;
- (c) the person who is at the time concerned the holder of the licence, where section 66(c) above applies;
- (d) the district council which passed the resolution, where section 66(d) above applies;
- (e) the person who is at the time concerned the holder of the licence, where section 66(e) above applies.

[601]

NOTES
Commencement: 29 April 1996.

68 Weight of material disposed of

(1)   The weight of the material disposed of on a taxable disposal shall be determined in accordance with regulations.

(2) The regulations may—
    (a) prescribe rules for determining the weight;
    (b) authorise rules for determining the weight to be specified by the Commissioners in a prescribed manner;
    (c) authorise rules for determining the weight to be agreed by the person liable to pay the tax and an authorised person.

(3) The regulations may in particular prescribe, or authorise the specification or agreement of, rules about—
    (a) the method by which the weight is to be determined;
    (b) the time by reference to which the weight is to be determined;
    (c) the discounting of constituents (such as water).

(4) The regulations may include provision that a specification authorised under subsection (2)(b) above may provide—
    (a) that it is to have effect only in relation to disposals of such descriptions as may be set out in the specification;
    (b) that it is not to have effect in relation to particular disposals unless the Commissioners are satisfied that such conditions as may be set out in the specification are met in relation to the disposals;
and the conditions may be framed by reference to such factors as the Commissioners think fit (such as the consent of an authorised person to the specification having effect in relation to disposals).

(5) The regulations may include provision that—
    (a) where rules are agreed as mentioned in subsection (2)(c) above, and
    (b) the Commissioners believe that they should no longer be applied because they do not give an accurate indication of the weight or they are not being fully observed or for some other reason,
the Commissioners may direct that the agreed rules shall no longer have effect.

(6) The regulations shall be so framed that where in relation to a given disposal—
    (a) no specification of the Commissioners has effect, and
    (b) no agreed rules have effect,
the weight shall be determined in accordance with rules prescribed in the regulations.

[602]

NOTES
Commencement: 29 April 1996.
Regulations: the Landfill Tax Regulations 1996, SI 1996/1527, as amended by SI 1996/2100, SI 1997/1431.

69 Taxable activities

(1) A person carries out a taxable activity if—
    (a) he makes a taxable disposal in respect of which he is liable to pay tax, or
    (b) he permits another person to make a taxable disposal in respect of which he (the first-mentioned person) is liable to pay tax.

(2) Where—
    (a) a taxable disposal is made, and
    (b) it is made without the knowledge of the person who is liable to pay tax in respect of it,
that person shall for the purposes of this section be taken to permit the disposal.

[603]

NOTES
Commencement: 29 April 1996.

70 Interpretation: other provisions

(1) Unless the context otherwise requires—
"accounting period" shall be construed in accordance with section 49 above;
"appeal tribunal" means a VAT and duties tribunal;
"authorised person" means any person acting under the authority of the Commissioners;
"the Commissioners" means the Commissioners of Customs and Excise;
"conduct" includes any act, omission or statement;
["the Environment Agency" means the body established by section 1 of the Environment Act 1995;]
"material" means material of all kinds, including objects, substances and products of all kinds;
"prescribed" means prescribed by an order or regulations under this Part;
"registrable person" has the meaning given by section 47(10) above;
["the Scottish Environment Protection Agency" means the body established by section 20 of the Environment Act 1995;]
"tax" means landfill tax;
"taxable disposal" has the meaning given by section 40 above.

(2) A landfill disposal is a disposal—
(a) of material as waste, and
(b) made by way of landfill.

[(2A) A local authority is—
(a) the council of a county, county borough, district, London borough, parish or group of parishes (or, in Wales, community or group of communities);
(b) the Common Council of the City of London;
(c) as respects the Temples, the Sub-Treasurer of the Inner Temple and the Under-Treasurer of the Middle Temple respectively;
(d) the council of the Isles of Scilly;
(e) any joint committee or joint board established by two or more of the foregoing;
(f) in relation to Scotland, a council constituted under section 2 of the Local Government etc (Scotland) Act 1994, any two or more such councils and any joint committee or joint board within the meaning of section 235(1) of the Local Government (Scotland) Act 1973.]]

(3) A reference to this Part includes a reference to any order or regulations made under it and a reference to a provision of this Part includes a reference to any order or regulations made under the provision, unless otherwise required by the context or any order or regulations.

(4) This section and sections 64 to 69 above apply for the purposes of this Part.

[604]

NOTES
Commencement: 1 August 1996 (sub-s (2A)); 29 April 1996 (remainder).
Sub-s (1): definitions "the Environment Agency" and "the Scottish Environment Protection Agency" inserted by the Landfill Tax (Contaminated Land) Order 1996, SI 1996/1529, art 5.
Sub-s (2A): inserted by SI 1996/1529, art 6.

Supplementary

71 Orders and regulations

(1) The power to make an order under section 57 above shall be exercisable by the Commissioners, and the power to make an order under any other provision of this Part shall be exercisable by the Treasury.

(2)   Any power to make regulations under this Part shall be exercisable by the Commissioners.

(3)   Any power to make an order or regulations under this Part shall be exercisable by statutory instrument.

(4)   An order to which this subsection applies shall be laid before the House of Commons; and unless it is approved by that House before the expiration of a period of 28 days beginning with the date on which it was made it shall cease to have effect on the expiration of that period, but without prejudice to anything previously done under the order or to the making of a new order.

(5)   In reckoning any such period as is mentioned in subsection (4) above no account shall be taken of any time during which Parliament is dissolved or prorogued or during which the House of Commons is adjourned for more than four days.

(6)   A statutory instrument containing an order or regulations under this Part (other than an order under section 57 above or an order to which subsection (4) above applies) shall be subject to annulment in pursuance of a resolution of the House of Commons.

(7)   Subsection (4) above applies to—
  (a)   an order under section 42(3) above providing for material which would otherwise be qualifying material not to be qualifying material;
  (b)   an order under section 46 above which produces the result that a disposal which would otherwise not be a taxable disposal is a taxable disposal;
  (c)   an order under section 63(5) above other than one which provides only that an earlier order under section 63(5) is not to apply to material;
  (d)   an order under section 65(5) above providing for anything which would otherwise not be a disposal of material by way of landfill to be such a disposal.

(8)   Any power to make an order or regulations under this Part—
  (a)   may be exercised as regards prescribed cases or descriptions of case;
  (b)   may be exercised differently in relation to different cases or descriptions of case.

(9)   An order or regulations under this Part may include such supplementary, incidental, consequential or transitional provisions as appear to the Treasury or the Commissioners (as the case may be) to be necessary or expedient.

(10) No specific provision of this Part about an order or regulations shall prejudice the generality of subsections (8) and (9) above.

[605]

NOTES
  Commencement: 29 April 1996.

72–196   (*Outside the scope of this work.*)

PART VII
MISCELLANEOUS AND SUPPLEMENTAL

Miscellaneous: indirect taxation

197 Setting of rates of interest

(1)   The rate of interest applicable for the purposes of an enactment to which this section applies shall be the rate which for the purposes of that enactment is provided for by regulations made by the Treasury under this section.

(2)   This section applies to—
  (a) paragraphs 7 and 9 of Schedule 6 to the Finance Act 1994 (interest payable to or by the Commissioners of Customs and Excise in connection with air passenger duty);
  (b) paragraphs 21 and 22 of Schedule 7 to that Act (interest on amounts of insurance premium tax and on amounts payable by the Commissioners in respect of that tax);
  (c) sections 74 and 78 of the Value Added Tax Act 1994 (interest on VAT recovered or recoverable by assessment and interest payable in cases of official error); . . .
  (d) paragraphs 26 and 29 of Schedule 5 to this Act (interest payable to or by the Commissioners in connection with landfill tax) [and
  (e) paragraph 17 of Schedule 5 to the Finance Act 1997 (interest on amounts repayable in respect of overpayments by the Commissioners in connection with excise duties, insurance premium tax and landfill tax).]

(3)   Regulations under this section may—
  (a) make different provision for different enactments or for different purposes of the same enactment,
  (b) either themselves specify a rate of interest for the purposes of an enactment or make provision for any such rate to be determined, and to change from time to time, by reference to such rate or the average of such rates as may be referred to in the regulations,
  (c) provide for rates to be reduced below, or increased above, what they otherwise would be by specified amounts or by reference to specified formulae,
  (d) provide for rates arrived at by reference to averages or formulae to be rounded up or down,
  (e) provide for circumstances in which changes of rates of interest are or are not to take place, and
  (f) provide that changes of rates are to have effect for periods beginning on or after a day determined in accordance with the regulations in relation to interest running from before that day, as well as in relation to interest running from, or from after, that day.

(4)   The power to make regulations under this section shall be exercisable by statutory instrument subject to annulment in pursuance of a resolution of the House of Commons.

(5)   Where—
  (a) regulations under this section provide, without specifying the rate determined in accordance with the regulations, for a new method of determining the rate applicable for the purposes of any enactment, or
  (b) the rate which, in accordance with regulations under this section, is the rate applicable for the purposes of any enactment changes otherwise than by virtue of the making of regulations specifying a new rate,

the Commissioners of Customs and Excise shall make an order specifying the new rate and the day from which, in accordance with the regulations, it has effect.

(6)   . . .

(7)   Subsections (1) and (6) above shall have effect for periods beginning on or after such day as the Treasury may by order made by statutory instrument appoint and shall have effect in relation to interest running from before that day, as well as in relation to interest running from, or from after, that day; and different days may be appointed under this subsection for different purposes.

NOTES
Commencement: 1 April 1997 (sub-ss (1), (6)); 29 April 1996 (remainder).

Sub-s (2): word omitted from para (c) repealed and para (e) added, by the Finance Act 1997, ss 50, 113, Sch 5, para 21, Sch 18, Pt V(1).

Sub-s (6): amends the Finance Act 1994, Sch 6, paras 7(1), (3), 9(1), Sch 7, paras 21(1), (3), 22(2), and the Value Added Tax Act 1994, ss 74(1), (2), (4), 78(3).

Orders: the Finance Act 1996, section 197, (Appointed Day) Order 1997, SI 1997/1015.

Regulations: the Air Passenger Duty and Other Indirect Taxes (Interest Rate) Regulations 1997, SI 1997/1016.

198–203 (*Relate to banks (s 198); quotation or listing of securities (s 199); domicile for tax purposes of overseas electors (s 200); enactment of Inland Revenue concessions (s 201); gilt stripping (s 202); modification of the Agriculture Act 1993 (s 203).*)

Supplemental

204, 205 (*Relate to interpretation (s 204); repeals (s 205).*)

206 Short title

This Act may be cited as the Finance Act 1996.

[607]

NOTES
Commencement: 29 April 1996.

(*Schs 1–4 outside the scope of this work.*)

SCHEDULE 5
LANDFILL TAX

Section 60

PART I
INFORMATION

General

1.—(1) Every person who is concerned (in whatever capacity) with any landfill disposal shall furnish to the Commissioners such information relating to the disposal as the Commissioners may reasonably require.

(2) The information mentioned in sub-paragraph (1) above shall be furnished within such time and in such form as the Commissioners may reasonably require.

Records

2.—(1) Regulations may require registrable persons to make records.

(2) Regulations under sub-paragraph (1) above may be framed by reference to such records as may be stipulated in any notice published by the Commissioners in pursuance of the regulations and not withdrawn by a further notice.

(3) Regulations may—
    (a)   require registrable persons to preserve records of a prescribed description (whether or not the records are required to be made in pursuance of regulations) for such period not exceeding six years as may be specified in the regulations;
    (b)   authorise the Commissioners to direct that any such records need only be preserved for a shorter period than that specified in the regulations;
    (c)   authorise a direction to be made so as to apply generally or in such cases as the Commissioners may stipulate.

(4) Any duty under regulations to preserve records may be discharged by the preservation of the information contained in them by such means as the Commissioners may approve; and where that information is so preserved a copy of any document forming part of the records shall (subject to the following provisions of this paragraph) be admissible in evidence in any proceedings, whether civil or criminal, to the same extent as the records themselves.

(5) The Commissioners may, as a condition of approving under sub-paragraph (4) above any means of preserving information contained in any records, impose such reasonable requirements as appear to them necessary for securing that the information will be as readily available to them as if the records themselves had been preserved.

(6) A statement contained in a document produced by a computer shall not by virtue of sub-paragraph (4) above be admissible in evidence—

    (a)   in criminal proceedings in England and Wales, except in accordance with sections 69 and 70 of the Police and Criminal Evidence Act 1984 and Part II of the Criminal Justice Act 1988;

  (b), (c)   (*apply to Scotland only*);

    (d)   in civil proceedings in Northern Ireland, except in accordance with sections 2 and 3 of the Civil Evidence Act (Northern Ireland) 1971;

    (e)   in criminal proceedings in Northern Ireland, except in accordance with Article 68 of the Police and Criminal Evidence (Northern Ireland) Order 1989 and Part II of the Criminal Justice (Evidence, Etc) (Northern Ireland) Order 1988.

(7) In the case of civil proceedings in England and Wales to which sections 5 and 6 of the Civil Evidence Act 1968 apply, a statement contained in a document produced by a computer shall not be admissible in evidence by virtue of sub-paragraph (4) above except in accordance with those sections.

Documents

3.—(1) Every person who is concerned (in whatever capacity) with any landfill disposal shall upon demand made by an authorised person produce or cause to be produced for inspection by that person any documents relating to the disposal.

(2) Where, by virtue of sub-paragraph (1) above, an authorised person has power to require the production of any documents from any person, he shall have the like power to require production of the documents concerned from any other person who appears to the authorised person to be in possession of them; but where any such other person claims a lien on any document produced by him, the production shall be without prejudice to the lien.

(3) The documents mentioned in sub-paragraphs (1) and (2) above shall be produced—

    (a)   at such place as the authorised person may reasonably require, and

    (b)   at such time as the authorised person may reasonably require.

(4) An authorised person may take copies of, or make extracts from, any document produced under sub-paragraph (1) or (2) above.

(5) If it appears to him to be necessary to do so, an authorised person may, at a reasonable time and for a reasonable period, remove any document produced under sub-paragraph (1) or (2) above and shall, on request, provide a receipt for any document so removed; and where a lien is claimed on a document produced under sub-paragraph (2) above the removal of the document under this sub-paragraph shall not be regarded as breaking the lien.

(6) Where a document removed by an authorised person under sub-paragraph (5) above is reasonably required for any purpose he shall, as soon as practicable, provide a copy of the document, free of charge, to the person by whom it was produced or caused to be produced.

(7) Where any documents removed under the powers conferred by this paragraph are lost or damaged the Commissioners shall be liable to compensate their owner for any expenses reasonably incurred by him in replacing or repairing the documents.

[608]

NOTES

Commencement: 29 April 1996.

Regulations: the Landfill Tax Regulations 1996, SI 1996/1527, as amended by SI 1996/2100, SI 1997/1431.

PART II
POWERS

Entry and inspection

4. For the purpose of exercising any powers under this Part of this Act an authorised person may at any reasonable time enter and inspect premises used in connection with the carrying on of a business.

Entry and search

5.—(1) Where—

    (a)   a justice of the peace is satisfied on information on oath that there is reasonable ground for suspecting that a fraud offence which appears to be of a serious nature is being, has been or is about to be committed on any premises or that evidence of the commission of such an offence is to be found there, or

    (b)   *(applies to Scotland only)*,

he may issue a warrant in writing authorising any authorised person to enter those premises, if necessary by force, at any time within one month from the time of the issue of the warrant and search them.

    (2)   A person who enters the premises under the authority of the warrant may—

    (a)   take with him such other persons as appear to him to be necessary;

    (b)   seize and remove any documents or other things whatsoever found on the premises which he has reasonable cause to believe may be required as evidence for the purposes of proceedings in respect of a fraud offence which appears to him to be of a serious nature;

    (c)   search or cause to be searched any person found on the premises whom he has reasonable cause to believe to be in possession of any such documents or other things;

but no woman or girl shall be searched except by a woman.

    (3)   The powers conferred by a warrant under this paragraph shall not be exercisable—

    (a)   by more than such number of authorised persons as may be specified in the warrant,

    (b)   outside such times of day as may be so specified, or

    (c)   if the warrant so provides, otherwise than in the presence of a constable in uniform.

    (4)   An authorised person seeking to exercise the powers conferred by a warrant under this paragraph or, if there is more than one such authorised person, that one of them who is in charge of the search shall provide a copy of the warrant endorsed with his name as follows—

    (a)   if the occupier of the premises concerned is present at the time the search is to begin, the copy shall be supplied to the occupier;

    (b)   if at that time the occupier is not present but a person who appears to the authorised person to be in charge of the premises is present, the copy shall be supplied to that person;

    (c)   if neither paragraph (a) nor paragraph (b) above applies, the copy shall be left in a prominent place on the premises.

    (5) In this paragraph "a fraud offence" means an offence under any provision of paragraph 15(1) to (5) below.

Arrest

6.—(1) Where an authorised person has reasonable grounds for suspecting that a fraud offence has been committed he may arrest anyone whom he has reasonable grounds for suspecting to be guilty of the offence.

    (2) In this paragraph "a fraud offence" means an offence under any provision of paragraph 15(1) to (5) below.

Order for access to recorded information etc

7.—(1) Where, on an application by an authorised person, a justice of the peace or, in Scotland, a justice (within the meaning of section 307 of the Criminal Procedure (Scotland) Act 1995) is satisfied that there are reasonable grounds for believing—

(a) that an offence in connection with tax is being, has been or is about to be committed, and

(b) that any recorded information (including any document of any nature whatsoever) which may be required as evidence for the purpose of any proceedings in respect of such an offence is in the possession of any person,

he may make an order under this paragraph.

(2) An order under this paragraph is an order that the person who appears to the justice to be in possession of the recorded information to which the application relates shall—

(a) give an authorised person access to it, and

(b) permit an authorised person to remove and take away any of it which he reasonably considers necessary,

not later than the end of the period of 7 days beginning with the date of the order or the end of such longer period as the order may specify.

(3) The reference in sub-paragraph (2)(a) above to giving an authorised person access to the recorded information to which the application relates includes a reference to permitting the authorised person to take copies of it or to make extracts from it.

(4) Where the recorded information consists of information contained in a computer, an order under this paragraph shall have effect as an order to produce the information in a form in which it is visible and legible and, if the authorised person wishes to remove it, in a form in which it can be removed.

(5) This paragraph is without prejudice to paragraphs 3 to 5 above.

Removal of documents etc

8.—(1) An authorised person who removes anything in the exercise of a power conferred by or under paragraph 5 or 7 above shall, if so requested by a person showing himself—

(a) to be the occupier of premises from which it was removed, or

(b) to have had custody or control of it immediately before the removal,

provide that person with a record of what he removed.

(2) The authorised person shall provide the record within a reasonable time from the making of the request for it.

(3) Subject to sub-paragraph (7) below, if a request for permission to be allowed access to anything which—

(a) has been removed by an authorised person, and

(b) is retained by the Commissioners for the purposes of investigating an offence,

is made to the officer in overall charge of the investigation by a person who had custody or control of the thing immediately before it was so removed or by someone acting on behalf of such a person, the officer shall allow the person who made the request access to it under the supervision of an authorised person.

(4) Subject to sub-paragraph (7) below, if a request for a photograph or copy of any such thing is made to the officer in overall charge of the investigation by a person who had custody or control of the thing immediately before it was so removed, or by someone acting on behalf of such a person, the officer shall—

(a) allow the person who made the request access to it under the supervision of an authorised person for the purpose of photographing it or copying it, or

(b) photograph or copy it, or cause it to be photographed or copied.

(5) Subject to sub-paragraph (7) below, where anything is photographed or copied under sub-paragraph (4)(b) above the officer shall supply the photograph or copy, or cause it to be supplied, to the person who made the request.

(6) The photograph or copy shall be supplied within a reasonable time from the making of the request.

(7) There is no duty under this paragraph to allow access to, or to supply a photograph or copy of, anything if the officer in overall charge of the investigation for the purposes of which it was removed has reasonable grounds for believing that to do so would prejudice—

(a) that investigation,

(b)   the investigation of an offence other than the offence for the purposes of the investigation of which the thing was removed, or

(c)   any criminal proceedings which may be brought as a result of the investigation of which he is in charge or any such investigation as is mentioned in paragraph (b) above.

(8)   Any reference in this paragraph to the officer in overall charge of the investigation is a reference to the person whose name and address are endorsed on the warrant concerned as being the officer so in charge.

9.—(1)   Where, on an application made as mentioned in sub-paragraph (2) below, the appropriate judicial authority is satisfied that a person has failed to comply with a requirement imposed by paragraph 8 above, the authority may order that person to comply with the requirement within such time and in such manner as may be specified in the order.

(2)   An application under sub-paragraph (1) above shall be made—

(a)   in the case of a failure to comply with any of the requirements imposed by sub-paragraphs (1) and (2) of paragraph 8 above, by the occupier of the premises from which the thing in question was removed or by the person who had custody or control of it immediately before it was so removed, and

(b)   in any other case, by the person who had such custody or control.

(3)   In this paragraph "the appropriate judicial authority" means—

(a)   in England and Wales, a magistrates' court;

(b)   (*applies to Scotland only*);

(c)   in Northern Ireland, a court of summary jurisdiction, as defined in Article 2(2)(a) of the Magistrates' Court (Northern Ireland) Order 1981.

(4)   In England and Wales and Northern Ireland, an application for an order under this paragraph shall be made by way of complaint; and sections 21 and 42(2) of the Interpretation Act (Northern Ireland) 1954 shall apply as if any reference in those provisions to any enactment included a reference to this paragraph.

Power to take samples

10.—(1)   An authorised person, if it appears to him necessary for the protection of the revenue against mistake or fraud, may at any time take, from material which he has reasonable cause to believe is intended to be, is being, or has been disposed of as waste by way of landfill, such samples as he may require with a view to determining how the material ought to be or to have been treated for the purposes of tax.

(2)   Any sample taken under this paragraph shall be disposed of in such manner as the Commissioners may direct.

[609]

NOTES

Commencement: 29 April 1996.

PART III
RECOVERY

General

11. Tax due from any person shall be recoverable as a debt due to the Crown.

12., 13.   . . .

Recovery of overpaid tax

14.—(1)   Where a person has paid an amount to the Commissioners by way of tax which was not tax due to them, they shall be liable to repay the amount to him.

(2)   The Commissioners shall only be liable to repay an amount under this paragraph on a claim being made for the purpose.

(3)   It shall be a defence, in relation to a claim under this paragraph, that repayment of an amount would unjustly enrich the claimant.

[(4) The Commissioners shall not be liable, on a claim made under this paragraph, to repay any amount paid to them more than three years before the making of the claim.]

(5) A claim under this paragraph shall be made in such form and manner and shall be supported by such documentary evidence as may be prescribed by regulations.

(6) Except as provided by this paragraph, the Commissioners shall not be liable to repay an amount paid to them by way of tax by virtue of the fact that it was not tax due to them.

[610]

NOTES

Commencement: 29 April 1996.

Para 12: partly amends the Insolvency Act 1986, s 386(1), the Insolvency (Northern Ireland) Order 1989, SI 1989/2405 (NI 19), and adds the Insolvency Act 1986, Sch 6, para 3B, SI 1989/2405, Sch 4, para 3B; remainder applies to Scotland only.

Para 13: repealed by the Finance Act 1997, s 113, Sch 18, Pt V(2).

Para 14: sub-para (4) substituted by the Finance Act 1997, s 50, Sch 5, para 5(3).

Regulations: the Landfill Tax Regulations 1996, SI 1996/1527, as amended by SI 1996/2100, SI 1997/1431.

PART IV
CRIMINAL PENALTIES

Criminal offences

15.—(1)   A person is guilty of an offence if—
    (a)   being a registrable person, he is knowingly concerned in, or in the taking of steps with a view to, the fraudulent evasion of tax by him or another registrable person, or
    (b)   not being a registrable person, he is knowingly concerned in, or in the taking of steps with a view to, the fraudulent evasion of tax by a registrable person.

(2) Any reference in sub-paragraph (1) above to the evasion of tax includes a reference to the obtaining of a payment under regulations under section 51(2)(c) or (d) or (f) of this Act.

(3) A person is guilty of an offence if with the requisite intent—
    (a)   he produces, furnishes or sends, or causes to be produced, furnished or sent, for the purposes of this Part of this Act any document which is false in a material particular, or
    (b)   he otherwise makes use for those purposes of such a document;
and the requisite intent is intent to deceive or to secure that a machine will respond to the document as if it were a true document.

(4) A person is guilty of an offence if in furnishing any information for the purposes of this Part of this Act he makes a statement which he knows to be false in a material particular or recklessly makes a statement which is false in a material particular.

(5) A person is guilty of an offence by virtue of this sub-paragraph if his conduct during any specified period must have involved the commission by him of one or more offences under the preceding provisions of this paragraph; and the preceding provisions of this sub-paragraph apply whether or not the particulars of that offence or those offences are known.

(6) A person is guilty of an offence if—
    (a)   he enters into a taxable landfill contract, or
    (b)   he makes arrangements for other persons to enter into such a contract,
with reason to believe that tax in respect of the disposal concerned will be evaded.

(7) A person is guilty of an offence if he carries out taxable activities without giving security (or further security) he has been required to give under paragraph 31 below.

(8) For the purposes of this paragraph a taxable landfill contract is a contract under which there is to be a taxable disposal.

Criminal penalties

16.—(1)   A person guilty of an offence under paragraph 15(1) above is liable—
    (a)   on summary conviction, to a penalty of the statutory maximum or of three times the amount of the tax, whichever is the greater, or to imprisonment for a term not exceeding six months or to both;
    (b)   on conviction on indictment, to a penalty of any amount or to imprisonment for a term not exceeding seven years or to both.

(2) The reference in sub-paragraph (1) above to the amount of the tax shall be construed, in relation to tax itself or a payment falling within paragraph 15(2) above, as a reference to the aggregate of—
- (a) the amount (if any) falsely claimed by way of credit, and
- (b) the amount (if any) by which the gross amount of tax was falsely understated.

(3) A person guilty of an offence under paragraph 15(3) or (4) above is liable—
- (a) on summary conviction, to a penalty of the statutory maximum (or, where sub-paragraph (4) below applies, to the alternative penalty there specified if it is greater) or to imprisonment for a term not exceeding six months or to both;
- (b) on conviction on indictment, to a penalty of any amount or to imprisonment for a term not exceeding seven years or to both.

(4) Where—
- (a) the document referred to in paragraph 15(3) above is a return required under this Part of this Act, or
- (b) the information referred to in paragraph 15(4) above is contained in or otherwise relevant to such a return,

the alternative penalty is a penalty equal to three times the aggregate of the amount (if any) falsely claimed by way of credit and the amount (if any) by which the gross amount of tax was understated.

(5) A person guilty of an offence under paragraph 15(5) above is liable—
- (a) on summary conviction, to a penalty of the statutory maximum (or, if greater, three times the amount of any tax that was or was intended to be evaded by his conduct) or to imprisonment for a term not exceeding six months or to both;
- (b) on conviction on indictment, to a penalty of any amount or to imprisonment for a term not exceeding seven years or to both;

and paragraph 15(2) and sub-paragraph (2) above shall apply for the purposes of this sub-paragraph as they apply respectively for the purposes of paragraph 15(1) and sub-paragraph (1) above.

(6) A person guilty of an offence under paragraph 15(6) above is liable on summary conviction to a penalty of level 5 on the standard scale or three times the amount of the tax, whichever is the greater.

(7) A person guilty of an offence under paragraph 15(7) above is liable on summary conviction to a penalty of level 5 on the standard scale.

(8) In this paragraph—
- (a) "credit" means credit for which provision is made by regulations under section 51 of this Act;
- (b) "the gross amount of tax" means the total amount of tax due before taking into account any deduction for which provision is made by regulations under section 51(2) of this Act.

Criminal proceedings etc

17. Sections 145 to 155 of the Customs and Excise Management Act 1979 (proceedings for offences, mitigation of penalties and certain other matters) shall apply in relation to offences under paragraph 15 above and penalties imposed under paragraph 16 above as they apply in relation to offences and penalties under the customs and excise Acts as defined in that Act.

[611]

NOTES
Commencement: 29 April 1996.

PART V
CIVIL PENALTIES

Evasion

18.—(1) Where—
- (a) for the purpose of evading tax, a registrable person does any act or omits to take any action, and
- (b) his conduct involves dishonesty (whether or not it is such as to give rise to criminal liability),

he is liable to a penalty equal to the amount of tax evaded, or (as the case may be) sought to be evaded, by his conduct; but this is subject to sub-paragraph (7) below.

(2) The reference in sub-paragraph (1)(a) above to evading tax includes a reference to obtaining a payment under regulations under section 51(2)(c) or (d) or (f) of this Act in circumstances where the person concerned is not entitled to the sum.

(3) The reference in sub-paragraph (1) above to the amount of tax evaded or sought to be evaded is a reference to the aggregate of—
    (a)   the amount (if any) falsely claimed by way of credit, and
    (b)   the amount (if any) by which the gross amount of tax was falsely understated.

(4) In this paragraph—
    (a)   "credit" means credit for which provision is made by regulations under section 51 of this Act;
    (b)   "the gross amount of tax" means the total amount of tax due before taking into account any deduction for which provision is made by regulations under section 51(2) of this Act.

(5) Statements made or documents produced by or on behalf of a person shall not be inadmissible in any such proceedings as are mentioned in sub-paragraph (6) below by reason only that it has been drawn to his attention—
    (a)   that, in relation to tax, the Commissioners may assess an amount due by way of a civil penalty instead of instituting criminal proceedings and, though no undertaking can be given as to whether the Commissioners will make such an assessment in the case of any person, it is their practice to be influenced by the fact that a person has made a full confession of any dishonest conduct to which he has been a party and has given full facilities for investigation, and
    (b)   that the Commissioners or, on appeal, an appeal tribunal have power under paragraph 25 below to reduce a penalty under this paragraph,

and that he was or may have been induced thereby to make the statements or produce the documents.

(6) The proceedings referred to in sub-paragraph (5) above are—
    (a)   any criminal proceedings against the person concerned in respect of any offence in connection with or in relation to tax, and
    (b)   any proceedings against him for the recovery of any sum due from him in connection with or in relation to tax.

(7) Where, by reason of conduct falling within sub-paragraph (1) above, a person is convicted of an offence (whether under this Part of this Act or otherwise) that conduct shall not also give rise to liability to a penalty under this paragraph.

19.—(1)   Where it appears to the Commissioners—
    (a)   that a body corporate is liable to a penalty under paragraph 18 above, and
    (b)   that the conduct giving rise to that penalty is, in whole or in part, attributable to the dishonesty of a person who is, or at the material time was, a director or managing officer of the body corporate (a named officer),
the Commissioners may serve a notice under this paragraph on the body corporate and on the named officer.

(2) A notice under this paragraph shall state—
    (a)   the amount of the penalty referred to in sub-paragraph (1)(a) above (the basic penalty), and
    (b)   that the Commissioners propose, in accordance with this paragraph, to recover from the named officer such portion (which may be the whole) of the basic penalty as is specified in the notice.

(3) Where a notice is served under this paragraph, the portion of the basic penalty specified in the notice shall be recoverable from the named officer as if he were personally liable under paragraph 18 above to a penalty which corresponds to that portion; and the amount of that penalty may be assessed and notified to him accordingly under paragraph 32 below.

(4) Where a notice is served under this paragraph—
    (a)   the amount which, under paragraph 32 below, may be assessed as the amount due by way of penalty from the body corporate shall be only so much (if any) of the

basic penalty as is not assessed on and notified to a named officer by virtue of sub-paragraph (3) above, and

(b)   the body corporate shall be treated as discharged from liability for so much of the basic penalty as is so assessed and notified.

(5)   No appeal shall lie against a notice under this paragraph as such but—

(a)   where a body corporate is assessed as mentioned in sub-paragraph (4)(a) above, the body corporate may require a review of the Commissioners' decision as to its liability to a penalty and as to the amount of the basic penalty as if it were specified in the assessment;

(b)   where an assessment is made on a named officer by virtue of sub-paragraph (3) above, the named officer may require a review of the Commissioners' decision that the conduct of the body corporate referred to in sub-paragraph (1)(b) above is, in whole or in part, attributable to his dishonesty and of their decision as to the portion of the penalty which the Commissioners propose to recover from him;

(c)   sections 55 and 56 of this Act shall apply accordingly.

(6)   In this paragraph a "managing officer", in relation to a body corporate, means any manager, secretary or other similar officer of the body corporate or any person purporting to act in any such capacity or as a director; and where the affairs of a body corporate are managed by its members, this paragraph shall apply in relation to the conduct of a member in connection with his functions of management as if he were a director of the body corporate.

Misdeclaration or neglect

20.—(1)   Where, for an accounting period—

(a)   a return is made which understates a person's liability to tax or overstates his entitlement to credit, or

(b)   an assessment is made which understates a person's liability to tax and, at the end of the period of 30 days beginning on the date of the assessment, he has not taken all such steps as are reasonable to draw the understatement to the attention of the Commissioners,

the person concerned is liable, subject to sub-paragraphs (3) and (4) below, to a penalty equal to 5 per cent of the amount of the understatement of liability or (as the case may be) overstatement of entitlement.

(2)   Where—

(a)   a return for an accounting period overstates or understates to any extent a person's liability to tax or his entitlement to credit, and

(b)   that return is corrected, in such circumstances and in accordance with such conditions as may be prescribed by regulations, by a return for a later accounting period which understates or overstates, to the corresponding extent, that liability or entitlement,

it shall be assumed for the purposes of this paragraph that the statement made by each such return is a correct statement for the accounting period to which the return relates.

(3)   Conduct falling within sub-paragraph (1) above shall not give rise to liability to a penalty under this paragraph if the person concerned furnishes full information with respect to the inaccuracy concerned to the Commissioners—

(a)   at a time when he has no reason to believe that enquiries are being made by the Commissioners into his affairs, so far as they relate to tax, and

(b)   in such form and manner as may be prescribed by regulations or specified by the Commissioners in accordance with provision made by regulations.

(4)   Where, by reason of conduct falling within sub-paragraph (1) above—

(a)   a person is convicted of an offence (whether under this Part of this Act or otherwise), or

(b)   a person is assessed to a penalty under paragraph 18 above,

that conduct shall not also give rise to liability to a penalty under this paragraph.

(5)   In this paragraph "credit" means credit for which provision is made by regulations under section 51 of this Act.

Registration

21.—(1)   A person who fails to comply with section 47(3) of this Act is liable to a penalty equal to 5 per cent of the relevant tax or, if it is greater or the circumstances are such that there is no relevant tax, to a penalty of £250; but this is subject to sub-paragraph (4) below.

(2)   In sub-paragraph (1) above "relevant tax" means the tax (if any) for which the person concerned is liable for the period which—

(a)   begins on the date with effect from which he is, in accordance with section 47 of this Act, required to be registered, and

(b)   ends on the date on which the Commissioners received notification of, or otherwise became aware of, his liability to be registered.

(3)   A person who fails to comply with section 47(4) of this Act is liable to a penalty of £250.

(4)   Where, by reason of conduct falling within sub-paragraph (1) above—

(a)   a person is convicted of an offence (whether under this Part of this Act or otherwise), or

(b)   a person is assessed to a penalty under paragraph 18 above,

that conduct shall not also give rise to liability to a penalty under this paragraph.

Information

22.—(1)   If a person—

(a)   fails to comply with any provision of paragraph 1 or 3 above, or

(b)   fails to make records as required by any provision of regulations made under paragraph 2 above,

he is liable to a penalty of £250; but this is subject to sub-paragraph (4) below.

(2)   Where—

(a)   a penalty (an initial penalty) is imposed on a person under sub-paragraph (1) above, and

(b)   the failure which led to the initial penalty continues after its imposition,

he is (subject to sub-paragraph (4) below) liable to a further penalty of £20 for each day during which (or any part of which) the failure continues after the day on which the initial penalty was imposed.

(3)   A person who fails to preserve records in compliance with any provision of regulations made under paragraph 2 above (read with that paragraph and any direction given under the regulations) is liable to a penalty of £250; but this is subject to sub-paragraph (4) below.

(4)   Where by reason of a failure falling within sub-paragraph (1) or (3) above—

(a)   a person is convicted of an offence (whether under this Part of this Act or otherwise), or

(b)   a person is assessed to a penalty under paragraph 18 above,

that failure shall not also give rise to liability to a penalty under this paragraph.

Breach of regulations

23.—(1)Where regulations made under this Part of this Act impose a requirement on any person, they may provide that if the person fails to comply with the requirement he shall be liable to a penalty of £250; but this is subject to sub-paragraphs (2) and (3) below.

(2)   Where by reason of any conduct—

(a)   a person is convicted of an offence (whether under this Part of this Act or otherwise), or

(b)   a person is assessed to a penalty under paragraph 18 above,

that conduct shall not also give rise to liability to a penalty under the regulations.

(3)   Sub-paragraph (1) above does not apply to any failure mentioned in paragraph 22 above.

Walking possession agreements

24.—(1) This paragraph applies where—
(a) in accordance with regulations under [section 51 of the Finance Act 1997 (enforcement by distress)] a distress is authorised to be levied on the goods and chattels of a person (a person in default) who has refused or neglected to pay any tax due from him or any amount recoverable as if it were tax due from him, and
(b) the person levying the distress and the person in default have entered into a walking possession agreement.

(2) For the purposes of this paragraph a walking possession agreement is an agreement under which, in consideration of the property distrained upon being allowed to remain in the custody of the person in default and of the delaying of its sale, the person in default—
(a) acknowledges that the property specified in the agreement is under distraint and held in walking possession, and
(b) undertakes that, except with the consent of the Commissioners and subject to such conditions as they may impose, he will not remove or allow the removal of any of the specified property from the premises named in the agreement.

(3) If the person in default is in breach of the undertaking contained in a walking possession agreement, he is liable to a penalty equal to half of the tax or other amount referred to in sub-paragraph (1)(a) above.

(4) This paragraph does not extend to Scotland.

Mitigation of penalties

25.—(1) Where a person is liable to a penalty under this Part of this Schedule the Commissioners or, on appeal, an appeal tribunal may reduce the penalty to such amount (including nil) as they think proper.

(2) Where the person concerned satisfies the Commissioners or, on appeal, an appeal tribunal that there is a reasonable excuse for any breach, failure or other conduct, that is a factor which (among other things) may be taken into account under sub-paragraph (1) above.

(3) In the case of a penalty reduced by the Commissioners under sub-paragraph (1) above an appeal tribunal, on an appeal relating to the penalty, may cancel the whole or any part of the reduction made by the Commissioners.

[612]

NOTES
Commencement: 29 April 1996.
Para 24: words in square brackets in sub-para (1) substituted by the Finance Act 1997, s 53(8), (9).
Regulations: the Landfill Tax Regulations 1996, SI 1996/1527, as amended by SI 1996/2100, SI 1997/1431.

PART VI
INTEREST

Interest on under-declared tax

26.—(1) Sub-paragraph (2) below applies where—
(a) under section 50(1) of this Act the Commissioners assess an amount of tax due from a registrable person for an accounting period and notify it to him, and
(b) the assessment is made on the basis that the amount (the additional amount) is due from him in addition to any amount shown in a return made in relation to the accounting period.

(2) The additional amount shall carry interest for the period which—
(a) begins with the day after that on which the person is required by provision made under section 49 of this Act to pay tax due from him for the accounting period, and
(b) ends with the day before the relevant day.

(3) For the purposes of sub-paragraph (2) above the relevant day is the earlier of—
(a) the day on which the assessment is notified to the person;
(b) the day on which the additional amount is paid.

(4) Sub-paragraph (5) below applies where under section 50(2) of this Act the Commissioners assess an amount as being tax due from a registrable person for an accounting period and notify it to him.

(5) The amount shall carry interest for the period which—
  (a) begins with the day after that on which the person is required by provision made under section 49 of this Act to pay tax due from him for the accounting period, and
  (b) ends with the day before the relevant day.

(6) For the purposes of sub-paragraph (5) above the relevant day is the earlier of—
  (a) the day on which the assessment is notified to the person;
  (b) the day on which the amount is paid.

(7) Interest under this paragraph shall be payable at the rate applicable under section 197 of this Act.

(8) Interest under this paragraph shall be paid without any deduction of income tax.

(9) Sub-paragraph (10) below applies where—
  (a) an amount carries interest under this paragraph (or would do so apart from that sub-paragraph), and
  (b) all or part of the amount turns out not to be due.

(10) In such a case—
  (a) the amount or part (as the case may be) shall not carry interest under this paragraph and shall be treated as never having done so, and
  (b) all such adjustments as are reasonable shall be made, including adjustments by way of repayment by the Commissioners where appropriate.

Interest on unpaid tax etc

27.—(1) Sub-paragraph (2) below applies where—
  (a) a registrable person makes a return under provision made under section 49 of this Act (whether or not he makes it at the time required by such provision), and
  (b) the return shows that an amount of tax is due from him for the accounting period in relation to which the return is made.

(2) The amount shall carry interest for the period which—
  (a) begins with the day after that on which the person is required by provision made under section 49 of this Act to pay tax due from him for the accounting period, and
  (b) ends with the day before that on which the amount is paid.

(3) Sub-paragraph (4) below applies where—
  (a) under section 50(1) of this Act the Commissioners assess an amount of tax due from a registrable person for an accounting period and notify it to him, and
  (b) the assessment is made on the basis that no return required by provision made under section 49 of this Act has been made by the person in relation to the accounting period.

(4) The amount shall carry interest for the period which—
  (a) begins with the day after that on which the person is required by provision made under section 49 of this Act to pay tax due from him for the accounting period, and
  (b) ends with the day before that on which the amount is paid.

(5) Sub-paragraph (6) below applies where—
  (a) under section 50(1) of this Act the Commissioners assess an amount of tax due from a registrable person for an accounting period and notify it to him, and
  (b) the assessment (the supplementary assessment) is made on the basis that the amount (the additional amount) is due from him in addition to any amount shown in a return, or in any previous assessment, made in relation to the accounting period.

(6) The additional amount shall carry interest for the period which—
  (a) begins with the day on which the supplementary assessment is notified to the person, and
  (b) ends with the day before that on which the additional amount is paid.

(7) Sub-paragraph (8) below applies where under section 50(2) of this Act the Commissioners assess an amount as being tax due from a registrable person for an accounting period and notify it to him.

(8) The amount shall carry interest for the period which—
    (a)   begins with the day on which the assessment is notified to the person, and
    (b)   ends with the day before that on which the amount is paid.

(9) Sub-paragraph (10) below applies where under paragraph 32 below the Commissioners—
    (a)   assess an amount due from a person by way of penalty under Part V of this Schedule and notify it to him, or
    (b)   assess an amount due from a person by way of interest under paragraph 26 above and notify it to him.

(10) The amount shall carry interest for the period which—
    (a)   begins with the day on which the assessment is notified to the person, and
    (b)   ends with the day before that on which the amount is paid.

(11) Interest under this paragraph shall be compound interest calculated—
    (a)   at the penalty rate, and
    (b)   with monthly rests;
and the penalty rate is the rate found by taking the rate at which interest is payable under paragraph 26 above and adding 10 percentage points to that rate.

(12) Interest under this paragraph shall be paid without any deduction of income tax.

(13) Where—
    (a)   the Commissioners assess and notify an amount as mentioned in sub-paragraph (5)(a) or (7) or (9)(a) or (b) above,
    (b)   they also specify a date for the purposes of this sub-paragraph, and
    (c)   the amount concerned is paid on or before that date,
the amount shall not carry interest by virtue of sub-paragraph (6) or (8) or (10) above (as the case may be).

(14) Sub-paragraph (15) below applies where—
    (a)   an amount carries interest under this paragraph (or would do so apart from that sub-paragraph), and
    (b)   all or part of the amount turns out not to be due.

(15) In such a case—
    (a)   the amount or part (as the case may be) shall not carry interest under this paragraph and shall be treated as never having done so, and
    (b)   all such adjustments as are reasonable shall be made, including adjustments by way of repayment by the Commissioners where appropriate.

28.—(1) Where a person is liable to pay interest under paragraph 27 above the Commissioners or, on appeal, an appeal tribunal may reduce the amount payable to such amount (including nil) as they think proper.

(2) Where the person concerned satisfies the Commissioners or, on appeal, an appeal tribunal that there is a reasonable excuse for the conduct giving rise to the liability to pay interest, that is a factor which (among other things) may be taken into account under sub-paragraph (1) above.

(3) In the case of interest reduced by the Commissioners under sub-paragraph (1) above an appeal tribunal, on an appeal relating to the interest, may cancel the whole or any part of the reduction made by the Commissioners.

Interest payable by Commissioners

29.—(1) Where, due to an error on the part of the Commissioners, a person—
    (a)   has paid to them by way of tax an amount which was not tax due and which they are in consequence liable to repay to him,
    (b)   has failed to claim payment of an amount to the payment of which he was entitled in pursuance of provision made under section 51(2)(c) or (d) or (f) of this Act, or
    (c)   has suffered delay in receiving payment of an amount due to him from them in connection with tax,

then, if and to the extent that they would not be liable to do so apart from this paragraph, they shall (subject to the following provisions of this paragraph) pay interest to him on that amount for the applicable period.

[(1A) In sub-paragraph (1) above—
- (a) the reference in paragraph (a) to an amount which the Commissioners are liable to repay in consequence of the making of a payment that was not due is a reference to only so much of that amount as is the subject of a claim that the Commissioners are required to satisfy or have satisfied; and
- (b) the amounts referred to in paragraph (c) do not include any amount payable under this paragraph.]

(2) The applicable period, in a case falling within sub-paragraph (1)(a) above, is the period—
- (a) beginning with the date on which the payment is received by the Commissioners, and
- (b) ending with the date on which they authorise payment of the amount on which the interest is payable.

(3) The applicable period, in a case falling within sub-paragraph (1)(b) or (c) above, is the period—
- (a) beginning with the date on which, apart from the error, the Commissioners might reasonably have been expected to authorise payment of the amount on which the interest is payable, and
- (b) ending with the date on which they in fact authorise payment of that amount.

[(4) In determining the applicable period for the purposes of this paragraph there shall be left out of account any period by which the Commissioners' authorisation of the payment of interest is delayed by the conduct of the person who claims the interest.

(4A) The reference in sub-paragraph (4) above to a period by which the Commissioners' authorisation of the payment of interest is delayed by the conduct of the person who claims it includes, in particular, any period which is referable to—
- (a) any unreasonable delay in the making of the claim for interest or in the making of any claim for the payment or repayment of the amount on which interest is claimed;
- (b) any failure by that person or a person acting on his behalf or under his influence to provide the Commissioners—
  - (i) at or before the time of the making of a claim, or
  - (ii) subsequently in response to a request for information by the Commissioners, with all the information required by them to enable the existence and amount of the claimant's entitlement to a payment or repayment, and to interest on that payment or repayment, to be determined; and
- (c) the making, as part of or in association with either—
  - (i) the claim for interest, or
  - (ii) any claim for the payment or repayment of the amount on which interest is claimed,
  of a claim to anything to which the claimant was not entitled.

(5) In determining for the purposes of sub-paragraph (4A) above whether any period of delay is referable to a failure by any person to provide information in response to a request by the Commissioners, there shall be taken to be so referable, except so far as may be provided for by regulations, any period which—
- (a) begins with the date on which the Commissioners require that person to provide information which they reasonably consider relevant to the matter to be determined; and
- (b) ends with the earliest date on which it would be reasonable for the Commissioners to conclude—
  - (i) that they have received a complete answer to their request for information;
  - (ii) that they have received all that they need in answer to that request; or
  - (iii) that it is unnecessary for them to be provided with any information in answer to that request.]

(7) The Commissioners shall only be liable to pay interest under this paragraph on a claim made in writing for that purpose.

[(8) A claim under this paragraph shall not be made more than three years after the end of the applicable period to which it relates.]

[(9) References in this paragraph—
(a)   to receiving payment of any amount from the Commissioners, or
(b)   to the authorisation by the Commissioners of the payment of any amount,

include references to the discharge by way of set-off (whether in accordance with regulations under paragraph 42 or 43 below or otherwise) of the Commissioners' liability to pay that amount.]

(10) Interest under this paragraph shall be payable at the rate applicable under section 197 of this Act.

30.—(1) Where—
(a)   any interest is payable by the Commissioners to a person on a sum due to him under this Part of this Act, and
(b)   he is a person to whom regulations under section 51 of this Act apply,

the interest shall be treated as an amount to which he is entitled by way of credit in pursuance of the regulations.

(2) Sub-paragraph (1) above shall be disregarded for the purpose of determining a person's entitlement to interest or the amount of interest to which he is entitled.

[613]

NOTES
Commencement: 29 April 1996.
Para 29: sub-para (1A) inserted, and sub-paras (8), (9) substituted, with retrospective effect, by the Finance Act 1997, s 50, Sch 5, para 11; sub-paras (4), (4A), (5) substituted, for paras (4)–(6) as originally enacted, in relation to determining whether any period beginning on or after 19 March 1997 is left out of account, by the Finance Act 1997, s 50, Sch 5, para 12.

PART VII
MISCELLANEOUS

Security for tax

31. Where it appears to the Commissioners requisite to do so for the protection of the revenue they may require a registrable person, as a condition of his carrying out taxable activities, to give security (or further security) of such amount and in such manner as they may determine for the payment of any tax which is or may become due from him.

Assessments to penalties etc

32.—(1) Where a person is liable—
(a)   to a penalty under Part V of this Schedule, or
(b)   for interest under paragraph 26 or 27 above,

the Commissioners may, subject to sub-paragraph (2) below, assess the amount due by way of penalty or interest (as the case may be) and notify it to him accordingly; and the fact that any conduct giving rise to a penalty under Part V of this Schedule may have ceased before an assessment is made under this paragraph shall not affect the power of the Commissioners to make such an assessment.

(2) In the case of the penalties and interest referred to in the following paragraphs of this sub-paragraph, the assessment under this paragraph shall be of an amount due in respect of the accounting period which in the paragraph concerned is referred to as the relevant period—
(a)   in the case of a penalty under paragraph 18 above relating to the evasion of tax, and in the case of interest under paragraph 27 above on an amount due by way of such a penalty, the relevant period is the accounting period for which the tax evaded was due;
(b)   in the case of a penalty under paragraph 18 above relating to the obtaining of a payment under regulations under section 51(2)(c) or (d) or (f) of this Act, and in the case of interest under paragraph 27 above on an amount due by way of such a penalty, the relevant period is the accounting period in respect of which the payment was obtained;

    (c)   in the case of interest under paragraph 26 above, and in the case of interest under paragraph 27 above on an amount due by way of interest under paragraph 26 above, the relevant period is the accounting period in respect of which the tax was due;

    (d)   in the case of interest under paragraph 27 above on an amount of tax, the relevant period is the accounting period in respect of which the tax was due.

(3) In a case where the amount of any penalty or interest falls to be calculated by reference to tax which was not paid at the time it should have been and that tax cannot be readily attributed to any one or more accounting periods, it shall be treated for the purposes of this Part of this Act as tax due for such period or periods as the Commissioners may determine to the best of their judgment and notify to the person liable for the tax and penalty or interest.

(4) Where a person is assessed under this paragraph to an amount due by way of any penalty or interest falling within sub-paragraph (2) above and is also assessed under subsection (1) or (2) of section 50 of this Act for the accounting period which is the relevant period under sub-paragraph (2) above, the assessments may be combined and notified to him as one assessment, but the amount of the penalty or interest shall be separately identified in the notice.

(5) Sub-paragraph (6) below applies in the case of an amount due by way of interest under paragraph 27 above.

(6) Where this sub-paragraph applies in the case of an amount—

    (a)   a notice of assessment under this paragraph shall specify a date, being not later than the date of the notice, to which the amount of interest which is assessed is calculated, and

    (b)   if the interest continues to accrue after that date, a further assessment or further assessments may be made under this paragraph in respect of amounts which so accrue.

(7) If, within such period as may be notified by the Commissioners to the person liable for the interest under paragraph 27 above, the amount referred to in paragraph 27(2), (4), (6), (8) or (10) above (as the case may be) is paid, it shall be treated for the purposes of paragraph 27 above as paid on the date specified as mentioned in sub-paragraph (6)(a) above.

(8) Where an amount has been assessed and notified to any person under this paragraph it shall be recoverable as if it were tax due from him unless, or except to the extent that, the assessment has subsequently been withdrawn or reduced.

(9) Subsection (8) of section 50 of this Act shall apply for the purposes of this paragraph as it applies for the purposes of that section.

Assessments: time limits

33.—(1) Subject to the following provisions of this paragraph, an assessment under—

    (a)   any provision of section 50 of this Act, or

    (b)   paragraph 32 above,

shall not be made more than six years after the end of the accounting period concerned or, in the case of an assessment under paragraph 32 above of an amount due by way of a penalty which is not a penalty referred to in sub-paragraph (2) of that paragraph, [three years] after the event giving rise to the penalty.

(2) Subject to sub-paragraph (5) below, an assessment under paragraph 32 above of—

    (a)   an amount due by way of any penalty referred to in sub-paragraph (2) of that paragraph, or

    (b)   an amount due by way of interest,

may be made at any time before the expiry of the period of two years beginning with the time when the amount of tax due for the accounting period concerned has been finally determined.

(3) In relation to an assessment under paragraph 32 above, any reference in sub-paragraph (1) or (2) above to the accounting period concerned is a reference to that period which, in the case of the penalty or interest concerned, is the relevant period referred to in sub-paragraph (2) of that paragraph.

(4) Subject to sub-paragraph (5) below, if tax has been lost—

    (a)   as a result of conduct falling within paragraph 18(1) above or for which a person has been convicted of fraud, or

    (b)   in circumstances giving rise to liability to a penalty under paragraph 21 above, an assessment may be made as if, in sub-paragraph (1) above, each reference to [three years] were a reference to twenty years.

(5) Where after a person's death the Commissioners propose to assess an amount as due by reason of some conduct of the deceased—
  (a) the assessment shall not be made more than three years after the death, and
  (b) if the circumstances are as set out in sub-paragraph (4) above, the modification of sub-paragraph (1) above contained in that sub-paragraph shall not apply but any assessment which (from the point of view of time limits) could have been made immediately after the death may be made at any time within three years after it.

Supplementary assessments

34. If, otherwise than in circumstances falling within subsection (5)(b) of section 50 of this Act, it appears to the Commissioners that the amount which ought to have been assessed in an assessment under any provision of that section or under paragraph 32 above exceeds the amount which was so assessed, then—
  (a) under the like provision as that assessment was made, and
  (b) on or before the last day on which that assessment could have been made,

the Commissioners may make a supplementary assessment of the amount of the excess and shall notify the person concerned accordingly.

Disclosure of information

35.—(1) Notwithstanding any obligation not to disclose information that would otherwise apply, the Commissioners may disclose information to—
  (a) the Secretary of State,
  (b) the Environment Agency,
  (c) the Scottish Environment Protection Agency,
  (d) the Department of the Environment for Northern Ireland,
  (e) a district council in Northern Ireland, or
  (f) an authorised officer of any person (a principal) mentioned in paragraphs (a) to (e) above,

for the purpose of assisting the principal concerned in the performance of the principal's duties.

(2) Notwithstanding any such obligation as is mentioned in sub-paragraph (1) above, any person mentioned in sub-paragraph (1)(a) to (f) above may disclose information to the Commissioners or to an authorised officer of the Commissioners for the purpose of assisting the Commissioners in the performance of duties in relation to tax.

(3) Information that has been disclosed to a person by virtue of this paragraph shall not be disclosed by him except—
  (a) to another person to whom (instead of him) disclosure could by virtue of this paragraph have been made, or
  (b) for the purpose of any proceedings connected with the operation of any provision of, or made under, any enactment in relation to the environment or to tax.

(4) References in the preceding provisions of this paragraph to an authorised officer of any person (the principal) are to any person who has been designated by the principal as a person to and by whom information may be disclosed by virtue of this paragraph.

(5) The Secretary of State shall notify the Commissioners in writing of the name of any person designated by the Secretary of State under sub-paragraph (4) above.

(6) No charge may be made for a disclosure made by virtue of this paragraph.

The register: publication

36.—(1) The Commissioners may publish, by such means as they think fit, information which—
  (a) is derived from the register kept under section 47 of this Act, and
  (b) falls within any of the descriptions set out below.

(2) The descriptions are—
  (a) the names of registered persons;

(b)   the addresses of any sites or other premises at which they carry on business;

(c)   the registration numbers assigned to them in the register;

(d)   the fact (where it is the case) that the registered person is a body corporate which under section 59 of this Act is treated as a member of a group;

(e)   the names of the other bodies corporate treated under that section as members of the group;

(f)   the addresses of any sites or other premises at which those other bodies carry on business.

(3) Information may be published in accordance with this paragraph notwithstanding any obligation not to disclose the information that would otherwise apply.

Evidence by certificate etc

37.—(1)   A certificate of the Commissioners—

(a)   that a person was or was not at any time registered under section 47 of this Act,

(b)   that any return required by regulations made under section 49 of this Act has not been made or had not been made at any time, or

(c)   that any tax shown as due in a return made in pursuance of regulations made under section 49 of this Act, or in an assessment made under section 50 of this Act, has not been paid,

shall be sufficient evidence of that fact until the contrary is proved.

(2) A photograph of any document furnished to the Commissioners for the purposes of this Part of this Act and certified by them to be such a photograph shall be admissible in any proceedings, whether civil or criminal, to the same extent as the document itself.

(3) Any document purporting to be a certificate under sub-paragraph (1) or (2) above shall be taken to be such a certificate until the contrary is proved.

Service of notices etc

38. Any notice, notification or requirement to be served on, given to or made of any person for the purposes of this Part of this Act may be served, given or made by sending it by post in a letter addressed to that person at his last or usual residence or place of business.

39.—(1)   This paragraph applies to directions, specifications and conditions which the Commissioners or an authorised person may give or impose under any provision of this Part.

(2) A direction, specification or condition given or imposed by the Commissioners may be withdrawn or varied by them.

(3) A direction, specification or condition given or imposed by an authorised person may be withdrawn or varied by him or by another authorised person.

(4) No direction, specification or condition shall have effect as regards any person it is intended to affect unless—

(a)   a notice containing it is served on him, or

(b)   other reasonable steps are taken with a view to bringing it to his attention.

(5) No withdrawal or variation of a direction, specification or condition shall have effect as regards any person the withdrawal or variation is intended to affect unless—

(a)   a notice containing the withdrawal or variation is served on him, or

(b)   other reasonable steps are taken with a view to bringing the withdrawal or variation to his attention.

40. . . .

Destination of receipts

41. All money and securities for money collected or received for or on account of the tax shall—

(a)   if collected or received in Great Britain, be placed to the general account of the Commissioners kept at the Bank of England under section 17 of the Customs and Excise Management Act 1979;

(b)   if collected or received in Northern Ireland, be paid into the Consolidated Fund of the United Kingdom in such manner as the Treasury may direct.

Set-off of amounts

42.—(1) Regulations may make provision in relation to any case where—

    (a) a person is under a duty to pay to the Commissioners at any time an amount or amounts in respect of landfill tax, and

    (b) the Commissioners are under a duty to pay to that person at the same time an amount or amounts in respect of any tax (or taxes) under their care and management.

(2) The regulations may provide that if the total of the amount or amounts mentioned in sub-paragraph (1)(a) above exceeds the total of the amount or amounts mentioned in sub-paragraph (1)(b) above, the latter shall be set off against the former.

(3) The regulations may provide that if the total of the amount or amounts mentioned in sub-paragraph (1)(b) above exceeds the total of the amount or amounts mentioned in sub-paragraph (1)(a) above, the Commissioners may set off the latter in paying the former.

(4) The regulations may provide that if the total of the amount or amounts mentioned in sub-paragraph (1)(a) above is the same as the total of the amount or amounts mentioned in sub-paragraph (1)(b) above no payment need be made in respect of the former or the latter.

[(4A) The regulations may provide for any limitation on the time within which the Commissioners are entitled to take steps for recovering any amount due to them in respect of landfill tax to be disregarded, in such cases as may be described in the regulations, in determining whether any person is under such a duty to pay as is mentioned in sub-paragraph (1)(a) above.]

(5) The regulations may include provision treating any duty to pay mentioned in sub-paragraph (1) above as discharged accordingly.

(6) References in sub-paragraph (1) above to an amount in respect of a particular tax include references not only to an amount of tax itself but also to other amounts such as interest and penalty.

(7) In this paragraph "tax" includes "duty".

43.—(1) Regulations may make provision in relation to any case where—

    (a) a person is under a duty to pay to the Commissioners at any time an amount or amounts in respect of any tax (or taxes) under their care and management, and

    (b) the Commissioners are under a duty to pay to that person at the same time an amount or amounts in respect of landfill tax.

(2) The regulations may provide that if the total of the amount or amounts mentioned in sub-paragraph (1)(a) above exceeds the total of the amount or amounts mentioned in sub-paragraph (1)(b) above, the latter shall be set off against the former.

(3) The regulations may provide that if the total of the amount or amounts mentioned in sub-paragraph (1)(b) above exceeds the total of the amount or amounts mentioned in sub-paragraph (1)(a) above, the Commissioners may set off the latter in paying the former.

(4) The regulations may provide that if the total of the amount or amounts mentioned in sub-paragraph (1)(a) above is the same as the total of the amount or amounts mentioned in sub-paragraph (1)(b) above no payment need be made in respect of the former or the latter.

[(4A) The regulations may provide for any limitation on the time within which the Commissioners are entitled to take steps for recovering any amount due to them in respect of any of the taxes under their care and management to be disregarded, in such cases as may be described in the regulations, in determining whether any person is under such a duty to pay as is mentioned in sub-paragraph (1)(a) above.]

(5) The regulations may include provision treating any duty to pay mentioned in sub-paragraph (1) above as discharged accordingly.

(6) References in sub-paragraph (1) above to an amount in respect of a particular tax include references not only to an amount of tax itself but also to other amounts such as interest and penalty.

(7) In this paragraph "tax" includes "duty".

Amounts shown as tax on invoices

44.—(1) Where—

    (a)   a registrable person issues an invoice showing an amount as tax chargeable on an event, and

    (b)   no tax is in fact chargeable on the event,

an amount equal to the amount shown as tax shall be recoverable from the person as a debt due to the Crown.

    (2) Where—

    (a)   a registrable person issues an invoice showing an amount as tax chargeable on a taxable disposal, and

    (b)   the amount shown as tax exceeds the amount of tax in fact chargeable on the disposal,

an amount equal to the excess shall be recoverable from the person as a debt due to the Crown.

    (3) References in this paragraph to an invoice are to any invoice, whether or not it is a landfill invoice within the meaning of section 61 of this Act.

Adjustment of contracts

45.—(1) This paragraph applies where—

    (a)   material undergoes a landfill disposal,

    (b)   a payment falls to be made under a disposal contract relating to the material, and

    (c)   after the making of the contract there is a change in the tax chargeable on the landfill disposal.

    (2) In such a case the amount of any payment mentioned in sub-paragraph (1)(b) above shall be adjusted, unless the disposal contract otherwise provides, so as to reflect the tax chargeable on the landfill disposal.

    (3) For the purposes of this paragraph a disposal contract relating to material is a contract providing for the disposal of the material, and it is immaterial—

    (a)   when the contract was made;

    (b)   whether the contract also provides for other matters;

    (c)   whether the contract provides for a method of disposal and (if it docs) what method it provides for.

    (4) The reference in sub-paragraph (1) above to a change in the tax chargeable is a reference to a change—

    (a)   to or from no tax being chargeable, or

    (b)   in the amount of tax chargeable.

46.—(1) This paragraph applies where—

    (a)   work is carried out under a construction contract,

    (b)   as a result of the work, material undergoes a landfill disposal,

    (c)   the contract makes no provision as to the disposal of such material, and

    (d)   the contract was made on or before 29th November 1994 (when the proposal to create tax was announced).

    (2) In such a case the amount of any payment which falls to be made—

    (a)   under the construction contract, and

    (b)   in respect of the work,

shall be adjusted, unless the contract otherwise provides, so as to reflect the tax (if any) chargeable on the disposal.

    (3) For the purposes of this paragraph a construction contract is a contract under which all or any of the following work is to be carried out—

    (a)   the preparation of a site;

    (b)   demolition;

    (c)   building;

    (d)   civil engineering.

Adjustment of rent etc

47.—(1) This paragraph applies where—
  (a) an agreement with regard to any sum payable in respect of the use of land (whether the sum is called rent or royalty or otherwise) provides that the amount of the sum is to be calculated by reference to the turnover of a business,
  (b) the agreement was made on or before 29th November 1994 (when the proposal to create tax was announced), and
  (c) the circumstances are such that (had the agreement been made after that date) it can reasonably be expected that it would have provided that tax be ignored in calculating the turnover.

(2) In such a case the agreement shall be taken to provide that tax be ignored in calculating the turnover.

[614]

NOTES
  Commencement: 29 April 1996.
  Para 33: words in square brackets in sub-paras (1), (4) substituted by the Finance Act 1997, s 50, Sch 5, para 6(1), (2)(c).
  Para 40: inserts the Income and Corporation Taxes Act 1988, s 827(1C).
  Paras 42, 43: sub-para (4A) inserted by the Finance Act 1997, s 50, Sch 5, para 13.
  Regulations: the Landfill Tax Regulations 1996, SI 1996/1527, as amended by SI 1996/2100, SI 1997/1431.

(Schs 6–41 outside the scope of this work.)

NOISE ACT 1996

(1996 c 37)

ARRANGEMENT OF SECTIONS

An Act to make provision about noise emitted from dwellings at night; about the forfeiture and confiscation of equipment used to make noise unlawfully; and for connected purposes

[18 July 1996]

Summary procedure for dealing with noise at night

1 Adoption of these provisions by local authorities

(1)   Sections 2 to 9 only apply to the area of a local authority if the authority have so resolved or an order made by the Secretary of State so provides.

(2)   If a local authority resolve to apply those sections to their area—
- (a)   those sections are to have effect there on and after a date specified in the resolution ("the commencement date"), which must be at least three months after the passing of the resolution, and
- (b)   the local authority must cause a notice to be published, in two consecutive weeks ending at least two months before the commencement date, in a local newspaper circulating in their area.

(3)   A notice published under subsection (2)(b) must—
- (a)   state that the resolution has been passed,
- (b)   give the commencement date, and
- (c)   set out the general effect of those sections.

(4)   An order under this section must not provide for those sections to have effect before the end of the period of three months beginning with the making of the order.

[615]

NOTES
Commencement: 23 July 1997.

2 Investigation of complaints of noise from a dwelling at night

(1)   A local authority must, if they receive a complaint of the kind mentioned in subsection (2), secure that an officer of the authority takes reasonable steps to investigate the complaint.

(2)   The kind of complaint referred to is one made by any individual present in a dwelling during night hours (referred to in this Act as "the complainant's dwelling") that excessive noise is being emitted from another dwelling (referred to in this group of sections as "the offending dwelling").

(3)   A complaint under subsection (2) may be made by any means.

(4)   If an officer of the authority is satisfied, in consequence of an investigation under subsection (1), that—
- (a)   noise is being emitted from the offending dwelling during night hours, and
- (b)   the noise, if it were measured from within the complainant's dwelling, would or might exceed the permitted level,

he may serve a notice about the noise under section 3.

(5)   For the purposes of subsection (4), it is for the officer of the authority dealing with the particular case—
- (a)   to decide whether any noise, if it were measured from within the complainant's dwelling, would or might exceed the permitted level, and
- (b)   for the purposes of that decision, to decide whether to assess the noise from within or outside the complainant's dwelling and whether or not to use any device for measuring the noise.

(6)   In this group of sections, "night hours" means the period beginning with 11 pm and ending with the following 7 am.

(7)   Where a local authority receive a complaint under subsection (2) and the offending dwelling is within the area of another local authority, the first local

authority may act under this group of sections as if the offending dwelling were within their area, and accordingly may so act whether or not this group of sections applies to the area of the other local authority.

(8)   In this section and sections 3 to 9, "this group of sections" means this and those sections.

[616]

NOTES

Commencement: 23 July 1997.

3 Warning notices

(1)   A notice under this section (referred to in this Act as "a warning notice") must—
- (a)   state that an officer of the authority considers—
  - (i)   that noise is being emitted from the offending dwelling during night hours, and
  - (ii)   that the noise exceeds, or may exceed, the permitted level, as measured from within the complainant's dwelling, and
- (b)   give warning that any person who is responsible for noise which is emitted from the dwelling, in the period specified in the notice, and exceeds the permitted level, as measured from within the complainant's dwelling, may be guilty of an offence.

(2)   The period specified in a warning notice must be a period—
- (a)   beginning not earlier than ten minutes after the time when the notice is served, and
- (b)   ending with the following 7 am.

(3)   A warning notice must be served—
- (a)   by delivering it to any person present at or near the offending dwelling and appearing to the officer of the authority to be responsible for the noise, or
- (b)   if it is not reasonably practicable to identify any person present at or near the dwelling as being a person responsible for the noise on whom the notice may reasonably be served, by leaving it at the offending dwelling.

(4)   A warning notice must state the time at which it is served.

(5)   For the purposes of this group of sections, a person is responsible for noise emitted from a dwelling if he is a person to whose act, default or sufferance the emission of the noise is wholly or partly attributable.

[617]

NOTES

Commencement: 23 July 1997.

4 Offence where noise exceeds permitted level after service of notice

(1)   If a warning notice has been served in respect of noise emitted from a dwelling, any person who is responsible for noise which—
- (a)   is emitted from the dwelling in the period specified in the notice, and
- (b)   exceeds the permitted level, as measured from within the complainant's dwelling,

is guilty of an offence.

(2)   It is a defence for a person charged with an offence under this section to show that there was a reasonable excuse for the act, default or sufferance in question.

(3)　A person guilty of an offence under this section is liable on summary conviction to a fine not exceeding level 3 on the standard scale.

[618]

NOTES

Commencement: 23 July 1997.

5 Permitted level of noise

(1)　For the purposes of this group of sections, the Secretary of State may by directions in writing determine the maximum level of noise (referred to in this group of sections as "the permitted level") which may be emitted during night hours from any dwelling.

(2)　The permitted level is to be a level applicable to noise as measured from within any other dwelling in the vicinity by an approved device used in accordance with any conditions subject to which the approval was given.

(3)　Different permitted levels may be determined for different circumstances, and the permitted level may be determined partly by reference to other levels of noise.

(4)　The Secretary of State may from time to time vary his directions under this section by further directions in writing.

[619]

NOTES

Commencement: 23 July 1997.

6 Approval of measuring devices

(1)　For the purposes of this group of sections, the Secretary of State may approve in writing any type of device used for the measurement of noise; and references in this group of sections to approved devices are to devices of a type so approved.

(2)　Any such approval may be given subject to conditions as to the purposes for which, and the manner and other circumstances in which, devices of the type concerned are to be used.

(3)　In proceedings for an offence under section 4, a measurement of noise made by a device is not admissible as evidence of the level of noise unless it is an approved device and any conditions subject to which the approval was given are satisfied.

[620]

NOTES

Commencement: 23 July 1997.

7 Evidence

(1)　In proceedings for an offence under section 4, evidence—
  (a) of a measurement of noise made by a device, or of the circumstances in which it was made, or
  (b) that a device was of a type approved for the purposes of section 6, or that any conditions subject to which the approval was given were satisfied,

may be given by the production of a document mentioned in subsection (2).

(2)　The document referred to is one which is signed by an officer of the local authority and which (as the case may be)—

(a) gives particulars of the measurement or of the circumstances in which it was made, or

(b) states that the device was of such a type or that, to the best of the knowledge and belief of the person making the statement, all such conditions were satisfied;

and if the document contains evidence of a measurement of noise it may consist partly of a record of the measurement produced automatically by a device.

(3)   In proceedings for an offence under section 4, evidence that noise, or noise of any kind, measured by a device at any time was noise emitted from a dwelling may be given by the production of a document—
    (a) signed by an officer of the local authority, and
    (b) stating that he had identified that dwelling as the source at that time of the noise or, as the case may be, the noise of that kind.

(4)   For the purposes of this section, a document purporting to be signed as mentioned in subsection (2) or (3)(a) is to be treated as being so signed unless the contrary is proved.

(5)   This section does not make a document admissible as evidence in proceedings for an offence unless a copy of it has, not less than seven days before the hearing or trial, been served on the person charged with the offence.

(6)   This section does not make a document admissible as evidence of anything other than the matters shown on a record produced automatically by a device if, not less than three days before the hearing or trial or within such further time as the court may in special circumstances allow, the person charged with the offence serves a notice on the prosecutor requiring attendance at the hearing or trial of the person who signed the document.

[621]

NOTES
    Commencement: 23 July 1997.

8 Fixed penalty notices

(1)   Where an officer of a local authority who is authorised for the purposes of this section has reason to believe that a person is committing or has just committed an offence under section 4, he may give that person a notice (referred to in this Act as a "fixed penalty notice") offering him the opportunity of discharging any liability to conviction for that offence by payment of a fixed penalty.

(2)   A fixed penalty notice may be given to a person—
    (a) by delivering the notice to him, or
    (b) if it is not reasonably practicable to deliver it to him, by leaving the notice, addressed to him, at the offending dwelling.

(3)   Where a person is given a fixed penalty notice in respect of such an offence—
    (a) proceedings for that offence must not be instituted before the end of the period of fourteen days following the date of the notice, and
    (b) he cannot be convicted of that offence if he pays the fixed penalty before the end of that period.

(4)   A fixed penalty notice must give such particulars of the circumstances alleged to constitute the offence as are necessary for giving reasonable information of the offence.

(5)   A fixed penalty notice must state—
    (a) the period during which, because of subsection (3)(a), proceedings will not be taken for the offence,

    (b) the amount of the fixed penalty, and
    (c) the person to whom and the address at which the fixed penalty may be paid.

(6)   Payment of the fixed penalty may (among other methods) be made by pre-paying and posting to that person at that address a letter containing the amount of the penalty (in cash or otherwise).

(7)   Where a letter containing the amount of the penalty is sent in accordance with subsection (6), payment is to be regarded as having been made at the time at which that letter would be delivered in the ordinary course of post.

(8)   The fixed penalty payable under this section is £100.

[622]

NOTES
Commencement: 23 July 1997.

9 Section 8: supplementary

(1)   If a form for a fixed penalty notice is specified in an order made by the Secretary of State, a fixed penalty notice must be in that form.

(2)   If a fixed penalty notice is given to a person in respect of noise emitted from a dwelling in any period specified in a warning notice—
    (a) no further fixed penalty notice may be given to that person in respect of noise emitted from the dwelling during that period, but
    (b) that person may be convicted of a further offence under section 4 in respect of noise emitted from the dwelling after the fixed penalty notice is given and before the end of that period.

(3)   The Secretary of State may from time to time by order amend section 8(8) so as to change the amount of the fixed penalty payable under that section.

(4)   Sums received by a local authority under section 8 must be paid to the Secretary of State.

(5)   In proceedings for an offence under section 4, evidence that payment of a fixed penalty was or was not made before the end of any period may be given by the production of a certificate which—
    (a) purports to be signed by or on behalf of the person having responsibility for the financial affairs of the local authority, and
    (b) states that payment of a fixed penalty was made on any date or, as the case may be, was not received before the end of that period.

[623]

NOTES
Commencement: 23 July 1997.

Seizure, etc of equipment used to make noise unlawfully

10 Powers of entry and seizure etc

(1)   The power conferred by subsection (2) may be exercised where an officer of a local authority has reason to believe that—
    (a) a warning notice has been served in respect of noise emitted from a dwelling, and
    (b) at any time in the period specified in the notice, noise emitted from the dwelling has exceeded the permitted level, as measured from within the complainant's dwelling.

(2) An officer of the local authority, or a person authorised by the authority for the purpose, may enter the dwelling from which the noise in question is being or has been emitted and may seize and remove any equipment which it appears to him is being or has been used in the emission of the noise.

(3) A person exercising the power conferred by subsection (2) must produce his authority, if he is required to do so.

(4) If it is shown to a justice of the peace on sworn information in writing that—
   (a) a warning notice has been served in respect of noise emitted from a dwelling,
   (b) at any time in the period specified in the notice, noise emitted from the dwelling has exceeded the permitted level, as measured from within the complainant's dwelling, and
   (c) entry of an officer of the local authority, or of a person authorised by the authority for the purpose, to the dwelling has been refused, or such a refusal is apprehended, or a request by an officer of the authority, or of such a person, for admission would defeat the object of the entry,

the justice may by warrant under his hand authorise the local authority, by any of their officers or any person authorised by them for the purpose, to enter the premises, if need be by force.

(5) A person who enters any premises under subsection (2), or by virtue of a warrant issued under subsection (4), may take with him such other persons and such equipment as may be necessary; and if, when he leaves, the premises are unoccupied, must leave them as effectively secured against trespassers as he found them.

(6) A warrant issued under subsection (4) continues in force until the purpose for which the entry is required has been satisfied.

(7) The power of a local authority under section 81(3) of the Environmental Protection Act 1990 to abate any matter, where that matter is a statutory nuisance by virtue of section 79(1)(g) of that Act (noise emitted from premises so as to be prejudicial to health or a nuisance), includes power to seize and remove any equipment which it appears to the authority is being or has been used in the emission of the noise in question.

(8) A person who wilfully obstructs any person exercising any powers conferred under subsection (2) or by virtue of subsection (7) is liable, on summary conviction, to a fine not exceeding level 3 on the standard scale.

(9) The Schedule to this Act (which makes further provision in relation to anything seized and removed by virtue of this section) has effect.

[624]

NOTES

   Commencement: 23 July 1997 (sub-ss (1)–(6), sub-ss (8), (9) certain purposes); 19 September 1996 (sub-s (7), sub-s (8), (9) remaining purposes).

General

11 Interpretation and subordinate legislation

(1) In this Act, "local authority" means—
   (a) in Greater London, a London borough council, the Common Council of the City of London and, as respects the Temples, the Sub-Treasurer of the Inner Temple and the Under-Treasurer of the Middle Temple respectively,
   (b) outside Greater London—
      (i) any district council,
      (ii) the council of any county so far as they are the council for any area for which there are no district councils,

    (iii) in Wales, the council of a county borough, and
  (c) the Council of the Isles of Scilly.

 (2) In this Act—
  (a) "dwelling" means any building, or part of a building, used or intended to be used as a dwelling,
  (b) references to noise emitted from a dwelling include noise emitted from any garden, yard, outhouse or other appurtenance belonging to or enjoyed with the dwelling.

 (3) The power to make an order under this Act is exercisable by statutory instrument which (except in the case of an order under section 14) shall be subject to annulment in pursuance of a resolution of either House of Parliament.

                            [625]

NOTES

Commencement: 23 July 1997 (certain purposes); 19 September 1996 (remaining purposes).

12 Protection from personal liability

 (1) A member of a local authority or an officer or other person authorised by a local authority is not personally liable in respect of any act done by him or by the local authority or any such person if the act was done in good faith for the purpose of executing powers conferred by, or by virtue, of this Act.

 (2) Subsection (1) does not apply to liability under section 19 or 20 of the Local Government Finance Act 1982 (powers of district auditor and court).

                            [626]

NOTES

Commencement: 23 July 1997 (certain purposes); 19 September 1996 (remaining purposes).

13 Expenses

There is to be paid out of money provided by Parliament any increase attributable to this Act in the sums payable out of money so provided under any other enactment.

                            [627]

NOTES

Commencement: 19 September 1996.

14 Short title, commencement and extent

 (1) This Act may be cited as the Noise Act 1996.

 (2) This Act is to come into force on such day as the Secretary of State may by order appoint, and different days may be appointed for different purposes.

 (3) This Act does not extend to Scotland.

 (4) In its application to Northern Ireland this Act has effect with the following modifications—
  (a) for any reference to a local authority there is substituted a reference to a district council,
  (b) for any reference to the area of a local authority there is substituted a reference to the district of a district council,
  (c) for any reference to the Secretary of State there is substituted a reference to the Department of the Environment for Northern Ireland,
  (d) any reference to an enactment includes reference to an enactment comprised in Northern Ireland legislation,

(e) in section 10(4) for the words "sworn information" there is substituted the words "a complaint made on oath and",
(f) in section 11 for subsection (3) there is substituted—

"(3) The power to make orders under this Act shall be exercisable by statutory rule for the purposes of the Statutory Rules (Northern Ireland) Order 1979, and any orders made under this Act shall (except in the case of an order under section 14) be subject to negative resolution within the meaning assigned by section 41(6) of the Interpretation Act (Northern Ireland) 1954 as if they were statutory instruments within the meaning of that Act.",

(g) in section 12 for subsection (2) there is substituted—

"(2) Subsection (1) does not apply to liability under section 81 or 82 of the Local Government Act (Northern Ireland) 1972 (powers of local government auditor and court).",

(h) the following provisions are omitted—
    (i) section 10(7),
    (ii) in section 10(8) the words "or by virtue of subsection (7)",
    (iii) section 11(1),
    (iv) in the Schedule, paragraph 1(a)(ii) and the word "and" immediately before it,
    (v) in the Schedule, in paragraph 1(b), the words "or section 81(3) of the Environmental Protection Act 1990 (as so extended)".

[628]

NOTES
Commencement: 23 July 1997 (sub-s (4)); 19 September 1996 (remainder).
Orders: the Noise Act 1996 (Commencement No 1) Order 1996, SI 1996/2219; the Noise Act 1996 (Commencement No 2) Order 1997, SI 1997/1695.

SCHEDULE
POWERS IN RELATION TO SEIZED EQUIPMENT

Section 10

Introductory

1. In this Schedule—
    (a) a "noise offence" means—
        (i) in relation to equipment seized under section 10(2) of this Act, an offence under section 4 of this Act, and
        (ii) in relation to equipment seized under section 81(3) of the Environmental Protection Act 1990 (as extended by section 10(7) of this Act), an offence under section 80(4) of that Act in respect of a statutory nuisance falling within section 79(1)(g) of that Act,
    (b) "seized equipment" means equipment seized in the exercise of the power of seizure and removal conferred by section 10(2) of this Act or section 81(3) of the Environmental Protection Act 1990 (as so extended),
    (c) "related equipment", in relation to any conviction of or proceedings for a noise offence, means seized equipment used or alleged to have been used in the commission of the offence,
    (d) "responsible local authority", in relation to seized equipment, means the local authority by or on whose behalf the equipment was seized.

Retention

2.—(1) Any seized equipment may be retained—
    (a) during the period of twenty-eight days beginning with the seizure, or
    (b) if it is related equipment in proceedings for a noise offence instituted within that period against any person, until—
        (i) he is sentenced or otherwise dealt with for the offence or acquitted of the offence, or
        (ii) the proceedings are discontinued.

(2) Sub-paragraph (1) does not authorise the retention of seized equipment if—

    (a)   a person has been given a fixed penalty notice under section 8 of this Act in respect of any noise,

    (b)   the equipment was seized because of its use in the emission of the noise in respect of which the fixed penalty notice was given, and

    (c)   that person has paid the fixed penalty before the end of the period allowed for its payment.

Forfeiture

3.—(1) Where a person is convicted of a noise offence the court may make an order ("a forfeiture order") for forfeiture of any related equipment.

(2) The court may make a forfeiture order whether or not it also deals with the offender in respect of the offence in any other way and without regard to any restrictions on forfeiture in any enactment.

(3) In considering whether to make a forfeiture order in respect of any equipment a court must have regard—

    (a)   to the value of the equipment, and

    (b)   to the likely financial and other effects on the offender of the making of the order (taken together with any other order that the court contemplates making).

(4) A forfeiture order operates to deprive the offender of any rights in the equipment to which it relates.

Consequences of forfeiture

4.—(1) Where any equipment has been forfeited under paragraph 3, a magistrates' court may, on application by a claimant of the equipment (other than the person in whose case the forfeiture order was made) make an order for delivery of the equipment to the applicant if it appears to the court that he is the owner of the equipment.

(2) No application may be made under sub-paragraph (1) by any claimant of the equipment after the expiry of the period of six months beginning with the date on which a forfeiture order was made in respect of the equipment.

(3) Such an application cannot succeed unless the claimant satisfies the court—

    (a)   that he had not consented to the offender having possession of the equipment, or

    (b)   that he did not know, and had no reason to suspect, that the equipment was likely to be used in the commission of a noise offence.

(4) Where the responsible local authority is of the opinion that the person in whose case the forfeiture order was made is not the owner of the equipment, it must take reasonable steps to bring to the attention of persons who may be entitled to do so their right to make an application under sub-paragraph (1).

(5) An order under sub-paragraph (1) does not affect the right of any person to take, within the period of six months beginning with the date of the order, proceedings for the recovery of the equipment from the person in possession of it in pursuance of the order, but the right ceases on the expiry of that period.

(6) If on the expiry of the period of six months beginning with the date on which a forfeiture order was made in respect of the equipment no order has been made under sub-paragraph (1), the responsible local authority may dispose of the equipment.

Return etc of seized equipment

5. If in proceedings for a noise offence no order for forfeiture of related equipment is made, the court (whether or not a person is convicted of the offence) may give such directions as to the return, retention or disposal of the equipment by the responsible local authority as it thinks fit.

6.—(1) Where in the case of any seized equipment no proceedings in which it is related equipment are begun within the period mentioned in paragraph 2(1)(a)—

    (a)   the responsible local authority must return the equipment to any person who—

        (i)   appears to them to be the owner of the equipment, and

        (ii)   makes a claim for the return of the equipment within the period mentioned in sub-paragraph (2), and

(b) if no such person makes such a claim within that period, the responsible local authority may dispose of the equipment.

(2) The period referred to in sub-paragraph (1)(a)(ii) is the period of six months beginning with the expiry of the period mentioned in paragraph 2(1)(a).

(3) The responsible local authority must take reasonable steps to bring to the attention of persons who may be entitled to do so their right to make such a claim.

(4) Subject to sub-paragraph (6), the responsible local authority is not required to return any seized equipment under sub-paragraph (1)(a) until the person making the claim has paid any such reasonable charges for the seizure, removal and retention of the equipment as the authority may demand.

(5) If—
  (a) equipment is sold in pursuance of—
        (i) paragraph 4(6),
        (ii) directions under paragraph 5, or
        (iii) this paragraph, and
  (b) before the expiration of the period of one year beginning with the date on which the equipment is sold any person satisfies the responsible local authority that at the time of its sale he was the owner of the equipment,

the authority is to pay him any sum by which any proceeds of sale exceed any such reasonable charges for the seizure, removal or retention of the equipment as the authority may demand.

(6) The responsible local authority cannot demand charges from any person under sub-paragraph (4) or (5) who they are satisfied did not know, and had no reason to suspect, that the equipment was likely to be used in the emission of noise exceeding the level determined under section 5.

[629]–[800]

NOTES
  Commencement: 23 July 1997 (certain purposes); 19 September 1996 (remaining purposes).

PART II
STATUTORY INSTRUMENTS

WATER RESOURCES (SUCCESSION TO LICENCES) REGULATIONS 1969

(SI 1969/976)

NOTES
Made: 17 July 1969.
Commencement: 6 August 1969.
Authority: Water Resources Act 1963, ss 32, 54, 134 (repealed); now take effect under the Water Resources Act 1991, s 50.

ARRANGEMENT OF REGULATIONS

1 Citation and commencement

These regulations may be cited as the Water Resources (Succession to Licences) Regulations 1969, and shall come into operation on 6th August 1969.

[801]

2 Interpretation

(1)   In these regulations, unless the context otherwise requires,—
"the Act" means the Water Resources Act 1963;
"the Minister" means the Minister of Housing and Local Government or the Secretary of State, according to circumstances, as section 1 of the Act provides;
"river authority" includes, in addition to a river authority established under the Act, any other body having river authority functions under Part IV of the Act in any area, and references (however expressed) to the area of a river authority shall be construed accordingly; and "the river authority", in relation to any matter, means the river authority, or other body having Part IV functions as aforesaid, for the area in which that matter arises;
"successor" means a person who becomes the occupier of any land formerly occupied by the holder of a licence under the Act to abstract water for use on specified land consisting of, or comprising, the land in question;
and, in relation to any successor and to his entitlement under the regulations,—
"the original holder" means the last preceding occupier of the land in question, who, immediately before he ceased to be the occupier, held a licence under the Act to abstract water for use on that land, with or without other land;
"the original licence" means the original holder's licence as it has effect for the purposes of the successor's entitlement at the time when he becomes the occupier of the land in question, or, if the relevant provisions of that licence are then contained in a new licence which has been substituted therefor in pursuance of the regulations, means that substituted licence;
"the original land" means all the land of which the original holder was the occupier immediately before the relevant event, in so far as it was, or formed part of, the land then specified in the original licence as the land on which water abstracted in pursuance of that licence was to be used;

"the relevant event" means the death of the original holder, or the other act or event by reason of which the original holder ceased to be the occupier of land consisting of, or comprising, the land of which the successor has become the occupier.

(2)   A reference in these regulations to any enactment shall be construed as a reference to that enactment as amended by any subsequent enactment and as including a reference to it as applied by or under any other enactment.

(3)   The Interpretation Act 1889 shall apply for the interpretation of these regulations as it applies for the interpretation of an Act of Parliament.

[802]

NOTES

Minister of Housing and Local Government: the functions of this Minister, in so far as they related to water supply in Wales, were transferred to the Secretary of State for Wales by SI 1965/319, and in so far as they related to England were transferred to the Secretary of State for the Environment by SI 1970/1681.

3 Service of documents

Any notice or other document required or authorised by these regulations to be given or served may be given or served in the manner prescribed by section 120 of the Act.

[803]

4 Rights of a successor on becoming the occupier of the whole of the original land

(1)   Subject to the following provisions of this regulation, where the original holder ceases to be the occupier of the whole of the original land and, whether immediately thereafter or subsequently, a successor becomes the occupier of the whole of that land but, by reason of the original land being only a part of the land specified in the original licence as the land on which water abstracted in pursuance of the licence is to be used, does not thereupon become the holder of the original licence by virtue of section 32(1) of the Act,—

    (a) the original holder (except where, being an individual, he has died) shall cease to be the holder of the original licence, and

    (b) the successor shall become the holder of that licence.

(2)   Where the preceding paragraph has effect, the successor shall cease to be the holder of the licence at the end of the period of one month beginning with the date on which he became the occupier of the original land, unless before the end of that period he has given notice to the river authority of the change in the occupation of that land.

(3)   Where, in the case of a change or proposed change in the occupation of land in the circumstances mentioned in paragraph (1) of this regulation, it is the intention of the parties, or of the one who is the original holder, that the original licence should be held by the original holder for purposes for which he could lawfully make use of it but for the operation of the said paragraph (1), then,—

    (a) if notice of that intention is given to the river authority by both the parties, and is not withdrawn, before the change in occupation takes place, paragraph (1) of this regulation shall not apply in relation to that change; and

    (b) if notice of that intention is given to the river authority by both the parties, and is not withdrawn, before the end of the period specified in paragraph (2) of this regulation (but not before the change in occupation takes place), or if such notice is given to the river authority by the original holder, and is not withdrawn, before the end of that period and the successor does not within that period give notice to the river authority for the purpose of the said paragraph (2), the original holder shall in either case become the holder of the original licence immediately after the successor has ceased, by virtue of that paragraph, to be the holder of it.

(4)   A successor who becomes the holder of the original licence by virtue of paragraph (1) of this regulation, and who does not cease to be the holder of the licence by virtue of paragraph (2), shall, in relation to any other person having a relevant entitlement under the next following regulation with respect to the same original licence, stand in the place of the original holder for the purpose of paragraph (3) of that regulation and shall for that purpose be entitled to apply for an appropriate new licence in pursuance of regulation 6 as if he were the original holder in the circumstances specified in regulation 6(1); and, if when the successor becomes the holder of the original licence as aforesaid there is an application made by the original holder with respect to the original licence for the purpose of regulation 5(3) which has not been disposed of, that application shall be deemed to have been adopted by the successor on becoming the holder of the original licence and may be determined accordingly: provided that reasonable notice shall be given to the successor before a decision is issued on the application as so adopted.

In this paragraph "a relevant entitlement" means an entitlement with respect to the original licence which a person acquires by becoming the occupier of land of which the original holder ceased to be the occupier on an occasion prior to the relevant event pursuant to which the successor becomes the holder of the original licence as aforesaid.

[804]

5 Rights of a successor on becoming the occupier of a part of the original land

(1)   Where the original holder ceases to be the occupier of the whole, or a part, of the original land and a successor becomes the occupier of a part of the original land within a period of two years beginning with the date of the relevant event, the successor, if he satisfies the conditions of section 27 of the Act (as modified by regulation 8), shall be entitled to apply, within a period of one month beginning with the date on which he becomes the occupier as aforesaid, for the grant of a new licence in accordance with the following provisions of these regulations.

(2)   Subject to the next following paragraph, a successor who accordingly applies for a new licence and who, when a decision falls to be made on the application, is the occupier of any of the land specified therein as land of which he has become the occupier in the circumstances mentioned in the preceding paragraph, shall be entitled to the grant of a new licence for the abstraction of water for use on land of which he is the occupier as aforesaid, containing provisions determined by reference to the provisions of the original licence in accordance with regulation 7 of these regulations.

(3)   It shall be a condition of the successor's entitlement under this regulation to the grant of a new licence that the original holder or, as the case may be, the holder for the time being of the original licence who stands in place of the original holder for this purpose by virtue of regulation 4(4), has duly made, and has not withdrawn, an application in pursuance of the next following regulation for the grant of an appropriate new licence in substitution for the original licence, or an application under section 42 of the Act for the revocation of the original licence or for its variation in such a manner as will secure that those of its provisions with respect to the abstraction of water which (with any modifications) are to be included in the new licence for which the successor has applied cease to have effect as provisions of the original licence.

This condition shall not apply where the original holder has ceased to be the holder of the original licence and there is for the time being no holder of that licence in the place of the original holder as aforesaid.

(4)   The Schedule hereto shall have effect in relation to applications for new licences in pursuance of this, or the next following, regulation.

[805]

6 Rights of the original holder with respect to the grant of a new licence

(1) Where a successor duly applies in pursuance of the last preceding regulation for the grant of a new licence, and the original holder continues to be the occupier of a part of the original land, the original holder, if he satisfies the conditions of section 27 of the Act (as modified by regulation 8), shall be entitled to apply for the grant of a new licence, in substitution for the original licence, in accordance with the following provisions of this regulation.

(2) On the grant of a new licence on the successor's application, the original holder, if he has duly applied, shall be entitled to the grant of a new licence, in substitution for the original licence, giving effect as nearly as may be to the provisions of the original licence (including any provision relating to the use of water on land of which the original holder is not the occupier) in so far as effect is not given to those provisions in the new licence granted to the successor.

[806]

7 Provisions of a new licence granted to a successor

(1) Subject to this regulation, the provisions of a new licence granted on the application of a successor in pursuance of regulation 5 shall be such as appear to the river authority to correspond as nearly as may be to the provisions of the original licence, modified so as to provide for the abstraction of water—

    (a) from any point of abstraction specified in the original licence which, having regard to section 27 of the Act (as modified by regulation 8) and to the provisions of the original licence, is available to the applicant for the purposes of the next following sub-paragraph; and

    (b) for use on any part of the original land occupied by the applicant, and for a purpose of the original licence appropriate to that part.

In the following provisions of these regulations, "the applicant's land" means that part of the original land which is occupied by the applicant and to which his application relates, and any reference, however expressed, to a point of abstraction available to the applicant is a reference to such a point of abstraction as is mentioned in sub-paragraph (a) of this paragraph.

(2) Subject to the next following paragraph, provision as to any quantity of water authorised to be abstracted in pursuance of the new licence shall be made as follows, that is to say:—

    (a) where the original licence specifies or otherwise limits a quantity of water to be abstracted during a period or periods so specified from any point available to the applicant, for use on the whole or a part of the applicant's land and not also on any other land, the new licence shall make the like provision;

    (b) where the original licence specifies or otherwise limits a quantity of water to be abstracted as aforesaid for use on the whole or a part of the applicant's land and also on other land, the new licence shall make the like provision with such modification as is required to secure that the quantity thereby authorised for use on the applicant's land, or, as the case may be, on the relevant part of that land, shall be an appropriate share of the relevant quantity provided for by the original licence, that is to say, either—

        (i) an amount which bears to the whole of the relevant quantity provided for by the original licence the same proportion as the area of the applicant's land, or of the relevant part of that land, bears to the area of the land on which that quantity was to be used in accordance with the original licence, or

        (ii) such other amount as the river authority (having regard to the provisions of the original licence, the manner in which any water abstracted has been used in accordance with that licence and any other material considerations) may determine to be the amount which would have been used on the land in question under the original licence if the original holder had continued to be the occupier of the applicant's land and had abstracted the whole of the relevant quantity.

(3)   Where—

(a) the original licence authorises the abstraction of water from a source of supply at two or more points of abstraction, not all of which have become available to the applicant as mentioned in paragraph (1) of this regulation, and

(b) the river authority are satisfied that, if the original holder had continued to be the occupier of the applicant's land, it would have been his practice in accordance with the original licence to use on that land water abstracted at any point of abstraction which has not become available to the applicant,

the river authority may, if the applicant so requests, provide in the new licence for the abstraction, at any point or points of abstraction specified in the original licence and available to the applicant as aforesaid, of a quantity or quantities of water not exceeding whichever is the smaller of—

(i) the corresponding quantity which, in the opinion of the authority, would have been abstracted and used on the applicant's land as mentioned in sub-paragraph (b) of this paragraph, and

(ii) the capacity of the existing means of abstraction at the relevant point or points, regard being had to any quantity of water to be authorised in pursuance of the foregoing paragraphs of this regulation.

(4)   In determining under this regulation what quantity of water is to be authorised in a new licence by reference to the provisions of the original licence, any relevant apportionment for the purposes of a licence previously granted hereunder by reference to the provisions of the same original licence shall (subject to the effect of any material revocation or variation) be deemed to be conclusive.

(5)   Any reference in this regulation to the river authority shall be construed as including a reference to the Minister on appeal.

                                                                              [807]

8 Application of provisions of Part IV of the Act

(1)   In relation to an application for a licence made by virtue of these regulations, or to a person entitled to make such an application, the provisions of Part IV of the Act shall have effect subject to the exceptions and modifications specified in this regulation.

(2)   Section 27 (which relates to entitlement to apply for a licence) shall have effect as if subsection (3) included a requirement that the occupation of, or right of access to, land mentioned in that subsection shall be such as to afford access to the relevant point or points of abstraction specified in the original licence.

(3)   Section 28 (which relates to notice of an application), section 29 (which relates to the determination of an application by the river authority), section 38 (which relates to the reference of applications to the Minister) and section 41 (which contains provisions supplementary to sections 38 to 40) shall not have effect.

(4)   Sections 23, 31 and 49 (which relate respectively to the restriction on abstracting water, the effect of a licence and penalties) shall each have effect with a modification providing—

(a) that, during the period beginning with the time at which any person other than the holder of the original licence becomes entitled to apply under these regulations for a licence and ending on the relevant date (as hereinafter defined), that person shall be deemed for the purposes of the section to be the holder of a licence containing such provisions as, having regard to all the circumstances of the case, could reasonably be expected to be included in any licence granted to him in virtue of his entitlement under the regulations, and

(b) that, for the purposes of the section, any licence granted on an application accordingly made by that person shall be treated as not having effect until the application has been disposed of.

In this paragraph "the relevant date" means, in a case where the relevant entitlement expires or is determined by virtue of a provision of these regulations, the date of that expiry or determination, and, in any other case, means the date on which the relevant application under the regulations for a licence is disposed of; and subsection (7) of section 56 of the Act (with the exception of paragraph (b) thereof) shall apply for determining when an application is to be taken to be disposed of for the purposes of this provision as it so applies for the purposes of section 56.

(5)   The last preceding paragraph shall apply in relation to section 26 as it applies in relation to the sections specified in that paragraph, with the substitution therein, for the words "during the period beginning with the time at which any person other than the holder of the original licence becomes entitled to apply", of the words "during the period beginning with the date on which any person other than the holder of the original licence entitled to do so duly applies."

[808]

SCHEDULE
APPLICATIONS FOR NEW LICENCES

Regulation 5(4)

1.—(1) An application in pursuance of these regulations for a licence to abstract water from a source of supply in a river authority area shall include the particulars and be verified by the evidence hereafter prescribed, and shall be made to the river authority in accordance with the provisions of this Schedule.

(2)   The application and any accompanying documents, together with such additional number of copies (not exceeding two) as the river authority may require, shall be addressed to the Clerk of the authority and posted to or delivered at the river authority's principal office or such other place as the authority may direct.

2.—(1) The application shall be accompanied by an ordnance map to a scale of not less than six inches to one mile for the purpose of showing the matters specified in the next sub-paragraph:

Provided that the river authority may dispense with this requirement, or may accept a map to a smaller scale, if on the request of the applicant they are satisfied in the circumstances of the case that a map is unnecessary or, as the case may be, that a smaller scale will suffice.

(2)   There shall be shown clearly on the map (if any):—
   (a)   the point or points of abstraction specified in the original licence (each with a reference number) at which the applicant proposes to abstract water;
   (b)   as respects each point of abstraction, the relevant land for the purposes of section 27 of the Act (as modified by regulation 8);
   (c)   the applicant's land (as defined in regulation 7(1)), distinguishing as may be necessary between parts of that land on which it is proposed to use water abstracted in pursuance of the licence for different purposes.

(3)   In this Schedule the expression "relevant land", used in connection with section 27 of the Act, means land contiguous to the existing point of abstraction at which the applicant proposes to abstract from an inland water, or land consisting of or comprising underground strata and with access to the existing point of abstraction at which he proposes to abstract from those strata, being in either case land in relation to which the applicant claims such rights of occupation or access, actual or prospective, as satisfy the relevant conditions of section 27 (as modified by regulation 8).

3.—(1) Subject to sub-paragraph (2) with respect to an application made by the holder of the original licence, the application shall include the following particulars:—
   (a)   The applicant's name and address, and the name and address of any other person authorised to act on the applicant's behalf in the matter.
   (b)   The source of supply to which the application relates.
   (c)   The serial number of the original licence by reference to which the application is made, and the name and address (if known) of the original holder.

    (d)   The name and address (if known) of any other person who to the applicant's knowledge has become the holder of the original licence.

    (e)   Particulars of the applicant's claim to be entitled to make the application, including—

        (i)   a description (by reference to the map, if any) of the applicant's land (as defined in regulation 7(1));

        (ii)   the date on which, and the manner in which, the applicant became the occupier of the relevant part of the original land, and (if different and so far as known to the applicant) the date on which, and the relevant event by reason of which, the original holder ceased to be the occupier of that part;

        (iii)   a statement showing how the applicant claims to be entitled to make the application in accordance with section 27 of the Act (as modified by regulation 8), with reference, where appropriate, to relevant land for the purpose of section 27 shown on the map.

    (f)   Particulars of the application, including—

        (i)   a brief description of the point or points of abstraction specified in the original licence at which the applicant proposes to abstract (with reference, where appropriate, to the point or points shown and numbered on the map);

        (ii)   the provisions which the applicant proposes the licence should contain, including provisions as to the quantity of water authorised to be abstracted during a period or periods specified at each point of abstraction or group of points of abstraction specified, and provisions as to the land on which and the purposes for which the water abstracted is to be used, all being provisions framed by reference to the corresponding provisions of the original licence;

        (iii)   a statement showing how the quantities of water specified have been assessed in accordance with the provisions of regulation 7.

    (2) In the case of an application by the original holder in pursuance of regulation 6, or by a person who has become the holder of the original licence and who is entitled to make such an application by virtue of regulation 4(4), sub-paragraph (1) of this paragraph shall have effect with the following modifications:—

    (a)   the particulars required at head (c) shall include the statement that the applicant is the original holder, or, as the case may be, that he has become the holder of the original licence by virtue of regulation 4;

    (b)   for the particulars required at head (d) there shall be substituted brief particulars sufficient to identify the application by a successor for a new licence (or, if there is more than one, each such application) in consequence of which the applicant is applying for a new licence;

    (c)   for the particulars required at head (e)(i) there shall be substituted a description of the part of the original land of which the original holder has continued to be the occupier, or, in the case of an application by a person who is the holder of the original licence by virtue of regulation 4(1), a description of the original land of which that person has become the occupier;

    (d)   the particulars required at head (e)(ii) shall not apply in the case of the original holder, and, in the case of a person who has become the holder of the original licence by virtue of regulation 4, there shall be substituted for those particulars the date on which, and the circumstances in which, he became the occupier of the whole of the original land;

    (e)   in head (f)(iii) for the words "in accordance with the provisions of regulation 7" there shall be substituted the words "having regard to the provisions of regulation 6".

4.—(1) The application shall be accompanied by evidence for the purpose of satisfying the river authority with respect to such of the following matters as are contained in the application, or shall include a statement as to the nature of any evidence which the applicant can produce for that purpose if the authority shall so require:—

    (a)   that the claim to have become the occupier of a part, or the whole, of the original land, and (in so far as material) to have done so at the time specified, is well founded;

    (b)   that the claim to be entitled to make the application in accordance with the provisions of section 27 of the Act (as modified by regulation 8) is well founded;

    (c)   in the case of a proposal that the new licence should authorise a quantity of water determined in accordance with regulation 7(2)(b)(ii), that the quantity proposed is the quantity which ought to be so determined;

    (d)   in the case of a request that, in accordance with regulation 7(3), there should be added to any quantity of water determined in accordance with regulation 7(2) a quantity which the original holder would have abstracted at a point of abstraction which has not become available to the applicant, that the circumstances are such as to enable the river authority to be satisfied with respect to the relevant matters specified in regulation 7(3).

(2) The application shall be accompanied by such information as the applicant is able to provide with respect to the following matters:—

(a) whether the holder (if any) of the original licence has applied, or is prepared to apply, for the grant of a new licence, or for the revocation or variation of the original licence, as mentioned in regulation 5(3);

(b) whether there is, or is likely to be, any related application for a new licence, made by another successor by reference to the same original licence, which might appropriately be considered together with the applicant's application.

5. Regulation 10 of the Water Resources (Licences) Regulations 1965 shall have effect in relation to the application as if it were an application for a licence of right and as if the period therein prescribed for dealing with the application were a period of 3 months; and regulation 12 of those Regulations shall have effect in relation to any appeal to the Minister in pursuance of the application, but, save as aforesaid, Part II of the said Regulations of 1965 shall not have effect in relation to applications made in pursuance of these regulations.

[809]

CONTROL OF NOISE (APPEALS) REGULATIONS 1975

(SI 1975/2116)

NOTES

Made: 11 December 1975.
Commencement: 1 January 1976.
Authority: Control of Pollution Act 1974, ss 70(2), (3), 104(1).

ARRANGEMENT OF REGULATIONS

PART I
INTRODUCTORY

PART I
INTRODUCTORY

1 Title and commencement

These regulations may be cited as the Control of Noise (Appeals) Regulations 1975 and shall come into operation on 1st January 1976.

[810]

2 Interpretation

(1)   The Interpretation Act 1889 shall apply for the interpretation of these regulations, as it applies for the interpretation of an Act of Parliament.

(2)   In these regulations, unless the context otherwise requires—
"the Act" means the Control of Pollution Act 1974, and any reference in these regulations to a numbered section shall be construed as a reference to the section bearing that number in the Act;
"best practicable means" shall be construed in accordance with section 72;
"person responsible" has the meaning given to it by section 73(1).

(3)   Any reference in these regulations to a numbered regulation shall be construed as a reference to the regulation bearing that number in these regulations.

[811]

PART II
APPEALS TO MAGISTRATES' COURTS

3 Interpretation of Part II

This part of these regulations relates only to appeals brought to magistrates' courts under Part III of the Act, and any reference in this part to an appeal or an appellant shall be construed accordingly.

[812]

4 (*Revoked by the Statutory Nuisance (Appeals) Regulations 1990, SI 1990/2276, reg 4(1).*)

5 Appeals under section 60(7)

(1)   The provisions of this regulation shall apply to an appeal brought by any person under subsection (7) of section 60 (control of noise on construction sites) against a notice served upon him by a local authority under that section.

(2)   The grounds on which a person served with such a notice may appeal under the said subsection (7) may include any of the following grounds which are appropriate in the circumstances of the particular case:—
(a) that the notice is not justified by the terms of section 60;
(b) that there has been some informality, defect or error in, or in connection with, the notice;
(c) that the authority have refused unreasonably to accept compliance with alternative requirements, or that the requirements of the notice are otherwise unreasonable in character or extent, or are unnecessary;
(d) that the time, or, where more than one time is specified, any of the times, within which the requirements of the notice are to be complied with is not reasonably sufficient for the purpose;
(e) that the notice should have been served on some person instead of the appellant, being a person who is carrying out, or going to carry out, the works, or is responsible for, or has control over, the carrying out of the works;
(f) that the notice might lawfully have been served on some person in addition to the appellant, being a person who is carrying out, or going to carry out, the works, or is responsible for, or has control over, the carrying out of the works, and that it would have been equitable for it to have been so served;
(g) that the authority have not had regard to some or all of the provisions of section 60(4).

(3)   If and so far as an appeal is based on the ground of some informality, defect or error in, or in connection with, the notice, the court shall dismiss the appeal, if it is satisfied that the informality, defect or error was not a material one.

(4)   Where the grounds upon which an appeal is brought include a ground specified in paragraph (2)(e) or (f) above, the appellant shall serve a copy of his

notice of appeal on any other person referred to, and in the case of any appeal to which this regulation applies he may serve a copy of his notice of appeal on any other person having an estate or interest in the premises in question.

(5) On the hearing of the appeal the court may—
    (a) quash the notice to which the appeal relates, or
    (b) vary the notice in favour of the appellant in such manner as it thinks fit, or
    (c) dismiss the appeal;

and a notice which is varied under sub-paragraph (b) above shall be final and shall otherwise have effect, as so varied, as if it had been so made by the local authority.

[813]

6 Appeals under section 61(7)

(1) The provisions of this regulation shall apply to an appeal brought by any person under subsection (7) of section 61 (prior consent for work on construction sites) in relation to a conditional consent given by a local authority under that section or in relation to an authority's refusal or failure to give a consent within the period specified in subsection (6) of that section.

(2) In this regulation, "conditional consent" means a consent given by a local authority under section 61 in respect of which the authority have attached any condition or imposed any limitation or qualification in pursuance of section 61(5)(a), (b) or (c); and "conditions" includes any limitation or qualification so imposed.

(3) The grounds on which a person to whom a local authority give a conditional consent may appeal under the said subsection (7) may include any of the following grounds which are appropriate in the circumstances of the particular case—
    (a) that any condition attached or imposed in relation to the consent (in this regulation referred to as "a relevant condition") is not justified by the terms of section 61;
    (b) that there has been some informality, defect or error in, or in connection with, the consent;
    (c) that the requirements of any relevant condition are unreasonable in character or extent, or are unnecessary;
    (d) that the time, or where more than one time is specified, any of the times, within which the requirements of any relevant condition are to be complied with is not reasonably sufficient for the purpose.

(4) If and so far as an appeal is based on the ground of some informality, defect or error in, or in connection with, the consent, the court shall dismiss the appeal, if it is satisfied that the informality, defect or error was not a material one.

(5) Where the appeal relates to a conditional consent given by a local authority, on the hearing of the appeal the court may—
    (a) vary the consent or any relevant condition in favour of the appellant in such manner as it thinks fit, or
    (b) quash any relevant condition, or
    (c) dismiss the appeal;

and a consent or condition which is varied under sub-paragraph (a) above shall be final and shall otherwise have effect, as so varied, as if it had been given, attached or imposed in that form by the authority.

(6) Where the appeal relates to a local authority's refusal or failure to give a consent within the period specified in section 61(6), on the hearing of the appeal the court shall afford to the appellant and to the authority an opportunity of making representations to it concerning the application under section 61(1) to which the appeal relates and concerning the terms and conditions of any consent which they consider to be appropriate thereto, and thereafter the court shall either—

(a) adjourn the appeal to enable the appellant to submit to the authority a new application under section 61(1) relating to the matters which are the subject of the appeal, or

(b) make an order giving consent to the application either unconditionally or subject to such conditions as it thinks fit, having regard to the provisions of section 61(4), (5) and (9), and any other matters which appear to it to be relevant,

and any consent given by an order made under sub-paragraph (b) above shall be final and shall otherwise have effect for the purpose of Part III of the Act as if it were a consent given by the local authority under section 61.

[814]

7 Appeals under section 66(7)

(1) The provisions of this regulation shall apply to an appeal brought by any person under subsection (7) of section 66 (reduction of noise levels) against a noise reduction notice served upon him by a local authority under that section.

(2) The grounds on which a person served with such a notice may appeal under the said subsection (7) may include any of the following grounds which are appropriate in the circumstances of the particular case:—

(a) that the notice is not justified by the terms of section 66;

(b) that there has been some informality, defect or error in, or in connection with, the notice;

(c) that the authority have refused unreasonably to accept compliance with alternative requirements, or that the requirements of the notice are otherwise unreasonable in character or extent, or are unnecessary;

(d) that the time, or, where more than one time is specified, any of the times, within which the requirements of the notice are to be complied with is not reasonably sufficient for the purpose;

(e) where the noise to which the notice relates is noise caused in the course of a trade or business, that the best practicable means have been used for preventing, or for counteracting the effect of, the noise;

(f) that the notice should have been served on some person instead of the appellant, being the person responsible for the noise;

(g) that the notice might lawfully have been served on some person in addition to the appellant, being a person also responsible for the noise and that it would have been equitable for it to have been so served.

(3) If and so far as an appeal is based on the ground of some informality, defect or error in, or in connection with, the notice, the court shall dismiss the appeal, if it is satisfied that the informality, defect or error was not a material one.

(4) Where the grounds upon which an appeal is brought include a ground specified in paragraph (2)(g) above, the appellant shall serve a copy of his notice of appeal on any other person referred to, and in the case of any appeal to which this regulation applies he may serve a copy of his notice of appeal on any other person having an estate or interest in the premises in question.

(5) On the hearing of the appeal the court may—

(a) quash the notice to which the appeal relates, or

(b) vary the notice in favour of the appellant in such manner as it thinks fit, or

(c) dismiss the appeal;

and a notice which is varied under sub-paragraph (b) above shall be final and shall otherwise have effect as so varied as if it had been so made by the local authority.

(6) Subject to paragraph (7) below, on the hearing of the appeal the court may make such order as it thinks fit—

(a) with respect to the person by whom any work is to be executed and the contribution to be made by any person towards the cost of the work, or

(b) as to the proportions in which any expenses which may become recoverable by the local authority under Part III of the Act are to be borne by the appellant and any other person.

(7)   In exercising its powers under paragraph (6) above, the court shall be satisfied, before it imposes any requirements thereunder on any person other than the appellant, that that person has received a copy of the notice of appeal in pursuance of paragraph (4) above.

[815]

PART III
APPEALS TO THE SECRETARY OF STATE

8 Interpretation of Part III

This part of these regulations relates only to appeals brought to the Secretary of State under Part III of the Act, and any reference in this part to an appeal or an appellant shall be construed accordingly.

[816]

9 Appeals under sections 64(3), 65(4) and 67(3)

(1)   Any person who brings an appeal under section 64(3), 65(4) or 67(3) shall give notice of appeal in writing, stating the grounds of the appeal, to the Secretary of State, and shall within seven days of giving that notice (or such longer period as the Secretary of State may at any time allow) send to him a copy of the following documents: —
(a) the application, if any, made to the local authority;
(b) any relevant plans and particulars submitted to them;
(c) any relevant record, consent determination, notice or other notification issued by the authority;
(d) all other relevant correspondence with the authority;
(e) a plan of the premises concerned (unless such a plan is included in the documents mentioned above).

(2)   The Secretary of State may, if he thinks fit, require the appellant or the local authority to submit within a specified period a further statement in writing in respect of the matters to which the appeal relates, and if, after considering the grounds of the appeal and any such further statement, the Secretary of State is satisfied that he is sufficiently informed for the purposes of reaching a decision as to those matters, he may decide the appeal without further investigation; but otherwise the Secretary of State shall cause a local inquiry to be held.

(3)   When he determines the appeal, the Secretary of State may allow or dismiss the appeal, or may reverse or vary any part of any record, consent, determination or decision of the local authority to which the appeal relates, or may deal with the application, if any, made by the appellant to the local authority as if it had been made in the first instance to the Secretary of State, and he may give the authority such directions as he thinks fit for giving effect to his determination.

(4)   At any time before the appeal is determined, the appellant may abandon it by giving notice in writing to the Secretary of State, and as soon as may be after he gives any such notice he shall send a copy thereof to the local authority.

[817]

PART IV
SUSPENSION OF NOTICES

10—(1) Subject to paragraph (2) of this regulation, where an appeal is brought against a notice served under section . . . 60, or 66 and—
(a) the noise to which the notice relates is noise caused in the course of the performance of some duty imposed by law on the appellant, or

(b) compliance with the notice would involve any person in expenditure on the carrying out of works before the hearing of the appeal,

the notice shall be suspended until the appeal has been abandoned or decided by the court.

(2)   A notice to which this regulation applies shall not be suspended if in the opinion of the local authority—
(a) the noise to which the notice relates—
  (i) is injurious to health, or
  (ii) is likely to be of a limited duration such that suspension of the notice would render the notice of no practical effect, or
(b) the expenditure which would be incurred by any person in the carrying out of works in compliance with the notice before any appeal has been decided would not be disproportionate to the public benefit to be expected in that period from such compliance,

and the notice includes a statement that it shall have effect notwithstanding any appeal to a magistrates' court which has not been decided by the court.

(3)   Save as provided in this regulation a notice under Part III of that Act shall not be suspended by reason only of the bringing of an appeal to a magistrates' court or the Secretary of State.

[818]

NOTES

Para (1): number omitted revoked by the Statutory Nuisance (Appeals) Regulations 1990, SI 1990/2276, reg 4(2).

TRADE EFFLUENTS (PRESCRIBED PROCESSES AND SUBSTANCES) REGULATIONS 1989

(SI 1989/1156)

NOTES

Made: 6 July 1989.

Commencement: 1 September 1989.

Authority: Water Act 1989, ss 74, 185(2) (s 74 of the 1989 Act was repealed by the Water Consolidation (Consequential Provisions) Act 1991, s 3, Sch 3, Pt I, and, by virtue of Sch 2, Pt I, para 1 to that Act, these regulations now take effect under the Water Industry Act 1991, s 138(1)).

ARRANGEMENT OF REGULATIONS

1 Citation and commencement

These Regulations may be cited as the Trade Effluents (Prescribed Processes and Substances) Regulations 1989 and shall come into force on 1st September 1989.

[819]

2 Interpretation

In these Regulations—
"the 1989 Act" means the Water Act 1989;
"asbestos" means any of the fibrous silicates, namely, crocidolite, actinolite, anthophyllite, chrysotile, amosite and tremolite; and
"background concentration", in relation to any substance, means such concentration of the substance as would, but for anything done on the premises in question, be present in the effluent discharged from those premises; and without prejudice to the generality of the foregoing, includes such concentrations of the substance as are present—
    (a) in water supplied to the premises;
    (b) in water abstracted for use in the premises; and
    (c) in precipitation onto the site within which the premises are situated.

[820]

3 Trade effluent containing prescribed substances

Section 74 of the 1989 Act (control of exercise of trade effluent functions in certain cases) shall apply to trade effluent in which any of the substances listed in Schedule 1 to these Regulations is present in a concentration greater than the background concentration.

[821]

4 Trade effluent derived from prescribed processes

Section 74 of the 1989 Act shall apply to trade effluent deriving from a process of a description mentioned in Schedule 2 to these Regulations if either asbestos or chloroform is present in that effluent in a concentration greater than the background concentration.

[822]

5 Variation of existing consents

(1) A sewerage undertaker shall, in the circumstances referred to in paragraph (2), notify the Secretary of State of its proposal to vary, by direction under section 60(1) of the Public Health Act 1961, the conditions attached to a consent having effect as if given by the undertaker under the Public Health (Drainage of Trade Premises) Act 1937 (consent to the discharge of trade effluent into a public sewer) [or to vary any agreement having effect as if entered into by the undertaker under section 7 of that Act (agreements for the reception and disposal of trade effluent)].

(2) The circumstances mentioned in paragraph (1) are that—
    (a) the consent [or agreement] has not been reviewed by the Secretary of State in accordance with paragraph 2 of Schedule 9 to the 1989 Act; and
    (b) if the proposed variation were made, the consent [or agreement] would authorise the discharge of effluent containing a concentration of a substance referred to in Schedule 1 to these Regulations in excess of the background concentration [or deriving from a process of a description mentioned in Schedule 2 to these Regulations where either asbestos or chloroform would be present in the effluent in a concentration greater than the background concentration].

(3) A notification under paragraph (1) shall be treated as a reference to the Secretary of State under paragraph 1 of the said Schedule 9 of the question whether the relevant operations should be prohibited; and paragraphs 3 and 4 of that Schedule shall have effect accordingly.

(4) Where the undertaker has notified the Secretary of State in accordance with paragraph (1)—

(a) it shall inform the owner or occupier of the trade premises in question of that notification; and

(b) it shall not vary the consent [or agreement before] the Secretary of State has given such a notice as is described in [paragraph 3] of the said Schedule 9.

(5)   The requirements imposed on a sewerage undertaker by this regulation shall be enforceable under section 20 of the 1989 Act by the Secretary of State.

[823]

NOTES
    Paras (1), (2): words in square brackets inserted by the Trade Effluents (Prescribed Processes and Substances) (Amendment) Regulations 1990, SI 1990/1629, reg 2(2), (3).
    Para (4): words in square brackets substituted by SI 1990/1629, reg 2(4).

SCHEDULE 1
PRESCRIBED SUBSTANCES

Regulation 3

Mercury and its compounds

Cadmium and its compounds

gamma-Hexachlorocyclohexane

DDT

Pentachlorophenol [and its compounds]

Hexachlorobenzene

Hexachlorobutadiene

Aldrin

Dieldrin

Endrin

Carbon Tetrachloride

Polychlorinated Biphenyls

Dichlorvos

1, 2-Dichloroethane

Trichlorobenzene

Atrazine

Simazine

Tributylin compounds

Triphenyltin compounds

Trifluralin

Fentirothion

Azinphos-methyl

Malathion

Endosulfan

[824]

NOTES
    Words in square brackets inserted by the Trade Effluents (Prescribed Processes and Substances) (Amendment) Regulations 1990, SI 1990/1629, reg 2(5).

SCHEDULE 2
PRESCRIBED PROCESSES

Regulation 4

Description of process

Any process for the production of chlorinated organic chemicals

Any process for the manufacture of paper pulp

. . .

Any process for the manufacture of asbestos cement

Any process for the manufacture of asbestos paper or board

[Any industrial process involving the use in any 12 month period of more than 100 kilograms of the product resulting from the crushing of asbestos ore]

[825]

NOTES
    Words omitted revoked and words in square brackets added by the Trade Effluents (Prescribed Processes and Substances) (Amendment) Regulations 1990, SI 1990/1629, reg 2(6).

CONTROL OF POLLUTION (SILAGE, SLURRY AND AGRICULTURAL FUEL OIL) REGULATIONS 1991

(SI 1991/324)

NOTES
    Made: 22 February 1991.
    Commencement: 1 September 1991.
    Authority: Water Act 1989, ss 110 (repealed), 185(2)(c)–(e); now take effect under the Water Resources Act 1991, s 92.

ARRANGEMENT OF REGULATIONS

1 Citation and commencement

These Regulations may be cited as the Control of Pollution (Silage, Slurry and Agricultural Fuel Oil) Regulations 1991 and shall come into force on 1st September 1991.

[826]

2 Interpretation

In these Regulations, unless the context otherwise requires—

"construct" includes install and cognate expressions shall be construed accordingly;

"fuel oil" means oil intended for use as a fuel for the production of heat or power but does not include oil intended for use exclusively as a fuel for heating a farmhouse or other residential premises on a farm and stored separately from other oil;

"livestock" means—

(a) any animals kept for the production of food or wool; or

(b) any birds kept for the production of food;

"reception pit" means a pit used for the collection of slurry before it is transferred into a slurry storage tank or for the collection of slurry discharged from such a tank;

["relevant substance" means slurry, fuel oil, a crop being made into silage or silage which is being stored;

"silage effluent" means effluent from silage or a crop being made into silage;

"silo" means any structure used for making or storing silage;]

"slurry" means—

(a) excreta produced by livestock whilst in a yard or building; or

(b) a mixture consisting wholly or mainly of such excreta, bedding, rainwater and washings from a building or yard used by livestock or any combination of these,

of a consistency that allows it to be pumped or discharged by gravity at any stage in the handling process;

"slurry storage system" means—

(a) a slurry storage tank;

(b) any reception pit and any effluent tank used in connection with the slurry storage tank; and

(c) any channels and pipes used in connection with the slurry storage tank, any reception pit or any effluent tank; and

"slurry storage tank" includes a lagoon, pit (other than a reception pit) or tower used for the storage of slurry.

[827]

NOTES

Definitions "relevant substance", "silage effluent" and "silo" substituted for original definition "relevant substance" by the Control of Pollution (Silage, Slurry and Agricultural Fuel Oil) (Amendment) Regulations 1997, SI 1997/547, reg 2(2).

---

3 Making of silage

(1)   [Subject to paragraph (1A) below,] no person shall have custody or control of any crop which is being made into silage [or any silage which is being stored] unless—

(a) [subject to paragraph (1B) below,] it is kept in a silo in relation to which the requirements of Schedule 1 are satisfied or which is an exempt structure by virtue of regulation 6 below; or

(b) it is compressed in the form of bales which are wrapped and sealed within impermeable membranes (or are enclosed in impermeable bags) and are stored at least 10 metres from any [inland freshwaters or coastal waters] which effluent escaping from the bales could enter[; or

(c) it is a crop being made into field silage or silage which is being stored on open land and—

(i) the Agency is given notice of the place where the silage is to be made or stored at least 14 days before it is first used for that purpose; and

(ii) the place is at least 10 metres from any inland freshwaters or coastal waters, and at least the specified distance from any protected water supply source, which silage effluent could enter if it escaped.]

[(1A) Paragraph (1) above shall not apply to silage whilst it is stored temporarily in a container, trailer or vehicle in connection with its transport about the farm or elsewhere.

(1B) The Agency may by notice relax the requirements of paragraph (1)(a) above subject to such conditions (if any) as are specified in the notice where a silo is used solely for the purpose of storing silage made elsewhere if it is satisfied that there is no significant risk of pollution of controlled waters from that use of the silo.

(1C) A water supply source is a protected water supply source if—
  (a) any relevant abstraction from the source is licensed under Part II of the Water Resources Act 1991; or
  (b) any relevant abstraction from the source is not so licensed but the person making or storing the silage was aware of the source's location before the making of the silage began or, in the case of silage made elsewhere, before it was stored on the land in question.

(1D) The specified distance in relation to a protected water supply source is 50 metres from the nearest relevant abstraction point.]

(2) No person having custody or control of any crop which is being, or has been, made into silage in the manner described in paragraph (1)(b) above shall open or remove the wrapping of any bales unless he does so at a place at least 10 metres from any [inland freshwaters or coastal waters] which silage effluent could enter as a result.

[(3) In this regulation—
  "field silage" means silage made on open land by a method which is different from that described in paragraph (1)(b) above;
  "relevant abstraction" means the abstraction of water from inland freshwaters or ground waters for use for—
    (a) human consumption or other domestic purposes within the meaning of section 218 of the Water Industry Act 1991; or
    (b) for manufacturing food or drink for human consumption;
  "water supply source" means inland freshwaters or ground waters from which any relevant abstraction is made or licensed to be made.]

[828]

NOTES
Para (1): words in first and fourth pairs of square brackets substituted, and words in second, third and fifth pairs of square brackets inserted, by the Control of Pollution (Silage, Slurry and Agricultural Fuel Oil) (Amendment) Regulations 1997, SI 1997/547, reg 2(3)(a).
Paras (1A)–(1D), (3): inserted by SI 1997/547, reg 2(3)(b), (d).
Para (2): words in square brackets substituted by SI 1997/547, reg 2(3)(c).

4 Storage of slurry

(1) Subject to paragraph (2) below, a person having custody or control of slurry shall store it only in a slurry storage system in relation to which the requirements of Schedule 2 are satisfied or which is an exempt structure by virtue of regulation 6 below.

(2) Paragraph (1) above shall not apply to slurry whilst it is stored temporarily in a tanker with a capacity not exceeding 18,000 litres which is used for transporting slurry on roads or about a farm.

[829]

5 Storage of fuel oil on farms

(1)   Subject to paragraph (2) below, no person shall have custody or control of fuel oil on a farm unless it is stored—
  (a) in a fuel storage tank within a storage area in relation to which the requirements of Schedule 3 are satisfied;
  (b) in drums within such a storage area;
  (c) temporarily in a tanker used for transporting fuel oil on roads or about the farm;
  (d) in a fuel storage tank which is an exempt structure by virtue of regulation 6 below; or
  (e) in an underground fuel storage tank.

(2)   Paragraph (1) above shall not apply if the total quantity of fuel stored on the farm does not exceed 1500 litres.

[830]

6 Exemptions

A silo, slurry storage system or fuel storage tank is for the time being an exempt structure if—
  (a) it was used before 1st March 1991 for the purpose of making silage, storing slurry or, as the case may be, storing fuel oil;
  (b) where it was not used before 1st March 1991 for that purpose, it was constructed before that date for such use; or
  (c) a contract for its construction was entered into before 1st March 1991 or its construction was commenced before that date and in either case was completed before 1st September 1991,

and it has not ceased to be an exempt structure by virtue of regulation 8(1) below.

[831]

7—(1) Subject to the following provisions of this regulation and regulation 8(2) below, regulation 3 above shall not apply where a person makes silage on a farm—
  (a) otherwise than in a silo;
  (b) by a method different from that described in regulation 3(1)(b) above,

and made the majority of his silage on that farm by that method in the period of 3 years immediately before 1st March 1991.

(2)   A person shall not be entitled to rely on the exemption conferred by paragraph (1) above—
  (a) unless he has given notice to the Authority before 1st September 1991 of his intention to do so and he keeps any crop which is being made into silage in a place at least 10 metres from any inland or coastal waters which silage effluent could enter if it were to escape;
  (b) . . .

[832]

NOTES
    Para (2): sub-para (b) revoked by the Control of Pollution (Silage, Slurry and Agricultural Fuel Oil) (Amendment) Regulations 1996, SI 1996/2044.

---

8 Loss of exemption

(1)   A structure which is an exempt structure by virtue of regulation 6 above shall cease to be an exempt structure if—
  (a) any requirement of a notice under regulation 9 below is not complied with within the period stated in the notice; or
  (b) at any time on or after 1st March 1991 it is substantially enlarged or substantially reconstructed unless a contract for the work was entered into

or the work was commenced before that date and in either case the work was completed before 1st September 1991.

(2) ...

(3)   Any reference in [paragraph (1)] above to the period stated in a notice is to that period as extended if it has been extended under regulation 9(4) below or by virtue of regulation 10(5) below; and any reference in those paragraphs to a requirement of a notice is to that requirement as modified if it has been modified under regulation 9(4) below.

[833]

NOTES

Para (2): revoked by the Control of Pollution (Silage, Slurry and Agricultural Fuel Oil) (Amendment) Regulations 1997, SI 1997/547, reg 2(4).

Para (3): words in square brackets substituted by SI 1997/547, reg 2(5).

---

9 Notice requiring works etc

[(1)   The Agency may serve notice on any person, who has custody or control of any relevant substance in circumstances in which these Regulations apply, requiring him to carry out such works, take such precautions or such other steps as are specified in the notice and which, in the opinion of the Agency, are appropriate, having regard to any requirements of these Regulations in relation to that substance, for reducing to a minimum any significant risk of pollution of controlled waters arising from the custody or control of that substance.]

(2)   The notice shall specify or describe the works, precautions or other steps which the person is required to carry out or take, state the period within which any such requirement is to be complied with and inform him of the effect in relation to the notice of regulation 10 below.

(3)   The period for compliance stated in the notice shall be such period as is reasonable in the circumstances and shall not in any case be less than 28 days.

(4)   The Authority may at any time—
  (a) withdraw the notice;
  (b) extend the period for compliance with any requirement of the notice;
  (c) with the consent of the person on whom the notice is served, modify the requirements of the notice,

and shall do so if so directed by the Secretary of State under regulation 10(4) below.

[834]

NOTES

Para (1): substituted by the Control of Pollution (Silage, Slurry and Agricultural Fuel Oil) (Amendment) Regulations 1997, SI 1997/547, reg 2(6).

---

10 Appeals against notices requiring works etc

(1)   A person served with a notice under regulation 9 above may within the period of 28 days beginning with the day on which that notice is served (or within such longer period as the Secretary of State may allow) appeal to the Secretary of State against the notice.

(2)   An appeal under this regulation shall be made by the appellant serving notice on the Secretary of State and the notice shall contain or be accompanied by a statement of the grounds of appeal.

(3)   Before determining an appeal under this regulation the Secretary of State shall, if requested to do so by the appellant or the Authority, afford them an

opportunity of appearing before and being heard by a person appointed by the Secretary of State for the purpose.

(4)   On determining an appeal under this regulation the Secretary of State shall have power to direct the Authority to withdraw the notice under regulation 9 above, to modify any of its requirements, to extend the period for compliance with any requirement or to dismiss the appeal.

(5)   The period for compliance with a notice under regulation 9 above shall, subject to any direction under paragraph (4) above, be extended [so that it expires] on the date on which the Secretary of State finally determines the appeal or, if the appeal is withdrawn, the date on which it is withdrawn.

[835]

NOTES

Para (5): words in square brackets substituted by the Control of Pollution (Silage, Slurry and Agricultural Fuel Oil) (Amendment) Regulations 1997, SI 1997/547, reg 2(7).

11 Notice of construction etc

A person who proposes to have custody or control of any relevant substance which is to be kept or stored on a farm in a silo, slurry storage system or, as the case may be, fuel storage area constructed, substantially enlarged or substantially reconstructed on or after 1st September 1991 shall serve notice on the Authority specifying the type of structure to be used and its location at least 14 days before it is to be used for such keeping or storage.

[836]

12 Criminal offences

(1)   A person who contravenes regulation 3(1) or (2), 4(1) or 5(1) above shall be guilty of an offence and liable—
(a)   on summary conviction, to a fine not exceeding the statutory maximum;
(b)   on conviction on indictment, to a fine.

(2)   A person who contravenes regulation 11 above shall be guilty of an offence and liable on summary conviction to a fine not exceeding level 2 on the standard scale.

[837]

SCHEDULE 1
REQUIREMENTS FOR SILOS

Regulation 3(1)(a)

1.   The requirements which have to be satisfied in relation to a silo are that—
(a)   it complies with the following provisions of this Schedule; or
(b)   it is designed and constructed in accordance with the standard on cylindrical forage tower silos published by the British Standards Institution and numbered BS 5061: 1974.

2.   The base of the silo shall extend beyond any walls of the silo and shall be provided at its perimeter with channels designed and constructed so as to collect any silage effluent which may escape from the silo and adequate provision shall be made for the drainage of that effluent from those channels to an effluent tank through a channel or pipe.

3.   The capacity of the effluent tank—
(a)   in the case of a silo with a capacity of less than 1500 cubic metres, shall be not less than 20 litres for each cubic metre of silo capacity; and
(b)   in the case of a silo with a capacity of 1500 cubic metres or more, shall be not less than 30 cubic metres plus 6.7 litres for each cubic metre of silo capacity in excess of 1500 cubic metres.

4.   The base of the silo, the base and walls of its effluent tank and channels and the walls of any pipes shall be impermeable.

5.   The base and any walls of the silo, its effluent tank and channels and the walls of any pipes shall, so far as reasonably practicable, be resistant to attack by silage effluent.

6.   No part of the silo, its effluent tank or channels or any pipes shall be situated within 10 metres of any [inland freshwaters or coastal waters] which silage effluent could enter if it were to escape.

7.   If the silo has retaining walls—
   (a)   the retaining walls shall be capable of withstanding minimum wall loadings calculated on the assumptions and in the manner indicated by paragraphs 13.9.1 to 13.9.9 of the code of practice on buildings and structures for agriculture published by the British Standards Institution and numbered BS 5502: Part 22: 1987;
   (b)   the silo shall at no time be loaded to a depth exceeding the maximum depth consistent with the design assumption made in respect of the loadings of the retaining walls; and
   (c)   notices shall be displayed on the retaining walls in accordance with paragraph 13.9.9 of that code of practice.

8.   Subject to paragraph 9 below, the silo, its effluent tank and channels and any pipes shall be designed and constructed so that with proper maintenance they are likely to satisfy the requirements of paragraphs 2 to 5 and, if applicable, 7(a) above for a period of at least 20 years.

9.   Where any part of an effluent tank is installed below ground level, the tank shall be designed and constructed so that without maintenance it is likely to satisfy the requirements of paragraphs 4 and 5 above for a period of at least 20 years.

[838]

NOTES
   Para 6: words in square brackets substituted by the Control of Pollution (Silage, Slurry and Agricultural Fuel Oil) (Amendment) Regulations 1997, SI 1997/547, reg 2(8).

SCHEDULE 2
REQUIREMENTS FOR SLURRY STORAGE SYSTEMS
Regulation 4(1)

1.   The requirements which have to be satisfied in relation to a slurry storage system are as follows.

2.   The base of the slurry storage tank, the base and walls of any effluent tank, channels and reception pit and the walls of any pipes shall be impermeable.

3.   The base and walls of the slurry storage tank, any effluent tank, channels and reception pit and the walls of any pipes shall be protected against corrosion in accordance with paragraph 7.2 of the code of practice on buildings and structures for agriculture published by the British Standards Institution and numbered BS 5502: Part 50: 1989.

4.   The base and walls of the slurry storage tank and of any reception pit shall be capable of withstanding characteristic loads calculated on the assumptions and in the manner indicated by paragraph 5 of that code of practice.

5.—(1)   Any facilities used for the temporary storage of slurry before it is transferred to a slurry storage tank shall have adequate capacity to store the maximum quantity of slurry which (disregarding any slurry which will be transferred directly into a slurry storage tank) is likely to be produced on the premises in any two day period [or such smaller capacity as the Agency may agree in writing is adequate to avoid any significant risk of pollution of controlled waters].

   (2)   Where slurry flows into a channel before discharging into a reception pit and the flow of slurry out of the channel is controlled by means of a sluice, the capacity of the reception pit shall be adequate to store the maximum quantity of slurry which can be released by opening the sluice.

6.—(1)   Subject to sub-paragraph (2) below, the slurry storage tank shall have adequate storage capacity for the likely quantities of slurry produced from time to time on the premises in question having regard to—

(a)   the proposed method of disposal of the slurry (including the likely rates and times of disposal); and

(b)   the matters mentioned in sub-paragraph (3) below.

(2)   Where it is proposed to dispose of the slurry on the premises by spreading it on the land nothing in sub-paragraph (1) above shall require the tank to have a greater storage capacity than is adequate, having regard to the matters mentioned in sub-paragraph (3) below, to store the maximum quantity of slurry which is likely to be produced in any continuous four month period.

(3)   The matters to which regard is to be had under sub-paragraphs (1) and (2) above are—

(a)   the storage capacity of any other slurry storage tank on the premises in question;

(b)   the likely quantities of rainfall (including any fall of snow, hail or sleet) which may fall or drain into the slurry storage tank during the likely maximum storage period; and

(c)   the need to make provision for not less than 750 millimetres of freeboard in the case of a tank with walls made of earth and 300 millimetres of freeboard in all other cases.

7.   No part of the slurry storage tank or any effluent tank, channels or reception pit shall be situated within 10 metres of any [inland freshwaters or coastal waters] which slurry could enter if it were to escape [unless such precautions are taken as the Agency may agree in writing are adequate to avoid any significant risk of pollution of controlled waters].

8.   The slurry storage tank and any effluent tank, channels, pipes and reception pit shall be designed and constructed so that with proper maintenance they are likely to satisfy the requirements of paragraphs 2 to 4 above for a period of at least 20 years.

9.   Where the walls of the slurry storage tank are not impermeable, the base of the tank shall extend beyond its walls and shall be provided with channels designed and constructed so as to collect any slurry which may escape from the tank and adequate provision shall be made for the drainage of the slurry from those channels to an effluent tank through a channel or pipe.

10.—(1)   Subject to sub-paragraph (2) below, where the slurry storage tank, any effluent tank or reception pit is fitted with a drainage pipe there shall be two valves in series on the pipe and each valve shall be capable of shutting off the flow of slurry through the pipe and shall be kept shut and locked in that position when not in use.

(2)   Sub-paragraph (1) above does not apply in relation to a slurry storage tank which drains through the pipe into another slurry storage tank of equal or greater capacity or where the tops of the tanks are at the same level.

11.   In the case of a slurry storage tank with walls which are made of earth the tank shall not be filled to a level which allows less than 750 millimetres of freeboard.

[839]

NOTES

Para 5: words in square brackets added by the Control of Pollution (Silage, Slurry and Agricultural Fuel Oil) (Amendment) Regulations 1997, SI 1997/547, reg 2(9)(a).

Para 7: words in first pair of square brackets substituted, words in second pair of square brackets added, by SI 1997/547, reg 2(9)(b).

SCHEDULE 3
REQUIREMENTS FOR FUEL OIL STORAGE AREAS

Regulation 5(1)(a)

1.   The requirements which have to be satisfied in relation to a fuel oil storage area are as follows.

2.   The fuel storage area shall be surrounded by a bund capable of retaining within the area—

(a)   in a case where there is only one fuel storage tank within the fuel storage area and fuel oil is not otherwise stored there, a volume of fuel oil not less than 110 per cent of the capacity of the tank;

(b)   in a case where there is more than one fuel storage tank within the fuel storage area and fuel oil is not otherwise stored there, a volume of fuel oil not less than whichever is the greater of—

> (i) 110 per cent of the capacity of the largest tank within the storage area; and
> (ii) 25 per cent of the total volume of such oil which could be stored in the tanks within the area;

(c) in a case where there is no fuel storage tank within the fuel storage area, a volume of fuel oil not less than 25 per cent of the total of such oil at any time stored within the area;

(d) in any other case, a volume of fuel oil not less than any of the following—

> (i) 110 per cent of the capacity of the fuel storage tank or, as the case may be, of the largest tank within the fuel storage area;
> (ii) where there is more than one fuel storage tank within the fuel storage area, 25 per cent of the total volume of such oil which could be stored in the tanks within the area;
> (iii) 25 per cent of the total volume of such oil at any time stored within the area.

3.   The bund and the base of the storage area shall be impermeable and shall be designed and constructed so that with proper maintenance they are likely to remain so for a period of at least 20 years.

4.   Every part of any fuel storage tank shall be within the bund.

5.   Any tap or valve permanently fixed to the tank through which fuel oil can be discharged to the open shall also be within the bund, shall be so arranged as to discharge vertically downwards and shall be shut and locked in that position when not in use.

6.   Where fuel from the tank is delivered through a flexible pipe which is permanently attached to the tank—

(a) it shall be fitted with a tap or valve at its end which closes automatically when not in use; and

(b) it shall be locked in a way which ensures that it is kept within the bund when not in use.

7.   No part of the fuel storage area or the bund enclosing it shall be situated within 10 metres of any [inland freshwaters or coastal waters] which fuel oil could enter if it were to escape.

[840]

NOTES
Para 7: words in square brackets substituted by the Control of Pollution (Silage, Slurry and Agricultural Fuel Oil) (Amendment) Regulations 1997, SI 1997/547, reg 2(10).

ENVIRONMENTAL PROTECTION (PRESCRIBED PROCESSES AND SUBSTANCES) REGULATIONS 1991

(SI 1991/472)

NOTES
Made: 6 March 1991.
Commencement: 1 April 1991 (England and Wales); 1 April 1992 (Scotland).
Authority: Environmental Protection Act 1990, s 2.

ARRANGEMENT OF REGULATIONS

1 Citation, application and commencement

(1) These Regulations may be cited as the Environmental Protection (Prescribed Processes and Substances) Regulations 1991.

(2) These Regulations shall come into force in England and Wales on 1st April 1991 and in Scotland on 1st April 1992.

[841]

2 Interpretation

In these Regulations—
    "the Act" means the Environmental Protection Act 1990;
    "background concentration" has the meaning given to that term in regulation 4(7);
    "Part A process" means a process falling within a description set out in Schedule 1 hereto under the heading "Part A" and "Part B process" means a process falling within a description so set out under the heading "Part B"; and
    "particulate matter" means grit, dust or fumes.

[842]

3 Prescribed Provisions

(1) Subject to the following provisions of these Regulations, the descriptions of processes set out in Schedule 1 hereto are hereby prescribed pursuant to section 2(1) of the Act as processes for the carrying on of which after the prescribed date an authorisation is required under section 6.

(2) Schedule 2 has effect for the interpretation of Schedule 1.

(3) In paragraph (1), the prescribed date means the appropriate date set out or determined in accordance with Schedule 3.

[843]

4 Exceptions

(1) Subject to paragraph (6), a process shall not be taken to be a Part A process if it has the following characteristics, namely—
    (i) that it cannot result in the release into the air of any substance prescribed by regulation 6(1) or there is no likelihood that it will result in the release into the air of any such substance except in a quantity which is so trivial that it is incapable of causing harm or its capacity to cause harm is insignificant; and
    [(ii) that it cannot result in the release into water of any substance prescribed by regulation 6(2) except—
        (a) in a concentration which is no greater than the background concentration; or
        (b) in a quantity which does not, in any 12 month period, exceed the background quantity by more than the amount specified in relation to the description of substance in column 2 of Schedule 5; and]

(iii) that it cannot result in the release into land of any substance prescribed by regulation 6(3) or there is no likelihood that it will result in the release into land of any such substance except in a quantity which is so trivial that it is incapable of causing harm or its capacity to cause harm is insignificant.

(2) Subject to paragraph (6), a process shall not be taken to be a Part B process unless it will, or there is a likelihood that it will, result in the release into the air of one or more substances prescribed by regulation 6(1) in a quantity greater than that mentioned in paragraph (1)(i) above.

(3) A process shall not be taken to fall within a description in Schedule 1 if it is carried on in a working museum to demonstrate an industrial process of historic interest or if it is carried on for educational purposes in a school as defined in section 114 of the Education Act 1944 or, in Scotland, section 135(1) of the Education (Scotland) Act 1980.

(4) The running on or within an aircraft, hovercraft, mechanically propelled road vehicle, railway locomotive or ship or other vessel of an engine which propels [or provides electricity for] it shall not be taken to fall within a description in Schedule 1.

[(4A) The running of an engine . . . in order to test it before installation or in the course of its development shall not be taken to fall within a description in Schedule 1.]

[(4B) The use of a fume cupboard shall not be taken to fall within a description in Schedule 1 if it is used as a fume cupboard in a laboratory for research or testing, and it is not—
    (a) a fume cupboard which is an industrial and continuous production process enclosure; or
    (b) a fume cupboard in which substances or materials are manufactured.

In this paragraph, "fume cupboard" has the meaning given by the British Standard 'Laboratory fume cupboards' published by the British Standards Institution numbered BS7258: Part 1: 1990.]

(5) A process shall not be taken to fall within a description in Schedule 1 if it is carried on as a domestic activity in connection with a private dwelling.

[(5A) . . .]

(6) Paragraphs (1) and (2) do not exempt any process described in Schedule 1 from the requirement for authorisation if the process may give rise to an offensive smell noticeable outside the premises where the process is carried on.

[(7) In these Regulations—
    "background concentration" means any concentration of the relevant substance which would be present in the release irrespective of any effect the process may have had on the composition of the release and, without prejudice to the generality of the foregoing, includes such concentration of the substance as is referred to in paragraph (8) below; and
    "background quantity" means such quantity of the relevant substance as is referred to in paragraph (8) below.

(8) The concentration or, as the case may be, quantity mentioned in paragraph (7) above is such concentration or quantity as is present in—
    (a) water supplied to the premises where the process is carried on;
    (b) water abstracted for use in the process; and
    (c) precipitation onto the premises on which the process is carried on.]

NOTES

Para (1): sub-para (ii) substituted by the Environmental Protection (Prescribed Processes and Substances Etc) (Amendment) Regulations 1994, SI 1994/1271, reg 4(1), Sch 2, para 1.

Para (4): words in square brackets inserted by SI 1994/1271, reg 4(1), Sch 2, para 2.

Para (4A): inserted by the Environmental Protection (Prescribed Processes and Substances) (Amendment) Regulations 1992, SI 1992/614, reg 2, Sch 1, para 2; words omitted revoked by SI 1994/1271, reg 4(1), Sch 2, para 3.

Para (4B): inserted by SI 1994/1271, reg 3, Sch 1, para 1.

Para (5A): inserted by SI 1992/614, reg 2, Sch 1, para 3; revoked by SI 1994/1271, reg 4(1), Sch 2, para 4.

Paras (7), (8): substituted, for para (7) as originally enacted, by SI 1994/1271, reg 4(1), Sch 2, para 5.

5 Enforcement

(1)   The descriptions of processes set out in Schedule 1 under the heading "Part A" are designated pursuant to section 2(4) of the Act for central control.

(2)   The descriptions of processes set out in Schedule 1 under the heading "Part B" are so designated for local control.

[845]

6 Prescribed substances: release into the air, water or land

(1)   The description of substances set out in Schedule 4 are prescribed pursuant to section 2(5) of the Act as substances the release of which into the air is subject to control under sections 6 and 7 of the Act.

(2)   The descriptions of substances set out in [column 1 of Schedule 5] are so prescribed as substances the release of which into water is subject to control under those sections.

(3)   The descriptions of substances set out in Schedule 6 are so prescribed as substances the release of which into land is subject to control under those sections.

[846]

NOTES

Para (2): words in square brackets substituted by the Environmental Protection (Prescribed Processes and Substances Etc) (Amendment) Regulations 1994, SI 1994/1271, reg 4(2).

SCHEDULE 1
DESCRIPTIONS OF PROCESSES

Regulation 3(1)

CHAPTER 1
[FUEL PRODUCTION PROCESSES, COMBUSTION PROCESSES (INCLUDING POWER GENERATION)] AND ASSOCIATED PROCESSES

Section 1.1 *Gasification and associated processes*

PART A

[(a)   Reforming natural gas.
(aa)   Refining natural gas if that process is related to another Part A process or is likely to involve the use in any 12 month period of 1000 tonnes or more of natural gas.]
(b)   Odorising natural gas or liquified petroleum gas [if that process is related to another Part A process].
(c)   Producing gas from coal, lignite, oil or other carbonaceous material or from mixtures thereof other than from sewage or the biological degradation of waste[, unless carried on as part of a process which is a combustion process (whether or not that process falls within Section 1.3 of this Schedule)].
(d)   Purifying or refining any product of any of the processes described in paragraphs (a), (b) or (c) or converting it into a different product.

In this Section, "carbonaceous material" includes such materials as charcoal, coke, peat and rubber.

[PART B

(a)   Odorising natural gas or liquified petroleum gas, except where that process is related to a Part A process.
(b)   Blending odorant for use with natural gas or liquified petroleum gas.
(c)   Any process for refining natural gas not falling within paragraph (aa) of Part A of this Section.]

[[In paragraph (c) of Part B of this Section, "refining natural gas"] does not include refining mains gas.]

Section 1.2 *Carbonisation and associated processes*

PART A

(a)   The pyrolysis, carbonisation, distillation, liquefaction, partial oxidation or other heat treatment of coal [(other than the drying of coal)], lignite, oil, other carbonaceous material (as defined in Section 1.1.) or mixtures thereof otherwise than with a view to gasification or making of charcoal.
(b)   The purification or refining of any of the products of a process mentioned in paragraph (a) or its conversion into a different product.

Nothing in paragraph (a) or (b) refers to the use of any substance as a fuel or its incineration as a waste or to any process for the treatment of sewage.

[In paragraph (a), the heat treatment of oil does not include heat treatment of waste oil or waste emulsions containing oil in order to recover the oil.]

PART B

Nil

Section 1.3 *Combustion processes*

PART A

[(a)   Burning any fuel in a combustion appliance with a net rated thermal input of 50 megawatts or more;]
(b)   . . .
(c)   burning any of the following in an appliance with a net rated thermal input of 3 megawatts or more otherwise than as a process which is related to a Part B process —
      (i)   waste oil;
      (ii)   recovered oil;
      (iii)   any fuel manufactured from, or comprising, any other waste.

[For the purposes of paragraph (a) above, where —
      (i)   two or more boilers or furnaces with an aggregate net rated thermal input of 50 megawatts or more (disregarding any boiler or furnace with a net rated thermal input of less than 3 megawatts); or
      (ii)   two or more gas turbines or compression ignition engines with an aggregate net rated thermal input of 50 megawatts or more (disregarding any such turbine or engine with a net rated thermal input of less than 3 megawatts),
are operated by the same person at the same location those boilers or furnaces or, as the case may be, those turbines or engines, shall be treated as a single combustion appliance with a net rated thermal input of 50 megawatts or more.]

[Nothing in this Part of this Section applies to the burning of any fuel in a boiler, furnace or other appliance with a net rated thermal input of less than 3 megawatts.]

PART B

The following processes [unless] carried on in relation to [and as part of] any Part A process —
      (a)   burning any fuel in a boiler or furnace with a net rated thermal input of not less than 20 megawatts (but less than 50 megawatts);
      (b)   burning any fuel in a gas turbine or compression ignition engine with a net rated thermal input of not less than 20 megawatts (but less than 50 megawatts);

(c)   burning as fuel, in an appliance with a net rated thermal input of less than 3 megawatts, waste oil or recovered oil;
(d)   burning in an appliance with a net rated thermal input of less than 3 megawatts solid fuel which has been manufactured from waste by a process involving the application of heat;
(e)   burning, in any appliance, fuel manufactured from, or including, waste (other than waste oil or recovered oil or such fuel as is mentioned in paragraph (d)) if the appliance has a net rated thermal input of less than 3 megawatts but at least 0.4 megawatts or is [used together with (whether or not it is operated simultaneously with)] other appliances [which each have a net rated thermal input of less than 3 megawatts and the aggregate net rated thermal input of all the appliances is at least 0.4 megawatts].

In paragraph (c) of Part A and paragraph (e) of Part B, "fuel" does not include gas produced by biological degradation of waste; and for the purposes of this Section—
"net rated thermal input" is the rate at which fuel can be burned at the maximum continuous rating of the appliance multiplied by the net calorific value of the fuel and expressed as megawatts thermal; and
"waste oil" means any mineral based lubricating or industrial oil which has become unfit for the use for which it was intended and, in particular, used combustion engine oil, gearbox oil, mineral lubricating oil, oil for turbines and hydraulic oil; and
"recovered oil" means waste oil which has been processed before being used.

Section 1.4 *Petroleum processes*

PART A

(a)   The loading, unloading or other handling of, the storage of, or the physical, chemical or thermal treatment of—
      (i)   crude oil;
      (ii) stabilised crude petroleum;
      (iii) crude shale oil;
      [(iv) if related to another process described in this paragraph, any associated gas or condensate.]
(b)   ...
(c)   Any process not falling within any other description in this Schedule by which the product of any process described in paragraph (a) . . . above is subject to further refining or conversion or is used (otherwise than as a fuel or solvent) in the manufacture of a chemical.

[PART B

The following processes unless falling within a description in Part A of this Section—
(a)   the storage of petrol in stationary storage tanks at a terminal, or the loading or unloading of petrol into or from road tankers, rail tankers or inland waterway vessels at a terminal;
(b)   the unloading of petrol into stationary storage tanks at a service station, other than an exempt service station, if the total quantity of petrol unloaded into such tanks at the service station in any 12 month period is likely to be equal to or greater than 100m to the power 3.

Paragraph 2(1) of Schedule 2 shall not apply to a process described in paragraph (b) of this Part of this Section.

In this Part of this Section—
"inland waterway vessel" means a vessel, other than a sea-going vessel, having a total dead weight of 15 tonnes or more;
"petrol" means any petroleum derivative, with or without additives, having a red vapour pressure of 27.6 kilopascals or more which is intended for use as a fuel for motor vehicles, other than liquefied petroleum gas;
"service station" means any premises where petrol is dispensed to motor vehicle fuel tanks from stationary storage tanks;
"exempt service station" means a service station—
      (a)   which was not in operation, and for the construction of which planning permission was not granted, before 31st December 1995;

(b)   at which the total quantity of petrol unloaded into stationary storage tanks does not exceed 500m to the power 3 in any 12 month period; and

(c)   which—

(i)   is situated in one of the following local government areas established by section 1 of the Local Government etc (Scotland) Act 1994—

—Argyll and Bute;

—Moray;

—Orkney Islands;

—Shetland Islands;

—Western Isles; or

(ii)   is situated in the local government area of Aberdeenshire established by that section and outside the Aberdeen area the boundary of which is shown as "The derogated boundary: Aberdeen area" on the maps contained in the volume of maps entitled "Volume of maps indicating the extent of derogated areas for new small petrol stations under the Environmental Protection (Prescribed Processes and Substances Etc) (Amendment) (Petrol Vapour Recovery) Regulations 1996" ("the Maps"); or

(iii)   is situated in the local government area of Highland established by that section and outside the Inverness area the boundary of which is shown on the Maps as "The derogated boundary: Inverness area"; or

(iv)   is situated in the local government area of Angus, Perth and Kinross or Stirling established by that section and to the north of the line shown on the Maps as "The derogated boundary: Central Scotland";

"terminal" means any premises which are used for the storage and loading of petrol into road tankers, rail tankers or inland waterway vessels;

and other expressions which are also used in European Parliament and Council Directive 94/63/EC on the control of volatile organic compound (VOC) emissions resulting from the storage of petrol and its distribution from terminals to service stations have the same meaning as in that Directive.]

CHAPTER 2
METAL PRODUCTION AND PROCESSING

Section 2.1 *Iron and steel*

PART A

(a)   Loading, unloading or otherwise handling or storing iron ore except in the course of mining operations.

(b)   Loading, unloading or otherwise handling or storing burnt pyrites.

(c)   Crushing, grading, grinding, screening, washing or drying iron ore or any mixture of iron ore and other materials.

(d)   Blending or mechanically mixing grades of iron ore or iron ore with other materials.

[(e)   Pelletising, calcining, roasting or sintering iron ore or any mixture of iron ore and other materials.]

(f)   Making, melting or refining iron, steel or any [ferrous alloy] in any furnace other than a furnace described in Part B of this Section.

(g)   Any process for the refining or making of iron, steel or any [ferrous alloy] in which air or oxygen or both are used unless related to a process described in Part B of this Section.

(h)   The desulphurisation of iron, steel or any [ferrous alloy] made by a process described in this Part of this Section.

(i)   Heating iron, steel or any [ferrous alloy] (whether in a furnace or other appliance) to remove grease, oil or any other non-metallic contaminant (including such operations as the removal by heat of plastic or rubber covering from scrap cable), if related to another process described in this Part of this Section.

(j)   Any foundry process (including ancillary foundry operations such as the manufacture and recovery of moulds, the reclamation of sand, fettling, grinding and shot-blasting) if related to another process described in this Part of this Section.

(k)   . . .

(l)   Handling slag in conjunction with a process described in paragraph (f) or (g).

[(m) Any process for rolling iron, steel or any ferrous alloy carried on in relation to any process described in paragraph (f) or (g), and any process carried on in conjunction with such rolling involving the scarfing or cutting with oxygen of iron, steel or any ferrous alloy.]

Nothing in paragraph (a) or (b) of this Part of this Section applies to the handling or storing of other minerals in association with the handling or storing of iron ore or burnt pyrites.

[A process does not fall within paragraph (a), (b), (c) or (d) of this Part of this Section unless—
(i)   it is carried on as part of or is related to a process falling within a paragraph of this Part of this Section other than paragraph (a), (b), (c) or (d); or
(ii) it consists of, forms part of or is related to a process which is likely to involve the unloading in any 12 month period of more than 500,000 tonnes of iron ore or burnt pyrites or, in aggregate, both.]

PART B

(a)   Making, melting or refining iron, steel or any [ferrous alloy] in—
(i)   an electric arc furnace with a designed holding capacity of less than 7 tonnes; or
(ii) a cupola[, crucible furnace, reverberatory furnace], rotary furnace, induction furnace or resistance furnace.

[(b) Any process for the refining or making of iron, steel or any ferrous alloy in which air or oxygen or both are used, if related to a process described in this Part of this Section.]

(c)   The desulphurisation of iron, steel or any [ferrous alloy], if the process does not fall within paragraph (h) of Part A of this Section.

(d)   Any such process as is described in paragraph (i) of Part A above, if not falling within that paragraph[; but a process does not fall within this paragraph if—
(i)   it is a process for heating iron, steel or any [ferrous alloy] in one or more furnaces or other appliances the primary combustion chambers of which have in aggregate a net rated thermal input of less than 0.2 megawatts;
(ii) it does not involve the removal by heat of plastic or rubber covering from scrap cable or of any asbestos contaminant; and
(iii) it is not related to any other process described in this Part of this Section.]

(e)   Any foundry process (including ancillary foundry operations such as the manufacture and recovery of moulds, the reclamation of sand, fettling, grinding, and shot-blasting) if related to another process described in this Part of this Section.

[(f) Any other process involving the casting of iron, steel or any ferrous alloy from deliveries of 50 tonnes or more at one time of molten metal.]

Any description of a process in this Section includes, where the process produces slag, the crushing, screening or grading or other treatment of the slag if that process is related to the process in question.

[In this Section "net rated thermal input" has the same meaning as in Section 1.3.]

[In this Section and Section 2.2, "ferrous alloy" means an alloy of which iron is the largest constituent, or equal to the largest constituent, by weight, whether or not that alloy also has a non-ferrous metal content greater than any percentage specified in Section 2.2 below, and "non-ferrous metal alloy" shall be construed accordingly.]

Section 2.2 *Non-ferrous metals*

PART A

(a)   The extraction or recovery from any material—
(i)   by chemical means or the use of heat of any non-ferrous metal or alloy of non-ferrous metal or any compound of a non-ferrous metal; or
(ii) by electrolytic means, of aluminium,
if the process may result in the release into the air of particulate matter or any metal, metalloid or any metal or metalloid compound or in the release into water of a substance described in Schedule 5 [and does not fall] within paragraph (b) of Part B of this Section.

(b)   The mining of zinc or tin where the process may result in the release into water of cadmium or any compound of cadmium.

(c)   The refining of any non-ferrous metal [(other than the electrolytic refining of copper)] or non-ferrous metal alloy except where the process is related to a process falling within a description in [paragraph (a), (c), or (d)] of Part B of this Section.

(d)   Any process other than a process described in [paragraph (b), (c) or (d) of Part B] of this Section for making or melting any non-ferrous metal or non-ferrous metal alloy in a furnace, bath or other holding vessel if the furnace, bath or vessel employed has a designed holding capacity of 5 tonnes or more.

[(e)   Any process for producing, melting or recovering by chemical means or by the use of heat lead or any lead alloy, if—

   (i)   the process may result in the release into the air of particulate matter or smoke which contains lead; and

   (ii)   in the case of lead alloy, the percentage by weight of lead in the alloy in molten form exceeds 23% if the alloy contains copper and 2% in other cases.]

[(ee)   Any process for . . . recovering any of the elements listed below if the process may result in the release into the air of particulate matter or smoke which contains any of those elements—

   gallium
   indium
   palladium
   tellurium
   thallium.]

[(f)   Any process for producing, melting or recovering (whether by chemical means or by electrolysis or by the use of heat) cadmium or mercury or any alloy containing more than 0.05 per cent by weight of either of those metals or of both of those metals in aggregate.]

(g)   Any manufacturing or repairing process involving the [manufacture or] use of beryllium or selenium or an alloy of one or both of those metals if the process may occasion the release into the air of any substance described in Schedule 4[; but a process does not fall within this paragraph by reason solely of its involving the melting of an alloy of beryllium if that alloy contains less than 0.1 per cent by weight of beryllium in molten form and the process falls within a description in [paragraph (a) or (d)] of Part B of this Section.]

(h)   The heating in a furnace or other appliance of any non-ferrous metal or non-ferrous metal alloy for the purpose of removing grease, oil or any other non-metallic contaminant (including such operations as the removal by heat of plastic or rubber covering from [scrap cable]), if related to another process described in this Part of this Section.

(i)   Any foundry process (including ancillary foundry operations such as the manufacture and recovery of moulds, the reclamation of sand, fettling, grinding and shot-blasting) if related to another process described in this Part of this Section.

(j)   . . .

[(k)   Pelletising, calcining, roasting or sintering any non-ferrous metal ore or any mixture of such ore and other materials.]

PART B

(a)   The making or melting of any non-ferrous metal or non-ferrous metal alloy [(other than tin or any alloy which, in molten form, contains 50 per cent or more by weight of tin)] in any furnace, bath or other holding vessel with a designed holding capacity of less than 5 tonnes (together with any incidental refining).

[(b)   The separation of copper, aluminium, magnesium or zinc from mixed scrap by differential melting.]

[(bb)   The fusion of calcined bauxite for the production of artificial corundum.]

(c)   Melting zinc or a zinc alloy in conjunction with a galvanising process.

[(d)   Melting zinc, aluminium or magnesium or an alloy of one or more of these metals in conjunction with a die-casting process.]

(e)   Any such process as is described in paragraph (h) of Part A above, if not related to another process described in that Part[; but a process does not fall within this paragraph if—

   (i)   it involves the use of one or more furnaces or other appliances the primary combustion chambers of which have in aggregate a net rated thermal input of less than 0.2 megawatts; and

   (ii)   it does not involve the removal by heat of plastic or rubber covering from scrap cable or of any asbestos contaminant.]

(f)   Any foundry process (including ancillary foundry operations such as the manufacture and recovery of moulds, the reclamation of sand, fettling, grinding and shot-blasting) if related to another process described in this Part of this Section.

[(g)   . . .

The processes described in [paragraphs (a), (c) and (d)] above include any related process for the refining of any non-ferrous metal or non-ferrous metal alloy.]

[In this Section "net rated thermal input" has the same meaning as in Section 1.3.]

[Nothing in this Section shall be taken to prescribe the processes of hand soldering or flow soldering.]

Section 2.3 . . .

CHAPTER 3
MINERAL INDUSTRIES

Section 3.1 *Cement and lime manufacture and associated processes*

PART A

(a)   Making cement clinker.

(b)   Grinding cement clinker.

(c)   Any of the following processes, where the process is related to a process described in paragraph (a) or (b), namely, blending cement; putting cement into silos for bulk storage; removing cement from silos in which it has been stored in bulk; and any process involving the use of cement in bulk, including the bagging of cement and cement mixtures, the batching of ready-mixed concrete and the manufacture of concrete blocks and other cement products.

(d)   The heating of calcium carbonate or calcium magnesium carbonate for the purpose of making lime [where the process is likely to involve the heating in any 12 month period of 5,000 tonnes or more of either substance or, in aggregate, of both.]

(e)   The slaking of lime for the purpose of making calcium hydroxide or calcium magnesium hydroxide where the process is related to a process described in paragraph (d) above.

PART B

(a)   Any of the following processes, if not related to a process falling within a description in Part A of this Section—

    (i)   storing, loading or unloading cement or cement clinker in bulk prior to further transportation in bulk;

    (ii)   blending cement in bulk or using cement in bulk other than at a construction site, including the bagging of cement and cement mixtures, the batching of ready-mixed concrete and the manufacture of concrete blocks and other cement products.

(b)   The slaking of lime for the purpose of making calcium hydroxide or calcium magnesium hydroxide unless related to [and carried on as part of] a process falling within another description in this Schedule.

[(c)   The heating of calcium carbonate or calcium magnesium carbonate for the purpose of making lime where the process is not likely to involve the heating in any 12 month period of 5,000 tonnes or more of either substance or, in aggregate, of both.]

Section 3.2 *Processes involving asbestos*

PART A

(a)   Producing raw asbestos by extraction from the ore except where the process is directly associated with the mining of the ore.

(b)   The manufacture and, where related to the manufacture, the industrial finishing of the following products where the use of asbestos is involved—

    asbestos cement
    asbestos cement products
    asbestos fillers

asbestos filters
asbestos floor coverings
asbestos friction products
asbestos insulating board
asbestos jointing, packaging and reinforcement material
asbestos packing
asbestos paper or card
asbestos textiles.

(c)   The stripping of asbestos from railway vehicles except—
   (i)   in the course of the repair or maintenance of the vehicle;
   (ii) in the course of recovery operations following an accident; or
   (iii) where the asbestos is permanently bonded in [cement or in any other material (including plastic, rubber or a resin)].

(d)   The destruction by burning of a railway vehicle if asbestos has been incorporated in, or sprayed on to, its structure.

PART B

The industrial finishing of any product mentioned in paragraph (b) of Part A of this Section if the process does not fall within that paragraph.

In this Section, "asbestos" means any of the following fibrous silicates—
actinolite, amosite, anthophyllite, chrysotile, crocidolite and tremolite.

Section 3.3 *Other mineral fibres*

PART A

Manufacturing—
   (i)   glass fibre;
   (ii) any fibre from any mineral other than asbestos.

PART B

Nil

Section 3.4 *Other mineral processes*

PART A

Nil

PART B

(a)   The crushing, grinding or other size reduction [(other than the cutting of stone)] or the grading, screening or heating of any designated mineral or mineral product except where—
   (i)   the process falls within a description in another Section of this Schedule;
   (ii) the process is related to [and carried on as part of] another process falling within such a description; or
   (iii) the operation of the process is unlikely to result in the release into the air of particulate matter.

(b)   Any of the following processes unless carried on at an exempt location or as part of a process falling within another description in this Schedule—
   (i)   crushing, grinding or otherwise breaking up coal or coke or any other coal product;
   (ii) screening, grading or mixing coal, or coke or any other coal product;
   (iii) loading or unloading [petroleum coke,] coal, coke or any other coal product except unloading on retail sale.

(c)   The crushing, grinding or other size reduction, with machinery designed for that purpose, of bricks, tiles or concrete.

(d)   Screening the product of any such process as is described in paragraph (c).

(e)   Coating roadstone with tar or bitumen.

[(f) Loading, unloading, or storing pulverised fuel ash in bulk prior to further transportation in bulk, unless carried on as part of or in relation to a process falling within another description in this Schedule.]

In this section—
   "coal" includes lignite;
   "designated mineral or mineral product" means—
>   (i)   clay, sand and any other naturally occurring mineral other than coal or lignite;
>   (ii)   metallurgical slag;
>   (iii) boiler or furnace ash produced from the burning of coal, coke or any other coal product;
>   (iv)   gypsum which is a by-product of any process; and
   ["exempt location" means—
>   (i)   any premises used for the sale of petroleum coke, coal, coke, or any coal product where the throughput of such substances at those premises in any 12 month period is in aggregate likely to be less than 10,000 tonnes; or
>   (ii)   any premises to which petroleum coke, coal, coke, or any coal product is supplied only for use there;]
   ["retail sale" means sale to the final consumer.]

Nothing in this Section applies to any process carried on underground.

Section 3.5 *Glass manufacture and production*

PART A

The manufacture of glass frit or enamel frit and its use in any process where that process is related to its manufacture [and the aggregate quantity of such substances manufactured in any 12 month period is likely to be 100 tonnes or more.]

PART B

(a)   The manufacture of glass at any location where the person concerned has the capacity to make 5,000 tonnes or more of glass in any 12 month period, and any process involving the use of glass which is carried on at any such location in conjunction with its manufacture.
(b)   The manufacture of glass where the use of lead or any lead compound is involved.
(c)   The making of any glass product where lead or any lead compound has been used in the manufacture of the glass except—
>   (i)   the making of products from lead glass blanks;
>   (ii) the melting, or mixing with another substance, of glass manufactured elsewhere to produce articles such as ornaments or road paint;
(d)   Polishing or etching glass or glass products in the course of any manufacturing process if—
>   (i)   hydrofluoric acid is used; or
>   (ii) hydrogen fluoride may be released into the air.
[(e) The manufacture of glass frit or enamel frit and its use in any process where that process is related to its manufacture if not falling within Part A of this Section.]

[Section 3.6 *Ceramic production*

PART A

Firing heavy clay goods or refractory material in a kiln where a reducing atmosphere is used for a purpose other than coloration.

PART B

(a)   Firing heavy clay goods or refractory material (other than heavy clay goods) in a kiln where the process does not fall within a description in Part A of this Section.
(b)   Vapour glazing earthenware or clay with salts.

In this Section—
   "clay" includes a blend of clay with ash, sand or other materials;
   "refractory material" means material (such as fireclay, silica, magnesite, chrome-magnesite, sillimanite, sintered alumina, beryllia and boron nitride) which is able to withstand high temperatures and to function as a furnace lining or in other similar high temperature applications.]

CHAPTER 4
THE CHEMICAL INDUSTRY

(See paragraph 4 of Schedule 2 as to cases where processes described in this chapter of the Schedule fall within two or more descriptions).

[Except where paragraph 2 or 8 of Schedule 2 applies, nothing in this chapter of this Schedule applies to the operation of waste treatment plant.]

Section 4.1 *Petrochemical processes*

PART A

(a)   Any process for the manufacture of [unsaturated hydrocarbons].
(b)   Any process for the manufacture of any chemical which involves the use of a product of a process described in paragraph (a).
(c)   Any process for the manufacture of any chemical which involves the use of a product of a process described in paragraph (b) otherwise than as a fuel or solvent.
[(d)   Any process for the polymerisation or co-polymerisation of any unsaturated hydrocarbons (other than the polymerisation or co-polymerisation of a pre-formulated resin or pre-formulated gel coat which contains any unsaturated hydrocarbons, or which contains any product of a process mentioned in paragraph (b) or (c) of Part A of this Section) which is likely to involve, in any 12 month period, the polymerisation or co-polymerisation of 50 tonnes or more of unsaturated hydrocarbons or of any such products or, in aggregate, of any combination of those materials and products.]
[(e)   Any process, if related to and carried on as part of a process falling within another paragraph of this Part of this Section, for the polymerisation or co-polymerisation of any pre-formulated resin or pre-formulated gel coat which contains any unsaturated hydrocarbons, or which contains any product of a process mentioned in paragraph (b) or (c) of Part A of this Section, which is likely to involve, in any 12 month period, the polymerisation or co-polymerisation of 100 tonnes or more of unsaturated hydrocarbons or of any such products or, in aggregate, of any combination of those materials and products.]

[PART B

Any process, unless related to and carried on as part of a process falling within Part A of this Section, for the polymerisation or co-polymerisation of any pre-formulated resin or pre-formulated gel coat which contains any unsaturated hydrocarbons, or which contains any product of a process mentioned in paragraph (b) or (c) of Part A of this Section, which is likely to involve, in any 12 month period, the polymerisation or co-polymerisation of 100 tonnes or more of unsaturated hydrocarbons or of any such products or, in aggregate, of any combination of those materials and products.]

[In this Section and in Section 4.2, "pre-formulated resin or pre-formulated gel coat" means any resin or gel coat which has been formulated before being introduced into the polymerisation or co-polymerisation process (whether or not the resin or gel coat contains a colour pigment, activator or catalyst).]

Section 4.2 *The manufacture and use of organic chemicals*

PART A

Any of the following processes unless falling within a description set out in Section 6.8—
[(a)   the manufacture of styrene or vinyl chloride;
[(aa)   the polymerisation or co-polymerisation of styrene or vinyl chloride (other than the polymerisation or co-polymerisation of a pre-formulated resin or pre-formulated gel coat which contains any styrene) where the process is likely to involve, in any 12 month period, the polymerisation or co-polymerisation of 50 tonnes or more of either of those materials or, in aggregate, of both;]]
[(ab)   any process, if related to and carried on as part of a process falling within another paragraph of this Part of this Section, for the polymerisation or co-polymerisation of any pre-formulated resin or pre-formulated gel coat which contains any styrene, which is likely to involve, in any 12 month period, the polymerisation or co-polymerisation of 100 tonnes or more of styrene;]

(b)   any process of manufacture involving the use of vinyl chloride;
(c)   the manufacture of acetylene, any aldehyde, amine, isocyanate, nitrile, [any carboxylic acid or any anhydride of carboxylic acid], any organic sulphur compound or any phenol, if the process may result in the release of any of those substances into the air;
[(d)   any process for the manufacture of a chemical involving the use of any substance mentioned in paragraph (c) if the process may result in the release of any such substance into the air;]
(e)   the manufacture or recovery of carbon disulphide;
(f)   any manufacturing process which may result in the release of carbon disulphide into the air;
[(g)   the manufacture or recovery of pyridine, or of any substituted pyridines;]
(h)   the manufacture of any organo-metallic compound;
(i)   the manufacture, purification or recovery of [any designated acrylate];
(j)   any process for the manufacture of a chemical [which is likely to involve the use in any 12 month period of 1 tonne or more of any designated acrylate or, in aggregate, of more than one such designated acrylate].

[In this Part of this Section, "designated acrylate" means any of the following, namely, acrylic acid, substituted acrylic acids, the esters of acrylic acid and the esters of substituted acrylic acids.]

[PART B

Any process, unless related to and carried on as part of a process falling within Part A of this Section, for the polymerisation or co-polymerisation of any pre-formulated resin or pre-formulated gel coat which contains any styrene, which is likely to involve, in any 12 month period, the polymerisation or co-polymerisation of 100 tonnes or more of styrene.]

Section 4.3 *Acid processes*

PART A

(a)   Any process for the manufacture, recovery, concentration or distillation of sulphuric acid or oleum.
(b)   Any process for the manufacture of any oxide of sulphur but excluding any combustion or incineration process other than the burning of sulphur.
(c)   Any process for the manufacture of a chemical which uses, or may result in the release into the air of, any oxide of sulphur but excluding any combustion or incineration process other than the burning of sulphur [and excluding also any process where such a release could only occur as a result of the storage and use of SO2 in cylinders].
(d)   Any process for the manufacture or recovery of nitric acid.
(e)   Any process for the manufacture of any acid-forming oxide of nitrogen.
(f)   Any other process (except the combustion or incineration of carbonaceous material as defined in Section 1.1. of this Schedule) [which is not described in Part B of this Section, does not fall within a description in Section 2.1 or 2.2 of this Schedule and is not treated as so falling by virtue of the rules in Schedule 2, and] which is likely to result in the release into the air of any acid-forming oxide of nitrogen.
(g)   Any process for the manufacture [or purification] of phosphoric acid.

[PART B

Any process for the surface treatment of metal which is likely to result in the release into the air of any acid-forming oxide of nitrogen and which does not fall within a description in Section 2.1 or 2.2 of this Schedule and is not treated as so falling by virtue of the rules in Schedule 2.]

Section 4.4 *Processes involving halogens*

PART A

The following processes if not falling within a description in any other Section of this Schedule—
(a)   any process for the manufacture of fluorine, chlorine, bromine or iodine or of any compound comprising only—

(i)   two or more of those halogens; or

(ii) any one or more of those halogens and oxygen;

(b)   any process of manufacture which involves the use of, or which is likely to result in the release into the air or into water of, any of those four halogens or any of the compounds mentioned in paragraph (a) other than the use of any of them as a pesticide (as defined in Schedule 6) in water;

(c)   any process for the manufacture of hydrogen fluoride, hydrogen chloride, hydrogen bromide or hydrogen iodide or any of their acids;

(d)   any process for the manufacture of chemicals which may result in the release into the air of any of the four compounds mentioned in paragraph (c);

(e)   any process of manufacture (other than the manufacture of chemicals) involving the use of any of the four compounds mentioned in paragraph (c) [or any of their acids] which may result in the release of any of those compounds into the air, other than the coating, plating or [surface treatment] of metal.

PART B

Nil

Section 4.5 *Inorganic chemical processes*

PART A

(a)   The manufacture of hydrogen cyanide or hydrogen sulphide other than in the course of fumigation.

(b)   Any manufacturing process involving the use of hydrogen cyanide or hydrogen sulphide.

(c)   Any process for the manufacture of a chemical which may result in the release into the air of hydrogen cyanide or hydrogen sulphide.

(d)   The production of [any compound containing any of the following]—

antimony
arsenic
beryllium
gallium
indium
lead
palladium
platinum
selenium
tellurium
thallium,

where the process may result in the release into the air of any of those elements or compounds or the release into water of any substance described in Schedule 5 [in a quantity which, in any 12 month period, exceeds the background quantity by more than the amount specified in relation to the description of substance in column 2 of that Schedule].

(e)   The recovery of any . . . compound referred to in paragraph (d) where the process may result in any such release as is mentioned in that paragraph.

(f)   The use in any process of manufacture, other than the application of a glaze or vitreous enamel, of any element or compound referred to in paragraph (d) where the process may result in such a release as is mentioned in that paragraph.

[(g) The production or recovery of any compound of cadmium or mercury.]

(h)   Any process of manufacture which involves the use of cadmium or mercury or of any compound of either of those elements or which may result in the release into the air of either of those elements or any of their compounds.

(i)   The production of any compound of—

chromium

. . .

manganese
nickel
zinc.

(j)   The manufacture of any metal carbonyl.

[(k) Any process for the manufacture of a chemical involving the use of a metal carbonyl.]

(l)   The manufacture or recovery of ammonia.
(m)   Any process for the manufacture of a chemical which involves the use of ammonia or may result in the release of ammonia into the air other than a process in which ammonia is used only as a refrigerant.
(n)   The production of phosphorous or of any oxide, hydride or halide of phosphorus.
(o)   Any process for the manufacture of a chemical which involves the use of phosphorus or any oxide, hydride or halide of phosphorus or which may result in the release into the air of phosphorus or of any such oxide, hydride or halide.
[(p)   The extraction of any magnesium compound from sea water.]

PART B

Nil

Section 4.6 *Chemical Fertiliser Production*

PART A

(a)   The manufacture of chemical fertilisers.
(b)   The conversion of chemical fertilisers into granules.

In this Section, "chemical fertilisers" means any inorganic chemical to be applied to the soil to promote plant growth; and "inorganic chemical" includes urea[; and "manufacture of chemical fertilisers" shall be taken to include any process for blending chemical fertilisers which is related to a process for their manufacture.]

PART B

Nil

Section 4.7 *Pesticide production*

[PART A

The manufacture or the formulation of chemical pesticides if the process may result in the release into water of any substance described in Schedule 5 [in a quantity which, in any 12 month period, exceeds the background quantity by more than the amount specified in relation to the description of substance in column 2 of that Schedule].]

PART B

Nil

In this Section "pesticide" has the same meaning as in Schedule 6.

Section 4.8 *Pharmaceutical production*

[PART A

The manufacture or the formulation of a medicinal product if the process may result in the release into water of any substance described in Schedule 5 [in a quantity which, in any 12 month period, exceeds the background quantity by more than the amount specified in relation to the description of substance in column 2 of that Schedule].]

PART B

Nil

In this Section, "medicinal product" means any substance or article (not being an instrument, apparatus or appliance) manufactured for use in one of the ways specified in section 130(1) of the Medicines Act 1968.

[Section 4.9 *The storage of chemicals in bulk*

PART A

Nil

PART B

The storage in a tank or tanks, other than as part of a Part A process, and other than in a tank for the time being forming part of a powered vehicle, of any of the substances listed below except where the total capacity of the tanks installed at the location in question in which the relevant substance may be stored is less than the figure specified below in relation to that substance;

any one or more designated acrylates	20 tonnes
acrylonitrile	20 tonnes
anhydrous ammonia	100 tonnes
anhydrous hydrogen fluoride	1 tonne
toluene di-isocyanate	20 tonnes
vinyl chloride monomer	20 tonnes
ethylene	8,000 tonnes

In this Section, "designated acrylate" has the same meaning as in Part A of Section 4.2.]

CHAPTER 5
WASTE DISPOSAL AND RECYCLING

Section 5.1 *Incineration*

PART A

(a)   The destruction by burning in an incinerator of any waste chemicals or waste plastic arising from the manufacture of a chemical or the manufacture of a plastic.
(b)   The destruction by burning in an incinerator, other than incidentally in the course of burning other waste, of any waste chemicals being, or comprising in elemental or compound form, any of the following—
bromine
cadmium
chlorine
fluorine
iodine
lead
mercury
nitrogen
phosphorus
sulphur
zinc.
(c)   The destruction by burning of any other waste, including animal remains, otherwise than by a process related to [and carried on as part of] a Part B process, on premises where there is plant designed to incinerate such waste at a rate of 1 tonne or more per hour.
(d)   The cleaning for reuse of metal containers used for the transport or storage of a chemical by burning out their residual content.

PART B

(a)   The destruction by burning in an incinerator other than an exempt incinerator of any waste, including animal remains, except where related to a Part A process.
(b)   The cremation of human remains.

In this section—
"exempt incinerator" means any incinerator on premises where there is plant designed to [incinerate waste, including animal remains] at a rate of not more than 50 kgs per hour, not being an incinerator employed to incinerate clinical waste, sewage sludge, sewage screenings or municipal waste (as defined in Article 1 of EC Directive 89/369/EEC); and for the purposes of this section, the weight of waste shall be determined by reference to its weight as fed into the incinerator;

["waste" means solid or liquid wastes or gaseous wastes (other than gas produced by
biological degradation of waste); and]

["clinical waste" means waste (other than waste consisting wholly of animal remains)
which falls within sub-paragraph (a) or (b) of the definition of such waste in
paragraph (2) of regulation 1 of the Controlled Waste Regulations 1992 (or would
fall within one of those sub-paragraphs but for paragraph (4) of that regulation).]

Section 5.2 *Recovery processes*

[PART A

(a)   The recovery by distillation of any oil or organic solvent.
(b)   The cleaning or regeneration of carbon, charcoal or ion exchange resins by removing
matter which is, or includes, any substance described in Schedule 4, 5 or 6.

Nothing in this Part of this Section applies to—
(i)   the distillation of oil for the production or cleaning of vacuum pump oil; or
(ii)   a process which is ancillary and related to another process which involves the
production or use of the substance which is recovered, cleaned or regenerated.]

PART B

Nil

Section 5.3 *The production of fuel from waste*

PART A

Making solid fuel from waste by any process involving the use of heat other than making
charcoal.

PART B

Nil

CHAPTER 6
OTHER INDUSTRIES

Section 6.1 *Paper and pulp manufacturing processes*

PART A

(a)   The making of paper pulp by a chemical method if the person concerned has the
capacity at the location in question to produce more than 25,000 tonnes of paper
pulp in any 12 month period.
(b)   Any process [associated with] making paper pulp or paper (including processes
connected with the recycling of paper such as de-inking) if the process may result in
the release into water of any substance described in Schedule 5 [in a quantity which,
in any 12 month period, exceeds the background quantity by more than the amount
specified in relation to the description of substance in column 2 of that Schedule].

In this paragraph, "paper pulp" includes pulp made from wood, grass, straw and similar
materials and references to the making of paper are to the making of any product using
paper pulp.

PART B

Nil

Section 6.2 *Di-isocyanate processes*

PART A
(a)   Any process for the manufacture of any di-isocyanate or a partly polymerised
di-isocyanate.
[(b)   Any manufacturing process involving the use of toluene di-isocyanate or partly
polymerised toluene di-isocyanate if—

<blockquote>
(i)   1 tonne or more of toluene di-isocyanate monomer is likely to be used in any 12 month period; and

(ii) the process may result in a release into the air which contains toluene di-isocyanate.]
</blockquote>

(c)   . . .

[(d) The flame bonding of polyurethane foams or polyurethane elastomers, and the hot wire cutting of such substances where such cutting is related to any other Part A process.]

[PART B

(a)   Any process not falling within any other description in this Schedule where the carrying on of the process by the person concerned at the location in question is likely to involve the use in any 12 month period of 5 tonnes or more of any di-isocyanate or of any partly polymerised di-isocyanate or, in aggregate, of both.

(b)   Any process not falling within any other description in this Schedule involving the use of toluene di-isocyanate or partly polymerised di-isocyanate if—

    (i)   less than 1 tonne of toluene di-isocyanate monomer is likely to be used in any 12 month period; and

    (ii) the process may result in a release into the air which contains toluene di-isocyanate.

(c)   The hot wire cutting of polyurethane foams or polyurethane elastomers, except where this process is related to any other Part A process.]

[Section 6.3 *Tar and bitumen processes*

PART A

Any process not falling within any other description in this Schedule involving—

(a)   the distillation of tar or bitumen in connection with any process of manufacture; or

(b)   the heating of tar or bitumen for the manufacture of electrodes or carbon-based refractory materials,

where the carrying on of the process by the person concerned at the location in question is likely to involve the use in any 12 month period of 5 tonnes or more of tar or of bitumen or, in aggregate, of both.

PART B

Any process not falling within Part A of this Section or within any other description in this Schedule involving—

(a)   the heating, but not the distillation, of tar or bitumen in connection with any process of manufacture; or

(b)   (unless the process is related to and carried on as part of a process falling within Part A of Section 1.4 of this Schedule) the oxidation of bitumen by blowing air through it,

where the carrying on of the process by the person concerned at the location in question is likely to involve the use in any 12 month period of 5 tonnes or more of tar or of bitumen or, in aggregate, of both.

In this Section the expressions "tar" and "bitumen" include pitch.]

Section 6.4 . . .

Section 6.5 *Coating Processes and Printing*

PART A

(a)   The application or removal of a coating material containing one or more tributyltin compounds or triphenyltin compounds, if carried out at a shipyard or boatyard where vessels of a length of 25 metres or more can be built or maintained or repaired.

(b)   The treatment of textiles if the process may result in the release into water of any substance described in Schedule 5 [in a quantity which, in any 12 month period, exceeds the background quantity by more than the amount specified in relation to the description of substance in column 2 of that Schedule].

(c)   . . .

[PART B

(a)   Any process (other than for the repainting or respraying of or of parts of aircraft or road or railway vehicles) for the application to a substrate of, or the drying or curing after such application of, printing ink or paint or any other coating material as, or in the course of, a manufacturing process where—
    (i)   the process may result in the release into the air of particulate matter or of any volatile organic compound; and
    (ii)   the carrying on of the process by the person concerned at the location in question is likely to involve the use in any 12 month period of—
        (aa)   20 tonnes or more applied in solid form of any printing ink, paint or other coating material; or
        (bb)   20 tonnes or more of any metal coatings which are sprayed on in molten form; or
        (cc)   25 tonnes or more of organic solvents in respect of any cold set web offset printing process or any sheet fed offset litho printing process or, in respect of any other process, 5 tonnes or more of organic solvents.

(b)   Any process for the repainting or respraying of or of parts of road vehicles if the process may result in the release into the air of particulate matter or of any volatile organic compound and the carrying on of the process by the person concerned at the location in question is likely to involve the use of 1 tonne or more of organic solvents in any 12 month period.

(c)   Any process for the repainting or respraying of or of parts of aircraft or railway vehicles if the process may result in the release into the air of particulate matter or of any volatile organic compound and the carrying on of the process by the person concerned at the location in question is likely to involve the use in any 12 month period of—
    (i)   20 tonnes or more applied in solid form of any paint or other coating material; or
    (ii)   20 tonnes or more of any metal coatings which are sprayed on in molten form; or
    (iii) 5 tonnes or more of organic solvents.]

[In this Section—
"aircraft" includes gliders and missiles;
"coating material" means paint, printing ink, varnish, lacquer, dye, any metal oxide coating, any adhesive coating, any elastomer coating, any metal or plastic coating and any other coating material]; and
[the amount of organic solvents used in a process shall be calculated as—
    (a)   the total input of organic solvents into the process, including both solvents contained in coating materials and solvents used for cleaning or other purposes; less
    (b)   any organic solvents that are removed from the process for re-use or for recovery for re-use.]

Section 6.6 *The manufacture of dyestuffs, printing ink and coating materials*

[PART A

Any process for the manufacture of dyestuffs if the process involves the use of hexachlorobenzene.]

PART B

Any process . . . —
    (a)   for the manufacture or formulation of printing ink or any other coating material containing, or involving the use of, an organic solvent, where the carrying on of the process by the person concerned at the location in question is likely to involve the use of 100 tonnes or more of organic solvents in any 12 month period;
    (b)   for the manufacture of any powder for [use as a coating material] where there is the capacity to produce 200 tonnes or more of such powder in any 12 month period.

In this Section, "coating material" has the same meaning as in Section 6.5[, and the amount of organic solvents used in a process shall be calculated as—

(a) the total input of organic solvents into the process, including both solvents contained in coating materials and solvents used for cleaning or other purposes; less

(b) any organic solvents (not contained in coating materials) that are removed from the process for re-use or for recovery for re-use.]

Section 6.7 *Timber processes*

PART A

(a) The curing or chemical treatment as part of a manufacturing process of timber or of products wholly or mainly made of wood if any substance described in Schedule 5 is used.

(b) . . .

PART B

The manufacture of products wholly or mainly of wood at any works if the process involves the sawing, drilling, sanding, shaping, turning, planing, curing or chemical treatment of wood [("relevant processes")] and the throughput of the works in any [12 month period is likely to exceed—

(i) 10,000 cubic metres, in the case of works at which wood is sawed but at which wood is not subjected to any other relevant processes or is subjected only to relevant processes which are exempt processes; or

(ii) 1,000 cubic metres in any other case.]

For the purposes of this paragraph—

[relevant processes other than sawing are "exempt processes" where, if no sawing were carried on at the works, the activities carried on there would be treated as not falling within this Part of this Section by virtue of regulation 4(2);]

"throughput" shall be calculated by reference to the amount of wood which is subjected to any [of the relevant processes]: but where, at the same works, wood is subject to two or more [relevant processes], no account shall be taken of the second or any subsequent process;

["wood" includes any product consisting wholly or mainly of wood;] and

"works" includes a sawmill or any other premises on which relevant processes are carried out on wood.

Section 6.8 *Processes involving rubber*

PART A

Nil

PART B

(a) The mixing, milling or blending of—

(i) natural rubber; or

(ii) synthetic [organic] elastomers,

if carbon black is used.

(b) Any process which converts the product of a process falling within paragraph (a) into a finished product if related to a process falling within that paragraph.

Section 6.9 *The treatment and processing of animal or vegetable matter*

PART A

Any of the following processes, unless falling within a description in another Section of the Schedule or an exempt process, namely, the processing in any way whatsoever, storing or drying by the application of heat of any dead animal (or part thereof) or any [vegetable matter] [if the process may result in the release into water of any substance described in Schedule 5 in a quantity which, in any 12 month period, exceeds the background quantity by more than the amount specified in relation to the description of substance in column 2 of that Schedule]: but excluding any process for the treatment of effluent so as to permit its discharge into controlled waters or into a sewer unless the treatment process involves the drying of any material with a view to its use as an animal feedstuff.

PART B

(a)   Any process mentioned in Part A, of this Section unless an exempt process—
- [(i)   where the process has the characteristics described in regulation 4(1)(ii) above; but]
- (ii)   may release into the air a substance described in Schedule 4 or any offensive smell noticeable outside the premises on which the process is carried on.

(b)   Breeding maggots in any case where 5 kg or more of animal or of vegetable matter or, in aggregate, of both are introduced into the process in any week.

In this Section—

"animal" includes a bird or a fish; and

"exempt process" means—
- (i)   any process carried on on a farm or agricultural holding other than the manufacture of goods for sale;
- (ii)   the manufacture or preparation of food or drink for human consumption but excluding—
  - (a)   the extraction, distillation or purification of animal or vegetable oil or fat otherwise than as a process incidental to the cooking of food for human consumption;
  - (b)   any process involving the use of green offal or the boiling of blood except the cooking of food (other than tripe) for human consumption;
  - (c)   the cooking of tripe for human consumption elsewhere than on premises on which it is to be consumed;
- [(iii)   the fleshing, cleaning and drying of pelts of fur-bearing mammals;]
- [(iv)   any process carried on in connection with the operation of a knacker's yard, as defined in article 3(1) of the Animal By-Products Order 1992;
- (v)   any process for the manufacture of soap not falling within a description in Part A of Section 4.2 of this Schedule;
- (vi)   the storage of vegetable matter otherwise than as part of any prescribed process;
- (vii)   the cleaning of shellfish shells;
- (viii)   the manufacture of starch;
- (ix)   the processing of animal or vegetable matter at premises for feeding a recognised pack of hounds registered under article 10 of the Animal By-Products Order 1992;
- (x)   the salting of hides or skins, unless related to any other prescribed process;
- (xi)   any process for composting animal or vegetable matter or a combination of both, except where that process is carried on for the purposes of cultivating mushrooms;
- (xii)   any process for cleaning, and any related process for drying or dressing, seeds, bulbs, corms or tubers;
- (xiii)   the drying of grain or pulses;
- (xiv)   any process for the production of cotton yarn from raw cotton or for the conversion of cotton yarn into cloth;]

["food" includes drink, articles and substances of no nutritional value which are used for human consumption, and articles and substances used as ingredients in the preparation of food;] and

"green offal" means the stomach and intestines of any animal, other than poultry or fish, and their contents.

[847]

NOTES

Chapter 1 heading: words in square brackets substituted by the Environmental Protection (Prescribed Processes and Substances) (Amendment) Regulations 1992, SI 1992/614, reg 2, Sch 1, para 4.

Section 1.1: in Part A, paras (a), (aa) substituted, for original para (a), words in second and third pairs of square brackets inserted, and Part B substituted, by the Environmental Protection (Prescribed Processes and Substances Etc) (Amendment) Regulations 1994, SI 1994/1271, reg 4(3), Sch 3, para 1, 2; words in fourth (outer) pair of square brackets inserted by SI 1994/1271, reg 4(3), Sch 3, para 3, words in fifth (inner) pair of square brackets substituted by the Environmental Protection (Prescribed Processes and Substances) (Amendment) Regulations 1995, SI 1995/3247, reg 2, Sch 1, para 1.

Section 1.2: words in first pair of square brackets inserted by SI 1994/1271, reg 4(3), Sch 3, para 4; words in second pair of square brackets inserted by SI 1992/614, reg 2, Sch 1, para 5.

Section 1.3: in Part A, para (a) substituted, para (b) revoked, and words in second pair of square brackets inserted, by SI 1995/3247, reg 2, Sch 1, para 2, words in final pair of square brackets inserted by

SI 1994/1271, reg 4(3), Sch 3, para 5; in Part B, words in first and final pairs of square brackets substituted by SI 1992/614, reg 2, Sch 1, para 7, words in second pair of square brackets inserted and words in third pair of square brackets substituted, by SI 1994/1271, regs 3, 4(3), Sch 1, para 2, Sch 3, para 6.

Section 1.4: in Part A, sub-para (a)(iv) substituted, para (b) revoked, and words omitted from para (c) revoked, by SI 1994/1271, reg 4(3), Sch 3, para 7; Part B substituted by the Environmental Protection (Prescribed Processes and Substances Etc) (Amendment) (Petrol Vapour Recovery) Regulations 1996, SI 1996/2678, reg 3.

Section 2.1: in Part A, para (e) substituted, words in square brackets in paras (f)–(i) substituted, para (k) revoked, para (m) inserted, and words in final pair of square brackets inserted, by SI 1994/1271, reg 4(3), Sch 3, para 8; in Part B, words in first, third and fourth pairs of square brackets substituted, words in second, seventh, eighth and final pair of square brackets inserted, words in fifth (outer) pair of square brackets inserted and words in square brackets therein substituted, by SI 1994/1271, regs 3, 4(3), Sch 1, paras 3, 4, Sch 3, paras 9, 10.

Section 2.2: in Part A, words in square brackets in para (a) substituted by SI 1995/3247, reg 2, Sch 1, para 3(a), words in first pair of square brackets in para (c) inserted by SI 1994/1271, reg 4(3), Sch 3, para 11(a), words in second pair of square brackets substituted by SI 1995/3247, reg 2, Sch 1, para 3(b), words in square brackets in para (d) substituted by SI 1995/3247, reg 2, Sch 1, para 3(c), para (e) substituted by SI 1994/1271, reg 4(3), Sch 3, para 11(c), para (ee) inserted by SI 1993/2405, reg 2(1) and words omitted therein revoked by SI 1994/1271, reg 4(3), Sch 3, para 11(d), para (f) substituted by SI 1994/1271, reg 4(3), Sch 3, para 11(e), words in first and second pair of square brackets in para (g) inserted by SI 1994/1271, reg 4(3), Sch 3, para 11(f), words "paragraph (a) or (d)" substituted by SI 1995/3247, reg 2, Sch 1, para 3(d), words in square brackets in para (h) substituted, and para (k) inserted, by SI 1994/1271, reg 4(3), Sch 3, para 11(g), (i), para (j) revoked by SI 1994/1271, reg 4(3), Sch 3, para 11(h); in Part B, words in square brackets in paras (a), (e) inserted, and para (bb) inserted, by SI 1994/1271, regs 3, 4(3), Sch 1, paras 5, 6, Sch 3, para 12(a), paras (b), (d) substituted by SI 1995/3247, reg 2, Sch 1, para 3(e), (f), para (g) inserted by SI 1994/1271, reg 4(3), Sch 3, para 12(b), revoked by SI 1995/3247, reg 2, Sch 1, para 3(g), words following para (g) inserted by SI 1994/1271, reg 4(3), Sch 3, para 12(b), words in square brackets therein substituted by SI 1995/3247, reg 2, Sch 1, para 3(h).

Section 2.3: revoked by SI 1994/1271, reg 4(3), Sch 3, para 14.

Section 3.1: words in square brackets inserted by SI 1994/1271, reg 4(3), Sch 3, paras 15, 16.

Section 3.2: words in square brackets substituted by SI 1994/1271, reg 4(3), Sch 3, para 17.

Section 3.4: words in first, second and third pairs of square brackets, para (f), and definition "retail sale" inserted, and definition "exempt location" substituted, by SI 1994/1271, regs 3, 4(3), Sch 1, para 7, Sch 3, paras 18, 19.

Section 3.5: words in square brackets inserted by SI 1994/1271, reg 4(3), Sch 3, paras 20, 21.

Section 3.6: substituted by SI 1994/1271, reg 4(3), Sch 3, para 22.

Chapter 4: words in first pair of square brackets inserted by SI 1994/1271, reg 4(3), Sch 3, para 23.

Section 4.1: in Part A, words in square brackets in para (a) substituted by SI 1994/1271, reg 4(3), Sch 3, para 24(a), para (d) inserted by SI 1994/1271, reg 4(3), Sch 3, para 24(b), substituted by SI 1995/3247, reg 2, Sch 1, para 4(a), para (e) inserted by SI 1995/3247, reg 2, Sch 1, para 4(b); Part B substituted, and words in final pair of square brackets inserted, by SI 1995/3247, reg 2, Sch 1, para 4(c), (d).

Section 4.2: in Part A, paras (a), (aa) substituted, for para (a) as originally enacted, by SI 1994/1271, reg 4(3), Sch 3, para 25, para (aa) further substituted by SI 1995/3247, reg 2, Sch 1, para 5(a), para (ab) inserted by SI 1995/3247, reg 2, Sch 1, para 5(b), words in square brackets in paras (c), (i), (j) substituted, paras (d), (g) substituted, and words in final pair of square brackets substituted, by SI 1994/1271, reg 4(3), Sch 3, para 25; Part B substituted by SI 1995/3247, reg 2, Sch 1, para 5(c).

Section 4.3: words in square brackets in Part A inserted, and Part B substituted, by SI 1994/1271, reg 4(3), Sch 3, paras 26, 27.

Section 4.4: words in first pair of square brackets inserted and words in second pair of square brackets substituted, by SI 1994/1271, reg 4(3), Sch 3, para 28.

Section 4.5: words in first pair of square brackets in para (d) substituted by SI 1993/2405, reg 2(2), words in final pair of square brackets inserted by SI 1995/3247, reg 2, Sch 1, para 6(a), paras (g), (k) substituted, words omitted from paras (e), (i) revoked, and para (p) inserted, by the Environmental Protection (Prescribed Processes and Substances) (Amendment) (No 2) Regulations 1993, SI 1993/2405, reg 2(2).

Section 4.6: words in square brackets inserted by SI 1994/1271, reg 4(3), Sch 3, para 29.

Section 4.7: Part A substituted by SI 1994/1271, reg 4(3), Sch 3, para 30; words in square brackets inserted by SI 1995/3247, reg 2, Sch 1, para 6(b).

Section 4.8: Part A substituted by SI 1994/1271, reg 4(3), Sch 3, para 31; words in square brackets inserted by SI 1995/3247, reg 2, Sch 1, para 6(c).

Section 4.9: substituted by SI 1994/1271, reg 4(3), Sch 3, para 32.

Section 5.1: in Part A words in square brackets in para (c) inserted by SI 1994/1271, reg 4(3), Sch 3, para 33; in Part B, definition "waste" and words in square brackets in definition "exempt incinerator" substituted, by SI 1992/614, reg 2, Sch 1, para 9, definition "clinical waste" substituted by SI 1994/1271, reg 3, Sch 1, para 8.

Section 5.2: Part A substituted by SI 1994/1271, reg 4(3), Sch 3, para 34.

Section 6.1: in Part A, words in first pair of square brackets in para (b) substituted by SI 1994/1271, reg 4(3), Sch 3, para 35, words in final pair of square brackets inserted by SI 1995/3247, reg 2, Sch 1, para 6(d).

Section 6.2: in Part A, paras (b), (d) substituted and para (c) revoked, and Part B substituted, by SI 1994/1271, reg 4(3), Sch 3, paras 36, 37.

Section 6.3: substituted by SI 1994/1271, reg 4(3), Sch 3, para 38.

Section 6.4: revoked by SI 1994/1271, reg 4(3), Sch 3, para 39.

Section 6.5: in Part A, words in square brackets in para (b) inserted by SI 1995/3247, reg 2, Sch 1, para 6(e), para (c) revoked by SI 1994/1271, reg 4(3), Sch 3, para 40; Part B substituted, and words in penultimate and final pair of square brackets substituted, by SI 1994/1271, regs 3, 4(3), Sch 1, para 10, Sch 3, paras 41, 42.

Section 6.6: Part A substituted, in Part B words omitted, words in square brackets substituted, and words in final pair of square brackets inserted, by SI 1994/1271, regs 3, 4(3), Sch 1, para 11, Sch 3, paras 43, 44.

Section 6.7: words omitted from Part A revoked, in Part B, words in second pair of square brackets substituted, words in third pair of square brackets inserted, and definition "wood" inserted, by SI 1994/1271, regs 3, 4(3), Sch 1, para 12, Sch 3, paras 45, 46; words in first pair of square brackets inserted, words in fourth and fifth pairs of square brackets substituted, by SI 1992/614, reg 2, Sch 1, para 11.

Section 6.8: word in square brackets inserted by SI 1994/1271, reg 3, Sch 1, para 13.

Section 6.9: words in first pair of square brackets substituted by SI 1992/614, reg 2, Sch 1, para 12; words in second pair of square brackets substituted by SI 1995/3247, reg 2, Sch 1, para 7; words in third pair of square brackets substituted, and words in fifth and final pair of square brackets inserted, by SI 1994/1271, regs 3, 4(3), Sch 1, para 14, Sch 3, para 47; words in fourth pair of square brackets inserted by the Environmental Protection (Prescribed Processes and Substances) (Amendment) Regulations 1993, SI 1993/1749, reg 2(2).

SCHEDULE 2
RULES FOR THE INTERPRETATION OF SCHEDULE 1

Regulation 3(2)

1. These rules apply for the interpretation of Schedule 1 subject to any specific provision to the contrary in that Schedule.

[2.—(1) Any description of a process includes any other process carried on at the same location by the same person as part of that process; but this rule does not apply in relation to any two or more processes described in different Sections of Schedule 1 which, accordingly, require distinct authorisation.

(2) For the purposes of this paragraph, two or more processes which are described in Part A of different Sections of Chapter 4 of Schedule 1 shall be treated as if they were described in the same Section.

2A. Notwithstanding the rule set out in paragraph 2, where a combustion process described in Part A of Section 1.3 of Schedule 1 is operated, or where one or more boilers, furnaces or other combustion appliances which are operated as part of a process so described are operated, as an inherent part of and primarily for the purpose of a process described in Part A of Section 1.1, Part A of Section 1.4[, [Part A of Section 2.1,] Part A of Section 6.3] or Part A of any Section of Chapter 4 of that Schedule ("the other process"), that combustion process or, as the case may be, the operation of those boilers, furnaces or appliances shall be treated as part of the other process and not as, or as part of, a separate combustion process.

[2B. Notwithstanding the rule set out in paragraph 2, where a process of reforming natural gas described in paragraph (a) of Part A of Section 1.1 of Schedule 1 is carried on as an inherent part of and primarily for the purpose of producing a feedstock for a process described in Part A of any Section of Chapter 4 of that Schedule ("the other process"), that reforming process shall be treated as part of the other process and not as a separate process.

2C. Notwithstanding the rule set out in paragraph 2, where the same person carries on at the same location two or more Part B processes described in the provisions of Schedule 1 mentioned in any one of the following sub-paragraphs, those processes shall be treated as requiring authorisation as a single process falling within Part B of the Section first mentioned in the relevant sub-paragraph—
    (a)   Section 2.1 and Section 2.2;
    (b)   Section 3.1 and Section 3.4;
    (c)   Section 3.6 and Section 3.4;
    (d)   Section 6.5 and Section 6.6;
    (e)   Section 6.7 and paragraph (e) of Part B of Section 1.3 insofar as it relates to any
           process for the burning of waste wood.]

3. Where a person carries on a process which includes two or more processes described in the same Section of Schedule 1 those processes shall be treated as requiring authorisation as a single process; and if the processes involved are described in both Part A and Part B of the same Section, they shall all be regarded as part of a Part A process and so subject to central control.

3A. Where a person carries on a process which includes two or more processes described in Part A of different Sections of Chapter 4 of Schedule 1, those processes shall be treated as a single process falling within a description determined in accordance with the rule set out in paragraph 4.

3B.—(1) Where paragraph 3A does not apply, but—

(a) two or more processes falling within descriptions in Part A of any Sections of Chapter 4 of Schedule 1 are carried on at the same location by the same person; and

(b) the carrying on of both or all of those processes at that location by that person is not likely to produce more than 250 tonnes of relevant products in any 12 month period,

those processes shall be treated as a single process falling within the description in whichever relevant Section is first mentioned in the sequence set out in paragraph 4.

(2) In sub-paragraph (1), "relevant products" means any products of the processes in question, other than—

(a) solid, liquid or gaseous waste;

(b) by-products, if the total value of all such by-products is insignificant in comparison to the total value of the output of the processes; or

(c) any substance or material retained in or added to the final product formulation, not as an active ingredient, but as a diluent, stabiliser or preservative or for a similar purpose.]

4. Where a process falls within two or more descriptions in Schedule 1, that process shall be regarded as falling only within that description which fits it most aptly: [but where two or more descriptions are equally apt and a process] falls within descriptions in different Sections of Chapter 4, it shall be taken to fall within the description in whichever relevant Section is first mentioned in the sequence, 4.5; 4.2; 4.1; 4.4; 4.3; 4.6; 4.7; 4.8; 4.9.

5. Notwithstanding the rules set out in paragraphs 2 and 3—

(a) the processes described in Part B of section 1.3 do not include the incidental storage, handling or shredding of tyres which are to be burned;

(b) the process described in paragraph (b) of Part B of Section 2.2 does not include the incidental storage or handling of scrap which is to be heated other than its loading into a furnace;

(c) the process described in paragraph (a) of Part B of Section 5.1 does not involve the incidental storage or handling of wastes and residues other than animal remains intended for burning in an incinerator used wholly or mainly for the incineration of such remains or residues from the burning of such remains in such an incinerator;

(d) the process described in Part B of Section 6.5 does not include the cleaning of used storage drums prior to painting and their incidental handling in connection with such cleaning;

[(e) any description of a Part B process includes any related process which would fall within paragraph (c) of Part A of Section 1.3 if it were not so related.]

[6. The following activities, that is to say—

(a) the unloading, screening, grading, mixing or otherwise handling of petroleum coke, coal, lignite, coke or any other coal product;

(b) the unloading of iron ore or burnt pyrites,

for use in a prescribed process by a person other than the person carrying on the process at the place where the process is carried on shall be treated as part of that process.]

7.—(1) Where by reason of the use at different times of different fuels or different materials or the disposal at different times of different wastes, processes of different descriptions are carried out with the same plant or machinery and those processes include one or more Part A processes and one or more other processes, the other processes shall be regarded as within the descriptions of the Part A processes.

(2) Where by reason of such use or disposal as is mentioned in paragraph (1), processes of different descriptions are carried out with the same plant or machinery and those processes

include one or more Part B processes and one or more other processes (but no Part A processes), all those processes shall be regarded as within the descriptions of the Part B processes.

[(3) Where by reason of such use or disposal as is mentioned in sub-paragraph (1), processes of different descriptions are carried out with the same plant and machinery and those processes include Part B processes falling within different Sections of Schedule 1 (but no Part A processes), those processes shall, notwithstanding the rule set out in paragraph 2, be treated as a single Part B process falling within the description in whichever of those Sections first appears in that Schedule.]

[7A. The reference to "any other process" in paragraph 2 and the references to "other processes" in paragraph 7 do not include references to a process (other than one described in Schedule 1) of loading or unloading any ship or other vessel.]

[8. Where in the course of, or as a process ancillary to, any prescribed process the person carrying on that process uses, treats or disposes of waste at the same location (whether as fuel or otherwise), the use, treatment or disposal of that waste shall, notwithstanding the rule set out in paragraph 2, be regarded as falling within the description of that process, whether the waste was produced by the person carrying on the process or acquired by him for such use, treatment or disposal.]

9.   References in Schedule 1 and this Schedule to related processes are references to separate processes carried on by the same person at the same location.

10. . . .

11. References to a process involving the release of a substance falling within a description in Schedule 4 or 5 hereto do not affect the application of paragraphs (1) and (2) of regulation 4.

[848]

NOTES

Paras 2, 3–3B: substituted, together with para 2A, for original paras 2, 3, by SI 1993/2405, reg 3.

Para 2A: substituted, together with paras 2, 3–3B, for original paras 2, 3, by SI 1993/2405, reg 3; words in first (outer) pair of square brackets inserted by SI 1994/1271, reg 4(4), Sch 4, para 1, words in second (inner) pair of square brackets inserted by SI 1995/3247, reg 2, Sch 1, para 8.

Paras 2B, 2C: inserted by SI 1994/1271, reg 3, Sch 1, para 15.

Para 4: words in square brackets substituted by SI 1992/614, reg 2, Sch 1, para 13(a).

Para 5: sub-para (e) inserted by SI 1994/1271, reg 4(4), Sch 4, para 2.

Para 6: substituted by SI 1995/3247, reg 2, Sch 1, para 9.

Para 7: sub-para (3) inserted by SI 1994/1271, reg 4(4), Sch 4, para 3.

Para 7A: inserted by SI 1992/614, reg 2, Sch 1, para 13(c).

Para 8: substituted by SI 1994/1271, reg 4(4), Sch 4, para 4.

Para 10: revoked by SI 1994/1271, reg 4(4), Sch 4, para 5.

SCHEDULE 3
DATE FROM WHICH AUTHORISATION IS REQUIRED UNDER SECTION 6 OF THE ACT

Regulation 3(1), (3)

PART I

1.   This Part of this Schedule applies in the case of a Part A process carried on in England or Wales.

2.   The prescribed date in the case of a Part A process is, except in the case of an existing process, 1st April 1991.

3.—(1)   In the case of an existing process, the prescribed date is—
    (i)   in a case falling within paragraph (2), the date at which the change mentioned in that paragraph is made unless later than the date applicable in accordance with sub-paragraph (ii);
    (ii)   where sub-paragraph (i) does not apply and subject to paragraph 5, the day after that on which the period for applying for authorisation in accordance with the Table in paragraph 4 expires.

(2) A case falls within this paragraph if the person carrying on the process makes a substantial change in the process on or after 1 April 1991 and that change—
    (i)   has not occasioned construction work which is in progress on that date; or
    (ii)   is not the subject of a contract for construction work entered into before that date.

4. Application for authorisation to carry on an existing process shall be made in the relevant period specified in the following Table—

TABLE

Any process falling within a description set out in—	Application to be made	
	Not earlier than	Not later than
Paragraph (a) of Section 1.3	1st April 1991	30th April 1991
Any other paragraph of Chapter 1	1st April 1992	30th June 1992
Section 2.1 or 2.3	1st January 1995	31st March 1995
Section 2.2	1st May 1995	31st July 1995
Chapter 3	1st December 1992	28th February 1993
Section 4.1, 4.2, 4.7 or 4.8	1st May 1993	[31st][October 1993]
[Section 4.3, 4.4 or paragraph (a) of Section 4.6]	1st November 1993	31st January 1994
[Section 4.5, paragraph (b) of Section 4.6, or Section 4.9]	1st May 1994	31st July 1994
Chapter 5	1st August 1992	31st October 1992
Chapter 6	1st November 1995	31st January 1996

5. Where paragraph 3(1)(ii) would otherwise apply and application is duly made in accordance with section 6 of the Act within the appropriate period specified in paragraph 4 for authorisation to carry on a process, the prescribed date as respects the carrying on by the applicant (or other person in his place) of the process to which the application relates is [the determination date for that process].

6. Subject to paragraph 7 below, references in this Part to an existing process are to a process—
    (i)   which was being carried on at some time in the 12 months immediately preceding 1st April 1991; or
    (ii)   which is to be carried on at a works, plant or factory or by means of mobile plant which was under construction or in course of manufacture or in the course of commission at that date, or the construction or supply of which was the subject of a contract entered into before that date.

7. A process shall cease to be an existing process for the purposes of this Part if at any time between 1st April 1990 and the last day by which an application is otherwise required to be made for authorisation for the carrying on of that process, the process ceases to be carried on and is not carried on again at the same location (or with the same mobile plant) within the following 12 months.

[8. In this Part and subsequent provisions of this Schedule—
    "the determination date" for a prescribed process is—
        (a)   in the case of a process for which an authorisation is granted, the date on which the enforcing authority grants it, whether in pursuance of the application or, on an appeal, of a direction to grant it;
        (b)   in the case of a process for which an authorisation is refused, the date of the refusal or, on an appeal, of the affirmation of the refusal;
    "substantial change" has the same meaning as in section 10 of the Act.]

NOTES
Para 4: date in square brackets substituted by the Environmental Protection (Prescribed Processes and Substances) (Amendment) Regulations 1993, SI 1993/1749, reg 2(3); section numbers in square brackets substituted by the Environmental Protection (Prescribed Processes and Substances) (Amendment) (No 2) Regulations 1993, SI 1993/2405, reg 4.
Para 5: words in square brackets substituted by the Environmental Protection (Amendment of Regulations) Regulations 1991, SI 1991/836, reg 2(2).
Para 8: substituted by SI 1991/836, reg 2(3).

PART II

9.   This Part of this Schedule applies in the case of a Part B process carried on in England or Wales.

10.   The prescribed date in the case of a Part B process is, except in the case of an existing process, the date specified in paragraph 12 below as the date from which application may be made for authorisation to carry on an existing process of the same description.

11.—(1)   In the case of an existing process, the prescribed date is, subject to paragraph 13,—
   (i)   in a case falling within paragraph (2), the date at which the change mentioned in that paragraph is made;
   (ii)   where sub-paragraph (i) does not apply, the day after that on which the period for applying for authorisation in accordance with the Table in paragraph 12 expires.

   (2)   A case falls within this paragraph if the person carrying on the process makes a substantial change in the process in the period specified in paragraph 12 in relation to the description of processes which comprise that process (when changed) and that change—
   (i)   has not occasioned construction work which is in progress at the beginning of that period; or
   (ii)   is not the subject of a contract for construction work entered into before the beginning of that period.

12. Application for authorisation for an existing process shall be made in the relevant period determined in accordance with the following Table—

TABLE

Any process falling within a description set out in—	Application to be made	
	Not earlier than	*Not later than*
Paragraph (a), (b), (c) or (e) of Section 1.3, Section 3.5, 3.6, 5.1 or 6.7 or paragraph (b) of Section 6.9	1st April 1991	30th September 1991
Section 2.1, 2.2, 3.1, 3.2 or 3.4	1st October 1991	31st March 1992
Paragraph (d) of Section 1.3, Section 6.2, 6.5, 6.6 or 6.8 or paragraph (a) of Section 6.9	1st April 1992	30th September 1992

13. Where application is duly made in accordance with section 6 of the Act for authorisation for the carrying on of an existing Part B process, the prescribed date as respects the carrying on by the applicant (or another person in his place) of the process to which the application relates is [the determination date for that process].

14. References in this Part to an existing process are to a process—
   (i)   which was being carried on at some time in the 12 months immediately preceding the earlier date mentioned in paragraph 12 in relation to the description of processes within which the process falls; or
   (ii)   which is to be carried on at a works, plant or factory or by means of mobile plant which was under construction or in course of manufacture or in the course of commission at that earlier date, or the construction or supply of which was the subject of a contract entered into before that date.

[850]

NOTES
Para 13: words in square brackets substituted by the Environmental Protection (Amendment of Regulations) Regulations 1991, SI 1991/836, reg 2(2).

PART III

15. This Part of this Schedule applies in the case of a Part A process carried on in Scotland.

16. The prescribed date in the case of a Part A process is, except in the case of an existing process, 1st April 1992.

17.—(1)   In the case of an existing process, the prescribed date is—
      (i)   in a case falling within paragraph (2), the date at which the change mentioned in that paragraph is made unless later than the date applicable in accordance with sub-paragraph (ii);
      (ii)   where sub-paragraph (i) does not apply and subject to paragraph 19, the day after than on which the period for applying for authorisation in accordance with the Table in paragraph 18 expires.

(2)   A case falls within this paragraph if the person carrying on the process makes a substantial change in the process on or after 1 April 1992 and that change—
      (i)   has not occasioned construction work which is in progress on that date; or
      (ii)   is not the subject of a contract for construction work entered into before that date.

18. Application for authorisation to carry on an existing process shall be made in the relevant period specified in the following Table—

TABLE

Any process falling within a description set out in—	Application to be made	
	Not earlier than	*Not later than*
Chapter 1	1st April 1992	30th June 1992
Section 2.1 or 2.3	1st January 1995	31st March 1995
Section 2.2	1st May 1995	31st July 1995
Chapter 3	1st December 1992	28th February 1993
Section 4.1, 4.2, 4.7 or 4.8	1st May 1993	[31st October 1993]
[Section 4.3, 4.4 or paragraph (a) of Section 4.6]	1st November 1993	31st January 1994
[Section 4.5, paragraph (b) of Section 4.6, or Section 4.9]	1st May 1994	31st July 1994
Chapter 5	1st August 1992	31st October 1992
Chapter 6	1st November 1995	31st January 1996

19. Where paragraph 17(1)(ii) would otherwise apply and application is duly made in accordance with Section 6 of the Act within the period specified in paragraph 18 for authorisation to carry on a process, the prescribed date as respects the carrying on by the applicant (or another person in his place) of the process to which the application relates is [the determination date for that process].

20. Subject to paragraph 21 below, references in this Part to an existing process are to a process—
      (i)   which was being carried on at some time in the 12 months immediately preceding 1st April 1992; or
      (ii)   which is to be carried on at a works, plant or factory or by means of mobile plant which was under construction or in course of manufacture or in the course of commission at that date, or, where construction or manufacture had not been begun before that date, the construction or supply of which was the subject of a contract entered into before that date.

21. A process shall cease to be an existing process for the purposes of this Part if at any time between 1st April 1992 and the last date by which an application is otherwise required to be made for authorisation for the carrying on of that process, the process ceases to be carried on and is not carried on again at the same location (or with the same mobile plant) within the following 12 months.

[851]

NOTES
    Para 18: date in square brackets substituted by the Environmental Protection (Prescribed Processes and Substances) (Amendment) Regulations 1993, SI 1993/1749, reg 2(3); section numbers in square brackets substituted by the Environmental Protection (Prescribed Processes and Substances) (Amendment) (No 2) Regulations 1993, SI 1993/2405, reg 4.
    Para 19: words in square brackets substituted by the Environmental Protection (Amendment of Regulations) Regulations 1991, SI 1991/836, reg 2(2).

PART IV

22. This Part of this Schedule applies in the case of a Part B process carried on in Scotland.

23. The prescribed date in the case of a Part B process is, except in the case of an existing process, the date specified in paragraph 25 below as the date from which application may be made for authorisation to carry on an existing process of the same description.

24.—(1)   In the case of an existing process the prescribed date is, subject to paragraph 26,—
        (i)   in a case falling within paragraph (2), the date at which the change mentioned in that paragraph is made;
        (ii)   where sub-paragraph (i) does not apply, the day after that on which the period for applying for authorisation in accordance with the Table in paragraph 25 expires.

    (2)   A case falls within this paragraph if the person carrying on the process makes a substantial change in the process in the period specified in paragraph 25 in relation to the description of processes which comprise that process (when changed) and that change—
        (i)   has not occasioned construction work which is in progress at the beginning of that period; or
        (ii)   is not the subject of a contract for construction work entered into before the beginning of that period.

25. Application for authorisation for an existing process shall be made in the relevant period specified in the following Table—

TABLE

	Application to be made	
Any process falling within a description set out in—	*Not earlier than*	*Not later than*
Paragraph (a), (b), (d) or (e) of Section 1.3, Section 3.2, 3.5, 3.6, 5.1 or 6.7 or paragraph (b) of Section 6.9	1st April 1992	31st July 1992
Paragraph (c) of Section 1.3	1st April 1992	30th September 1992
Section 2.1, 2.2, 3.1 or 3.4	1st August 1992	30th November 1992
Section 6.2, 6.5, 6.6 or 6.8 or paragraph (a) of Section 6.9	1st December 1992	31st March 1993

26. Where application is duly made in accordance with section 6 of the Act for authorisation for the carrying on of an existing Part B process, the prescribed date as respects the carrying on by the applicant (or another person in his place) of the process to which the application relates is [the determination date for that process].

27. References in this Part to an existing process are to a process—
        (i)   which was being carried on at some time in the 12 months immediately preceding the earlier date mentioned in paragraph 25 in relation to the description of processes within which the process falls; or

(ii)   which is to be carried on at a works, plant or factory or by means of mobile plant which was under construction or in course of manufacture or in the course of commission at that earlier date, or the construction or supply of which was the subject of a contract entered into before that date.

[852]

NOTES
Para 26: words in square brackets substituted by the Environmental Protection (Amendment of Regulations) Regulations 1991, SI 1991/836, reg 2(2).

SCHEDULE 4
RELEASE INTO THE AIR: PRESCRIBED SUBSTANCES

Regulation 6(1)

Oxides of sulphur and other sulphur compounds

Oxides of nitrogen and other nitrogen compounds

Oxides of carbon

Organic compounds and partial oxidation products

Metals, metalloids and their compounds

Asbestos (suspended particulate matter and fibres), glass fibres and mineral fibres

Halogens and their compounds

Phosphorus and its compounds

Particulate matter.

[853]

SCHEDULE 5
[RELEASE INTO WATER: PRESCRIBED SUBSTANCES

Regulations 4(1), 6(2)

[(1) Substance	(2) Amount in excess of background quantity released in any 12 month period
	(Grammes)
Mercury and its compounds	200 (expressed as metal)
Cadmium and its compounds	1000 (expressed as metal)
All isomers of hexachlorocyclohexane	20
All isomers of DDT	5
Pentachlorophenol and its compounds	350 [(expressed as PCP)]
Hexachlorobenzene	5
Hexachlorobutadiene	20
Aldrin	2
Dieldrin	2
Endrin	1
Polychlorinated Biphenyls	1
Dichlorvos	0.2
1,2-Dichloroethane	2000
All isomers of trichlorobenzene	75

[(1) Substance	(2) Amount in excess of background quantity released in any 12 month period
	(Grammes)
Atrazine	350*
Simazine	350*
Tributyltin compounds	4 [(expressed as TBT)]
Triphenyltin compounds	4 [(expressed as TPT)]
Trifluralin	20
Fenitrothion	2
Azinphos-methyl	2
Malathion	2
Endosulfan	0.5

*Where both Atrazine and Simazine are released, the figure in aggregate is 350 grammes.)]

[854]

NOTES

Commencement: 1 December 1994.

Schedule substituted by the Environmental Protection (Prescribed Processes and Substances Etc) (Amendment) Regulations 1994, SI 1994/1271, reg 4(5), Sch 5.

Words in square brackets inserted by the Environmental Protection (Prescribed Processes and Substances) (Amendment) Regulations 1995, SI 1995/3247, reg 2, Sch 1, para 10.

SCHEDULE 6

RELEASE INTO LAND: PRESCRIBED SUBSTANCES

Regulation 6(3)

Organic solvents

Azides

Halogens and their covalent compounds

Metal carbonyls

Organo-metallic compounds

Oxidising agents

Polychlorinated dibenzofuran and any congener thereof

Polychlorinated dibenzo-p-dioxin and any congener thereof

Polyhalogenated biphenyls, terphenyls and naphthalenes

Phosphorus

Pesticides, that is to say, any chemical substance or preparation prepared or used for destroying any pest, including those used for protecting plants or wood or other plant products from harmful organisms; regulating the growth of plants; giving protection against harmful creatures; rendering such creatures harmless; controlling organisms with harmful or unwanted effects on water systems, buildings or other structures, or on manufactured products; or protecting animals against ectoparasites.

Alkali metals and their oxides and alkaline earth metals and their oxides.

[855]

ENVIRONMENTAL PROTECTION (APPLICATIONS, APPEALS AND REGISTERS) REGULATIONS 1991

(SI 1991/507)

NOTES
Made: 6 March 1991.
Commencement: 1 April 1991 (England and Wales); 1 April 1992 (Scotland).
Authority: Environmental Protection Act 1990, ss 10(8), 11(1), (3)–(7), 15(10), 20(1)–(3), (10), 22(6), Sch 1, paras 1–3, 6, 7 (s 20(3) is repealed and s 22(6) is substituted by the Environment Act 1995, s 120(1), (3), Sch 22, paras 57(3), 58(3), Sch 24).

1 Citation, commencement and interpretation

(1) These Regulations may be cited as the Environmental Protection (Applications, Appeals and Registers) Regulations 1991 and shall come into force in England and Wales on 1st April 1991 and in Scotland on 1st April 1992.

(2) In these Regulations, "the 1990 Act" means the Environmental Protection Act 1990.

[856]

2 Applications for an authorisation

(1) An application to an enforcing authority for an authorisation under section 6 of the 1990 Act shall be in writing and, subject to paragraphs (2) and (3) below, shall contain the following information—
  (a) the name of the applicant, his telephone number and address and, if different, any address to which correspondence relating to the application should be sent and, if the applicant is a body corporate, the address of its registered or principal office [and, if that body corporate is a subsidiary of a holding company (within the meaning of section 736 of the Companies Act 1985), the name of the ultimate holding company and the address of its registered or principal office];
  (b) in a case where the prescribed process will not be carried on by means of mobile plant—
    (i) the name of any local authority in whose area the prescribed process will be carried on;
    (ii) the address of the premises where the prescribed process will be carried on;

(iii) a map or plan showing the location of those premises; and
(iv) if only part of those premises will be used for carrying on the process, a plan or other means of identifying that part;

(c) in a case where the prescribed process will be carried on by means of mobile plant—
    (i) the name of the local authority in whose area the applicant has his principal place of business; and
    (ii) the address of that place of business;

(d) a description of the prescribed process;

(e) a list of prescribed substances (and any other substances which might cause harm if released into any environmental medium) which will be used in connection with, or which will result from, the carrying on of that process;

(f) a description of the techniques to be used for preventing the release into any environmental medicum of such substances, for reducing the release of such substances to a minimum and for rendering harmless any such substances which are released;

(g) details of any proposed release of such substances into any environmental medium and an assessment of the environmental consequences;

(h) proposals for monitoring any release of such substances, the environmental consequences of any such release and the use of any techniques described in accordance with sub-paragraph (f) above;

(i) the matters on which the applicant relies to establish that the objectives mentioned in section 7(2) of the 1990 Act (including the objective referred to in section 7(7) will be achieved and that he will be able to comply with the general condition implied by section 7(4);

(j) any additional information which he wishes the enforcing authority to take into account in considering his application.

(2) Paragraph (1) above shall apply in relation to an application to a local enforcing authority for an authorisation in respect of a prescribed process designated for local control (other than that mentioned in paragraph (3) below) as if the words in brackets in sub-paragraph (i) were omitted and references to the release of substances into any environmental medium were references to the release of substances into the air.

(3) Paragraph (1) above shall apply in relation to an application to a local enforcing authority for an authorisation to carry on any prescribed process involving only the burning of waste oil in an appliance with a net rated thermal input of less than 0.4 megawatts as if the following sub-paragraphs were substituted for sub-paragraphs (d) to (i)—

    "(d) the name and number of the appliance (if any) and the name of its manufacturer;

    (e) the net rated thermal input of the appliance and whether or not it is constructed or adapted so as to comply with the specification for fixed, flued fan-assisted heaters in Part 2 of the specification for oil-burning air heaters published by the British Standards Institution and numbered BS 4256 1972;

    (f) details of the type of fuel to be used and its source;

    (g) details of the height and location of any chimney through which waste gases produced by the appliance would be carried away;

    (h) details of the efflux velocity of the waste gases leaving such a chimney produced by the appliance in normal operation;

    (i) details of the location of the fuel storage tanks of the appliance;".

(4) In this regulation—

"net rated thermal point" is the rate at which fuel can be burned at the maximum continuous rating of the appliance multiplied by the net calorific value of the fuel and expressed as megawatts thermal;

"waste oil" means any mineral based lubricating or industrial oil which—
  (a) has become unfit for the use for which it was intended and, in particular, used combustion engine oil, gearbox oil, mineral lubricating oil, oil for turbines and hydraulic oil; and
  (b) is generated only as a result of activities carried out by the applicant on the premises where the process is to be carried on.

[857]

NOTES

Para (1): words in square brackets in sub-para (a) inserted by the Environmental Protection (Applications, Appeals and Registers) (Amendment) Regulations 1996, SI 1996/667, reg 2, Schedule, para 1.

3 Variation of conditions of an authorisation

(1) Any notice given to an enforcing authority under section 11(1)(a) of the 1990 Act of a proposed relevant change in a prescribed process shall be in writing.

(2) An application to an enforcing authority under any provision of section 11 of the 1990 Act for the variation of the conditions of an authorisation shall be in writing.

(3) A person making—
  (a) a request to an enforcing authority under section 11(1)(b) of the 1990 Act for a determination of the matters mentioned in section 11(2); or
  (b) an application to such an authority under any provision of section 11 for the variation of the conditions of an authorisation,

shall furnish the authority with his name, address and telephone number and shall also furnish the authority—
  (i) in a case where the prescribed process will not be carried on by means of mobile plant, with the address of the premises where the prescribed process will be carried on;
  (ii) in a case where the process will be carried on by means of mobile plant, with the address of his principal place of business;
  (iii) in all cases, with a statement of any changes as respects any information supplied under regulation 2(1)(a) to (c) above;
  [(iv) in a case where the holder of the authorisation is a body corporate which is a subsidiary of a holding company (within the meaning of section 736 of the Companies Act 1985) and the information has not already been supplied under regulation 2(1)(a) above, with the name of the ultimate holding company and the address of its registered or principal office.]

(4) Subject to paragraph (5) below, a person making—
  (a) a request to an enforcing authority under section 11(1)(b) of the 1990 Act for a determination of the matters mentioned in section 11(2); or
  (b) an application to such an authority under section 11(5) for the variation of the conditions of an authorisation,

shall also furnish the authority with—
  (i) a description of any proposed change in the manner in which the prescribed process will be carried on;
  (ii) a statement of any changes as respects the matters dealt with in regulation 2(1)(e) to (i) above which would result if any proposed change in the manner of carrying on the prescribed process were made;
  (iii) any additional information which he wishes the authority to take into account in considering his application; and
  (iv) in the case of an application under section 11(5) of the 1990 Act, an indication of the variations which he wishes the authority to make.

(5) Paragraph (4) above shall apply in relation to a process mentioned in regulation 2(3) above as if sub-paragraph (ii) were omitted.

(6)   A person making an application to an enforcing authority under section 11(3)(b) or (4)(b) of the 1990 Act . . . for the variation of the conditions of an authorisation shall also furnish the authority with—
 (a)   an indication of the variations which he wishes the authority to make;
 (b)   a statement of any changes in any information supplied to the authority under paragraph (3) above; and
 (c)   any additional information which he wishes the authority to take into account in considering his application.

(7)   A person making an application to an enforcing authority for the variation of the conditions of an authorisation under section 11(6) of the 1990 Act shall also furnish the authority with—
 (a)   an indication of the variations which he wishes the authority to make; and
 (b)   any additional information which he wishes the authority to take into account in considering his application.

[858]

NOTES
     Para (3): sub-para (iv) inserted by the Environmental Protection (Applications, Appeals and Registers) (Amendment) Regulations 1996, SI 1996/667, reg 2, Schedule, para 2.
     Para (6): words omitted revoked by the Environmental Protection (Amendment of Regulations) Regulations 1991, SI 1991/836, reg 3.

4 Consultation

(1)   Subject to regulations 6 and 7(2) below, [and except in the case of a prescribed process to which regulation 6A below applies,] the persons to be consulted under paragraph 2, 6 or 7 of Schedule 1 to the 1990 Act are—
 (a)   the Health and Safety Executive, in all cases [except, in the case of a prescribed process designated for local control, where the enforcing authority has, within the period specified in paragraph (2) below, notified the Health and Safety Executive that the application has been made or, as the case may be, that notification has been given pursuant to section 10(5) of the 1990 Act];
 (b)   the Minister of Agriculture, Fisheries and Food, in the case of all prescribed processes designated for central control which will be carried on in England;
 (c)   the Secretary of State for Wales, in the case of all prescribed processes designated for central control which will be carried on in Wales;
 (d)   the Secretary of State for Scotland, in the case of all prescribed processes designated for central control which will be carried on in Scotland;
 (e)   . . .
 (f)   the sewerage undertaker or, in relation to Scotland, the [sewerage authority], in the case of all prescribed processes designated for central control which may involve the release of any substance into a sewer vested in the undertaker or [the authority];
 (g)   the Nature Conservancy Council for England, [Scottish Natural Heritage] or the Countryside Council for Wales—
    (i)   in the case of all prescribed processes designated for central control which may involve a release of any substance;
    (ii) in the case of all prescribed processes designated for local control which may involve a release of any substance into the air,
     which may affect a site of special scientific interest within [the body's] area;
 (h)   the harbour authority, in the case of all prescribed processes designated for central control which may involve a release of any substance into a harbour managed by the harbour authority;
 (i)   . . .

[(j) the local authority in whose area the process will be carried on, in the case of all prescribed processes (other than those which will be carried on by means of mobile plant) designated for central control, or in respect of which a direction under section 4(4) of the 1990 Act is in force, which will be carried on in England and Wales;

(k) the local authority in whose area the process will be carried on, in the case of all prescribed processes (other than those which will be carried on by means of mobile plant) which will be carried on in Scotland;

(l) the local fisheries committee, in the case of all prescribed processes designated for central control which may involve a release of any substance directly into relevant territorial waters or coastal waters within the sea fisheries district of that committee.]

[(1A) The petroleum licensing authority in whose area the process will be carried on (if it is not the enforcing authority) is hereby prescribed as a person to be consulted under paragraph 2(1), 6(2) or 7(2) of Schedule 1 to the 1990 Act in the case of a prescribed process to which regulation 6A below applies, except where the enforcing authority has, within the period specified in paragraph (2) below, notified that authority that the application has been made or, as the case may be, that notification has been given pursuant to section 10(5) of the 1990 Act.]

(2)   Subject to regulation 7(5)(a) below, the period for notification under paragraph 2(1), 6(2) or 7(2) of Schedule 1 to the 1990 Act shall be the period of 14 days beginning with—
(a) in the case of a notification under paragraph 2(1), the day on which the enforcing authority receives the application for an authorisation;
(b) in the case of a notification under paragraph 6(2), the day on which the authority notifies the holder of an authorisation in accordance with section 10(5) of that Act; and
(c) in the case of a notification under paragraph 7(2), the day on which the authority receives the application for a variation of an authorisation.

(3)   In paragraph (1)(h) above and regulation 7(3)(c) below, "harbour authority" has the same meaning as in section 57(1) of the Harbours Act 1964.

[(4)   In paragraph (1)(f) above "sewerage authority" shall be construed in accordance with section 62 of the Local Government etc (Scotland) Act 1994.

(5)   In paragraph (1)(j) above "local authority" means—
(a) in England—
  (i)   the council of a county, so far as it is the council of an area for which there are no district councils;
  (ii) a district council;
  (iii) the council of a London borough;
  (iv) the Council of the Isles of Scilly;
  (v)   the Common Council of the City of London and, as respects the Temples, the Sub-Treasurer of the Inner Temple and the Under-Treasurer of the Middle Temple respectively;
(b) in Wales, the council of a county or county borough.

(6)   In paragraph (1)(k) above "local authority" means a council for an area constituted under section 2 of the Local Government etc (Scotland) Act 1994.

(7)   In paragraph (1)(l) above "relevant territorial waters" and "coastal waters" have the same meaning as in Part III of the Water Resources Act 1991.]

[(8)   In paragraph (1A) above "petroleum licensing authority" means a local authority empowered to grant petroleum spirit licences under the Petroleum (Consolidation) Act 1928.]

NOTES

Para (1): words in first pair of square brackets inserted by the Environmental Protection (Prescribed Processes and Substances Etc) (Amendment) (Petrol Vapour Recovery) Regulations 1996, SI 1996/2678, reg 2(a); words in square brackets in sub-para (a) inserted, sub-paras (j), (k), (l) inserted, words in square brackets in sub-paras (f), (g) substituted, and sub-paras (e), (i) revoked, by the Environmental Protection (Applications, Appeals and Registers) (Amendment) Regulations 1996, SI 1996/667, reg 2, Schedule, para 3(1)(a)–(f), (2).

Paras (1A), (8): inserted by SI 1996/2678, reg 2(b), (c).

Paras (4)–(7): added by SI 1996/667, reg 2, Schedule, para 3(1)(g), (2).

5 Advertisements

(1) Subject to paragraph (4) and [regulations 6 and 6A] below, an advertisement—
  (a) by an applicant under paragraph 1(2) of Schedule 1 to the 1990 Act; or
  (b) by the holder of an authorisation under paragraph 6(2) or 7(2) of that Schedule,

shall be published in one or more newspapers circulating in the locality in which the prescribed process will be carried on [and also, in the case of a prescribed process designated for central control—
  (i) if the process will be carried on in England and Wales otherwise than by means of mobile plant, or will be carried on by means of mobile plant by a person whose principal place of business in Great Britain is in England and Wales, in the London Gazette;
  (ii) if the process will be carried on in Scotland otherwise than by means of mobile plant, or will be carried on by means of mobile plant by a person whose principal place of business in Great Britain is in Scotland, in the Edinburgh Gazette.]

(2) Subject to regulation 7(5)(b) below, any such advertisement as is mentioned in paragraph (1) above shall be published within a period of 28 days beginning 14 days after—
  (a) in the case of an advertisement under paragraph 1(2) of Schedule 1 to the 1990 Act, the day on which the application for an authorisation is made;
  (b) in the case of an advertisement under paragraph 6(2) of that Schedule, the day on which the holder of the authorisation is notified in accordance with section 10(5) of that Act;
  (c) in the case of an advertisement under paragraph 7(2) of that Schedule, the day on which the application for a variation is made.

(3) Subject to regulation 7(4) below, any such advertisement as is mentioned in paragraph (1) above shall—
  (a) state the name of the applicant or, as the case may be, of the holder of the authorisation;
  (b) [except in the case of a prescribed process which will be carried on by means of mobile plant] give the address of the premises on which the prescribed process will be carried on;
  (c) describe briefly the prescribed process;
  (d) state where any register which contains particulars of the application or of the action to be taken may be inspected and that it may be inspected free of charge; and
  (e) explain that any person may make representations in writing to the enforcing authority within the period of 28 days beginning with the date of the advertisement and give the authority's address;
  [(f) explain that any such representations made by any person will be entered in a public register unless that person requests in writing that they should not be so placed, and that where such a request is made there will be included in the register a statement indicating only that representations have been made which have been the subject of such a request.]

(4) [The requirement in paragraph (1) of this regulation to publish an advertisement in one or more newspapers circulating in the locality in which the prescribed process will be carried on does not apply] in relation to any prescribed process which will be carried on by means of mobile plant.

[860]

NOTES

Para (1): words in first pair of square brackets substituted by the Environmental Protection (Prescribed Processes and Substances Etc) (Amendment) (Petrol Vapour Recovery) Regulations 1996, SI 1996/2678, reg 2(d); words in final pair of square brackets inserted by the Environmental Protection (Applications, Appeals and Registers) (Amendment) Regulations 1996, SI 1996/667, reg 2, Schedule, para 4(1)(a), (2).

Para (3): words in square brackets in sub-para (b) inserted, and sub-para (f) inserted, by SI 1996/667, reg 2, Schedule, para 4(1)(b), (c), (2).

Para (4): words in square brackets substituted by SI 1996/667, reg 2, Schedule, para 4(1)(d), (2).

6 Exemption for waste oil burners

(1) The requirements of paragraph 1(2), 2, 6 or 7 of Schedule 1 to the 1990 Act shall not apply in relation to any process involving only the burning of waste oil in an appliance with a net rated thermal input of less than 0.4 megawatts.

(2) In this regulation—
"net rated thermal input" has the same meaning as in regulation 2(4) above; and
"waste oil" means any mineral based lubricating or industrial oil which has become unfit for the use for which it was intended and, in particular, used combustion engine oil, gearbox oil, mineral lubricating oil, oil for turbines and hydraulic oil.

[861]

[6A Exemption for service stations

(1) This regulation applies to a prescribed process falling within paragraph (b) of Part B of Section 1.4 of Schedule 1 to the Environmental Protection (Prescribed Processes and Substances) Regulations 1991.

(2) The following requirements shall not apply in relation to a process to which this regulation applies—
(a) the requirement in paragraph 1(2) of Schedule 1 to the 1990 Act to advertise an application for an authorisation;
(b) the requirement in paragraph 6(2) of that Schedule to advertise the action to be taken by the holder of an authorisation in consequence of a variation;
(c) the requirement in paragraph 7(2) of that Schedule to advertise an application for a variation of an authorisation.]

[862]

NOTES

Commencement: 1 December 1996.

Inserted by the Environmental Protection (Prescribed Processes and Substances Etc) (Amendment) (Petrol Vapour Recovery) Regulations 1996, SI 1996/2678, reg 2(e).

7 National Security and confidential information

(1) This regulation applies where in relation to an application or an authorisation—
(a) a direction given by the Secretary of State under section 21(2) of the 1990 Act applies;
(b) notice is given to the Secretary of State under section 21(4) of that Act;
(c) an application is made to an enforcing authority under section 22(2) of that Act; or
(d) an objection is made to such an authority under section 22(4) of that Act.

(2)   Subject to paragraph (3) below, the requirements of paragraph 2(1), 6(2) or 7(2) of Schedule 1 to the 1990 Act shall not apply in so far as they would require a person mentioned in regulation 4(1)(f), (g), or (h) above to be consulted on information which is not to be included in the register by virtue of section 21 or 22 of that Act.

(3)   Information which is not to be included in the register by virtue of section 22 of the 1990 Act shall not be excluded by paragraph (2) above if—
  (a) in the case of any person mentioned in regulation 4(1)(f) above, it is information about the release of any substance into a sewer vested in that person;
  (b) in the case of any person mentioned in regulation 4(1)(g) above, it is information about the release of any substance—
    (i) designated for central control;
    (ii) designated for local control which may involve a release of any substance into the air,
    which may affect a site of special scientific interest in that person's area; or
  (c) in the case of any person mentioned in regulation 4(1)(h) above, it is information about the release of any substance into a harbour managed by a harbour authority.

(4)   The requirements of paragraph 1(2), 6(2) or 7(2) of Schedule 1 to the 1990 Act shall not apply in so far as they would require the advertisement of information mentioned in regulation 5(3) above which is not to be included in the register by virtue of section 21 or 22 of that Act.

(5)   Where a matter falls to be determined under section 21 or 22 of the 1990 Act—
  (a) the period for notification under paragraph 2(1), 6(2) or 7(2) of Schedule 1 to that Act shall be the period of 14 days beginning 14 days after the day on which the matters to be determined under section 21 or 22 of that Act are finally disposed of;
  (b) the period within which an advertisement is to be published in the manner specified in regulation 5(1) above shall be the period of 28 days beginning 14 days after the day on which the matters to be determined under section 21 or 22 of the 1990 Act are finally disposed of.

(6)   For the purposes of paragraph (5) above, the matters to be determined under section 21 or 22 of the 1990 Act are finally disposed of—
  (a) on the date on which the Secretary of State determines under section 21 of that Act whether or not information is to be included in the register;
  (b) on the date on which the enforcing authority is treated under section 22(3) of that Act as having made a determination;
  (c) in a case where the enforcing authority determines under section 22(2) or (4) of that Act that the information in question is commercially confidential, on the date of the authority's determination;
  (d) in a case where the enforcing authority determines under section 22(2) or (4) of that Act that the information in question is not commercially confidential, on the date on which the period for bringing an appeal expires without an appeal being brought or, if such an appeal is brought within that period, on the date of the Secretary of State's final determination of the appeal or, as the case may be, the date on which the appellant withdraws his appeal.

[863]

8 Transitional applications

Where an application for an authorisation is transmitted under paragraph 3(1) of Schedule 1 to the 1990 Act to the Secretary of State for determination, a request by the applicant or the enforcing authority concerned that the Secretary of State exercise one of the powers under paragraph 3(3) of that Schedule shall be made to him in writing within the period of 21 days beginning with the day on which the applicant is informed that the application is being transmitted to the Secretary of State.

[864]

9 Notice of appeal

(1)   A person who wishes to appeal to the Secretary of State under section 15 or 22(5) of the 1990 Act shall give to the Secretary of State written notice of the appeal together with the documents specified in paragraph (2) below and shall at the same time send to the enforcing authority a copy of that notice together with the documents specified in paragraph (2)(a) and (f) below.

(2)   The documents mentioned in paragraph (1) above are—
    (a) statement of the grounds of appeal;
    (b) a copy of any relevant application;
    (c) a copy of any relevant authorisation;
    (d) a copy of any relevant correspondence between the appellant and the enforcing authority;
    (e) a copy of any decision or notice which is the subject-matter of the appeal;
    (f) a statement indicating whether the appellant wishes the appeal to be in the form of a hearing or to be disposed of on the basis of written representations.

(3)   If the appellant wishes to withdraw an appeal he shall do so by notifying the Secretary of State in writing and shall send a copy of that notification to the enforcing authority.

[865]

10 Time limit for bringing appeal

(1)   Subject to paragraph (2) below, notice of appeal in accordance with regulation 9(1) above is to be given—
    (a) in the case of an appeal by a person who has been refused the grant of an authorisation under section 6 of the 1990 Act, before the expiry of the period of six months beginning with—
       (i) the date of the decision which is the subject-matter of the appeal; or
      (ii) in the case of an appeal against a deemed refusal of an application for an authorisation, the date on which the application is deemed under the provisions of paragraph 5(2) of Schedule 1 to the 1990 Act to have been refused;
    (b) in the case of an appeal by a person who is aggrieved by the conditions attached to his authorisation or who has been refused a variation of an authorisation on an application under section 11 of the 1990 Act, before the expiry of the period of six months beginning with the date of the decision which is the subject-matter of the appeal;
    (c) in the case of an appeal in respect of a decision of an enforcing authority to revoke an authorisation, before the date on which the revocation of the authorisation takes effect;
    (d) in the case of an appeal by a person on whom a variation notice, an enforcement notice or a prohibition notice is served, before the expiry of the period of two months beginning with the date of the notice which is the subject-matter of the appeal;
    (e) in the case of an appeal in respect of a decision of an enforcing authority that information is not commercially confidential, before the expiry of the period of 21 days beginning with the date of the notice of determination.

(2)   The Secretary of State may in a particular case allow notice of appeal to be given after the expiry of the periods mentioned in paragraph (1)(a), (b) or (d) above.

[866]

11 Action upon receipt of notice of appeal

(1)   Subject to paragraph (4) below, the enforcing authority shall, within 14 days of receipt of the copy of the notice of appeal in accordance with regulation 9(1) above—

(a) in the case of an appeal by a person in respect of a decision of an enforcing authority to revoke an authorisation or on whom a variation notice, an enforcement notice or a prohibition notice is served, give written notice of it to any person who appears to the enforcing authority likely to have a particular interest in the subject-matter of the appeal; and

(b) in any other case given written notice of it—

(i) to any person who made representations to the authority with respect to the grant or variation of the authorisation; and

(ii) to any person who was required to be consulted on the application under paragraph [2 or 7] of Schedule 1 to the 1990 Act pursuant to regulation 4(1) above.

(2)   A notice under paragraph (1) above shall—

(a) state that an appeal has been lodged;

(b) give the name of the appellant and—

(i) where the prescribed process will not be carried on by means of mobile plant, the address of the premises where the prescribed process will be carried on;

(ii) where the prescribed process will be carried on by means of mobile plant, the address of this principal place of business;

(c) describe the application or authorisation to which the appeal relates;

(d) . . .

(e) state that representations with respect to the appeal may be made to the Secretary of State in writing by any recipient of the notice within a period of 21 days beginning with the date of the notice[, and that copies of any representations so made will be furnished to the appellant and to the enforcing authority]; and

[(ea) explain that any such representations made by any person will be entered in a public register unless that person requests in writing that they should not be so placed, and that where such a request is made there will be included in the register a statement indicating only that representations have been made which have been the subject of such a request;]

(f) state that if a hearing is to be held wholly or partly in public, a person mentioned in paragraph (1)(a) or b(i) above who makes representations with respect to the appeal and any person mentioned in paragraph (1)(b)(ii) above will be notified of the date of the hearing.

(3)   The enforcing authority shall, within 14 days of sending a notice under paragraph (1) above, . . . notify the Secretary of State of the persons to whom and the date on which the notice was sent.

[(3A) In the event of an appeal being withdrawn, the enforcing authority shall give written notice of the withdrawal to every person to whom notice was given under paragraph (1) above.]

(4)   The preceding provisions of this regulation do not apply in the case of an appeal brought under section 22(5) of the 1990 Act.

[867]

NOTES

Para (1): words in square brackets in sub-para (b) substituted by the Environmental Protection (Applications, Appeals and Registers) (Amendment) Regulations 1996, SI 1996/667, reg 2, Schedule, para 5(1)(a), (2).

Para (2): sub-para (d) revoked, words in square brackets in sub-para (e) inserted, and sub-para (ea) inserted, by SI 1996/667, reg 2, Schedule, para 5(1)(b)–(d), (2).

Para (3): words omitted revoked by SI 1996/667, reg 2, Schedule, para 5(1)(e), (2).

Para (3A): inserted by SI 1996/667, reg 2, Schedule, para 5(1)(f), (2).

12 Written representations

(1) Where the appellant informs the Secretary of State that he wishes the appeal to be disposed of on the basis of written representations, the enforcing authority shall submit any written representations to the Secretary of State not later than 28 days after receiving a copy of the documents mentioned in regulation 9(2)(a) and (f) above.

(2) The appellant shall make any further representations by way of reply to any representations from the enforcing authority not later than 17 days after the date of submission of those representations by the enforcing authority.

(3) Any representations made by the appellant or the enforcing authority shall be dated and submitted to the Secretary of State on the date they bear.

(4) When the enforcing authority or the appellant submits any representations to the Secretary of State they shall at the same time send a copy of them to the other party.

(5) The Secretary of State shall send to the appellant and the enforcing authority a copy of any representations made to him by the persons mentioned in regulation 11(1) above and shall allow the appellant and the enforcing authority a period of not less than 14 days in which to make representations thereon.

(6) The Secretary of State may in a particular case—
    (a) set later time limits than those mentioned in this regulation;
    (b) require exchanges of representations between the parties in addition to those mentioned in paragraphs (1) and (2) above.

[868]

13 Hearings

(1) The Secretary of State shall give the appellant and the enforcing authority at least 28 days written notice (or such shorter period of notice as they may agree) of the date, time and place fixed for the holding of any hearing in respect of an appeal under section 15 or 22(5) of the 1990 Act.

(2) Subject to paragraph (4) and (5) below, in the case of a hearing which is to be held wholly or partly in public, the Secretary of State shall, at least 21 days before the date fixed for the holding of the hearing, publish a copy of the notice mentioned in paragraph (1) above—
    (a) in a case where the prescribed process will not be carried on by means of mobile plant, in a newspaper circulating in the locality in which the prescribed process which is the subject of the appeal will be carried on; and
    (b) in a case where the appeal is in respect of a decision of an enforcement authority to revoke an authorisation or against a variation notice, an enforcement notice or a prohibition notice in respect of a prescribed process was carried on by means of mobile plant, in a newspaper circulating in the locality in which the prescribed process was carried on at the time when the notice of revocation, variation notice, enforcement notice or prohibition notice was served,

and shall serve a copy of the notice mentioned in paragraph (1) above on every person mentioned in regulation 11(1)(a) and (b)(i) above who has made representations in writing to the Secretary of State and on any person who was required under regulation 11(1)(b)(ii) above to be notified of the appeal.

(3) The Secretary of State may vary the date fixed for the holding of any hearing and paragraphs (1) and (2) above shall apply to the variation of a date as they applied to the date originally fixed.

(4) The Secretary of State may also vary the time or place for the holding of a hearing but shall give such notice of any such variation as appears to him to be reasonable.

(5)   Paragraph (2) above shall not apply in the case of a hearing in respect of an appeal brought under section 22(5) of the 1990 Act.

(6)   The persons entitled to be heard at a hearing are—
   (a) the appellant;
   (b) the enforcing authority; and
   (c) any person required under regulation 11(1)(b)(ii) above to be notified of the appeal.

(7)   Nothing in paragraph (6) above shall prevent the person appointed to conduct the hearing of the appeal from permitting any other person to be heard at the hearing and such permission shall not be unreasonably withheld.

(8)   After the conclusion of a hearing, the person appointed to conduct the hearing shall[, unless he has been appointed under section 114(1) of the Environment Act 1995 to determine the appeal,] make a report in writing to the Secretary of State which shall include his conclusions and his recommendations or his reasons for not making any recommendations.

[869]

NOTES
   Para (8): words in square brackets inserted by the Environmental Protection (Applications, Appeals and Registers) (Amendment) Regulations 1996, SI 1996/667, reg 2, Schedule, para 6.

---

14 Notification of determination

(1)   The Secretary of State shall notify the appellant in writing of his determination of the appeal and shall provide him with a copy of any report mentioned in regulation 13(8) above.

(2)   The Secretary of State shall at the same time send—
   (a) a copy of the documents mentioned in paragraph (1) above to the enforcing authority and to any persons required under regulation 11(1)(b)(ii) above to be notified of the appeal; and
   (b) a copy of his determination of the appeal to a person mentioned in regulation 11(1)(a) and (b)(i) above who made representations to the Secretary of State and, if a hearing was held, to any other person who made representations in relation to the appeal at the hearing.

[870]

15 Registers

[Subject to sections 21 and 22 of the 1990 Act, a register maintained by an enforcing authority under section 20 of that Act shall be maintained in accordance with regulation 15A below and shall contain—
   (a) all particulars of any application for an authorisation, or for a variation of the conditions of an authorisation, made to the authority;
   (b) all particulars of any advertisement published pursuant to regulation 5 above;
   (c) all particulars of any notice to the applicant by the authority under paragraph 1(3) of Schedule 1 to that Act and of any information furnished in response to such a notice;
  [(ca) all particulars of any representations made by any person required to be consulted under paragraph 2, 6 or 7 of Schedule 1 to the 1990 Act pursuant to regulation 4(1) above;]
   (d) all particulars of any representations made by any person in response to an advertisement published pursuant to regulation 5 above which contains the explanation required by paragraph (3)(f) of that regulation, or a notice given pursuant to regulation 11(1) above which contains the explanation required

by paragraph (2)(ea) of that regulation, other than representations which the person who made them requested should not be placed in the register;

(e) in a case where any such representations are omitted from the register at the request of the person who made them, a statement by the authority that such representations have been made which have been the subject of such a request (but such statement shall not identify the person who made the representations in question);

(f) all particulars of any authorisation granted by the authority;

(g) all particulars of any written notice of the transfer of an authorisation given to the authority pursuant to section 9(2) of that Act;

(h) all particulars of any notification given to the holder of an authorisation by the authority under section 10(5) of that Act;

(i) all particulars of any revocation of an authorisation effected by the authority;

(j) all particulars of any variation notice, enforcement notice or prohibition notice issued by the authority;

(k) all particulars of any notice issued by the authority withdrawing an enforcement notice or a prohibition notice;

(l) all particulars of any notice of appeal under section 15 of that Act against a decision by the authority, the documents relating to the appeal mentioned in regulation 9(2)(a), (d) and (e) above, any written notification of the Secretary of State's determination of such an appeal and any report accompanying any such written notification;

(m) details of any conviction of any person for any offence under section 23(1) of that Act which relates to the carrying on of a prescribed process under an authorisation granted by the authority, or without such an authorisation in circumstances where one is required by section 6(1) of the 1990 Act, including the name of the offender, the date of conviction, the penalty imposed and the name of the Court;

(n) all particulars of any monitoring information relating to the carrying on of a prescribed process under an authorisation granted by the authority obtained by the authority as a result of its own monitoring or furnished to the authority in writing by virtue of a condition of the authorisation or section 19(2) of that Act;

(o) in a case where any such monitoring information is omitted from the register by virtue of section 22 of that Act, a statement by the authority, based on the monitoring information from time to time obtained by or furnished to them, indicating whether or not there has been compliance with any relevant condition of the authorisation;

(p) all particulars of any other information furnished to the authority on or after 1st April 1996 in compliance with a condition of the authorisation, a variation notice, enforcement notice or prohibition notice, or section 19(2) of that Act;

(q) all particulars of any report published by an enforcing authority relating to an assessment of the environmental consequences of the carrying on of a prescribed process in the locality of premises where the prescribed process is carried on under an authorisation granted by the authority; and

(r) all particulars of any direction (other than a direction under section 21(2) of that Act) given to the authority by the Secretary of State under any provision of Part I of that Act.]

[871]

NOTES

Commencement: 1 April 1996.

Substituted by the Environmental Protection (Applications, Appeals and Registers) (Amendment) Regulations 1996, SI 1996/667, reg 2, Schedule, para 7.

Para (ca): inserted by the Environmental Protection (Applications, Appeals and Registers) (Amendment No 2) Regulations 1996, SI 1996/979, reg 2.

[15A—(1) Where an advertisement is required to be published in accordance with regulation 5 above—

(a) in the case of an advertisement under paragraph 1(2) or 7(2) of Schedule 1 to the 1990 Act, the particulars referred to in paragraph (a) of regulation 15 above shall be entered in the register not later than 14 days after the receipt by the enforcing authority of the application to which the advertisement relates;

(b) in the case of an advertisement under paragraph 6(2) of that Schedule, the particulars referred to in paragraph (h) of regulation 15 above shall be entered in the register not later than 14 days after the giving of the notification under section 10(5) of the 1990 Act.

(2)   Where an application for an authorisation is withdrawn by the applicant at any time before it is determined, all particulars relating to that application which are already in the register shall be removed from that register not less than two months and not more than three months after the date of withdrawal of the application, and no further particulars relating to that application shall be entered in the register.

(3)   Where, by virtue of any regulations made under section 2(1) of the 1990 Act a description of process ceases to be a prescribed process, all particulars relating to processes of that description shall be removed from the register not less than two months and not more than three months after the date on which that description of process ceases to be prescribed.]

[872]

NOTES
  Commencement: 1 April 1996.
  Inserted by the Environmental Protection (Applications, Appeals and Registers) (Amendment) Regulations 1996, SI 1996/667, reg 2, Schedule, para 8.

16   [A register maintained by a local enforcing authority in England and Wales which is not a port health authority shall (in addition to the particulars required by regulation 15 above) contain all particulars of such information contained in any register maintained by the Environment Agency as relates to the carrying on in the area of the local enforcing authority of prescribed processes in relation to which that Agency has functions under Part I of the 1990 Act.]

[873]

NOTES
  Commencement: 1 April 1996.
  Substituted by the Environmental Protection (Applications, Appeals and Registers) (Amendment) Regulations 1996, SI 1996/667, reg 2, Schedule, para 9.

17   [Nothing in regulation 15 or 16 above shall require an enforcing authority to keep in a register maintained by them—

(a) monitoring information relating to a particular process four years after that information was entered in the register; or

(b) information relating to a particular process which has been superseded by later information relating to that process four years after that later information was entered in the register,

but nothing in this regulation shall apply to any aggregated monitoring data relating to overall emissions of any substance or class of substances from prescribed processes generally or from any class of prescribed process.]

[874]

NOTES
  Commencement: 1 April 1996.
  Substituted by the Environmental Protection (Applications, Appeals and Registers) (Amendment) Regulations 1996, SI 1996/667, reg 2, Schedule, para 10.

DISPOSAL OF CONTROLLED WASTE (EXCEPTIONS) REGULATIONS 1991

(SI 1991/508)

NOTES

Made: 6 March 1991.

Commencement: 1 April 1991 (England and Wales); 1 April 1992 (Scotland).

Authority: Control of Pollution Act 1974, ss 3(1), 4(3), 104(1)(a), 105(1) (ss 3, 4 repealed with savings by the Environmental Protection Act 1990, s 162(2), Sch 16, Pt II; for savings see the Environmental Protection Act 1990 (Commencement No 15) Order 1994, SI 1994/1096 at **[966]**).

1 Citation and commencement

(1)   These Regulations may be cited as the Disposal of Controlled Waste (Exceptions) Regulations 1991.

(2)   These Regulations shall come into force in England and Wales on 1 April 1991 and in Scotland on 1 April 1992.

[875]

2 Exceptions from section 3(1) of the Control of Pollution Act 1974

(1)   Subject to paragraph (2), section 3(1) of the Control of Pollution Act 1974 shall not apply as respects any deposit of controlled waste on land or the use of any plant or equipment for the purpose of disposing of, or dealing with, controlled waste so far as that deposit or use—
   (a) is, or forms part of, a process which is for the time being designated pursuant to section 2(4) of the Environmental Protection Act 1990 for central control, the carrying on of which is for the time being authorised under section 6 of that Act; or
   (b) is an activity described in the Schedule hereto constituting, or forming part of, a process for the time being so designated for local control, the carrying on of which is so authorised.

(2)   Paragraph (1) does not exempt the final disposal of controlled waste by deposit in or on land.

[876]

SCHEDULE
ACTIVITIES REFERRED TO IN REGULATION 2(1)

Regulation 2(1)

1. In this Schedule, "Schedule 1" means Schedule 1 to the Environmental Protection (Prescribed Processes and Substances) Regulation 1991.

2. Using untreated straw, poultry litter or wood as a fuel so far as it constitutes a process or part of a process within a description in Part B of Section 1.3 of Schedule 1 and any related activity so far as it constitutes a process or part of a process within such a description.

3. Using tyres as a fuel and any related fuel feeding so far as it constitutes a process or part of a process falling within the said Part B of Section 1.3.

4. The operation of a scrap metal furnace and the loading or unloading of such a furnace so far as those activities form part of a process described in paragraph (b) of Part B of Section 2.2 of Schedule 1.

5. Pulverising bricks, tiles or concrete so far as those activities form a process or part of a process described in paragraph (c) of Part B of Section 3.4 of Schedule 1.

6. Depositing glass as part of a process described in Part B of Section 3.5 of Schedule 1.

7.   Incinerating waste as a process or part of a process described in paragraph (a) of Part B of Section 5.1 of Schedule 1; depositing animal remains at the site of an incinerator for burning as mentioned in that paragraph and any other operation ancillary to the burning of animal remains which forms part of a process so described.

[877]

ENVIRONMENTAL PROTECTION (AUTHORISATION OF PROCESSES) (DETERMINATION OF PERIODS) ORDER 1991

(SI 1991/513)

NOTES
Made: 7 March 1991.
Commencement: 1 April 1991 (England and Wales); 1 April 1992 (Scotland).
Authority: Environmental Protection Act 1990, Sch 1, para 5(3).

1 Citation, commencement and interpretation

(1)   This Order may be cited as the Environmental Protection (Authorisation of Processes) (Determination Periods) Order 1991 and shall come into force in England and Wales on 1st April 1991 and in Scotland on 1st April 1992.

(2)   In this Order "the 1990 Act" means the Environmental Protection Act 1990.

[878]

2 Extension of period for consideration of applications in cases involving information affecting national security or certain confidential information

(1)   Subject to article 3(6) below, in the case of an application to which paragraph (2) below applies, for the period mentioned in paragraph 5(1) of Schedule 1 to the 1990 Act there shall be substituted the period mentioned in paragraph (3) below.

(2)   This paragraph applies to an application for an authorisation to carry on a process in relation to which—
- (a)   a matter falls to be determined by the Secretary of State under section 21(2) or (4) of the 1990 Act;
- (b)   an application is made to an enforcing authority under section 22(2) of that Act; or
- (c)   an objection is made to such an authority under section 22(4) of that Act.

(3)   The period to be substituted in paragraph 5(1) of Schedule 1 to the 1990 Act is the period of four months beginning with the day on which the matters to be determined under section 21 or 22 of that Act are finally disposed of or such longer period as the enforcing authority may agree with the applicant.

(4)   For the purposes of paragraph (3) above and article 3(6) below, the matters to be determined under section 21 or 22 of the 1990 Act are finally disposed of—
- (a)   on the date on which the Secretary of State determines under section 21 whether or not the information in question is to be included in the register;
- (b)   on the date on which the enforcing authority is treated under section 22(3) as having made a determination;
- (c)   in a case where the enforcing authority determines under section 22(2) that the information in question is commercially confidential, on the date of the authority's determination;
- (d)   in a case where the enforcing authority determines under section 22(2) or (4) that the information in question is not commercially confidential, on the date on which the period for bringing an appeal expires without an appeal being brought or, if such an appeal is brought within that period, on the date of the Secretary of State's final determination of the appeal or, as the case may be, the date on which the appellant withdraws his appeal.

[879]

3 Extension of period for consideration of applications by local authorities

(1)   Subject to paragraph (6) below, in the case of an application to which paragraph (2) below applies, for the period mentioned in paragraph 5(1) of Schedule 1 to the 1990 Act there shall be substituted—
(a) in England and Wales, the period of eighteen months;
(b) in Scotland, the period of fifteen months,
beginning with the day on which the enforcing authority received the application or within such longer period as it may agree with the applicant.

(2)   This paragraph applies to an application for an authorisation to carry on a process which—
(a) falls within the description set out in paragraph (c) of Part B of section 1.3 in Schedule 1 to the Environmental Protection (Prescribed Processes and Substances) Regulations 1991 (burning waste oil to produce energy);
(b) involves only the use of one or more appliances having a net rated thermal input, or aggregate net rated thermal input, not exceeding 0.4 megawatts; and
(c) is an existing process for which the prescribed date is, in the case of a process carried on in England or Wales, that referred to in paragraph 11(1)(ii) of Schedule 3 to those Regulations and, in the case of a process carried on in Scotland, that referred to in paragraph 24(1)(ii) of that Schedule.

(3)   Subject to paragraph (6) below, in the case of an application to which paragraph (4) below applies, for the period mentioned in paragraph 5(1) of Schedule 1 to the 1990 Act there shall be substituted, the period of fourteen days beginning with the day on which the enforcing authority received the application or within such longer period as it may agree with the applicant.

(4)   This paragraph applies to an application for an authorisation to carry on any process which—
(a) is not an existing process;
(b) falls within paragraph (2)(a) and (b) above; and
(c) does not involve the burning of waste oil generated otherwise than as a result of activities carried on by the applicant on the premises where the process is to be carried on.

(5)   Subject to paragraph (6) below, in the case of an application for an authorisation to carry on any existing process subject to local control which is described in paragraph (2)(c) above but does not fall within paragraph (2)(a) and (b) above [or paragraph (5A) below], for the period mentioned in paragraph 5(1) of Schedule 1 to the 1990 Act there shall be substituted—
(a) in England and Wales, the period of twelve months;
(b) in Scotland, the period of nine months,
beginning with the day on which the enforcing authority received the application or within such longer period as it may agree with the applicant.

[(5A) Subject to paragraph (6) below, in the case of an application for an authorisation to carry on a process subject to local control in respect of which paragraph 5, 6 or 7 of Schedule 6 to the Environmental Protection (Prescribed Processes and Substances Etc) (Amendment) Regulations 1994 applies but which does not fall within paragraph (2)(a) and (b) above, for the period mentioned in paragraph 5(1) of Schedule 1 to the 1990 Act there shall be substituted the period of nine months beginning with the day on which the enforcing authority received the application or such longer period as it may agree with the applicant.]

(6)   In the case of an application to which [paragraph (2), (4), (5) or (5A)] above applies and to which article 2(2) above also applies, the period mentioned in [paragraph (1), (3), (5) and (5A)] above shall begin with the day on which the matters to be determined under section 21 or 22 of the 1990 Act are finally disposed of.

(7)   In this article, "existing process" has the same meaning as in the Environmental Protection (Prescribed Processes and Substances) Regulations 1991.

[880]

NOTES
Para (5): words in square brackets inserted by the Environmental Protection (Authorisation of Processes) (Determination Periods) (Amendment) Order 1994, SI 1994/2847, art 2(2).
Para (5A): inserted by SI 1994/2847, art 2(3).
Para (6): words in square brackets substituted by SI 1994/2847, art 2(4).

CONTROLLED WASTE (REGISTRATION OF CARRIERS AND SEIZURE OF VEHICLES) REGULATIONS 1991

(SI 1991/1624)

NOTES
Made: 17 July 1991.
Commencement: 14 October 1991.
Authority: Control of Pollution (Amendment) Act 1989, ss 1(3)(a), 2, 3, 4(6), 5(3), (6)(a), 6(1)(c), (5)–(7), 8(2), 9(1).

ARRANGEMENT OF REGULATIONS

1 Citation, commencement and interpretation

(1)   These Regulations may be cited as the Controlled Waste (Registration of Carriers and Seizure of Vehicles) Regulations 1991 and shall come into force on 14th October 1991.

(2)   In these Regulations—
    "the 1989 Act" means the Control of Pollution (Amendment) Act 1989;
    "another relevant person" has the meaning given by section 3(5) of the 1989 Act;
    "date of expiry" means, in relation to a carrier's registration, the date on which
        the period of three years mentioned in regulation 11(2) expires;
    "disposed of", in relation to an appeal, has the meaning given by section 4(8) of
        the 1989 Act;
    "notice" means notice in writing;
    "prescribed offence" means an offence under an enactment listed in Schedule 1;
    "relevant period" has the meaning given by section 4(1) of the 1989 Act.

(3)   For the purposes of these Regulations, an application for registration or for the renewal of a registration as a carrier of controlled waste shall be treated as pending—
    (a) whilst it is being considered by the regulation authority; or
    (b) if it has been refused or the relevant period from the making of the application has expired without the applicant having been registered, whilst either—
        (i) the period for appealing in relation to that application has not expired; or
        (ii) the application is the subject of an appeal which has not been disposed of.

[881]

2 Exemption from registration

(1)   The following persons shall not be required for the purposes of section 1 of the 1989 Act to be registered carriers of controlled waste—
    (a) an authority which is a waste collection authority, waste disposal authority or waste regulation authority for the purposes of Part II of the Environmental Protection Act 1990;
    (b) the producer of the controlled waste in question except where it is building or demolition waste;
    [(c) any wholly owned subsidiary of the British Railways Board which has applied in accordance with these Regulations for registration as a carrier of controlled waste but only—
        (i) if it is registered under paragraph 12 of Schedule 4 to the Waste Management Licensing Regulations 1994; and
        (ii) whilst its application is pending;]
    (d) a ferry operator in relation to the carriage on the ferry of any vehicle carrying controlled waste;
    (e) the operator of a vessel, aircraft, hovercraft, floating container or vehicle in relation to its use, after it has been loaded with waste in circumstances in which a licence under Part II of the Food and Environment Protection Act 1985 is needed or would be needed but for an order under section 7 of that Act, for transporting the waste in order to carry out any operation mentioned in section 5 or 6 of that Act;
    (f) a charity;
    (g) a voluntary organisation within the meaning of section 48(11) of the Local Government Act 1985 or section 83(2D) of the Local Government (Scotland) Act 1973;
    (h) a person who before 1st April 1992 applies in accordance with these Regulations for registration as a carrier of controlled waste but only whilst his application is pending;

[(i) a person who—
    (i) is the holder of a knacker's yard licence or a licence under article 5(2)(c) or 6(2)(d) of the Animal By-Products Order 1992; or
    (ii) has obtained an approval under article 8 of that Order; or
    (iii) is registered under article 9 or 10 of that Order,
in relation to the transport of animal by-products in accordance with Schedule 2 to that Order in connection with the activity to which the licence, approval or registration relates.]

(2)   In this regulation—
["animal by-products" has the same meaning as in article 3(1) of the Animal By-Products Order 1992;]
"building or demolition waste" means waste arising from works of construction or demolition, including waste arising from work preparatory thereto;
["construction" includes improvement, repair or alteration;]
["knacker's yard licence"—
    (a) in relation to England and Wales, has the same meaning as in section 34 of the Slaughterhouses Act 1974;
    (b) in relation to Scotland, means a licence under section 6 of the Slaughter of Animals (Scotland) Act 1980;]
["registered broker of controlled waste" has the same meaning as in regulation 20 of, and Schedule 5 to, the Waste Management Licensing Regulations 1994;]
"vessel" has the same meaning as in section 742 of the Merchant Shipping Act 1894;
["wholly owned subsidiary" has the same meaning as in section 736 of the Companies Act 1985.]

[882]

NOTES
Para (1): sub-para (c) substituted, and sub-para (i) inserted, by the Waste Management Licensing Regulations 1994, SI 1994/1056, reg 23(2), (3).
Para (2): definitions "animal by-products", "knacker's yard licence", "registered broker of controlled waste" and "wholly owned subsidiary" inserted by SI 1994/1056, reg 23(4); definition "construction" inserted by the Controlled Waste Regulations 1992, SI 1992/588, reg 10.

3 Registers

(1)   It shall be the duty of each regulation authority to establish and maintain a register of carriers of controlled waste and—
    (a) to secure that the register is open for inspection . . . by members of the public free of charge at all reasonable hours; and
    (b) to afford to members of the public reasonable facilities for obtaining copies of entries in the register on payment of reasonable charges.

(2)   A register under this regulation may be kept in any form but shall be indexed and arranged so that members of the public can readily trace information contained in it.

[883]

NOTES
Para (1): words omitted revoked by the Environment Act 1995 (Consequential Amendments) Regulations 1996, SI 1996/593, reg 3, Sch 2, para 9(2).

4 Applications for registration

(1)   An application for registration or for the renewal of a registration as a carrier of controlled waste shall be made to the regulation authority for the area in which the applicant has or proposes to have his principal place of business in Great Britain;

but if the applicant does not have or propose to have a place of business in Great Britain the applicant may apply to any regulation authority.

(2)   Subject to paragraphs (3) to (5), a person shall not make an application for registration or for the renewal of a registration whilst—
   (a) a previous application of his is pending; or
   (b) he is registered.

(3)   Paragraph (2) shall not prevent a person from applying for the renewal of a registration where his application is made within the period of six months mentioned in regulation 11(4).

(4)   An application for registration or for the renewal of a registration in respect of a business which is or is to be carried on by a partnership shall be made by all of the partners or prospective partners.

(5)   A prospective partner in a business carried on by a partnership whose members are already registered may make an application for registration as a partner in that business to the regulation authority with whom the business is registered.

(6)   An application for registration shall be made on a form corresponding to the form in Part I of Schedule 2, or on a form substantially to the like effect, and shall contain the information required by that form.

(7)   An application for the renewal of a registration shall be made on a form corresponding to the form in Part II of Schedule 2, or on a form substantially to the like effect, and shall contain the information required by that form.

(8)   A regulation authority shall provide a copy of the appropriate application form free of charge to any person requesting one.

(9)   [Subject to paragraph 3(11)(a) and (b) of Schedule 5 of the Waste Management Licensing Regulations 1994,] a regulation authority shall charge an applicant in respect of their consideration of his application—
   (a) in the case of an application for registration, £95;
   (b) in the case of an application for the renewal of a registration, £65;
   [(c) in the case of an application by a registered broker of controlled waste for registration as a carrier of controlled waste, £25,]
and the applicant shall pay the charge when he makes his application.

(10) A regulation authority shall, on receipt of an application for registration or for the renewal of a registration, ensure that the register contains a copy of the application.

(11) A regulation authority may remove from their register a copy of an application included under paragraph (10) at any time more than six years after the application was made.

[884]

NOTES
   Para (9): words in first pair of square brackets, and sub-para (c), inserted by the Waste Management Licensing Regulations 1994, SI 1994/1056, reg 23(5), (6).

---

5 Refusal of applications

(1)   Subject to section 3(6) of the 1989 Act, a regulation authority may refuse an application for registration or for the renewal of a registration if, and only if—
   (a) there has, in relation to that application, been a contravention of any of the requirements of regulation 4; or
   (b) the applicant or another relevant person has been convicted of a prescribed offence and, in the opinion of the authority, it is undesirable for the applicant to be authorised to transport controlled waste.

(2)   Where a regulation authority decide to refuse an application for registration or for the renewal of a registration, the authority shall give notice to the applicant informing him that his application is refused and of the reasons for their decision.

(3)   If an appeal is made under section 4(1) of the 1989 Act in accordance with these Regulations, the regulation authority shall, as soon as reasonably practicable, make appropriate entries in their register indicating when the appeal was made and the result of the appeal.

(4)   If no such appeal is made, the regulation authority shall, as soon as reasonably practicable make an appropriate entry in their register indicating that the application has not been accepted and that no appeal has been made.

(5)   A regulation authority may remove an entry made under paragraph (3) or (4) at any time more than six years after the application in question was made.

[885]

6 Registration as a carrier

(1)   On accepting a person's application for registration or on being directed under section 4(3) of the 1989 Act to register a person following an appeal in respect of such an application, the regulation authority shall make an entry in their register—

(a) showing that person as a registered carrier of controlled waste and allocating him a registration number (which may include any letter);

(b) specifying the date on which the registration takes effect and its date of expiry;

(c) stating any business name of his and the address of his principal place of business (together with any telephone, telex or fax number of his) and, in the case of an individual, his date of birth;

(d) in the case of a body corporate, listing the names of each director, manager, secretary or other similar officer of that body and their respective dates of birth;

(e) in the case of a company registered under the Companies Acts, specifying its registered number and, in the case of a company incorporated outside Great Britain, the country in which it was incorporated;

(f) in a case where the person who is registered or another relevant person has been convicted of a prescribed offence, giving the person's name, details of the offence, the date of conviction, the penalty imposed, the name of the Court and, in the case of an individual, his date of birth; and

(g) in a case where the person who is registered or any company in the same group of companies as that person is the holder of a waste management licence or a disposal licence, stating the name of the holder of the licence and the name of the authority which granted it.

(2)   In the case of a business which is or is to be carried on by a partnership, all the partners shall be registered under one entry and only one registration number shall be allocated to the partnership.

(3)   On making an entry in their register under paragraph (1) the regulation authority shall—

(a) issue to the registered person or partnership a certificate of registration free of charge which shall be in the form set out in Schedule 3, or in a form substantially to the like effect, and shall contain the information required by that form; and

(b) provide him or them free of charge with a copy of the entry in the register.

(4)   In this regulation—

"Companies Acts" has the same meaning as in section 744 of the Companies Act 1985;

"business name" means a name under which a person carries on business and by virtue of which the Business Names Act 1985 applies;

"disposal licence" has the same meaning as in section 30(1) of the Control of Pollution Act 1974;

"group" has the same meaning as in section 53(1) of the Companies Act 1989; and

"waste management licence" has the same meaning as in section 35 of the Environmental Protection Act 1990.

[886]

7 Amendment of entries

(1)   On accepting a person's application for the renewal of a registration or on being directed under section 4(3) of the 1989 Act to register a person following an appeal in respect of such an application, the regulation authority shall amend the relevant entry in the register—

(a) to show the date on which the renewal takes effect and the revised date of expiry of the registration;

(b) to record any other change disclosed as a result of the application; and

(c) to note in the register the date on which the amendments are made.

(2)   The regulation authority shall at the same time as amending the register—

(a) issue to the registered person or partnership an amended certificate of registration free of charge which shall be in the form set out in Schedule 3, or in a form substantially to the like effect, and shall contain the information required by that form;

(b) provide him or them free of charge with a copy of the amended entry in the register.

[887]

8 Change of circumstances and registration of additional partners

(1)   A person who is registered shall notify the regulation authority which maintain the relevant register of any change of circumstances affecting information in the entry relating to him.

(2)   On—

(a) being notified of any change of circumstances in accordance with paragraph (1);

(b) accepting a prospective partner's application for registration in relation to a business carried on by a partnership whose members are already registered; or

(c) being directed under section 4(3) of the 1989 Act to register a prospective partner,

the regulation authority shall—

(i) amend the relevant entry to reflect the change of circumstances or the registration of the prospective partner;

(ii) note in the register the date on which the amendment is made;

(iii) if the amendment of the register affects information contained in the certificate of registration, issue to the registered person or partnership free of charge an amended certificate of registration which shall be in the form set out in Schedule 3, or in a form substantially to the like effect, and shall contain the information required by that form;

(iv) provide him or them free of charge with a copy of the amended entry in the register.

[888]

9 Copies of certificates of registration

(1)   The regulation authority shall, on payment of their reasonable charges, provide a person who is registered with such copies of his certificate of registration as he may request.

(2)   The regulation authority shall ensure that the copies of the certificate are numbered and marked so as to show that they are copies and that they have been provided by the authority under this regulation.

[889]

10 Revocation of registration

(1)   Subject to section 3(6) of the 1989 Act, a regulation authority may revoke a person's registration as a carrier of controlled waste if, and only if—
  (a) that person or another relevant person has been convicted of a prescribed offence; and
  (b) in the opinion of the authority, it is undesirable for the registered carrier to continue to be authorised to transport controlled waste.

(2)   Where a regulation authority decide to revoke a person's registration as a carrier of controlled waste, they shall give notice to the carrier informing him of the revocation and of the reasons for their decision.

[890]

11 Duration of registration

(1)   This regulation is subject to—
  (a) section 3(2) of the 1989 Act (which ensures that a registration ceases to have effect if the registered carrier gives written notice requiring the removal of his name from the register); and
  (b) section 4(7) and (8) of the 1989 Act (which extend the period during which the registration has effect where an appeal under that section is made).

(2)   Subject to paragraphs (4) to (6), a person's registration as a carrier of controlled waste shall cease to have effect on the expiry of the period of three years beginning with the date of the registration or, if it has been renewed, beginning with the date on which it was renewed or, as the case may be, last renewed.

(3)   The regulation authority shall, no later than six months before the expiry of the period of three years mentioned in paragraph (2), serve on a registered person—
  (a) a notice informing him of the date on which that period expires and of the effect of paragraph (4); and
  (b) an application form for the renewal of his registration and a copy of his current entry in the register.

(4)   Where an application for the renewal of a registration is made within the last six months of the period of three years mentioned in paragraph (2), the registration shall, notwithstanding the expiry of that period, continue in force—
  (a) until the application is withdrawn or accepted; or
  (b) if the regulation authority refuse the application or the relevant period from the making of the application has expired without the applicant having been registered, until—
    (i)   the expiry of the period for appealing; or
    (ii) where the applicant indicates within that period that he does not intend to make or continue with an appeal, the date on which such an indication is given.

(5)   Where a regulation authority revoke a person's registration, the registration shall, notwithstanding the revocation, continue in force until—

    (a) the expiry of the period for appealing against the revocation; or

    (b) where that person indicates within that period that he does not intend to make or continue with an appeal, the date on which such an indication is given.

(6)   A registration in respect of a business which is carried on by a partnership shall cease to have effect if any of the partners ceases to be registered or if any person who is not registered becomes a partner.

(7)   The duration of a registration in respect of a business which is carried on by a partnership shall not be affected if a person ceases to be a partner or if a prospective partner is registered under regulation 8(2) in relation to the partnership.

(8)   Where a regulation authority accept an application for the renewal of a registration within the period of three years mentioned in paragraph (2), the renewal shall for the purposes of these Regulations take effect at the expiry of that period.

[891]

12 Alteration of register to reflect cessation of registration

(1)   Where by virtue of regulation 11 or section 3(2) or 4(7) and (8) of the 1989 Act a registration ceases to have effect, the regulation authority shall record this fact in the appropriate entry in their register and the date on which it occurred.

(2)   The regulation authority may remove the appropriate entry from their register at any time more than six years after the registration ceases to have effect.

[892]

13 Duty to return certificates etc

Where—

    (a) a person's registration as a carrier of controlled waste ceases to have effect by virtue of regulation 11 or section 3(2) or 4(7) and (8) of the 1989 Act; or

    (b) a person is issued with an amended certificate under regulation 7(2) or 8(2),

he shall immediately return to the regulation authority his certificate of registration, or, as the case may be, his previous certificate of registration, together with any copies of it issued by that authority.

[893]

14 Production of authority

(1)   Where a person is required by virtue of section 5 of the 1989 Act to produce an authority for transporting controlled waste and does not do so by producing it forthwith to the person requiring its production, he shall produce it at or send it to [an office] of the regulation authority for the area in which he is stopped no later than seven days after the day on which he was required to produce it.

(2)   A copy of a person's certificate of registration as a carrier of controlled waste shall for the purposes of section 5 of the 1989 Act be authority for transporting controlled waste if it was provided by the regulation authority under regulation 9.

[894]

NOTES

    Para (1): words in square brackets substituted by the Environment Act 1995 (Consequential Amendments) Regulations 1996, SI 1996/593, reg 3, Sch 2, para 9(3).

---

15 Appeals

(1)   Notice of an appeal to the Secretary of State under section 4(1) or (2) of the 1989 Act shall be given in writing by the appellant to the Secretary of State.

(2)   The notice of appeal shall be accompanied by the following—
- (a) a statement of the grounds of appeal;
- (b) in the case of an appeal under section 4(1) of the 1989 Act, a copy of the relevant application;
- (c) in the case of an appeal under section 4(2) of the 1989 Act, a copy of the appellant's entry in the register;
- (d) a copy of any relevant correspondence between the appellant and the regulation authority;
- (e) a copy of any notice given to the appellant under regulation 5(2) or 10(2);
- (f) a statement indicating whether the appellant wishes the appeal to be conducted by written representations or by a hearing.

(3)   The appellant shall at the same time as giving notice of appeal to the Secretary of State serve on the regulation authority a copy of the notice and a copy of the documents mentioned in paragraph (2)(a) and (f).

[895]

16 Time limit for bringing an appeal

Notice of appeal is to be given before the expiry of the period of 28 days beginning with—
- (a) in the case of an appeal under section 4(1)(a) of the 1989 Act, the date on which the appellant is given notice by the regulation authority that his application has been refused; or
- (b) in the case of an appeal under section 4(1)(b) of the 1989 Act, the date on which the relevant period from the making of the application expired without the appellant having been registered; or
- (c) in the case of an appeal under section 4(2) of the 1989 Act, the date on which the appellant is given notice by the regulation authority that his registration as a carrier of controlled waste has been revoked,

or before such later date as the Secretary of State may allow.

[896]

17 Hearings

(1)   If either party to an appeal requests a hearing or the Secretary of State so decides, the appeal shall be or continue in the form of a hearing before a person appointed for the purpose by the Secretary of State.

(2)   The person holding the hearing shall after its conclusion make a written report to the Secretary of State which shall include his conclusions and recommendations or his reasons for not making any recommendations.

[897]

18 Notification of determination

(1)   The Secretary of State shall notify the appellant in writing of his determination of the appeal and of his reasons for it and, if a hearing is held, shall also provide him with a copy of the report of the person who conducted the hearing.

(2)   The Secretary of State shall at the same time send a copy of those documents to the regulation authority.

[898]

19 Prescribed information

The prescribed information for the purposes of section 6(1)(c) of the 1989 Act is the name and address of the person who was using the vehicle at the time when the offence was committed.

[899]

20 Prescribed steps to be taken before applying for a warrant to seize property

(1)   The prescribed steps for the purposes of section 6(1)(c) of the 1989 Act are as follows.

(2)   The regulation authority shall—
(a)   in the case of a vehicle with a GB registration mark, obtain from the Secretary of State the name and address of the person shown in his records, at the time when the offence was committed, as the keeper and user of the vehicle;
(b)   in the case of a vehicle with a Northern Ireland registration mark, provide the Secretary of State for Transport with details of the registration mark and of the time when the offence was committed and a brief description of the vehicle. request his help in finding the person who was the owner of the vehicle at that time and explain the reason for making the request; and
(c)   in any other case, provide the chief officer of the police force in whose area the offence was committed with details of the foreign registration mark (if any) and of the time when the offence was committed and a brief description of the vehicle, request his help in finding the person who was the owner of the vehicle at that time and explain the reason for making the request.

(3)   The regulation authority shall serve notice under section 71(2) of the Environmental Protection Act 1990 on any person who they consider (whether as a result of action taken under paragraph (2) or otherwise) may be able to provide them with the name and address of the person who was using the vehicle at the time when the offence was committed, requiring him, if he is able to do so, to provide them with the name and address of that person.

(4)   In this regulation—
"GB registration mark" means a registration mark issued in relation to a vehicle under the Vehicles (Excise) Act 1971;
"Northern Ireland registration mark" means a mark indicating registration in Northern Ireland;
"foreign registration mark" means a mark indicating registration in some country other than Great Britain or Northern Ireland;
"owner" includes a person entitled to possession of a vehicle under a hiring agreement or hire purchase agreement.

[900]

21 Removal of vehicles seized

(1)   A vehicle seized under section 6 of the 1989 Act on behalf of a regulation authority may be removed under subsection (5) of that section in the following manner.

(2)   The vehicle may be driven, towed or removed by such other means as are reasonable in the circumstances and any necessary steps may be taken in relation to the vehicle in order to facilitate its removal.

(3)   Contents of the vehicle may be removed separately in cases where—
(a)   it is reasonable to do so to facilitate removal of the vehicle;
(b)   there is good reason for storing them at a different place from the vehicle; or
(c)   their condition requires them to be disposed of without delay.

[901]

22 Return of property seized

(1)   Unless the relevant property has already been disposed of under regulation 23, a regulation authority shall return any property seized under section 6 of the 1989 Act to a person who—
   (a) produces satisfactory evidence of his entitlement to it and of his identity and address; or
   (b) where he seeks to recover the property as the agent of another person, produces satisfactory evidence of his identity, his address and his authority to act on behalf of his principal and of his principal's identity, address and entitlement to the property; and
   (c) where the property is a vehicle and the person seeking its return (or in a case falling within sub-paragraph (b), his principal) purports to be the keeper or the user of the vehicle, produces the registration book for the vehicle.

(2)   Where the person claiming to be entitled to a vehicle establishes his entitlement, he shall be treated for the purposes of this regulation as also entitled to its contents unless and to the extent that another person has claimed them or part of them.

(3)   Where there is more than one claim to the property, the regulation authority shall determine which person is entitled to it on the basis of the evidence provided to them.

[902]

23 Disposal of property seized

(1)   The regulation authority may sell, destroy or deposit at any place property seized under section 6 of the 1989 Act if—
   (a) the authority have published a notice in a newspaper circulating in the area in which the property was seized—
      (i) giving the authority's name, a brief description of the property seized and the vehicle's registration mark (if any);
      (ii) indicating the time and place at which, and the powers under which, it was seized on behalf of the authority;
      (iii) stating that it may be claimed at the place and at the times specified in the notice and that, if no-one establishes within the period specified in the notice that he is entitled to the return of the property, the authority intend to dispose of it after the expiry of that period unless its condition requires its earlier disposal;
   (b) the authority have served a copy of the notice on—
      (i) any person on whom a notice under section 71(2) of the Environmental Protection Act 1990 has been served by virtue of regulation 20(3) in relation to the relevant vehicle;
      (ii) the chief officer of the police force in whose area the property was seized;
      (iii) the Secretary of State for Transport;
      (iv) HP Information plc; and
   (c) either—
      (i) the period of 28 days, beginning with the date on which notice is published under sub-paragraph (a) or, if later, a copy of that notice is served under sub-paragraph (b), has expired without any obligation arising under regulation 22 for the regulation authority to return the property to any person; or
      (ii) the condition of the property requires it to be disposed of without delay.

(2)   The period specified in a notice under paragraph (1)(a)(iii) shall be the period mentioned in paragraph (1)(c)(i).

[903]

24 Notice of disposal of a vehicle

After disposing of any vehicle under regulation 23, the regulation authority shall serve notice of the disposal on the following persons—
(a) the chief officer of the police force in whose area it was seized;
(b) the Secretary of State for Transport; and
(c) HP Information plc.

[904]

25 Application of proceeds of sale

(1) The proceeds of sale of any property sold by a regulation authority under regulation 23 shall be applied towards meeting expenses incurred by the authority in exercising their functions by virtue of section 6 of the 1989 Act and, in so far as they are not so applied, in meeting any claim to the proceeds of sale made and established in accordance with paragraph (2).

(2) A claim to the proceeds of sale of any property shall be established if the claimant provides the regulation authority with satisfactory evidence that he would have been entitled to the return of the property under regulation 22 if the property had not been sold.

[905]

26 Service of notices

Any notice or other document required by these Regulations to be served on or given to a person may be served or given in accordance with section 160 of the Environmental Protection Act 1990.

[906]

SCHEDULE 1
PRESCRIBED OFFENCES: RELEVANT ENACTMENTS
Regulation 1(2)

Section 22 of the Public Health (Scotland) Act 1897.

Section 95(1) of the Public Health Act 1936.

Section 60 of the Transport Act 1968.

Sections 3, 5(6), 16(4), 18(2), 31(1), 32(1), 34(5), 78, 92(6) and 93(3) of the Control of Pollution Act 1974.

Section 2 of the Refuse Disposal (Amenity) Act 1978.

The Control of Pollution (Special Waste) Regulations 1980.

Section 9(1) of the Food and Environment Protection Act 1985.

The Transfrontier Shipment of Hazardous Waste Regulations 1988.

The Merchant Shipping (Prevention of Pollution by Garbage) Regulations 1988.

Sections 1, 5, 6(9) and 7(3) of the Control of Pollution (Amendment) Act 1989.

Sections 107, 118(4) and 175(1) of the Water Act 1989.

Sections 23(1), 33, 34(6), 44, 47(6), 57(5), 59(5), 63(2), 69(9), 70(4), 71(3) and 80(4) of the Environmental Protection Act 1990.

[The Transfrontier Shipment of Waste Regulations 1994.]

[The Special Waste Regulations 1996.]

[907]

NOTES
Entry in first pair of square brackets inserted by the Transfrontier Shipment of Waste Regulations 1994, SI 1994/1137, reg 19(1); entry in final pair of square brackets added by the Special Waste Regulations 1996, SI 1996/972, reg 22.

SCHEDULE 2
APPLICATION FORMS

Regulation 4(6), (7)

PART I
APPLICATION FOR REGISTRATION AS A CARRIER OF CONTROLLED WASTE

Please read the guidance notes before completing this form

1. Full name of applicant (*note 1*)

     Former name (if applicable)

     Date of birth (if applicable)

2. Name under which applicant carries on business
     (if different from 1)

3. Address for correspondence

     Post Code

4. Address of principal place of business
     (if different from 3)

     Post Code

5. Telephone/Telex/Fax number

Tel.	Telex	Fax

6. If applicant has previously been a registered carrier, give:

     (a) registration number or numbers

     (b) name of regulation authority or authorities

7. If applicant is a company registered under the Companies
Acts, give:

     (a) company's registered number

     (b) address of registered office

     Post Code

     (c) in the case of a company incorporated outside
         Great Britain, the country in which
         it was incorporated

8. If applicant is a registered company or other body corporate, for each director, manager, secretary or other similar officer, give:

Full name	Position held	Address	Date of birth

9. If applicant is a prospective partner in a business carried on by a partnership whose members are already registered carriers, give:

    (a) full name of partnership

    (b) registration number of partnership

10. Has the applicant or another relevant person (*note 2*) been convicted of any offence listed in the Controlled Waste (Registration of Carriers and Seizure of Vehicles) Regulations 1991 (*notes 3 and 4*)?

        Yes ☐   No ☐

If **Yes**, give full details of each offence—

Full name of person convicted	Position held	Name of Court	Date of conviction	Offence and penalty imposed

If details of any conviction have been given, use the following space to provide the regulation authority with any additional information which you wish the authority to take into account in determining whether or not it is undesirable for the applicant to be authorised to transport controlled waste—

11. Is the applicant or another company in the same group (within the meaning of section 53(1) of the Companies Act 1989) the holder of a disposal licence or a waste management licence?

        Yes ☐   No ☐

If **Yes**, give details of licence:

Full name of holder of licence	Date of birth (if applicable)	Date of issue of licence	Name of authority which issued the licence

Declaration

I declare that I have personally checked the information given in this application form and that it is true to the best of my knowledge, information and belief. I understand that registration may be refused if false or incomplete information is given and that untrue statements may result in prosecution and could lead to revocation of registration.

Signature: Date:

Position held:

Have you enclosed the fee of £95? (*note 5*)   Yes ☐

GUIDANCE NOTES

1. In the case of a partnership or proposed partnership, each partner must apply for registration and his details must be included in this application form.

2. Details of an offence listed in the Controlled Waste (Registration of Carriers and Seizure of Vehicles) Regulations 1991 must be given if the applicant was convicted of the offence or if the person convicted of the offence ("the relevant person")—

    (a)   committed it in the course of his employment by the applicant;

    (b)   committed it in the course of the carrying on of any business by a partnership one of the members of which was the applicant;

    (c)   was a body corporate and at the time when the offence was committed the applicant was a director, manager, secretary or other similar officer of that body;

    (d)   was a director, manager, secretary or other similar officer of the applicant (where the applicant is a body corporate);

    (e)   was a body corporate and at the time when the offence was committed a director, manager, secretary or other similar officer of the applicant held such an office in the body corporate which committed the offence.

3. The offences listed in the Controlled Waste (Registration of Carriers and Seizure of Vehicles) Regulations 1991 are offences under any of the following provisions—

    section 22 of the Public Health (Scotland) Act 1987;

    section 95(1) of the Public Health Act 1936;

    section 60 of the Transport Act 1968;

    sections 3, 5(6), 16(4), 18(2), 31(1), 32(1), 34(5), 78, 92(6) and 93(3) of the Control of Pollution Act 1974;

    section 2 of the Refuse Disposal (Amenity) Act 1978;

    the Control of Pollution (Special Waste) Regulations 1980;

    section 9(1) of the Food and Environment Protection Act 1985;

    the Transfrontier Shipment of Hazardous Waste Regulations 1988;

    the Merchant Shipping (Prevention of Pollution by Garbage) Regulations 1988;

    sections 1, 5, 6(9) and 7(3) of the Control of Pollution (Amendment) Act 1989;

    section 107, 118(4) and 175(1) of the Water Act 1989;

    sections 23(1), 33, 34(6), 44, 47(6), 57(5), 59(5), 63(2), 69(9), 70(4), 71(3) and 80(4) of the Environmental Protection Act 1990.

    [the Transfrontier Shipment of Waste Regulations 1994.]

4. Details of a conviction need not be given when under the terms of the Rehabilitation of Offenders Act 1974 the conviction is spent.

5. The fee of £95 must be sent with the application. The regulation authority may refuse the application if the fee is not enclosed.

[908]

NOTES

    Note 3: words in square brackets added by the Transfrontier Shipment of Waste Regulations 1994, SI 1994/1137, reg 19(2).

PART II
APPLICATION FOR RENEWAL OF REGISTRATION AS A CARRIER OF
CONTROLLED WASTE

Please read the guidance notes before completing this form

1.   Full name of applicant (*note 1*)

       Former name (if applicable)

       Date of birth (if applicable)

2.   Address for correspondence

                                         Post Code

3. Telephone/Telex/Fax number

Tel.	Telex	Fax

4. Registration number as a carrier

5. Has the applicant or another relevant person (*note 2*) been convicted of any offence listed in the Controlled Waste (Registration of Carriers and Seizure of Vehicles) Regulations 1991

(*notes 3 and 4*)? Yes ☐ No ☐

If **Yes**, give full details of each offence—

Full name of person convicted	Position held	Name of Court	Date of conviction	Offence and penalty imposed

If details of any conviction have been given, use the following space to provide the regulation authority with any additional information which you wish the authority to take into account in determining whether or not it is undesirable for the applicant to be authorised to transport controlled waste—

6. Give details of any changes in any other information in the applicant's existing entry in the register (*note 5*)—

Declaration

I declare that I have personally checked the information given in this application form and that it is true to the best of my knowledge, information and belief. I understand that registration may be refused if false or incomplete information is given and that untrue statements may result in prosecution and could lead to revocation of registration.

Signature: Date:

Position held:

Have you enclosed the fee of £65? (*note 6*) Yes ☐

GUIDANCE NOTES

1. In the case of a partnership, each partner must apply for registration and his details must be included in this application form.

2. Details of an offence listed in the Controlled Waste (Registration of Carriers and Seizure of Vehicles) Regulations 1991 must be given if the applicant was convicted of the offence or if the person convicted of the offence ("the relevant person")—

(a) committed it in the course of his employment by the applicant;

(b) committed it in the course of the carrying on of any business by a partnership one of the members of which was the applicant;

(c) was a body corporate and at the time when the offence was committed the applicant was a director, manager, secretary or other similar officer of that body;

(d) was a director, manager, secretary or other similar officer of the applicant (where the applicant is a body corporate);

(e) was a body corporate and at the time when the offence was committed a director, manager, secretary or other similar officer of the applicant held such an office in the body corporate which committed the offence.

3. The offences listed in the Controlled Waste (Registration of Carriers and Seizure of Vehicles) Regulations 1991 are offences under any of the following provisions—

section 22 of the Public Health (Scotland) Act 1987;

section 95(1) of the Public Health Act 1936;

section 60 of the Transport Act 1968;

sections 3, 5(6), 16(4), 18(2), 31(1), 32(1), 34(5), 78, 92(6) and 93(3) of the Control of Pollution Act 1974;

section 2 of the Refuse Disposal (Amenity) Act 1978;

the Control of Pollution (Special Waste) Regulations 1980;

section 9(1) of the Food and Environment Protection Act 1985;

the Transfrontier Shipment of Hazardous Waste Regulations 1988;

the Merchant Shipping (Prevention of Pollution by Garbage) Regulations 1988;

sections 1, 5, 6(9) and 7(3) of the Control of Pollution (Amendment) Act 1989;

sections 107, 118(4) and 175(1) of the Water Act 1989;

sections 23(1), 33, 34(6), 44, 47(6), 57(5), 59(5), 63(2), 69(9), 70(4), 71(3) and 80(4) of the Environmental Protection Act 1990;

[the Transfrontier Shipment of Waste Regulations 1994.]

4. Details of a conviction need not be given when under the terms of the Rehabilitation of Offenders Act 1974 the conviction is spent.

5. Check the information in the copy of the current entry in the register sent with the regulation authority's reminder that registration needs to be renewed or, if no such copy has been received, ask the authority for one.

6. The fee of £65 must be sent with the application. The regulation authority may refuse the application if the fee is not enclosed.

[909]

NOTES

Note 3: words in square brackets added by the Transfrontier Shipment of Waste Regulations 1994, SI 1994/1137, reg 19(2).

SCHEDULE 3
CERTIFICATE OF REGISTRATION UNDER THE CONTROL OF POLLUTION (AMENDMENT) ACT 1989

Regulations 6(3), 7(2), 8(2)

Regulation Authority
Name:
Address:
Post Code:
Tel.:   Telex: Fax:

The following information is hereby certified by the above-mentioned authority to be information which at the date of this certificate† is entered in the register which they maintain under regulation 3 of the Controlled Waste (Registration of Carriers and Seizure of Vehicles) Regulations 1991—

Name(s) of registered carrier:

Registration number:

Business name (if any):

Address of registered carrier's

principal place of business:

Tel.: Telex: Fax:

Date of registration:

Date of expiry of registration:*

Date on which last amendment (if any) was made to the carrier's entry in the register:

Signature of authorised officer
of the regulation authority: Date:

† You can check whether there has been any change in the information contained in this certificate by contacting the regulation authority named above.

* Registration will expire on this date unless—
  (a) it is revoked before expiry;
  (b) the carrier requests the removal of his name from the register at an earlier time;
  (c) an application for renewal is made within the six months ending on the expiry date and the application is still outstanding, or is the subject of an appeal, on that date;
  (d) in the case of a registered partnership, if any of the partners ceases to be registered or if anyone who is not registered becomes a partner.

[910]

ENVIRONMENTAL PROTECTION (DUTY OF CARE) REGULATIONS 1991

(SI 1991/2839)

NOTES
Made: 16 December 1991.
Commencement: 1 April 1992.
Authority: Environmental Protection Act 1990, s 34(5).

1 Citation, commencement and interpretation

(1) These Regulations may be cited as the Environmental Protection (Duty of Care) Regulations 1991 and shall come into force on 1st April 1992.

(2) In these Regulations—
"the 1990 Act" means the Environmental Protection Act 1990;
"transferor" and "transferee" mean respectively, in relation to a transfer of controlled waste by a person who is subject to the duty imposed by section 34(1) of the 1990 Act, the person who in compliance with that section transfers a written description of the waste and the person who receives that description.

[911]

2 Transfer notes

(1)   [Subject to paragraph (3),] the transferor and the transferee shall, at the same time as the written description of the waste is transferred, ensure that such a document as is described in paragraph (2) ("a transfer note") is completed and signed on their behalf.

(2)   A transfer note shall—
  (a) identify the waste to which it relates and state—
    (i) its quantity and whether on transfer it is loose or in a container;
    (ii) if in a container, the kind of container; and
    (iii) the time and place of transfer;
  (b) give the name and address of the transferor and the transferee;
  (c) state whether or not the transferor is the producer or importer of the waste and, if so, which;
  (d) if the transfer is to a person for authorised transport purposes, specify which of those purposes; and
  (e) state as respects the transferor and the transferee which, if any, of the categories of person shown in column 1 of the following Table describes him and provide any relevant additional information specified in column 2 of the Table.

TABLE

Category of person	Additional information
An authority which is a waste collection authority for the purposes of Part II of the 1990 Act.	
A person who is the holder of a waste management licence under section 35 of the 1990 Act or of a disposal licence under section 5 of the Control of Pollution Act 1974.	If the waste is to be kept, treated or disposed of by that person, the relevant licence number and the name of the licensing authority.
A person to whom section 33(1) of the 1990 Act does not apply by virtue of regulations under subsection (3) of that section.	
A person registered as a carrier of controlled waste under section 2 of the Control of Pollution (Amendment) Act 1989.	The name of the waste regulation authority with whom he is registered and his registration number.
A person who is not required to be so registered by virtue of regulations under section 1(3) of that Act.	
A waste disposal authority in Scotland.	

[(3)   Paragraph (1) shall not apply where the waste transferred is special waste within the meaning of the Special Waste Regulations 1996 and the consignment note and, where appropriate, schedule required by those Regulations are completed and dealt with in accordance with those Regulations.]

[912]

NOTES
Commencement: 1 September 1996 (para (3)); 1 April 1992 (remainder).
Para (1): words in square brackets inserted by the Special Waste Regulations 1996, SI 1996/972, reg 23(a).
Para (3): added by SI 1996/972, reg 23(b).

3 Duty to keep copies of written descriptions of waste and transfer notes

The transferor and the transferee shall each keep the written description of the waste and the transfer note or copies thereof for a period of two years from the transfer of the controlled waste.

[913]

4 Duty to furnish documents

A person who has been served by a waste regulation authority with a notice in writing specifying or describing any document and requiring its production shall, if the document is one which at that time he is under a duty to keep under regulation 3, furnish the authority with a copy of it at the authority's office specified in the notice and within the period (not being less than 7 days) so specified.

[914]

TRADE EFFLUENTS (PRESCRIBED PROCESSES AND SUBSTANCES) REGULATIONS 1992

(SI 1992/339)

NOTES
Made: 20 February 1992.
Commencement: 20 March 1992.
Authority: Water Industry Act 1991, s 138(1).

1 Citation and commencement

These Regulations may be cited as the Trade Effluents (Prescribed Processes and Substances) Regulations 1992 and shall come into force on 20th March 1992.

[915]

2 Trade effluent derived from prescribed processes

Trade effluent which derives from any process which occasions liquid discharges containing trichloroethylene or perchloroethylene in quantities of thirty kilogrammes per year or more shall be special category effluent for the purposes of Chapter III of Part IV of the Water Industry Act 1991.

[916]

CONTROLLED WASTE REGULATIONS 1992

(SI 1992/588)

NOTES
Made: 9 March 1992.
Commencement: 1 April 1992 (regs 1–9, Schs 1–4); 1 June 1992 (reg 10).
Authority: Control of Pollution (Amendment) Act 1989, ss 1(3)(a), 8(2), 9(1); Environmental Protection Act 1990, ss 33(3), 45(3), 75(7)(d), (8), 96.

ARRANGEMENT OF REGULATIONS

1 Citation, commencement and interpretation

(1)   These Regulations may be cited as the Controlled Waste Regulations 1992 and shall come into force on 1st April 1992 save for regulation 10, which shall come into force on 1st June 1992.

(2)   In these Regulations—
"the Act" means the Environmental Protection Act 1990;
"the 1989 Regulations" means the Sludge (Use in Agriculture) Regulations 1989;
"camp site" means land on which tents are pitched for the purposes of human
    habitation and land the use of which is incidental to land on which tents are
    so pitched;
"charity" means any body of persons or trust established for charitable
    purposes only;
"clinical waste" means—
    (a) any waste which consists wholly or partly of human or animal tissue,
        blood or other body fluids, excretions, drugs or other pharmaceutical
        products, swabs or dressings, or syringes, needles or other sharp
        instruments, being waste which unless rendered safe may prove
        hazardous to any person coming into contact with it; and
    (b) any other waste arising from medical, nursing, dental, veterinary,
        pharmaceutical or similar practice, investigation, treatment, care, teaching
        or research, or the collection of blood for transfusion, being waste which
        may cause infection to any person coming into contact with it;
"composite hereditament" has the same meaning as in section 64(9) of the
    Local Government Finance Act 1988;
"construction" includes improvement, repair or alteration;
["Directive waste" has the meaning given by regulation 1(3) of the Waste
    Management Licensing Regulations 1994;]
"part residential subjects" has the same meaning as in [section 99(1) of the
    Local Government Finance Act 1992];
"scrap metal" has the same meaning as in section 9(2) of the Scrap Metal
    Dealers Act 1964;
"septic tank sludge" and "sludge" have the same meaning as in regulation 2(1)
    of the 1989 Regulations; and
"vessel" includes a hovercraft within the meaning of section 4(1) of the
    Hovercraft Act 1968.

(3)   Any reference in these Regulations to a section is, except where the context otherwise requires, a reference to a section of the Act.

(4)   References in these Regulations to waste—
    (a) do not include waste from any mine or quarry or waste from premises used
        for agriculture within the meaning of the Agriculture Act 1947 or, in
        Scotland, the Agriculture (Scotland) Act 1948;
    (b) except so far as otherwise provided, do not include sewage (including
        matter in or from a privy).

NOTES

Para (2): definition "Directive waste" inserted, and words in square brackets in definition "part residential subjects" substituted, by the Waste Management Licensing Regulations 1994, SI 1994/1056, reg 24(2).

2 Waste to be treated as household waste

(1) [Subject to paragraph (2) and regulation 3 and 7A,] waste of the descriptions set out in Schedule 1 shall be treated as household waste for the purposes of Part II of the Act.

(2) Waste of the following descriptions shall be treated as household waste for the purposes only of section 34(2) (household waste produced on domestic property)—
   (a) waste arising from works of construction or demolition, including waste arising from work preparatory thereto; and
   (b) septic tank sludge.

[918]

NOTES

Para (1): words in square brackets substituted by the Waste Management Licensing Regulations 1994, SI 1994/1056, reg 24(3).

3 Waste not to be treated as household waste

(1) Waste of the following descriptions shall not be treated as household waste for the purposes of section 33(2) (treatment, keeping or disposal of household waste within the curtilage of a dwelling)—
   (a) any mineral or synthetic oil or grease;
   (b) asbestos; and
   (c) clinical waste.

(2) Scrap metal shall not be treated as household waste for the purposes of section 34 [at any time before [1st October 1995]].

[919]

NOTES

Para (2): words in first (outer) pair of square brackets substituted by the Controlled Waste (Amendment) Regulations 1993, SI 1993/566, reg 2, words in second (inner) pair of square brackets substituted by the Waste Management Licensing (Amendment etc) Regulations 1995, SI 1995/288, reg 2(1).

4 Charges for the collection of household waste

The collection of any of the types of household waste set out in Schedule 2 is prescribed for the purposes of section 45(3) as a case in respect of which a charge for collection may be made.

[920]

5 Waste to be treated as industrial waste

(1) Subject to paragraph (2) and [regulations 7 and 7A], waste of the descriptions set out in Schedule 3 shall be treated as industrial waste for the purposes of Part II of the Act.

(2) Waste of the following descriptions shall be treated as industrial waste for the purposes of Part II of the Act (except section 34(2))—
   (a) waste arising from works of construction or demolition, including waste arising from work preparatory thereto;
   (b) septic tank sludge not falling within [regulation 7(1)(a) or (c)].

[921]

NOTES
Words in square brackets substituted by the Waste Management Licensing Regulations 1994, SI 1994/1056, reg 24(4), (5).

6 Waste to be treated as commercial waste

Subject to [regulations 7 and 7A], waste of the descriptions set out in Schedule 4 shall be treated as commercial waste for the purposes of Part II of the Act.

[922]

NOTES
Words in square brackets substituted by the Waste Management Licensing Regulations 1994, SI 1994/1056, reg 24(6).

7 Waste not to be treated as industrial or commercial waste

(1)   Waste of the following descriptions shall not be treated as industrial waste or commercial waste for the purposes of Part II of the Act—
   (a) sewage, sludge or septic tank sludge which is treated, kept or disposed of (otherwise than by means of mobile plant) within the curtilage of a sewage treatment works as an integral part of the operation of those works;
   (b) sludge which is supplied or used in accordance with the 1989 Regulations;
   (c) septic tank sludge which is used [on agricultural land within the meaning of] the 1989 Regulations.

(2)   Scrap metal shall not be treated as industrial waste or commercial waste for the purposes of section 34 [at any time before [1st October 1995]].

[(3)   Animal by-products which are collected and transported in accordance with Schedule 2 to the Animal By-Products Order 1992 shall not be treated as industrial waste or commercial waste for the purposes of section 34 (duty of care etc as respects waste).

(4)   In this regulation, "animal by-products" has the same meaning as in article 3(1) of the Animal By-Products Order 1992.]

[923]

NOTES
Para (1): words in square brackets in sub-para (c) substituted by the Waste Management Licensing (Amendment etc) Regulations 1995, SI 1995/288, reg 2(2).
Para (2): words in first (outer) pair of square brackets substituted by the Controlled Waste (Amendment) Regulations 1993, SI 1993/566, reg 2, words in second (inner) pair of square brackets substituted by SI 1995/288, reg 2(1).
Paras (3), (4): added by the Waste Management Licensing Regulations 1994, SI 1994/1056, reg 24(7).

[7A Waste not to be treated as household, industrial or commercial waste

For the purposes of Part II of the Act, waste which is not Directive waste shall not be treated as household waste, industrial waste or commercial waste.]

[924]

NOTES
Commencement: 1 May 1994.
Inserted by the Waste Management Licensing Regulations 1994, SI 1994/1056, reg 24(8).

8 Application of Part II of the Act to litter and refuse

Part II of the Act shall have effect as if—
   (a) references to controlled waste included references to litter and refuse to which section 96 applies;

(b) references to controlled waste of a description set out in the first column of Table A below included references to litter and refuse of a description set out in the second column thereof;

(c) references to controlled waste collected under section 45 included references to litter and refuse collected under sections 89(1)(a) and (c) and 92(9); and

(d) references to controlled waste collected under section 45 which is waste of a description set out in the first column of Table B below included references to litter and refuse of a description set out in the second column thereof.

TABLE A

Description of waste	Description of litter and refuse
Household waste.	Litter and refuse collected under section 89(1)(a), (c) and (f).
Industrial waste.	Litter and refuse collected under section 89(1)(b) and (e).
Commercial waste.	Litter and refuse collected under sections 89(1)(d) and (g), 92(9) and 93.

TABLE B

Description of waste	Description of litter and refuse
Household waste.	Litter and refuse collected under section 89(1)(a) and (c).
Commercial waste.	Litter and refuse collected under section 92(9).

[925]

9 Exceptions from section 33(1) of the Act

(1)   Subject to the following provisions of this regulation, section 33(1) shall not apply—

(a) . . .

(b) as respects the use of land by a waste disposal authority in accordance with a resolution under section 11 of that Act.

(2)   Paragraph (1)(b) shall cease to apply in relation to a waste disposal authority in England and Wales as from the date on which the restriction imposed by section 51(1) applies to that authority in accordance with section 77(6) and (7).

[926]

NOTES
Para (1): sub-para (a) revoked by the Waste Management Licensing (Amendment etc) Regulations 1995, SI 1995/288, reg 2(3).

10 Amendment of the Controlled Waste (Registration of Carriers and Seizure of Vehicles) Regulations 1991

(1) . . .

(2)   Paragraph (1) does not apply to a person who before 1st June 1992 applies in accordance with the Controlled Waste (Registration of Carriers and Seizure of Vehicles) Regulations 1991 for registration as a carrier of controlled waste whilst his application is pending for the purposes of those Regulations.

[927]

NOTES
Para (1): amends the Controlled Waste (Registration of Carriers and Seizure of Vehicles) Regulations 1991, SI 1991/1624, reg 2(2).

SCHEDULE 1
WASTE TO BE TREATED AS HOUSEHOLD WASTE

Regulation 2(1)

1. Waste from a hereditament or premises exempted from local non-domestic rating by virtue of—
   (a)   in England and Wales, paragraph 11 of Schedule 5 to the Local Government Finance Act 1988 (places of religious worship etc.);
   (b)   in Scotland, section 22 of the Valuation and Rating (Scotland) Act 1956 (churches etc).

2. Waste from premises occupied by a charity and wholly or mainly used for charitable purposes.

3. Waste from any land belonging to or used in connection with domestic property, a caravan or a residential home.

4. Waste from a private garage which either has a floor area of 25 square metres or less or is used wholly or mainly for the accommodation of a private motor vehicle.

5. Waste from private storage premises used wholly or mainly for the storage of articles of domestic use.

6. Waste from a moored vessel used wholly for the purposes of living accommodation.

7. Waste from a camp site.

8. Waste from a prison or other penal institution.

9. Waste from a hall or other premises used wholly or mainly for public meetings.

10. Waste from a royal palace.

11. Waste arising from the discharge by a local authority of its duty under section 89(2).

[928]

SCHEDULE 2
TYPES OF HOUSEHOLD WASTE FOR WHICH A CHARGE FOR COLLECTION MAY BE MADE

Regulation 4

1.   Any article of waste which exceeds 25 kilograms in weight.

2.   Any article of waste which does not fit, or cannot be fitted into—
   (a)   a receptacle for household waste provided in accordance with section 46; or
   (b)   where no such receptacle is provided, a cylindrical container 750 millimetres in diameter and 1 metre in length.

3.   Garden waste.

4.   Clinical waste from a domestic property, a caravan or from a moored vessel used wholly for the purposes of living accommodation.

5.   Waste from a residential hostel, a residential home or from premises forming part of a university, school or other educational establishment or forming part of a hospital or nursing home.

6.   Waste from domestic property or a caravan used in the course of a business for the provision of self-catering holiday accommodation.

7.   Dead domestic pets.

8.   Any substances or articles which, by virtue of a notice served by a collection authority under section 46, the occupier of the premises may not put into a receptacle for household waste provided in accordance with that section.

9.   Litter and refuse collected under section 89(1)(f).

10. Waste from—
   (a)   in England and Wales, domestic property forming part of a composite hereditament;
   (b)   in Scotland, the residential part of part residential subjects.

11. Any mineral or synthetic oil or grease.

12. Asbestos.

13. Waste from a caravan which in accordance with any licence or planning permission regulating the use of the caravan site on which the caravan is stationed is not allowed to be used for human habitation throughout the year.

14. Waste from a camp site, other than from any domestic property on that site.

15. Waste from premises occupied by a charity and wholly or mainly used for charitable purposes, unless it is waste falling within paragraph 1 of Schedule 1.

16. Waste from a prison or other penal institution.

17. Waste from a hall or other premises used wholly or mainly for public meetings.

18. Waste from a royal palace.

[929]

SCHEDULE 3
WASTE TO BE TREATED AS INDUSTRIAL WASTE
Regulation 5(1)

1. Waste from premises used for maintaining vehicles, vessels or aircraft, not being waste from a private garage to which paragraph 4 of Schedule 1 applies.

2. Waste from a laboratory.

3.—(1) Waste from a workshop or similar premises not being a factory within the meaning of section 175 of the Factories Act 1961 because the people working there are not employees or because the work there is not carried on by way of trade or for purposes of gain.

(2) In this paragraph, "workshop" does not include premises at which the principal activities are computer operations or the copying of documents by photographic or lithographic means.

4. Waste from premises occupied by a scientific research association approved by the Secretary of State under section 508 of the Income and Corporation Taxes Act 1988.

5. Waste from dredging operations.

6. Waste arising from tunnelling or from any other excavation.

7. Sewage not falling within a description in regulation 7 which—
    (a) is treated, kept or disposed of in or on land, other than by means of a privy, cesspool or septic tank;
    (b) is treated, kept or disposed of by means of mobile plant; or
    (c) has been removed from a privy or cesspool.

8. Clinical waste other than—
    (a) clinical waste from a domestic property, caravan, residential home or from a moored vessel used wholly for the purposes of living accommodation;
    (b) waste collected under section 22(3) of the Control of Pollution Act 1974 [or section 25(2) of the Local Government and Planning (Scotland) Act 1982]; or
    (c) waste collected under sections 89, 92(9) or 93.

9. Waste arising from any aircraft, vehicle or vessel which is not occupied for domestic purposes.

10. Waste which has previously formed part of any aircraft, vehicle or vessel and which is not household waste.

11. Waste removed from land on which it has previously been deposited and any soil with which such waste has been in contact, other than—
    (a) waste collected under section 22(3) of the Control of Pollution Act 1974 [or section 25(2) of the Local Government and Planning (Scotland) Act 1982]; or
    (b) waste collected under sections 89, 92(9) or 93.

12. Leachate from a deposit of waste.

13. Poisonous or noxious waste arising from any of the following processes undertaken on premises used for the purposes of a trade or business—
  (a)   mixing or selling paints;
  (b)   sign writing;
  (c)   laundering or dry cleaning;
  (d)   developing photographic film or making photographic prints;
  (e)   selling petrol, diesel fuel, paraffin, kerosene, heating oil or similar substances; or
  (f)   selling pesticides, herbicides or fungicides.

14. Waste from premises used for the purposes of breeding, boarding, stabling or exhibiting animals.

15.—(1)   Waste oil, waste solvent or (subject to regulation 7(2)) scrap metal, other than—
  (a)   waste from a domestic property, caravan or residential home;
  (b)   waste falling within paragraphs 3 to 6 of Schedule 1.

  (2)   In this paragraph—
  "waste oil" means mineral or synthetic oil which is contaminated, spoiled or otherwise unfit for its original purpose; and
  "waste solvent" means solvent which is contaminated, spoiled or otherwise unfit for its original purpose.

16. Waste arising from the discharge by the Secretary of State of his duty under section 89(2).

17. Waste imported into Great Britain.

18.—(1)   Tank washings or garbage landed in Great Britain.

  (2)   In this paragraph—
  ["tank washings" has the same meaning as in paragraph 36 of Schedule 3 to the Waste Management Licensing Regulations 1994;] and
  "garbage" has the same meaning as in regulation 1(2) of the Merchant Shipping (Reception Facilities for Garbage) Regulations 1988.

[930]

NOTES
  Paras 8, 11: words in square brackets inserted by the Waste Management Licensing Regulations 1994, SI 1994/1056, reg 24(9).
  Para 18: definition "tank washings" in sub-para (2) substituted by the Special Waste Regulations 1996, SI 1996/972, reg 24.

SCHEDULE 4
WASTE TO BE TREATED AS COMMERCIAL WASTE

Regulation 6

1.   Waste from an office or showroom.

2.   Waste from a hotel within the meaning of—
  (a)   in England and Wales, section 1(3) of the Hotel Proprietors Act 1956; and
  (b)   in Scotland, section 139(1) of the Licensing (Scotland) Act 1976.

3.   Waste from any part of a composite hereditament, or, in Scotland, of part residential subjects, which is used for the purposes of a trade or business.

4.   Waste from a private garage which either has a floor area exceeding 25 square metres or is not used wholly or mainly for the accommodation of a private motor vehicle.

5.   Waste from premises occupied by a club, society or any association of persons (whether incorporated or not) in which activities are conducted for the benefit of the members.

6.   Waste from premises (not being premises from which waste is by virtue of the Act or of any other provision of these Regulations to be treated as household waste or industrial waste) occupied by—
  (a)   a court;
  (b)   a government department;
  (c)   a local authority;
  (d)   a body corporate or an individual appointed by or under any enactment to discharge any public functions; or
  (e)   a body incorporated by a Royal Charter.

7. Waste from a tent pitched on land other than a camp site.

8. Waste from a market or fair.

9. Waste collected under section 22(3) of the Control of Pollution Act 1974 [or section 25(2) of the Local Government and Planning (Scotland) Act 1982].

[931]

NOTES
Para 9: words in square brackets added by the Waste Management Licensing Regulations 1994, SI 1994/1056, reg 24(9).

ENVIRONMENTAL INFORMATION REGULATIONS 1992

(SI 1992/3240)

NOTES
Made: 18 December 1992.
Commencement: 31 December 1992.
Authority: European Communities Act 1972, s 2(2).

1 Citation, commencement and extent

(1) These Regulations may be cited as the Environmental Information Regulations 1992.

(2) These Regulations shall come into force on 31st December 1992.

(3) These Regulations shall extend to Great Britain only.

[932]

2 Construction of Regulations

(1) These Regulations apply to any information which—
 (a) relates to the environment;
 (b) is held by a relevant person in an accessible form and otherwise than for the purposes of any judicial or legislative functions; and
 (c) is not (apart from these Regulations) either—
  (i) information which is required, in accordance with any statutory provision, to be provided on request to every person who makes a request; or
  (ii) information contained in records which are required, in accordance with any statutory provision, to be made available for inspection by every person who wishes to inspect them.

(2) For the purposes of these Regulations information relates to the environment if, and only if, it relates to any of the following, that is to say—
 (a) the state of any water or air, the state of any flora or fauna, the state of any soil or the state of any natural site or other land;
 (b) any activities or measures (including activities giving rise to noise or any other nuisance) which adversely affect anything mentioned in sub-paragraph (a) above or are likely adversely to affect anything so mentioned;
 (c) any activities or administrative or other measures (including any environmental management programmes) which are designed to protect anything so mentioned.

(3) For the purposes of these Regulations the following are relevant persons, that is to say—
 (a) all such Ministers of the Crown, Government departments, local authorities and other persons carrying out functions of public administration at a

national, regional or local level as, for the purposes of or in connection with their functions, have responsibilities in relation to the environment; and

(b) any body with public responsibilities for the environment which does not fall within sub-paragraph (a) above but is under the control of a person falling within that sub-paragraph.

(4)   In these Regulations—

"information" includes anything contained in any records;

"records" includes registers, reports and returns, as well as computer records and other records kept otherwise than in a document; and

"statutory provision" means any provision made by or under any enactment.

[933]

3 Obligation to make environmental information available

(1)   Subject to the following provisions of these Regulations, a relevant person who holds any information to which these Regulations apply shall make that information available to every person who requests it.

(2)   It shall be the duty of every relevant person who holds information to which these Regulations apply to make such arrangements for giving effect to paragraph (1) above as secure—

(a) that every request made for the purposes of that paragraph is responded to as soon as possible;

(b) that no such request is responded to more than two months after it is made; and

(c) that, where the response to such a request contains a refusal to make information available, the refusal is in writing and specifies the reasons for the refusal.

(3)   Arrangements made by a relevant person for giving effect to paragraph (1) above may include provision entitling that person to refuse a request for information in cases where a request is manifestly unreasonable or is formulated in too general a manner.

(4)   The arrangements made by a relevant person for giving effect to paragraph (1) above may—

(a) include provision for the imposition of a charge on any person in respect of the costs reasonably attributable to the supply of information to that person in pursuance of that paragraph; and

(b) make the supply of any information in pursuance of that paragraph conditional on the payment of such a charge.

(5)   The obligation of a relevant person to make information available in pursuance of paragraph (1) above shall not require him to make it available except in such form, and at such times and places, as may be reasonable.

(6)   Without prejudice to any remedies available apart from by virtue of this paragraph in respect of any failure by a relevant person to comply with the requirements of these Regulations, the obligation of such a person to make information available in pursuance of paragraph (1) above shall be a duty owed to the person who has requested the information.

(7)   Subject to regulation 4 below, where any statutory provision or rule of law imposes any restriction or prohibition on the disclosure of information by any person, that restriction or prohibition shall not apply to any disclosure of information in pursuance of these Regulations.

[934]

4 Exceptions to right to information

(1)   Nothing in these Regulations shall—

(a) require the disclosure of any information which is capable of being treated as confidential; or

(b) authorise or require the disclosure of any information which must be so treated.

(2) For the purposes of these Regulations information is to be capable of being treated as confidential if, and only if, it is—
- (a) information relating to matters affecting international relations, national defence or public security;
- (b) information relating to, or to anything which is or has been the subject-matter of, any legal or other proceedings (whether actual or prospective);
- (c) information relating to the confidential deliberations of any relevant person or to the contents of any internal communications of a body corporate or other undertaking or organisation;
- (d) information contained in a document or other record which is still in the course of completion; or
- (e) information relating to matters to which any commercial or industrial confidentiality attaches or affecting any intellectual property.

(3) For the purposes of these Regulations information must be treated as confidential if, and only if, in the case of any request made to a relevant person under regulation 3 above—
- (a) it is capable of being so treated and its disclosure in response to that request would (apart from regulation 3(7) above) contravene any statutory provision or rule of law or would involve a breach of any agreement;
- (b) the information is personal information contained in records held in relation to an individual who has not given his consent to its disclosure;
- (c) the information is held by the relevant person in consequence of having been supplied by a person who—
  - (i) was not under, and could not have been put under, any legal obligation to supply it to the relevant person;
  - (ii) did not supply it in circumstances such that the relevant person is entitled apart from these Regulations to disclose it; and
  - (iii) has not consented to its disclosure;

  or
- (d) the disclosure of the information in response to that request would, in the circumstances, increase the likelihood of damage to the environment affecting anything to which the information relates.

(4) Nothing in this regulation shall authorise a refusal to make available any information contained in the same record as, or otherwise held with, other information which is withheld by virtue of this regulation unless it is incapable of being separated from the other information for the purpose of making it available.

(5) In this regulation "legal or other proceedings" includes any disciplinary proceedings, the proceedings at any local or other public inquiry and the proceedings at any hearing conducted by a person appointed under any enactment for the purpose of affording an opportunity to persons to make representations or objections with respect to any matter.

[935]

5 Existing rights to information

Where any information which is not information to which these Regulations apply is required under any statutory provision to be made available to any person, the arrangements made by any relevant person for giving effect to the requirements of that provision shall be such as to secure—
- (a) that every request for information relating to the environment which is made for the purposes of that provision is responded to as soon as possible;
- (b) that no such request is responded to more than two months after it is made;
- (c) that, where the response to such a request contains a refusal to make information available, the refusal is in writing and specifies the reasons for the refusal; and

(d) that no charge that exceeds a reasonable amount is made for making information relating to the environment available in accordance with that provision.

[936]

WASTE MANAGEMENT LICENSING REGULATIONS 1994

(SI 1994/1056)

NOTES

Made: 12 April 1994.

Commencement: 1 May 1994 (regs 1–3, 6–20, Schs 1–5); 10 August 1994 (regs 4, 5).

Authority: European Communities Act 1972, s 2(2); Control of Pollution Act 1974, ss 30(4), 104(1); Control of Pollution (Amendment) Act 1989, ss 1(3)(a), 2, 8(2), 9(1); Environmental Protection Act 1990, ss 29(10), 33(3), 35(6), 36(1), 39(3), 40(3), 43(8), 45(3), 50(3), 54(14), 64(1), (4), (8), 74(6), 75(8), 156 (s 50 of the 1990 Act is repealed by the Environment Act 1995, s 120(1), (3), Sch 22, para 78, Sch 24, subject to savings: see the Environment Act 1995 (Commencement No 5) Order 1996, SI 1996/186; s 54 of the 1990 Act is repealed by s 120(3) of, and Sch 24 to, the 1995 Act, as from a day to be appointed).

1 Citation, commencement, interpretation and extent

(1)   These Regulations may be cited as the Waste Management Licensing Regulations 1994 and, except for regulations 4 and 5, shall come into force on 1st May 1994.

(2)   Regulations 4 and 5 shall come into force on 10th August 1994.

(3)   In these Regulations, unless the context otherwise requires—
"the 1990 Act" means the Environmental Protection Act 1990;
"the 1991 Regulations" means the Environmental Protection (Prescribed Processes and Substances) Regulations 1991;
"construction work" includes the repair, alteration or improvement of existing works;
"the Directive" means Council Directive 75/442/EEC on waste as amended by Council Directives 91/156/EEC and 91/692/EEC;
"Directive waste" means any substance or object in the categories set out in Part II of Schedule 4 which the producer or the person in possession of it discards or intends or is required to discard but with the exception of anything excluded from the scope of the Directive by Article 2 of the Directive, "discard" has the same meaning as in the Directive, and "producer" means anyone whose activities produce Directive waste or who carries out preprocessing, mixing or other operations resulting in a change in its nature or composition;
"disposal" means any of the operations listed in Part III of Schedule 4, and any reference to waste being disposed of is a reference to its being submitted to any of those operations;
"disposal licence" and "disposal authority" have the meaning given by sections 3(1) and 30(2) to (2D) respectively of the Control of Pollution Act 1974;
"enforcing authority" and "local enforcing authority" have the meaning given by section 1(7) and (8) of the 1990 Act;
"exempt activity" means any of the activities set out in Schedule 3;
"inland waters"—
    (a) in England and Wales, has the meaning given by section 221(1) of the Water Resources Act 1991;
    (b) in Scotland, has the meaning given by section 30A of the Control of Pollution Act 1974 except that it includes any loch or pond whether or not it discharges into a river or watercourse;
"operational land" has the meaning given by sections 263 and 264 of the Town and Country Planning Act 1990 or, in Scotland, sections 211 and 212 of the Town and Country Planning (Scotland) Act 1972;
"recovery" means any of the operations listed in Part IV of Schedule 4, and any reference to waste being recovered is a reference to its being submitted to any of those operations;
"scrap metal" has the meaning given by section 9(2) of the Scrap Metal Dealers Act 1964;
["special waste" has the meaning given by regulation 2 of the Special Waste Regulations 1996, except that it does not include radioactive waste within the meaning of the Radioactive Substances Act 1993;]
"waste" means Directive waste;
"waste management licence" has the meaning given by section 35(1) of the 1990 Act, and "site licence" has the meaning given by section 35(12) of the 1990 Act;
"waste oil" means any mineral-based lubricating or industrial oil which has become unfit for the use for which it was originally intended and, in particular, used combustion engine oil, gearbox oil, mineral lubricating oil, oil for turbines and hydraulic oil;

"waste regulation authority", "waste disposal authority" and "waste collection authority" have the meaning given by section 30 of the 1990 Act; and "work" includes preparatory work.

(4) Any reference in these Regulations to carrying on business as a scrap metal dealer has the meaning given by section 9(1) of the Scrap Metal Dealers Act 1964, and any reference, in relation to Scotland, to carrying on business as a metal dealer has the meaning given by section 37(2) of the Civic Government (Scotland) Act 1982.

(5) Regulations 13, 14 and 15, and Schedule 4, shall apply in relation to land in the area of a waste disposal authority in Scotland which is occupied by the authority as if—
    (a) references to a waste management licence were references to a resolution under section 54 of the 1990 Act;
    (b) references to an application being made for a waste management licence were references to consideration being given to passing such a resolution;
    (c) references to granting or issuing a waste management licence were references to passing, and references to rejecting an application were references to not passing, such a resolution;
    (d) references to the terms or conditions of a waste management licence were references to the terms or conditions specified in such a resolution; and
    (e) references to varying or revoking a waste management licence under section 37 or 38 of the 1990 Act were references to varying or rescinding such a resolution under section 54(8) of that Act.

(6) These Regulations do not extend to Northern Ireland.

[(7) The provisions of section 160 of the 1990 Act shall apply to—
    (a) the service or giving of any notice required or authorised by these Regulations to be served on or given to a person; or
    (b) the sending or giving of any document required or authorised by these Regulations to be sent or given to a person,

as if the service or giving of any such notice or, as the case may be, the sending or giving of any such document, was required or authorised by or under that Act.]

[937]

NOTES

Commencement: 1 April 1995 (para (7)); 1 May 1994 (remainder).

Para (3): definition "special waste" substituted by the Special Waste Regulations 1996, SI 1996/972, reg 25, Sch 3.

Para (7): added by the Waste Management Licensing (Amendment etc) Regulations 1995, SI 1995/288, reg 3(2).

---

2 Application for a waste management licence or for the surrender or transfer of a waste management licence

(1) An application for a waste management licence shall be made in writing.

(2) An application for the surrender of a site licence shall be made in writing and shall, subject to paragraphs (3) and (4) below, include the information and be accompanied by the evidence prescribed by Schedule 1.

(3) Nothing in paragraph (2) above shall require the information prescribed by paragraphs 3 to 6 of Schedule 1 to be provided to the waste regulation authority if the information has previously been provided by the applicant to the authority or a predecessor of the authority in connection with a waste management licence, or a disposal licence under section 5 of the Control of Pollution Act 1974, in respect of the site in question or any part of it.

(4) Insofar as the information prescribed by paragraphs 4, 5(a) and 6(a) of Schedule 1 relates to activities carried on, or works carried out, at the site at a time prior to the applicant's first involvement with the site, paragraph (2) above only requires that information to be included in the application so far as it is known to

either the applicant or, where the applicant is a partnership or body corporate, to any of the partners or, as the case may be, to any director, manager, secretary or other similar officer of the body corporate.

(5)   An application for the transfer of a waste management licence shall be made in writing and shall include the information prescribed by Schedule 2.

[938]

3 Relevant offences

An offence is relevant for the purposes of section 74(3)(a) of the 1990 Act if it is an offence under any of the following enactments—

    (a) section 22 of the Public Health (Scotland) Act 1897;

    (b) section 95(1) of the Public Health Act 1936;

    (c) section 3, 5(6), 16(4), 18(2), 31(1), 32(1), 34(5), 78, 92(6) or 93(3) of the Control of Pollution Act 1974;

    (d) section 2 of the Refuse Disposal (Amenity) Act 1978;

    (e) the Control of Pollution (Special Waste) Regulations 1980;

    (f) section 9(1) of the Food and Environment Protection Act 1985;

    (g) the Transfrontier Shipment of Hazardous Waste Regulations 1988;

    (h) the Merchant Shipping (Prevention of Pollution by Garbage) Regulations 1988;

    (i) section 1, 5, 6(9) or 7(3) of the Control of Pollution (Amendment) Act 1989;

    (j) section 107, 118(4) or 175(1) of the Water Act 1989;

    (k) section 23(1), 33, 34(6), 44, 47(6), 57(5), 59(5), 63(2), 69(9), 70(4), 71(3) or 80(4) of the 1990 Act;

    (l) section 85, 202 or 206 of the Water Resources Act 1991;

  (m) section 33 of the Clean Air Act 1993;

  [(n) the Transfrontier Shipment of Waste Regulations 1994]

  [(n) the Special Waste Regulations 1996].

[939]

NOTES

    First para (n): added by the Transfrontier Shipment of Waste Regulations 1994, SI 1994/1137, reg 19(3).
    Second para (n): added by the Special Waste Regulations 1996, SI 1996/972, reg 25, Sch 3.

4 Technical competence

(1)   Subject to paragraph (2) and regulation 5 below, a person is technically competent for the purposes of section 74(3)(b) of the 1990 Act in relation to a facility of a type listed in Table 1 below if, and only if, he is the holder of one of the certificates awarded by the Waste Management Industry Training and Advisory Board specified in that Table as being a relevant certificate of technical competence for that type of facility.

[Table 1

Type of facility	*Relevant certificate of technical competence*
A landfill site which receives special waste.	Managing landfill operations: special waste (level 4).
A landfill site which receives biodegradable waste or which for some other reason requires substantial engineering works to protect the environment but which in either case does not receive special waste.	1 Managing landfill operations: biodegradable waste (level 4); or 2 Managing landfill operations: special waste (level 4).
Any other type of landfill site with a total capacity exceeding 50,000 cubic metres.	1 Landfill operations: inert waste (level 3); or 2 Managing landfill operations: biodegradable waste (level 4); or 3 Managing landfill operations: special waste (level 4).

Type of facility	Relevant certificate of technical competence
A site on which waste is burned in an incinerator designed to incinerate waste at a rate of more than 50 kilograms per hour but less than 1 tonne per hour.	Managing incinerator operations: special waste (level 4).
A waste treatment plant where clinical or special waste is subjected to a chemical or physical process.	1 Managing treatment operations: clinical or special waste (level 4); or 2 *Managing treatment operations: special waste (level 4) (see note).*
A waste treatment plant where biodegradable waste, but no clinical or special waste, is subjected to a chemical or physical process.	1 Managing treatment operations: biodegradable waste (level 4); or 2 Managing treatment operations: clinical or special waste (level 4); or 3 *Managing treatment operations: special waste (level 4) (see note).*
A waste treatment plant where waste, none of which is bio-degradable, clinical or special waste, is subjected to a chemical or physical process.	1 Treatment operations: inert waste (level 3); or 2 Managing treatment operations: biodegradable waste (level 4); or 3 Managing treatment operations: clinical or special waste (level 4); or 4 *Managing treatment operations: special waste (level 4) (see note).*
A transfer station where— (a) clinical or special waste is dealt with; and (b) the total quantity of waste at the station at any time exceeds 5 cubic metres.	1 Managing transfer operations: clinical or special waste (level 4); or 2 *Managing transfer operations: special waste (level 4) (see note).*
A transfer station where— (a) biodegradable waste, but no clinical or special waste, is dealt with; and (b) the total quantity of waste at the station at any time exceeds 5 cubic metres.	1 Managing transfer operations: biodegradable waste (level 4); or 2 Managing transfer operations: clinical or special waste (level 4); or 3 *Managing transfer operations: special waste (level 4) (see note).*
Any other type of waste transfer station where the total quantity of waste at the station at any time exceeds 50 cubic metres.	1 Transfer operations: inert waste (level 3); or 2 Managing transfer operations: biodegradable waste (level 4); or 3 Managing transfer operations: clinical or special waste (level 4); or 4 *Managing transfer operations: special waste (level 4) (see note).*
A civic amenity site.	1 Civic amenity site operations (level 3); or 2 Managing transfer operations: biodegradable waste (level 4); or 3 Managing transfer operations: clinical or special waste (level 4); or 4 *Managing transfer operations: special waste (level 4) (see note).*

Note: The certificates shown in italics will cease to be awarded on 9th October 1997.]

(2)   Paragraph (1) above does not apply in relation to a facility which is used exclusively for the purposes of—

    (a) carrying on business as a scrap metal dealer or, in Scotland, as a metal dealer; or

    (b) dismantling motor vehicles.

(3)   In this regulation—

"civic amenity site" means a place provided under section 1 of the Refuse Disposal (Amenity) Act 1978 or by virtue of section 51(1)(b) of the 1990 Act;

"clinical waste" has the meaning given by regulation 1(2) of the Controlled Waste Regulations 1992; and

["landfill site" does not include a site used only for the burial of dead domestic pets;]

"transfer station" means a facility where waste is unloaded in order to permit its preparation for further transport for treatment, keeping or disposal elsewhere.

[940]

NOTES

Para (1): Table 1 substituted by the Waste Management Licensing (Amendment) Regulations 1997, SI 1997/2203, reg 2.

Para (3): definition "landfill site" inserted by the Waste Management Regulations 1996, SI 1996/634, reg 2(2)(b).

By virtue of the Waste Management Licensing (Amendment etc) Regulations 1995, SI 1995/288, reg 4, transitional provisions relating to technical competence have effect. Reg 4 provides as follows—

"(1)   Where before 10th July 1995 a person has applied to the Waste Management Industry Training and Advisory Board for a certificate of technical competence and at any time in the 23 months ending on that date he acted as the manager of a facility of a type listed in Table 1 in the Principal Regulations for which the certificate is a relevant certificate, then, until 10th August 1999, regulation 4 of the Principal Regulations shall not apply to him in relation to either—

(a)   any facility of that type; or

(b)   a facility of any other type if—

(i)   the certificate is a relevant certificate for that other type of facility; and

(ii)   the entry for that other type of facility appears, in Table 1 in the Principal Regulations, after the entry in that Table for the type of facility in respect of which he acted as the manager,

and he shall be treated as technically competent for the purposes of section 74(3)(b) of the 1990 Act in relation to any such facility.

(2)   A person shall be treated as the manager of a facility for the purposes of paragraph (1) above if at the relevant time he was the manager of activities which were carried on at that facility and either—

(a)   those activities involved the recovery or disposal of waste as or as part of a process designated for central control under section 2(4) of the 1990 Act and were authorised by an authorisation granted under Part I of that Act; or

(b)   those activities involved the disposal of waste as or as part of a process designated for local control under section 2(4) of the 1990 Act and falling within paragraph (a) of Part B of Section 5.1 (incineration) of Schedule 1 to the 1991 Regulations and were authorised by an authorisation granted under Part I of that Act.

(3)   Where at any time in the 15 months ending on 31st July 1995 a person has acted as the manager of a facility the operation of which at that time was not in breach of section 33(1)(a) or (b) of the 1990 Act solely by virtue of the exemption provided by regulation 17 of, and paragraph 43 of Schedule 3 to, the Principal Regulations, then, until the date specified in paragraph (4) below, regulation 4 of the Principal Regulations shall not apply to him in relation to that facility and he shall be treated as technically competent for the purposes of section 74(3)(b) of the 1990 Act in relation to that facility.

(4)   The date referred to in paragraph (3) above as being specified in this paragraph is 31st July 1995 except in the following cases—

(a)   where the facility is of a type listed in Table 1 in the Principal Regulations, and the person has applied on or before 31st July 1995 to the Waste Management Industry Training and Advisory Board for a certificate of technical competence which is a relevant certificate, then the specified date is 10th August 1999;

(b)   where the facility is not of a type listed in Table 1 in the Principal Regulations, and an application is made on or before 31st July 1995 for a waste management licence which, if granted, would authorise the operation of the facility, then the specified date is the day after the day upon which the licence is granted or, if the application is (or is deemed to be) rejected, the day after—

(i)   the day on which the period for appealing expires without any appeal having been made; or

(ii)   the day on which any appeal is withdrawn or finally determined.

[(5)   In their application in relation to the manager of a facility at which activities falling within paragraph 8 or 9 of Part III of Schedule 4 to the Principal Regulations are carried on, paragraphs (3) and (4) above shall have effect as if—

(a)   in paragraph (3), for the words "the 15 months ending on 31st July 1995" there were substituted the words ["the 29 months ending on 30th September 1996"];

(b)   in paragraph (4), for the words "31st July 1995" in each place where they occur there were substituted the words ["30th September 1996"].]"

(SI 1995/288, reg 4(5) added by SI 1995/1950, reg 3; words in square brackets therein substituted by SI 1996/634, reg 3.)

5 Technical competence—transitional provisions

(1) [Subject to paragraph (4),] where before 10th August 1994 a person has applied to the Waste Management Industry Training and Advisory Board for a certificate of technical competence and at any time in the 12 months ending on that date he acted as the manager of a facility of a type listed in Table 1 above for which the certificate is a relevant certificate, then, until 10th August 1999, regulation 4 shall not apply to him in relation to either—

(a) any facility of that type; or

(b) a facility of any other type if—

(i) the certificate is a relevant certificate for that other type of facility; and

(ii) the entry for that other type of facility appears, in Table 1 above, after the entry in that Table for the type of facility in respect of which he acted as the manager,

and he shall be treated as technically competent for the purposes of section 74(3)(b) of the 1990 Act in relation to any such facility.

(2) [Subject to paragraph (4),] where a person is 55 or over on 10th August 1994 and in the 10 years ending on that date he has had at least 5 years experience as the manager of a facility of a type listed in Table 1 above, then, until 10th August 2004, regulation 4 shall not apply to him in relation to either—

(a) any facility of that type; or

(b) a facility of any other type if each certificate which is a relevant certificate for the type of facility in relation to which he has had such experience as manager is also a relevant certificate for that other type of facility,

and he shall be treated as technically competent for the purposes of section 74(3)(b) of the 1990 Act in relation to any such facility.

(3) A person shall be treated as the manager of a facility for the purposes of paragraph (1) or (2) above if at the relevant time he was the manager of activities which were carried on at that facility and which were authorised by a disposal licence under section 5 of the Control of Pollution Act 1974, a resolution under section 11 of that Act or under section 54 of the 1990 Act, or a waste management licence.

[(4) Subject to paragraphs (6) and (7), in their application in relation to a person mentioned in paragraph (5), paragraphs (1) and (2) shall apply as if the following dates were substituted for the dates in those paragraphs which are specified—

(a) in paragraph (1)

(i) for "10th August 1994", "1st October 1996";

(ii) for "10th August 1999", "1st October 2001"; and

(b) in paragraph (2),

(i) for "10th August 1994", "1st October 1996";

(ii) for "10th August 2004", "1st October 2006".

(5) The person mentioned in paragraph (4) is the manager of a facility at which activities were authorised by a resolution under section 11 of the Control of Pollution Act 1974.

(6) Paragraph (4) does not apply to a person who is to be treated as technically competent by virtue of other provisions than those in that paragraph.

(7) Paragraph (4) does not apply in Scotland.]

[941]

NOTES

Commencement: 1 April 1996 (paras (4)–(7)); 10 August 1994 (remainder).

Paras (1), (2): words in square brackets inserted, in relation to England and Wales, by the Waste Management Regulations 1996, SI 1996/634, reg 2(3)(a), (b).

Paras (4)–(7): added, in relation to England and Wales, by SI 1996/634, reg 2(3)(c).

6 Notice of appeal

(1) A person who wishes to appeal to the Secretary of State under section 43 or 66(5) of the 1990 Act (appeals to the Secretary of State from decisions with respect to waste management licences or from determinations that information is not commercially confidential) shall do so by notice in writing.

(2) The notice shall be accompanied by—
  (a) a statement of the grounds of appeal;
  (b) where the appeal relates to an application for a waste management licence or for the modification, surrender or transfer of a waste management licence, a copy of the appellant's application and any supporting documents;
  (c) where the appeal relates to a determination under section 66(2) or (4) of the 1990 Act that information is not commercially confidential, the information in question;
  (d) where the appeal relates to an existing waste management licence (including a waste management licence which has been suspended or revoked), a copy of that waste management licence;
  (e) a copy of any correspondence relevant to the appeal;
  (f) a copy of any other document relevant to the appeal including, in particular, any relevant consent, determination, notice, planning permission, established use certificate or certificate of lawful use or development; and
  (g) a statement indicating whether the appellant wishes the appeal to be in the form of a hearing or to be determined on the basis of written representations.

(3) The appellant shall serve a copy of his notice of appeal on the waste regulation authority together with copies of the documents mentioned in paragraph (2) above.

(4) If the appellant wishes to withdraw an appeal, he shall do so by notifying the Secretary of State in writing and shall send a copy of that notification to the waste regulation authority.

[942]

7 Time limit for making an appeal

(1) Subject to paragraph (2) below, notice of appeal shall be given—
  (a) in the case of an appeal under section 43 of the 1990 Act, before the expiry of the period of 6 months beginning with—
    (i) the date of the decision which is the subject of the appeal; or
    (ii) the date on which the waste regulation authority is deemed by section 36(9), 37(6), 39(10) or 40(6) of the 1990 Act to have rejected the application;
  (b) in the case of an appeal under section 66(5) of the 1990 Act, before the expiry of the period of 21 days beginning with the date on which the determination which is the subject of the appeal is notified to the person concerned.

(2) The Secretary of State may in relation to an appeal under section 43 of the 1990 Act at any time allow notice of appeal to be given after the expiry of the period mentioned in paragraph (1)(a) above.

[943]

8 Reports of hearings

The person hearing an appeal under section 43(2)(c) of the 1990 Act shall, unless he has been appointed to determine the appeal under [section 114(1)(a) of the Environment Act 1995], make a written report to the Secretary of State which shall include his conclusions and recommendations or his reasons for not making any recommendations.

[944]

NOTES
  Words in square brackets substituted by the Environment Act (Consequential Amendments) Regulations 1996, SI 1996/593, reg 3, Sch 2, para 10(2).

9 Notification of determination

(1)   The Secretary of State or other person determining an appeal shall notify the appellant in writing of his decision and of his reasons.

(2)   If the Secretary of State determines an appeal after a hearing under section 43(2)(c) of the 1990 Act, he shall provide the appellant with a copy of any report made to him under regulation 8.

(3)   The Secretary of State or other person determining an appeal shall, at the same time as notifying the appellant of his decision, send the waste regulation authority a copy of any document sent to the appellant under this regulation.

[945]

10 Particulars to be entered in public registers

(1)   Subject to sections 65 and 66 of the 1990 Act and regulation 11, a register maintained by a waste regulation authority under section 64(1) of the 1990 Act shall contain full particulars of—
  (a) current or recently current waste management licences ("licences") granted by the authority and any associated working plans;
  (b) current or recently current applications to the authority for licences, or for the transfer or modification of licences, including details of—
      (i) documents submitted by applicants containing supporting information;
      (ii) written representations considered by the authority under section 36(4)(b), (6)(b) or (7)(b) or 37(5) of the 1990 Act;
      (iii) decisions of the Secretary of State under section 36(5), or, in Scotland, section 36(6), of the 1990 Act;
      (iv) notices by the authority rejecting applications;
      (v) emergencies resulting in the postponement of references under section 37(5)(a) of the 1990 Act;
  (c) notices issued by the authority under section 37 of the 1990 Act effecting the modification of licences;
  (d) notices issued by the authority under section 38 of the 1990 Act effecting the revocation or suspension of licences or imposing requirements on the holders of licences;
  (e) notices of appeal under section 43 of the 1990 Act relating to decisions of the authority and other documents relating to such appeals served on or sent to the authority under regulation 6(3) or (4) or 9(3);
  (f) convictions of holders of licences granted by the authority for any offence under Part II of the 1990 Act (whether or not in relation to a licence) including the name of the offender, the date of conviction, the penalty imposed and the name of the Court;
  (g) reports produced by the authority in discharge of any functions under section 42 of the 1990 Act, including details of—
      (i) any correspondence with the [Environment Agency] or river purification authority as a result of section 42(2) of the 1990 Act;
      (ii) remedial or preventive action taken by the authority under section 42(3) of the 1990 Act;
      (iii) notices issued by the authority under section 42(5) of the 1990 Act;
  (h) any monitoring information relating to the carrying on of any activity under a licence granted by the authority which was obtained by the authority as a result of its own monitoring or was furnished to the authority in writing by virtue of any condition of the licence or section 71(2) of the 1990 Act;
  (i) directions given by the Secretary of State to the authority under section 35(7), 37(3), 38(7), 42(8), 50(9), 54(11) or (15), 58 or 66(7) of the 1990 Act;
  (j) any summary prepared by the authority of the amount of special waste produced or disposed of in their area;

(k) registers and records provided to the authority under regulation 13(5) or 14(1) of the Control of Pollution (Special Waste) Regulations 1980 [or regulation 15(5) or 16(1) of the Special Waste Regulations 1996];

(l) applications to the authority under section 39 of the 1990 Act for the surrender of licences, including details of—

    (i) documents submitted by applicants containing supporting information and evidence;

    (ii) information and evidence obtained under section 39(4) of the 1990 Act;

    (iii) written representations considered by the authority under section 39(7)(b) or (8)(b) of the 1990 Act;

    (iv) decisions by the Secretary of State under section 39(7) or (8) of the 1990 Act; and

    (v) notices of determination and certificates of completion issued under section 39(9) of the 1990 Act;

(m) written reports under section 70(3) of the 1990 Act by inspectors appointed by the authority [or written reports under section 109(2) of the Environment Act 1995 by persons authorised by the authority under section 108(1) or (2) of that Act where the articles or substances seized and rendered harmless are waste];

(n) in Scotland, resolutions made by the authority under section 54 of the 1990 Act, including details of—

    (i) proposals made in relation to land in the area of the authority by a waste disposal authority under section 54(4) of the 1990 Act;

    (ii) statements made and written representations considered by the authority under section 54(4) of the 1990 Act;

    (iii) requests made to, and disagreements with, the authority which are referred to the Secretary of State under section 54(7) of the 1990 Act and his decisions on such references;

    (iv) emergencies resulting in the postponement of references under section 54(4) of the 1990 Act.

(2) The register shall also contain the following—

(a) where an inspector appointed by the authority exercises any power under section 69(3) of the 1990 Act, a record showing when the power was exercised and indicating what information was obtained, and what action was taken, on that occasion;

[(aa) where a person authorised by the authority exercises any power under section 108(4) of the Environment Act 1995 in connection with the authority's functions under Part II of the Environmental Protection Act 1990, a record showing when the power was exercised and indicating what information was obtained, and what action was taken, on that occasion;]

(b) where any information is excluded from the register by virtue of section 66 of the 1990 Act and the information shows whether or not there is compliance with any condition of a waste management licence, a statement based on that information indicating whether or not there is compliance with that condition.

(3) A register maintained under section 64(4) of the 1990 Act by a waste collection authority in England [or Wales] . . . shall contain full particulars of the following information contained in any register maintained under section 64(1) of the 1990 Act, to the extent that it relates to the treatment, keeping or disposal of controlled waste in the area of the authority—

(a) current or recently current waste management licences;

(b) notices issued under section 37 of the 1990 Act effecting the modification of waste management licences;

(c) notices issued under section 38 of the 1990 Act effecting the revocation or suspension of waste management licences;

(d) certificates of completion issued under section 39(9) of the 1990 Act.

(4)   For the purposes of this regulation, waste management licences are "recently" current for the period of twelve months after they cease to be in force, and applications for waste management licences, or for the transfer or modification of such licences, are "recently" current if they relate to a waste management licence which is current or recently current or, in the case of an application which is rejected, for the period of twelve months beginning with the date on which the waste regulation authority gives notice of rejection or, as the case may be, on which the application is deemed by section 36(9), 37(6) or 40(6) of the 1990 Act to have been rejected.

[946]

NOTES

Para (1): words in square brackets substituted by the Environment Act 1995, s 120, Sch 22, para 233(1); words in square brackets in sub-para (k) inserted by the Special Waste Regulations 1996, SI 1996/972, reg 25, Sch 3; words in square brackets in sub-para (m) inserted by the Environment Act (Consequential Amendments) Regulations 1996, SI 1996/593, reg 3, Sch 2, para 10(3)(a).

Para (2): sub-para (aa) inserted by SI 1996/593, reg 3, Sch 2, para 10(3)(b).

Para (3): words in square brackets inserted, and words omitted revoked, by SI 1996/593, reg 3, Sch 2, para 10(3)(c).

11 Information to be excluded or removed from a register

(1)   Nothing in regulation 10(1)(g) or (m) or (2) shall require a register maintained by a waste regulation authority under section 64(1) of the 1990 Act to contain information relating to, or to anything which is the subject-matter of, any criminal proceedings (including prospective proceedings) at any time before those proceedings are finally disposed of.

(2)   Nothing in regulation 10 shall require a register maintained by a waste regulation authority or waste collection authority under section 64 of the 1990 Act to contain—

(a)   any such monitoring information as is mentioned in regulation 10(1)(h) after 4 years have elapsed from that information being entered in the register; or

(b)   any information which has been superseded by later information after 4 years have elapsed from that later information being entered in the register.

[946A]

[12 Mobile plant

(1)   Plant of the following descriptions, if it is designed to move or be moved by any means from place to place with a view to being used at each such place or, if not so designed, is readily capable of so moving or being so moved, but no other plant, shall be treated as being mobile plant for the purposes of Part II of the 1990 Act—

(a)   an incinerator which is an exempt incinerator for the purposes of Section 5.1 of Schedule 1 to the 1991 Regulations;

(b)   plant for—

(i)   the recovery, by filtration or heat treatment, of waste oil from electrical equipment; or

(ii)   the destruction by dechlorination of waste polychlorinated biphenyls or terphenyls (PCBs or PCTs);

(c)   plant for the vitrification of waste;

(d)   plant for the treatment by microwave of clinical waste.

[(e)   plant for the treatment of waste soil.]

(2)   For the purposes of paragraph (1)(d) above, "clinical waste" has the meaning given by regulation 1(2) of the Controlled Waste Regulations 1992.]

[947]

NOTES

Commencement: 1 April 1995.

Substituted by the Waste Management Licensing (Amendment etc) Regulations 1995, SI 1995/288, reg 3(3).

Para (1): sub-para (e) inserted by the Waste Management Regulations 1996, SI 1996/634, reg 2.

13 Health at work

No conditions shall be imposed in any waste management licence for the purpose only of securing the health of persons at work (within the meaning of Part I of the Health and Safety at Work etc Act 1974).

[948]

14 Waste oils

(1)   Where a waste management licence or disposal licence authorises the regeneration of waste oil, it shall include conditions which ensure that base oils derived from regeneration do not constitute a toxic and dangerous waste and do not contain PCBs or PCTs at all or do not contain them in concentrations beyond a specified maximum limit which in no case is to exceed 50 parts per million.

(2)   Where a waste management licence or disposal licence authorises the keeping of waste oil, it shall include conditions which ensure that it is not mixed with toxic and dangerous waste or PCBs or PCTs.

(3)   In this regulation—
"PCBs or PCTs" means polychlorinated biphenyls, polychlorinated terphenyls and mixtures containing one or both of such substances; and
"toxic and dangerous waste" has the meaning given by Article 1(b) of Council Directive 78/319/EEC.

[949]

15 Groundwater

(1)   Where a waste regulation authority proposes to issue a waste management licence authorising—
  (a) any disposal or tipping for the purpose of disposal of a substance in list I which might lead to an indirect discharge into groundwater of such a substance;
  (b) any disposal or tipping for the purpose of disposal of a substance in list II which might lead to an indirect discharge into groundwater of such a substance;
  (c) a direct discharge into groundwater of a substance in list I; or
  (d) a direct discharge into groundwater of a substance in list II,
the authority shall ensure that the proposed activities are subjected to prior investigation.

(2)   The prior investigation referred to in paragraph (1) above shall include examination of the hydrogeological conditions of the area concerned, the possible purifying powers of the soil and sub-soil and the risk of pollution and alteration of the quality of the groundwater from the discharge and shall establish whether the discharge of substances into groundwater is a satisfactory solution from the point of view of the environment.

(3)   A waste management licence shall not be issued in any case within paragraph (1) above until the waste regulation authority has checked that the groundwater, and in particular its quality, will undergo the requisite surveillance.

(4)   In a case within paragraph (1)(a) or (c) above—
  (a) where the waste regulation authority is satisfied, in the light of the investigation, that the groundwater which may be affected by a direct or indirect discharge of a substance in list I is permanently unsuitable for other uses, especially domestic and agricultural, the waste management licence may only be issued if the authority is also satisfied that—
    (i) the presence of that substance once discharged into groundwater will not impede exploitation of ground resources; and

(ii) all technical precautions will be taken to ensure that no substance in list I can reach other aquatic systems or harm other ecosystems; and

(b) where the waste regulation authority is not satisfied, in the light of the investigation, that the groundwater which may be affected by such a discharge is permanently unsuitable for other uses, especially domestic and agricultural, a waste management licence may only be issued if it is made subject to such conditions as the authority, in the light of the investigations, is satisfied will ensure the observance of all technical precautions necessary to prevent any discharges into groundwater of substances in list I.

(5)   In a case within paragraph (1)(b) or (d) above, if a waste management licence is issued, it shall be issued subject to such conditions as the waste regulation authority, in the light of the investigation, is satisfied will ensure the observance of all technical precautions for preventing groundwater pollution by substances in list II.

(6)   Where a waste management licence is granted in any case within paragraph (1)(a) or (b) above, the licence shall be granted on such terms and subject to such conditions as specify—

(a) the place where any disposal or tipping which might lead to a discharge into groundwater of any substances in list I or II is to be done;

(b) the methods of disposal or tipping which may be used;

(c) the essential precautions which must be taken, paying particular attention to the nature and concentration of the substances present in the matter to be disposed of or tipped, the characteristics of the receiving environment and the proximity of the water catchment areas, in particular those for drinking, thermal and mineral water;

(d) the maximum quantity permissible, during one or more specified periods of time, of matter containing substances in list I or II and, where possible, of those substances themselves, to be disposed of or tipped and the appropriate requirements as to the concentration of those substances;

(e) the technical precautions required by paragraph (4)(b) or (5) above;

(f) if necessary, the measures for monitoring the groundwater, and in particular its quality.

(7)   Where a waste management licence is granted in any case within paragraph (1)(c) or (d) above, the licence shall be granted on such terms and subject to such conditions as specify—

(a) the place where any substances in list I or II are to be discharged into groundwater;

(b) the method of discharge which may be used;

(c) the essential precautions which must be taken, paying particular attention to the nature and concentration of the substances present in the effluents, the characteristics of the receiving environment and the proximity of the water catchment areas, in particular those for drinking, thermal and mineral water;

(d) the maximum quantity of a substance in list I or II permissible in an effluent during one or more specified periods of time and the appropriate requirements as to the concentration of those substances;

(e) the arrangements enabling effluents discharged into groundwater to be monitored;

(f) if necessary, the measures for monitoring the groundwater, and in particular its quality.

(8)   Any authorisation granted by a waste management licence for an activity within paragraph (1) above shall be granted for a limited period only.

(9)   Any authorisation granted by a waste management licence for an activity within paragraph (1) above shall be reviewed at least every 4 years.

(10) Waste regulation authorities shall review all waste management licences current on 1st May 1994 which authorise any activity within paragraph (1) above and shall, so far as may be necessary to give effect to Council Directive 80/68/EEC, exercise their powers under sections 37 and 38 of the 1990 Act (variation and revocation etc of waste management licences) in relation to any such authorisation.

(11) The foregoing provisions of this regulation apply, with any necessary modifications, to the granting or review by disposal authorities of disposal licences under Part I of the Control of Pollution Act 1974 as they apply to the granting or review by waste regulation authorities of waste management licences.

(12) Expressions used both in this regulation and in Council Directive 80/68/EEC have for the purposes of this regulation the same meaning as in that Directive.

[950]

16 Exclusion of activities under other control regimes from waste management licensing

(1) Subject to paragraph (2) below, section 33(1)(a), (b) and (c) of the 1990 Act shall not apply in relation to the carrying on of any of the following activities—

(a) the [deposit in or on land,] recovery or disposal of waste under an authorisation granted under Part I of the 1990 Act where the activity is or forms part of a process designated for central control under section 2(4) of the 1990 Act;

(b) the disposal of waste under an authorisation granted under Part I of the 1990 Act where the activity is or forms part of a process within paragraph (a) of Part B of Section 5.1 (incineration) of Schedule 1 to the 1991 Regulations insofar as the activity results in releases of substances into the air;

(c) the disposal of liquid waste under a consent under Chapter II of Part III of the Water Resources Act 1991 or under Part II of the Control of Pollution Act 1974; and

(d) the recovery or disposal of waste where the activity is or forms part of an operation which is for the time being either—

(i) the subject of a licence under Part II of the Food and Environment Protection Act 1985; or

(ii) carried on in circumstances where such a licence would be required but for an order under section 7 of that Act.

(2) Paragraph (1)(a) and (b) above does not apply insofar as the activity involves the final disposal of waste by deposit in or on land.

[951]

NOTES

Para (1): words in square brackets in sub-para (a) inserted by the Waste Management Licensing (Amendment etc) Regulations 1995, SI 1995/288, reg 3(4).

---

17 Exemptions from waste management licensing

(1) Subject to the following provisions of this regulation and to any conditions or limitations in Schedule 3, section 33(1)(a) and (b) of the 1990 Act shall not apply in relation to the carrying on of any exempt activity set out in that Schedule.

[(1A) Paragraph (1) above does not apply to the carrying on of an exempt activity falling within paragraph 45(1), (2) or (5) of Schedule 3 where the carrying on of that activity is authorised by a waste management licence granted upon an application made after 31st March 1995 under section 36 of the 1990 Act.]

(2) In the case of an exempt activity set out in paragraph 4, 7, 9, 11, 13, 14, 15, 17, 18, 19, 25, 37, [40, 41 or 45] of Schedule 3, paragraph (1) above only applies if—

(a) the exempt activity is carried on by or with the consent of the occupier of the land where the activity is carried on; or

(b) the person carrying on the exempt activity is otherwise entitled to do so on that land.

(3)   Unless otherwise indicated in Schedule 3, paragraph (1) above does not apply to the carrying on of an exempt activity insofar as it involves special waste.

[(3A) Paragraph (1) does not apply to the carrying on of an exempt activity insofar as it involves the carrying out, by an establishment or undertaking, of their own waste disposal at the place of production if the waste being disposed of is special waste.]

(4)   Paragraph (1) above only applies in relation to an exempt activity involving the disposal or recovery of waste by an establishment or undertaking if the type and quantity of waste submitted to the activity, and the method of disposal or recovery, are consistent with the need to attain the objectives mentioned in paragraph 4(1)(a) of Part I of Schedule 4.

(5)   For the purposes of Schedule 3, a container, lagoon or place is secure in relation to waste kept in it if all reasonable precautions are taken to ensure that the waste cannot escape from it and members of the public are unable to gain access to the waste, and any reference to secure storage means storage in a secure container, lagoon or place.

[952]

NOTES

Commencement: 1 September 1996 (para (3A)); 1 April 1995 (para (1A)); 1 May 1994 (remainder).

Para (1A): inserted by the Waste Management Licensing (Amendment etc) Regulations 1995, SI 1995/288, reg 3(5).

Para (2): words in square brackets substituted by SI 1995/288, reg 3(6).

Para (3A): inserted by the Special Waste Regulations 1996, SI 1996/972, reg 25, Sch 3.

18 Registration in connection with exempt activities

(1)   Subject to [paragraphs (1A), (1B) and (7)] below, it shall be an offence for an establishment or undertaking to carry on, after 31st December 1994, an exempt activity involving the recovery or disposal of waste without being registered with the appropriate registration authority.

[(1A) In the case of an exempt activity falling within paragraph 45(1) or (2) of Schedule 3, paragraph (1) above shall have effect as if "30th September 1995" were substituted for "31st December 1994".

(1B) Paragraph (1) above shall not apply in the case of an exempt activity to which a resolution under section 54 of the 1990 Act relates and which is carried on in accordance with the conditions, specified in the resolution, which relate to it.]

(2)   It shall be the duty of each appropriate registration authority to establish and maintain a register for the purposes of paragraph (1) above of establishments and undertakings carrying on exempt activities involving the recovery or disposal of waste in respect of which it is the appropriate registration authority.

(3)   Subject to paragraph (4) below, the register shall contain the following particulars in relation to each such establishment or undertaking—

(a) the name and address of the establishment or undertaking;

(b) the activity which constitutes the exempt activity; and

(c) the place where the activity is carried on.

(4)   [Subject to paragraphs (4A) and (4B) below,] the appropriate registration authority shall enter the relevant particulars in the register in relation to an

establishment or undertaking if it receives notice of them in writing or otherwise becomes aware of those particulars.

[(4A) Paragraph (4) above shall not apply in the case of an exempt activity falling within paragraph 45(1) or (2) of Schedule 3 and, in such a case, the appropriate registration authority shall enter the relevant particulars in the register in relation to an establishment or undertaking only if—
  (a) it receives notice of them in writing;
  (b) that notice is provided to it by that establishment or undertaking;
  (c) that notice is accompanied by a plan of each place at which any such exempt activity is carried on showing—
    (i) the boundaries of that place;
    (ii) the locations within that place at which the exempt activity is to be carried on;
    (iii) the location and specifications of any such impermeable pavements, drainage systems or hardstandings as are mentioned in paragraph 45(1)(c) or (2)(f) or (g) of Schedule 3; and
    (iv) the location of any such secure containers as are mentioned in paragraph 45(2)(e) of Schedule 3;
    and
  (d) that notice is also accompanied by payment of a fee of [£400] in respect of each place where any such exempt activity is carried on.

(4B) Where any fee payable under paragraph 45(3)(d) of Schedule 3 is not received by the appropriate registration authority within 2 months of the due date for its payment as ascertained in accordance with paragraph 45(4) of Schedule 3—
  (a) in a case where the establishment or undertaking is registered for exempt activities falling within paragraph 45(1) or (2) in respect of only one place, or where it is so registered in respect of more than one place and the fee in respect of each such place is then unpaid, the registration of the establishment or undertaking shall be cancelled and the authority shall remove from its register the relevant entry in respect of the establishment or undertaking;
  (b) in any other case, the registration of the establishment or undertaking in respect of those activities shall be cancelled insofar as it relates to any place in respect of which the fee is then unpaid and the authority shall amend the relevant entry in its register accordingly,

and where the authority removes or amends an entry from or in its register by virtue of this paragraph it shall notify the establishment or undertaking in writing of the removal or amendment.]

(5) For the purposes of paragraph (4) above, the appropriate registration authority shall be taken to be aware of the relevant particulars in relation to an exempt activity mentioned in paragraph (10)(a), (b) or (c) below.

(6) A person guilty of an offence under paragraph (1) above shall be liable on summary conviction to a fine [not exceeding—
  (a) in the case of an exempt activity falling within paragraph 45(1) or (2) of Schedule 3, level 2 on the standard scale; and
  (b) in any other case, £10].

(7) The preceding provisions of this regulation shall not apply in the case of an exempt activity to which paragraph 7(3)(c) of Schedule 3 applies, but the appropriate registration authority shall enter in its register the particulars furnished to it pursuant to that provision.

(8) Each appropriate registration authority shall secure that any register maintained by it under this regulation is open to inspection . . . by members of the public free of charge at all reasonable hours and shall afford to members of the

public reasonable facilities for obtaining, on payment of reasonable charges, copies of entries in the register.

(9)   Registers under this regulation may be kept in any form.

(10)   For the purposes of this regulation, the appropriate registration authority is—
   (a)   in the case of an exempt activity falling within—
      (i)   paragraph 1, 2, 3 or 24 of Schedule 3; or
     (ii)   paragraph 4 of Schedule 3 if it involves the coating or spraying of metal containers as or as part of a process within Part B of Section 6.5 (coating processes and printing) of Schedule 1 to the 1991 Regulations and the process is for the time being the subject of an authorisation granted under Part I of the 1990 Act, or if it involves storage related to that process; or
    (iii)   paragraph 12 of Schedule 3 if it involves the composting of biodegradable waste as or as part of a process within paragraph (a) of Part B of Section 6.9 (treatment or processing of animal or vegetable matter) of Schedule 1 to the 1991 Regulations, the compost is to be used for the purpose of cultivating mushrooms and the process is for the time being the subject of an authorisation granted under Part I of the 1990 Act, or if it involves storage related to that process,
the local enforcing authority responsible for granting the authorisation under Part I of the 1990 Act for the prescribed process involving the exempt activity, or to which the exempt activity relates;
   (b)   in a case falling within paragraph 16 of Schedule 3, the issuing authority responsible for granting the licence under article 7 or 8 of the Diseases of Animals (Waste Food) Order 1973 under which the exempt activity is carried on;
      (i)   where the exempt activity is carried on by virtue of a licence under article 5(2)(c) or 6(2)(d), or an approval under article 8, of the Animal By-Products Order 1992, the Minister;
     (ii)   where the exempt activity is carried on by virtue of a registration under article 9 or 10 of that Order, the appropriate Minister;
    (iii)   where the exempt activity is carried on at a knacker' s yard in respect of which the occupier holds a licence under section 1 of the Slaughterhouses Act 1974 authorising the use of that yard as a knacker's yard or, in Scotland, in respect of which a licence has been granted under section 6 of the Slaughter of Animals (Scotland) Act 1980, the local authority;
and in this sub-paragraph "the Minister" and "the appropriate Minister" have the meaning given by section 86(1) of the Animal Health Act 1981, and "knacker's yard" and "local authority" have the meaning given by section 34 of the Slaughterhouses Act 1974 or, in Scotland, have the meaning given by section 22 of the Slaughter of Animals (Scotland) Act 1980;
   (d)   in any other case, the waste regulation authority for the area in which the exempt activity is carried on.

[953]

NOTES

Commencement: 1 April 1995 (paras (1A), (1B), (4A), (4B)); 1 May 1994 (remainder).

Paras (1), (6): words in square brackets substituted by the Waste Management Licensing (Amendment etc) Regulations 1995, SI 1995/288, reg 3(7), (11).

Paras (1A), (1B), (4B): inserted by SI 1995/288, reg 3(8), (10).

Para (4): words in square brackets inserted by SI 1995/288, reg 3(9).

Para (4A): inserted by SI 1995/288, reg 3(10); sum in square brackets substituted by the Waste Management Regulations 1996, SI 1996/634, reg 2(5).

Para (8): words omitted revoked by the Environment Act (Consequential Amendments) Regulations 1996, SI 1996/593, reg 3, Sch 2, para 10(4).

19 Waste Framework Directive

Schedule 4 (which implements certain provisions of Council Directive 75/442/EEC on waste) shall have effect.

[954]

20 Registration of brokers

(1)   Subject to paragraphs (2) to (4) below, it shall be an offence for an establishment or undertaking after 31st December 1994 to arrange (as dealer or broker) for the disposal or recovery of controlled waste on behalf of another person unless it is a registered broker of controlled waste.

(2)   Paragraph (1) above shall not apply in relation to an arrangement under which an establishment or undertaking will itself carry out the disposal or recovery of the waste and either—

(a)   it is authorised to carry out the disposal or recovery of the waste by a waste management licence, an authorisation under Part I of the 1990 Act, a consent under Chapter II of Part III of the Water Resources Act 1991 or under Part II of the Control of Pollution Act 1974 or a licence under Part II of the Food and Environment Protection Act 1985; or

(b)   the recovery of the waste is covered by an exemption conferred by—

(i)   regulation 17(1) of, and Schedule 3 to, these Regulations; or

(ii)   article 3 of the Deposits in the Sea (Exemptions) Order 1985.

(3)   Paragraph (1) above shall not apply in relation to an arrangement for the disposal or recovery of controlled waste made by a person who is registered as a carrier of controlled waste, or who is registered for the purposes of paragraph 12(1) of Part I of Schedule 4, if as part of the arrangement he transports the waste to or from any place in Great Britain.

(4)   Paragraph (1) above shall not apply to an establishment or undertaking which—

(a)   is a charity;

(b)   is a voluntary organisation within the meaning of section 48(11) of the Local Government Act 1985 or section 83(2D) of the Local Government (Scotland) Act 1973;

(c)   is an authority which is a waste collection authority, waste disposal authority or waste regulation authority; or

(d)   applies before 1st January 1995 in accordance with Schedule 5 for registration as a broker of controlled waste but only whilst its application is pending (and paragraph 1(4) and (5) of Part I of Schedule 5 shall apply for the purpose of determining whether an application is pending).

(5)   A person guilty of an offence under this section shall be liable on summary conviction to a fine not exceeding level 5 on the standard scale.

(6)   Section 157 of the 1990 Act shall apply in relation to an offence under this section as it applies in relation to an offence under that Act.

(7)   Schedule 5 (which makes provision for the registration of brokers of controlled waste) shall have effect.

(8)   Sections 68(3) to (5), 69 and 71(2) and (3) of the 1990 Act (power to appoint inspectors, powers of entry and power to obtain information) shall have effect as if the provisions of this regulation and Schedule 5 were provisions of Part II of that Act.

[955]

21–24 (*Reg 24 amends the Deposits in the Sea (Exemptions) Order 1985, SI 1985/1699, art 3, and adds arts 4, 5, thereto; s 22 amends the Collection and Disposal of Waste Regulations 1988, SI 1988/819, regs 3, 6, 7, and inserts reg 7A therein; reg 23 amends the Controlled Waste (Registration of Carriers and Seizure of Vehicles) Regulations 1991, SI 1991/1624, regs 2, 4 at* **[882]**, **[884]**; *reg 24 amends the Controlled Waste Regulations 1992, SI 1992/588, regs 1, 2, 5–7, Sch 3, paras 8, 11, Sch 4, para 9, and inserts reg 7A therein at* **[917]–[931]**.)

SCHEDULE 1
INFORMATION AND EVIDENCE REQUIRED IN RELATION TO AN APPLICATION FOR THE SURRENDER OF A SITE LICENCE

Regulations 2(2), (3), (4)

1. The full name, address and daytime telephone, fax and telex number (if any) of the holder of the site licence and, where the holder employs an agent in relation to the application, of that agent.

2. The number (if any) of the site licence, and the address or a description of the location of the site.

3. A map or plan—
    (a) showing the location of the site;
    (b) indicating whereabouts on the site the different activities mentioned in paragraph 4 were carried on; and
    (c) indicating relevant National Grid references.

4. A description of the different activities involving the treatment, keeping or disposal of controlled waste which were carried on at the site (whether or not in pursuance of the licence), an indication of when those activities were carried on and an estimate of the total quantities of the different types of waste which were dealt with at the site.

5. Where the site is a landfill or lagoon—
    (a) particulars of all significant engineering works carried out for the purpose of preventing or minimising pollution of the environment or harm to human health as a result of activities carried on at the site, including—
        (i) an indication of when those works were carried out and a copy of all relevant plans or specifications; and
        (ii) details of works of restoration carried out after completion of operations at the site;
    (b) geological, hydrological and hydrogeological information relating to the site and its surrounds, including information about the flows of groundwater;
    (c) monitoring data on the quality of surface water or groundwater which could be affected by the site and on the production of any landfill gas or leachate at the site and information about the physical stability of the site; and
    (d) where special waste has been deposited at the site, a copy of the records and plans relating to the deposits kept under regulation 14 of the Control of Pollution (Special Waste) Regulations 1980;

and any estimate under paragraph 4 of the total quantities of the different types of waste dealt with at the site shall, in particular, differentiate between biodegradable waste, non-biodegradable waste and special waste.

6. Where the site is not a landfill or lagoon—
    (a) details of the contaminants likely to be present at the site having reg~~~ f~~~ ~~~~ and
        (i) the different activities involving the treatment, keep~~~~~ Such numbers, and at waste carried on at the site (whether or ~~~~~ indication of the locations high concentrations; and
        (ii) the nature of the different typ~~~~~ples were taken.
    (b) a report which— ~~~~ ~~ishes the waste regulation authority to take
        (i) records th~

SCHEDULE 2
INFORMATION REQUIRED IN RELATION TO AN APPLICATION FOR THE TRANSFER OF A WASTE MANAGEMENT LICENCE

Regulation 2(5)

1.   The full name, address and daytime telephone, fax and telex number (if any) of the holder of the waste management licence and, where the application is made by an agent of the holder, of the agent.

2.   The number (if any) of the waste management licence and, except in the case of mobile plant, the address or a description of the location of the licensed premises.

3.   In the case of mobile plant, sufficient information to identify the plant.

4.   Where the proposed transferee is an individual, his full name, date of birth, address and daytime telephone, fax and telex number (if any).

5.   Where the proposed transferee is a registered company or other body corporate—
    (a)   its name and, in the case of a registered company, its registered number;
    (b)   the address, telephone, fax and telex number (if any) of its registered or principal office;
    (c)   the full name, position, address and date of birth of each director, manager, secretary or other similar officer of the proposed transferee.

6.   Where the proposed transferee is a partnership—
    (a)   the name of the partnership;
    (b)   its address, telephone, fax and telex number (if any);
    (c)   the full name, address and date of birth of each partner.

7.   If the proposed transferee has a business name different from any name of the transferee mentioned above, the transferee's business name.

8.   Where the proposed transferee has appointed an agent to deal with the transfer, the agent's full name, address and daytime telephone, fax and telex number (if any).

9.   Details of any conviction of the proposed transferee or of another relevant person for any offence which is relevant for the purposes of section 74(3)(a) of the 1990 Act, including the date of conviction, the penalty imposed and the name of the Court.

10. The full name of the person who is to manage the activities which are authorised by the waste management licence and information to establish that he is technically competent for the purposes of section 74(3)(b) of the 1990 Act, including—
    (a)   details of any relevant certificate of technical competence (within the meaning of regulation 4) he holds; or
    (b)   in a case where the transferee relies on regulation 5(1) or (2), sufficient information to establish that that provision applies.

11. Details of the financial provision which the proposed transferee has made or proposes to make to discharge the obligations arising from the waste management licence.

12. Any other information which the applicant wishes the waste regulation authority to take into account.

[957]

SCHEDULE 3
ACTIVITIES EXEMPT FROM WASTE MANAGEMENT LICENSING

Regulations 1(3), 17

1.—(1) The ... as part of a p... Schedule 1 to the ... does not exceed 600,... ...thorisation granted under Part I of the 1990 Act, of waste glass ... of Section 3.5 (glass manufacture and production) of

(2)   The storage, at the ... intended to be so used. ...tal quantity of waste glass so used in that process ...welve months.

2.—(1) The operation, under an aut... metal furnace with a designed holding c... ...ed on, of any such waste which is

...90 Act, of a scrap ...hat it is or

forms part of a process within paragraph (a), (b) or (d) of Part B of Section 2.1 (iron and steel), or paragraph (a), (b) or (e) of Part B of Section 2.2 (non-ferrous metals), of Schedule 1 to the 1991 Regulations.

(2) The loading or unloading of such a furnace in connection with its operation in a manner covered by the exemption conferred by sub-paragraph (1) above.

(3) The storage, at the place where such a furnace is located (but not in cases where that place is used for carrying on business as a scrap metal dealer or, in Scotland, as a metal dealer), of scrap metal intended to be submitted to an operation covered by the exemption conferred by sub-paragraph (1) above.

3.   The carrying on of any of the following operations—
    (a)   burning as a fuel, under an authorisation granted under Part I of the 1990 Act, of—
          (i)   straw, poultry litter or wood;
          (ii) waste oil [(including waste oil which is special waste)]; or
          (iii) solid fuel which has been manufactured from waste by a process involving the application of heat,
        to the extent that it is or forms part of a process within Part B of any Section of Schedule 1 to the 1991 Regulations;
    (b)   the secure storage on any premises of any wastes mentioned in sub-paragraph (a) above, other than waste oil, which are intended to be burned as mentioned in that sub-paragraph, and the feeding of such wastes into an appliance in which they are to be so burned;
    (c)   the secure storage of waste oil [(including waste oil which is special waste)] at the place where it is produced for a period not exceeding twelve months if the waste oil is intended to be submitted to an operation covered by the exemption conferred by sub-paragraph (a) above;
    (d)   burning as a fuel, under an authorisation granted under Part I of the 1990 Act, of tyres to the extent that it is or forms part of a process within Part B of Section 1.3 of Schedule 1 to the 1991 Regulations, and the shredding and feeding of tyres into an appliance in which they are to be so burned;
    (e)   the storage in a secure place on any premises of tyres where—
          (i)   the tyres are intended to be submitted to an operation covered by the exemption conferred by sub-paragraph (d) above;
          (ii) the tyres are stored separately;
          (iii) none of the tyres is stored on the premises for longer than twelve months; and
          (iv) the number of the tyres stored on the premises at any one time does not exceed 1,000.

4.—(1) The cleaning, washing, spraying or coating of waste consisting of packaging or containers so that it or they can be reused if the total quantity of such waste so dealt with at any place does not exceed 1,000 tonnes in any period of seven days.

(2) The storage of waste in connection with the carrying on of any activities described in sub-paragraph (1) above if that storage is at the place where the activity is carried on unless—
    (a)   the total quantity of such waste stored at that place exceeds 1,000 tonnes; or
    (b)   more than 1 tonne of metal containers used for the transport or storage of any chemical are dealt with in any period of seven days.

5.—(1) Burning waste as a fuel in an appliance if the appliance has a net rated thermal input of less than 0.4 megawatts or, where the appliance is used together with [(whether or not it is operated simultaneously with)] other appliances, the aggregate net rated thermal input of all the appliances is less than 0.4 megawatts.

(2) The secure storage of waste intended to be submitted to such burning.

(3) In this paragraph, "net rated thermal input" means the rate at which fuel can be burned at the maximum continuous rating of the appliance multiplied by the net calorific value of the fuel and expressed as megawatts thermal.

6.—(1) Burning waste oil as a fuel in an engine of an aircraft, hovercraft, mechanically propelled vehicle, railway locomotive, ship or other vessel if the total amount burned of such waste does not exceed 2,500 litres an hour in any one engine.

(2) The storage, in a secure container, of waste oil intended to be so burned.

7.—(1) The spreading of any of the wastes listed in Table 2 on land which is used for agriculture.

(2) The spreading of any of the wastes listed in Part I of Table 2 on—
  (a) operational land of a railway, light railway, internal drainage board or the [Environment Agency]; or
  (b) land which is a forest, woodland, park, garden, verge, landscaped area, sports ground, recreation ground, churchyard or cemetery.

Table 2

PART I
  Waste soil or compost.
  Waste wood, bark or other plant matter.

PART II
  Waste food, drink or materials used in or resulting from the preparation of food or drink.
  Blood and gut contents from abattoirs.
  Waste lime.
  Lime sludge from cement manufacture or gas processing.
  Waste gypsum.
  Paper waste sludge, waste paper and de-inked paper pulp.
  Dredgings from any inland waters.
  Textile waste.
  Septic tank sludge.
  Sludge from biological treatment plants.
  Waste hair and effluent treatment sludge from a tannery.

(3) Sub-paragraphs (1) and (2) above only apply if—
  (a) no more than 250 tonnes or, in the case of dredgings from inland waters, 5,000 tonnes of waste per hectare are spread on the land in any period of twelve months;
  (b) the activity in question results in benefit to agriculture or ecological improvement; and
  (c) where the waste is to be spread by an establishment or undertaking on land used for agriculture, it furnishes to the waste regulation authority in whose area the spreading is to take place the particulars listed in sub-paragraph (4) below—
    (i) in a case where there is to be a single spreading, in advance of carrying out the spreading; or
    (ii) in a case where there is to be regular or frequent spreading of waste of a similar composition, every six months or, where the waste to be spread is of a description different from that last notified, in advance of carrying out the spreading.

(4) The particulars referred to in sub-paragraph (3)(c) above are—
  (a) the establishment or undertaking's name and address, and telephone or fax number (if any);
  (b) a description of the waste, including the process from which it arises;
  (c) where the waste is being or will be stored pending spreading;
  (d) an estimate of the quantity of the waste or, in such a case as is mentioned in sub-paragraph (3)(c)(ii) above, an estimate of the total quantity of waste to be spread during the next six months; and
  (e) the location, and intended date or, in such a case as is mentioned in sub-paragraph (3)(c)(ii) above, the frequency, of the spreading of the waste.

(5) Subject to sub-paragraph (6) below, the storage, at the place where it is to be spread, of any waste (other than septic tank sludge) intended to be spread in reliance upon the exemption conferred by sub-paragraph (1) or (2) above.

(6) Sub-paragraph (5) above does not apply to the storage of waste in liquid form unless it is stored in a secure container or lagoon and no more than 500 tonnes is stored in any one container or lagoon.

(7) The storage, in a secure container or lagoon (or, in the case of dewatered sludge, in a secure place), of septic tank sludge intended to be spread in reliance upon the exemption conferred by sub-paragraph (1) above.

(8) In this paragraph and paragraph 8, "agriculture" has the same meaning as in the Agriculture Act 1947 or, in Scotland, the Agriculture (Scotland) Act 1948.

(9) In this paragraph and paragraph 30, "internal drainage board" has the meaning given by section 1(1) of the Land Drainage Act 1991 and, for the purposes of the definition of operational land, an internal drainage board shall be deemed to be a statutory undertaker.

(10) In this paragraph and paragraphs 8 and 10, "septic tank sludge" has the meaning given by regulation 2(1) of the Sludge (Use in Agriculture) Regulations 1989.

8.—(1) The storage, in a secure container or lagoon (or, in the case of dewatered sludge, in a secure place) on land used for agriculture, of sludge which is to be used in accordance with the 1989 Regulations.

(2) The spreading of sludge on land which is not agricultural land within the meaning of the 1989 Regulations if—
  (a)   it results in ecological improvement; and
  (b)   it does not cause the concentration in the soil of any of the elements listed in column 1 of the soil table set out in Schedule 2 to the 1989 Regulations to exceed the limit specified in column 2 of the table.

(3) The storage, in a secure container or lagoon (or, in the case of dewatered sludge, in a secure place), of sludge intended to be spread in reliance upon the exemption conferred by sub-paragraph (2) above.

(4) In this paragraph, "the 1989 Regulations" means the Sludge (Use in Agriculture) Regulations 1989 and "used", in relation to sludge, has the meaning given by regulation 2(1) of the 1989 Regulations.

(5) In this paragraph, and in paragraphs 9 and 10, "sludge" has the meaning given by regulation 2(1) of the 1989 Regulations.

9.—(1) Subject to sub-paragraph (3) below, the spreading of waste consisting of soil, rock, ash or sludge, or of waste from dredging any inland waters or arising from construction or demolition work, on any land in connection with the reclamation or improvement of that land if—
  (a)   by reason of industrial or other development the land is incapable of beneficial use without treatment;
  (b)   the spreading is carried out in accordance with a planning permission for the reclamation or improvement of the land and results in benefit to agriculture or ecological improvement; and
  (c)   no more than 20,000 cubic metres per hectare of such waste is spread on the land.

(2) The storage, at the place where it is to be spread, of any such waste which is intended to be spread in reliance upon the exemption conferred by sub-paragraph (1) above.

(3) Sub-paragraph (1) above does not apply to the disposal of waste at a site designed or adapted for the final disposal of waste by landfill.

10.—(1) Any recovery operation carried on within the curtilage of a sewage treatment works in relation to sludge or septic tank sludge brought from another sewage treatment works if the total quantity of such waste brought to the works in any period of twelve months does not exceed 10,000 cubic metres.

(2) The treatment within the curtilage of a water treatment works of waste arising at the works from water treatment if the total quantity of such waste which is treated at the works in any period of twelve months does not exceed 10,000 cubic metres.

(3) The storage of waste intended to be submitted to the activities mentioned in sub-paragraph (1) or (2) above if that storage is at the place where those activities are to be carried on.

11. Carrying on at any place, in respect of a kind of waste listed in Table 3, any of the activities specified in that Table in relation to that kind of waste where—
  (a)   the activity is carried on with a view to the recovery or reuse of the waste (whether or not by the person carrying on the activity listed in that Table); and
  (b)   the total quantity of any particular kind of waste dealt with at that place does not in any period of seven days exceed the limit specified in relation to that kind of waste in that Table.

Table 3

Kind of waste	Activities	Limit (tonnes per week)
Waste paper or cardboard	Baling, sorting or shredding	3,000
Waste textiles	Baling, sorting or shredding	100
Waste plastic	Baling, sorting, shredding, densifying or washing	100
Waste glass	Sorting, crushing or washing	1,000
Waste steel cans, aluminium cans or aluminium foil	Sorting, crushing, pulverising, shredding, compacting or baling	100
Waste food or drink cartons	Sorting, crushing, pulverising, shredding, compacting or baling	100

12.—(1) Composting biodegradable waste at the place where the waste is produced or where the compost is to be used, or at any other place occupied by the person producing the waste or using the compost, if the total quantity of waste being composted at that place at any time does not exceed—

    (a)   in the case of waste composted or to be composted for the purposes of cultivating mushrooms, 10,000 cubic metres; and

    (b)   in any other case, 1,000 cubic metres.

(2) The storage of biodegradable waste which is to be composted if that storage is at the place where the waste is produced or is to be composted.

(3) In this paragraph, "composting" includes any other biological transformation process that results in materials which may be spread on land for the benefit of agriculture or ecological improvement.

13.—(1) The manufacture from—

    (a)   waste which arises from demolition or construction work or tunnelling or other excavations; or

    (b)   waste which consists of ash, slag, clinker, rock, wood, bark, paper, straw or gypsum, of timber products, straw board, plasterboard, bricks, blocks, roadstone or aggregate.

(2) The manufacture of soil or soil substitutes from any of the wastes listed in sub-paragraph (1) above if—

    (a)   the manufacture is carried out at the place where either the waste is produced or the manufactured product is to be applied to land; and

    (b)   the total amount manufactured at that place on any day does not exceed 500 tonnes.

(3) The treatment of waste soil or rock which, when treated, is to be spread on land under paragraph 7 or 9, if—

    (a)   it is carried out at the place where the waste is produced or the treated product is to be spread; and

    (b)   the total amount treated at that place in any day does not exceed 100 tonnes.

(4) The storage of waste which is to be submitted to any of the activities mentioned in sub-paragraphs (1) to (3) above if—

    (a)   the waste is stored at the place where the activity is to be carried on; and

    (b)   the total quantity of waste stored at that place does not exceed—

        (i)   in the case of the manufacture of roadstone from road planings, 50,000 tonnes; and

        (ii)   in any other case, 20,000 tonnes.

14.—(1) The manufacture of finished goods from any of the following kinds of waste, namely waste metal, plastic, glass, ceramics, rubber, textiles, wood, paper or cardboard.

(2) The storage of any such waste intended to be used in reliance upon the exemption conferred by sub-paragraph (1) above if—

    (a)   the waste is stored at the place of manufacture; and

    (b)   the total amount of any particular kind of waste stored at that place at any time does not exceed 15,000 tonnes.

15.—(1)The beneficial use of waste if—
  (a)   it is put to that use without further treatment; and
  (b)   that use of the waste does not involve its disposal.

(2)   The storage of waste intended to be used in reliance upon the exemption conferred by sub-paragraph (1) above insofar as that storage does not amount to disposal of the waste.

(3)   This paragraph does not apply to the use or storage of waste if that activity is covered by an exemption conferred by paragraph 7, 8, 9, 19 or 25, or would be so covered but for any condition or limitation to which that exemption is subject by virtue of any provision contained in the paragraph by which that exemption is conferred.

16. The carrying on, in accordance with the conditions and requirements of a licence granted under article 7 or 8 of the Diseases of Animals (Waste Food) Order 1973, of any activity authorised by the licence.

17.—(1) The storage in a secure place on any premises of waste of a kind described in Table 4 below if—
  (a)   the total quantity of that kind of waste stored on those premises at any time does not exceed the quantity specified in that Table;
  (b)   the waste is to be reused, or used for the purposes of—
    (i)   an activity described in paragraph 11; or
    (ii)   any other recovery operation;
  (c)   each kind of waste listed in the Table stored on the premises is kept separately; and
  (d)   no waste is stored on the premises for longer than twelve months.

Table 4

Kind of waste	Maximum total quantity
Waste paper or cardboard	15,000 tonnes
Waste textiles	1,000 tonnes
Waste plastics	500 tonnes
Waste glass	5,000 tonnes
Waste steel cans, aluminium cans or aluminium foil	500 tonnes
Waste food or drink cartons	500 tonnes
Waste articles which are to be used for construction work which are capable of being so used in their existing state	100 tonnes
Solvents (including solvents which are special waste)	5 cubic metres
Refrigerants and halons (including refrigerants and halons which are special waste)	18 tonnes
Tyres	1,000 tyres
[waste mammalian protein	60,000 tonnes
waste mammalian tallow	45,000 tonnes]

(2)   In this paragraph, "refrigerants" means dichlorodifluoromethane, chlorotrifluoromethane, dichlorotetrafluoroethane, chloropentafluoroethane, bromotrifluoromethane, chlorodifluoromethane, chlorotetrafluoroethane, trifluoromethane, difluoromethane, pentafluoroethane, tetrafluoroethane, chlorodifluoroethane, difluoroethane, trichlorofluoromethane, trichlorotrifluoroethane, dichlorotrifluoroethane, dichlorofluoroethane and mixtures containing any of those substances.

[(3) In this paragraph—
    "mammalian protein" means proteinaceous material and "mammalian tallow" means fat, which in each case is derived from the whole or part of any dead mammal by a process of crushing, cooking or grinding.]

18.—(1) The storage on any premises in a secure container or containers of waste of a kind described in sub-paragraph (2) below if—

    (a)   the storage capacity of the container or containers does not exceed 400 cubic metres in total;

    (b)   in the case of waste oil, the storage capacity of any container or containers used for its storage does not exceed 3 cubic metres in total, and provision is made to prevent oil escaping into the ground or a drain;

    (c)   there are no more than 20 containers on those premises;

    (d)   the waste will be reused, or used for the purposes of—

        (i)   any activity described in paragraph 11 carried on at those premises; or

        (ii)   any other recovery activity;

    (e)   each kind of waste described in sub-paragraph (2) below stored on the premises is kept separately;

    (f)   no waste is stored on the premises for longer than twelve months; and

    (g)   the person storing the waste is the owner of the container or has the consent of the owner.

(2) Sub-paragraph (1) above applies to the following kinds of waste—

    (a)   any waste described in paragraph 17 other than waste solvents, refrigerants or halons;

    (b)   waste oil [(including waste oil which is special waste)].

19.—(1) The storage on a site of waste which arises from demolition or construction work or tunnelling or other excavations or which consists of ash, slag, clinker, rock, wood or gypsum, if—

    (a)   the waste in question is suitable for use for the purposes of relevant work which will be carried on at the site; and

    (b)   in the case of waste which is not produced on the site, it is not stored there for longer than three months before relevant work starts.

(2) The use of waste of a kind mentioned in sub-paragraph (1) above for the purposes of relevant work if the waste is suitable for use for those purposes.

(3) The storage on a site of waste consisting of road planings which are to be used for the purposes of relevant work carried on elsewhere if—

    (a)   no more than 50,000 tonnes of such waste are stored at the site; and

    (b)   the waste is stored there for no longer than 3 months.

(4) In this paragraph, "relevant work" means construction work, including the deposit of waste on land in connection with—

    (a)   the provision of recreational facilities on that land; or

    (b)   the construction, maintenance or improvement of a building, highway, railway, airport, dock or other transport facility on that land,

but not including either any deposit of waste in any other circumstances or any work involving land reclamation.

20.—(1) Laundering or otherwise cleaning waste textiles with a view to their recovery or reuse.

(2) The storage of waste textiles at the place where they are to be so laundered or cleaned.

21.—(1) Chipping, shredding, cutting or pulverising waste plant matter (including wood or bark), or sorting and baling sawdust or wood shavings, on any premises if—

    (a)   those activities are carried on for the purposes of recovery or reuse; and

    (b)   no more than 1,000 tonnes of such waste are dealt with on those premises in any period of seven days.

(2) The storage of waste in connection with any activity mentioned in sub-paragraph (1) above at the premises where it is carried on if the total amount of waste stored at those premises does not at any time exceed 1,000 tonnes.

22.—(1) The recovery, at any premises, of silver from waste produced in connection with printing or photographic processing if no more than 50,000 litres of such waste are dealt with on those premises in any day.

(2) The storage, at those premises, of waste which is to be submitted to such a recovery operation as is mentioned in sub-paragraph (1) above.

23.—(1) The keeping or treatment of animal by-products in accordance with the Animal By-Products Order 1992.

(2) In this paragraph, "animal by-products" has the same meaning as in article 3(1) of the Animal By-Products Order 1992.

24.—(1) Crushing, grinding or other size reduction of waste bricks, tiles or concrete, under an authorisation granted under Part I of the 1990 Act, to the extent that it is or forms part of a process within paragraph (c) of Part B of Section 3.4 (other mineral processes) of Schedule 1 to the 1991 Regulations.

(2) Where any such crushing, grinding or other size reduction is carried on otherwise than at the place where the waste is produced, the exemption conferred by sub-paragraph (1) above only applies if those activities are carried on with a view to recovery or reuse of the waste.

(3) The storage, at the place where the process is carried on, of any such waste which is intended to be so crushed, ground or otherwise reduced in size, if the total quantity of such waste so stored at that place at any one time does not exceed 20,000 tonnes.

25.—(1) Subject to sub-paragraphs (2) to (4) below, the deposit of waste arising from dredging inland waters, or from clearing plant matter from inland waters, if either—
  (a) the waste is deposited along the bank or towpath of the waters where the dredging or clearing takes place; or
  (b) the waste is deposited along the bank or towpath of any inland waters so as to result in benefit to agriculture or ecological improvement.

(2) The total amount of waste deposited along the bank or towpath under sub-paragraph (1) above on any day must not exceed 50 tonnes for each metre of the bank or towpath along which it is deposited.

(3) Sub-paragraph (1) above does not apply to waste deposited in a container or lagoon.

(4) Sub-paragraph (1)(a) above only applies to an establishment or undertaking where the waste deposited is the establishment or undertaking's own waste.

(5) The treatment by screening or dewatering of such waste as is mentioned in sub-paragraph (1) above—
  (a) on the bank or towpath of the waters where either the dredging or clearing takes place or the waste is to be deposited, prior to its being deposited in reliance upon the exemption conferred by the foregoing provisions of this paragraph;
  (b) on the bank or towpath of the waters where the dredging or clearing takes place, or at a place where the waste is to be spread, prior to its being spread in reliance upon the exemption conferred by paragraph 7(1) or (2); or
  (c) in the case of waste from dredging, on the bank or towpath of the waters where the dredging takes place, or at a place where the waste is to be spread, prior to its being spread in reliance upon the exemption conferred by paragraph 9(1).

26.—(1) The recovery or disposal of waste, at the place where it is produced, as an integral part of the process that produces it.

(2) The storage, at the place where it is produced, of waste which is intended to be so recovered or disposed of.

(3) Sub-paragraph (1) above does not apply to the final disposal of waste by deposit in or on land.

27.—(1) Baling, compacting, crushing, shredding or pulverising waste at the place where it is produced.

(2) The storage, at the place where it is produced, of waste which is to be submitted to any of those operations.

[28. The storage of returned goods that are waste, and the secure storage of returned goods that are special waste, pending recovery or disposal, for a period not exceeding one month, by their manufacturer, distributor or retailer.]

29.—(1) The disposal of waste at the place where it is produced, by the person producing it, by burning it in an incinerator which is an exempt incinerator for the purposes of Section 5.1 (incineration) of Schedule 1 to the 1991 Regulations.

(2) The secure storage at that place of any such waste intended to be submitted to such burning.

30.—(1) Subject to sub-paragraph (2) below, burning waste on land in the open if—
    (a) the waste consists of wood, bark or other plant matter;
    (b) it is produced on land which is operational land of a railway, light railway, tramway, internal drainage board or the [Environment Agency], or which is a forest, woodland, park, garden, verge, landscaped area, sports ground, recreation ground, churchyard or cemetery, or it is produced on other land as a result of demolition work;
    (c) it is burned on the land where it is produced; and
    (d) the total quantity burned in any period of 24 hours does not exceed 10 tonnes.

(2) Sub-paragraph (1) above only applies to the burning of waste by an establishment or undertaking where the waste burned is the establishment or undertaking's own waste.

(3) The storage pending its burning, on the land where it is to be burned, of waste which is to be burned in reliance upon the exemption conferred by sub-paragraph (1) above.

31. The discharge of waste onto the track of a railway from a sanitary convenience or sink forming part of a vehicle used for the carriage of passengers on the railway if the discharge in question does not exceed 25 litres.

32. The burial on premises of waste arising from the use on those premises of a sanitary convenience which is equipped with a removable receptacle if the total amount buried in any period of twelve months does not exceed 5 cubic metres.

33.—(1) The keeping or deposit of waste consisting of excavated materials arising from peatworking at the place where that activity takes place.

(2) Sub-paragraph (1) above only applies to the keeping or deposit of waste by an establishment or undertaking where the waste kept or deposited is the establishment or undertaking's own waste.

34.—(1) The keeping or deposit on land at the place where it is produced of spent ballast if the land is operational land of a railway, light railway or tramway and the total amount kept or deposited at that place does not exceed 10 tonnes for each metre of track from which the ballast derives.

(2) Sub-paragraph (1) above only applies to the keeping or deposit of waste by an establishment or undertaking where the waste kept or deposited is the establishment or undertaking's own waste.

35.—(1) The deposit of waste consisting of excavated material from a borehole or other excavation made for the purpose of mineral exploration if—
    (a) it is deposited in or on land at the place where it is excavated; and
    (b) the total quantity of waste so deposited over any period of 24 months does not exceed 45,000 cubic metres per hectare.

(2) Sub-paragraph (1) above only applies if—
    (a) the drilling of the borehole or the making of any other excavation is development for which planning permission is granted by article 3 of, and Class A or B of Part 22 of Schedule 2 to, the Town and Country Planning General Development Order 1988 or, in Scotland, which is permitted by Class 53, 54 or 61 of Schedule 1 to the Town and Country Planning (General Permitted Development) (Scotland) Order 1992; and
    (b) the conditions subject to which the development is permitted are observed.

(3) Expressions used in this paragraph which are also used in the Town and Country Planning General Development Order 1988 or, in Scotland, the Town and Country Planning (General Permitted Development) (Scotland) Order 1992, shall have the same meaning as in the relevant Order.

36.—(1) The temporary storage of waste consisting of garbage, including any such waste which is special waste, at reception facilities provided within a harbour area in accordance with the Merchant Shipping (Reception Facilities for Garbage) Regulations 1988, where such storage is incidental to the collection or transport of the waste and so long as—
    (a) the amount of garbage so stored within a harbour area at any time does not exceed 20 cubic metres for each ship from which garbage has been landed; and
    (b) no garbage is so stored for more than seven days.

(2) The temporary storage of waste consisting of tank washings, including any such waste which is special waste, at reception facilities provided within a harbour area in accordance with the Prevention of Pollution (Reception Facilities) Order 1984, where such storage is incidental to the collection or transport of the waste and so long as—

(a)　the amount of tank washings consisting of dirty ballast so stored within a harbour area at any time does not exceed 30% of the total deadweight of the ships from which such washings have been landed; .

(b)　the amount of tank washings consisting of waste mixtures containing oil so stored within a harbour area at any time does not exceed 1% of the total deadweight of the ships from which such washings have been landed.

(3)　In this paragraph—

"garbage" has the same meaning as in the Merchant Shipping (Reception Facilities for Garbage) Regulations 1988;

"harbour area" has the same meaning as in the Dangerous Substances in Harbour Areas Regulations 1987;

"ship" means a vessel of any type whatsoever operating in the marine environment including submersible craft, floating craft and any structure which is a fixed or floating platform; and

"tank washings" means waste residues from the tanks (other than the fuel tanks) or holds of a ship or waste arising from the cleaning of such tanks or holds.

37.—(1) Subject to sub-paragraph (2) below, the burial of a dead domestic pet in the garden of a domestic property where the pet lived.

(2)　This paragraph does not apply if—

(a)　the dead domestic pet may prove hazardous to anyone who may come into contact with it; or

(b)　the burial is carried out by an establishment or undertaking and the pet did not die at the property.

38. The deposit or storage of samples of waste, including samples of waste which is special waste, which are being or are to be subjected to testing and analysis, at any place where they are being or are to be tested or analysed, if the samples are taken—

(a)　in the exercise of any power under the Radioactive Substances Act 1993, the Sewerage (Scotland) Act 1968, the Control of Pollution Act 1974, the 1990 Act, the Water Industry Act 1991 or the Water Resources Act 1991;

(b)　by or on behalf of the holder of a waste management licence in pursuance of the conditions of that licence;

(c)　by or on behalf of a person carrying on in relation to the waste an activity described in this Schedule or in regulation 16(1);

(d)　by or on behalf of the owner or occupier of the land from which the samples are taken;

(e)　by or on behalf of any person to whom section 34 of the 1990 Act applies in connection with his duties under that section; or

(f)　for the purposes of research.

39.—(1) The secure storage at a pharmacy, pending their disposal there or elsewhere, of waste medicines (including those which are special waste) which have been returned to the pharmacy from households or by individuals if—

(a)　the total quantity of such returned waste medicines at the pharmacy does not exceed 5 cubic metres at any time; and

(b)　any waste medicine so returned to the pharmacy is not stored there for longer than six months.

(2)　The storage at the premises of a medical, nursing or veterinary practice of waste (including special waste) produced in carrying on that practice if—

(a)　the total quantity of that waste at the premises does not at any time exceed 5 cubic metres; and

(b)　no such waste is stored at those premises for longer than three months.

40.—(1) The storage of non-liquid waste at any place other than the premises where it is produced if—

(a)　it is stored in a secure container or containers, does not at any time exceed 50 cubic metres in total and is not kept for a period longer than 3 months;

(b)　the person storing the waste is the owner of the container or has the consent of the owner;

(c)   the place where it is stored is not a site designed or adapted for the reception of waste with a view to its being disposed of or recovered elsewhere; and

(d)   such storage is incidental to the collection or transport of the waste.

[(1A) Sub-paragraph (1) above does not apply to the storage of waste at a place designed or adapted for the recovery of scrap metal or the dismantling of waste motor vehicles.]

(2) The temporary storage of scrap rails on operational land of a railway, light railway or tramway if the total quantity of that waste in any one place does not at any time exceed 10 tonnes and the storage is incidental to the collection or transport of the scrap rails.

41.—(1) The temporary storage of waste, pending its collection, on the site where it is produced.

[(1A) Sub-paragraph (1) above does not apply to the storage of waste at a place designed or adapted for the recovery of scrap metal or the dismantling of waste motor vehicles.]

(2) Sub-paragraph (1) above shall apply to special waste if—
(a)   it is stored on the site for no more than twelve months;
(b)   in the case of liquid waste, it is stored in a secure container and the total volume of that waste does not at any time exceed 23,000 litres; and
(c)   in any other case, either—
   (i)   it is stored in a secure container and the total volume of that waste does not at any time exceed 80 cubic metres; or
   (ii) it is stored in a secure place and the total volume of that waste does not at any time exceed 50 cubic metres.

42.—(1) The treatment, keeping or disposal by any person at any premises of waste (including special waste) consisting of scrap metal or waste motor vehicles which are to be dismantled if—
(a)   he was carrying on the activity in question at those premises before [1st April 1995]; and
(b)   he has applied, before that date, for a disposal licence under Part I of the Control of Pollution Act 1974 authorising that activity and that application is pending on that date.

(2) The exemption conferred by sub-paragraph (1) above, in relation to the carrying on of an activity at any premises, shall cease to have effect in relation to the carrying on of that activity at those premises on the date on which the licence applied for is granted or, if the application is (or is deemed to be) rejected, on the date on which—
(a)   the period for appealing expires without an appeal being made; or
(b)   any appeal is withdrawn or finally determined.

43.—(1) The treatment, keeping or disposal by any person at any premises of waste (including special waste) if—
(a)   he was carrying on the activity in question at those premises before 1st May 1994; and
(b)   before that date no disposal licence was required under Part I of the Control of Pollution Act 1974 for that activity.

(2) Subject to sub-paragraph (3) below, the exemption conferred by sub-paragraph (1) above, in relation to an activity carried on by a person at any premises, [shall—
(a)   after [30th September 1996], in the case of an activity falling within paragraph 8 or 9 of Part III of Schedule 4;
(b)   after 31st July 1995, in any other case,

cease to have effect] in relation to the carrying on of that activity at those premises unless on or before that date he applies for a waste management licence in relation to the activity in question.

(3) Where a person makes such an application as is mentioned in sub-paragraph (2) above, the exemption conferred by sub-paragraph (1) above shall continue to have effect in relation to the activity in question until the date on which the licence applied for is granted or, if the application is (or is deemed to be) rejected, until the date on which—
(a)   the period for appealing expires without an appeal being made; or
(b)   any appeal is withdrawn or finally determined.

[44.—(1)Heating iron, steel or any ferrous-alloy, non-ferrous metal or non-ferrous metal alloy, in one or more furnaces or other appliances the primary combustion chambers of which have in aggregate a net rated thermal input of less than 0.2 megawatts, for the purpose of removing grease, oil or any other non-metallic contaminant.

(2) Sub-paragraph (1) does not apply to the removal by heat of plastic or rubber covering from scrap cable or of any asbestos contaminant.

(3) In the case of a process involving the heating of iron, steel or any ferrous-alloy, sub-paragraph (1) does not apply if that process is related to a process described in any of paragraphs (a) to (h), or (j) to (m), of Part A or paragraphs (a) to (c), or (e) or (f), of Part B of Section 2.1 of Schedule 1 to the 1991 Regulations.

(4) In the case of a process involving the heating of any non-ferrous metal or non-ferrous metal alloy, sub-paragraph (1) does not apply if that process is related to a process described in any of paragraphs (a) to (g), or (i) to (k), of Part A of Section 2.2 of Schedule 1 to the 1991 Regulations.

(5) The secure storage of waste intended to be submitted to heating to which sub-paragraph (1) applies if the waste or, as the case may be, any container in which the waste is stored, is stored on an impermeable pavement which is provided with a sealed drainage system.

(6) In this paragraph, "net rated thermal input" means the rate at which fuel can be burned at the maximum continuous rating of the appliance multiplied by the net calorific value of the fuel and expressed as megawatts thermal.

(7) In this paragraph, "ferrous alloy" means an alloy of which iron is the largest constituent, or equal to the largest constituent, by weight, whether or not that alloy also has a non-ferrous metal content greater than any percentage specified in Section 2.2 of Schedule 1 to the 1991 Regulations, and "non-ferrous metal alloy" shall be construed accordingly.

45.—(1) Subject to sub-paragraph (3) below, the carrying on, at any secure place designed or adapted for the recovery of scrap metal or the dismantling of waste motor vehicles, in respect of a kind of waste described in Table 4A, of any of the activities specified in that Table in relation to that kind of waste if—

  (a) the total quantity of any particular kind of waste so dealt with at that place does not in any period of seven days exceed the limit specified in relation to that kind of waste in that Table;
  (b) the activity is carried on with a view to the recovery of the waste (whether or not by the person carrying on the activity listed in that Table);
  (c) every part of that place upon which the activity is carried out is surfaced with an impermeable pavement provided with a sealed drainage system; and
  (d) the plant or equipment used in carrying on the activity is maintained in reasonable working order.

Table 4A

Kind of Waste	Activities	Seven day limit
Ferrous metals or ferrous alloys in metallic non-dispersible form (but not turnings, shavings or chippings of those metals or alloys)	Sorting; grading; baling; shearing by manual feed; compacting; crushing; cutting by hand-held equipment	8,000 tonnes
The following non-ferrous metals, namely copper, aluminium, nickel, lead, tin, tungsten, cobalt, molybdenum, vanadium, chromium, titanium, zirconium, manganese or zinc, or non-ferrous alloys, in metallic non-dispersible form, of any of those metals (but not turnings, shavings or chippings of those metals or alloys)	Sorting; grading; baling; shearing by manual feed; compacting; crushing; cutting by hand-held equipment	400 tonnes
Turnings, shavings or chippings of any of the metals or alloys listed in either of the above categories	Sorting; grading; baling; shearing by manual feed; compacting; crushing; cutting by hand-held equipment	300 tonnes

Kind of Waste	Activities	Seven day limit
Motor vehicles (including any substance which is special waste and which forms part of, or is contained in, a vehicle and was necessary for the normal operation of the vehicle)	Dismantling, rebuilding, restoring or reconditioning, but, in relation to lead acid batteries, only their removal from motor vehicles	40 vehicles
Lead acid motor vehicle batteries (including those whose contents are special waste), whether or not forming part of, or contained in, a motor vehicle	Sorting (including removal from motor vehicles)	20 tonnes

(2) Subject to sub-paragraph (3) below, the storage, at any secure place designed or adapted for the recovery of scrap metal or the dismantling of waste motor vehicles, of waste of a kind listed in Table 4B if—

(a) the waste is to be submitted to any of the activities specified in Table 4A in relation to that kind of waste, or to a recycling or reclamation operation authorised by a waste management licence or an authorisation under Part I of the 1990 Act;

(b) the total quantity of waste of that kind stored at that place does not exceed the maximum total quantity specified in Table 4B in relation to that kind of waste;

(c) no waste is stored at that place for a period exceeding 12 months;

(d) each kind of waste is either stored separately or is kept in separate containers, but in a case where a consignment consisting of more than one kind of waste is delivered to that place it may be stored unseparated at that place pending sorting for a period not exceeding 2 months;

(e) in the case of waste which is liquid or consists of motor vehicle batteries, it is stored in a secure container;

(f) in the case of waste motor vehicles from which all fluids have been drained, they are, unless stored on a hardstanding, stored on an impermeable pavement;

(g) subject to paragraph (f) above, the waste or, as the case may be, any container in which it is stored, is stored on an impermeable pavement which is provided with a sealed drainage system; and

(h) the height of any pile or stack of waste does not exceed 5 metres.

Table 4B

Kind of waste	Maximum total quantity
Ferrous metals or ferrous alloys in metallic non-dispersible form (but not turnings, shavings or chippings of those metals or alloys)	50,000 tonnes
The following non-ferrous metals, namely copper, aluminium, nickel, lead, tin, tungsten, cobalt, molybdenum, vanadium, chromium, titanium, zirconium, manganese or zinc, or non-ferrous alloys, in metallic non-dispersible form, of any of those metals (but not turnings, shavings or chippings of those metals or alloys)	1,500 tonnes
Turnings, shavings or chippings of any of the metals or alloys listed in either of the above categories	1,000 tonnes
Motor vehicles (including any substance which is special waste and which forms part of, or is contained in, a vehicle and was necessary for the normal operation of the vehicle):	
— where any such vehicle is stored on a hardstanding which is not an impermeable pavement:	100 vehicles
— where all such vehicles are stored on an impermeable pavement:	1,000 vehicles

Kind of waste	Maximum total quantity
Lead acid motor vehicle batteries (including those whose contents are special waste) whether or not forming part of, or contained in, a motor vehicle	40 tonnes

(3) Sub-paragraph (1) or (2) above only applies to the carrying on of an activity at a place if—
   (a) the person responsible for the management of that place—
      (i) has established administrative arrangements to ensure that—
         (A) waste accepted at that place is of a kind listed in Table 4A or, as the case may be, Table 4B; and
         (B) no waste is accepted at that place in such a quantity as would cause there to be a breach of any of the terms and conditions of the exemption;
      and
      (ii) carries out a monthly audit to confirm compliance with the terms and conditions of the exemption;
   (b) the records required by paragraph 14 of Part I of Schedule 4 are kept in such a form as to show, for each month, the total quantity of each kind of waste recovered during that month at that place, and details of the total quantity of each kind of waste recovered at that place during the preceding 12 months are sent annually to the appropriate registration authority with the annual fee referred to in paragraph (d) below;
   (c) an up to date plan of that place containing the details referred to in regulation 18(4A)(c)(i) to (iv) is sent annually to the appropriate registration authority with the annual fee referred to in paragraph (d) below; and
   (d) a fee of [£150] is paid annually in respect of that place to the appropriate registration authority by the due date which shall be ascertained in accordance with sub-paragraph (4) below.

(4) For the purposes of ascertaining the due date in any year for payment of the fee referred in sub-paragraph (3)(d) above in respect of any place—
   (a) the appropriate registration authority shall serve notice in accordance with the following provisions of this sub-paragraph on the establishment or undertaking from which notice has been received by the authority under regulation 18(4A) in respect of that place;
   (b) a notice required by paragraph (a) above shall be served not later than one month before the anniversary of the date when the notice, plan and fee referred to in regulation 18(4A) were received by the authority in respect of that place and shall specify—
      (i) the amount of the payment due,
      (ii) the method of payment,
      (iii) the date of such anniversary,
      (iv) that payment is due on that date or, if later, upon the day falling one month after the date of the notice, and
      (v) the effect of payment not being made by the date on which it is due,

and the due date for payment of the annual fee for that year by that establishment or undertaking in respect of that place shall be the date specified for payment in the notice.

(5) The temporary storage of waste (in this sub-paragraph referred to as "the non-scrap waste"), pending its collection, at a secure place designed or adapted for the recovery of scrap metal or the dismantling of waste motor vehicles if—
   (a) the non-scrap waste is not of a kind described in Table 4B;
   (b) the non-scrap waste was delivered to that place as part of a consignment of waste of which—
      (i) at least 70 per cent by weight was waste consisting of waste motor vehicles; or
      (ii) at least 95 per cent by weight was waste of any kind described in Table 4B other than waste motor vehicles,
      and is capable of being separated from that waste by sorting or hand dismantling;
   (c) the non-scrap waste is stored at that place for no more than 3 months;
   (d) in a case where the non-scrap waste is liquid, it is stored in a secure container; and

    (e)   the non-scrap waste or, as the case may be, the container in which the non-scrap waste is stored, is stored on an impermeable pavement which is provided with a sealed drainage system.

(6) In Table 4A, "shearing" means the cold cutting of metal by purpose-made shears.

(7) For the purposes of this paragraph and paragraph 44 above, "sealed drainage system", in relation to an impermeable pavement, means a drainage system with impermeable components which does not leak and which will ensure that—

    (a)   no liquid will run off the pavement otherwise than via the system; and

    (b)   except where they may be lawfully discharged, all liquids entering the system are collected in a sealed sump.]

[958]

NOTES

Commencement: 1 September 1996 (para 28); 1 April 1995 (paras 44, 45); 1 May 1994 (remainder).

Paras 3, 18: words in square brackets inserted by the Special Waste Regulations 1996, SI 1996/972, reg 25, Sch 3.

Para 5: words in square brackets in sub-para (1) inserted by the Waste Management Licensing (Amendment etc) Regulations 1995, SI 1995/288, reg 3(12).

Paras 7, 30: words in square brackets substituted by the Environment Act 1995, s 120, Sch 22, para 233(1).

Para 17: words in square brackets in Table 4 inserted, and sub-para (3) inserted, by the Waste Management Licensing (Amendment) Regulations 1996, SI 1996/1279, reg 2.

Para 28: substituted by SI 1996/972, reg 25, Sch 3.

Paras 40, 41: sub-para (1A) inserted by SI 1995/288, reg 3(13).

Para 42: words in square brackets substituted by SI 1995/288, reg 3(14).

Para 43: words in first (outer) pair of square brackets in Table 4 substituted by the Waste Management Licensing (Amendment No 2) Regulations 1995, SI 1995/1950, reg 2, words in second (inner) pair of square brackets substituted by the Waste Management Regulations 1996, SI 1996/634, reg 2(6).

Para 44: added by SI 1995/288, reg 3(16).

Para 45: added by SI 1995/288, reg 3(16); words in square brackets in sub-para (3) substituted by SI 1996/634, reg 2(7).

SCHEDULE 4

WASTE FRAMEWORK DIRECTIVE ETC

Regulations 1(3), 19

PART I

GENERAL

1. Interpretation of Schedule 4

In this Schedule, unless the context otherwise requires—

    "competent authority" has the meaning given by paragraph 3;

    "development", "development plan", "government department" and "planning permission" have the same meaning as in the Town and Country Planning Act 1990 or, in Scotland, as in the Town and Country Planning (Scotland) Act 1972;

    "licensing authority" and "the Ministers" have the meaning given by section 24(1) of the Food and Environment Protection Act 1985;

    "local planning authority" and "the planning Acts" have the same meaning as in the Town and Country Planning Act 1990;

    "permit" means a waste management licence, a disposal licence, an authorisation under Part I of the 1990 Act, a resolution under section 54 of the 1990 Act, a licence under Part II of the Food and Environment Protection Act 1985 or a consent under Chapter II of Part III of the Water Resources Act 1991 or under Part II of the Control of Pollution Act 1974 (and, in relation to a permit, "grant" includes give, issue or pass, "modify" includes vary, and cognate expressions shall be construed accordingly);

    "plan-making provisions" means paragraph 5 below, section 50 of the 1990 Act . . . Part II of the Town and Country Planning Act 1990 or, in Scotland, Part II of the Town and Country Planning (Scotland) Act 1972 [and section 44A of the Environmental Protection Act 1990 or, in Scotland, section 44B of that Act];

"planning authority" means the local planning authority, the person appointed under paragraph 1 of Schedule 6 to the Town and Country Planning Act 1990 or, as the case may be, the government department responsible for discharging a function under the planning Acts or, in Scotland, the planning authority (as defined in section 172 of the Local Government (Scotland) Act 1973), the person appointed under paragraph 1 of Schedule 7 to the Town and Country Planning (Scotland) Act 1972, or, as the case may be, the government department responsible for discharging a function under the Town and Country Planning (Scotland) Act 1972, and the Secretary of State shall be treated as a planning authority in respect of his functions under the planning Acts or, in Scotland, the Town and Country Planning (Scotland) Act 1972;

"pollution control authority" means any competent authority other than a planning authority;

. . . . .

"specified action" means any of the following—
  (a) determining—
      (i) an application for planning permission; or
      (ii) an appeal made under section 78 of the Town and Country Planning Act 1990 or, in Scotland, under section 33 of the Town and Country Planning (Scotland) Act 1972, in respect of such an application;
  (b) deciding whether to take any action under section 141(2) or (3) or 177(1)(a) or (b) of the Town and Country Planning Act 1990, or under section 196(5) of that Act as originally enacted, or under section 35(5) of the Planning (Listed Buildings and Conservation Areas) Act 1990 or, in Scotland, under section 85(5)(a), (b) or (c), 91(3) (as enacted prior to its repeal) or 172(2) or (3) of, or paragraph 2(6) of Schedule 17 to, the Town and Country Planning (Scotland) Act 1972;
  (c) deciding whether to direct under section 90(1), (2) or (2A) of the Town and Country Planning Act 1990 or, in Scotland, section 37(1) of the Town and Country Planning (Scotland) Act 1972 or paragraph 7(1) of Schedule 8 to the Electricity Act 1989, that planning permission shall be deemed to be granted;
  (d) deciding whether—
      (i) in making or confirming a discontinuance order, to include in the order any grant of planning permission; or
      (ii) to confirm (with or without modifications) a discontinuance order insofar as it grants planning permission,
      and, for the purposes of this sub-paragraph, "discontinuance order" means an order under section 102 of the Town and Country Planning Act 1990 (including an order made under that section by virtue of section 104 of that Act), or under paragraph 1 of Schedule 9 to that Act (including an order made under that paragraph by virtue of paragraph 11 of that Schedule), or, in Scotland, an order under section 49 of the Town and Country Planning (Scotland) Act 1972 (including an order made under that section by virtue of section 260 of that Act);
  (e) discharging functions under Part II of the Town and Country Planning Act 1990 or, in Scotland, Part II of the Town and Country Planning (Scotland) Act 1972.

2. Duties of competent authorities

(1) Subject to the following provisions of this paragraph, the competent authorities shall discharge their specified functions, insofar as they relate to the recovery or disposal of waste, with the relevant objectives.

(2) Nothing in sub-paragraph (1) above requires a planning authority to deal with any matter which the relevant pollution control authority has power to deal with.

(3) In a case where the recovery or disposal of waste is or forms part of a prescribed process designated for local control under Part I of the 1990 Act, and either requires a waste management licence or is covered by an exemption conferred by regulation 17(1) of, and Schedule 3 to, these Regulations, nothing in sub-paragraph (1) above shall require a competent authority to discharge its functions under—

(a)   Part I of the 1990 Act in order to control pollution of the environment due to the release of substances into any environmental medium other than the air; or

(b)   Part II of the 1990 Act in order to control pollution of the environment due to the release of substances into the air resulting from the carrying on of the prescribed process.

(4)   In sub-paragraph (3) above, "prescribed process", "designated for local control", "pollution of the environment due to the release of substances into the air" and "pollution of the environment due to the release of substances into any environmental medium other than the air" have the meaning which they have in Part I of the 1990 Act.

3. Meaning of "competent authority" etc

(1)   For the purposes of this Schedule, "competent authority" means any of the persons or bodies listed in column (1) of Table 5 below and, subject to sub-paragraph (2) below, in relation to a competent authority "specified function" means any function of that authority listed in column (2) of that Table opposite the entry for that authority.

Table 5

Competent authorities	Specified functions
(1)	(2)
Any planning authority.	The taking of any specified action.
A waste regulation authority, the Secretary of State or a person appointed under [section 114(1)(a) of the Environment Act 1995].	Their respective functions under Part II of the 1990 Act in relation to waste management licences, including preparing plans or modifications of them under section 50 of the 1990 Act [and preparing the strategy, or any modification of it, under section 44A or 44B of that Act].
A disposal authority or the Secretary of State.	Their respective functions under Part I of the Control of Pollution Act 1974 in relation to disposal licences and resolutions under section 11 of that Act.
A licensing authority or the Ministers.	Their respective functions under Part II of the Food and Environment Protection Act 1985, or under paragraph 5 below.
An enforcing authority, the Secretary of State or a person appointed under [section 114(1)(a) of the Environment Act 1995].	Their respective functions under Part I of the 1990 Act in relation to prescribed processes except when— (a) the process is designated for local control; and (b) it is an exempt activity carried out subject to the conditions and limitations specified in Schedule 3.
The [Environment Agency] or the Secretary of State.	Their respective functions in relation to the giving of consents under Chapter II of Part III of the Water Resources Act 1991 (offences in relation to pollution of water resources) for any discharge of waste in liquid form other than waste waters.
In Scotland, [the Scottish Environment Protection Agency] or the Secretary of State.	Their respective functions in relation to the giving of consents under Part II of the Control of Pollution Act 1974 (pollution of water) for any discharge of waste in liquid form other than waste waters.

(2)   In Table 5 above, references to functions do not include functions of making, revoking, amending, revising or re-enacting orders, regulations or schemes where those functions are required to be discharged by statutory instrument.

4. Relevant objectives

(1) For the purposes of this Schedule, the following objectives are relevant objectives in relation to the disposal or recovery of waste—
- (a) ensuring that waste is recovered or disposed of without endangering human health and without using processes or methods which could harm the environment and in particular without—
  - (i) risk to water, air, soil, plants or animals; or
  - (ii) causing nuisance through noise or odours; or
  - (iii) adversely affecting the countryside or places of special interest;
- (b) implementing, so far as material, any plan made under the plan-making provisions.

(2) The following additional objectives are relevant objectives in relation to the disposal of waste—
- (a) establishing an integrated and adequate network of waste disposal installations, taking account of the best available technology not involving excessive costs; and
- (b) ensuring that the network referred to at paragraph (a) above enables—
  - (i) the European Community as a whole to become self-sufficient in waste disposal, and the Member States individually to move towards that aim, taking into account geographical circumstances or the need for specialised installations for certain types of waste; and
  - (ii) waste to be disposed of in one of the nearest appropriate installations, by means of the most appropriate methods and technologies in order to ensure a high level of protection for the environment and public health.

(3) The following further objectives are relevant objectives in relation to functions under the plan-making provisions—
- (a) encouraging the prevention or reduction of waste production and its harmfulness, in particular by—
  - (i) the development of clean technologies more sparing in their use of natural resources;
  - (ii) the technical development and marketing of products designed so as to make no contribution or to make the smallest possible contribution, by the nature of their manufacture, use or final disposal, to increasing the amount or harmfulness of waste and pollution hazards; and
  - (iii) the development of appropriate techniques for the final disposal of dangerous substances contained in waste destined for recovery; and
- (b) encouraging—
  - (i) the recovery of waste by means of recycling, reuse or reclamation or any other process with a view to extracting secondary raw materials; and
  - (ii) the use of waste as a source of energy.

5. Preparation of offshore waste management plan

(1) Subject to sub-paragraph (2) below, it shall be the duty of a licensing authority to prepare a statement ("the plan") containing the authority's policies in relation to the recovery or disposal of waste for attaining the relevant objectives in those parts of United Kingdom waters and United Kingdom controlled waters for which the authority is the licensing authority.

(2) Two or more licensing authorities may join together to prepare a single statement covering the several parts of United Kingdom waters and United Kingdom controlled waters for which they are the licensing authorities.

(3) The plan shall relate in particular to—
- (a) the type, quantity and origin of waste to be recovered or disposed of;
- (b) general technical requirements;
- (c) any special arrangements for particular wastes; and
- (d) suitable disposal sites or installations.

(4) The licensing authority shall make copies of the plan available to the public on payment of reasonable charges.

(5) In this paragraph, "United Kingdom waters" and "United Kingdom controlled waters" have the meaning given by section 24(1) of the Food and Environment Protection Act 1985.

6. Matters to be covered by permits

When a pollution control authority grants or modifies a permit, and the activities authorised by the permit include the disposal of waste, the pollution control authority shall ensure that the permit covers—
- (a) the types and quantities of waste,
- (b) the technical requirements,
- (c) the security precautions to be taken,
- (d) the disposal site, and
- (e) the treatment method.

7. Modifications of provisions relating to development plans

(1) Subject to sub-paragraph (2) below, sections 12(3A), 31(3) and 36(3) of the Town and Country Planning Act 1990 or, in Scotland, sections 5(3)(a) and 9(3)(a) of the Town and Country Planning (Scotland) Act 1972, shall have effect as if the policies referred to in those sections also included policies in respect of suitable waste disposal sites or installations.

(2) In the case of the policies referred to in section 36(3) of the Town and Country Planning Act 1990, sub-paragraph (1) above shall have effect subject to the provisions of section 36(5) of that Act.

(3) Section 38(1) of the Town and Country Planning Act 1990 shall have effect as if the definition of waste policies included detailed policies in respect of suitable disposal sites or installations for the carrying on of such development as is referred to in that definition.

8. Modifications of Part I of the Environmental Protection Act 1990

(1) Subject to section 28(1) of the 1990 Act, Part I of the 1990 Act shall have effect in relation to prescribed processes involving the disposal or recovery of waste with such modifications as are needed to allow an enforcing authority to exercise its functions under that Part for the purpose of achieving the relevant objectives.

(2) Nothing in sub-paragraph (1) above requires an enforcing authority granting an authorisation in relation to such a process to take account of the relevant objectives insofar as they relate to the prevention of detriment to the amenities of the locality in which the process is (or is to be) carried on if planning permission, resulting from the taking of a specified action by a planning authority after 30th April 1994, is or, before the process is carried on, will be in force.

9. Modifications of Part II of the Environmental Protection Act 1990

(1) Part II of the 1990 Act shall have effect subject to the following modifications.

(2) Any reference to waste shall include a reference to Directive waste.

(3) In sections 33(1)(a) and (5), 54(1)(a), (2), (3) and (4)(d) and 69(2), any reference to the deposit of waste in or on land shall include a reference to any operation listed in Part III or IV of this Schedule involving such a deposit.

(4) In sections 33(1)(b), 54(1)(b), (2), (3) and (4)(d) and 69(2), any reference to the treatment or disposal, or to the treatment, keeping or disposal, of controlled waste shall be taken to be a reference to submitting controlled waste to any of the operations listed in Part III or IV of this Schedule other than an operation mentioned in sub-paragraph (3) above.

(5) In sections 33(1)(c) and 35, any reference to the treatment or disposal, or to the treatment, keeping or disposal, of controlled waste shall include a reference to submitting controlled waste to any of the operations listed in Part III or Part IV of this Schedule.

(6) Section 33(2) shall not apply to the treatment, keeping or disposal of household waste by an establishment or undertaking.

(7) In section 36(3), the reference to planning permission shall be taken to be a reference to planning permission resulting from the taking of a specified action by a planning authority after 30th April 1994.

(8) In section 50(3), any reference to the disposal of waste shall include a reference to the recovery of waste.

[(9) In subsection (1) of section 62, any reference to the treatment, keeping or disposal of such waste as is referred to in that subsection shall include a reference to submitting such waste to any of the operations listed in Part III or IV of this Schedule.

(10) In subsection (2) of section 62, any reference to the treatment, keeping or disposal of special waste shall include a reference to submitting special waste to any of the operations listed in Part III or IV of this Schedule.]

10. Modifications of Part I of the Control of Pollution Act 1974

(1) Part I of the Control of Pollution Act 1974 shall have effect, in a case where the planning permission referred to in section 5(3) of that Act does not result from the taking of a specified action by a planning authority after 30th April 1994, as if the duty imposed upon the disposal authority by that subsection was a duty not to reject the application unless the authority is satisfied that its rejection is necessary for the purpose of preventing—
  (a)   pollution of the environment;
  (b)   danger to public health; or
  (c)   serious detriment to the amenities of the locality.

(2) In sub-paragraph (1) above, "pollution of the environment" has the same meaning as in Part II of the 1990 Act.

(3) Part I of the Control of Pollution Act 1974 shall have effect as if any reference in that Part to waste included a reference to Directive waste.

11. References to "waste" in Planning and Water legislation

In the Town and Country Planning Act 1990, the Town and Country Planning (Scotland) Act 1972, Part II of the Control of Pollution Act 1974 and Chapter II of Part III of the Water Resources Act 1991, any reference to "waste" shall include a reference to Directive waste.

12. Registration by professional collectors and transporters of waste, and by dealers and brokers

(1) Subject to sub-paragraph (3) below, it shall be an offence for an establishment or undertaking falling within sub-paragraph (a), (c), (f) or (g) of regulation 2(1) of the Controlled Waste (Registration of Carriers and Seizure of Vehicles) Regulations 1991 after 31st December 1994 to collect or transport waste on a professional basis unless it is registered in accordance with the provisions of this paragraph.

(2) Subject to sub-paragraph (3) below, it shall be an offence for an establishment or undertaking falling within sub-paragraph (a), (b) or (c) of regulation 20(4) after 31st December 1994 to arrange for the recovery or disposal of waste on behalf of another person unless it is registered in accordance with the provisions of this paragraph.

(3) Sub-paragraphs (1) and (2) above do not apply in cases where the establishment or undertaking is carrying on the activities therein mentioned pursuant to, and in accordance with the terms and conditions of, a permit.

(4) An establishment or undertaking shall register with the waste regulation authority in whose area its principal place of business in Great Britain is located or, where it has no place of business in Great Britain, with any waste regulation authority.

(5) Each waste regulation authority shall establish and maintain a register of establishments and undertakings registering with it under the provisions of this paragraph.

(6) The register shall contain the following particulars in relation to each such establishment or undertaking—
  (a)   the name of the establishment or undertaking;
  (b)   the address of its principal place of business; and
  (c)   the address of any place at or from which it carries on its business.

(7) The waste regulation authority shall enter the relevant particulars in the register in relation to an establishment or undertaking if it receives notice of them in writing or otherwise becomes aware of those particulars.

(8) A person guilty of an offence under sub-paragraph (1) or (2) above shall be liable on summary conviction to a fine not exceeding level 2 on the standard scale.

(9) Each waste regulation authority shall secure that any register maintained by it under this paragraph is open to inspection . . . by members of the public free of charge at all reasonable hours and shall afford to members of the public reasonable facilities for obtaining, on payment of reasonable charges, copies of entries in the register.

(10) Registers under this paragraph may be kept in any form.

(11) In this paragraph, "registered carrier" and "controlled waste" have the same meaning as they have in the Control of Pollution (Amendment) Act 1989, "registered broker" has the same meaning as in regulation 20 and Schedule 5, and "collect" and "transport" have the same meaning as they have in Article 12 of the Directive.

13. Duty to carry out appropriate periodic inspections

(1) [Subject to sub-paragraphs (3) to (5) below,] any establishment or undertaking which carries out the recovery or disposal of controlled waste, or which collects or transports controlled waste on a professional basis, or which arranges for the recovery or disposal of controlled waste on behalf of others (dealers or brokers), [and producers of special waste,] shall be subject to appropriate periodic inspections by the competent authorities.

(2) [Section] 71(2) and (3) of the 1990 Act (. . . power to obtain information) shall have effect as if the provisions of this paragraph were provisions of Part II of that Act and as if, in those sections, references to a waste regulation authority were references to a competent authority.

[(2A) Section 108 of the Environment Act 1995 (powers of entry) shall apply as if the competent authority was an enforcing authority and its functions under this paragraph were pollution control functions.]

[(3) Subject to sub-paragraph (4) below, in a case where an establishment or undertaking is carrying on an exempt activity in reliance upon an exemption conferred by regulation 17(1) of, and paragraph 45(1) or (2) of Schedule 3 to, these Regulations, a competent authority which is a waste regulation authority shall discharge its duty under sub-paragraph (1) in respect of any place where such an activity is so carried on by—
  (a) carrying out an initial inspection of that place within two months of having received in respect of that place the notice, plan and fee referred to in regulation 18(4A); and
  (b) thereafter carrying out periodic inspections of that place at intervals not exceeding 12 months.

(4) Where the notice, plan and fee referred to in paragraph (a) of sub-paragraph (3) above are received by the authority before 1st October 1995, that paragraph shall have effect as if for the reference to carrying out an initial inspection within two months of the receipt of such notice, plan and fee there were substituted a reference to carrying out such an inspection within nine months of their receipt.

(5) In the case of any such place as is mentioned in sub-paragraph (3) above, but without prejudice to any duties of waste regulation authorities imposed otherwise than by this paragraph, sub-paragraph (1) above does not require (but does permit) a competent authority which is a waste regulation authority to carry out the periodic inspections referred to in sub-paragraph (3)(b) above at intervals of less than 10 months.]

14. Record keeping

(1) Subject to [paragraph 45(3)(b) of Schedule 3 and] sub-paragraph (2) below, an establishment or undertaking which carries out the disposal or recovery of controlled waste shall—
  (a) keep a record of the quantity, nature, origin and, where relevant, the destination, frequency of collection, mode of transport and treatment method of any waste which is disposed of or recovered; and
  (b) make that information available, on request, to the competent authorities [or, in the case of special waste, to a previous holder; and for this purpose "holder", in respect of any such waste, means the producer or the person in possession of it].

[(1A) Where special waste is recovered or disposed of by an establishment or undertaking, it shall keep a record of the carrying out and supervision of the operation and, in the case of a disposal operation, of the after-care of the disposal site.]

(2) [Subject to sub-paragraph (3) below,] sub-paragraph (1) above does not apply where the disposal or recovery of the waste is covered by an exemption conferred by—

(a)　regulation 17(1) of, and Schedule 3 to, these Regulations; or

(b)　article 3 of the Deposits in the Sea (Exemptions) Order 1985.

[(3) Sub-paragraph (1) above does apply to an activity subject to an exemption conferred by regulation 17(1) of, and paragraph 45(1) or (2) of Schedule 3 to, these Regulations.]

[(4) Subject to sub-paragraph (5) below, it shall be an offence for an establishment or undertaking to fail to comply with any of the foregoing provisions of this paragraph insofar as that provision imposes any requirement or obligation upon it.

(5) Paragraph (2) of regulation 18 of the Special Waste Regulations 1996 (defence in cases of emergency etc) shall apply to a person charged with an offence under sub-paragraph (4) above as it applies to a person charged with an offence under paragraph (1) of that regulation.

(6) A person who, in purported compliance with a requirement to furnish any information imposed by or under any of the provisions of this paragraph, makes a statement which he knows to be false or misleading in a material particular, or recklessly makes any statement which is false or misleading in a material particular, commits an offence.

(7) A person who intentionally makes a false entry in any record required to be kept by virtue of any of the provisions of this paragraph commits an offence.

(8) Paragraphs (5) to (9) of regulation 18 of the Special Waste Regulations 1996 (offence where act or default causes offence by another, offences by bodies corporate and penalties) shall apply to an offence under this paragraph as they apply to an offence under that regulation.]

[959]

NOTES

Para 1: word omitted from definition "plan-making provisions" revoked, and words in square brackets substituted, by the Environment Act (Consequential Amendments) Regulations 1996, SI 1996/593, reg 3, Sch 2, para 10(5)(a); definition omitted revoked by SI 1996/973, reg 2, Schedule, para 17(3)(a).

Para 3: in Table 5 words in first and third pairs of square brackets substituted, and words in second pair of square brackets inserted, by SI 1996/593, reg 3, Sch 2, para 10(5)(b), words in fourth pair of square brackets substituted by the Environment Act 1995, s 120, Sch 22, para 233(1), words in final pair of square brackets substituted by SI 1996/973, reg 2, Schedule, para 17(3)(b).

Para 9: sub-paras (9), (10) inserted by SI 1996/972, reg 25, Sch 3.

Para 12: words omitted from sub-para (9) revoked by SI 1996/593, reg 3, Sch 2, para 10(c).

Para 13: words in first pair of square brackets in sub-para (1) inserted by the Waste Management Licensing (Amendment etc) Regulations 1995, SI 1995/288, reg 3(17), words in second pair of square brackets in sub-para (1) inserted by SI 1996/972, reg 25, Sch 3; word in square brackets in sub-para (2) substituted, and words omitted from sub-para (2A) revoked, and sub-para (2A) inserted, by SI 1996/593, reg 3, Sch 2, para 10(d); sub-paras (3)–(5) inserted by SI 1995/288, reg 3(18).

Para 14: words in first pair of square brackets in sub-para (1) inserted by SI 1995/288, reg 3, words in second pair of square brackets in sub-para (1) inserted by SI 1996/972, reg 25, Sch 3; sub-paras (1A), (4)–(8) inserted by SI 1996/972, reg 25, Sch 3; words in square brackets in sub-para (2) inserted, and sub-para (3) inserted, by SI 1995/288, reg 3.

Modification: para 4(1)(b) shall have effect as if the reference to any plan made under the plan making provisions included plans made under the Transfrontier Shipment of Waste Regulations 1994, reg 11, by the Transfrontier Shipment of Waste Regulations 1994, SI 1994/1137, reg 11(6).

PART II
SUBSTANCES OR OBJECTS WHICH ARE WASTE WHEN DISCARDED ETC

1.　Production or consumption residues not otherwise specified in this Part of this Schedule (Q1).

2.　Off-specification products (Q2).

3.　Products whose date for appropriate use has expired (Q3).

4.　Materials spilled, lost or having undergone other mishap, including any materials, equipment, etc, contaminated as a result of the mishap (Q4).

5.　Materials contaminated or soiled as a result of planned actions (eg residues from cleaning operations, packing materials, containers, etc) (Q5).

6.　Unusable parts (eg reject batteries, exhausted catalysts, etc) (Q6).

7. Substances which no longer perform satisfactorily (eg contaminated acids, contaminated solvents, exhausted tempering salts, etc) (Q7).

8. Residues of industrial processes (eg slags, still bottoms, etc) (Q8).

9. Residues from pollution abatement processes (eg scrubber sludges, baghouse dusts, spent filters, etc) (Q9).

10. Machining or finishing residues (eg lathe turnings, mill scales, etc) (Q10).

11. Residues from raw materials extraction and processing (eg mining residues, oil field slops, etc) (Q11).

12. Adulterated materials (eg oils contaminated with PCBs, etc) (Q12).

13. Any materials, substances or products whose use has been banned by law (Q13).

14. Products for which the holder has no further use (eg agricultural, household, office, commercial and shop discards, etc) (Q14).

15. Contaminated materials, substances or products resulting from remedial action with respect to land (Q15).

16. Any materials, substances or products which are not contained in the above categories (Q16).

(Note:—the reference in brackets at the end of each paragraph of this Part of this Schedule is the number of the corresponding paragraph in Annex 1 to the Directive.)

[960]

PART III
WASTE DISPOSAL OPERATIONS

1. Tipping of waste above or underground (eg landfill, etc) (D1).

2. Land treatment of waste (eg biodegradation of liquid or sludge discards in soils, etc) (D2).

3. Deep injection of waste (eg injection of pumpable discards into wells, salt domes or naturally occurring repositories, etc) (D3).

4. Surface impoundment of waste (eg placement of liquid or sludge discards into pits, ponds or lagoons, etc) (D4).

5. Specially engineered landfill of waste (eg placement of waste into lined discrete cells which are capped and isolated from one another and the environment, etc) (D5).

6. Release of solid waste into a water body except seas or oceans (D6).

7. Release of waste into seas or oceans including seabed insertion (D7).

8. Biological treatment of waste not listed elsewhere in this Part of this Schedule which results in final compounds or mixtures which are disposed of by means of any of the operations listed in this Part of this Schedule (D8).

9. Physico-chemical treatment of waste not listed elsewhere in this Part of this Schedule which results in final compounds or mixtures which are disposed of by means of any of the operations listed in this Part of this Schedule (eg evaporation, drying, calcination, etc) (D9).

10. Incineration of waste on land (D10).

11. Incineration of waste at sea (D11).

12. Permanent storage of waste (eg emplacement of containers in a mine, etc) (D12).

13. Blending or mixture of waste prior to the waste being submitted to any of the operations listed in this Part of this Schedule (D13).

14. Repackaging of waste prior to the waste being submitted to any of the operations listed in this Part of this Schedule (D14).

15. Storage of waste pending any of the operations listed in this Part of this Schedule, but excluding temporary storage, pending collection, on the site where the waste is produced (D15).

(Note:— the reference in brackets at the end of each paragraph of this Part of this Schedule is the number of the corresponding paragraph in Annex IIA to the Directive.)

[961]

PART IV
WASTE RECOVERY OPERATIONS

1. Reclamation or regeneration of solvents (R1).

2. Recycling or reclamation of organic substances which are not used as solvents (R2).

3. Recycling or reclamation of metals and metal compounds (R3).

4. Recycling or reclamation of other inorganic materials (R4).

5. Regeneration of acids or bases (R5).

6. Recovery of components used for pollution abatement (R6).

7. Recovery of components from catalysts (R7).

8. Re-refining, or other reuses, of oil which is waste (R8).

9. Use of waste principally as a fuel or for other means of generating energy (R9).

10. Spreading of waste on land resulting in benefit to agriculture or ecological improvement, including composting and other biological transformation processes, except in the case of waste excluded under Article 2(1)(b)(iii) of the Directive (R10).

11. Use of wastes obtained from any of the operations listed in paragraphs 1 to 10 of this Part of this Schedule (R11).

12. Exchange of wastes for submission to any of the operations listed in paragraphs 1 to 11 of this Part of this Schedule (R12).

13. Storage of waste consisting of materials intended for submission to any operation listed in this Part of this Schedule, but excluding temporary storage, pending collection, on the site where it is produced (R13).

(Note:—the reference in brackets at the end of each paragraph of this Part of this Schedule is the number of the corresponding paragraph in Annex IIB to the Directive.)

[962]

SCHEDULE 5
REGISTRATION OF BROKERS OF CONTROLLED WASTE
Regulation 20(7)

PART I
GENERAL

1. Interpretation

(1) In this Schedule—
"the Carriers Regulations" means the Controlled Waste (Registration of Carriers and Seizure of Vehicles) Regulations 1991;
"date of expiry", in relation to a broker's registration, in a case to which sub-paragraph (2) or (3) of paragraph 7 applies, has the meaning given by that sub-paragraph, and in any other case means the date on which the period of three years mentioned in paragraph 7(1) expires;
"notice" means notice in writing;
"relevant offence" means an offence under any of the enactments listed in regulation 3; and
"relevant period" means two months or, except in the case of an application for the renewal of his registration by a person who is already registered, such longer period as may be agreed between the applicant and the waste regulation authority.

(2) In determining for the purposes of paragraph 3(13) or 5(1) whether it is desirable for any individual to be or to continue to be authorised to arrange (as dealer or broker) for the disposal or recovery of controlled waste on behalf of other persons, a waste regulation authority shall have regard, in a case in which a person other than the individual has been convicted of a relevant offence, to whether that individual has been a party to the carrying on of a business in a manner involving the commission of relevant offences.

(3) In relation to any applicant for registration or registered broker, another relevant person shall be treated for the purposes of paragraph 3(13) or 5(1) as having been convicted of a relevant offence if—

    (a)   any person has been convicted of a relevant offence committed by him in the course of his employment by the applicant or registered broker or in the course of the carrying on of any business by a partnership one of the members of which was the applicant or registered broker;

    (b)   a body corporate has been convicted of a relevant offence committed at a time when the applicant or registered broker was a director, manager, secretary or other similar officer of that body corporate; or

    (c)   where the applicant or registered broker is a body corporate, a person who is a director, manager, secretary or other similar officer of that body corporate—

        (i)   has been convicted of a relevant offence; or

        (ii)   was a director, manager, secretary or other similar officer of another body corporate at a time when a relevant offence for which that other body corporate has been convicted was committed.

(4) For the purposes of this Schedule, an application for registration or for the renewal of a registration as a broker of controlled waste shall be treated as pending—

    (a)   whilst it is being considered by the waste regulation authority; or

    (b)   if it has been refused or the relevant period from the making of the application has expired without the applicant having been registered, whilst either—

        (i)   the period for appealing in relation to that application has not expired; or

        (ii)   the application is the subject of an appeal which has not been disposed of.

(5) For the purposes of this Schedule, an appeal is disposed of when any of the following occurs—

    (a)   the appeal is withdrawn;

    (b)   the appellant is notified by the Secretary of State or the waste regulation authority in question that his appeal has been dismissed; or

    (c)   the waste regulation authority complies with any direction of the Secretary of State to renew the appellant's registration or to cancel the revocation.

(6) . . .

2. Registers

(1) It shall be the duty of each waste regulation authority to establish and maintain a register of brokers of controlled waste and—

    (a)   to secure that the register is open for inspection . . . by members of the public free of charge at all reasonable hours; and

    (b)   to afford to members of the public reasonable facilities for obtaining copies of entries in the register on payment of reasonable charges.

(2) A register under this paragraph may be kept in any form.

3. Applications for registration

(1) An application for registration or for the renewal of a registration as a broker of controlled waste shall be made to the waste regulation authority for the area in which the applicant has or proposes to have his principal place of business in Great Britain; but if the applicant does not have or propose to have a place of business in Great Britain, the applicant may apply to any waste regulation authority.

(2) Subject to sub-paragraphs (3) to (5) below, a person shall not make an application for registration or for the renewal of a registration whilst—

    (a)   a previous application of his is pending; or

    (b)   he is registered.

(3) Sub-paragraph (2) above shall not prevent a person from applying for the renewal of a registration where his application is made within the period of six months mentioned in paragraph 7(5).

(4) An application for registration or for the renewal of a registration in respect of a business which is or is to be carried on by a partnership shall be made by all of the partners or prospective partners.

(5) A prospective partner in a business carried on by a partnership whose members are already registered may make an application for registration as a partner in that business to the waste regulation authority with whom the business is registered.

(6) An application for registration shall be made on a form corresponding to the form in Part II of this Schedule, or on a form substantially to the like effect, and shall contain the information required by that form.

(7) An application for the renewal of a registration shall be made on a form corresponding to the form in Part III of this Schedule, or on a form substantially to the like effect, and shall contain the information required by that form.

(8) Where an applicant wishes to apply to be registered both as a carrier and as a broker of controlled waste, he may, instead of making the application on the forms provided for by regulation 4(6) of the Carriers Regulations and sub-paragraph (6) above, make a combined application on a form containing the information required by those forms.

(9) Where an applicant wishes to apply both for the renewal of his registration as a carrier of controlled waste and for the renewal of his registration as a broker of controlled waste, he may, instead of making an application on the forms provided for by regulation 4(7) of the Carriers Regulations and sub-paragraph (7) above, make a combined application on a form containing the information required by those forms.

(10) A waste regulation authority shall provide a copy of the appropriate application form free of charge to any person requesting one.

(11) A waste regulation authority shall charge an applicant in respect of its consideration of his application—
    (a)   subject to paragraph (c) below, in the case of either an application for registration as a broker of controlled waste or a combined application for registration as both a carrier and broker of controlled waste, £95;
    (b)   in the case of either an application for the renewal of a registration as a broker of controlled waste or a combined application for renewal of registration both as a carrier and as a broker of controlled waste, £65;
    (c)   in the case of an application by a registered carrier of controlled waste for registration as a broker of controlled waste, £25,

and the applicant shall pay the charge when he makes his application.

(12) A waste regulation authority shall, on receipt of an application for registration or for the renewal of a registration, ensure that the register contains a copy of the application.

(13) A waste regulation authority may refuse an application for registration or for the renewal of a registration if, and only if—
    (a)   there has, in relation to that application, been a contravention of any of the requirements of the preceding provisions of this paragraph; or
    (b)   the applicant or another relevant person has been convicted of a relevant offence and, in the opinion of the authority, it is undesirable for the applicant to be authorised to arrange (as dealer or broker) for the disposal or recovery of controlled waste on behalf of other persons.

(14) Where a waste regulation authority decides to refuse an application for registration or for the renewal of a registration, the authority shall give notice to the applicant informing him that his application is refused and of the reasons for its decision.

(15) If an appeal is made under and in accordance with paragraph 6, the waste regulation authority shall, as soon as reasonably practicable, make appropriate entries in its register indicating when the appeal was made and the result of the appeal.

(16) If no such appeal is made, the waste regulation authority shall, as soon as reasonably practicable, make an appropriate entry in its register indicating that the application has not been accepted and that no appeal has been made.

(17) A waste regulation authority may remove from its register—
    (a)   a copy of an application included under sub-paragraph (12) above; or
    (b)   an entry made under sub-paragraph (15) or (16) above,

at any time more than six years after the application in question was made.

4. Registration as a broker and amendment of entries

(1) On accepting a person's application for registration or on being directed under paragraph 6(9) to register a person following an appeal in respect of such an application, the waste regulation authority shall make an entry in its register—

(a)   showing that person as a registered broker of controlled waste and allocating him a registration number (which may include any letter);

(b)   specifying the date on which the registration takes effect and its date of expiry;

(c)   stating any business name of his and the address of his principal place of business (together with any telephone, telex or fax number of his) and, in the case of an individual, his date of birth;

(d)   in the case of a body corporate, listing the names of each director, manager, secretary or other similar officer of that body and their respective dates of birth;

(e)   in the case of a company registered under the Companies Acts, specifying its registered number and, in the case of a company incorporated outside Great Britain, the country in which it was incorporated;

(f)   in a case where the person who is registered or another relevant person has been convicted of a relevant offence, giving the person's name, details of the offence, the date of conviction, the penalty imposed, the name of the Court and, in the case of an individual, his date of birth; and

(g)   in a case where the person who is registered or any company in the same group of companies as that person is the holder of a waste management licence, stating the name of the holder of the licence and the name of the authority which granted it.

(2) In the case of a business which is, or is to be, carried on by a partnership, all the partners shall be registered under one entry and only one registration number shall be allocated to the partnership.

(3) On making an entry in its register under sub-paragraph (1) above the waste regulation authority shall provide the registered person or partnership free of charge with a copy of the entry in the register.

(4) On accepting a person's application for the renewal of a registration or on being directed under paragraph 6(9) to register a person following an appeal in respect of such an application, the waste regulation authority shall amend the relevant entry in the register—

(a)   to show the date on which the renewal takes effect and the revised date of expiry of the registration;

(b)   to record any other change disclosed as a result of the application; and

(c)   to note in the register the date on which the amendments are made.

(5) The waste regulation authority shall at the same time as amending the register under sub-paragraph (4) above provide the registered person or partnership free of charge with a copy of the amended entry in the register.

(6) A person who is registered shall notify the waste regulation authority which maintains the relevant register of any change of circumstances affecting information in the register relating to him.

(7) On—

(a)   being notified of any change of circumstances in accordance with sub-paragraph (6) above;

(b)   accepting a prospective partner's application for registration in relation to a business carried on by a partnership whose members are already registered; or

(c)   being directed under paragraph 6(9) to register a prospective partner,

the waste regulation authority shall—

(i)   amend the relevant entry to reflect the change of circumstances or the registration of the prospective partner;

(ii)   note in the register the date on which the amendment is made;

(iii)   provide the registered person or partnership free of charge with a copy of the amended entry in the register.

(8) In this regulation—

"Companies Acts" has the meaning given by section 744 of the Companies Act 1985;

"business name" means a name under which a person carries on business and by virtue of which the Business Names Act 1985 applies; and

"group" has the meaning given by section 53(1) of the Companies Act 1989.

5. Revocation of registration

(1) A waste regulation authority may revoke a person's registration as a broker of controlled waste if, and only if—

    (a)   that person or another relevant person has been convicted of a relevant offence; and

    (b)   in the opinion of the authority, it is undesirable for the registered broker to continue to be authorised to arrange (as dealer or broker) for the disposal or recovery of controlled waste on behalf of other persons.

(2) Where a waste regulation authority decides to revoke a person's registration as a broker of controlled waste, it shall give notice to the broker informing him of the revocation and the reasons for its decision.

6. Appeals

(1) Where a person has applied to a waste regulation authority to be registered as a broker of controlled waste in accordance with paragraph 3, he may appeal to the Secretary of State if—

    (a)   his application is refused; or

    (b)   the relevant period from the making of the application has expired without his having been registered.

(2) A person whose registration as a broker of controlled waste has been revoked may appeal against the revocation to the Secretary of State.

(3) Notice of an appeal to the Secretary of State under sub-paragraph (1) or (2) above shall be given by the appellant to the Secretary of State.

(4) The notice of appeal shall be accompanied by the following—

    (a)   a statement of the grounds of appeal;

    (b)   in the case of an appeal under sub-paragraph (1) above, a copy of the relevant application;

    (c)   in the case of an appeal under sub-paragraph (2) above, a copy of the appellant's entry in the register;

    (d)   a copy of any relevant correspondence between the appellant and the waste regulation authority;

    (e)   a copy of any notice given to the appellant under paragraph 3(14) or 5(2);

    (f)   a statement indicating whether the appellant wishes the appeal to be in the form of a hearing or to be determined on the basis of written representations.

(5) The appellant shall at the same time as giving notice of appeal to the Secretary of State serve on the waste regulation authority a copy of the notice and a copy of the documents referred to in sub-paragraph (4)(a) and (f) above.

(6) Notice of appeal is to be given before the expiry of the period of 28 days beginning with—

    (a)   in the case of an appeal under sub-paragraph (1)(a) above, the date on which the appellant is given notice by the waste regulation authority that his application has been refused;

    (b)   in the case of an appeal under sub-paragraph (1)(b) above, the date on which the relevant period from the making of the application expired without the appellant having been registered; or

    (c)   in the case of an appeal under sub-paragraph (2) above, the date on which the appellant is given notice by the waste regulation authority that his registration as a broker of controlled waste has been revoked,

or before such later date as the Secretary of State may at any time allow.

(7) If either party to an appeal requests a hearing or the Secretary of State so decides, the appeal shall be or continue in the form of a hearing before a person appointed for the purpose by the Secretary of State.

(8) The person holding such a hearing shall after its conclusion make a written report to the Secretary of State which shall include his conclusions and recommendations or his reasons for not making any recommendations.

(9) On an appeal under this paragraph the Secretary of State may, as he thinks fit, either dismiss the appeal or give the waste regulation authority in question a direction to register the appellant or, as the case may be, to cancel the revocation.

(10) The Secretary of State shall—
    (a)   notify the appellant in writing of his determination of the appeal and of his reasons for it and, if a hearing is held, shall also provide him with a copy of the report of the person who conducted the hearing; and
    (b)   at the same time send a copy of those documents to the waste regulation authority.

(11) Where on an appeal made by virtue of sub-paragraph (1)(b) above the Secretary of State dismisses an appeal, he shall direct the waste regulation authority in question not to register the appellant.

(12) It shall be the duty of a waste regulation authority to comply with any direction under this paragraph.

[(13) This paragraph is subject to 114 of the Environment Act 1995 (delegation or reference of appeals).]

7. Duration of registration

(1) Subject to the following provisions of this paragraph, a person's registration as a broker of controlled waste shall cease to have effect on the expiry of the period of three years beginning with the date of the registration or, if it has been renewed, beginning with the date on which it was renewed or, as the case may be, last renewed.

(2) Where a registered carrier of controlled waste is registered as a broker of controlled waste otherwise than by way of renewal of an existing registration as a broker, and his registration as a carrier will expire within three years of the date of his registration as a broker, if at the time of making his application for registration as a broker he so requests, his registration as a broker shall expire on the same date as his registration as a carrier.

(3) Where a registered broker of controlled waste is registered as a carrier of controlled waste otherwise than by way of renewal of an existing registration as a carrier, and his registration as a broker will expire within three years of the date of his registration as a carrier, if on the next application for renewal of his registration as a broker which he makes after having been registered as a carrier he so requests, his renewed registration as a broker shall expire on the same date as his registration as a carrier.

(4) Registration as a registered broker shall cease to have effect if the registered broker gives notice requiring the removal of his name from the register.

(5) The waste regulation authority shall, no later than six months before the date of expiry of a broker's registration, serve on a registered broker—
    (a)   a notice informing him of the date of expiry and of the effect of sub-paragraph (6) below; and
    (b)   an application form for the renewal of his registration and a copy of his current entry in the register.

(6) Where an application for the renewal of a registration is made within the last six months prior to its date of expiry, the registration shall, notwithstanding the passing of the expiry date, continue in force—
    (a)   until the application is withdrawn or accepted; or
    (b)   if the waste regulation authority refuse the application or the relevant period from the making of the application has expired without the applicant having been registered, until—
        (i)   the expiry of the period for appealing; or
        (ii) where the applicant indicates within that period that he does not intend to make or continue with an appeal, the date on which such an indication is given.

(7) Where a waste regulation authority revokes a broker's registration, the registration shall, notwithstanding the revocation, continue in force until—
    (a)   the expiry of the period for appealing against the revocation; or
    (b)   where that person indicates within that period that he does not intend to make or continue with an appeal, the date on which such an indication is given.

(8) Where an appeal is made under and in accordance with the provisions of paragraph 6—
    (a) by a person whose appeal is in respect of such an application for the renewal of his registration as was made, in accordance with paragraph 3, at a time when he was already registered; or
    (b) by a person whose registration has been revoked,

that registration shall continue in force after its date of expiry or, as the case may be, notwithstanding the revocation, until the appeal is disposed of.

(9) A registration in respect of a business which is carried on by a partnership shall cease to have effect if any of the partners ceases to be registered or if any person who is not registered becomes a partner.

(10) The duration of a registration in respect of a business which is carried on by a partnership shall not be affected if a person ceases to be a partner or if a prospective partner is registered under paragraph 4(7) in relation to the partnership.

(11) Where a waste regulation authority accepts an application for the renewal of a broker's registration before the expiry date, the renewal shall for the purposes of this Schedule take effect from the expiry date.

8. Cessation of registration

Where by virtue of paragraph 6(11) or 7 a registration ceases to have effect, the waste regulation authority—
    (a) shall record this fact in the appropriate entry in its register and the date on which it occurred;
    (b) may remove the appropriate entry from its register at any time more than six years after the registration ceases to have effect.

[963]

NOTES
Para 1: sub-para (6) revoked by the Waste Management Licensing (Amendment etc) Regulations 1995, SI 1995/288, reg 3(22).
Para 2: words omitted revoked by the Environment Act (Consequential Amendments) Regulations 1996, SI 1996/593, reg 3, Sch 2, para 10(6)(a).
Para 6: sub-para (13) inserted by SI 1996/593, reg 3, Sch 2, para 10(6)(b).

PART II
FORM OF APPLICATION FOR REGISTRATION AS A BROKER OF CONTROLLED WASTE

Please read the guidance notes before completing this form

1. Full name of applicant (*note 1*)

Former name (if applicable)

Date of birth (if applicable)

2. Name under which applicant carries on business (if different from 1)

3. Address for correspondence

Post Code

4. Address of principal place of business (if different from 3)

Post Code

5.   Telephone/Telex/Fax number

Tel		Telex		Fax	

6.   If applicant has previously been a registered broker give:

(a) registration number or numbers

(b) name of waste regulation authority or authorities

7.   If applicant is a company registered under the Companies Act, give:

(a) company's registered number

(b) address of registered office

Post Code

(c) in the case of a company incorporated outside Great Britain, the country in which it was incorporated

8.   If applicant is a registered company or other body corporate, for each director, manager, secretary or other similar officer, give:

Full name	Position held	Address	Date of birth

9.   If applicant is a prospective partner in a business carried on by a partnership whose members are already registered brokers, give:

(a)   full name of partnership

(b)   registration number of partnership

10. Has the applicant or another relevant person *(note 2)* been convicted of any offence listed in regulation 3 of the Waste Management Licensing Regulations 1994 *(notes 3 and 4)*?

Yes ☐   No ☐

If **Yes**, give full details of each offence—

Full name of person convicted	Position held	Name of Court	Date of conviction	Offence and penalty imposed

If details of any conviction have been given, use the following space to provide the waste regulation authority with any additional information which you wish the authority to take into account in determining whether or not it is undesirable for the applicant to be authorised to arrange (as dealer or broker) for the disposal or recovery of controlled waste on behalf of other persons.

11. If the applicant is already a registered carrier of controlled waste, does he want his registration as a broker to expire on the same date as that on which his registration as a carrier expires (instead of lasting for 3 years)?

Yes   ☐   No   ☐

12. Is the applicant or another company in the same group (within the meaning of section 53(1) of the Companies Act 1989) the holder of a waste management licence?

Yes   ☐   No   ☐

    If **Yes**, give details of licence—

Full name of holder of licence	*Date of birth (if applicable)*	*Date of issue of licence*	*Name of authority which issued the licence*

Declaration

I declare that I have personally checked the information given in this application form and that it is true to the best of my knowledge, information and belief. I understand that registration may be refused if false or incomplete information is given and that untrue statements may result in prosecution and could lead to revocation of registration.

Signature: Date:

Position held:

Have you enclosed the fee of £95 (or where you are already a registered carrier of controlled waste, £25)? *(note 5)*

                                      Yes   ☐

GUIDANCE NOTES

1. In the case of a partnership or proposed partnership, each partner must apply for registration and his details must be included in this application form.

2. Details of an offence listed in regulation 3 of the Waste Management Licensing Regulations 1994 must be given if the applicant was convicted of the offence or if the person convicted of the offence ("the relevant person")—

    (a)   committed it in the course of his employment by the applicant;
    (b)   committed it in the course of the carrying on of any business by a partnership one of the members of which was the applicant;
    (c)   was a body corporate and at the time when the offence was committed the applicant was a director, manager, secretary or other similar officer of that body;
    (d)   was a director, manager, secretary or other similar officer of the applicant (where the applicant is a body corporate);

(e) was a body corporate and at the time when the offence was committed a director, manager, secretary or other similar officer of the applicant held such an office in the body corporate which committed the offence.

3. The offences listed in regulation 3 of the Waste Management Licensing Regulations 1994 are offences under any of the following provisions—

section 22 of the Public Health (Scotland) Act 1897;
section 95(1) of the Public Health Act 1936;
section 3, 5(6), 16(4), 18(2), 31(1), 32(1), 34(5), 78, 92(6) or 93(3) of the Control of Pollution Act 1974;
section 2 of the Refuse Disposal (Amenity) Act 1978;
the Control of Pollution (Special Waste) Regulations 1980;
section 9(1) of the Food and Environment Protection Act 1985;
the Transfrontier Shipment of Hazardous Waste Regulations 1988;
the Merchant Shipping (Prevention of Pollution by Garbage) Regulations 1988;
section 1, 5, 6(9) or 7(3) of the Control of Pollution (Amendment) Act 1989;
section 107, 118(4) or 175(1) of the Water Act 1989;
section 23(1), 33, 34(6), 44, 47(6), 57(5), 59(5), 63(2), 69(9), 70(4), 71(3) or 80(4) of the Environmental Protection Act 1990;
section 85, 202 or 206 of the Water Resources Act 1991;
section 33 of the Clean Air Act 1993;
[the Transfrontier Shipment of Waste Regulations 1994]
[the Special Waste Regulations 1996].

4. Details of a conviction need not be given where under the terms of the Rehabilitation of Offenders Act 1974 the conviction is spent.

5. The fee of £95 (or, if you are already a registered carrier of controlled waste, £25) must be sent with the application. The regulation authority may refuse the application if the fee is not enclosed.

[964]

NOTES

Guidance Note 3: words in first pair of square brackets inserted by the Transfrontier Shipment of Waste Regulations 1994, SI 1994/1137, reg 19(4); words in second pair of square brackets inserted by the Special Waste Regulations 1996, SI 1996/972, reg 25, Sch 3.

PART III
FORM OF APPLICATION FOR RENEWAL OF REGISTRATION AS A BROKER OF CONTROLLED WASTE

Please read the guidance notes before completing this form

1. Full name of applicant *(note 1)*

    Former name (if applicable)

    Date of birth (if applicable)

2. Address for correspondence

    Post Code

3. Telephone/Telex/Fax number   Tel   Telex   Fax

4. Registration number as broker

5. Has the applicant or another relevant person *(note 2)* been convicted of any offence listed in regulation 3 of the Waste Management Licensing Regulations 1994 *(notes 3 and 4)*?

    Yes ☐   No ☐

If **Yes**, give full details of each offence—

Full name of person convicted	Position held	Name of Court	Date of conviction	Offence and penalty imposed

If details of any convictions have been given, use the following space to provide the waste regulation authority with any additional information which you wish the authority to take into account in determining whether or not it is undesirable for the applicant to be authorised to arrange (as dealer or broker) for the disposal or recovery of controlled waste on behalf of others—

6. Give details of any changes in any other information in the applicant's existing entry in the register *(note 5)*.

7. If the applicant has been registered as a carrier of controlled waste since the commencement of his current registration as a broker, does he want his renewed registration as a broker to expire when his registration as a carrier expires (instead of it lasting for 3 years)?

Yes ☐   No ☐

Declaration

I declare that I have personally checked the information given in this application form and that it is true to the best of my knowledge, information and belief. I understand that registration may be refused if false or incomplete information is given and that untrue statements may result in prosecution and could lead to revocation of registration.

Signature: Date:

Position held:

Have you enclosed the fee of £65? *(note 6)*   Yes   ☐

GUIDANCE NOTES

1. In the case of a partnership, each partner must apply for registration and his details must be included in this application form.

2. Details of an offence listed in regulation 3 of the Waste Management Licensing Regulations 1994 must be given if the applicant was convicted of the offence or if the person convicted of the offence ("the relevant person")—

    (a)   committed it in the course of his employment by the applicant;
    (b)   committed it in the course of the carrying on of any business by a partnership one of the members of which was the applicant;
    (c)   was a body corporate and at the time when the offence was committed the applicant was a director, manager, secretary or other similar officer of that body;
    (d)   was a director, manager, secretary or other similar officer of the applicant (where the applicant is a body corporate);
    (e)   was a body corporate and at the time when the offence was committed a director, manager, secretary or other similar officer of the applicant held such an office in the body corporate which committed the offence.

3. The offences listed in regulation 3 of the Waste Management Licensing Regulations 1994 are offences under any of the following provisions—

    section 22 of the Public Health (Scotland) Act 1897;
    section 95(1) of the Public Health Act 1936;
    section 3, 5(6), 16(4), 18(2), 31(1), 32(1), 34(5), 78, 92(6) or 93(3) of the Control of Pollution Act 1974;
    section 2 of the Refuse Disposal (Amenity) Act 1978;
    the Control of Pollution (Special Waste) Regulations 1980;

section 9(1) of the Food and Environment Protection Act 1985;
the Transfrontier Shipment of Hazardous Waste Regulations 1988;
the Merchant Shipping (Prevention of Pollution by Garbage) Regulations 1988;
section 1, 5, 6(9) or 7(3) of the Control of Pollution (Amendment) Act 1989;
section 107, 118(4) or 175(1) of the Water Act 1989;
section 23(1), 33, 34(6), 44, 47(6), 57(5), 59(5), 63(2), 69(9), 70(4), 71(3) or 80(4) of
    the Environmental Protection Act 1990;
section 85, 202 or 206 of the Water Resources Act 1991;
section 33 of the Clean Air Act 1993;
[the Transfrontier Shipment of Waste Regulations 1994]
[the Special Waste Regulations].

4. Details of a conviction need not be given where under the terms of the Rehabilitation of Offenders Act 1974 the conviction is spent.

5. Check the information in the copy of the current entry in the register sent with the regulation authority's reminder that registration needs to be renewed or, if no such copy has been received, ask the authority for one.

6. The fee of £65 must be sent with the application. The regulation authority may refuse the application if the fee is not enclosed.

[965]–[968]

NOTES
    Guidance Note 3: words in first pair of square brackets inserted by the Transfrontier Shipment of Waste Regulations 1994, SI 1994/1137, reg 19(4); words in second pair of square brackets inserted by the Special Waste Regulations 1996, SI 1996/972, reg 25, Sch 3.

TRANSFRONTIER SHIPMENT OF WASTE REGULATIONS 1994

(SI 1994/1137)

NOTES
    Made: 22 April 1994.
    Commencement: 6 May 1994.
    Authority: European Communities Act 1972, s 2(2); Control of Pollution (Amendment) Act 1989, ss 2, 3, 9(1); Environmental Protection Act 1990, s 74(6).

ARRANGEMENT OF REGULATIONS

1 Citation and commencement

These Regulations may be cited as the Transfrontier Shipment of Waste Regulations 1994 and shall come into force on 6th May 1994.

[969]

2 Interpretation

(1)   In these Regulations "the principal Regulation" means Council Regulation (EEC) No 259/93 on the supervision and control of shipments of waste within, into and out of the European Community.

(2)   Unless the context otherwise requires—
  (a) expressions used in these Regulations shall have the meaning they bear in the principal Regulation; and
  (b) any reference in these Regulations to an Article is to an Article of the principal Regulation, including that Article as applied by any other provision of the principal Regulation.

[970]

3 Competent authorities of dispatch and destination

The following authorities shall be the competent authorities of dispatch and destination in relation to their areas for the purpose of the principal Regulation—
  (a) in Great Britain, waste regulation authorities within the meaning of section 30 of the Environmental Protection Act 1990;
  (b) in Northern Ireland, district councils within the meaning of section 1 of the Local Government Act (Northern Ireland) 1972.

[971]

4 Competent authority of transit

The Secretary of State shall be the competent authority of transit for the purpose of the principal Regulation.

[972]

5 Correspondent

The Secretary of State shall be the correspondent for the purpose of the principal Regulation.

[973]

6 Transmission of notification by competent authority of dispatch

(1)   If a competent authority of dispatch decides, in relation to the notifications referred to in Article 3(1), 6(1) or 15(1) relating to shipments of waste dispatched from its area, or in relation to any class of such notifications, to transmit the notification itself to the competent authority of destination, with copies to the consignee and to any competent authority of transit, it shall give notice by advertisement of that decision.

(2)   A notice of a decision under paragraph (1) above shall describe the notifications to which the competent authority's decision applies and the decision which is the subject of the notice shall take effect 2 weeks after the publication of the last of the notices required to be published.

(3)   Where a decision under paragraph (1) above takes effect, a notifier who intends to make a shipment of waste which requires a notification to which the competent authority's decision applies shall send the required notification to the authority which published the notice and shall not send copies of that notification to any other competent authority or to the consignee.

(4)   Subject to paragraph (5) below, a competent authority which receives a notification in accordance with paragraph (3) above shall, within 3 working days of receiving the notification, transmit it to the competent authority of destination, with copies to the consignee and any competent authority of transit.

(5)   Where the notification relates to the shipment of waste for disposal, paragraph (4) above shall not apply if the competent authority of dispatch has immediate objections to raise against the shipment in accordance with Article 4(3).

(6)   A competent authority which has published notice of a decision in accordance with this regulation may withdraw it at any time by giving notice by advertisement of the withdrawal and the withdrawal shall take effect 2 weeks after the publication of the last of the notices required to be published.

(7)   In this regulation "notice by advertisement" means—
  (a)   in relation to notice by a competent authority in England or Wales, a notice published in the London Gazette and [in such other manner as the authority consider appropriate for bringing the matters to which it relates to the attention of persons likely to be affected by them];
  (b)   in relation to notice by a competent authority in Scotland, a notice published in the Edinburgh Gazette and [in such other manner as the authority consider appropriate for bringing the matters to which it relates to the attention of persons likely to be affected by them]; and
  (c)   in relation to notice by a competent authority in Northern Ireland, a notice published in the Belfast Gazette and in at least 3 local newspapers circulating in the area of that authority.

                                                                              [974]

NOTES
    Para (7): words in square brackets in paras (a), (b) substituted by the Environment Act 1995 (Consequential Amendments) Regulations 1996, SI 1996/593, reg 3, Sch 2, para 11(2).

7 Financial guarantees or equivalent insurance

(1)   No person shall ship waste into or out of the United Kingdom unless a certificate has been issued in relation to the shipment under this regulation.

(2)   An application for a certificate under this regulation shall be made to the authority which is the competent authority of dispatch, destination or transit in the United Kingdom (as the case may be) in relation to the shipment.

(3)   A competent authority which receives an application under paragraph (2) above shall issue the certificate requested if it is satisfied that there is in force in respect of the shipment, or will be at the time the waste is shipped into or out of the United Kingdom (as the case may be), a financial guarantee or equivalent insurance satisfying the requirements of Article 27.

(4)   A competent authority shall make its decision on an application under paragraph (2) above—
  (a)   in respect of a shipment to which Article 3 applies, within 20 days following receipt of the application if it is a competent authority of dispatch or transit or within 30 days if it is a competent authority of destination;
  (b)   in respect of a shipment to which Article 6 applies, within 30 days following receipt of the application;
  (c)   in respect of a shipment to which Article 15 applies, within 70 days following receipt of the application;
  (d)   in respect of a shipment to which Article 20 applies, within 60 days following receipt of the application if it is a competent authority of transit or 70 days if it is a competent authority of destination;

(e) in respect of a shipment to which Article 23 applies, within 60 days following receipt of the application if it is the last competent authority of transit within the Community or otherwise within 20 days.

(5) A certificate issued under this regulation shall certify that the competent authority is satisfied as mentioned in paragraph (3) above.

[975]

8 Power of competent authority of dispatch to ensure return of waste

(1) Where a competent authority of dispatch is required by Article 25(1) or 26(2) to ensure that waste is returned to the United Kingdom it may serve a notice on the notifier concerned under paragraph (2) below.

(2) A notice served under this paragraph shall require the notifier to return the waste to an area within the United Kingdom specified in the notice by a date so specified.

(3) The date specified in a notice under paragraph (2) above shall allow the notifier a reasonable time to comply with the notice, having regard, in particular, to the location of the waste at the time the notice is served.

(4) Where a notifier fails to comply with a notice served on him under paragraph (2) above, the competent authority may serve a further notice on the notifier stating that the authority intends to act as the agent of the notifier to effect the return of the waste to the United Kingdom in order to fulfil the obligations of the authority under Article 25(1) or 26(2), as the case may be.

(5) Where a competent authority serves a notice under paragraph (4) above it may act as the agent of the notifier so far as is necessary to effect the return of the waste as mentioned in that paragraph and the notifier shall provide the competent authority with such information and assistance as the authority may reasonably request in writing to enable it to effect the return of the waste.

(6) Where a competent authority acts under paragraph (5) above it shall be deemed to be the duly authorised agent of the notifier acting within the scope of its authority.

[976]

9 Power of competent authority of destination to ensure disposal of waste

(1) Where a competent authority of destination is required by Article 26(3) to ensure the disposal or recovery of waste in an environmentally sound manner it may serve a notice on the consignee concerned under paragraph (2) below.

(2) A notice served under this paragraph shall require the consignee to ensure the disposal or recovery of waste in an environmentally sound manner in accordance with the notice and by a date specified in the notice.

(3) The date specified in a notice under paragraph (2) above shall allow the consignee a reasonable time to comply with the notice.

(4) Where a consignee fails to comply with a notice served on him under paragraph (2) above the competent authority may serve a further notice on the consignee stating that the powers set out in paragraph (6) below will be exercised on behalf of the authority so far as is necessary to enable it to effect the disposal or recovery of the waste in order to fulfil its obligations under Article 26(3).

(5) The powers referred to in paragraph (4) above shall be exercised on behalf of the competent authority, . . . by a person authorised in writing by the authority to exercise those powers ("authorised person").

(6)   Pursuant to a notice served under paragraph (4) above, an . . . authorised person may, on production of his authority—

(a) enter any land which he has reason to believe it is necessary for him to enter and on entering any land take with him—

(i) any person duly authorised by the competent authority and, if he has reasonable cause to apprehend any serious obstruction in the execution of the powers conferred by this regulation, a constable; and

(ii) any equipment or materials required for any purpose for which the power of entry is being exercised;

(b) make such examination and investigation as may in any circumstances be necessary;

(c) remove any waste from the land, or arrange for its removal, for the purpose of its disposal or recovery;

(d) dispose of or recover waste, or arrange for its disposal or recovery.

(7)   An . . . authorised person may exercise any of the powers set out in paragraph (6) above so far as is necessary to enable him to effect the disposal or recovery of the waste in order to fulfil the obligations of the competent authority under Article 26(3) and the consignee shall provide the . . . authorised person and the competent authority with such information and assistance as the . . . authorised person or the authority may reasonably request in writing to enable the competent authority to fulfil those obligations.

[977]

NOTES

Paras (5)–(7): words omitted revoked by the Environment Act 1995 (Consequential Amendments) Regulations 1996, SI 1996/593, reg 3, Sch 2, para 11(3).

10 Power of customs officer to detain shipment

(1)   On a request made upon him by a competent authority of dispatch or destination in the United Kingdom for the purpose of facilitating the exercise of any functions conferred on it by the principal Regulation or these Regulations, a customs officer may detain, for not more than 3 working days, waste specified in that request which has been imported into the United Kingdom or brought to a place for the purpose of being exported from the United Kingdom.

(2)   Anything detained under this regulation shall be dealt with during the period of its detention in such manner as the Commissioners of Customs and Excise may direct.

(3)   In this regulation and in regulation 12 below "customs officer" means any officer within the meaning of the Customs and Excise Management Act 1979.

[978]

11 Objections to shipments of waste in accordance with a waste management plan made by the Secretary of State

(1)   The Secretary of State shall prepare a waste management plan ("the plan") in accordance with Article 7 of Council Directive 75/442/EEC which shall contain his policies in relation to the import and export of waste for recovery or disposal into and out of the United Kingdom.

(2)   Any provision in the plan relating to the prevention of imports or exports of waste for disposal shall be in accordance with the principles referred to in Article 4(3)(a)(i), but shall be subject to Article 4(3)(a)(ii) and (iii).

(3)   For the purpose of preventing movements of waste which are not in accordance with the plan—

(a) a competent authority of destination shall, within the applicable time limit, object to any shipment of waste notified under Article 3(1) or 20(1), which the plan indicates should not be imported into the United Kingdom;

(b) a competent authority of dispatch shall, within the applicable time limit, object to any shipment of waste notified under Article 3(1) or 15(1), which the plan indicates should not be exported from the United Kingdom.

(4) In the case of shipments of waste to which Article 7(4) applies, competent authorities of destination and dispatch shall, within the applicable time limit, raise reasoned objections under the first indent of Article 7(4)(a) to prevent movements of waste which are not in accordance with the plan.

(5) It shall be the duty of the Secretary of State—

(a) to send a copy of the plan to each competent authority of dispatch and destination; and

(b) to make copies of the plan available to the public on payment of such reasonable charges as he thinks fit.

(6) Paragraph 4(1)(b) of Schedule 4 to the Waste Management Licensing Regulations 1994 shall have effect as if the reference to any plan made under the plan-making provisions included a reference to a plan made under this regulation.

[979]

12 Offences

(1) Any person who contravenes a provision of the principal Regulation in the United Kingdom so that waste is shipped in circumstances which are deemed to be illegal traffic under Article 26 commits an offence.

(2) Any person who transports, recovers, disposes of, or otherwise handles waste in the United Kingdom in contravention of a condition imposed under the principal Regulation on the shipment of waste commits an offence.

(3) Any consignee who, in relation to waste shipped to the United Kingdom, fails to send a certificate of disposal or recovery pursuant to Article 5(6), 8(6) or 20(9) (as the case may be) within the time limit set out in the applicable Article, or sends a certificate which is false in a material particular, commits an offence.

(4) Any person who contravenes regulation 7 of these Regulations commits an offence.

(5) Any person who supplies information which is false in a material particular to a competent authority in the United Kingdom for the purpose of obtaining a certificate under regulation 7 of these Regulations commits an offence.

(6) Any person who, in the United Kingdom, mixes wastes which are the subject of different notifications during shipment contrary to Article 29 commits an offence.

(7) Any notifier who ships waste from the United Kingdom without having entered into a contract with the consignee in accordance with Article 3(6), 6(6) or 15(4) where required to do so by the principal Regulation commits an offence.

(8) Any notifier who ships waste from the United Kingdom which is required to be accompanied by the information set out in Article 11, signed as required by that Article, and which is not so accompanied whilst in the United Kingdom, commits an offence.

(9) Any person who fails to comply with a notice served on him under regulation 8(2) or 9(2) of these Regulations commits an offence.

(10) Any person who intentionally obstructs an inspector or authorised person in the exercise of his powers under regulation 9 of these Regulations or a customs

officer in the exercise of his powers under regulation 10 of these Regulations commits an offence.

(11) Where the commission by any person of an offence under this regulation is due to the act or default of some other person, that other person shall be guilty of the offence, and a person may be charged with and convicted of an offence by virtue of this paragraph whether or not proceedings are taken against the first-mentioned person.

[980]

13 Offences by corporations etc

(1)   Where an offence under regulation 12 above which has been committed by a body corporate is proved to have been committed with the consent or connivance of, or to have been attributable to any neglect on the part of, a director, manager, secretary or other similar officer of the body corporate, or any other person purporting to act in any such capacity, he, as well as the body corporate, shall be guilty of that offence and shall be liable to be proceeded against and punished accordingly.

(2)   Where the affairs of a body corporate are managed by its members, paragraph (1) above shall apply in relation to the acts or defaults of a member in connection with his functions of management as if he were a director of the body corporate.

(3)   Where, in Scotland, an offence under regulation 12 above which has been committed by a Scottish partnership or an unincorporated association (other than a partnership) is proved to have been committed with the consent or connivance of, or to have been attributable to any neglect on the part of, a partner in the partnership or, as the case may be, a person concerned in the management or control of the association, he, as well as the partnership or association, shall be guilty of that offence and shall be liable to be proceeded against and punished accordingly.

[981]

14 Defences

(1)   In any proceedings for an offence under regulation 12 above it shall be a defence for the person charged to prove that he took all reasonable steps and exercised all due diligence to avoid the commission of the offence.

(2)   In any proceedings for an offence under regulation 12(2) above, it shall be a defence for the person charged to prove that he was not reasonably able to comply with the condition concerned by reason of an emergency.

(3)   In any proceedings for an offence under regulation 12(3) above on the grounds that the consignee has not sent a certificate of disposal or recovery (as the case may be) within the applicable time limit, it shall be a defence for the consignee to prove—
    (a) that he was not able to send the certificate within that time limit because he had not been able to dispose of or recover the waste in time as a result of an emergency; and
    (b) that he disposed of or recovered the waste as soon as was reasonably practicable or that he is taking all reasonable steps to ensure that the waste is disposed of or recovered as soon as is reasonably practicable.

[982]

15 Penalties

(1)   Subject to paragraph (2) below, a person who commits an offence under regulation 12 above shall be liable on summary conviction to a fine not exceeding—
    (a) in Great Britain, the statutory maximum;
    (b) in Northern Ireland, £2,000;
or on conviction on indictment to imprisonment for a term not exceeding two years, or a fine, or both.

(2)   A person who commits an offence under paragraph (8) of regulation 12 above shall be liable on summary conviction to a fine not exceeding—
   (a) in Great Britain, level 3 on the standard scale;
   (b) in Northern Ireland, £400.

[983]

16 Provision of information etc

For the purpose of performing any of his functions under the principal Regulation the Secretary of State may, by notice in writing, require any competent authority in the United Kingdom to furnish such information and documents as may be specified in the notice.

[984]

17 Notices

(1)   Any notice which is authorised to be served on a notifier under regulation 8 above or on a consignee under regulation 9 above may be served on the person in question either by delivering it to him, or by leaving it at his proper address, or by sending it by post to him at that address.

(2)   Any such notice may—
   (a) in the case of a body corporate, be served on the secretary or clerk of that body; and
   (b) in the case of a partnership, be served on a partner or a person having the control or management of that partnership business.

(3)   For the purpose of this regulation and section 7 of the Interpretation Act 1978 (service of documents by post) in its application to this regulation, the proper address of any person on whom a notice is to be served shall be the address given for him on the consignment note relating to the shipment of waste in connection with which the notice is to be served.

[985]

18, 19   *(Reg 18(1), (2) revoked by the Special Waste Regulations 1996, SI 1996/972, reg 26(1)(d); reg 18(3), (4) amend the Pollution Control (Special Waste) Regulations (Northern Ireland) 1981, SI 1981/252, reg 18, and substitute reg 8 of those Regulations; reg 19(1), (2) amend the Controlled Waste (Registration of Carriers and Seizure of Vehicles) Regulations 1991, SI 1991/1624, Schs 1, 2 at* **[907]**, **[908]***; reg 19(3), (4) amend the Waste Management Licensing Regulations 1994, SI 1994/1056, reg 3, Sch 5, Pts II, III at* **[939]**, **[964]**, **[965]***.)*

20 Registration of dealers and brokers

(1)   The register established and maintained by a waste regulation authority pursuant to paragraph 12(5) of Part I of Schedule 4 to the Waste Management Licensing Regulations 1994 shall also be a register of establishments or undertakings registering with the authority under this regulation.

(2)   The register shall contain the following particulars in relation to each such establishment or undertaking—
   (a) the name of the establishment or undertaking;
   (b) the address of its principal place of business; and
   (c) the address of any place at or from which it carries on business.

(3)   The waste regulation authority shall enter the relevant particulars in the register in relation to an establishment or undertaking which arranges (as dealer or broker) for the disposal or the recovery of waste if it becomes aware of them as a result of either—

(a) that establishment or undertaking applying, before 1st January 1995, to the authority under paragraph 3 of Part I of Schedule 5 to the Waste Management Licensing Regulations 1994 to be registered as a broker of controlled waste; or

(b) the authority being otherwise notified in writing before 1st January 1995 of those particulars.

(4) An establishment or undertaking registering under paragraph (3)(b) above shall register with the waste regulation authority in whose area its principal place of business in Great Britain is located or, where it has no place of business in Great Britain, with any waste regulation authority.

(5) In the case of an establishment or undertaking registered by virtue of paragraph (3)(a) above, its registration under this regulation shall have effect only for so long as its application to be registered as a broker of controlled waste is pending.

(6) In the case of an establishment or undertaking registered by virtue of paragraph (3)(b) above, its registration under this regulation shall cease to have effect on 1st January 1995 unless—

(a) it has before that date applied to be registered as a broker of controlled waste; and

(b) immediately before that date that application is pending,

in which event its registration under this regulation shall continue to have effect for so long as its application to be registered as a broker of controlled waste is pending.

(7) For the purposes of this regulation, paragraph 1(4) and(5) of Part I of Schedule 5 to the Waste Management Licensing Regulations 1994 shall apply for the purpose of determining whether an application to be registered as a broker of controlled waste is pending.

(8) Where a registration under this regulation ceases to have effect, the waste regulation authority—

(a) shall record this fact in the appropriate entry in its register and the date on which it occurred; and

(b) may remove the appropriate entry from its register at any time more than three years after the registration ceases to have effect.

(9) In this regulation, "waste regulation authority" has the meaning given by section 30 of the Environmental Protection Act 1990.

[986]

21 Revocations

(1) Subject to paragraph (2) below, the Transfrontier Shipment of Hazardous Waste Regulations 1988, the Control of Pollution (Special Waste) (Amendment) Regulations 1988 and the Transfrontier Shipment of Hazardous Waste Regulations (Northern Ireland) 1989 are hereby revoked.

(2) The Transfrontier Shipment of Hazardous Waste Regulations 1988 and the Transfrontier Shipment of Hazardous Waste Regulations (Northern Ireland) 1989 shall continue to apply in relation to shipments of waste effected before 6th November 1994 under an acknowledgement of receipt issued under Articles 4 and 5 of Council Directive 84/631/EEC on the supervision and control within the European Community of the transfrontier shipment of hazardous waste before these Regulations come into force.

[987]

CONSERVATION (NATURAL HABITATS, &C) REGULATIONS 1994

(SI 1994/2716)

NOTES
Made: 20 October 1994.
Commencement: 30 October 1994.
Authority: European Communities Act 1972, s 2(2).

ARRANGEMENT OF REGULATIONS

PART I
INTRODUCTORY PROVISIONS

PART II
CONSERVATION OF NATURAL HABITATS AND HABITATS OF SPECIES

European sites

Register of European sites

Management agreements

Control of potentially damaging operations

Special nature conservation orders

Byelaws

PART III
PROTECTION OF SPECIES

PART IV
ADAPTATION OF PLANNING AND OTHER CONTROLS

PART V
SUPPLEMENTARY PROVISIONS

PART I
INTRODUCTORY PROVISIONS

1 Citation and commencement

(1)   These Regulations may be cited as the Conservation (Natural Habitats, &c) Regulations 1994.

(2)   These Regulations shall come into force on the tenth day after that on which they are made.

[988]

2 Interpretation and application

(1)   In these Regulations—
"agriculture Minister" means the Minister of Agriculture, Fisheries and Food or the Secretary of State;
"competent authority" shall be construed in accordance with regulation 6;
"destroy", in relation to an egg, includes doing anything to the egg which is calculated to prevent it from hatching, and "destruction" shall be construed accordingly;
"enactment" includes a local enactment and an enactment contained in subordinate legislation within the meaning of the Interpretation Act 1978;
"European site" has the meaning given by regulation 10 and "European marine site" means a European site which consists of, or so far as it consists of, marine areas;
"functions" includes powers and duties;
"the Habitats Directive" has the meaning given by regulation 3(1);
"land" includes land covered by water and as respects Scotland includes salmon fishings;
"livestock" includes any animal which is kept—
     (a) for the provision of food, skins or fur,
     (b) for the purpose of its use in the carrying on of any agricultural activity, or
     (c) for the provision or improvement of shooting or fishing;
"local planning authority" means—
     (a) in England and Wales, except as otherwise provided, any authority having any function as a local planning authority or mineral planning authority under the Town and Country Planning Act 1990, and
     (b) in Scotland, a planning authority within the meaning of section 172(1) of the Local Government (Scotland) Act 1973;
"management agreement" means an agreement entered into, or having effect as if entered into, under regulation 16;
"marine area" means any land covered (continuously or intermittently) by tidal waters or any part of the sea in or adjacent to Great Britain up to the seaward limit of territorial waters;
"Natura 2000" means the European network of special areas of conservation, and special protection areas under the Wild Birds Directive, provided for by Article 3(1) of the Habitats Directive;
"nature conservation body", and "appropriate nature conservation body" in relation to England, Wales or Scotland, have the meaning given by regulation 4;

"occupier", for the purposes of Part III (protection of species), includes, in relation to any land other than the foreshore, any person having any right of hunting, shooting, fishing or taking game or fish;

"planning authority", in Scotland, means a planning authority within the meaning of section 172(1) of the Local Government (Scotland) Act 1973;

"the register" means the register of European sites in Great Britain provided for by regulation 11;

"relevant authorities", in relation to marine areas and European marine sites, shall be construed in accordance with regulation 5;

"statutory undertaker" has the same meaning as in the National Parks and Access to the Countryside Act 1949;

"the Wild Birds Directive" means Council Directive 79/409/EEC on the conservation of wild birds.

(2)	Unless the context otherwise requires, expressions used in these Regulations and in the Habitats Directive have the same meaning as in that Directive.

The following expressions, in particular, are defined in Article 1 of that Directive—

"priority natural habitat types" and "priority species";

"site" and "site of Community importance"; and

"special area of conservation".

(3)	In these Regulations, unless otherwise indicated—
(a)	any reference to a numbered regulation or Schedule is to the regulation or Schedule in these Regulations which bears that number, and
(b)	any reference in a regulation or Schedule to a numbered paragraph is to the paragraph of that regulation or Schedule which bears that number.

(4)	Subject to regulation 68 (which provides for Part IV to be construed as one with the Town and Country Planning Act 1990), these Regulations apply to the Isles of Scilly as if the Isles were a county and the Council of the Isles were a county council.

(5)	For the purposes of these Regulations the territorial waters of the United Kingdom adjacent to Great Britain shall be treated as part of Great Britain and references to England, Wales and Scotland shall be construed as including the adjacent territorial waters.

For the purposes of this paragraph—
(a)	territorial waters include any waters landward of the baselines from which the breadth of the territorial sea is measured; and
(b)	any question as to whether territorial waters are to be treated as adjacent to England, Wales or Scotland shall be determined by the Secretary of State or, for any purpose in relation to which the Minister of Agriculture, Fisheries and Food has responsibility, by the Secretary of State and that Minister acting jointly.

[989]

NOTES
Habitats Directive: Council Directive 92/43/EEC: OJ L206, 22.7.92, p 7.
Council Directive 79/409/EEC: OJ L103, 25.4.79, p 1.

3 Implementation of Directive

(1)	These Regulations make provision for the purpose of implementing, for Great Britain, Council Directive 92/43/EEC on the conservation of natural habitats and of wild fauna and flora (referred to in these Regulations as "the Habitats Directive").

(2)   The Secretary of State, the Minister of Agriculture, Fisheries and Food and the nature conservation bodies shall exercise their functions under the enactments relating to nature conservation so as to secure compliance with the requirements of the Habitats Directive.

Those enactments include—
>   Part III of the National Parks and Access to the Countryside Act 1949,
>   section 49A of the Countryside (Scotland) Act 1967 (management agreements),
>   section 15 of the Countryside Act 1968 (areas of special scientific interest),
>   Part I and sections 28 to 38 of the Wildlife and Countryside Act 1981,
>   sections 131 to 134 of the Environmental Protection Act 1990,
>   sections 2, 3, 5, 6, 7 and 11 of the Natural Heritage (Scotland) Act 1991, and
>   these Regulations.

(3)   In relation to marine areas any competent authority having functions relevant to marine conservation shall exercise those functions so as to secure compliance with the requirements of the Habitats Directive.

This applies, in particular, to functions under the following enactments—
>   the Sea Fisheries Acts within the meaning of section 1 of the Sea Fisheries (Wildlife Conservation) Act 1992,
>   the Dockyard Ports Regulation Act 1865,
>   section 2(2) of the Military Lands Act 1900 (provisions as to use of sea, tidal water or shore),
>   the Harbours Act 1964,
>   Part II of the Control of Pollution Act 1974,
>   sections 36 and 37 of the Wildlife and Countryside Act 1981 (marine nature reserves),
>   sections 120 to 122 of the Civic Government (Scotland) Act 1982 (control of the seashore, adjacent waters and inland waters),
>   the Water Resources Act 1991,
>   the Land Drainage Act 1991, and
>   these Regulations.

(4)   Without prejudice to the preceding provisions, every competent authority in the exercise of any of their functions, shall have regard to the requirements of the Habitats Directive so far as they may be affected by the exercise of those functions.

[990]

4 Nature conservation bodies

In these Regulations "nature conservation body" means the Nature Conservancy Council for England, the Countryside Council for Wales or Scottish Natural Heritage; and references to "the appropriate nature conservation body", in relation to England, Wales or Scotland, shall be construed accordingly.

[991]

5 Relevant authorities in relation to marine areas and European marine sites

For the purposes of these Regulations the relevant authorities, in relation to a marine area or European marine site, are such of the following as have functions in relation to land or waters within or adjacent to that area or site—
>   (a)   a nature conservation body;
>   (b)   a county council, [county council borough,] district council, London borough council or, in Scotland, a regional, islands or district council;
>   (c)   the [Environment Agency], a water undertaker or sewerage undertaker, or an internal drainage board;

    (d) a navigation authority within the meaning of the Water Resources Act 1991;

    (e) a harbour authority within the meaning of the Harbours Act 1964;

    (f) a lighthouse authority;

    (g) [the Scottish Environment Protection Agency] or a district salmon fishery board;

    (h) a local fisheries committee constituted under the Sea Fisheries Regulation Act 1966 or any authority exercising the powers of such a committee.

[992]

NOTES

Words in first pair of square brackets inserted by the Local Government Reorganisation (Wales) (Consequential Amendments) Order 1996, SI 1996/525, art 3, Schedule, para 18(1); words in second pair of square brackets substituted by the Environment Act 1995, s 120, Sch 22, para 233(1); words in final pair of square brackets substituted by SI 1996/973, reg 2, Schedule, para 18.

6 Competent authorities generally

(1)   For the purposes of these Regulations the expression "competent authority" includes any Minister, government department, public or statutory undertaker, public body of any description or person holding a public office.

The expression also includes any person exercising any function of a competent authority in the United Kingdom.

(2)   In paragraph (1)—

    (a) "public body" includes any local authority, joint board or joint committee; and

    (b) "public office" means—

        (a) an office under Her Majesty,

        (b) an office created or continued in existence by a public general Act of Parliament, or

        (c) an office the remuneration in respect of which is paid out of money provided by Parliament.

(3)   In paragraph (2)(a)—

"local authority"—

    (a) in relation to England, means a county council, district council or London borough council, the Common Council of the City of London, the sub- treasurer of the Inner Temple, the under treasurer of the Middle Temple or a parish council,

    (b) in relation to Wales, means a county council, [county borough] council or community council, and

    (c) in relation to Scotland, means a regional, islands or district council;

"joint board" and "joint committee" in relation to England and Wales mean—

    (a) a joint or special planning board constituted for a National Park by order under paragraph 1 or 3 of Schedule 17 to the Local Government Act 1972, or a joint planning board within the meaning of section 2 of the Town and Country Planning Act 1990, and

    (b) a joint committee appointed under section 102(1)(b) of the Local Government Act 1972,

and in relation to Scotland have the same meaning as in the Local Government (Scotland) Act 1973.

[993]

NOTES

Para (3): in definition "local authority" words in square brackets substituted by the Local Government Reorganisation (Wales) (Consequential Amendments) Order 1996, SI 1996/525, art 3, Schedule, para 18(2).

Modification: para (3)(b) modified, in relation to a National Park authority in Wales, by the National Park Authorities (Wales) Order 1995, SI 1995/2803, art 18, Sch 5, para 20.

Modification: para (3) modified, in relation to a National Park authority in England, by the National Park Authorities (England) Order 1996, SI 1996/1243, art 18, Sch 5, para 14.

PART II
CONSERVATION OF NATURAL HABITATS AND HABITATS OF SPECIES

European sites

7 Selection of sites eligible for identification as of Community importance

(1)   On the basis of the criteria set out in Annex III (Stage 1) to the Habitats Directive, and relevant scientific information, the Secretary of State shall propose a list of sites indicating with respect to each site—
   (a) which natural habitat types in Annex I to the Directive the site hosts, and
   (b) which species in Annex II to the Directive that are native to Great Britain the site hosts.

(2)   For animal species ranging over wide areas these sites shall correspond to the places within the natural range of such species which present the physical or biological factors essential to their life and reproduction.

For aquatic species which range over wide areas, such sites shall be proposed only where there is a clearly identifiable area representing the physical and biological factors essential to their life and reproduction.

(3)   Where appropriate the Secretary of State may propose modification of the list in the light of the results of the surveillance referred to in Article 11 of the Habitats Directive.

(4)   The list shall be transmitted to the Commission on or before 5th June 1995, together with information on each site including—
   (a) a map of the site,
   (b) its name, location and extent, and
   (c) the data resulting from application of the criteria specified in Annex III (Stage 1),
provided in a format established by the Commission.

[994]

8 Adoption of list of sites: designation of special areas of conservation

(1)   Once a site of Community importance in Great Britain has been adopted in accordance with the procedure laid down in paragraph 2 of Article 4 of the Habitats Directive, the Secretary of State shall designate that site as a special area of conservation as soon as possible and within six years at most.

(2)   The Secretary of State shall establish priorities for the designation of sites in the light of—
   (a) the importance of the sites for the maintenance or restoration at a favourable conservation status of—
      (i) a natural habitat type in Annex I to the Habitats Directive, or
      (ii) a species in Annex II to the Directive,
      and for the coherence of Natura 2000; and
   (b) the threats of degradation or destruction to which those sites are exposed.

[995]

9 Consultation as to inclusion of site omitted from the list

If consultation is initiated by the Commission in accordance with Article 5(1) of the Habitats Directive with respect to a site in Great Britain hosting a priority natural habitat type or priority species and—
   (a) the Secretary of State agrees that the site should be added to the list transmitted in accordance with regulation 7, or

    (b) the Council, acting on a proposal from the Commission in pursuance of paragraph 2 of Article 5 of the Habitats Directive, so decides,

the site shall be treated as added to the list as from the date of that agreement or decision.

[996]

10 Meaning of "European site" in these Regulations

    (1)   In these Regulations a "European site" means—
    (a) a special area of conservation,
    (b) a site of Community importance which has been placed on the list referred to in the third sub-paragraph of Article 4(2) of the Habitats Directive,
    (c) a site hosting a priority natural habitat type or priority species in respect of which consultation has been initiated under Article 5(1) of the Habitats Directive, during the consultation period or pending a decision of the Council under Article 5(3), or
    (d) an area classified pursuant to Article 4(1) or (2) of the Wild Birds Directive.

    (2)   Sites which are European sites by virtue only of paragraph (1)(c) are not within regulations 20(1) and (2), 24 and 48 (which relate to the approval of certain plans and projects); but this is without prejudice to their protection under other provisions of these Regulations.

[997]

Register of European sites

11 Duty to compile and maintain register of European sites

    (1)   The Secretary of State shall compile and maintain, in such form as he thinks fit, a register of European sites in Great Britain.

    (2)   He shall include in the register—
    (a) special areas of conservation, as soon as they are designated by him;
    (b) sites of Community importance as soon as they are placed on the list referred to in the third sub-paragraph of Article 4(2) of the Habitats Directive, until they are designated as special areas of conservation;
    (c) any site hosting a priority natural habitat type or priority species in respect of which consultation is initiated under Article 5(1) of the Habitats Directive, during the consultation period or pending a Council decision under Article 5(3); and
    (d) areas classified by him pursuant to Article 4(1) or (2) of the Wild Birds Directive, as soon as they are so classified or, if they have been classified before the commencement of these Regulations, as soon as practicable after commencement.

    (3)   He may, if appropriate, amend the entry in the register relating to a European site.

    (4)   He shall remove the relevant entry—
    (a) if a special area of conservation is declassified by the Commission under Article 9 of the Habitats Directive; or
    (b) if a site otherwise ceases to fall within any of the categories listed in paragraph (2) above.

    (5)   He shall keep a copy of the register available for public inspection at all reasonable hours and free of charge.

[998]

12 Notification to appropriate nature conservation body

(1)   The Secretary of State shall notify the appropriate nature conservation body as soon as may be after including a site in the register, amending an entry in the register or removing an entry from the register.

(2)   Notification of the inclusion of a site in the register shall be accompanied by a copy of the register entry.

(3)   Notification of the amendment of an entry in the register shall be accompanied by a copy of the amended entry.

(4)   Each nature conservation body shall keep copies of the register entries relating to European sites in their area available for public inspection at all reasonable hours and free of charge.

[999]

13 Notice to landowners, relevant authorities, &c

(1)   As soon as practicable after a nature conservation body receive notification under regulation 12 they shall give notice to—
  (a) every owner or occupier of land within the site,
  (b) every local planning authority in whose area the site, or any part of it, is situated, and
  (c) such other persons or bodies as the Secretary of State may direct.

(2)   Notice of the inclusion of a site in the register, or of the amendment of an entry in the register, shall be accompanied by a copy of so much of the relevant register entry as relates to land owned or occupied by or, as the case may be, to land within the area of, the person or authority to whom the notice is given.

(3)   The Secretary of State may give directions as to the form and content of notices to be given under this regulation.

[1000]

14 Local registration: England and Wales

An entry in the register relating to a European site in England and Wales is a local land charge.

[1001]

15   (*Applies to Scotland only.*)

Management agreements

16 Management agreements

(1)   The appropriate nature conservation body may enter into an agreement (a "management agreement") with every owner, lessee and occupier of land forming part of a European site, or land adjacent to such a site, for the management, conservation, restoration or protection of the site, or any part of it.

(2)   A management agreement may impose such restrictions as may be expedient for the purposes of the agreement on the exercise of rights over the land by the persons who can be bound by the agreement.

(3)   A management agreement—
  (a) may provide for the management of the land in such manner, the carrying out thereon of such work and the doing thereon of such other things as may be expedient for the purposes of the agreement;
  (b) may provide for any of the matters mentioned in sub-paragraph (a) being carried out, or for the costs thereof being defrayed, either by the said owner

or other persons or by the appropriate nature conservation body, or partly in one way and partly in another;

(c) may contain such other provisions as to the making of payments by the appropriate nature conservation body, and in particular for the payment by them of compensation for the effect of the restrictions mentioned in paragraph (2), as may be specified in the agreement.

(4) Where land in England and Wales is subject to a management agreement, the appropriate nature conservation body shall, as respects the enforcement of the agreement against persons other than the original contracting party, have the like rights as if—

(a) they had at all material times been the absolute owners in possession of ascertained land adjacent to the land subject to the agreement and capable of being benefited by the agreement, and

(b) the management agreement had been expressed to be for the benefit of that adjacent land;

and section 84 of the Law of Property Act 1925 (which enables the Lands Tribunal to discharge or modify restrictive covenants) shall not apply to the agreement.

(5) A management agreement affecting land in Scotland may be registered either—

(a) in a case where the land affected by the agreement is registered in that register, in the Land Register of Scotland, or

(b) in any other case, in the General Register of Sasines;

and, on being so recorded, it shall be enforceable at the instance of the appropriate nature conservation body against any person having an interest in the land and against any person deriving title from him:

Provided that a management agreement shall not be so enforceable against a third party who has *bona fide* onerously acquired right (whether completed by infeftment or not) to his interest in the land prior to the agreement being recorded as aforesaid, or against any person deriving title from such third party.

[1002]

17 Continuation in force of existing agreement, &c

(1) Any agreement previously entered into under—

(a) section 16 of the National Parks and Access to the Countryside Act 1949 (nature reserves),

(b) section 15 of the Countryside Act 1968 (areas of special scientific interest), or

(c) section 49A of the Countryside (Scotland) Act 1967 (management agreements),

in relation to land which on or after the commencement of these Regulations becomes land within a European site, or adjacent to such a site, shall have effect as if entered into under regulation 16 above.

Regulation 32(1)(b) (power of compulsory acquisition in case of breach of agreement) shall apply accordingly.

(2) Any other thing done or deemed to have been done under any provision of Part III or VI of the National Parks and Access to the Countryside Act 1949, or under section 49A of the Countryside (Scotland) Act 1967, in respect of any land prior to that land becoming land within a European site, or adjacent to such a site, shall continue to have effect as if done under the corresponding provision of these Regulations.

For the purposes of this paragraph Part III of the 1949 Act shall be deemed to include section 15 of the Countryside Act 1968 and anything done or deemed to be done under that section and to which this paragraph applies shall have effect as if done or deemed to be done under section 16 of the 1949 Act.

(3)   Any reference in an outlying enactment to a nature reserve within the meaning of section 15 of the National Parks and Access to the Countryside Act 1949 shall be construed as including a European site.

For this purpose an "outlying enactment" means an enactment not contained in, or in an instrument made under, the National Parks and Access to the Countryside Act 1949 or the Wildlife and Countryside Act 1981.

[1003]

Control of potentially damaging operations

18 Notification of potentially damaging operations

(1)   Any notification in force in relation to a European site under section 28 of the Wildlife and Countryside Act 1981 (areas of special scientific interest) specifying—
- (a) the flora, fauna, or geological or physiographical features by reason of which the land is of special interest, and
- (b) any operations appearing to the appropriate nature conservation body to be likely to damage that flora or fauna or those features,

shall have effect for the purposes of these Regulations.

(2)   The appropriate nature conservation body may, for the purpose of securing compliance with the requirements of the Habitats Directive, at any time amend the notification with respect to any of the matters mentioned in paragraph (1)(a) or (b).

(3)   Notice of any amendment shall be given—
- (a) to every owner and occupier of land within the site who in the opinion of the appropriate nature conservation body may be affected by the amendment, and
- (b) to the local planning authority;

and the amendment shall come into force in relation to an owner or occupier upon such notice being given to him.

(4)   The provisions of—
- (a) section 28(11) of the Wildlife and Countryside Act 1981 (notification to be local land charge in England and Wales), and
- (b) section 28(12) to (12B) of that Act (local registration of notification in Scotland),

apply, with the necessary modifications, in relation to an amendment of a notification under this regulation as in relation to the original notification.

[1004]

19 Restriction on carrying out operations specified in notification

(1)   The owner or occupier of any land within a European site shall not carry out, or cause or permit to be carried out, on that land any operation specified in a notification in force in relation to the site under regulation 18, unless—
- (a) one of them has given the appropriate nature conservation body written notice of a proposal to carry out the operation, specifying its nature and the land on which it is proposed to carry it out, and
- (b) one of the conditions specified in paragraph (2) is fulfilled.

(2)   Those conditions are—
- (a) that the operation is carried out with the written consent of the appropriate nature conservation body;
- (b) that the operation is carried out in accordance with the terms of a management agreement;
- (c) that four months have expired from the giving of the notice under paragraph (1)(a).

(3)   A person who, without reasonable excuse, contravenes paragraph (1) commits an offence and is liable on summary conviction to a fine not exceeding level 4 on the standard scale.

(4)   For the purposes of paragraph (3) it is a reasonable excuse for a person to carry out an operation—
  (a) that the operation was an emergency operation particulars of which (including details of the emergency) were notified to the appropriate nature conservation body as soon as practicable after the commencement of the operation; or
  (b) that the operation was authorised by a planning permission granted on an application under Part III of the Town and Country Planning Act 1990 or Part III of the Town and Country Planning (Scotland) Act 1972.

(5)   The appropriate nature conservation body has power to enforce this regulation; but nothing in this paragraph shall be construed as authorising the institution of proceedings in Scotland for an offence.

(6)   Proceedings in England and Wales for an offence under this regulation shall not, without the consent of the Director of Public Prosecutions, be taken by a person other than the appropriate nature conservation body.

[1005]

20 Supplementary provisions as to consents

(1)   Where it appears to the appropriate nature conservation body that an application for consent under regulation 19(2)(a) relates to an operation which is or forms part of a plan or project which—
  (a) is not directly connected with or necessary to the management of the site, and
  (b) is likely to have a significant effect on the site (either alone or in combination with other plans or projects),
they shall make an appropriate assessment of the implications for the site in view of that site's conservation objectives.

(2)   In the light of the conclusions of life assessment, they may give consent for the operation only after having ascertained that the plan or project will not adversely affect the integrity of the site.

(3)   The above provisions do not apply in relation to a site which is a European site by reason only of regulation 10(1)(c) (site protected in accordance with Article 5(4)).

(4)   Where in any case, whether in pursuance of this regulation or otherwise, the appropriate nature conservation body have not given consent for an operation, but they consider that there is a risk that the operation may nevertheless be carried out, they shall notify the Secretary of State.

(5)   They shall take such steps as are requisite to secure that any such notification is given at least one month before the expiry of the period mentioned in regulation 19(2)(c) (period after which operation may be carried out in absence of consent).

[1006]

21 Provision as to existing notices and consents

(1)   Any notice or consent previously given under section 28(5)(a) or (6)(a) of the Wildlife and Countryside Act 1981 in relation to land which on or after the commencement of these Regulations becomes land within a European site shall have effect, subject as follows, as if given under regulation 19(1)(a) or (2)(a) above.

(2)   The appropriate nature conservation body shall review any such consent as regards its compatibility with the conservation objectives of the site, and may modify or withdraw it.

(3)   Notice of any such modification or withdrawal of consent shall be given to every owner and occupier of land within the site who in the opinion of the appropriate nature conservation body may be affected by it; and the modification or withdrawal shall come into force in relation to an owner or occupier upon such notice being given to him.

(4)   The modification or withdrawal of a consent shall not affect anything done in reliance on the consent before the modification or withdrawal takes effect.

(5)   Where or to the extent that an operation ceases to be covered by a consent by reason of the consent being modified or withdrawn, the period after which in accordance with regulation 19(2)(c) the operation may be carried out in the absence of consent shall be four months from the giving of notice of the modification or withdrawal under paragraph (3) above.

(6)   Regulation 20(4) and (5) (provisions as to notification of Secretary of State) apply in such a case, with the following modifications—
  (a) for the reference to consent not having been given substitute a reference to consent being modified or withdrawn;
  (b) for the reference to the period specified in regulation 19(2)(c) substitute a reference to the period specified in paragraph (5) above.

[1007]

Special nature conservation orders

22 Power to make special nature conservation order

(1)   The Secretary of State may, after consultation with the appropriate nature conservation body, make in respect of any land within a European site an order (a "special nature conservation order") specifying operations which appear to him to be likely to destroy or damage the flora, fauna, or geological or physiographical features by reason of which the land is a European site.

(2)   A special nature conservation order may be amended or revoked by a further order.

(3)   Schedule 1 has effect with respect to the making, confirmation and coming into operation of special nature conservation orders and amending or revoking orders.

(4)   A special nature conservation order in relation to land in England and Wales is a local land charge.

(5)   (*Applies to Scotland only.*)

(6)   A report submitted by a nature conservation body to the Secretary of State under paragraph 20 of Schedule 6 to the Environmental Protection Act 1990 or section 10(2) of the Natural Heritage (Scotland) Act 1991 shall set out particulars of any land in their area as respects which a special nature conservation order has come into operation during the year to which the report relates.

[1008]

23 Restriction on carrying out operations specified in order

(1)   No person shall carry out on any land within a European site in respect of which a special nature conservation order is in force any operation specified in the order, unless the operation is carried out, or caused or permitted to be carried out, by the owner or occupier of the land and—

(a) one of them has, after the making of the order, given the appropriate nature conservation body written notice of a proposal to carry out the operation, specifying its nature and the land on which it is proposed to carry it out, and

(b) one of the conditions specified in paragraph (2) is fulfilled.

(2) Those conditions are—

(a) that the operation is carried out with the written consent of the appropriate nature conservation body;

(b) that the operation is carried out in accordance with the terms of a management agreement.

(3) A person who, without reasonable excuse, contravenes paragraph (1) commits an offence and is liable—

(a) on summary conviction, to a fine not exceeding the statutory maximum;

(b) on conviction on indictment, to a fine.

(4) For the purposes of paragraph (3) it is a reasonable excuse for a person to carry out an operation—

(a) that the operation was an emergency operation particulars of which (including details of the emergency) were notified to the appropriate nature conservation body as soon as practicable after the commencement of the operation; or

(b) that the operation was authorised by a planning permission granted on an application under Part III of the Town and Country Planning Act 1990 or Part III of the Town and Country Planning (Scotland) Act 1972.

[1009]

24 Supplementary provisions as to consents

(1) Where it appears to the appropriate nature conservation body that an application for consent under regulation 23(2)(a) relates to an operation which is or forms part of a plan or project which—

(a) is not directly connected with or necessary to the management of the site, and

(b) is likely to have a significant effect on the site (either alone or in combination with other plans or projects),

they shall make an appropriate assessment of the implications for the site in view of that site's conservation objectives.

(2) In the light of the conclusions of the assessment, they may give consent for the operation only after having ascertained that the plan or project will not adversely affect the integrity of the site.

(3) Where the appropriate nature conservation body refuse consent in accordance with paragraph (2) they shall give reasons for their decision.

(4) The owner or occupier of the land in question may—

(a) within two months of receiving notice of the refusal of consent, or

(b) if no notice of a decision is received by him within three months of an application for consent being made,

by notice in writing to the appropriate nature conservation body require them to refer the matter forthwith to the Secretary of State.

(5) If on the matter being referred to the Secretary of State he is satisfied that, there being no alternative solutions, the plan or project must be carried out for imperative reasons of overriding public interest (which, subject to paragraph (6), may be of a social or economic nature), he may direct the appropriate nature conservation body to give consent to the operation.

(6)   Where the site concerned hosts a priority natural habitat type or a priority species the reasons referred to in paragraph (5) must be either—
    (a)   reasons relating to human health, public safety or beneficial consequences of primary importance to the environment, or
    (b)   other reasons which in the opinion of the European Commission are imperative reasons of overriding public interest.

(7)   Where the Secretary of State directs the appropriate nature conservation body to give consent under this regulation, he shall secure that such compensatory measures are taken as are necessary to ensure that the overall coherence of Natura 2000 is protected.

(8)   This regulation does not apply in relation to a site which is a European site by reason only of regulation 10(1)(c) (site protected in accordance with Article 5(4)).

[1010]

25 Compensation for effect of order

(1)   Where a special nature conservation order is made, the appropriate nature conservation body shall pay compensation to any person having at the time of the making of the order an interest in land comprised in an agricultural unit comprising land to which the order relates who, on a claim made to the appropriate nature conservation body within the time and in the manner prescribed by regulations, shows that the value of his interest is less than it would have been if the order had not been made.

(2)   For this purpose an "agricultural unit" means land which is occupied as a unit for agricultural purposes, including any dwelling-house or other building occupied by the same person for the purpose of farming the land.

(3)   No claim for compensation shall be made under this regulation in respect of an order unless the Secretary of State has given notice under paragraph 6(1) or (2) of Schedule 1 of his decision in respect of the order.

[1011]

26 Restoration where order contravened

(1)   Where a person is convicted of an offence under regulation 23, the court by which he is convicted may, in addition to dealing with him in any other way, make an order requiring him to carry out, within such period as may be specified in the order, such operations for the purpose of restoring the land to its former condition as may be so specified.

(2)   An order under this regulation made on conviction on indictment shall be treated for the purposes of section 30 of the Criminal Appeal Act 1968 (effect of appeals on orders for the restitution of property) as an order for the restitution of property.

(3)   In the case of an order under this regulation made by a magistrates' court the period specified in the order shall not begin to run—
    (a)   in any case until the expiration of the period for the time being prescribed by law for the giving of notice of appeal against a decision of a magistrates' court;
    (b)   where notice of appeal is given within the period so prescribed, until determination of the appeal.

(4)   At any time before an order under this regulation has been complied with or fully complied with, the court by which it was made may, on the application of the person against whom it was made, discharge or vary the order if it appears to the court that a change in circumstances has made compliance or full compliance with the order impracticable or unnecessary.

(5)   If a person fails without reasonable excuse to comply with an order under this regulation, he commits an offence and is liable on summary conviction to a fine not exceeding level 5 on the standard scale; and if the failure continues after conviction, he may be proceeded against for a further offence from time to time until the order is complied with.

(6)   If, within the period specified in an order under this regulation, any operations specified in the order have not been carried out, the appropriate nature conservation body may enter the land and carry out those operations and recover from the person against whom the order was made any expenses reasonably incurred by them in doing so.

(7)   (*Applies to Scotland only.*)

[1012]

27 Continuation in force of existing orders, &c

(1)   Where an order is in force under section 29 of the Wildlife and Countryside Act 1981 (special protection for certain areas of special scientific interest) in relation to land which on or after the commencement of these Regulations becomes land within a European site, the order shall have effect as if made under regulation 22 above.

(2)   Any notice previously given under section 29(4)(a) (notice by owner or occupier of proposal to carry out operation) shall have effect as if given under regulation 23(1)(a) and, if the appropriate nature conservation body have neither given nor refused consent, shall be dealt with under these Regulations.

(3)   Any consent previously given under section 29(5)(a) shall be reviewed by the appropriate nature conservation body as regards its compatibility with the conservation objectives of the site, and may be modified or withdrawn.

(4)   Notice of any such modification or withdrawal of consent shall be given to every owner and occupier of land within the site who in the opinion of the appropriate nature conservation body may be affected by it; and the modification or withdrawal shall come into force in relation to an owner or occupier upon such notice being given to him.

(5)   The modification or withdrawal of a consent shall not affect anything done in reliance on the consent before the modification or withdrawal takes effect.

(6)   Section 29(5)(c), (6) and (7) shall cease to apply and the carrying out, or continuation, of any operation on land within a European site which is not otherwise authorised in accordance with these Regulations shall be subject to the prohibition in regulation 23(1).

[1013]

Byelaws

28 Power to make byelaws

(1)   The appropriate nature conservation body may make byelaws for the protection of a European site under section 20 of the National Parks and Access to the Countryside Act 1949 (byelaws for protection of nature reserves).

(2)   Without prejudice to the generality of paragraph (1), byelaws under that section as it applies by virtue of this regulation may make provision of any of the following kinds.

(3)   They may—
  (a) provide for prohibiting or restricting the entry into, or movement within, the site of persons, vehicles, boats and animals;
  (b) prohibit or restrict the killing, taking, molesting or disturbance of living creatures of any description in the site, the taking, destruction or disturbance of eggs of any such creature, the taking of, or interference with, vegetation of any description in the site, or the doing of anything in the site which will interfere with the soil or damage any object in the site;
  (c) contain provisions prohibiting the depositing of rubbish and the leaving of litter in the site;
  (d) prohibit or restrict, or provide for prohibiting or restricting, the lighting of fires in the site or the doing of anything likely to cause a fire in the site.

(4)   They may prohibit or restrict any activity referred to in paragraph (3) within such area surrounding or adjoining the site as appears to the appropriate nature conservation body requisite for the protection of the site.

(5)   They may provide for the issue, on such terms and subject to such conditions as may be specified in the byelaws, of permits authorising—
  (a) entry into the site or any such surrounding or adjoining area as is mentioned in paragraph (4), or
  (b) the doing of anything within the site, or any such surrounding or adjoining area,

where such entry, or doing that thing, would otherwise be unlawful under the byelaws.

(6)   They may be made so as to relate either to the whole or to any part of the site, or of any such surrounding or adjoining area as is mentioned in paragraph (4), and may make different provision for different parts thereof.

(7)   This regulation does not apply in relation to a European marine site (but see regulation 36).

[1014]

29 Byelaws: limitation on effect

Byelaws under section 20 of the National Parks and Access to the Countryside Act 1949 as it applies by virtue of regulation 28 shall not interfere with—
  (a) the exercise by any person of a right vested in him as owner, lessee or occupier of land in the European site, or in any such surrounding or adjoining area as is mentioned in paragraph (4) of that regulation;
  (b) the exercise of any public right of way;
  (c) the exercise of any functions of statutory undertakers;
  (d) the exercise of any functions of an internal drainage board, a district salmon fishery board or the Commissioners appointed under the Tweed Fisheries Act 1969; or
  (e) the running of a telecommunications code system or the exercise of any right conferred by or in accordance with the telecommunications code on the operator of any such system.

[1015]

30 Compensation for effect of byelaws

Where the exercise of any right vested in a person, whether by reason of his being entitled to any interest in land or by virtue of a licence or agreement, is prevented or hindered by the coming into operation of byelaws under section 20 of the National Parks and Access to the Countryside Act 1949 as it applies by virtue of regulation 28, he shall be entitled to receive from the appropriate nature conservation body compensation in respect thereof.

[1016]

31 Continuation in force of existing byelaws

Any byelaws in force under section 20 of the National Parks and Access to the Countryside Act 1949 in relation to land which on or after the commencement of these Regulations becomes land within a European site, or adjacent to such a site, shall have effect as if made under the said section 20 as it applies by virtue of regulation 28 and shall be construed as if originally so made.

[1017]

Powers of compulsory acquisition

32 Powers of compulsory acquisition

(1)   Where the appropriate nature conservation body are satisfied—
  (a) that they are unable, as respects any interest in land within a European site, to conclude a management agreement on terms appearing to them to be reasonable, or
  (b) where they have entered into a management agreement as respects such an interest, that a breach of the agreement has occurred which prevents or impairs the satisfactory management of the European site,

they may acquire that interest compulsorily.

(2)   Such a breach as is mentioned in paragraph (1)(b) shall not be treated as having occurred by virtue of any act or omission capable of remedy unless there has been default in remedying it within a reasonable time after notice given by the appropriate nature conservation body requiring the remedying thereof.

(3)   Any dispute arising whether there has been such a breach of a management agreement shall be determined—
  (a) in the case of land in England and Wales, by an arbitrator appointed by the Lord Chancellor;
  (b) in the case of land in Scotland, by an arbiter appointed by the Lord President of the Court of Session.

[1018]

Special provisions as to European marine sites

33 Marking of site and advice by nature conservation bodies

(1)   The appropriate nature conservation body may install markers indicating the existence and extent of a European marine site.

This power is exercisable subject to the obtaining of any necessary consent under section 34 of the Coast Protection Act 1949 (restriction of works detrimental to navigation).

(2)   As soon as possible after a site becomes a European marine site, the appropriate nature conservation body shall advise other relevant authorities as to—
  (a) the conservation objectives for that site, and
  (b) any operations which may cause deterioration of natural habitats or the habitats of species, or disturbance of species, for which the site has been designated.

[1019]

34 Management scheme for European marine site

(1)   The relevant authorities, or any of them, may establish for a European marine site a management scheme under which their functions (including any power to make byelaws) shall be exercised so as to secure in relation to that site compliance with the requirements of the Habitats Directive.

(2)   Only one management scheme may be made for each European marine site.

(3)   A management scheme may be amended from time to time.

(4)   As soon as a management scheme has been established, or is amended, a copy of it shall be sent by the relevant authority or authorities concerned to the appropriate nature conservation body.

[1020]

35 Direction to establish or amend management scheme

(1)   The relevant Minister may give directions to the relevant authorities, or any of them, as to the establishment of a management scheme for a European marine site.

(2)   Directions may, in particular—
  (a) require conservation measures specified in the direction to be included in the scheme;
  (b) appoint one of the relevant authorities to co-ordinate the establishment of the scheme;
  (c) set time limits within which any steps are to be taken;
  (d) provide that the approval of the Minister is required before the scheme is established; and
  (e) require any relevant authority to supply to the Minister such information concerning the establishment of the scheme as may be specified in the direction.

(3)   The relevant Minister may give directions to the relevant authorities, or any of them, as to the amendment of a management scheme for a European marine site, either generally or in any particular respect.

(4)   Any direction under this regulation shall be in writing and may be varied or revoked by a further direction.

(5)   In this regulation "the relevant Minister" means, in relation to a site in England, the Secretary of State and the Minister of Agriculture, Fisheries and Food acting jointly and in any other case the Secretary of State.

[1021]

36 Byelaws for protection of European marine site

(1)   The appropriate nature conservation body may make byelaws for the protection of a European marine site under section 37 of the Wildlife and Countryside Act 1981 (byelaws for protection of marine nature reserves).

(2)   The provisions of subsections (2) to (11) of that section apply in relation to byelaws made by virtue of this regulation with the substitution for the references to marine nature reserves of references to European marine sites.

(3)   Nothing in byelaws made by virtue of this regulation shall interfere with the exercise of any functions of a relevant authority, any functions conferred by or under an enactment (whenever passed) or any right of any person (whenever vested).

[1022]

Miscellaneous

37 Nature conservation policy in planning contexts

(1)   For the purposes of the planning enactments mentioned below, policies in respect of the conservation of the natural beauty and amenity of the land shall be taken to include policies encouraging the management of features of the landscape which are of major importance for wild flora and fauna.

Such features are those which, by virtue of their linear and continuous structure (such as rivers with their banks or the traditional systems of marking field boundaries) or their function as stepping stones (such as ponds or small woods), are essential for the migration, dispersal and genetic exchange of wild species.

(2)   The enactments referred to in paragraph (1) are—
   (a)   in the Town and Country Planning Act 1990, section 12(3A) (unitary development plans), section 31(3) (structure plans) and section 36(3) (local plans);
   (b)   in the Town and Country Planning (Scotland) Act 1972, section 5(3)(a) (structure plans) and section 9(3)(a) (local plans).

[1023]

PART III
PROTECTION OF SPECIES

Protection of animals

38 European protected species of animals

The species of animals listed in Annex IV(a) to the Habitats Directive whose natural range includes any area in Great Britain are listed in Schedule 2 to these Regulations.

References in these Regulations to a "European protected species" of animal are to any of those species.

[1024]

39 Protection of wild animals of European protected species

(1)   It is an offence—
   (a)   deliberately to capture or kill a wild animal of a European protected species;
   (b)   deliberately to disturb any such animal;
   (c)   deliberately to take or destroy the eggs of such an animal; or
   (d)   to damage or destroy a breeding site or resting place of such an animal.

(2)   It is an offence to keep, transport, sell or exchange, or offer for sale or exchange, any live or dead wild animal of a European protected species, or any part of, or anything derived from, such an animal.

(3)   Paragraphs (1) and (2) apply to all stages of the life of the animals to which they apply.

(4)   A person shall not be guilty of an offence under paragraph (2) if he shows—
   (a)   that the animal had not been taken or killed, or had been lawfully taken or killed, or
   (b)   that the animal or other thing in question had been lawfully sold (whether to him or any other person).

For this purpose "lawfully" means without any contravention of these Regulations or Part I of the Wildlife and Countryside Act 1981.

(5)   In any proceedings for an offence under this regulation, the animal in question shall be presumed to have been a wild animal unless the contrary is shown.

(6)   A person guilty of an offence under this regulation is liable on summary conviction to a fine not exceeding level 5 on the standard scale.

[1025]

40 Exceptions from regulation 39

(1)   Nothing in regulation 39 shall make unlawful—
  (a) anything done in pursuance of a requirement by the agriculture Minister under section 98 of the Agriculture Act 1947 or section 39 of the Agriculture (Scotland) Act 1948 (prevention of damage by pests); or
  (b) anything done under, or in pursuance of an order made under, the Animal Health Act 1981.

(2)   Nothing in regulation 39(1)(b) or (d) shall make unlawful anything done within a dwelling-house.

(3)   Notwithstanding anything in regulation 39, a person shall not be guilty of an offence by reason of—
  (a) the taking of a wild animal of a European protected species if he shows that the animal had been disabled otherwise than by his unlawful act and was taken solely for the purpose of tending it and releasing it when no longer disabled;
  (b) the killing of such an animal if he shows that the animal has been so seriously disabled otherwise than by his unlawful act that there was no reasonable chance of its recovering; or
  (c) any act made unlawful by that regulation if he shows that the act was the incidental result of a lawful operation and could not reasonably have been avoided.

(4)   A person shall not be entitled to rely on the defence provided by paragraph (2) or (3)(c) as respects anything done in relation to a bat otherwise than in the living area of a dwelling-house unless he had notified the appropriate nature conservation body of the proposed action or operation and allowed them a reasonable time to advise him as to whether it should be carried out and, if so, the method to be used.

(5)   Notwithstanding anything in regulation 39 a person—
  (a) being the owner or occupier, or any person authorised by the owner or occupier, of the land on which the action authorised is taken, or
  (b) authorised by the local authority for the area within which the action authorised is taken,

shall not be guilty of an offence by reason of the killing or disturbing of an animal of a European protected species if he shows that his action was necessary for the purpose of preventing serious damage to livestock, foodstuffs, crops, vegetables, fruit, growing timber or any other form of property or fisheries.

(6)   A person may not rely on the defence provided by paragraph (5) as respects action taken at any time if it had become apparent before that time that the action would prove necessary for the purpose mentioned in that paragraph and either—
  (a) a licence under regulation 44 authorising that action had not been applied for as soon as reasonably practicable after that fact had become apparent, or
  (b) an application for such a licence had been determined.

(7)   In paragraph (5) "local authority" means—
  (a) in relation to England and Wales, a county, [county borough,] district or London borough council and includes the Common Council of the City of London, and
  (b) in Scotland, a regional, islands or district council.

[1026]

NOTES

   Para (7): words in square brackets in sub-para (a) inserted by the Local Government Reorganisation (Wales) (Consequential Amendments) Order 1996, SI 1996/525, art 3, Schedule, para 18(3).

41 Prohibition of certain methods of taking or killing wild animals

(1)   This regulation applies in relation to the taking or killing of a wild animal—
    (a) of any of the species listed in Schedule 3 to these Regulations (which shows the species listed in Annex V(a) to the Habitats Directive, and to which Article 15 applies, whose natural range includes any area of Great Britain), or
    (b) of a European protected species, where the taking or killing of such animals is permitted in accordance with these Regulations.

(2)   It is an offence to use for the purpose of taking or killing any such wild animal—
    (a) any of the means listed in paragraph (3) or (4) below, or
    (b) any form of taking or killing from the modes of transport listed in paragraph (5) below.

(3)   The prohibited means of taking or killing of mammals are—
    (a) blind or mutilated animals used as live decoys;
    (b) tape recorders;
    (c) electrical and electronic devices capable of killing or stunning;
    (d) artificial light sources;
    (e) mirrors and other dazzling devices;
    (f) devices for illuminating targets;
    (g) sighting devices for night shooting comprising an electronic image magnifier or image converter;
    (h) explosives;
    (i) nets which are non-selective according to their principle or their conditions of use;
    (j) traps which are non-selective according to their principle or their conditions of use;
    (k) crossbows;
    (l) poisons and poisoned or anaesthetic bait;
    (m) gassing or smoking out;
    (n) semi-automatic or automatic weapons with a magazine capable of holding more than two rounds of ammunition.

(4)   The prohibited means of taking or killing fish are—
    (a) poison;
    (b) explosives.

(5)   The prohibited modes of transport are—
    (a) aircraft;
    (b) moving motor vehicles.

(6)   A person guilty of an offence under this regulation is liable on summary conviction to a fine not exceeding level 5 on the standard scale.

[1027]

Protection of plants

42 European protected species of plants

The species of plants listed in Annex IV(b) to the Habitats Directive whose natural range includes any area in Great Britain are listed in Schedule 4 to these Regulations.

References in these Regulations to a "European protected species" of plant are to any of those species.

[1028]

43 Protection of wild plants of European protected species

(1) It is an offence deliberately to pick, collect, cut, uproot or destroy a wild plant of a European protected species.

(2) It is an offence to keep, transport, sell or exchange, or offer for sale or exchange, any live or dead wild plant of a European protected species, or any part of, or anything derived from, such a plant.

(3) Paragraphs (1) and (2) apply to all stages of the biological cycle of the plants to which they apply.

(4) A person shall not be guilty of an offence under paragraph (1), by reason of any act made unlawful by that paragraph if he shows that the act was an incidental result of a lawful operation and could not reasonably have been avoided.

(5) A person shall not be guilty of an offence under paragraph (2) if he shows that the plant or other thing in question had been lawfully sold (whether to him or any other person).

For this purpose "lawfully" means without any contravention of these Regulations or Part I of the Wildlife and Countryside Act 1981.

(6) In any proceedings for an offence under this regulation, the plant in question shall be presumed to have been a wild plant unless the contrary is shown.

(7) A person guilty of an offence under this section is liable on summary conviction to a fine not exceeding level 4 on the standard scale.

[1029]

Power to grant licences

44 Grant of licences for certain purposes

(1) Regulations 39, 41 and 43 do not apply to anything done for any of the following purposes under and in accordance with the terms of a licence granted by the appropriate authority.

(2) The purposes referred to in paragraph (1) are—
   (a) scientific or educational purposes;
   (b) ringing or marking, or examining any ring or mark on, wild animals;
   (c) conserving wild animals or wild plants or introducing them to particular areas;
   (d) protecting any zoological or botanical collection;
   (e) preserving public health or public safety or other imperative reasons of overriding public interest including those of a social or economic nature and beneficial consequences of primary importance for the environment;
   (f) preventing the spread of disease; or
   (g) preventing serious damage to livestock, foodstuffs for livestock, crops, vegetables, fruit, growing timber or any other form of property or to fisheries.

(3) The appropriate authority shall not grant a licence under this regulation unless they are satisfied—
   (a) that there is no satisfactory alternative, and
   (b) that the action authorised will not be detrimental to the maintenance of the population of the species concerned at a favourable conservation status in their natural range.

(4) For the purposes of this regulation "the appropriate authority" means—
   (a) in the case of a licence under any of sub-paragraphs (a) to (d) of paragraph (2), the appropriate nature conservation body; and
   (b) in the case of a licence under any of sub-paragraphs (e) to (g) of that paragraph, the agriculture Minister.

(5)   The agriculture Minister shall from time to time consult with the nature conservation bodies as to the exercise of his functions under this regulation; and he shall not grant a licence of any description unless he has been advised by the appropriate nature conservation body as to the circumstances in which, in their opinion, licences of that description should be granted.

[1030]

45 Licences: supplementary provisions

(1)   A licence under regulation 44—
  (a) may be, to any degree, general or specific;
  (b) may be granted either to persons of a class or to a particular person; and
  (c) may be subject to compliance with any specified conditions.

(2)   For the purposes of a licence under regulation 44 the definition of a class of persons may be framed by reference to any circumstances whatever including, in particular, their being authorised by any other person.

(3)   A licence under regulation 44 may be modified or revoked at any time by the appropriate authority; but otherwise shall be valid for the period stated in the licence.

(4)   A licence under regulation 44 which authorises any person to kill wild animals shall specify the area within which and the methods by which the wild animals may be killed and shall not be granted for a period of more than two years.

(5)   It shall be a defence in proceedings for an offence under section 8(b) of the Protection of Animals Act 1911 or section 7(b) of the Protection of Animals (Scotland) Act 1912 (which restrict the placing on land of poison and poisonous substances) to show that—
  (a) the act alleged to constitute the offence was done under and in accordance with the terms of a licence under regulation 44, and
  (b) any conditions specified in the licence were complied with.

(6)   The appropriate authority may charge for a licence under regulation 44 such reasonable sum (if any) as they may determine.

[1031]

46 False statements made for obtaining licence

(1)   A person commits an offence who, for the purposes of obtaining, whether for himself or another, the grant of a licence under regulation 44—
  (a) makes a statement or representation, or furnishes a document or information, which he knows to be false in a material particular, or
  (b) recklessly makes a statement or representation, or furnishes a document or information, which is false in a material particular.

(2)   A person guilty of an offence under this regulation is liable on summary conviction to a fine not exceeding level 4 on the standard scale.

[1032]

PART IV
ADAPTATION OF PLANNING AND OTHER CONTROLS

Introductory

47 Application of provisions of this Part

(1)   The requirements of—
  (a) regulations 48 and 49 (requirement to consider effect on European sites), and

(b) regulations 50 and 51 (requirement to review certain existing decisions and consents, &c),

apply, subject to and in accordance with the provisions of regulations 54 to 85, in relation to the matters specified in those provisions.

(2) Supplementary provision is made by—
    (a) regulation 52 (co-ordination where more than one competent authority involved), and
    (b) regulation 53 (compensatory measures where plan or project is agreed to notwithstanding a negative assessment of the implications for a European site).

[1033]

General provisions for protection of European sites

48 Assessment of implications for European site

(1) A competent authority, before deciding to undertake, or give any consent, permission or other authorisation for, a plan or project which—
    (a) is likely to have a significant effect on a European site in Great Britain (either alone or in combination with other plans or projects), and
    (b) is not directly connected with or necessary to the management of the site,

shall make an appropriate assessment of the implications for the site in view of that site's conservation objectives.

(2) A person applying for any such consent, permission or other authorisation shall provide such information as the competent authority may reasonably require for the purposes of the assessment.

(3) The competent authority shall for the purposes of the assessment consult the appropriate nature conservation body and have regard to any representations made by that body within such reasonable time as the authority may specify.

(4) They shall also, if they consider it appropriate, take the opinion of the general public; and if they do so, they shall take such steps for that purpose as they consider appropriate.

(5) In the light of the conclusions of the assessment, and subject to regulation 49, the authority shall agree to the plan or project only after having ascertained that it will not adversely affect the integrity of the European site.

(6) In considering whether a plan or project will adversely affect the integrity of the site, the authority shall have regard to the manner in which it is proposed to be carried out or to any conditions or restrictions subject to which they propose that the consent, permission or other authorisation should be given.

(7) This regulation does not apply in relation to a site which is a European site by reason only of regulation 10(1)(c) (site protected in accordance with Article 5(4)).

[1034]

49 Considerations of overriding public interest

(1) If they are satisfied that, there being no alternative solutions, the plan or project must be carried out for imperative reasons of overriding public interest (which, subject to paragraph (2), may be of a social or economic nature), the competent authority may agree to the plan or project notwithstanding a negative assessment of the implications for the site.

(2) Where the site concerned hosts a priority natural habitat type or a priority species, the reasons referred to in paragraph (1) must be either—

    (a) reasons relating to human health, public safety or beneficial consequences of primary importance to the environment, or

    (b) other reasons which in the opinion of the European Commission are imperative reasons of overriding public interest.

(3)   Where a competent authority other than the Secretary of State desire to obtain the opinion of the European Commission as to whether reasons are to be considered imperative reasons of overriding public interest, they shall submit a written request to the Secretary of State—

    (a) identifying the matter on which an opinion is sought, and

    (b) accompanied by any documents or information which may be required.

(4)   The Secretary of State may thereupon, if he thinks fit, seek the opinion of the Commission; and if he does so, he shall upon receiving the Commission's opinion transmit it to the authority.

(5)   Where an authority other than the Secretary of State propose to agree to a plan or project under this regulation notwithstanding a negative assessment of the implications for a European site, they shall notify the Secretary of State.

Having notified the Secretary of State, they shall not agree to the plan or project before the end of the period of 21 days beginning with the day notified to them by the Secretary of State as that on which their notification was received by him, unless the Secretary of State notifies them that they may do so.

(6)   In any such case the Secretary of State may give directions to the authority prohibiting them from agreeing to the plan or project, either indefinitely or during such period as may be specified in the direction.

This power is without prejudice to any other power of the Secretary of State in relation to the decision in question.

[1035]

50 Review of existing decisions and consents, &c

(1)   Where before the date on which a site becomes a European site or, if later, the commencement of these Regulations, a competent authority have decided to undertake, or have given any consent, permission or other authorisation for, a plan or project to which regulation 48(1) would apply if it were to be reconsidered as of that date, the authority shall as soon as reasonably practicable, review their decision or, as the case may be, the consent, permission or other authorisation, and shall affirm, modify or revoke it.

(2)   They shall for that purpose make an appropriate assessment of the implications for the site in view of that site's conservation objectives; and the provisions of regulation 48(2) to (4) shall apply, with the appropriate modifications, in relation to such a review.

(3)   Subject to the following provisions of this Part, any review required by this regulation shall be carried out under existing statutory procedures where such procedures exist, and if none exist the Secretary of State may give directions as to the procedure to be followed.

(4)   Nothing in this regulation shall affect anything done in pursuance of the decision, or the consent, permission or other authorisation, before the date mentioned in paragraph (1).

[1036]

51 Consideration on review

(1)   The following provisions apply where a decision, or a consent, permission or other authorisation, falls to be reviewed under regulation 50.

(2)   Subject as follows, the provisions of regulation 48(5) and (6) and regulation 49 shall apply, with the appropriate modifications, in relation to the decision on the review.

(3)   The decision, or the consent, permission or other authorisation, may be affirmed if it appears to the authority reviewing it that other action taken or to be taken by them, or by another authority, will secure that the plan or project does not adversely affect the integrity of the site.

Where that object may be attained in a number of ways, the authority or authorities concerned shall seek to secure that the action taken is the least onerous to those affected.

(4)   The Secretary of State may issue guidance to authorities for the purposes of paragraph (3) as to the manner of determining which of different ways should be adopted for securing that the plan or project does not have any such effect, and in particular—

    (a) the order of application of different controls, and

    (b) the extent to which account should be taken of the possible exercise of other powers;

and the authorities concerned shall have regard to any guidance so issued in discharging their functions under that paragraph.

(5)   Any modification or revocation effected in pursuance of this regulation shall be carried out under existing statutory procedures where such procedures exist.

If none exist, the Secretary of State may give directions as to the procedure to be followed.

[1037]

52 Co-ordination where more than one competent authority involved

(1)   The following provisions apply where a plan or project—

    (a) is undertaken by more than one competent authority,

    (b) requires the consent, permission or other authorisation of more than one competent authority, or

    (c) is undertaken by one or more competent authorities and requires the consent, permission or other authorisation of one or more other competent authorities.

(2)   Nothing in regulation 48(1) or 50(2) requires a competent authority to assess any implications of a plan or project which would be more appropriately assessed under that provision by another competent authority.

(3)   The Secretary of State may issue guidance to authorities for the purposes of regulations 48 to 51 as to the circumstances in which an authority may or should adopt the reasoning or conclusions of another competent authority as to whether a plan or project—

    (a) is likely to have a significant effect on a European site, or

    (b) will adversely affect the integrity of a European site;

and the authorities involved shall have regard to any guidance so issued in discharging their functions under those regulations.

(4)   In determining whether a plan or project should be agreed to under regulation 49(1) (considerations of overriding public interest) a competent authority other than the Secretary of State shall seek and have regard to the views of the other competent authority or authorities involved.

[1038]

53 Compensatory measures

Where in accordance with regulation 49 (considerations of overriding public interest)—

(a) a plan or project is agreed to, notwithstanding a negative assessment of the implications for a European site, or

(b) a decision, or a consent, permission or other authorisation, is affirmed on review, notwithstanding such an assessment,

the Secretary of State shall secure that any necessary compensatory measures are taken to ensure that the overall coherence of Natura 2000 is protected.

[1039]

Planning

54 Grant of planning permission

(1) Regulations 48 and 49 (requirement to consider effect on European site) apply, in England and Wales, in relation to—

(a) granting planning permission on an application under Part III of the Town and Country Planning Act 1990;

(b) granting planning permission, or upholding a decision of the local planning authority to grant planning permission (whether or not subject to the same conditions and limitations as those imposed by the local planning authority), on determining an appeal under section 78 of that Act in respect of such an application;

(c) granting planning permission under—

(i) section 141(2)(a) of that Act (action by Secretary of State in relation to purchase notice),

(ii) section 177(1)(a) of that Act (powers of Secretary of State on appeal against enforcement notice), or

(iii) section 196(5) of that Act as originally enacted (powers of Secretary of State on reference or appeal as to established use certificate);

(d) directing under section 90(1), (2) or (2A) of that Act (development with government authorisation), or under section 5(1) of the Pipe-lines Act 1962, that planning permission shall be deemed to be granted;

(e) making—

(i) an order under section 102 of that Act (order requiring discontinuance of use or removal of buildings or works), including an order made under that section by virtue of section 104 (powers of Secretary of State), which grants planning permission, or

(ii) an order under paragraph 1 of Schedule 9 to that Act (order requiring discontinuance of mineral working), including an order made under that paragraph by virtue of paragraph 11 of that Schedule (default powers of Secretary of State), which grants planning permission,

or confirming any such order under section 103 of that Act;

(f) directing under—

(i) section 141(3) of that Act (action by Secretary of State in relation to purchase notice), or

(ii) section 35(5) of the Planning (Listed Buildings and Conservation Areas) Act 1990 (action by Secretary of State in relation to listed building purchase notice),

that if an application is made for planning permission it shall be granted.

(2) Regulations 48 and 49 (requirement to consider effect on European site) apply, in Scotland, in relation to—

(a) granting planning permission on an application under Part III of the Town and Country Planning (Scotland) Act 1972;

(b) granting planning permission, or upholding a decision of the planning authority to grant planning permission (whether or not subject to the same conditions and limitations as those imposed by the local planning authority), on determining an appeal under section 33 (appeals) of that Act in respect of such an application;

(c) granting planning permission under—
  (i) section 172(2) of that Act (action by Secretary of State in relation to purchase notice),
  (ii) section 85(5) of that Act (powers of Secretary of State on appeal against enforcement notice), or
  (iii) section 91(3) of that Act as originally enacted (powers of Secretary of State on reference or appeal as to established use certificate);

(d) directing under sections 37(1) (development with government authorisation) of that Act, or under section 5(1) of the Pipe-lines Act 1962 or paragraph 7 of Schedule 8 to the Electricity Act 1989, that planning permission shall be deemed to be granted;

(e) making an order under section 49 of that Act (order requiring discontinuance of use or removal of buildings or works), including an order made under that section by virtue of section 260 (default powers of Secretary of State), which grants planning permission, or confirming any such order;

(f) directing under—
  (i) section 172(3) of that Act (powers of Secretary of State in relation to purchase notice), or
  (ii) paragraph 2(6) of Schedule 17 to that Act (powers of Secretary of State in relation to listed building purchase notice),
  that if an application is made for planning permission it shall be granted.

(3) Where regulations 48 and 49 apply, the competent authority may, if they consider that any adverse effects of the plan or project on the integrity of a European site would be avoided if the planning permission were subject to conditions or limitations, grant planning permission or, as the case may be, take action which results in planning permission being granted or deemed to be granted subject to those conditions or limitations.

(4) Where regulations 48 and 49 apply, outline planning permission shall not be granted unless the competent authority are satisfied (whether by reason of the conditions and limitations to which the outline planning permission is to be made subject, or otherwise) that no development likely adversely to affect the integrity of a European site could be carried out under the permission, whether before or after obtaining approval of any reserved matters.

In this paragraph "outline planning permission" and "reserved matters" have the same meaning as in section 92 of the Town and Country Planning Act 1990 or section 39 of the Town and Country Planning (Scotland) Act 1972.

[1040]

55 Planning permission: duty to review

(1) Subject to the following provisions of this regulation, regulations 50 and 51 (requirement to review certain decisions and consents, &c) apply to any planning permission or deemed planning permission, unless—
  (a) the development to which it related has been completed, or
  (b) it was granted subject to a condition as to the time within which the development to which it related was to be begun and that time has expired without the development having been begun, or
  (c) it was granted for a limited period and that period has expired.

(2) Regulations 50 and 51 do not apply to planning permission granted or deemed to have been granted—

   (a) by a development order (but see regulations 60 to 64 below);

   (b) by virtue of the adoption of a simplified planning zone scheme or of alterations to such a scheme (but see regulation 65 below);

   (c) by virtue of the taking effect of an order designating an enterprise zone under Schedule 32 to the Local Government, Planning and Land Act 1980, or by virtue of the approval of a modified enterprise zone scheme (but see regulation 66 below).

  (3)   Planning permission deemed to be granted by virtue of—

   (a) a direction under section 90(1) of the Town and Country Planning Act 1990 or section 37(1) of the Town and Country Planning (Scotland) Act 1972 in respect of development for which an authorisation has been granted under section 1 or 3 of the Pipe-lines Act 1962,

   (b) a direction under section 5(1) of the Pipe-lines Act 1962,

   (c) a direction under section 90(1) of the Town and Country Planning Act 1990 or section 37(1) of the Town and Country Planning (Scotland) Act 1972 in respect of development for which a consent has been given under section 36 or 37 of the Electricity Act 1989,

   (d) a direction under section 90(2) of the Town and Country Planning Act 1990 or paragraph 7 of Schedule 8 to the Electricity Act 1989, or

   (e) a direction under section 90(2A) of the Town and Country Planning Act 1990 (which relates to development in pursuance of an order under section 1 or 3 of the Transport and Works Act 1992),

shall be reviewed in accordance with the following provisions of this Part in conjunction with the review of the underlying authorisation, consent or order.

  (4)   In the case of planning permission deemed to have been granted in any other case by a direction under section 90(1) of the Town and Country Planning Act 1990 or section 37(1) of the Town and Country Planning (Scotland) Act 1972, the local planning authority shall—

   (a) identify any such permission which they consider falls to be reviewed under regulations 50 and 51, and

   (b) refer the matter to the government department which made the direction;

and the department shall, if it agrees that the planning permission does fall to be so reviewed, thereupon review the direction in accordance with those regulations.

  (5)   Save as otherwise expressly provided, regulations 50 and 51 do not apply to planning permission granted or deemed to be granted by a public general Act of Parliament.

  (6)   Subject to paragraphs (3) and (4), where planning permission granted by the Secretary of State falls to be reviewed under regulations 50 and 51—

   (a) it shall be reviewed by the local planning authority, and

   (b) the power conferred by section 97 of the Town and Country Planning Act 1990 or section 42 of the Town and Country Planning (Scotland) Act 1972 (revocation or modification of planning permission) shall be exercisable by that authority as in relation to planning permission granted on an application under Part III of that Act.

In a non-metropolitan county in England . . . the function of reviewing any such planning permission shall be exercised by the district planning authority unless it relates to a county matter (within the meaning of Schedule 1 to the Town and Country Planning Act 1990) in which case it shall be exercised by the county planning authority.

[1041]

NOTES

   Para (6): words omitted revoked by the Local Government Reorganisation (Wales) (Consequential Amendments) Order 1996, SI 1996/525, art 3, Schedule, para 18(4).

---

56 Planning permission: consideration on review

(1)   In reviewing any planning permission or deemed planning permission in pursuance of regulations 50 and 51, the competent authority shall, in England and Wales—

(a) consider whether any adverse effects could be overcome by planning obligations under section 106 of the Town and Country Planning Act 1990 being entered into, and

(b) if they consider that those effects could be so overcome, invite those concerned to enter into such obligations;

and so far as the adverse effects are not thus overcome the authority shall make such order under section 97 of that Act (power to revoke or modify planning permission), or under section 102 of or paragraph 1 of Schedule 9 to that Act (order requiring discontinuance of use, &c), as may be required.

(2)   In reviewing any planning permission or deemed planning permission in pursuance of regulations 50 and 51, the competent authority shall, in Scotland—

(a) consider whether any adverse effects could be overcome by an agreement under section 50 (agreements regulating development or use of land) of the Town and Country Planning (Scotland) Act 1972 being entered into, and

(b) if they consider that those effects could be so overcome, invite those concerned to enter into such an agreement;

and so far as the adverse effects are not thus overcome, the authority shall make such order under section 42 of that Act (power to revoke or modify planning permission), or under section 49 of that Act (orders requiring discontinuance of use, &c) as may be required.

(3)   Where the authority ascertain that the carrying out or, as the case may be, the continuation of the development would adversely affect the integrity of a European site, they nevertheless need not proceed under regulations 50 and 51 if and so long as they consider that there is no likelihood of the development being carried out or continued.

[1042]

57 Effect of orders made on review: England and Wales

(1)   An order under section 97 of the Town and Country Planning Act 1990 (power to revoke or modify planning permission) made pursuant to regulation 55 shall take effect upon service of the notices required by section 98(2) of that Act or, where there is more than one such notice and those notices are served at different times, upon the service of the last such notice to be served.

(2)   Where the Secretary of State determines not to confirm such an order, the order shall cease to have effect from the time of that determination, and the permission revoked or modified by the order shall thereafter have effect as if the order had never been made, and—

(a) any period specified in the permission for the taking of any action, being a period which had not expired prior to the date upon which the order took effect under paragraph (1) above, shall be extended by a period equal to that during which the order had effect; and

(b) there shall be substituted for any date specified in the permission as being a date by which any action should be taken, not being a date falling prior to the date upon which the order took effect under paragraph (1) above, such date as post-dates the specified date by a period equal to that during which the order had effect.

(3)   An order under section 102 of, or under paragraph 1 of Schedule 9 to, the Town and Country Planning Act 1990 (order requiring discontinuance of use, &c) made pursuant to regulation 55 shall insofar as it requires the discontinuance of a

use of land or imposes conditions upon the continuance of a use of land, take effect upon service of the notices required by section 103(3) or, where there is more than one such notice and those notices are served at different times, upon service of the last such notice to be served.

(4)   Where the Secretary of State determines not to confirm any such order, the order shall cease to have effect from the time of that determination and the use which by the order was discontinued or upon whose continuance conditions were imposed—
   (a)   may thereafter be continued as if the order had never been made, and
   (b)   shall be treated for the purposes of the Town and Country Planning Act 1990 as if it had continued without interruption or modification throughout the period during which the order had effect.

(5)   An order under section 97 of that Act (power to revoke or modify planning permission) made in pursuance of regulation 55 shall not affect so much of the development authorised by the permission as was carried out prior to the order taking effect.

(6)   An order under section 102 of, or under paragraph 1 of Schedule 9 to, that Act (order requiring discontinuance of use, &c) made in pursuance of regulation 55 shall not affect anything done prior to the site becoming a European site or, if later, the commencement of these Regulations.

[1043]

58 (*Applies to Scotland only.*)

59 Planning permission: supplementary provisions as to compensation

(1)   Where the Secretary of State determines not to confirm—
   (a)   an order under section 97 of the Town and Country Planning Act 1990 (revocation or modification of planning permission) which has taken effect under regulation 57(1), or
   (b)   an order under section 42 of the Town and Country Planning (Scotland) Act 1972 (revocation or modification of planning permission) which has taken effect under regulation 58(1),

any claim for compensation under section 107 of the Act of 1990 or section 153 of the Act of 1972 shall be limited to any loss or damage directly attributable to the permission being suspended or temporarily modified for the duration of the period between the order so taking effect and the Secretary of State determining not to confirm the order.

(2)   Where the Secretary of State determines not to confirm—
   (a)   an order under section 102 of the Town and Country Planning Act 1990 (order requiring discontinuance of use, &c) which has taken effect under regulation 57(3) above, or
   (b)   an order under section 49 of the Town and Country Planning (Scotland) Act 1972 (order requiring discontinuance of use, &c) which has taken effect under regulation 58(3) above,

any claim for compensation under section 115 of the Act of 1990 or section 159 of the Act of 1972 shall be limited to any loss or damage directly attributable to any right to continue a use of the land being, by virtue of the order, suspended or subject to conditions for the duration of the period between the order so taking effect and the Secretary of State determining not to confirm the order.

(3)   Where compensation is payable in respect of—
   (a)   an order under section 97 of the Town and Country Planning Act 1990, or
   (b)   any order mentioned in section 115(1) of that Act (compensation in respect of orders under s 102, &c), or to which that section applies by virtue of section 115(5),

and the order has been made pursuant to regulation 50, the question as to the amount of the compensation shall be referred, by the authority liable to pay the compensation, to and be determined by the Lands Tribunal unless and to the extent that in any particular case the Secretary of State has indicated in writing that such a reference and determination may be dispensed with.

(4) Where compensation is payable in respect of—
  (a) an order under section 42 of the Town and Country Planning (Scotland) Act 1972 (revocation or modification of planning permission), or
  (b) any order mentioned in section 153(1) of that Act (compensation in respect of orders under s 49),

and the order has been made pursuant to regulation 50, the question as to the amount of the compensation shall be referred, by the authority liable to pay the compensation, to and be determined by the Lands Tribunal for Scotland unless and to the extent that in any particular case the Secretary of State has indicated in writing that such a reference and determination may be dispensed with.

[1044]

60 General development orders

(1) It shall be a condition of any planning permission granted by a general development order, whether made before or after the commencement of these Regulations, that development which—
  (a) is likely to have a significant effect on a European site in Great Britain (either alone or in combination with other plans or projects), and
  (b) is not directly connected with or necessary to the management of the site,

shall not be begun until the developer has received written notification of the approval of the local planning authority under regulation 62.

(2) It shall be a condition of any planning permission granted by a general development order made before the commencement of these Regulations that development which—
  (a) is likely to have a significant effect on a European site in Great Britain (either alone or in combination with other plans or projects), and
  (b) is not directly connected with or necessary to the management of the site,

and which was begun but not completed before the commencement of these Regulations, shall not be continued until the developer has received written notification of the approval of the local planning authority under regulation 62.

(3) Nothing in this regulation shall affect anything done before the commencement of these Regulations.

[1045]

61 General development orders: opinion of appropriate nature conservation body

(1) Where it is intended to carry out development in reliance on the permission granted by a general development order, application may be made in writing to the appropriate nature conservation body for their opinion whether the development is likely to have such an effect as is mentioned in regulation 60(1)(a) or (2)(a).

The application shall give details of the development which is intended to be carried out.

(2) On receiving such an application, the appropriate nature conservation body shall consider whether the development is likely to have such an effect.

(3) Where they consider that they have sufficient information to conclude that the development will, or will not, have such an effect, they shall in writing notify the applicant and the local planning authority of their opinion.

(4)   If they consider that they have insufficient information to reach either of those conclusions, they shall notify the applicant in writing indicating in what respects they consider the information insufficient; and the applicant may supply further information with a view to enabling them to reach a decision on the application.

(5)   The opinion of the appropriate nature conservation body, notified in accordance with paragraph (3), that the development is not likely to have such an effect as is mentioned in regulation 60(1)(a) or (2)(a) shall be conclusive of that question for the purpose of reliance on the planning permission granted by a general development order.

[1046]

62 General development orders: approval of local planning authority

(1)   Where it is intended to carry out development in reliance upon the permission granted by a general development order, application may be made in writing to the local planning authority for their approval.

(2)   The application shall—
  (a) give details of the development which is intended to be carried out; and
  (b) be accompanied by—
    (i) a copy of any relevant notification by the appropriate nature conservation body under regulation 61, and
    (ii) any fee required to be paid.

(3)   For the purposes of their consideration of the application the local planning authority shall assume that the development is likely to have such an effect as is mentioned in regulation 60(1)(a) or (2)(a).

(4)   The authority shall send a copy of the application to the appropriate nature conservation body and shall take account of any representations made by them.

(5)   If in their representations the appropriate nature conservation body state their opinion that the development is not likely to have such an effect as is mentioned in regulation 60(1)(a) or (2)(a), the local planning authority shall send a copy of the representations to the applicant; and the sending of that copy shall have the same effect as a notification by the appropriate nature conservation body of its opinion under regulation 61(3).

(6)   In any other case the local planning authority shall, taking account of any representations made by the appropriate nature conservation body, make an appropriate assessment of the implications of the development for the European site in view of that site's conservation objectives.

  In the light of the conclusions of the assessment the authority shall approve the development only after having ascertained that it will not adversely affect the integrity of the site.

[1047]

63 General development orders: supplementary

(1)   The local planning authority for the purposes of regulations 60 to 62 shall be the authority to whom an application for approval under regulation 62 would fall to be made if it were an application for planning permission.

(2)   The fee payable in connection with an application for such approval is—
  (a) £25 in the case of applications made before 3rd January 1995, and
  (b) £30 in the case of applications made on or after that date.

(3)   Approval required by regulation 60 shall be treated—

(a) for the purposes of the provisions of the Town and Country Planning Act 1990, or the Town and Country Planning (Scotland) Act 1972, relating to appeals, as approval required by a condition imposed on a grant of planning permission; and

(b) for the purposes of the provisions of any general development order relating to the time within which notice of a decision should be made, as approval required by a condition attached to a grant of planning permission.

[1048]

64 Special development orders

(1) A special development order made after the commencement of these Regulations may not grant planning permission for development which—

(a) is likely to have a significant effect on a European site in Great Britain (either alone or in combination with other plans or projects), and

(b) is not directly connected with or necessary to the management of the site;

and any such order made before the commencement of these Regulations shall, on and after that date, cease to have effect to grant such permission, whether or not the development authorised by the permission has been begun.

(2) Nothing in this regulation shall affect anything done before the commencement of these Regulations.

[1049]

65 Simplified planning zones

The adoption or approval of a simplified planning zone scheme after the commencement of these Regulations shall not have effect to grant planning permission for development which—

(a) is likely to have a significant effect on a European site in Great Britain (either alone or in combination with other plans or projects), and

(b) is not directly connected with or necessary to the management of the site;

and every simplified planning zone scheme already in force shall cease to have effect to grant such permission, whether or not the development authorised by the permission has been begun.

[1050]

66 Enterprise zones

An order designating an enterprise zone, or the approval of a modified scheme, if made or given after the commencement of these Regulations, shall not have effect to grant planning permission for development which—

(a) is likely to have a significant effect on a European site in Great Britain (either alone or in combination with other plans or projects), and

(b) is not directly connected with or necessary to the management of the site;

and where the order or approval was made or given before that date, the permission granted by virtue of the taking effect of the order or the modifications shall, from that date, cease to have effect to grant planning permission or such development, whether or not the development authorised by the permission has been begun.

[1051]

67 Simplified planning zones and enterprise zones: supplementary provisions as to compensation

(1) Where in England and Wales—

(a) planning permission is withdrawn by regulation 65 or 66, and

(b) development authorised by the permission had been begun but not completed before the commencement of these Regulations, and

(c) on an application made under Part III of the Town and Country Planning Act 1990 before the end of the period of 12 months beginning with the date of commencement of these Regulations, planning permission for the development is refused or is granted subject to conditions other than those imposed by the scheme,

section 107(1)(a) of that Act (compensation in respect of abortive expenditure) shall apply as if the permission granted by the scheme had been granted by the local planning authority under Part III of that Act and had been revoked or modified by an order under section 97 of that Act.

(2)   Where in Scotland—
    (a) planning permission is withdrawn by regulation 65 or 66, and
    (b) development authorised by the permission had been begun but not completed before the commencement of these Regulations, and
    (c) on an application made under Part III of the Town and Country Planning (Scotland) Act 1972 before the end of the period of 12 months beginning with the date of commencement of these Regulations, planning permission for the development is refused or is granted subject to conditions other than those imposed by the scheme,

section 153(1)(a) of that Act (compensation in respect of abortive expenditure) shall apply as if the permission granted by the scheme had been granted by the local planning authority under Part III of that Act and had been revoked or modified by an order under section 42 of that Act.

(3)   Paragraphs (1) and (2) above do not apply in relation to planning permission for the development of operational land by statutory undertakers.

[1052]

68 Construction as one with planning legislation

Regulations 54 to 67 shall be construed as one—
    (a) in England and Wales, with the Town and Country Planning Act 1990; and
    (b) in Scotland, with the Town and Country Planning (Scotland) Act 1972.

[1053]

Highways and roads

69 Construction or improvement of highways or roads

(1)   Regulations 48 and 49 (requirement to consider effect on European site) apply in relation to any plan or project—
    (a) by the Secretary of State—
       (i) to construct a new highway or to improve, within the meaning of the Highways Act 1980, an existing highway, or
       (ii) to construct a new road or to improve, within the meaning of the Roads (Scotland) Act 1984, an existing road; or
    (b) by a local highway authority or local roads authority, to carry out within the boundaries of a road any works required for the improvement of the road.

(2)   Regulations 50 and 51 (requirement to review certain decisions and consents, &c) apply to any such plan or project as is mentioned in paragraph (1) unless the works have been completed before the site became a European site or, if later, the commencement of these Regulations.

[1054]

70 Cycle tracks and other ancillary works

As from the commencement of these Regulations, section 3(10) of the Cycle Tracks Act 1984 and section 152(4) of the Roads (Scotland) Act 1984 shall cease to have effect to deem planning permission to be granted for development which—
  (a) is likely to have a significant effect on a European site in Great Britain (either alone or in combination with other plans or projects), and
  (b) is not directly connected with or necessary to the management of the site,

whether or not the development authorised by the permission has been begun.

[1055]

Electricity

71 Consents under Electricity Act 1989: application of general requirements

  (1)   Regulations 48 and 49 (requirement to consider effect on European site) apply in relation to the granting of—
  (a) consent under section 36 of the Electricity Act 1989 to construct, extend or operate a generating station, or
  (b) consent under section 37 of that Act to install an electric line above ground.

  (2)   Where in such a case the Secretary of State considers that any adverse effects of the plan or project on the integrity of a European site would be avoided if the consent were subject to conditions, he may grant consent subject to those conditions.

  (3)   Regulations 50 and 51 (requirement to review existing decisions and consents, &c) apply to such a consent as is mentioned in paragraph (1) unless—
  (a) the works to which the consent relates have been completed before the site became a European site or, if later, the commencement of these Regulations, or
  (b) the consent was granted subject to a condition as to the time within which the works to which it relates were to be begun and that time has expired without them having been begun, or
  (c) it was granted for a limited period and that period has expired.

  Where the consent is for, or includes, the operation of a generating station, the works shall be treated as completed when, in reliance on the consent, the generating station is first operated.

  (4)   Where on the review of such a consent the Secretary of State considers that any adverse effects on the integrity of a European site of the carrying out or, as the case may be, the continuation of the plan or project would be avoided by a variation of the consent, he may vary the consent accordingly.

  (5)   In conjunction with the review of any such consent the Secretary of State shall review any direction deeming planning permission to be granted for the plan or project and may vary or revoke it.

[1056]

72 Consents under the Electricity Act 1989: procedure on review

  (1)   Where the Secretary of State decides in pursuance of regulation 71 to revoke or vary a consent under the Electricity Act 1989, or a direction deeming planning permission to be granted, he shall serve notice on—
  (a) the person to whom the consent was granted or, as the case may be, in whose favour the direction was made,
  (b) in the case of a consent under section 36 of the Electricity Act 1989, any other person proposing to operate the generating station in question, and

(c) any other person who in his opinion will be affected by the revocation or variation,

informing them of the decision and specifying a period of not less than 28 days within which any person on whom the notice is served may make representations to him.

(2) The Secretary of State shall also serve notice on—
  (a) the relevant planning authority within tic meaning of paragraph 2(6) of Schedule 8 to the Electricity Act 1989, and
  (b) the appropriate nature conservation body,

informing them of the decision and inviting their representations within the specified period.

(3) The Secretary of State shall consider whether to proceed with the revocation or variation, and shall have regard to any representations made to him in accordance with paragraph (1) or (2).

(4) If within the specified period a person on whom notice was served under paragraph (1), or the relevant planning authority, so requires, the Secretary of State shall before deciding whether to proceed with the revocation or variation give—
  (a) to them, and
  (b) to any other person on whom notice under paragraph (1) or (2) was required to be served,

an opportunity of appearing before, and being heard by, a person appointed by the Secretary of State for the purpose.

[1057]

73 Consents under Electricity Act 1989: effect of review

(1) The revocation or variation pursuant to regulation 71 of a consent under section 36 or 37 of the Electricity Act 1989, or a direction deeming planning permission to be granted, shall take effect upon service of the notices required by regulation 72(1) or, where there is more than one such notice and those notices are served at different times, from the date on which the last of them was served.

(2) Where the Secretary of State decides not to proceed with the revocation or variation, the consent or direction shall have effect again from the time of that decision, and shall thereafter have effect as if—
  (a) any period specified in the consent or direction for the taking of any action, being a period which had not expired prior to the date mentioned in paragraph (1), were extended by a period equal to that during which the revocation or variation had effect; and
  (b) there were substituted for any date specified in the consent or direction as being a date by which any action should be taken, not being a date falling prior to that date mentioned in paragraph (1), such date as post-dates the specified date by a period equal to that during which the revocation or variation had effect.

(3) The revocation or variation pursuant to regulation 71 of a consent under section 36 or 37 of the Electricity Act 1989, or a direction deeming planning permission to be granted, shall not affect anything done under the consent or direction prior to the revocation or variation taking effect.

[1058]

74 Consents under Electricity Act 1989: compensation for revocation or variation

(1) Where a direction deeming planning permission to be granted is revoked or varied pursuant to regulation 71, that permission shall be treated—

(a) for the purposes of Part IV of the Town and Country Planning Act 1990 (compensation) as having been revoked or modified by order under section 97 of that Act, or

(b) for the purposes of Part VIII of the Town and Country Planning (Scotland) Act 1972 (compensation) as having been revoked or modified by order under section 42 of that Act.

(2)   Where a consent under section 36 or 37 of the Electricity Act 1989 is revoked or varied pursuant to regulation 71, Part IV of the Town and Country Planning Act 1990 or Part VIII of the Town and Country Planning (Scotland) Act 1972 (compensation) shall apply as if—

(a) the consent had been planning permission granted on an application under that Act and had been revoked or modified by order under section 97 of the 1990 Act or section 42 of the 1972 Act; and

(b) each of those Parts provided that the Secretary of State was the person liable to pay any compensation provided for by that Part.

This paragraph shall not have effect to confer any right to compensation for any expenditure, loss or damage for which compensation is payable by virtue of paragraph (1) above.

(3)   Where the Secretary of State decides not to proceed with the revocation or variation of a consent under section 36 or 37 of the Electricity Act 1989, or a direction deeming planning permission to be granted, any claim for compensation by virtue of this regulation shall be limited to any loss or damage directly attributable to the consent or direction ceasing to have effect or being varied for the duration of the period between the revocation or variation taking effect under regulation 73(1) and the Secretary of State deciding not to proceed with it.

(4)   Where compensation is payable by virtue of this regulation, the question as to the amount of the compensation shall be referred to and determined by the Lands Tribunal, or the Lands Tribunal for Scotland, unless and to the extent that in any particular case the Secretary of State has indicated in writing that such a reference and determination may be dispensed with.

[1059]

Pipe-lines

75 Authorisations under the Pipe-lines Act 1962: application of general requirements

(1)   Regulations 48 and 49 (requirement to consider effect on European site) apply in relation to the granting of a pipe-line construction or diversion authorisation under the Pipe-lines Act 1962.

(2)   Where in such a case the Secretary of State considers that any adverse effects of the plan or project on the integrity of a European site would be avoided by granting an authorisation for the execution of works for the placing of the proposed pipe-line or, as the case may be, the portion of the pipe-line to be diverted, along a modified route, he may, subject to the provisions of Schedule 1 to the Pipe-lines Act 1962, grant such an authorisation.

(3)   Regulations 50 and 51 (requirement to review existing decisions and consents, &c) apply to a pipe-line construction or diversion authorisation under the Pipe-lines Act 1962 unless—

(a) the works to which the authorisation relates have been completed before the site became a European site or, if later, the commencement of these Regulations, or

(b) the authorisation was granted subject to a condition as to the time within which the works to which it relates were to be begun and that time has expired without them having been begun, or

(c) it was granted for a limited period and that period has expired.

(4)   Where on the review of such an authorisation the Secretary of State considers that any adverse effects on the integrity of a European site of the carrying out or, as the case may be, the continuation of the plan or project would be avoided by a variation of the authorisation, he may vary it accordingly.

(5)   In conjunction with the review of any such authorisation the Secretary of State shall review any direction deeming planning permission to be granted for the plan or project and may vary or revoke it.

[1060]

76 Authorisations under the Pipe-lines Act 1962: procedure on review

(1)   Where the Secretary of State decides in pursuance of regulation 75 to revoke or vary an authorisation under the Pipe-lines Act 1962, or a direction deeming planning permission to be granted, he shall serve notice on—
  (a) the person to whom the authorisation was granted or, as the case may be, in whose favour the direction was made, and
  (b) any other person who in his opinion will be affected by the revocation or variation,

informing them of the decision and specifying a period of not less than 28 days within which any person on whom the notice is served may make representations to him.

(2)   The Secretary of State shall also serve notice on—
  (a) the local planning authority, and
  (b) the appropriate nature conservation body,

informing them of the decision and inviting their representations within the specified period.

(3)   The Secretary of State shall consider whether to proceed with the revocation or variation, and shall have regard to any representations made to him in accordance with paragraph (1) or (2).

(4)   If within the specified period a person on whom notice was served under paragraph (1), or the local planning authority, so requires, the Secretary of State shall before deciding whether to proceed with the revocation or variation give—
  (a) to them, and
  (b) to any other person on whom notice under paragraph (1) or (2) was required to be served,

an opportunity of appearing before, and being heard by, a person appointed by the Secretary of State for the purpose.

[1061]

77 Authorisations under the Pipe-lines Act 1962: effect of review

(1)   The revocation or variation pursuant to regulation 75 of an authorisation under the Pipe-lines Act 1962, or of a direction deeming planning permission to be granted, shall take effect upon service of the notices required by regulation 76(1) or, where there is more than one such notice and those notices are served at different times, upon the service of the last such notice to be served.

(2)   Where the Secretary of State decides not to proceed with the revocation or variation, the authorisation or direction shall have effect again from the time of that decision, and shall thereafter have effect as if—
  (a) any period specified in the authorisation or direction for the taking of any action, being a period which had not expired prior to the date mentioned in paragraph (1), were extended by a period equal to that during which the revocation or variation had effect; and
  (b) there were substituted for any date specified in the authorisation or direction as being a date by which any action should be taken, not being a

date falling prior to that date mentioned in paragraph (1), such date as post-dates the specified date by a period equal to that during which the revocation or variation had effect.

(3)   The revocation or variation pursuant to regulation 75 of an authorisation under the Pipe-lines Act 1962, or a direction deeming planning permission to be granted, shall not affect anything done under the authorisation or direction prior to the revocation or variation taking effect.

[1062]

78 Authorisations under the Pipe-lines Act 1962: compensation for revocation or variation

(1)   Where a direction deeming planning permission to be granted is revoked or varied pursuant to regulation 75, that permission shall be treated—
- (a) for the purposes of Part IV of the Town and Country Planning Act 1990 (compensation) as having been revoked or modified by order under section 97 of that Act, or
- (b) for the purposes of Part VIII of the Town and Country Planning (Scotland) Act 1972 (compensation) as having been revoked or modified by order under section 42 of that Act.

(2)   Where an authorisation under the Pipe-lines Act 1962 is revoked or varied pursuant to regulation 75, Part IV of the Town and Country Planning Act 1990 or Part VIII of the Town and Country Planning (Scotland) Act 1972 (compensation) shall apply as if—
- (a) the authorisation had been planning permission granted on an application under that Act and had been revoked or modified by order under section 97 of the 1990 Act or section 42 of the 1972 Act; and
- (b) each of those Parts provided that the Secretary of State was the person liable to pay any compensation provided for by that Part.

This paragraph shall not have effect to confer any right to compensation for any expenditure, loss or damage for which compensation is payable by virtue of paragraph (1) above.

(3)   Where the Secretary of State decides not to proceed with the revocation or variation of an authorisation under the Pipe-lines Act 1962, or a direction deeming planning permission to be granted, any claim for compensation by virtue of this regulation shall be limited to any loss or damage directly attributable to the authorisation or direction ceasing to have effect or being varied for the duration of the period between the revocation or variation taking effect under regulation 77(1) and the Secretary of State deciding not to proceed with it.

(4)   Where compensation is payable by virtue of this regulation, the question as to the amount of the compensation shall be referred to and determined by the Lands Tribunal, or the Lands Tribunal for Scotland, unless and to the extent that in any particular case the Secretary of State has indicated in writing that such a reference and determination may be dispensed with.

[1063]

Transport and works

79 Orders under the Transport and Works Act 1992: application of general requirements

(1)   Regulations 48 and 49 (requirement to consider effect on European site) apply in relation to the making of an order under section 1 or 3 of the Transport and Works Act 1992.

(2)   Where in such a case the Secretary of State considers that any adverse effects of the plan or project on the integrity of a European site would be avoided by making modifications to the proposals, he may make an order subject to those modifications.

(3)   Regulations 50 and 51 (requirement to review existing decisions and consents, &c) apply to an order under section 1 or 3 of the Transport and Works Act 1992 unless the works to which the order relates have been completed before the site became a European site.

(4)   Where on the review of such an order the Secretary of State considers that any adverse effects on the integrity of a European site of the carrying out or, as the case may be, the continuation of the plan or project would be avoided by a variation of the order, he may vary it accordingly.

(5)   In conjunction with the review of any such order the Secretary of State shall review any direction deeming planning permission to be granted for the plan or project and may vary or revoke it.

[1064]

80 Orders under the Transport and Works Act 1992: procedure on review

(1)   Where the Secretary of State decides in pursuance of regulation 79 to revoke or vary an order under the Transport and Works Act 1992, or a direction deeming planning permission to be granted, he shall serve notice on—
   (a) the person (if any) on whose application the order was made or, as the case may be, in whose favour the direction was made, and
   (b) any other person who in his opinion will be affected by the revocation or variation,

informing them of the decision and specifying a period of not less than 28 days within which any person on whom the notice is served may make representations to him.

(2)   The Secretary of State shall also serve notice on—
   (a) the local planning authority, and
   (b) the appropriate nature conservation body,

informing them of the decision and inviting their representations within the specified period.

(3)   The Secretary of State shall consider whether to proceed with the revocation or variation, and shall have regard to any representations made to him in accordance with paragraph (1) or (2).

(4)   If within the specified period a person on whom notice was served under paragraph (1), or the local planning authority, so requires, the Secretary of State shall before deciding whether to proceed with the revocation or variation of the order or direction give—
   (a) to them,
   (b) to any other person on whom notice under paragraph (1) or (2) was required to be served,

an opportunity of appearing before, and being heard by, a person appointed by the Secretary of State for the purpose.

[1065]

81 Orders under the Transport and Works Act 1992: effect of review

(1)   The revocation or variation pursuant to regulation 79 of an order under the Transport and Works Act 1992, or of a direction deeming planning permission to be granted, shall take effect upon service of the notices required by regulation 80(1) or,

where there is more than one such notice and those notices are served at different times, upon the service of the last such notice to be served.

(2) Where the Secretary of State decides not to proceed with the revocation or variation, the order or direction shall have effect again from the time of that decision, and shall thereafter have effect as if—

 (a) any period specified in the order or direction for the taking of any action, being a period which had not expired prior to the date mentioned in paragraph (1), were extended by a period equal to that during which the revocation or variation had effect; and

 (b) there were substituted for any date specified in the order or direction as being a date by which any action should be taken, not being a date falling prior to that date mentioned in paragraph (1), such date as post-dates the specified date by a period equal to that during which the revocation or variation had effect.

(3) The revocation or variation pursuant to regulation 79 of an order under section 1 or 3 of the Transport and Works Act 1992, or of a direction deeming planning permission to be granted, shall not affect anything done under the order or direction prior to the revocation or variation taking effect.

                        [1066]

82 Orders under the Transport and Works Act 1992: compensation for revocation or variation

(1) Where a direction deeming planning permission to be granted is revoked or varied pursuant to regulation 79, that permission shall be treated for the purposes of Part IV of the Town and Country Planning Act 1990 (compensation) as having been revoked or modified by order under section 97 of that Act.

(2) Where an order under section 1 or 3 of the Transport and Works Act 1992 is revoked or varied pursuant to regulation 79, Part IV of the Town and Country Planning Act 1990 shall apply as if—

 (a) the order had been planning permission granted on an application under that Act and had been revoked or modified by order under section 97 of that Act; and

 (b) that Part provided that the Secretary of State was the person liable to pay any compensation provided for by that Part.

 This paragraph shall not have effect to confer any right to compensation for any expenditure, loss or damage for which compensation is payable by virtue of paragraph (1) above.

(3) Where the Secretary of State decides not to proceed with the revocation or variation of an order under section 1 or 3 of the Transport and Works Act 1992, or a direction deeming planning permission to be granted, any claim for compensation by virtue of this regulation shall be limited to any loss or damage directly attributable to the order or direction ceasing to have effect or being varied for the duration of the period between the revocation or variation taking effect under regulation 81(1) and the Secretary of State deciding not to proceed with it.

(4) Where compensation is payable by virtue of this regulation, the question as to the amount of the compensation shall be referred to and determined by the Lands Tribunal unless and to the extent that in any particular case the Secretary of State has indicated in writing that such a reference and determination may be dispensed with.

                        [1067]

Environmental controls

83 Authorisations under Part I of the Environmental Protection Act 1990

(1)   Regulations 48 and 49 (requirement to consider effect on European site) apply in relation to the granting of an authorisation under Part I of the Environmental Protection Act 1990 (integrated pollution control and local authority air pollution control).

(2)   Where in such a case the competent authority consider that any adverse effects of the plan or project on the integrity of a European site would be avoided if the authorisation were subject to conditions, they may grant an authorisation, or cause an authorisation to be granted, subject to those conditions.

(3)   Regulations 50 and 51 (requirement to review existing decisions and consents, &c) apply to any such authorisation as is mentioned in paragraph (1).

(4)   Where on the review of such an authorisation the competent authority consider that any adverse effects on the integrity of a European site of the carrying out or, as the case may be, the continuation of activities authorised by it would be avoided by a variation of the authorisation, they may vary it, or cause it to be varied, accordingly.

(5)   Where any question arises as to agreeing to a plan or project, or affirming an authorisation on review, under regulation 49 (considerations of overriding public interest), the competent authority shall refer the matter to the Secretary of State who shall determine the matter in accordance with that regulation and give directions to the authority accordingly.

[1068]

84 Licences under Part II of the Environmental Protection Act 1990

(1)   Regulations 48 and 49 (requirement to consider effect on European site) apply in relation to—
    (a) the granting of a waste management licence under Part II of the Environmental Protection Act 1990,
    (b) the passing of a resolution under section 54 of that Act (provisions as to land occupied by disposal authorities themselves), and
    (c) the granting of a disposal licence under Part I of the Control of Pollution Act 1974 and the passing of a resolution under section 11 of that Act.

(2)   Where in such a case the competent authority consider that any adverse effects of the plan or project on the integrity of a European site would be avoided by making any licence subject to conditions, they may grant a licence, or cause a licence to be granted, or, as the case may be, pass a resolution, subject to those conditions.

(3)   Regulations 50 and 51 (requirement to review existing decisions and consents, &c) apply to any such licence or resolution as is mentioned in paragraph (1).

(4)   Where on the review of such a licence or resolution the competent authority consider that any adverse effects on the integrity of a European site of the carrying out or, as the case may be, the continuation of the activities authorised by it would be avoided by a variation of the licence or resolution, they may vary it, or cause it to be varied, accordingly.

[1069]

85 Discharge consents under water pollution legislation

(1)   Regulations 48 and 49 (requirement to consider effect on European site) apply in relation to the giving of consent under—

(a) Chapter II of Part III to the Water Resources Act 1991 (control of pollution of water resources), or

(b) Part II of the Control of Pollution Act 1974 (which makes corresponding provision for Scotland).

(2) Where in such a case the competent authority consider that any adverse effects of the plan or project on the integrity of a European site would be avoided by making any consent subject to conditions, they may give consent, or cause it to be given, subject to those conditions.

(3) Regulations 50 and 51 (requirement to review existing decisions and consents, &c) apply to any such consent as is mentioned in paragraph (1).

(4) Where on the review of such a consent the competent authority consider that any adverse effects on the integrity of a European site of the carrying out or, as the case may be, the continuation of the activities authorised by it would be avoided by a variation of the consent, they may vary it, or cause it to be varied, accordingly.

[1070]

PART V
SUPPLEMENTARY PROVISIONS

Supplementary provisions as to management agreements

86 Powers of limited owners, &c to enter into management agreements

(1) In the case of settled land in England and Wales—
  (a) the tenant for life may enter into a management agreement relating to the land, or any part of it, either for consideration or gratuitously;
  (b) the Settled Land Act 1925 shall apply as if the power conferred by sub-paragraph (a) had been conferred by that Act; and
  (c) for the purposes of section 72 of that Act (which relates to the mode of giving effect to a disposition by a tenant for life and to the operation thereof), and of any other relevant statutory provision, entering into a management agreement shall be treated as a disposition.

The above provisions of this paragraph shall be construed as one with the Settled Land Act 1925.

(2) Section 28 of the Law of Property Act 1925 (which confers the powers of a tenant for life on trustees for sale) shall apply as if the power of a tenant for life under paragraph (1)(a) above had been conferred by the Settled Land Act 1925.

(3) A university or college to which the Universities and College Estates Act 1925 applies may enter into a management agreement relating to any land belonging to it in England and Wales either for consideration or gratuitously.

That Act shall apply as if the power conferred by this paragraph had been conferred by that Act.

(4) In the case of glebe land or other land belonging to an ecclesiastical benefice—
  (a) the incumbent of the benefice, and
  (b) in the case of land which is part of the endowment of any other ecclesiastical corporation, the corporation,

may with the consent of the Church Commissioners enter into a management agreement either for consideration or gratuitously.

The Ecclesiastical Leasing Acts shall apply as if the power conferred by this paragraph had been conferred by those Acts, except that the consent of the patron of an ecclesiastical benefice shall not be requisite.

(5)   In the case of any land in Scotland, any person being—
   (a) the liferenter, or
   (b) the heir of entail,

in possession of the land shall have power to enter into a management agreement relating to the land or any part of it.

(6)   The Trusts (Scotland) Act 1921 shall have effect as if among the powers conferred on trustees by section 4 of that Act (which relates to the general powers of trustees) there were included a power to enter into management agreements relating to the trust estate or any part of it.

[1071]

Supplementary provisions as to potentially damaging operations

87 Carrying out of operation after expiry of period

(1)   If before the expiry of the period of four months referred to in regulation 19(2)(c) the relevant person agrees in writing with the appropriate nature conservation body that, subject as follows, the condition specified in that provision shall not apply in relation to the operation in question, then, subject as follows, regulation 19(2) shall as from the date of the agreement have effect in relation to the operation (as regards both the owner or the occupier of the land in question) as if sub-paragraph (c) were omitted.

(2)   If after such an agreement has been made the relevant person (whether a party to the agreement or not) gives written notice to the appropriate nature conservation body that he wishes to terminate the agreement, then as from the giving of the notice regulation 19(2) shall have effect in relation to the operation in question (as regards both the owner and the occupier of the land in question) as if paragraph (c) specified the condition that one month, or any longer period specified in the notice, has expired from the giving of the notice under this paragraph.

(3)   In paragraphs (1) and (2) above "the relevant person"—
   (a) in a case where the notice under regulation 19(1)(a) was given by the owner of the land in question, means the owner of that land;
   (b) in a case where that notice was given by the occupier of that land, means the occupier of that land.

[1072]

88 Duties of agriculture Ministers with respect to European sites

(1)   Where an application for a farm capital grant is made as respects expenditure incurred or to be incurred for the purpose of activities on land within a European site, the Minister responsible for determining the application—
   (a) shall, so far as may be consistent with the purposes of the grant provisions, so exercise his functions thereunder as to further the conservation of the flora, fauna, or geological or physiographical features by reason of which the land is a European site; and
   (b) where the appropriate nature conservation body have objected to the making of the grant on the ground that the activities in question have destroyed or damaged or will destroy or damage that flora or fauna or those features, shall not make the grant except after considering the objection and, in the case of land in England, after consulting with the Secretary of State.

(2)   Where in consequence of an objection by the appropriate nature conservation body, an application for a grant as respects expenditure to be incurred is refused on the ground that the activities in question will have such an effect as is mentioned in paragraph (1)(b), the appropriate nature conservation body shall, within three months of their receiving notice of the Minister's decision, offer to

enter into, in the terms of a draft submitted to the applicant, a management agreement—
> (a) imposing restrictions as respects those activities, and
> (b) providing for the making by them of payments to the applicant.

(3)   In this regulation—
"farm capital grant" means—
> (a) a grant under a scheme made under section 29 of the Agriculture Act 1970, or
> (b) a grant under regulations made under section 2(2) of the European Communities Act 1972 to a person carrying on an agricultural business within the meaning of those regulations in respect of expenditure incurred or to be incurred for the purposes of or in connection with that business, being expenditure of a capital nature or incurred in connection with expenditure of a capital nature; and

"grant provisions" means—
> (i) in the case of such a grant as is mentioned in paragraph (a) above, the scheme under which the grant is made and section 29 of the Agriculture Act 1970, and
> (ii) in the case of such a grant as is mentioned in paragraph (b) above, the regulations under which the grant is made and the Community instrument in pursuance of which the regulations were made.

[1073]

89 Payments under certain agreements offered by authorities

(1)   This regulation applies where the appropriate nature conservation body offers to enter into a management agreement providing for the making of payments by them to—
> (a) a person who has given notice under regulation 19(1)(a) or 23(1)(a), or
> (b) a person whose application for a farm capital grant within the meaning of regulation 88 has been refused in consequence of an objection by that body.

(2)   Subject to paragraph (3), the said payments shall be of such amounts as may be determined by the offeror in accordance with guidance given—
> (a) in England, by the Minister of Agriculture, Fisheries and Food and the Secretary of State, or
> (b) in Wales or Scotland, by the Secretary of State.

(3)   If the offeree so requires within one month of receiving the offer, the determination of those amounts shall be referred to an arbitrator to be appointed, in default of agreement, by the Secretary of State.

(4)   Where the amounts determined by the arbitrator exceed those determined by the offeror, the offeror shall—
> (a) amend the offer so as to give effect to the arbitrator's determination, or
> (b) except in the case of an offer made to a person whose application for a farm capital grant has been refused in consequence of an objection by the offeror, withdraw the offer.

(5)   In the application of this regulation in Scotland references to an arbitrator shall be construed as references to an arbiter.

[1074]

90 Powers of entry

(1)   A person authorised in writing by the appropriate nature conservation body may, at any reasonable time and (if required to do so) upon producing evidence that he is so authorised, enter any land—

(a) to ascertain whether a special nature conservation order should be made in relation to that land, or if an offence under regulation 23 is being, or has been, committed on that land; or

(b) to ascertain the amount of any compensation payable under regulation 25 in respect of an interest in that land.

But nothing in this paragraph shall authorise any person to enter a dwelling.

(2) A person shall not demand admission as of right to any land which is occupied unless either—

(a) 24 hours' notice of the intended entry has been given to the occupier, or

(b) the purpose of the entry is to ascertain if an offence under regulation 23 is being, or has been, committed on that land.

(3) A person who intentionally obstructs a person in the exercise of his powers under this regulation commits an offence and is liable on summary conviction to a fine not exceeding level 3 on the standard scale.

[1075]

91 Compensation: amount and assessment

(1) The following provisions have effect as to compensation under regulation 25(1) (effect of special nature conservation order: decrease in value of agricultural unit).

(2) The amount of the compensation shall be the difference between the value of the interest in question and what it would have been had the order not been made.

(3) For this purpose—

(a) an interest in land shall be valued as at the time when the order is made; and

(b) where a person, by reason of his having more than one interest in land, makes more than one claim in respect of the same order, his various interests shall be valued together.

(4) Section 10 of the Land Compensation Act 1973 (mortgages, trusts for sale and settlements) or section 10 of the Land Compensation (Scotland) Act 1973 apply in relation to compensation under regulation 25(1) as in relation to compensation under Part I of that Act.

(5) For the purposes of assessing compensation under regulation 25(1), the rules set out in section 5 of the Land Compensation Act 1961 or section 12 of the Land Compensation (Scotland) Act 1963 have effect, so far as applicable and subject to any necessary modifications, as they have effect for the purpose of assessing compensation for the compulsory acquisition of an interest in land.

[1076]

92 Compensation: other supplementary provisions

(1) The following provisions have effect in relation to compensation under regulation 25 (compensation for effect of special nature conservation order).

(2) The compensation shall carry interest, at the rate for the time being prescribed under section 32 of the Land Compensation Act 1961 or section 40 of the Land Compensation (Scotland) Act 1963, from the date of the claim until payment.

(3) Except in so far as may be provided by regulations, any question of disputed compensation shall be referred to and determined by the Lands Tribunal or the Lands Tribunal for Scotland.

(4) In relation to the determination of any such question, the provisions of sections 2 and 4 of the Land Compensation Act 1961 or sections 9 and 11 of the Land Compensation (Scotland) Act 1963 (procedure and costs) shall apply, subject to any necessary modifications and to the provisions of any regulations.

[1077]

93 Compensation: procedural provisions

(1)   The power to make regulations under section 30 of the Wildlife and Countryside Act 1981 (provisions as to compensation where order made under section 29 of that Act) shall be exercisable so as to make provision for the purposes of these Regulations corresponding to those for which provision may be made under that section.

(2)   The references in regulation 25 to matters being prescribed by regulations, and in regulation 92(3) and (4) to matters being provided by regulations, are to their being so prescribed or provided.

(3)   Any regulations in force under section 30 on the commencement of these Regulations shall have effect for the purposes of these Regulations as if made under that section as applied by this regulation.

[1078]

Supplementary provisions as to byelaws

94 Procedure for making byelaws, penalties, &c

(1)   Sections 236 to 238 of the Local Government Act 1972 or sections 201 to 204 of the Local Government (Scotland) Act 1973 (procedure, &c for byelaws; offences against byelaws; evidence of byelaws) apply to all byelaws made under section 20 of the National Parks and Access to the Countryside Act 1949 as it applies by virtue of regulation 28 as if the appropriate nature conservation body were a local authority within the meaning of that Act.

(2)   In relation to byelaws so made the confirming authority for the purposes of the said section 236 or section 201 shall be the Secretary of State.

(3)   The appropriate nature conservation body shall have power to enforce byelaws made by them:

Provided that nothing in this paragraph shall be construed as authorising the institution of proceedings in Scotland for an offence.

[1079]

95 Powers of entry

(1)   For the purpose of surveying land, or of estimating its value, in connection with any claim for compensation payable under regulation 30 in respect of that or any other land, an officer of the Valuation Office or person duly authorised in writing by the authority from whom the compensation is claimed may enter upon the land.

(2)   A person authorised under this regulation to enter upon any land shall, if so required, produce evidence of his authority before entering.

(3)   A person shall not under this regulation demand admission as of right to any land which is occupied unless at least 14 days' notice in writing of the intended entry has been given to the occupier.

(4)   A person who intentionally obstructs a person in the exercise of his powers under this regulation commits an offence and is liable on summary conviction to a fine not exceeding level 3 on the standard scale.

[1080]

96 Compensation: England and Wales

(1)   The following provisions have effect as to compensation under regulation 30 (compensation for effect of byelaws) in respect of land in England and Wales.

(2)   Any dispute arising on a claim for any such compensation shall be determined by the Lands Tribunal.

(3)   For the purposes of any such reference to the Lands Tribunal, section 4 of the Land Compensation Act 1961 (which relates to costs) has effect with the substitution for references to the acquiring authority of references to the authority from whom the compensation in question is claimed.

(4)   Rules (2) to (4) of the Rules set out in section 5 of that Act (which provides rules for valuation of a compulsory acquisition) apply to the calculation of any such compensation, in so far as it is calculated by reference to the depreciation of the value of an interest in land.

(5)   In the case of an interest in land subject to a mortgage—
  (a) any such compensation in respect of the depreciation of that interest shall be calculated as if the interest were not subject to the mortgage;
  (b) a claim or application for the payment of any such compensation may be made by any person who when the byelaws giving rise to the compensation were made was the mortgagee of the interest, or by any person claiming under such a person, but without prejudice to the making of a claim or application by any other person;
  (c) a mortgagee shall not be entitled to any such compensation in respect of his interest as such; and
  (d) any compensation payable in respect of the interest subject to the mortgage shall be paid to the mortgagee or, where there is more than one mortgagee, to the first mortgagee, and shall in either case be applied by him as if it were proceeds of sale.

[1081]

97 (*Applies to Scotland only.*)

Supplementary provisions as to compulsory acquisition

98 Supplementary provisions as to acquisition of land

(1)   The powers of compulsory acquisition conferred on the appropriate nature conservation body by regulation 32 are exercisable in any particular case on their being authorised so to do by the Secretary of State.

(2)   In that regulation and in this regulation "land" includes any interest in land.

  For this purpose "interest", in relation to land, includes any estate in land and any right over land, whether the right is exercisable by virtue of the ownership of an interest in land or by virtue of a licence or agreement, and in particular includes sporting rights.

(3)   The Acquisition of Land Act 1981 applies in relation to any acquisition under these Regulations of land in England and Wales, and the Compulsory Purchase Act 1965 applies with any necessary modifications in relation to the acquisition of any interest in land in England and Wales.

(4)   In relation to the compulsory acquisition of land in Scotland, the Acquisition of Land (Authorisation Procedure) (Scotland) Act 1947 shall apply as if these Regulations had been in force immediately before the commencement of that Act and as if in paragraph (a) of subsection (1) of section 1 thereof, in Part I of the First Schedule thereto and in the Second Schedule thereto references to a local authority included Scottish Natural Heritage:

  Provided that section 2 of the said Act (which confers temporary powers for the speedy acquisition of land in urgent cases) shall not apply to any such compulsory acquisition as is mentioned in this paragraph.

The provisions of the Lands Clauses Acts incorporated with these Regulations by virtue of paragraph 1 of the Second Schedule to the Acquisition of Land (Authorisation Procedure) (Scotland) Act 1947, as applied by this paragraph, shall apply with the necessary modifications in relation to the compulsory acquisition of any interest in land, being an interest not falling within the definition of "lands" contained in the Lands Clauses Acts.

[1082]

99 Powers of entry

(1) For the purpose of surveying land in connection with the acquisition thereof or of any interest therein, whether by agreement or compulsorily, in the exercise of any power conferred by these Regulations, a person duly authorised in writing by the authority having power so to acquire the land or interest may enter upon the land.

(2) A person authorised under this regulation to enter upon any land shall, if so required, produce evidence of his authority before entering.

(3) A person shall not under this regulation demand admission as of right to any land which is occupied unless at least 14 days' notice in writing of the intended entry has been given to the occupier.

(4) A person who intentionally obstructs a person in the exercise of his powers under this regulation commits an offence and is liable on summary conviction to a fine not exceeding level 3 on the standard scale.

[1083]

Supplementary provisions as to protection of species

100 Attempts and possession of means of committing offence

(1) A person who attempts to commit an offence under Part III of these Regulations is guilty of an offence and punishable in like manner as for that offence.

(2) A person who, for the purposes of committing an offence under Part III of these Regulations, has in his possession anything capable of being used for committing the offence is guilty of an offence and punishable in like manner as for that offence.

(3) References below to an offence under Part III include an offence under this regulation.

[1084]

101 Enforcement

(1) If a constable suspects with reasonable cause that any person is committing or has committed an offence under Part III of these Regulations, the constable may without warrant—

(a) stop and search that person if the constable suspects with reasonable cause that evidence of the commission of the offence is to be found on that person;

(b) search or examine any thing which that person may then be using or have in his possession if the constable suspects with reasonable cause that evidence of the commission of the offence is to be found on that thing;

(c) seize and detain for the purposes of proceedings under that Part any thing which may be evidence of the commission of the offence or may be liable to be forfeited under regulation 103.

(2) If a constable suspects with reasonable cause that any person is committing an offence under Part III of these Regulations, he may, for the purposes of exercising

the powers conferred by paragraph (1) or arresting a person in accordance with section 25 of the Police and Criminal Evidence Act 1984 for such an offence, enter any land other than a dwelling-house.

(3)   If a justice of the peace is satisfied by information on oath that there are reasonable grounds for suspecting that an offence under regulation 39, 41 or 43 has been committed and that evidence of the offence may be found on any premises, he may grant a warrant to any constable (with or without other persons) to enter upon and search those premises for the purpose of obtaining that evidence.

In the application of this paragraph to Scotland, the reference to a justice of the peace includes a sheriff.

[1085]

102 Proceedings for offences: venue, time limits

(1)   An offence under Part III of these Regulations shall, for the purposes of conferring jurisdiction, be deemed to have been committed in any place where the offender is found or to which he is first brought after the commission of the offence.

(2)   Summary proceedings for—
    (a) any offence under regulation 39(1) involving the taking or killing of a wild animal, and
    (b) any offence under regulation 43(1),

may be brought within a period of six months from the date on which evidence sufficient in the opinion of the prosecutor to warrant the proceedings came to his knowledge.

But no such proceedings shall be brought by virtue of this paragraph more than two years after the commission of the offence.

(3)   For the purposes of paragraph (2) a certificate signed by or on behalf of the prosecutor and stating the date on which such evidence as aforesaid came to his knowledge shall be conclusive evidence of that fact; and a certificate stating that matter and purporting to be so signed shall be deemed to be so signed unless the contrary is proved.

[1086]

103 Power of court to order forfeiture

(1)   The court by which a person is convicted of an offence under Part III of these Regulations—
    (a) shall order the forfeiture of any animal, plant or other thing in respect of which the offence was committed; and
    (b) may order the forfeiture of any vehicle, animal, weapon or other thing which was used to commit the offence.

(2)   In paragraph (1)(b) "vehicle" includes aircraft, hovercraft and boat.

[1087]

104 Saving for other protective provisions

Nothing in these Regulations shall be construed as excluding the application of the provisions of Part I of the Wildlife and Countryside Act 1981 (protection of wildlife) in relation to animals or plants also protected under Part III of these Regulations.

[1087A]

General supplementary provisions

105 Powers of drainage authorities

(1)   Where the appropriate nature conservation body or any other person enter into an agreement with a drainage authority for the doing by that authority of any work on land in a European site, no limitation imposed by law on the capacity of the drainage authority by virtue of its constitution shall operate so as to prevent the authority carrying out the agreement.

(2)   In paragraph (1) "drainage authority" means the [Environment Agency] or an internal drainage board.

[1088]

NOTES

Para (2): words in square brackets substituted by the Environment Act 1995, s 120, Sch 22, para 233(1).

106 Offences by bodies corporate, &c

(1)   Where an offence under these Regulations committed by a body corporate is proved to have been committed with the consent or connivance of, or to be attributable to any neglect on the part of, a director, manager, secretary or other similar officer of the body corporate, or a person purporting to act in any such capacity, he as well as the body corporate is guilty of the offence and liable to be proceeded against and punished accordingly.

For this purpose "director", in relation to a body corporate whose affairs are managed by its members, means any member of the body.

(2)   Where an offence under these Regulations committed by a Scottish partnership is proved to have been committed with the consent or connivance of, or to be attributable to neglect on the part of, a partner, he (as well as the partnership) is guilty of the offence and liable to be proceeded against and punished accordingly.

[1089]

107 Local inquiries

(1)   The Secretary of State may cause a local inquiry to be held for the purposes of the exercise of any of his functions under these Regulations.

(2)   The provisions of section 250(2) to (5) of the Local Government Act 1972 or section 210(4) to (8) of the Local Government (Scotland) Act 1973 (local inquiries: evidence and costs) apply in relation to an inquiry held under this regulation.

[1090]

108 Service of notices

(1)   Section 329 of the Town and Country Planning Act 1990 or section 269 of the Town and Country Planning (Scotland) Act 1972 (service of notices) apply to notices and other documents required or authorised to be served under these Regulations.

(2)   Paragraph (1) does not apply to the service of any notice required or authorised to be served under the Acquisition of Land Act 1981 or the Acquisition of Land (Authorisation Procedure) (Scotland) Act 1947, as applied by these Regulations.

[1091]

SCHEDULE 1
PROCEDURE IN CONNECTION WITH ORDERS UNDER REGULATION 22
Regulation 22(3)

Coming into operation

1.—(1) An original order or a restrictive amending order takes effect on its being made.

(2) The Secretary of State shall consider every such order, and the order shall cease to have effect nine months after it is made unless he has previously given notice under paragraph 6 that he has considered it and does not propose to amend or revoke it, or has revoked it.

(3) Subject to paragraphs 3(1) and 4(4), a revoking order, or an amending order which is not restrictive, does not take effect until confirmed by the Secretary of State.

(4) An amending or revoking order requiring confirmation shall stand revoked if the Secretary of State gives notice under paragraph 6 below that it is not to be confirmed.

Publicity for orders

2.—(1) The Secretary of State shall, where an order has been made, give notice setting out the order (or describing its general effect) and stating that it has taken effect or, as the case may be, that it has been made and requires confirmation.

(2) The notice shall—
    (a) name a place in the area in which the land to which the order relates is situated where a copy of the order may be inspected free of charge at all reasonable hours; and
    (b) specify the time (not being less than 28 days from the date of the first publication of the notice) within which, and the manner in which, representations or objections with respect to the order may be made.

(3) The notice shall be given—
    (a) by publication in the Gazette and also at least one local newspaper circulating in the area in which the land to which the order relates is situated;
    (b) by serving a like notice—
        (i) on every owner and occupier of that land (subject to sub-paragraph (4) below); and
        (ii) on the local planning authority within whose area the land is situated.

(4) The Secretary of State may, in any particular case, direct that it shall not be necessary to comply with sub-paragraph (3)(b)(i); but if he so directs in the case of any land, then in addition to publication the notice shall be addressed to "The owners and any occupiers" of the land (describing it) and a copy or copies of the notice shall be affixed to some conspicuous object or objects on the land.

Unopposed orders

3.—(1) Where an order has taken effect immediately and no representations or objections are duly made in respect of it or any so made are withdrawn, the Secretary of State shall, as soon as practicable after considering the order, decide either to take no action on it or to make an order amending or revoking it.

An amending or revoking order under this sub-paragraph takes effect immediately and does not require confirmation nor shall any representation or objection with respect to it be entertained.

(2) Where an order requiring confirmation is made and no representations or objections are duly made in respect of it, or any so made are withdrawn, the Secretary of State may confirm the order (with or without modification).

Opposed orders

4.—(1) If any representation or objection duly made with respect to an order is not withdrawn, then, as soon as practicable in the case of an order having immediate effect and before confirming an order requiring confirmation, the Secretary of State shall either—
    (a) cause a local inquiry to be held; or
    (b) afford any person by whom a representation or objection has been duly made and not withdrawn an opportunity of being heard by a person appointed by the Secretary of State for the purpose.

(2) On considering any representations or objections duly made and the report of any person appointed to hold the inquiry or to hear representations or objections, the Secretary of State—

    (a)   if the order has already taken effect, shall decide either to take no action on the order, or to make an order amending or revoking it as he thinks appropriate in the light of the report, representations or objections; and

    (b)   if the order requires confirmation, may confirm it (with or without modifications).

(3) The provisions of section 250(2) to (5) of the Local Government Act 1972 or section 210(4) to (8) of the Local Government (Scotland) Act 1973 (local inquiries: evidence and costs) apply in relation to an inquiry held under this paragraph.

(4) An amending or revoking order made by virtue of sub-paragraph (2) above takes effect immediately and does not require confirmation nor shall any representation or objection with respect to it be entertained.

Restriction on power to amend orders or confirm them with modifications

5. The Secretary of State shall not by virtue of paragraphs 3(1) or 4(2) amend an order which has taken effect, or confirm any other order with modifications, so as to extend the area to which the order applies.

Notice of final decision on order

6.—(1) The Secretary of State shall as soon as practicable after making an order by virtue of paragraphs 3(1) or 4(2) give notice—

    (a)   setting out the order (or describing its effect) and stating that it has taken effect; and

    (b)   naming a place in the area in which the land to which the order relates is situated where a copy of the order may be inspected free of charge at all reasonable hours.

(2) The Secretary of State shall give notice of any of the following decisions of his as soon as practicable after making the decision—

    (a)   a decision under paragraph 3(1) or 4(2) to take no action on an order which has already taken effect;

    (b)   a decision to confirm or not to confirm an order requiring confirmation under this Schedule.

(3) A notice under this paragraph of a decision to confirm an order shall—

    (a)   set out the order as confirmed (or describe its general effect) and state the day on which the order took effect; and

    (b)   name a place in the area in which the land to which the order relates is situated where a copy of the order as confirmed may be inspected free of charge at all reasonable hours.

(4) Notice under this paragraph shall be given by publishing it in accordance with paragraph 2(3) and serving a copy of it on any person on whom a notice was required to be served under paragraph 2(3) or (4).

Proceedings for questioning validity of orders

7.—(1) This paragraph applies to any order which has taken effect and as to which the Secretary of State has given notice under paragraph 6 of a decision of his to take no action or to amend the order in accordance with paragraph 4; and in this paragraph "the relevant notice" means that notice.

(2) If any person is aggrieved by an order to which this paragraph applies and desires to question its validity on the ground that it is not within the powers of regulation 22, or that any of the requirements of this Schedule have not been complied with in relation to it, he may within six weeks from the date of the relevant notice make an application to the court under this paragraph.

(3) On any such application the court may, if satisfied that the order is not within those powers or that the interests of the applicant have been substantially prejudiced by a failure to comply with any of those requirements—

    (a)   in England and Wales, quash the order, or any provision of the order, either generally or in so far as it affects the interests of the applicant; or

    (b)   in Scotland, make such declarator as seems to the court to be appropriate.

(4) Except as provided by this paragraph, the validity of an order shall not be questioned in any legal proceedings whatsoever.

(5) In this paragraph "the court" means the High Court in relation to England and Wales and the Court of Session in relation to Scotland.

Interpretation

8. In this Schedule—
    "amending order" and "revoking order" mean an order which amends or, as the case may be, revokes a previous order;
    "the Gazette" means—
        (a) if the order relates in whole or in part to land in England and Wales, the London Gazette; and
        (b) if the order relates in whole or in part to land in Scotland, the Edinburgh Gazette;
    "order" means an order under regulation 22;
    "original order" means an order other than an amending or revoking order; and
    "restrictive amending order" means an amending order which extends the area to which a previous order applies.

[1092]

SCHEDULE 2
EUROPEAN PROTECTED SPECIES OF ANIMALS

Regulation 38

Common name	Scientific name
Bats, Horseshoe (all species)	Rhinolophidae
Bats, Typical (all species)	Vespertilionidae
Butterfly, Large Blue	Maculinea arion
Cat, Wild	Felis silvestris
Dolphins, porpoises and whales (all species)	Cetacea
Dormouse	Muscardinus avellanarius
Lizard, Sand	Lacerta agilis
Newt, Great Crested (or Warty)	Triturus cristatus
Otter, Common	Lutra lutra
Snake, Smooth	Coronella austriaca
Sturgeon	Acipenser sturio
Toad, Natterjack	Bufo calamita
Turtles, Marine	Caretta caretta
	Chelonia mydas
	Lepidochelys kempii
	Eretmochelys imbricata
	Dermochelys coriacea

NOTE. The common name or names given in the first column of this Schedule are included by way of guidance only; in the event of any dispute or proceedings, the common name or names shall not be taken into account.

[1093]

SCHEDULE 3
ANIMALS WHICH MAY NOT BE TAKEN OR KILLED IN CERTAIN WAYS

Regulation 41(1)(a)

Common name	Scientific name
Barbel	Barbus barbus
Grayling	Thymallus thymallus
Hare, Mountain	Lepus timidus
Lamprey, River	Lampetra fluviatilis
Marten, Pine	Martes martes
Polecat	Mustela putorius (otherwise known as Putorius putorius)
Salmon, Atlantic	Salmo salar (only in fresh water)
Seal, Bearded	Erignathus barbatus
Seal, Common	Phoca vitulina
Seal, Grey	Halichoerus grypus
Seal, Harp	Phoca groenlandica (otherwise known as Pagophilus groenlandicus)
Seal, Hooded	Cystophora cristata
Seal, Ringed	Phoca hispida (otherwise known as Pusa hispida)
Shad, Allis	Alosa alosa
Shad, Twaite	Alosa fallax
Vendace	Coregonus albula
Whitefish	Coregonus lavaretus

NOTE. The common name or names given in the first column of this Schedule are included by way of guidance only; in the event of any dispute or proceedings, the common name or names shall not be taken into account.

[1094]

SCHEDULE 4
EUROPEAN PROTECTED SPECIES OF PLANTS

Regulation 42

Common name	Scientific name
Dock, Shore	Rumex rupestris
Fern, Killarney	Trichomanes speciosum
Gentian, Early	Gentianella anglica
Lady's-slipper	Cypripedium calceolus
Marshwort, Creeping	Apium repens
Naiad, slender	Najas flexilis
Orchid, Fen	Liparis loeselii
Plantain, Floating-leaved water	Luronium natans
Saxifrage, Yellow Marsh	Saxifraga hirculus

NOTE. The common name or names given in the first column of this Schedule are included by way of guidance only; in the event of any dispute or proceedings, the common name or names shall not be taken into account.

[1095]

STATUTORY NUISANCE (APPEALS) REGULATIONS 1995

(SI 1995/2644)

NOTES
Made: 9 October 1995.
Commencement: 8 November 1995.
Authority: Environmental Protection Act 1990, Sch 3, para 1(4).

1 Citation, commencement and interpretation

(1)   These Regulations may be cited as the Statutory Nuisance (Appeals) Regulations 1995 and shall come into force on 8th November 1995.

(2)   In these Regulations—
"the 1974 Act" means the Control of Pollution Act 1974;
"the 1990 Act" means the Environmental Protection Act 1990; and
"the 1993 Act" means the Noise and Statutory Nuisance Act 1993.

[1096]

2 Appeals under section 80(3) of the 1990 Act

(1)   The provisions of this regulation apply in relation to an appeal brought by any person under section 80(3) of the 1990 Act (appeals to magistrates) against an abatement notice served upon him by a local authority.

(2)   The grounds on which a person served with such a notice may appeal under section 80(3) are any one or more of the following grounds that are appropriate in the circumstances of the particular case—
  (a) that the abatement notice is not justified by section 80 of the 1990 Act (summary proceedings for statutory nuisances);
  (b) that there has been some informality, defect or error in, or in connection with, the abatement notice, or in, or in connection with, any copy of the abatement notice served under section 80A(3) (certain notices in respect of vehicles, machinery or equipment);
  (c) that the authority have refused unreasonably to accept compliance with alternative requirements, or that the requirements of the abatement notice are otherwise unreasonable in character or extent, or are unnecessary;
  (d) that the time, or where more than one time is specified, any of the times, within which the requirements of the abatement notice are to be complied with is not reasonably sufficient for the purpose;
  (e) where the nuisance to which the notice relates—
    (i) is a nuisance falling within section 79(1)(a), (d), (e), (f) or (g) of the 1990 Act and arises on industrial, trade, or business premises, or
    (ii) is a nuisance falling within section 79(1)(b) of the 1990 Act and the smoke is emitted from a chimney, or
    (iii) is a nuisance falling within section 79(1)(ga) of the 1990 Act and is noise emitted from or caused by a vehicle, machinery or equipment being used for industrial, trade or business purposes,
    that the best practicable means were used to prevent, or to counteract the effects of, the nuisance;
  (f) that, in the case of a nuisance under section 79(1)(g) or (ga) of the 1990 Act (noise emitted from premises), the requirements imposed by the abatement notice by virtue of section 80(1)(a) of the Act are more onerous than the requirements for the time being in force, in relation to the noise to which the notice relates, of—
    (i) any notice served under section 60 or 66 of the 1974 Act (control of noise on construction sites and from certain premises), or

      (ii) any consent given under section 61 or 65 of the 1974 Act (consent for work on construction sites and consent for noise to exceed registered level in a noise abatement zone), or

      (iii) any determination made under section 67 of the 1974 Act (noise control of new buildings);

    (g) that, in the case of a nuisance under section 79(1)(ga) of the 1990 Act (noise emitted from or caused by vehicles, machinery or equipment), the requirements imposed by the abatement notice by virtue of section 80(1)(a) of the Act are more onerous than the requirements for the time being in force, in relation to the noise to which the notice relates, of any condition of a consent given under paragraph 1 of Schedule 2 to the 1993 Act (loudspeakers in streets or roads);

    (h) that the abatement notice should have been served on some person instead of the appellant, being—

      (i) the person responsible for the nuisance, or

      (ii) the person responsible for the vehicle, machinery or equipment, or

      (iii) in the case of a nuisance arising from any defect of a structural character, the owner of the premises, or

      (iv) in the case where the person responsible for the nuisance cannot be found or the nuisance has not yet occurred, the owner or occupier of the premises;

    (i) that the abatement notice might lawfully have been served on some person instead of the appellant being—

      (i) in the case where the appellant is the owner of the premises, the occupier of the premises, or

      (ii) in the case where the appellant is the occupier of the premises, the owner of the premises,

and that it would have been equitable for it to have been so served;

    (j) that the abatement notice might lawfully have been served on some person in addition to the appellant, being—

      (i) a person also responsible for the nuisance, or

      (ii) a person who is also owner of the premises, or

      (iii) a person who is also an occupier of the premises, or

      (iv) a person who is also the person responsible for the vehicle, machinery or equipment,

and that it would have been equitable for it to have been so served.

    (3)   If and so far as an appeal is based on the ground of some informality, defect or error in, or in connection with, the abatement notice, or in, or in connection with, any copy of the notice served under section 80A(3), the court shall dismiss the appeal if it is satisfied that the informality, defect or error was not a material one.

    (4)   Where the grounds upon which an appeal is brought include a ground specified in paragraph (2)(i) or (j) above, the appellant shall serve a copy of his notice of appeal on any other person referred to, and in the case of any appeal to which these regulations apply he may serve a copy of his notice of appeal on any other person having an estate or interest in the premises, vehicle, machinery or equipment in question.

    (5)   On the hearing of the appeal the court may—

    (a) quash the abatement notice to which the appeal relates, or

    (b) vary the abatement notice in favour of the appellant in such manner as it thinks fit, or

    (c) dismiss the appeal;

and an abatement notice that is varied under sub-paragraph (b) above shall be final and shall otherwise have effect, as so varied, as if it had been so made by the local authority.

(6)   Subject to paragraph (7) below, on the hearing of an appeal the court may make such order as it thinks fit—

(a) with respect to the person by whom any work is to be executed and the contribution to be made by any person towards the cost of the work, or

(b) as to the proportions in which any expenses which may become recoverable by the authority under Part III of the 1990 Act are to be borne by the appellant and by any other person.

(7)   In exercising its powers under paragraph (6) above the court—

(a) shall have regard, as between an owner and an occupier, to the terms and conditions, whether contractual or statutory, of any relevant tenancy and to the nature of the works required, and

(b) shall be satisfied before it imposes any requirement thereunder on any person other than the appellant, that that person has received a copy of the notice of appeal in pursuance of paragraph (4) above.

[1097]

3 Suspension of notice

(1)   Where—

(a) an appeal is brought against an abatement notice served under section 80 or section 80A of the 1990 Act, and—

(b) either—

(i) compliance with the abatement notice would involve any person in expenditure on the carrying out of works before the hearing of the appeal, or

(ii) in the case of a nuisance under section 79(1)(g) or (ga) of the 1990 Act, the noise to which the abatement notice relates is noise necessarily caused in the course of the performance of some duty imposed by law on the appellant, and

(c) either paragraph (2) does not apply, or it does apply but the requirements of paragraph (3) have not been met,

the abatement notice shall be suspended until the appeal has been abandoned or decided by the court.

(2)   This paragraph applies where—

(a) the nuisance to which the abatement notice relates—

(i) is injurious to health, or

(ii) is likely to be of a limited duration such that suspension of the notice would render it of no practical effect, or

(b) the expenditure which would be incurred by any person in the carrying out of works in compliance with the abatement notice before any appeal has been decided would not be disproportionate to the public benefit to be expected in that period from such compliance.

(3)   Where paragraph (2) applies the abatement notice—

(a) shall include a statement that paragraph (2) applies, and that as a consequence it shall have effect notwithstanding any appeal to a magistrates' court which has not been decided by the court, and

(b) shall include a statement as to which of the grounds set out in paragraph (2) apply.

[1098]

4 (*Revokes the Statutory Nuisance (Appeals) Regulations 1990, SI 1990/2276, and the Statutory Nuisance (Appeals) (Amendment) Regulations 1990, SI 1990/2483.*)

ENVIRONMENTAL PROTECTION (CONTROLS ON SUBSTANCES THAT DEPLETE THE OZONE LAYER) REGULATIONS 1996

(SI 1996/506)

NOTES
Made: 1 March 1996.
Commencement: 29 March 1996.
Authority: European Communities Act 1972, s 2(2); Environmental Protection Act 1990, s 140(1), (2), (3)(b)–(d), (4), (9).

ARRANGEMENT OF REGULATIONS

1 Citation, commencement and extent

(1)   These Regulations may be cited as the Environmental Protection (Controls on Substances that Deplete the Ozone Layer) Regulations 1996 and shall come into force on 29th March 1996.

(2)   These Regulations shall apply to Northern Ireland in so far as they relate to importation.

[1099]

2 Interpretation

(1)   In these Regulations—
   "the 1974 Act" means the Health and Safety at Work etc Act 1974;
   "authorised person" means a person authorised by the Secretary of State for
      any purpose of these Regulations;
   "customs officer" means any officer within the meaning of the Customs and
      Excise Management Act 1979;
   "health and safety inspector" means an inspector appointed under section 19 of
      the 1974 Act;
   "the principal Regulation" means Council Regulation (EC) No 3093/94 on
      substances that deplete the ozone layer.

(2)   Unless the context otherwise requires—
   (a) expressions used in these Regulations shall have the meaning they bear in
      the principal Regulation; and
   (b) any reference in these Regulations to an Article is to an Article of the
      principal Regulation.

[1100]

3 The competent authority

The Secretary of State shall be the competent authority for the purposes of the principal Regulation.

[1101]

4 Direction

The Secretary of State directs that any prohibition on importation into the United Kingdom imposed by Article 5(5) shall be treated as imposed under section 140(1)(a) of the Environmental Protection Act 1990 and the power conferred on him by regulation 8 shall be exercisable accordingly.

[1102]

5 Prohibitions and restrictions on importation, landing and unloading

(1)   No person shall import into the United Kingdom a controlled substance unless a licence, permitting the release for free circulation in the Community or inward processing of that controlled substance, has been issued by the Commission under Article 6(1).

(2)   No person shall import into the United Kingdom a controlled substance whose release for free circulation in the Community is prohibited by Article 8.

(3)   No person shall import into the United Kingdom a product whose release for free circulation in the Community is prohibited by Article 9.

(4)   Subject to paragraph (5), no person shall knowingly land or unload a controlled substance, a product or equipment which has been imported contrary to paragraphs (1) to (3) above or Article 5(5).

(5)   Paragraph (4) shall not apply to an authorised person who is exercising any of the powers prescribed in regulation 9 for the purpose of carrying these Regulations into effect.

[1103]

6 Duty with respect to Articles 14 and 15

It shall be the duty of any person having control of the controlled substances mentioned in Articles 14 and 15 to comply with those provisions.

[1104]

7 Power of customs officer to detain controlled substances and products

(1)   A customs officer may detain a controlled substance or product imported, landed or unloaded in contravention of regulation 5, or equipment imported in contravention of Article 5(5).

(2)   Anything detained under this regulation shall be dealt with during the period of its detention in such a manner as the Commissioners of Customs and Excise may direct.

[1105]

8 Powers of the Secretary of State

The Secretary of State may require a person who has imported, landed or unloaded a controlled substance or product in contravention of regulation 5, or imported equipment in contravention of Article 5(5)—

    (a) to dispose of it without causing pollution of the environment or harm to human health or to the health of animals or plants or otherwise to render it harmless, or

(b) to remove it from the United Kingdom,

and such a person shall comply with that requirement.

9 Powers of authorised persons

(1) Subject to paragraph (9) below, an authorised person may, on production (if so required) of his authority, exercise any of the powers in paragraph (2) below for the purpose of carrying these Regulations into effect.

(2) The powers of an authorised person are—
   (a) at any reasonable time to enter premises, other than premises used wholly or mainly for residential purposes, which he has reason to believe it is necessary for him to enter;
   (b) on entering any premises by virtue of sub-paragraph (a) above to take with him—
      (i) if the authorised person has reasonable cause to apprehend any serious obstruction in the execution of his duty, a constable; and
      (ii) any equipment or materials required for any purpose for which the power of entry is being exercised;
   (c) to make such examination and investigation as may in any circumstances be necessary;
   (d) as regards any premises which he has power to enter, to direct that those premises or any part of them, or anything in them, shall be left undisturbed (whether generally or in particular respects) for so long as is reasonably necessary for the purpose of any examination or investigation under sub-paragraph (c) above;
   (e) to take such measurements and photographs and make such recordings as he considers necessary for the purpose of any examination or investigation under sub-paragraph (c) above;
   (f) to take samples of any articles or substances found in or on any premises which he has power to enter;
   (g) in the case of any article or substance found in or on any premises which he has power to enter, being an article or substance which appears to him to have caused or to be likely to cause pollution of the environment or harm to human health or to the health of animals or plants, to cause it to be dismantled or subjected to any process or test (but not so as to damage or destroy it unless this is necessary);
   (h) in the case of any such article or substance as is mentioned in sub-paragraph (g) above, to take possession of it and detain it for so long as is necessary for all or any of the following purposes, namely—
      (i) to examine it and do to it anything which he has power to do under that sub-paragraph;
      (ii) to ensure that it is not tampered with before his examination of it is completed;
      (iii) to ensure that it is available for use as evidence in any proceedings for an offence under regulation 11 below;
   (i) to require any person whom he has reasonable cause to believe to be able to give any information relevant to any examination or investigation under sub-paragraph (c) above to answer (in the absence of anyone, other than someone nominated by that person to be present and anyone whom the authorised person may allow to be present) such questions as the authorised person thinks fit to ask and to sign a declaration of the truth of his answers;
   (j) to require the production of, or where the information is recorded in computerised form, the furnishing of extracts from, any records which it is necessary for him to see for the purposes of any examination or investigation under sub-paragraph (c) above and to inspect and take copies of, or of any entry in, the records;

    (k) to require any person to afford him such facilities and assistance with respect to any matters or things within that person's control or in relation to which that person has responsibilities as are necessary to enable the authorised person to exercise any of the powers conferred on him by this regulation.

(3)   Where an authorised person proposes to exercise the power conferred by paragraph (2)(g) above in the case of an article or substance found in or on any premises, he shall, if so requested by a person who at the time is present on and has responsibilities in relation to those premises, cause anything which is to be done by virtue of that power to be done in the presence of that person.

(4)   Before exercising the power conferred by paragraph (2)(g) above in the case of any article or substance, an authorised person shall consult such persons as appear to him appropriate for the purpose of ascertaining what dangers, if any, there may be in doing anything which he proposes to do under the power.

(5)   Where under the power conferred by paragraph (2)(h) above an authorised person takes possession of any article or substance found on any premises, he shall leave there, either with a responsible person or, if that is impracticable, fixed in a conspicuous position, a notice giving particulars of that article or substance sufficient to identify it and stating that he has taken possession of it under that power; and before taking possession of any such substance under that power an authorised person shall, if it is practical for him to do so, take a sample of it and give to a responsible person at the premises a portion of the sample marked in a manner sufficient to identify it.

(6)   No answer given by a person in pursuance of a requirement imposed under paragraph (2)(i) shall be admissible in evidence in England, Wales or Northern Ireland against that person in any proceedings, or in Scotland against that person in any criminal proceedings.

(7)   Nothing in this regulation shall be taken to compel the production by any person of a document of which he would on grounds of legal professional privilege be entitled to withhold production on an order for discovery in an action in the High Court or, in relation to Scotland, on an order for the production of documents in an action in the Court of Session.

(8)   No person shall—
    (a) intentionally prevent any other person from appearing before an authorised person under paragraph (2)(i) or from answering any question to which an authorised person may by virtue of paragraph (2)(i) require an answer;
    (b) intentionally obstruct an authorised person in the exercise or performance of his powers or duties; or
    (c) falsely pretend to be an authorised person.

(9)   The reference to "these Regulations" in paragraph (1) above does not include a reference to regulation 6, in so far as that regulation relates to Article 15(1) and (2).

[1107]

10 Enforcement of Articles 5(1) to (4) and regulation 6, in so far as that regulation relates to Article 15(1) and (2)

Sections 18 to 26 of the 1974 Act and regulations made under section 18 of that Act shall apply to any requirement or prohibition imposed upon any person by Article 5(1) to (4) and regulation 6, in so far as that regulation relates to Article 15(1) and (2), as if the requirement or prohibition were imposed by regulations made under section 15 of that Act.

[1108]

11 Offences

(1) Any person who uses, or causes or permits another person to use, a hydrochlorofluorocarbon in contravention of Article 5(1) to (4) commits an offence.

(2) Any person who supplies, or causes or permits another person to supply equipment in contravention of Article 5(5) commits an offence.

(3) Any person who contravenes, or causes or permits another person to contravene, regulation 5 commits an offence.

(4) Any person who knowingly supplies information that is false in a material particular for the purpose of obtaining a licence issued by the Commission under Article 6(1) commits an offence.

(5) Any person who fails to discharge a duty to which he is subject by virtue of regulation 6 commits an offence.

(6) Any person who intentionally obstructs a customs officer in the exercise of his powers under regulation 7 commits an offence.

(7) Any person who fails to comply with regulation 8 or causes or permits another person to fail to comply with that regulation commits an offence.

(8) Any person who—
    (a) without reasonable excuse fails to comply with any requirement imposed under regulation 9(2), or
    (b) makes a statement which he knows to be false or misleading in a material particular, where the statement is made in purported compliance with a requirement to furnish information imposed under regulation 9(2)(i),

commits an offence.

(9) Any person who contravenes, or causes or permits another person to contravene, regulation 9(8) commits an offence.

(10) Where a health and safety inspector, under sections 20 and 21 of the 1974 Act, exercises his powers for the purposes of enforcing Articles 5(1) to (4) and regulation 6, in so far as that regulation relates to Article 15(1) and (2), any person who—
    (a) fails to comply with an improvement notice served under section 21 of the 1974 Act including any such notice as modified on appeal,
    (b) without reasonable excuse fails to comply with any requirement imposed under section 20 of the 1974 Act,
    (c) prevents any other person from appearing before or from answering any question to which a health and safety inspector, by virtue of section 20 of the 1974 Act, may require an answer, or
    (d) intentionally obstructs a health and safety inspector in the exercise or performance of his powers or duties under section 20 of the 1974 Act,

commits an offence.

[1109]

12 Offences by corporations etc

(1) Where an offence under regulation 11 above which has been committed by a body corporate is proved to have been committed with the consent or connivance of, or to have been attributable to any neglect on the part of, a director, manager, secretary or other similar officer of the body corporate, or any other person purporting to act in any such capacity, he, as well as the body corporate, shall be guilty of that offence and shall be liable to be proceeded against and punished accordingly.

(2)   Where the affairs of a body corporate are managed by its members, paragraph (1) above shall apply in relation to the acts or defaults of a member in connection with his functions of management as if he were a director of the body corporate.

(3)   Where, in Scotland, an offence under regulation 11 above which has been committed by a Scottish partnership or an unincorporated association (other than a partnership) is proved to have been committed with the consent or connivance of, or to have been attributable to any neglect on the part of, a partner in the partnership or, as the case may be, a person concerned in the management or control of the association, he, as well as the partnership or association, shall be guilty of that offence and shall be liable to be proceeded against and punished accordingly.

[1110]

13 Penalties

A person who—
   (a) commits an offence under regulation 11(1) to (5), (7), (8)(b) and (10)(a) shall be liable, on summary conviction, to a fine not exceeding level 5 on the standard scale or, on conviction on indictment, to a fine
   (b) commits an offence under regulation 11(6), (8)(a), (9) and (10)(b) to (d) shall be liable, on summary conviction, to a fine not exceeding level 5 on the standard scale.

[1111]

14 (*Amends the Environmental Protection (Non-Refillable Refrigerant Containers) Regulations 1994, SI 1994/199, regs 7, 8.*)

ENVIRONMENTAL LICENCES (SUSPENSION AND REVOCATION) REGULATIONS 1996

(SI 1996/508)

NOTES
Made: 29 February 1996.
Commencement: 1 April 1996.
Authority: Environment Act 1995, s 41(6), (10).

ARRANGEMENT OF REGULATIONS

1 Citation and commencement

These Regulations may be cited as the Environmental Licences (Suspension and Revocation) Regulations 1996 and shall come into force on 1st April 1996.

[1112]

2 Interpretation

In these Regulations—
   "holder" in relation to an environmental licence means the person liable to pay any charges due and payable in respect of the subsistence of that licence.

[1113]

3 Notice demanding payment

The appropriate procedure, where a new Agency proposes to suspend or revoke an environmental licence under section 41(6) of the Environment Act 1995, is as follows—

(a) before taking any action under regulation 5 below to suspend or revoke an environmental licence, the new Agency shall first serve on the holder of the environmental licence a notice demanding payment within twenty-eight days after the service of the notice of any charges due and payable in respect of the subsistence of the licence; and

(b) the new Agency shall allow the period of twenty-eight days to expire before taking further action to suspend or revoke the environmental licence.

[1114]

4 Contents of notice demanding payment

A notice demanding the payment of any charges which is served for the purposes of regulation 3 shall state—

(a) that the environmental licence may be suspended or revoked if the charges are not paid within twenty-eight days after the service of the notice; and

(b) the effect of suspension or revocation.

[1115]

5 Notice of suspension or revocation

(1) Suspension or revocation of a licence under section 41(6) of the Environment Act 1995 shall be effected by the service of a notice of suspension or revocation on the holder of the environmental licence.

(2) A notice of suspension or revocation shall—

(a) set out the reason for the suspension or revocation and the date and time at which it will take effect; and

(b) in the case of a suspension of an environmental licence, set out the circumstances in which the suspension may be lifted.

[1116]

WASTE MANAGEMENT REGULATIONS 1996

(SI 1996/634)

NOTES
Made: 7 March 1996.
Commencement: 30 March 1996 (regs 2(6), 3); 1 April 1996 (remainder).
Authority: European Communities Act 1972, s 2(2); the Environmental Protection Act 1990, ss 29(10), 33(3), 52(8), 74(6).

1 Citation, commencement and extent

(1) These Regulations may be cited as the Waste Management Regulations 1996 and, except for regulations 2(6) and 3, shall come into force on 1st April 1996.

(2) Regulations 2(6) and 3 shall come into force on 30th March 1996.

(3) Regulation 2(3) does not extend to Scotland.

[1117]

2, 3 *(S 2 amends the Waste Management Licensing Regulations 1994, SI 1994/1056, regs 4, 5, 12, 18(4A), Sch 3, para 43(2), Sch 3, para 45(3) at* **[940]–[958]***; s 3 amends the Waste Management Licensing (Amendment etc) Regulations 1995, SI 1995/288, reg 4(5).)*

4 Pre-qualification technical competence

(1)   Where—

    (a) a person has applied to the Waste Management Industry Training and Advisory Board for a certificate of technical competence in relation to one of the types of facility mentioned in paragraph (2);

    (b) an application has been made for a waste management licence to authorise activities whose management is intended to be in that person's hands;

    (c) the activities mentioned in sub-paragraph (b) are to be carried on at a facility of the same type as that in relation to which the application mentioned in sub-paragraph (a) was made; and

    (d) the relevant Agency as defined in paragraph (3) is satisfied that, but for regulation 4 of the Waste Management Licensing Regulations 1994, he would be a technically competent person;

then, in relation to the facility in respect of which the application mentioned in sub-paragraph (b) was made and until the expiry of two years from the grant of a licence pursuant to that application, regulation 4 of those Regulations shall not apply to that person and he shall be treated as technically competent for the purposes of section 74(3)(b) of the Environmental Protection Act 1990.

(2)   The types of facility mentioned in paragraph (1)(a) are all those listed in Table 1 of regulation 4(1) of the Waste Management Licensing Regulations 1994 other than any type of landfill site.

(3)   The relevant Agency mentioned in paragraph (1)(d) is:

    (a) in relation to England and Wales, the Environment Agency established by section 1 of the Environment Act 1995; and

    (b) in relation to Scotland, the Scottish Environment Protection Agency established by section 20 of that Act.

[1118]

5 Transitional provision for certificates of technical competence: waste treatment plants

(1)   Paragraph (2) of this regulation applies to a person who has made an application to the Waste Management Industry Training and Advisory Board for a "Treatment operations: inert waste (level 3)" certificate of technical competence before 10th August 1994, in a case where that application has not been determined.

(2)   Unless he notifies the Board in writing that he does not wish this regulation to apply to him, the person mentioned in paragraph (l) shall be treated for the purposes of regulation 5 of the Waste Management Licensing Regulations 1994 as if the certificate for which he applied was a "Managing treatment operations: special waste (level 4)" certificate of technical competence.

(3)   Paragraph (4) of this regulation applies to a person who has made an application to the Waste Management Industry Training and Advisory Board for a "Treatment operations: inert waste (level 3)" certificate of technical competence before 1st April 1996, in a case where that application has not been determined.

(4)   Unless he notifies the Board in writing that he does not wish this regulation to apply to him, the person mentioned in paragraph (3) shall be treated for the purposes of regulation 4 of the Waste Management Licensing (Amendment etc) Regulations 1995 as if the certificate for which he applied was a "Managing treatment operations: special waste (level 4)" certificate of technical competence.

[1119]

6 (*Revoked by the Waste Management (Miscellaneous Provisions) Regulations 1997, SI 1997/351, reg 4(d).*)

SPECIAL WASTE REGULATIONS 1996

(SI 1996/972)

NOTES
Made: 28 March 1996.
Commencement: 1 September 1996.
Authority: European Communities Act 1972, s 2(2); Control of Pollution Act 1974, ss 3(1), 17, 30(4), (5), 104(1); Environmental Protection Act 1990, ss 33(3), 34(5), 62(1)–(3), 74(6), 75(8), 78.

ARRANGEMENT OF REGULATIONS

1 Citation, commencement, extent, application and interpretation

(1)   These Regulations may be cited as the Special Waste Regulations 1996 and shall come into force on 1st September 1996.

(2)   These Regulations do not extend to Northern Ireland.

(3)   These Regulations do not apply in relation to any special waste in respect of which, in accordance with regulation 26 below, the Control of Pollution (Special Waste) Regulations 1980 continue to have effect.

(4)   In these Regulations, unless the context otherwise requires—
"the 1990 Act" means the Environmental Protection Act 1990;
"the 1994 Regulations" means the Waste Management Licensing Regulations 1994;
"Agency" means—
    (a)   in relation to places, premises and sites in England and Wales, the Environment Agency established by section 1 of the Environment Act 1995; and
    (b)   in relation to places, premises and sites in Scotland, the Scottish Environment Protection Agency established by section 20 of that Act;

"the approved classification and labelling guide" means the document entitled "Approved guide to the classification and labelling of substances and preparations dangerous for supply (Second edition)" approved by the Health and Safety Commission on 18th October 1994 for the purposes of the Chemicals (Hazard Information and Packaging for Supply) Regulations 1994;

"the approved supply list" means the document entitled "Approved Supply List ([3rd Edition])—Information approved for the classification and labelling of substances and preparations dangerous for supply" approved by the Health and Safety Commission on [24th January 1996] for the purposes of the Chemicals (Hazard Information and Packaging for Supply) Regulations 1994;

"carrier", in relation to a consignment of special waste, means the person who collects that waste from the premises at which it is being held and transports it to another place;

"carrier's round" in relation to consignments of special waste, means a journey made by a carrier during which he collects more than one consignment of special waste and transports all consignments collected to the same consignee who is specified in the consignment note;

"carrier's schedule" means a schedule prepared in accordance with regulation 8;

"consignee", in relation to a consignment of special waste, means the person to whom that waste is to be transported;

"consignment note", in relation to a consignment of special waste, means a note in a form corresponding to the form set out in Schedule 1 to these Regulations, or in a form substantially to the like effect, and giving at any time the details required by these Regulations to be shown in respect of that consignment (including, where the consignment is one in a succession of consignments, any details required to be shown in respect of other consignments in the succession);

"consignor", in relation to a consignment of special waste, means the person who causes that waste to be removed from the premises at which it is being held;

"controlled waste" has the same meaning as in Part II of the 1990 Act;

"conveyance" includes a vehicle designed to carry goods by road or rail and a vessel designed to carry goods by water;

"harbour area" has the same meaning as in the Dangerous Substances in Harbour Areas Regulations 1987;

"the Hazardous Waste Directive" means Council Directive 91/689/EEC on hazardous waste, as amended by Council Directive 94/31/EC;

["household waste" means waste which is household waste for the purposes of Part II of the 1990 Act or which is treated as household waste for those purposes by virtue of regulation 2(1) of the Controlled Waste Regulations 1992, other than—
  (a) asbestos;
  (b) waste from a laboratory;
  (c) waste from a hospital, other than waste from a self-contained part of a hospital which is used wholly for the purposes of living accommodation.]

"premises" includes any ship;

"relevant code", in relation to a consignment note or carrier's schedule, means the code assigned in accordance with regulation 4 to the consignment of special waste to which the consignment note or carrier's schedule relates or, where the consignment is one in a carrier's round, to the consignments in that round;

"risk phrase" means the risk phrase shown under Part III of the approved supply list;

"ship" means a vessel of any type whatsoever operating in the marine environment including submersible craft, floating craft and any structure which is a fixed or floating platform;

"special waste" has the meaning given by regulation 2 of these Regulations; and "waste management licence" has the meaning given by section 35(1) of the 1990 Act.

[1120]

NOTES

Para (4): words in square brackets in definition "the approved supply list" substituted, and definition "household waste" substituted, by the Special Waste (Amendment) Regulations 1996, SI 1996/2019, reg 2, Schedule, para 2.

[2 Meaning of special waste

(1)   Any controlled waste, other than household waste,—
    (a) to which a six-digit code is assigned in the list set out in Part I of Schedule 2 to these Regulations (which reproduces the list of hazardous waste annexed to Council Decision 94/904/EC establishing a list of hazardous waste pursuant to Article 1(4) of the Hazardous Waste Directive); and
    (b) which displays any of the properties specified in Part II of that Schedule (which reproduces Annex III to the Hazardous Waste Directive),

is special waste.

(2)   Any other controlled waste, other than household waste, which—
    (a) displays the property H3-A (first indent), H4, H5, H6, H7 or H8 specified in Part II of Schedule 2 to these Regulations; or
    (b) is a medicinal product, as defined in section 130 of the Medicines Act 1968 (meaning of "medicinal product" etc), of a description, or falling within a class, specified in an order under section 58 of that Act (medicinal products on prescription only),

is special waste.

(3)   For the purposes of paragraphs (1) and (2) waste shall be treated as displaying none of the properties H4 to H8 specified in Part II of Schedule 2 to these Regulations if it satisfies none of the criteria set out in Part III of that Schedule.

(4)   Part IV of Schedule 2 to these Regulations (which contains rules for the interpretation of that Schedule) shall have effect.]

[1121]

NOTES

Substituted by the Special Waste (Amendment) Regulations 1996, SI 1996/2019, reg 2, Schedule, para 3.

3 Certain radioactive waste to be special waste

Section 62 (special provision with respect to certain dangerous and intractable waste) of the 1990 Act shall have effect, without modification, so as to empower the Secretary of State to make provision for waste which would be controlled waste but for the fact that it is radioactive waste within the meaning of the Radioactive Substances Act 1993; and paragraphs (1) and (2) of regulation 2 shall apply to any such waste as if it were controlled waste.

[1122]

4 Coding of consignments

(1)   [Subject to paragraph (3),] an Agency shall assign or supply forthwith to any person, on request, for the purpose of assigning to a consignment of special waste or, where the consignment is one in a carrier's round, to the consignments in that round, a code unique to that consignment or round, as the case may be.

(2)   A code assigned or supplied in accordance with paragraph (1) may consist of letters, numbers or symbols, or any combination of letters, numbers and symbols, or a bar code which enables the consignment or carrier's round, as the case may be, to be identified electronically.

[(3)   The Agency need not assign or supply a code for a consignment or round until any fee required in respect of it under regulation 14(1) has been paid.]

[1123]

NOTES
   Para (1): words in square brackets inserted by the Special Waste (Amendment) Regulations 1996, SI 1996/2019, reg 2, Schedule, para 4(a).
   Para (3): added by SI 1996/2019, reg 2, Schedule, para 4(b).

5 Consignment notes: standard procedure

(1)   Except in a case to which regulation 6, 8 or 9 applies, this regulation applies where a consignment of special waste is to be removed from the premises at which it is being held.

(2)   Before the consignment is removed—
  (a) five copies of the consignment note shall be prepared, and, on each copy, Parts A and B shall be completed and the relevant code entered;
  (b) the consignor shall ensure that one of those copies (on which Parts A and B have been completed and the relevant code entered) is furnished to the Agency for the place to which the consignment is to be transported;
  (c) the carrier shall complete Part C on each of the four remaining copies; and
  (d) the consignor—
    (i) shall complete Part D on each of those copies;
    (ii) shall retain one copy (on which Parts A to D have been completed and the relevant code entered); and
    (iii) shall give the three remaining copies (on which Parts A to D have been completed and the relevant code entered) to the carrier.

(3)   The carrier shall ensure that the copies which he has received—
  (a) travel with the consignment; and
  (b) are given to the consignee on delivery of the consignment.

(4)   Subject to regulation 10, on receiving the consignment the consignee shall—
  (a) complete Part E on the three copies of the consignment note given to him;
  (b) retain one copy;
  (c) give one copy to the carrier; and
  (d) forthwith furnish one copy to the Agency for the place to which the consignment has been transported.

(5)   The carrier shall retain the copy of the consignment note given to him by the consignee.

[1124]

6 Consignment notes: cases in which pre-notification is not required

(1)   For the purposes of regulation 7, except in a case to which regulation 8 applies, this regulation applies—
  (a) subject to paragraph (2)(a), to the removal, from the premises at which it is being held, of each of the second and any subsequent consignment of special waste in a succession of consignments of special waste,
  (b) subject to paragraph (2)(b), to the removal as a consignment of special waste of a product or material for the purposes of the return by the person to whom the product or material had been supplied to the person who supplied it to him or who manufactured it,

(c) subject to paragraph (2)(c), to the removal of a consignment of special waste where the consignor and the consignee are bodies corporate belonging to the same group,

(d) to the removal from a ship in a harbour area of a consignment of special waste to a conveyance for transportation to a place outside that area, and

(e) to the removal of a consignment of special waste which consists entirely of lead acid motor vehicle batteries.

(2)   This regulation does not apply unless—

(a) in the case mentioned in paragraph (1)(a), in respect of each consignment—

(i) the waste is of the same description as the waste in the first of the consignments in the succession;

(ii) the consignor is the same person;

(iii) the consignee is the same person;

(iv) the premises from which the consignment is removed are the same;

(v) the place to which the consignment is transported is the same; and

(vi) the removal of the consignment takes place within one year of the removal of the first consignment in the succession;

(b) in the case mentioned in paragraph (1)(b), the person to whom the product or material was supplied is satisfied that, as supplied, the product or material fails to meet any specification which he expected it to meet;

(c) in the case mentioned in paragraph (1)(c), the removal is for the purposes of an operation within either paragraph 15 of Part III, or paragraph 13 of Part IV, of Schedule 4 to the 1994 Regulations, and the consignee either—

(i) is the holder of a waste management licence which authorises the relevant operation; or

(ii) carries on any activity to which section 33(1)(a) and (b) of the 1990 Act does not apply by virtue of regulation 16 or 17 of the 1994 Regulations.

(3)   In paragraph (1)(c) "group", in relation to a body corporate, means that body corporate, any other body corporate which is its holding company or subsidiary and any other body corporate which is a subsidiary of that holding company; and for these purposes—

"body corporate" does not include a corporation sole or a Scottish partnership, but includes a company incorporated elsewhere than in Great Britain; and

"holding company" and "subsidiary" have the meaning given by section 736 of the Companies Act 1985.

[1125]

7 Consignment notes: procedure where pre-notification is not required

Paragraph (2), with the exception of sub-paragraph (b), and paragraphs (3) to (5) of regulation 5 shall apply in cases to which regulation 6 applies as if—

(a) "four" were substituted for "five" in sub-paragraph (a) of paragraph (2);

(b) references to the consignor were references—

(i) in relation to the case mentioned in regulation 6(1)(b), to the person to whom the product or material was supplied; and

(ii) in relation to the case mentioned in regulation 6(1)(d), to the master of the ship; and

(c) references to the consignee were references, in relation to the case mentioned in regulation 6(1)(b), to the person to whom the product or material is to be returned.

[1126]

8 Consignment notes: carrier's rounds

(1)　This regulation applies to a carrier's round or to a succession of such rounds by the same carrier starting and ending within a twelve month period in respect of which—
- (a) every consignor is a person specified in the consignment note or in the schedule prepared in accordance with paragraph (2)(b)(iii) or whose particulars are notified in writing to the Agency not less than 72 hours before the removal of the first waste on the carrier's round;
- (b) the premises from which the special waste is removed are:
  - (i) specified in the consignment note or in the schedule prepared in accordance with paragraph (2)(b)(iii) or notified in writing to the Agency not less than 72 hours before the removal of the first waste on the carrier's round; and
  - (ii) so located that the Agency for each of those premises is the same;
- (c) the special waste is of a description specified in the consignment note; and
- (d) in the case of a single round other than a round that satisfies the requirements of regulation 14(2)(a), the time between the collection of the first consignment and delivery to the consignee is no more than 24 hours.

(2)　Before the first removal of waste, the carrier shall,
- (a) on any carrier's round which is not in a succession or on the first round in such a succession, ensure that
  - (i) Parts A and B of the consignment note are completed and that the relevant code is entered;
  - (ii) [except where the special waste to be collected on the carrier's round consists entirely of lead acid motor vehicle batteries,] one copy of the consignment note is furnished to the Agency for the place to which the special waste is to be transported;
- (b) on every round—
  - (i) prepare [three] copies of the consignment note in addition to one copy for each consignor from whom waste is to be collected during the round;
  - (ii) complete on those copies Parts A and B, the carrier's particulars and particulars of transport in Part C, the code assigned or supplied under regulation 4 in respect of the round and, if it is a second or subsequent round, the code in respect of the first round; and
  - (iii) ensure that four copies of a schedule are prepared in the form set out in Part II of Schedule 1 to these Regulations, or in a form substantially to the like effect, in addition to one consignor's copy for each site from which waste is to be collected during that round.

[(2A) In a case where waste of more than one description is specified in the consignment note, either—
- (a) the schedule referred to in paragraph (2)(b)(iii) shall contain a separate entry for each description of waste to be collected from each consignor showing the description of waste to which that entry relates; or
- (b) each entry in the schedule shall show the different descriptions of the waste to be collected and, for each such description, the quantity of the waste to be collected.]

(3)　The consignor shall, before the removal of waste from a site, complete on all the copies that part of the schedule indicated on it as for completion by him.

(4)　The carrier shall ensure, before the removal of the waste, that—
- (a) the part of the schedule indicated on it as for completion by him is completed on all the copies [and includes a record of the time at which it is completed]; and
- (b) he has all copies of the schedule (on which the part to be completed by the consignor has been completed) except the copy to be retained by the consignor under paragraph (5).

(5)   The consignor shall retain in respect of each site one copy of the consignment note and of that part of the schedule on which the parts to be completed by him and by the carrier have been completed.

[(5A) Before the removal of the last consignment of waste on the carrier's round, the carrier shall complete Part C on the three copies of the consignment note retained by him.]

(6)   The carrier shall ensure that the copies of the consignment note and of the schedule which he has received—

(a) . . .

(b) travel with the waste to which they refer;

(c) are given to the consignee on delivery of the waste.

(7)   Subject to regulation 10, on receiving the waste collected on each round, the consignee shall—

(a) complete Part E on the three copies of the consignment note given to him;

(b) retain one copy of the consignment note and one copy of the schedule;

(c) give to the carrier a copy of the consignment note and a copy of the schedule; and

(d) forthwith furnish to the Agency for the place to which the consignment has been transported one copy of the consignment note and one copy of the schedule.

(8)   The carrier shall retain the copies given to him in accordance with paragraph (7)(c).

[1127]

NOTES

Para (2): words in square brackets in sub-para (a)(ii) inserted, and word in square brackets in sub-para (a)(ii) substituted, by the Special Waste (Amendment) Regulations 1996, SI 1996/2019, reg 2, Schedule, para 5(a), (b).

Paras (2A), (5A): inserted by SI 1996/2019, reg 2, Schedule, para 5(c), (e).

Para (4): words in square brackets in sub-para (a) inserted by SI 1996/2019, reg 2, Schedule, para 5(d).

Para (6): sub-para (a) revoked by SI 1996/2019, reg 2, Schedule, para 5(f).

---

9 Consignment notes: removal of ships' waste to reception facilities

(1)   This regulation applies where special waste is removed from a ship in a harbour area to—

(a) reception facilities provided within that harbour area; or

(b) by pipeline to any such facilities provided outside a harbour area.

(2)   Before the waste is removed from the ship—

(a) three copies of the consignment note shall be prepared and Parts A and B shall be completed and the relevant code entered on each of those copies;

(b) the operator of the facilities shall complete Part C on each of those copies; and

(c) the master of the ship—

(i) shall ensure that Part D is completed on each of those copies;

(ii) shall retain one copy (on which Parts A to D have been completed); and

(iii) shall give the two remaining copies (on which Parts A to D have been completed) to the operator of the facilities.

(3)   On receiving a consignment of special waste the operator of the facilities shall—

(a) complete Part E on the copies of the consignment note which he has received;

(b) retain one copy; and

(c) forthwith furnish the other copy to the Agency for the place where the facilities are situated.

[1128]

10 Consignment notes etc: duty of consignee not accepting delivery of a consignment

(1)   This regulation applies where the consignee does not accept delivery of a consignment of special waste.

(2)   In a case to which this regulation applies the requirements of regulation 5(4) (including that paragraph as applied in cases to which regulation 6 applies) or 8(7), as the case may be, shall not apply to the consignee.

(3)   If, in a case to which this regulation applies, copies of the consignment note have been given to the consignee he shall—
  (a) indicate on Part E of each copy that he does not accept the consignment and the reasons why he does not accept the consignment;
  (b) retain one copy;
  (c) ensure that one copy, accompanied by one copy of any carrier's schedule given to him in accordance with regulation 8, are furnished forthwith to the Agency for the place to which the special waste has been transported; and
  (d) ensure that the other copy is returned to the carrier forthwith.

(4)   If, in a case to which this regulation applies, no copies of the consignment note have been given to the consignee he shall ensure that a written explanation of his reasons for not accepting delivery, including such details of the consignment and of the carrier as are known to him, is furnished forthwith to the Agency for the place to which the special waste has been transported.

(5)   In a case to which this regulation applies—
  (a) on being informed that the consignee will not accept delivery of the consignment, the carrier shall inform the Agency and seek instructions from the consignor;
  (b) the consignor shall forthwith inform the carrier and the Agency of his intentions as regards the consignment; and
  (c) the carrier shall take all reasonable steps to ensure that the consignor's intentions are fulfilled.

(6)   For the purposes of paragraph (5), the consignor may propose one of the following, namely—
  (a) the delivery of the consignment to the premises from which it had been collected;
  (b) the delivery of the consignment to the premises at which it had been produced;
  (c) the delivery of the consignment to other specified premises in respect of which there is held any waste management licence necessary to authorise the receipt of the waste.

[1129]

11 Consignment notes: duties of the Agencies

(1)   Subject to paragraph (2), where—
  (a) an Agency ("the receiving Agency") has been furnished with a copy of a consignment note under regulation 5, 7, 8, 9 or 10 or with a copy of the explanation under regulation 10(4); and
  (b) the other Agency is the Agency for the premises from which the special waste was removed,

the receiving Agency shall, within two weeks of receipt, send to the other Agency one copy of the consignment note or explanation as the case may be.

(2)   Where copies have been furnished—
  (a) under regulation 7 in a case to which regulation 6 applies by virtue of paragraph (1)(d) of that regulation, or
  (b) under regulation 9(3)(c),

paragraph (1) shall have effect as if the reference to the premises from which the special waste was removed were a reference to the harbour area in which the special waste was removed from the ship.

[1130]

12 Consignment notes: provisions as to furnishing

(1)   Subject to paragraphs (2), (3) and (6), a copy of a consignment note required by regulation 5 or 8 to be furnished to an Agency must be furnished not more than one month and not less than 72 hours before the removal of the consignment.

(2)   Subject to paragraphs (3) and (6), a copy of a consignment note required to be furnished by regulation 8(2)(a)(ii) shall be furnished not less than 72 hours before the removal of the first consignment to which the consignment note relates.

(3)   The copy of the consignment note mentioned in paragraphs (1) and (2) may be furnished to the Agency within 72 hours before the removal where—
    (a) the consignment is to be delivered to other specified premises pursuant to a proposal under regulation 10(6)(c);
    (b) the consignment cannot lawfully remain where it is for 72 hours.

(4)   The requirements of paragraphs (1) and (2) shall be treated as satisfied if—
    (a) a facsimile of the copy is furnished to the Agency by telephonic, electronic or other similar means of transmission in compliance with the time limits set out in those paragraphs, and
    (b) the copy is furnished to the Agency before or, in accordance with paragraph (5) below, forthwith upon removal of the consignment.

(5)   A copy of a consignment note or a written explanation of reasons for refusing to accept delivery of any special waste is furnished to an Agency in accordance with this paragraph if it, and any document required to be furnished with it, is—
    (a) delivered to the Agency, or
    (b) posted to the Agency by pre-paid first class post,
within one day of the receipt, removal or refusal to accept delivery of the special waste in question, as the case may be.

(6)   In reckoning any period of hours for the purposes of paragraphs (1), (2) and (3), the hours of any Saturday, Sunday, Good Friday, Christmas Day, bank holiday or other public holiday shall be disregarded.

[1131]

13 Consignment notes: importers and exporters

(1)   Subject to paragraphs (3) and (4), regulations 5 to 12 shall apply to special waste imported into Great Britain from Northern Ireland or Gibraltar as if—
    (a) any reference to the consignor were a reference to the person importing the special waste;
    (b) any reference to the premises at which the special waste is being held and from which it is removed were a reference to the place where it first enters Great Britain; and
    (c) the special waste is removed from that place at the time when it first enters Great Britain.

(2)   Subject to paragraph (4), these Regulations shall apply to special waste exported from Great Britain to Northern Ireland or Gibraltar as if—
    (a) any reference to the consignee were a reference to the person exporting the waste; and
    (b) the consignment of special waste is received by that person at the place where and the time when it leaves Great Britain.

(3)   Paragraph (1) does not apply in a case to which either regulation 6(1)(d) or regulation 9 applies.

(4)   Nothing in regulations 5 to 12 shall apply in relation to shipments of waste to which the provisions of Council Regulation (EEC) No 259/93, other than Title III of that Regulation, apply.

[1132]

14 Fees

(1)   Subject to paragraph (2), [in connection with the assignment or supply of] a code for a consignment or a carrier's round in accordance with regulation 4(1), an Agency shall require payment of a fee of—
   (a) £10 in respect of a code relating to a consignment, or a round, which consists entirely of lead acid motor vehicle batteries;
   (b) £15 in other cases.

(2)   An Agency shall not require payment of a fee where the code is assigned or supplied in connection with:
   (a) a second or subsequent carrier's round in a succession of [such rounds in which a single vehicle is used and in respect of which]—
      (i)   the carrier is also the consignee in relation to every consignment in all the rounds;
      (ii) no more than one consignment is collected from any consignor during the succession;
      (iii) the total weight of special waste collected in each round does not exceed 400 kg; and
      (iv) the time between the collection of the first consignment on the first round in the succession and the delivery of the last consignment to the place to which it is to be transported is no more than one week;
   (b) the removal of a single consignment of special waste for the purposes set out in regulation 6(1)(b) provided that the person to whom the product or material was supplied is satisfied that it fails to meet any specification which he expected it to meet; or
   (c) the removal of special waste from a ship in a harbour area—
      (i)   to a conveyance for transportation to a place outside that area;
      (ii) to reception facilities provided within the same harbour area; or
      (iii) by pipeline to reception facilities provided outside the harbour area.

[(3)   Where an Agency assigns or supplies a code under regulation 4(1) without the fee required under this regulation having been paid to it, the person who requested the assignment or supply shall be required to pay the fee to that Agency within the period of two months beginning with the date on which the request was made.]

[1133]

NOTES

   Paras (1), (2): words in square brackets substituted by the Special Waste (Amendment) Regulations 1996, SI 1996/2019, reg 2, Schedule, para 6(a), (b).
   Para (3): added by SI 1996/2019, reg 2, Schedule, para 6(c).

---

15 Registers

(1)   At each site from which any consignment of special waste has been removed, the consignor shall keep a register containing—
   (a) a copy of the consignment note; and
   (b) where the consignment is one to which regulation 8 applies, a copy of that part of the carrier's schedule retained under regulation 8(5),
applicable to each consignment removed from that site.

(2)   Every carrier shall keep a register containing—
  (a) a copy of the consignment note; and
  (b) where the consignment is one to which regulation 8 applies, a copy of the carrier's schedule,
applicable to each consignment which he has transported.

(3)   At each site at which any consignment of special waste has been received, the consignee shall keep a register containing—
  (a) a copy of the consignment note; and
  (b) where the consignment is one to which regulation 8 applies, a copy of the carrier's schedule,
applicable to each consignment, other than a consignment to which regulation 10 applies, received at that site.

(4)   A consignment note or carrier's schedule required by paragraph (1) or (2) to be kept in a register shall be retained in the register for not less than three years from the date on which the waste to which it relates was removed from the premises at which it was being held.

(5)   Subject to paragraphs (6) and (7), consignment notes and carrier's schedules required by paragraph (3) to be kept by a person shall be retained until his waste management licence for the site in question is surrendered or revoked entirely, at which time he shall send the register to the Agency for the site; and that Agency shall retain the register for not less than three years after its receipt.

(6)   Where, by virtue of regulation 16(1)(a) or (b) of the 1994 Regulations, section 33(1)(a), (b) and (c) of the 1990 Act does not apply to any of the activities carried on at a site at which special waste is received, paragraph (5) shall have effect as if any reference to the surrender or revocation of a person's waste management licence were a reference to the surrender or revocation of his authorisation under Part I of the 1990 Act for the site in question.

(7)   Where, in circumstances other than those mentioned in paragraph (6), section 33(1)(a) and (b) of the 1990 Act does not apply to any of the activities carried on at a site at which special waste is received, each consignment note and carrier's schedule required to be kept in a register shall be kept in that register for not less than three years from the date on which the consignment of special waste to which it relates was received at the site to which it was transported.

(8)   Insofar as is consistent with the foregoing provisions of this regulation, registers under this regulation may be kept in any form.

[1134]

16 Site records

(1)   Any person who makes a deposit of special waste in or on any land shall record the location of each such deposit, shall keep such records until his waste management licence is surrendered or revoked and shall then send the records to the Agency for the site.

(2)   Such records shall comprise either—
  (a) a site plan marked with a grid, or
  (b) a site plan with overlays on which deposits are shown in relation to the contours of the site.

(3)   Deposits shall be described in such records by reference to the register of consignment notes kept under regulation 15, save that where waste is disposed of—
  (a) by pipeline, or
  (b) within the curtilage of the premises at which it is produced,
the deposits shall be described by reference to a record of the quantity and composition of the waste and the date of its disposal.

(4)   In the case of liquid wastes discharged without containers into underground strata or disused workings the record shall comprise only a written statement of the quantity and composition of special waste so discharged and the date of its disposal.

(5)   Every record made pursuant to regulation 14 of the Control of Pollution (Special Waste) Regulations 1980 shall—
  (a) be kept with the records referred to in paragraph (1) above for so long as is mentioned in that paragraph, and
  (b) shall accompany those records when they are sent to the Agency in accordance with that paragraph.

[1135]

17 Restrictions on mixing special waste

(1)   Subject to paragraph (2), an establishment or undertaking which carries out the disposal or recovery of special waste, or which collects or transports special waste, shall not—
  (a) mix different categories of special waste; or
  (b) mix special waste with waste which is not special waste.

(2)   Paragraph (1) above shall not apply if the mixing—
  (a) is authorised by a waste management licence or under an authorisation granted under Part I of the 1990 Act; or
  (b) is an activity to which, by virtue of regulation 17 of the 1994 Regulations, section 33(1)(a) and (b) of the 1990 Act does not apply.

[1136]

18 Offences

(1)   Subject to paragraph (2) below, it shall be an offence for a person (other than a member, officer or employee of an Agency who is acting as authorised by that Agency,) to fail to comply with any of the foregoing provisions of these Regulations insofar as that provision imposes any obligation or requirement upon him.

(2)   It shall be a defence for a person charged with an offence under paragraph (1) to prove that he was not reasonably able to comply with the provision in question by reason of an emergency or grave danger and that he took all steps as were reasonably practicable in the circumstances for—
  (a) minimising any threat to the public or the environment; and
  (b) ensuring that the provision in question was complied with as soon as reasonably practicable after the event.

(3)   A person who, in purported compliance with a requirement imposed by or under any of the foregoing provisions of these Regulations to furnish any information, makes a statement which he knows to be false or misleading in a material particular, or recklessly makes any statement which is false or misleading in a material particular, commits an offence.

(4)   A person who intentionally makes a false entry in any record or register required to be kept by virtue of any of the foregoing provisions of these Regulations commits an offence.

(5)   Where the commission by any person of an offence under this regulation is due to the act or default of some other person, that other person may be charged with and convicted of an offence by virtue of this paragraph whether or not proceedings are taken against the first-mentioned person.

(6)   Where an offence under this regulation which has been committed by a body corporate is proved to have been committed with the consent or connivance of, or to have been attributable to, any neglect on the part of a director, manager, secretary or other similar officer of the body corporate, or any person who was purporting to act in any such capacity, he, as well as the body corporate, shall be liable to be proceeded against and punished accordingly.

(7) Where the affairs of a body corporate are managed by its members, paragraph (6) shall apply in relation to the acts or defaults of a member in connection with his functions of management as if he were a director of the body corporate.

(8) Where, in Scotland, an offence under this regulation which has been committed by a partnership or an unincorporated association (other than a partnership) is proved to have been committed with the consent or connivance of, or to have been attributable to any neglect on the part of, a partner in the partnership or, as the case may be, a person concerned in the management or control of the association, he, as well as the partnership or association, shall be liable to be proceeded against and punished accordingly.

(9) A person who commits an offence under this regulation shall be liable—
  (a) on summary conviction, to a fine not exceeding level 5 on the standard scale;
  (b) on conviction on indictment, to a fine or to imprisonment for a term not exceeding two years, or to both.

[1137]

19 Responsibilities of the Agencies

The Agencies shall be responsible for supervising the persons and activities subject to any provision of these Regulations.

[1138]

20 Transitional provisions for certificates of technical competence

(1) This regulation applies in relation to—
  (a) waste defined as special waste under regulation 2 of these Regulations which was not so defined under regulation 2 of the Control of Pollution (Special Waste) Regulations 1980 ("waste now defined as special waste"); and
  (b) persons to be treated as technically competent for the purposes of section 74(3)(b) of the 1990 Act—
    (i) pursuant to regulation 4 of the 1994 Regulations; or
    (ii) pursuant to regulation [5(1)] of the 1994 Regulations, or to regulation 4(1) or (3) of the Waste Management Licensing (Amendment etc) Regulations 1995.

(2) For the purposes only of operations concerning waste now defined as special waste and provided that both the conditions set out in paragraph (3) are satisfied, the persons referred to in paragraph (1)(b) shall continue to be treated as technically competent—
  (a) in the case of those referred to in paragraph (1)(b)(i), until 10th August 2000; and
  (b) in the case of those referred to in paragraph (1)(b)(ii), in accordance with the Regulations mentioned there, except that paragraph (1) of regulation 5 of the 1994 Regulations and paragraphs (1) and (4) of regulation 4 of the Waste Management Licensing (Amendment etc) Regulations 1995 shall have effect as if for the date "10th August 1999" there were substituted the date "10th August 2000".

(3) The conditions referred to in paragraph (2) are that:
  (a) before 1st March 1997, the person applies to the Waste Management Industry Training and Advisory Board for a certificate of technical competence at Level 4 in respect of special waste; and
  (b) before 1st September 1996, the person was entitled to act as the manager of a facility in respect of which there was in force a waste management licence authorising activities concerning waste now defined as special waste.

[1139]

NOTES

Para (1): number in square brackets substituted by the Special Waste (Amendment) Regulations 1997, SI 1997/251, reg 2(a).

[20A Transitional provisions and "grandfather rights"

A person who by virtue of paragraph (2) of regulation 5 of the 1994 Regulations is treated as being technically competent for the purposes of section 74(3)(b) of the 1990 Act, shall continue to be so treated in accordance with paragraphs (2) and (4) of that regulation as if waste now defined as special waste within the meaning of regulation 20(1)(a) were not special waste.]

[1140]

NOTES

Commencement: 28 February 1997.
Inserted by the Special Waste (Amendment) Regulations 1997, SI 1997/251, reg 2(b).

21–26 *(S 21(1) amends the Town and Country Planning (Assessment of Environmental Effects) Regulations 1988, SI 1988/1199, reg 2; s 21(2) applies to Scotland only; s 22 amends the Controlled Waste (Registration of Carriers and Seizure of Vehicles) Regulations 1991, SI 1991/1624, Sch 1 at* **[907]**; *s 23 amends the Environmental Protection (Duty of Care) Regulations 1991, SI 1991/2839, reg 2 at* **[912]**; *s 24 amends the Controlled Waste Regulations 1992, SI 1992/588, Sch 3, para 18(2) at* **[930]**; *s 25 introduces Sch 3 to the regulations; s 26 revokes the Control of Pollution (Special Waste) Regulations 1980, SI 1980/1709, subject to savings provisions, the Control of Pollution (Landed Ships' Waste) Regulations 1987, SI 1987/402, the Control of Pollution (Landed Ships' Waste) (Amendment) Regulations 1989, SI 1989/65, the Transfrontier Shipment of Waste Regulations 1994, SI 1994/1137, reg 18(1), (2).)*

(Sch 1 sets out the Form of Consignment Note and the Form of Schedule; they are not reproduced for the purposes of this work.)

SCHEDULE 2
SPECIAL WASTE

Regulation 2

PART I
HAZARDOUS WASTE LIST

Waste code (6 digits)/Chapter Heading (2 and 4 digits)	Description
02	WASTE FROM AGRICULTURAL, HORTICULTURAL, HUNTING, FISHING AND AQUACULTURE PRIMARY PRODUCTION, FOOD PREPARATION AND PROCESSING
0201	PRIMARY PRODUCTION WASTE
020105	agrochemical wastes
03	WASTES FROM WOOD PROCESSING AND THE PRODUCTION OF PAPER, CARDBOARD, PULP, PANELS AND FURNITURE
0302	WOOD PRESERVATION WASTE
030201	non-halogenated organic wood preservatives
030202	organochlorinated wood preservatives
030203	organometallic wood preservatives
030204	inorganic wood preservatives
04	WASTES FROM THE LEATHER AND TEXTILE INDUSTRIES

Waste code (6 digits)/Chapter Heading (2 and 4 digits)	Description
0401	WASTES FROM THE LEATHER INDUSTRY
040103	degreasing wastes containing solvents without a liquid phase
0402	WASTES FROM TEXTILE INDUSTRY
040211	halogenated wastes from dressing and finishing
05	WASTES FROM PETROLEUM REFINING, NATURAL GAS PURIFICATION AND PYROLYTIC TREATMENT OF COAL
0501	OILY SLUDGES AND SOLID WASTES
050103	tank bottom sludges
050104	acid alkyl sludges
050105	oil spills
050107	acid tars
050108	other tars
0504	SPENT FILTER CLAYS
050401	spent filter clays
0506	WASTE FROM THE PYROLYTIC TREATMENT OF COAL
050601	acid tars
050603	other tars
0507	WASTE FROM NATURAL GAS PURIFICATION
050701	sludges containing mercury
0508	WASTES FROM OIL REGENERATION
050801	spent filter clays
050802	acid tars
050803	other tars
050804	aqueous liquid waste from oil regeneration
06	WASTES FROM INORGANIC CHEMICAL PROCESSES
0601	WASTE ACIDIC SOLUTIONS
060101	sulphuric acid and sulphurous acid
060102	hydrochloric acid
060103	hydrofluoric acid
060104	phosphoric and phosphorous acid
060105	nitric acid and nitrous acid
060199	waste not otherwise specified
0602	ALKALINE SOLUTIONS
060201	calcium hydroxide
060202	soda
060203	ammonia
060299	wastes not otherwise specified
0603	WASTE SALTS AND THEIR SOLUTIONS
060311	salts and solutions containing cyanides

Waste code (6 digits)/Chapter Heading (2 and 4 digits)	Description
0604	METAL-CONTAINING WASTES
060402	metallic salts (except 0603)
060403	wastes containing arsenic
060404	wastes containing mercury
060405	wastes containing heavy metals
0607	WASTES FROM HALOGEN CHEMICAL PROCESSES
060701	wastes containing asbestos from electrolysis
060702	activated carbon from chlorine production
0613	WASTES FROM OTHER INORGANIC CHEMICAL PROCESSES
061301	inorganic pesticides, biocides and wood preserving agents
061302	spent activated carbon (except 060702)
07	WASTES FROM ORGANIC CHEMICAL PROCESSES
0701	WASTE FROM THE MANUFACTURE, FORMULATION, SUPPLY AND USE (MFSU) OF BASIC ORGANIC CHEMICALS
070101	aqueous washing liquids and mother liquors
070103	organic halogenated solvents, washing liquids and mother liquors
070104	other organic solvents, washing liquids and mother liquors
070107	halogenated still bottoms and reaction residues
070108	other still bottoms and reaction residues
070109	halogenated filter cakes, spent absorbents
070110	other filter cakes, spent absorbents
0702	WASTE FROM THE MFSU OF PLASTICS, SYNTHETIC RUBBER AND MAN-MADE FIBRES
070201	aqueous washing liquids and mother liquors
070203	organic halogenated solvents, washing liquids and mother liquors
070204	other organic solvents, washing liquids and mother liquors
070207	halogenated still bottoms and reaction residues
070208	other still bottoms and reaction residues
070209	halogenated filter cakes, spent absorbents
070210	other filter cakes, spent absorbents
0703	WASTE FROM THE MFSU FOR ORGANIC DYES AND PIGMENTS (EXCLUDING 0611)
070301	aqueous washing liquids and mother liquors
070303	organic halogenated solvents, washing liquids and mother liquors
070304	other organic solvents, washing liquids and mother liquors
070307	halogenated still bottoms and reaction residues
070308	other still bottoms and reaction residues
070309	halogenated filter cakes, spent absorbents
070310	other filter cakes, spent absorbents

Waste code (6 digits)/Chapter Heading (2 and 4 digits)	Description
0704	WASTE FROM THE MFSU FOR ORGANIC PESTICIDES (EXCEPT 020105)
070401	aqueous washing liquids and mother liquors
070403	organic halogenated solvents, washing liquids and mother liquors
070404	other organic solvents, washing liquids and mother liquors
070407	halogenated still bottoms and reaction residues
070408	other still bottoms and reaction residues
070409	halogenated filter cakes, spent absorbents
070410	other filter cakes, spent absorbents
0705	WASTE FROM THE MFSU OF PHARMACEUTICALS
070501	aqueous washing liquids and mother liquors
070503	organic halogenated solvents, washing liquids and mother liquors
070504	other organic solvents, washing liquids and mother liquors
070507	halogenated still bottoms and reaction residues
070508	other still bottoms and reaction residues
070509	halogenated filter cakes, spent absorbents
070510	other filter cakes, spent absorbents
0706	WASTE FROM THE MFSU OF FATS, GREASE, SOAPS, DETERGENTS, DISINFECTANTS AND COSMETICS
070601	aqueous washing liquids and mother liquors
070603	organic halogenated solvents, washing liquids and mother liquors
070604	other organic solvents, washing liquids and mother liquors
070607	halogenated still bottoms and reaction residues
070608	other still bottoms and reaction residues
070609	halogenated filter cakes, spent absorbents
070610	other filter cakes, spent absorbents
0707	WASTE FROM THE MFSU OF FINE CHEMICALS AND CHEMICAL PRODUCTS NOT OTHERWISE SPECIFIED
070701	aqueous washing liquids and mother liquors
070703	organic halogenated solvents, washing liquids and mother liquors
070704	other organic solvents, washing liquids and mother liquors
070707	halogenated still bottoms and reaction residues
070708	other still bottoms and reaction residues
070709	halogenated filter cakes, spent absorbents
070710	other filter cakes, spent absorbents
08	WASTES FROM THE MANUFACTURE, FORMULATION, SUPPLY AND USE (MFSU) OF COATINGS (PAINTS, VARNISHES AND VITREOUS ENAMELS), ADHESIVE, SEALANTS AND PRINTING INKS
0801	WASTES FROM MFSU OF PAINT AND VARNISH
080101	waste paints and varnish containing halogenated solvents
080102	waste paints and varnish free of halogenated solvents
080106	sludges from paint or varnish removal containing halogenated solvents
080107	sludges from paint or varnish removal free of halogenated solvents

Waste code (6 digits)/Chapter Heading (2 and 4 digits)	Description
0803	WASTES FROM MFSU OF PAINT AND VARNISH
080301	waste ink containing halogenated solvents
080302	waste ink free of halogenated solvents
080305	ink sludges containing halogenated solvents
080306	ink sludges free of halogenated solvents
0804	WASTES FROM MFSU OF ADHESIVE AND SEALANTS (INCLUDING WATER-PROOFING PRODUCTS)
080401	waste adhesives and sealants containing halogenated solvents
080402	waste adhesives and sealants free of halogenated solvents
080405	adhesives and sealants sludges containing halogenated solvents
080406	adhesives and sealants sludges free of halogenated solvents
09	WASTES FROM THE PHOTOGRAPHIC INDUSTRY
0901	WASTES FROM PHOTOGRAPHIC INDUSTRY
090101	water based developer and activator solutions
090102	water based offset plate developer solutions
090103	solvent based developer solutions
090104	fixer solutions
090105	bleach solutions and bleach fixer solutions
090106	waste containing silver from on-site treatment of photographic waste
10	INORGANIC WASTES FROM THERMAL PROCESSES
1001	WASTES FROM POWER STATION AND OTHER COMBUSTION PLANTS (EXCEPT 1900)
100104	oil fly ash
100109	sulphuric acid
1003	WASTES FROM ALUMINIUM THERMAL METALLURGY
100301	tars and other carbon-containing wastes from anode manufacture
100303	skimmings
100304	primary smelting slags/white drosses
100307	spent pot lining
100308	salt slags from secondary smelting
100309	black drosses from secondary smelting
100310	waste from treatment of salt slags and black drosses treatment
1004	WASTES FROM LEAD THERMAL METALLURGY
100401	slags (1st and 2nd smelting)
100402	dross and skimmings (1st and 2nd smelting)
100403	calcium arsenate
100404	flue gas dust
100405	other particulates and dust
100406	solid waste from gas treatment
100407	sludges from gas treatment

Waste code (6 digits)/Chapter Heading (2 and 4 digits)	Description
1005	WASTES FROM ZINC THERMAL METALLURGY
100501	slags (1st and 2nd smelting)
100502	dross and skimmings (1st and 2nd smelting)
100503	flue gas dust
100505	solid waste from gas treatment
100506	sludges from gas treatment
1006	WASTES FROM COPPER THERMAL METALLURGY
100603	flue gas dust
100605	waste from electrolytic refining
100606	solid waste from gas treatment
100607	sludges from gas treatment
11	INORGANIC WASTE WITH METALS FROM METAL TREATMENT AND THE COATING OF METALS; NON-FERROUS HYDRO-METALLURGY
1101	LIQUID WASTES AND SLUDGES FROM METAL TREATMENT AND COATING OF METALS (eg GALVANIC PROCESSES, ZINC COATING PROCESSES, PICKLING PROCESSES, ETCHING, PHOSPHATIZING, ALKALINE DE-GREASING)
110101	cyanidic (alkaline) wastes containing heavy metals other than chromium
110102	cyanidic (alkaline) wastes which do not contain heavy metals
110103	cyanide-free wastes containing chromium
110105	acidic pickling solutions
110106	acids not otherwise specified
110107	alkalis not otherwise specified
110108	phosphatizing sludges
1102	WASTES AND SLUDGES FROM NON-FERROUS HYDROMETALLURGICAL PROCESSES
110202	sludges from zinc hydrometallurgy (including jarosite, goethite)
1103	SLUDGES AND SOLIDS FROM TEMPERING PROCESSES
110301	wastes containing cyanide
110302	other wastes
12	WASTES FROM SHAPING AND SURFACE TREATMENT OF METALS AND PLASTICS
1201	WASTES FROM SHAPING (INCLUDING FORGING, WELDING, PRESSING, DRAWING, TURNING, CUTTING AND FILING)
120106	waste machining oils containing halogens (not emulsioned)
120107	waste machining oils free of halogens (not emulsioned)
120108	waste machining emulsions containing halogens
120109	waste machining emulsions free of halogens
120110	synthetic machining oils
120111	machining sludges
120112	spent waxes and fats

Waste code (6 digits)/Chapter Heading (2 and 4 digits)	Description
1203	WASTES FROM WATER AND STEAM DEGREASING PROCESSES (EXCEPT 1100)
120301	aqueous washing liquids
120302	steam degreasing wastes
13	OIL WASTES (EXCEPT EDIBLE OILS, 0500 AND 1200)
1301	WASTE HYDRAULIC OILS AND BRAKE FLUIDS
130101	hydraulic oils, containing PCBs or PCTs
130102	other chlorinated hydraulic oils (not emulsions)
130103	non-chlorinated hydraulic oils (not emulsions)
130104	chlorinated emulsions
130105	non-chlorinated emulsions
130106	hydraulic oils containing only mineral oil
130107	other hydraulic oils
130108	brake fluids
1302	WASTE ENGINE, GEAR AND LUBRICATING OILS
130201	chlorinated engine, gear and lubricating oils
130202	non-chlorinated engine, gear and lubricating oils
130203	other machine, gear and lubricating oils
1303	WASTE INSULATING AND HEAT TRANSMISSION OILS AND OTHER LIQUIDS
130301	insulating or heat transmission oils and other liquids containing PCBs or PCTs
130302	other chlorinated insulating and heat transmission oils and other liquids
130303	non-chlorinated insulating and heat transmission oils and other liquids
130304	synthetic insulating and heat transmission oils and other liquids
130305	mineral insulating and heat transmission oils
1304	BILGE OILS
130401	bilge oils from inland navigation
130402	bilge oils from jetty sewers
130403	bilge oils from other navigation
1305	OIL/WATER SEPARATOR CONTENTS
130501	oil/water separator solids
130502	oil/water separator sludges
130503	interceptor sludges
130504	desalter sludges or emulsions
130505	other emulsions
1306	OIL WASTE NOT OTHERWISE SPECIFIED
130601	oil waste not otherwise specified

Waste code (6 digits)/Chapter Heading (2 and 4 digits)	Description
14	WASTES FROM ORGANIC SUBSTANCES EMPLOYED AS SOLVENTS (EXCEPT 0700 AND 0800)
1401	WASTES FROM METAL DEGREASING AND MACHINERY MAINTENANCE
140101	chlorofluorocarbons
140102	other halogenated solvents and solvent mixes
140103	other solvents and solvent mixes
140104	aqueous solvent mixes containing halogens
140105	aqueous solvent mixes free of halogens
140106	sludges or solid wastes containing halogenated solvents
140107	sludges or solid wastes free of halogenated solvents
1402	WASTES FROM TEXTILE CLEANING AND DEGREASING OF NATURAL PRODUCTS
140201	halogenated solvents and solvent mixes
140202	solvent mixes or organic liquids free of halogenated solvents
140203	sludges or solid wastes containing halogenated solvents
140204	sludges or solid wastes containing other solvents
1403	WASTES FROM THE ELECTRONIC INDUSTRY
140301	chlorofluorocarbons
140302	other halogenated solvents
140303	solvents and solvent mixes free of halogenated solvents
140304	sludges or solid wastes containing halogenated solvents
140305	sludges or solid wastes containing other solvents
1404	WASTES FROM COOLANTS, FOAM/AEROSOL PROPELLANTS
140401	chlorofluorocarbons
140402	other halogenated solvents and solvent mixes
140403	other solvents and solvent mixes
140404	sludges or solid wastes containing halogenated solvents
140405	sludges or solid wastes containing other solvents
1405	WASTES FROM SOLVENT AND COOLANT RECOVERY (STILL BOTTOMS)
140501	chlorofluorocarbons
140502	halogenated solvents and solvent mixes
140503	other solvents and solvent mixes
140504	sludges containing halogenated solvents
140505	sludges containing other solvents
16	WASTES NOT OTHERWISE SPECIFIED IN THE CATALOGUE
1602	DISCARDED EQUIPMENT AND SHREDDER RESIDUES
160201	transformers and capacitors containing PCBs or PCTs

Waste code (6 digits)/Chapter Heading (2 and 4 digits)	Description
1604	WASTE EXPLOSIVES
160401	waste ammunition
160402	fireworks waste
160403	other waste explosives
1606	BATTERIES AND ACCUMULATORS
160601	lead batteries
160602	Ni-Cd batteries
160603	mercury dry cells
160606	electrolyte from batteries and accumulators
1607	WASTE FROM TRANSPORT AND STORAGE TANK CLEANING (EXCEPT 0500 AND 1200)
160701	waste from marine transport tank cleaning, containing chemicals
160702	waste from marine transport tank cleaning, containing oil
160703	waste from railway and road transport tank cleaning, containing oil
160704	waste from railway and road transport tank cleaning, containing chemicals
160705	waste from storage tank cleaning, containing chemicals
160706	waste from storage tank cleaning, containing oil
17	CONSTRUCTION AND DEMOLITION WASTE (INCLUDING ROAD CONSTRUCTION)
1706	INSULATION MATERIALS
170601	insulation materials containing asbestos
18	WASTES FROM HUMAN OR ANIMAL HEALTH CARE AND/OR RELATED RESEARCH (EXCLUDING KITCHEN AND RESTAURANT WASTES WHICH DO NOT ARISE FROM IMMEDIATE HEALTH CARE)
1801	WASTE FROM NATAL CARE, DIAGNOSIS, TREATMENT OR PREVENTION OF DISEASE IN HUMANS
180103	other wastes whose collection and disposal is subject to special requirements in view of the prevention of infection
1802	WASTE FROM RESEARCH, DIAGNOSIS, TREATMENT OR PREVENTION OF DISEASE INVOLVING ANIMALS
180202	other wastes whose collection and disposal is subject to special requirements in view of the prevention of infection
180204	discarded chemicals
19	WASTES FROM WASTE TREATMENT FACILITIES, OFF-SITE WASTE WATER TREATMENT PLANTS AND THE WATER INDUSTRY
1901	WASTES FROM INCINERATION OR PYROLYSIS OF MUNICIPAL AND SIMILAR COMMERCIAL, INDUSTRIAL AND INSTITUTIONAL WASTES
190103	fly ash
190104	boiler dust
190105	filter cake from gas treatment
190106	aqueous liquid waste from gas treatment and other aqueous liquid wastes
190107	solid waste from gas treatment
190110	spent activated carbon from flue gas treatment

Waste code (6 digits)/Chapter Heading (2 and 4 digits)	Description
1902	WASTES FROM SPECIFIC PHYSICO/CHEMICAL TREATMENTS OF INDUSTRIAL WASTES (eg DECHROMATATION, DECYANIDATION, NEUTRALIZATION)
190201	metal hydroxide sludges and other sludges from metal insolubilization treatment
1904	VITRIFIED WASTES AND WASTES FROM VITRIFICATION
190402	fly ash and other flue gas treatment wastes
190403	non-vitrified solid phase
1908	WASTES FROM WASTE WATER TREATMENT PLANTS NOT OTHERWISE SPECIFIED
190803	grease and oil mixture from oil/waste water separation
190806	saturated or spent ion exchange resins
190807	solutions and sludges from regeneration of ion exchangers
20	MUNICIPAL WASTES AND SIMILAR COMMERCIAL, INDUSTRIAL AND INSTITUTIONAL WASTES INCLUDING SEPARATELY COLLECTED FRACTIONS
2001	SEPARATELY COLLECTED FRACTIONS
200112	paint, inks, adhesives and resins
200113	solvents
200117	photo chemicals
200119	pesticides
200121	fluorescent tubes and other mercury containing waste

[1141]

PART II
HAZARDOUS PROPERTIES

H1   "Explosive": substances and preparations which may explode under the effect of flame or which are more sensitive to shocks or friction than dinitrobenzene.

H2   "Oxidizing": substances and preparations which exhibit highly exothermic reactions when in contact with other substances, particularly flammable substances.

H3–A   "Highly flammable":

— liquid substances and preparations having a flash point below 21°C (including extremely flammable liquids), or

— substances and preparations which may become hot and finally catch fire in contact with air at ambient temperature without any application of energy, or

— solid substances and preparations which may readily catch fire after brief contact with a source of ignition and which continue to burn or to be consumed after removal of the source of ignition, or

— gaseous substances and preparations which are flammable in air at normal pressure, or

— substances and preparations which, in contact with water or damp air, evolve highly flammable gases in dangerous quantities.

H3–B	"Flammable": liquid substances and preparations having a flash point equal to or greater than 21°C and less than or equal to 55°C.
H4	"Irritant": non-corrosive substances and preparations which, through immediate, prolonged or repeated contact with the skin or mucous membrane, can cause inflammation.
H5	"Harmful": substances and preparations which, if they are inhaled or ingested or if they penetrate the skin, may involve limited health risks.
H6	"Toxic": substances and preparations (including very toxic substances and preparations) which, if they are inhaled or ingested or if they penetrate the skin, may involve serious, acute or chronic health risks and even death.
H7	"Carcinogenic": substances and preparations which, if they are inhaled or ingested or if they penetrate the skin, may induce cancer or increase its incidence.
H8	"Corrosive": substances and preparations which may destroy living tissue on contact.
H9	"Infectious": substances containing viable micro-organisms or their toxins which are known or reliably believed to cause disease in man or other living organisms.
H10	"Teratogenic": substances and preparations which, if they are inhaled or ingested or if they penetrate the skin, may induce non-hereditary congenital malformations or increase their incidence.
H11	"Mutagenic": substances and preparations which, if they are inhaled or ingested or if they penetrate the skin, may induce hereditary genetic defects or increase their incidence.
H12	Substances and preparations which release toxic or very toxic gases in contact with water, air or an acid.
H13	Substances and preparations capable by any means, after disposal, of yielding another substance, eg a leachate, which possesses any of the characteristics listed above.
H14	"Ecotoxic": substances and preparations which present or may present immediate or delayed risks for one or more sectors of the environment.

[1142]

PART III
THRESHOLDS FOR CERTAIN HAZARDOUS PROPERTIES

In the waste—
— the total concentration of substances classified as irritant and having assigned to them any of the risk phrases R36 ("irritating to the eyes"), R37 ("irritating to the respiratory system") or R38 ("irritating to the skin") is equal to or greater than 20%;
— the total concentration of substances classified as irritant and having assigned to them the risk phrase R41 ("risk of serious damage to eyes") is equal to or greater than 10%;
— the total concentration of substances classified as harmful is equal to or greater than 25%;
— the total concentration of substances classified as very toxic is equal to or greater than 0.1%;
— the total concentration of substances classified as toxic is equal to or greater than 3%;
— the total concentration of substances classified as carcinogenic and placed by the approved classification and labelling guide in category 1 or 2 of that classification is equal to or greater than 0.1%;
— the total concentration of substances classified as corrosive and having assigned to them the risk phrase R34 ("causes burns") is equal to or greater than 5%; and
— the total concentration of substances classified as corrosive and having assigned to them the risk phrase R35 ("causes severe burns") is equal to or greater than 1%.

[1143]

PART IV
[RULES FOR THE INTERPRETATION OF THIS SCHEDULE]

[1. Except in the case of a substance listed in the approved supply list, the test methods to be used for the purposes of deciding which (if any) of the properties mentioned in Part II of this Schedule are to be assigned to a substance are those described in Annex V to Council Directive 67/548/EEC, as amended by Commission Directive 92/69/EEC.

2. Any reference in Part III of this Schedule to a substance being classified as having a hazardous property, having assigned to it a particular risk phrase, or being placed within a particular category of a classification is a reference to that substance being so classified, having that risk phrase assigned to it or being placed in that category—

    (i)   in the case of a substance listed in the approved supply list, on the basis of Part V of that list;

    (ii) in the case of any other substance, on the basis of the criteria laid down in the approved classification and labelling guide.

3. Any reference in Part III of this Schedule to the total concentration of any substances being equal to or greater than a given percentage is a reference to the proportion by weight of those substances in any waste being equal to or, as the case may be, greater than that percentage.]

[1144]

NOTES

    Part added by the Special Waste (Amendment) Regulations 1996, SI 1996/2019, reg 2, Schedule, para 7.

(Sch 3 amends the Waste Management Licensing Regulations 1994, SI 1994/1056, regs 1(3), 3, 10(1), 17, Sch 3, paras 3, 18, 28, Sch 4, paras 9, 13(1), 14, Sch 5.)

CONTROL OF POLLUTION (APPLICATIONS, APPEALS AND REGISTERS) REGULATIONS 1996

(SI 1996/2971)

NOTES

    Made: 26 November 1996.

    Commencement: 31 December 1996.

    Authority: Water Resources Act 1991, ss 90A(1), 91(2K), 91(3) (as originally enacted), 99, 190(1), 191B(6), (9), 219(2), Sch 10, paras 1(1)(b), (2), 2(1), (2), (4), (7), 3(5), 5(3), (5), 6(4), (5), 10(2), and paras 1(7), 3(3), 4(3), (5), (9) of that Schedule (as originally enacted).

ARRANGEMENT OF REGULATIONS

1 Citation, commencement and interpretation

(1)   These Regulations may be cited as the Control of Pollution (Applications, Appeals and Registers) Regulations 1996 and shall come into force on 31st December 1996.

(2)   In these Regulations—
"discharge consent" has the same meaning as in section 91(8) of the Water Resources Act 1991;
"register" means a register maintained by the Agency under section 190 of that Act (pollution control registers).

[1145]

2 Advertisements

(1)   Subject to regulation 4, an application for—
(a) a discharge consent or the variation of a discharge consent;
(b) a consent for the purposes of section 89(4)(a) of the Water Resources Act 1991 (consents for the deposit of solid refuse from mines or quarries on land near inland freshwaters); or
(c) a consent for the purposes of section 90(1) or (2) of that Act (consents for the removal of deposits or for the cutting or uprooting of vegetation in or near inland freshwaters),
shall be advertised in accordance with the following provisions of this regulation and regulation 3.

(2)   Notice of the application shall be published—
(a) in one or more newspapers circulating in—
(i)   the locality in which the activities which are the subject matter of the application are proposed to be carried on; and
(ii) the locality in which the controlled waters which may be affected by the proposed activities are situated; and
(b) in the London Gazette.

(3)   Subject to paragraph (4) below, the notice shall—
(a) state the name of the applicant;
(b) specify where the activities which are the subject matter of the application are proposed to be carried on;
(c) describe briefly the nature of the proposed activities;
(d) state where the register containing information about the application may be inspected, the times at which the register is open for inspection and that the register may be inspected free of charge; and
(e) explain that any person may make representations in writing to the Agency, specify when the period allowed for making representations ends and give the address of the Agency to which representations are to be sent.

(4)   Nothing in paragraph (3) above shall require the disclosure of any information which is not to be included in a register by virtue of section 191A or 191B of the Water Resources Act 1991 (exclusion from registers of information affecting national security and of certain confidential information).

[1146]

3 Timing of advertisements

(1)   An application to which regulation 2 applies shall be advertised in accordance with paragraph (2) of that regulation within the period of 28 days beginning 14 days after the relevant date.

(2)   Subject to paragraphs (3) to (5) below, the relevant date in relation to an application shall be the date on which the application is received by the Agency.

(3)   In a case where the Agency has notified the applicant within 14 days of the receipt of the application that it refuses to proceed with the application until information required by section 90A(4) of; or paragraph 1(3) or (4) of Schedule 10 to, the Water Resources Act 1991 (duty to provide Agency with information) is provided, the relevant date shall be the date on which the Agency is finally provided with the information required.

(4)   In a case where a matter falls to be determined under section 191A of the Water Resources Act 1991 (exclusion from registers of information affecting national security), the relevant date shall be the date on which the Secretary of State notifies the applicant of his determination.

(5)   In a case where a matter falls to be determined under section 191B of the Water Resources Act 1991 (exclusion from registers of certain confidential information), the relevant date shall be—
  (a) if the Agency is treated by virtue of section 191B(3) of that Act as having determined that the information in question is commercially confidential, the date on which the period of 14 days mentioned in section 191B(3) expires;
  (b) if the Agency determines under section 191B(2) or (4) of that Act that the information in question is commercially confidential, the date on which the Agency notifies the applicant of its determination;
  (c) if the Agency determines under section 191B(2) or (4) of that Act that the information in question is not commercially confidential—
    (i)   the date on which the period for appealing expires without an appeal having been made;
    (ii) the date on which the Secretary of State notifies the applicant of his final determination of the appeal; or
    (iii) the date on which the appeal is withdrawn.

(6)   Where the relevant date for the purposes of this regulation in relation to an application is later than the date on which the application is received, a period of four months beginning with the relevant date shall be substituted for the period of four months specified in paragraph 3(2) of Schedule 10 to the Water Resources Act 1991 (failure to determine application within four months or longer period agreed with applicant).

[1147]

4 Exemption from advertising requirements

The Agency may determine that an application is not required to be advertised if it appears to the Agency that it is appropriate to dispense with advertising the application because—
  (a) section 191A of the Water Resources Act 1991 (exclusion from registers of information affecting national security) applies; or
  (b) the Agency considers that the activities which are the subject matter of the application are unlikely to have an appreciable effect on controlled waters in the locality in which those activities are proposed to be carried on; or
  (c) the application is made before 1st April 1997 and it relates to discharges of a kind which the applicant, or a predecessor of his, was authorised to make by virtue of a consent to which paragraph 21 of Schedule 23 to the Environment Act 1995 applied but notice in accordance with sub-paragraph (2)(b)(ii) of that paragraph was not given by him or his predecessor,

and, in any case where the Agency so determines, the application shall be exempt from the requirements of section 90A(1)(b) of, or, as the case may be, paragraph 1(1)(b) of Schedule 10 to, the Water Resources Act 1991 (requirement to advertise applications).

[1148]

5 Consultation

(1)   Subject to paragraph (3) below, the persons to be consulted under paragraph 2 of Schedule 10 to the Water Resources Act 1991 (consultation in connection with applications) in relation to an application for, or for the variation of, a discharge consent are—

(a) every local authority or water undertaker within whose area any of the proposed discharges are to be made;

(b) each of the Ministers if any of the proposed discharges are to be made into coastal waters, relevant territorial waters or waters outside the seaward limits of relevant territorial waters;

(c) the harbour authority within the meaning of section 57(1) of the Harbours Act 1964 if any of the proposed discharges are to be made into a harbour managed by the authority; and

(d) the local fisheries committee, if any of the proposed discharges are to be made into relevant territorial waters or coastal waters within the sea fisheries district of that committee.

(2)   The specified period for notification of those persons under paragraph 2 of Schedule 10 to the Water Resources Act 1991 (consultation in connection with applications) is the period of 14 days beginning with the relevant date and, for this purpose, "relevant date" has the same meaning as in regulation 3.

(3)   The requirements of paragraph 2 of Schedule 10 to the Water Resources Act 1991 (consultation in connection with applications) shall not apply in relation to any of the bodies mentioned in paragraph (1)(a), (c) or (d) above—

(a) in so far as they would require the disclosure of any information which is not to be included in a register by virtue of section 191A or 191B of the Water Resources Act 1991 (exclusion from registers of information affecting national security and of certain confidential information);

(b) in relation to an application for, or for the variation of, a discharge consent which need not be advertised as a result of an exemption under regulation 4.

(4)   A period of six weeks beginning with the last date on which the making of the application was advertised in pursuance of paragraph 1(1)(b) of Schedule 10 to the Water Resources Act 1991 shall be substituted for the period specified in paragraph 2(6)(b) of that Schedule (period allowed for making representations).

[1149]

6 Transmitted applications

(1)   The following provisions of this regulation shall apply where an application for, or for the variation of, a discharge consent is transmitted to the Secretary of State under paragraph 5(1) of Schedule 10 to the Water Resources Act 1991 (reference to the Secretary of State of certain applications for consent).

(2)   Paragraph 2 of Schedule 10 to the Water Resources Act 1991 (consultation in connection with applications) shall apply subject to the modification that representations made to the Agency within the period allowed for making representations shall, instead of being considered by the Agency, be sent by the Agency to the Secretary of State and shall be considered by him along with any representations made by the Agency.

(3)   Any request to be heard by the applicant or the Agency with respect to the application shall be made in writing to the Secretary of State within the period of 28 days beginning with the day on which the applicant is informed by the Agency of the transmission of his application to the Secretary of State.

[1150]

7 Discharge consents without applications

The provisions of Schedule 1 to these Regulations shall apply where the Agency gives a discharge consent under paragraph 6 of Schedule 10 to the Water Resources Act 1991 (discharge consents without applications).

[1151]

8 Appeals

(1) A person who wishes to appeal to the Secretary of State under section 91 or 191B(5) of the Water Resources Act 1991 (appeals in respect of consents under Chapter II of Part III and appeals in relation to information which the Agency has determined is not commercially confidential) shall give the Secretary of State notice of the appeal.

(2) The notice of appeal shall—
  (a) specify the grounds of appeal; and
  (b) indicate whether the appellant wishes the appeal to be determined on the basis of a hearing or written representations.

(3) The notice of appeal shall be accompanied by copies of any application, consent, correspondence, decision, notice or other document relevant to the appeal.

(4) At the same time as the appellant gives notice of the appeal to the Secretary of State, the appellant shall send the Agency a copy of his notice of appeal, together with a list of the documents provided to the Secretary of State under paragraph (3) above.

(5) If the appellant wishes at any time to withdraw his appeal he shall do so by notice informing the Secretary of State and shall send a copy of the notice to the Agency.

[1152]

9 Time limit for bringing appeal

(1) Subject to the following provisions of this regulation, notice of appeal in accordance with regulation 8(1) shall be given—
  (a) in the case of an appeal against the revocation of a consent, before the revocation takes effect;
  (b) in the case of an appeal against an enforcement notice, before the expiry of the period of 21 days beginning with the date on which the enforcement notice is received;
  (c) in the case of an appeal against a determination under section 191B(2) or (4) of the Water Resources Act 1991 (exclusion from registers of certain confidential information) that information is not commercially confidential, before the expiry of the period of 21 days beginning with the date on which the appellant is notified of the determination; and
  (d) in any other case, before the expiry of the period of three months beginning with—
    (i) the date on which the appellant is notified of the decision which is the subject matter of the appeal; or
    (ii) if paragraph 3(2) of Schedule 10 to the Water Resources Act 1991 (failure to determine application within 4 months or longer period agreed with applicant) applies, the date on which the applicable period under paragraph 3(2) expires.

(2) Subject to paragraph (3) below, the Secretary of State may allow notice of appeal to be given after the expiry of the relevant period mentioned in paragraph (1) above.

(3)   Paragraph (2) above shall not apply in the case of an appeal against—
  (a) a decision to revoke a discharge consent;
  (b) a decision to modify the conditions of any such consent;
  (c) a decision to provide that any such consent which was unconditional shall
       be subject to conditions;
  (d) a determination under section 191B(2) or (4) of the Water Resources Act
       1991 (exclusion from registers of certain confidential information) that
       information is not commercially confidential.

[1153]

10 Action upon receipt of notice of appeal

(1)   Subject to paragraph (5) below, the Agency shall, within 14 days of receipt
of the copy of the notice of appeal in accordance with regulation 8(4)—
  (a) in the case of an appeal against a decision—
       (i) to revoke a discharge consent; or
       (ii) to modify the conditions of any such consent, or to provide that any
            such consent which was unconditional shall be subject to conditions,
            unless in either case the decision was made in response to an
            application for a variation,
       give notice of the appeal to any person who appears to the Agency likely to
       have a particular interest in its subject matter; and
  (b) in any other case give notice of the appeal—
       (i) to any person who made representations or objections to the Agency
            with respect to the grant or variation of the consent; and
       (ii) to any person who was required to be consulted in relation to the grant
            or variation of the consent under paragraph 2(1) or 6(4) of Schedule 10
            to the Water Resources Act 1991 pursuant to regulation 5(1) or
            paragraph 3(1) of Schedule 1 to these Regulations.

(2)   A notice under paragraph (1) above shall—
  (a) inform the person on whom it is served that an appeal to the Secretary of
       State has been made; and
  (b) state—
       (i)   that any representations made to the Secretary of State in writing by
             the recipient of the notice will be considered by the Secretary of State
             if they are made within the period of 21 days beginning with the date
             of receipt of the notice;
       (ii) that copies of the representations will be sent to the appellant and the
             Agency;
       (iii) that copies of the representations will be placed on registers
             maintained under section 190 of the Water Resources Act 1991
             (pollution control registers);
       (iv) that any person who makes any such representations will be informed
             about the hearing of the appeal if there is to be a hearing held wholly
             or partly in public,
       and shall be accompanied by a copy of the notice of appeal.

(3)   The Agency shall, within 14 days of sending a notice under paragraph (1)
above, notify the Secretary of State of the name and address of every person who
was sent such a notice in relation to the appeal and the date on which it was sent.

(4)   Where an appeal is withdrawn after a notice under paragraph (1) above has
been sent, the Agency shall inform every person who was sent such a notice in
relation to the appeal.

(5)   This regulation shall not apply in relation to an appeal under section 91(1)(h)
or 191B(5) of the Water Resources Act 1991 (appeals against enforcement notices and
appeals against determinations that information is not commercially confidential).

[1154]

11 Written representations

(1)   Where the appellant informs the Secretary of State that he wishes the appeal to be disposed of on the basis of written representations, the Agency shall submit any written representations to the Secretary of State—

    (a) in the case of an appeal against an enforcement notice, not later than 14 days after receiving a copy of the notice of appeal in accordance with regulation 8(4); and

    (b) in all other cases, not later than 28 days after receiving a copy of the notice of appeal in accordance with regulation 8(4).

(2)   The appellant shall make any further representations by way of reply not later than 14 days after receiving the Agency's representations under paragraph (1) above.

(3)   The Secretary of State shall send to the appellant and the Agency copies of any representations made to him in relation to the appeal under regulation 10 and shall allow them each a period of 14 days from the date of the receipt of those copies in which to make representations thereon.

(4)   The Secretary of State may in any particular case—

    (a) set shorter or longer time limits than those mentioned in this regulation;

    (b) allow the parties to make representations in addition to those mentioned in paragraphs (1) to (3) above.

(5)   Any representations made by a party to the appeal shall be dated with the date on which they are submitted to the Secretary of State.

(6)   Where either party to the appeal submits any representations to the Secretary of State they shall at the same time send a copy to the other party.

[1155]

12 Hearings

(1)   The Secretary of State shall give the appellant and the Agency at least 28 days notice (unless they agree to a shorter period of notice) of the date, time and place fixed for a hearing in relation to an appeal under section 91 or 191B(5) of the Water Resources Act 1991 (appeals in respect of consents under Chapter II of Part III and appeals in relation to information which the Agency has determined is not commercially confidential).

(2)   Subject to paragraph (4) and (5) below, in the case of a hearing which is to be held wholly or partly in public, the Secretary of State shall, at least 21 days before the date fixed for the hearing—

    (a) publish a copy of the notice given under paragraph (1) above in a newspaper circulating in the locality which he considers may be affected by any matter which falls to be determined in relation to the appeal; and

    (b) serve a copy of the notice given under paragraph (1) above on every person who has made representations or objections in writing to the Secretary of State under regulation 10 in relation to the appeal.

(3)   The Secretary of State may vary the date fixed for the hearing and paragraphs (1) and (2) above shall apply, with necessary modifications, to the variation of the date.

(4)   The Secretary of State may also vary the time or place for the holding of a hearing but shall give such notice of any such variation as appears to him to be reasonable.

(5)   Paragraph (2) above shall not apply in the case of a hearing in relation to an appeal under section 191B(5) of the Water Resources Act 1991 (appeals in relation to information which the Agency has determined is not commercially confidential).

(6)   The persons entitled to be heard at a hearing are—
   (a) the appellant;
   (b) the Agency; and
   (c) any person required under regulation 10(1)(b)(ii) to be notified of the appeal.

(7)   Nothing in paragraph (6) above shall prevent the person appointed to conduct the hearing of the appeal from permitting any other person to be heard at the hearing and such permission shall not be unreasonably withheld.

(8)   After the conclusion of a hearing, the person appointed to conduct the hearing shall, unless he was appointed under section 114(1)(a) of the Environment Act 1995 (power of Secretary of State to delegate his functions of determining appeals), make a report in writing to the Secretary of State which shall include his conclusions and his recommendations or his reasons for not making any recommendations.

[1156]

13 Notification of determination

(1)   The Secretary of State shall notify the appellant in writing of his determination of the appeal and shall provide him with a copy of any report mentioned in regulation 12(8).

(2)   The Secretary of State shall at the same time send—
   (a) a copy of the documents mentioned in paragraph (1) above to the Agency and to any persons required under regulation 10(1)(b)(ii) to be notified of the appeal; and
   (b) a copy of his determination of the appeal to any other person who made representations to the Secretary of State under regulation 10 and, if a hearing was held, to any other person who made representations in relation to the appeal at the hearing.

[1157]

14 Consents for discharges by the Agency

(1)   Section 88 of the Water Resources Act 1991 (defence to principal offences in respect of authorised discharges) shall have effect in relation to cases in which consents for the purposes of subsection (1)(a) of that section are required by the Agency as if for subsection (2) there were substituted—

   "(2) Schedule 2 to the Control of Pollution (Applications, Appeals and Registers) Regulations 1996 shall apply with respect to the making of applications by the Agency for consents under this Chapter for the purposes of subsection (1)(a) above and with respect to the giving, revocation and modification of such consents."

(2)   Schedule 2 to these Regulations (which deals with consents for discharges by the Agency) shall have effect.

[1158]

15 Pollution control registers

Subject to sections 191A and 191B of the Water Resources Act 1991 and regulations 16 and 17, registers maintained by the Agency under section 190 of that Act (pollution control registers) shall contain full particulars of—
   (a) notices of water quality objectives and other notices served under section 83 of that Act;
   (b) applications made for consents, or for the variation of consents, under Chapter II of Part III of that Act, together with information provided in connection with such applications;

(c) consents given under that Chapter, the conditions to which the consents are subject and any variation of the consents;

(d) the date and time of each sample of water or effluent taken by the Agency for the purposes of the water pollution provisions of that Act (including details of the place where it was taken) and the result of the analysis of each sample and the steps, if any, taken in consequence by the Agency;

(e) information corresponding to that mentioned in paragraph (d) above with respect to samples of water or effluent taken by any other person, and the analysis of those samples, acquired by the Agency from that person under arrangements made by the Agency for the purposes of any of the water pollution provisions of that Act, including any steps taken by that person in consequence of the results of the analysis of any sample;

(f) prohibition notices served under section 86(1) of that Act;

(g) enforcement notices served under section 90B of that Act;

(h) revocations of discharge consents under paragraph 7 of Schedule 10 to that Act;

(i) notices of appeal under section 91 of that Act, correspondence provided to the Secretary of State under regulation 8(3), the decisions or notices which are the subject matter of the appeals, representations made under regulation 10, written notifications of the Secretary of State's determination of appeals and reports accompanying any such notification;

(j) directions given by the Secretary of State in relation to the Agency's functions under the water pollution provisions of that Act, with the exception of directions under section 191A(2) of that Act (directions in relation to information affecting national security);

(k) convictions, for offences under Part III of that Act, of persons who have the benefit of discharge consents, including the name of the offender, the date of conviction, the penalty imposed, the costs, if any, awarded against the offender and the name of the Court;

(l) returns and other information about the nature, origin, composition, temperature, volume and rate of discharges provided to the Agency in pursuance of conditions of discharge consents; and

(m) information which was entered on the registers under the Control of Pollution (Registers) Regulations 1989.

[1159]

16 Entry of particulars on register, removal of certain particulars and indexing of registers

(1)   Subject to sections 191A and 191B of the Water Resources Act 1991 and paragraph (2) below, where registers are by virtue of regulation 15 to contain any particulars, those particulars shall be entered on the registers—

(a) if they relate to an application or notice which is to be advertised under regulation 2(2), paragraph 1(1) of Schedule 1 or paragraph 1(2) of Schedule 2, before the beginning of the period of 28 days during which the application or notice is required to be advertised;

(b) if they relate to an enforcement notice served under section 90B of that Act, not later than 7 days after it is served;

(c) in all other cases, not later than 28 days after those particulars become available to the Agency.

(2)   Where an application for a consent, or for the variation of a consent, is withdrawn at any time before it is determined—

(a) no further particulars relating to the application shall be entered on the registers after the application is withdrawn; and

(b) all particulars relating to the application shall be removed from the registers not less than 2 months, and not more than 3 months, after the application is withdrawn.

(3)   The Agency shall keep records in each register showing the dates on which particulars are entered on that register.

(4)   Each register shall be indexed in a way which facilitates access to particulars entered on it.

[1160]

17 Period after which information may be removed from pollution control registers

(1)   Nothing in regulation 15 shall require the Agency to keep on a register—
   (a) monitoring information more than four years after that information was entered on the register; or
   (b) other information which has been superseded by later information more than four years after that later information was entered on the register.

(2)   In this regulation "monitoring information" means information entered on the register by virtue of regulation 15(d), (e) or (l).

[1161]

18 Revocation of existing regulations

(1)   ...

(2)   Subject to paragraph (3) below, nothing in paragraph (1)(a) or (b) above shall affect—
   (a) the application of the Control of Pollution (Discharges by the National Rivers Authority) Regulations 1989, and regulations 2 to 6 of the Control of Pollution (Consents for Discharges etc) (Secretary of State Functions) Regulations 1989, in relation to any application made under paragraph 1 of Schedule 10 to the Water Resources Act 1991 (applications for discharge consents) before 31st December 1996 or any consent given under paragraph 5 of that Schedule (discharge consents granted without applications) before that date; or
   (b) the application of regulations 2 and 7 of the Control of Pollution (Consents for Discharges etc) (Secretary of State Functions) Regulations 1989 (appeals in respect of consents under Chapter II of Part III of that Act), in relation to any appeal under that section made in relation to a decision taken before 31st December 1996.

(3)   Paragraph (2)(a) above shall not apply in relation to an application made under paragraph 1 of Schedule 10 to the Water Resources Act 1991 before 31st December 1996 if—
   (a) the application relates to discharges of a kind which the applicant, or a predecessor of his, was authorised to make by virtue of a consent to which paragraph 21 of Schedule 23 to the Environment Act 1995 (transitional provisions in relation to discharge consents) applied; and
   (b) notice in accordance with sub-paragraph (2)(b)(ii) of that paragraph was not given by him or his predecessor.

[1162]

NOTES

   Para (1): sub-paras (a)–(c) revoke respectively the Control of Pollution (Consents for Discharges etc) (Secretary of State Functions) Regulations 1989, SI 1989/1151, the Control of Pollution (Discharges by the National Rivers Authority) Regulations 1989, SI 1989/1157, the Control of Pollution (Registers) Regulations 1989, SI 1989/1160.

SCHEDULE 1
DISCHARGE CONSENTS WITHOUT APPLICATIONS

Regulation 7

1 Advertisements

(1) Notice of any discharge consent given by the Agency under paragraph 6 of Schedule 10 to the Water Resources Act 1991 (discharge consents without applications) shall be published—
  (a)   in one or more newspapers circulating in—
      (i)   the locality in which the discharges are made; and
      (ii)   the locality in which the controlled waters which may be affected by the discharges are situated; and
  (b)   in the London Gazette.

(2) Subject to sub-paragraph (3) below, the notice shall—
  (a)   state the name of the person to whom the discharge consent was given;
  (b)   specify where the discharges are made;
  (c)   describe briefly the nature of the discharges;
  (d)   state where the register containing information about the discharges may be inspected, the times at which the register is open for inspection and that the register may be inspected free of charge;
  (e)   explain that any person may make representations in writing to the Agency, specify when the period allowed for making representations ends and give the address of the Agency to which representations are to be sent.

(3) Nothing in sub-paragraph (1) or (2) above shall require the disclosure of any information which is not to be included in a register by virtue of section 191A or 191B of the Water Resources Act 199 (exclusion from registers of information affecting national security and of certain confidential information).

2 Timing of advertisements

(1) In the case of any discharge consent to which paragraph 1 above applies, advertisements required by sub-paragraph (1) of that paragraph shall be published within the period of 28 days beginning with the relevant date.

(2) Subject to sub-paragraphs (3) and (4), the relevant date in relation to any such discharge consent shall be the date on which it comes into force.

(3) In a case where a matter falls to be determined under section 191A of the Water Resources Act 1991 (exclusion from registers of information affecting national security), the relevant date shall be the date on which the Secretary of State notifies the applicant of his determination.

(4) In a case where a matter falls to be determined under section 191B of the Water Resources Act 1991 (exclusion from registers of certain confidential information), the relevant date shall be—
  (a)   if the Agency determines under section 191B(4) of that Act that the information in question is commercially confidential, the date on which the Agency notifies the applicant of its decision;
  (b)   if the Agency determines under section 191B(4) of that Act that the information in question is not commercially confidential—
      (i)   the date on which the period for appealing expires without an appeal having been made;
      (ii)   the date on which the Secretary of State notifies the applicant of his final determination of the appeal; or
      (iii)   the date on which the appeal is withdrawn.

3 Consultation

(1) Subject to sub-paragraph (4) below, copies of the discharge consent shall be sent, within the period of 28 days beginning with the relevant date, to—
  (a)   every local authority or water undertaker within whose area any of the discharges are made;
  (b)   each of the Ministers if any of the discharges are made into coastal waters, relevant territorial waters or waters outside the seaward limits of relevant territorial waters;

(c)   the harbour authority within the meaning of section 57(1) of the Harbours Act 1964 if any of the discharges are made into a harbour managed by the authority; and

(d)   the local fisheries committee, if any of the discharges are made into relevant territorial waters or coastal waters within the sea fisheries district of that committee.

(2)   The Agency need only consider representations or objections under paragraph 6(5) of Schedule 10 to the Water Resources Act 1991 which have not been withdrawn if they were made in writing to the Agency within the period allowed under sub-paragraph (3) below.

(3)   The period allowed for making representations or objections is—

(a)   in the case of a person who is required to be consulted under sub-paragraph (1) above, the period of six weeks beginning with the date on which a copy of the discharge consent is sent to him; and

(b)   in the case of any other person, the period of six weeks beginning with the last date on which the making of the application was advertised under paragraph 1(1) above.

(4)   Nothing in sub-paragraph (1) above shall require the disclosure in relation to any of the bodies mentioned in sub-paragraph (1)(a), (c) or (d) of any information which is not to be included in a register by virtue of section 191A or 191B of the Water Resources Act 1991 (exclusion from registers of information affecting national security and of certain confidential information).

(5)   In this paragraph, "the relevant date", in relation to a discharge consent, has the same meaning as it has in paragraph 2 above.

[1163]

SCHEDULE 2
DISCHARGE CONSENTS FOR THE AGENCY

Regulation 14(2)

1 Application for consent

(1)   An application by the Agency for a consent, for the purposes of section 88(1)(a) of the Water Resources Act 1991, for any discharges shall be made to the Secretary of State in writing accompanied by such information as he may require; and shall be advertised by the Agency in accordance with sub-paragraphs (2) and (3) below.

(2)   Notice of the application shall be published within the period of 28 days beginning with the date on which the application is received—

(a)   in one or more newspapers circulating in—
    (i)   the locality in which the proposed discharges are to be made; and
    (ii)   the locality in which the controlled waters likely to be affected by the proposed discharges are situated; and

(b)   in the London Gazette.

(3)   The notice shall—

(a)   state that the application is made by the Agency;

(b)   specify where the discharges are proposed to be made;

(c)   describe briefly the nature of the proposed discharges;

(d)   state where the register containing information about the application may be inspected, the times at which the register is open for inspection and that the register may be inspected free of charge; and

(e)   explain that any person may make representations in writing to the Secretary of State, specify when the period allowed for making representations ends and give the address of the Secretary of State to which representations are to be sent.

(4)   The Secretary of State may give the Agency notice requiring it to provide him with such further information of any description specified in the notice as he may require for the purpose of determining the application.

(5)   An application made in accordance with this paragraph which relates to proposed discharges at two or more places may be treated by the Secretary of State as separate applications for consents for discharges at each of those places.

2 Consultation in connection with applications

(1) The Agency shall, within the period of 28 days beginning with the date on which any application under paragraph 1 above is made, give notice of the application, together with a copy of the application, to—

(a) every local authority or water undertaker within whose area any of the proposed discharges are to be made;

(b) the Minister if any of the proposed discharges are to be made into coastal or relevant territorial waters, or waters outside the seaward limits of relevant territorial waters, which are in or adjacent to England;

(c) the harbour authority within the meaning of section 57(1) of the Harbours Act 1964 if any of the proposed discharges are to be made into a harbour managed by the authority; and

(d) the local fisheries committee, if any of the proposed discharges are to be made into relevant territorial waters or coastal waters within the sea fisheries district of that committee.

(2) Any representations made by any persons within the period allowed under sub-paragraph (3) below and not withdrawn shall he considered by the Secretary of State in determining the application.

(3) The period allowed for making representations is—

(a) in the case of persons given notice of the application under sub-paragraph (1) above, the period of six weeks beginning with the date on which the notice was given under that sub-paragraph; and

(b) in the case of other persons, the period of six weeks beginning with the last date on which the making of the application was advertised under paragraph 1(2) above.

3 Consideration and determination of applications

(1) On an application under paragraph 1 above the Secretary of State shall be under a duty, if the requirements of that paragraph and paragraph 2 above are complied with, to consider whether to give the consent applied for, either unconditionally or subject to conditions, or to refuse it.

(2) The conditions subject to which a consent may be given under this paragraph shall be such conditions as the Secretary of State may think fit and, in particular, may include conditions—

(a) as to the places at which the discharges to which the consent relates may be made and as to the design and construction of any outlets for the discharges;

(b) as to the nature, origin, composition, temperature, volume and rate of the discharges and as to the periods during which the discharges may be made;

(c) as to the steps to be taken, in relation to the discharges or by way of subjecting any substance likely to affect the description of matter discharged to treatment or any other process, for minimising the polluting effects of the discharges on any controlled waters;

(d) as to the provision of facilities for taking samples of the matter discharged and, in particular, as to the provision, maintenance and use of manholes, inspection chambers, observation wells and boreholes in connection with the discharges;

(e) as to the provision, maintenance and testing of meters for measuring or recording the volume and rate of the discharges and apparatus for determining the nature, composition and temperature of the discharges;

(f) as to the keeping of records of the nature, origin, composition, temperature, volume and rate of the discharges and, in particular, of records of readings of meters and other recording apparatus provided in accordance with any other condition attached to the consent; and

(g) as to the making of returns and the giving of other information to the Secretary of State about the nature, origin, composition, temperature, volume and rate of the discharges;

and it is hereby declared that a consent may be given under this paragraph subject to different conditions in respect of different periods.

(3) Before determining an application, the Secretary of State may, and shall, if the Agency request him to do so—

(a) cause a local inquiry to be held with respect to the application; or

(b) afford the Agency an opportunity of appearing before, and being heard by, a person appointed by the Secretary of State for the purpose.

4 Revocation of consents and alteration and imposition of conditions

(1) The Secretary of State may from time to time review any consent given under paragraph 3 above and the conditions (if any) to which the consent is subject.

(2) Where the Secretary of State has reviewed a consent under this paragraph, he may by a notice served on the Agency—

(a) revoke the consent;
(b) make modifications of the conditions of the consent; or
(c) in the case of an unconditional consent, provide that it shall he subject to such conditions as may be specified in the notice.

5 Applications for variation

(1) The Agency may make an application in writing to the Secretary of State for the variation of a consent given under paragraph 3 above; and any such application shall be accompanied by such information as the Secretary of State may require.

(2) The provisions of paragraphs 1 to 3 above shall apply (with the necessary modifications) to applications under sub-paragraph (1) above, and to the variation of consents in pursuance of such applications, as they apply to applications for, and the grant of, consents.

6 Transfer of consents

(1) A consent under paragraph 3 may be transferred by the Agency to a person who proposes to carry on making the discharges in place of the Agency.

(2) A consent under paragraph 3 above which is transferred to a person under this paragraph shall have effect on and after the date of the transfer as if it had been granted to that person under paragraph 3 of Schedule 10 to the Water Resources Act 1991, subject to such modifications as the Agency may specify in writing.

(3) Where a consent under paragraph 3 above is transferred under sub-paragraph (1) above, the Agency shall give notice of that fact to the Secretary of State.

[1164]

LANDFILL TAX REGULATIONS 1996

(SI 1996/1527)

NOTES

Made: 12 June 1996.
Commencement: 1 August 1996.
Authority: Finance Act 1996, ss 47(9), 48(1), (2), 49, 51(1)–(6), 52(1)–(3), 53(1)–(4), 58(1), (4)–(6), 61(2), 62(1)–(3), (5), (6), 68(1)–(6), Sch 5, paras 2(1)–(3), 13(1), (6), 14(5), 20(3), 23(1), 42(1)–(5), 43(1)–(5).

ARRANGEMENT OF REGULATIONS

PART I
PRELIMINARY

PART II
REGISTRATION AND PROVISION FOR SPECIAL CASES

PART X
DETERMINATION OF WEIGHT OF MATERIAL DISPOSED OF

PART XI
SET-OFF OF AMOUNTS

PART XII
DISTRESS AND DILIGENCE

PART I
PRELIMINARY

1 Citation and commencement

These Regulations may be cited as the Landfill Tax Regulations 1996 and shall come into force on 1st August 1996.

[1165]

2 Interpretation

(1)   In these Regulations—
"accounting period" means—
   (a) in the case of a registered person, each period of three months ending on the dates notified to him by the Commissioners, whether by means of a registration certificate issued by them or otherwise;
   (b) in the case of a registrable person who is not registered, each quarter; or
   (c) in the case of any registrable person, such other period in relation to which he is required by or under regulation 11 to make a return;
   and, in every case, the first accounting period of a registrable person shall begin on the effective date of registration;
"the Act" means the Finance Act 1996;
"Collector" means a Collector, Deputy Collector or Assistant Collector of Customs and Excise;
"credit", except where the context otherwise requires, means credit which a person is entitled to claim under Part IV of these Regulations;
"disposal" means a landfill disposal (which expression has the meaning given in section 70(2) of the Act) made on or after 1st October 1996 and "disposed of" shall be construed accordingly;
"effective date of registration" means the date determined in accordance with section 47 of the Act upon which the person was or should have been registered;
"landfill invoice" means an invoice of the description in regulation 37;
"landfill site" has the meaning given in section 66 of the Act;
"landfill tax account" has the meaning given in regulation 12;
"landfill tax bad debt account" has the meaning given in regulation 26;

> "quarter" means a period of three months ending at the end of March, June, September or December;
>
> "registered person" means a person who is registered under section 47 of the Act and "register" and "registration" shall be construed accordingly;
>
> "registrable person" has the meaning given in section 47(10) of the Act;
>
> "registration number" means the identifying number allocated to a registered person and notified to him by the Commissioners;
>
> "return" means a return which is required to be made in accordance with regulation 11;
>
> "taxable business" means a business or part of a business in the course of which taxable activities are carried out;
>
> "transfer note" has the same meaning as in the Environmental Protection (Duty of Care) Regulations 1991;
>
> "working day" means any day of the week except Saturday and Sunday and a bank holiday or public holiday, in either case, for England.

(2) In these Regulations any question whether a person is connected with another shall be determined in accordance with section 839 of the Taxes Act 1988.

(3) Any reference in these Regulations to "this Part" is a reference to the Part of these Regulations in which that reference is made.

(4) Any reference in these Regulations to a form prescribed in the Schedule to these Regulations shall include a reference to a form which the Commissioners are satisfied is a form to the like effect.

[1166]

3 Designation, direction or approval

Any designation, direction or approval by the Commissioners under or for the purposes of these Regulations shall be made or given by a notice in writing.

[1167]

PART II
REGISTRATION AND PROVISION FOR SPECIAL CASES

4 Notification of liability to be registered

(1) A person who is required by section 47(3) of the Act to notify the Commissioners of his intention to carry out taxable activities shall do so on the form numbered 1 in the Schedule to these Regulations.

(2) Where the notification referred to in this regulation is made by a person who operates or intends to operate more than one landfill site, it shall include the particulars set out on the form numbered 2 in the Schedule to these Regulations.

(3) Where the notification referred to in this regulation is made by a partnership, it shall include the particulars set out on the form numbered 3 in the Schedule to these Regulations.

(4) The notification referred to in this regulation shall be made within 30 days of the earliest date after 1st August 1996 on which the person either forms or continues to have the intention to carry out taxable activities.

[1168]

5 Changes in particulars

(1) A person who has made a notification under regulation 4, whether or not it was made in accordance with paragraph (4) of that regulation, shall, within 30 days of—

(a) discovering any inaccuracy in; or
(b) any change occurring which causes to become inaccurate,

any of the information which was contained in or provided with the notification, notify the Commissioners in writing and furnish them with full particulars.

(2) Without prejudice to paragraph (1) above, a registrable person shall, within 30 days of any change occurring in any of the circumstances referred to in paragraph (4) below, notify the Commissioners in writing and furnish them with particulars of—
(a) the change; and
(b) the date on which the change occurred.

(3) A registrable person who discovers that any information contained in or provided with a notification under paragraph (1) or (2) above was inaccurate shall, within 30 days of his discovering the inaccuracy, notify the Commissioners in writing and furnish them with particulars of—
(a) the inaccuracy;
(b) the date on which the inaccuracy was discovered;
(c) how the information was inaccurate; and
(d) the correct information.

(4) The circumstances mentioned in paragraph (2) above are the following circumstances relating to the registrable person or any taxable business carried on by him:
(a) his name, his trading name (if different), his address and the landfill sites he operates;
(b) his status, namely whether he carries on business as a sole proprietor, body corporate, partnership or other unincorporated body;
(c) in the case of a partnership, the name and address of any partner.

(5) Any person failing to comply with a requirement imposed in any of paragraphs (1) to (3) above shall be liable to a penalty of £250.

(6) Where in relation to a registered person the Commissioners are satisfied that any of the information recorded in the register is or has become inaccurate they may correct the register accordingly.

(7) For the purposes of paragraph (6) above, it is immaterial whether or not the registered person has notified the Commissioners of any change which has occurred in accordance with paragraphs (1) to (3) above.

[1169]

6 Notification of cessation of taxable activities

A person who is required by section 47(4) of the Act to notify the Commissioners of his having ceased to have the intention to carry out taxable activities shall, within 30 days of his so having ceased, notify the Commissioners in writing and shall therein inform them of—
(a) the date on which he ceased to have the intention of carrying out taxable activities; and
(b) if different, the date on which he ceased to carry out taxable activities.

[1170]

7 Transfer of a going concern

(1) Where—
(a) a taxable business is transferred as a going concern;
(b) the registration of the transferor has not already been cancelled;
(c) as a result of the transfer of the business the registration of the transferor is to be cancelled and the transferee has become liable to be registered; and
(d) an application is made on the form numbered 4 in the Schedule to these Regulations by both the transferor and the transferee,

the Commissioners may with effect from the date of the transfer cancel the registration of the transferor and register the transferee with the registration number previously allocated to the transferor.

(2)   An application under paragraph (1) above shall be treated as the notification referred to in regulation 6.

(3)   Where the transferee of a business has been registered under paragraph (1) above with the registration number previously allocated to the transferor—
- (a) any liability of the transferor existing at the date of the transfer to make a return or account for or pay any tax under Part III of these Regulations shall become the liability of the transferee;
- (b) any entitlement of the transferor, whether or not existing at the date of the transfer, to credit or payment under Part IV of these Regulations shall become the entitlement of the transferee.

(4)   In addition to the provisions set out in paragraph (3) above, where the transferee of a business has been registered under paragraph (1) above with the registration number previously allocated to the transferor during an accounting period subsequent to that in which the transfer took place (but with effect from the date of the transfer) and any—
- (a) return has been made;
- (b) tax has been accounted for; or
- (c) entitlement to credit has been claimed,

by either the transferor or the transferee, it shall be treated as having been done by the transferee.

(5)   Where—
- (a) a taxable business is transferred as a going concern;
- (b) the transferee removes material as described in regulation 21(2) or (4); and
- (c) the transferor has paid tax on the disposal concerned,

then, whether or not the transferee has been registered under paragraph (1) above with the registration number previously allocated to the transferor, any entitlement to credit arising under Part V of these Regulations shall become the entitlement of the transferee.

[1171]

8 Representation of unincorporated body

(1)   Where anything is required to be done by or under the Act (whether by these Regulations or otherwise) by or on behalf of an unincorporated body other than a partnership, it shall be the joint and several responsibility of—
- (a) every member holding office as president, chairman, treasurer, secretary or any similar office; or
- (b) if there is no such office, every member holding office as a member of a committee by which the affairs of the body are managed; or
- (c) if there is no such office or committee, every member;

but, subject to paragraph (2) below, if it is done by any of the persons referred to above that shall be sufficient compliance with any such requirement.

(2)   Where an unincorporated body other than a partnership is required to make any notification such as is referred to in regulations 4 to 6, it shall not be sufficient compliance unless the notification is made by a person upon whom a responsibility for making it is imposed by paragraph (1) above.

(3)   Where anything is required to be done by or under the Act (whether by these Regulations or otherwise) by or on behalf of a partnership, it shall be the joint and several responsibility of every partner; but if it is done by one partner or, in the case of a partnership whose principal place of business is in Scotland, by any other

person authorised by the partnership with respect thereto that shall be sufficient compliance with any such requirement.

[1172]

9 Bankruptcy or incapacity of registrable persons

(1) If a registrable person becomes bankrupt or incapacitated, the Commissioners may, from the date on which he became bankrupt or incapacitated, as the case may be, treat as a registrable person any person carrying on any taxable business of his; and any legislation relating to landfill tax shall apply to any person so treated as though he were a registered person.

(2) Any person carrying on such business as aforesaid shall, within 30 days of commencing to do so, inform the Commissioners in writing of that fact and the date of the bankruptcy order or of the nature of the incapacity and the date on which it began.

(3) Where the Commissioners have treated a person carrying on a business as a registrable person under paragraph (1) above, they shall cease so to treat him if—
  (a) the registration of the registrable person is cancelled, whether or not any other person is registered with the registration number previously allocated to him;
  (b) the bankruptcy is discharged or the incapacity ceases; or
  (c) he ceases carrying on the business of the registrable person.

(4) In relation to a registrable person which is a company, the references in this regulation to the registrable person becoming incapacitated shall be construed as references to its going into liquidation or receivership or to an administration order being made in relation to it; and references to the incapacity ceasing shall be construed accordingly.

[1173]

PART III
ACCOUNTING, PAYMENT AND RECORDS

10 Interpretation

In this Part, "accounting period" has the meaning given in regulation 2(1).

[1174]

11 Making of returns

(1) Subject to paragraph (3) below and save as the Commissioners may otherwise allow, a registrable person shall, in respect of each accounting period, make a return to the Controller, Central Collection Unit (LT), on the form numbered 5 in the Schedule to these Regulations.

(2) Subject to paragraph (3) below, a registrable person shall make each return not later than the last working day of the month next following the end of the period to which it relates.

(3) Where the Commissioners consider it necessary in the circumstances of any particular case, they may—
  (a) vary the length of any accounting period or the date on which it begins or ends or by which any return must be made;
  (b) allow or direct the registrable person to make a return in accordance with sub-paragraph (a) above;
  (c) allow or direct a registrable person to make returns to a specified address,

and any person to whom the Commissioners give any direction such as is referred to in this regulation shall comply therewith.

[1175]

12 Landfill tax account

(1)   Every registrable person shall make and maintain an account to be known as "the landfill tax account".

(2)   The landfill tax account shall be in such form and contain such particulars as may be stipulated in a notice published by the Commissioners and not withdrawn by a further notice.

[1176]

13 Correction of errors

(1)   In this regulation—
"overdeclaration" means, in relation to any return, the amount (if any) which was wrongly treated as tax due for the accounting period concerned and which caused the amount of tax which was payable to be overstated, or the entitlement to a payment under regulation 20 to be understated (or both) or would have caused such an overstatement or understatement were it not for the existence of an underdeclaration in relation to that return;
"underdeclaration" means, in relation to any return, the aggregate of—
   (a) the amount (if any) of tax due for the accounting period concerned which was not taken into account; and
   (b) the amount (if any) which was wrongly deducted as credit,
and which caused the amount of tax which was payable to be understated, or the entitlement to a payment under regulation 20 to be overstated (or both) or would have caused such an understatement or overstatement were it not for the existence of an overdeclaration in relation to that return.

(2)   This regulation applies where a registrable person has made a return which was inaccurate as the result of an overdeclaration or underdeclaration.

(3)   Where in any accounting period a registrable person has discovered one or more overdeclarations, he may enter the overdeclarations in the return for the accounting period in which they were discovered by including their amount in the box opposite the legend "Overdeclarations from previous periods (no limit)".

(4)   Where in any accounting period—
   (a) a registrable person discovers one or more underdeclarations; and
   (b) having treated the amount of those underdeclarations as reduced by the amount of any overdeclarations for the same accounting periods, the total of those underdeclarations does not exceed £2,000,
he may enter the underdeclarations in his return for the accounting period in which they were discovered by including their amount in the box opposite the legend "Underdeclarations from previous periods (must not exceed £2,000, see general notes)".

(5)   Where a registrable person enters an amount in a return in accordance with paragraph (3) or (4) above he shall calculate the tax payable by him or the payment to which he is entitled accordingly.

(6)   Where an amount has been entered in accordance with this regulation in a return which has been made—
   (a) the return shall be regarded as correcting any earlier return to which that amount relates; and
   (b) the registrable person shall be taken to have furnished information with respect to the inaccuracy in the prescribed form and manner for the purposes of paragraph 20 of Schedule 5 to the Act.

(7)   No amount shall be entered in a return in respect of any overdeclaration or underdeclaration except in accordance with this regulation; and as regards any underdeclaration that cannot be corrected under paragraph (4) above a person shall

not be taken to have furnished information with respect to an inaccuracy in the prescribed form and manner for the purposes of paragraph 20 of Schedule 5 to the Act unless he provides such information to the Commissioners in writing.

[1177]

14 Claims for overpaid tax

Except where the amount to which the claim relates has been entered in a return in accordance with regulation 13 or is included in an amount so entered, any claim under paragraph 14 of Schedule 5 to the Act shall be made in writing to the Commissioners and shall, by reference to such documentary evidence as is in the possession of the claimant, state the amount of the claim and the method by which that amount was calculated.

[1178]

15 Payment of tax

Save as the Commissioners may otherwise allow or direct, any person required to make a return shall pay to the Controller, Central Collection Unit (LT), such amount of tax as is payable by him in respect of the accounting period to which the return relates no later than the last day on which he was required to make the return.

[1179]

16 Records

(1) Every registrable person shall, for the purpose of accounting for tax, preserve the following—
  (a) his business and accounting records;
  (b) his landfill tax account;
  (c) transfer notes and any other original or copy records in relation to material brought onto or removed from the landfill site (including any record made for the purpose of Part IX of these Regulations);
  (d) all invoices (including landfill invoices) and similar documents issued to him and copies of such invoices and similar documents issued by him;
  (e) all credit or debit notes or other documents received by him which evidence an increase or decrease in the amount of any consideration for a relevant transaction, and copies of such documents that are issued by him;
  (f) such other records as the Commissioners may specify in a notice published by them and not withdrawn by a further notice.

(2) Subject to paragraphs (3) and (4) below, every registrable person shall preserve the records specified in paragraph (1) above for a period of six years.

(3) Subject to paragraph (4) below, a registrable person who has made a landfill tax bad debt account shall preserve that account for a period of five years from the date of the claim made under Part VI of these Regulations.

(4) The Commissioners may direct that registrable persons shall preserve the records specified in paragraph (1) above for a shorter period than that specified in this regulation; and such direction may be made so as to apply generally or in such cases as the Commissioners may stipulate.

(5) In paragraph (1) above—
  (a) the reference to material being brought onto a landfill site is a reference to material that is brought onto the site for the purpose of a relevant transaction;
  (b) the reference to material being removed from a landfill site is a reference to material being removed that has at some previous time fallen wholly or partly within paragraph (a) above.

(6)   In this regulation "relevant transaction" means a disposal or anything that would be a disposal but for the fact that the material is not disposed of as waste.

[1180]

PART IV
CREDIT: GENERAL

17 Interpretation

In this Part—
  "relevant accounting period" means—
    (a) in the case of an entitlement to credit arising under Part V of these Regulations, the accounting period in which the reuse condition or, as the case may be, the enforced removal condition was satisfied;
    (b) in the case of an entitlement to credit arising under Part VI of these Regulations, the accounting period in which the period of one year from the date of the issue of the landfill invoice expired;
    (c) in the case of an entitlement arising under Part VII of these Regulations, the accounting period in which the qualifying contribution was made;
  "relevant amount" means the amount of the credit as determined in accordance with Part V, VI or VII of these Regulations, as the case may be;
  "relevant tax" means the tax, if any, that was required to have been paid as a condition of the entitlement to credit.

[1181]

18 Scope

(1)   This Part applies to entitlements to credit arising under Part V, VI or VII of these Regulations.

(2)   No credit arising under any provision of these Regulations may be claimed except in accordance with this Part.

[1182]

19 Claims in returns

(1)   Subject to paragraphs (2) and (3) below, a person entitled to credit may claim it by deducting its amount from any tax due from him for the relevant accounting period or any subsequent accounting period and, where he does so, he shall make his return for that accounting period accordingly.

(2)   Where the entitlement to credit arises under Part VII of these Regulations paragraph (1) above shall apply as if there were substituted for "or any subsequent accounting period" the words "or any subsequent accounting period in the same contribution year as determined in relation to that person under regulation 31".

(3)   The Commissioners may make directions generally or with regard to particular cases prescribing rules in accordance with which credit may or shall be held over to be credited in an accounting period subsequent to the relevant accounting period; and where such a direction has been made that credit, subject to any subsequent such direction varying or withdrawing the rules, may only be claimed in accordance with those rules.

[1183]

20 Payments in respect of credit

(1)   Subject to paragraph (5) below, where the total credit claimed by a registrable person in accordance with this Part exceeds the total of the tax due from

him for the accounting period, the Commissioners shall pay to him an amount equal to the excess.

(2)   Where the Commissioners have cancelled the registration of a person in accordance with section 47(6) of the Act, and he is not a registrable person, he shall make any claim in respect of credit to which this Part applies by making an application in writing.

(3)   A person making an application under paragraph (2) above shall furnish to the Commissioners full particulars in relation to the credit claimed, including (but not restricted to)—
  (a) except in the case of an entitlement to credit arising under Part VII of these Regulations, the return in which the relevant tax was accounted for;
  (b) except in the case of an entitlement to credit arising under Part VII of these Regulations, the amount of the tax and the date and manner of its payment;
  (c) the events by virtue of which the entitlement to credit arose.

(4)   Subject to paragraph (5) below, where the Commissioners are satisfied that a person who has made a claim in accordance with paragraphs (2) and (3) above is entitled to credit, and that he has not previously had the benefit of that credit, they shall pay to him an amount equal to the credit.

(5)   The Commissioners shall not be liable to make any payment under this regulation unless and until the person has made all the returns which he was required to make.

[1184]

PART V
CREDIT: PERMANENT REMOVALS ETC

21 Entitlement to credit

(1)   An entitlement to credit arises under this Part where—
  (a) a registered person has accounted for an amount of tax and, except where the removal by virtue of which sub-paragraph (b) below is satisfied takes place in the accounting period in which credit arising under this Part is claimed in accordance with Part IV of these Regulations, he has paid that tax; and
  (b) in relation to the disposal on which that tax was charged, either—
    (i) the reuse condition has been satisfied; or
    (ii) the enforced removal condition has been satisfied.

(2)   The reuse condition is satisfied where—
  (a) the disposal has been made with the intention that the material comprised in it—
    (i) would be recycled or incinerated, or
    (ii) removed for use (other than by way of a further disposal) at a place other than a relevant site;
  (b) that material, or some of it, has been recycled, incinerated or permanently removed from the landfill site, as the case may be, in accordance with that intention;
  (c) that recycling, incineration or removal—
    (i) has taken place no later than one year after the date of the disposal; or
    (ii) where water had been added to the material in order to facilitate its disposal, has taken place no later than five years after the date of the disposal; and
  (d) the registered person has, before the disposal, notified the Commissioners in writing that he intends to make one or more removals of material in relation to which sub-paragraphs (a) to (c) above will be satisfied.

(3)   For the purpose of paragraph (2)(a)(ii) above a relevant site is the landfill site at which the disposal was made or any other landfill site.

(4)   The enforced removal condition is satisfied where—

(a) the disposal is in breach of the terms of the licence or resolution, as the case may be, by virtue of which the land constitutes a landfill site;

(b) the registered person has been directed to remove the material comprised in the disposal, or some of it, by a relevant authority and he has removed it, or some of it; and

(c) a further taxable disposal of the material has been made and, except where the registered person is the person liable for the tax chargeable on that further disposal, he has paid to the site operator an amount representing that tax.

(5)   For the purpose of paragraph (4)(b) above the following are relevant authorities—

(a) the Environment Agency;

(b) the Scottish Environment Protection Agency;

(c) the Department of the Environment for Northern Ireland;

(d) a district council in Northern Ireland.

(6)   The amount of the credit arising under this Part shall be equal to the tax that was charged on the disposal; except that where only some of the material comprised in that disposal is removed, the amount of the credit shall be such proportion of that tax as the material removed forms of the total of the material.

[1185]

PART VI
CREDIT: BAD DEBTS

22 Interpretation

In this Part—

"claim" means a claim in accordance with Part IV of these Regulations for an amount of credit arising under this Part and "claimant" shall be construed accordingly;

"customer" means a person for whom a taxable activity is carried out by the claimant;

"outstanding amount" means, in relation to any claim—

(a) if at the time of the claim the claimant has received no payment in respect of the amount written off in his accounts, the amount so written off; or

(b) if at that time he has received a payment, the amount by which the amount written off exceeds the payment (or the aggregate of the payments);

"relevant disposal" means any taxable disposal upon which a claim is based;

"security" means—

(a) in relation to England, Wales and Northern Ireland, any mortgage, charge, lien or other security; and

(b) in relation to Scotland, any security (whether heritable or moveable), any floating charge and any right of lien or preference and right of retention (other than a right of compensation or set-off).

[1186]

23 Scope

An entitlement to credit arises under this Part where—

(a) a registered person has carried out a taxable activity for a consideration in money for a customer with whom he is not connected;

(b) he has accounted for and paid tax on the disposal concerned;
(c) the whole or any part of the consideration for the disposal has been written off in his accounts as a bad debt;
(d) he has issued a landfill invoice in respect of the disposal which shows the amount of tax chargeable;
(e) that invoice was issued—
　　(i) within 14 days of the date of the disposal, or
　　(ii) within such other period as may have been specified in a direction of the Commissioners made under section 61(3) of the Act;
(f) a period of one year (beginning with the date of the issue of that invoice) has elapsed; and
(g) the following provisions of this Part have been complied with.

[1187]

24 Amount of credit

The credit arising under this Part shall be of an amount equal to such proportion of the tax charged on the relevant disposal as the outstanding amount forms of the total consideration.

[1188]

25 Evidence required in support of claim

The claimant, before he makes a claim, shall hold in respect of each relevant disposal—
(a) a copy of the landfill invoice issued by him;
(b) records or any other documents showing that he has accounted for and paid tax on the disposal; and
(c) records or any other documents showing that the consideration has been written off in his accounts as a bad debt.

[1189]

26 Records required to be kept

(1) Any person who makes a claim shall make a record of that claim.

(2) The record referred to in paragraph (1) above shall contain the following information in respect of each claim made:
(a) in respect of each relevant disposal—
　　(i) the amount of tax charged;
　　(ii) the return in which that tax was accounted for and when it was paid;
　　(iii) the date and identifying number of the landfill invoice that was issued;
　　(iv) any consideration that has been received (whether before the claim was made or subsequently);
　　(v) the details of any transfer note;
(b) the outstanding amount;
(c) the amount of the claim;
(d) the return in which the claim was made.

(3) Any records made in pursuance of this regulation shall be kept in a single account known as "the landfill tax bad debt account".

[1190]

27 Attribution of payments

(1) Where—
(a) the claimant has carried out a taxable activity for a customer;
(b) there exist one or more other matters in respect of which the claimant is entitled to a debt owed by the customer (whether they involve a taxable disposal or not and whether they are connected with waste or not); and
(c) a payment has been received by the claimant from the customer,

the payment shall be attributed to the taxable activity and the other matters in accordance with the rule set out in paragraphs (2) and (3) below (and the debts arising in respect of the taxable activity and the other matters are collectively referred to in those paragraphs as debts).

(2)   The payment shall be attributed to the debt which arose earliest and, if not wholly attributed to that debt, thereafter to debts in the order of the dates on which they arose, except that attribution under this paragraph shall not be made if the payment was allocated to a debt by the customer at the time of payment and the debt was paid in full.

(3)   Where—
   (a) the earliest debt and the other debts to which the whole of the payment could be attributed arose on the same day; or
   (b) the debts to which the balance of the payment could be attributed in accordance with paragraph (2) above arose on the same day,

the payment shall be attributed to those debts by multiplying, for each such debt, the payment made by a fraction of which the numerator is the amount remaining unpaid in respect of that debt and the denominator is the amount remaining unpaid in respect of all those debts.

[1191]

28 Repayment of credit

(1)   Where a claimant—
   (a) has benefited from an amount of credit to which he was entitled under this Part; and
   (b) either—
      (i) a payment for the relevant disposal is subsequently received; or
      (ii) a payment is, by virtue of regulation 27, treated as attributed to the relevant disposal,

he shall repay to the Commissioners such amount as equals the amount of the credit, or the balance thereof, multiplied by a fraction of which the numerator is the amount so received or attributed, and the denominator is the amount of the outstanding consideration,

(2)   Where the claimant—
   (a) fails to comply with the requirements of regulation 26; or
   (b) in relation to the documents mentioned in that regulation, fails to comply with either—
      (i) regulation 16; or
      (ii) any obligation arising under paragraph 3 of Schedule 5 to the Act,

he shall repay to the Commissioners the amount of the claim to which the failure to comply relates.

[1192]

29 Writing off debts

(1)   This regulation shall apply for the purpose of determining whether, and to what extent, the consideration is to be taken to have been written off as a bad debt.

(2)   The whole or any part of the consideration for a taxable activity shall be taken to have been written off as a bad debt where—
   (a) the claimant has written it off in his accounts as a bad debt; and
   (b) he has made an entry in relation to that activity in the landfill tax bad debt account in accordance with regulation 26 (and this shall apply regardless of whether a claim can be made in relation to that activity at that time).

(3)   Where the claimant owes an amount of money to the customer which can be set off, the consideration written off in the landfill tax bad debt account shall be reduced by the amount so owed.

(4)   Where the claimant holds in relation to the customer an enforceable security, the consideration written off in the landfill tax bad debt account shall be reduced by the value of the security.

[1193]

PART VII
CREDIT: BODIES CONCERNED WITH THE ENVIRONMENT

30 Interpretation and general provisions

(1)   In this Part—
"approved body" means a body approved for the time being under regulation 34;
"approved object" has the meaning given in regulation 33;
"income" includes interest;
"qualifying contribution" has the meaning given in regulation 32;
"the regulatory body" means such body, if any, as in relation to which an approval of the Commissioners under regulation 35 has effect for the time being;
"running costs" includes any cost incurred in connection with the management and administration of a body or its assets.

(2)   A body shall only be taken to spend a qualifying contribution in the course or furtherance of its approved objects—
   (a) in a case where the contribution is made subject to a condition that it may only be invested for the purpose of generating income, where the body so spends all of that income;
   (b) in a case not falling within sub-paragraph (a) above, where the body becomes entitled to income, where it so spends both the whole of the qualifying contribution and all of that income;
   (c) in a case not falling within either of sub-paragraphs (a) and (b) above, where the body so spends the whole of the qualifying contribution; or
   (d) where—
      (i) it transfers any qualifying contribution or income derived therefrom to another approved body, and
      (ii) that transfer is subject to a condition that the sum transferred shall be spent only in the course or furtherance of that other body's approved objects.

(3)   Any approval, or revocation of such approval, by the Commissioners or the regulatory body shall be given by notice in writing to the body affected and shall take effect from the date the notice is given or such later date as the Commissioners or, as the case may be, the regulatory body may specify in it.

[1194]

31 Entitlement to credit

(1)   Subject to the following provisions of this regulation, an entitlement to credit arises under this Part in respect of qualifying contributions made by registered persons.

(2)   Subject to paragraph (3) below, a person shall be entitled to credit in respect of 90 per cent of the amount of each qualifying contribution made by him in any accounting period; and for this purpose a qualifying contribution made—
   (a) in the first accounting period following the end of a contribution year;
   (b) before the return for the previous accounting period has been made; and
   (c) before the period within which that return is required to be made has expired, shall be treated as having been made in the accounting period mentioned in sub-paragraph (b) above (and not in the accounting period in which it was in fact made).

(3)   In respect of the qualifying contributions made in each contribution year, a person shall not be entitled to credit of an amount greater than 20 per cent of his relevant tax liability.

(4)   For the purpose of paragraphs (2) and (3) above the contribution year of a person is his first contribution year and each period of 12 months ending on the anniversary of the end of his first contribution year; but this is subject to paragraph (6) below.

(5)   The reference in paragraph (4) above to the first contribution year of a person is a reference to—
  (a)   the period of 12 months beginning with his effective date of registration; or
  (b)   where that period of 12 months does not end on the last day of an accounting period, the period beginning with his effective date of registration and ending on the last day of the accounting period in which the 12 month period ends.

  (6)   Where—
  (a)   the Commissioners vary the length of a person's accounting period under regulation 11(3);
  (b)   as a consequence of the variation the end of any contribution year of his other than the first contribution year would not coincide with the end of an accounting period,
the contribution year thus affected shall end on the same day as the end of the accounting period in which that contribution year would apart from this regulation end; and each of the person's subsequent contribution years shall end on the anniversary of the end of that contribution year (subject to any subsequent application of this paragraph).

(7)   Subject to paragraphs (8) and (10) below, the reference in paragraph (3) above to the relevant tax liability of a person is a reference to the aggregate of—
  (a)   the tax payable by him, if any, in respect of the accounting period in relation to which that liability falls to be determined; and
  (b)   the tax payable by him, if any, in respect of any earlier accounting period or periods which fall within the same contribution year as that accounting period;
and where in respect of any accounting period he is entitled to a payment under regulation 20 the aggregate of the tax payable by him in respect of the accounting periods mentioned in sub-paragraphs (a) and (b) above shall be reduced by the amount of that payment.

(8)   Where paragraph (5)(b) above applies so that the first contribution year of a person exceeds 12 months his relevant tax liability for that contribution year shall be taken to be such amount as is found by multiplying the tax payable by him in respect of that accounting period by a fraction the numerator of which is 12 and the denominator of which is the number of months comprised in the period.

(9)   For the purpose of determining the number of months comprised in an accounting period as described in paragraph (8) above—
  (a)   if the period does not begin on the first day of a month, it shall be taken to begin on the nearest first day of a month;
  (b)   if the period does not end on the last day of a month, it shall be taken to end on the nearest last day of a month;
  (c)   if the period begins or ends on the sixteenth day of a month comprising thirty-one days, it shall be taken to begin on the first day of the following month or, as the case may be, end on the last day of the preceding month;
  (d)   if the period begins or ends on the fifteenth day of February when it contains twenty-nine days, it shall be taken to begin on the first day of March or, as the case may be, end on the last day of January.

(10) For the purposes of paragraphs (7) and (8) above any entitlement to credit arising under this Part shall be disregarded in determining the tax payable by a person in respect of any period.

[1195]

32 Qualifying contributions

(1) A payment is a qualifying contribution if—
   (a) it is made by a registered person to an approved body;
   (b) it is made subject to a condition that the body shall spend the sum paid or any income derived from it or both only in the course or furtherance of its approved objects;
   (c) the requirements of paragraph (2) below have been complied with in relation to that payment; and
   (d) it is not repaid to him in the same accounting period as that in which it was made.

(2) A person claiming credit arising under this Part shall make a record containing the following information—
   (a) the amount and date of each payment he has made to an approved body;
   (b) the name and enrolment number of that body.

(3) Where any qualifying contribution or income derived therefrom is transferred to a body as described in regulation 30(2)(d)—
   (a) the body to whom the sum is transferred shall be treated for the purposes of this Part as having received qualifying contributions of that amount; and
   (b) that body shall be treated accordingly as having received qualifying contributions from the person or persons from whom the body making the transfer in fact received them (but this shall not give rise to any further entitlement to credit in respect of those contributions).

[1196]

33 Bodies eligible for approval

(1) A body is within this regulation if—
   (a) it is—
      (i) a body corporate, or
      (ii) a trust, partnership or other unincorporated body;
   (b) its objects are or include any of the objects within paragraph (2) below (approved objects);
   (c) it is precluded from distributing and does not distribute any profit it makes or other income it receives;
   (d) it applies any profit or other income to the furtherance of its objects (whether or not approved objects);
   (e) it is precluded from applying any of its funds for the benefit of any of the persons who have made qualifying contributions to it, except that such persons may benefit where they belong to a class of persons that benefits generally; and
   (f) it is not controlled by one or more
      (i) local authorities,
      (ii) bodies corporate controlled by one or more local authorities, or
      (iii) registered persons.

(2) The objects of a body are approved objects insofar as they are any of the following objects—
   (a) in relation to any land the use of which for any economic, social or environmental purpose has been prevented or restricted because of the carrying on of an activity on the land which has ceased—
      (i) reclamation, remediation or restoration; or

     (ii) any other operation intended to facilitate economic, social or environmental use;

    but this is subject to paragraph (3) below;

(b) in relation to any land the condition of which, by reason of the carrying on of an activity on the land which has ceased, is such that pollution (whether of that land or not) is being or may be caused—

     (i) any operation intended to prevent or reduce any potential for pollution; or

     (ii) any operation intended to remedy or mitigate the effects of any pollution that has been caused,

    but this is subject to paragraph (3) below;

(c) for the purpose of encouraging the use of more sustainable waste management practices—

     (i) research and development;

     (ii) education; or

     (iii) collection and dissemination of information about waste management practices generally;

(d) where it is for the protection of the environment, the provision, maintenance or improvement of—

     (i) a public park; or

     (ii) another public amenity,

    in the vicinity of a landfill site, provided the conditions in paragraph (6) below are satisfied;

(e) where it is for the protection of the environment, the maintenance, repair or restoration of a building or other structure which—

     (i) is a place of religious worship or of historic or architectural interest,

     (ii) is open to the public, and

     (iii) is situated in the vicinity of a landfill site,

    provided the conditions in paragraph (6) below are satisfied;

(f) the provision of financial, administration and other similar services to bodies which are within this regulation and only such bodies.

(3) An object shall not be, or shall no longer be, regarded as falling within paragraph (2)(a) or (b) above if the reclamation, remediation, restoration or other operation—

(a) is such that any benefit from it will accrue to any person who has carried out or knowingly permitted the activity which has ceased;

(b) involves works which are required to be carried out by a notice or order within paragraph (4) below; or

(c) is wholly or partly required to be carried out by a relevant condition.

(4) The notices and order mentioned in paragraph (3) above are—

(a) a works notice served under section 46A of the Control of Pollution Act 1974;

(b) an enforcement notice served under section 13 of the Environmental Protection Act 1990;

(c) a prohibition notice served under section 14 of the Environmental Protection Act 1990;

(d) an order under section 26 of the Environmental Protection Act 1990;

(e) a remediation notice served under section 78E of the Environmental Protection Act 1990;

(f) an enforcement notice served under section 90B of the Water Resources Act 1991;

(g) a works notice served under section 161A of the Water Resources Act 1991;

(5) In paragraph (2)(c) above "waste management practices" includes waste minimisation, minimisation of pollution and harm from waste, reuse of waste, waste recovery activities and the clearing of pollutants from contaminated land.

(6)   The conditions mentioned in sub-paragraphs (d) and (e) of paragraph (2) above are—
    (a) in a case falling within sub-paragraph (d), that the provision of the park or amenity is not required by a relevant condition; and
    (b) in a case falling within either of those sub-paragraphs, that the park, amenity, building or structure (as the case may be) is not to be operated with a view to profit.

(7)   Where the objects of a body are or include any of the objects set out in paragraph (2) above, the following shall also be regarded as objects within that paragraph—
    (a) the use of qualifying contributions in paying the running costs of the body, but this is subject to paragraph (8) below;
    (b) where the regulatory body has made the approval of the body subject to a condition to that effect, the use of qualifying contributions in paying a contribution to the running costs of the regulatory body.

(8)   The use of qualifying contributions in paying the running costs of the body shall only be regarded as an approved object if the body determines so to use no more than such proportion of the total of qualifying contributions, together with any income derived from them, (or, in the case of a contribution within regulation 30(2)(a), only that income) as the proportion of that total forms of the total funds at its disposal and does not in fact use a greater amount.

(9)   For the purposes of paragraph (1) above a local authority, body corporate or registered person (in each case, "the person") shall be taken to control a body where—
    (a) in the case of a body which is a body corporate, the person is empowered by statute to control that body's activities or if he is that body's holding company within the meaning of section 736 of the Companies Act 1985, and an individual shall be taken to control a body corporate if he, were he a company, would be that body's holding company within the meaning of that Act;
    (b) in the case of a body which is a trust or a partnership, where—
        (i)   the person, taken together with any nominee of his, or
        (ii) any nominee of the person, taken together with any nominee of that nominee or any other nominee of the person,
    forms a majority of the total number of trustees or partners, as the case may be;
    (c) in the case of any other body, where the person, whether directly or through any nominee, has the power—
        (i)   to appoint or remove any officer of the body;
        (ii) to determine the objects of the body;
        (iii) to determine how any of the body's funds may be applied.

(10) For the purposes of paragraphs (3) and (6) above a condition is relevant if it is—
    (a) a condition of any planning permission or other statutory consent or approval granted on the application of any person making a qualifying contribution to the body, or
    (b) a term of an agreement made under section 106 of the Town and Country Planning Act 1990 to which such a person is a party.

[1197]

34 Functions of the regulatory body

(1)   The regulatory body—
    (a) may approve a body which is within regulation 33;
    (b) may require any person applying for approval to pay an application fee;

(c) without prejudice to the generality of sub-paragraph (d) below, may require approved bodies to pay a contribution to the running costs of the regulatory body and such contribution may be required to be paid periodically;

(d) may, either at the time of granting the approval or subsequently, make the approval subject to such conditions as it thinks fit, including conditions relating to the records and accounts the body shall keep;

(e) may revoke the approval;

(f) shall maintain a roll of bodies which it has approved;

(g) shall allocate an identifying number (the enrolment number) to each such body;

(h) shall remove from the roll any body whose approval it has revoked;

(i) shall satisfy itself, by reference to such records or other documents or information it thinks fit, that the qualifying contributions received by the body have been spent by it only in the course or furtherance of its approved objects; and

(j) shall publish information regarding which bodies it has approved and which approvals it has revoked.

(2) Where—

(a) the Commissioners revoke their approval of the regulatory body without approving another body with effect from the day after the revocation takes effect; and

(b) they have not given notice in writing to each body which has been enrolled (and which has not been removed from the roll), no later than the date such revocation takes effect, that they will not be performing any of the functions specified in paragraph (1) above,

the approval of all such bodies shall be deemed to have been revoked on the day the Commissioners revoked their approval.

[1198]

35 Functions of the Commissioners

(1) The Commissioners—

(a) may approve a body for the purposes of this Part;

(b) may, either at the time of granting the approval or subsequently, make the approval subject to such conditions as they think fit;

(c) may revoke the approval;

(d) shall not approve a body without first revoking the approval for any other body with effect from a time earlier than that for which the new approval is to take effect;

(e) for any time as regards which no approval has effect, may perform any of the functions specified in regulation 34(1);

(f) may disclose to the body information which relates to the tax affairs of registered persons and which is relevant to the credit scheme established by this Part; and

(g) having regard to any information received from the body, may serve notices under regulation 36.

(2) Without prejudice to the generality of paragraph (1)(c) above, the Commissioners may revoke their approval of a body where it appears to them—

(a) that the body is in breach of any condition imposed under paragraph (1)(b) above; or

(b) that it is necessary to do so for the proper operation of the credit scheme established by this Part.

[1199]

36 Repayment of credit

(1)   Where a person has benefited from an amount of credit to which he was entitled under this Part and the Commissioners serve upon him a notice in relation to a qualifying contribution paid to an approved body—
  (a) specifying that—
     (i) they are not satisfied that the contribution has been spent by the body only in the course or furtherance of its approved objects; or
     (ii) they are not satisfied that any income derived from the contribution has been so spent by the body;
  (b) specifying a breach of a condition to which the approval of the body was made subject and which occurred before the contribution was spent by the body; or
  (c) specifying that—
     (i) the approval of the body has been revoked; and
     (ii) the contribution had not been spent by the body before that revocation took effect,

he shall repay to the Commissioners the credit claimed in respect of the qualifying contribution.

(2)   For the purpose of paragraph (1) above where—
  (a) repayment is required in relation to credit that has been claimed in respect of more than one qualifying contribution in an accounting period; and
  (b) regulation 31(3) applied so that the amount of credit was restricted,

the person shall be deemed to have claimed credit in respect of such proportion of each contribution made in that accounting period as the total credit claimed in accordance with that regulation forms of the total of the contributions made.

(3)   Where—
  (a) a person has benefited from an amount of credit to which he was entitled under this Part; and
  (b) the whole or a part of the qualifying contribution in respect of which the entitlement to credit arose has been repaid to him,

he shall pay to the Commissioners an amount equal to 90 per cent of the amount repaid to him.

(4)   Paragraph (5) below applies where—
  (a) a person has benefited from an amount of credit to which he was entitled under this Part; and
  (b) he is entitled to a payment under regulation 20 in respect of a later accounting period in the same contribution year as the accounting period in respect of which that credit was claimed.

(5)   Where this paragraph applies the person shall pay to the Commissioners an amount equal to the difference between—
  (a) the aggregate of—
     (i) the amount of the credit from which he has benefited, and
     (ii) any other amounts of credit arising under this Part which he is or was entitled to claim,
    in respect of that contribution year; and
  (b) the amount of credit which he would have been entitled to claim if he had in fact claimed the aggregate amount mentioned in sub-paragraph (a) above in the return for the accounting period in respect of which he was entitled to the payment under regulation 20.

(6)   Where—
  (a) a person has benefited from an amount of credit to which he was entitled under this Part;
  (b) he acquires an asset from a body to which he has made a qualifying contribution for—

(i) no consideration, or
(ii) a consideration which is less than the open market value of the asset,

he shall pay to the Commissioners an amount equal to 90 per cent of the amount by which the open market value exceeds the consideration; but this is subject to paragraph (7) below.

(7)   A person required to pay an amount to the Commissioners by paragraph (6) above—
    (a) shall not be required to pay more than the total amount of relevant credit;
    (b) shall not be entitled to claim any further amounts of credit in respect of qualifying contributions made by him to the body in question on or after the date on which he acquired the asset.

(8)   For the purposes of paragraphs (6) and (7) above—
    (a) "asset" includes land, goods or services and any interest in any of these;
    (b) the open market value of an asset is the amount of the consideration in money that would be payable for the asset by a person standing in no such relationship with any person as would affect that consideration;
    (c) "relevant credit" means credit arising under this Part—
        (i) from which a person has benefited, and
        (ii) which has arisen in respect of qualifying contributions made by him to the body in question or treated by virtue of regulation 32(3) as having been received by that body from him.

[1200]

PART VIII
LANDFILL INVOICES

37 Contents of a landfill invoice

(1)   An invoice is a landfill invoice if it contains the following information—
    (a) an identifying number;
    (b) the date of its issue;
    (c) the date of the disposal or disposals in respect of which it is issued or, where a series of disposals is made for the same person, the dates between which the disposals were made;
    (d) the name, address and registration number of the person issuing it;
    (e) the name and address of the person to whom it is issued;
    (f) the weight of the material disposed of;
    (g) a description of the material disposed of;
    (h) the rate of tax chargeable in relation to the disposal or, if the invoice relates to more than one disposal and the rate of tax for each of them is not the same, the rate of tax chargeable for each disposal;
    (i) the total amount payable for which the invoice is issued; and
    (j) where the amount of tax is shown separately, a statement confirming that that tax may not be treated as the input tax of any person.

(2)   In paragraph (1)(j) above "input tax" has the same meaning as in section 24(1) of the Value Added Tax Act 1994.

[1201]

PART IX
TEMPORARY DISPOSALS

38 Scope and effect

(1)   A disposal to which this Part applies—
    (a) shall not be treated as made at the time when apart from this Part it would be regarded as made; and

    (b) shall be treated as having been made—
        (i) when it is treated as being an exempt disposal by virtue of regulation 39, or
       (ii) to the extent that it is not so treated, at the time when it is treated as having been made by virtue of regulation 40.

(2)   This Part applies to a disposal where—
    (a) an authorised person has designated an area (the designated area) for the purpose of this Part;
    (b) material is disposed of in the designated area at a time when the designation has effect;
    (c) the disposal is a temporary one pending all of the material being put to a qualifying use within the relevant period; and
    (d) such other conditions as the Commissioners or an authorised person may specify for the purpose of this Part, whether generally or with regard to particular cases, are satisfied.

(3)   A designation ceases to have effect if—
    (a) notice to that effect is given in writing by the Commissioners or by an authorised person;
    (b) any period for which the designation was to have effect by virtue of a condition specified in relation thereto expires;
    (c) any disposal to which this Part does not apply (whether because it is not temporary or for some other reason) is made in the designated area; or
    (d) a disposal is treated by virtue of regulation 40 as having been made at a certain time and all of the material comprised in that disposal is not removed from the designated area within seven days of that time.

(4)   A use is a qualifying use if thereby the material is—
    (a) recycled or incinerated;
    (b) used (other than by way of a further disposal) at a place other than a relevant site; or
    (c) sorted pending—
        (i) its use at a place other than a relevant site, or
       (ii) its disposal,
    being a use or disposal, as the case may be, within the relevant period.

(5)   For the purposes of paragraph (4) above—
    (a) a use is not a qualifying use if it would constitute a breach of any condition relating to the use of the material to be disposed of which has been specified in relation to that designated area or generally;
    (b) a relevant site is the landfill site at which the disposal was made or any other landfill site;
    (c) the relevant period is the period of one year commencing with the date of the disposal or such other period as the Commissioners or an authorised person may approve or direct.

                                                          [1202]

39 Disposals to be treated as exempt

(1)   Where there is a disposal to which this Part applies and—
    (a) the material comprised in the disposal has been put to a qualifying use within the relevant period, if it would otherwise be a taxable disposal that disposal shall be treated as not being a taxable disposal (shall be treated as being an exempt disposal); but this is subject to paragraph (2) below;
    (b) some of the material comprised in a disposal has been put to a qualifying use within the relevant period (and some has not), the disposal shall be treated as being an exempt disposal to the extent of the part so dealt with and the remaining part shall be treated in accordance with regulation 40.

(2)   A disposal shall not be treated as being an exempt disposal unless the landfill site operator concerned has made and, in relation to that disposal, maintained the record specified in paragraph (3) below (the temporary disposal record).

(3)   The temporary disposal record mentioned in paragraph (2) above is a record, in relation to the designated area, of—
    (a) the weight and description of all material disposed of;
    (b) the intended destination of all such material and, where any material has been removed, the actual destination of that material; and
    (c) the weight and description of any material removed.

[1203]

40 Disposals to be treated as made at certain times

(1)   Where in the case of a disposal to which this Part applies the disposal is not wholly treated as being an exempt disposal it shall, to the extent that it is not so treated, be treated as having been made at the earliest of the following times—
    (a) when the relevant period has expired;
    (b) when the designation ceases to have effect;
    (c) when there has been a breach of any condition specified by the Commissioners or an authorised person;
    (d) when there has been a failure to make the temporary disposal record;
    (e) when there has been a failure to maintain the temporary disposal record;
    (f) when any of the material concerned is used (other than by way of a further disposal) at the same or another landfill site (but not in the same designated area).

(2)   The reference in paragraph (1)(e) above to a failure to maintain the temporary disposal record is a reference to an omission to enter in a record that has been made the information specified in regulation 39(3) in relation to any disposal made after the record was made.

[1204]

PART X
DETERMINATION OF WEIGHT OF MATERIAL DISPOSED OF

41 Scope

This Part applies for the purpose of determining the weight of material comprised in a disposal; and references in this Part to weight shall be construed as references to the weight of such material.

[1205]

42 Basic method

(1)   Except where regulation 43 or 44 applies and subject to paragraph (2) below, a registrable person shall determine weight by weighing the material concerned.

(2)   The weighing of the material shall be carried out at the time of the disposal; and for this purpose any time at which section 61 of the Act or Part IX of these Regulations require the disposal to be treated as made shall be disregarded.

[1206]

43 Specified methods

(1)   Except where regulation 44 applies, this regulation applies where the Commissioners have specified rules for determining weight in a notice published by them and not withdrawn by a further notice.

(2)   A specification made by the Commissioners as described in paragraph (1) above may make provision for—

   (a) the method by which weight is to be determined;

   (b) the time by reference to which weight is to be determined.

(3)   A specification made by the Commissioners as described in paragraph (1) above may provide—

   (a) that it is to have effect only in relation to disposals of such descriptions as may be set out in the specification;

   (b) that it is not to have effect in relation to particular disposals unless the Commissioners are satisfied that such conditions as may be set out in the specification are met in relation to the disposals.

(4)   Where this regulation applies the registrable person shall determine weight in accordance with the rules in the specification (and not in accordance with the rule in regulation 42).

[1207]

44 Agreed methods

(1)   This regulation applies where—

   (a) the registrable person and an authorised person have agreed in writing that weight shall be determined in accordance with rules other than those described in regulation 42 or specified under regulation 43; and

   (b) a direction under paragraph (3) below has not been made.

(2)   Rules may be agreed under this regulation as regards—

   (a) the method by which weight is to be determined;

   (b) the time by reference to which weight is to be determined;

   (c) the discounting of water forming a constituent of material disposed of, but this is subject to paragraph (5) below.

(3)   Where rules have been agreed under this regulation and the Commissioners believe that they should no longer be applied because they do not give an accurate indication of the weight or they are not being fully observed or for some other reason they may direct that the agreed rules shall no longer have effect.

(4)   Where this regulation applies the registrable person shall determine weight in accordance with the rules agreed (and not in accordance with the rule in regulation 42 or 43).

(5)   Subject to paragraphs (6) to (8) below, rules may be agreed regarding the discounting of water if, and only if—

   (a) no water is present in the material naturally and the water is present because—

      (i) it has been added for the purpose of enabling the material to be transported for disposal;

      (ii) it has been used for the purpose of extracting any mineral; or

      (iii) it has arisen, or has been added, in the course of an industrial process; or

   (b) the material is the residue from the treatment of effluent or sewage by a water treatment works.

(6)   Rules may not be agreed under paragraph (5) above where any of the material is capable of escaping from the landfill site concerned by leaching unless—

   (a) it is likely to do so in the form of water only; or

   (b) the leachate is to be collected on the site concerned and treated in order to eliminate any potential it has to cause harm.

(7)   Where the material falls within paragraph (5)(a) above rules may not be agreed under paragraph (5) above unless the total water which has been added, or (in

a case falling within paragraph (5)(a)(iii) above) has arisen or has been added or both, constitutes 25 per cent or more of the weight at the time of the disposal.

(8)   Where the material falls within paragraph (5)(b) above rules may not be agreed under paragraph (5) above except for the discounting of water which has been added prior to disposal (and not of water which is present in the material naturally).

(9)   For the purposes of paragraph (8) above any water which has been extracted prior to disposal shall be deemed to be water that has been added, except that where the water extracted exceeds the quantity of water added that excess shall be deemed to have been present naturally.

[1208]

PART XI
SET-OFF OF AMOUNTS

45 Landfill tax amount owed to Commissioners

(1)   Subject to regulation 47, this regulation applies where—
   (a) a person is under a duty to pay to the Commissioners at any time an amount or amounts in respect of landfill tax; and
   (b) the Commissioners are under a duty to pay to that person at the same time an amount or amounts in respect of any tax or taxes under their care and management.

(2)   Where the total of the amount or amounts mentioned in paragraph (1)(a) above exceeds the total of the amount or amounts mentioned in paragraph (1)(b) above, the latter shall be set off against the former.

(3)   Where the total of the amount or amounts mentioned in paragraph (1)(b) above exceeds the total of the amount or amounts mentioned in paragraph(1)(a) above, the Commissioners may set off the latter in paying the former.

(4)   Where the total of the amount or amounts mentioned in paragraph (1)(a) above is the same as the total of the amount or amounts mentioned in paragraph (1)(b) above, no payment need be made in respect of either.

(5)   Where this regulation applies and an amount has been set off in accordance with any of paragraphs (2) to (4) above, the duty of both the person and the Commissioners to pay the amount or amounts concerned shall be treated as having been discharged accordingly.

(6)   References in paragraph (1) above to an amount in respect of a particular tax include references not only to an amount of tax itself but also to amounts of penalty, surcharge or interest.

(7)   In this regulation "tax" includes "duty".

[1209]

46 Landfill tax amount owed by Commissioners

(1)   Subject to regulation 47, this regulation applies where—
   (a) a person is under a duty to pay to the Commissioners at any time an amount or amounts in respect of any tax or taxes under their care and management; and
   (b) the Commissioners are under a duty to pay to that person at the same time an amount or amounts in respect of landfill tax.

(2)   Where the total of the amount or amounts mentioned in paragraph (1)(a) above exceeds the total of the amount or amounts mentioned in paragraph (1)(b) above, the latter shall be set off against the former.

(3)   Where the total of the amount or amounts mentioned in paragraph (1)(b) above exceeds the total of the amount or amounts mentioned in paragraph (1)(a) above, the Commissioners may set off the latter in paying the former.

(4)   Where the total of the amount or amounts mentioned in paragraph (1)(a) above is the same as the total of the amount or amounts mentioned in paragraph (1)(b) above, no payment need be made in respect of either.

(5)   Where this regulation applies and an amount has been set off in accordance with any of paragraphs (2) to (4) above, the duty of both the person and the Commissioners to pay the amount or amounts concerned shall be treated as having been discharged accordingly.

(6)   Paragraphs (6) and (7) of regulation 45 shall apply in relation to this regulation as they apply in relation to that regulation.

[1210]

47 No set-off where insolvency procedure applied

(1)   Neither regulation 45 nor 46 shall require any such amount as is mentioned in paragraph (1)(b) of those regulations (in either case, "the credit") to be set against any such sum as is mentioned in paragraph (1)(a) of those regulations (in either case, "the debit") in any case where—
    (a) an insolvency procedure has been applied to the person entitled to the credit;
    (b) the credit became due after that procedure was so applied;
    (c) the liability to pay the debit either arose before that procedure was so applied or (having risen afterwards) relates to, or to matters occurring in the course of—
        (i) the carrying on of any business; or
        (ii) in the case of any sum such as is mentioned in regulation 46(1)(b), the carrying out of taxable activities,
    at times before the procedure was so applied.

(2)   Subject to paragraph (3) below, the following are the times when an insolvency procedure is to be taken, for the purposes of this regulation, to have been applied to any person, that is to say—
    (a) when a bankruptcy order, winding-up order, administration order or award of sequestration is made in relation to that person;
    (b) when that person is put into administrative receivership;
    (c) when that person, being a corporation, passes a resolution for voluntary winding-up;
    (d) when any voluntary arrangement approved in accordance with Part I or Part VIII of the Insolvency Act 1986, or Part II or Chapter II of Part VIII of the Insolvency (Northern Ireland) Order 1989, comes into force in relation to that person;
    (e) when a deed of arrangement registered in accordance with the Deeds of Arrangement Act 1914 or Chapter I of Part VIII of that Order of 1989 takes effect in relation to that person;
    (f) when that person's estate becomes vested in any other person as that person's trustee under a trust deed.

(3)   References in this regulation, in relation to any person, to the application of an insolvency procedure to that person shall not include—
    (a) the making of a bankruptcy order, winding-up order, administration order or award of sequestration at a time when any such arrangements or deed as is mentioned in paragraph (2)(d) to (f) above is in force in relation to that person;
    (b) the making of a winding-up order at any of the following times—
        (i) immediately upon the discharge of an administration order made in relation to that person;

    (ii) when that person is being wound-up voluntarily;
    (iii) when that person is in administrative receivership; or
  (c) the making of an administration order in relation to that person at any time when that person is in administrative receivership.

(4) For the purposes of this regulation a person shall be regarded as being in administrative receivership throughout any continuous period for which (disregarding any temporary vacancy in the office of receiver) there is an administrative receiver of that person, and the reference in paragraph (2) above to a person being put into administrative receivership shall be construed accordingly.

[1211]

PART XII
DISTRESS AND DILIGENCE

[**A48** In this Part—
    "Job Band" followed by a number between "1" and "12" means the band for the purposes of pay and grading in which the job an officer performs is ranked in the system applicable to Customs and Excise.]

[1212]

NOTES

Inserted by the Landfill Tax (Amendment) Regulations 1996, SI 1996/2100, reg 3.

48 (*Revoked by the Distress for Customs and Excise Duties and Other Indirect Taxes Regulations 1997, SI 1997/1431, reg 3(1), Sch 3.*)

49 Diligence

In Scotland the following provisions shall have effect—
  (a) where the Commissioners are empowered to apply to the sheriff for a warrant to authorise a sheriff officer to recover any amount of tax or sum recoverable as if it were tax remaining due and unpaid, any application, and any certificate required to accompany that application, may be made on their behalf by a Collector or an officer of rank not below that of Higher Executive Officer;
  (b) where during the course of a poinding and sale in accordance with Schedule 5 to the Debtors (Scotland) Act 1987 the Commissioners are entitled as a creditor to do any act, then any such act, with the exception of the exercise of the power contained in paragraph 18(3) of that Schedule, may be done on their behalf by a Collector or an officer of rank not below that of Higher Executive Officer.

[1213]

LANDFILL TAX (QUALIFYING MATERIAL) ORDER 1996

(SI 1996/1528)

NOTES

Made: 12 June 1996.
Commencement: 1 October 1996.
Authority: Finance Act 1996, ss 42(3), 63(5), (6).

1 This Order may be cited as the Landfill Tax (Qualifying Material) Order 1996 and shall come into force on 1st October 1996.

[1214]

2   Subject to articles 3 to 5 below, the material listed in column 2 of the Schedule to this Order is qualifying material for the purpose of section 42 of the Act.

[1215]

3   The Schedule to this Order shall be construed in accordance with the notes contained in it.

[1216]

4   The material listed in column 2 of the Schedule to this Order must not be treated as qualifying material unless any condition set out alongside the description of the material in column 3 of that Schedule is satisfied.

[1217]

5   Where the owner of the material immediately prior to the disposal and the operator of the landfill site at which the disposal is made are not the same person, material must not be treated as qualifying material unless it satisfies the relevant condition.

[1218]

6   In the case of a disposal at a landfill site in Great Britain, the relevant condition is that a transfer note includes in relation to each type of material of which the disposal consists—
   (a) a description of the material—
       (i)   which accords with its description in column 2 of the Schedule to this Order, or
       (ii) where a note contained in that Schedule lists the material (other than by way of exclusion), which accords with that description, or
       (iii) which is some other accurate description; or
   (b) where the material is water within Group 9 of the Schedule to this Order—
       (i)   the description "water", and
       (ii) a description of the material held in suspension which, if that material had been disposed of separately, would comply with the requirements of paragraph (a) above.

[1219]

7   In the case of a disposal at a landfill site in Northern Ireland, the relevant condition is that any document produced to evidence the transfer of the material includes, in relation to each type of material of which the disposal consists, a description of that material as specified in paragraph (a) or, as the case may be, paragraph (b) of article 6 above.

[1220]

8   In article 6 above "transfer note" has the same meaning as in the Environmental Protection (Duty of Care) Regulations 1991.

[1221]

SCHEDULE

Article 2

Column 1	Column 2	Column 3
Group	Description of material	Conditions
Group 1	Rocks and soils	Naturally occurring
Group 2	Ceramic or concrete materials	
Group 3	Minerals	Processed or prepared, not used
Group 4	Furnace slags	

Column 1	Column 2	Column 3
Group 5	Ash	
Group 6	Low activity inorganic compounds	
Group 7	Calcium sulphate	Disposed of either at site not licensed to take putrescible waste or in containment cell which takes only calcium sulphate
Group 8	Calcium hydroxide and brine	Deposited in brine cavity
Group 9	Water	Containing other qualifying material in suspension

Notes:

(1) Group 1 includes clay, sand, gravel, sandstone, limestone, crushed stone, china clay, construction stone, stone from the demolition of buildings or structures, slate, topsoil, peat, silt and dredgings.

(2) Group 2 comprises only the following—
  (a) glass;
  (b) ceramics;
  (c) concrete.

(3) For the purposes of Note (2) above—
  (a) glass includes fritted enamel, but excludes glass fibre and glass-reinforced plastic;
  (b) ceramics includes bricks, bricks and mortar, tiles, clay ware, pottery, china and refractories;
  (c) concrete includes reinforced concrete, concrete blocks, breeze blocks and aircrete blocks, but excludes concrete plant washings.

(4) Group 3 comprises only the following—
  (a) moulding sands;
  (b) clays;
  (c) mineral absorbents;
  (d) man-made mineral fibres;
  (e) silica;
  (f) mica;
  (g) mineral abrasives.

(5) For the purposes of Note (4) above—
  (a) moulding sands excludes sands containing organic binders;
  (b) clays includes moulding clays and clay absorbents, including Fuller's earth and bentonite;
  (c) man-made mineral fibres includes glass fibres, but excludes glass-reinforced plastic and asbestos.

(6) Group 4 includes—
  (a) vitrified wastes and residues from thermal processing of minerals where, in either case, the residue is both fused and insoluble;
  (b) slag from waste incineration.

(7) Group 5—
  (a) comprises only bottom ash and fly ash from wood, coal or waste combustion; and
  (b) excludes fly ash from municipal, clinical and hazardous waste incinerators and sewage sludge incinerators.

(8) Group 6 comprises only titanium dioxide, calcium carbonate, magnesium carbonate, magnesium oxide, magnesium hydroxide, iron oxide, ferric hydroxide, aluminium oxide, aluminium hydroxide and zirconium dioxide.

(9) Group 7 includes gypsum and calcium sulphate based plasters, but excludes plasterboard.

PRODUCER RESPONSIBILITY OBLIGATIONS (PACKAGING WASTE) REGULATIONS 1997

(SI 1997/648)

NOTES

Made: 5 March 1997.
Commencement: 6 March 1997.
Authority: Environment Act 1995, ss 93, 94, 95.
These Regulations implement European Parliament and Council Directive 94/62/EEC on packaging and packaging waste, Art 6(1) (not reproduced in this work).

ARRANGEMENT OF REGULATIONS

PART I
GENERAL

PART II
PRODUCERS AND OBLIGATIONS

PART III
REGISTRATION

PART IV
REGISTRATION OF SCHEMES—APPEALS

PART V
RECORDS, RETURNS AND CERTIFICATE

PART VI
AGENCIES' POWERS AND DUTIES

PART I
GENERAL

1   Citation and commencement

These Regulations may be cited as the Producer Responsibility Obligations
(Packaging Waste) Regulations 1997 and shall come into force on the day after the
day on which they are made.

[1223]

2   Interpretation and notices

(1)   In these Regulations—
   "the Act" means the Environment Act 1995;
   "the 1990 Act" means the Environmental Protection Act 1990;
   "the Director" means the Director General of Fair Trading;
   "energy recovery" means the use of combustible packaging waste as a means to
      generate energy through direct incineration with or without other waste but
      with recovery of the heat;

"organic recycling" means the aerobic (composting) or anaerobic (biomethanization) treatment, under controlled conditions and using micro-organisms, of the biodegradable parts of packaging waste, which produces stabilized organic residues or methane; for the purposes of these Regulations landfill shall not be considered a form of organic recycling;

"packaging" means all products made of any materials of any nature to be used for the containment, protection, handling, delivery and presentation of goods, from raw materials to processed goods, from the producer to the user or the consumer, including non-returnable items used for the same purposes but only where the products are—

(a) sales packaging or primary packaging, that is to say packaging conceived so as to constitute a sales unit to the final user or consumer at the point of purchase;

(b) grouped packaging or secondary packaging, that is to say packaging conceived so as to constitute at the point of purchase a grouping of a certain number of sales units whether the latter is sold as such to the final user or consumer or whether it serves only as a means to replenish the shelves at the point of sale; it can be removed from the product without affecting its characteristics; or

(c) transport packaging or tertiary packaging, that is to say packaging conceived so as to facilitate handling and transport of a number of sales units or grouped packagings in order to prevent physical handling and transport damage; for the purposes of these Regulations transport packaging does not include road, rail, ship and air containers;

"packaging materials" means materials used in the manufacture of packaging and includes raw materials and processed materials prior to their conversion into packaging;

"packaging waste" means any packaging or packaging material covered by the definition of waste in article 1 of Directive 75/442 EC ("the Waste Directive") which, together with Annex 1 to that Directive, is reproduced in Part I of Schedule 3 to these Regulations, other than production residues and, by virtue of article 2(1)(b)(i) of the Waste Directive, radioactive waste;

"preceding year" has the meaning given in regulation 3;

"producer" has the meaning given in regulation 3 and the classes of producer are those set out in column 4 of the Table in Schedule 1;

"producer responsibility obligations" are the producer registration, recovery and recycling, and certifying obligations specified in regulation 3;

"recovery" means any of the applicable operations provided for in Annex IIB to the Waste Directive, reproduced in Part II of Schedule 3;

"recycling" means the reprocessing in a production process of the waste materials for the original purpose or for other purposes including organic recycling but excluding energy recovery;

"relevant year" has the meaning given in regulation 3;

"reprocessor" means a person who, in the ordinary course of conduct of a trade, occupation or profession, carries out the activities of recovery or recycling;

"reuse" means any operation by which packaging, which has been conceived and designed to accomplish within its life cycle a minimum number of trips or rotations, is refilled or used for the same purpose for which it was conceived, with or without the support of auxiliary products present on the market enabling the packaging to be refilled; such reused packaging will become packaging waste when no longer subject to reuse;

"scheme" means a scheme which is (or, if it were to be registered in accordance with these Regulations would be) a scheme whose members for the time being are, by virtue of these Regulations and their membership of that scheme, exempt from the requirement to comply with their producer responsibility obligations and "registered scheme" means a scheme which is registered with the appropriate Agency in accordance with these Regulations;

"transit packaging" means—

    (a) grouped packaging or secondary packaging, as defined in paragraph (b) of the definition of packaging in this regulation; or

    (b) transport packaging or tertiary packaging as defined in paragraph (c) of that definition of packaging; and

"year" means a calendar year beginning on 1st January.

(2)   Where notices are to be served on a producer under regulations 6(6), 10, and 11(3), information is to be provided by a producer under regulations 7 and 8, fees are to be paid by a producer under regulation 9(2), and records and returns are to be maintained and furnished by a producer under regulation 22, they shall be served on, provided, paid, or maintained and furnished, by—

    (a) in the case of a partnership with a principal place of business in England and Wales, the partner notified under regulation 6(4)(e), or in accordance with the undertaking referred to in regulation 7(a)(ii), or

    (b) in the case of a partnership with a principal place of business in Scotland, by a partner acting on behalf of the partnership,

and references in these Regulations to the producer shall be read accordingly.

(3)   Where the operator of a scheme is a partnership, or where this is not the case but there is more than one operator of a scheme—

    (a) notices to be served on the operator of the scheme under regulations 12(6), 16, 17(3), 31(5) and (10), shall be served on the partner or operator, respectively, notified under regulation 12(3)(h), or in accordance with the condition referred to in regulation 13(d)(ii); and

    (b) where information is to be provided by the operator of the scheme under regulations 13 and 14, fees are to be paid by the operator of the scheme under regulation 15(3), records and returns are to be maintained and furnished by the operator of the scheme under regulation 24, and appeals may be made by the operator of the scheme under regulation 18, they shall be provided, paid, or maintained and furnished, and such appeals may only be made, by the partner or operator, respectively, notified under regulation 12(3)(h), or in accordance with the condition referred to in regulation 13(d)(ii),

and references in these Regulations to the operator of the scheme shall be read accordingly.

[1224]

PART II
PRODUCERS AND OBLIGATIONS

3 Producers and producer responsibility obligations

(1)   This regulation is subject to regulations 4, 29 and 30.

(2)   In respect of a year a person is a producer of a class specified in an entry in column 4 of the Table set out in Schedule 1 if—

    (a) in that year and the preceding year he performs the relevant functions of the class of producer specified in Column 1 of that Table in relation to that entry;

    (b) in the preceding year he made supplies of the materials or products specified in Column 2 of that Table in relation to that entry of a class in Column 3 of that Table in relation to that entry; and

    (c) in relation to that year he satisfies the threshold tests as provided by paragraph 3 of that Schedule,

and the other provisions of that Schedule shall also have effect for the purposes of determining whether a person is a producer of any class.

(3)   Where in respect of a year a person is a producer and satisfies the provisions of Columns 1 to 3 of the Table in Schedule 1 in relation to more than one class of producer specified in an entry in Column 4 of that Table, whether or not in relation to the same materials or products specified in Column 2 of that Table, or the same transaction or process, for that year that person belongs to each such class.

(4)   For the purposes of these Regulations—

    (a) "relevant year" is the year referred to in paragraph (2) above, that is to say a year in respect of which a person is a producer; and

    (b) "preceding year" is the year immediately preceding a relevant year.

(5)   A person who is a producer in respect of a year has producer responsibility obligations in respect of that year, that is to say he shall—

    (a) be registered as provided in regulation 5 (in these Regulations referred to as the "producer registration obligation"); and

    (b) for the year 1998 and subsequent years—

        (i) take reasonable steps to recover and recycle packaging waste (in these Regulations referred to as the "recovery and recycling obligations") in relation to each of the classes of producer to which the producer belongs, calculated as provided in Schedule 2, and

        (ii) furnish a certificate of compliance in respect of his recovery and recycling obligations in accordance with regulation 23 (in these Regulations referred to as the "certifying obligation").

(6)   The recovery and recycling obligations of producers are to enable the United Kingdom to attain the recovery and recycling targets for Member States set out in article 6(1) of Directive 94/62/EC and those targets are set out in Schedule 10.

[1225]

4   Exclusions and limitations

(1)   Where a producer is a member of a registered scheme throughout a relevant year—

    (a) the producer is exempt from complying with his producer responsibility obligations for the relevant year; and

    (b) the recovery and recycling obligations with which, but for his membership of the scheme, the producer would have had to comply in relation to the relevant year shall be performed through the scheme.

(2)   These Regulations do not apply to a charity within the meaning given in section 506 of the Income and Corporation Taxes Act 1988.

(3)   The producer responsibility obligations of the producer class of wholesaler apply only in respect of the year 2000 and subsequent years.

(4)   A special producer as defined in Part III of Schedule 3 shall have producer responsibility obligations as provided in Part IV of that Schedule and shall provide records and returns to the appropriate Agency in accordance with Part V of that Schedule.

[1226]

PART III
REGISTRATION

5   Producer registration obligation

Subject to regulations 4(3) and (4), 29 and 30, a producer shall be registered with an appropriate Agency in respect of a relevant year, or any part of that year, during which he is not a member of a registered scheme.

[1227]

6   Application for producer registration

(1)   Subject to paragraph (3) below, a producer who is required by regulation 5 to be registered and who is not registered shall, on or before 1st April in a relevant year, make an application for producer registration to the appropriate Agency, being—

    (a) the Agency, where at the beginning of the relevant year the applicant's registered office or principal place of business is in England or Wales;

    (b) SEPA, where at the beginning of the relevant year the applicant's registered office or principal place of business is in Scotland; or

    (c) either the Agency or SEPA where at the beginning of the relevant year the applicant does not have a registered office or principal place of business in Great Britain.

(2)   Where the producer is a partnership, where the principal place of business of the partnership is in England or Wales, the application shall be made by all the partners, and where the principal place of business of the partnership is in Scotland, the application shall be made by any partner acting on behalf of the partnership.

(3)   Where—

    (a) the relevant year is the year 1997, the application for registration shall be made on or before 31st August 1997; or

    (b) any of the following occurs in a relevant year—

        (i) the application for registration of a scheme of which the applicant was a member is refused,

        (ii) the registration of a scheme of which the applicant was a member is cancelled,

        (iii) the applicant's membership of a scheme is discontinued,

        (iv) the applicant becomes a producer in respect of that year, or

        (v) an application to register made within the time limit in paragraph (1) or sub-paragraph (a), above, is refused,

    an application for registration shall be made within 28 days of the occurrence.

(4)   An application for producer registration shall—

    (a) be made in writing;

    (b) contain the initial information set out in Part I of Schedule 4;

    (c) subject to paragraphs (7) and (8) below, be accompanied by the further information specified in, and provided on a form corresponding to, the form set out in Part II of Schedule 4, or provided on a form substantially to that effect;

    (d) be accompanied by the fee referred to in regulation 9; and

    (e) where the applicant is a partnership whose principal place of business is in England and Wales, be accompanied by a statement as to which partner is able to accept notices and act on behalf of the partnership as provided in regulation 2(2).

(5)   An application for producer registration shall be granted where—

    (a) the producer has complied with paragraph (4)(a), (b), (d) and (e) above and, where applicable, paragraph (8) below;

    (b) the Agency is satisfied that the information provided in accordance with paragraph (4)(c) above, or (8) below, has been provided in accordance with paragraph (7) below; and

    (c) the producer has given the undertakings referred to in regulation 7, which have been required by the appropriate Agency;

and shall otherwise be refused.

(6)   Where an application for producer registration is granted—

    (a) the appropriate Agency shall, within 28 days of it being granted confirm to the producer in writing that he is registered with it; and

    (b) the producer shall be treated as having been registered from the beginning of the relevant year or, where the producer has applied to be registered for part of a year, from the date specified in the confirmation, until any cancellation of the producer's registration in accordance with regulation 11.

(7)   The further information shall—
    (a) where the application for registration, or compliance with regulation 8, is in respect of any of the years 1997, 1998 or 1999, be provided using the producer's reasonable estimates of the information required; and
    (b) where the application for registration, or compliance with regulation 8, is in respect of the year 2000 or any subsequent year, the information provided shall be as accurate as reasonably possible.

(8)   Where the application to register is made in one of the circumstances set out in paragraph (3)(b) above, the further information referred to in paragraph (4)(c) above need not accompany the application but shall be provided within 56 days of the application being made.

[1228]

7 Requirements for producer registration

As requirements for producer registration the appropriate Agency may require the applicant to undertake that he will—
    (a) inform the appropriate Agency of—
        (i) any change in the circumstances of the producer which relate to the registration of the producer, and where the producer is a partnership, any change of partners;
        (ii) any change in the person who is the partner who is able to accept notices and act on behalf of the partnership as stated as required in regulation 6(4)(e);
      (iii) any material change in the initial information provided in accordance with regulation 6(4)(b), or
      (iv) any material change in the further information provided in accordance with regulation 6(4)(c), or (8), as the case may be, or regulation 8, within 28 days of the occurrence of any such change;
    (b) comply with the requirements of regulation 8;
    (c) provide records and returns to the appropriate Agency as required by regulation 22; and
    (d) apply to the appropriate Agency to cancel his registration where he has become a member of a registered scheme or has ceased to be a producer in respect of a year.

[1229]

8 Continuation of producer registration

On or before 1st April in a relevant year a producer who is registered shall provide to the appropriate Agency—
    (a) in accordance with regulation 6(7), the further information referred to in regulation 6(4)(c); and
    (b) the fee referred to in regulation 9.

[1230]

9 Forms and fees for producer registration

(1)   The appropriate Agency shall provide a copy of any form referred to in regulation 6 free of charge to any person requesting one.

(2)   The fee which is to be charged by an appropriate Agency on an application for producer registration or continuation of producer registration is £750.

[1231]

10 Refusal to register producers

Any decision of the appropriate Agency under regulation 6(5) to refuse to register a producer shall be notified within 28 days of the decision to the producer in writing together with the reasons for the decision and a statement as to the offence specified in regulation 34(1)(a).

[1232]

11 Cancellation of registration of producers

(1) An appropriate Agency may cancel the registration with it of a producer where—
   (a) the information or the fee required by regulation 8 are not provided;
   (b) it appears to the appropriate Agency that—
      (i) the producer is in breach of any of the undertakings referred to in regulation 7 and given by him to that Agency,
      (ii) the producer knowingly supplied false information in connection with his application for registration, or with compliance with any undertaking referred to in regulation 7, or with regulation 8; or
      (iii) information provided pursuant to regulation 8 was not provided in accordance with regulation 6(7).

(2) An appropriate Agency shall cancel the registration with it of a producer where it is notified that the producer has become a member of a registered scheme or has otherwise ceased to be subject to the producer registration obligation in respect of a year.

(3) Before cancellation of a registration under paragraphs (1) or (2) above, an appropriate Agency shall serve on the producer concerned written notice of—
   (a) its decision to cancel;
   (b) the reasons for the decision; and
   (c) the date when cancellation will take effect, not being earlier than—
      (i) in the case of cancellation under paragraph (1) above, 28 days from the date of the notice, and
      (ii) in the case of cancellation under paragraph (2) above, 5 days from the date of the notice.

[1233]

12 Application for registration of a scheme

(1) Subject to paragraph (8) below, an application for registration of a scheme in relation to a year shall be made by the operator of the scheme, on or before 1st April in the year, to the appropriate Agency, being—
   (a) the Agency, where at the date of the application the registered office or principal place of business of the operator of the scheme is in England or Wales;
   (b) SEPA, where at the date of the application the registered office or principal place of business of the operator of the scheme is in Scotland; or
   (c) either the Agency or SEPA, where at the date of the application the operator of the scheme does not have a registered office or principal place of business in Great Britain, or there is more than one operator of the scheme and such operators have registered offices or principal places of business in England and Wales, and in Scotland.

(2) Where the operator of the scheme is a partnership the application for registration shall, where at the date of the application the principal place of business of the partnership is in England and Wales, be made by all the partners, and where at that date the principal place of business of the partnership is in Scotland, be made by any partner acting on behalf of the partnership.

(3)   An application for registration of a scheme shall—
   (a) be made in writing;
   (b) contain the initial information set out in Part III of Schedule 4;
   (c) subject to paragraph (7) below, be accompanied by the further information specified in, and provided on a form corresponding to, the form set out in Part II of Schedule 4, or provided on a form substantially to that effect, for each class of producer, and aggregating the information in relation to all of the scheme's members who belong to that class;
   (d) be accompanied by a published statement as provided in Part IV of Schedule 4;
   (e) be accompanied by an operational plan for the scheme as provided in Part IV of Schedule 4;
   (f) be accompanied by an undertaking by the operator of the scheme that the conditions referred to in regulation 13 will be complied with;
   (g) be accompanied by a fee calculated as provided in regulation 15; and
   (h) where the operator of the scheme is a partnership whose principal place of business is in England and Wales, or where there is more than one operator of the scheme, be accompanied by a statement as to which partner or operator, respectively, is able to accept notices or act on behalf of all the partners, or all the operators of the scheme, as the case may be, as provided in regulation 2(3).

(4)   A scheme shall not be registered unless it has been approved by the Secretary of State and the operator of the scheme has been notified under regulation 31(5) that it meets the requirements of competition scrutiny referred to in regulation 31, and the operator of the scheme shall supply evidence of that approval and notification to the appropriate Agency—
   (a) where such approval or notification is obtained before making the application to register the scheme, at the time of the application; or
   (b) where such approval or notification is obtained after the application to register is made, as soon as possible after receipt.

(5)   An application for registration shall be granted where—
   (a) the operator has complied with paragraphs (3)(a), (b), (d), (f), (g) and (h), and (4) above;
   (b) the appropriate Agency is satisfied that the information provided in accordance with paragraph (3)(c) above has been provided in accordance with paragraph (7) below; and
   (c) the appropriate Agency is satisfied as to the contents of the operational plan provided as required by paragraph (3) above and shall otherwise be refused.

(6)   Where an application for registration of a scheme is granted—
   (a) the appropriate Agency shall, within 28 days of it being granted confirm to the operator of the scheme in writing that the scheme is registered with it; and
   (b) the scheme shall be treated as registered from the beginning of the year of application until any cancellation of the scheme's registration in accordance with regulation 17, except that for the purposes of regulations 32 and 33 the scheme shall be treated as registered from the date of confirmation until any such cancellation.

(7)   The further information shall—
   (a) where the application for registration, or compliance with regulation 14, is in relation to any of the years 1997, 1998 or 1999 be provided using the reasonable estimates of the operator of the scheme; and
   (b) where the application for registration, or compliance with regulation 14, is in relation to the year 2000 or any subsequent year, be as accurate as reasonably possible.

(8)   Where an application for registration is made in the year 1997 the application shall be made on or before 31st August 1997.

[1234]

13   Conditions of registration of a scheme

Registration of a scheme shall be subject to the following conditions—

    (a) that the recovery and recycling obligations of all of its members referred to in regulation 4(1)(b) will be performed through the scheme;

    (b) that the operator of the scheme will provide information at the request of the appropriate Agency with regard to the obligations referred to in paragraph (a) above;

    (c) that the operator of the scheme will notify the appropriate Agency in writing at intervals as required by the Agency of any change in the membership of the scheme and that any such notification will be accompanied by the additional fee calculated as provided in regulation 15(3);

    (d) that the operator of the scheme will inform the appropriate Agency in writing of—

        (i) any change in the person who is the operator of the scheme, and in the case where the operator of the scheme is a partnership, or where there is more than one operator of a scheme, any change of partners or operators,

        (ii) any change in the person who is the partner or operator who is able to accept notices and act on behalf of the partners or operators as stated as provided in regulation 12(3)(h),

        (iii) any material change in the initial information provided in accordance with regulation 12(3)(b), or

        (iv) any material change in the further information provided in accordance with regulations 12(3)(c) or 14,

    within 28 days of the occurrence of any such change;

    (e) that the operator of the scheme will comply with the requirements of regulation 14;

    (f) that the operator of the scheme will provide records and returns to the appropriate Agency as required by regulation 24; and

    (g) that the operator of the scheme will inform the appropriate Agency in writing if the Secretary of State withdraws approval of the scheme or notifies the operator under regulation 31(10) that he has ceased to be satisfied that the scheme meets the requirements of competition scrutiny.

[1235]

14   Continuation of registration of a scheme

On or before 1st April in a relevant year and in respect of a scheme which is registered, the operator of the scheme shall provide to the appropriate Agency—

    (a) in accordance with regulation 12(7), the further information referred to in regulation 12(3)(c); and

    (b) a fee calculated as provided in regulation 15.

[1236]

15   Forms and fees for registration of a scheme

(1)   The appropriate Agency shall provide a copy of any form referred to in regulation 12 free of charge to any person requesting one.

(2)   The fee which is to be charged by an appropriate Agency on an application for registration of a scheme, and under regulation 14, is calculated as follows—

$$A \times B = F$$

where—

A   is the number of members of the scheme at the date of the application, or the date of compliance with regulation 14, whichever is applicable,

B   is an amount calculated by reference to the number of members of the scheme at that date as follows—

2 to 500 members	£600
501 to 1500 members	£450
1501 to 3000 members	£300
Over 3000 members	£100, and

F is the fee.

(3)   The fee which is to be paid by an operator of a scheme in compliance with the condition referred to in regulation 13(c) is calculated as follows—

$$A \times B = AF$$

where—

A   is the number of new members of the scheme which are the subject of the notification,

B   is the amount referred to in B in paragraph (2) above except that it is calculated by reference to the number of members of the scheme at the date of notification to the appropriate Agency, and

AF is the fee.

[1237]

16 Refusal to register a scheme

Any decision of the appropriate Agency under regulation 12(5) to refuse to register a scheme shall be notified, within 28 days of the decision, to the operator of the scheme in writing together with—

(a) the reasons for the decision;

(b) a statement as to the right of appeal under Part IV of these Regulations; and

(c) a statement as to the offence specified in regulation 34(1)(a).

[1238]

17 Cancellation of registration of a scheme

(1)   Subject to the right of appeal under Part IV of these Regulations, the appropriate Agency may cancel the registration with it of a scheme where—

(a) the information or the fee required by regulation 14 are not provided; or

(b) it appears to the appropriate Agency that—

(i)   any of the conditions referred to in regulation 13 has been broken,

(ii) the operator knowingly supplied false information in connection with the application for registration, or with compliance with the conditions referred to in regulation 13, or with regulation 14, or

(iii) information provided pursuant to regulation 14 was not provided in accordance with regulation 12(7).

(2)   An appropriate Agency shall cancel the registration with it of a scheme if the Secretary of State withdraws his approval of the scheme or gives notice under regulation 31(10) that he has ceased to be satisfied that the scheme meets the requirements of competition scrutiny.

(3)   Before the cancellation of a registration an appropriate Agency shall serve on the operator of the scheme written notice of—

(a) its decision under paragraph (1) or (2) above to cancel the registration;

(b) the reasons for the decision;

    (c) where the decision is made under paragraph (1) above, the right of appeal under Part IV of these Regulations; and

    (d) the date when cancellation will take effect, not being earlier than—

        (i) in the case of cancellation under paragraph (1) above, the expiration of the time limit for an appeal against the notice provided for in paragraph 2 of Schedule 5, or

        (ii) in the case of cancellation under paragraph (2) above, 5 days from the date of the notice.

[1239]

PART IV
REGISTRATION OF SCHEMES—APPEALS

18   Right of appeal

The operator of a scheme may appeal to the Secretary of State against a decision of the appropriate Agency—

    (a) to refuse registration under regulation 12(5), except where the refusal arises from failure to comply with regulation 12(4); or

    (b) to cancel registration under regulation 17(1).

[1240]

19   Procedure of appeals

  (1) Where an appeal is made to the Secretary of State, he may—

    (a) appoint any person to exercise on his behalf, with or without payment, the function of determination of the appeal; or

    (b) refer any matter involved in the appeal to such person as the Secretary of State may appoint for the purpose, with or without payment.

  (2) If the operator of the scheme so requests, or the Secretary of State so decides, the appeal shall be or continue in the form of a hearing (which may, if the person hearing the appeal so decides, be held or held to any extent in private).

  (3) Schedule 5 shall have effect with respect to the procedure on any such appeal.

[1241]

20   Determination of appeals

Where, on such an appeal, the Secretary of State determines that the decision of the appropriate Agency shall be altered it shall be the duty of the appropriate Agency to give effect to the determination.

[1242]

21   Status pending appeal

Where an appeal is pending in a case falling within regulation 17(1), the decision to cancel registration shall be ineffective until the appeal is disposed of; and if the appeal is dismissed or withdrawn the decision shall become effective from the end of the day on which the appeal is dismissed or withdrawn.

[1243]

PART V
RECORDS, RETURNS AND CERTIFICATE

22   Producers—records and returns

  (1) A producer who is subject to the certifying obligation shall maintain, and retain for at least 4 years after the record is made, records of the information referred

to in paragraph (2) below and shall, at the same time as he furnishes a certificate of compliance to the appropriate Agency in accordance with regulation 23, make a return to that Agency of that information.

    (2)   The information is, in respect of the year 1998 and subsequent years—
        (a) the amount in tonnes, to the nearest tonne, of packaging waste provided to a reprocessor by or on behalf of the producer;
        (b) the amount in tonnes, to the nearest tonne, of each packaging material comprised in the packaging waste referred to in sub-paragraph (a) above, received by a reprocessor from the producer or a person acting on the producer's behalf; and
        (c) the dates on which, and the name and address of the reprocessor to which, the packaging waste referred to in sub-paragraph (a) above, was so provided.

    (3)   For the purposes of paragraph (2) above, for the year 1998 and subsequent years, packaging materials means the materials mentioned in paragraph 6(1)(b) of Schedule 2.

[1244]

23 Producers—certifying obligation

    (1)   Subject to regulations 4 and 29, a producer shall furnish in accordance with this regulation a certificate of compliance to the appropriate Agency.

    (2)   A certificate of compliance shall be furnished as evidence of whether or not the producer has complied with its recovery and recycling obligations for a relevant year and shall be furnished on or before 31st January in the year immediately following the relevant year.

    (3)   The provisions of Schedule 6 shall apply as regards the information to be contained in a certificate of compliance.

[1245]

24 Schemes—records and returns

    (1)   The operator of a scheme shall maintain, and retain for at least 4 years after they are made, records of the information referred to in paragraphs (2) and (3) below, and make returns of the information referred to in paragraph (3) below to the appropriate Agency upon request.

    (2)   In respect of the year 1997 the information is, for each producer which is a member of the scheme in that year, the information referred to in regulations 12(3)(c) and 14, together with any changes notified in accordance with the condition referred to in regulation 13(d)(iv).

    (3)   In respect of the year 1998 and subsequent years the information is, in addition to the information referred to in paragraph (2) above—
        (a) the amount in tonnes, to the nearest tonne, of packaging waste provided to a reprocessor through the scheme;
        (b) the amount in tonnes, to the nearest tonne, of each packaging material comprised in the packaging waste referred to in sub-paragraph (a) above, provided to a reprocessor through the scheme; and
        (c) the dates on which, and the name and address of the reprocessor to which, the packaging waste referred to in sub-paragraph (a) above was so provided.

    (4)   For the purposes of paragraph (3) above, for the year 1998 and subsequent years packaging materials means the materials mentioned in paragraph 6(1)(b) of Schedule 2.

[1246]

PART VI
AGENCIES' POWERS & DUTIES

25 Monitoring

(1)   An appropriate Agency shall monitor in accordance with this regulation—
  (a) compliance with their producer responsibility obligations by persons who are or may be producers; and
  (b) the discharge through schemes registered with it of the obligations of their members referred to in regulation 4(1)(b).

(2)   The duty referred to in paragraph (1) above includes a duty to monitor—
  (a) the registration of producers as required by regulation 5;
  (b) the accuracy of the initial information and the further information provided by producers and referred to in regulations 6 and 8, together with any changes notified in accordance with the undertakings referred to in regulation 7(a)(iii) and (iv);
  (c) the accuracy of the returns furnished to the Agency by a producer under regulation 22 or Part V of Schedule 3;
  (d) the accuracy of the information contained in certificates of compliance furnished to the Agency under regulation 23;
  (e) the accuracy of the initial information and the further information provided by an operator of a scheme and referred to in regulations 12 and 14, together with any changes notified in accordance with the conditions referred to in regulation 13(d)(iii) and (iv); and
  (f) the accuracy of the returns provided to the Agency by an operator of a scheme under regulation 24.

[1247]

26 Public register

(1)   The appropriate Agency shall maintain and make available in accordance with this regulation a register relating to the producers and schemes registered with it in accordance with regulations 5 to 16 and containing—
  (a) the information relating to producer registration prescribed in paragraph 1 of Schedule 7; and
  (b) the information relating to registration of schemes prescribed in paragraph 2 of Schedule 7.

(2)   The appropriate Agency shall—
  (a) secure that the register is open for inspection at its principal office by members of the public free of charge at all reasonable hours; and
  (b) permit members of the public to obtain copies of entries in the register on payment of reasonable charges.

(3)   The register may be kept in any form but shall be indexed and arranged so that members of the public can readily trace information contained in it.

(4)   An appropriate Agency shall amend the relevant entry in the register to record any change to the information entered and shall note the date on which the amendment is made.

(5)   Nothing in this regulation shall require a register maintained by an appropriate Agency to contain information relating to, or to anything which is the subject-matter of, any criminal proceedings (including prospective proceedings) at any time before those proceedings are finally disposed of.

(6)   Nothing in this regulation shall require a register maintained by an appropriate Agency to contain any information which has been superseded by later information after 4 years have elapsed from that later information being entered in the register.

[1248]

27   Approval of persons to issue certificates of compliance

For the purposes of issuing certificates of compliance an appropriate Agency may approve—
  (a) where the producer is an individual, that individual;
  (b) where the producer is a partnership, a partner; or
  (c) where the producer is a company, a director of that company.

[1249]

28   Entry and inspection

(1)   A person who appears suitable to an appropriate Agency may be authorised in writing by that Agency for the purposes of its functions under these Regulations to exercise the powers of entry and inspection referred to in paragraph (2) below.

(2)   The powers of entry and inspection are those set out in section 108(4)(a) to (l) of the Act (powers of enforcing authorities and persons authorised by them) and for this purpose section 108(4) shall be read as if references to the authorised person were references to the appropriate Agency's servant or agent and as if—
  (a) the words "(or, in an emergency, at any time and, if need be, by force)" in section 108(4)(a) were omitted;
  (b) the power set out in section 108(4)(b) were omitted;
  (c) the reference to measurements in section 108(4)(e) were omitted;
  (d) the reference in section 108(4)(f) to articles or substances in relation to which samples may be taken were to records and packaging and packaging materials and as if the power in that paragraph to take samples of the air, water or land in, on, or in the vicinity of, the premises were omitted;
  (e) the power set out in section 108(4)(g) were omitted;
  (f) the reference in section 108(4)(h) to any article or substance were to any sample as is mentioned in paragraph (d) above and as if the reference to an offence in section 108(4)(h)(iii) were to an offence under regulation 34 of these Regulations;
  (g) the reference to records in section 108(4)(k)(i) were to the records and returns required to be kept and provided to the appropriate Agency under regulations 22 and 24 and Part V of Schedule 3; and
  (h) the reference to the power in section 108(1) were to the power conferred by this regulation.

(3)   The provisions of section 108(6) and (7) of the Act shall apply to the powers conferred by paragraphs (1) and (2) above as they apply to the powers conferred by section 108(4) of the Act, but as if any reference to an authorised person were to the appropriate Agency's servant or agent, and as if—
  (a) in section 108(6) and (7) the words "except in an emergency" were omitted; and
  (b) in section 108(6) the words "or to take heavy equipment on to any premises" were omitted.

(4)   The provisions of section 108(12) and (13) of the Act shall apply to the powers conferred by paragraphs (1) and (2) above as they apply to the powers conferred by section 108(4) of the Act.

(5)   The provisions of paragraphs 2 to 6 of Schedule 18 to the Act (supplemental provisions with respect to powers of entry) shall apply to the powers conferred by this regulation as they apply to the powers conferred by section 108 of the Act, but as if any reference—
  (a) to a designated person were to a person authorised in writing by an appropriate Agency to exercise on its behalf any power conferred by this regulation;
  (b) to a relevant power were to a power conferred by this regulation, including a power exercisable by virtue of a warrant under the provisions of that Schedule as applied by this paragraph;

(c) in paragraph 2(3) to subsection (6) of section 108 of the Act were to paragraph (2) of this regulation;

(d) in paragraph 4(1) to section 108(12) of the Act were to paragraph (4) of this regulation; and

(e) in paragraph 6(1) to section 108(4)(a) or (b) or (5) of the Act were to paragraph (1)(a) or (b) of this regulation.

(6)   In this regulation "warrant" means a warrant under the provisions set out in Schedule 18 to the Act as applied by paragraph (5) above.

[1250]

PART VII
GROUPS OF COMPANIES AND MID-YEAR CHANGES

29   Groups of companies

The provisions of Schedule 8 shall apply with regard to groups of companies as defined in that Schedule.

[1251]

30   Mid-year changes

The provisions of Schedule 9 shall apply with regard to changes in a year in respect of a person who is a producer in respect of that year and any change in membership of a group of companies or of a scheme by such a producer, or other event affecting a producer in the relevant year.

[1252]

PART VIII
COMPETITION SCRUTINY

31   Competition scrutiny

(1)   For the purposes of this regulation, the requirements of competition scrutiny in relation to a scheme are that—

(a) the scheme does not have, and is not likely to have, the effect of restricting, distorting or preventing competition or, where it appears to the Secretary of State that the scheme has or is likely to have any such effect, the effect is or is likely to be no greater than is necessary for achieving the environmental or economic benefits mentioned in section 93(6) of the Act; and

(b) the scheme does not lead, and is not likely to lead, to an abuse of market power.

(2)   An operator who intends to apply for registration of a scheme under regulation 12 shall apply to the Director for the purpose of competition scrutiny, and shall submit with the application the information referred to in regulation 12(3)(h) and the information set out in Part III of Schedule 4.

(3)   The Director shall advise the Secretary of State whether, in the Director's opinion, the Secretary of State may be satisfied that the scheme meets the requirements of competition scrutiny.

(4)   For the purpose of the Director's advice under paragraph (3) above or (8) below as to whether, in his opinion, a scheme may meet or no longer meets the requirements of competition scrutiny, the words "where it appears to the Director" shall be substituted for the words "where it appears to the Secretary of State" in paragraph (1)(a) above.

(5)   If, after considering the advice of the Director, the Secretary of State decides that he is satisfied that the scheme meets the requirements of competition scrutiny,

he shall give notice in writing to the appropriate Agency, and to the operator of the scheme to that effect.

(6)   The Secretary of State shall send a copy of any notice given under paragraph (5) above to the Director.

(7)   The Director shall keep under review the operation of—
   (a) any registered scheme; and
   (b) any scheme in respect of which an application for registration is pending and the Secretary of State has given notice under paragraph (5) above.

(8)   Subject to paragraph (9) below, if at any time the Director is of the opinion that any scheme whose operation he is keeping under review no longer meets the requirements of competition scrutiny, he shall advise the Secretary of State of his opinion and the reasons therefor.

(9)   Paragraph (8) above shall not require the Director to repeat advice in respect of any scheme which he has previously given under paragraphs (3) or (8) above in respect of that scheme unless there has been a material change of circumstances since the advice was given.

(10) If at any time after giving a notice under paragraph (5) above the Secretary of State decides, after considering any advice on the matter from the Director, that he has ceased to be satisfied that the scheme meets the requirements of competition scrutiny, he shall give notice to the appropriate Agency and to the operator of the scheme to that effect.

(11) The Secretary of State shall send a copy of any notice given under paragraph (10) above to the Director.

(12) For the purposes of, or otherwise in connection with, competition scrutiny, the Director may, by notice in writing, require any person to provide within a specified time such information as may be specified or described in the notice and which that person has, or which he may at any future time acquire, relating to any scheme or to any acts or omissions of an operator of such a scheme or of any person dealing with such an operator.

[1253]

PART IX
THE RESTRICTIVE TRADE PRACTICES ACT 1976

32 The 1976 Act

(1)   In this Part "the 1976 Act" means the Restrictive Trade Practices Act 1976.

(2)   The 1976 Act shall not apply to any agreement for the constitution of a body (whether corporate or unincorporated) which operates a registered scheme by reason of—
   (a) any term of the agreement; or
   (b) any implied term deemed to be contained in the agreement by virtue of section 8(2) or section 16(3) of the 1976 Act;
being in either case a term which is required or contemplated by that scheme.

(3)   Where an agreement ceases by virtue of this regulation to be subject to registration under the 1976 Act—
   (a) the Director shall remove from the register maintained by him under the 1976 Act any particulars which are entered or filed in that register in respect of the agreement; and
   (b) any proceedings in respect of the agreement which are pending before the Restrictive Practices Court shall be discontinued.

(4) Where an agreement which has been exempt from registration under the 1976 Act by virtue of paragraph (2) above ceases to be exempt in consequence of the cancellation of the registration of a scheme under regulation 17, the time within which particulars of the agreement are to be furnished in accordance with section 24 of and Schedule 2 to the 1976 Act shall be the period of one month beginning with the day on which the agreement ceased to be exempt from registration under the 1976 Act.

[1254]

33 Agreements to which the 1976 Act applies

(1) In this regulation, "the Court", "information provision" and "restriction" have the same meanings as they have in the 1976 Act.

(2) This regulation applies to an agreement to which the 1976 Act applies—
  (a) at least one of the parties to which is an operator of a registered scheme; and
  (b) which is made for the purposes of that scheme.

(3) If it appears to the Secretary of State—
  (a) that the restrictions in an agreement to which this regulation applies do not have and are not intended or likely to have the effect of restricting, distorting or preventing competition; or
  (b) in a case where all or any of those restrictions have, or are intended or likely to have, that effect, that the effect is not greater than is necessary for achieving the environmental or economic benefits mentioned in section 93(6) of the Act;

he may give a direction to the Director requiring him not to make an application to the Court under Part 1 of the 1976 Act in respect of the agreement.

(4) If it appears to the Secretary of State that one or more (but not all) of the restrictions in an agreement to which this regulation applies—
  (a) do not have, and are not intended or likely to have, the effect mentioned in paragraph (3) above; or
  (b) if they have, or arc intcnded or likely to have, that effect, that the effect is not greater than is necessary for achieving the benefits mentioned in paragraph (3) above,

he may make a declaration to that effect and give notice of it to the Director and to the Court.

(5) The Court shall not in any proceedings begun by an application made after notice has been given to it of a declaration under this regulation make any finding or exercise any power under Part 1 of the 1976 Act in relation to a restriction in respect of which the declaration has effect.

(6) Before making an application to the Court under Part 1 of the 1976 Act in respect of an agreement to which this regulation applies, the Director shall—
  (a) notify the Secretary of State of his intention to do so and give him particulars of the agreement together with such other information as he considers will assist the Secretary of State in deciding whether to exercise his powers under this regulation, or as the Secretary of State may request; and
  (b) advise the Secretary of State as to his opinion—
    (i) of the effects or likely effects on competition of the restrictions in the agreement, and
    (ii) as to whether any such effects are necessary for achieving the benefits mentioned in paragraph (3) above.

(7) The Director shall not make an application to the Court under Part 1 of the 1976 Act in respect of an agreement to which this regulation applies unless the

Secretary of State has either notified him that he does not intend to give a direction or make a declaration under this regulation or has given him notice of a declaration in respect of it.

(8)   The Secretary of State may—
(a) revoke a direction or declaration under this regulation;
(b) vary any such declaration; or
(c) give a direction or make a declaration notwithstanding a previous notification to the Director that he did not intend to give a direction or make a declaration,

if he is satisfied that there has been a material change of circumstances since the direction, declaration or notification was given.

(9)   The Secretary of State shall give notice to the Director of the revocation of a direction and to the Director and the Court of the revocation or variation of a declaration; and no such variation shall have effect so as to restrict the powers of the Court in any proceedings begun by an application already made by the Director.

(10)   A direction or declaration under this regulation shall cease to have effect if the agreement in question ceases to be an agreement to which this regulation applies.

(11)   This regulation applies to information provisions as it applies to restrictions.
[1255]

PART X
OFFENCES

34   Offences and penalties

(1)   Subject to paragraph 5 of Schedule 8, a producer who contravenes a requirement of—
(a) subject to paragraph (2) below, regulation 3(5)(a);
(b) regulation 3(5)(b)(i); or
(c) regulation 3(5)(b)(ii),
is guilty of an offence.

(2)   A producer is not guilty of an offence under paragraph (1)(a) above in respect of any period during which, under regulation 6(6), he is treated as having been registered.

(3)   A person who—
(a) furnishes a certificate of compliance under regulation 23 and either—
(i) knows the information provided in or in connection with the certificate to be false or misleading in a material particular, or
(ii) furnishes such information recklessly and it is false or misleading in a material particular;
(b) fails without reasonable excuse to furnish any information required by the Director in accordance with regulation 31(12); or
(c) furnishes any information to the appropriate Agency in connection with its functions under these Regulations, or to the Secretary of State or to the Director in connection with the functions of either of them under Part VIII of these Regulations, and either—
(i) knows the information to be false or misleading in a material particular, or
(ii) furnishes such information recklessly and it is false or misleading in a material particular,
is guilty of an offence.

(4)   A person who intentionally delays or obstructs a person authorised by an appropriate Agency in the exercise of powers referred to in regulation 28 is guilty of an offence.

(5)   A person guilty of an offence under any of paragraphs (1) to (4) above shall be liable—
    (a)   on summary conviction to a fine not exceeding the statutory maximum; or
    (b)   on conviction on indictment, to a fine.

[1256]

SCHEDULE 1
PRODUCERS

Regulation 3(2) and (3)

Column 1	Column 2	Column 3	Column 4
Relevant function performed in Years 1 and 2	Subject matter of supply in Year 1	Class of supply in Year 1	Class of producer in Year 2
Manufacturer	Packaging materials	A B or C	Manufacturer
Convertor, subject to paragraph 1(2)	Packaging or packaging materials	A B or C	Convertor
Packer/filler	Packaging or packaging materials	A B or C	Packer/filler
Importer	Packaging or packaging materials	A B or C	Importer
Wholesaler	Packaging	D	Wholesaler
Seller	Packaging	E	Seller
Manufacturer, Convertor, Packer/filler, Wholesaler, or Importer	Transit packaging	B or F	Secondary provider

1.—(1) For the purposes of Column 1 in the above Table—
    (a)   "relevant function" means the performance by a person of the functions of one of the following—
        (i)   manufacturer,
        (ii)   convertor,
        (iii)   packer/filler,
        (iv)   importer,
        (v)   wholesaler, or
        (vi)   seller,
        either himself or through an agent acting on his behalf, and in the course of business;
    (b)   "convertor" means a person who uses or modifies packaging materials in the production or formation packaging;
    (c)   "importer" means a person who imports packaging or packaging materials into the United Kingdom;
    (d)   "manufacturer" means a person who manufactures raw materials for packaging;
    (e)   "packer/filler" means a person who puts goods into packaging;
    (f)   "seller" means any person who supplies packaging to a user or a consumer of that packaging, whether or not the filling has taken place at the time of the supply;
    (g)   "wholesaler" means a person who supplies packaging to a seller but who does not carry out the functions of a packer/filler in relation to that packaging;

    (h)   "Year 1" means the preceding year; and

    (j)   "Year 2" means the relevant year.

    (2) Where a person performs the functions of a convertor and a packer/filler at the same time, and as part of the same packing/filling process, and in relation to the same packaging, as regards supplies of packaging or packaging materials made to or by him in connection with those functions, or that process, he is treated for the purposes of these Regulations as a producer of the class of packer/filler only.

    (3) For the purposes of this Schedule a person acts "in the course of business" if he acts in the ordinary course of conduct of a trade, occupation or profession.

2. For the purposes of Column 3 of the above Table, and Schedule 2—

    (a)   "Class A supply" means a deemed supply;

    (b)   "Class B supply" means a supply, other than solely for the purpose of transport, to a person who acts as a distributor, that is to say who, in relation to the packaging or packaging materials supplied, neither performed the functions of one of the classes of producer, nor was the user or consumer;

    (c)   "Class C supply" means a supply, other than a Class F supply, to a person for the application by that person of a relevant function other than that of an importer;

    (d)   "Class D supply" means a supply to a seller who, at the time of the supply, was not a producer;

    (e)   "Class E supply" means a supply, other than a supply of transit packaging in respect of which a Class F supply has already been made, to a user or consumer other than a person who performed a relevant function;

    (f)   "Class F supply" means a supply—

        (i)   to a person who performed a relevant function,

        (ii) to a user or consumer, or

        (iii) to a person who acts as a distributor,

        using the transit packaging supplied to perform the functions of a packer/filler and seller; and

    (g)   "supply" means doing any of the following, either himself or through an agent acting on his behalf, in relation to packaging or packaging materials owned by the supplier—

        (i)   selling, hiring out or lending,

        (ii) providing in exchange for any consideration (including trading stamps within the meaning of section 10 of the Trading Stamps Act 1964) other than money,

        (iii) providing in or in connection with the performance of any statutory function, or

        (iv) giving as a prize or otherwise making a gift,

        and "deemed supply" means a supply which is deemed to occur when a person who has carried out a relevant function then performs another such function in relation to the same packaging or packaging materials.

3. A person satisfies the threshold tests if—

    (a)   his turnover—

        (i)   where the obligation year is 1997, 1998 or 1999, in the last financial year in respect of which audited accounts are available before the relevant date, was more than £5,000,000, and

        (ii) where the obligation year is the year 2000 or any subsequent year, in the last financial year in respect of which audited accounts are available before the relevant date, was more than £1,000,000; and

    (b)   in the calculation year the person handled in aggregate more than 50 tonnes of packaging or packaging materials.

4.—(1) For the purposes of paragraph 3 above—

    (a)   "financial year" in relation to a person—

        (i)   where the person is a company is determined as provided in section 223(1) to (3) of the Companies Act 1985, and

        (ii) in any other case has the meaning given in section 223(4) of the Companies Act 1985, but as if the reference there to an undertaking were a reference to that person;

    (b)   "obligation year" means a year in respect of which it is being considered whether a person is a producer and "calculation year" means a year immediately before an obligation year;

    (c)   "relevant date" means—
- (i)   subject to sub-paragraph (iii) below, where the obligation year is 1997, 31st August 1997,
- (ii)   subject to sub-paragraph (iii) below, where the obligation year is 1998 or any subsequent year, 1st April in the year, and
- (iii)   where an application for registration is made in a circumstance set out in regulation 6(3), or as required by paragraph 11 of Schedule 9, the date of the application;

    (d)   a person's "turnover" means his turnover as defined in section 262(1) of the Companies Act 1985 but as if the references to a company were references to that person; and

    (e)   the references to audited accounts being available are, where the person is a company, the annual accounts delivered to the registrar under section 242 of the Companies Act 1985.

(2) For the purposes of paragraph 3 above, and Schedule 2, the amount of packaging or packaging materials handled is the amount in respect of which the producer made a supply referred to in Column 3 of the Table, other than a Class A supply, calculated in tonnes to the nearest tonne by—
- (a)   including packaging or packaging materials so supplied which were imported into the United Kingdom by the producer, either himself or through an agent acting on his behalf; and
- (b)   excluding—
  - (i)   any packaging or packaging materials so supplied which were exported from the United Kingdom by the producer, either himself or through an agent acting on his behalf, or which to the producer's reasonable knowledge were otherwise exported from the United Kingdom,
  - (ii)   production residues, and
  - (iii)   reused packaging.

[1257]

SCHEDULE 2
RECOVERY AND RECYCLING OBLIGATIONS

Regulation 3(5)(b)(i)

1. A producer's obligations to recover and recycle packaging waste in a relevant year are, in relation to each class of producer to which he belongs—
- (a)   to recover an amount of packaging waste as provided in paragraph 2(1) below;
- (b)   to recover by recycling a proportion of that packaging waste, as provided in paragraph 2(2) below; and
- (c)   as part of the obligation to recover packaging waste as provided in sub-paragraph (a) above, to recover by recycling an amount of packaging materials which is packaging waste, as provided in paragraph 2(3) below,

and are calculated by aggregating his obligations in relation to each class of producer to which he belongs in respect of that year.

2.—(1) The amount of packaging waste to be recovered by a producer in relation to a class of producer to which he belongs is calculated as follows—

$$P \times C \times X = Z$$

where—
    P is the amount in tonnes to the nearest tonne of packaging and packaging materials handled by the producer in the preceding year,
    C is the percentage prescribed in paragraph 3 below in relation to the class of producer,
    X is the percentage prescribed in paragraph 4 below as the recovery target for the relevant year, and
    Z is the amount by tonnage of packaging waste which is to be recovered within the relevant year.

(2) The proportion of the packaging waste referred to in sub-paragraph (1) above which is to be recovered by recycling is, for the year 2001 and subsequent years, in relation to a class of producer to which the producer belongs, not less than 50% of the amount by tonnage of packaging waste represented by "Z" in sub-paragraph (1) above.

(3) The obligations of a producer to recover by recycling an amount of packaging materials which is packaging waste in relation to a class of producer to which he belongs are calculated in relation to each packaging material which he handled in the preceding year, as follows—

$$M \times C \times Y = Q$$

where—

M is the amount in tonnes to the nearest tonne of the packaging material handled by the producer in the preceding year,

C is the percentage prescribed in paragraph 3 below in relation to the class of producer,

Y is the percentage prescribed in paragraph 5 below as the recycling target for the relevant year, and

Q is the amount by tonnage of packaging waste of that packaging material which is to be recycled in the relevant year.

3.—(1) The following percentages are prescribed as the percentages for the following classes of producer—

(a)	manufacturer	6%;
(b)	convertor	11%;
(c)	packer/filler	36%;
(d)	seller or wholesaler	47%; and
(e)	secondary provider	83%.

(2) The following percentages are prescribed for the class of importer—

(a) the manufacturer's percentage, that is 6%—

    (i) on Class A supplies, where the importer also carries out the functions of a convertor,

    (ii) on Class B supplies, where the relevant packaging or packaging materials are supplied, by the distributor who receives them, to a convertor, and

    (iii) on Class C supplies to a convertor;

(b) the manufacturer's and the convertor's percentages aggregated, that is 6% + 11% = 17%—

    (i) on Class A supplies, where the importer also carries out the functions of a packer/filler,

    (ii) on Class B supplies, where the relevant packaging or packaging materials are supplied, by the distributor who receives them, to a packer/filler, and

    (iii) on Class C supplies to a packer/filler;

(c) the manufacturer's, the convertor's and the packer/filler's percentages aggregated, that is 6% + 11% + 36% = 53%—

    (i) on Class A supplies where the importer also carries out the functions of a seller,

    (ii) on Class B supplies where the relevant packaging or packaging materials are supplied, by the distributor who receives them, to a seller, and

    (iii) on Class C supplies to a seller; and

(d) the manufacturer's, the convertor's, the packer/filler's and the seller's percentages aggregated, that is 6% + 11% + 36% + 47% = 100%—

    (i) on Class F supplies, and

    (ii) on Class A supplies, where the importer is also the final user or consumer.

4. The following is prescribed as the recovery target "X"—

    (a) for the years 1998 and 1999, 38%;

    (b) for the year 2000, 43%; and

    (c) for any subsequent year, 52%.

5. The following is prescribed as the recycling target "Y"—

    (a) for the years 1998 and 1999, 7%;

    (b) for the year 2000, 11%; and

    (c) for any subsequent year, 16%.

6.—(1) In this Schedule—

    (a) for the purposes of paragraph 2(1) above and for the years 1998 and 1999 "packaging materials" means any of the following—

        (i)   glass,
        (ii) aluminium,
        (iii) steel,
        (iv) paper/fibreboard, or
        (v) plastic;

   (b)   for the purposes of paragraph 2(1) above, and for the year 2000 and subsequent years, "packaging materials" means any of the materials referred to in sub-paragraph (a) above together with wood and other packaging materials; and

   (c)   for the purposes of paragraph 2(3) above "packaging materials" means any of the materials referred to in sub-paragraph (a) above.

(2) For the purposes of sub-paragraph (1) above, packaging materials composed of a combination of the materials there referred to are to be treated as made of the material which is predominant by weight.

[1258]

SCHEDULE 3

(Pts I, II set out Council Directive 75/442/EEC, Art 1, Annex I, Annex IIB at **[1301]**, **[1322]**, **[1324]**.*)*

PART III
DEFINITION OF SPECIAL PRODUCERS

Regulation 4(4)

3.   A special producer is a producer who in the preceding year handled—
   (a)   primary packaging, that is to say packaging within part (a) of the definition of packaging in regulation 2, any of which, in his reasonable opinion, when discarded was—
        (i)   likely to be special waste as defined in regulation 2 of the Special Waste Regulations 1996; or
        (ii) likely to have been used to contain or used in connection with the containment of such waste; or
   (b)   packaging which is a package within the meaning given in regulation 2 of the Carriage of Dangerous Goods (Classification, Packaging and Labelling) and Use of Transportable Pressure Receptacles Regulations 1996 and which in his reasonable opinion was likely to be subject to the requirements of regulations 8 to 10 of those Regulations (particulars to be shown on packages containing dangerous goods) other than any package referred to in regulation 8(5) of those Regulations.

[1259]

PART IV
SPECIAL PRODUCERS—OBLIGATIONS

Regulation 4(4)

4.   For the purposes of the provision of further information by a special producer under regulations 6(4), or (8), if applicable, and 8, such information shall only be in respect of packaging or packaging materials other than packaging referred to in Part III of this Schedule.

5.   For the purposes of the calculation of the recovery and recycling obligations of a special producer, Schedule 2 to these Regulations shall apply and item "P" in that Schedule shall be the amount by tonnage of packaging and packaging materials handled by the producer in the preceding year other than packaging referred to in Part III of this Schedule.

[1260]

PART V
SPECIAL PRODUCERS—RECORDS AND RETURNS

Regulation 4(4)

6.   A special producer shall, in relation to any relevant year—
   (a)   make records and returns as required under regulation 22 in relation to the packaging and packaging materials referred to in paragraph 4 above, and in relation to such packaging and packaging materials when it becomes waste; and

(b)   in addition to any records and returns he is required to make under regulation 22 maintain, and retain for at least 4 years after the record is made, records of the information referred to in paragraph 7 below in respect of each relevant year, and shall make a return to the appropriate Agency of that information on or before 31st January in the year immediately following the relevant year.

7.   The information is—
(a)   the amount in tonnes to the nearest tonne of packaging handled by the producer in the preceding year;
(b)   the amount in tonnes to the nearest tonne of the packaging referred to in sub-paragraph (a) above which was packaging referred to in Part III of this Schedule; and
(c)   any steps taken by the producer to promote or increase the recovery of the packaging referred to in sub-paragraph (b) above when it becomes waste.

8.   In relation to a special producer the reference in regulation 7(c) to regulation 22 shall be read as a reference to regulation 22 and this Part of this Schedule.

[1261]

SCHEDULE 4
INFORMATION

Regulations 6, 8, 12, 14, 31

PART I
INFORMATION TO BE CONTAINED IN APPLICATION FOR PRODUCER REGISTRATION

Regulation 6(4)

1.   The address and telephone number of the registered office of the producer or, if not a company, the principal place of business of the producer.

2.   The business name of the producer if different from that referred to in paragraph 1 above.

3.   The address for service of notices on the producer if different from that referred to in paragraph 1 above.

[1262]

PART II
PRODUCER AND SCHEME REGISTRATION
FURTHER INFORMATION

Regulations 6, 8, 12 and 14

FOR PROVISION OF FURTHER INFORMATION BY OBLIGATED PRODUCERS AND ON BEHALF OF SCHEMES AS REQUIRED UNDER REGULATIONS 6, 8, 12 AND 14 OF THE PRODUCER RESPONSIBILITY OBLIGATIONS (PACKAGING WASTE) REGULATIONS 1997

EA/SEPA reference number: ....

Please complete in black ink. "Producers" are obligated businesses, that is companies, partnerships, sole traders etc.

As indicated below parts of the form are optional but will assist in any future review of your sector's obligations.

Please supply DATA IN METRIC TONNES and for PREVIOUS YEAR

SECTION 1

Name of Business: ....

Address of registered office or   ....
principal place of business:
....

....

Post Code: ....

Telephone number: ....

Fax number: ....

Name and position of Contact: ....

Where a group registration, ...
name of group to which
companies belong, if any:

Tick main activity performed with regard to packaging:

Manufacturing of packaging raw materials	
Conversion	
Packing/filling	
Wholesaling*	
Selling	
Importing	

*Wholesalers who perform no other activity are obligated with effect from 1 January 2000 only.

SECTION 2

1. In accordance with regulations 6(7) and 12(7) you are required in the initial years to give <u>reasonable estimates in tonnes per annum</u> and in subsequent years to give information which is as accurate as reasonably possible in terms of the activities and materials set out in the following tables. You should attach a short description of how the data was obtained (Section 4). Tables <u>1–5</u> are (where applicable) required under Regulations 6 and 12. Tables <u>6–8</u> are optional but will assist in any future review of your sector's obligations.

2. Schedule 1 paragraph 2(f) and Schedule 2 paragraph 3(1)(e) apply an obligation of 83% to transit or "secondary provider" packaging. This is the sum of the packer/filler and seller obligations on the transit packaging you use to pack and sell goods to customers (36% + 47% = 83%). Transit packaging should therefore be included in Tables 1 and 2a according to the activities performed on it.

3. Imports carry a cumulative or "rolled up" obligation depending on the stage at which they are imported (see Schedules 1 and 2).

4. Composite packaging should be included according to the predominant material by total weight.

5. Where an entry amounts to less than 1 tonne, it does not need to be recorded separately but should be aggregated with the principal packaging material handled by the business.

6. In calculating tonnages of packaging handled you may use your own information or any ready reckoner or guidance published by or in association with the Environment Agencies.

Table 1: Packaging/Packaging Materials Supplied

	Paper	Glass	Metals		Plastic	Wood	Other
			Al	Steel			
Raw material manufacturing							
Conversion							
Pack/filling							
Selling							

Table 2a: [where applicable] Packaging/Packaging Materials Exported by the Producer

	Paper	Glass	Metals		Plastic	Wood	Other
			Al	Steel			
Raw material manufacture							
Conversion							
Pack/filling							
Selling							

Table 2b: [where applicable and if known] Packaging/Packaging Materials Exported by a Third Party

	Paper	Glass	Metals		Plastic	Wood	Other
			Al	Steel			
Raw material manufacture							
Conversion							
Pack/filling							
Selling							

Table 3: [where applicable] Tonnage of Packaging/Packaging Materials Imported for the purpose of the named activity

	Paper	Glass	Metals		Plastic	Wood	Other
			Al	Steel			
Conversion							
Pack/filling							
Selling							
Transit packing round imports							

As of 1 January 1999 and in subsequent years (see below for 1997 and 1998), you will be required to calculate and declare your obligation to recover and recycle, and fill in Table 4 below. **IT SHOWS YOUR OBLIGATION. IT IS FOR THE CURRENT YEAR AND IS BASED ON DATA FROM THE PREVIOUS YEAR.**

Summary Table 4: Statement of Obligations

Recovery Obligation			
Of which, Recycling Obligation for	paper		
	glass		
	Metals	Aluminium	
		Steel	
	plastic		

SECTION 3

Table 5 Optional: Re-Use

You do not have to answer this question, but if you can, please note below the tonnage of reused packaging excluded by material.

Paper		
Glass		
Metals	Aluminium	
	Steel	
Plastics		
Wood from 1.1.2000		
Other from 1.1.2000		

Table 6 Optional: Composites

You do not have to answer this question, but if you can, please note below the tonnage of packaging included in your obligated tonnage that was composite packaging, for each material.

Paper		
Glass		
Metals	Aluminium	
	Steel	
Plastics		
Wood from 1.1.2000		
Other from 1.1.2000		

Table 7 Optional IN 1997 AND 1998 ONLY: please provide an assessment of your levels of recovery and recycling (by material) of packaging waste in years 1996 and 1997 respectively:

Recovery			
Recycling	paper		
	glass		
	Metals	Aluminium	
		Steel	
	plastic		

SECTION 4

Basis of Assessment

How did you arrive at this assessment? Data from your own systems? Data from a Materials Organisation, from a Trade Association or Guidance from the Environment Agencies? Data from your suppliers? Other source?—please specify, using a separate sheet if necessary.

```
┌──────────────────────────────────────────────────────────────────┐
│                                                                    │
│                                                                    │
│                                                                    │
│                                                                    │
│                                                                    │
│                                                                    │
└──────────────────────────────────────────────────────────────────┘
```

Please return completed form by [   ] to the Agency with which you are registering. You must retain a copy for yourself.

Environment Agency	Scottish Environment Protection Agency
Hampton House	Erskine Court
20 Albert Embankment	The Castle Business Park
London SE1 7TJ	Stirling FK9 4TR
Fax: 0171 840 6147	Fax: 01786 446885

[1263]

PART III

INFORMATION TO BE INCLUDED IN APPLICATION FOR REGISTRATION OF A SCHEME OR COMPETITION SCRUTINY

Regulations 12(3)(b) and 31(2)

4. The name of the scheme.

5. The name of the operator, and where the operator is a partnership whose principal place of business is in Scotland, the names of all the partners.

6. The address and telephone number of the registered office of the operator or, if not a company, the principal place of business of the operator, and, if more than one, all the operators.

7. The address for service of notices if different from that referred to in paragraph 6 above.

8. The names and addresses of the registered offices, or, if not companies, the principal places of business, of the scheme's members.

9. Full particulars of the agreement for the constitution of the scheme including any rules or regulations to be observed by its members.

[1264]

PART IV

STATEMENT OF THE SCHEME'S POLICIES AND SCHEME'S OPERATIONAL PLAN

Regulation 12(3)(d) and (e)

10. The matters to be contained in the statement with regard to the scheme's policies referred to in regulation 12(3)(d) are—
   (a)   the steps intended to be taken through the scheme to increase the use of recycled packaging waste in the manufacture of packaging, packaging materials or other products or materials supplied by its members; and
   (b)   the principal methods by which packaging waste is to be recovered and recycled through the scheme, together with information about the steps the user or consumer may take to assist the scheme in applying these methods.

11. The matters to be contained in the scheme's operational plan referred to in regulation 12(3)(e) are matters which demonstrate—

(a) that sufficient financial resources and technical expertise will be available to enable the recovery and recycling obligations of the scheme's members referred to in regulation 4(1)(b) to be discharged through the scheme;

(b) that the arrangements for recovery and recycling through a scheme take account of any statement which, where the scheme is to be registered with the Agency, contains the Secretary of State's policies in relation to the recovery and disposal of waste in England and Wales, and which is made under section 44A of the 1990 Act, and, where the scheme is to be registered with SEPA, contains that Agency's policies in relation to the recovery and disposal of waste in Scotland, and which is made under section 44B of the 1990 Act;

(c) that there are arrangements in place to enable the operator to supply further information as required under regulation 14;

(d) how the recovery and recycling obligations of its members referred to in regulation 4(1)(b) will be performed as regards each of the packaging materials relevant to those obligations including —

   (i) the names and addresses of the reprocessors it is intended to use,

   (ii) the names of any waste collection or disposal authorities from whom packaging waste is intended to be obtained,

   (iii) the proportions in which the packaging waste which is to be recovered and recycled is to be obtained from the waste of a producer who is a member of the scheme, other industrial or commercial waste, household waste or other waste,

   (iv) the amounts to the nearest tonne of packaging waste it is proposed to recover in the three years immediately following registration, and

   (v) the amounts to the nearest tonne of each such packaging material which it is proposed to recycle in the three years immediately following registration; and

(e) the steps it is proposed to take to recover and recycle any of the packaging materials relevant to the recovery and recycling obligations of the scheme's members in order not to adversely affect the interests of any member of the scheme, or any other producer, whose recovery and recycling obligations are predominantly in relation to another such packaging material.

12.—(1) For the purposes of paragraph 11(d)(ii) above "waste collection authority" and "waste disposal authority" shall have the meanings given in section 30 of the 1990 Act.

(2) For the purposes of paragraph 11(d)(iii) above "houschold waste", "industrial waste" and "commercial waste" shall have the same meanings as in section 75 of the 1990 Act.

[1265]

SCHEDULE 5
PROCEDURE ON APPEALS

Regulation 19

1.—(1) An operator of a scheme who wishes to appeal to the Secretary of State under regulation 18 shall do so by notice in writing given or sent to the Secretary of State.

(2) The notice shall be accompanied by —

(a) a statement of the grounds of appeal;

(b) where the appeal relates to refusal of registration under regulation 16, a copy of the appellant's application and any supporting documents;

(c) where the appeal relates to cancellation of registration under regulation 17(1), a copy of the notification of the decision and any supporting documents;

(d) a copy of any correspondence relevant to the appeal;

(e) a copy of any other document relevant to the appeal; and

(f) a statement indicating whether the appellant wishes the appeal to be in the form of a hearing or to be determined on the basis of written representations.

(3) The appellant shall serve a copy of his notice of appeal on the appropriate Agency together with copies of the documents mentioned in sub-paragraph (2) above.

2.—(1) Subject to sub-paragraph (2) below, notice of appeal shall be given before the expiry of the period of 6 months beginning with the date of the decision which is the subject of the appeal.

(2) The Secretary of State may at any time allow notice of an appeal to be given after the expiry of the period mentioned in sub-paragraph (1) above.

3. Where under regulation 19(2) the appeal is by way of a hearing, the person hearing the appeal shall, unless he has been appointed to determine an appeal under regulation 19(1)(a), make a written report to the Secretary of State which shall include his conclusions and recommendations or his reasons for not making any recommendations.

4.—(1) The Secretary of State or other person determining an appeal shall notify the appellant in writing of his decision and of his reasons.

(2) If the Secretary of State determines an appeal after a hearing under regulation 19(2) he shall provide the appellant with a copy of any report made to him under paragraph 3 above.

(3) The Secretary of State or other person determining an appeal shall, at the same time as notifying the appellant of his decision, send the appropriate Agency a copy of any document sent to the appellant under this paragraph.

[1266]

SCHEDULE 6
INFORMATION IN CERTIFICATE OF COMPLIANCE

Regulation 23

The information to be contained in a certificate of compliance is as follows—
- (a) the name and address of the approved person who is issuing the certificate;
- (b) the date of the certificate;
- (c) the producer in respect of whom the approved person is issuing the certificate ("the relevant producer");
- (d) the initial and further information provided by the relevant producer to the appropriate Agency in accordance with regulations 6(4)(b), 6(4)(c) or (8), as the case may be, and regulation 8, together with any changes made to such information and provided to the appropriate Agency in accordance with the undertakings referred to in regulations 7(a)(iii) and (iv);
- (e) a statement by the approved person that the certificate has been issued in accordance with any guidance issued by the appropriate Agency under section 94(4) of the Act; and
- (f) certification by the approved person as to whether the relevant producer has complied with his recovery and recycling obligations.

[1267]

SCHEDULE 7
PUBLIC REGISTER

Regulation 26

Information regarding producer registration

1   The information to be contained in the register shall be—
- (a) for the years 1997 and 1998, the name and address of the registered office or principal place of business of the producer registered; and
- (b) for the year 1999 and subsequent years, the information referred to in sub-paragraph (a) above together with a statement in relation to each producer registered and each relevant year as to whether a certificate of compliance has been furnished.

Information regarding scheme registration

2   The information to be contained in the register shall be—
- (a) for the years 1997 and 1998—
  - (i) the name of the scheme,
  - (ii) the name and address of the registered office or principal place of business of each operator of the scheme, and
  - (iii) the name and address of the registered office or principal place of business of the members of the scheme; and

(b)   for the year 1999 and subsequent years, the information referred to in sub-paragraph (a) above together with a statement in relation to each scheme member and each year as to whether the scheme has discharged the recovery and recycling obligations of its members referred to in regulation 4(1)(b).

[1268]

SCHEDULE 8
GROUPS OF COMPANIES

Regulation 29

1.   This Schedule applies in relation to a relevant year—
    (a)   where a holding company and one or more of its subsidiaries, or two or more subsidiary companies of the same holding company (in either case referred to in this Schedule and Schedule 9 as "a group of companies") each satisfies the provisions of Columns 1 to 3 of the Table in Schedule 1 in relation to a class or classes of producer; and
    (b)   where the aggregate of the turnovers, and the aggregate of the amounts of packaging or packaging materials handled by each such company, are sufficient to satisfy the threshold tests as provided by paragraph 3 of Schedule 1.

2.   Subject to regulation 4, in respect of a year each company referred to in paragraph 1 above is a producer of a class specified in an entry in Column 4 of the Table set out in Schedule 1 if—
    (a)   in that year and the preceding year he performs the relevant functions specified in Column 1 of that Table in relation to that entry; and
    (b)   in the preceding year he made supplies of the materials or products specified in Column 2 of that Table in relation to that entry of a class specified in Column 3 of that Table in relation to that entry;

and the other provisions of that Schedule, other than paragraph 3, shall also have effect for the purposes of determining to which class of producer such a company belongs.

3.   For the purposes of this Schedule and Schedule 9 "subsidiary" and "holding company" have the same meanings as they have in section 736(1) of the Companies Act 1985.

4.   Subject to regulation 4, companies who are producers and are in a group of companies shall comply with their producer registration obligations for a relevant year by either—
    (a)   being registered for that year with the appropriate Agency as required by regulation 5, in which case each company so registered has its own recovery, recycling and certifying obligations; or
    (b)   the holding company and one or more of the subsidiaries being registered together for that year with the appropriate Agency, (in this Schedule and Schedule 9 referred to as a "group registration") in which case paragraphs 5 and 6 below shall apply.

5.   Where there is a group registration—
    (a)   the subsidiary companies in the group registration are exempt from complying with their producer responsibility obligations for the relevant year;
    (b)   the holding company has a producer registration obligation for the relevant year which is an obligation to make the group registration and for this purpose regulations 5 to 11, and Parts I and II of Schedule 4, shall be read as if—
       (i)   references to the applicant or the producer were references to the holding company,
      (ii)   references to information to be provided regarding the producer were to information to be provided regarding each company in the group registration, and
     (iii)   the references in regulations 6(4)(d) and 9(2) to a fee for producer registration were read as references to a fee for group registration;
    (c)   the holding company has recovery and recycling obligations for the relevant year which are the aggregate of its own obligations in respect of that year, if any, and the obligations which the subsidiary companies in the group registration would have had but for the group registration;
    (d)   the holding company shall furnish records and returns and provide a certificate of compliance, and references in regulation 23 and Schedule 6—
       (i)   to a producer shall be read as references to the holding company, and

      (ii)   to information shall be read as references to information regarding each company in the group registration; and

  (e)   regulation 34(1) (offences) shall not apply to the companies in the group and paragraphs 6 and 7 below shall apply instead.

6.   Where in accordance with this Schedule there is a group registration the holding company is guilty of an offence if—

  (a)   it does not comply with its recovery and recycling obligations referred to in paragraph 5(c) above; or

  (b)   it does not furnish a certificate of compliance in accordance with paragraph 5(d) above.

7.   A person guilty of an offence under paragraph 6 above shall be liable—

  (a)   on summary conviction to a fine not exceeding the statutory maximum; or

  (b)   on conviction on indictment, to a fine.

8.   This Schedule is subject to the provisions of Schedule 9.

[1269]

SCHEDULE 9
MID-YEAR CHANGES

Regulation 30

PART I
SCHEME MEMBERSHIP

1.   Subject to paragraph 4 below, where a person who is a producer in respect of a year becomes a member of a registered scheme during that year, the recovery and recycling obligations of the producer for that year, referred to in regulation 4(1)(b), shall be performed through the scheme.

2.   Subject to paragraph 3 below, where a person who is a producer in respect of a year ceases to be a member of a registered scheme during that year, he shall comply with his recovery and recycling obligations for that year, calculated as provided in regulation 3 and Schedule 2.

3.   Where a person who is a producer in respect of a year ceases to be a member of a registered scheme, because the registration of the scheme has been cancelled in accordance with regulation 17, during that year he shall comply with a proportion of his recovery and recycling obligations for the year, calculated as follows—

$$\frac{D}{E}$$

where—

    D is the number of days in the relevant year from the date when such membership ceased, and

    E is the number of days in the relevant year.

4.   Where a person who is a producer in respect of a year ceases to be a member of one registered scheme ("the first scheme") and becomes a member of another registered scheme ("the second scheme") during that year, the first scheme shall not be required to perform any of the producer's recovery and recycling obligations, referred to in regulation 4(1)(b), and all such obligations shall be performed through the second scheme.

[1270]

PART II
GROUP MEMBERSHIP

5.   This Part applies where—

  (a)   a company joins a group of companies and becomes a company to which paragraph 1 of Schedule 8 applies; or

  (b)   a holding company or subsidiary company to which paragraph 1 of Schedule 8 applies ceases to belong to a group of companies.

6.   Where paragraph 5(a) above applies the company shall either—

(a) be registered separately with the appropriate Agency as required by regulation 5; or

(b) be registered with the appropriate Agency as part of a group registration under Schedule 8 and for the purposes of this paragraph—

　(i) such registration is effected upon notice being given by the holding company to the appropriate Agency of the change in the group registration, and

　(ii) where prior to joining the group of companies the company was registered with an appropriate Agency, the Agency shall cancel the company's registration on receipt of that notice and regulations 11(2) and (3) shall apply to that cancellation.

7. Where—

(a) paragraph 5(a) above applies;

(b) in relation to the obligation year the company itself satisfies the threshold tests; and

(c) the company is registered as part of a group registration;

the holding company shall comply with the requirements of the company's recovery and recycling obligations for the year in which it joins the group.

8. Where—

(a) paragraph 5(a) above applies;

(b) in relation to the obligation year the company itself satisfies the threshold tests; and

(c) the company is registered separately with the appropriate Agency;

the company shall comply with its recovery and recycling obligations for the year in which it joins the group.

9. Where—

(a) paragraph 5(a) above applies;

(b) in relation to the obligation year the company itself does not satisfy the threshold tests; and

(c) the company is registered as part of a group registration;

the holding company shall comply with a proportion of the requirements of the company's recovery and recycling obligations for the year in which it joins the group, such proportion being calculated as provided in paragraph 17(1) below.

10. Where—

(a) paragraph 5(a) above applies;

(b) in relation to the obligation year the company itself does not satisfy the threshold tests; and

(c) the company is registered separately with the appropriate Agency;

the company shall comply with a proportion of its recovery and recycling obligations for the year in which it joins the group, such proportion being calculated as provided in paragraph 17(1) below.

11. Where—

(a) paragraph 5(b) above applies; and

(b) in relation to the obligation year the company itself satisfies the threshold tests;

it shall register with the appropriate Agency as required by regulation 5 within 28 days of ceasing to be a member of a group and regulations 6 to 11 shall apply as if this were an occurrence specified in regulation 6(3).

12. Where—

(a) paragraph 5(b) above applies;

(b) in relation to the obligation year the company itself satisfies the threshold tests; and

(c) the company was registered as part of a group registration;

the following shall apply—

　(i) the holding company shall comply with a proportion, calculated as provided in paragraph 17(1) below, of the requirements of the company's recovery and recycling obligations for the year in which it ceases to be a member of the group, and

    (ii)   the company shall comply with a proportion of its recovery and recycling obligations for that year, such proportion being calculated as provided in paragraph 17(1) below, except that for this purpose G is the number of days in the relevant year during which the company was not a member of the group.

13. Where—
    (a)   paragraph 5(b) above applies;
    (b)   in relation to the obligation year the company itself satisfies the threshold tests; and
    (c)   the company is registered separately with the appropriate Agency;

the company shall comply with its recovery and recycling obligations for the year in which it ceases to be a member of the group.

14. Where—
    (a)   paragraph 5(b) above applies;
    (b)   in relation to the obligation year the company itself does not satisfy the threshold tests; and
    (c)   the company was registered as part of a group registration;

the holding company shall comply with a proportion of the requirements of the company's recovery and recycling obligations for the year in which it ceases to be a member of the group, such proportion being calculated as provided in paragraph 17(1) below.

15. Where—
    (a)   paragraph 5(b) above applies;
    (b)   in relation to the obligation year the company itself does not satisfy the threshold tests; and
    (c)   the company was registered separately with the appropriate Agency;

the holding company shall comply with a proportion of the requirements of the company's recovery and recycling obligations for the year in which it ceases to be a member of the group, such proportion being calculated as provided in paragraph 17(1) below.

16. Where in a relevant year paragraph 5 above applies to a company as a result of that company ceasing to be a member of one group ("the first group") and becoming a member of another group ("the second group")—
    (a)   where in relation to each group the company is registered as part of a group registration, each holding company shall comply with the requirements of a proportion of the company's recovery and recycling obligations, such proportion being calculated as provided in paragraph 17(2) below;
    (b)   where in relation to each group the company is registered separately with the appropriate Agency, the company shall comply with its recovery and recycling obligations for the year;
    (c)   where in relation to the first group the company was registered as part of a group registration and in relation to the second group the company is registered separately with the appropriate Agency, the holding company in relation to the first group, and the company, shall each comply with a proportion of the company's recovery and recycling obligations, such proportion being calculated as provided in paragraph 17(2) below; or
    (d)   where in relation to the first group the company was registered separately with the appropriate Agency and in relation to the second group the company is registered as part of a group registration, the company, and the holding company in relation to the second group, shall each comply with a proportion of the company's recovery and recycling obligations, such proportion being calculated as provided in paragraph 17(2) below.

17.—(1) The proportion referred to in paragraphs 9, 10, 12(c)(i) and (ii), 14 and 15 above shall be calculated as follows—

$$\frac{G}{H}$$

where—
    G is the number of days in the relevant year during which the company was a member of the group, and
    H is the number of days in the relevant year.

(2) The proportion referred to in paragraph 16(a), (c) and (d) above shall be calculated as provided in sub-paragraph (1) above except that for this purpose G is the number of days in the relevant year during which the company was a member of the group in relation to which the calculation is being made.

18. For the purposes of this Part of this Schedule —
   (a)   the "threshold tests" means the threshold tests provided in paragraph 3 of Schedule 1; and
   (b)   "obligation year" has the meaning given in that Schedule for the purposes of the definition of the threshold tests.

[1271]

PART III
INCAPACITY

19. Where in a relevant year a producer dies or becomes bankrupt or incapacitated ("the first producer") that person shall cease to have any producer responsibility obligations for that year and any person who carries on the activities of the first producer following that event shall be treated as a producer and shall have the producer responsibility obligations of the producer for that year.

20. Any person carrying on the activities of the first producer referred to in paragraph 19 above shall within 28 days of commencing to do so —
   (a)   inform the appropriate Agency in writing of that fact and the date of the death, the date of bankruptcy or the nature of the incapacity and the date on which it began; and
   (b)   apply to be registered as required by regulation 5 and for this purpose the requirement in regulation 6(4)(d) (payment of a fee) shall not apply.

21. In relation to a producer which is a company, the references to a person becoming bankrupt or incapacitated in paragraph 19 above shall be construed as references to it going into liquidation or receivership or to an administration order being made in relation to it.

[1272]

SCHEDULE 10
UNITED KINGDOM'S RECOVERY AND RECYCLING TARGETS
Regulation 3(6)

The United Kingdom's recovery and recycling targets are —
   (a)   no later than the year 2001 between 50 per cent as a minimum and 65 per cent as a maximum by weight of the packaging waste is to be recovered; and
   (b)   within this general target and with the same time limit between 25 per cent as a minimum and 45 per cent as a maximum by weight of the totality of packaging materials contained in packaging waste are to be recycled with a minimum of 15 per cent by weight for each packaging material.

[1273]–[1300]

PART III
EC MATERIAL

COUNCIL DIRECTIVE
of 15 July 1975

on waste

(75/442/EEC)

NOTES

Date of publication in OJ: OJ L194, 25.7.75, p 39.

[THE COUNCIL OF THE EUROPEAN COMMUNITIES—

Having regard to the Treaty establishing the European Economic Community, and in particular Article 130s thereof;

Having regard to the proposal from the Commission;[1]

Having regard to the opinion of the European Parliament;[2]

Having regard to the opinion of the Economic and Social Committee;[3]

Whereas Directive 75/442/EEC[4] established a set of Community rules on waste disposal; whereas these must be amended to take account of experience gained in the implementation of this Directive by the Member States; whereas the amendments take as a base a high level of environmental protection;

Whereas the Council undertook to amend Directive 75/442/EEC in its resolution of 7 May 1990 on waste policy;[5]

Whereas common terminology and a definition of waste are needed in order to improve the efficiency of waste management in the Community;

Whereas, in order to achieve a high level of environmental protection, the Member States must, in addition to taking action to ensure the responsible removal and recovery of waste, take measures to restrict the production of waste particularly by promoting clean technologies and products which can be recycled and re-used, taking into consideration existing or potential market opportunities for recovered waste;

Whereas, moreover, any disparity between Member States' laws on waste disposal and recovery can affect the quality of the environment and interfere with the functioning of the internal market;

Whereas it is desirable to encourage the recycling of waste and re-use of waste as raw materials; whereas it may be necessary to adopt specific rules for re-usable waste;

Whereas it is important for the Community as a whole to become self-sufficient in waste disposal and it is desirable for Member States individually to aim at such self-sufficiency;

Whereas, in order to achieve the abovementioned objectives, waste management plans should be drawn up in the Member States;

Whereas movements of waste should be reduced and whereas Member States may take the necessary measures to that end in their management plans;

Whereas, to ensure a high level of protection and effective control, it is necessary to provide for authorisation and inspection of undertakings which carry out waste disposal and recovery;

Whereas, subject to certain conditions, and provided that they comply with environmental protection requirements, some establishments which process their waste themselves or carry out waste recovery may be exempt from permit requirements; whereas such establishments should be subject to registration;

Whereas, in order that waste can be monitored from its production to its final deposal, other undertakings involved with waste, such as waste collectors, carriers and brokers should also be subject to authorisation or registration and appropriate inspection;

Whereas a committee should be set up to assist the Commission in implementing this Directive and adapting it to scientific and technical progress,]

NOTES

[1]   OJ C295, 19.11.88, p 3 and OJ C326, 30.12.89, p 6.

[2]   OJ C158, 26.6.89, p 232 and opinion delivered on 22 February 1991.

[3]   OJ C56, 6.3.89, p 2.

[4]   OJ L194, 25.7.75, p 47.

[5]   OJ C122, 18.5.90, p 2.

This Preamble is substituted by virtue of Council Directive 91/156/EEC.

HAS ADOPTED THIS DIRECTIVE—

[Article 1

For the purposes of this Directive—
> (a) "waste" shall mean any substance or object in the categories set out in Annex I which the holder discards or intends or is required to discard.
>
>> The Commission, acting in accordance with the procedure laid down in Article 18, will draw up, not later than 1 April 1993, a list of wastes belonging to the categories listed in Annex I. This list will be periodically reviewed and, if necessary, revised by the same procedure;
>
> (b) "producer" shall mean anyone whose activities produce waste ("original producer") and/or anyone who carries out pre-processing, mixing or other operations resulting in a change in the nature or composition of this waste;
> (c) "holder" shall mean the producer of the waste or the natural or legal person who is in possession of it;
> (d) "management" shall mean the collection, transport, recovery and disposal of waste, including the supervision of such operations and after-care of disposal sites;
> (e) "disposal" shall mean any of the operations provided for in Annex IIA;
> (f) "recovery" shall mean any of the operations provided for in Annex IIB;
> (g) "collection" shall mean the gathering, sorting and/or mixing of waste for the purpose of transport.]

[1301]

NOTES

Arts 1–12 substituted by Arts 1–18 and Arts 13–15 renumbered as Arts 19–21 by Council Directive 91/156/EEC of 18 March 1991, Art 1.

[Article 2

> 1. The following shall be excluded from the scope of this Directive—
> (a) gaseous effluents emitted into the atmosphere;
> (b) where they are already covered by other legislation—
>> (i) radioactive waste;
>> (ii) waste resulting from prospecting, extraction, treatment and storage of mineral resources and the working of quarries;
>> (iii) animal carcases and the following agricultural waste: faecal matter and other natural, non-dangerous substances used in farming;
>> (iv) waste waters, with the exception of waste in liquid form;
>> (v) decommissioned explosives.

2. Specific rules for particular instances or supplementing those of this Directive on the management of particular categories of waste may be laid down by means of individual Directives.]

[1302]

NOTES

Substituted as noted to Art 1 at **[1301]**.

[Article 3

> 1. Member States shall take appropriate measures to encourage—
> (a) firstly, the prevention or reduction of waste production and its harmfulness, in particular by—
>> — the development of clean technologies more sparing in their use of natural resources,
>> — the technical development and marketing of products designed so as to make no contribution or to make the smallest possible contribution, by the nature of their manufacture, use or final disposal, to increasing the amount or harmfulness of waste and pollution hazards,

— the development of appropriate techniques for the final disposal of dangerous substances contained in waste destined for recovery;

(b) secondly—

(i) the recovery of waste by means of recycling, re-use or reclamation or any other process with a view to extracting secondary raw materials, or

(ii) the use of waste as a source of energy.

2. Except where Council Directive 83/189/EEC of 28 March 1983 laying down a procedure for the provision of information in the field of technical standards and regulations[1] applies, Member States shall inform the Commission of any measures they intend to take to achieve the aims set out in paragraph 1. The Commission shall inform the other Member States and the committee referred to in Article 18 of such measures.]

[1303]

NOTES

[1] OJ L109, 26.4.83, p 8.

Substituted as noted to Art 1 at **[1301]**.

[Article 4

Member States shall take the necessary measures to ensure that waste is recovered or disposed of without endangering human health and without using processes or methods which could harm the environment, and in particular—

— without risk to water, air, soil and plants and animals,

— without causing a nuisance through noise or odours,

— without adversely affecting the countryside or places of special interest.

Member States shall also take the necessary measures to prohibit the abandonment, dumping or uncontrolled disposal of waste.]

[1304]

NOTES

Substituted as noted to Art 1 at **[1301]**.

[Article 5

1. Member States shall take appropriate measures, in co-operation with other Member States where this is necessary or advisable, to establish an integrated and adequate network of disposal installations, taking account of the best available technology not involving excessive costs. The network must enable the Community as a whole to become self-sufficient in waste disposal and the Member States to move towards that aim individually, taking into account geographical circumstances or the need for specialised installations for certain types of waste.

2. The network must also enable waste to be disposed of in one of the nearest appropriate installations, by means of the most appropriate methods and technologies in order to ensure a high level of protection for the environment and public health.]

[1305]

NOTES

Substituted as noted to Art 1 at **[1301]**.

[Article 6

Member States shall establish or designate the competent authority or authorities to be responsible for the implementation of this Directive.]

[1306]

NOTES

Substituted as noted to Art 1 at **[1301]**.

[Article 7

1.   In order to attain the objectives referred to in Article 3, 4 and 5, the competent authority or authorities referred to in Article 6 shall be required to draw up as soon as possible one or more waste management plans. Such plans shall relate in particular to—
— the type, quantity and origin of waste to be recovered or disposed of,
— general technical requirements,
— any special arrangements for particular wastes,
— suitable disposal sites or installations.

Such plans may, for example, cover—
— the natural or legal persons empowered to carry out the management of waste,
— the estimated costs of the recovery and disposal operations,
— appropriate measures to encourage rationalisation of the collection, sorting and treatment of waste.

2.   Member States shall collaborate as appropriate with the other Member States concerned and the Commission to draw up such plans. They shall notify the Commission thereof.

3.   Member States may take the measures necessary to prevent movements of waste which are not in accordance with their waste management plans. They shall inform the Commission and the Member States of any such measures.]

[1307]

NOTES
Substituted as noted to Art 1 at **[1301]**.

[Article 8

Member States shall take the necessary measures to ensure that any holder of waste—
— has it handled by a private or public waste collector or by an undertaking which carries out the operations listed in Annex IIA or B, or
— recovers or disposes of it himself in accordance with the provisions of this Directive.]

[1308]

NOTES
Substituted as noted to Art 1 at **[1301]**.

[Article 9

1.   For the purposes of implementing Articles 4, 5 and 7, any establishment or undertaking which carries out the operations specified in Annex IIA must obtain a permit from the competent authority referred to in Article 6.

Such permit shall cover—
— the types and quantities of waste,
— the technical requirements,
— the security precautions to be taken,
— the disposal site,
— the treatment method.

2.   Permits may be granted for a specified period, they may be renewable, they may be subject to conditions and obligations, or, notably, if the intended method of disposal is unacceptable from the point of view of environmental protection, they may be refused.]

[1309]

NOTES
Substituted as noted to Art 1 at **[1301]**.

[Article 10

For the purposes of implementing Article 4, any establishment or undertaking which carries out the operations referred to in Annex IIB must obtain a permit.]

[1310]

NOTES
Substituted as noted to Art 1 at **[1301]**.

[Article 11

1.   Without prejudice to Council Directive 78/319/EEC of 20 March 1978 on toxic and dangerous waste,[1] as last amended by the Act of Accession of Spain and Portugal, the following may be exempted from the permit requirement imposed in Article 9 or Article 10—
   (a) establishments or undertakings carrying out their own waste disposal at the place of production;
        and
   (b) establishments or undertakings that carry out waste recovery.

   This exemption may apply only—
   — if the competent authorities have adopted general rules for each type of activity laying down the types and quantities of waste and the conditions under which the activity in question may be exempted from the permit requirements,
      and
   — if the types or quantities of waste and methods of disposal or recovery are such that the conditions imposed in Article 4 are complied with.

2.   The establishments or undertakings referred to in paragraph 1 shall be registered with the competent authorities.

3.   Member States shall inform the Commission of the general rules adopted pursuant to paragraph 1.]

[1311]

NOTES
[1]   OJ L377, 31.12.91, p 48.
Substituted as noted to Art 1 at **[1301]**.

[Article 12

Establishments or undertakings which collect or transport waste on a professional basis or which arrange for the disposal or recovery of waste on behalf of others (dealers or brokers), where not subject to authorisation, shall be registered with the competent authorities.]

[1312]

NOTES
Substituted as noted to Art 1 at **[1301]**.

[Article 13

Establishments or undertakings which carry out the operations referred to in Articles 9 to 12 shall be subject to appropriate periodic inspections by the competent authorities.]

[1313]

NOTES
Substituted as noted to Art 1 at **[1301]**.

[Article 14

All establishments or undertakings referred to in Articles 9 and 10 shall—
— keep a record of the quantity, nature, origin, and, where relevant, the destination, frequency of collection, mode of transport and treatment method in respect of the waste referred to in Annex I and the operations referred to in Annex IIA or B,
— make this information available, on request, to the competent authorities referred to in Article 6.

Member States may also require producers to comply with the provisions of this Article.]

[1314]

NOTES
Substituted as noted to Art 1 at [1301].

[Article 15

In accordance with the "polluter pays" principle, the cost of disposing of waste must be borne by—
— the holder who has waste handled by a waste collector or by an undertaking as referred to in Article 9,
and/or
— the previous holders or the producer of the product from which the waste came.]

[1315]

NOTES
Substituted as noted to Art 1 at [1301].

[Article 16

At intervals of three years Member States shall send information to the Commission on the implementation of this Directive, in the form of a sectoral report which shall also cover other pertinent Community Directives. This report shall be drawn up on the basis of a questionnaire or outline drafted by the Commission in accordance with the procedure laid down in Article 6 of Directive 91/692/EEC.[1] The questionnaire or outline shall be sent to the Member States six months before the start of the period covered by the report. The report shall be made to the Commission within nine months of the end of the three-year period covered by it.

The first report shall cover the period 1995 to 1997 inclusive.

The Commission shall publish a Community report on the implementation of the Directive within nine months of receiving the reports from the Member States.]

[1316]

NOTES
[1]   OJ L377, 31.12.91, p 48.
Originally substituted as noted to Art 1 at [1301]; further substituted by Council Directive 91/692/EEC of 23 December 1991, Art 5, Annex VI.

[Article 17

The amendments necessary for adapting the Annexes to this Directive to scientific and technical progress shall be adopted in accordance with the procedure laid down in Article 18.]

[1317]

NOTES
Substituted as noted to Art 1 at [1301].

[Article 18

The Commission shall be assisted by a committee composed of the representatives of the Member States and chaired by the representative of the Commission.

The representative of the Commission shall submit to the committee a draft of the measures to be taken. The committee shall deliver its opinion on the draft within the time limit which the chairman may lay down according to the urgency of the matter. The Opinion shall be delivered by the majority laid down in Article 148(2) of the EEC Treaty in the case of decisions which the Council is required to adopt on a proposal from the Commission. The votes of the representatives of the Member States within the committee shall be weighted in the manner set out in that Article. The chairman shall not vote.

The Commission shall adopt the measures envisaged if they are in accordance with the opinion of the committee.

If the measures envisaged are not in accordance with the opinion of the committee, or if no opinion is delivered, the Commission shall, without delay, submit to the Council a proposal relating to the measures to be taken. The Council shall act by a qualified majority.

If, on the expiry of a period of three months from the date of referral to the Council, the Council has not acted, the proposed measures shall be adopted by the Commission.]

[1318]

NOTES

Substituted as noted to Art 1 at **[1301]**.

Article [19]

Member States shall bring into force the measures needed in order to comply with this Directive within 24 months of its notification and shall forthwith inform the Commission thereof.

[1319]

NOTES

Renumbered as noted to Art 1 at **[1301]**.

Article [20]

Member States shall communicate to the Commission the texts of the main provisions of national law which they adopt in the field covered by this Directive.

[1320]

NOTES

Renumbered as noted to Art 1 at **[1301]**.

Article [21]

This Directive is addressed to the Member States.

[1321]

NOTES

Renumbered as noted to Art 1 at **[1301]**.

Done at Brussels, 15 July 1975.

[ANNEX I
CATEGORIES OF WASTE

Q1 Production or consumption residues not otherwise specified below

Q2 Off-specification products

Q3 Products whose date for appropriate use has expired

Q4 Materials spilled, lost or having undergone other mishap, including any materials, equipment, etc, contaminated as a result of the mishap

Q5 Materials contaminated or soiled as a result of planned actions (eg residues from cleaning operations, packing materials, containers, etc)

Q6 Unusable parts (eg reject batteries, exhausted catalysts, etc)

Q7 Substances which no longer perform satisfactorily (eg contaminated acids, contaminated solvents, exhausted tempering salts, etc)

Q8 Residues of industrial processes (eg slags, still bottoms, etc)

Q9 Residues from pollution abatement processes (eg scrubber sludges, baghouse dusts, spent filters, etc)

Q10 Machining/finishing residues (eg lathe turnings, mill scales, etc)

Q11 Residues from raw materials extraction and processing (eg mining residues, oil field slops, etc)

Q12 Adulterated materials (eg oils contaminated with PCBs, etc)

Q13 Any materials, substances or products whose use has been banned by law

Q14 Products for which the holder has no further use (eg agricultural, household, office, commercial and shop discards, etc)

Q15 Contaminated materials, substances or products resulting from remedial action with respect to land

Q16 Any materials, substances or products which are not contained in the above categories.]

[1322]

NOTES
Added by Council Directive 91/156/EEC of 18 March 1991, Art 1.

[ANNEX IIA
DISPOSAL OPERATIONS

NB: This Annex is intended to list disposal operations such as they occur in practice. In accordance with Article 4 waste must be disposed of without endangering human health and without the use of processes or methods likely to harm the environment.

D1 Deposit into or onto land (eg landfill, etc)

D2 Land treatment (eg biodegradation of liquid or sludgy discards in soils, etc)

D3 Deep injection (eg injection of pumpable discards into wells, salt domes or naturally occurring repositories, etc)

D4 Surface impoundment (eg placement of liquid or sludgy discards into pits, ponds or lagoons, etc)

D5 Specially engineered landfill (eg placement into lined discrete cells which are capped and isolated from one another and the environment, etc)

D6 Release into a water body except seas/oceans

D7 Release into seas/oceans including sea-bed insertion

D8 Biological treatment not specified elsewhere in this Annex which results in final compounds or mixtures which are discarded by means of any of the operations numbered D1 to D12

D9 Physico-chemical treatment not specified elsewhere in this Annex which results in final compounds or mixtures which are discarded by means of any of the operations numbered D1 to D12 (eg evaporation, drying, calcination, etc)

D10 Incineration on land

D11 Incineration at sea

D12 Permanent storage (eg emplacement of containers in a mine, etc)

D13   Blending or mixture prior to submission to any of the operations numbered D1 to D12

D14   Repackaging prior to submission to any of the operations numbered D1 to D13

D15   Storage pending any of the operations numbered D1 to D14, excluding temporary storage, pending collection, on the site where it is produced.]

[1323]

NOTES

Added by Council Directive 91/156/EEC of 18 March 1991, Art 1; substituted by Commission Decision 96/350/EC of 24 May 1996, Art 1.

[ANNEX IIB
RECOVERY OPERATIONS

NB: This Annex is intended to list recovery operations as they occur in practice. In accordance with Article 4 waste must be recovered without endangering human health and without the use of processes or methods likely to harm the environment.

R1   Use principally as a fuel or other means to generate energy

R2   Solvent reclamation/regeneration

R3   Recycling/reclamation of organic substances which are not used as solvents (including composting and other biological transformation processes)

R4   Recycling/reclamation of metals and metal compounds

R5   Recycling/reclamation of other inorganic materials

R6   Regeneration of acids or bases

R7   Recovery of components used for pollution abatement

R8   Recovery of components from catalysts

R9   Oil re-refining or other reuses of oil

R10   Land treatment resulting in benefit to agriculture or ecological improvement

R11   Use of wastes obtained from any of the operations numbered R1 to R10

R12   Exchange of wastes for submission to any of the operations numbered R1 to R11

R13   Storage of wastes pending any of the operations numbered R1 to R12 (excluding temporary storage, pending collection, on the site where it is produced.)]

[1324]

NOTES

Added by Council Directive 91/156/EEC of 18 March 1991, Art 1; substituted by Commission Decision 96/350/EC of 24 May 1996, Art 1.

COUNCIL DIRECTIVE
of 4 May 1976

on pollution caused by certain dangerous substances discharged into the aquatic environment of the Community

(76/464/EEC)

NOTES

Date of publication in OJ: OJ L129, 18.5.76, p 23.

THE COUNCIL OF THE EUROPEAN COMMUNITIES—

Having regard to the Treaty establishing the European Economic Community, and in particular Articles 100 and 235 thereof,

Having regard to the proposal from the Commission,

Having regard to the opinion of the European Parliament,[1]

Having regard to the opinion of the Economic and Social Committee,[2]

Whereas there is an urgent need for general and simultaneous action by the Member States to protect the aquatic environment of the Community from pollution, particularly that caused by certain persistent, toxic and bioaccumulable substances;

Whereas several conventions or draft conventions, including the Convention for the prevention of marine pollution from land-based sources, the draft Convention for the protection of the Rhine against chemical pollution and the draft European Convention for the protection of international watercourses against pollution, are designed to protect international watercourses and the marine environment from pollution; whereas it is important to ensure the co-ordinated implementation of these conventions;

Whereas any disparity between the provisions on the discharge of certain dangerous substances into the aquatic environment already applicable or in preparation in the various Member States may create unequal conditions of competition and thus directly affect the functioning of the common market; whereas it is therefore necessary to approximate laws in this field, as provided for in Article 100 of the Treaty;

Whereas it seems necessary for this approximation of laws to be accompanied by Community action so that one of the aims of the Community in the sphere of protection of the environment and improvement of the quality of life can be achieved by more extensive rules; whereas certain specific provisions to this effect should therefore be laid down; whereas Article 235 of the Treaty should be invoked as the powers required for this purpose have not been provided for by the Treaty;

Whereas the programme of action of the European Communities on the environment,[3] provides for a number of measures to protect fresh water and sea water from certain pollutants;

Whereas in order to ensure effective protection of the aquatic environment of the Community, it is necessary to establish a first list, called List I, of certain individual substances selected mainly on the basis of their toxicity, persistence, and bioaccumulation, with the exception of those which are biologically harmless or which are rapidly converted into substances which are biologically harmless, and a second list, called List II, containing substances which have a deleterious effect on the aquatic environment, which can, however, be confined to a given area and which depend on the characteristics and location of the water into which they are discharged; whereas any discharge of these substances should be subject to prior authorisation which specifies emission standards;

Whereas pollution through the discharge of the various dangerous substances within List I must be eliminated; whereas the Council should, within specific time limits and on a proposal from the Commission, adopt limit values which the emission standards should not exceed, methods of measurement, and the time limits with which existing dischargers should comply;

Whereas the Member States should apply these limit values, except where a Member State can prove to the Commission, in accordance with a monitoring procedure set up by the Council, that the quality objectives established by the Council, on a proposal from the Commission, are being met and continuously maintained throughout the area which might be affected by the discharges because of the action taken, among others, by that Member State;

Whereas it is necessary to reduce water pollution caused by the substances within List II; whereas to this end the Member States should establish programmes which incorporate quality objectives for water drawn up in compliance with Council Directives where they exist; whereas the emission standards applicable to such substances should be calculated in terms of these quality objectives;

Whereas, subject to certain exceptions and modifications, this Directive should be applied to discharges into ground water pending the adoption of specific Community rules in the matter;

Whereas one or more Member States may be able, individually or jointly, to take more stringent measures than those provided for under this Directive;

Whereas an inventory of discharges of certain particularly dangerous substances into the aquatic environment of the Community should be drawn up in order to know where they originated;

Whereas it may be necessary to revise and, where required, supplement Lists I and II on the basis of experience, if appropriate, by transferring certain substances from List II to List I,

NOTES

1 OJ C5, 8.1.75, p 62.
2 OJ C108, 15.5.75, p 76.
3 OJ C112, 20.12.73, p 1.

HAS ADOPTED THIS DIRECTIVE—

Article 1

1.   Subject to Article 8, this Directive shall apply to—
— inland surface water,
— territorial waters,
— internal coastal waters,
— ground water.

2.   For the purposes of this Directive—
    (a) "inland surface water" means all static or flowing fresh surface water situated in the territory of one or more Member States;
    (b) "internal coastal waters" means waters on the land-ward side of the base line from which the breadth of territorial waters is measured, extending, in the case of watercourses, up to the fresh-water limit;
    (c) "fresh-water limit" means the place in the watercourse where, at low tide and in a period of low fresh-water flow, there is an appreciable increase in salinity due to the presence of sea-water;
    (d) "discharge" means the introduction into the waters referred to in paragraph 1 of any substances in List I or List II of the Annex, with the exception of—
        — discharges of dredgings,
        — operational discharges from ships in territorial waters,
        — dumping from ships in territorial waters;
    (e) "pollution" means the discharge by man, directly or indirectly, of substances or energy into the aquatic environment, the results of which are such as to cause hazards to human health, harm to living resources and to aquatic ecosystems, damage to amenities or interference with other legitimate uses of water.

[1325]

Article 2

Member States shall take the appropriate steps to eliminate pollution of the waters referred to in Article 1 by the dangerous substances in the families and groups of substances in List I of the Annex and to reduce pollution of the said waters by the dangerous substances in the families and groups of substances in List II of the Annex, in accordance with this Directive, the provisions of which represent only a first step towards this goal.

[1326]

Article 3

With regard to the substances belonging to the families and groups of substances in List I, hereinafter called "substances within List I"—
    1   all discharges into the waters referred to in Article 1 which are liable to contain any such substance shall require prior authorisation by the competent authority of the Member State concerned;
    2   the authorisation shall lay down emission standards with regard to discharges of any such substance into the waters referred to in Article 1 and, where this is necessary for the implementation of this Directive, to discharges of any such substance into sewers;
    3   in the case of existing discharges of any such substance into the waters referred to in Article 1, the dischargers must comply with the conditions laid down in the authorisation within the period stipulated therein. This period may not exceed the limits laid down in accordance with Article 6(4);
    4   authorisations may be granted for a limited period only. They may be renewed, taking into account any charges in the limit values referred to in Article 6.

[1327]

Article 4

1.   Member States shall apply a system of zero-emission to discharges into ground water of substances within List I.

2.   Member States shall apply to ground water the provisions of this Directive relating to the substances belonging to the families and groups of substances in List II, hereinafter called "substances within List II".

3.   Paragraphs 1 and 2 shall apply neither to domestic effluents nor to discharges injected into deep, saline and unusable strata.

4.   The provisions of this Directive relating to ground water shall no longer apply upon the implementation of a separate Directive on ground water.

[1328]

Article 5

1.   The emission standards laid down in the authorisations granted pursuant to Article 3 shall determine —
  - (a) the maximum concentration of a substance permissible in a discharge. In the case of dilution the limit value provided for in Article 6(1)(a) shall be divided by the dilution factor;
  - (b) the maximum quantity of a substance permissible in a discharge during one or more specified periods of time. This quantity may, if necessary, also be expressed as a unit of weight of the pollutant per unit of the characteristic element of the polluting activity (eg unit of weight per unit of raw material or per product unit).

2.   For each authorisation, the competent authority of the Member State concerned may, if necessary, impose more stringent emission standards than those resulting from the application of the limit values laid down by the Council pursuant to Article 6, taking into account in particular the toxicity, persistence, and bioaccumulation of the substance concerned in the environment into which it is discharged.

3.   If the discharger states that he is unable to comply with the required emission standards, or if this situation is evident to the competent authority in the Member State concerned, authorisation shall be refused.

4.   Should the emission standards not be complied with, the competent authority in the Member State concerned shall take all appropriate steps to ensure that the conditions of authorisation are fulfilled and, if necessary, that the discharge is prohibited.

[1329]

Article 6

1.   The Council, acting on a proposal from the Commission, shall lay down the limit values which the emission standards must not exceed for the various dangerous substances included in the families and groups of substances within List I. These limit values shall be determined by —
  - (a) the maximum concentration of a substance permissible in a discharge, and
  - (b) where appropriate, the maximum quantity of such a substance expressed as a unit of weight of the pollutant per unit of the characteristic element of the polluting activity (eg unit of weight per unit of raw material or per product unit).

Where appropriate, limit values applicable to industrial effluents shall be established according to sector and type of product.

The limit values applicable to the substances within List I shall be laid down mainly on the basis of—
— toxicity,
— persistence,
— bioaccumulation,
taking into account the best technical means available.

2.   The Council, acting on a proposal from the Commission, shall lay down quality objectives for the substances within List I.

These objectives shall be laid down principally on the basis of the toxicity, persistence and accumulation of the said substances in living organisms and in sediment, as indicated by the latest conclusive scientific data, taking into account the difference in characteristics between salt-water and fresh water.

3.   The limit values established in accordance with paragraph 1 shall apply except in the cases where a Member State can prove to the Commission, in accordance with a monitoring procedure set up by the Council on a proposal from the Commission, that the quality objectives established in accordance with paragraph 2, or more severe Community quality objectives, are being met and continuously maintained throughout the area which might be affected by the discharges because of the action taken, among others, by that Member State.

The Commission shall report to the Council the instances where it has had recourse to the quality objectives method. Every five years the Council shall review, on the basis of a Commission proposal and in accordance with Article 148 of the Treaty, the instances where the said method has been applied.

4.   For those substances included in the families and groups of substances referred to in paragraph 1, the deadlines referred to in point 3 of Article 3 shall be laid down by the Council in accordance with Article 12, taking into account the features of the industrial sectors concerned and, where appropriate, the types of products.

[1330]

Article 7

1.   In order to reduce pollution of the waters referred to in Article 1 by the substances within List II, Member States shall establish programmes in the implementation of which they shall apply in particular the methods referred to in paragraphs 2 and 3.

2.   All discharges into the waters referred to in Article 1 which are liable to contain any of the substances within List II shall require prior authorisation by the competent authority in the Member State concerned, in which emission standards shall be laid down. Such standards shall be based on the quality objectives, which shall be fixed as provided for in paragraph 3.

3.   The programmes referred to in paragraph 1 shall include quality objectives for water; these shall be laid down in accordance with Council Directives, where they exist.

4.   The programmes may also include specific provisions governing the composition and use of substances or groups of substances and products and shall take into account the latest economically feasible technical developments.

5.   The programmes shall set deadlines for their implementation.

6.   Summaries of the programmes and the results of their implementation shall be communicated to the Commission.

7.   The Commission, together with the Member States, shall arrange for regular comparisons of the programmes in order to ensure sufficient co-ordination in their

implementation. If it sees fit, it shall submit relevant proposals to the Council to this end.

[1331]

Article 8

Member States shall take all appropriate steps to implement measures adopted by them pursuant to this directive in such a way as not to increase the pollution of waters to which Article 1 does not apply. They shall in addition prohibit all acts which intentionally or unintentionally circumvent the provisions of this Directive.

[1332]

Article 9

The application of the measures taken pursuant to this Directive may on no account lead, either directly or indirectly, to increased pollution of the waters referred to in Article 1.

[1333]

Article 10

Where appropriate, one or more Member States may individually or jointly take more stringent measures than those provided for under this Directive.

[1334]

Article 11

The competent authority shall draw up an inventory of the discharges into the waters referred to in Article 1 which may contain substances within List I to which emission standards are applicable.

[1335]

Article 12

1.   The Council, acting unanimously, shall take a decision within nine months on any Commission proposal made pursuant to Article 6 and on the proposals concerning the methods of measurement applicable.

 Proposals concerning an initial series of substances as well as the methods of measurement applicable and the deadlines referred to in Article 6(4) shall be submitted by the Commission within a maximum period of two years following notification of this Directive.

2.   The Commission shall, where possible within 27 months following notification of this Directive, forward the first proposals made pursuant to Article 7(7). The Council, acting unanimously, shall take a decision within nine months.

[1336]

Article 13

[1.   At intervals of three years the Member States shall send information to the Commission on the implementation of this Directive, in the form of a sectoral reports which shall also cover other pertinent Community Directives. This report shall be drawn up on the basis of a questionnaire or outline drafted by the Commission in accordance with the procedure laid down in Article 6 of Directive 91/692/EEC.[1] The questionnaire or outline shall be sent to the Member States six months before the start of the period covered by the report. The report shall be sent to the Commission within nine months of the end of the three-year period covered by it.

 The first report shall cover the period from 1993 to 1995 inclusive.

The Commission shall publish a Community report on the implementation of the Directive within nine months of receiving the reports from the Member States.]

2.   Information acquired as a result of the application of this Article shall be used only for the purpose for which it was requested.

3.   The Commission and the competent authorities of the Member States, their officials and other servants shall not disclose information acquired by them pursuant to this Directive and of a kind covered by the obligation of professional secrecy.

4.   The provisions of paragraphs 2 and 3 shall not prevent publication of general information or surveys which do not contain information relating to particular undertakings or associations of undertakings.

[1337]

NOTES
    [1]   OJ L377, 31.12.91, p 48.
    Para (1): substituted by Council Directive 91/692/EEC of 23 December 1991, Art 2(1), Annex I.

Article 14

The Council, acting on a proposal from the Commission, which shall act on its own initiative or at the request of a Member State, shall revise and, where necessary, supplement Lists I and II on the basis of experience, if appropriate, by transferring certain substances from List II to List I.

[1338]

Article 15

This Directive is addressed to the Member States.

[1339]

Done at Brussels, 4 May 1976.

ANNEX
List I of families and groups of substances

List I contains certain individual substances which belong to the following families and groups of substances, selected mainly on the basis of their toxicity, persistence and bioaccumulation, with the exception of those which are biologically harmless or which are rapidly converted into substances which are biologically harmless—
    1.   organohalogen compounds and substances which may form such compounds in the aquatic environment,
    2.   organophosphorus compounds,
    3.   organotin compounds,
    4.   substances in respect of which it has been proved that they possess carcinogenic properties in or via the aquatic environment,[1]
    5.   mercury and its compounds,
    6.   cadmium and its compounds,
    7.   persistent mineral oils and hydrocarbons of petroleum origin,
          and for the purposes of implementing Articles 2, 8, 9 and 14 of this Directive—
    8.   persistent synthetic substances which may float, remain in suspension or sink and which may interfere with any use of the waters.

NOTES
    [1]   Where certain substances in List II are carcinogenic, they are included in category 4 of this list.

List II of families and groups of substances

List II contains—
    —   substances belonging to the families and groups of substances in List I for which the limit values referred to in Article 6 of the Directive have not been determined,

— certain individual substances and categories of substances belonging to the families and groups of substances listed below,

and which have a deleterious effect on the aquatic environment, which can, however, be confined to a given area and which depend on the characteristics and location of the water into which they are discharged.

Families and groups of substances referred to in the second indent

1.   The following metalloids and metals and their compounds—

1. zinc	6. selenium	11. tin	16. vanadium
2. copper	7. arsenic	12. barium	17. cobalt
3. nickel	8. antimony	13. beryllium	18. thalium
4. chromium	9. molybdenum	14. boron	19. tellurium
5. lead	10. titanium	15. uranium	20. silver

2.   Biocides and their derivatives not appearing in List I.

3.   Substances which have a deleterious effect on the taste and/or smell of the products for human consumption derived from the aquatic environment,

and compounds liable to give rise to such substances in water.

4.   Toxic or persistent organic compounds of silicon, and substances which may give rise to such compounds in water, excluding those which are biologically harmless or are rapidly converted in water into harmless substances.

5.   Inorganic compounds of phosphorus and elemental phosphorus.

6.   Non persistent mineral oils and hydrocarbons of petroleum origin.

7.   Cyanides, fluorides.

8.   Substances which have an adverse effect on the oxygen balance, particularly—

ammonia, nitrites.

Statement on Article 8

With regard to the discharge of waste water into the open sea by means of pipelines, Member States undertake to lay down requirements which shall, be not less stringent than those imposed by this Directive.

[1340]

COUNCIL DIRECTIVE
of 2 April 1979

on the conservation of wild birds

(79/409/EEC)

NOTES

Date of publication in OJ: OJ L103, 25.4.79, p 1.

THE COUNCIL OF THE EUROPEAN COMMUNITIES:

Having regard to the Treaty establishing the European Economic Community, and in particular Article 235 thereof,

Having regard to the proposal from the Commission,[1]

Having regard to the opinion of the European Parliament,[2]

Having regard to the opinion of the Economic and Social Committee,[3]

Whereas the Council declaration of 22 November 1973 on the programme of action of the European Communities on the environment[4] calls for specific action to protect birds, supplemented by the resolution of the Council of the European Communities and of the representatives of the Governments of the Member States meeting within the Council of 17 May 1977 on the continuation and implementation of a European Community policy and action programme on the environment;[5]

Whereas a large number of species of wild birds naturally occurring in the European territory of the Member States are declining in number, very rapidly in some cases; whereas this decline represents a serious threat to the conservation of the natural environment, particularly because of the biological balances threatened thereby;

Whereas the species of wild birds naturally occurring in the European territory of the Member States are mainly migratory species; whereas such species constitute a common heritage and whereas effective bird protection is typically a trans-frontier environment problem entailing common responsibilities;

Whereas the conditions of life for birds in Greenland are fundamentally different from those in the other regions of the European territory of the Member States on account of the general circumstances and in particular the climate, the low density of population and the exceptional size and geographical situation of the island;

Whereas therefore this Directive should not apply to Greenland;

Whereas the conservation of the species of wild birds naturally occurring in the European territory of the Member States is necessary to attain, within the operation of the common market, of the Community's objectives regarding the improvement of living conditions, a harmonious development of economic activities throughout the Community and a continuous and balanced expansion, but the necessary specific powers to act have not been provided for in the Treaty;

Whereas the measures to be taken must apply to the various factors which may affect the numbers of birds, namely the repercussions of man's activities and in particular the destruction and pollution of their habitats, capture and killing by man and the trade resulting from such practices; whereas the stringency of such measures should be adapted to the particular situation of the various species within the framework of a conservation policy;

Whereas conservation is aimed at the long-term protection and management of natural resources as an integral part of the heritage of the peoples of Europe; whereas it makes it possible to control natural resources and governs their use on the basis of the measures necessary for the maintenance and adjustment of the natural balances between species as far as is reasonably possible;

Whereas the preservation, maintenance or restoration of a sufficient diversity and area of habitats is essential to the conservation of all species of birds; whereas certain species of birds should be the subject of special conservation measures concerning their habitats in order to ensure their survival and reproduction in their area of distribution; whereas such measures must also take account of migratory species and be co-ordinated with a view to setting up a coherent whole;

Whereas, in order to prevent commercial interests from exerting a possible harmful pressure on exploitation levels it is necessary to impose a general ban on marketing and to restrict all derogation to those species whose biological status so permits, account being taken of the specific conditions obtaining in the different regions;

Whereas, because of their high population level, geographical distribution and reproductive rate in the Community as a whole, certain species may be hunted, which constitutes acceptable exploitation; where certain limits are established and respected, such hunting must be compatible with maintenance of the population of these species at a satisfactory level;

Whereas the various means, devices or methods of large-scale or non-selective capture or killing and hunting with certain forms of transport must be banned because of the excessive pressure which they exert or may exert on the numbers of the species concerned;

Whereas, because of the importance which may be attached to certain specific situations, provision should be made for the possibility of derogations on certain European Communities conditions and subject to monitoring by the Commission;

Whereas the conservation of birds and, in particular, migratory birds still presents problems which call for scientific research; whereas such research will also make it possible to assess the effectiveness of the measures taken;

Whereas care should be taken in consultation with the Commission to see that the introduction of any species of wild bird not naturally occurring in the European territory of the Member States does not cause harm to local flora and fauna;

Whereas the Commission will every three years prepare and transmit to the Member States a composite report based on information submitted by the Member States on the application of national provisions introduced pursuant to this Directive;

Whereas it is necessary to adapt certain Annexes rapidly in the light of technical and scientific progress; whereas, to facilitate the implementation of the measures needed for this purpose, provision should be made for a procedure establishing close co-operation between the Member States and the Commission in a Committee for Adaptation to Technical and Scientific Progress,

NOTES
1   OJ C24, 1.2.77, p 3; OJ C201, 23.8.77, p 2.
2   OJ C163, 11.7.77, p 28.
3   OJ C152, 29.6.77, p 3.
4   OJ C112, 20.12.73, p 40.
5   OJ C139, 13.6.77, p 1.

HAS ADOPTED THIS DIRECTIVE—

Article 1

1.   This Directive relates to the conservation of all species of naturally occurring birds in the wild state in the European territory of the Member States to which the Treaty applies. It covers the protection, management and control of these species and lays down rules for their exploitation.

2.   It shall apply to birds, their eggs, nests and habitats.

3.   This Directive shall not apply to Greenland.

[1341]

Article 2

Member States shall take the requisite measures to maintain the population of the species referred to in Article 1 at a level which corresponds in particular to ecological, scientific and cultural requirements, while taking account of economic and recreational requirements, or to adapt the population of these species to that level.

[1342]

Article 3

1.   In the light of the requirements referred to in Article 2, Member States shall take the requisite measures to preserve, maintain or re-establish a sufficient diversity and area of habitats for all the species of birds referred to in Article 1.

2.   The preservation, maintenance and re-establishment of biotopes and habitats shall include primarily the following measures—
    (a) creation of protected areas;
    (b) upkeep and management in accordance with the ecological needs of habitats inside and outside the protected zones;
    (c) re-establishment of destroyed biotopes;
    (d) creation of biotopes.

[1343]

Article 4

1.   The species mentioned in Annex I shall be the subject of special conservation measures concerning their habitat in order to ensure their survival and reproduction in their area of distribution.

In this connection, account shall be taken of—
    (a) species in danger of extinction;
    (b) species vulnerable to specific changes in their habitat;
    (c) species considered rare because of small populations or restricted local distribution;
    (d) other species requiring particular attention for reasons of the specific nature of their habitat.

Trends and variations in population levels shall be taken into account as a background for evaluations.

Member States shall classify in particular the most suitable territories in number and size as special protection areas for the conservation of these species, taking into account their protection requirements in the geographical sea and land area where this Directive applies.

2.   Member States shall take similar measures for regularly occurring migratory species not listed in Annex I, bearing in mind their need for protection in the geographical sea and land area where this Directive applies, as regards their breeding, moulting and wintering areas and staging posts along their migration routes. To this end, Member States shall pay particular attention to the protection of wetlands and particularly to wetlands of international importance.

3.   Member States shall send the Commission all relevant information so that it may take appropriate initiatives with a view to the co-ordination necessary to ensure that the areas provided for in paragraphs 1 and 2 above form a coherent whole which meets the protection requirements of these species in the geographical sea and land area where this Directive applies.

4.   In respect of the protection areas referred to in paragraphs 1 and 2 above, Member States shall take appropriate steps to avoid pollution or deterioration of habitats or any disturbances affecting the birds, in so far as these would be significant having regard to the objectives of this Article. Outside these protection areas, Member States shall also strive to avoid pollution or deterioration of habitats.
[1344]

NOTES
   Obligations arising under the first sentence of para 4 are replaced by obligations arising under Council Directive 92/43/EC, Art 6(2), (3), (4), see further Art 7 thereof at **[1423]**.

Article 5

Without prejudice to Articles 7 and 9, Member States shall take the requisite measures to establish a general system of protection for all species of birds referred to in Article 1, prohibiting in particular—
   (a) deliberate killing or capture by any method;
   (b) deliberate destruction of, or damage to, their nests and eggs or removal of their nests;
   (c) taking their eggs in the wild and keeping these eggs even if empty;
   (d) deliberate disturbance of these birds particularly during the period of breeding and rearing, in so far as disturbance would be significant having regard to the objectives of this Directive;
   (e) keeping birds of species the hunting and capture of which is prohibited.
[1345]

Article 6

1.   Without prejudice to the provisions of paragraphs 2 and 3, Member States shall prohibit, for all the bird species referred to in Article 1, the sale, transport for sale, keeping for sale and the offering for sale of live or dead birds and of any readily recognisable parts or derivatives of such birds.

2.   The activities referred to in paragraph 1 shall not be prohibited in respect of the species referred to in Annex III/1, provided that the birds have been legally killed or captured or otherwise legally acquired.

3.   Member States may, for the species listed in Annex III/2, allow within their territory the activities referred to in paragraph 1, making provision for certain restrictions, provided the birds have been legally killed or captured or otherwise legally acquired.

Member States wishing to grant such authorisation shall first of all consult the Commission with a view to examining jointly with the latter whether the marketing of specimens of such species would result or could reasonably be expected to result in the population levels, geographical distribution or reproductive rate of the species being endangered throughout the Community. Should this examination prove that the intended authorisation will, in the view of the Commission, result in any one of the aforementioned species being thus endangered or in the possibility of their being thus endangered, the Commission shall forward a reasoned recommendation to the Member State concerned stating its opposition to the marketing of the species in question. Should the Commission consider that no such risk exists, it will inform the Member State concerned accordingly.

The Commission's recommendation shall be published in the *Official Journal of the European Communities*.

Member States granting authorisation pursuant to this paragraph shall verify at regular intervals that the conditions governing the granting of such authorisation continue to be fulfilled.

4.	The Commission shall carry out studies on the biological status of the species listed in Annex III/3 and on the effects of marketing on such status.

It shall submit, at the latest four months before the time limit referred to in Article 18(1) of this Directive, a report and its proposals to the Committee referred to in Article 16, with a view to a decision on the entry of such species in Annex III/2.

Pending this decision, the Member States may apply existing national rules to such species without prejudice to paragraph 3 hereof.

[1346]

Article 7

1.	Owing to their population level, geographical distribution and reproductive rate throughout the Community, the species listed in Annex II may be hunted under national legislation. Member States shall ensure that the hunting of these species does not jeopardise conservation efforts in their distribution area.

2.	The species referred to in Annex II/1 may be hunted in the geographical sea and land area where this Directive applies.

3.	The species referred to in Annex II/2 may be hunted only in the Member States in respect of which they are indicated.

4.	Member States shall ensure that the practice of hunting, including falconry if practised, as carried on in accordance with the national measures in force, complies with the principles of wise use and ecologically balanced control of the species of birds concerned and that this practice is compatible as regards the population of these species, in particular migratory species, with the measures resulting from Article 2. They shall see in particular that the species to which hunting laws apply are not hunted during the rearing season nor during the various stages of reproduction. In the case of migratory species, they shall see in particular that the species to which hunting regulations apply are not hunted during their period of reproduction or during their return to their rearing grounds. Member States shall send the Commission all relevant information on the practical application of their hunting regulations.

[1347]

Article 8

1.	In respect of the hunting, capture or killing of birds under this Directive, Member States shall prohibit the use of all means, arrangements or methods used for the large-scale or non-selective capture or killing of birds or capable of causing the local disappearance of a species, in particular the use of those listed in Annex IV(a).

2.   Moreover, Member States shall prohibit any hunting from the modes of transport and under the conditions mentioned in Annex IV(b).

[1348]

Article 9

1.   Member States may derogate from the provisions of Articles 5, 6, 7 and 8, where there is no other satisfactory solution, for the following reasons—
   (a) in the interests of public health and safety,
          — in the interests of air safety,
          — to prevent serious damage to crops, livestock, forests, fisheries and water,
          — for the protection of flora and fauna;
   (b) for the purposes of research and teaching, of re-population, of re-introduction and for the breeding necessary for these purposes;
   (c) to permit, under strictly supervised conditions and on a selective basis, the capture, keeping or other judicious use of certain birds in small numbers.

2.   The derogations must specify—
   — the species which are subject to the derogations,
   — the means, arrangements or methods authorised for capture or killing,
   — the conditions of risk and the circumstances of time and place under which such derogations may be granted,
   — the authority empowered to declare that the required conditions obtain and to decide what means, arrangements or methods may be used, within what limits and by whom,
   — the controls which will be carried out.

3.   Each year the Member States shall send a report to the Commission on the implementation of this Article.

4.   On the basis of the information available to it, and in particular the information communicated to it pursuant to paragraph 3, the Commission shall at all times ensure that the consequences of these derogations are not incompatible with this Directive. It shall take appropriate steps to this end.

[1349]

Article 10

1.   Member States shall encourage research and any work required as a basis for the protection, management and use of the population of all species of bird referred to in Article 1.

2.   Particular attention shall be paid to research and work on the subjects listed in Annex V. Member States shall send the Commission any information required to enable it to take appropriate measures for the co-ordination of the research and work referred to in this Article.

[1350]

Article 11

Member States shall see that any introduction of species of bird which do not occur naturally in the wild state in the European territory of the Member States does not prejudice the local flora and fauna. In this connection they shall consult the Commission.

[1351]

Article 12

1.   Member States shall forward to the Commission every three years, starting from the date of expiry of the time limit referred to in Article 18(1), a report on the implementation of national provisions taken thereunder.

2.   The Commission shall prepare every three years a composite report based on the information referred to in paragraph 1. That part of the draft report covering the information supplied by a Member State shall be forwarded to the authorities of the Member State in question for verification. The final version of the report shall be forwarded to the Member States.

[1352]

Article 13

Application of the measures taken pursuant to this Directive may not lead to deterioration in the present situation as regards the conservation of species of birds referred to in Article 1.

[1353]

Article 14

Member States may introduce stricter protective measures than those provided for under this Directive.

[1354]

Article 15

Such amendments as are necessary for adapting Annexes I and V to this Directive to technical and scientific progress and the amendments referred to in the second paragraph of Article 6(4) shall be adopted in accordance with the procedure laid down in Article 17.

[1355]

Article 16

1.   For the purposes of the amendments referred to in Article 15 of this Directive, a Committee for the Adaptation to Technical and Scientific Progress (hereinafter called "the Committee"), consisting of representatives of the Member States and chaired by a representative of the Commission, is hereby set up.

2.   The Committee shall draw up its rules of procedure.

[1356]

Article 17

1.   Where the procedure laid down in this Article is to be followed, matters shall be referred to the Committee by its chairman, either on his own initiative or at the request of the representative of a Member State.

2.   The Commission representative shall submit to the Committee a draft of the measures to be taken. The Committee shall deliver its opinion on the draft within a time limit set by the chairman having regard to the urgency of the matter. It shall act by a majority of [54] votes, the votes of the Member States being weighted as provided in Article 148(2) of the Treaty. The chairman shall not vote.

3.   (a) The Commission shall adopt the measures envisaged where they are in accordance with the opinion of the Committee.

     (b) Where the measures envisaged are not in accordance with the opinion of the Committee, or if no opinion is delivered, the Commission shall without delay submit a proposal to the Council concerning the measures to be adopted. The Council shall act by a qualified majority.

     (c) If, within three months of the proposal being submitted to it, the Council has not acted, the proposed measures shall be adopted by the Commission.

[1357]

NOTES
Para (2): figure in square brackets substituted by the Act of Accession of Spain and Portugal 1985.

Article 18

1.   Member States shall bring into force the laws, regulations and administrative provisions necessary to comply with this Directive within two years of its notification. They shall forthwith inform the Commission thereof.

2.   Member States shall communicate to the Commission the texts of the main provisions of national law which they adopt in the field governed by this Directive.

[1358]

Article 19

This Directive is addressed to the Member States.

[1359]

Done at Luxembourg, 2 April 1979.

(The Annexes to this Directive are not reproduced.)

COUNCIL DIRECTIVE
of 17 December 1979

on the protection of groundwater against pollution caused by certain dangerous substances

(80/68/EEC)

NOTES
Date of publication in OJ: OJ L20, 26.1.80, p 43.

THE COUNCIL OF THE EUROPEAN COMMUNITIES:

Having regard to the Treaty establishing the European Economic Community, and in particular Articles 100 and 235 thereof,

Having regard to the proposal from the Commission,[1]

Having regard to the opinion of the European Parliament,[2]

Having regard to the opinion of the Economic and Social Committee,[3]

Whereas there is an urgent need for action to protect the groundwater of the Community from pollution, particularly that caused by certain toxic, persistent and bioaccumulable substances;

Whereas the 1973 programme of action of the European Communities on the environment,[4] supplemented by that of 1977,[5] provides for a number of measures to protect groundwater from certain pollutants;

Whereas Article 4 of Council Directive 76/464/EEC of 4 May 1976 on pollution caused by certain dangerous substances discharged into the aquatic environment of the Community[6] provides for the implementation of a separate Directive on groundwater;

Whereas any disparity between the provisions on the discharge of certain dangerous substances into groundwater already applicable or in preparation in the Member States may create unequal conditions of competition and thus directly affect the functioning of the common market; whereas it is therefore necessary to approximate laws in this field, as provided for in Article 100 of the Treaty;

Whereas it is necessary for this approximation of laws to be accompanied by Community action in the sphere of environmental protection and improvement of the quality of life; whereas certain specific provisions to this effect should therefore be laid down; whereas Article 235 of the Treaty should be invoked as the requisite powers have not been provided for by the Treaty;

Whereas the following should be excluded from the scope of this Directive: domestic effluent from certain isolated dwellings and discharges containing substances in lists I or II in very small quantities and concentrations, on account of the low risk of pollution and the difficulty of controlling the discharge of such effluent; whereas discharges of matter containing radioactive substances, which will be dealt with in a specific Community instrument, should also be excluded;

Whereas to ensure the effective protection of groundwater in the Community it is necessary to prevent the discharge of substances in list I and limit the discharge of substances in list II;

Whereas a distinction should be drawn between direct discharges of dangerous substances into groundwater and actions likely to result in indirect discharges;

Whereas, with the exception of direct discharges of substances in list I, which are automatically prohibited, all discharges must be made subject to a system of authorisation; whereas such authorisations may only be delivered after a survey of the receiving environment;

Whereas provision should be made for exceptions to the rules prohibiting discharges into groundwater of substances in list I, after a survey has been made of the receiving environment and prior authorisation given, provided that the discharge is made into groundwater permanently unsuitable for any other use, particularly domestic or agricultural purposes;

Whereas artificial recharges of groundwater intended for public water supplies should be made subject to special rules;

Whereas the competent authorities of the Member States should monitor compliance with the conditions laid down in the authorisations and the effects of discharges on groundwater;

Whereas an inventory should be kept of authorisation of discharges into groundwater of substances in list I and of direct discharges into groundwater of substances in list II, and an inventory of authorisations for artificial recharges for the purpose of groundwater management;

Whereas, to the extent that the Hellenic Republic is to become a member of the European Economic Community on 1 January 1981 in accordance with the Act concerning the conditions of accession of the Hellenic Republic and the adjustments to the Treaties, it appears necessary that, for that State, the period granted to Member States to bring into force the laws, regulations and administrative provisions necessary to comply with this Directive should be extended from two to four years, bearing in mind the inadequacy of that State's technical and administrative infrastructure,

NOTES

[1] OJ C37, 14.2.78, p 3.
[2] OJ C296, 11.12.78, p 35.
[3] OJ C283, 27.11.78, p 39.
[4] OJ C112, 20.12.73, p 3.
[5] OJ C139, 13.6.77, p 3.
[6] OJ L129, 18.5.76, p 23.

HAS ADOPTED THIS DIRECTIVE—

Article 1

1.   The purpose of this Directive is to prevent the pollution of groundwater by substances belonging to the families and groups of substances in lists I or II in the Annex, hereinafter referred to as "substances in lists I or II", and as far as possible to check or eliminate the consequences of pollution which has already occurred.

2.   For the purposes of this Directive—
  (a) "groundwater" means all water which is below the surface of the ground in the saturation zone and in direct contact with the ground or subsoil;
  (b) "direct discharge" means the introduction into groundwater of substances in lists I or II without percolation through the ground or subsoil;
  (c) "indirect discharge" means the introduction into groundwater of substances in lists I or II after percolation through the ground or subsoil;
  (d) "pollution" means the discharge by man, directly or indirectly, of substances or energy into groundwater, the results of which are such as to endanger human health or water supplies, harm living resources and the aquatic ecosystem or interfere with other legitimate uses of water.

[1360]

Article 2

This Directive shall not apply to—
- (a) discharges of domestic effluents from isolated dwellings not connected to a sewerage system and situated outside areas protected for the abstraction of water for human consumption;
- (b) discharges which are found by the competent authority of the Member State concerned to contain substances in lists I or II in a quantity and concentration so small as to obviate any present or future danger of deterioration in the quality of the receiving groundwater;
- (c) discharges of matter containing radioactive substances.

[1361]

Article 3

Member States shall take the necessary steps to—
- (a) prevent the introduction into groundwater of substances in list I; and
- (b) limit the introduction into groundwater of substances in list II so as to avoid pollution of this water by these substances.

[1362]

Article 4

1.	To comply with the obligation referred to in Article 3(a), Member States—
- — shall prohibit all direct discharge of substances in list I,
- — shall subject to prior investigation any disposal or tipping for the purpose of disposal of these substances which might lead to indirect discharge. In the light of that investigation, Member States shall prohibit such activity or shall grant authorisation provided that all the technical precautions necessary to prevent such discharge are observed,
- — shall take all appropriate measures they deem necessary to prevent any indirect discharge of substances in list I due to activities on or in the ground other than those mentioned in the second indent. They shall notify such measures to the Commission, which, in the light of this information, may submit proposals to the Council for revision of this Directive.

2.	However, should prior investigation reveal that the groundwater into which the discharge of substances in list I is envisaged is permanently unsuitable for other uses, especially domestic or agricultural, the Member States may authorise the discharge of these substances provided that their presence does not impede exploitation of ground resources.

These authorisations may be granted only if all technical precautions have been taken to ensure that these substances cannot reach other aquatic systems or harm other ecosystems.

3.	Member States may, after prior investigation, authorise discharges due to re-injection into the same aquifer of water used for geothermal purposes, water pumped out of mines and quarries or water pumped out for civil engineering works.

[1363]

Article 5

1.	To comply with the obligation referred to in Article 3(b), Member States shall make subject to prior investigation—
- — all direct discharge of substances in list II, so as to limit such discharges,
- — the disposal or tipping for the purpose of disposal of these substances which might lead to indirect discharge.

In the light of that investigation, Member States may grant an authorisation, provided that all the technical precautions for preventing groundwater pollution by these substances are observed.

2.   Furthermore, Member States shall take the appropriate measures they deem necessary to limit all indirect discharge of substances in list II, due to activities on or in the ground other than those mentioned in the first paragraph.

[1364]

Article 6

Notwithstanding Articles 4 and 5, artificial recharges for the purpose of groundwater management shall be subject to a special authorisation issued by the Member States on a case-by-case basis. Such authorisation shall be granted only if there is no risk of polluting the groundwater.

[1365]

Article 7

The prior investigations referred to in Articles 4 and 5 shall include examination of the hydrogeological conditions of the area concerned, the possible purifying powers of the soil and subsoil and the risk of pollution and alteration of the quality of the groundwater from the discharge and shall establish whether the discharge of substances into groundwater is a satisfactory solution from the point of view of the environment.

[1366]

Article 8

The authorisations referred to in Articles 4, 5 and 6 may not be issued by the competent authorities of the Member States until it has been checked that the groundwater, and in particular its quality, will undergo the requisite surveillance.

[1367]

Article 9

When direct discharge is authorised in accordance with Article 4(2) and (3) or Article 5, or when waste water disposal which inevitably causes indirect discharge is authorised in accordance with Article 5, the authorisation shall specify in particular—
— the place of discharge,
— the method of discharge,
— essential precautions, particular attention being paid to the nature and concentration of the substances present in the effluents, the characteristics of the receiving environment and the proximity of water catchment areas, in particular those for drinking, thermal and mineral water,
— the maximum quantity of a substance permissible in an effluent during one or more specified periods of time and the appropriate requirements as to the concentration of these substances,
— the arrangements enabling effluents discharged into groundwater to be monitored;
— if necessary, measures for monitoring groundwater, and in particular its quality.

[1368]

Article 10

When disposal or tipping for the purpose of disposal which might lead to indirect discharge is authorised in accordance with Articles 4 or 5, authorisation shall specify in particular—
— the place where such disposal or tipping is done,
— the methods of disposal or tipping used,

— essential precautions, particular attention being paid to the nature and concentration of the substances present in the matter to be tipped or disposed of, the characteristics of the receiving environment and the proximity of water catchment areas, in particular those for drinking, thermal and mineral water,

— the maximum quantity permissible, during one or more specified periods of time, of the matter containing substances in lists I or II and, where possible, of those substances themselves, to be tipped or disposed of and the appropriate requirements as to the concentration of those substances,

— in the cases referred to in Article 4(1) and Article 5(1) the technical precautions to be implemented to prevent any discharge into groundwater of substances in list I and any pollution of such water by substances in list II,

— if necessary, the measures for monitoring the groundwater, and in particular its quality.

[1369]

Article 11

The authorisations referred to in Articles 4 and 5 may be granted for a limited period only, and will be reviewed at least every four years. They may be renewed, amended or withdrawn.

[1370]

Article 12

1.   If the person requesting an authorisation as referred to in Articles 4 or 5 states that he is unable to comply with the conditions laid down, or if this situation is evident to the competent authority in the Member State concerned, authorisation shall be refused.

2.   Should the conditions laid down in an authorisation not be complied with, the competent authority in the Member State concerned shall take appropriate steps to ensure that these conditions are fulfilled; if necessary, it shall withdraw the authorisation.

[1371]

Article 13

The competent authorities of the Member States shall monitor compliance with the conditions laid down in the authorisations and the effects of discharges on groundwater.

[1372]

Article 14

As regards discharges of the substances in lists I or II already occurring at the time of notification of this Directive, the Member States may stipulate a period not exceeding four years after entry into force of the provisions referred to in Article 21(1), on expiry of which the discharges in question must comply with this Directive.

[1373]

Article 15

The competent authorities of the Member States shall keep an inventory of the authorisations referred to in Article 4 of discharges of substances in list I, the authorisations referred to in Article 5 of direct discharges of substances in list II and the authorisations referred to in Article 6.

[1374]

Article 16

[1.   At intervals of three years the Member States shall send information to the Commission on the implementation of this Directive, in the form of a sectoral reports which shall also cover other pertinent Community Directives. This report shall be drawn up on the basis of a questionnaire or outline drafted by the Commission in accordance with the procedure laid down in Article 6 of Directive 91/692.[1] The questionnaire or outline shall be sent to the Member States six months before the start of the period covered by the report. The report shall be sent to the Commission within nine months of the end of the three-year period covered by it.

The first report shall cover the period from 1993 to 1995 inclusive.

The Commission shall publish a Community report on the implementation of the Directive within nine months of receiving the reports from the Member States.]

2.   Information acquired as a result of the application of this Article shall be used only for the purpose for which it was requested.

3.   The Commission and the competent authorities of the Member States, their officials and other servants shall not disclose information acquired by them pursuant to this Directive and of a kind covered by the obligation of professional secrecy.

4.   The provisions of paragraphs 2 and 3 shall not prevent publication of general information or surveys which do not contain information relating to particular undertakings or associations of undertakings.

[1375]

NOTES
   [1]   OJ L377, 31.12.91, p 48.
   Para (1): substituted by Council Directive 91/692/EEC of 23 December 1991, Art 2(1), Annex I.

Article 17

With regard to discharges into transfrontier groundwater, the competent authority of the Member State which intends to grant authorisation for such discharges shall inform the other Member States concerned before an authorisation is issued. At the request of one of the Member States concerned and before an authorisation is issued, consultations shall be held in which the Commission may participate.

[1376]

Article 18

The application of the measures taken pursuant to this Directive may on no account lead, either directly or indirectly, to pollution of the water referred to in Article 1.

[1377]

Article 19

Where appropriate, one or more Member States may individually or jointly take more stringent measures than those provided for under this Directive.

[1378]

Article 20

The Council, acting on a proposal from the Commission, shall, in the light of experience, revise and, if necessary, supplement lists I and II, where appropriate, by transferring certain substances from list II to list I.

[1379]

Article 21

1.   The Member States shall bring into force the laws, regulations and administrative provisions necessary to comply with this Directive within two years of its notification. They shall immediately inform the Commission thereof.

However, this period shall be increased to four years for the Hellenic Republic, subject to its accession on 1 January 1981.

2.   The Member States shall communicate to the Commission the texts of the main provisions of national law which they adopt in the field covered by this Directive.

3.   Once the measures referred to in paragraph 1 have been implemented by a Member State, the provisions of Directive 76/464/EEC relating to groundwater shall no longer apply in respect of that Member State.

[1380]

Article 22

This Directive is addressed to the Member States.

[1381]

Done at Brussels, 17 December 1979.

ANNEX

List I of families and groups of substances

List I contains the individual substances which belong to the families and groups of substances enumerated below, with the exception of those which are considered inappropriate to list I on the basis of a low risk of toxicity, persistence and bioaccumulation.

Such substances which with regard to toxicity, persistence and bioaccumulation are appropriate to list II are to be classed in list II.

1.   Organohalogen compounds and substances which may form such compounds in the aquatic environment

2.   Organophosphorus compounds

3.   Organotin compounds

4.   Substances which possess carcinogenic mutagenic or teratogenic properties in or via the aquatic environment[1]

5.   Mercury and its compounds

6.   Cadmium and its compounds

7.   Mineral oils and hydrocarbons

8.   Cyanides.

Notes
[1]   Where certain substances in list II are carcinogenic, mutagenic or teratogenic, they are included in category 4 of this list.

List II of families and groups of substances

List II contains the individual substances and the categories of substances belonging to the families and groups of substances listed below which could have a harmful effect on groundwater.

1. The following metalloids and metals and their compounds—

1. Zinc	11. Tin
2. Copper	12. Barium
3. Nickel	13. Beryllium
4. Chrome	14. Boron
5. Lead	15. Uranium
6. Selenium	16. Vanadium
7. Arsenic	17. Cobalt
8. Antimony	18. Thallium
9. Molybdenum	19. Tellurium
10. Titanium	20. Silver

2. Biocides and their derivatives not appearing in list I.

3. Substances which have a deleterious effect on the taste and/or odour of groundwater, and compounds liable to cause the formation of such substances in such water and to render it unfit for human consumption.

4. Toxic or persistent organic compounds of silicon, and substances which may cause the formation of such compounds in water, excluding those which are biologically harmless or are rapidly converted in water into harmless substances.

5. Inorganic compounds of phosphorus and elemental phosphorus.

6. Fluorides.

7. Ammonia and nitrites.

[1382]

COUNCIL DIRECTIVE
of 28 June 1984

on the combating of air pollution from industrial plants

(84/360/EEC)

NOTES

Date of publication in OJ: OJ L188, 16.7.84, p 20.

THE COUNCIL OF THE EUROPEAN COMMUNITIES—

Having regard to the Treaty establishing the European Economic Community, and in particular Articles 100 and 235 thereof,

Having regard to the proposal from the Commission,[1]

Having regard to the opinion of the European Parliament,[2]

Having regard to the opinion of the Economic and Social Committee,[3]

Whereas the 1973,[4] 1977[5] and 1983[6] action programmes of the European Communities on the environment stress the importance of the prevention and reduction of air pollution;

Whereas the 1973 and 1977 action programmes in particular provide not only for the objective evaluation of the risks to human health and to the environment from air pollution but also for the formulation of quality objectives and the setting of quality standards, especially for a number of air pollutants regarded as the most hazardous;

Whereas the Council has already adopted several Directives under these programmes;

Whereas, moreover, under Decision 81/462/EEC[7] the Community is a party to the Convention on long-range transboundary air pollution;

Whereas the 1983 action programme, the general guidelines of which have been approved by the Council of the European Communities and by the representatives of the Member States meeting within the Council, envisages that the Commission will continue its efforts to establish air quality standards and that where appropriate emission standards for certain types of source should be laid down;

Whereas all the Member States have laws, regulations and administrative provisions concerning the combating of air pollution from stationary industrial plants; whereas several Member States are in the process of amending the existing provisions;

Whereas the disparities between the provisions concerning the combating of air pollution from industrial installations currently in force, or in the process of amendment, in the different Member States are liable to create unequal conditions of competition and thus have a direct effect on the functioning of the common market; whereas, therefore, approximation of the law in this field is required, as provided for by Article 100 of the Treaty;

Whereas one of the essential tasks of the Community is to promote throughout the Community a harmonious development of economic activities and a continuous and balanced expansion, tasks which are inconceivable in the absence of a campaign to combat pollution and nuisances or of an improvement in the quality of life and in the protection of the environment;

Whereas the Community should and must help increase the effectiveness of action undertaken by the Member States to combat air pollution from stationary industrial plants;

Whereas in order to achieve this end certain principles aiming at the implementation of a series of measures and procedures designed to prevent and reduce air pollution from industrial plants within the Community should be introduced;

Whereas the Community's endeavours to introduce these principles can be only gradual, bearing in mind the complexity of the situations and the fundamental principles on which the various national policies are based;

Whereas initially a general framework should be introduced to permit the Member States to adapt, where necessary, their existing rules to the principles adopted at Community level; whereas the Member States should therefore introduce a system of prior authorisation for the operation and substantial alteration of stationary industrial plants which can cause air pollution;

Whereas, moreover, the competent national authorities cannot grant such authorisation unless a number of conditions have been fulfilled, including the requirements that all appropriate preventive measures are taken, and that the operation of the plant does not result in a significant level of air pollution;

Whereas it should be possible to apply special provisions in particularly polluted areas and in areas in need of special protection;

Whereas the rules applicable to the authorisation procedures and to the determination of emissions must satisfy certain requirements;

Whereas in certain situations the competent authorities must explore the need to impose further requirements, which, however, must not result in excessive costs for the undertaking concerned;

Whereas the provisions taken pursuant to this Directive are to be applied gradually to existing plants, taking due account of technical factors and the economic effects;

Whereas provision must be made for co-operation between the Member States themselves and with the Commission to facilitate implementation of the measures designed to prevent and to reduce air pollution and to develop preventive technology,

NOTES

[1]   OJ C139, 27.5.83, p 5.
[2]   OJ C342, 19.12.83, p 160.
[3]   OJ C23, 30.1.84, p 27.
[4]   OJ C112, 20.12.73, p 1.
[5]   OJ C139, 13.6.77, p 1.
[6]   OJ C46, 17.2.83, p 1.
[7]   OJ L171, 27.6.81, p 11.

HAS ADOPTED THIS DIRECTIVE—

Article 1

The purpose of this Directive is to provide for further measures and procedures designed to prevent or reduce air pollution from industrial plants within the Community, particularly those belonging to the categories set out in Annex I.

[1383]

Article 2

For the purposes of this Directive—

1. "Air pollution" means the introduction by man, directly or indirectly, of substances or energy into the air resulting in deleterious effects of such a nature as to endanger human health, harm living resources and ecosystems and material property and impair or interfere with amenities and other legitimate uses of the environment.
2. "Plant" means any establishment or other stationary plant used for industrial or public utility purposes which is likely to cause air pollution.
3. "Existing plant" means a plant in operation before 1 July 1987 or built or authorised before that date.
4. "Air quality limit values" means the concentration of polluting substances in the air during a specified period which is not to be exceeded.
5. "Emission limit values" means the concentration and/or mass of polluting substances in emissions from plants during a specified period which is not to be exceeded.

[1384]

Article 3

1. Member States shall take the necessary measures to ensure that the operation of plants belonging to the categories listed in Annex I requires prior authorisation by the competent authorities. The necessity to meet the requirements prescribed for such authorisation must be taken into account at the plant's design stage.

2. Authorisation is also required in the case of substantial alteration of all plants which belong to the categories listed in Annex I or which, as a result of the alteration, will fall within those categories.

3. Member States may require other categories of plants to be subject to authorisation or, where national legislation so provides, prior notification.

[1385]

Article 4

Without prejudice to the requirements laid down by national and Community provisions with a purpose other than that of this Directive, an authorisation may be issued only when the competent authority is satisfied that—

1. all appropriate preventive measures against air pollution have been taken, including the application of the best available technology, provided that the application of such measures does not entail excessive costs;
2. the use of plant will not cause significant air pollution particularly from the emission of substances referred to in Annex II;
3. none of the emission limit values applicable will be exceeded;
4. all the air quality limit values applicable will be taken into account.

[1386]

Article 5

Member States may—

— define particularly polluted areas for which emission limit values more stringent than those referred to in Article 4 may be fixed,
— define areas to be specially protected for which air quality limit values and emission limit values more stringent than those referred to in Article 4 may be fixed,
— decide that, within the abovementioned areas, specified categories of plants set out in Annex I may not be built or operated unless special conditions are complied with.

[1387]

Article 6

Applications for authorisation shall include a description of the plant containing the necessary information for the purposes of the decision whether to grant authorisation in accordance with Articles 3 and 4.

[1388]

Article 7

Subject to the provisions regarding commercial secrecy, Member States shall exchange information among themselves and with the Commission regarding their experience and knowledge of measures for prevention and reduction of air pollution, as well as technical processes and equipment and air quality and emission limit values.

[1389]

Article 8

1.   The Council, acting unanimously on a proposal from the Commission, shall if necessary fix emission limit values based on the best available technology not entailing excessive costs, and taking into account the nature, quantities and harmfulness of the emissions concerned.

2.   The Council, acting unanimously on a proposal from the Commission, shall stipulate suitable measurement and assessment techniques and methods.

[1390]

Article 9

1.   Member States shall take the necessary measures to ensure that applications for authorisation and the decisions of the competent authorities are made available to the public concerned in accordance with procedures provided for in the national law.

2.   Paragraph 1 shall apply without prejudice to specific national or Community provisions concerning the assessment of the environmental effects of public and private projects and subject to observance of the provisions regarding commercial secrecy.

[1391]

Article 10

The Member States shall make available to the other Member States concerned, as a basis for all necessary consultation within the framework of their bilateral relations, the same information as is furnished to their own nationals.

[1392]

Article 11

Member States shall take the necessary measures to ensure that emissions from plants are determined for the purpose of monitoring compliance with the obligations referred to in Article 4. The determination methods must be approved by the competent authorities.

[1393]

Article 12

The Member States shall follow developments as regards the best available technology and the environmental situation.

In the light of this examination they shall, if necessary, impose appropriate conditions on plants authorised in accordance with this Directive, on the basis both of those developments and of the desirability of avoiding excessive costs for the plants in question, having regard in particular to the economic situation of the plants belonging to the category concerned.

[1394]

Article 13

In the light of an examination of developments as regards the best available technology and the environmental situation, the Member States shall implement policies and strategies, including appropriate measures, for the gradual adaptation of existing plants belonging to the categories given in Annex I to the best available technology, taking into account in particular—
— the plant's technical characteristics,
— its rate of utilisation and length of its remaining life,
— the nature and volume of polluting emissions from it,
— the desirability of not entailing excessive costs for the plant concerned, having regard in particular to the economic situation of undertakings belonging to the category in question.

[1395]

Article 14

Member States may, in order to protect public health and the environment, adopt provisions stricter than those provided for in this Directive.

[1396]

Article 15

The Directive does not apply to industrial plants serving national defence purposes.

[1397]

[Article 15a

At intervals of three years the Member States shall send information to the Commission on the implementation of this Directive, in the form of a sectoral report which shall also cover other pertinent Community Directives. This report shall be drawn up on the basis of a questionnaire or outline drafted by the Commission in accordance with the procedure laid down in Article 6 of Directive 91/692/EEC.[1] The questionnaire or outline shall be sent to the Member States six months before the start of the period covered by the report. The report shall be sent to the Commission within nine months of the end of the three-year period covered by it.

The first report shall cover the period from 1994 to 1996 inclusive.

The Commission shall publish a Community report on the implementation of the Directive within nine months of receiving the reports from the Member States.]

[1398]

NOTES
[1] OJ L377, 31.12.91 p 48.
Inserted by Council Directive 91/692/EEC of 23 December 1991, Art 4, Annex III.

Article 16

1. Member States shall bring into force the laws, regulations and administrative provisions necessary to comply with this Directive not later than 30 June 1987.

2. Member States shall communicate to the Commission the texts of the provisions of national law which they adopt in the field governed by this Directive.

[1399]

Article 17

This Directive is addressed to the Member States.

[1400]

Done at Luxembourg, 28 June 1984.

ANNEX I
CATEGORIES OF PLANTS[1]

(covered by Article 3)

1 Energy industry

1.1 Coke ovens

1.2 Oil refineries (excluding undertakings manufacturing only lubricants from crude oil)

1.3 Coal gasification and liquefaction plants

1.4 Thermal power stations (excluding nuclear power stations) and other combustion installations with a nominal heat output of more than 50 MW.

2 Production and processing of metals

2.1 Roasting and sintering plants with a capacity of more than 1 000 tonnes of metal ore per year

2.2 Integrated plants for the production of pig iron and crude steel

2.3 Ferrous metal foundries having melting installations with a total capacity of over 5 tonnes

2.4 Plants for the production and melting of non-ferrous metals having installations with a total capacity of over 1 tonne for heavy metals or 0,5 tonne for light metals.

3 Manufacture of non-metallic mineral products

3.1 Plants for the production of cement and rotary kiln lime production

3.2 Plants for the production and processing of asbestos and manufacture of asbestos-based products

3.3 Plants for the manufacture of glass fibre or mineral fibre

3.4 Plants for the production of glass (ordinary and special) with a capacity of more than 5 000 tonnes per year

3.5 Plants for the manufacture of coarse ceramics notably refractory bricks, stoneware pipes, facing and floor bricks and roof tiles.

4 Chemical industry

4.1 Chemical plants for the production of olefins, derivatives of olefins, monomers and polymers

4.2 Chemical plants for the manufacture of other organic intermediate products

4.3 Plants for the manufacture of basic inorganic chemicals.

5 Waste disposal

5.1 Plants for the disposal of toxic and dangerous waste by incineration

5.2 Plants for the treatment by incineration of other solid and liquid waste.

6   Other industries

Plants for the manufacture of paper pulp by chemical methods with a production capacity of 25000 tonnes or more per year.

[1401]

Notes
¹ The thresholds given in this Annex refer to production capacities.

ANNEX II
LIST OF MOST IMPORTANT POLLUTING SUBSTANCES
(within the meaning of Article 4(2))

1. Sulphur dioxide and other sulphur compounds

2. Oxides of nitrogen and other nitrogen compounds

3. Carbon monoxide

4. Organic compounds, in particular hydrocarbons (except methane)

5. Heavy metals and their compounds

6. Dust; asbestos (suspended particulates and fibres), glass and mineral fibres

7. Chlorine and its compounds

8. Fluorine and its compounds

[1402]

COUNCIL DIRECTIVE
of 12 December 1991

on hazardous waste

(91/689/EEC)

NOTES
Date of publication in OJ: OJ L377, 31.12.91, p 20.

THE COUNCIL OF THE EUROPEAN COMMUNITIES—

Having regard to the Treaty establishing the European Economic Community, and in particular Article 103s thereof,

Having regard to the proposal from the Commission,[1]

Having regard to the opinion of the European Parliament,[2]

Having regard to the opinion of the Economic and Social Committee,[3]

Whereas Council Directive 78/319/EEC of 20 March 1978 on toxic and dangerous waste,[4] established Community rules on the disposal of dangerous waste; whereas in order to take account of experience gained in the implementation of that Directive by the Member States, it is necessary to amend the rules and to replace Directive 78/319/EEC by this Directive;

Whereas the Council resolution of 7 May 1990 on waste policy[5] and the action programme of the European Communities on the environment, which was the subject of the resolution of the Council of the European Communities and of the representatives of the Government of the Member States, meeting within the Council, of 19 October 1987 on the continuation and implementation of a European Community policy and action programme on the environment (1987 to 1992),[6] envisage Community measures to improve the conditions under which hazardous wastes are disposed of and managed;

Whereas the general rules applying to waste management which are laid down by Council Directive 75/442/EEC of 15 July 1975 on waste,[7] as amended by Directive 91/156/EEC,[8] also apply to the management of hazardous waste;

Whereas the correct management of hazardous waste necessitates additional, more stringent rules to take account of the special nature of such waste;

Whereas it is necessary, in order to improve the effectiveness of the management of hazardous waste in the Community, to use a precise and uniform definition of hazardous waste based on experience;

Whereas it is necessary to ensure that disposal and recovery of hazardous waste is monitored in the fullest manner possible;

Whereas it must be possible rapidly to adapt the provisions of this Directive to scientific and technical progress; whereas the Committee set up by Directive 75/442/EEC must also be empowered to adapt the provisions of this Directive to such progress,

NOTES
1. OJ C295, 19.11.88, p 8 and OJ C42, 22.2.90, p 19.
2. OJ C158, 26.6.89, p 238.
3. OJ C56, 6.3.89, p 2.
4. OJ L84, 31.3.78, p 43.
5. OJ C122, 18.5.90, p 2.
6. OJ C238, 7.12.87, p 1.
7. OJ L194, 25.7.75, p 39.
8. OJ L78, 26.3.91, p 32.

HAS ADOPTED THIS DIRECTIVE—

Article 1

1.   The object of this Directive, drawn up pursuant to Article 2(2) of Directive 75/442/EEC, is to approximate the laws of the Member States on the controlled management of hazardous waste.

2.   Subject to this Directive, Directive 75/442/EEC shall apply to hazardous waste.

3.   The definition of "waste" and of the other terms used in this Directive shall be those in Directive 75/442/EEC.

4.   For the purpose of this Directive "hazardous waste" means—
— wastes featuring on a list to be drawn up in accordance with the procedure laid down in Article 18 of Directive 75/442/EEC on the basis of Annexes I and II to this Directive, not later than six months before the date of implementation of this Directive. These wastes must have one or more of the properties listed in Annex III. The list shall take into account the origin and composition of the waste and, where necessary, limit values of concentration. This list shall be periodically reviewed and if necessary by the same procedure,
— any other waste which is considered by a Member State to display any of the properties listed in Annex III. Such cases shall be notified to the Commission and reviewed in accordance with the procedure laid down in Article 18 of Directive 75/442/EEC with a view to adaptation of the list.

5.   Domestic waste shall be exempted from the provisions of this Directive. The Council shall establish, upon a proposal from the Commission, specific rules taking into consideration the particular nature of domestic waste not later than the end of 1992.

[1403]

Article 2

1.   Member States shall take the necessary measures to require that on every site where tipping (discharge) of hazardous waste takes place the waste is recorded and identified.

2.   Member States shall take the necessary measures to require that establishments and undertakings which dispose of, recover, collect or transport

hazardous waste do not mix different categories of hazardous waste or mix hazardous waste with non-hazardous waste.

3. By way of derogation from paragraph 2, the mixing of hazardous waste with other hazardous waste or with other waste, substances or materials may be permitted only where the conditions laid down in Article 4 of Directive 75/442/EEC are complied with and in particular for the purpose of improving safety during disposal or recovery. Such an operation shall be subject to the permit requirement imposed in Articles 9, 10 and 11 of Directive 75/442/EEC.

4. Where waste is already mixed with other waste, substances or materials, separation must be effected, where technically and economically feasible, and where necessary in order to comply with Article 4 of Directive 75/442/EEC.

[1404]

Article 3

1. The derogation referred to in Article 11(1)(a) of Directive 75/442/EEC from the permit requirement for establishments or undertakings which carry out their own waste disposal shall not apply to hazardous waste covered by this Directive.

2. In accordance with Article 11(1)(b) of Directive 75/442/EEC, a Member State may waive Article 10 of that Directive for establishments or undertakings which recover waste covered by this Directive —
   — if the Member State adopts general rules listing the type and quantity of waste and laying down specific conditions (limit values for the content of hazardous substances in the waste, emission limit values, type of activity) and other necessary requirements for carrying out different forms of recovery, and
   — if the types or quantities of waste and methods of recovery are such that the conditions laid down in Article 4 of Directive 75/442/EEC are complied with.

3. The establishments or undertakings referred to in paragraph 2 shall be registered with the competent authorities.

4. If a Member State intends to make use of the provisions of paragraph 2, the rules referred to in that paragraph shall be sent to the Commission not later than three months prior to their coming into force. The Commission shall consult the Member States. In the light of these consultations the Commission shall propose that the rules be finally agreed upon in accordance with the procedure laid down in Article 18 of Directive 75/442/EEC.

[1405]

Article 4

1. Article 13 of Directive 75/442/EEC shall also apply to producers of hazardous waste.

2. Article 14 of Directive 75/442/EEC shall also apply to producers of hazardous waste and to all establishments and undertakings transporting hazardous waste.

3. The records referred to in Article 14 of Directive 75/442/EEC must be preserved for at least three years except in the case of establishments and undertakings transporting hazardous waste which must keep such records for at least 12 months. Documentary evidence that the management operations have been carried out must be supplied at the request of the competent authorities or of a previous holder.

[1406]

Article 5

1.   Member States shall take the necessary measures to ensure that, in the course of collection, transport and temporary storage, waste is properly packaged and labelled in accordance with the international and Community standards in force.

2.   In the case of hazardous waste, inspections concerning collection and transport operations made on the basis of Article 13 of Directive 75/442/EEC shall cover more particularly the origin and destination of such waste.

3.   Where hazardous waste is transferred, it shall be accompanied by an identification form containing the details specified in Section A of Annex I to Council Directive 84/631/EEC of 6 December 1984 on the supervision and control within the European Community of the transfrontier shipment of hazardous waste,[1] as last amended by Directive 86/279/EEC.[2]

[1407]

NOTES
[1]   OJ L326, 13.12.84, p 31.
[2]   OJ L181, 4.7.86, p 13.

Article 6

1.   As provided in Article 7 of Directive 75/442/EEC, the competent authorities shall draw up, either separately or in the framework of their general waste management plans, plans for the management of hazardous waste and shall make these plans public.

2.   The Commission shall compare these plans, and in particular the methods of disposal and recovery. It shall make this information available to the competent authorities of the Member States which ask for it.

[1408]

Article 7

In cases of emergency or grave danger, Member States shall take all necessary steps, including, where appropriate, temporary derogations from this Directive, to ensure that hazardous waste is so dealt with as not to constitute a threat to the population or the environment. The Member State shall inform the Commission of any such derogations.

[1409]

Article 8

1.   In the context of the report provided for in Article 16(1) of Directive 75/442/EEC, and on the basis of a questionnaire drawn up in accordance with that Article, the Member States shall send the Commission a report on the implementation of this Directive.

2.   In addition to the consolidated report referred to in Article 16(2) of Directive 75/442/EEC, the Commission shall report to the European Parliament and the Council every three years on the implementation of this Directive.

3.   In addition, by 12 December 1994, the Member States shall send the Commission the following information for every establishment or undertaking which carries out disposal and/or recovery of hazardous waste principally on behalf of third parties and which is likely to form part of the integrated network referred to in Article 5 of Directive 75/442/EEC—
—   name and address,
—   the method used to treat waste,
—   the types and quantities of waste which can be treated.

Once a year, Member States shall inform the Commission of any changes in this information.

The Commission shall make this information available on request to the competent authorities in the Member States.

The format in which this information will be supplied to the Commission shall be agreed upon in accordance with the procedure laid down in Article 18 of Directive 75/442/EEC.

[1410]

Article 9

The amendments necessary for adapting the Annexes to this Directive to scientific and technical progress and for revising the list of wastes referred to in Article 1(4) shall be adopted in accordance with the procedure laid down in Article 18 of Directive 75/442/EEC.

[1411]

Article 10

[1.   Member States shall bring into force the laws, regulations and administrative provisions necessary for them to comply with this Directive by 27 June 1995. They shall immediately inform the Commission thereof.]

2.   When Member States adopt these measures, they shall contain a reference to this Directive or shall be accompanied by such reference on the occasion of their official publication. The methods of making such a reference shall be laid down by the Member States.

3.   Member States shall communicate to the Commission the texts of the main provisions of national law which they adopt in the field governed by this Directive.

[1412]

NOTES

Para 1: substituted by Council Directive 94/31/EEC of 27 June 1994, Art 1.

[Article 11

Directive 78/319/EEC shall be repealed with effect from 27 June 1995.]

[1413]

NOTES

Substituted by Council Directive 94/31/EEC of 27 June 1994, Art 1.

Article 12

This Directive is addressed to the Member States.

[1414]

Done at Brussels, 12 December 1991.

ANNEX I
CATEGORIES OR GENERIC TYPES OF HAZARDOUS WASTE LISTED ACCORDING TO THEIR NATURE OR THE ACTIVITY WHICH GENERATED THEM[1] (WASTE MAY BE LIQUID, SLUDGE OR SOLID IN FORM)

ANNEX I.A.

Wastes displaying any of the properties listed in Annex III and which consist of —

1   anatomical substances; hospital and other clinical wastes;
2   pharmaceuticals, medicines and veterinary compounds;
3   wood preservatives;
4   biocides and phyto-pharmaceutical substances;
5   residue from substances employed as solvents;

6   halogenated organic substances not employed as solvents excluding inert polymerised materials;
7   tempering salts containing cyanides;
8   mineral oils and oily substances (eg cutting sludges, etc);
9   oil/water, hydrocarbon/water mixtures, emulsions;
10   substances containing PCBs and/or PCTs (eg dielectrics etc);
11   tarry materials arising from refining, distillation and any pyrolytic treatment (eg still bottoms, etc);
12   inks, dyes, pigments, paints, lacquers, varnishes;
13   resins, latex, plasticisers, glues/adhesives;
14   chemical substances arising from research and development or teaching activities which are not identified and/or are new and whose effects on man and/or the environment are not known (eg laboratory residues, etc);
15   pyrotechnics and other explosive materials;
16   photographic chemicals and processing materials;
17   any material contaminated with any congener of polychlorinated dibenzo-furan;
18   any material contaminated with any congener of polychlorinated dibenzo-p-dioxin.

ANNEX I.B.

Wastes which contain any of the constituents listed in Annex II and having any of the properties listed in Annex III and consisting of—

19   animal or vegetable soaps, fats, waxes;
20   non-halogenated organic substances not employed as solvents;
21   inorganic substances without metals or metal compounds;
22   ashes and/or cinders;
23   soil, sand, clay including dredging spoils;
24   non-cyanidic tempering salts;
25   metallic dust, powder;
26   spent catalyst materials;
27   liquids or sludges containing metals or metal compounds;
28   residue from pollution control operations (eg baghouse dusts, etc) except (29), (30) and (33);
29   scrubber sludges;
30   sludges from water purification plants;
31   decarbonisation residue;
32   ion-exchange column residue;
33   sewage sludges, untreated or unsuitable for use in agriculture;
34   residue from cleaning of tanks and/or equipment;
35   contaminated equipment;
36   contaminated containers (eg packaging, gas cylinders, etc) whose contents included one or more of the constituents listed in Annex II;
37   batteries and other electrical cells;
38   vegetable oils;
39   materials resulting from selective waste collections from households and which exhibit any of the characteristics listed in Annex III;
40   any other wastes which contain any of the constituents listed in Annex II and any of the properties listed in Annex III.

[1415]

Notes
[1]   Certain duplications of entries found in Annex II are intentional.

ANNEX II
CONSTITUENTS OF THE WASTES IN ANNEX I.B. WHICH RENDER THEM HAZARDOUS WHEN THEY HAVE THE PROPERTIES DESCRIBED IN ANNEX III[1]

Wastes having as constituents—
C1   beryllium; beryllium compounds;
C2   vanadium compounds;
C3   chromium (VI) compounds;

C4	cobalt compounds;
C5	nickel compounds;
C6	copper compounds;
C7	zinc compounds;
C8	arsenic; arsenic compounds;
C9	selenium; selenium compounds;
C10	silver compounds;
C11	cadmium; cadmium compounds;
C12	tin compounds;
C13	antimony; antimony compounds;
C14	tellurium; tellurium compounds;
C15	barium compounds; excluding barium sulfate;
C16	mercury; mercury compounds;
C17	thallium; thallium compounds;
C18	lead; lead compounds;
C19	inorganic sulphides;
C20	inorganic fluorine compounds, excluding calcium fluoride;
C21	inorganic cyanides;
C22	the following alkaline or alkaline earth metals: lithium, sodium, potassium, calcium, magnesium in uncombined form;
C23	acidic solutions or acids in solid form;
C24	basic solutions or bases in solid form;
C25	asbestos (dust and fibres);
C26	phosphorus: phosphorus compounds, excluding mineral phosphates;
C27	metal carbonyls;
C28	peroxides;
C29	chlorates;
C30	perchlorates;
C31	azides;
C32	PCBs and/or PCTs;
C33	pharmaceutical or veterinary compounds;
C34	biocides and phyto-pharmaceutical substances (eg pesticides, etc);
C35	infectious substances;
C36	creosotes;
C37	isocyanates; thiocyanates;
C38	organic cyanides (eg nitriles, etc);
C39	phenols; phenol compounds;
C40	halogenated solvents;
C41	organic solvents, excluding halogenated solvents;
C42	organohalogen compounds, excluding inert polymerised materials and other substances referred to in this Annex;
C43	aromatic compounds; polycyclic and heterocyclic organic compounds;
C44	aliphatic amines;
C45	aromatic amines;
C46	ethers;
C47	substances of an explosive character, excluding those listed elsewhere in this Annex;
C48	sulphur organic compounds;
C49	any congener of polychlorinated dibenzo-furan;
C50	any congener of polychlorinated dibenzo-p-dioxin;
C51	hydrocarbons and their oxygen; nitrogen and/or sulphur compounds not otherwise taken into account in this Annex.

[1416]

Notes
[1] Certain duplications of generic types of hazardous wastes listed in Annex I are intentional.

ANNEX III
PROPERTIES OF WASTES WHICH RENDER THEM HAZARDOUS

H1 "Explosive": substances and preparations which may explode under the effect of flame or which are more sensitive to shocks or friction than dinitrobenzene.

H2   "Oxidising": substances and preparations which exhibit highly exothermic reactions when in contact with other substances, particularly flammable substances.

H3–A "Highly flammable":
— liquid substances and preparations having a flash point below 21°C (including extremely flammable liquids), or
— substances and preparations which may become hot and finally catch fire in contact with air at ambient temperature without any application of energy, or
— solid substances and preparations which may readily catch fire after brief contact with a source of ignition and which continue to burn or to be consumed after removal of the source of ignition, or
— gaseous substances and preparations which are flammable in air at normal pressure, or
— substances and preparations which, in contact with water or damp air, evolve highly flammable gases in dangerous quantities.

H3–B "Flammable": liquid substances and preparations having a flash point equal to or greater than 21°C and less than or equal to 55°C.

H4   "Irritant": non-corrosive substances and preparations which, through immediate, prolonged or repeated contact with the skin or mucous membrane, can cause inflammation.

H5   "harmful": substances and preparations which, if they are inhaled or ingested or if they penetrate the skin, may involve limited health risks.

H6   "Toxic": substances and preparations (including very toxic substances and preparations) which, if they are inhaled or ingested or if they penetrate the skin, may involve serious, acute or chronic health risks and even death.

H7   "Carcinogenic": substances and preparations which, if they are inhaled or ingested or if they penetrate the skin, may induce cancer or increase its incidence.

H8   "Corrosive": substances and preparations which may destroy living tissue on contacts.

H9   "Infectious": substances containing viable micro-organisms or their toxins which are known or reliably believed to cause disease in man or other living organisms.

H10   "Teratogenic": substances and preparations which, if they are inhaled or ingested or if they penetrate the skin, may induce non-hereditary congenital malformations or increase their incidence.

H11   "Mutagenic": substances and preparations which, if they are inhaled or ingested or if they penetrate the skin, may induce hereditary genetic defects or increase their incidence.

H12   Substances and preparations which release toxic or very toxic gases in contact with water, air or an acid.

H13   Substances and preparations capable by any means, after disposal, of yielding another substance, eg a leachate, which possesses any of the characteristics listed above.

H14   "Ecotoxic": substances and preparations which present or may present immediate or delayed risks for one or more sectors of the environment.

Notes

1. Attribution of the hazard properties "toxic" (and "very toxic"), "harmful", "corrosive" and "irritant" is made on the basis of the criteria laid down by Annex VI, part IA and part IIB, of Council Directive 67/548/EEC of 27 June 1967 on the approximation of laws, regulations and administrative provisions relating to the classification, packaging and labelling of dangerous substances,[1] in the version as amended by Council Directive 79/831/EEC.[2]

2. With regard to attribution of the properties "carcinogenic", "teratogenic" and "mutagenic", and reflecting the most recent findings, additional criteria are contained in the Guide to the classification and labelling of dangerous substances and preparations of Annex VI (part IID) to Directive 67/548/EEC in the version as amended by Commission Directive 83/467/EEC.[3]

Test methods

The test methods serve to give specific meaning to the definitions given in Annex III.

The methods to be used are those described in Annex V to Directive 67/548/EEC, in the version as amended by Commission Directive 84/449/EEC,[4] or by subsequent Commission Directives adapting Directive 67/548/EEC to technical progress. These methods are themselves based on the work and recommendations of the competent international bodies, in particular the OECD.

NOTES
1   OJ L196, 16.8.67, p 1.
2   OJ L259, 15.10.79, p 10.
3   OJ L257, 16.9.83, p 1.
4   OJ L251, 19.9.89, p 1.

COUNCIL DIRECTIVE

of 21 May 1992

on the conservation of natural habitats and of wild fauna and flora

(92/43/EEC)

NOTES
Date of publication in OJ: OJ L206, 22.7.92, p 7.

THE COUNCIL OF THE EUROPEAN COMMUNITIES—

Having regard to the Treaty establishing the European Economic Community, and in particular Article 130s thereof,

Having regard to the proposal from the Commission,[1]

Having regard to the opinion of the European Parliament,[2]

Having regard to the opinion of the Economic and Social Committee,[3]

Whereas the preservation, protection and improvement of the quality of the environment, including the conservation of natural habitats and of wild fauna and flora, are an essential objective of general interest pursued by the Community, as stated in Article 130r of the Treaty;

Whereas the European Community policy and action programme on the environment (1987 to 1992)[4] makes provision for measures regarding the conservation of nature and natural resources;

Whereas, the main aim of this Directive being to promote the maintenance of biodiversity, taking account of economic, social, cultural and regional requirements, this Directive makes a contribution to the general objective of sustainable development; whereas the maintenance of such biodiversity may in certain cases require the maintenance, or indeed the encouragement, of human activities;

Whereas, in the European territory of the Member States, natural habitats are continuing to deteriorate and an increasing number of wild species are seriously threatened; whereas given that the threatened habitats and species form part of the Community's natural heritage and the threats to them are often of a transboundary nature, it is necessary to take measures at Community level in order to conserve them;

Whereas, in view of the threats to certain types of natural habitat and certain species, it is necessary to define them as having priority in order to favour the early implementation of measures to conserve them;

Whereas, in order to ensure the restoration or maintenance of natural habitats and species of Community interest at a favourable conservation status, it is necessary to designate special areas of conservation in order to create a coherent European ecological network according to a specified timetable;

Whereas all the areas designated, including those classified now or in the future as special protection areas pursuant to Council Directive 79/409/EEC of 2 April 1979 on the conservation of wild birds,[5] will have to be incorporated into the coherent European ecological network;

Whereas it is appropriate, in each area designated, to implement the necessary measures having regard to the conservation objectives pursued;

Whereas sites eligible for designation as special areas of conservation are proposed by the Member States but whereas a procedure must nevertheless be laid down to allow the designation in exceptional cases of a site which has not been proposed by a Member State but which the Community considers essential for either the maintenance or the survival of a priority natural habitat type or a priority species;

Whereas an appropriate assessment must be made of any plan or programme likely to have a significant effect on the conservation objectives of a site which has been designated or is designated in future;

Whereas it is recognised that the adoption of measures intended to promote the conservation of priority natural habitats and priority species of Community interest is a common responsibility of all Member States; whereas this may, however, impose an excessive financial burden on certain Member States given, on the one hand, the uneven distribution of such habitats and species throughout the Community and, on the other hand, the fact that the "polluter pays" principle can have only limited application in the special case of nature conservation;

Whereas it is therefore agreed that, in this exceptional case, a contribution by means of Community co-financing should be provided for within the limits of the resources made available under the Community's decisions;

Whereas land-use planning and development policies should encourage the management of features of the landscape which are of major importance for wild fauna and flora;

Whereas a system should be set up for surveillance of the conservation status of the natural habitats and species covered by this Directive;

Whereas a general system of protection is required for certain species of flora and fauna to complement Directive 79/409/EEC; whereas provision should be made for management measures for certain species, if their conservation status so warrants, including the prohibition of certain means of capture or killing, whilst providing for the possibility of derogations on certain conditions;

Whereas, with the aim of ensuring that the implementation of this Directive is monitored, the Commission will periodically prepare a composite report based, inter alia, on the information sent to it by the Member States regarding the application of national provisions adopted under this Directive;

Whereas the improvement of scientific and technical knowledge is essential for the implementation of this Directive; whereas it is consequently appropriate to encourage the necessary research and scientific work;

Whereas technical and scientific progress mean that it must be possible to adapt the Annexes; whereas a procedure should be established whereby the Council can amend the Annexes;

Whereas a regulatory committee should be set up to assist the Commission in the implementation of this Directive and in particular when decisions on Community co-financing are taken;

Whereas provision should be made for supplementary measures governing the reintroduction of certain native species of fauna and flora and the possible introduction of non-native species;

Whereas education and general information relating to objectives of this Directive are essential for ensuring its effective implementation,

NOTES
[1] OJ C247, 21.9.88, p 3 and OJ C195, 3.8.90, p 1.
[2] OJ C75, 20.3.91, p 12.
[3] OJ C31, 6.2.91, p 25.
[4] OJ C328, 7.12.87, p 1.
[5] OJ L103, 25.4.79, p 1. Directive as last amended by Directive 91/244/EEC (OJ L115, 8.5.91, p 41).

HAS ADOPTED THIS DIRECTIVE—

DEFINITIONS

Article 1

For the purpose of this Directive—
  (a) *conservation* means a series of measures required to maintain or restore the natural habitats and the populations of species of wild fauna and flora at a favourable status as defined in (e) and (i);
  (b) *natural habitats* means terrestrial or aquatic areas distinguished by geographic, abiotic and biotic features, whether entirely natural or semi-natural;
  (c) *natural habitat types of Community interest* means those which, within the territory referred to in Article 2—
    (i) are in danger of disappearance in their natural range; or
    (ii) have a small natural range following their regression or by reason of their intrinsically restricted area; or

(iii) present outstanding examples of typical characteristics of one or more of the [six] following biogeographical regions: Alpine, Atlantic, [Boreal] Continental, Macaronesian and Mediterranean.

Such habitat types are listed or may be listed Annex I;

(d) *priority natural habitat types* means natural habitat types in danger of disappearance, which are present on the territory referred to in Article 2 and for the conservation of which the Community has particular responsibility in view of the proportion of their natural range which falls within the territory referred to in Article 2; these priority natural habitat types are indicated by an asterisk (*) in Annex I;

(e) *conservation status of a natural habitat* means the sum of the influences acting on a natural habitat and its typical species that may affect its long-term natural distribution, structure and functions as well as the long-term survival of its typical species within the territory referred to in Article 2.

The conservation status of a natural habitat will be taken as "favourable" when—

— its natural range and areas it covers within that range are stable or increasing, and

— the specific structure and functions which are necessary for its long-term maintenance exist and are likely to continue to exist for the foreseeable future, and

— the conservation status of its typical species is favourable as defined in (i);

(f) *habitat of a species* means an environment defined by specific abiotic and biotic factors, in which the species lives at any stage of its biological cycle;

(g) *species of Community interest* means species which, within the territory referred to in Article 2, are—

(i) endangered, except those species whose natural range is marginal in that territory and which are not endangered or vulnerable in the western palearctic region; or

(ii) vulnerable, ie believed likely to move into the endangered category in the near future if the causal factors continue operating; or

(iii) rare, ie with small populations that are not at present endangered or vulnerable, but are at risk. The species are located within restricted geographical areas or are thinly scattered over a more extensive range; or

(iv) endemic and requiring particular attention by reason of the specific nature of their habitat and/or the potential impact of their exploitation on their habitat and/or the potential impact of their exploitation on their conservation status.

Such species are listed or may be listed in Annex II and/or Annex IV or V;

(h) *priority species* means species referred to in (g)(i) for the conservation of which the Community has particular responsibility in view of the proportion of their natural range which falls within the territory referred to in Article 2; these priority species are indicated by an asterisk (*) in Annex II;

(i) *conservation status of a species* means the sum of the influences acting on the species concerned that may affect the long-term distribution and abundance of its populations within the territory referred to in Article 2;

The *conservation status will* be taken as "favourable" when—

— population dynamics data on the species concerned indicate that it is maintaining itself on a long-term basis as a viable component of its natural habitats, and

— the natural range of the species is neither being reduced nor is likely to be reduced for the foreseeable future, and

— there is, and will probably continue to be, a sufficiently large habitat to maintain its populations on a long-term basis;

(j) *site* means a geographically defined area whose extent is clearly delineated;

(k) *site of Community importance* means a site which, in the biogeographical region or regions to which it belongs, contributes significantly to the maintenance or restoration at a favourable conservation status of a natural habitat type in Annex I or of a species in Annex II and may also contribute significantly to the coherence of Natura 2000 referred to in Article 3, and/ or contributes significantly to the maintenance of biological diversity within the biogeographic region or regions concerned.

For animal species ranging over wide areas, sites of Community importance shall correspond to the places within the natural range of such species which present the physical or biological factors essential to their life and reproduction;

(l) *special area of conservation* means a site of Community importance designated by the Member States through a statutory, administrative and/or contractual act where the necessary conservation measures are applied for the maintenance or restoration, at a favourable conservation status, of the natural habitats and/or the populations of the species for which the site is designated;

(m) *specimen* means any animal or plant, whether alive or dead, of the species listed in Annex IV and Annex V, any part or derivative thereof, as well as any other goods which appear, from an accompanying document, the packaging or a mark or label, or from any other circumstances, to be parts or derivatives of animals or plants of those species;

(n) *the committee* means the committee set up pursuant to Article 20.

[1418]

NOTES

Para 1: figure in square brackets substituted and word in square brackets inserted by the 1994 Act of Accession of the Kingdom of Norway, the Republic of Austria, the Republic of Finland and the Kingdom of Sweden, Annex I(VIII)(E), para 4(a), as adjusted by Council Decision 95/1/EC, Annex I(VIII)(E)(4), para 4(a).

Article 2

1.   The aim of this Directive shall be to contribute towards ensuring bio-diversity through the conservation of natural habitats and of wild fauna and flora in the European territory of the Member States to which the Treaty applies.

2.   Measures taken pursuant to this Directive shall be designed to maintain or restore, at favourable conservation status, natural habitats and species of wild fauna and flora of Community interest.

3.   Measures taken pursuant to this Directive shall take account of economic, social and cultural requirements and regional and local characteristics.

[1419]

CONSERVATION OF NATURAL HABITATS AND HABITATS OF SPECIES

Article 3

1.   A coherent European ecological network of special areas of conservation shall be set up under the title Natura 2000. This network, composed of sites hosting the natural habitat types listed in Annex I and habitats of the species listed in Annex II, shall enable the natural habitat types and the species' habitats concerned to be maintained or, where appropriate, restored at a favourable conservation status in their natural range.

The Natura 2000 network shall include the special protection areas classified by the Member States pursuant to Directive 79/409/EEC.

2.   Each Member State shall contribute to the creation of Natura 2000 in proportion to the representation within its territory of the natural habitat types and the habitats of species referred to in paragraph 1. To that effect each Member State shall designate, in accordance with Article 4, sites as special areas of conservation taking account of the objectives set out in paragraph 1.

3.   Where they consider it necessary, Member States shall endeavour to improve the ecological coherence of Natura 2000 by maintaining, and where appropriate developing, features of the landscape which are of major importance for wild fauna and flora, as referred to in Article 10.

[1419A]

Article 4

1.   On the basis of the criteria set out in Annex III (Stage 1) and relevant scientific information, each Member State shall propose a list of sites indicating which natural habitat types in Annex I and which species in Annex II that are native to its territory the sites host. For animal species ranging over wide areas these sites shall correspond to the places within the natural range of such species which present the physical or biological factors essential to their life and reproduction. For aquatic species which range over wide areas, such sites will be proposed only where there is a clearly identifiable area representing the physical and biological factors essential to their life and reproduction. Where appropriate, Member States shall propose adaptation of the list in the light of the results of the surveillance referred to in Article 11.

The list shall be transmitted to the Commission, within three years of the notification of this Directive, together with information on each site. That information shall include a map of the site, its name, location, extent and the data resulting from application of the criteria specified in Annex III (Stage 1) provided in a format established by the Commission in accordance with the procedure laid down in Article 21.

2.   On the basis of the criteria set out in Annex III (Stage 2) and in the framework both of each of the five biogeographical regions referred to in Article 1(c)(iii) and of the whole of the territory referred to in Article 2(1), the Commission shall establish, in agreement with each Member State, a draft list of sites of Community importance drawn from the Member States' lists identifying those which host one or more priority natural habitat types or priority species.

Member States whose sites hosting one or more priority natural habitat types and priority species represent more than 5% of their national territory may, in agreement with the Commission, request that the criteria listed in Annex III (Stage 2) be applied more flexibly in selecting all the sites of Community importance in their territory.

The list of sites selected as sites of Community importance, identifying those which host one or more priority natural habitat types or priority species, shall be adopted by the Commission in accordance with the procedure laid down in Article 21.

3.   The list referred to in paragraph 2 shall be established within six years of the notification of this Directive.

4.   Once a site of Community importance has been adopted in accordance with the procedure laid down in paragraph 2, the Member State concerned shall designate that site as a special area of conservation as soon as possible and within six years at most, establishing priorities in the light of the importance of the sites for the maintenance or restoration, at a favourable conservation status, of a natural habitat type in Annex I or a species in Annex II and for the coherence of Natura 2000, and in the light of the threats of degradation or destruction to which those sites are exposed.

5.   As soon as a site is placed on the list referred to in the third subparagraph of paragraph 2 it shall be subject to Article 6(2), (3) and (4).

[1420]

Article 5

1.   In exceptional cases where the Commission finds that a national list as referred to in Article 4(1) fails to mention a site hosting a priority natural habitat type or priority species which, on the basis of relevant and reliable scientific information, it considers to be essential for the maintenance of that priority natural habitat type or for the survival of that priority species, a bilateral consultation procedure shall be initiated between that Member State and the Commission for the purpose of comparing the scientific data used by each.

2.   If, on expiry of a consultation period not exceeding six months, the dispute remains unresolved, the Commission shall forward to the Council a proposal relating to the selection of the site as a site of Community importance.

3.   The Council, acting unanimously, shall take a decision within three months of the date of referral.

4.   During the consultation period and pending a Council decision, the site concerned shall be subject to Article 6(2).

[1421]

Article 6

1.   For special areas of conservation, Member States shall establish the necessary conservation measures involving, if need be, appropriate management plans specifically designed for the sites or integrated into other development plans, and appropriate statutory, administrative or contractual measures which correspond to the ecological requirements of the natural habitat types in Annex I and the species in Annex II present on the sites.

2.   Member States shall take appropriate steps to avoid, in the special areas of conservation, the deterioration of natural habitats and the habitats of species as well as disturbance of the species for which the areas have been designated, in so far as such disturbance could be significant in relation to the objectives of this Directive.

3.   Any plan or project not directly connected with or necessary to the management of the site but likely to have a significant effect thereon, either individually or in combination with other plans or projects, shall be subject to appropriate assessment of its implications for the site in view of the site's conservation objectives. In the light of the conclusions of the assessment of the implications for the site and subject to the provisions of paragraph 4, the competent national authorities shall agree to the plan or project only after having ascertained that it will not adversely affect the integrity of the site concerned and, if appropriate, after having obtained the opinion of the general public.

4.   If, in spite of a negative assessment of the implications for the site and in the absence of alternative solution, a plan or project must nevertheless be carried out for imperative reasons of overriding public interest, including those of a social or economic nature, the Member State shall take all compensatory measures necessary to ensure that the overall coherence of Natura 2000 is protected. It shall inform the Commission of the compensatory measures adopted.

Where the site concerned hosts a priority natural habitat type and/or a priority species, the only considerations which may be raised are those relating to human health or public safety, to beneficial consequences of primary importance for the environment or, further to an opinion from the Commission, to other imperative reasons of overriding public interest.

[1422]

Article 7

Obligations arising under Article 6(2), (3) and (4) of this Directive shall replace any obligations arising under the first sentence of Article 4(4) of Directive 79/409/EEC in respect of areas classified pursuant to Article 4(1) or similarly recognised under Article 4(2) thereof, as from the date of implementation of this Directive or the date of classification or recognition by a Member State under Directive 79/409/EEC, where the latter date is later.

[1423]

Article 8

1.   In parallel with their proposals for sites eligible for designation as special areas of conservation, hosting priority natural habitat types and/or priority species, the Member States shall send, as appropriate, to the Commission their estimates relating to the Community co-financing which they consider necessary to allow them to meet their obligations pursuant to Article 6(1).

2.   In agreement with each of the Member States concerned, the Commission shall identify, for sites of Community importance for which co-financing is sought, those measures essential for the maintenance or re-establishment at a favourable conservation status of the priority natural habitat types and priority species on the sites concerned, as well as the total cost arising from those measures.

3.   The Commission, in agreement with the Member States concerned, shall assess the financing, including co-financing, required for the operation of the measures referred to in paragraph 2, taking into account, amongst other things, the concentration on the Member State's territory of priority natural habitat types and/or priority species and the relative burdens which the required measures entail.

4.   According to the assessment referred to in paragraphs 2 and 3, the Commission shall adopt, having regard to the available sources of funding under the relevant Community instruments and according to the procedure set out in Article 21, a prioritised action framework of measures involving co-financing to be taken when the site has been designated under Article 4(4).

5.   The measures which have not been retained in the action framework for lack of sufficient resources, as well as those included in the abovementioned action framework which have not received the necessary co-financing or have only been partially co-financed, shall be reconsidered in accordance with the procedure set out in Article 21, in the context of the two-yearly review of the action framework and may, in the meantime, be postponed by the Member States pending such review. This review shall take into account, as appropriate, the new situation of the site concerned.

6.   In areas where the measures dependent on co-financing are postponed, Member States shall refrain from any new measures likely to result in deterioration of those areas.

[1424]

Article 9

The Commission, acting in accordance with the procedure laid down in Article 21, shall periodically review the contribution of Natura 2000 towards achievement of the objectives set out in Article 2 and 3. In this context, a special area of conservation may be considered for declassification where this is warranted by natural developments noted as a result of the surveillance provided for in Article 11.

[1425]

Article 10

Member States shall endeavour, where they consider it necessary, in their land-use planning and development policies and, in particular, with a view to improving the ecological coherence of the Natura 2000 network, to encourage the management of features of the landscape which are of major importance for wild fauna and flora.

Such features are those which, by virtue of their linear and continuous structure (such as rivers with their banks or the traditional systems for marking field boundaries) or their function as stepping stones (such as ponds or small woods), are essential for the migration, dispersal and genetic exchange of wild species.

[1426]

Article 11

Member States shall undertake surveillance of the conservation status of the natural habitats and species referred to in Article 2 with particular regard to priority natural habitat types and priority species.

[1427]

PROTECTION OF SPECIES

Article 12

1.   Member States shall take the requisite measures to establish a system of strict protection for the animal species listed in Annex IV(a) in their natural range, prohibiting—
    (a) all forms of deliberate capture or killing of specimens of these species in the wild;
    (b) deliberate disturbance of these species, particularly during the period of breeding, rearing, hibernation and migration;
    (c) deliberate destruction or taking of eggs from the wild;
    (d) deterioration or destruction of breeding sites or resting places.

2.   For these species, Member States shall prohibit the keeping, transport and sale or exchange, and offering for sale or exchange, of specimens taken from the wild, except for those taken legally before this Directive is implemented.

3.   The prohibition referred to in paragraph 1(a) and (b) and paragraph 2 shall apply to all stages of life of the animals to which this Article applies.

4.   Member States shall establish a system to monitor the incidental capture and killing of the animal species listed in Annex IV(a). In the light of the information gathered, Member States shall take further research or conservation measures as required to ensure that incidental capture and killing does not have a significant negative impact on the species concerned.

[1428]

Article 13

1.   Member States shall take the requisite measures to establish a system of strict protection for the plant species listed in Annex IV(b), prohibiting—
    (a) the deliberate picking, collecting, cutting, uprooting or destruction of such plants in their natural range in the wild;
    (b) the keeping, transport and sale or exchange and offering for sale or exchange of specimens of such species taken in the wild, except for those taken legally before this Directive is implemented.

2.   The prohibitions referred to in paragraph 1(a) and (b) shall apply to all stages of the biological cycle of the plants to which this Article applies.

[1429]

Article 14

1. If, in the light of the surveillance provided for in Article 11, Member States deem it necessary, they shall take measures to ensure that the taking in the wild of specimens of species of wild fauna and flora listed in Annex V as well as their exploitation is compatible with their being maintained at a favourable conservation status.

2. Where such measures are deemed necessary, they shall include continuation of the surveillance provided for in Article 11. Such measures may also include in particular—
— regulations regarding access to certain property,
— temporary or local prohibition of the taking of specimens in the wild and exploitation of certain populations,
— regulation of the periods and/or methods of taking specimens,
— application, when specimens are taken, of hunting and fishing rules which take account of the conservation of such populations,
— establishment of a system of licences for taking specimens or of quotas,
— regulation of the purchase, sale, offering for sale, keeping for sale or transport for sale of specimens,
— breeding in captivity of animal species as well as artificial propagation of plant species, under strictly controlled conditions, with a view to reducing the taking of specimens of the wild,
— assessment of the effect of the measures adopted.

[1430]

Article 15

In respect of the capture or killing of species of wild fauna listed in Annex V(a) and in cases where, in accordance with Article 16, derogations are applied to the taking, capture or killing of species listed in Annex IV(a), Member States shall prohibit the use of all indiscriminate means capable of causing local disappearance of, or serious disturbance to, populations of such species, and in particular—
(a) use of the means of capture and killing listed in Annex VI(a);
(b) any form of capture and killing from the modes of transport referred to in Annex VI(b).

[1431]

Article 16

1. Provided that there is no satisfactory alternative and the derogation is not detrimental to the maintenance of the populations of the species concerned at a favourable conservation status in their natural range, Member States may derogate from the provisions of Articles 12, 13, 14 and 15(a) and (b)—
(a) in the interest of protecting wild fauna and flora and conserving natural habitats;
(b) to prevent serious damage, in particular to crops, livestock, forests, fisheries and water and other types of property;
(c) in the interests of public health and public safety, or for other imperative reasons of overriding public interest, including those of a social or economic nature and beneficial consequences of primary importance for the environment;
(d) for the purpose of research and education, of repopulating and re-introducing these species and for the breedings operations necessary for these purposes, including the artificial propagation of plants;
(e) to allow, under strictly supervised conditions, on a selective basis and to a limited extent, the taking or keeping of certain specimens of the species listed in Annex IV in limited numbers specified by the competent national authorities.

2.   Member States shall forward to the Commission every two years a report in accordance with the format established by the Committee on the derogations applied under paragraph 1. The Commission shall give its opinion on these derogations within a maximum time limit of 12 months following receipt of the report and shall give an account to the Committee.

3.   The reports shall specify—
   (a) the species which are subject to the derogations and the reason for the derogation, including the nature of the risk, with, if appropriate, a reference to alternatives rejected and scientific data used;
   (b) the means, devices or methods authorised for the capture or killing of animal species and the reasons for their use;
   (c) the circumstances of when and where such derogations are granted;
   (d) the authority empowered to declare and check that the required conditions obtain and to decide what means, devices or methods may be used, within what limits and by what agencies, and which persons are to carry out the task;
   (e) the supervisory measures used and the results obtained.

[1432]

INFORMATION

Article 17

1.   Every six years from the date of expiry of the period laid down in Article 23, Member States shall draw up a report on the implementation of the measures taken under this Directive. This report shall include in particular information concerning the conservation measures referred to in Article 6(1) as well as evaluation of the impact of those measures on the conservation status of the natural habitat types of Annex I and the species in Annex II and the main results of the surveillance referred to in Article 11. The report, in accordance with the format established by the committee, shall be forwarded to the Commission and made accessible to the public.

2.   The Commission shall prepare a composite report based on the reports referred to in paragraph 1. This report shall include an appropriate evaluation of the progress achieved and, in particular, of the contribution of Natura 2000 to the achievement of the objectives set out in Article 3. A draft of the part of the report covering the information supplied by a Member State shall be forwarded to the Member State in question for verification. After submission to the committee, the final version of the report shall be published by the Commission, not later than two years after receipt of the reports referred to in paragraph 1, and shall be forwarded to the Member States, the European Parliament, the Council and the Economic and Social Committee.

3.   Member States may mark areas designated under this Directive by means of Community notices designed for that purpose by the committee.

[1433]

RESEARCH

Article 18

1.   Member States and the Commission shall encourage the necessary research and scientific work having regard to the objectives set out in Article 2 and the obligation referred to in Article 11. They shall exchange information for the purposes of proper co-ordination of research carried out at Member State and at Community level.

2.   Particular attention shall be paid to scientific work necessary for the implementation of Articles 4 and 10, a transboundary co-operative research between Member States shall be encouraged.

[1434]

PROCEDURE FOR AMENDING THE ANNEXES

Article 19

Such amendments as are necessary for adapting Annexes II, III, V and VI to technical and scientific progress shall be adopted by the Council acting by qualified majority on a proposal from the Commission.

Such amendments as are necessary for adapting Annex IV to technical and scientific progress shall be adopted by the Council acting unanimously on a proposal from the Commission.

[1435]

COMMITTEE

Article 20

The Commission shall be assisted by a committee consisting of representatives of the Member States and chaired by a representative of the Commission.

[1436]

Article 21

1.   The representative of the Commission shall submit to the committee a draft of the measures to be taken. The committee shall deliver its opinion on the draft within a time limit which the Chairman may lay down according to the urgency of the matter. The opinion shall be delivered by the majority laid down in Article 148(2) of the Treaty in the case of decisions which the Council is required to adopt on a proposal from the Commission. The votes of the representatives of the Member States within the committee shall be weighted in the manner set out in that Article. The Chairman shall not vote.

2.   The Commission shall adopt the measures envisaged if they are in accordance with the opinion of the committee.

If the measures envisaged are not in accordance with the opinion of the committee, or if no opinion is delivered, the Commission shall, without delay, submit to the Council a proposal relating to the measures to be taken. The Council shall act by a qualified majority.

If, on the expiry of three months from the date of referral to the Council, the Council has not acted, the proposed measures shall be adopted by the Commission.

[1437]

SUPPLEMENTARY PROVISIONS

Article 22

In implementing the provisions of this Directive, Member States shall—
  (a) study the desirability of re-introducing species in Annex IV that are native to their territory where this might contribute to their conservation, provided that an investigation, also taking into account experience in other Member States or elsewhere, has established that such re-introduction contributes effectively to re-establishing these species at a favourable conservation status and that it takes place only after proper consultation of the public concerned;
  (b) ensure that the deliberate introduction into the wild of any species which is not native to their territory is regulated so as not to prejudice natural habitats within their natural range or the wild native fauna and flora and, if they consider it necessary, prohibit such introduction. The results of the assessment undertaken shall be forwarded to the committee for information;
  (c) promote education and general information on the need to protect species of wild fauna and flora and to conserve their habitats and natural habitats.

[1438]

FINAL PROVISIONS

Article 23

1.   Member States shall bring into force the laws, regulations and administrative provisions necessary to comply with this Directive within two years of its notification. They shall forthwith inform the Commission thereof.

2.   When Member States adopt such measures, they shall contain a reference to this Directive or be accompanied by such reference on the occasion of their official publication. The methods of making such a reference shall be laid down by the Member States.

3.   Member States shall communicate to the Commission the main provisions of national law which they adopt in the field covered by this Directive.

[1439]

Article 24

This Directive is addressed to the Member States.

[1440]

Done at Brussels, 21 May 1992.

ANNEX I
NATURAL HABITAT TYPES OF COMMUNITY INTEREST WHOSE CONSERVATION REQUIRES THE DESIGNATION OF SPECIAL AREAS OF CONSERVATION

NOTES

Main headings and sub-headings only are reproduced in this Annex.

Interpretation

Code: The hierarchical classification of habitats produced through the Corine programme[1] (Corine biotopes project) is the reference work for this Annex. Most types of natural habitat quoted are accompanied by the corresponding Corine code listed in the Technical Handbook, Volume 1, pp. 73–109, Corine/Biotope/89/2.2, 19 May 1988, partially updated 14 February 1989.

. . .

---

[1]   Corine: Council Decision 85/338/EEC of 27 June 1985 (OJ L176, 6.7.85, p 14).
Material omitted outside the scope of this work.

COASTAL AND HALOPHYTIC HABITATS

Open sea and tidal areas
Sea cliffs and shingle or stony beaches
Atlantic and continental salt marshes and salt meadows
Mediterranean and thermo-Atlantic salt marshes and salt meadows
Salt and gypsum continental steppes

COASTAL SAND DUNES AND CONTINENTAL DUNES

Sea dunes of the Atlantic, North Sea and Baltic coasts
Sea dunes of the Mediterranean coast
Continental dunes, old and decalcified

FRESHWATER HABITATS

Standing water
Running water

TEMPERATE HEATH AND SCRUB

SCLEROPHYLLOUS SCRUB (MATORRAL)

Sub-Mediterranean and temperate
Mediterranean arborescent matorral
Thermo-Mediterranean and pre-steppe brush
Phrygana

NATURAL AND SEMI-NATURAL GRASSLAND FORMATIONS

Natural grasslands
Semi-natural dry grasslands and scrubland facies
Sclerophyllous grazed forests (dehesas)
Semi-natural tall-herb humid meadows
Mesophile grasslands

RAISED BOGS AND MIRES AND FENS

Sphagnum acid bogs
Calcareous fens
[Aapa mires]

ROCKY HABITATS AND CAVES

Scree
Chasmophytic vegetation on rocky slopes
Other rocky habitats

FORESTS

[Boreal forests]
Forests of temperate Europe
Mediterranean deciduous forests
Mediterranean sclerophyllous forests
Alpine and subalpine coniferous forests
Mediterranean mountainous coniferous forests

[1441]

NOTES
Words in square brackets inserted by the 1994 Act of Accession of the Kingdom of Norway, the Republic of Austria, the Republic of Finland and the Kingdom of Sweden, Annex I(VIII)(E), para 4(b), as adjusted by Council Decision 95/1/EC, Annex I(VIII)(E)(4), para 4(b).

(Annexes II–IV are not reproduced)

COUNCIL REGULATION

of 1 February 1993

on the supervision and control of shipments of waste within, into and out of the European Community

(259/93/EEC)

NOTES
Date of publication in OJ: OJ L30, 6.2.93, p 1.

THE COUNCIL OF THE EUROPEAN COMMUNITIES—

Having regard to the Treaty establishing the European Economic Community, and in particular Article 130s thereof,

Having regard to the proposal from the Commission,[1]
Having regard to the opinion of the European Parliament,[2]
Having regard to the opinion of the Economic and Social Committee,[3]

Whereas the Community has signed the Basle Convention of 22 March 1989 on the control of transboundary movements of hazardous wastes and their disposal;

Whereas provisions concerning waste are contained in Article 39 of the ACP–EEC Convention of 15 December 1989;

Whereas the Community has approved the Decision of the OECD Council of 30 March 1992 on the control of transfrontier movements of wastes destined for recovery operations;

Whereas, in the light of the foregoing, Directive 84/631/EEC,[4] which organises the supervision and control of transfrontier shipments of hazardous waste, needs to be replaced by a Regulation;

Whereas the supervision and control of shipments of waste within a Member State is a national responsibility; whereas, however, national systems for the supervision and control of shipments of waste within a Member State should comply with minimum criteria in order to ensure a high level of protection of the environment and human health;

Whereas it is important to organise the supervision and control of shipments of wastes in a way which takes account of the need to preserve, protect and improve the quality of the environment;

Whereas Council Directive 75/442/EEC of 15 July 1975 on waste[5] lays down in its Article 5(1) that an integrated and adequate network of waste disposal installations, to be established by Member States through appropriate measures, where necessary or advisable in co-operation with other Member States, must enable the Community as a whole to become self-sufficient in waste disposal and the Member States to move towards that aim individually, taking into account geographical circumstances or the need for specialised installations for certain types of waste; whereas Article 7 of the said Directive requests the drawing up of waste management plans, if appropriate in co-operation with the Member States concerned, which shall be notified to the Commission, and stipulates that Member States may take measures necessary to prevent movements of waste which are not in accordance with their waste management plans and that they shall inform the Commission and the other Member States of any such measures;

Whereas it is necessary to apply different procedures depending on the type of waste and its destination, including whether it is destined for disposal or recovery;

Whereas shipments of waste must be subject to prior notification to the competent authorities enabling them to be duly informed in particular of the type, movement and disposal or recovery of the waste, so that these authorities may take all necessary measures for the protection of human health and the environment, including the possibility of raising reasoned objections to the shipment;

Whereas Member States should be able to implement the principles of proximity, priority for recovery and self-sufficiency at Community and national levels—in accordance with Directive 75/442/EEC—by taking measures in accordance with the Treaty to prohibit generally or partially or to object systematically to shipments of waste for disposal, except in the case of hazardous waste produced in the Member State of dispatch in such a small quantity that the provision of new specialised disposal installations within that State would be uneconomic; whereas the specific problem of disposal of such small quantities requires co-operation between the Member States concerned and possible recourse to a Community procedure;

Whereas exports of waste for disposal to third countries must be prohibited in order to protect the environment of those countries; whereas exceptions shall apply to exports to EFTA countries which are also Parties to the Basle Convention;

Whereas exports of waste for recovery to countries to which the OECD Decision does not apply must be subject to conditions providing for environmentally sound management of waste;

Whereas agreements or arrangements on exports of waste for recovery with countries to which the OECD Decision does not apply must be subject to periodic review by the Commission leading, if appropriate, to a proposal by the Commission to reconsider the conditions under which such exports take place, including the possibility of a ban;

Whereas shipments of waste for recovery listed on the green list of the OECD Decision shall be generally excluded from the control procedures of this Regulation since such waste should not normally present a risk to the environment if properly recovered in the country of #IO116,9# destination; whereas some exceptions to this exclusion are necessary in accordance with Community legislation and the OECD Decision; whereas some exceptions are also necessary in order to facilitate the tracking of such shipments within the Community and to take account of exceptional cases; whereas such waste shall be subject to Directive 75/442/EEC;

Whereas exports of waste for recovery listed on the OECD green list to countries to which the OECD Decision does not apply must be subject to consultation by the Commission with the country of destination; whereas it may be appropriate in the light of such consultation that the Commission make proposals to the Council;

Whereas exports of waste for recovery to countries which are not parties to the Basle Convention must be subject to specific agreements between these countries and the Community; whereas Member States must, in exceptional cases, be able to conclude after the date of application of this Regulation bilateral agreements for the import of specific waste before the Community has concluded such agreements, in the case of waste for recovery in order to avoid any interruption of waste treatment and in the case of waste for disposal where the country of dispatch does not have or cannot reasonably acquire the technical capacity and necessary facilities to dispose of the waste in an environmentally sound manner;

Whereas provision must be made for the waste to be taken back or to be disposed of or recovered in an alternative and environmentally sound manner if the shipment cannot be completed in accordance with the terms of the consignment note or the contract;

Whereas, in the event of illegal traffic, the person whose action is the cause of such traffic must take back and/or dispose of or recover the waste in an alternative and environmentally sound manner; whereas, should he fail to do so, the competent authorities of dispatch or destination, as appropriate, must themselves intervene;

Whereas it is important for a system of financial guarantees or equivalent insurance to be established;

Whereas Member States must provide the Commission with information relevant to the implementation of this Regulation;

Whereas the documents provided for by this Regulation must be established and the Annexes adapted within a Community procedure,

NOTES

[1] OJ C115, 6.5.92, p 4.

[2] OJ C94, 13.4.92, p 276 and opinion delivered on 20 January 1993 (not yet published in the Official Journal).

[3] OJ C269, 14.10.91, p 10.

[4] OJ L326, 13.12.84, p 31. Directive as last amended by Directive 91/692/EEC (OJ L377, 31.12.91, p 48).

[5] OJ L194, 25.7.75, p 39. Directive as amended by Directive 91/156/EEC (OJ L78, 26.3.91, p 32).

HAS ADOPTED THIS REGULATION—

TITLE I
SCOPE AND DEFINITIONS

Article 1

1. This Regulation shall apply to shipments of waste within, into and out of the Community.

2. The following shall be excluded from the scope of this Regulation—
   (a) the offloading to shore of waste generated by the normal operation of ships and offshore platforms, including waste water and residues, provided that such waste is the subject of a specific binding international instrument;
   (b) shipments of civil aviation waste;
   (c) shipments of radioactive waste as defined in Article 2 of Directive 92/3/Euratom of 3 February 1992 on the supervision and control of shipments of radioactive waste between Member States and into and out of the Community;[1]
   (d) shipments of waste mentioned in Article 2(1)(b) of Directive 75/442/ EEC, where they are already covered by other relevant legislation;
   (e) shipments of waste into the Community in accordance with the requirements of the Protocol on Environmental Protection to the Antarctic Treaty.

3.—(a) Shipments of waste destined for recovery only and listed in Annex II shall also be excluded from the provisions of this Regulation except as provided for in subparagraphs (b), (c), (d) and (e), in Article 11 and in Article 17(1), (2) and (3).

(b) Such waste shall be subject to all provisions of Directive 75/442/EEC. It shall in particular be—
   — destined for duly authorised facilities only, authorised according to Article 10 and 11 of Directive 75/442/EEC,
   — subject to all provisions of Articles 8, 12, 13 and 14 of Directive 75/442/EEC.

(c) However, certain wastes listed in Annex II may be controlled, if, among other reasons, they exhibit any of the hazardous characteristics listed in Annex III of Council Directive 91/689/EEC,[2] as if they had been listed in Annex III or IV.

These wastes and the decision about which of the two procedures should be followed shall be determined in accordance with the procedure laid down in Article 18 of Directive 75/442/EEC. Such wastes shall be listed in Annex II(a).

(d) In exceptional cases, shipments of wastes listed in Annex II may, for environmental or public health reasons, be controlled by Member States as if they had been listed in Annex III or IV.

Member States which make use of this possibility shall immediately notify the Commission of such cases and inform other Member States, as appropriate, and give reasons for their decision. The Commission, in accordance with the procedure laid down in Article 18 of Directive 75/442/ EEC, may confirm such action including, where appropriate, by adding such wastes to Annex II.A.

(e) Where waste listed in Annex II is shipped in contravention of this Regulation or of Directive 75/442/EEC, Member States may apply appropriate provisions of Articles 25 and 26 of this Regulation.

[1442]

NOTES
[1]   OJ L35, 12.2.92, p 24.
[2]   OJ L377, 31.12.91, p 20.

Article 2

For the purposes of this Regulation—
   (a) *waste* is as defined in Article 1(a) of Directive 75/442/EEC;
   (b) *competent authorities* means the competent authorities designated by either the Member States in accordance with Article 36 or non-Member States;
   (c) *competent authority of dispatch* means the competent authority, designated by the Member States in accordance with Article 36, for the area from which the shipment is dispatched or designated by non-Member States;
   (d) *competent authority of destination* means the competent authority, designated by the Member States in accordance with Article 36, for the area in which the shipment is received, or in which waste is loaded on board before disposal at sea without prejudice to existing conventions on disposal at sea or designated by non-Member States;
   (e) *competent authority of transit* means the single authority designated by Member States in accordance with Article 36 for the State through which the shipment is in transit;
   (f) *correspondent* means the central body designated by each Member State and the Commission, in accordance with Article 37;
   (g) *notifier* means any natural person or corporate body to whom or to which the duty to notify is assigned, that is to say the person referred to hereinafter who proposes to ship waste or have waste shipped—

(i)   the person whose activities produced the waste (original producer); or
(ii)   where this is not possible, a collector licensed to this effect by a Member State or a registered or licensed dealer or broker who arranges for the disposal or the recovery of waste; or
(iii) where these persons are unknown or are not licensed, the person having possession or legal control of the waste (holder); or
(iv)   in the case of import into or transit through the Community of waste, the person designated by the laws of the State of dispatch or, when this designation has not taken place, the person having possession or legal control of the waste (holder);

(h)   *consignee* means the person or undertaking to whom or to which the waste is shipped for recovery or disposal;

(i)   *disposal* is as defined in Article 1(e) of Directive 75/442/EEC;

(j)   *authorised centre* means any establishment or undertaking authorised or licensed pursuant to Article 6 of Directive 75/439/EEC[1], Articles 9, 10 and 11 of Directive 75/442/EEC and Article 6 of Directive 76/403/ EEC;[2]

(k)   *recovery* is as defined in Article 1(f) of Directive 75/442/EEC;

(l)   *State of dispatch* means any State from which a shipment of waste is planned or made;

(m)   *State of destination* means any State to which a shipment of waste is planned or made for disposal or recovery, or for loading on board before disposal at sea without prejudice to existing conventions on disposal at sea;

(n)   *State of transit* means any State, other than the State of dispatch or destination, through which a shipment of waste is planned or made;

(o)   *consignment note* means the standard consignment note to be drawn up in accordance with Article 42;

(p)   *the Basle Convention* means the Basle Convention of 22 March 1989 on the control of transboundary movements of hazardous wastes and their disposal;

(q)   *the fourth Lomé Convention* means the Lomé Convention of 15 December 1989;

(r)   *the OECD Decision* means the decision of the OECD Council of 30 March 1992 on the control of transfrontier movements of wastes destined for recovery operations.

[1443]

NOTES
[1] OJ L194, 25.7.75, p 23. Directive as last amended by Directive 91/692/EEC (OJ L377, 31.12.91, p 48).
[2] OJ L108, 26.4.76, p 41.

TITLE II
SHIPMENTS OF WASTE BETWEEN MEMBER STATES

CHAPTER A
WASTE FOR DISPOSAL

Article 3

1.   Where the notifier intends to ship waste for disposal from one Member State to another Member State and/or pass it in transit through one or several other Member States, and without prejudice to Articles 25(2) and 26(2), he shall notify the competent authority of destination and send a copy of the notification to the competent authorities of dispatch and of transit and to the consignee.

2.   Notification shall mandatorily cover any intermediate stage of the shipment from the place of dispatch to its final destination.

3.   Notification shall be effected by means of the consignment note which shall be issued by the competent authority of dispatch.

4.   In making notification, the notifier shall complete the consignment note and shall, if requested by competent authorities, supply additional information and documentation.

5.   The notifier shall supply on the consignment note information with particular regard to—
— the source, composition and quantity of the waste for disposal including, in the case of Article 2(g)(ii), the producer's identity and, in the case of waste from various sources a detailed inventory of the waste and, if known, the identity of the original producers,
— the arrangements for routing and for insurance against damage to third parties,
— the measures to be taken to ensure safe transport and, in particular, compliance by the carrier with the conditions laid down for transport by the Member States concerned,
— the identity of the consignee of the waste, the location of the disposal centre and the type and duration of the authorisation under which the centre operates. The centre must have adequate technical capacity for the disposal of the waste in question under conditions presenting no danger to human health or to the environment,
— the operations involving disposal as referred to in Annex II.A to Directive 75/442/EEC.

6.   The notifier must make a contract with the consignee for the disposal of the waste.

The contract may include some or all of the information referred to in paragraph 5.

The contract must include the obligation—
— of the notifier, in accordance with Articles 25 and 26(2), to take the waste back if the shipment has not been completed as planned or if it has been effected in violation of this Regulation,
— of the consignee, to provide as soon as possible and no later than 180 days following the receipt of the waste a certificate to the notifier that the waste has been disposed of in an environmentally sound manner.

A copy of this contract must be supplied to the competent authority on request.

Should the waste be shipped between two establishments under the control of the same legal entity, this contract may be replaced by a declaration by the entity in question undertaking to dispose of the waste.

7.   The information given in accordance with paragraphs 4 to 6 shall be treated confidentially in accordance with existing national regulations.

8.   A competent authority of dispatch may, in accordance with national legislation, decide to transmit the notification itself instead of the notifier to the competent authority of destination, with copies to the consignee and to the competent authority of transit.

The competent authority of dispatch may decide not to proceed with notification if it has itself immediate objections to raise against the shipment in accordance with Article 4(3). It shall immediately inform the notifier of these objections.

[1444]

Article 4

1.   On receipt of the notification, the competent authority of destination shall, within three working days, send an acknowledgement to the notifier and copies thereof to the other competent authorities concerned and to the consignee.

2.—(a) The competent authority of destination shall have 30 days following dispatch of the acknowledgement to take its decision authorising the shipment, with or without conditions, or refusing it. It may also request additional information.

It shall give its authorisation only in the absence of objections on its part or on the part of the other competent authorities. The authorisation shall be subject to any transport conditions referred to in (d).

The competent authority of destination shall take its decision not earlier than 21 days following the dispatch of the acknowledgement. It may, however, take its decision earlier if it has the written consent of the other competent authorities concerned.

The competent authority of destination shall send its decision to the notifier in writing, with copies to the other competent authorities concerned.

(b) The competent authorities of dispatch and transit may raise objections within 20 days following the dispatch of the acknowledgement. They may also request additional information. These objections shall be conveyed in writing to the notifier, with copies to the other competent authorities concerned.

(c) The objections and conditions referred to in (a) and (b) shall be based on paragraph 3.

(d) The competent authorities of dispatch and transit may, within 20 days following the dispatch of the acknowledgement, lay down conditions in respect of the transport of waste within their jurisdiction.

These conditions must be notified to the notifier in writing, with copies to the competent authorities concerned, and entered in the consignment note. They may not be more stringent than those laid down in respect of similar shipments occurring wholly within their jurisdiction and shall take due account of existing agreements, in particular relevant international conventions.

3.—(a)(i) In order to implement the principles of proximity, priority for recovery and self-sufficiency at Community and national levels in accordance with Directive 75/442/EEC, Member States may take measures in accordance with the Treaty to prohibit generally or partially or to object systematically to shipments of waste. Such measures shall immediately be notified to the Commission, which will inform the other Member States.

(ii) In the case of hazardous waste (as defined in Article 1(4) of Directive 91/689/EEC) produced in a Member State of dispatch in such a small quantity overall per year that the provision of new specialised disposal installations within that State would be uneconomic, (i) shall not apply.

(iii) The Member State of destination shall co-operate with the Member State of dispatch which considers that (ii) applies, with a view to resolving the issue bilaterally. If there is no satisfactory solution, either Member State may refer the matter to the Commission, which will determine the issue in accordance with the procedure laid down in Article 18 of Directive 75/442/EEC.

(b) The competent authorities of dispatch and destination, while taking into account geographical circumstances or the need for specialised installations for certain types of waste, may raise reasoned objections to planned shipments if they are not in accordance with Directive 75/442/EEC, especially Articles 5 and 7—

(i) in order to implement the principle of self-sufficiency at Community and national levels;

    (ii) in cases where the installation has to dispose of waste from a nearer source and the competent authority has given priority to this waste;

    (iii) in order to ensure that shipments are in accordance with waste management plans.

(c) Furthermore, the competent authorities of dispatch, destination and transit may raise reasoned objections to the planned shipment if—

— it is not in accordance with national laws and regulations relating to environmental protection, public order, public safety or health protection,

— the notifier or the consignee was previously guilty of illegal trafficking. In this case, the competent authority of dispatch may refuse all shipments involving the person in question in accordance with national legislation, or

— the shipment conflicts with obligations resulting from international conventions concluded by the Member State or Member States concerned.

4.   If, within the time limits laid down in paragraph 2, the competent authorities are satisfied that the problems giving rise to their objections have been solved and that the conditions in respect of the transport will be met they shall immediately inform the notifier in writing, with copies to the consignee and to the other competent authorities concerned.

  If there is subsequently any essential change in the conditions of the shipment, a new notification must be made.

5.   The competent authority of destination shall signify its authorisation by appropriately stamping the consignment note.

[1445]

Article 5

1.   The shipment may be effected only after the notifier has received authorisation from the competent authority of destination.

2.   Once the notifier has received authorisation, he shall insert the date of shipment and otherwise complete the consignment note and send copies to the competent authorities concerned three working days before the shipment is made.

3.   A copy or, if requested by the competent authorities, a specimen of the consignment note, together with the stamp of authorisation, shall accompany each shipment.

4.   All undertakings involved in the operation shall complete the consignment note at the points indicated, sign it and retain a copy thereof.

5.   Within three working days following receipt of the waste for disposal, the consignee shall send copies of the completed consignment note, except for the certificate referred to in paragraph 6, to the notifier and the competent authorities concerned.

6.   As soon as possible and not later than 180 days following the receipt of the waste, the consignee shall, under his responsibility, send a certificate of disposal to the notifier and the other competent authorities concerned. This certificate shall be part of or attached to the consignment note which accompanies the shipment.

[1446]

CHAPTER B
WASTE FOR RECOVERY

Article 6

1.   Where the notifier intends to ship waste for recovery listed in Annex III from one Member State to another Member State and/or pass it in transit through one or

several other Member States, and without prejudice to Articles 25(2) and 26(2), he shall notify the competent authority of destination and send copies of the notification to the competent authorities of dispatch and transit and to the consignee.

2.   Notification shall mandatorily cover any intermediary stage of the shipment from the place of dispatch to its final destination.

3.   Notification shall be effected by means of the consignment note which shall be issued by the competent authority of dispatch.

4.   In making notification, the notifier shall complete the consignment note and shall, if requested by competent authorities, supply additional information and documentation .

5.   The notifier shall supply on the consignment note information with particular regard to—
  — the source, composition and quantity of the waste for recovery, including the producer's identity and, in the case of waste from various sources, a detailed inventory of the waste and, if known, the identity of the original producer,
  — the arrangements for routing and for insurance against damage to third parties,
  — the measures to be taken to ensure safe transport and, in particular, compliance by the carrier with the conditions laid down for transport by the Member States concerned,
  — the identity of the consignee of the waste, the location of the recovery centre and the type and duration of the authorisation under which the centre operates. The centre must have adequate technical capacity for the recovery of the waste in question under conditions presenting no danger to human health or to the environment,
  — the operations involving recovery as contained in Annex II.B to Directive 75/442/EEC,
  — the planned method of disposal for the residual waste after recycling has taken place,
  — the amount of the recycled material in relation to the residual waste,
  — the estimated value of the recycled material.

6.   The notifier must conclude a contract with the consignee for the recovery of the waste.

The contract may include some or all of the information referred to in paragraph 5.

The contract must include the obligation—
  — of the notifier, in accordance with Articles 25 and 26(2), to take the waste back if the shipment has not been completed as planned or if it has been effected in violation of this Regulation,
  — of the consignee to provide, in the case of retransfer of the waste for recovery to another Member State or to a third country, the notification of the initial country of dispatch,
  — of the consignee to provide, as soon as possible and not later than 180 days following the receipt of the waste, a certificate to the notifier that the waste has been recovered in an environmentally sound manner.

A copy of this contract must be supplied to the competent authority on request.

Should the waste be shipped between two establishments under the control of the same legal entity, this contract may be replaced by a declaration by the entity in question undertaking to recover the waste.

7.   The information given in accordance with paragraphs 4 to 6 shall be treated confidentially in accordance with existing national regulations.

8.   A competent authority of dispatch may, in accordance with national legislation, decide to transmit the notification itself instead of the notifier to the competent authority of destination, with copies to the consignee and to the competent authority of transit.

[1447]

Article 7

1.   On receipt of the notification the competent authority of destination shall send, within three working days, an acknowledgement to the notifier and copies thereof to the other competent authorities and to the consignee.

2.   The competent authorities of destination, dispatch and transit shall have 30 days following dispatch of the acknowledgement to object to the shipment. Such objection shall be based on paragraph 4. Any objection must be provided in writing to the notifier and to other competent authorities concerned within the 30-day period.

The competent authorities concerned may decide to provide written consent in a period less than the 30 days.

Written consent or objection may be provided by post, or by telefax followed by post. Such consent shall expire within one year unless otherwise specified.

3.   The competent authorities of dispatch, destination and transit shall have 20 days following the dispatch of the acknowledgement in which to lay down conditions in respect of the transport of waste within their jurisdiction.

These conditions must be notified to the notifier in writing, with copies to the competent authorities concerned, and entered in the consignment note. They may not be more stringent that those laid down in respect of similar shipments occurring wholly within their jurisdiction and shall take due account of existing agreements, in particular relevant international conventions.

4.(a)   The competent authorities of destination and dispatch may raise reasoned objections to the planned shipment—
  — in accordance with Directive 75/442/EEC, in particular Article 7 thereof, or
  — if it is not in accordance with national laws and regulations relating to environmental protection, public order, public safety or health protection, or
  — if the notifier or the consignee has previously been guilty of illegal trafficking. In this case, the competent authority of dispatch may refuse all shipments involving the person in question in accordance with national legislation, or
  — if the shipment conflicts with obligations resulting from international conventions concluded by the Member State or Member States concerned, or
  — if the ratio of the recoverable and non-recoverable waste, the estimated value of the materials to be finally recovered or the cost of the recovery and the cost of the disposal of the non recoverable fraction do not justify the recovery under economic and environmental considerations.
 (b)   The competent authorities of transit may raise reasoned objections to the planned shipment based on the second, third and fourth indents of (a).

5.   If within the time limit laid down in paragraph 2 the competent authorities are satisfied that the problems giving rise to their objections have been solved and that the conditions in respect of the transport will be met, they shall immediately inform the notifier in writing, with copies to the consignee and to the other competent authorities concerned.

If there is subsequently any essential change in the conditions of the shipment, a new notification must be made.

6. In case of prior written consent, the competent authority shall signify its authorisation by appropriately stamping the consignment note.

[1448]

Article 8

1. The shipment may be effected after the 30-day period has passed if no objection has been lodged. Tacit consent, however, expires within one year from that date.

Where the competent authorities decide to provide written consent, the shipment may be effected immediately after all necessary consents have been received.

2. The notifier shall insert the date of shipment and otherwise complete the consignment note and send copies to the competent authorities concerned three working days before the shipment is made.

3. A copy or, if requested by the competent authorities, a specimen of the consignment note shall accompany each shipment.

4. All undertakings involved in the operation shall complete the consignment note at the points indicated, sign it and retain a copy thereof.

5. Within three working days following receipt of the waste for recovery, the consignee shall send copies of the completed consignment note, except for the certificate referred to in paragraph 6, to the notifier and to the competent authorities concerned.

6. As soon as possible and not later than 180 days following receipt of the waste the consignee, under his responsibility, shall send a certificate of recovery of the waste to the notifier and the other competent authorities concerned. This certificate shall be part of or attached to the consignment note which accompanies the shipment.

[1449]

Article 9

1. The competent authorities having jurisdiction over specific recovery facilities may decide, notwithstanding Article 7, that they will not raise objections concerning shipments of certain types of waste to a specific recovery facility. Such decisions may be limited to a specific period of time; however, they may be revoked at any time.

2. Competent authorities which select this option shall inform the Commission of the recovery facility name, address, technologies employed, waste types to which the decision applies and the period covered. Any revocations must also be notified to the Commission.

The Commission shall send this information without delay to the other competent authorities concerned in the Community and to the OECD Secretariat.

3. All intended shipments to such facilities shall require notification to the competent authorities concerned, in accordance with Article 6. Such notification shall arrive prior to the time the shipment is dispatched.

The competent authorities of the Member States of dispatch and transit may raise objections to any such shipment, based on Article 7(4), or impose conditions in respect of the transport.

4. In instances where competent authorities acting under terms of their domestic laws are required to review the contract referred to in Article 6(6), these

authorities shall so inform the Commission. In such cases, the notification plus the contracts or portions thereof to be reviewed must arrive seven days prior to the time the shipment is dispatched in order that such review may be appropriately performed.

5.   For the actual shipment, Article 8(2) to (6) shall apply.

[1450]

Article 10

Shipments of waste for recovery listed in Annex IV and of waste for recovery which has not yet been assigned to Annex II, Annex III or Annex IV shall be subject to the same procedures as referred to in Articles 6 to 8 except that the consent of the competent authorities concerned must be provided in writing prior to commencement of shipment.

[1451]

Article 11

1.   In order to assist the tracking of shipments of waste for recovery listed in Annex II, they shall be accompanied by the following information, signed by the holder—
    (a)   the name and address of the holder;
    (b)   the usual commercial description of the waste;
    (c)   the quantity of the waste;
    (d)   the name and address of the consignee;
    (e)   the operations involving recovery, as listed in Annex II.B to Directive 75/442/EEC;
    (f)   the anticipated date of shipment.

2.   The information specified in paragraph 1 shall be treated confidentially in accordance with existing national regulations.

[1452]

CHAPTER C
SHIPMENT OF WASTE FOR DISPOSAL AND RECOVERY BETWEEN MEMBER STATES WITH TRANSIT VIA THIRD STATES

Article 12

Without prejudice to Articles 3 to 10, where a shipment of waste takes place between Member States with transit via one or more third States,
    (a)   the notifier shall send a copy of the notification to the competent authority(ies) of the third State(s);
    (b)   the competent authority of destination shall ask the competent authority in the third State(s) whether it wishes to send its written consent to the planned shipment—
       — in the case of parties to the Basle Convention, within 60 days, unless it has waived this right in accordance with the terms of that Convention, or
       — in the case of countries not parties to the Basle Convention, within a period agreed between the competent authorities.

In both cases the competent authority of destination shall, where appropriate, wait for consent before giving its authorisation.

[1453]

TITLE III
SHIPMENTS OF WASTE WITHIN MEMBER STATES

Article 13

1.   Titles II, VII and VIII shall not apply to shipments within a Member State.

2.   Member States shall, however, establish an appropriate system for the supervision and control of shipments of waste within their jurisdiction. This system should take account of the need for coherence with the Community system established by this Regulation.

3.   Member States shall inform the Commission of their system for the supervision and control of shipments of waste. The Commission shall inform the other Member States thereof.

4.   Member States may apply the system provided for in Titles II, VII and VIII within their jurisdiction.

[1454]

TITLE IV
EXPORTS OF WASTE

CHAPTER A
WASTE FOR DISPOSAL

Article 14

1.   All exports of waste for disposal shall be prohibited, except those to EFTA countries which are also parties to the Basle Convention.

2.   However, without prejudice to Articles 25(2), and 26(2), exports of waste for disposal to an EFTA country shall also be banned—
   (a) where the EFTA country of destination prohibits imports of such wastes or where it has not given its written consent to the specific import of this waste;
   (b) if the competent authority of dispatch in the Community has reason to believe that the waste will not be managed in accordance with environmentally sound methods in the EFTA country of destination concerned.

3.   The competent authority of dispatch shall require that any waste for disposal authorised for export to EFTA countries be managed in an environmentally sound matter throughout the period of shipment and in the State of destination.

[1455]

Article 15

1.   The notifier shall send the notification to the competent authority of dispatch by means of the consignment note in accordance with Article 3(5), with copies to the other competent authorities concerned and to the consignee. The consignment note shall be issued by the competent authority of dispatch.

On receipt of the notification, the competent authority of dispatch shall within three working days send the notifier a written acknowledgement of the notification, with copies to the other competent authorities concerned.

2.   The competent authority of dispatch shall have 70 days following dispatch of the acknowledgement to take its decision authorising the shipment, with or without conditions, or refusing it. It may also request additional information.

It shall give its authorisation only in the absence of objections on its part or on the part of the other competent authorities and if it has received from the notifier the copies referred to in paragraph 4. The authorisation shall, where applicable, be subject to any transport conditions referred to in paragraph 5.

The competent authority of dispatch shall take its decision no earlier than 61 days following the dispatch of the acknowledgement.

It may, however, take its decision earlier if it has the written consent of the other competent authorities.

It shall send a certified copy of the decision to the other competent authorities concerned, to the customs office of departure from the Community and to the consignee.

3.   The competent authorities of dispatch and transit in the Community may, within 60 days following the dispatch of the acknowledgement, raise objections based on Article 4(3). They may also request additional information. Any objection must be provided in writing to the notifier, with copies to the other competent authorities concerned.

4.   The notifier shall provide to the competent authority of dispatch a copy of—
  (a) the written consent of the EFTA country of destination to the planned shipment;
  (b) the confirmation from the EFTA country of destination of the existence of a contract between the notifier and the consignee specifying environmentally sound management of the waste in question; a copy of the contract must be supplied, if requested.
  The contract shall also specify that the consignee be required to provide—
    — within three working days following the receipt of the waste for disposal, copies of the fully completed consignment note, except for the certification referred to in the second indent, to the notifier and to the competent authority concerned,
    — as soon as possible and not later than 180 days following the receipt of the waste, a certificate of disposal under his responsibility to the notifier and to the competent authority concerned. The form of this certificate shall be part of the consignment note which accompanies the shipment.

  The contract shall, in addition, stipulate that if a consignee issues an incorrect certificate with the consequence that the financial guarantee is released he shall bear the costs arising from the duty to return the waste to the area of jurisdiction of the competent authority of dispatch and its disposal in an alternative and environmentally sound manner;
  (c) written consent to the planned shipment from the other State(s) of transit, unless this (these) State(s) is (are) a Party (Parties) to the Basle Convention and has (have) waived this in accordance with the terms of that Convention.

5.   The competent authorities of transit in the Community shall have 60 days following the dispatch of the acknowledgement in which to lay down conditions in respect of the shipments of waste in their area of jurisdiction.

These conditions, which shall be forwarded to the notifier, with copies to the other competent authorities concerned, may not be more stringent than those laid down in respect of similar shipments effected wholly within the area of jurisdiction of the competent authority in question.

6.   The competent authority of dispatch shall signify its authorisation by appropriately stamping the consignment note.

7. The shipment may be effected only after the notifier has received authorisation from the competent authority of dispatch.

8. Once the notifier has received authorisation, he shall insert the date of shipment and otherwise complete the consignment note and send copies to the competent authorities concerned three working days before the shipment is made. A copy or, if requested by the competent authorities, a specimen of the consignment note, together with the stamp of authorisation, shall accompany each shipment.

All undertakings involved in the operation shall complete the consignment note at the points indicated, sign it and retain a copy thereof.

A specimen of the consignment note shall be delivered by the carrier to the last customs office of departure when the waste leaves the Community.

9. As soon as the waste has left the Community, the customs office of departure shall send a copy of the consignment note to the competent authority which issued the authorisation.

10. If, 42 days after the waste has left the Community, the competent authority which gave the authorisation has received no information from the consignee about his receipt of the waste, it shall inform without delay the competent authority of destination.

It shall take action in a similar way if, 180 days after the waste has left the Community, the competent authority which gave the authorisation has not received from the consignee the certificate of disposal referred to in paragraph 4.

11. A competent authority of dispatch may, in accordance with national legislation, decide to transmit the notification itself instead of the notifier, with copies to the consignee and the competent authority of transit.

The competent authority of dispatch may decide to proceed with any notification if it has itself immediate objections to raise against the shipment in accordance with Article 4(3). It shall immediately inform the notifier of these objections.

12. The information given in paragraphs 1 to 4 shall be treated confidentially in accordance with existing national regulations.

[1456]

CHAPTER B
WASTE FOR RECOVERY

Article 16

[1. All exports for recovery of waste listed in Annex V for recovery shall be prohibited except those to—
  (a) countries to which the OECD Decision applies;
  (b) other countries—
      — which are Parties to the Basle Convention and/or with which the Community, or the Community and its Member States, have concluded bilateral or multilateral or regional agreements or arrangements in accordance with Article 11 of the Basle Convention and paragraph 2 of this Article. Any such exports shall however be prohibited from 1 January 1998 onwards,
      — with which individual Member States have concluded bilateral agreements and arrangements prior to the date of application of this Regulation, insofar as these are compatible with Community legislation and in accordance with Article 11 of the Basle Convention and paragraph 2 of this Article. These agreements and arrangements shall be notified to the Commission within three months of the date of application of this Regulation or of the date that such agreements are

brought into effect, whichever is earlier, and shall expire when agreements or arrangements are concluded in accordance with the first indent. Any such exports shall however be prohibited as from 1 January 1998 onwards.

The Commission, in accordance with the procedure laid down in Article 18 of Directive 75/442/EEC shall, as soon as possible, and at the latest before 1 January 1998, review and amend Annex V to this Regulation taking into full consideration those wastes featuring on the list of wastes adopted in accordance with Article 1(4) of Council Directive 91/689/EEC of 12 December 1991 on hazardous waste* and any lists of wastes characterised as hazardous for the purposes of the Basle Convention.

Annex V shall be reviewed and further amended as appropriate under the same procedure. In particular, the Commission shall review the Annex in order to give effect to decisions of the Parties to the Basle Convention as to what waste should be characterised as hazardous for the purposes of the Convention and to amendments of the list of wastes adopted in accordance with Article 1(4) of Direction 91/689/EEC.]

2.   The agreements and arrangements referred to in paragraph 1(b) shall guarantee an environmentally sound management of the waste in accordance with Article 11 of the Basle Convention and shall, in particular—

  (a) guarantee that the recovery operation is carried out in an authorised centre which complies with the requirements for environmentally sound management;

  (b) fix the conditions for the treatment of the non-recoverable components of the waste and, if appropriate, oblige the notifier to take them back;

  (c) enable, if appropriate, the examination of the compliance of the agreements on the spot in agreement with the countries concerned;

  (d) be subject to periodic review by the Commission and for the first time not later than 31 December 1996, taking into account the experience gained and the ability of the countries concerned to carry out recovery activities in a manner which provides full guarantees of environmentally sound management. The Commission shall inform the European Parliament and the Council about the results of this review. If such a review leads to the conclusion that environmental guarantees are insufficient, the continuation of waste exports under such terms shall, on a proposal from the Commission, be reconsidered, including the possibility of a ban.

3.   However, without prejudice to Article 25(2) and 26(2), exports of waste for recovery to the countries referred to in paragraph 1 shall be prohibited—

  (a) where such a country prohibits all imports of such wastes or where it has not given its consent to their specific import;

  (b) if the competent authority of dispatch has reason to believe that the waste will not be managed in accordance with environmentally sound methods in such a country.

4.   The competent authority of dispatch shall require that any waste for recovery authorised for export be managed in an environmentally sound manner throughout the period of shipment and in the State of destination.

[1457]

NOTES

  *   OJ L377, 31.12.91, p 20. Directive as amended by Directive 94/31/EC (OJ L168, 2.7.94, p 28).
     Para 1: substituted by Council Regulation 120/97/EC of 20 January 1997, Art 1.

Article 17

1.   In respect of waste listed in Annex II, the Commission shall notify prior to the date of application of this Regulation to every country to which the OECD

Decision does not apply the list of waste included in that Annex and request written confirmation that such waste is not subject to control in the country of destination and that the latter will accept categories of such waste to be shipped without recourse to the control procedures which apply to Annex III or IV or that it indicate where such waste should be subject to either those procedures or the procedure laid down in Article 15.

If such confirmation is not received six months before the date of application of this Regulation, the Commission shall make appropriate proposals to the Council.

2.   Where waste listed in Annex II is exported, it shall be destined for recovery operations within a facility which under applicable domestic law is operating or is authorised to operate in the importing country. Furthermore, a surveillance system based on prior automatic export licensing shall be established in cases to be determined in accordance with the procedure laid down in Article 18 of Directive 75/442/EEC.

Such a system shall in each case provide that a copy of the export licence be forwarded without delay to the authorities of the country in question.

3.   Where such waste is subject to control in the country of destination or upon request of such a country in accordance with paragraph 1 or where a country of destination has notified under Article 3 of the Basle Convention that it regards certain kinds of waste listed in Annex II is hazardous, exports of such waste to that country shall be subjected to control. The Member State of export or the Commission shall notify all such cases to the committee established pursuant to Article 18 of Directive 75/442/EEC; the Commission shall determine in consultation with the country of destination which of the control procedures shall apply, that is those applicable to Annex III or IV or the procedure laid down in Article 15.

4.   Where waste listed in Annex III is exported from the Community for recovery to countries and through countries to which the OECD Decision applies, Article 6, 7, 8 and 9(1), (3), (4) and (5) shall apply, the provisions concerning the competent authorities of dispatch and transit applying only to the competent authorities in the Community.

5.   In addition, the competent authorities of the exporting and Community-transit countries shall be informed of the decision referred to in Article 9.

6.   Where the waste for recovery listed in Annex IV and waste for recovery which has not yet been assigned to Annex II, III or IV is exported for recovery to countries and through countries to which the OECD Decision applies, Article 10 shall apply by analogy.

7.   In addition, where waste is exported in accordance with paragraphs 4 to 6—
   — a specimen of the consignment note shall be delivered by the carrier to the last customs office of departure when the waste leaves the Community,
   — as soon as the waste has left the Community, the customs office of departure shall send a copy of the consignment note to the competent authority of export,
   — if, 42 days after the waste has left the Community, the competent authority of export has received no information from the consignee about this receipt of the waste, it shall inform without delay the competent authority of destination,
   — the contract shall stipulate that, if a consignee issues an incorrect certificate with the consequence that the financial guarantee is released, he shall bear the costs arising from the duty to return the waste to the area of jurisdiction of the competent authority of dispatch and its disposal or recovery in an alternative and environmentally sound manner.

8.   Where waste for recovery listed in Annex III and IV and waste for recovery which has not yet been assigned to Annex II, III or IV is exported to and through countries to which the OECD Decision does not apply—

— Article 15, except for paragraph 3, shall apply by analogy,
— reasoned objections may be raised in accordance with Article 7(4) only,

save as otherwise provided for in bilateral or multilateral agreements entered into in accordance with Article 16(1)(b) and on the basis of the control procedure of either paragraph 4 or 6 of this Article or Article 15.

[1458]

CHAPTER C
EXPORT OF WASTE TO ACP STATES

Article 18

1.   All exports of waste to ACP States shall be prohibited.

2.   This prohibition does not prevent a Member State to which an ACP State has chosen to export waste for processing from returning the processed waste to the ACP State of origin.

3.   In case of re-export to ACP States, a specimen of the consignment note, together with the stamp of authorisation, shall accompany each shipment.

[1459]

TITLE V
IMPORTS OF WASTE INTO THE COMMUNITY

CHAPTER A
IMPORTS OF WASTE FOR DISPOSAL

Article 19

1.   All imports into the Community of waste for disposal shall be prohibited except those from—
  (a) EFTA countries which are Parties to the Basle Convention;
  (b) other countries—
      — which are Parties to the Basle Convention, or
      — with which the Community, or the Community and its Member States, have concluded bilateral or multilateral agreements or arrangements compatible with Community legislation and in accordance with Article 11 of the Basle Convention guaranteeing that the disposal operations carried out in an authorised centre and complies with the requirements for environmentally sound management, or
      — with which individual Member States have concluded bilateral agreements or arrangements prior to the date of application of this Regulation, compatible with Community legislation and in accordance with Article 11 of the Basle Convention, containing the same guarantees as referred to above and guaranteeing that the waste originated in the country of dispatch and that disposal will be carried out exclusively in the Member State which has concluded the agreement or arrangement. These agreements or arrangements shall be notified to the Commission within three months of the date of application of the Regulation or of their date of application, whichever is the earlier, and shall expire when agreements or arrangements are concluded in accordance with the second indent, or
      — with which individual Member States conclude bilateral agreements or arrangements after the date of application of this Regulation in the circumstances of paragraph 2.

2.   The Council hereby authorises individual Member States to conclude bilateral agreements and arrangements after the date of application of this Regulation in exceptional cases for the disposal of specific waste, where such waste will not be managed in an environmentally sound manner in the country of dispatch. These agreements and arrangements shall comply with the conditions set out in paragraph 1(b), third indent and shall be notified to the Commission prior to their conclusion.

3.   The countries referred to in paragraph 1(b) shall be required to present a duly motivated request beforehand to the competent authority of the Member State of destination on the basis that they do no have and cannot reasonable acquire the technical capacity and the necessary facilities in order to dispose of the waste in an environmentally sound manner.

4.   The competent authority of destination shall prohibit the bringing of waste into its area of jurisdiction if it has reason to believe that the waste will not be managed in an environmentally sound manner in its area.

[1460]

Article 20

1.   Notification shall be made to the competent authority of destinations by means of the consignment note in accordance with Article 3(5) with copies to the consignee of the waste and to the competent authorities of transit. The consignment note shall be issued by the competent authority of destination.

On receipt of the notification, the competent authority of destination shall, within three working days, send a written acknowledgement to the notifier, with copies to the competent authorities of transit in the Community.

2.   The competent authority of destination shall authorise the shipment only in the absence of objections on its part or from the other competent authorities concerned. The authorisation shall be subject to any transport conditions referred to in paragraph 5.

3.   The competent authorities of destination and transit in the Community may, within 60 days of dispatch of the copy of the acknowledgement, raise objections based on Article 4(3).

They may also request additional information. These objections shall be conveyed in writing to the notifier, with copies to the other competent authorities concerned in the Community;

4.   The competent authority of destination shall have 70 days following dispatch of the acknowledgement to take its decision authorising the shipment, with or without conditions, or refusing it. It may also request additional information.

It shall send certified copies of the decision to the competent authorities of transit in the Community, the consignee and the customs office of entry into the Community.

The competent authority of destination shall take its decision no earlier than 61 days following the dispatch of the acknowledgement. It may, however, take its decision earlier if it has the written consent of the other competent authorities.

The competent authority of destination shall signify its authorisation by appropriately stamping the consignment note.

5.   The competent authority of destination and transit in the Community shall have 60 days following dispatch of the acknowledgement to lay down conditions in respect of the shipment of the waste. These conditions, which must be conveyed to the notifier, with copies to the competent authorities concerned, may not be more stringent than those laid down in respect of similar shipments occurring wholly within the jurisdiction of the competent authority in question.

6.   The shipment may be effected only after the notifier has received authorisation from the competent authority of destination.

7.   Once the notifier has received authorisation, he shall insert the date of the shipment and otherwise complete the consignment note and send copies to the competent authorities concerned three working days before the shipment is made. A specimen of the consignment note shall be delivered by the carrier to the customs office of entry into the Community.

A copy or, if requested by the competent authorities, a specimen of the consignment note, together with the stamp of authorisation, shall accompany each shipment.

All undertakings involved in the operation shall complete the consignment note at the points indicated, sign it and retain a copy.

8.   Within three working days following receipt of the waste for disposal, the consignee shall send copies of completed consignment note, except for the certificate referred to in paragraph 9, to the notifier and the competent authorities concerned;

9.   As soon as possible and not later than 180 days following the receipt of the waste, the consignee shall under his responsibility, send a certificate of disposal to the notifier and the other competent authority concerned. This certificate shall be part of or attached to the consignment note which accompanies the shipment.

[1461]

CHAPTER B
IMPORTS OF WASTE FOR RECOVERY

Article 21

1.   All imports of waste for recovery into the Community shall be prohibited, except those from—
   (a) countries to which the OECD decision applies;
   (b) other countries—
      — which are Parties to the Basle Convention and/or with which the Community, or the Community and its Member States, have concluded bilateral or multilateral or regional agreements or arrangements compatible with Community legislation and in accordance with Article 11 of the Basle Convention, guaranteeing that the recovery operation is carried out in an authorised centre and complies with the requirements for environmentally sound management, or
      — with which individual Member States have concluded bilateral agreements or arrangements prior to the date of application of this Regulation, where these are compatible with Community legislation and in accordance with Article 11 of the Basle Convention, containing the same guarantees as referred to above. These agreements or arrangements shall be notified to the Commission within three months of the date of application of this Regulation or of their date of application, whichever is the earlier, and shall expire when agreements or arrangements are concluded in accordance with the first indent, or
      — with which individual Member States conclude bilateral agreements or arrangements after the date of application of this Regulation in the circumstances of paragraph 2.

2.   The Council hereby authorises individual Member States to conclude after the date of applications of this Regulation bilateral agreements and arrangements in exceptional cases for the recovery of specific waste, where a Member State deems such agreements or arrangements necessary to avoid any interruption of waste treatment before the Community has concluded those agreements and arrangements.

Such agreements and arrangements shall also be compatible with Community legislation and in accordance with Article 11 of the Basle Convention; they shall be notified to the Commission prior to their conclusion and shall expire when agreements or arrangements are concluded in accordance with paragraph 1(b), first indent.

[1462]

Article 22

1.   Where waste is imported for recovery from countries and through countries to which the OECD Decision applies, the following control procedures shall apply by analogy—
    (a) for waste listed in Annex III: Articles 6, 7, 8, 9(1), (3), (4) and (5), and 17(5);
    (b) for waste listed in Annex IV and waste which has not yet been assigned to Annex II, III or IV: Article 10.

2.   Where waste for recovery listed in Annexes III and IV and waste which has not yet been assigned to Annex II, III or IV is imported from and through countries to the OECD Decision does not apply—
    — Article 20 shall apply by analogy,
    — reasoned objections may be raised in accordance with Article 7(4) only,

save as otherwise provided for the bilateral or multilateral agreements entered into in accordance with Article 21(1)(b) and on the basis of the control procedures of either paragraph 1 of this Article or Article 20.

[1463]

TITLE VI
TRANSIT OF WASTE FROM OUTSIDE AND THROUGH THE COMMUNITY FOR DISPOSAL OR RECOVERY OUTSIDE THE COMMUNITY

CHAPTER A
WASTE FOR DISPOSAL AND RECOVERY (EXCEPT TRANSIT COVERED BY ARTICLE 24)

Article 23

1.   Where waste for disposal and, except in cases covered by Article 24, recovery is shipped through (a) Member State(s), notification shall be effected by means of the consignment note to the last competent authority of transit within the Community, with copies to the consignee, the other competent authorities concerned and the customs offices of entry into and departure from the Community.

2.   The last competent authority of transit within the Community shall promptly inform the notifier of receipt of the notification. The other competent authorities in the Community shall, on the basis of paragraph 5, convey their reactions to the last competent authority of transit in the Community, which shall then respond in writing to the notifier within 60 days, consenting to the shipment with or without reservations; or imposing, if appropriate, conditions laid down by the other competent authorities of transit, or withholding information. Any refusal or reservations must be justified. The competent authority shall send a certified copy of the decision to both the other competent authorities concerned and the customs offices of entry into and departure from the Community.

3.   Without prejudice to Articles 25(2) and 26(2), the shipment shall be admitted into the Community only if the notifier has received the written consent of the last competent authority of transit. This authority shall signify its consent by appropriately stamping the consignment note.

4.   The competent authorities of transit within the Community shall have 20 days following notification to lay down, if appropriate, any conditions attached to the transport of the waste.

These conditions, which must be conveyed to the notifier, with copies to the competent authorities concerned, may not be more stringent than those laid down in respect of similar shipments occurring wholly within the jurisdiction of the competent authority in question.

5.   The consignment note shall be issued by the last competent authority of transit within the Community.

6.   Once the notifier has received authorisation, he shall complete the consignment note and send copies to the competent authorities concerned three working days before the shipment is made.

A specimen of the consignment note, together with the stamp of authorisation, shall accompany each shipment.

A specimen of the consignment note shall be supplied by the carrier to the customs office of departure when the waste leaves the Community.

All undertakings involved in the operation shall complete the consignment note at the points indicated, sign it and retain a copy thereof.

7.   As soon as the waste has left the Community, the customs office of departure shall send a copy of the consignment note to the last competent authority of transit within the Community.

Furthermore, at the latest 42 days after the waste has left the Community, the notifier shall declare or certify to that competent authority, with copies to the other competent authorities of transit, that it has arrived at its intended destination.

[1464]

CHAPTER B
TRANSIT OF WASTE FOR RECOVERY FROM AND TO A COUNTRY TO WHICH THE OECD DECISION APPLIES

Article 24

1.   Transit of waste for recovery listed in Annexes III and IV from a country and transferred for recovery to a country to which the OECD Decision applies through (a) Member State(s) requires notification to all competent authorities of transit of the Member State(s) concerned.

2.   Notification shall be effected by means of the consignment note.

3.   On receipt of the notification the competent authority(ies) of transit shall send an acknowledgement to the notifier and to the consignee within three working days.

4.   This competent authority(ies) of transit may raise reasoned objections to the planned shipment based on Article 7(4). Any objection must be provided in writing to the notifier and to the competent authorities of transit of the other Member States concerned within 30 days of dispatch of the acknowledgement.

5.   The competent authority of transit may decide to provide written consent in less than 30 days.

In the case of transit of waste listed in Annex IV and waste which has not yet been assigned to Annex II, III or IV, consent must be given in writing prior to commencement of the shipment.

6.   The shipment may be effected only in the absence of any objection.

[1465]

TITLE VII
COMMON PROVISIONS

Article 25

1.　　Where a shipment of waste to which the competent authorities concerned have consented cannot be completed in accordance with the terms of the consignment note or the contract referred to in Articles 3 and 6, the competent authority of dispatch shall, within 90 days after it has been informed thereof, ensure that the notifier returns the waste to its area of jurisdiction or elsewhere within the State of dispatch unless it is satisfied that the waste can be disposed of or recovered in an alternative and environmentally sound manner.

2.　　In cases referred to in paragraph 1, a further notification shall be made. No Member State of dispatch or Member State of transit shall oppose the return of this waste at the duly motivated request of the competent authority of destination and with an explanation of the reason.

3.　　The obligation of the notifier and the subsidiary obligation of the State of dispatch to take the waste back shall end when the consignee has issued the certificate referred to in Articles 5 and 8.

[1466]

Article 26

1.　　Any shipment of waste effected—
  (a) without notification to all competent authorities concerned pursuant to the provisions of this Regulation; or
  (b) without the consent of the competent authorities concerned pursuant to the provisions of this Regulation; or
  (c) with consent obtained from the competent authorities concerned through falsification, misrepresentation or fraud; or
  (d) which is not specified in a material way in the consignment note; or
  (e) which results in disposal or recovery in contravention of Community or international rules; or
  (f) contrary to Articles 14, 16, 19 and 21
shall be deemed to be illegal traffic.

2.　　If such illegal traffic is the responsibility of the notifier of the waste, the competent authority of dispatch shall ensure that the waste in question is—
  (a) taken back by the notifier or, if necessary, by the competent authority itself, into the State of dispatch or if impracticable;
  (b) otherwise disposed of or recovered in an environmentally sound manner, within 30 days from the time when the competent authority was informed of the illegal traffic or within such other period of time as may be agreed by the competent authorities concerned.

In this case a further notification shall be made. No Member State of dispatch or Member State of transit shall oppose the return of this waste at the duly motivated request of the competent authority of destination and with an explanation of the reason.

3.　　If such illegal traffic is the responsibility of the consignee, the competent authority of destination shall ensure that the waste in question is disposed of in an environmentally sound manner by the consignee or, if impracticable, by the competent authority itself within 30 days from the time it was informed of the illegal traffic or within any such other period of time as may be agreed by the competent authorities concerned. To this end, they shall co-operate, as necessary, in the disposal or recovery of the waste in an environmentally sound manner.

4.   Where responsibility for the illegal traffic cannot be imputed to either the notifier or the consignee, the competent authorities shall co-operate to ensure that the waste in question is disposed of or recovered in an environmentally sound manner. Guidelines for this co-operation shall be established in accordance with the procedure laid down in Article 18 of Directive 75/442/EEC.

5.   Member States shall take appropriate legal action to prohibit and punish illegal traffic.

[1467]

Article 27

1.   All shipments of waste covered within the scope of this Regulation shall be subject to the provision of a financial guarantee or equivalent insurance covering costs for shipment, including cases referred to in Articles 25 and 26, and for disposal or recovery.

2.   Such guarantees shall be returned when proof has been furnished, by means of—

— the certificate of disposal or recovery, that the waste has reached its destination and has been disposed of or recovered in an environmentally sound manner,

— Control copy T 5 drawn up pursuant to Commission Regulation (EEC) No 2823/87[1] that, in the case of transit through the Community, the waste has left the Community.

3.   Each Member State shall inform the Commission of the provision which it makes in national law pursuant to this Article. The Commission shall forward this information to all Member States.

[1468]

NOTES

   [1]   OJ L270, 23.9.87, p 1.

Article 28

1.   While respecting the obligations imposed on him by the applicable Articles 3, 6, 9, 15, 17, 20, 22, 23 and 24, the notifier may use a general notification procedure where waste for disposal or recovery having the same physical and chemical characteristics is shipped periodically to the same consignee following the same route. If, in the case of unforeseen circumstances, this route cannot be followed, the notifier shall inform the competent authorities concerned as soon as possible or before the shipment starts if the need for route modification is already known at this time.

Where the route modification is known before the shipment starts and this involves other competent authorities than those concerned in the general notification, this procedure shall not be used.

2.   Under a general notification procedure, a single notification may cover several shipments of waste over a maximum period of one year. The indicated period may be shortened by agreement between the competent authorities concerned.

3.   The competent authorities concerned shall make their agreement to the use of this general notification procedure subject to the subsequent supply of additional information. If the composition of the waste is not as notified or if the conditions imposed on its shipment are not respected, the competent authorities concerned shall withdraw their consent to this procedure by means of official notice to the notifier. Copies of this notice shall be sent to the other competent authorities concerned.

4.   General notification shall be made by means of the consignment note.

[1469]

Article 29

Wastes which are the subject of different notifications shall not be mixed during shipment.

[1470]

Article 30

1.   Member States shall take the measures needed to ensure that waste is shipped in accordance with the provisions of this Regulation. Such measures may include inspections of establishments and undertakings, in accordance with Article 13 of Directive 75/442/EEC, and spot checks of shipments.

2.   Checks may take place in particular—
— at the point of origin, carried out with the producer, holder or notifier,
— at the destination, carried out with the final consignee,
— at the external frontiers of the Community,
— during the shipment within the Community.

3.   Checks may include the inspection of documents, the confirmation of identity and, if appropriate, the physical control of the waste.

[1471]

Article 31

1.   The consignment note shall be printed and completed and any further documentation and information referred to in Article 4 and 6 shall be supplied in a language which is acceptable to the competent authority of—
— dispatch, as referred to in Articles 3, 7, 15 and 17, in the case of both a shipment of waste within the Community and the export of waste,
— destination, as referred to in Articles 20 and 22, in the case of the import of waste,
— transit, as referred to in Articles 23 and 24.

A translation shall be supplied by the notifier at the request of the other competent authorities concerned in a language acceptable to them.

2.   Further details may be determined in accordance with the procedure laid down in Article 18 of Directive 75/442/EEC.

[1472]

TITLE VIII
OTHER PROVISIONS

Article 32

The provisions of the international transport conventions listed in Annex I to which the Member States are parties shall be complied with in so far as they cover the waste to which this Regulation refers.

[1473]

Article 33

1.   Appropriate administrative costs of implementing the notification and supervision procedure and usual costs of appropriate analyses and inspections may be charged to the notifier.

2.   Costs arising from the return of waste, including shipment, disposal or recovery of the waste in an alternative and environmentally sound manner pursuant to Articles 25(1) and 26(2), shall be charged to the notifier or, if impracticable, to the Member States concerned.

3.   Costs arising from disposal or recovery in an alternative and environmentally sound manner pursuant to Article 26(3) shall be charged to the consignee.

4.   Costs arising from disposal or recovery, including possible shipment pursuant to Article 26(4), shall be charged to the notifier and/or the consignee depending upon the decision by the competent authorities involved.

[1474]

Article 34

1.   Without prejudice to the provisions of Article 26 and to Community and national provisions concerning civil liability and irrespective of the point of disposal or recovery of the waste, the producer of that waste shall take all the necessary steps to dispose of or recover or to arrange for disposal or recovery of the waste so as to protect the quality of the environment in accordance with Directives 75/442/EEC and 91/689/EEC.

2.   Member States shall take all necessary steps to ensure that the obligations laid down in paragraph 1 are carried out.

[1475]

Article 35

All documents sent to or by the competent authorities shall be kept in the Community for at least three years by the competent authorities, the notifier and the consignee.

[1476]

Article 36

Member States shall designate the competent authority or authorities for the implementation of this Regulation. A single competent authority of transit shall be designated by each Member State.

[1477]

Article 37

1.   Member States and the Commission shall each designate at least one correspondent responsible for informing or advising persons or undertakings who or which make enquiries. The Commission correspondent shall forward to the correspondents of the Member States any questions put to him which concern the latter, and vice versa.

2.   The Commission shall, if requested by Member States or if otherwise appropriate, periodically hold a meeting of the correspondents to examine with them the questions raised by the implementation of this Regulation.

[1478]

Article 38

1.   Member States shall notify the Commission not later than three months before the date of application of Regulation of the name(s), address(es) and telephone and telex/telefax number(s) of the competent authorities and of the correspondents, together with the stamp of the competent authorities.

Member States shall notify the Commission annually of any changes in this information.

2.   The Commission shall send the information without delay to the other Member States and to the Secretariat of the Basle Convention.

The Commission shall furthermore send to Member States the waste management plans referred to in Article 7 of Directive 75/442/EEC.

[1479]

Article 39

1.   Member States may designate customs offices of entry into and departure from the Community for shipments of waste entering and leaving the Community and inform the Commission thereof.

 The Commission shall publish the list of these offices in the Official Journal of the European Communities and, if appropriate, update this list.

2.   If Member States decide to designate the custom offices referred to in paragraph 1, no shipment of waste shall be allowed to use any other frontier crossing points within a Member State for entering or leaving the Community.

[1480]

Article 40

Member States, as appropriate and necessary in liaison with the Commission, shall co-operate with other parties to the Basle Convention and inter-State organisations directly or through the Secretariat of the Basle Convention, inter alia, via the exchange of information, the promotion of environmentally sound technologies and the development of appropriate codes of good practice.

[1481]

Article 41

1.   Before the end of each calendar year, Member States shall draw up a report in accordance with Article 13(3) of the Basle Convention and send it to the Secretariat of the Basle Convention and a copy thereof to the Commission.

2.   The Commission shall, based on these reports, establish every three years a report on the implementation of this Regulation by the Community and its Member States. It may request to this end additional information in accordance with Article 6 of Directive 91/692/EEC.[1]

[1482]

NOTES
[1]   OJ L377, 31.12.91, p 48.

Article 42

1.   The Commission shall draw up not later than three months before the date of application of this Regulation and adapt if appropriate afterwards, in accordance with the procedure laid down in Article 18 of Directive 75/442/EEC, the standard consignment note, including the form of the certificate of disposal and recovery (either integral to the consignment note or, meanwhile, attached to the existing consignment note under Directive 84/631/EEC) taking account in particular of—
 —   the relevant Articles of this Regulation,
 —   the relevant international Conventions and agreements.

2.   The existing form of the consignment note shall apply by analogy until the new consignment note has been drawn up. The form of the certificate of disposal and recovery to be attached to the existing consignment note shall be drawn up as soon as possible.

3.   Without prejudice to the procedure laid down in Article 1(3)(c) and (d) regarding Annex II.A, Annexes II, III and IV shall be adapted by the Commission in accordance with the procedure laid down in Article 18 of Directive 75/442/EEC only to reflect changes already agreed under the review mechanism of the OECD.

4.   The procedure referred to in paragraph 1 shall apply also to define environmentally sound management, taking into account the relevant international conventions and agreements.

[1483]

Article 43

Directive 84/631/EEC is hereby repealed with effect from the date of application of this Regulation. Any shipment pursuant to Articles 4 and 5 of that Directive shall be completed not later than six months from the date of application of this Regulation.

[1484]

Article 44

This Regulation shall enter into force on the third day following its publication in the Official Journal of the European Communities.

It shall apply 15 months after publication.

This Regulation shall be binding in its entirety and directly applicable in all Member States.

[1485]

Done at Brussels, 1 February 1993.

ANNEX I
LIST OF INTERNATIONAL TRANSPORT CONVENTIONS REFERRED TO IN ARTICLE 32[1]

1.   ADR—

      European Agreement concerning the international carriage of dangerous goods by road (1957).

2.   Cotif—

      Convention concerning the international carriage of dangerous goods by rail (1985).

      RID—

      Regulation on the international carriage by rail of dangerous goods (1985).

3.   Solas Convention—

      International Convention for the safety of life at sea (1974).

4.   IMDG Code[2]

      International maritime dangerous goods code.

5.   Chicago Convention—

      Convention on international civil aviation (1944), Annex 18 to which deals with the carriage of dangerous goods by air (TI: Technical instructions for the safe transport of dangerous goods by air).

6.   Marpol Convention—

      International Convention for the prevention of pollution from ships (1973 to 1978).

7.   ADNR—

      Regulations of the carriage of dangerous substances on the Rhine (1970).

---

[1]   This list contains those Conventions in force at the time of adoption of this Regulation.
[2]   Since 1 January 1985, the IMDG code has been incorporated in the Solas Convention.

[1486]

[ANNEX II
GREEN LIST OF WASTES*

Regardless of whether or not wastes are included on this list, they may not be moved as green wastes if they are contaminated by other materials to an extent which (a) increases the risks associated with the waste sufficiently to render it appropriate for inclusion in the amber or red lists, or (b) prevents the recovery of the waste in an environmentally sound manner.

NOTES
    *   Wherever possible, the code number of the Harmonised Commodity Description and Coding System, established by the Brussels Convention of 14 June 1983 under the auspices of the Customs Cooperation Council (Harmonised System) is listed opposite an entry. This code may apply to both wastes and products. This Regulation does not include items which are not wastes. Therefore, the code—used by customs officials in order to facilitate their procedures as well as by others—is only provided here to help in identifying wastes that are listed and subject to this Regulation. However, corresponding official Explanatory Notes as issued by the Customs Cooperation Council should be used as interpretative guidance to identify wastes covered by genetic headings. The indicative 'ex' identifies a specific item contained within a heading of the Harmonised System code.

    The code in bold in the first column is the OECD code: it consists of two letters (one for the list: **Green**, **A**mber or **R**ed and one for the category of waste: A, B, C ...) followed by a number.

GA. METAL AND METAL-ALLOY WASTES IN METALLIC, NON-DISPERSIBLE FORM**

The following waste and scrap of precious metals and their alloys:

GA 010 ex 7112 10	Of gold
GA 020 ex 7112 20	Of platinum (the expression 'platinum' includes platinum, iridium, osmium, palladium, rhodium and ruthenium)
GA 030 ex 7112 90	Of other precious metal, eg silver
	NB: Mercury is specifically excluded as a contaminant of these metals or their alloys or amalgams.

The following ferrous waste and scrap of iron or steel:

GA 040	7204 10	Waste and scrap of cast iron
GA 050	7204 21	Waste and scrap of stainless steel
GA 060	7204 29	Waste and scrap of other alloy steels
GA 070	7204 30	Waste and scrap of tinned iron or steel
GA 080	7204 41	Turnings, shavings, chips, milling waste, filings, trimmings and stampings, whether or not in bundles
GA 090	7204 49	Other ferrous waste and scrap
GA 100	7204 50	Re-melting scrap ingots
GA 110 ex 7302 10		Used iron and steel rails

The following waste and scrap of non-ferrous metals and their alloys:

GA 120	7404 00	Copper waste and scrap
GA 130	7503 00	Nickel waste and scrap
GA 140	7602 00	Aluminium waste and scrap
GA 150	7802 00	Lead waste and scrap
GA 160	7902 00	Zinc waste and scrap
GA 170	8002 00	Tin waste and scrap
GA 180 ex 8101 91		Tungsten waste and scrap

GA 190 ex 8102 91	Molybdenum waste and scrap	
GA 200 ex 8103 10	Tantalum waste and scrap	
GA 210 8104 20	Magnesium waste and scrap	
GA 220 ex 8105 10	Cobalt waste and scrap	
GA 230 ex 8106 00	Bismuth waste and scrap	
GA 240 ex 8107 10	Cadmium waste and scrap	
GA 250 ex 8108 10	Titanium waste and scrap	
GA 260 ex 8109 10	Zirconium waste and scrap	
GA 270 ex 8110 00	Antimony waste and scrap	
GA 280 ex 8111 00	Manganese waste and scrap	
GA 290 ex 8112 11	Beryllium waste and scrap	
GA 300 ex 8112 20	Chromium waste and scrap	
GA 310 ex 8112 30	Germanium waste and scrap	
GA 320 ex 8112 40	Vanadium waste and scrap	
ex 8112 91	Wastes and scrap of:	
GA 330	—Hafnium	
GA 340	—Indium	
GA 350	—Niobium	
GA 360	—Rhenium	
GA 370	—Gallium	
GA 380	—Thallium	
GA 390 ex 2844 30	Thorium waste and scrap	
GA 400 ex 2804 90	Selenium waste and scrap	
GA 410 ex 2804 50	Tellurium waste and scrap	
GA 420 ex 2805 30	Rare earths waste and scrap	

NOTES

    ** 'Non-dispersible' does not include any wastes in the form of powder, sludge, dust or solid items containing encased hazardous waste liquids.

GB. METAL BEARING WASTES ARISING FROM MELTING, SMELTING AND REFINING OF METALS

GB 010 2620 11	Hard zinc spelter	
GB 020	Zinc containing drosses:	
GB 021	—Galvanizing slab zinc top dross (> 90% Zn)	
GB 022	—Galvanizing slab zinc bottom dross (> 92% Zn)	
GB 023	—Zinc die cast dross (> 85% Zn)	
GB 024	—Hot dip galvanizers slab zinc dross (batch) (> 92% Zn)	
GB 025	—Zinc skimmings	
GB 030	Aluminium skimmings	
GB 040 ex 2620 90	Slags from precious metals and copper processing for further refining	
GB 050 ex 2620 90	Tantalum bearing tin slags with less than 0,5% tin	

GC. OTHER WASTES CONTAINING METALS

GC 010	Electrical assemblies consisting only of metals or alloys
GC 020	Electronic scrap (eg printed circuit boards, electronic components, wire, etc) and reclaimed electronic components suitable for base and precious metal recovery
GC 030 ex 8908 00	Vessels and other floating structures for breaking up, properly emptied of any cargo and other materials arising from the operation of the vessel which may have been classified as a dangerous substance or waste
GC 040	Motor vehicle wrecks, drained of liquids
GC 050	Spent catalysts:
GC 051	—Fluid catalytic cracking (FCC) catalysts
GC 052	—Precious metal bearing catalysts
GC 053	—Transition metal catalysts (eg chromium, cobalt, copper, iron, nickel, manganese, molybdenum, tungsten, vanadium, zinc)
GC 070 ex 2619 00	Slag arising from the manufacture of iron and carbon steel (including low alloy steel) excluding those slags which have been specifically produced to meet both national and relevant international requirements and standards*
GC 080	Mill scale (ferrous metal)

NOTES
* This entry covers the use of such slags as a source of titanium dioxide and vanadium.

GD. WASTES FROM MINING OPERATIONS: THESE WASTES TO BE IN NON-DISPERSIBLE FORM

GD 010 ex 2504 90	Natural graphite waste
GD 020 ex 2514 00	Slate waste, whether or not roughly trimmed or merely cut, by sawing or otherwise
GD 030 2525 30	Mica waste
GD 040 ex 2529 30	Leucite, nepheline and nepheline synite waste
GD 050 ex 2529 10	Feldspar waste
GD 060 ex 2529 21 ex 2529 22	Fluospar waste
GD 070 ex 2811 22	Silica wastes in solid form excluding those used in foundry operations

GE. GLASS WASTE IN NON-DISPERSIBLE FORM

GE 010 ex 7001 00	Cullet and other waste and scrap of glass except for glass from cathode-ray tubes and other activated glasses
GE 020	Fibre glass wastes

GF. CERAMIC WASTES IN NON-DISPERSIBLE FORM

GF 010	Ceramic wastes which have been fired after shaping, including ceramic vessels (before and/or after use)
GF 020 ex 8113 00	Cermet waste and scrap (metal ceramic composites)
GF 030	Ceramic based fibres not elsewhere specified or included

GG. OTHER WASTES CONTAINING PRINCIPALLY INORGANIC CONSTITUENTS, WHICH MAY CONTAIN METALS AND ORGANIC MATERIALS

GG 010	Partially refined calcium sulphate produced from flue gas desulphurization (FGD)
GG 020	Waste gypsum wallboard or plasterboard arising from the demolition of buildings
GG 030 ex 2621	Bottom ash and slag tap from coal-fired power plants
GG 040 ex 2621	Coal-fired power plants fly ash
GG 050	Anode butts of petroleum coke and/or bitumen
GG 060 ex 2803	Spent activated carbon
GG 080 ex 2621 00	Slag from copper production, chemical stabilised, having a high iron content (above 20%) and processed according to industrial specifications (eg DIN 4301 and DIN 8201) mainly for construction and abrasive applications
GG 090	Sulphur in solid form
GG 100	Limestone from the production of calcium cyanamide (having a pH less than 9)
GG 110 ex 2621 00	Neutralised red mud from alumina production
GG 120	Sodium, potassium, calcium chlorides
GG 130	Carborundum (silicon carbide)
GG 140	Broken concrete
GG 150 ex 2620 90	Lithium-tantalum and lithium-niobium containing glass scraps

GH. SOLID PLASTIC WASTES

Including, but not limited to:

GH 010 3915	Waste, parings and scrap of plastics of:
GH 011 ex 3915 10	—Polymers of ethylene
GH 012 ex 3915 20	—Polymers of styrene
GH 013 ex 3915 30	—Polymers of vinyl chloride
GH 014 ex 3915 90	—Polymerised or co-polymers: for example:

       —Polypropylene

       —Polyethylene terephthalate

       —Acrylonitrile copolymer

       —Butadiene copolymer

       —Styrene copolymer

       —Polyamides

       —Polybutylene terephthalates

    —Polycarbonates

    —Polyphenylene sulphides

    —Acrylic polymers

    —Paraffins (C10–C13)*

    —Polyurethane (not containing chlorofluorocarbons)

    —Polysiloxalanes (silicones)

    —Polymethyl methacrylate

    —Polyvinyl alcohol

    —Polyvinyl butyral

    —Polyvinyl acetate

    —Polymers of fluorinated ethylene (Teflon, PTFE)

GH 015 ex 3915 90   —Resins or condensation products, for example:

    —Urea formaldehyde resins

    —Phenol formaldehyde resins

    —Melamine formaldehyde resins

    —Epoxy resins

    —Alkyd resins

    —Polyamides

NOTES

(*) These cannot be polymerised and are used as plasticizers.

GI. PAPER, PAPERBOARD AND PAPER PRODUCT WASTES

GI 010	4707	Waste and scrap of paper or paperboard:
GI 011	4707 10	—Of unbleached kraft paper or paperboard or of corrugated paper or paperboard
GI 012	4707 20	—Of other paper or paperboard, made mainly of bleached chemical pulp, not coloured in the mass
GI 013	4707 30	—Of paper or paperboard made mainly of mechanical pulp (for example, newspapers, journals and similar printed matter)
GI 014	4707 90	—Other, including but not limited to:

    1. Laminated paperboard

    2. Unsorted waste and scrap

GJ. TEXTILE WASTES

GJ 010	5003	Silk waste (including cocoons unsuitable for reeling, yarn waste and garnetted stock)
GJ 011	5003 10	—Not carded or combed
GJ 012	5003 90	—Other
GJ 020	5103	Waste of wool or of fine or coarse animal hair, including yarn waste but excluding garnetted stock
GJ 021	5103 10	—Noils of wool or of fine animal hair
GJ 022	5103 20	—Other waste of wool or of fine animal hair

GJ 023	5103 30	—Waste of coarse animal hair
GJ 030	5202	Cotton waste (including yarn waste and garnetted stock)
GJ 031	5202 10	—Yarn waste (including thread waste)
GJ 032	5202 91	—Garnetted stock
GJ 033	5202 99	— Other
GJ 040	5301 30	Flax tow and waste
GJ 050 ex	5302 90	Tow and waste (including yarn waste and garnetted stock) of true hemp (*Cannabis sativa* L.)
GJ 060 ex	5303 90	Tow and waste (including yarn waste and garnetted stock) of jute and other textile bast fibres (excluding flax, true hemp and ramie)
GJ 070 ex	5304 90	Tow and waste (including yarn waste and garnetted stock) of sisal and other textile fibres of the genus Agave
GJ 080 ex	5305 19	Tow, noils and waste (including yarn waste and garnetted stock) of coconut
GJ 090 ex	5305 29	Tow, noils and waste (including yarn waste and garnetted stock) of abaca (Manila hemp of *Musa textilis* Nee)
GJ 100 ex	5305 99	Tow, noils and waste (including yarn waste and garnetted stock) of ramie and other vegetable textile fibres, not elsewhere specified or included
GJ 110	5505	Waste (including noils, yarn waste and garnetted stock) of man-made fibres
GJ 111	5505 10	—Of synthetic fibres
GJ 112	5505 20	—Of artificial fibres
GJ 120	6309 00	Worn clothing and other worn textile articles
GJ 130 ex	6310	Used rags, scrap twine, cordage, rope and cables and worn out articles of twine, cordage, rope or cables of textile materials
GJ 131 ex	6310 10	— Sorted
GJ 132 ex	6310 90	— Other

GK. RUBBER WASTES

GK 010	4004 00	Waste, parings and scrap of rubber (other than hard rubber) and granules obtained therefrom
GK 020	4012 20	Used pneumatic tyres
GK 030 ex	4017 00	Waste and scrap of hard rubber (for example, ebonite)

GL. UNTREATED CORK AND WOOD WASTES

GL 010 ex	4401 30	Wood waste and scrap, whether or not agglomerated in logs, briquettes, pellets or similar forms
GL 020	4501 90	Cork waste; crushed, granulated or ground cork

GM. WASTES ARISING FROM AGRO-FOOD INDUSTRIES

GM 070 ex	2307	Wine lees
GM 080 ex	2308	Dried and sterilised vegetable waste, residues and by-products, whether or not in the form of pellets, of a kind used in animal feeding, not elsewhere specified or included

GM 090	1522	Degras; residues resulting from the treatment of fatty substances or animal or vegetable waxes
GM 100	0506 90	Waste of bones and horn-cones, unworked, defatted, simply prepared (but not cut to shape), treated with acid or degelatinized
GM 110 ex 0511 90		Fish waste
GM 120	1802 00	Cocoa shells, husks, skins and other cocoa waste
GM 130		Waste from the agro-food industry excluding by-products which meet national and international requirements and standards for human or animal consumption

GN. WASTES ARISING FROM TANNING AND FELLMONGERY OPERATIONS AND LEATHER USE

GN 010 ex 0502 00	Waste of pigs', hogs' or boars' bristles and hair or of badger hair and other brush-making hair
GN 020 ex 0503 00	Horsehair waste, whether or not put up as a layer with or without supporting material
GN 030 ex 0505 90	Waste of skins and other parts of birds, with their feathers or down, of feathers and parts of feathers (whether or not with trimmed edges) and down, not further worked than cleaned, disinfected or treated for preservation
GN 040 ex 4110 00	Parings and other waste of leather or of composition leather, not suitable for the manufacture of leather articles, excluding leather sludges

GO. OTHER WASTES CONTAINING PRINCIPALLY ORGANIC CONSTITUENTS, WHICH MAY CONTAIN METALS AND INORGANIC MATERIALS

GO 010 ex 0501 00	Waste of human hair
GO 020	Waste straw
GO 030	Deactivated fungus mycelium from penicillin production to be used as animal feed
GO 040	Waste photographic film base and waste photographic film not containing silver
GO 050	Single-use cameras without batteries]

[1487]

NOTES

Substituted by Commission Decision 96/660/EC of 14 November 1996, Art1.

[ANNEX III
AMBER LIST OF WASTES*

Regardless of whether or not wastes are included on this list, they may not be moved as amber wastes if they are contaminated by other materials to an extent which (a) increases the risks associated with the waste sufficiently to render it appropriate for inclusion in the red list, or (b) prevents the recovery of the waste in an environmentally sound manner.

NOTES

  *   Wherever possible, the code number of the Harmonised Commodity Description and Coding System, established by the Brussels Convention of 14 June 1983 under the auspices of the Customs Cooperation Council (Harmonised System) is listed opposite an entry. This code may apply to both wastes and products. This Regulation does not include items which are not wastes. Therefore, the code—used by customs officials in order to facilitate their procedures as well as by others—is only provided here to help in identifying wastes that are listed and subject to this Regulation.

However, corresponding official Explanatory Notes as issued by the Customs Cooperation Council should be used as interpretative guidance to identify wastes covered by generic headings.

The indicative "ex" identifies a specific item contained within a heading of the Harmonised System code.

The code in bold in the first column is the OECD: it consists of two letters (one for the list: **G**reen, **A**mber or **R**ed and one for the category of waste: A, B, C, ...) followed by a number.

AA. METAL BEARING WASTES

AA 010 ex 2619 00	Dross, scalings and other wastes from the manufacture of iron and steel**
AA 020 ex 2620 19	Zinc ashes and residues**
AA 030 2620 20	Lead ashes and residues**
AA 040 ex 2620 30	Copper ashes and residues**
AA 050 ex 2620 40	Aluminium ashes and residues**
AA 060 ex 2620 50	Vanadium ashes and residues**
AA 070 2620 90	Ashes and residues** containing metals or metal compounds not elsewhere specified or included
AA 080	Thallium waste and residues**
AA 090 ex 2804 80	Arsenic waste and residues**
AA 100 ex 2805 40	Mercury waste and residues**
AA 110	Residues from alumina production not elsewhere specified or included
AA 120	Galvanic sludges
AA 130	Liquors from the pickling of metals
AA 140	Leaching residues from zinc processing, dusts and sludges such as jarosite, hematite, goethite, etc.
AA 150	Precious metal bearing residues in solid form which contain traces of inorganic cyanides
AA 160	Precious metal ash, sludge, dust and other residues such as:
AA 161	—Ash from incineration of printed circuit boards
AA 162	—Photographic film ash
AA 170	Lead-acid batteries, whole or crushed
AA 180	Used batteries or accumulators, whole or crushed, other than lead-acid batteries, and waste and scrap arising from the production of batteries and accumulators, not otherwise specified or included

NOTES

** This listing includes wastes in the form of ash, residue, slag, dross, skimming, scaling, dust, powder, sludge and cake, unless a material is expressly listed elsewhere.

AB. WASTES CONTAINING PRINCIPALLY INORGANIC CONSTITUENTS, WHICH MAY CONTAIN METALS AND ORGANIC MATERIALS

AB 010 2621 00	Slag, ash and residues,** not elsewhere specified or included
AB 020	Residues arising from the combustion of municipal/household wastes
AB 030	Wastes from non-cyanide based systems which arise from surface treatment of metals

AB 040 ex 7001 00	Glass waste from cathode-ray tubes and other activated glasses
AB 050 ex 2529 21	Calcium fluoride sludge
AB 060	Other inorganic fluorine compounds in the form of liquids or sludges
AB 070	Sands used in foundry operations
AB 080	Waste catalysts not on the green list
AB 090	Waste hydrates of aluminium
AB 100	Waste alumina
AB 110	Basic solutions
AB 120	Inorganic halide compounds, not elsewhere specified or included
AB 130	Used blasting grit
AB 140	Gypsum arising from chemical industry processes
AB 150	Unrefined calcium sulphite and calcium sulphate from flue gas desulphurization (FGD)

NOTES

** This listing includes wastes in the form of ash, residue, slag, dross, skimming, scaling, dust, powder, sludge and cake, unless a material is expressly listed elsewhere.

AC. WASTES CONTAINING PRINCIPALLY ORGANIC CONSTITUENTS, WHICH MAY CONTAIN METALS AND INORGANIC MATERIALS

AC 010 ex 2713 90	Waste from the production/processing of petroleum coke and bitumen, excluding anode butts
AC 020	Asphalt cement wastes
AC 030	Waste oils unfit for their originally intended use
AC 040	Leaded petrol (gasoline) sludges
AC 050	Thermal (heat transfer) fluids
AC 060	Hydraulic fluids
AC 070	Brake fluids
AC 080	Antifreeze fluids
AC 090	Waste from production, formulation and use of resins, latex, plasticizers, glues and adhesives
AC 100 ex 3915 90	Nitrocellulose
AC 110	Phenols, phenol compounds including chlorophenol in the form of liquids or sludges
AC 120	Polychlorinated naphtalenes
AC 130	Ethers
AC 140	Triethylamine catalyst for setting foundry sands
AC 150	Chlorofluorocarbons
AC 160	Halons
AC 170	Treated cork and wood wastes
AC 180 ex 4110 00	Leather dust, ash, sludges and flours
AC 190	Fluff—light fraction from automobile shredding

AC 200	Organic phosphorous compounds
AC 210	Non-halogenated solvents
AC 220	Halogenated solvents
AC 230	Halogenated or unhalogenated non-aqueous distillation residues arising from organic solvent recovery operations
AC 240	Wastes arising from the production of aliphatic halogenated hydrocarbons (such as chloromethanes, dichloro-ethane, vinyl chloride, vinylidene chloride, allyl chloride and epichlohydrin)
AC 250	Surface active agents (surfactants)
AC 260	Liquid pig manure; faeces
AC 270	Sewage sludge

AD. WASTES WHICH MAY CONTAIN EITHER INORGANIC OR ORGANIC CONSTITUENTS

AD 010	Wastes from the production and preparation of pharmaceutical products
AD 020	Wastes from the production, formulation and use of biocides and phytopharmaceuticals
AD 030	Wastes from the manufacture, formulation and use of wood preserving chemicals
	Wastes that contain, consist of or are contaminated which any of the following:
AD 040	—Inorganic cyanides, excepting precious metal-bearing residues in solid form containing traces of inorganic cyanides
AD 050	-—Organic cyanides
AD 060	Waste oils/water, hydrocarbons/water mixtures, emulsions
AD 070	Wastes from production, formulation and use of inks, dyes, pigments, paints, lacquers, varnish
AD 080	Wastes of an explosive nature, when not subject to specific other legislation
AD 090	Wastes from production, formulation and use of reprographic and photographic chemicals and materials not elsewhere specified or included
AD 100	Wastes from non-cyanide based systems which arise from surface treatment of plastics
AD 110	Acidic solutions
AD 120	Ion exchange resins
AD 130	Single-use cameras with batteries
AD 140	Wastes from industrial pollution control devices for cleaning of industrial off-gases, not elsewhere specified or included
AD 150	Naturally occurring organic material used as a filter medium (such as bio-filters)
AD 160	Municipal/household wastes]

[1488]

NOTES
Substituted by Commission Decision 94/721/EC of 21 October 1994, Art 1.

[ANNEX IV
RED LIST OF WASTES

"Containing" or "contained with", when used in this list, means that the substance referred to is present to an extent which (a) renders the waste hazardous, or (b) renders it not suitable for submission to a recovery operation.

RA. WASTES CONTAINING PRINCIPALLY ORGANIC CONSTITUENTS, WHICH MAY CONTAIN METALS AND INORGANIC MATERIALS

RA 010 — Wastes, substances and articles containing, consisting of or contaminated with polychlorinated biphenyl (PCB) and/or polychlorinated terphenyl (PCT) and/or polybrominated biphenyl (PBB), including any other polybrominated analogues of these compounds, at a concentration level of 50 mg/kg or more

RA 020 — Waste tarry residues (excluding asphalt cements) arising from refining, distillation and any pyrolitic treatment

RB. WASTES CONTAINING PRINCIPALLY INORGANIC CONSTITUENTS, WHICH MAY CONTAIN METALS AND ORGANIC MATERIALS

RB 010 — Asbestos (dusts and fibres)

RB 020 — Ceramic-based fibres of physico-chemical characteristics similar to those of asbestos

RC. WASTES WHICH MAY CONTAIN EITHER INORGANIC OR ORGANIC CONSTITUENTS

Wastes that contain, consist of or are contaminated with any of the following:

RC 010 — —Any congenor of polychlorinated dibenzo-furan

RC 020 — — Any congenor of polychlorinated dibenzo-dioxin

RC 030 — Leaded anti-knock compounds sludges

RC 040 — Peroxides other than hydrogen peroxide]

[1489]

NOTES
Substituted by Commission Decision 94/721/EC of 21 October 1994, Art 1.

[ANNEX V

Wastes listed in Annex III to this Regulation

Wastes listed in Annex IV to this Regulation]

[1490]

NOTES
Added by Council Regulation 120/97/EC of 20 January 1997, Art 2.

COUNCIL REGULATION

of 15 December 1994

on substances that deplete the ozone layer

(3093/94/EC)

THE COUNCIL OF THE EUROPEAN UNION—

Having regard to the Treaty establishing the European Community, and in particular Article 103s(1) thereof,

Having regard to the proposal from the Commission,[1]

Having regard to the opinion of the Economic and Social Committee,[2]

Acting in accordance with the procedure laid down in Article 189c of the Treaty,[3]

Whereas it is established that continued emissions of ozone-depleting substances at current levels cause significant damage to the ozone layer;

Whereas Council Regulation (EEC) No 594/91 of 4 March 1991 on substances that deplete the ozone layer[4] was amended by Regulation (EEC) No 3952/92;[5] whereas on the occasion of this amendment it is desirable, in the interests of clarity, to recast that Regulation;

Whereas in view of the Community's responsibilities for the environment and trade, all Member States and the Community have become Parties to the Vienna Convention for the Protection of the Ozone Layer and the Montreal Protocol on Substances that Deplete the Ozone Layer as amended by the Parties to the Protocol at their second meeting in London;

Whereas, in the light of recent scientific evidence, at their fourth meeting in Copenhagen, at which the Community and the Member States played a leading role, the Parties to the Montreal Protocol adopted a second amendment to the Protocol comprising additional measures for the protection of the ozone layer;

Whereas it is necessary for action to be taken at Community level to carry out the Community's obligations under the Convention and the second amendment to the Protocol, in particular to control the production and supply of methyl bromide and hydrobromofluorocarbons and the supply and use of hydrochlorofluorocarbons within the Community;

Whereas in the light of scientific evidence in particular it is appropriate in certain cases to introduce control measures which are more severe than those of the second amendment to the Protocol;

Whereas a periodical review of the permitted uses of ozone-depleting substances by means of the committee procedure is desirable;

Whereas it is necessary to keep under review the evolution of the market in ozone-depleting substances, particularly in order to ensure sufficient supply for essential uses, and the state of development of appropriate substitutes, but also to keep to a minimum the imports of virgin, recovered and reclaimed ozone-depleting substances released for free circulation in the European Community;

Whereas it is appropriate to take all precautionary measures practicable to prevent leakages of ozone-depleting substances and to promote the recovery of such substances after use for recycling or safe destruction,

---

NOTES

[1]　OJ C232, 28.8.1993, p 6.

[2]　OJ C52, 19.2.1994, p8.

[3]　European Parliament opinion of 8 February 1994 (OJ C61, 28.2.1994, p114). Council common position of 27 July 1994 (OJ C301, 27.10.1994, p 1). European Parliament decision of 17 November 1994 (not yet published in the Official Journal).

[4]　OJ L67, 14.3.1991, p 1.

[5]　OJ L405, 31.12.1992, p 41.

HAS ADOPTED THIS REGULATION—

CHAPTER I
INTRODUCTORY PROVISIONS

Article 1

Scope

This Regulation shall apply to the production, importation, exportation, supply, use and recovery of chlorofluorocarbons, other fully halogenated chlorofluorocarbons, halons, carbon tetrachloride, 1,1,1-trichloroethane, methyl bromide, hydrobromofluorocarbons and hydrochlorofluorocarbons. It shall also apply to the reporting of information on these substances.

[1491]

Article 2

Definitions

For the purposes of this Regulation—
  - 'Protocol' shall mean the Montreal Protocol on Substances that Deplete the Ozone Layer, whether in the original 1987 version as adjusted in 1990 and 1992, the amended 1990 version as adjusted in 1992, or the amended 1992 version,
  - 'Party' shall mean any Party to the Protocol,
  - 'State not Party to the Protocol' shall, with respect to a particular controlled substance, include any State or regional economic-integration organisation that has not agreed to be bound by the control measures applicable to that substance,
  - 'controlled substances' shall mean chlorofluorocarbons, other fully halogenated chlorofluorocarbons, halons, carbon tetrachloride, 1,1,1-trichloroethane, methyl bromide, hydrobromofluorocarbons and hydrochlorofluorocarbons, whether alone or in a mixture. This definition shall not cover any controlled substance which is in a manufactured product other than a container used for the transportation or storage of that substance, or insignificant quantities of any controlled substance, originating from inadvertent or coincidental production during a manufacturing process, from unreacted feedstock, or from use as a processing agent which is present in chemical substances as trace impurities, or that is emitted during product manufacture or handling;
  - 'chlorofluorocarbons' shall mean the controlled substances listed in Group I of Annex I, including their isomers,
  - 'other fully halogenated chlorofluorocarbons' shall mean the controlled substances listed in Group II of Annex I, including their isomers,
  - 'halons' shall mean the controlled substances listed in Group III of Annex I, including their isomers,
  - 'carbon tetrachloride' shall mean the controlled substance specified in Group IV of Annex I,
  - '1,1,1-trichloroethane' shall mean the controlled substance specified in Group V of Annex I,
  - 'methyl bromide' shall mean the controlled substance specified in Group VI of Annex I,
  - 'hydrobromofluorocarbons' shall mean the controlled substances listed in Group VII of Annex I, including their isomers,
  - 'hydrochlorofluorocarbons' shall mean the controlled substances listed in Group VIII of Annex I, including their isomers,
  - 'producer' shall mean any natural or legal person manufacturing controlled substances within the Community,

— 'production' shall mean the amount of controlled substances produced, less the amount destroyed by technologies approved by the Parties and less the amount entirely used as feedstock in the manufacture of other chemicals. No amount recovered and reclaimed shall be considered as 'production',
— 'undertaking' shall mean any natural or legal person who produces, recycles for placing on the market or uses controlled substances for industrial or commercial purposes in the Community, who releases such imported substances for free circulation in the Community, or who exports such substances from the Community for industrial or commercial purposes,
— 'ozone-depleting potential' shall mean the figure specified in the final column of Annex I representing the potential effect of each controlled substance on the ozone layer,
— 'calculated level' shall mean a quantity determined by multiplying the quantity of each controlled substance by its ozone-depleting potential as specified in Annex I and by adding together, for each group of controlled substances in Annex I separately, the resulting figures,
— 'industrial rationalisation' shall mean the transfer either between Parties or within a Member State of all or a portion of the calculated level of production of one producer to another, for the purpose of optimising economic efficiency or responding to anticipated shortfalls in supply as a result of plant closures,
— 'recovery' shall mean the collection and the storage of controlled substances from, for example, machinery, equipment and containment vessels during servicing or before disposal,
— 'recycling' shall mean the reuse of a recovered controlled substance following a basic cleaning process such as filtering and drying. For refrigerants, recycling normally involves recharge back into equipment as is often carried out on site,
— 'reclamation' shall mean the reprocessing and upgrading of a recovered controlled substance through such processes as filtering, drying, distillation and chemical treatment in order to restore the substance to a specified standard of performance, which often involves processing off site at a central facility.

[1492]

CHAPTER II
PHASE-OUT SCHEDULE

Article 3

Control of production of controlled substances

1.　　Subject to paragraphs 8 to 12, each producer shall ensure that—
— the calculated level of his production of chlorofluorocarbons in the period 1 January to 31 December 1994 does not exceed 15% of the calculated level of his production of chlorofluorocarbons in 1986,
— he produces no chlorofluorocarbons after 31 December 1994.

However, subject to paragraphs 8 to 12, each producer in a Member State in which the calculated level of production of chlorofluorocarbons was less than 15 000 tonnes in 1986 shall ensure that—
— the calculated level of his production of chlorofluorocarbons in the period 1 January to 31 December 1994 and in the following 12-month period does not exceed 15% of the calculated level of his production in 1986,
— he produces no chlorofluorocarbons after 31 December 1995.

In the light of the nominations made by Member States the Commission shall, in accordance with the procedure laid down in Article 16, apply the criteria set out in

Decision IV/25 of the Parties to the Montreal Protocol in order to determine every year any essential uses for which the production and importation of chlorofluorocarbons may be permitted in the Community after 31 December 1994 and those users who may take advantage of those essential uses for their own account. Such production and importation shall be allowed only if no adequate alternatives or recycled chlorofluorocarbons are available from any of the Parties to the Protocol.

The Commission shall issue licences to those users identified as laid down in the third subparagraph and shall notify them of the use for which they have authorisation and the substances and the quantities of them that they are authorised to use.

A producer may be authorised by the competent authority of the Member State in which his relevant production is situated to produce chlorofluorocarbons after 31 December 1994 for the purpose of meeting the licensed demands presented by users identified as laid down in the third subparagraph. The competent authority of the Member State concerned shall notify the Commission in advance of its intention of issuing any such authorisation.

    2.   Subject to paragraphs 8 to 12, each producer shall ensure that—
- the calculated level of his production of other fully halogenated chlorofluorocarbons in the period 1 January to 31 December 1994 does not exceed 15% of the calculated level of his production of other fully halogenated chlorofluorocarbons in 1989,
- he produces no other fully halogenated chlorofluorocarbons after 31 December 1994.

In the light of the nominations made by Member States the Commission shall, in accordance with the procedure laid down in Article 16, apply the criteria set out in Decision IV/25 of the Parties to the Montreal Protocol in order to determine every year any essential uses for which the production and importation of other fully halogenated chlorofluorocarbons may be permitted in the Community after 31 December 1994 and those users who may take advantage of those essential uses for their own account. Such production and importation shall be allowed only if no adequate alternatives or recycled other fully halogenated chlorofluorocarbons are available from any of the Parties to the Protocol.

The Commission shall issue licences to those users identified as laid down in the second subparagraph and shall notify them of the use for which they have authorisation and the substances and the quantities of them that they are authorised to use.

A producer may be authorised by the competent authority of the Member State in which his relevant production is situated to produce other fully halogenated chlorofluorocarbons after 31 December 1994 for the purpose of meeting the licenced demands presented by users identified as laid down in the second subparagraph. The competent authority of the Member State concerned shall notify the Commission in advance of its intention of issuing any such authorisation.

    3.   Subject to paragraphs 8 to 12, each producer shall ensure that he produces no halons after 31 December 1993.

In the light of the nominations made by Member States the Commission shall, in accordance with the procedure laid down in Article 16, apply the criteria set out in Decision IV/25 of the Parties to the Montreal Protocol in order to determine every year any essential uses for which the production and importation of halons may be permitted in the Community after 31 December 1993 and those users who may take advantage of those essential uses for their own account. Such production and importation shall be allowed only if no adequate alternatives or recycled halons are available from any of the Parties to the Protocol.

The Commission shall issue licences to those users identified as laid down in the second subparagraph and shall notify them of the use for which they have authorisation and the substances and the quantities of them that they are authorised to use.

A producer may be authorised by the competent authority of the Member State in which his relevant production is situated to produce halons after 31 December 1993 for the purpose of meeting the licensed demands presented by users identified as laid down in the second subparagraph. The competent authority of the Member State concerned shall notify the Commission in advance of its intention of issuing any such authorisation.

4.   Subject to paragraphs 8 to 12, each producer shall ensure that—
   — the calculated level of his production of carbon tetrachloride in the period 1 January to 31 December 1994 does not exceed 15% of the calculated level of his production of carbon tetrachloride in 1989,
   — he produces no carbon tetrachloride after 31 December 1994.

In the light of the nominations made by Member States the Commission shall, in accordance with the procedure laid down in Article 16, apply the criteria set out in Decision IV/25 of the Parties to the Montreal Protocol in order to determine every year any essential uses for which the production and importation of carbon tetrachloride may be permitted in the Community after 31 December 1994 and those users who may take advantage of those essential uses for their own account. Such production and importation shall be allowed only if no adequate alternatives or recycled carbon tetrachloride are available from any of the Parties to the Protocol.

The Commission shall issue licences to those users identified as laid down in the second subparagraph and shall notify them of the use for which they have authorisation and the substances and the quantities of them that they are authorised to use.

A producer may be authorised by the competent authority of the Member State in which his relevant production is situated to produce carbon tetrachloride after 31 December 1994 for the purpose of meeting the licensed demands presented by users identified as laid down in the second subparagraph. The competent authority of the Member State concerned shall notify the Commission in advance of its intention of issuing any such authorisation.

5.   Subject to paragraphs 8 to 12, each producer shall ensure that—
   — the calculated level of his of 1,1,1-trichloroethane in the period 1 January to 31 December 1994 and in the following 12-month period does not exceed 50% of the calculated level of his production of 1,1,1-trichloroethane in 1989,
   — he produces no 1,1,1-trichloroethane after 31 December 1995.

In the light of the nominations made by Member States the Commission shall, in accordance with the procedure laid down in Article 16, apply the criteria set out in Decision IV/25 of the Parties to the Montreal Protocol in order to determine every year any essential uses for which the production and importation of 1,1,1-trichloroethane may be permitted in the Community after 31 December 1995 and those users who may take advantage of those essential uses for their own account. Such production and importation shall be allowed only if no adequate alternatives or recycled 1,1,1-trichloroethane are available from any of the Parties to the Protocol.

The Commission shall issue licences to those users identified as laid down in the second subparagraph and shall notify them of the use for which they have authorisation and the substances and the quantities of them that they are authorised to use.

A producer may be authorised by the competent authority of the Member State in which his relevant production is situated to produce 1,1,1-trichloroethane after 31 December 1995 for the purpose of meeting the licensed demands presented by users identified as laid down in the second subparagraph. The competent authority of the Member State concerned shall notify the Commission in advance of its intention of issuing any such authorisation.

6.   Subject to paragraphs 8 to 12, each producer shall ensure that—

— the calculated level of his production of methyl bromide in the period 1 January to 31 December 1995 and in each 12-month period thereafter does not exceed the calculated level of his production of methyl bromide in 1991,
— the calculated level of his production of methyl bromide in the period 1 January to 31 December 1998 and in each 12-month period thereafter does not exceed 75% of the calculated level of his production of methyl bromide in 1991.

The calculated level of each producer's production of methyl bromide under this paragraph shall not include the amount he produces for quarantine and pre-shipment applications.

7. Subject to paragraphs 10 to 12, each producer shall ensure that he produces no hydrobromofluorocarbons after 31 December 1995.

In the light of the nominations made by Member States the Commission shall, in accordance with the procedure laid down in Article 16, apply the criteria set out in Decision IV/25 of the Parties to the Montreal Protocol in order to determine every year any essential uses for which the production and importation of hydrobromofluorocarbons may be permitted in the Community after 31 December 1995 and those users who may take advantage of those essential uses for their own account. Such production and importation shall be allowed only if no adequate alternatives or recycled hydrobromofluorocarbons are available from any of the Parties to the Protocol.

The Commission shall issue licences to those users identified as laid down in the second subparagraph and shall notify them of the use for which they have authorisation and the substances and the quantities of them that they are authorised to use.

A producer may be authorised by the competent authority of the Member State in which his relevant production is situated to produce hydrobromofluorocarbons after 31 December 1995 for the purpose of meeting the licensed demands presented by users identified as laid down in the second subparagraph. The competent authority of the Member State concerned shall notify the Commission in advance of its intention of issuing any such authorisation.

8. To the extent permitted by the Protocol, the competent authority of the Member State in which a producer's relevant production is situated may authorise him to exceed the calculated levels of production laid down in paragraphs 1 to 6 in order to satisfy the basic domestic needs of Parties pursuant to Article 5 of the Protocol, provided that the additional calculated levels of production of the Member State concerned do not exceed those permitted for that purpose by Articles 2A to 2E and 2H of the Protocol for the periods in question. The competent authority of the Member State concerned shall notify the Commission in advance of its intention of issuing any such authorisation.

9. To the extent permitted by the Protocol, the competent authority of the Member State in which a producer's relevant production is situated may authorise him to exceed the calculated levels of production laid down in paragraphs 1 to 5 and 7 in order to satisfy any essential uses of Parties at their request. The competent authority of the Member State concerned shall notify the Commission in advance of its intention of issuing any such authorisation.

10. To the extent permitted by the Protocol, the competent authority of the Member State in which a producer's relevant production is situated may authorise him to exceed the calculated levels of production laid down in paragraphs 1 to 9 for the purpose of industrial rationalisation within the Member State concerned, provided that the calculated levels of production of that Member State do not exceed the sum of the calculated levels of production of its domestic producers as laid down

in paragraphs 1 to 9 for the periods in question. The competent authority of the Member State concerned shall notify the Commission in advance of its intention of issuing any such authorisation.

11.   To the extent permitted by the Protocol, the Commission may, in agreement with the competent authority of the Member State in which a producer's relevant production is situated, authorise him to exceed the calculated levels of production laid down in paragraphs 1 to 10 for the purpose of industrial rationalisation between Member States, provided that the combined calculated levels of production of the Member States concerned do not exceed the sum of the calculated levels of production of their domestic producers as laid down in paragraphs 1 to 10 for the periods in question. The agreement of the competent authority of the Member State in which it is intended to reduce production shall also be required.

12.   To the extent permitted by the Protocol, the Commission may, in agreement with both the competent authority of the Member State in which a producer's relevant production is situated and the government of the third Party concerned, authorise a producer to combine the calculated levels of production laid down in paragraphs 1 to 11 with the calculated levels of production allowed to a producer in a third Party under the Protocol and that producer's national legislation for the purpose of industrial rationalisation with a third Party, provided that the combined calculated levels of production by the two producers do not exceed the sum of the calculated levels of production allowed to the Community producer under paragraphs 1 to 11 and the calculated levels of production allowed to the third Party producer under the Protocol and his national legislation.

[1493]

Article 4

Control of the supply of controlled substances

1.   Subject to paragraph 10, each producer shall ensure that—
— the calculated level of chlorofluorocarbons which he places on the market or uses for his own account in the period 1 January to 31 December 1994 does not exceed 15% of the calculated level of chlorofluorocarbons which he placed on the market or used for his own account in 1986,
— he does not place any chlorofluorocarbons on the market or use any for his own account after 31 December 1994.

The competent authority of the Member State in which a producer's production is situated may authorise him to place chlorofluorocarbons on the market after 31 December 1994 for the purpose of meeting the licensed demands of those users identified as laid down in Article 3(1).

2.   Subject to paragraph 10, each producer shall ensure that—
— the calculated level of other fully halogenated chlorofluorocarbons which he places on the market or uses for his own account in the period 1 January to 31 December 1994 does not exceed 15% of the calculated level of other fully halogenated chlorofluorocarbons which he placed on the market or used for his own account in 1989,
— he does not place any other fully halogenated chlorofluorocarbons on the market or use any for his own account after 31 December 1994.

The competent authority of the Member State in which a producer's production is situated may authorise him to place other fully halogenated chlorofluorocarbons on the market after 31 December 1994 for the purpose of meeting the licensed demands of those users identified as laid down in Article 3(2).

3.   Subject to paragraph 10, each producer shall ensure that he does not place any halons on the market or use any for his own account after 31 December 1993.

The competent authority of the Member State in which a producer's production is situated may authorise him to place halons on the market after 31 December 1993 for the purpose of meeting the licensed demands of those users identified as laid down in Article 3(3).

4. Subject to paragraph 10, each producer shall ensure that—
— the calculated level of carbon tetrachloride which he places on the market or uses for his own account in the period 1 January to 31 December 1994 does not exceed 15% of the calculated level of carbon tetrachloride which he placed on the market or used for his own account in 1989,
— he does not place any carbon tetrachloride on the market or use any for his own account after 31 December 1994.

The competent authority of the Member State in which a producer's production is situated may authorise him to place carbon tetrachloride on the market after 31 December 1994 for the purpose of meeting the licensed demands of those users identified as laid down in Article 3(4).

5. Subject to paragraph 10, each producer shall ensure that—
— the calculated level of 1,1,1-trichchlorethane which he places on the market or uses for his own account in the period 1 January to 31 December 1994 and in the following 12-month period does not exceed 50% of the calculated level of 1,1,1-trichloroethane which he placed on the market or used for his own account in 1989,
— he does not place any 1,1,1-trichloroethane on the market or use any for his own account after 31 December 1995.

The competent authority of the Member State in which a producer's production is situated may authorise him to place 1,1,1-trichloroethane on the market after 31 December 1995 for the purpose of meeting the licensed demands of those users identified as laid down in Article 3(5).

6. Subject to paragraph 10, each producer shall ensure that—
— the calculated level of methyl bromide which he places on the market or uses for his own account in the period 1 January to 31 December 1995 and in each 12-month period thereafter does not exceed the calculated level of methyl bromide which he placed on the market or used for his own account in 1991,
— the calculated level of methyl bromide which he places on the market or uses for his own account in the period 1 January to 31 December 1998 and in each 12-month period thereafter does not exceed 75% of the calculated level of methyl bromide which he placed on the market or used for his own account in 1991,

The calculated level of methyl bromide which each producer places on the market or uses for his own account under this paragraph shall not include any amounts he places on the market or uses for his own account for quarantine and pre-shipment application.

7. Subject to paragraph 10, each producer shall ensure that he does not place any hydrobromofluorocarbons on the market or use any for his own account after 31 December 1995.

The competent authority of the Member State in which a producer's production is situated may authorise him to place hydrobromofluorocarbons on the market after 31 December 1995 for the purpose of meeting the licensed demands of those users identified as laid down in Article 3(7).

8. Subject to paragraph 10—
— the calculated level of hydrochlorofluorocarbons which producers and importers place on the market or use for their own account in the period 1 January to 31 December 1995 and in each 12-month period thereafter shall not exceed the sum of—

— 2.6% of the calculated level of chlorofluorocarbons which producers and importers placed on the market or used for their own account in 1989, and

— the calculated level of hydrochlorofluorocarbons which producers and importers placed on the market or used for their own account in 1989.

To this end the Commission shall, in accordance with the procedure laid down in Article 16, assign a quota to each producer or importer when the total quantity which producers and importers place on the market or use for their own account reaches 80% of the quantity defined by the sum described above or at the latest on 1 January 2000, whichever comes first,

— the calculated level of hydrochlorofluorocarbons which a producer or importer places on the market or uses for his own account in the period 1 January to 31 December 2004 and in each 12-month period thereafter shall not exceed 65% of the quota assigned,

— the calculated level of hydrochlorofluorocarbons which a producer or importer places on the market or uses for his own account in the period 1 January to 31 December 2007 and in each 12-month period thereafter shall not exceed 40% of the quota assigned,

— the calculated level of hydrochlorofluorocarbons which a producer or importer places on the market or uses for his own account in the period 1 January to 31 December 2010 and in each 12-month period thereafter shall not exceed 20% of the quota assigned,

— the calculated level of hydrochlorofluorocarbons which a producer or importer places on the market or uses for his own account in the period 1 January to 31 December 2013 and in each 12-month period thereafter shall not exceed 5% of the quota assigned,

— no producer or importer shall place hydrochlorofluorocarbons on the market or use any for his own account after 31 December 2014.

The Commission may, in accordance with the procedure laid down in Article 16, revise the assigned quotas for hydrochlorofluorocarbons to the extent permitted by this Regulation.

9.   The quantities referred to in paragraphs 1 to 7 shall apply to the amounts of virgin substances which a producer places on the market or uses for his own account within the Community.

The quantities referred to in paragraph 8 shall apply to the amounts of virgin substances which a producer or importer places on the market or uses for his own account within the Community and which were produced in or imported into the Community.

10.   Any producer entitled to place a group of substances referred to in this Article on the market or use them for his own account may transfer his right in respect of all or any quantities of that group of substances fixed in accordance with this Article to any other producer of that group of substances within the Community. A producer acquiring such rights shall immediately notify the Commission. The transfer of the right to place on the market or use shall not imply the further right to produce.

At the request of a producer, the Commission may adopt measures to respond to any shortfalls in that producer's right to place hydrochlorofluorocarbons on the market or use them for his own account to the extent permitted by the Protocol.

[1494]

Article 5

Control of the use of hydrochlorofluorocarbons

1.   From the first day of the sixth month following that of the entry into force of this Regulation, the use of hydrochlorofluorocarbons shall be prohibited except—

— as solvents,
— as refrigerants,
— for the production of rigid insulating foams and integral-skin foams for use in safety applications,
— in laboratory uses, including research and development,
— as feedstock in the manufacture of other chemicals and
— as carrier gas for sterilisation substances in closed systems.

2.   From 1 January 1996 the use of hydrochlorofluorocarbons shall be prohibited—

— in non-contained solvent uses including open-top cleaners and open-top dewatering systems without cold areas, in adhesives and mould-release agents when not employed in closed equipment, for drain cleaning where hydrochlorofluorocarbons are not recovered and aerosols, apart from use as solvents for reagents in fingerprint development on porous surfaces such as paper and apart from use as fixing agents for laser printers produced before 1 January 1996,
— in equipment produced after 31 December 1995 for the following uses—
    (a) as refrigerants in non-confined direct-evaporation systems;
    (b) as refrigerants in domestic refrigerators and freezers;
    (c) in car air conditioning;
    (d) in road public-transport air conditioning.

3.   From 1 January 1998 the use of hydrochlorofluorocarbons in equipment produced after 31 December 1997 for the following uses shall be prohibited—

— in rail public-transport air conditioning,
— as carrier gas for sterilisation substances in closed systems.

4.   From 1 January 2000 the use of hydrochlorofluorocarbons in equipment produced after 31 December 1999 for the following uses shall be prohibited—

— as refrigerants in public and distribution cold stores and warehouses,
— as refrigerants for equipment of 150 kw and over, shaft input,

except where codes, safety regulations or other such constraints prevent the use of ammonia.

5.   The importing, release for free circulation and placing on the market of equipment for which a use restriction is in force under this Article shall be prohibited from the date on which that use restriction comes into force. Equipment shown to be manufactured before the date of that use restriction shall not be covered by this prohibition.

6.   The Commission may, in accordance with the procedure laid down in Article 16 and in the light of technical progress, add to, delete items from or amend the list set out in paragraphs 1 to 4.

[1495]

CHAPTER III
TRADE

Article 6

Licences to import from third countries

1.   The release for free circulation in the Community or inward processing of controlled substances shall be subject to the presentation of an import licence, whether the substances are virgin, recovered or reclaimed. Such licences shall be issued by the Commission after verification of compliance with Articles 6, 7, 8 and 12. The Commission shall forward a copy of each licence to the competent authority of the Member State into which the substances concerned are to be imported. Each Member State shall appoint a competent authority for that purpose.

2.   A request for a licence shall state—
    (a) the names and the addresses of the importer and the exporter;
    (b) the country of exportation;
    (c) a description of each controlled substance including—
         — the commercial description,
         — the heading and the CN code;
         — the nature of the substance (virgin, recovered or reclaimed),
         — the quantity of the substance in kilograms;
    (d) the purpose of the proposed import (destruction by technologies approved by the Parties, recycling, feedstock use or other use of the controlled substance);
    (e) the place and date of the proposed importation, if known.

3.   The Commission may require a certificate attesting to the nature of substances to be imported.

[1496]

Article 7

Imports of controlled substances from third countries

1.   Without prejudice to Article 4(8) and unless the substances are intended for destruction by a technology approved by the Parties, for feedstock use in the manufacture of other chemicals or for quarantine and preshipment, the release for free circulation in the Community of controlled substances imported from third countries shall be subject to quantitiative limits. Those limits shall be determined in accordance with the procedure laid down in Article 16.

2.   The Community shall open the quotas set out in Annex II or in Article 4(8) which shall be applicable for each 12-month period laid down in the Annex or in Article 4(1) and allocate them to undertakings in accordance with the procedure laid down in Article 16.

3.   The Commission may, in accordance with the procedure laid down in Article 16, alter the quotas set out in Annex II.

4.   The Commission may allow the importation into the Community of controlled substances over and above the quantities set out in Article 4(8) and Annex II to meet the licensed demands of users identified as laid down in Articles 3(1) to (5) and (7).

5.   The Commission may authorise undertakings to release for free circulation in the Community controlled substances which are intended for destruction by a technology approved by the Parties, for feedstock use in the manufacture of other chemicals or for quarantine and preshipment in accordance with the procedure laid down in Article 16.

[1497]

Article 8

Imports of controlled substances from a State not Party

1.   The release for free circulation in the Community of virgin, recovered or reclaimed chlorofluorocarbons, other fully halogenated chlorofluorocarbons, halons, carbon tetrachloride or 1,1,1-trichloroethane imported from any State not Party shall be prohibited.

2.   One year after the date of the entry into force of the second amendment to the Protocol, the release for free circulation in the Community of virgin, recovered or reclaimed hydrobromofluorocarbons imported from any State not Party shall be

prohibited. The Commission shall publish the date of the entry into force of that amendment in the *Official Journal of the European Communities*.

[1498]

Article 9

Imports of products containing controlled substances from a State not Party

1. Subject to the decision referred to in paragraph 4, the release for free circulation in the Community of products containing chlorofluorocarbons or halons imported from any State not Party shall be prohibited.

2. Subject to the decision referred to in paragraph 4, the release for free circulation in the Community of products containing other fully halogenated chlorofluorocarbons, carbon tetrachloride or 1,1,1-trichloroethane imported from any State not Party shall be prohibited.

3. Subject to the decision referred to in paragraph 4, the release for free circulation in the Community of products containing hydrobromofluorocarbons imported from any State not Party shall be prohibited.

4. The Commission may, in accordance with the procedure laid down in Article 16, add to, delete items from or amend the list set out in Annex V in the light of the lists established by the Parties.

[1499]

Article 10

Imports of products produced using controlled substances from a State not Party

In the light of the decision of the Parties, the Council shall, on a proposal from the Commission, adopt rules applicable to the release for free circulation in the Community of products imported from any State not Party, produced from controlled substances, which can be positively identified as such but do not contain such controlled substances. The identification of such products shall comply with periodical technical advice given to the Parties. The Council shall act by a qualified majority.

[1500]

Article 11

Exports of controlled substances to a State not Party

1. Exports of virgin, recovered or reclaimed chlorofluorocarbons, other fully halogenated chlorofluorocarbons, halons, carbon tetrachloride or 1,1,1-trichloroethane from the Community to any State not Party shall be prohibited.

2. One year after the date published in the *Official Journal of the European Communities* pursuant to Article 8 (2), exports of virgin, recovered or reclaimed by hydrobromofluorocarbons from the Community to any State not Party shall be prohibited.

[1501]

Article 12

Exceptional authorisation to trade with a State not Party

By way of derogation from Articles 8, 9 (1), (2) and (3) and 11, trade with any State not Party in controlled substances and products which contain or are produced by means of one or more such substances may be authorised by the Commission, to the extent that the State not Party is determined by a meeting of the Parties to be in full compliance with Articles 2, 2A to 2E, 2G and 4 of the Protocol and has submitted data to that effect as specified in Article 7 of the Protocol. The Commission shall act in accordance with the procedure laid down in Article 16.

[1502]

Article 13

Trade with a territory not covered by the Protocol

1.   Subject to any decision taken under paragraph 2, Articles 8, 9 and 11 shall apply to any territory not covered by the Protocol as they apply to any State not Party.

2.   Where the authorities of a territory not covered by the Protocol are in full compliance with Articles 2, 2A to 2E, 2G and 4 of the Protocol and have submitted data to that effect as specified in Article 7 of the Protocol, the Commission may decide that some or all of the provisions of Articles 8, 9 and 11 shall not apply in respect of that territory.

The Commission shall take its decision in accordance with the procedure laid down in Article 16.

[1503]

CHAPTER IV
EMISSION CONTROL

Article 14

Recovery of used controlled substances

From the first day of the fourth month following that of the entry into force of this Regulation, chlorofluorocarbons, fully halogenated chlorofluorocarbons, halons, carbon tetrachloride, 1,1,1-trichloroethane, hydrobromofluorocarbons and hydrochlorofluorocarbons contained in—

— commercial and industrial refrigeration equipment and air-conditioning equipment,
— equipment containing solvents, and
— fire protection systems

shall be recovered if practicable for destruction by technologies approved by the Parties or by any other environmentally acceptable destruction technology, or for recycling or reclamation during the servicing and maintenance of equipment or before the dismantling or disposal of equipment. Member States may define the minimum qualification requirements for the servicing personnel involved.

This provision shall be without prejudice to Council Directive 75/442/EEC of 15 July 1975[1] on waste or to Member States' measures transposing its provisions.

Before 31 December 1994 the Commission shall submit to the Council and the European Parliament a report on the implementation of the provisions of this Article by the Member States.

[1504]

NOTES
[1]   OJ L194, 25.7.1975, p.39. Directive as amended by Directive 91/156/EEC (OJ L78, 26.3.1991, p 32) and by Directive 91/692/EEC (OJ L377, 31.12.1991, p 48).

Article 15

Leakages of controlled substances

1.   From the first day of the fourth month following that of the entry into force of this Regulation, all precautionary measures practicable shall be taken to prevent leakages of chlorofluorocarbons, other fully halogenated chlorofluorocarbons, halons, carbon tetrachloride, 1,1,1-trichloroethane, hydrobromofluorocarbons and hydrochlorofluorocarbons from commercial and industrial air-conditioning and refrigeration equipment, from fire-protection systems and from equipment containing solvents during manufacture, installation, operation and servicing. Member States may define the minimum qualification requirements for the servicing personnel involved.

2.   From the first day of the fourth month following that of the entry into force of this Regulation, all precautionary measures practicable shall be taken to prevent leakages of methyl bromide from fumigation installations and operations in which methyl bromide is used. Member States may define the minimum qualification requirements for the servicing personnel involved .

3.   From the first day of the fourth month following that of the entry into force of this Regulation, all precautionary measures practicable shall be taken to prevent leakages of controlled substances used as feedstock in the manufacture of other chemicals.

4.   From the first day of the fourth month following that of the entry into force of this Regulation, all precautionary measures practicable shall be taken to prevent any leakage of controlled substances inadvertently produced in the course of the manufacture of other chemicals.

[1505]

CHAPTER V
MANAGEMENT, REPORTING AND FINAL PROVISIONS

Article 16

Management

The Commission shall be assisted by a committee composed of representatives of the Member States and chaired by a representative of the Commission.

The representative of the Commission shall submit to the committee a draft of the measures to be taken. The committee shall deliver its opinion on that draft within a time limit which the chairman may lay down according to the urgency of the matter. Each opinion shall be delivered by the majority laid down in Article 148(2) of the Treaty for decisions which the Council is required to adopt on a proposal from the Commission. The votes of the representatives of the Member States within the committee shall be weighted in the manner laid down in that Article. The chairman shall not vote.

The Commission shall adopt measures which shall apply immediately. If, however, those measures are not in accordance with the committee's opinion the Commission shall communicate them to the Council forthwith. In that event, the Commission may defer application of the measures on which it has decided for up to one month after the date of that communication.

The Council may, acting by a qualified majority, take a different decision within the time limit laid down in the third paragraph.

[1506]

Article 17

Reporting

1.—(a) Every year before 31 March, starting in 1995, each producer, importer and exporter of controlled substances shall communicate to the Commission, sending a copy to the competent authority of the Member State concerned—
- his total production,
- his production to meet the licensed demands of users identified as laid down in Articles 3(1) to (5) and (7),
- any increase in his production under Article 3(8) to satisfy the basic domestic needs of Parties pursuant to Article 5 of the Protocol,
- any increase in his production under Article 3(9) to satisfy any essential uses of Parties,
- any increase in his production under Article 3(10), (11) and (12) authorised in connection with industrial rationalisation,
- any quantities recycled,
- any quantities destroyed by means of technologies approved by the Parties,
- any stocks,
- any quantities of imported virgin substances released for free circulation in the Community with separate figures for States Party and States not Party,
- any imports into the Community to meet the licensed demands of users identified as laid down in Article 3(1) to (5) and (7),
- any exports of production from the Community, with separate figures for States Party and States not Party,
- any production placed on the market or used for the producer's own account within the Community,
- any quantities used for feedstock,

for each controlled substance in respect of the period 1 January to 31 December of the preceding year.

Notwithstanding the above obligations, the communication referred to in this paragraph for the period 1 January to 31 December 1993 shall be effected no later than the last day of the fourth month following that of the entry into force of this Regulation.

(b) For the purposes of Article 4(8) on the last day of the quarter following that of the entry into force of this Regulation, and on the last day of each quarter thereafter, each producer or importer of hydrochlorofluorocarbons shall communicate to the Commission, sending a copy to the competent authority of the Member State concerned—
- his production of hydrochlorofluorocarbons placed on the market or used for his own account within the Community,
- his imports of hydrochlorofluorocarbons into the Community.

2.   Every year before 31 March, beginning in 1996 for chlorofluorocarbons, other fully halogenated chlorofluorocarbons, halons and carbon tetrachloride and 1997 for 1,1,1-trichloroethane and hydrobromofluorocarbons, each user identified as laid down in Articles 3(1) to (5) and (7) shall communicate to the Commission, sending a copy to the competent authority of the Member States in which he uses them, his use and the quantities he has used of those substances for which he has received authorisation under the relevant paragraphs of Article 3.

3.   Each producer, importer and exporter of methyl bromide in 1991 shall communicate to the Commission, sending a copy to the competent authority of the Member State concerned, the information referred to in paragraph 1 in respect of that year not later than the last day of the fourth month following that of the entry into force of this Regulation. Each producer, importer and exporter shall also indicate any quantities which relate to quarantine and pre-shipment uses.

4. The Commission shall take appropriate steps to protect the confidentiality of the information submitted.

[1507]

Article 18

Inspection

1. In carrying out the tasks assigned to it by this Regulation, the Commission may obtain all the information from the governments and competent authorities of the Member States and from undertakings.

2. When requesting information from an undertaking the Commission shall at the same time forward a copy of the request to the competent authority of the Member State within the territory of which the undertaking's seat is situated, together with a statement of the reasons why that information is required.

3. The competent authorities of the Member States shall carry out the investigations which the Commission considers necessary under this Regulation.

4. Subject to the agreement of the Commission and of the competent authority of the Member State within the territory of which the investigations are to be made, the officials of the Commission shall assist the officials of that authority in the performance of their duties.

5. The Commission shall take appropriate steps to protect the confidentiality of information obtained under this Article.

[1508]

Article 19

Sanctions

Each Member State shall determine the penalties to be imposed in the event of any failure to comply with this Regulation or with any national measures taken to implement it.

[1509]

Article 20

1. Regulation (EEC) No 594/91 shall be repealed.

2. References to the Regulation repealed under paragraph 1 shall be construed as references to this Regulation.

[1510]

Article 21

Entry into force

This Regulation shall enter into force on the day following that of its publication in the *Official Journal of the European Communities.*

This Regulation shall be binding in its entirety and directly applicable in all Member States.

[1511]

Done at Brussels, 15 December 1994.

ANNEX I
SUBSTANCES COVERED

Group	Substance		Ozone depleting potential[1]
Group I	$CFCl_3$	(CFC- 11)	1,0
	CF_2Cl_2	(CFC- 12)	1,0
	$C_2F_3Cl_3$	(CFC-113)	0,8
	$C_2F_4Cl_2$	(CFC-114)	1,0
	C_2F_5Cl	(CFC-115)	0,6
Group II	CF_3Cl	(CFC- 13)	1,0
	C_2FCl_5	(CFC-111)	1,0
	$C_2F_2Cl_4$	(CFC-112)	1,0
	C_3FCl_7	(CFC-211)	1,0
	$C_3F_2Cl_6$	(CFC-212)	1,0
	$C_3F_3Cl_5$	(CFC-213)	1,0
	$C_3F_4Cl_4$	(CFC-214)	1,0
	$C_3F_5Cl_3$	(CFC-215)	1,0
	$C_3F_6Cl_2$	(CFC-216)	1,0
	C_3F_7Cl	(CFC-217)	1,0
Group III	CF_2BrCl	(halon-1211)	3,0
	CF_3Br	(halon-1301)	10,0
	$C_2F_4Br_2$	(halon-2402)	6,0
Group IV	CCl_4	(carbon tetrachloride)	1,1
Group V	$C_2H_3Cl_3{}^2$	(1,1,1-trichloroethane)	0,1
Group VI	CH_3Br	(methyl bromide)	0,7
Group VII	$CHFBr_2$		1,00
	CHF_2Br		0,74
	CH_2FBr		0,73
	C_2HFBr_4		0,8
	$C_2HF_2Br_3$		1,8
	$C_2HF_3Br_2$		1,6
	C_2HF_4Br		1,2
	$C_2H_2FBr_3$		1,1
	$C_2H_2F_2Br_2$		1,5
	$C_2H_2F_3Br$		1,6
	$C_2H_3FBr_2$		1,7
	$C_2H_3F_2Br$		1,1
	C_2H_4FBr		0,1
	C_3HFBr_6		1,5
	$C_3HF_2Br_5$		1,9
	$C_3HF_3Br_4$		1,8
	$C_3HF_4Br_3$		2,2

Group	Substance		Ozone depleting potential[1]
Group VII *contd*	$C_3HF_5Br_2$		2,0
	C_3HF_6Br		3,3
	$C_3H_2FBr_5$		1,9
	$C_3H_2F_2Br_4$		2,1
	$C_3H_2F_3Br_3$		5,6
	$C_3H_2F_4Br_2$		7,5
	$C_3H_2F_5Br$		1,4
	$C_3H_3FBr_4$		1,9
	$C_3H_3F_2Br_3$		3,1
	$C_3H_3F_3Br_2$		2,5
	$C_3H_3F_4Br$		4,4
	$C_3H_4FBr_3$		0,3
	$C_3H_4F_2Br_2$		1,0
	$C_3H_4F_3Br$		0,8
	$C_3H_5FBr_2$		0,4
	$C_3H_5F_2Br$		0,8
	C_3H_6FBr		0,7
Group VIII	$CHFCl_2$	(HCFC- 21)	0,040
	CHF_2Cl	(HCFC- 22)	0,055
	CH_2FCl	(HCFC- 31)	0,020
	C_2HFCl_4	(HCFC-121)	0,040
	$C_2HF_2Cl_3$	(HCFC-122)	0,080
	C_2HFCl_2	(HCFC-123)[3]	0,020
	C_2HF_4Cl	(HCFC-124)[3]	0,022
	$C_2H_2FCl_3$	(HCFC-131)	0,050
	$C_2H_2F_2Cl_2$	(HCFC-132)	0,050
	$C_2H_2F_3Cl$	(HCFC-133)	0,060
	$C_2H_3FCl_2$	(HCFC-141)	0,070
	CH_3FCl_2	(HCFC-141b)[3]	0,110
	$C_2H_3F_2Cl$	(HCFC-142)	0,070
	CH_3F_2Cl	(HCFC-142b)[3]	0,065
	C_2H_4FCl	(HCFC-151)	0,005
	C_3HFCl_6	(HCFC-221)	0,070
	$C_3HF_2Cl_5$	(HCFC-222)	0,090
	$C_3HF_3Cl_4$	(HCFC-223)	0,080
	$C_3HF_4Cl_3$	(HCFC-224)	0,090
	$C_3HF_5Cl_2$	(HCFC-225)	0,070
	$CF_3CF_2CHCl_2$	(HCFC-225ca)[3]	0,025
	CF_2ClF_2CHClF	(HCFC-225cb)[3]	0,033

Group	Substance		Ozone depleting potential[1]
Group VIII *contd*	C_3HF_6Cl	(HCFC-226)	0,100
	$C_3H_2FCl_5$	(HCFC-231)	0,090
	$C_3H_2F_2Cl_4$	(HCFC-232)	0,100
	$C_3H_2F_3Cl_3$	(HCFC-233)	0,230
	$C_3H_2F_4Cl_2$	(HCFC-234)	0,280
	$C_3H_2F_5Cl$	(HCFC-235)	0,520
	$C_3H_3FCl_4$	(HCFC-241)	0,090
	$C_3H_3F_2Cl_3$	(HCFC-242)	0,130
	$C_3H_3F_3Cl_2$	(HCFC-243)	0,120
	$C_3H_3F_4Cl$	(HCFC-244)	0,140
	$C_3H_4FCl_3$	(HCFC-251)	0,010
	$C_3H_4F_2Cl_2$	(HCFC-252)	0,040
	$C_3H_4F_3Cl$	(HCFC-253)	0,030
	$C_3H_5FCl_2$	(HCFC-261)	0,020
	$C_3H_5F_2Cl$	(HCFC-262)	0,020
	C_3H_6FCl	(HCFC-271)	0,030

[1]　These ozone-depleting potentials are estimates based on existing knowledge and will be reviewed and revised periodically in the light of decisions taken by the Parties to the Montreal Protocol on Substances that Deplete the Ozone Layer.

[2]　This formula does not refer to 1,1,2-trichloroethane.

[3]　Identifies the most commercially-viable substance as prescribed in the Protocol.

[1512]

ANNEX II
QUANTITATIVE LIMITS ON IMPORTS FROM THIRD COUNTRIES
(calculated levels expressed in tonnes)

Substance For 12-month periods from 1 January to 31 December	Group I	Group II	Group III	Group IV	Group V	Group VI	Group VII
1993	1161	14	700	1 288	2 378		
1994	348	4	0	386	1 189		
1995	0	0		0	1 189	11 530	
1996					0	11 530	0
1997						11530	
1998						8 648	
1999						8 648	
2000						8 648	
2001						8 648	
2002						8 648	
2003						8 648	
2004						8 648	
2005						8 648	

Substance For 12-month periods from 1 January to 31 December	Group I	Group II	Group III	Group IV	Group V	Group VI	Group VII
2006						8 648	
2007						8 648	
2008						8 648	
2009						8 648	
2010						8 648	
2011						8 648	
2012						8 648	
2013						8 648	
2014						8 648	
2015						8 648	
thereafter						8 648	

[1513]

ANNEX III
COMBINED NOMENCLATURE (CN) CODES AND DESCRIPTIONS FOR THE
SUBSTANCES REFERRED TO IN ANNEXES I AND II

CN code	Description
2903 40 10	— — — Trichlorofluoromethane
2903 40 20	— — — Dichlorodifluoromethane
2903 40 30	— — — Trichlorotrifluoroethane
2903 40 40	— — — Dichlorotetrafluoroethane
2903 40 50	— — — Chloropentafluoroethane
2903 40 61	— — — — Chlorotrifluoromethane, Pentachlorofluoroethane, Tetrachlorodifluoroethane, Heptachlorofluoropropane, Hexachlorodifluoropropane, Pentachlorotrifluoropropane, Tetrachlorotetrafluoropropane, Trichloropentafluoropropane, Dichlorohexafluoropropane or Chloroheptafluoropropane
2903 40 70	— — — Bromotrifluoromethane
2903 40 80	— — — Dibromotetrafluoroethane
2903 40 91	— — — Bromochlorodifluoromethane
2903 14 00	— — Carbon tetrachloride
2903 19 10	— — — 1,1,1-Trichloroethane
2903 30 33	— — — Bromomethane (methyl bromide)
ex 2903 40 98	— — — Hydrobromofluorocarbons
ex 2903 40 69	— — — Hydrochlorofluorocarbons
ex 3823 90 96	— — — — Mixtures containing substances falling within codes 2903 40 10, 2903 40 20, 2903 40 30, 2903 40 40, 2903 40 50 or 2903 40 61
ex 3823 90 97	— — — — Mixtures containing substances falling within codes 2903 40 70, 2903 40 80, 2903 40 91 or 3823 90 96
ex 3823 90 98	— — — Mixtures containing substances falling within codes 2903 14 00 or 2903 19 10

[1514]

ANNEX IV
TOTAL QUANTITATIVE LIMITS ON PRODUCERS' AND IMPORTERS' PLACING HYDROCHLOROFLUOROCARBONS ON THE MARKET AND USING THEM FOR THEIR OWN ACCOUNT IN THE COMMUNITY

For the 12-month period from 1 January to 31 December	Group VIII[1]	
	Limit in ODP tonnes	Percentage of limit
1995	7 655	100%
1996	7 655	100%
1997	7 655	100%
1998	7 655	100%
1999	7 655	100%
2000	7 655	100%
2001	7 655	100%
2002	7 655	100%
2003	7 655	100%
2004	4 975	65%
2005	4 975	65%
2006	4 975	65%
2007	3 062	40%
2008	3 062	40%
2009	3 062	40%
2010	1 531	20%
2011	1 531	20%
2012	1 531	20%
2013	383	5%
2014	383	5%
2015	0	0%

[1]   The limits consists of 2.6% of the CFC and 100% of the HCFC marketed by producers or used for their own account in 1989.

[1515]

ANNEX V
COMBINED NOMENCLATURE (CN) CODES FOR PRODUCTS CONTAINING CONTROLLED SUBSTANCES[1]

[1]   These customs codes are given for the guidance of the Member States' customs authorities.

1.   Automobiles and truck air-conditioning units

CN codes
8701 20 10 — 8701 90 90
8702 10 11 — 8702 90 90
8703 10 10 — 8703 90 90
8704 10 11 — 8704 90 90
8705 10 00 — 8705 90 90
8706 00 11 — 8706 00 99

2.   Domestic and commercial refrigeration and air-conditioning/heat-pump equipment

Refrigerators—

CN codes
8418 10 10 — 8418 29 00
8418 50 11 — 8418 50 19
8418 61 10 — 8418 69 99

Freezers—

CN codes
8418 10 10 — 8418 29 00
8418 30 10 — 8418 30 99
8418 40 10 — 8418 40 99
8418 50 11 — 8418 50 19
8418 61 10 — 8418 61 90
8418 69 10 — 8418 69 99

Dehumidifiers—

CN codes
8415 10 00 — 8415 83 90
8424 89 00
8479 89 10
8479 89 80

Water coolers—

CN codes
8419 60 00
8419 89 80

Ice machines—

CN codes
8418 10 10 — 8414 29 00
8418 30 10 — 8418 30 99
8418 40 10 — 8418 40 99
8418 50 11 — 8418 50 19
8418 61 10 — 8418 61 90
8418 69 10 — 8418 69 99
8479 89 80

Air-conditioning and heat-pump units—

CN codes
8415 10 00 — 8415 83 90
8418 61 10 — 8418 61 90
8418 69 10 — 8418 69 99
8418 99 10 — 8418 99 90

3.   Aerosol products, except medical aerosols

Food products—

CN codes
0404 90 11 — 0404 90 99
1517 90 10 — 1517 90 99
2106 90 91
2106 90 99

Paints and varnishes, prepared water pigments and dyes—

CN codes
3208 10 10 — 3208 10 90
3208 20 10 — 3208 20 90
3208 90 10 — 3208 90 99
3209 10 00 — 3209 90 00
3210 00 10 — 3210 00 90
3212 90 90

Perfumery, cosmetic or toilet preparations—

CN codes
3303 00 10 — 3303 00 90
3304 30 00
3304 99 00
3305 10 00 — 3305 90 90
3306 10 00 — 3306 90 00
3307 10 00 — 3307 30 00
3307 49 00
3307 90 00

Surface-active preparations—

CN codes
3402 20 10 — 3402 20 90

Lubricating preparations—

CN codes
3403 11 00
3403 19 10 — 3403 19 99
3403 91 00
3403 99 10 — 3403 99 90.

Household preparations—

CN codes
3405 10 00
3405 20 00
3405 30 00
3405 40 00
3405 90 10 — 3405 90 90

Articles of combustible materials—

CN codes
3606 10 00

Insecticides, rodenticides, fungicides, herbicides, etc.—

CN codes
3808 10 10 — 3808 10 90
3808 20 10 — 3808 20 80
3808 30 11 — 3808 30 90
3808 40 10 — 3808 40 90
3808 90 10 — 3808 90 90

Finishing agents, etc—

CN codes
3809 10 10 — 3809 10 90
3809 91 00 — 3809 93 00

Organic composite solvents, etc—

CN codes
3814 00 10 — 3814 00 90

Prepared de-icing fluids—

CN codes
3820 00 00

Products of the chemical or allied industries

CN codes
3823 90 10
3823 90 60
3823 90 70
3823 90 81 — 3823 90 98

Silicones in primary forms—

CN codes
3910 00 00

Arms—

CN codes
9304 00 00

4.   Portable fire extinguishers

CN codes
8424 10 10 — 8424 10 99

5.   Insulation boards, panels and pipe covers

CN codes
3917 21 10 — 3917 40 90
3920 10 21 — 3920 99 90
3921 11 00 — 3921 90 90
3925 10 00 — 3925 90 80
3926 90 10 — 3926 90 99

6.   Pre-polymers

CN codes
3901 10 10 — 3911 90 90

[1516]

INDEX

References are to paragraph numbers

BEST PRACTICABLE MEANS
  meaning, 14
BIRDS, 30–37
  areas of special protection, 32, 33
  captive, protection of, 37
  captive, registration of, 36
  eggs, protection of, 30, 31, 33
  eggs, sale of, 35
  nests, protection of, 30, 31, 33
  wild, prohibition of certain methods of killing
      or taking, 34
  wild, protection of, 30, 31, 33
  wild, sale of, 35

CABLE BURNING, 429
CHIMNEYS, 411–413
  height, 411–413
    applications for approval, 412
  meaning, 460
CLEAN AIR, 398–470
  administration, 445–458
  application of Part XII, Public Health Act 1936,
      458
  cumulative penalties on continuance of certain
      offences, 446
  default powers, 456
  definitions, 460
  duty to notify occupiers of offences, 447
  enforcement, 445–458
    general provisions, 451
  fumes and gases, 443
  inquiries, 455
  Isles of Scilly, 461
  joint exercise of local authority functions,
      457
  offence due to act or default of another, 449
  offences committed by bodies corporate, 448
  orders, 459
  power of county court to authorise works and
      order payments, 450
  power of local authorities to obtain information,
      454
  power to give effect to international
      agreements, 444
  regulations, 459
  rights of entry and inspection, 452, 453
  transitional provisions, 467–469
  unjustified disclosures of information, 445
CLINICAL WASTE
  meaning, 917
CLOSED LANDFILLS
  duty of waste regulation authorities, 146
CODES OF GOOD AGRICULTURAL
      PRACTICE, 364
COLLIERY SPOILBANKS
  air pollution, 438
COMMERCIAL WASTE
  meaning, 155
  receptacles for, 137
  waste not to be treated as, 923, 924
  waste to be treated as, 922, 931

CONSERVATION
  natural habitats, 988–1095. *See also* NATURAL
      HABITATS
  competent authorities, 993
  definitions, 989
  European sites, 994–1001
  Habitats Directive, 990
  relevant authorities
    European marine sites, 992
    marine areas, 992
CONSTRUCTION SITES
  noise, 2, 3
CONTAMINATED LAND, 159–184
  appropriate agency to have regard to guidance
      by Secretary of State, 179, 182
  determination of appropriate person to bear
      responsibility, 164
  duty of enforcing authority to require
      remediation, 163
  identification, 160
  Isles of Scilly, 181
  meaning, 159
  powers of enforcing authority to carry out
      remediation, 171
  radioactivity, 184
  recovery of cost of mediation, 172
  registers, 174
    confidential information, 176
    national security, 175
  remediation notices
    appeals against, 169
    offences of not complying with, 170
    prohibitions on, 166
    registers, 174
    restrictions on, 166
  reports by appropriate Agency on state of, 177
  restrictions on liability relating to pollution of
      controlled waters, 167
  rights of entry
    compensation for, 165
    grant of, 165
  security for cost of remediation, 172
  significant harm, 180
  site-specific guidance, 178
  special sites. *See* SPECIAL SITE
  substances escaping to other land, 168
CONTROL OF POLLUTION, 1–18, 20–29,
      81–92
  appeals, 1152–1157
    action upon receipt of notice, 1154
    advertisements, 1146
      exemptions, 1148
      timing of, 1147
    consultation, 1149
    discharge consents without, 1151, 1163
    hearings, 1156
    notification of determination, 1157
    time limit for bringing, 1153
    transmitted, 1150
    written representations, 1155
  appeals to Court of Session, 17

References are to paragraph numbers

References are to paragraph numbers

References are to paragraph numbers

References are to paragraph numbers

References are to paragraph numbers

References are to paragraph numbers

References are to paragraph numbers

References are to paragraph numbers

References are to paragraph numbers